The Essential World of Psychology

Y0-CQO-097

Samuel E. Wood
Lindenwood University

Ellen Green Wood
St. Louis Community College
Meramec

ALLYN AND BACON

BOSTON LONDON TORONTO SYDNEY TOKYO SINGAPORE

Executive Editor: Carolyn Merrill
Vice President, Director of Field Marketing: Joyce Nilsen
Senior Development Editor: Sue Gleason
Development Editor: Jodi Devine
Editorial Assistant: Lara Zeises
Senior Editorial Production Administrator: Susan McIntyre
Editorial Production Service: Lifland et al., Bookmakers
Text Designer: Delgado Design
Photo Researcher: Kathy Smith
Composition Buyer: Linda Cox
Manufacturing Buyer: Megan Cochran
Cover Administrator: Linda Knowles
Electronic Composition: Christine Thompson

Copyright © 2000 by Allyn & Bacon
A Pearson Education Company
Needham Heights, MA 02494
Internet: www.abacon.com

Library of Congress Cataloging-in-Publication Data

Wood, Samuel E.
    The essential world of psychology / Samuel E. Wood, Ellen Green
  Wood.
      p.   cm.
  Includes bibliographical references and index.
  ISBN 0-205-28641-0
  1. Psychology.   I. Wood, Ellen R. Green.   II. Title.
BF121.W656   1999
150—dc21   99–25033
                                                  CIP

Printed in the United States of America
10 9 8 7 6 5 4 3 2 1 VHP 03 02 01 00 99

We dedicate this book with affection to our siblings and their spouses:

Margie (Wood) Ison & Jim
Richard S. Rosenthal & Rosemary
Dr. Albert L. Wood & Pat
and the late Judy Wood

Contents

CHAPTER 3

Sensation and Perception 64

CHAPTER 4

States of Consciousness 100

CONTENTS

CHAPTER 6

Memory 167

CHAPTER 5

Learning 132

CHAPTER 7

Cognition,
Language, and
Creativity 199

CONTENTS

CHAPTER 8

Human Development 239

CHAPTER 9

Motivation and Emotion 288

CHAPTER 10

Personality Theory and Assessment 324

CONTENTS

Health and Stress 357

Psychological Disorders 390

Therapies 423

CHAPTER 14

Social Psychology 454

Introduction to Social Psychology 455

Social Perception 456

Impression Formation: Sizing Up the Other Person 456
Attribution: Explaining Behavior 457

Attraction 458

Factors Influencing Attraction: Magnets That Draw People Together 458

An Invitation to the Student

We all learn best when we can apply new concepts to the world we know. *The Essential World of Psychology* allows you to do just that. Highly interactive *and* active, clearly written, and thoroughly up to date, this textbook will encourage you to think for yourself as you learn about, relate to, and apply the psychological principles that affect your life.

So that you can make the most of all the material in the following pages, this textbook package incorporates a number of helpful features and ancillary items.

A Clear, Engaging Writing Style

The writing style is conversational, and the text uses numerous everyday examples and realistic analogies to help you grasp even the most complex concepts.

A chapter opening vignette draws you into each chapter's topics with a dramatic real-life story—one you'll find memorable and directly related to the chapter's content.

You'll be especially interested in the stories of the McCaughey septuplets, world champion chess player Garry Kasparov's loss to the supercomputer Deep Blue, and men tried for crimes they did not commit because of faulty eyewitness testimony.

Hypnosis: The Power of Suggestion

Have you ever been hypnotized? Many people are fascinated by this unusual, somewhat mysterious phenomenon. **Hypnosis** may be defined as a procedure through which one person, the hypnotist, uses the power of suggestion to induce changes in thoughts, feelings, sensations, perceptions, or behavior in another person, the subject. Under hypnosis, people suspend their usual rational and logical ways of thinking and perceiving and allow themselves to experience distortions in perceptions, memories, and thinking. They may experience positive hallucinations, in which they see, hear, touch, smell, or taste things that are not present in the environment. Or they may have negative hallucinations, in which they fail to perceive things that are actually present.

About 80–95% of people are hypnotizable to some degree, but only 5% can reach the deepest levels of the hypnotic state (Nash & Baker, 1984). The ability to become completely absorbed in imaginative activities is characteristic of highly hypnotizable people (Nadon et al., 1991). Silva and Kirsch (1992) found that individuals' fantasy-proneness and their expectation of responding to hypnotic suggestions were predictors of hypnotizability.

There are many misconceptions about hypnosis, some of which probably stem from its long association

What is hypnosis, and when is it most useful?

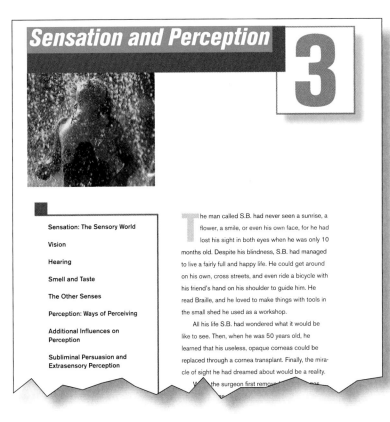

Sensation and Perception

3

- Sensation: The Sensory World
- Vision
- Hearing
- Smell and Taste
- The Other Senses
- Perception: Ways of Perceiving
- Additional Influences on Perception
- Subliminal Persuasion and Extrasensory Perception

The man called S.B. had never seen a sunrise, a flower, a smile, or even his own face, for he had lost his sight in both eyes when he was only 10 months old. Despite his blindness, S.B. had managed to live a fairly full and happy life. He could get around on his own, cross streets, and even ride a bicycle with his friend's hand on his shoulder to guide him. He read Braille, and he loved to make things with tools in the small shed he used as a workshop.

All his life S.B. had wondered what it would be like to see. Then, when he was 50 years old, he learned that his useless, opaque corneas could be replaced through a cornea transplant. Finally, the miracle of sight he had dreamed about would be a reality.

When the surgeon first removed

Interact with Your Textbook

What better way to learn new material—to make it fresh, interesting, and memorable—than to demonstrate for yourself the principles discussed? The unique *Try It!* features encourage you to learn by doing. The highly praised *Try Its!* provide simple experiments that you can perform without elaborate equipment, usually as you read.

Link It! icons appear at appropriate places in the margins of the book to alert you that related or updated information is available at the book's web site or through related links.

Finally, you'll have a chance to relate psychological principles to your own life in the *Apply It!* section at the end of each chapter. Each *Apply It!* helps you apply psychology to problems and issues that may affect your personal life. Among the wide range of topics addressed are these:

- Handedness—Does It Make a Difference?
- How to Win the Battle against Procrastination
- Building a Good Relationship
- The Quest for Happiness
- Learning to Be Optimistic

A Formula for Success

This textbook is organized to help you maximize your learning by following five steps: *Survey, Question, Read, Recite,* and *Review.* Together, these are known as the *SQ3R method.* You will learn and remember more if, instead of simply reading each chapter, you follow these steps. Here's how they work.

Survey   First, scan the chapter you are going to read. The *chapter outline* helps you preview the content and its organization.

Read all the section headings and the *learning objective questions,* which are designed to focus your attention on key information that you should learn and remember.

Glance at the illustrations and tables, including the *Review & Reflect* tables. Then read the chapter's *Summary and Review.* This survey process gives you an overview of the chapter.

Question   Before you actually read each section in a chapter, turn its heading into one or more questions. Some sections provide a learning objective question, but you can also jot down questions of your own. For example, one heading in Chapter 1 is "The Goals of Psychology." The learning objective question is "What are the four goals of psychology?" You might add this question: "What is meant by 'control' as a goal of psychology?" Asking such questions helps focus your reading.

Read   Read the section. As you read, try to answer the learning objective question *and* your own question(s). After reading the section, stop. If the section is very long or if the material seems especially difficult or complex, you should stop after reading only one or two paragraphs.

Recite   After reading part or all of a section, try to answer the learning objective question and your own question(s). To better grasp each topic, write a short summary of the material. If you have trouble summarizing a topic or answering the questions, scan or read the section once more before trying again.

When you have mastered one section, move on to the next. If the text does not include a learning objective question, formulate your own. Then read and recite, answering your question or writing a brief summary as before.

Review   When you have finished a chapter, turn to the *Summary and Review*. Review the *Key Terms*. If you don't know the meaning of a term, turn to the page where that term is defined in the margin. The *marginal definitions* provide a ready reference for important key terms that appear in boldface print in the text. All of these terms and definitions also appear in the *Glossary* at the end of the book. Phonetic pronunciations are provided for potentially hard-to-pronounce terms.

Next, review each learning objective question in the *Summary and Review* and answer it in your own words. The answers that are provided are only condensed reminders, and you should be able to expand on them.

Finally, each chapter ends with its own **Study Guide**, which contains five sections. Four of the sections are the same in every chapter: Chapter Review, Fill In the Blank, Comprehensive Practice Test, and Critical Thinking. However, the second section in each Study Guide is different, providing an exercise that is best suited to help you review the material in that particular chapter; examples include Identify the Concept, Important Psychologists, and Complete the Diagrams. An answer key is provided at the end of the text.

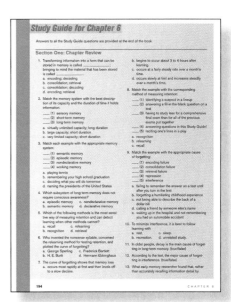

And for Some Extra Practice . . .

Several items that supplement this textbook may be available at your school's bookstore. Check with your instructor.

Practice Tests   Multiple-choice tests for all chapters provide answers and include some actual test items from this book's test bank to prepare you to take the real thing.

PSYCH-ED! Core Concepts in Psychology   This CD-ROM is an exciting and revolutionary addition to the study of introductory psychology. It offers a unique chapter review format, enhanced with video, sound, and animations.

Companion Web Site   The Internet and the World Wide Web provide an opportunity for you and your instructor to access and interact with an almost endless amount of information. Visit this textbook's web site (http://www.abacon.com/woodessentials) for a wealth of material related to introductory psychology. Interact with an online study guide, explore other web sites related to key topics, or just browse. The *Link It!* icons in the text indicate related material on the web site and provide updates and interesting web links.

Additional student resources include *Studying Psychology: A Manual for Success,* by Robert T. Brown; *Evaluating Psychological Information: Sharpening Your Critical Thinking Skills,* 3rd edition, by James Bell; *Psychology and Culture,* edited by Lonner and Malpass; *Majoring in Psych?* by Betsy Morgan; and *Psychologically Speaking,* by Donovan and Rosato. Your instructor can tell you more about these and other supplements to accompany *The Essential World of Psychology.*

To the Instructor

Our goals for this book are to introduce the essentials of psychology accurately and clearly to students, via an interesting and memorable format. We present the principles of psychology using a clear and engaging writing style and a pedagogically sound learning format that is accessible and appealing to students.

We are sensitive to the complexities of the teaching/learning process, having taught thousands of students their first course in psychology. However, we realize that a semester is usually not long enough to cover all the topics in an introductory psychology text; therefore, we introduce our essentials version in order to meet the demands of instructors who wish to offer a briefer course but still teach with a thoroughly researched, up-to-date, accessible, and interactive text. In addition to including many of the pedagogical features from *The World of Psychology,* Third Edition, *The Essential World of Psychology* introduces a comprehensive Study Guide at the end of every chapter.

To accomplish our goals, we set the following objectives:

To Maintain a Clear, Understandable Writing Style That Students Will Find Interesting

First and foremost, a textbook is a teaching instrument. A good psychology textbook must communicate clearly to a diverse audience of various ages and levels of academic ability. Our text is appealing to accomplished students, yet accessible to students whose academic skills are yet to be fully developed.

We explain concepts in much the same way as we do in our own psychology classes. Throughout the text we strive for flow and continuity by using a dialogic style that avoids abrupt shifts in thought. In addition, this text is filled with everyday examples pertinent to students' lives.

To Write a Textbook That Encourages Students to Become Active Participants in the Learning Process

Reading about psychology is not enough. Students should be able to practice what they have learned, where appropriate. Many of the principles we teach can be demonstrated, without elaborate equipment and sometimes as the student reads. What better way to teach new material and make it fresh, interesting, and memorable than to have students demonstrate principles for themselves using an important and innovative element of the book: *Try It!* boxes. The *Try Its!* personalize psychology and make it come alive.

Student involvement is also promoted through the extensive use of rhetorical questions and by casting the student in the role of the participant in selected studies (for example, as the "teacher" in the Milgram experiment). Thus, students who use *The Essential World of Psychology* become active participants in the learning process rather than simply passive recipients of information.

To Provide a Series of High-Interest Features That Will Appeal to Today's Students

Every chapter opens with a real-life vignette to capture student interest and build motivation. We have also included special features at the end of each chapter, called *Apply It!,* which show the practical applications of the principles of psychology.

To Promote and Nurture Critical Thinking

Critical thinking does not consist of being critical of all viewpoints other than one's own. Rather, critical thinking is a process of evaluating claims, propositions, or conclusions objectively, to determine whether they follow logically from the evidence presented. Critical thinkers are open-minded, objective, and unbiased, and they maintain a skeptical attitude that leads them to search for alternative explanations.

Critical thinking is too important to leave to chance. The first *Apply It!* section, "Study Skills and Critical Thinking," provides students with an understanding of what critical thinking entails. In addition to promoting critical thinking throughout the text, we have also developed a systematic method of nurturing it. A *Critical Thinking* section at the end of each chapter's Study Guide features three types of questions:

1. Evaluation questions teach students to think critically as they evaluate psychological theories, techniques, approaches, perspectives, and research studies.

2. Point/counterpoint questions require students to comprehend, to analyze, and to formulate convincing arguments on *both* sides of important issues in psychology.

3. Real-life application questions allow students to apply psychological principles and concepts to their own lives and the everyday world.

To Help Students Understand and Appreciate Human Diversity and More Fully Comprehend the Part Multicultural Issues Play in Modern Psychology

To promote understanding of human diversity, we integrate coverage of diversity issues throughout the book. This material covers a wide range of multicultural issues, among them "Bias in Psychological Research," "Cultural Differences in the Perception of Visual Illusions," "Culture and Altered States of Consciousness," "Memory and Culture," "Expectations, Effort, and Academic Achievement—A Cross-Cultural Comparison," "Cultural Rules for Displaying Emotion," and "Therapy and Race, Ethnicity, and Gender." In addition, human diversity has been considered in relation to dozens of other topics throughout the text.

To Achieve a Balance between Psychological Principles and Applications

To present psychological principles alone may leave students wondering what psychology has to do with their own lives. This text has a relevant *Apply It!* section at the end of each chapter to help students apply psychology to their personal lives and to contemporary social and cultural issues or problems. *Apply It!* topics include "Stimulating Creativity," "Building a Good Relationship," "The Quest for Happiness," and "Learning to Be Optimistic."

To Be Current in Our Coverage While Preserving the Classic Contributions in the Field

Advances in scientific knowledge occur at an ever-increasing pace, and modern authors must keep abreast. This textbook introduces students to the most up-to-date research in many rapidly changing areas, including cognitive psychology and neuroscience, gender differences, adolescent drug use, sexual orientation, death and bereavement, and behavioral genetics. Topics include functional MRI (fMRI), melatonin as a sleep aid, "designer drugs," binge drinking on college campuses, hormones and memory, emotional intelligence, and the information-processing approach to cognitive development.

Yet we do not pursue newness for its own sake. We also discuss studies that have stood the test of time, and we explore classic contributions to psychology in depth.

To Provide Instructors with a Complete, Coordinated Teaching Package of the Highest Quality

The Instructor's Resource Manual (IRM), prepared by Fred Whitford, of Montana State University, provides lecture examples, demonstrations, diversity topics, and more than 150 ready-to-duplicate handouts.

The Essential World of Psychology is also supported by a comprehensive test bank (approximately 2,300 questions) and a computerized test item file (for Macintosh, DOS, and Windows), prepared by Greg Cook, University of Wisconsin–Whitewater. Items have been class-tested and validated at Montana State University.

Also available to instructors are a superb set of acetate transparencies, a Power-Point Presentation created specifically for this edition by Jerry Newall of Citrus College, a Digital Media Archive, Allyn and Bacon's Interactive Video and User's Guide, an exclusive Video Disc series, an extensive video library, and much more. Please see your Allyn and Bacon sales representative for more information about these and other ancillary materials.

Acknowledgments

We are indebted to an incredible group of people at Allyn and Bacon for their contributions to *The Essential World of Psychology*. First, we want to thank Carolyn Merrill, Executive Editor. We are so impressed with her professional talents and her creativity that we hardly know where to begin to acknowledge her contribution. Carolyn is the prime mover of this book. She is a tireless worker, and her editorial excellence and good taste are reflected everywhere in the text. In publishing, in particular, there is so much to do and so little time in which to do it. Carolyn does it all, and we have been moved (literally) by her power to motivate. Finally, Carolyn's exceptional personal qualities—her great warmth, integrity, good humor, and ability to empathize—all have made her someone whom we greatly admire and also cherish as a friend.

Our developmental editor, Jodi Devine, did a remarkable job in helping to prepare *The Essential World of Psychology*. Working against an unusually tight schedule, she never slowed her pace or lost patience. Jodi carefully scrutinized the manuscript and provided invaluable suggestions for changes and deletions. We are deeply indebted to her.

Although the production process that transforms a manuscript into a finished book is long and complex, our book was in the superbly capable hands of Susan McIntyre, Senior Editorial Production Administrator. Susan is a perfectionist who manages the many stages of the production process with great skill and precision. Fully aware of Susan's commitment to excellence, we were confident that all the parts of the process would come together smoothly.

We were exceedingly fortunate to have worked with Jane Hoover and Quica Ostrander of Lifland et al., Bookmakers. Jane skillfully and painstakingly guided and coordinated the day-to-day activities of the production process. She is a consummate professional who read all of the text revisions and scrutinized every figure and table to make sure they came together with clarity and precision. Quica, our meticulous copyeditor, carefully considered every word, made many useful suggestions, and never wavered in her attention to detail. We appreciate her contribution.

Production is one component of a successful book; marketing is another. We want to express our deep appreciation to Sandi Kirshner, Senior Vice President, Executive Publisher, who brings to her craft infectious enthusiasm and creative insight, and who is a wellspring of innovative ideas. In our travels with Joyce Nilsen, Vice President, Director of Field Marketing, we have seen her competence firsthand and learned the secret of her success. Joyce is a master of human relations with a rare ability to empathize with professors and sales representatives alike—truly understanding their wants and needs and skillfully solving problems. We also extend our thanks to Lou Kennedy, Vice President, Director of Advertising, for her outstanding role in developing the brochures, catalogs, and other materials for presenting the book and its ancillary materials.

No psychology text is considered complete without an accompanying package of ancillary materials. We are grateful to Dan Kelts of Illinois Central College for the outstanding and creative chapter Study Guides, extensive class testing of the text and learning package, and enthusiastic support of the book. Fred Whitford of Montana State University prepared the excellent *Instructor's Resource Manual*. Greg Cook, University of Wisconsin–Whitewater, prepared a comprehensive *Test Bank*.

We remain deeply indebted to our trusted colleague and friend Ward Moore, Senior Publisher's Representative, for initially bringing our manuscript to the attention of Allyn and Bacon.

All of the professionals at Allyn and Bacon work hard to maintain a standard of excellence in producing fine books. This certainly includes Bill Barke, President of Allyn and Bacon, who has kept in close touch with our book from its inception. We extend our sincere appreciation to Bill for his confidence in us and for his commitment to this project.

To Our Reviewers

Numerous reviewers were invaluable as we wrote the first three editions of *The World of Psychology*. Their help provided a solid foundation for the creation of *The Essential World of Psychology*. First, we extend our sincere appreciation to several people who adopted and reviewed the entire second edition and provided us with a wealth of valuable feedback and helpful suggestions for fine-tuning our book:

Edward Brady, Belleville Community College
David Gersh, Houston Community College–Central
Audry Guild, Houston Community College
Thomas Tutko, San Jose State University
Janet Weigel, Black Hawk College

We thank the following expert reviewers: Betsy Berger, Kansas State University; A. Jerry Bruce, Sam Houston State University; Randy Fisher, University of Central Florida; Grace Galliano, Kennesaw State University; Beverly Kopper, University of Northern Iowa; Edward Merrill, University of Alabama–Tuscaloosa.

We also thank the following survey respondents, who provided feedback for the third edition: Yukie Aida, Austin Community College–Rio Grande; Kristin Anderson, Houston Community College–Southwest; Elizabeth A. Baldwin, Austin Community College–Southwest; Joyce Bishop, Golden West College; Sandra Y. Boyd, Houston Community College–Central; Maria G. Cisneros-Solis, Austin Community College–Rio Grande; Michael R. Cline, J. Sargent Reynolds Community College; Herbert Coleman, Austin Community College–Rio Grande; Pat Crane, San Antonio College; Linda E. Flickinger, St. Clair County Community College; John H. Forthman, San Antonio College; Laura Freberg, California Polytechnic State University; Patricia Kennedy Furr, Austin Community College–Northridge; David Gersh, Houston Community College–Central; Irene Gianakos, Kent State University; Joanne C. Hsu, Houston Community College; Jennifer Jacobs, Indiana University–Southeast; Chris Jenkins-Burk, Sandhills Community College; Susan S. Maher, Austin Community College–Southwest; Duane G. McClearn, Elon College; Jim Mullen, Pierce College; Ramona Parrish, Guilford Technical Community College; Gary W. R. Patton, Indiana University of Pennsylvania; Robert J. Pellegrini, San Jose State University; Vicky Phares, University of South Florida; Paula Pile, Greensboro College; Murray Preston-Smith, Houston Community College–Southwest; George

D. Ritchie, Guilford Technical Community College; Karen Saenz, Houston Community College; Rita S. Santanello, Belleville Area College; Joyce Schaeuble, Sacramento City College; Diane Silver, Austin Community College–Northridge; Jeanne Spaulding, Houston Community College–Northwest; L. K. Springer, Glendale Community College; Jean E. Stiles, Glendale Community College; Jonathan Stone, Dutchess Community College; Deborah Van Marche, Glendale Community College; Ken R. Vincent, Houston Community College–Northwest; Andrea Wagonblast, Bowling Green State University; Marie Waung, University of Michigan–Dearborn; Janet Weigel, Black Hawk College; Gordon Whitman, Sandhills Community College; Diane E. Wille, Indiana University Southeast; Joseph A. Zizzi, Mohawk Valley Community College.

About the Authors

Samuel E. Wood received his doctorate
from the University of Florida. He has taught at
West Virginia University and the University of
Missouri–St. Louis and was a member of the
doctoral faculty at both universities. From 1984
to 1996, he served as president of the Higher
Education Center, a consortium of 14 colleges
and universities in the St. Louis area. He was a
co-founder of the Higher Education Cable TV

channel (HEC-TV) in St. Louis and served as its president and CEO from its found-
ing in 1987 until 1996. Dr. Wood is currently assistant to the president and adjunct
professor of psychology at Lindenwood University.

Ellen Green Wood received her doctorate in educational psychology from St. Louis
University and is currently an adjunct professor of psychology at St. Louis Community
College at Meramec. Previously she taught in the clinical experiences program in
education at Washington University and at the University of Missouri–St. Louis. In
addition to her teaching, Dr. Wood has developed and taught seminars on critical
thinking. She received the Telecourse Pioneer Award from 1982 through 1988 for
her contributions to the field of distance learning.

Together, Sam and Evie Wood have more than 30 years of experience teaching
introductory psychology to thousands of students of all ages, backgrounds, and abilities. *The Essential World of Psychology* is the direct result of their teaching experience.

1 Introduction to Psychology

Early in 1998, seven babies named Kenneth, Nathan, Brandon, Joel, Alexis, Natalie, and Kelsey left the hospital where they were born and went home. There was nothing unusual about this—except that all seven had the same mother and were born at the same time. These babies were the world's first surviving set of septuplets.

"They are beautiful babies," said a public relations agent representing the family. "There is something fragile but something very, very strong about them— how delicate they look and how perfectly formed. I was awestruck to see the seven in a row."

More than 40 medical professionals—including perinatologists, neonatologists, respiratory therapists, neonatal nurse practitioners, and nurses—were on call for the births, which took place on November 19, 1997. The babies, each weighing only about 2 pounds, were immediately placed in intensive care but were soon breathing on their own and gaining weight on schedule.

The babies' parents, Kenny and Bobbi McCaughey of Carlisle, Iowa, had been unable to have children until Bobbi began taking a fertility drug. Their first child, Mikayla, was born less than 2 years before the septuplets arrived. When informed that the second pregnancy would result in multiple births, the McCaugheys refused to abort some of the fetuses to improve the chances of the others. They decided, as they put it, to prepare for "a miracle."

The couple received much support from other residents of their small town (population about 3,500). A local construction company built a new house for the family using donations from many other Iowa builders and suppliers. Members of the family's church helped keep the pregnancy secret in order to deflect the media spotlight as long as possible. Other townspeople donated bassinets, diapers, and baby clothes. Friends and neighbors have helped to care for the infants.

Even with the support and aid from their community, Bobbi and Kenny McCaughey face difficult adjustments and hard work. Just feeding and diapering seven infants is almost a full-time job, and giving them the attention they need to develop into healthy, happy adults will be a major challenge.

Many people were fascinated by the story of the world's first surviving septuplets. From an event such as this spring countless questions having to do with the world of psychology. How will the McCaugheys cope with the stress of caring for seven infants at the same time? What are the physical and psychological effects of stress, and what are some effective ways to cope with it? How much sleep will the McCaugheys be able to get in a house full of infants, and how does sleep deprivation affect people? And what about the heartwarming outpouring of emotional and material support from the local community? What motivates people to help others through such acts of kindness? As for the babies themselves, what developmental risks are associated with very low birthweight? How will the septuplets differ physically, mentally, and psychologically throughout childhood, adolescence, and adulthood? Will their IQs be similar? How much will their personalities differ?

For psychologists, the McCaughey septuplets offer an unmatched opportunity to study human growth and development. But the world of psychology you are about to enter will introduce you to a range of issues far broader than those involving the "magnificent seven."

PSYCHOLOGY: AN INTRODUCTION

Many people who consider the field of psychology conjure up images of mental disorders and abnormal behavior. Psychologists do study the strange and unusual, but they are interested in the normal and commonplace as well.

Just what is psychology? Psychology has changed over the years, and so has its definition. In the late 19th century, mental processes were considered to be the appropriate subject matter of psychology. Later there was a movement to restrict psychology to the study of observable behavior alone. Today the importance of both areas is recognized, and **psychology** is now defined as the scientific study of behavior and mental processes.

psychology: The scientific study of behavior and mental processes.

Answer true or false for each statement in the *Try It!* to see how much you already know about some of the topics we will explore in *The World of Psychology*. (You'll find the answers below.)

Try It!

Indicate whether each statement is true (T) or false (F).

____ 1. Memory is more accurate under hypnosis.

____ 2. All people dream during a night of normal sleep.

____ 3. As the number of bystanders at an emergency increases, the time it takes for the victim to get help decreases.

____ 4. Humans do not have a maternal instinct.

____ 5. Older adults tend to express less satisfaction with life in general than younger adults do.

____ 6. Eyewitness testimony is often unreliable.

____ 7. Children with high IQs tend to be less able physically than their peers.

____ 8. Creativity and high intelligence do not necessarily go together.

____ 9. When it comes to close personal relationships, opposites attract.

____ 10. The majority of teenagers have good relationships with their parents.

Psychology: Science or Common Sense?

What is the scientific method?

When students begin their first course in psychology, many of them consider it more common sense than science. Will you be studying a collection of common-sense notions this semester? Or can we make a valid claim that psychology is a science? For the *Try It!* common sense might have led you astray. All of the odd-numbered items are false, and all of the even-numbered items are true.

Many people also believe that whether a field of study is considered a science depends on the nature of its body of knowledge. Physics, for example, is a science, and so is chemistry. But neither qualifies as a science solely because of its subject matter. A science is a science not because of the nature of its body of knowledge, but because the scientific method is used to acquire that body of knowledge.

The Scientific Method: A Method for All Sciences   The **scientific method** consists of the orderly, systematic procedures that researchers follow as they identify a research problem, design a study to investigate the problem, collect and analyze data, draw conclusions, and communicate their findings.

Scientists do not simply pull a research problem out of thin air. In most cases they have a well-established body of theory to guide their research. A **theory** is a general principle or set of principles proposed to explain how a number of separate facts are related. A theory enables researchers to fit many separate facts into a larger framework and thus imposes order on what would otherwise be a disconnected jumble of data. The value of a theory rests on how well it accounts for the accumulated research findings in a given area and how accurately it can predict new findings.

The scientific method is the best method known for acquiring knowledge because the information derived from it is least compromised by biases, preconceptions, personal beliefs, and emotions (Christensen, 1997). The knowledge gained is dependable because it is based on empirical evidence—data collected and measurements made directly by the researcher. Many scientific studies are published in professional journals so that they can be evaluated by other researchers.

Link It!

scientific method: The orderly, systematic procedures researchers follow as they identify a research problem, design a study to investigate the problem, collect and analyze data, draw conclusions, and communicate their findings.

theory: A general principle or set of principles proposed to explain how a number of separate facts are related.

Important, as well, are the values and attitudes scientists hold as they conduct their research. Researchers must strive to be open-minded—ready to consider new and variant explanations of behavior and mental processes. But they must also be skeptical, refusing to accept the ideas or conclusions of others in the absence of convincing evidence. Researchers must even be willing to alter or abandon their own deeply held beliefs and conclusions when faced with substantial evidence to the contrary.

What are the goals researchers in psychology seek to accomplish as they apply the scientific method in their research?

The Goals of Psychology

What are the four goals of psychology?

The goals of psychology are the description, explanation, prediction, and control of behavior and mental processes. Psychological researchers always seek to accomplish one or more of these goals when they plan and conduct their studies.

Description is usually the first step in understanding any behavior or mental process. To attain this goal, researchers tell what occurred by describing the behavior or mental process of interest as accurately and completely as possible. The second goal, *explanation*, requires an understanding of the conditions under which a given behavior or mental process occurs. Such an understanding often enables researchers to state the causes of the behavior or mental process they are studying. But researchers do not reach the goal of explanation until their results have been tested, retested, and confirmed. The goal of *prediction* is met when researchers can specify the conditions under which a behavior or event is likely to occur. Then, if researchers can identify all the antecedent (prior) conditions required for a behavior or event to occur, they can predict the behavior or event. The goal of *control* is accomplished when researchers know how to apply a principle or change a condition to prevent unwanted occurrences or to bring about desired outcomes. For example, a therapy could be designed to prevent anxiety attacks.

The two types of research psychologists pursue to accomplish their goals are (1) basic, or pure, research and (2) applied research. The purpose of **basic research** is to seek new knowledge and to explore and advance general scientific understanding. Basic research explores such topics as the nature of memory, brain function, motivation, and emotional expression. **Applied research** is conducted specifically for the purpose of solving practical problems and improving the quality of life. Applied research focuses on such concerns as methods to improve memory or increase motivation, therapies to treat psychological disorders, ways to decrease stress, and so on. Applied research is primarily concerned with the fourth goal—control—because it specifies ways and means of changing behavior.

Critical Thinking: Thinking Like a Scientist

basic research: Research conducted to advance knowledge rather than for its practical application.

applied research: Research conducted to solve practical problems.

critical thinking: The process of objectively evaluating claims, propositions, or conclusions to determine whether they follow logically from the evidence presented.

descriptive research methods: Research methods that yield descriptions of behavior rather than causal explanations.

naturalistic observation: A research method in which the researcher observes and records behavior in its natural setting, without attempting to influence or control it.

Living in the "information age" means being bombarded daily with information on every conceivable subject. The critical thinking skills scientists use are necessary to sift through all of this information, pick out the true and useful, discard the false and misleading, and make intelligent decisions. **Critical thinking** is the process of objectively evaluating claims, propositions, or conclusions to determine whether they follow logically from the evidence presented.

Critical thinkers share some important characteristics:

■ They are independent thinkers. Critical thinkers do not automatically accept and believe what they read or hear. They carefully analyze and evaluate the evidence and the reasoning presented. They are able to recognize manipulative emotional appeals, spot unsupported assumptions, and detect faulty logic.

■ They are willing to suspend judgment. Critical thinkers do not make snap judgments; they gather and consider the most relevant and up-to-date information on all sides of an issue before taking a position.

■ They are willing to modify or abandon prior judgments, including deeply held beliefs. Critical thinkers evaluate new evidence or experience that contradicts their existing beliefs. If they find it valid, they modify their beliefs to accommodate it.

To think critically about information you encounter in this text and in the popular media, it is important to (1) understand the various research methods psychologists use to achieve their goals, (2) know the advantages and limitations of these methods, and (3) be able to identify the elements that distinguish good research.

Link It!

DESCRIPTIVE RESEARCH METHODS

The goals of psychological research—description, explanation, prediction, and control—are typically accomplished in stages. In the early stages of research, descriptive research methods are usually the most appropriate. **Descriptive research methods** yield descriptions rather than explanations of the causes of behavior. Naturalistic observation, the case study, and the survey are examples of descriptive research methods.

Naturalistic Observation: Caught in the Act of Being Themselves

Naturalistic observation is a research method in which the researchers observe and record behavior in its natural setting without attempting to influence or control it. Ethologists are researchers who study the behavior patterns of animals in their natural environment. They might observe their subjects through high-powered telescopes or from blinds that they build to conceal themselves.

Often human subjects are not aware that they are being observed. This can be accomplished by means of one-way mirrors, a technique researchers often use to observe children in nursery schools or special classrooms. You may have seen episodes of *60 Minutes* or *20/20* or reruns of *Candid Camera* in which hidden cameras or tape recorders were used to gather information from unsuspecting subjects "caught in the act of being themselves."

What is naturalistic observation, and what are some of its advantages and limitations?

The major advantage of naturalistic observation is the opportunity to study behavior in normal settings. Here behavior occurs more naturally and spontaneously than it would under artificial and contrived laboratory conditions. Sometimes naturalistic observation is the only feasible way to study certain phenomena that would be either impossible or unethical to set up as an experiment, such as how people typically react during disasters like earthquakes or fires.

Naturalistic observation has its limitations, however. Researchers must wait for events to occur; they cannot speed up or slow down the process. And because they have no control over the situation, researchers cannot reach conclusions about cause-and-effect relationships. Another potential problem in naturalistic observation is *observer bias*, which can result when researchers' expectations about a situation cause them to see what they expect to see or to make incorrect inferences about the behavior they observe. The accuracy of observations can be improved substantially when two or more observers view the same behavior or when the behavior is videotaped.

Although naturalistic observation allows researchers to study behavior in everyday settings, observer bias may cause them to see what they expect to see.

Another method of observation takes place not in its natural setting, but in the laboratory. There researchers can exert more control and use more precise equipment to measure responses. Much of what is known about sleep or the human sexual response, for example, has been learned through laboratory observation.

The Case Study Method: Studying a Few Individuals in Depth

What is the case study method, and for what purposes is it particularly well suited?

The **case study**, or case history, is another descriptive research method used by psychologists. In a case study, a single individual or a small number of persons are studied in great depth, usually over an extended period of time. A case study involves the use of observation, interviews, and sometimes psychological testing. The case study is exploratory in nature, and its purpose is to provide a detailed description of some behavior or disorder. This method is particularly appropriate for studying people who have uncommon psychological or physiological disorders or brain injuries. You may have read the book or seen the movie *Sybil*, the case study of a young woman who had multiple personalities. Much of what is known about unusual psychological disorders such as multiple personality, now known as dissociative identity disorder, comes from the in-depth analyses provided by case studies.

Case studies have provided the foundation for psychological theories. The theory of Sigmund Freud is based primarily on case studies of his own patients.

Although the case study has proven useful in advancing knowledge in several areas of psychology, it has certain limitations. Researchers cannot establish the cause of behaviors observed in a case study, and observer bias is a potential problem. Moreover, because so few individuals are studied, researchers do not know how applicable, or generalizable, their findings may be to larger groups or to different cultures.

Survey Research: The Art of Sampling and Questioning

What are the methods and purposes of survey research?

The **survey** is a method in which researchers use interviews and/or questionnaires to gather information about the attitudes, beliefs, experiences, or behaviors of a group of people. The results of carefully conducted surveys have provided much of the information available about the incidence of drug use, about sexual behaviors of particular segments of the population, and about the incidence of various mental disorders. But survey results are strongly affected by wording, context, and format (Schwarz, 1999).

What is a representative sample, and why is it essential in a survey?

Selecting a Sample   Researchers in psychology rarely conduct experiments or surveys using all members of the group they would like to study. For example, researchers interested in studying the sexual behavior of American women do not attempt to study every woman in the United States. Instead of studying the whole **population** (the entire group of interest to researchers and to which they wish to apply their findings), the researchers select a sample for study. A **sample** is a part of a population that is selected and studied in order to reach conclusions about the entire population of interest.

Perhaps you have seen a carton of ice cream that contains three separate flavors packed side by side—chocolate, strawberry, and vanilla. To properly sample the carton, you would need a small amount of ice cream containing all three flavors in the same proportions as in the whole carton—a representative sample. A **representative sample** is one that mirrors the population of interest—that is, it includes important subgroups in the same proportions as they are found in that population. A *biased sample*, on the other hand, does not adequately reflect the larger population.

The most common method for obtaining a sample that is representative is to select a random sample from a list of all members of the population of interest. Participants are selected in such a way that every member of the larger population has an equal chance of being included in the sample. To obtain random samples, researchers use a procedure based on chance, such as pulling names out of a hat or using a table of random numbers generated by a computer. By using highly sophisticated polling techniques, organizations such as Gallup and Roper can accurately represent the views of the American public with carefully chosen samples as small as 1,000 people (O'Brien, 1996).

Interviews and Questionnaires: Researchers using the survey method rely on information gathered through *interviews, questionnaires,* or some combination of the two. But the validity or truthfulness of the responses can be affected by personal characteristics of the interviewers, such as their gender, age, racial or ethnic background, religion, social class, accent, and vocabulary. In general, male interviewers obtain less information than do female interviewers. And people are most inhibited when they give personal information to interviewers who are of the same age but the opposite sex. Skilled survey researchers, therefore, must select interviewers who have personal characteristics that are appropriate for the intended respondents.

Surveys that use questionnaires can be completed more quickly and less expensively than those involving interviews. The largest survey ever taken of the sexual behavior of American women was conducted by *Cosmopolitan* magazine (Wolfe, 1981). About 106,000 women—3.5% of *Cosmopolitan* readers—completed and returned a questionnaire that had appeared in the magazine. Two-thirds of the respondents claimed to have had 5 to 25 sexual partners, and a high percentage reported having had intercourse with more than one partner on the same day. Do these results reflect the sexual behavior of American women in general?

The number of people who respond to a survey is not the most critical element. A researcher can generalize findings from a sample *only* if it is representative of the entire population of interest. The *Cosmopolitan* survey was a biased sample: The readers of *Cosmopolitan* magazine do not represent a cross-section of American women. Furthermore, the response rate was only 3.5% of the magazine's readers and, therefore, probably didn't even reflect the behavior of that group as a whole. It is possible that those women who chose to respond to the survey were more sexually active—or less sexually active—than the average reader.

The critical point to remember is that surveys based on questionnaires appearing in magazines or on phone-in responses by TV viewers are not scientific. If a sample is not representative, it doesn't matter how many people are in that sample.

Advantages and Disadvantages of Survey Research   If worded and conducted properly, surveys can provide highly accurate information. They can also track changes in attitudes or behavior over time. For example, Johnston, O'Malley, and Bachmann (1997) have tracked drug use among high school students since 1975. But such large-scale surveys can be costly and time-consuming.

The major limitation of the survey is that the respondents may provide inaccurate information. False information can result from a faulty memory or a desire to please the interviewer. Respondents may try to present themselves in a good light (called the *social desirability response*), or they may even deliberately attempt to mislead the researcher. Finally, when respondents answer questions about sensitive subjects, such as sexual behavior and the use of alcohol and drugs, they are often less candid in face-to-face interviews than in self-administered questionnaires (Tourangeau et al., 1997).

THE EXPERIMENTAL METHOD: SEARCHING FOR CAUSES

The descriptive research methods (naturalistic observation, the case study, and the survey) are all well suited for satisfying the first goal of psychology—description. But at some point researchers usually seek to determine the causes of behavior and various other psychological phenomena. What, for example, are the causes of depression, insomnia, stress, forgetting, and aggression?

The results of carefully conducted surveys have provided valuable information about a wide variety of human behaviors.

case study: An in-depth study of one or a few individuals consisting of information gathered through observation, interview, and perhaps psychological testing.

survey: A method in which researchers use interviews and/or questionnaires to gather information about the attitudes, beliefs, experiences, or behaviors of a group of people.

population: The entire group of interest to researchers and to which they wish to generalize their findings; the group from which a sample is selected.

sample: The portion of any population that is selected for study and from which generalizations are made about the larger population.

representative sample: A sample of participants selected from the larger population in such a way that important subgroups within the population are included in the sample in the same proportions as they are found in the larger population.

What is the main advantage of the experimental method?

experimental method: The research method in which researchers randomly assign participants to groups and control all conditions other than one or more independent variables, which are then manipulated to determine their effect on some behavioral measure—the dependent variable in the experiment.

hypothesis: A prediction about the relationship between two or more variables.

independent variable: In an experiment, the factor or condition that the researcher manipulates in order to determine its effect on another behavior or condition known as the dependent variable.

dependent variable: The variable that is measured at the end of an experiment and is presumed to vary as a result of manipulations of the independent variable.

experimental group: In an experiment, the group that is exposed to the independent variable, or the treatment.

control group: In an experiment, a group that is similar to the experimental group and is exposed to the same experimental environment but is not exposed to the independent variable; used for purposes of comparison.

The **experimental method**, or the experiment, is the *only* research method that can be used to identify cause–effect relationships. An experiment is designed to test a **hypothesis**—a prediction about a cause–effect relationship between two or more conditions or variables. A *variable* is any condition or factor that can be manipulated, controlled, or measured. One variable of interest to you is the grade you will receive in this psychology course. Another variable that probably interests you is the amount of time you will spend studying for this course. Do you suppose there is a cause–effect relationship between the amount of time students spend studying and the grades they receive?

Consider two other variables—alcohol consumption and aggression. Alcohol consumption and aggressive behavior are often observed together. We can assume that there is likely to be more aggression among drinkers in a lively tavern than among a gathering of nondrinkers in a discussion group. But can we assume that the alcohol consumption itself causes the aggressive behavior?

Alan Lang and his colleagues (1975) conducted an experiment to determine if alcohol consumption itself increases aggression or if the beliefs or expectations about the effects of alcohol cause the aggressive behavior. Participants in the experiment were 96 male college students who were classified as heavy social drinkers. Half the students were given plain tonic to drink; the other half were given a vodka-and-tonic drink in amounts sufficient to raise their blood alcohol level to .10, which, in many states, is the legal limit of intoxication. Participants were assigned to four groups:

Group 1: Expected alcohol/Received only tonic
Group 2: Expected alcohol/Received alcohol mixed with tonic
Group 3: Expected tonic/Received alcohol mixed with tonic
Group 4: Expected tonic/Received only tonic

You might think that heavy social drinkers could detect the difference between plain tonic and a one-to-five mixture of vodka and tonic. But during pilot testing, drinkers could distinguish between the two with no more than 50% accuracy (Marlatt & Rohsenow, 1981).

After the students had consumed the designated amount, the researchers had a confederate—an accomplice who posed as a participant—purposely provoke half of the students by belittling their performance on a difficult task. All the students then participated in a learning experiment in which the same confederate posed as the learner. The subjects were told to administer an electric shock to the confederate each time he made a mistake on a decoding task. Each participant was allowed to determine the intensity and duration of the "shock." (Although the students believed they were shocking the confederate, no shocks were actually delivered.) The researchers measured the aggressiveness of the students in terms of the duration and the intensity of the shocks they chose to deliver.

As you might imagine, the students who had been provoked gave the confederate stronger shocks than those who had not been provoked. But the students who drank the alcohol were not necessarily the most aggressive. Regardless of the actual content of their drinks, the participants who thought they were drinking alcohol gave significantly stronger shocks, whether provoked or not, than those who assumed they were drinking only tonic (see Figure 1.1). The researchers concluded that it was the expectation of drinking alcohol, not the alcohol itself, that caused the aggression.

Independent and Dependent Variables

What is the difference between the independent variable and the dependent variable?

In all experiments there are two types of variables. First, there are one or more **independent variables**—variables that the researcher manipulates in order to determine whether they cause any change in another behavior or condition. Sometimes the independent variable is referred to as the *treatment*. In the Lang experiment there were two independent variables—the alcoholic content of the drink and the expectation of drinking alcohol.

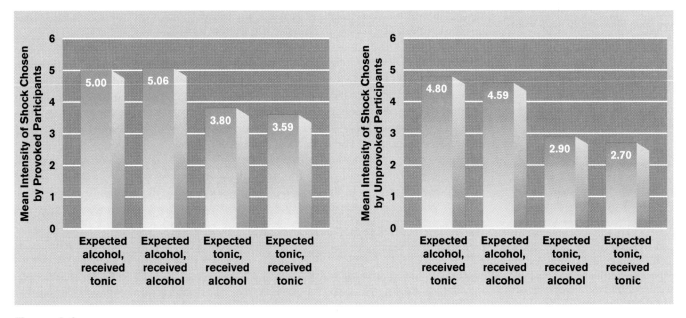

Figure 1.1

Mean Intensity of Shock Chosen by Provoked and Unprovoked Participants

In the Lang experiment, participants who thought they were drinking alcohol chose to give significantly stronger shocks, whether provoked or not, than those who believed they were drinking only tonic. (Data from Lang et al., 1975.)

The second type of variable found in all experiments is the **dependent variable**. It is measured at the end of the experiment and is presumed to vary (increase or decrease) as a result of the manipulations of the independent variable(s). The dependent variable is presumed to depend on or to be affected by changes in the independent variable. Researchers must provide operational definitions of all variables in an experiment—that is, they must specify precisely how the variables will be observed and measured. In the Lang study the dependent variable—aggression—was operationally defined as the intensity and duration of the "shocks" the participants chose to deliver to the confederate.

Experimental and Control Groups: The Same Except for the Treatment

Most experiments are conducted using two or more groups of participants. There must always be at least one **experimental group**—a group of participants who are exposed to the independent variable, or the treatment. The Lang experiment used three experimental groups:

How do the experimental and control groups differ?

Group 1: Expected alcohol/Received only tonic
Group 2: Expected alcohol/Received alcohol mixed with tonic
Group 3: Expected tonic/Received alcohol mixed with tonic

In most experiments it is desirable to have a **control group**—a group that is similar to the experimental group and used for purposes of comparison. The control group is exposed to the same experimental environment as the experimental group but is not given the treatment. The fourth group in the Lang study was not exposed to either of the two independent variables; that is, this group did not expect alcohol and did not receive alcohol. Because this group was similar to the experimental groups and was exposed to the same experimental environment, it served as a con-

selection bias: The assignment of participants to experimental or control groups in such a way that systematic differences among the groups are present at the beginning of the experiment.

random assignment: In an experiment, the assignment of participants to experimental and control groups by using a chance procedure, which guarantees that each has an equal probability of being placed in any of the groups; a control for selection bias.

placebo effect: The phenomenon that occurs when a person's response to a treatment or response on the dependent variable in an experiment is due to expectations regarding the treatment rather than to the treatment itself.

trol group. In an experiment, all groups, including the control group, are measured on the dependent variable at the end of the experiment.

Sometimes an experiment is affected by *confounding variables*—factors or conditions other than the independent variable that are not equivalent across groups and that could cause differences among the groups on the dependent variable. By conducting their experiment in a laboratory, Lang and his colleagues were able to control the experimental environment to eliminate such possible confounding variables as frustration, pain, and extreme noise or heat, which could have increased aggressive responses. The researchers altered only the independent variables—the students' expectations and the content of their drinks. That way, the researchers could be reasonably sure that the manipulation of those independent variables caused the differences in the degree of aggression among the groups.

Generalizing the Experimental Findings: Do the Findings Apply to Other Groups?

What should be concluded from the Lang experiment? Can we conclude that people in general tend to be more aggressive when they believe they are under the influence of alcohol? Before reaching such a conclusion, we must consider several factors: (1) All participants in this experiment were male college students. We cannot be sure that the same results would have occurred if females or males of other ages had been included. (2) The participants in this experiment were classified as heavy social drinkers. Would the same results have occurred if nondrinkers, moderate social drinkers, or alcoholics had been included? To apply this experiment's findings to other groups, researchers would have to replicate, or repeat, the experiment using different populations of subjects. (3) The amount of alcohol given to the students was just enough to bring their blood alcohol level to .10. We cannot be sure that the same results would have occurred if they had consumed more or less alcohol.

Potential Problems in Experimental Research

If an experiment is properly designed and conducted, the researcher should be able to attribute changes in the dependent variable to the manipulations of the independent variable. But several factors other than the independent variables can cause changes in the dependent variable and, therefore, destroy the validity of an experiment. Three of these potential problems (confounding variables) are selection bias, the placebo effect, and experimenter bias.

What is selection bias, and what technique do researchers use to control for it?

Selection Bias   Selection bias occurs when participants are assigned to groups in such a way that systematic differences among the groups are present at the beginning of the experiment. If selection bias occurs, then differences at the end of the experiment may not reflect the manipulation of the independent variable but may be due to preexisting differences in the groups.

To control for selection bias, researchers must use **random assignment**. This means selecting participants by using a chance procedure (such as drawing the names of participants out of a hat) to guarantee that all participants have an equal probability of being assigned to any of the groups. Random assignment maximizes the likelihood that the groups will be as similar as possible at the beginning of the experiment. If there were preexisting differences in the level of aggressiveness of students in Lang's alcohol experiment, random assignment should have spread those differences across groups.

What is the placebo effect, and how do researchers control for it?

The Placebo Effect   Another factor that can influence the outcome of an experiment is the placebo effect. The **placebo effect** occurs when a participant's response to a treatment is due to his or her expectations about the treatment rather than to the treatment itself. Suppose a drug is prescribed for a patient and the patient reports improvement. The improvement could be a direct result of the drug, or it could be a result of the patient's expectation that the drug will work. Studies have shown that sometimes remarkable improvement in patients can be attributed solely to the power of suggestion—the placebo effect.

A researcher must use a control group to test whether results in an experiment are due to the treatment or to the placebo effect. So participants in the control group are given a fake treatment. In drug experiments, the control group is usually given a **placebo**—an inert, or harmless, substance such as a sugar pill or an injection of saline solution. To control for the placebo effect, researchers do not let participants know whether they are in the experimental group (receiving the treatment) or in the control group (receiving the placebo). If participants getting the real drug or treatment show a significantly greater improvement than those receiving the placebo, then the improvement can be attributed to the drug rather than to the power of suggestion. In the Lang experiment, some students who expected alcohol mixed with tonic were given only tonic. The tonic without alcohol functioned as a placebo. This enabled the researchers to measure the effect of the power of suggestion alone in producing aggression.

The placebo effect can invalidate the results of experiments when researchers do not take participants' expectations into account. But what about the expectations of those who conduct the experiments—the researchers themselves?

Experimenter Bias   The expectations of the experimenter can influence the outcome of an experiment. **Experimenter bias** occurs when researchers' preconceived notions or expectations become a self-fulfilling prophecy and cause the researchers to find what they expect to find. A researcher's expectations can be communicated to participants, perhaps unintentionally, through tone of voice, gestures, or facial expression, which may influence the participants' behavior. Expectations can also influence a researcher's interpretation of the experimental results, even if no influence occurred during the experiment.

To control for experimenter bias, researchers must not know which participants are assigned to the experimental and control groups until after the research data are collected and recorded. (Obviously, someone assisting the researcher does know.) When neither the participants nor the experimenter knows which participants are getting the treatment and which are in the control group, the experiment is using the **double-blind technique**.

Advantages and Limitations of the Experimental Method

The overwhelming advantage of the experiment is its ability to reveal cause–effect relationships. This benefit is possible because researchers are able to exercise strict control over the experimental setting. This allows them to rule out factors other than the independent variable as possible reasons for differences in the dependent variable. But often the more control the experimenter exercises, the more unnatural and contrived the research setting becomes and the less generalizable findings may be to the real world. When participants know that they are taking part in an experiment, their behavior may be different from what it would be in a more natural setting. When a natural setting is considered to be an important factor in a study, researchers may choose to use a *field experiment*—an experiment conducted in a real-life setting. Although some control over the experimental environment is sacrificed, the advantage is more natural behavior on the part of the participants.

A major limitation of the experimental method is that in many areas of interest to psychologists this method is either unethical or not possible. Some treatments cannot be given to human participants because their physical or psychological health would be endangered, or their constitutional rights violated.

placebo (pluh-SEE-bo): Some inert substance, such as a sugar pill or an injection of saline solution, given to the control group in an experiment as a control for the placebo effect.

experimenter bias: A phenomenon that occurs when the researcher's preconceived notions in some way influence the participants' behavior and/or the interpretation of experimental results.

double-blind technique: An experimental procedure in which neither the participants nor the experimenter knows who is in the experimental or control groups until after the results have been gathered; a control for experimenter bias.

What is experimenter bias, and how is it controlled?

OTHER RESEARCH METHODS

The Correlational Method: Discovering Relationships, Not Causes

What is the correlational method, and when is it used?

Does stress cause illness? Does smoking cause cancer? Does heavy marijuana use cause students to lose interest in school and get lower grades? Researchers would like to have answers to these questions, but none of them can be studied using the experimental method. It is often illegal and always unethical to assign people randomly to experimental conditions that could be harmful. For example, to find out if smoking marijuana causes a decline in academic achievement, no researcher would randomly assign high school students to an experimental study that would require students in the experimental groups to smoke marijuana. Can you imagine a principal notifying parents that their son or daughter had been chosen to smoke marijuana for 2 years in order to further scientific knowledge?

When, for ethical reasons, an experimental study cannot be performed to determine cause–effect relationships, the **correlational method** is usually used. This research method determines the correlation, or degree of relationship, between two characteristics, events, or behaviors. A group is selected for study, and the variables of interest are measured for each participant in the study. For example, the variables might be amount of marijuana previously used and grade point average. Then the researcher applies a statistical formula to obtain a correlation coefficient.

What is a correlation coefficient?

The Correlation Coefficient   A **correlation coefficient** is a numerical value indicating the degree and direction of the relationship between two variables. A correlation coefficient ranges from +1.00 (a perfect positive correlation) to .00 (no relationship) to –1.00 (a perfect negative correlation). The number in a correlation coefficient indicates the relative *strength* of the relationship between two variables—the higher the number, the stronger the relationship. Therefore, a correlation of –.85 is higher than a correlation of +.64.

The sign of a correlation coefficient (+ or –) indicates whether the two variables vary in the same or opposite directions. A positive correlation indicates that two variables vary in the same direction. For example, there is a positive though weak correlation between stress and illness. When stress increases, illness is likely to increase; when stress decreases, illness tends to decrease. A negative correlation means that an increase in the value of one variable is associated with a decrease in the value of the other variable. There is a negative correlation between the number of cigarettes people smoke and the number of years they can expect to live.

Correlations are useful in making predictions—the stronger the relationship between the variables, the better the prediction. A perfect correlation (+1.00 or –1.00) would enable you to make completely accurate predictions. For more information on correlations, see the Appendix.

Psychological Tests: Assessing the Individual

Psychologists have developed a wide range of tests for measuring intelligence, scholastic achievement, aptitudes, creativity, vocational interests, personality traits, and psychiatric problems. As a student, you have taken some of these tests—IQ tests, SAT or ACT, Iowa Test of Basic Skills or California Achievement Test, Kuder Preference Test or Strong Interest Inventory, to name a few. Psychological tests are used in schools, in the workplace, and in therapeutic settings. These tests are used to evaluate or compare individuals, to measure changes in behavior, and to make predictions about behavior. Test results also provide information that can be used in educational decision making, personnel selection, and vocational guidance. But psychological tests are useless unless they have proven reliability and validity.

correlational method: A research method used to establish the degree of relationship (correlation) between two characteristics, events, or behaviors.

correlation coefficient: A numerical value that indicates the strength and direction of the relationship between two variables; ranges from +1.00 (a perfect positive correlation) to –1.00 (a perfect negative correlation).

reliability: The ability of a test to yield nearly the same scores when the same people are tested and then retested using the same test or an alternate form of the test.

validity: The ability of a test to measure what it is intended to measure.

Reliability refers to the consistency of a test. A reliable test will yield nearly the same score time after time if the same person is tested and then retested. **Validity** is a test's ability to measure what it is intended to measure. Just as a clock is a valid instrument only for measuring time, so a psychological test must be able to measure accurately and adequately the specific area it is designed to measure—vocational aptitude or scholastic achievement, for example. (Reliability and validity will be discussed in more detail in Chapter 7.)

Psychologists often use testing in conjunction with their research. For example, tests may be administered as part of a case study, and the dependent variable in an experiment might be the score on a psychological test. Tests are also used in correlation studies. For instance, researchers may statistically compare individuals' SAT scores with their college grades to determine the correlation between the scores and grades.

replication: The process of repeating a study with different participants and preferably a different investigator to verify research findings.

meta-analysis: A complex statistical procedure used to combine the results from many studies on the same topic in order to determine the degree to which a hypothesis can be supported.

Meta-Analysis: Combining the Results of Many Studies

To verify research findings, it is necessary that studies be replicated. **Replication** is the repeating of studies with the same procedures, but with different participants and preferably different investigators. If the results of a study are scientifically valid, a careful replication of the study should yield similar results.

What is meta-analysis?

But what if some replications find evidence of strong support for a hypothesis, while others find evidence to the contrary? Fortunately, there is a way researchers can average or combine the results of all such studies and reach conclusions about what the weight of evidence shows in the particular area of research.

Using a complex statistical technique known as **meta-analysis**, researchers can combine the results from many separate studies on the same topic to determine the strength of support for a hypothesis. For example, Janet Hyde and Marcia Lynn (1988) used meta-analysis to examine 165 studies reporting test results on verbal ability for about 1.5 million males and females. Their meta-analysis revealed no significant gender differences in verbal ability.

Review & Reflect 1.1 (on page 14) summarizes the different types of research methods we've discussed in this chapter.

PARTICIPANTS IN PSYCHOLOGICAL RESEARCH

Ethics in Research: Protecting the Participants

In 1992 the American Psychological Association (APA) adopted a new set of ethical standards governing research with human participants so as to safeguard their rights while supporting the goals of scientific inquiry. Following are some of the main provisions of the code: Participation in research must be strictly voluntary, and participants must give *informed consent*. This means that they must be informed in advance about (1) the nature of the research, (2) any factors—risks, discomfort, or unpleasant emotional experiences—that might affect their willingness to participate, and (3) their freedom to decline to participate or to withdraw from the research at any time.

What are some ethical guidelines governing the use of human participants in research?

What about deception? Is it ethical for researchers to lie to participants or otherwise mislead them in order to conduct their studies? Clearly, without deception some research, such as the Lang experiment, could not be conducted, or the knowledge gained. Psychologist Diane Baumrind (1985) opposes research using deception because of the potential harm to the participants. She also believes that such practices will damage the reputation of psychology and psychologists and cause people to lose confidence in the profession.

Today the APA's code of ethical standards allows deception (1) if it is justified by the value of the potential findings, provided that equally effective procedures that do not involve deception cannot be used; (2) if participants are not deceived

Method	Description	Advantages	Limitations
Naturalistic observation	Observation and recording of behavior in its natural setting. Subjects may or may not know that they are being observed.	Provides descriptive information. Can provide basis for hypotheses to be tested later. Behavior studied in everyday setting is more natural.	Researchers' expectations can distort observations (observer bias). Presence of researcher may influence behavior of subjects. Researcher has little or no control over conditions.
Case study	In-depth study of one or a few individuals using observation, interview, and/or psychological testing.	Source of information for rare or unusual conditions or events. Can provide basis for hypotheses to be tested later.	May not be representative of condition or event. Time-consuming. Subject to misinterpretation by researcher.
Survey	Interviews and/or questionnaires used to gather information about attitudes, beliefs, experiences, or behaviors of a group of people.	Can provide accurate information about large numbers of people. Can track changes in attitudes and behavior over time.	Responses may be inaccurate. Sample may not be representative. Characteristics of interviewer may influence responses.
Experimental method	Random assignment of participants to groups. Manipulation of the independent variable(s) and measurement of its effect on the dependent variable.	Enables identification of cause–effect relationships.	Laboratory setting may inhibit natural behavior of participants. Findings may not be generalizable to the real world. In some cases, experiment is unethical.
Correlational method	Method used to determine the relationship (correlation) between two events, characteristics, or behaviors.	Can assess strength of relationship between variables. Provides basis for prediction.	Does not demonstrate cause and effect.
Psychological tests	Tests used for measuring intelligence, scholastic achievement, aptitudes, vocational interests, personality traits, or psychiatric problems.	Provide data for educational and vocational decision making, personnel selection, research, and psychological assessment.	Tests may not be reliable or valid.
Meta-analysis	Statistical method of combining the results from many research studies to determine whether a hypothesis is supported.	Provides an overall estimate of the combined effects of many studies on the same topic.	Findings can be no more reliable than the research on which they are based.

about "physical risks, discomfort, or unpleasant emotional experiences" that might affect their willingness to participate; and (3) if participants are debriefed as soon as possible after the experiment. The debriefing sessions provide information about the nature of the research and clear up any misconceptions about what occurred. In the Lang study, debriefing interviews informed students of the deception and revealed to them that no electric shocks were actually used.

Human Participants in Psychological Research: The Challenge of Diversity

Each year the population of the United States becomes more diverse, and this trend will continue. Projections by the U.S. Bureau of the Census (1997) indicate that the percentage of non-Hispanic Whites in the United States is expected to decrease from 72% in the year 2000 to 53% in 2050. During this same period the percentage of Asian Americans in the overall population is projected to increase from 4.1% to 11.4%; that of African Americans, from 12.2% to 13.6%; and that of Hispanic Americans, from 11.4% to 24.5%. Because of a longer life expectancy, the percentage of older adults in the U.S. population is also rising.

Is this diversity reflected in the participants in psychological studies? The answer is no. For practical reasons, the majority of studies with human participants in the last 30 years have used college students. Psychology studies have also used disproportionate numbers of males (Gannon et al., 1992) and of Whites (Graham, 1992).

Heavy reliance on college students presents a problem. College students are a relatively select group in terms of age, socioeconomic class, and educational level. Thus, they are not representative of the general population. However, studies that investigate basic psychological processes such as sensation, perception, and memory are likely to be relatively generalizable, because these processes probably function in similar ways in most adults. But there is great cultural and individual variation in human social behavior and thus a problem in generalizing the results of many studies with college students to other segments of the population. To adequately understand human behavior, researchers must not only know how people are alike but also understand and appreciate how they differ.

Because college students are a convenient group for professors to study, research results often do not reflect the characteristics of the more diverse general population.

Bias in Psychological Research

Several researchers have cited evidence of bias in psychological research, including gender bias (Gannon et al., 1992), racial bias, and age bias.

In their studies of gender bias in psychological research, Ader and Johnson (1994) found that bias is still very much in evidence in reports of research findings and in discussion of single-sex studies. When conducting research in which all of the participants are of one sex, these authors ask, why do researchers consider it important to specify the gender of the sample clearly when it is female, but not when the sample is exclusively male? Such a practice, say Ader and Johnson, reveals a "tendency to consider male participants 'normative,' and results obtained from them generally applicable, whereas female participants are somehow 'different,' and results obtained from them are specific to female participants" (pp. 217–218). On a positive note, however, these researchers report that over the decades, gender bias in the sampling and selection of research participants has decreased.

Investigating race bias, Sandra Graham (1992) reported finding a decline in research on African Americans in psychological journals. And prominent among the research articles that she did find was what she termed a methodological flaw—failure to include socioeconomic status—in research comparing White and African Americans. Graham points out that African Americans are overrepresented among those who are economically disadvantaged. She maintains that socioeconomic status should be incorporated into research designs "to disentangle race and social class effects" in studies that compare White and African Americans (p. 634).

Ageism is another continuing source of bias, especially apparent in the language used in psychological research (Schaie, 1993). For example, the titles of research on aging tend to focus heavily on loss, deterioration, decline, and dependency. Moreover, researchers are too likely to understate the great diversity among the older adults they study. According to Schaie (1993), "most research on adulthood shows that differences between those in their 60s and those in their 80s are far greater than those between 20- and 60-year-olds" (p. 50). Researchers should guard against descriptions or conclusions implying that all members of a given age group are defined by deterioration, forgetfulness, and deficits.

The Use of Animals in Research

Why are animals used in research?

Link It!

Where would psychology be today without the laboratory rat, Pavlov's salivating dogs, the pigeon, and the many other species of animals used to advance scientific knowledge? Yet animals are used in only 7–8% of psychological experiments, and 95% of the animals used are rodents (Gallup & Suarez, 1985).

Why are animals used in research? There are at least six reasons. Animals are used in experimental studies because (1) they provide a simpler model for studying processes that operate similarly in humans; (2) researchers can exercise far more control over animal subjects and thus be more certain of their conclusions; (3) a wider range of medical and other manipulations can be used with animals; (4) it is easier to study the entire life span and even multiple generations in some animal species; (5) animals are more economical to use and are available at the researchers' convenience; and (6) some researchers simply want to learn more about the animals themselves.

Animal research has yielded much knowledge about the brain and the physiology of vision, hearing, and the other senses (Domjan & Purdy, 1995). It has also increased knowledge in the areas of learning, motivation, stress, memory, and the effects on the unborn of various drugs ingested during pregnancy. Almost half of the research funded by the National Institutes of Health is conducted on animals (Cork et al., 1997). And virtually all of the marvels of modern medicine are due at least in part to experimentation using animals.

The APA has always supported the use of animals in research, and its code of ethics supports the humane treatment of animals. According to the association's guidelines governing animal research, researchers must do everything possible to minimize discomfort, pain, and illness in animal subjects (APA, 1992b).

Nevertheless, a storm of controversy surrounds the research use of animals. Many animal rights advocates want all animal research stopped immediately. Some have even broken into laboratories, freed laboratory animals, destroyed records, and wrecked equipment and other property. Books on animal rights devote an average of 63.3% of their content to the use of animals in research (Nicholl & Russell, 1990). Yet, of the 6,309 million animals killed each year in the United States, only 0.3% are used in research and education, while 96.5% are used for food, 2.6% are killed by hunters, 0.4% are killed in animal shelters, and 0.2% are used for fur garments (Christensen, 1997).

In a recent survey of almost 4,000 randomly selected members of the APA, "80% of respondents expressed general support for psychological research on animals" (Plous, 1996, p. 1177). Among the general public, support for animal research is higher when the research is tied to human health and highest when the animals involved in such research are rats and mice rather than dogs, cats, or primates (Plous, 1996).

Overall, the animal rights controversy has served to increase concern for the treatment of animals as research subjects, and today "the number of animals used in laboratory experiments is going down" (Mukerjee, 1997, p. 86). The book *Animal Experimentation* (Orlans et al., 1998) has well-balanced coverage of this controversial subject.

Most psychologists recognize that many scientific advances would not have been possible without animal research. Where do you stand on this issue?

EXPLORING PSYCHOLOGY'S ROOTS

If you were to trace the development of psychology from the beginning, you would need to stretch far back to the earliest pages of recorded history, even beyond the early Greek philosophers, such as Aristotle and Plato. People have always had questions about human nature and human behavior. For centuries these questions were the subject of speculation and were considered to be in the realm of philosophy. It was not until experimental methods were applied to the study of psychological processes that psychology became recognized as a formal academic discipline.

The Founding of Psychology

Three German physiologists—Ernst Weber, Gustav Fechner, and Hermann von Helmholtz—pioneered in the application of experimental methods to the study of psychological processes, and they profoundly influenced the early development of psychology. But it is Wilhelm Wundt (1832–1920) who is generally thought of as the "father of psychology."

Wundt established a psychological laboratory at the University of Leipzig in Germany in 1879. This event is considered to mark the birth of psychology as a formal academic discipline. Wundt's primary purpose was to identify the elements of consciousness and to discover the laws that govern how those elements are connected. He believed that consciousness could be reduced to its basic elements, just as water (H_2O) can be broken down into its constitutent elements—hydrogen (H) and oxygen (O). For Wundt pure sensations—such as sweetness, coldness, or redness—were the basic elements of consciousness. And these pure sensations, he believed, combined to form perceptions.

But conscious experience can be observed only by the person having that experience. Therefore, research on the experience necessarily involves self-observation, or introspection. *Introspection* as a research method involves looking inward to examine one's own conscious experience and then reporting that experience. Wundt's advanced psychology students were rigorously trained in introspection. It is said that they had to introspect their way through some 10,000 separate practice experiences before their reports could be considered valid.

What is Wundt's legacy? Wundt put great emphasis on the use of precise measurements and the necessity of replicating research findings (Viney, 1993). And although his laboratory work was limited mainly to sensory processes, perception, and reaction time, he did have a larger vision of the field of psychology—a vision that included studies of social and cultural influences on human thought (Benjafield, 1996). Wundt clearly earned a place as a major figure in psychology. In fact, he was placed first by historians of the field in a ranking of the most eminent psychologists of all time (Korn et al., 1991).

Wundt's most famous student, Englishman Edward Bradford Titchener (1867–1927), took the new field to the United States, where he set up a psychological laboratory at Cornell University. He gave the name **structuralism** to this first school of thought in psychology, which aimed at analyzing the basic elements, or the structure, of conscious mental experience.

Structuralism was most severely criticized for its primary method, introspection. Introspection was not objective, even though it involved observation, measurement, and experimentation. When different introspectionists were exposed to the same stimulus, such as the click of a metronome, they frequently reported different experiences. Structuralism was not long considered to be a viable approach. Later schools of thought in psychology were established, partly in reaction against structuralism, which did not survive after the death of its most ardent spokesperson, E. B. Titchener.

What was Wundt's contribution to psychology?

Link It!

What were the goals and method of structuralism, the first school of psychology?

structuralism: The first formal school of psychology, aimed at analyzing the basic elements, or structure, of conscious mental experience through the use of introspection.

Functionalism: The First American School of Psychology

What was the goal of the early school of psychology known as functionalism?

As structuralism was losing its influence in the United States in the early 20th century, a new school of psychology called functionalism was taking shape. **Functionalism** was concerned not with the structure of consciousness, but with how mental processes function—that is, how humans and animals use mental processes in adapting to their environment.

The famous American psychologist William James (1842–1910) was an advocate of functionalism even though he did much of his writing before this school of psychology appeared. James's best-known work is his highly regarded and frequently quoted textbook *Principles of Psychology*, published more than a century ago (1890). James taught that mental processes are fluid and that they have continuity, rather than a rigid or fixed structure as the structuralists suggested. James spoke of the "stream of consciousness," which he said functioned to help humans adapt to their environment.

Functionalism broadened the scope of psychology to include the study of behavior as well as mental processes. It also allowed the study of children, animals, and the mentally impaired, groups that could not be studied by the structuralists because they could not be trained to use introspection. Functionalism also focused on an applied, more practical use of psychology by encouraging the study of educational psychology, individual differences, and industrial psychology (adaptation in the workplace).

Gestalt Psychology: The Whole Is More Than the Sum of Its Parts

What is the emphasis of Gestalt psychology?

Link It!

Gestalt psychology made its appearance in Germany in 1912. The Gestalt psychologists, notably Max Wertheimer, Kurt Koffka, and Wolfgang Köhler, objected to the central idea of structuralism—that we can best understand conscious experience by reducing it to its basic elements. **Gestalt psychology** emphasized that individuals perceive objects and patterns as whole units, and that the whole thus perceived is more than the sum of its parts. The German word *Gestalt* roughly means "whole, form, or pattern."

To support the Gestalt theory, Wertheimer, the leader of the Gestalt psychologists, presented his famous experiment demonstrating the phi phenomenon. In this experiment two light bulbs are placed a short distance apart in a dark room. The first light is flashed on and then turned off just as the second light is flashed on. As this pattern of flashing the lights on and off continues, an observer sees what looks like a single light moving back and forth from one position to another. Here, said the Gestaltists, is proof that people perceive wholes or patterns, not collections of separate and independent sensations.

When the Nazis came to power in Germany in the 1930s, the Gestalt school disbanded as its most prominent members emigrated to the United States. But even today Gestalt psychology continues to exert an influence, particularly in the fields of perception and learning.

Behaviorism: Never Mind the Mind

How did behaviorism differ from previous schools of psychology?

Psychologist John B. Watson (1878–1958) looked at the study of psychology as defined by the structuralists and functionalists and disliked virtually everything he saw. In Watson's view the study of mental processes, the concepts of mind and consciousness, and the primary investigative technique of introspection were not scientific. Watson pointed out that each person's introspection is strictly individual. He further maintained that self-reflection and internal ruminations cannot be observed, verified, understood, or communicated in objective, scientific terms. In his article "Psychology as the Behaviorist Views It" (1913), Watson argued that all the strictly subjective techniques and concepts in psychology must be thrown out. Watson did not deny the existence of conscious thought or experience. He simply did not view them as appropriate subject matter for psychology.

Watson proposed a radically new approach to psychology. This new school of psychology, called **behaviorism**, redefined psychology as the "science of behavior." Behaviorism confined itself to the study of behavior because it was observable and measurable and, therefore, objective and scientific. Behaviorism also emphasized that behavior is determined primarily by factors in the environment.

Behaviorism soon became the most influential school of thought in American psychology and remained so until the 1960s. It is still a major force in modern psychology, in large part because of the profound influence of B. F. Skinner (1904–1990). Skinner agreed with Watson that concepts such as mind, consciousness, and feelings were neither objective nor measurable and, therefore, were not the appropriate subject matter of psychology. Furthermore, Skinner argued that these concepts are not needed in order to explain behavior. One can explain behavior, he claimed, by analyzing the conditions that were present before a behavior occurs and by analyzing the consequences that follow the behavior. Skinner's research emphasized the importance of reinforcement in learning and in shaping and maintaining behavior. Any behavior that is reinforced—followed by a pleasant or rewarding consequence—is more likely to be performed again.

Because the strict behaviorist position of Skinner and others ignores inner, mental processes like thoughts and feelings, behaviorism has been a continuing target of criticism. Today many behaviorists do not take as extreme a view of behavior as Skinner himself did. Although they still emphasize the central importance of the study of behavior, they are also willing to consider what mental processes contribute to behavior.

Psychoanalysis: It's What's Down Deep That Counts

Whereas the behaviorists completely rejected unobservable mental forces in explaining behavior, this is precisely where Sigmund Freud looked in formulating his theory. Freud emphasized the importance of unseen, unconscious mental forces as the key to understanding human nature and behavior.

Sigmund Freud (1856–1939), whose life and work you will study in Chapter 13, developed a theory of human behavior based largely on case studies of his patients. Freud's theory, **psychoanalysis**, maintains that human mental life is like an iceberg. The smallest, visible part of the iceberg represents the conscious mental experience of the individual. But underwater, hidden from view, floats a vast store of unconscious impulses, thoughts, wishes, and desires, such as disturbing sexual and aggressive impulses. Freud insisted that individuals do not consciously control their thoughts, feelings, and behavior, which are instead determined by these unconscious forces.

The overriding importance that Freud placed on sexual and aggressive impulses caused much controversy both inside and outside the field of psychology. The most notable of Freud's famous students—Carl Jung, Alfred Adler, and Karen Horney—broke away from their mentor and developed their own theories of personality. These three are often collectively referred to as *neo-Freudians*.

Although Freud continues to have an impact on the popular culture, the volume of research on psychoanalysis has declined steadily (Robins et al., 1999). When they think of Freud, many people picture a psychiatrist using psychoanalysis with a patient on the familiar couch. The general public has heard of such concepts as the unconscious, repression, rationalization, and the Freudian slip. Such familiarity has made Sigmund Freud a larger-than-life figure rather than an obscure Austrian doctor resting within the dusty pages of history.

Humanistic Psychology: Looking at Human Potential

Humanistic psychology emerged in part as a reaction against behaviorism and psychoanalysis, the two major forces in psychology in the United States. Abraham Maslow (1908–1970) called humanistic psychology the third force in psychology.

functionalism: An early school of psychology that was concerned with how mental processes help humans and animals adapt to their environments.

Gestalt psychology (geh-SHTALT): The school of psychology that emphasizes that individuals perceive objects and patterns as whole units and that the perceived whole is more than the sum of its parts.

behaviorism: The school of psychology founded by John B. Watson that views observable, measurable behavior as the appropriate subject matter for psychology and emphasizes the key role of environment as a determinant of behavior.

psychoanalysis (SY-ko-ah-NAL-ih-sis): The term Freud used for both his theory of personality and his therapy for the treatment of psychological disorders; the unconscious is the primary focus of psychoanalytic theory.

What is the role of the unconscious in psychoanalysis, Freud's approach to psychology?

Link It!

What is the focus of humanistic psychology?

Humanistic psychology focuses on the uniqueness of human beings and their capacity for choice, growth, and psychological health. The humanists reject the behaviorist notion that people have no free will and are shaped and controlled strictly by the environment. Humanists also reject Freud's theory that people are determined and driven from within, acting and marching to the dark drums of the unconscious; they point out that Freud based his theory primarily on data from his disturbed patients.

Maslow and other prominent humanistic psychologists, such as Carl Rogers (1902–1987), emphasized a much more positive view of human nature. They maintained that people are innately good and that they possess free will. The humanists believe that people are capable of making conscious, rational choices, which can lead to growth and psychological health.

Maslow proposed a theory of motivation that consists of a hierarchy of needs. He considered the need for self-actualization (developing to one's fullest potential) to be the highest need on the hierarchy. Carl Rogers developed his client-centered therapy and, with other humanists, popularized encounter groups and other techniques as part of the human potential movement.

Cognitive Psychology: Focusing on Mental Processes

What is the focus of cognitive psychology?

Cognitive psychology is a specialty that focuses on mental processes such as memory, problem solving, concept formation, reasoning and decision making, language, and perception. Cognitive psychology grew and developed partly in response to strict behaviorism. Cognitive psychologists see humans not as passive recipients who are pushed and pulled by environmental forces, but as active participants who seek out experiences, who alter and shape them, and who use mental processes to transform information in the course of their own cognitive development. So how people perceive and explain an event, whether accurate or not, affects how they will respond to that event.

Beginning in the 1950s, a combination of forces—linguistics, computer science, neuroscience, and psychology—enabled researchers to undertake a more scientific approach to the study of mental structures and processes (Haberlandt, 1997). Cognitive psychology was influenced by the pioneering work of linguist Noam Chomsky, whose research laid important groundwork for investigating mental processes through the experimental study of language.

The advent of the computer provided cognitive psychologists with a new way to conceptualize mental structures and processes, known as the *information-processing approach*. According to this view, the brain processes information in sequential stages, or levels—in much the same way as a computer does serial processing. But as modern technology changed computers and computer programs, cognitive psychologists changed their cognitive models. "Increasingly, parallel processing models are developed in addition to stage models of processing" (Haberlandt, 1997, p. 22). Some cognitive psychologists have extended their study of human mental processes to work on artificial intelligence. In this research, sophisticated computers are used to simulate the intellectual processes of the human brain.

Unlike the early behaviorists, researchers today *can* observe some mental processes directly. Thanks to modern brain-imaging techniques such as the PET scan, combined with sophisticated computer technology, researchers can observe the action of specific clusters of brain cells (neurons) involved in carrying out various mental processes (Raichle, 1994). Such mental activities as thinking, remembering, solving a problem, listening to a melody, speaking, viewing images and colors, and so on have all been "observed," providing a rich body of knowledge that cognitive psychologists use in their work. Today cognitive psychology is the most prominent school of thought in the field (Robins et al., 1999).

Review & Reflect 1.2 summarizes the major schools of thought in psychology.

humanistic psychology: The school of psychology that focuses on the uniqueness of human beings and their capacity for choice, growth, and psychological health.

cognitive psychology: A specialty that studies mental processes such as memory, problem solving, decision making, perception, language, and other forms of cognition; often uses the information-processing approach.

Review&Reflect 1.2 Schools of Thought in Psychology

School	Description
Structuralism E. B. Titchener	The first formal school of psychology. Focused on analyzing the basic elements or structure of conscious mental experience through the use of introspection.
Functionalism William James	The first American school of psychology. Concerned with the study of mental processes and their role in facilitating adaptation to the environment. Broadened the scope of psychology to include the study of behavior as well as mental processes, and the study of children, the mentally impaired, and animals.
Gestalt psychology Max Wertheimer Kurt Koffka Wolfgang Köhler	Emphasizes that individuals perceive objects and patterns as whole units. The perceived whole is more than the sum of its parts and is not best understood by analysis of its elemental parts (as suggested by the structuralists).
Behaviorism John Watson B. F. Skinner	Views observable, measurable behavior rather than internal mental processes as the appropriate subject matter of psychology. Stresses the key roles of learning and the environment in determining behavior.
Psychoanalysis Sigmund Freud	Emphasizes the roles of unconscious mental forces and conflicts in determining behavior.
Humanistic psychology Abraham Maslow Carl Rogers	Focuses on the uniqueness of human beings and their capacity for choice, growth, and psychological health. Called the third force in psychology (behaviorism and psychoanalysis being the other two forces).
Cognitive psychology	Focuses on mental processes such as memory, problem solving, reasoning and decision making, language, and perception. Uses the information-processing approach.

Women and Minorities: Pioneers in Psychology

From its beginning until the mid–20th century, psychology was shaped and dominated largely by White European and American males. The reason for this longstanding domination was the thinking of the times. For centuries conventional thought had held that higher education was the exclusive domain of White males, that women should rear the children and be the homemakers, and that minorities were best suited for manual labor. And, as Thomas Paine observed in his influential book *Common Sense*, "A long habit of not thinking a thing *wrong*, gives it a superficial appearance of being *right*." However, beginning in the late 19th century, women and minorities overcame these prejudices to make notable achievements in and contributions to the study of psychology.

Christine Ladd-Franklin (1847–1930) completed the requirements for a PhD at Johns Hopkins University in the mid-1880s but had to wait over 40 years before receiving her degree in 1926, when the university first agreed to grant it to women. Ladd-Franklin formulated a well-regarded, evolutionary theory of color vision.

Mary Whiton Calkins (1863–1930) completed the requirements for a doctorate at Harvard in 1895. And even though William James described her as one of his most capable students, Harvard refused to grant the degree to a woman. Undeterred, Calkins established a psychology laboratory at Wellesley College and developed the paired-associates test, an important research technique for the study of memory. She became the first female president of the American Psychological Association in 1905.

Margaret Floy Washburn (1871–1939) received her PhD in psychology from Cornell University and later taught at Vassar College. She wrote several books, among them *The Animal Mind* (1908), an influential book on animal behavior, and *Movement and Mental Imagery* (1916).

Francis Cecil Sumner (1895–1954) was a self-taught scholar. Without benefit of a formal high school education, he became, in 1920, the first African American to earn a PhD in psychology, from Clark University. This feat was accomplished "in spite of innumerable social and physical factors mitigating against such achievements by black people in America" (Guthrie, 1998, p. 177). Sumner translated more than 3,000 articles from German, French, and Spanish. He chaired the psychology department at Howard University and is known as the "father" of African American psychology.

Albert Sidney Beckham (1897–1964), another African American psychologist, conducted some impressive early studies on intelligence and showed how it is related to success in numerous occupational fields. Beckham also established the first psychological laboratory at a Black institution of higher learning—Howard University.

A more recent African American pioneer, psychologist Kenneth Clark, achieved national recognition for his writings on the harmful effects of racial segregation. His work affected the Supreme Court ruling that declared racial segregation in the schools to be unconstitutional. His wife, Mamie Phipps Clark, also achieved recognition when the couple published their works on racial identification and self-esteem, writings that have become classics in the field.

Hispanic American Jorge Sanchez conducted studies on bias in intelligence testing. He pointed out that both cultural differences and language differences militate against Hispanic students in their performance on IQ tests.

These psychologists and others persevered to blaze the trail for the women and minorities who would follow.

PSYCHOLOGY TODAY

Modern Perspectives in Psychology: Current Views on Behavior and Thinking

Modern psychologists are not easily categorized into specific schools of thought. There are no structuralists roaming the halls of psychology departments, and no professors calling themselves functionalists. Today, rather than discussing schools of psychology, it is more appropriate to refer to psychological perspectives—points of view used for explaining people's behavior and thinking, whether normal or abnormal. Many psychologists take an eclectic position, choosing a combination of approaches to explain a particular behavior or psychological problem.

Psychologists who adopt the **biological perspective** emphasize the role of biological processes and heredity as the key to understanding behavior and thinking. To explain thinking, emotion, and behavior, both normal and abnormal, biologically oriented psychologists study the structures of the brain and central nervous system, the functioning of the neurons, the delicate balance of neurotransmitters and hormones, and the impact of genes. For example, too much or too little of different neurotransmitters in the brain is related to various psychological disorders, such as schizophrenia and depression. Drugs already used in treating some of these disorders are designed to restore the brain's biochemical balance. Researchers and theo-

What are seven major perspectives in psychology today?

biological perspective: A perspective that emphasizes the role of biological processes and heredity as the key to understanding behavior.

22

CHAPTER 1

rists who adopt the biological perspective are often referred to as physiological psychologists, psychobiologists, or neuropsychologists. And many of them are working under the umbrella of a new interdisciplinary field known as neuroscience. **Neuroscience** combines the work of psychologists, biologists, biochemists, medical researchers, and others in the study of the structure and function of the nervous system. The continuing development of medical technology in recent decades has spurred the research efforts of physiological psychologists, and many important findings in psychology have resulted from their work.

The psychoanalytic (psychodynamic) perspective in psychology is derived from the theory developed by Sigmund Freud. But the psychoanalytic approach has been modified considerably over the past several decades by psychologists known as neo-Freudians. The **psychoanalytic perspective** emphasizes the role of unconscious motivation and early childhood experiences in determining behavior and thought.

In contrast to the biological approach and the psychoanalytic approach, the **behavioral perspective** looks outward, emphasizing learning and the role of environmental factors in shaping behavior. Behavioral psychologists analyze these environmental factors in order to understand the causes of behavior and to establish programs of behavior modification to change problem behaviors.

The **cognitive perspective** considers the role of mental processes to be key. The cognitive approach maintains that a given stimulus does not simply cause a given response. Rather, the individual consciously perceives, remembers, thinks, organizes, analyzes, decides, and then responds. To explain behavior more fully, according to cognitive psychologists, it is necessary to consider such cognitive processes as perception, thinking, memory, language, and others.

Humanistic psychologists reject with equal vigor (1) the pessimistic view of the psychoanalytic approach, that human behavior is determined primarily by unconscious forces, and (2) the behaviorist view that behavior is determined by factors in the environment. The **humanistic perspective** views humans as capable of making rational, conscious choices. It emphasizes the importance of people's own subjective experiences as the key to understanding their behavior. The humanistic approach unashamedly admits the inherent subjective nature of its position.

The **evolutionary perspective** focuses on how humans have evolved and adapted behaviors required for survival over the long course of evolution (Archer, 1996). Evolutionary psychologists study how inherited tendencies and dispositions in humans influence a wide range of behaviors—from how we select mates, to what level of intellectual performance we demonstrate, and even to why we help others of our species. But most evolutionary psychologists recognize that genes alone do not control an individual's ultimate destiny. Inherited tendencies are *not* set in concrete.

The **sociocultural perspective** emphasizes social and cultural influences on human behavior and stresses the importance of understanding those influences when interpreting the behavior of others. Gergen and others (1996) have claimed that there is a "desperate need" for culturally sensitive research about people's behavior in such areas as health, "birth control, child abuse, drug addiction, ethnic and religious conflict, and the effects of technology on society" (p. 502).

Review & Reflect 1.3 (on page 24) gives a brief summary of these seven perspectives in psychology today.

Psychologists at Work

Psychologists have many different orientations toward the practice of psychology. Some psychologists teach at colleges and universities; others have private clinical practices and counsel patients. Psychologists work in hospitals and other medical facilities, in elementary and secondary schools, and in business and industry. Wherever you find human activity, you are very likely to encounter psychologists.

neuroscience: A field that combines the work of psychologists, biologists, biochemists, medical researchers, and others in the study of the structure and function of the nervous system.

psychoanalytic perspective (SY-ko-AN-il-IT-ik): A perspective initially proposed by Freud that emphasizes the importance of the unconscious and of early childhood experiences as the keys to understanding behavior and thought.

behavioral perspective: A perspective that emphasizes the role of environment in shaping behavior.

cognitive perspective: A perspective that emphasizes the role of mental processes that underlie behavior.

humanistic perspective: A perspective that emphasizes the importance of an individual's subjective experience as a key to understanding behavior.

evolutionary perspective: A perspective that focuses on how humans have evolved and adapted behaviors required for survival against various environmental pressures over the long course of evolution.

sociocultural perspective: A perspective that emphasizes social and cultural influences on human behavior and stresses the importance of understanding those influences when interpreting the behavior of others.

What are some specialists in psychology, and in what settings are they employed?

Perspective	Emphasis
Biological	The role of biological processes and structures, as well as heredity, in explaining behavior
Psychoanalytic	The role of unconscious motivation and early childhood experiences in determining behavior and thought
Behavioral	The role of environment in shaping and controlling behavior
Cognitive	The role of mental processes—perception, thinking, and memory—that underlie behavior
Humanistic	The importance of an individual's subjective experience as a key to understanding his or her behavior
Evolutionary	The roles of inherited tendencies that have proven adaptive in humans
Sociocultural	The roles of social and cultural influences on behavior

Psychologists work in a wide range of settings—including clinics, laboratories, businesses, and schools. This developmental psychologist is observing a kindergarten classroom.

There are many specialties within the field of psychology. A few of them are briefly described here.

Clinical psychologists specialize in the diagnosis and treatment of mental and behavioral disorders. Some clinical psychologists also conduct research in these areas. Most clinical psychologists work in clinics, hospitals, and private practice, and many hold professorships at colleges and universities.

Counseling psychologists help people who have adjustment problems (marital, social, or behavioral) that are less severe than those generally handled by clinical psychologists. Counseling psychologists may also provide academic or vocational counseling. *Counselors* usually work in a nonmedical setting such as a school or university, or they may have a private practice. About 60% of all psychologists in the United States may be classified as either clinical or counseling psychologists.

Physiological psychologists, also called neuropsychologists, study the relationship between physiological processes and behavior. They study the structure and function of the brain and central nervous system, the role of the neurotransmitters and hormones, and other aspects of body chemistry to determine how physical and chemical processes affect behavior in both people and animals.

Experimental psychologists specialize in the use of experimental research methods. They conduct experiments in most fields of specialization in psychology—learning, memory, sensation, perception, motivation, emotion, and other areas. Some experimental psychologists study the brain and nervous system and how they affect behavior; their work overlaps with that of physiological psychologists. Experimental psychologists usually work in a laboratory, where they can exert precise control over the humans or animals they are studying. Many experimental psychologists are faculty members who teach and conduct their research in college or university laboratories.

Developmental psychologists study how people grow, develop, and change throughout the life span. Some developmental psychologists specialize in a particular age group, such as infancy, childhood (child psychologists), adolescence, or old age (gerontologists). Others may concentrate on a specific aspect of human development such as physical, language, cognitive, or moral development.

Educational psychologists specialize in the study of teaching and learning. They may help train teachers and other educational professionals or conduct research in teaching and classroom behavior. Some help prepare school curricula, develop achievement tests, or conduct evaluations of teaching and learning.

While most other psychologists are concerned with what makes the individual function, *social psychologists* investigate how the individual feels, thinks, and behaves in a social setting—in the presence of others.

Industry and business have found that expertise in psychology pays off in the workplace. *Industrial/organizational (I/O) psychologists* study the relationships between people and their work environments.

Figure 1.2 shows the percentages of psychologists who work in the specialties discussed in this section. As you can see, psychology is an enormously broad and diverse field of study.

Figure 1.2

What Psychologists Do

Clinical psychologists make up the largest percentage of members of the American Psychological Association who work in the field of psychology. (Data provided by the APA, 1995.)

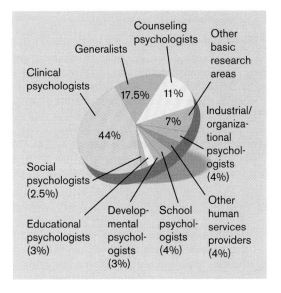

Apply It!

Study Skills and Critical Thinking

Studying—where, when, and how. Many years of research on memory have revealed a number of techniques you can use to help you study more efficiently and retain more of what you learn. More techniques will be presented in Chapter 6, but these will get you started.

- Establish a quiet place, free of distractions, where you do nothing else but study. You can condition yourself to associate this environment with studying, so that entering the room or area will be your cue to begin work. Moreover, you will be less tempted to do other things while you are there. Turn off the television, the radio, or the stereo, and have an answering machine take your calls.

- Schedule your study time. Research on memory has proven that spaced learning is more effective than massed practice (cramming). Instead of studying for 5 hours straight, try five study sessions of 1 hour each.

- Consider what your assignments are for the next several weeks. In order to be prepared for each class meeting, set yourself specific goals each week and for individual study sessions. Your goals should be challenging but not overwhelming. If the task for an individual study session is doable, it will be easier to sit down and face it. And completing the task that you have set for yourself will give you a sense of accomplishment.

- The more active a role you play in the learning process, the more you will remember. Spend some of your study time *reciting* the material rather than *rereading* it. One effective method is to use index cards as flash cards. Write a key term on the front of each card. On the back, list information from the text and lectures pertaining to that term. You should also have an index card for each study question, with the answer on the back of the card. Use these cards to help you prepare for tests. Test yourself before your professor does.

- *Overlearning* means studying beyond the point at which you can just barely recite the information you are trying to memorize. For best results, don't stop studying at this point. Review the information again and again until it is firmly locked in memory. If you are subject to test anxiety, overlearning will help. Overlearned information is more likely to survive an attack of nerves.

- Forgetting takes place most rapidly within the first 24 hours after you study. No matter how much time you have spent studying for a test, *always* review shortly before you take it. Refreshing your memory will raise your grade.

- Sleeping immediately after you study will help you retain more of what you have learned. If you can't study before you go to sleep, at least review what you studied earlier in the day. This is a good time to go through your index cards. (When you read Chapter 6, you will learn why sleep facilitates memory and why following the other suggestions will help you remember more of what you study.)

Being a good consumer of psychological research. If you were thinking of buying a car, you probably wouldn't look in a junkyard or take the first car you saw. Similarly, when studying psychology, you must be a wise consumer in order to get accurate information—to become a critical thinker.

Some publications are more scientifically respectable than others—for example, *Science News* and *Psychology Today* are more credible than *The National Enquirer* and *Cosmopolitan*. Science writers have more experience reading and understanding research and usually give more accurate reports of research results than general reporters do. Science writers tend to write more objectively than nonscience writers and are less likely to suggest that researchers' findings are the last word on the subject. General reporters, on the other hand, are more likely to make sweeping statements and extreme claims: "The most important study of our time," "Amazing new cure," "Dramatic results show . . . ."

James Bell (1991) suggests that to evaluate information you must be able to answer three key questions: "Who says so? What do they say? How do they know?" (p. 36). To critically evaluate research, you need to know who conducted the study and the methodology used. You need a description of the participants—their number, how they were selected, whether they were human or animal, and, if they were human, their age, gender, and any other characteristics that are relevant to evaluating the researchers' conclusions.

Critical thinkers are those who determine whether the methodology used by the researchers would enable them to reach their conclusions, whether those conclusions are logical, whether they are supported by the data, and whether there are alternative explanations for the findings.

Critical thinkers carefully consider the biases of writers and researchers. Do they have "axes to grind"? Are they presenting information that can be confirmed as factual or merely expressing their own opinions?

Critical thinkers understand that testimonials and accounts of personal experience are no substitute for scientific evidence. Don't be convinced by testimonials ("I've used this headache remedy for years, and it has always worked for me") or anecdotal accounts ("My Uncle Joe lived to be 95, and he smoked three packs of cigarettes a day").

Finally, critical thinkers do not accept the results of one study as definitive evidence. They want to know whether the research has been replicated and what other studies have been published on the subject. As a critical thinker, you would not modify your life based on one study you read. "One study does not a finding make" (Weeks, as quoted in Schmitz, 1991, p. 44).

SUMMARY AND REVIEW

PSYCHOLOGY: AN INTRODUCTION

What is the scientific method?

The scientific method consists of the orderly, systematic procedures researchers follow as they identify a research problem, design a study to investigate the problem, collect and analyze data, draw conclusions, and communicate their findings.

What are the four goals of psychology?

The four goals of psychology are the description, explanation, prediction, and control of behavior and mental processes.

Key Terms
psychology (p. 2); scientific method (p. 3); theory (p. 3); basic research (p. 4); applied research (p. 4); critical thinking (p. 4)

DESCRIPTIVE RESEARCH METHODS

What is naturalistic observation, and what are some of its advantages and limitations?

In naturalistic observation, researchers observe and record the behavior of subjects in a natural setting without attempting to influence or control it. Limitations include the researcher's lack of control over the observed situation, and the potential for observer bias.

What is the case study method, and for what purposes is it particularly well suited?

The case study is an in-depth study of one or several individuals through observation, interview, and sometimes psychological testing. It is particularly appropriate for studying people with rare psychological or physiological disorders.

What are the methods and purposes of survey research?

In survey research, investigators use interviews and/or questionnaires to gather information about the attitudes, beliefs, experiences, or behaviors of a group of people.

What is a representative sample, and why is it essential in a survey?

A representative sample is a sample of participants selected from the population of interest in such a way that important subgroups within the whole population are included in the same proportions in the sample. A sample must be representative for the findings to be applied to the larger population.

Key Terms

descriptive research methods (p. 5); naturalistic observation (p. 5); case study (p. 6); survey (p. 6); population (p. 6); sample (p. 6); representative sample (p. 6)

THE EXPERIMENTAL METHOD: SEARCHING FOR CAUSES

What is the main advantage of the experimental method?

The experimental method is the only research method that can be used to identify cause–effect relationships.

What is the difference between the independent variable and the dependent variable?

In an experiment an independent variable is a condition or factor manipulated by the researcher to determine its effect on the dependent variable. The dependent variable, measured at the end of the experiment, is presumed to vary as a result of the manipulations of the independent variable.

How do the experimental and control groups differ?

The experimental group is exposed to the independent variable. The control group is similar to the experimental group and is exposed to the same experimental environment but is not exposed to the independent variable.

What is selection bias, and what technique do researchers use to control for it?

Selection bias occurs when there are systematic differences within the groups before the experiment begins. Random assignment maximizes the probability that groups are similar at the beginning of the experiment.

What is the placebo effect, and how do researchers control for it?

The placebo effect occurs when a person's expectations influence the outcome of a treatment or experiment. To control for the placebo effect, the researcher must ensure that participants do not know if they are members of the experimental group (receiving the treatment) or of the control group (receiving the placebo).

What is experimenter bias, and how is it controlled?

Experimenter bias occurs when the researcher's expectations affect the outcome of the experiment. It is controlled by using the double-blind technique, in which neither the experimenter nor the participants know who is in the experimental group and who is in the control group.

Key Terms

experimental method (p. 8); hypothesis (p. 8); independent variable (p. 8); dependent variable (p. 9); experimental group (p. 9); control group (p. 9); selection bias (p. 10); random assignment (p. 10); placebo effect (p. 10); placebo (p. 11); experimenter bias (p. 11); double-blind technique (p. 11)

OTHER RESEARCH METHODS

What is the correlational method, and when is it used?

The correlational method is a research method that determines the correlation, or degree of relationship, between two variables. It is often used when it is either impossible or unethical to conduct an experimental study.

What is a correlation coefficient?

A correlation coefficient is a numerical value that indicates the strength and direction of the relationship between two variables.

What is meta-analysis?

Meta-analysis is a complex statistical procedure researchers use to combine the results from many research studies on a particular topic in order to determine the degree to which a specific hypothesis can be supported.

Key Terms

correlational method (p. 12); correlation coefficient (p. 12); reliability (p. 13); validity (p. 13); replication (p. 13); meta-analysis (p. 13)

PARTICIPANTS IN PSYCHOLOGICAL RESEARCH

What are some ethical guidelines governing the use of human participants in research?

Participation must be strictly voluntary. Participants must give informed consent, must be free to withdraw from the study at any time, and must be debriefed as soon as possible after they participate.

Why are animals used in research?

Animals provide a simpler model for studying similar processes in humans. Researchers can exercise more control over animals and use a wider range of medical and other manipulations. It is easier to study the entire life span and even several generations in some species. And animals are readily available and more economical to study.

EXPLORING PSYCHOLOGY'S ROOTS

What was Wundt's contribution to psychology?

Wundt, considered the father of psychology, established the first psychological laboratory in 1879 and launched the study of psychology as a formal academic discipline.

What were the goals and method of structuralism, the first school of psychology?

Structuralism's main goal was to analyze the basic elements, or structure, of conscious mental experience through the use of introspection.

What was the goal of the early school of psychology known as functionalism?

Functionalism was concerned with how mental processes help humans and animals adapt to their environment.

What is the emphasis of Gestalt psychology?

Gestalt psychology emphasizes that individuals perceive objects and patterns as whole units and that the perceived whole is more than the sum of its parts.

How did behaviorism differ from previous schools of psychology?

Behaviorism, the school of psychology founded by John B. Watson, views observable, measurable behavior as the only appropriate subject matter for psychology. Behaviorism also emphasizes the environment as the key determinant of behavior.

What is the role of the unconscious in psychoanalysis, Freud's approach to psychology?

According to Freud's theory of psychoanalysis, an individual's thoughts, feelings, and behavior are determined primarily by the unconscious—unseen mental forces that one cannot control.

What is the focus of humanistic psychology?

Humanistic psychology focuses on the uniqueness of human beings and their capacity for choice, growth, and psychological health.

What is the focus of cognitive psychology?

Cognitive psychology is a specialty that focuses on mental processes such as memory, problem solving, concept formation, reasoning and decision making, language, and perception.

Key Terms
structuralism (p. 17); functionalism (p. 18); Gestalt psychology (p. 18); behaviorism (p. 19); psychoanalysis (p. 19); humanistic psychology (p. 20); cognitive psychology (p. 20)

PSYCHOLOGY TODAY

What are seven major perspectives in psychology today?

Seven major perspectives in psychology today are (1) the biological perspective, which emphasizes the role of biological processes and heredity as the keys to understanding behavior and thought; (2) the psychoanalytic perspective, which focuses on the role of the unconscious and early childhood experiences; (3) the behavioral perspective, which emphasizes learning and the role of environmental factors in shaping behavior; (4) the cognitive perspective, which stresses the role of the mental processes (perceiving, thinking, remembering, etc.); (5) the humanistic perspective, which emphasizes the importance of an individual's subjective experience; (6) the evolutionary perspective, which looks at the inherited tendencies that have proved adaptive in humans; and (7) the sociocultural perspective, which emphasizes the role of social and cultural influences on behavior.

What are some specialists in psychology, and in what settings are they employed?

There are clinical and counseling psychologists, physiological psychologists, experimental psychologists, developmental psychologists, educational and school psychologists, social psychologists, and industrial/organizational psychologists. Psychologists are found in many different settings—in colleges and universities, in elementary and secondary schools, in medical settings, in business and industry, and in private practice.

Key Terms
biological perspective (p. 22); neuroscience (p. 23); psychoanalytic perspective (p. 23); behavioral perspective (p. 23); cognitive perspective (p. 23); humanistic perspective (p. 23); evolutionary perspective (p. 23); sociocultural perspective (p. 23)

Answers to all the Study Guide questions are provided at the end of the book.

Section One: Chapter Review

1. The orderly, systematic procedures scientists follow in acquiring a body of knowledge is the _____.

2. The four goals of psychology are _____, _____, _____, and _____.

3. Basic research is designed to solve practical problems. (true/false)

4. Which descriptive research method would be best for studying each topic?
   _____ (1) attitudes toward exercise
   _____ (2) gender differences in how people position themselves and their belongings in a library
   _____ (3) physiological changes that occur during sleep
   _____ (4) the physical and emotional effects of a rare brain injury
   a. naturalistic observation
   b. laboratory observation
   c. case study
   d. survey

5. When conducting a survey, a researcher can compensate for a sample that is not representative by using a sample that is very large. (true/false)

6. The experimental method is the *only* research method that can be used to identify cause–effect relationships between variables. (true/false)

7. A researcher investigates the effectiveness of a new antidepressant drug. She randomly assigns depressed patients to two groups. Group 1 is given the drug, and Group 2 is given a placebo. At the end of the experiment, the level of depression of all participants is measured as a score on a test called a depression inventory. Match the elements of this experiment with the appropriate term.
   _____ (1) score on depression inventory
   _____ (2) the antidepressant drug
   _____ (3) Group 1
   _____ (4) Group 2
   a. experimental group
   b. control group
   c. independent variable
   d. dependent variable

8. The placebo effect occurs when a participant responds according to
   a. the hypothesis.
   b. the actual treatment.
   c. how other participants behave.
   d. his or her expectations.

9. The results of an experiment can be influenced by the expectations of either the participants or the researcher. (true/false)

10. Random assignment is used to control for
    a. experimenter bias.   c. selection bias.
    b. the placebo effect.   d. participant bias.

11. The correlational method is used to demonstrate cause–effect relationships. (true/false)

12. Which of the following correlation coefficients indicates the strongest relationship?
    a. +.65   c. .00
    b. −.78   d. +.25

13. There is a (positive/negative) correlation between the amount of fat people eat and their body weight.

14. Test X has turned out to be a poor predictor of college GPA. Therefore, you can say that Test X is not (reliable/valid) for predicting GPA in college.

15. Psychological tests are sometimes used in case studies, experiments, and correlational studies. (true/false)

16. What is the term for a statistical procedure used to combine the results from many research studies to determine whether a specific hypothesis is supported?
    a. combinational analysis
    b. multiple analysis
    c. statistical summation
    d. meta-analysis

17. Psychologists are required to debrief participants thoroughly after a research study when the study
    a. violates participants' rights to privacy.
    b. deceives participants about the true purpose of the research.
    c. exposes participants to unreasonable risk or harm.
    d. wastes taxpayers' money on trivial questions.

18. Which of the following groups has *not* been over-represented as participants in psychological research?
    a. whites   c. females
    b. males   d. college students

19. Which of the following was *not* identified in the text as a source of bias in psychological research?
    a. age   c. race
    b. gender d. religion

20. Investigators use animals in psychological research to learn more about humans. (true/false)

21. The American Psychological Association (APA) has guidelines for ethical treatment for human participants but not for animal subjects. (true/false)

22. Match the school of psychology with its major emphasis.
    ___ (1) the scientific study of behavior
    ___ (2) the perception of whole units or patterns
    ___ (3) the unconscious
    ___ (4) analysis of the basic elements of conscious mental experience
    ___ (5) the uniqueness of human beings and their capacity for conscious choice and growth
    ___ (6) the function of conscious mental experience
    ___ (7) the study of mental processes
    a. Gestalt psychology
    b. structuralism
    c. functionalism
    d. psychoanalysis
    e. humanistic psychology

f. behaviorism
g. cognitive psychology

23. Match the major figure(s) with the appropriate school of psychology.
    ___ (1) James   a. humanistic psychology
    ___ (2) Freud   b. structuralism
    ___ (3) Watson   c. functionalism
          and Skinner d. psychoanalysis
    ___ (4) Titchener e. behaviorism
    ___ (5) Maslow
          and Rogers

24. Match the psychological perspective with its major emphasis.
    ___ (1) the role of biological processes and heredity
    ___ (2) the role of learning and environmental factors
    ___ (3) the role of mental processes
    ___ (4) the role of the unconscious and early childhood experience
    ___ (5) the importance of the individual's own subjective experience
    ___ (6) the role of social and cultural influences
    ___ (7) the role of inherited tendencies that have proved adaptive in humans
    a. psychoanalytic
    b. biological
    c. behavioral
    d. cognitive
    e. humanistic
    f. evolutionary
    g. sociocultural

Section Two: Who Said This?

Read each statement below and then, in the blank that follows, identify the person mentioned in Chapter 1 who would be most likely to make the statement.

1. I did research on *operant conditioning* and the effects of *reinforcement* on behavior. _____

2. I established the first psychological laboratory in Leipzig, Germany. _____

3. I wrote *Principles of Psychology* and advocated *functionalism.* _____

4. I became known as the father of *behaviorism.* _____

5. I proposed a *theory of motivation* that consists of a hierarchy of needs. _____

6. I was the first African American to earn a PhD in psychology. _____

7. I became the first female president of the American Psychological Association. _____

Section Three: Fill In the Blank

1. A _____ is a general principle or set of principles proposed to explain how a number of separate facts are related.

2. Dr. Smith is interested in using _____ _____ to study cooperative versus competitive play in children in nursery school. To accomplish this, she is going to observe and record children's play behaviors at nursery school without attempting to influence or control the behaviors.

3. Dr. Jones is interested in learning about college students in the United States who begin their education after the age of 30. He knows that there are many such students and that he will not be able to study them all, so he decides to carefully define this _____ (the group to which he hopes to generalize his findings) and then study a _____ _____ of these students. He hopes this approach will allow him to make accurate generalizations.

4. A psychologist believes there is an important relationship between test anxiety and test performance. Her _____ predicts that higher levels of anxiety will interfere with test performance.

5. To test her prediction, the psychologist in question 4 randomly assigns psychology students to two different groups. One group is told that the test they are about to take will determine over half of their semester grade. The other group is told that the test will have no bearing on their grade but will help the psychologist prepare better lectures. The psychologist believes the two groups will have different levels of anxiety and that the first group will perform less well than the second group on a standardized psychology test. In this experiment, the _____ variable is the pretest instructions, and the _____ variable is the test scores.

6. In an experiment, the _____ group is exposed to the same experimental environment as the experimental group but is not exposed to the independent variable.

7. Correlations can be useful in allowing you to make _____ but should not be used to draw conclusions about _____ and _____.

8. The first formal school of psychology was known as _____, and members of this school were interested in analyzing the basic elements, or structure, of conscious mental experience.

9. Another early school of psychology was _____. Psychologists who used this approach were interested in how mental processes help humans and animals adapt to their environments.

10. The school of psychology that emphasizes the role of unconscious mental forces and conflicts in determining behavior is known as _____.

11. The _____ perspective in psychology studies the role of mental processes—perception, thinking, and memory—in behavior.

12. According to the text, _____ psychologists make up the largest percentage of members of the American Psychological Association.

13. Sigmund Freud is associated with the _____ perspective in psychology.

Section Four: Comprehensive Practice Test

1. Which of the following psychological perspectives likened human mental life to an iceberg?
   a. behaviorism   c. humanistic psychology
   b. psychoanalysis   d. structuralism

2. _____ is the approach to psychology that arose from the belief that the study of the mind and consciousness was not scientific.
   a. Structuralism   c. Humanism
   b. Behaviorism   d. Psychoanalysis

3. The _____ perspective in psychology would explain behavior by referring to the operation of the brain and the central nervous system.
   a. evolutionary   c. behavioral
   b. structuralist   d. biological

4. A _____ psychologist specializes in the diagnosis and treatment of mental and behavior disorders.
   a. social   c. clinical
   b. developmental   d. cognitive

5. "The whole is perceived as greater than the sum of its parts" is a statement you would be most likely to hear from a _____ psychologist.
   a. behavioral   c. Gestalt
   b. cognitive   d. developmental

6. Description, explanation, prediction, and control of behavior and mental processes are the _____ of psychology.
   a. reasons   c. perspectives
   b. goals   d. methods

7. In an experiment, a researcher would use the double-blind approach to control for
   _____.
   a. experimenter bias   c. selection bias
   b. placebo bias   d. random bias

8. Jack believes that he did not do well on his test because the test had nothing to do with the subject matter of the class. Jack doubts the _____ of the test.
   a. reliability   c. standardization
   b. meta-analysis   d. validity

9. If a researcher wants to establish evidence for a cause–effect relationship between variables, he should use _____.
   a. naturalistic observation
   b. correlation
   c. the experimental method
   d. the survey method

10. Which of the following psychologists is associated with the humanistic perspective?
    a. Maslow   c. Watson
    b. Darwin   d. Freud

11. A social psychologist would be most interested in how individuals behave in isolated settings, such as when they are alone at home. (true/false)

12. Basic research is aimed at solving practical problems and improving the quality of life. (true/false)

13. Watson would suggest that Freud's psychological approach is invalid because of Freud's emphasis on unconscious motivation and other mental events. (true/false)

14. In an experiment, the experimental group is exposed to all aspects of the treatment except the independent variable. (true/false)

15. Structuralism used introspection to study the basic elements of conscious mental experience. (true/false)

16. Combining the results of many research studies to determine whether a hypothesis is supported is known as meta-analysis. (true/false)

17. A test gives very different results for the same test taker each time it is administered. This test would be said to have poor reliability. (true/false)

18. The best way to establish a cause–effect relationship between variables is to use the case study method because that method gives a researcher an in-depth knowledge of the subject matter from spending so much time with just a few participants. (true/false)

19. A researcher is studying the relationship between styles of computer keyboards and typing accuracy. In this case, the dependent variable is the different types of computer keyboards included in the study. (true/false)

20. You would probably expect to find a negative correlation between the number of alcoholic drinks consumed and the number of accidents a participant has while being tested on an experimental driving simulator. (true/false)

Section Five: Critical Thinking

1. Consider three of the major forces in psychology: behaviorism, psychoanalysis, and humanistic psychology. Which appeals to you most and which least, and why?

2. This chapter discussed deception in research and described a study that used deception to examine the effects of alcohol consumption and expectations on aggression. Prepare convincing arguments to support each of these opinions:

   a. Deception is justified in research studies
   b. Deception is not justified in research studies.

3. In this chapter you've learned something about experimental research and survey research. How can you use this new knowledge to evaluate research results you may read or hear about?

Biology and Behavior

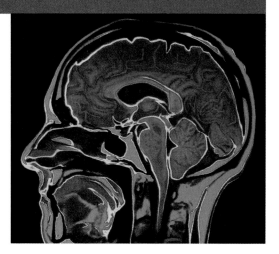

On September 13, 1848, Phineas Gage, a 25-year-old foreman on a railroad construction crew, was using dynamite to blast away rock and dirt. Suddenly an unplanned explosion almost took Gage's head off, sending a 3½-foot-long, 13-pound metal rod under his left cheekbone and out through the top of his skull.

Much of the brain tissue in Gage's frontal lobe was torn away, along with flesh, pieces of his skull, and other bone fragments. This should have been the end of Phineas Gage, but it wasn't. He regained consciousness within a few minutes and was loaded onto a cart and wheeled to his hotel nearly a mile away. He got out with a little help, walked up the stairs, entered his room, and walked to his bed. He was still conscious when the doctor arrived nearly 2 hours later.

Gage recovered and returned home in about 5 weeks, but he was not the same man. Before the accident, he was described as a hard worker who was polite, dependable, and well liked. But the new Phineas Gage, without part of his frontal lobe, was found to be loud-mouthed and profane, rude and impulsive, and contemptuous toward others. He no longer planned realistically for the future and was no longer motivated and industrious, as he once had been. Gage lost his job as foreman and joined P. T. Barnum's circus as a sideshow exhibit at carnivals and county fairs. (Adapted from Harlow, 1848.)

neuron (NEW-ron): A specialized cell that conducts impulses through the nervous system and contains three major parts—a cell body, dendrites, and an axon.

cell body: The part of the neuron, containing the nucleus, that carries out the metabolic functions of the neuron.

dendrites (DEN-drytes): The branchlike extensions of a neuron that receive signals from other neurons.

axon (AK-sahn): The slender, tail-like extension of the neuron that transmits signals to the dendrites or cell body of other neurons or to muscles or glands.

More than 150 years have passed since the heavy metal rod tore through Phineas Gage's brain. During that time much has been learned about the human brain—some of it puzzling and mysterious, all of it fascinating. How can the brain sustain such massive damage as in the case of Gage, who survived, while a small bullet fired through the brain in any one of a number of different places can result in instant death? In this chapter you will learn how tough and resilient, yet how fragile and vulnerable this remarkable 3-pound organ really is.

Chapter 1, the introduction to *The World of Psychology*, defined *psychology* as the scientific study of behavior and mental processes. Before you can gain an understanding and an appreciation of human behavior and mental processes, we must first explore the all-important biological connection. Every thought you think, every emotion you feel, every sensation you experience, every decision you reach, every move you make—in short, all of human behavior—is rooted in a biological event. Therefore, in this chapter, we study biology and behavior. The story begins where the action begins, in the smallest functional unit of the brain—the nerve cell, or neuron.

THE NEURONS AND THE NEUROTRANSMITTERS

The Neurons: The Nervous System's Messenger Cells

What is a neuron, and what are its three parts?

All our thoughts, feelings, and behavior can ultimately be traced to the activity of **neurons**—the specialized cells that conduct impulses through the nervous system. Most experts estimate that there may be as many as 100 billion neurons in the brain (Swanson, 1995). This would mean that you have about 17 times as many neurons as there are people living on the earth right now.

Neurons perform several important tasks: (1) Afferent (sensory) neurons relay messages from the sense organs and receptors—eyes, ears, nose, mouth, and skin—to the brain or spinal cord. (2) Efferent (motor) neurons convey signals from the brain and spinal cord to the glands and the muscles, enabling the body to move. (3) Interneurons, thousands of times more numerous than motor or sensory neurons, carry information between neurons in the brain and between neurons in the spinal cord.

Although no two neurons are exactly alike, nearly all are made up of three important parts: the **cell body** (soma), dendrites, and the axon. The cell body contains the nucleus and carries out the metabolic, or life-sustaining, functions of the neuron. Branching out from the cell body are the **dendrites**, which look much like the leafless branches of a tree. The dendrites are the primary receivers of signals from other neurons, but the cell body can also receive signals directly. And dendrites do not merely receive signals from other neurons and relay them to the cell body. Scientists now know that dendrites relay messages backward—from the cell body to their own branches (a process called *back propagating*). These backward messages may shape the dendrites' responses to future signals they receive (Magee & Johnston, 1997; Sejnowski, 1997).

The **axon** is the slender, tail-like extension of the neuron that sprouts into many branches, each ending in a bulbous axon terminal. The axon terminals transmit sig-

This scanning electron micrograph shows numerous axon terminals (the orange button-shaped structures) that could synapse with the cell body of the neuron (shown in green).

34

Figure 2.1

The Structure of a Typical Neuron

A typical neuron has three important parts: (1) a cell body, which carries out the metabolic functions of the neuron; (2) branched fibers called dendrites, which are the primary receivers of the impulses from other neurons; and (3) a slender, tail-like extension called an axon, the transmitting end of the neuron, which sprouts into many branches, each ending in an axon terminal. The photograph shows human neurons greatly magnified.

nals to the dendrites or cell bodies of other neurons, and to muscles, glands, and other parts of the body. In humans, some axons are only thousandths of an inch long. Others can be up to a meter, long enough to reach from the brain to the tip of the spinal cord, or from the spinal cord to remote parts of the body. Figure 2.1 shows a neuron's structure.

Remarkably, the billions of neurons that send and receive signals are not physically connected. The axon terminals are separated from the receiving neurons by tiny, fluid-filled gaps called *synaptic clefts*. The **synapse** is the junction where the axon terminal of a sending (presynaptic) neuron communicates with a receiving (postsynaptic) neuron across the synaptic cleft. There may be as many as 100 trillion synapses in the human nervous system (Swanson, 1995). And a single neuron may synapse with thousands of other neurons (Kelner, 1997). A technique that has recently been developed to monitor the action at the synapses may soon enable researchers to visualize the activity of all the synapses of a single neuron (Miesenbock & Rothman, 1997).

If neurons are not physically connected, how do they communicate? How do they send and receive their messages?

The Neural Impulse: The Beginning of Thought and Action   Cells in the brain, the spinal cord, and the muscles generate electrical potentials. Every time you move a muscle, experience a sensation, or have a thought or a feeling, a small but measurable electrical impulse is present.

How does this biological electricity work? Even though the impulse that travels down the axon is electrical, the axon does not transmit it the way a wire conducts an electrical current. What actually moves through the axon is a change in the permeability of the cell membrane. This process allows ions (electrically charged atoms or molecules) to move into and out of the axon through ion channels in the membrane.

Body fluids contain ions, some with positive charges and others with negative charges. Inside the axon, there are normally more negative than positive ions. When at rest (not firing), the axon membrane carries a negative electrical potential of about –70 millivolts (70 thousandths of a volt) relative to the fluid outside the cell. This slight negative charge is referred to as the neuron's **resting potential**.

When the excitatory effects on a neuron reach a certain threshold, ion channels begin to open in the cell membrane of the axon at the point closest to the cell body, allowing positive ions to flow into the axon. This inflow of positive ions causes the membrane potential to change abruptly, to a positive value of about +50 millivolts (Pinel, 1997). This sudden reversal of the resting potential, which lasts for about 1 millisecond (1 thousandth of a second), is the **action potential**. Then the ion channels admitting positive ions close, and other ion channels open, forcing some positive ions out of the axon. As a result, the original negative charge, or resting potential, is

What is a synapse?

What is the action potential?

synapse (SIN-aps): The junction where the axon of a sending neuron communicates with a receiving neuron across the synaptic cleft.

resting potential: The membrane potential of a neuron at rest, about –70 millivolts.

action potential: The firing of a neuron that results when the charge within the neuron becomes more positive than the charge outside the cell's membrane.

restored. The opening and closing of ion channels continues segment by segment down the length of the axon, causing the action potential to move along the axon.

The action potential operates according to the "all or none" law—a neuron either fires completely or does not fire at all. Immediately after a neuron fires, it enters a *refractory period*, during which it cannot fire again for 1 to 2 milliseconds. But this rest period is often very short: When stimulated, neurons can fire up to 1,000 times per second.

How can the brain tell the difference between a very strong and a very weak stimulus?

Consider this important question: If a neuron only fires or does not fire, how can we tell the difference between a very strong and a very weak stimulus? A jarring blow and a soft touch? A blinding light and a dim one? A shout and a whisper? The answer lies in the number of neurons firing at the same time and their rate of firing. A weak stimulus may cause relatively few neurons to fire, while a strong stimulus may trigger thousands of neurons to fire at the same time. Also, a weak stimulus may be signaled by neurons firing very slowly; a stronger stimulus may incite neurons to fire hundreds of times per second.

Nerve impulses travel at speeds from about 1 meter per second to approximately 100 meters per second (about 224 miles per hour). The most important factor in speeding the impulse on its way is the **myelin sheath**—a white, fatty coating wrapped around some axons that acts as insulation. If you look again at Figure 2.1, you will see that the coating has numerous gaps, called *nodes of Ranvier*. The electrical impulse is retriggered or regenerated at each node (or naked gap) on the axon. This regeneration speeds the impulse up to 100 times faster than impulses in axons without myelin sheaths.

Neurotransmitters: The Chemical Messengers of the Brain

What are neurotransmitters, and what role do they play in the transmission of signals from one neuron to another?

Once a neuron fires, how does it get its message across the synaptic cleft and on to other neurons? Messages are transmitted between neurons by one or more of a large group of chemical substances known as **neurotransmitters**.

Where are the neurotransmitters located? Inside the axon terminal are many small, sphere-shaped containers with thin membranes called *synaptic vesicles*, which hold the neurotransmitters. When an action potential arrives at the axon terminal, synaptic vesicles move toward the cell membrane, fuse with it, and release their neurotransmitter molecules. This process is shown in Figure 2.2.

The Receptor: Locks for Neurotransmitter Keys   Once released, neurotransmitters do not simply flow into the synaptic cleft and stimulate all the adjacent neurons. Each neurotransmitter has a distinctive molecular shape, and **receptors** on the surfaces of dendrites and cell bodies also have distinctive shapes. Neurotransmitters can affect only those neurons that have receptors designed to receive molecules of their particular shape. In other words, each receptor is somewhat like a locked door that only certain neurotransmitter keys can unlock.

However, the binding of neurotransmitters with receptors is not as fixed and rigid a process as keys fitting locks, or jigsaw puzzle pieces interlocking. Receptors in the brain are living matter; they can expand and contract their enclosed volumes. Consequently, the interaction where the neurotransmitter and the receptor meet is controlled not by the direct influence of one on the other, but by their *mutual* influence on each other. In such a dynamic interplay, a certain neurotransmitter may be competing for the same receptor with another neurotransmitter of a slightly different shape. The receptor will admit only one of the competing neurotransmitters— the one that fits it most perfectly. Thus, a receptor may receive a neurotransmitter at one time, but not at other times if another neurotransmitter molecule is present whose "affinity with the receptor is even stronger. As in dating and mating, what is finally settled for is always a function of what is available" (Restak, 1993, p. 28).

The Action of Neurotransmitters   When neurotransmitters bind with receptors on the dendrites or cell bodies of receiving neurons, their action is either excitatory (influencing the neurons to fire) or inhibitory (influencing them not to fire).

myelin sheath (MY-uh-lin): The white, fatty coating wrapped around some axons that acts as insulation and enables impulses to travel much faster.

neurotransmitter (NEW-ro-TRANS-mit-er): A chemical that is released into the synaptic cleft from the axon terminal of a sending neuron, crosses a synapse, and binds to appropriate receptor sites on the dendrites or cell body of a receiving neuron, influencing the cell either to fire or not to fire.

receptors: Protein molecules on the dendrite or cell body of a neuron that will interact only with specific neurotransmitters.

reuptake: The process by which neurotransmitter molecules are taken from the synaptic cleft back into the axon terminal for later use, thus terminating their excitatory or inhibitory effect on the receiving neuron.

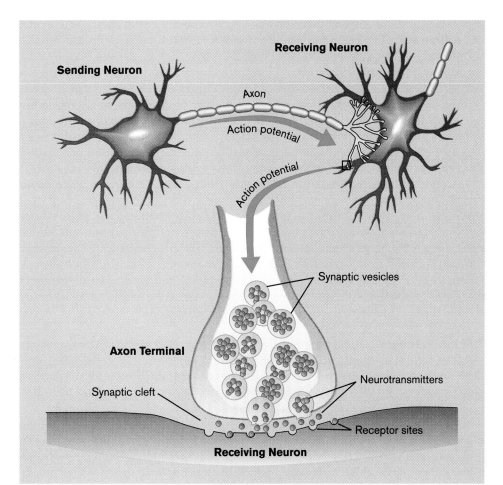

Figure 2.2

Synaptic Transmission

Sending neurons transmit their messages to receiving neurons by electrochemical action. When a neuron fires, the action potential arrives at the axon terminal and triggers the release of neurotransmitters from the synaptic vesicles. Neurotransmitters flow into the synaptic cleft and move toward the receiving neuron, which has numerous receptor sites. The receptors will bind only with neurotransmitters having distinctive molecular shapes that match their own. Neurotransmitters influence the receiving neuron only to fire or not to fire.

Because a single neuron may synapse with thousands of other neurons at the same time, there will always be both excitatory and inhibitory influences on receiving neurons. For the neuron to fire, the excitatory influences must exceed the inhibitory influences of neurotransmitter substances by a sufficient amount (the threshold).

For many years researchers believed that each individual neuron responded to only one neurotransmitter. But it is now known that individual neurons may respond to several different neurotransmitters, suggesting a greater flexibility of response, even at the level of a single neuron.

You may wonder how the synaptic vesicles can continue to pour out neurotransmitters, yet have a ready supply so that the neuron can respond to continuing stimulation. First, the cell body of the neuron is always working to manufacture more of the neurotransmitter substance. Second, unused neurotransmitters in the synaptic cleft may be broken down into their component molecules and reclaimed by the axon terminal to be recycled and used again. Third, by an important process called **reuptake**, the neurotransmitter substance is taken back into the axon terminal, intact and ready for immediate use. This terminates the neurotransmitter's excitatory or inhibitory effect on the receiving neuron.

The Variety of Neurotransmitters

Substances that act as neurotransmitters are manufactured in the brain, the spinal cord, the glands, and a few other parts of the body. Each kind of neurotransmitter affects the activity of the brain in a different way. Some neurotransmitters are always excitatory, and others are always inhibitory; however, some neurotransmitters can be either excitatory or inhibitory depending on the receptor with which

What are some of the ways in which neurotransmitters affect behavior, and what are some of the major neurotransmitters?

they bind. Researchers long believed that an individual neuron could secrete only one neurotransmitter. But it has been demonstrated that some neurons may secrete several different neurotransmitters (Changeux, 1993).

Acetylcholine   The neurotransmitter **acetylcholine** (ACh) exerts excitatory effects on the skeletal muscle fibers, causing them to contract so that the body can move. But it has an inhibitory effect on the muscle fibers in the heart. How can the same neurotransmitter excite some postsynaptic membranes and inhibit others? In such cases it is not the neurotransmitter itself that produces the effect, but the differing nature of the receptors on the postsynaptic (receiving) neuron that determines the effect.

Acetylcholine is involved in a variety of functions, including learning and memory, and in rapid eye movement (REM) sleep, during which dreaming occurs. Recent studies of acetylcholine and memory indicate that acetylcholine plays an excitatory role in stimulating the neurons involved in learning new information. At the same time, acetylcholine performs an inhibitory function in preventing "previously learned memories from interfering with the learning of new memories" (Hasselmo & Bower, 1993, p. 218). The severe memory loss of people suffering from Alzheimer's disease is associated with significantly reduced levels of acetylcholine in the brain. We will discuss Alzheimer's disease more fully in Chapter 8.

The Monoamines   An important class of neurotransmitters called *monoamines* includes four neurotransmitters—dopamine, norepinephrine (noradrenalin), epinephrine (adrenalin), and serotonin. Like acetylcholine, **dopamine** (DA) produces both excitatory and inhibitory effects and is involved in several functions, including learning, attention, movement, and reinforcement. A deficiency in dopamine is related to Parkinson's disease, a condition characterized by tremors and rigidity in the limbs. An oversensitivity to dopamine is thought to be related to some cases of schizophrenia, a severe psychotic disorder you will learn more about in Chapter 12. Many people with schizophrenia are helped by antipsychotic drugs, which reduce the effects of dopamine in the brain.

Norepinephrine (NE) has an effect on eating habits (it stimulates the intake of carbohydrates) and plays a major role in alertness and wakefulness. *Epinephrine* affects the metabolism of glucose and causes the nutrient energy stored in muscles to be released during strenuous exercise. Epinephrine also acts as a neurotransmitter in the brain but plays a minor role compared to norepinephrine.

Serotonin produces inhibitory effects at most of the receptors with which it interacts. It plays an important role in regulating mood, sleep, impulsivity, aggression, and appetite (Greden, 1994). A deficiency in serotonin has been associated with such behaviors as suicide (Nordström et al., 1994) and impulsive violence (Sandou et al., 1994). Both serotonin and norepinephrine are related to positive moods, and a deficiency in them has been linked to depression. Some antidepressant drugs relieve the symptoms of depression by blocking the reuptake of serotonin or norepinephrine, thus increasing the neurotransmitter's availability in the synapses.

Amino Acids   Researchers believe that eight or more *amino acids* also serve as neurotransmitters. Two of particular importance are found more commonly than any other transmitter substances in the central nervous system. They are glutamate (glutamic acid) and GABA (gamma-aminobutyric acid). *Glutamate* is the primary excitatory neurotransmitter in the brain (Riedel, 1996). It may be released by about 40% of neurons and is active in areas of the brain involved in learning, thought, and emotions (Coyle & Draper, 1996).

GABA is the main inhibitory neurotransmitter in the brain (Miles, 1999). It is thought to facilitate the control of anxiety in humans. Tranquilizers, barbiturates, and alcohol appear to have a calming and relaxing effect because they bind with one type of GABA receptor and thus increase GABA's anxiety-controlling effect. An abnormality in the neurons that secrete GABA is believed to be one of the causes of

acetylcholine (ah-SEET-ul-KOH-leen): A neurotransmitter that plays a role in learning, memory, and rapid eye movement (REM) sleep and causes the skeletal muscle fibers to contract.

dopamine (DOE-pah-meen): A neurotransmitter that plays a role in learning, attention, and movement; a deficiency of dopamine is associated with Parkinson's disease, and an oversensitivity to it is associated with some cases of schizophrenia.

norepinephrine (nor-EP-ih-NEF-rin): A neurotransmitter affecting eating and sleep; a deficiency of norepinephrine is associated with depression.

serotonin (ser-oh-TOE-nin): A neurotransmitter that plays an important role in regulating mood, sleep, aggression, and appetite; a serotonin deficiency is associated with anxiety, depression, and suicide.

endorphins (en-DOOR-fins): Chemicals produced naturally by the brain that reduce pain and positively affect mood.

central nervous system (CNS): The brain and the spinal cord.

spinal cord: An extension of the brain, reaching from the base of the brain through the neck and spinal column, that transmits messages between the brain and the peripheral nervous system.

Neurotransmitter	Functions
Acetylcholine (ACh)	Affects movement, learning, memory, REM sleep
Dopamine (DA)	Affects movement, attention, learning, reinforcement
Norepinephrine (NE)	Affects eating, alertness, wakefulness
Epinephrine	Affects metabolism of glucose, energy release during exercise
Serotonin	Affects mood, sleep, appetite, impulsivity, aggression
GABA	Neural inhibition in the central nervous system
Endorphins	Relief from pain; feelings of pleasure and well-being

Link It!

epilepsy, a serious neurological disorder in which neural activity can become so heightened that seizures result.

Endorphins   Over 25 years ago, Candace Pert and others (1974) demonstrated that a localized region of the brain contains neurons with receptors that respond to the opiates—drugs such as opium, morphine, and heroin. Later it was learned that the brain itself produces its own opiatelike substances, known as **endorphins**. Endorphins provide relief from pain or the stress of vigorous exercise and produce feelings of pleasure and well-being. "Runner's high" is attributed to the release of endorphins. (See Chapter 3 for more information on endorphins.)

Review & Reflect 2.1 summarizes the major neurotransmitters and their functions.

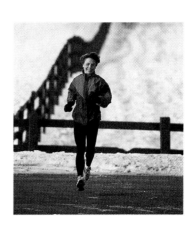

Ultramarathoners often experience runner's high—a euphoric feeling that results from the release of endorphins and that helps these athletes overcome fatigue and pain.

THE CENTRAL NERVOUS SYSTEM

We have discussed how neurons function individually and in groups through electrochemical action. But human functioning involves much more than the action of individual neurons. Collections of neurons, brain structures, and organ systems also play essential roles in the body. The nervous system is divided into two parts: (1) the **central nervous system (CNS)**, which is composed of the brain and the spinal cord, and (2) the peripheral nervous system, which connects the central nervous system to all other parts of the body (see Figure 2.3, on p. 40).

The Spinal Cord: An Extension of the Brain

The **spinal cord** can best be thought of as an extension of the brain. Like the brain, it has gray matter as well as white matter. A cylinder of neural tissue about the diameter of your little finger, the spinal cord reaches from the base of the brain, through the neck, and down the hollow center of the spinal column. The spinal cord is protected by

Why is an intact spinal cord important to normal functioning?

Figure 2.3
Divisions of the Human Nervous System

The human nervous system is divided into two parts: (1) the central nervous system, consisting of the brain and the spinal cord, and (2) the peripheral nervous system.

bone and also by spinal fluid, which serves as a shock absorber. The spinal cord literally links the body with the brain. It transmits messages between the brain and the peripheral nervous system. Thus, sensory information can reach the brain, and messages from the brain can be sent to the muscles, the glands, and other parts of the body.

Although the spinal cord and the brain usually function together, the spinal cord can act without help from the brain to protect the body from injury. A simple withdrawal reflex triggered by a painful stimulus—from touching a hot stove burner, for example—involves three types of neurons. Sensory neurons in your fingers detect the painful stimulus and relay this information to interneurons in the spinal cord. These interneurons activate motor neurons that control the muscles in your arm, and you jerk your hand away. All this happens within a fraction of a second, without any involvement of the brain. The brain, however, quickly becomes aware and involved when the pain signal reaches it. At that point you might plunge your hand into cold water to relieve the pain.

The Brainstem: The Most Primitive Part of the Brain

What are the crucial functions handled by the brainstem?

The **brainstem** begins at the site where the spinal cord enlarges as it enters the skull. The brainstem includes the medulla, the pons, and the reticular formation, as shown in Figure 2.4. The brainstem handles functions that are so critical to physical survival that damage to it is life-threatening. The **medulla** is the part of the brainstem that controls heartbeat, breathing, blood pressure, coughing, and swallowing. Fortunately, the medulla handles these functions automatically, so you do not have to decide consciously to breathe or remember to keep your heart beating.

Extending through the central core of the brainstem into the pons is another important structure, the **reticular formation**, sometimes called the *reticular activating system* (RAS). Find it in Figure 2.4. The reticular formation plays a crucial role in arousal and attention (Kinomura et al., 1996; Steriade, 1996). Every day your sense organs are bombarded with stimuli, but you cannot possibly pay attention to everything you see or hear. The reticular formation screens messages entering the brain. It blocks some messages and sends others on to higher brain centers for processing.

The reticular formation also determines how alert we are. When it slows down, we doze off or go to sleep. But like an alarm clock, it also can jolt us into consciousness. Thanks to the reticular formation, important messages get through even when we are asleep. That is why parents may be able to sleep through a thunderstorm but will awaken to the slightest cry of their baby. (The next time you sleep through your alarm and are late for class, blame it on your reticular formation.)

brainstem: The structure that begins at the point where the spinal cord enlarges as it enters the brain and that includes the medulla, the pons, and the reticular formation.

medulla (muh-DUL-uh): The part of the brainstem that controls heartbeat, blood pressure, breathing, coughing, and swallowing.

reticular formation: A structure in the brainstem that plays a crucial role in arousal and attention and that screens sensory messages entering the brain.

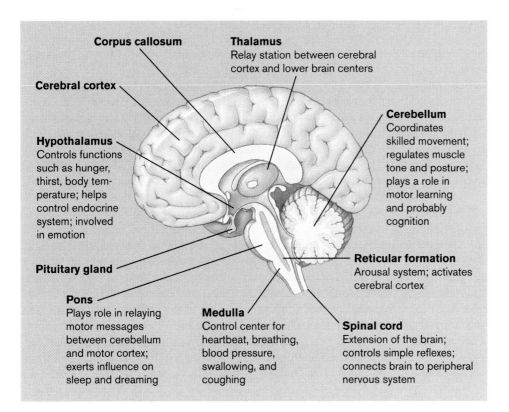

Figure 2.4

Major Structures of the Human Brain

Some of the major structures of the brain are shown in the drawing, and a brief description of the function of each is provided. The brainstem contains the medulla, the reticular formation, and the pons.

In the figure:

Corpus callosum

Thalamus
Relay station between cerebral cortex and lower brain centers

Cerebral cortex

Hypothalamus
Controls functions such as hunger, thirst, body temperature; helps control endocrine system; involved in emotion

Pituitary gland

Pons
Plays role in relaying motor messages between cerebellum and motor cortex; exerts influence on sleep and dreaming

Medulla
Control center for heartbeat, breathing, blood pressure, swallowing, and coughing

Cerebellum
Coordinates skilled movement; regulates muscle tone and posture; plays a role in motor learning and probably cognition

Reticular formation
Arousal system; activates cerebral cortex

Spinal cord
Extension of the brain; controls simple reflexes; connects brain to peripheral nervous system

The Cerebellum: A Must for Graceful Movement

The **cerebellum** makes up about 10% of the brain's volume and, with its two hemispheres, resembles the larger cerebrum that lies above it (Swanson, 1995). Look again at Figure 2.4. The cerebellum is critically important to the body's ability to execute smooth, skilled movements; it also regulates muscle tone and posture. Furthermore, it has been found to play a role in motor learning and in retaining memories of motor activities (Lalonde & Botez, 1990). The cerebellum coordinates and orchestrates the series of movements necessary to perform many simple activities—such as walking in a straight line or touching your finger to the tip of your nose—without studied, conscious effort. For people who have damage to their cerebellum or who are temporarily impaired by too much alcohol, such simple acts may be difficult or impossible to perform. Recent studies suggest that the cerebellum may be involved in cognitive as well as motor functions (Allen et al., 1997; Fiez, 1996).

What are the primary functions of the cerebellum?

The Thalamus: The Brain's Relay Station

The **thalamus** lies above the brainstem and consists of two egg-shaped structures. It serves as the relay station for virtually all the information that flows into and out of the higher brain centers, including sensory information from all the senses except smell. (You'll learn more about the sense of smell in Chapter 3.) Incoming sensory information from the eyes, ears, skin, or taste buds travels first to parts of the thalamus or hypothalamus and then to the proper area of the cortex that handles vision, hearing, taste, or touch. Pain signals connect directly with the thalamus, which sends the pain message to the appropriate sensory areas of the cerebral cortex.

The thalamus, or at least one small part of it, apparently affects our ability to learn new information, especially if it is verbal. This structure also plays a role in the production of language (Metter, 1991). Another function of the thalamus is the regulation of sleep cycles, which is thought to be accomplished in cooperation with the pons and the reticular formation.

What is the primary role of the thalamus?

cerebellum (sehr-uh-BELL-um): The brain structure that executes smooth, skilled body movements and regulates muscle tone and posture.

thalamus (THAL-uh-mus): The structure, located above the brainstem, that acts as a relay station for information flowing into or out of the higher brain centers.

What are some of the
processes regulated by the
hypothalamus?

hypothalamus (HY-po-THAL-uh-mus): A small but influential brain structure that controls the pituitary gland and regulates hunger, thirst, sexual behavior, body temperature, and a wide variety of emotional behaviors.

limbic system: A group of structures in the brain, including the amygdala and hippocampus, that are collectively involved in emotion, memory, and motivation.

amygdala (ah-MIG-da-la): A structure in the limbic system that plays an important role in emotion, particularly in response to aversive stimuli.

hippocampus (hip-po-CAM-pus): A structure in the limbic system that plays a central role in the formation of long-term memories.

What is the role of the limbic system?

The Hypothalamus: A Master Regulator

Nestled directly below the thalamus and weighing only about 2 ounces, the **hypothalamus** is, ounce for ounce, the most influential structure in the brain. It regulates hunger, thirst, sexual behavior, and a wide variety of emotional behaviors. The hypothalamus also regulates internal body temperature, starting the process that causes us to perspire when we are too hot and to shiver to conserve body heat when we are too cold. It also houses the biological clock—the mechanism responsible for the timing of the sleep/wakefulness cycle and the daily fluctuation in more than 100 body functions (Ginty et al., 1993). As small as it is, the hypothalamus maintains nearly all bodily functions except blood pressure, heart rhythm, and breathing.

The physiological changes in the body that accompany strong emotion are initiated by neurons concentrated primarily in the hypothalamus. You have felt these physical changes—sweaty palms, a pounding heart, or a lump in your throat.

The electrical stimulation of parts of the hypothalamus has elicited some unusual reactions in animals. Long ago, researcher José Delgado (1969) implanted an electrode in a particular spot in the hypothalamus of a bull, specifically bred for bull fighting in Spain. Delgado stood calmly in the ring as the bull charged toward him. He then pressed a remote control box that stimulated an area of the bull's hypothalamus. The bull stopped abruptly in its tracks. (Fortunately for Delgado, the batteries in the remote were working.) Apparently, aggression in animals can be turned on or off by stimulating specific areas of the hypothalamus. Not only that, even the sensations of pleasure can be produced if the right place on the hypothalamus is stimulated (Olds, 1956).

The Limbic System: Primitive Emotion and Memory

The **limbic system** is a group of structures in the brain, including the amygdala and the hippocampus, that are collectively involved in emotional expression, memory, and motivation. The **amygdala** plays an important role in emotion, particularly in response to aversive stimuli (LeDoux, 1994). It is heavily involved in the learning of fear responses and helps in the formation of vivid memories of emotional events, which enable humans and other animals to avoid dangerous situations and unpleasant consequences (Cahill et al., 1995; LeDoux, 1995). The mere sight of frightened faces excites the firing of neurons in the amygdala (Morris et al., 1996). Damage to the amygdala can impair a person's ability to recognize facial expressions and tones of voice that are associated with fear and anger (Scott et al., 1997).

The **hippocampus**, an important brain structure of the limbic system located in the interior temporal lobes, plays a central role in memory (see Figure 2.5). If your

Figure 2.5

The Principal Structures in the Limbic System

The amygdala plays an important role in emotion; the hippocampus is essential in the formation of conscious memory.

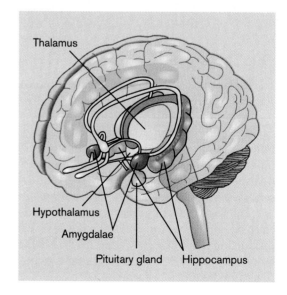

hippocampal region—the hippocampus and the underlying cortical areas—were destroyed, you would not be able to store or recall any new personal or cognitive information (Eichenbaum, 1997; Gluck & Myers, 1997; Vargha-Khadem et al., 1997). Yet memories already stored before destruction of the region would remain intact. Besides its critically important role in memory, researchers have discovered that the hippocampus is an essential part of a cortical network that detects and responds to unexpected or novel stimuli (Knight, 1996). The hippocampus also plays a role in the brain's internal representation of space in the form of neural "maps" that help us learn our way about in new environments and remember where we have been (Wilson & McNaughton, 1993). You will learn more about the central role of the hippocampal region in the formation of memories in Chapter 6.

THE CEREBRAL HEMISPHERES

The most extraordinary and the most essentially human part of the magnificent 3-pound human brain is the cerebrum and its cortex. Like a walnut, which has two matched halves connected to each other, the **cerebrum** is composed of two **cerebral hemispheres**—a left and a right hemisphere resting side by side (see Figure 2.6). The two hemispheres are physically connected at the bottom by a thick band of nerve fibers called the **corpus callosum**. This connection makes possible the transfer of information and the coordination of activity between the hemispheres. In general, the right cerebral hemisphere controls movement and feeling on the left side of the body. The left hemisphere controls the right side of the body. In over 95% of people, the left hemisphere also controls the language functions (Hellige, 1990). The size of the corpus callosum is related to higher-order cognitive functioning (Giedd, 1999).

The cerebral hemispheres have a thin outer covering about ⅛ inch thick called the **cerebral cortex**, which is primarily responsible for the higher mental processes

cerebrum (seh-REE-brum): The largest structure of the human brain, consisting of the two cerebral hemispheres connected by the corpus callosum and covered by the cerebral cortex.

cerebral hemispheres (seh-REE-brul): The right and left halves of the cerebrum, covered by the cerebral cortex and connected by the corpus callosum.

corpus callosum (KOR-pus kah-LO-sum): The thick band of nerve fibers that connects the two cerebral hemispheres and makes possible the transfer of information and the synchronization of activity between them.

cerebral cortex (seh-REE-brul KOR-tex): The gray, convoluted covering of the cerebral hemispheres that is responsible for higher mental processes such as language, memory, and thinking.

What are the cerebral hemispheres, the corpus callosum, and the cerebral cortex?

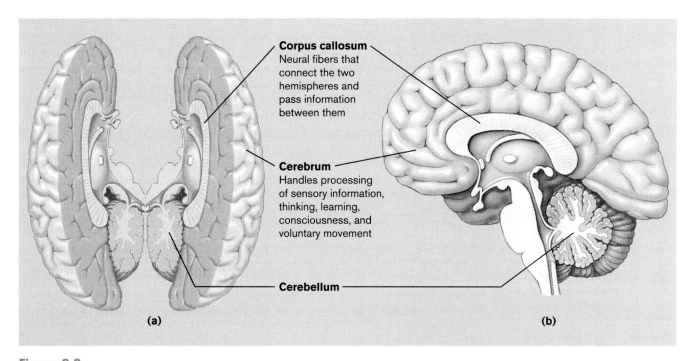

Corpus callosum
Neural fibers that connect the two hemispheres and pass information between them

Cerebrum
Handles processing of sensory information, thinking, learning, consciousness, and voluntary movement

Cerebellum

(a)   (b)

Figure 2.6
Two Views of the Cerebral Hemispheres

(a) The two hemispheres rest side by side like two matched halves, physically connected by the corpus callosum. (b) An inside view of the right hemisphere.

The two cerebral hemispheres show up clearly in this view looking down on an actual brain.

of language, memory, and thinking. The presence of the cell bodies of billions of neurons in the cortex gives it a grayish appearance. Thus, the cortex is often referred to as *gray matter*. Immediately beneath the cortex are the white myelinated axons (referred to as *white matter*) that connect the neurons of the cortex with those of other brain regions. If the human cortex were spread out flat, it would measure about 2 feet by 3 feet. Because the cortex is roughly three times the size of the cerebrum itself, it does not fit smoothly around the cerebrum. It is arranged in numerous folds or wrinkles called *convolutions*. About two-thirds of the cortex is hidden from view in the folds. The cortex of less intelligent animals is much smaller in proportion to total brain size and, therefore, is much less convoluted.

The cerebral cortex contains three types of areas: (1) sensory input areas, where vision, hearing, touch, pressure, and temperature register; (2) motor areas, which control voluntary movement; and (3) **association areas,** which house memories and are involved in thought, perception, and language.

The Lobes of the Brain

In each cerebral hemisphere there are four lobes—the frontal lobe, the parietal lobe, the occipital lobe, and the temporal lobe. Find them in Figure 2.7.

The Frontal Lobes: For Moving, Speaking, and Thinking   The frontal lobes are by far the largest of the brain's lobes. Beginning at the front of the brain, the **frontal lobes** extend to the top center of the skull. They contain the motor cortex, Broca's area, and the frontal association areas.

In 1870 two physicians, Fritsch and Hitzig, used a probe to apply a weak electrical current to the cortex of a dog. (The brain itself is insensitive to pain, so probing the brain causes no discomfort.) When they stimulated various points on the cortex along the rear of the frontal lobe, specific parts of the dog's body moved. Fritsch and Hitzig had discovered the **motor cortex**—the area that controls voluntary body movement (refer to Figure 2.7). The right motor cortex controls movement on the left side of the body, and the left motor cortex controls movement on the right side of the body.

In 1937 Canadian neurosurgeon Wilder Penfield applied electrical stimulation to the motor cortex of conscious human patients undergoing neurosurgery. He mapped the primary motor cortex in humans. Penfield noted that the parts of the body capable of the most finely coordinated movements, such as the fingers, lips, and tongue, have a larger share of the motor cortex.

What happens when part of the motor cortex is damaged? Depending on the severity of the damage, some degree of impairment of coordination can result. Sometimes damage in the motor cortex can cause the grand mal seizures of epilepsy. On the other hand, if an arm or leg is amputated, many of the neurons in the corresponding area of the motor cortex will eventually be dedicated to another function (Murray, 1995).

In 1861 Paul Broca performed autopsies on two patients—one who had been totally without speech, and another who could say only four words (Jenkins et al., 1975). Broca found that both patients had damage in the left hemisphere, slightly in front of the part of the motor cortex that controls movement of the jaw, lips, and tongue. Broca was among the first scientists to demonstrate the existence of localized functions in the cerebral cortex. He concluded that the site of damage, now called **Broca's area,** was the part of the brain responsible for speech production (refer to Figure 2.7). Broca's area is involved in directing the pattern of muscle movement required to produce the speech sounds.

If Broca's area is damaged, **Broca's aphasia** may result. **Aphasia** is a general term for a loss or impairment of the ability to use or understand language, resulting from damage to the brain. Characteristically, patients with Broca's aphasia know

What are some of the main areas within the frontal lobes, and what are their functions?

association areas: Areas of the cerebral cortex that house memories and are involved in thought, perception, learning, and language.

frontal lobes: The lobes that control voluntary body movements, speech production, and such functions as thinking, motivation, planning for the future, impulse control, and emotional responses.

motor cortex: The strip of tissue at the rear of the frontal lobes that controls voluntary body movement.

Broca's area (BRO-kuz): The area in the frontal lobe, usually in the left hemisphere, that controls the production of speech sounds.

Broca's aphasia (BRO-kuz uh-FAY-zyah): An impairment in the physical ability to produce speech sounds, or in extreme cases an inability to speak at all; caused by damage to Broca's area.

aphasia (uh-FAY-zyah): A loss or impairment of the ability to understand or communicate through the written or spoken word, which results from damage to the brain.

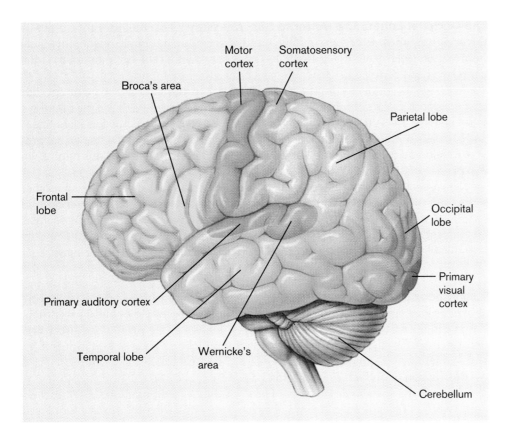

Figure 2.7

The Cerebral Cortex of the Left Hemisphere

This illustration of the left cerebral hemisphere shows the four lobes: (1) the frontal lobe, including the motor cortex and Broca's area; (2) the parietal lobe, with the somatosensory cortex; (3) the occipital lobe, with the primary visual cortex; and (4) the temporal lobe, with the primary auditory cortex and Wernicke's area.

what they want to say but can speak very little or not at all. If they are able to speak, their words are produced very slowly, with great effort, and are poorly articulated. Broca's aphasia, then, is a deficit in producing language, not in understanding it.

Much of the frontal lobes consists of association areas involved in thinking, motivation, planning for the future, impulse control, and emotional responses (Stuss et al., 1992). Damage to the frontal association areas produces deficiencies in the ability to plan and anticipate the consequences of actions. Sometimes pronounced changes in emotional responses occur when the frontal lobes are damaged. Phineas Gage, discussed in the story that opened this chapter, represents one case in which damage to the frontal lobes drastically altered impulse control and emotional responses.

The Parietal Lobes: Vital to the Sense of Touch   The **parietal lobes** are involved in the reception and processing of touch stimuli. The front strip of brain tissue in the parietal lobes is the **somatosensory cortex**, the site where touch, pressure, temperature, and pain register in the cortex (refer to Figure 2.7). The somatosensory cortex also makes you aware of movement in your body and the positions of your body parts at any given moment.

The two halves of the somatosensory cortex in the left and right parietal lobes are wired to opposite sides of the body. A person with damage to the somatosensory cortex of one hemisphere loses some sensitivity to touch on the opposite side of the body. If the damage is severe enough, the person might not be able to feel the difference between sandpaper and silk, or the affected part of the body might feel numb.

Other parts of the parietal lobes are responsible for spatial orientation and sense of direction. There are association areas in the parietal lobes that house memories of how objects feel, a fact that explains why we can identify objects by touch. People with damage to these areas could hold a pencil, scissors, or a ball in their hand but not be able to identify the object by touch alone.

What are the primary functions of the parietal lobes in general and the somatosensory cortex in particular?

parietal lobes (puh-RY-uh-tul): The lobes that contain the somatosensory cortex (where touch, pressure, temperature, and pain register) and other areas that are responsible for body awareness and spatial orientation.

somatosensory cortex (so-MAT-oh-SENS-or-ee): The strip of tissue at the front of the parietal lobes where touch, pressure, temperature, and pain register in the cerebral cortex.

What are the primary functions of the occipital lobes in general and the primary visual cortex in particular?

The Occipital Lobes: The Better to See You With   At the rear of the brain lie the **occipital lobes**, which are involved in the reception and interpretation of visual information (refer back to Figure 2.7). At the very back of the occipital lobes is the **primary visual cortex**, the site where vision registers in the cortex.

Each eye is connected to the primary visual cortex in both the right and left occipital lobes. Look straight ahead and draw an imaginary line down the middle of what you see. Everything to the left of the line is referred to as the left visual field and registers in the right visual cortex. Everything to the right of the line is the right visual field and registers in the left visual cortex. A person who sustains damage to one primary visual cortex will still have partial vision in both eyes.

The association areas in the occipital lobes are involved in the interpretation of visual stimuli. The association areas hold memories of past visual experiences and enable us to recognize what is familiar among the things we see. When these areas are damaged, people can lose their ability to identify objects visually, although they are still able to identify the same objects by touch or through some other sense.

What are the major areas within the temporal lobes, and what are their functions?

The Temporal Lobes: Hearing's Here   The **temporal lobes**, located slightly above the ears, are involved in the reception and interpretation of auditory stimuli. The site in the cortex where hearing registers is known as the **primary auditory cortex**. The primary auditory cortex in each temporal lobe receives sound inputs from both ears. Injury to one of these areas results in reduced hearing in both ears, and the destruction of both areas causes total deafness.

Adjacent to the primary auditory cortex in the left temporal lobe is **Wernicke's area**, which is the language area involved in comprehending the spoken word and in formulating coherent written and spoken language (refer back to Figure 2.7). In about 95% of people, Wernicke's area is in the left hemisphere. When you listen to someone speak, the sound registers first in the primary auditory cortex. The sound is then sent to Wernicke's area, where the speech sounds are unscrambled into meaningful patterns of words. Wernicke's area is also activated in deaf individuals when they watch a person using sign language (Nishimura et al., 1999). Wernicke's area is also involved when you select the words to use in speech and written expression.

Wernicke's aphasia is a type of aphasia resulting from damage to Wernicke's area. Although speech is fluent and words are clearly articulated, the actual message does not make sense to others (Maratsos & Matheney, 1994). The content may be vague or bizarre and may contain inappropriate words, parts of words, or a gibberish of nonexistent words. People with Wernicke's aphasia are not aware that anything is wrong with their speech.

Another type of aphasia is *auditory aphasia*, or word deafness. It can occur if there is damage to the nerves connecting the primary auditory cortex with Wernicke's area. The person is able to hear normally but may not understand spoken language—just as when you hear a foreign language spoken, and perceive the sounds but have no idea what the speaker is saying.

The remainder of the temporal lobes consist of the association areas that house memories and are involved in the interpretation of auditory stimuli. For example, the association area where your memories of various sounds are stored enables you to recognize the sounds of running water, fire engine sirens, dogs barking, and so on. There is also a special association area where familiar melodies are stored.

occipital lobes (ahk-SIP-uh-tul): The lobes that contain the primary visual cortex, where vision registers, and the association areas involved in the interpretation of visual information.

primary visual cortex: The area at the rear of the occipital lobes where vision registers in the cerebral cortex.

temporal lobes: The lobes that contain the primary auditory cortex, Wernicke's area, and association areas for interpreting auditory information.

primary auditory cortex: The part of the temporal lobes where hearing registers in the cerebral cortex.

Wernicke's area: The language area in the temporal lobe involved in comprehension of the spoken word and in formulation of coherent speech and written language.

Wernicke's aphasia: Aphasia that results from damage to Wernicke's area and in which the person's spoken language is fluent, but the content is either vague or incomprehensible to the listener.

lateralization: The specialization of one of the cerebral hemispheres to handle a particular function.

Specialized Functions of the Left Hemisphere: Language, First and Foremost

Although they may look very much alike, the two cerebral hemispheres make different but complementary contributions to people's mental and emotional lives. Research has shown that some **lateralization** of the hemispheres exists; that is, each hemisphere is specialized, to some extent, to handle certain functions. Yet functions are usually not handled exclusively by one hemisphere; the two hemispheres always work together.

In 95% of right-handers and in about 62% of left-handers, the **left hemisphere** handles most of the language functions, including speaking, writing, reading, and understanding the spoken word. But American sign language (ASL), used by deaf persons, is processed by both hemispheres (Neville et al., 1998). The left hemisphere is also specialized for mathematical abilities, particularly calculation, and it processes information in an analytical and sequential, or step-by-step, manner. Logic is primarily a left hemisphere specialty.

The left hemisphere coordinates complex movements by directly controlling the right side of the body and by indirectly controlling the movements of the left side of the body. The left hemisphere accomplishes this by sending orders across the corpus callosum to the right hemisphere so that the proper movements will be coordinated and executed smoothly. (Remember that the cerebellum also plays an important role in helping coordinate complex movements.)

Specialized Functions of the Right Hemisphere: The Leader in Visual-Spatial Tasks

The **right hemisphere** is generally considered to be the hemisphere more adept at visual-spatial relations. Artists, sculptors, architects, and do-it-yourselfers have strong visual-spatial skills. When you put together a jigsaw puzzle, draw a picture, or assemble a piece of furniture according to instructions, you are calling primarily on your right hemisphere.

The right hemisphere processes information holistically rather than part by part or piece by piece, as the left hemisphere does. Auditory, visual, and tactile stimuli register in both hemispheres, but the right hemisphere appears to be more specialized than the left for complex perceptual tasks. Consequently, the right hemisphere is better at pattern recognition, whether of familiar voices, melodies, or visual patterns.

The right hemisphere also makes an important contribution to the understanding of language. Van Lancker (1987) points out that "although the left hemisphere knows best what is being said, the right hemisphere figures out how it is meant and who is saying it" (p. 13). It is the right hemisphere that is able to understand familiar idiomatic expressions such as "He is turning over a new leaf." A person whose right hemisphere is damaged may understand only the literal meaning of the statement.

To experience an effect of the specialization of the cerebral hemispheres, try your hand at the *Try It!*

left hemisphere: The hemisphere that controls the right side of the body, coordinates complex movements, and, in 95% of people, controls the production of speech and written language.

right hemisphere: The hemisphere that controls the left side of the body and that, in most people, is specialized for visual-spatial perception and for interpreting nonverbal behavior.

What are the specialized functions of the left hemisphere?

What are the specialized functions of the right hemisphere?

Try It!

Get a meter stick or yardstick. Try balancing it vertically on the end of your left index finger. Then try balancing it on your right index finger. Most people are better with their dominant hand—the right hand for right-handers, for example. Is this true for you?

Now try this: Begin reciting the alphabet out loud as fast as you can while balancing the stick with your *left* hand. Do you have less trouble this time? Why should that be? The right hemisphere controls the act of balancing with the left hand. However, your left hemisphere, though poor at controlling the left hand, still tries to coordinate your balancing efforts. When you distract the left hemisphere with a steady stream of talk, the right hemisphere can orchestrate more efficient balancing with your left hand without interference.

Pick out the happy face and the sad face (from Jaynes, 1976).

Even though the faces in the drawings are mirror images, right-handed people tend to see the face at the left as the happier face. If you are right-handed, you are likely to perceive the emotional tone revealed by the part of a face to your left as you view it (McGee & Skinner, 1987). The right hemisphere processes information from the left visual field, so right-handed people tend to be more emotionally affected by the left side of the faces they view.

Creativity and intuition are typically considered right hemisphere specialties, but the left hemisphere shares these functions. The right hemisphere controls singing and seems to be more specialized for musical ability in untrained musicians (Kinsella et al., 1988). But in trained musicians, both hemispheres play important roles in musical ability. In fact, parts of the left auditory cortex are significantly larger in musicians with perfect pitch, indicating the involvement of the left hemisphere (Schlaug et al., 1995).

Patients with right hemisphere damage may have difficulty with spatial orientation, such as in finding their way around even in familiar surroundings. They may also have attentional deficits and be unaware of objects in the left visual field, a condition called *unilateral neglect* (Halligan & Marshall, 1994). Patients with this condition may eat only the food on the right side of the plate, read only the words on the right half of a page, and even groom only the right half of their bodies (Bisiach, 1996). And remarkably, some patients may even deny that the arm on the side opposite the brain damage belongs to them (Posner, 1996).

The right hemisphere is also more active in the recognition and expression of emotion (Borod, 1992). It even responds to the emotional message conveyed by another's tone of voice (Heilman et al., 1975). Reading and interpreting nonverbal behavior, such as gestures and facial expressions, is primarily a right hemisphere task. Look at the two faces in the *Try It!*

Evidence also continues to accumulate that brain mechanisms responsible for negative emotions reside in the right hemisphere, while those responsible for positive emotions are located in the left hemisphere (Hellige, 1993). Recent research shows that patients suffering from major depression experience decreased activity in the left prefrontal cortex, where positive emotions are produced (Drevets et al., 1997).

The Split Brain: Separate Halves or Two Separate Brains?

What is the significance of the split-brain operation?

The fact that parts of the human brain are specialized for some functions does not mean that some people are left-brained, while others are right-brained. Unless the hemispheres have been surgically separated, they do not operate in isolation and cannot be educated separately. Even though each contributes its own important specialized functions, the cerebral hemispheres are always in intimate and immediate contact, thanks to the corpus callosum.

There have been rare cases of people who have been born with no corpus callosum or who have had their corpus callosum severed in a drastic surgical procedure called the **split-brain operation**. Neurosurgeons Joseph Bogen and Philip Vogel (1963) found that patients with severe epilepsy, suffering frequent and uncontrollable grand mal seizures, could be helped by surgery that severed their corpus callosum. The split-brain operation surgically separates the hemispheres, making the transfer of information between them impossible. The patient is then left with two independently functioning hemispheres. The operation has been quite successful, completely eliminating the seizures in some patients. And the surgery causes no major changes in personality, intelligence, or behavior.

Research with split-brain patients by Roger Sperry (1964) and colleagues Michael Gazzaniga (1970, 1989) and Jerre Levy (1985) has expanded knowledge of the unique capabilities of the individual hemispheres. Sperry (1968) found that when the brain was surgically separated, each hemisphere continued to have individual and private experiences, sensations, thoughts, and perceptions. However, most sensory experiences are shared almost simultaneously because each ear and eye has direct sensory connections to both hemispheres. For his work, Sperry won the Nobel Prize in Medicine in 1981.

split-brain operation: An operation, performed in severe cases of epilepsy, in which the corpus callosum is cut, separating the cerebral hemispheres and usually lessening the severity and frequency of grand mal seizures.

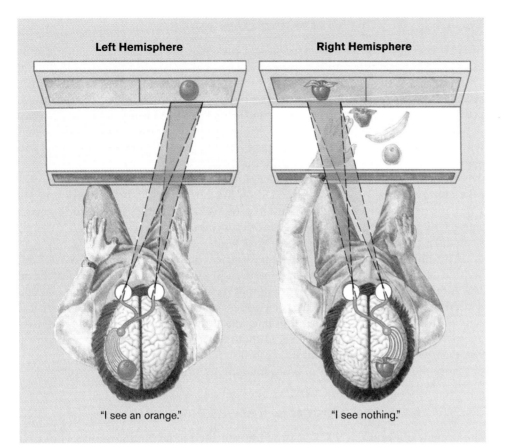

Left Hemisphere   **Right Hemisphere**

"I see an orange."   "I see nothing."

Figure 2.8

Testing a Split-Brain Person

Using special equipment, researchers are able to study the independent functioning of the hemispheres in split-brain persons. In this experiment, when a visual image (an orange) is flashed on the right side of the screen, it is transmitted to the left (talking) hemisphere. When asked what he sees, the split-brain patient replies, "I see an orange." When an image (an apple) is flashed on the left side of the screen, it is transmitted only to the right (nonverbal) hemisphere. Because the split-brain patient's left (language) hemisphere did not receive the image, he replies, "I see nothing." But he can pick out the apple by touch if he uses his left hand, proving that the right hemisphere "saw" the apple. (Based on Gazzaniga, 1983.)

Sperry's research revealed some fascinating findings. Look at Figure 2.8. In this illustration, a split-brain patient sits in front of a screen that separates the right and left fields of vision. If an orange is flashed to the right field of vision, it will register in the left (verbal) hemisphere. If asked what he saw, the patient will readily reply, "I saw an orange." Suppose that instead an apple is flashed to the left visual field and is relayed to the right (nonverbal) hemisphere. The patient will reply, "I saw nothing."

Why could the patient report that he saw the orange but not the apple? Sperry maintains that in split-brain patients, only the verbal left hemisphere can report what it sees. In these experiments, the left hemisphere does not see what is flashed to the right hemisphere, and the right hemisphere is unable to report verbally what it has viewed. But did the right hemisphere actually see the apple that was flashed in the left visual field? Yes, because with his left hand (which is controlled by the right hemisphere), the patient can pick out from behind a screen the apple or any other object shown to the right hemisphere. The right hemisphere knows and remembers what it sees just as well as the left, but unlike the left hemisphere, the right cannot name what it has seen. (In these experiments, images must be flashed for no more than ¹⁄₁₀ or ²⁄₁₀ of a second so that the patients do not have time to refixate their eyes and send the information to the opposite hemisphere.)

DISCOVERING THE BRAIN'S MYSTERIES

Modern researchers need not rely solely on autopsies or wait for injuries to learn more about the brain. Today researchers are unlocking the mysteries of the human brain using the electroencephalograph (EEG), the microelectrode, and modern scanning techniques such as the CT scan, magnetic resonance imaging (MRI), the PET scan, functional MRI, and others.

What are some methods that researchers have used to learn about brain function?

The EEG and the Microelectrode

What is an electroencephalogram (EEG), and what are three of the brain-wave patterns it reveals?

The electroencephalograph (EEG) uses electrodes placed on the scalp to amplify and record electrical activity in the brain.

electroencephalogram (EEG) (ee-lek-tro-en-SEFF-uh-lo-gram): A record of brain-wave activity made by the electroencephalograph.

beta wave (BAY-tuh): The brain wave associated with mental or physical activity.

alpha wave: The brain wave associated with deep relaxation.

delta wave: The brain wave associated with slow-wave (deep) sleep.

microelectrode: An electrical wire so small that it can be used either to monitor the electrical activity of a single neuron or to stimulate activity within it.

CT scan (computerized axial tomography): A brain-scanning technique involving a rotating X-ray scanner and a high-speed computer analysis that produces slice-by-slice, cross-sectional images of the structure of the brain.

magnetic resonance imaging (MRI): A diagnostic scanning technique that produces high-resolution images of the structures of the brain.

PET scan (positron-emission tomography): A brain-imaging technique that reveals activity in various parts of the brain, based on the amount of oxygen and glucose consumed.

In 1924 Austrian psychiatrist Hans Berger invented the electroencephalograph, a machine that amplifies a million times the electrical activity occurring in the brain. This electrical activity, detected by electrodes placed at various points on the scalp, provides the power to drive a pen across paper, producing a record of brain-wave activity called an **electroencephalogram (EEG)**. The **beta wave** is the brain-wave pattern associated with mental or physical activity. The **alpha wave** is associated with deep relaxation, and the **delta wave** with slow-wave (deep) sleep. (You will learn more about these brain-wave patterns in Chapter 4.)

An EEG computerized imaging technique shows the different levels of electrical activity occurring every millisecond on the surface of the brain (Gevins et al., 1995). It can show an epileptic seizure in progress and can be used to study neural activity in people with learning disabilities, schizophrenia, Alzheimer's disease, sleep disorders, and other neurological problems.

Although the EEG is able to detect electrical activity in different areas of the brain, it cannot reveal what is happening in individual neurons. The microelectrode can. A **microelectrode** is a wire so small that it can be inserted near or into a single neuron without damaging it. Microelectrodes can be used to monitor the electrical activity of a single neuron or to stimulate activity within it. Researchers have used microelectrodes to discover the exact functions of single cells within the primary visual cortex and the primary auditory cortex.

Since the 1970s, a number of brain-imaging techniques have been developed.

The CT Scan and Magnetic Resonance Imaging

The patient undergoing a **CT scan (computerized axial tomography)** is placed inside a large, doughnut-shaped structure where an X-ray tube encircles the entire head. The tube rotates in a complete circle and shoots X rays through the brain as it does so. A series of computerized, cross-sectional images reveal the structures within the brain (or other parts of the body) as well as abnormalities and injuries, including tumors and evidence of old or more recent strokes.

Another technique, **MRI (magnetic resonance imaging)**, produces clearer and more detailed images without exposing patients to the hazards of X-ray photography. MRI can be used to find abnormalities in the central nervous system and in other systems of the body. Although the CT scan and MRI do a remarkable job of showing what the brain looks like both inside and out, they cannot reveal what the brain is doing. But other technological marvels can.

The PET Scan, fMRI, and Other Imaging Techniques

The **PET scan (positron-emission tomography)** is a powerful technique for identifying malfunctions that cause physical and psychological disorders and also for studying normal brain activity. The PET scan can map the patterns of blood flow, oxygen use, and glucose consumption (the food of the brain). It can also show the action of drugs and other biochemical substances in the brain and other bodily organs (Farde, 1996).

Still, the PET scan can detect only *changes* in blood flow and in oxygen and glucose consumption as they occur in the various brain areas. But many parts of the brain are always active, even when a person is doing nothing observable. How do researchers separate the activity of specific brain locations responsible for seeing, speaking, reading, and so on from the other unrelated brain areas that are active at the same time? Thanks to sophisticated computing techniques, researchers can subtract all other brain activity from the activity involved in the specific mental tasks subjects are performing (Raichle, 1994b).

A newer technique, **functional MRI (fMRI)** has several important advantages over PET: (1) It can image *both* brain structure and brain activity; (2) it requires no

MRI (left) is a powerful tool for revealing what the brain looks like. Unlike PET, however, it cannot show what the brain is doing. PET scans (right) show activity in specific areas of the brain.

injections (of radioactive or other material); (3) it can image locations of activity more precisely than PET can; and (4) it can detect changes that take place in less than a second, compared to around a minute for PET ("Brain Imaging," 1997).

Brain-imaging techniques have helped neuroscientists develop an impressive store of knowledge about how the normal brain performs a variety of cognitive tasks and what functions are disrupted by particular types of brain damage. These techniques can also show abnormal brain patterns peculiar to certain psychiatric disorders and reveal where and how various drugs affect the brain (Tamminga & Conley, 1997). And some neuroscientists are combining virtual reality with fMRI to study how the brain responds to situations and environments that would be impossible to observe using conventional imaging techniques (Travis, 1996).

BRAIN DAMAGE: CAUSES AND CONSEQUENCES

Let's reconsider the question posed at the beginning of this chapter. How can someone like Phineas Gage, whose brain sustained such massive damage, survive, while a small bullet fired into a person's brain in a particular place can result in instant death? The precise location of a brain injury is the most important factor in determining whether a person lives or dies. Had the metal rod torn through Gage's brainstem, that would have been the end of him. Brain damage has many causes. Stroke, head injuries, diseases, tumors, and the abuse of drugs can leave people with a variety of disabilities.

In the United States, a stroke is the most common cause of injury to the adult brain and the third most common cause of death. A **stroke** occurs when a blood clot or plug of fat blocks an artery and cuts off the blood supply to an area of the brain or when a blood vessel bursts, often as a result of high blood pressure. High doses of stimulants such as amphetamines and cocaine also increase the risk of stroke. Of some 500,000 people who suffer strokes each year in the United States, about 150,000 die (Gorman, 1996). Another 100,000 to 150,000 are severely and permanently disabled (Zivin & Choi, 1991). Stroke patients may be left with impaired intellect, loss of coordination or sensation, or paralysis. Many stroke survivors suffer from depression (Angeleri et al., 1997), and about 25% have aphasia.

Each year more than 373,000 Americans survive injuries that leave them with significant brain damage (Ryan, 1997). Impaired motor coordination and language ability are often the most obvious results of head injury. Even more devastating is the loss of intellectual functioning—concentration, memory, reasoning, judgment, and problem-solving and decision-making abilities. Social behavior is frequently affected, as in the case of Phineas Gage, who became irritable, verbally abusive, and irresponsible. The precise disability depends largely on the area of the brain that is affected and the severity of the damage. Many people who suffer injuries to the head develop epilepsy—a chronic brain disorder that results in recurring seizures and frequently a loss or impairment of consciousness.

Recovering from Brain Damage

We have been taught that we are all born with a full supply of neurons and that those that are destroyed are never replaced. But new research indicates that "the human hippocampus, at least, can regenerate neurons" (Jones, 1999, p. 216). Damaged neurons can sprout new dendrites and reestablish connections with other neurons to assume some of the functions of the brain cells that were lost. Axons, too, are able to regenerate and grow (Fawcett, 1992).

Some abilities lost through brain damage can be regained if areas near the damaged site take over the lost function. The ability of the brain to reorganize and to compensate for brain damage is termed **plasticity.** Recent studies show that experience stimulates multiple changes in the brain, including longer dendrites, increased synapse formation, and more glial activity (Kolb & Whishaw, 1998). Plasticity is greatest in young children, whose hemispheres have not yet completely lateralized. Some individuals who have had an entire hemisphere removed early in life because of uncontrollable epilepsy have still achieved near-normal intellectual functioning.

A stroke victim may be able to recover some lost abilities with the help of a physical therapist and perhaps an interactive computer program.

What must occur in the brain for there to be some recovery from brain damage?

What is the peripheral nervous system?

plasticity: The ability of the brain to reorganize and compensate for brain damage.

peripheral nervous system (PNS) (peh-RIF-er-ul): The nerves connecting the central nervous system to the rest of the body.

THE PERIPHERAL NERVOUS SYSTEM

The **peripheral nervous system (PNS)** is made up of all the nerves that connect the central nervous system to the rest of the body. Without the peripheral nervous system, the brain and spinal cord, encased in their bone coverings, would be isolated and unable to send information to or receive information from other parts of the body. The peripheral nervous system has two subdivisions—the somatic nervous system and the autonomic nervous system. Figure 2.9 shows the subdivisions within the peripheral nervous system.

The *somatic nervous system* consists of (1) all the sensory nerves, which transmit information from the sense receptors—eyes, ears, nose, tongue, and skin—to the central nervous system; and (2) all the motor nerves, which relay messages from the central nervous system to all the skeletal muscles of the body. In short, the nerves of the somatic nervous system make it possible for us to sense our environment and to move, and they are primarily under conscious control.

The word *autonomic* is sometimes misread as "automatic," and that is not a bad synonym—because the *autonomic nervous system* operates quite well automatically, without any conscious control or awareness on our part. It transmits messages between the central nervous system and the glands, the cardiac (heart) muscle, and the smooth muscles, which are not normally under voluntary control (such as those in the large arteries and the gastrointestinal system).

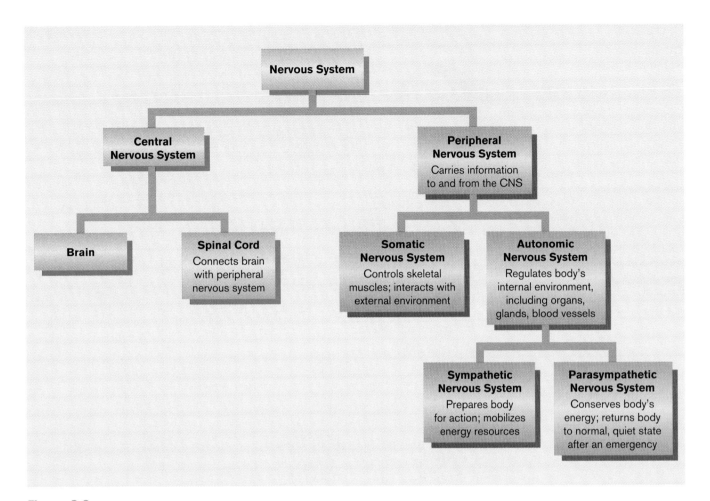

Figure 2.9
The Human Nervous System

The nervous system is divided into two parts: the central nervous system and the peripheral nervous system. The diagram shows the relationships among the parts of the nervous system and provides a brief description of the functions of those parts.

The autonomic nervous system is further divided into two parts—the sympathetic and the parasympathetic nervous systems. Any time we are under stress or faced with an emergency, the **sympathetic nervous system** automatically mobilizes the body's resources, preparing us for action. This physiological arousal produced by the sympathetic nervous system was named the *fight-or-flight response* by Walter Cannon (1929, 1935). If an ominous-looking stranger started following you down a dark, deserted street, your sympathetic nervous system would automatically set to work. Your heart would begin to pound, your pulse rate would increase rapidly, your breathing would quicken, and your digestive system would nearly shut down. Blood flow to your skeletal muscles would be enhanced, and all of your bodily resources would be made ready to handle the emergency—*run!*

But once the emergency is over, something must happen to bring these heightened bodily functions back to normal. The **parasympathetic nervous system** does just that. As a result of its action, your heart stops pounding and slows to normal, your pulse rate and breathing slow down, and your digestive system resumes its normal functioning. As shown in Figure 2.10 (on page 54), the sympathetic and parasympathetic branches act as opposing but complementary forces in the autonomic nervous system. Their balanced functioning is essential for health and survival.

What are the roles of the sympathetic and parasympathetic nervous systems?

sympathetic nervous system: The division of the autonomic nervous system that mobilizes the body's resources during stress, emergencies, or heavy exertion, preparing the body for action.

parasympathetic nervous system: The division of the autonomic nervous system that is associated with relaxation and the conservation of energy and that brings the heightened bodily responses back to normal following an emergency.

Figure 2.10

The Autonomic Nervous System

The autonomic nervous system consists of (1) the sympathetic nervous system, which mobilizes the body's resources during emergencies or during stress, and (2) the parasympathetic nervous system, which is associated with relaxation and which brings the heightened bodily responses back to normal after an emergency. This diagram shows the opposite effects of the sympathetic and parasympathetic nervous systems on various parts of the body.

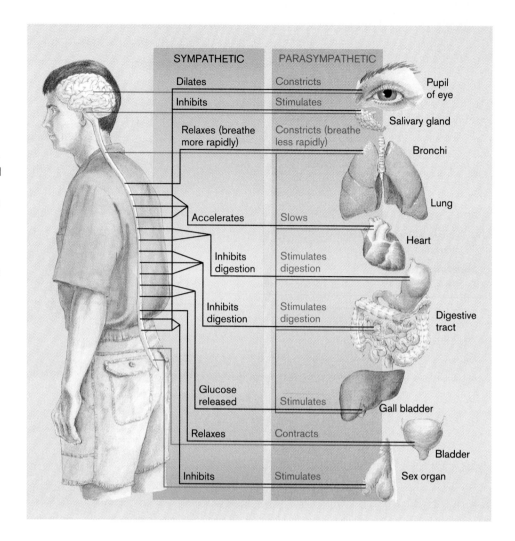

What is the endocrine system, and what are some of the glands within it?

THE ENDOCRINE SYSTEM

We have seen how certain chemical substances, the neurotransmitters, exert their influence on the 100 billion or so neurons in the nervous system. There is another system in which chemical substances stimulate and regulate many other important functions in the body. The **endocrine system** is a series of ductless glands, located in various parts of the body, that manufacture and secrete chemical substances known as **hormones**. Hormones are manufactured and released in one part of the body but have an effect on other parts of the body. Released into the bloodstream to travel throughout the circulatory system, each hormone performs its assigned job only when it connects with the body cells that have receptors for it. Some of the same chemical substances that are neurotransmitters act as hormones as well—norepinephrine and vasopressin, to name two. Figure 2.11 shows the glands in the endocrine system and their locations in the body.

The **pituitary gland** rests in the brain just below the hypothalamus and is controlled by it (see Figure 2.11). The pituitary is considered to be the master gland of the body because it releases the hormones that "turn on," or activate, the other glands in the endocrine system—a big job for a tiny structure about the size of a pea. The pituitary also produces the hormone that is responsible for body growth (Howard et al., 1996). Too little of this powerful substance will make a person a dwarf, too much will produce a giant.

The *thyroid gland* rests in the front, lower part of the neck just below the voice box (larynx). The thyroid produces the important hormone thyroxin, which regulates the rate at which food is metabolized, or transformed into energy. The *pancreas* regulates the body's blood sugar levels by releasing the hormones insulin and glucagon into the bloodstream. In people with diabetes, too little insulin is produced. Without insulin to break down the sugars in food, the blood-sugar levels can get dangerously high.

The two **adrenal glands**, which rest just above the kidneys (as shown in Figure 2.11), produce epinephrine and norepinephrine. By activating the sympathetic nervous system, these two hormones play an important role in the body's response to stress. The adrenal glands also release the corticoids, which control the important salt balance in the body, and small amounts of the sex hormones.

The *gonads* are the sex glands—the ovaries in females and the testes in males (see Figure 2.11). Activated by the pituitary gland, the gonads release the sex hormones that make reproduction possible and that are responsible for the secondary sex characteristics—pubic and underarm hair in both sexes, breasts in females, and facial hair and a deepened voice in males. Androgens, the male sex hormones, influence sexual motivation. Estrogen and progesterone, the female sex hormones, help regulate the menstrual cycle. Although both males and females have androgens and estrogens, males have considerably more androgens, and females have considerably more estrogens. (The sex hormones and their effects are discussed in more detail in Chapter 8.)

Biology and behavior are intimately related. However, there is much more to the scientific study of behavior and mental processes than can be revealed by studying the biological connection alone. Later chapters of this book will expand on other aspects of behavior and mental processes.

endocrine system (EN-duh-krin): A system of ductless glands in various parts of the body that manufacture and secrete hormones into the bloodstream or lymph fluids, thus affecting cells in other parts of the body.

hormone: A substance manufactured and released in one part of the body that affects other parts of the body.

pituitary gland: The endocrine gland located in the brain and often called the "master gland," which releases hormones that control other endocrine glands and also releases a growth hormone.

adrenal glands (ah-DREE-nal): A pair of endocrine glands that release hormones that prepare the body for emergencies and stressful situations and also release small amounts of the sex hormones.

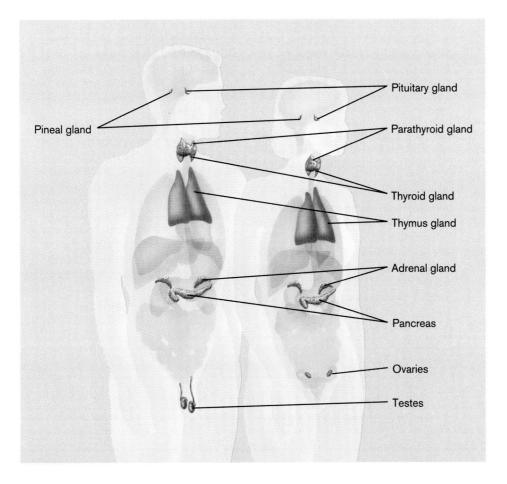

Pituitary gland

Pineal gland

Parathyroid gland

Thyroid gland

Thymus gland

Adrenal gland

Pancreas

Ovaries

Testes

Figure 2.11

The Endocrine System

The endocrine system is a series of glands, which manufacture and secrete hormones. The hormones travel through the circulatory system and have important effects on many bodily functions.

Handedness–Does It Make a Difference?

If you are left-handed, you are in good company. Alexander the Great, Michelangelo, Leonardo da Vinci, Benjamin Franklin, and Albert Einstein are among the better-known lefties from the past. Among left-handers in more recent times are Martina Navratilova, Whoopi Goldberg, and Tom Cruise.

The majority of people–about 90% of the world's population–are right-handed. Left-handedness occurs more often in males than in females. People who are left-handed are generally also left-footed, and to a lesser extent left-eyed and left-eared as well.

Is handedness inherited or is it learned? Scientists have long wondered why such a small percentage of human beings are left-handed. Some researchers propose a genetic cause (Annett, 1985; Levy & Nagylaki, 1972); others claim that handedness is for the most part environmentally influenced (Blau, 1946; Provins, 1997). No theory yet proposed is able to explain all the facts, although there is strong evidence of a genetic element in handedness. Hepper and others (1990) found that a hand preference is already apparent in the womb. Of the fetuses they observed, 94.6% were sucking their right thumb and only 5.4% were sucking their left thumb.

Geschwind and Behan (1982) found further evidence for a genetic contribution to handedness. According to Geschwind, a genetically based excess of testosterone, or an increased sensitivity to it, slows the growth of the left hemisphere and thereby allows greater development of the right hemisphere, which may lead to left-handedness.

Differences between lefties and righties. Investigators have identified a number of physiological differences between left-handed and right-handed people. On the average, the corpus callosum of left-handers is 11% larger and contains up to 2.5 million more nerve fibers than that of right-handers (Witelson, 1985). In about 60% of left-handers, language functions are controlled by the left hemisphere; in 25%, by the right hemisphere; and in about 15%, by both hemispheres. In general, the two sides of the brain are less specialized in left-handers (Hellige et al., 1994). Thus left-handers tend to experience less language loss following an injury to either hemisphere (Geschwind, 1979); and they are more likely to recover, because the undamaged hemisphere can more easily take over the speech functions.

But there are also disadvantages. Left-handers are 12 times more likely than right-handers to stutter and have learning disabilities such as dyslexia. Left-handers are also 2½ times more likely to have autoimmune diseases such as allergies, and they are more likely to suffer from migraine headaches, epilepsy, mental retardation, depression, and other mental disorders. A disproportionate number of premature and low-birthweight infants are left-handed (Geschwind and Behan, 1982).

Left in a right-handed world. Left-handedness is also associated with a variety of positive traits. Benbow and Stanley (1983) found that over 20% of 12- and 13-year-olds with exceptionally high scores on the math portion of the SAT were left-handers. Left-handers are also overrepresented among musicians, artists, engineers, mathematicians, and major-league baseball players. And in the 1990s, it is clear that left-handedness has been no barrier to being elected to the highest office in the land. George Bush and Bill Clinton are both left-handed.

Left-handers are five times more likely to suffer serious accidents than right-handers, but this is probably because they must function in a world designed for right-handers (Coren, 1989). For example, the seats found in many college classrooms have a large writing surface at the end of the right arm, allowing right-handed people to rest their arms while writing. Left-handed people are cramped by this arrangement, which forces them to sit at an awkward angle and keep both arms on the writing surface. In cars with a standard shift, the gear shift is located on the right side of the driver's seat. The markings on measuring cups, thermometers, and other measuring devices cannot be read unless the object is held in the right hand. The bias toward right-handedness even extends to feet: The arrangement of pedals in a car favors right-footed people.

Most left-handed people are able to adapt to these conditions. Some actually become ambidextrous as a result of using both hands for certain activities (working with tools, for example). Eating and writing, however, are rarely performed with the "other" hand. Fortunately some items–tools and sports equipment–are designed specifically for left-handers.

Most children show a consistent preference for one hand by the age of 5; some, however, begin to favor one hand by 18 months. Some left-handed children have been trained to eat or write with their right hand. But most experts on child development agree that it is harmful to interfere with the hand preference of a young child. It can cause emotional distress and may lead to speech or reading problems.

SUMMARY AND REVIEW

THE NEURONS AND THE NEUROTRANSMITTERS

What is a neuron, and what are its three parts?

A neuron is a specialized cell that conducts messages through the nervous system. Its three main parts are the cell body, the dendrites, and the axon.

What is a synapse?

A synapse is the junction where the axon terminal of a sending neuron communicates with a receiving neuron across the synaptic cleft.

What is the action potential?

The action potential is the firing of a neuron that results when the charge within the neuron becomes more positive than the charge outside the cell's membrane.

How can the brain tell the difference between a very strong and a very weak stimulus?

A strong stimulus will cause many more neurons to fire and to fire much more rapidly than a weak stimulus will.

What are neurotransmitters, and what role do they play in the transmission of signals from one neuron to another?

Neurotransmitters are chemicals released into the synaptic cleft from the axon terminal of the sending neuron. They cross the synaptic cleft and bind to receptors on the receiving neuron, influencing the cell to fire or not to fire.

What are some of the ways in which neurotransmitters affect behavior, and what are some of the major neurotransmitters?

Neurotransmitters regulate the actions of glands and muscles, affect learning and memory, promote sleep, stimulate mental and physical alertness, and influence moods and emotions ranging from depression to euphoria. Some of the major neurotransmitters are acetylcholine, dopamine, norepinephrine, serotonin, glutamate, GABA, and endorphins.

Key Terms

neuron (p. 34); cell body (p. 34); dendrites (p. 34); axon (p. 34); synapse (p. 35); resting potential (p. 35); action potential (p. 35); myelin sheath (p. 36); neurotransmitter (p. 36); receptors (p. 36); reuptake (p. 37); acetylcholine (p. 38); dopamine (p. 38); norepinephrine (p. 38); serotonin (p. 38); endorphins (p. 39)

THE CENTRAL NERVOUS SYSTEM

Why is an intact spinal cord important to normal functioning?

The spinal cord is an extension of the brain connecting it to the peripheral nervous system. The spinal cord must be intact so that sensory information can reach the brain and messages from the brain can reach the muscles and glands.

What are the crucial functions handled by the brainstem?

The brainstem contains (1) the medulla, which controls heartbeat, breathing, blood pressure, coughing, and swallowing, and (2) the reticular formation, which plays a crucial role in arousal and attention.

What are the primary functions of the cerebellum?

The cerebellum allows the body to execute smooth, skilled movements and regulates muscle tone and posture.

What is the primary role of the thalamus?

The thalamus acts as a relay station for information flowing into and out of the higher brain centers.

What are some of the processes regulated by the hypothalamus?

The hypothalamus controls the pituitary gland and regulates hunger, thirst, sexual behavior, body temperature, and a variety of emotional behaviors.

What is the role of the limbic system?

The limbic system is a group of structures in the brain, including the amygdala and the hippocampus, which are collectively involved in emotion, memory, and motivation.

Key Terms

central nervous system (p. 39); spinal cord (p. 39); brainstem (p. 40); medulla (p. 40); reticular formation (p. 40); cerebellum (p. 41); thalamus (p. 41); hypothalamus (p. 42); limbic system (p. 42); amygdala (p. 42); hippocampus (p. 42)

THE CEREBRAL HEMISPHERES

What are the cerebral hemispheres, the corpus callosum, and the cerebral cortex?

The cerebral hemispheres are the two halves of the cerebrum, connected by the corpus callosum and covered by the cerebral cortex, which is responsible for higher mental processes such as language, memory, and thinking.

What are some of the main areas within the frontal lobes, and what are their functions?

The frontal lobes contain (1) the motor cortex, which controls voluntary motor activity; (2) Broca's area, which functions in speech production; and (3) the frontal association areas, which are involved in thinking, motivation, planning for the future, impulse control, and emotional responses.

What are the primary functions of the parietal lobes in general and the somatosensory cortex in particular?

The parietal lobes are involved in the reception and processing of touch stimuli. They contain the somatosensory cortex, where touch, pressure, temperature, and pain register.

What are the primary functions of the occipital lobes in general and the primary visual cortex in particular?

The occipital lobes are involved in the reception and interpretation of visual information. They contain the primary visual cortex, where vision registers in the cerebral cortex.

What are the major areas within the temporal lobes, and what are their functions?

The temporal lobes contain (1) the primary auditory cortex, where hearing registers in the cortex; (2) Wernicke's area, which is involved in comprehending the spoken word and in formulating coherent speech and written language; and (3) association areas, where memories are stored and auditory stimuli are interpreted.

What are the specialized functions of the left hemisphere?

The left hemisphere controls the right side of the body, coordinates complex movements, and handles most of the language functions, including speaking, writing, reading, and understanding the spoken word.

What are the specialized functions of the right hemisphere?

The right hemisphere controls the left side of the body; is specialized for visual-spatial perception, singing, and interpreting nonverbal behavior; and is more active in the recognition and expression of emotion.

What is the significance of the split-brain operation?

In the split-brain operation a surgeon cuts the corpus callosum, which prevents the transfer of any information between the cerebral hemispheres. Research on split-brain patients has extended scientific knowledge of the functions of the hemispheres.

Key Terms
cerebrum (p. 43); cerebral hemispheres (p. 43); corpus callosum (p. 43); cerebral cortex (p. 43); association areas (p. 44); frontal lobes (p. 44); motor cortex (p. 44); Broca's area (p. 44); Broca's aphasia (p. 44); aphasia (p. 44); parietal lobes (p. 45); somatosensory cortex (p. 45); occipital lobes (p. 46); primary visual cortex (p. 46); temporal lobes (p. 46); primary auditory cortex (p. 46); Wernicke's area (p. 46); Wernicke's aphasia (p. 46); lateralization (p. 46); left hemisphere (p. 47); right hemisphere (p. 47); split-brain operation (p. 48)

DISCOVERING THE BRAIN'S MYSTERIES

What are some methods that researchers have used to learn about brain function?

Researchers have learned about brain function from clinical studies of patients, through electrical stimulation of the brain, and from studies using the EEG, microelectrodes, CT scan, MRI, PET scan, and fMRI.

What is an electroencephalogram (EEG), and what are three of the brain-wave patterns it reveals?

An electroencephalogram (EEG) is a record of brain-wave activity. Three normal brain-wave patterns are the beta wave, the alpha wave, and the delta wave.

Key Terms
electroencephalogram (EEG) (p. 50); beta wave (p. 50); alpha wave (p. 50); delta wave (p. 50); microelectrode (p. 50); CT scan (p. 50); MRI (p. 50); PET scan (p. 50); fMRI (p. 50)

BRAIN DAMAGE: CAUSES AND CONSEQUENCES

Why is a stroke so serious?

In the United States, stroke is the most common cause of damage to the adult brain and the third leading cause of death. It leaves many of its victims with paralysis and/or aphasia.

What must occur in the brain for there to be some recovery from brain damage?

For some recovery from brain damage to occur, (1) damaged neurons must sprout new dendrites and reestablish connections with other neurons, (2) areas near the damaged site must take over the lost function, or (3) the undamaged hemisphere must assume the lost language function (as in aphasia).

Key Terms
stroke (p. 51); plasticity (p. 52)

THE PERIPHERAL NERVOUS SYSTEM

What is the peripheral nervous system?

The peripheral nervous system connects the central nervous system to the rest of the body. It has two subdivisions: (1) the somatic nervous system, which consists of the nerves that make it possible for the body to sense and move; and (2) the autonomic nervous system.

What are the roles of the sympathetic and parasympathetic nervous systems?

The autonomic nervous system has two parts: (1) the sympathetic nervous system, which mobilizes the body's resources during emergencies or during stress; and (2) the parasympathetic nervous system, which is associated with relaxation and brings the heightened bodily responses back to normal after an emergency.

Key Terms
peripheral nervous system (p. 52); sympathetic nervous system (p. 53); parasympathetic nervous system (p. 53)

THE ENDOCRINE SYSTEM

What is the endocrine system, and what are some of the glands within it?

The endocrine system is a system of glands in various parts of the body that manufacture hormones and secrete them into the bloodstream. The hormones then affect cells in other parts of the body. The pituitary gland releases hormones that control other glands in the endocrine system and also releases a growth hormone. The thyroid gland produces thyroxin, which regulates metabolism. The pancreas produces insulin and regulates blood sugar. The adrenal glands release epinephrine and norepinephrine, which prepare the body for emergencies and stressful situations; those glands also release small amounts of the sex hormones. The gonads are the sex glands, which produce the sex hormones and make reproduction possible.

Key Terms
endocrine system (p. 54); hormone (p. 54); pituitary gland (p. 54); adrenal glands (p. 55)

Study Guide for Chapter 2

Answers to all the Study Guide questions are provided at the end of the book.

Section One: Chapter Review

1. The branchlike extensions of neurons that act as the *primary* receivers of signals from other neurons are the
   a. dendrites.   c. neurotransmitters.
   b. axons.   d. cell bodies.

2. The junction where the axon of a sending neuron communicates with a receiving neuron is called the
   a. reuptake site.   c. synapse.
   b. receptor site.   d. axon terminal.

3. When a neuron fires, neurotransmitters are released from the synaptic vesicles in the _____ terminal into the synaptic cleft.
   a. dendrite   c. receptor
   b. cell body's   d. axon

4. The (resting, action) potential is the firing of a neuron that results when the charge within the neuron becomes more positive than the charge outside the cell membrane.

5. Receptor sites on the receiving neuron
   a. receive any available neurotransmitter molecules.
   b. receive only neurotransmitter molecules of specific shapes.
   c. can only be influenced by neurotransmitters from a single neuron.
   d. are located only on the dendrites.

6. Which of the following substances cross the synaptic cleft and enter receptor sites on the dendrites and cell bodies of receiving neurons?
   a. sodium ions
   b. potassium ions
   c. neurotransmitters
   d. synapse modulators

7. Endorphins, norepinephrine, dopamine, and serotonin are all examples of
   a. hormones.
   b. neurotransmitters.
   c. neuropeptides.
   d. neuromodulators.

8. The brain and the spinal cord make up the peripheral nervous system. (true/false)

9. The hypothalamus regulates all the following except
   a. internal body temperature.
   b. coordinated movement.
   c. hunger and thirst.
   d. sexual behavior.

10. The part of the limbic system primarily involved in the formation of memories is the (amygdala, hippocampus).

11. Match the brain structure with its description.
    ____ (1) connects the brain with the peripheral nervous system
    ____ (2) controls heart rate, breathing, and blood pressure
    ____ (3) consists of the medulla, the pons, and the reticular formation
    ____ (4) influences attention and arousal
    ____ (5) coordinates complex body movements
    ____ (6) serves as a relay station for sensory information flowing into the brain
    a. medulla
    b. spinal cord
    c. reticular formation
    d. thalamus
    e. cerebellum
    f. brainstem

12. What is the thick band of fibers connecting the two cerebral hemispheres?
    a. cortex   c. cerebrum
    b. corpus callosum d. motor cortex

13. The ⅛-inch outer covering of the cerebrum is the
    a. cerebral cortex.   c. myelin sheath.
    b. cortex callosum.   d. white matter.

14. Match the lobes with the brain areas they contain.
    ____ (1) primary auditory cortex, Wernicke's area
    ____ (2) primary visual cortex
    ____ (3) Broca's area, motor cortex
    ____ (4) somatosensory cortex
    a. frontal lobes
    b. parietal lobes
    c. occipital lobes
    d. temporal lobes

15. Match the specialized area with the appropriate description of function.
    ____ (1) site where hearing registers
    ____ (2) site where vision registers
    ____ (3) site where touch, pressure, and temperature register
    ____ (4) speech production
    ____ (5) voluntary movement
    ____ (6) formulation and understanding of the spoken and written word
    ____ (7) thinking, motivation, impulse control

    a. primary visual cortex   f. Wernicke's area
    b. motor cortex   g. Broca's area
    c. frontal association area
    d. primary auditory cortex
    e. somatosensory cortex

16. Match the hemisphere with the specialized abilities usually associated with it.
    ____ (1) visual-spatial skills
    ____ (2) speech
    ____ (3) recognition and expression of emotion
    ____ (4) singing
    ____ (5) mathematics

    a. right hemisphere
    b. left hemisphere

17. Which of these statements is *not* true of the split-brain operation?
    a. It is used on people with severe epilepsy.
    b. It provides a means of studying the functions of the individual hemispheres.
    c. It causes major changes in intelligence, personality, and behavior.
    d. It makes transfer of information between hemispheres impossible.

18. The CT scan and MRI are used to
    a. show the amount of activity in various parts of the brain.
    b. produce images of the brain's structures.
    c. measure electrical activity in the brain.
    d. observe neural communication at synapses.

19. Which of the following reveals the electrical activity of the brain by producing a record of brain waves?
    a. electroencephalograph   c. PET scan
    b. CT scan   d. MRI

20. Which of the following reveals brain activity and function, rather than the structure of the brain?
    a. CT scan   b. EEG   c. PET scan   d. MRI

21. Which of the following reveals both brain structure and brain activity?
    a. MRI   b. PET scan   c. fMRI   d. CT scan

22. Match the brain-wave pattern with the state associated with it.
    ____ (1) slow-wave (deep) sleep
    ____ (2) deep relaxation while awake
    ____ (3) physical or mental activity

    a. beta wave
    b. delta wave
    c. alpha wave

23. Which of the following is *not* true of stroke?
    a. Stroke is the main cause of injury to the adult brain.
    b. Stroke can cause paralysis and total loss of language ability.
    c. Stroke is caused when the blood supply to part of the brain is cut off.
    d. Although stroke causes many disabilities, it is not life-threatening.

24. Plasticity of the brain increases with age. (true/false)

25. The _____ nervous system connects the brain and spinal cord to the rest of the body.
    a. central   c. somatic
    b. peripheral   d. autonomic

26. The _____ nervous system mobilizes the body's resources during times of stress; the _____ nervous system brings the heightened bodily responses back to normal when the emergency is over.
    a. somatic; autonomic
    b. autonomic; somatic
    c. sympathetic; parasympathetic
    d. parasympathetic; sympathetic

27. The endocrine glands secrete _____ directly into the _____.
    a. hormones; bloodstream
    b. enzymes; digestive tract
    c. enzymes; bloodstream
    d. hormones; digestive tract

28. Match the endocrine gland with the appropriate description.
    ____ (1) keeps body's metabolism in balance
    ____ (2) acts as a master gland that activates the other glands
    ____ (3) regulates the blood sugar
    ____ (4) makes reproduction possible
    ____ (5) releases hormones that prepare the body for emergencies

    a. pituitary gland   d. thyroid gland
    b. adrenal glands   e. pancreas
    c. gonads

Section Two: Label the Brain

Identify each of the numbered parts of the brain diagram.

1. _____

2. _____

3. _____

4. _____

5. _____

6. _____

7. _____

8. _____

9. _____

Section Three: Fill In the Blank

1. In most cases, the _____ is the part of the neuron that receives chemical messages from other neurons.

2. Dopamine, serotonin, and acetylcholine are all examples of _____.

3. The amygdala and the hippocampus are structures in the _____ system.

4. The _____ _____ is at the back of the occipital lobe.

5. The somatosensory cortex is located in the _____ lobe.

6. Phineas Gage suffered damage to his _____ lobe.

7. Broca's area and Wernicke's area are important for language and are located in the _____ hemisphere.

8. The longest part of a neuron is called the _____.

9. The central nervous system is composed of the _____ and the_____.

10. The fight-or-flight response is related to the activity of the _____ division of the autonomic nervous system.

11. The _____ is often referred to as the body's thermostat—it monitors and regulates internal body temperature.

12. The _____ _____ occurs when the neuron ion channels open and allow a sudden influx of positive ions into the axon.

13. _____ aphasia is an impairment in the ability to produce speech sounds, or in extreme cases, an inability to speak at all.

14. The limbic system structure thought to play a central role in the formation of memories is the _____.

15. The primary auditory cortex is located in the _____ lobes.

16. You can write notes in class or execute other smooth, skilled body movements because of the action of the _____.

17. The somatic and the autonomic nervous systems are the two primary divisions of the _____ nervous system.

Section Four: Comprehensive Practice Test

1. Phineas Gage changed from a polite, dependable, well-liked railroad foreman to a rude and impulsive person who could no longer plan realistically for the future after he suffered serious damage to his
   a. occipital lobe.
   c. medulla.
   b. frontal lobe.
   d. cerebellum.

2. Afferent is to efferent as
   a. sensory is to sensation.
   b. sensation is to perception.
   c. motor is to sensory.
   d. sensory is to motor.

3. A deficiency in _____ has been associated with Parkinson's disease, a disease characterized by tremors and rigidity in the limbs.
   a. dopamine
   c. acetylcholine
   b. norepinephrine
   d. GABA

4. Neurons can conduct messages faster if they have
   a. an axon with a myelin sheath.
   b. a positive resting potential.
   c. more than one cell body.
   d. fewer dendrites.

5. The electrical charge inside a neuron is about −70 millivolts, and is known as the _____ potential.
   a. action
   c. resting
   b. refractory
   d. impulse

6. The nervous system is divided into the _____ and the _____ systems.
   a. somatic; autonomic
   b. central; peripheral
   c. brain; spinal cord
   d. sympathetic; parasympathetic

7. The structure that is located above the brainstem and serves as a relay station for information to and from the higher brain centers is the
   a. pituitary gland.
   c. thalamus.
   b. hypothalamus.
   d. hippocampus.

8. The structure that is located in the brain stem and is important for basic life functions such as heartbeat and breathing is the
   a. pons.
   c. hypothalamus.
   b. medulla.
   d. anygdala.

9. The _____ is sometimes referred to as the body's thermostat because it controls temperature, hunger, thirst, and emotional behaviors.
   a. corpus callosum
   c. cerebellum
   b. pituitary gland
   d. hypothalamus

10. The lobe that contains the primary visual cortex is the
    a. parietal lobe.
    c. temporal lobe.
    b. occipital lobe.
    d. frontal lobe.

11. The primary motor cortex is located in the _____ lobe.
    a. frontal
    c. temporal
    b. occipital
    d. occulovisual

12. The pituitary gland, known as the master gland, is part of the _____ system.
    a. somatic
    c. endocrine
    b. peripheral nervous
    d. central nervous

13. The adrenal glands control salt balance in the body through the release of
    a. insulin.
    c. androgens.
    b. corticoids.
    d. endorphins.

14. A researcher interested in getting information about the brain's activity based on the amount of oxygen and glucose consumed should use a(n)
    a. MRI.
    c. PET scan.
    b. EEG.
    d. CT scan.

15. The _____ nervous system controls skeletal muscles and allows the body to interact with the external environment.
    a. autonomic
    c. sympathetic
    b. parasympathetic
    d. somatic

16. Damage to Broca's area will result in a type of aphasia in which patients know what they want to say but cannot speak. (true/false)

17. A person who loves music and art likely has a more dominant left hemisphere. (true/false)

18. In the United States, stroke is the _____ common cause of injury to the adult brain.
    a. most
    c. third-most
    b. second-most
    d. least

19. The functional MRI (fMRI) reveals both brain structure and brain activity. (true/false)

Section Five: Critical Thinking

1. Using your knowledge about how the human brain has been studied in the past and is studied today, point out the advantages and the disadvantages of the older investigative methods—the case study, the autopsy, and the study of people with brain injuries or who have had brain surgery (including the split-brain operation). Follow the same procedure to discuss the more modern techniques—EEG, CT scan, MRI, PET scan, and fMRI.

2. A continuing controversial issue is the ethical question of whether animals should be used in biological research. Review the chapter and find each instance of animals being used to advance scientific knowledge of the brain. Using what you have read in this chapter and any other information you have acquired, prepare arguments to support both of the following positions:
   a. The use of animals in research projects is ethical and justifiable because of the possible benefits to humankind.
   b. The use of animals in research projects is not ethical or justifiable on the grounds of possible benefits to humankind.

3. How would your life change if you had a massive stroke affecting your left hemisphere? How would it change if the stroke damaged your right hemisphere? Which stroke would be more tragic for you, and why?

Sensation and Perception

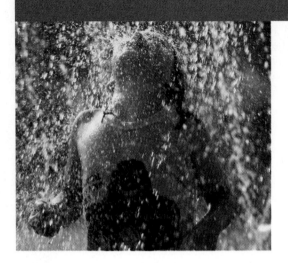

The man called S.B. had never seen a sunrise, a flower, a smile, or even his own face, for he had lost his sight in both eyes when he was only 10 months old. Despite his blindness, S.B. had managed to live a fairly full and happy life. He could get around on his own, cross streets, and even ride a bicycle with his friend's hand on his shoulder to guide him. He read Braille, and he loved to make things with tools in the small shed he used as a workshop.

All his life S.B. had wondered what it would be like to see. Then, when he was 50 years old, he learned that his useless, opaque corneas could be replaced through a cornea transplant. Finally, the miracle of sight he had dreamed about would be a reality.

When the surgeon first removed the bandages from S.B.'s eyes, people and objects were little more than large blurs to him. But the operation was successful, and after a few days S.B. could see quite well. He could walk up and down the hospital corridors without using a cane or holding onto the wall. Soon he was able to see and recognize objects by sight that he already knew well by touch. But all was not well.

S.B. had difficulty recognizing unfamiliar objects and things he had never touched. He never learned to read by sight, although he could recognize numbers and capital letters. S.B. had trouble perceiving distance. From the window of his hospital room he watched the cars and trucks pass in the street below. He thought his feet would touch the ground if he hung from the windowsill with his hands, yet his window was nearly 60 feet above the ground.

S.B.'s story did not have a happy ending. The world looked drab to him, and he was upset by the imperfections he saw. Objects he had once imagined to be perfect now had disappointing defects. He could no longer cross streets because seeing cars whizzing by terrified him. Often he would not even bother to turn on the lights at night, for he preferred to sit in his more comfortable world of darkness. As time passed, S.B. became more and more depressed and withdrawn. Within 3 years after the cornea transplant, he died. (Adapted from Gregory, 1978.)

Are you surprised that the miracle in S.B.'s life, the gift of sight, turned out to be hardly a gift at all? The surgeons were able to give him the sensation of sight but, sadly, not the 50 years of visual perceptual experience he had missed.

Sensation and perception are intimately related in everyday experience, but they are not the same. **Sensation** is the process through which the senses detect visual, auditory, and other sensory stimuli and transmit them to the brain. **Perception** is the process by which sensory information is actively organized and interpreted by the brain. Sensation furnishes the raw material of sensory experience, while perception provides the finished product.

To a large extent humans must learn to perceive, and people whose sight has been restored differ greatly in their ability to develop useful perception. S.B.'s life shows dramatically the great gap between sensation (the reception of sensory information) and perception (the process of giving it meaning). For many who regain their vision, it is truly a remarkable gift; but for others like S.B., gaining sight can be a major disappointment.

In this chapter we will explore the world of sensation, with a focus on the five primary senses—vision, hearing, touch, taste, and smell—along with such secondary senses as balance and pain. You will learn how the senses detect sensory information and how this sensory information is actively organized and interpreted by the brain. We begin with a closer look at sensation.

What is the difference between sensation and perception?

SENSATION: THE SENSORY WORLD

Our senses serve as ports of entry for all information about the world. Virtually everything we experience is detected initially by our senses. Yet it is amazing how little of the sensory world we actually sense. For example, we can see only a thin slice of the vast spectrum of electromagnetic energy. We cannot perceive microwaves, X rays, or ultraviolet light. We are unable to hear the ultrasonic sound of a dog whistle and can detect a scant 20% of the sounds a dolphin or a bat can hear. Nor can we sense the outline of a warm-blooded animal from its infrared heat pat-

sensation: The process through which the senses pick up visual, auditory, and other sensory stimuli and transmit them to the brain; sensory information that has registered in the brain but has not been interpreted.

perception: The process by which sensory information is actively organized and interpreted by the brain.

Along the U.S.–Mexican border, infrared-sensitive cameras are used to allow police to "see" illegal entrants in the dark. Their body heat is what makes the two people show up in this infrared photo.

What is the difference between the absolute threshold and the difference threshold?

tern at night, as rattlesnakes and other pit vipers can. Yet all of these sensory stimuli exist in the real, physical world.

No matter which of the senses are compared, humans are not at the top of the list for quality or sensitivity. Some animals have a superior sense of hearing (bats and dolphins); others have sharper vision (hawks); still others have a superior sense of smell (bloodhounds); and so on. Nevertheless, humans have remarkable sensory abilities and superior abilities of perception.

The Absolute Threshold: To Sense or Not to Sense

What is the softest sound you can hear, the dimmest light you can see, the most diluted substance you can taste? What is the lightest touch you can feel, the faintest odor you can smell? Researchers in sensory psychology and psychophysics have performed many experiments over the years to answer these questions. Their research has established measures for the senses known as *absolute thresholds*. Just as the threshold of a doorway is the dividing point between being outside a room and inside, the **absolute threshold** of a sense marks the difference between not being able to perceive a stimulus and being just barely able to perceive it. Psychologists have arbitrarily defined this absolute threshold as the minimum amount of sensory stimulation that can be detected 50% of the time. The absolute thresholds established for the five primary senses in humans are (1) for vision, a candle flame 30 miles away on a clear night; (2) for hearing, a watch ticking 20 feet away; (3) for taste, 1 teaspoon of sugar dissolved in 2 gallons of water; (4) for smell, a single drop of perfume in a three-room house; and (5) for touch, a bee's wing falling a distance of 1 centimeter onto the cheek.

Important as it is, the absolute threshold, once crossed, says nothing about the broad range of sensory experiences. To sense or not to sense—that is the only question the absolute threshold answers. But read on—there are other questions to be answered.

The Difference Threshold: Detecting Differences

If you are listening to music, the very fact that you can hear it means that the absolute threshold has been crossed. But how much must the volume be turned up or down for you to notice a difference? The **difference threshold** is a measure of the smallest increase or decrease in a physical stimulus that is required to produce the **just noticeable difference (JND)**. The JND is the smallest change in sensation that a person is able to detect 50% of the time. If you were holding a 5-pound weight and 1 pound were added, you could easily notice the difference. But if you were holding 100 pounds and 1 additional pound were added, you could not sense the difference. Why not?

More than 150 years ago, researcher Ernst Weber (1795–1878) observed that the JND for all the senses depends on a proportion or percentage of change rather than a fixed amount of change. This observation became known as **Weber's law**. A weight you are holding must increase or decrease by a ratio of ⅟₅₀, or 2%, for you to notice the difference. According to Weber's law, the greater the original stimulus, the more it must be increased or decreased for the difference to be noticeable.

The difference threshold is not the same for all the senses. A very large (⅕, or 20%) difference is necessary for some changes in taste to be detected. In contrast, if you were listening to music, you would notice a difference if a tone became slightly higher or lower in pitch by only about 0.33%.

Aren't some people more sensitive to sensory changes than others? Yes, the difference thresholds for the various senses are not the same for all people. In fact, there are great individual differences. Expert wine tasters would know if a particular vintage was a little too sweet, even if its sweetness varied by only a fraction of the 20% necessary for changes in taste. Actually, Weber's law best fits people with average sensitivities, and sensory stimuli that are neither very strong (loud thunder) nor very weak (a faint whisper).

absolute threshold: The minimum amount of sensory stimulation that can be detected 50% of the time.

difference threshold: The smallest increase or decrease in a physical stimulus required to produce a difference in sensation that is noticeable 50% of the time.

just noticeable difference (JND): The smallest change in sensation that a person is able to detect 50% of the time.

Weber's law: The law stating that the just noticeable difference (JND) for all the senses depends on a proportion or percentage of change in a stimulus rather than on a fixed amount of change.

Signal Detection Theory

You may have realized that the classic methods in psychophysics for measuring sensory thresholds have a serious limitation. They focus exclusively on the physical stimulus—how strong or weak it is or how much the stimulus must change for the difference to be noticed. But even within the same individual, sensory capabilities are sharper and duller from time to time and under different conditions. Factors that affect a person's ability to detect a sensory signal are, in addition to the strength of the stimulus, the person's motivation to detect it, previous experience, expectation that it will occur, and alertness or level of fatigue.

Another approach takes these factors into account. **Signal detection theory** is the view that the detection of a sensory stimulus involves both discriminating that stimulus from background "noise" and deciding whether the stimulus is actually present. Deciding that a stimulus is present depends partly on the probability that the stimulus will occur and partly on the potential gain or loss associated with deciding whether it is present or absent.

Signal detection theory has special relevance to people in many occupations—air traffic controllers, police officers, military personnel on guard duty, medical professionals, poultry inspectors, to name a few. Whether these professionals detect certain stimuli can have important consequences for the health and welfare of vast numbers of people (Swets, 1992).

Transduction: Transforming Sensory Stimuli into Neural Impulses

You may be surprised to learn that our eyes do not actually see; nor do our ears hear. The sense organs provide only the beginning point of sensation that must be completed by the brain. As you learned in Chapter 2, specific clusters of neurons in specialized parts of the brain must be stimulated for us to see, hear, taste, and so on. Yet the brain itself cannot respond directly to light, sound waves, odors, and tastes. How, then, does it get the message? The answer is through the sensory receptors.

The body's sense organs are equipped with specialized cells called **sensory receptors,** which detect and respond to one type of sensory stimuli—light, sound waves, odors, and so on. Then, through a process known as **transduction,** the receptors change or convert the sensory stimulation into neural impulses, the electrochemical language of the brain. The neural impulses are then transmitted to precise locations in the brain, such as the primary visual cortex for vision or the primary auditory cortex for hearing. You experience a sensation only when the appropriate part of the brain is stimulated. The sense receptors provide the essential link between the physical sensory world and the brain.

Sensory Adaptation

All of our senses are more receptive, more finely tuned, to changes in sensory stimuli than to sameness. After a time the sensory receptors become accustomed to constant, unchanging levels of stimuli—sights, sounds, smells—so that we notice them less and less, or not at all. This process of becoming less sensitive to an unchanging sensory stimulus over time is known as **sensory adaptation**.

You have undoubtedly noticed the distinctive odor of your home when you first walk through the door, but after a few minutes you are not aware of it. A continuous odor will stimulate the smell receptors to respond only for a while. Then, if there is no change in the odors, the receptors will

signal detection theory: The view that detection of a sensory stimulus involves both discriminating a stimulus from background "noise" and deciding whether the stimulus is actually present.

sensory receptors: Specialized cells in each sense organ that detect and respond to sensory stimuli—light, sound, odors, etc.—and transduce (convert) the stimuli into neural impulses.

transduction: The process by which sensory receptors convert sensory stimuli—light, sound, odors, etc.—into neural impulses.

sensory adaptation: The process of becoming less sensitive to an unchanging sensory stimulus over time.

Link It!

How are sensory stimuli in the environment experienced as sensations?

People who swim in icy water experience a degree of sensory adaptation, which helps their bodies adjust to the frigid temperature.

steadily diminish their firing rate, and smell adaptation will occur. However, sensory adaptation is not likely to occur in the presence of a very strong stimulus—such as the smell of ammonia, an ear-splitting sound, or the taste of rancid food.

Even though it reduces our sensory awareness, sensory adaptation enables us to shift our attention to what is most important at any given moment. We don't need to constantly sense the feel of the clothing on our bodies, the background noises around us, or any persistent odors in our environment. Thanks to sensory adaptation, we can give full concentration to new incoming stimuli.

VISION

For most people, vision is the most valued sensory experience, and it is the sense that has been most investigated. But, before looking at *how* we see, let's consider *what* we see. We cannot see any object unless light is reflected from it or given off by it.

Light: What We See

Light is one form of electromagnetic rays made up of tiny particles called *photons*, which travel in waves. But light is only a small portion of the spectrum of electromagnetic waves (see Figure 3.1). Cosmic rays, gamma rays, X rays, and ultraviolet rays have wavelengths too short for human eyes to perceive. And the wavelengths of infrared rays, microwaves, radar waves, radio and TV waves, and AC circuits are too long. Our eyes can respond only to a very narrow band of electromagnetic waves, a band called the **visible spectrum**.

The length of a light wave primarily determines the color the human eye perceives. The shortest light waves we can see appear violet, while the longest visible waves appear red. *What* we see is confined to the visible spectrum, but *how* we see depends on the many parts of the eye and brain that bring us the world of sight.

The Eye: Window to the Visual Sensory World

For most of us, the eyes are the most important sensory connection to the world. Vision provides most of the information on which the brain feeds. Look at the parts of the eye shown in Figure 3.2 as you read about the role each structure plays in vision.

visible spectrum: The narrow band of electromagnetic waves, 380–760 nm in length, that are visible to the human eye.

cornea (KOR-nee-uh): The transparent covering on the front surface of the eyeball that bends light rays inward through the pupil.

lens: The transparent structure behind the iris that changes shape as it focuses images on the retina.

accommodation: The action of the lens in changing shape as it focuses objects on the retina, becoming more spherical for near objects and flatter for far objects.

retina: The membrane at the back of the eye that contains the rods and the cones and onto which the incoming image is projected by the lens.

Figure 3.1

The Electromagnetic Spectrum

Human eyes can perceive only a very thin band of electromagnetic waves known as the visible spectrum.

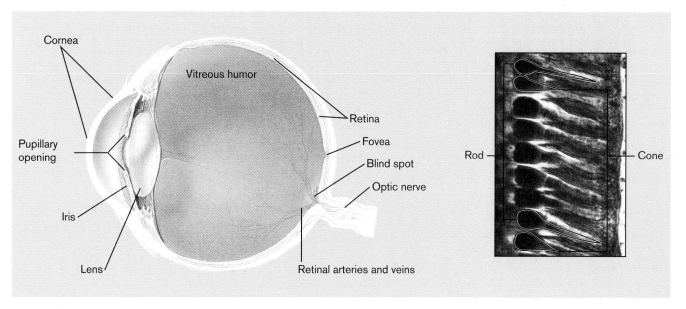

Figure 3.2
The Major Parts of the Human Eye

The Cornea, Iris, and Pupil   The globe-shaped human eyeball measures about 1 inch in diameter. Bulging from its front surface is the **cornea**—the tough, transparent, protective layer covering the front of the eye. About the size of a dime, the cornea performs the first step in vision by bending the light rays inward. It herds the light rays through the pupil—the small, dark opening in the center of the iris.

The iris is the circular, colored part of the eye, which researchers have found to be even more unique to individuals than their fingerprints (Johnson, 1996). Two muscles in the iris dilate and contract the pupil and thus regulate the amount of light entering the eye. Although the pupil never closes completely, in very bright light it can contract to the size of the head of a pin; in very dim light it can dilate to the size of a pencil eraser.

From Lens to Retina: Focusing Images   Suspended just behind the iris and the pupil, the **lens** is composed of many thin layers and looks like a transparent disc. The lens performs the task of focusing on objects closer than 20 feet. It flattens as it focuses on objects viewed at a distance, but it becomes more spherical, bulging in the center, as it focuses on close objects. This flattening and bulging action of the lens is known as **accommodation**. With age, the lens loses some elasticity. Hence, it loses the ability to change its shape to accommodate for near vision, a condition called *presbyopia* ("old eyes"). This is why many people over age 40 must hold a book or newspaper at arm's length or use reading glasses to magnify the print.

The lens focuses the incoming image onto the **retina**—a membrane about the size of a small postage stamp and as thin as onion skin, located on the inner surface of the eyeball. The retina contains the sensory receptors for vision. The image projected onto the retina is upside down and reversed left to right. You can demonstrate this for yourself in the *Try It!*

How do the cornea, the iris, and the pupil function in vision?

What are the lens and the retina?

Take an ordinary teaspoon—one in which you can see your reflection. Looking at the bottom (the convex surface) of the spoon, you will see an image of your face that is right side up—the way the image enters the eye. Turn the spoon over and look at the inside (the concave surface), and you will see your face upside down and reversed left to right—the way the image appears on the retina. The brain, however, perceives images right side up.

What roles do the rods and cones play in vision?

rods: The light-sensitive receptors in the retina that allow humans to see in black, white, and shades of gray in dim light.

cones: The receptor cells in the retina that enable humans to see color and fine detail in adequate light, but that do not function in dim light.

fovea (FO-vee-uh): A small area of the retina, ⅟₅₀ of an inch in diameter, that provides the clearest and sharpest vision because it has the largest concentration of cones.

dark adaptation: The eye's increasing ability to see in dim light.

optic nerve: The nerve that carries visual information from the retina to the brain.

hue: The property of light commonly referred to as color (red, blue, green, etc.), determined primarily by the wavelength of light reflected from a surface.

saturation: The degree to which light waves producing a color are of the same wavelength; the purity of a color.

The Rods and Cones: Receptors for Light and Color   At the back of the retina is a layer of light-sensitive receptor cells—the **rods** and the **cones**. Named for their shapes, the rods look like slender cylinders, and the cones appear shorter and more rounded. There are about 120 million rods and 6 million cones in each retina.

The cones are the receptor cells that enable us to see color and fine detail in adequate light. Color vision is made possible by three classes of cones: receptors that are sensitive to long (red), medium (green), and short (blue) wavelengths (Roorda & Williams, 1999). The bipolar cells and the ganglion cells in the retina begin the work that the brain completes in computing the perceived colors and analyzing the relative activity in the three types of cones (Masland, 1996; Nathans, 1989). You will read more about color vision later in this chapter.

If someone were to plot an imaginary line through the middle of your pupil, the line would strike the center of the retina in the **fovea**, a small pit-like area about the size of the period at the end of this sentence (refer to Figure 3.2). When you look directly at an object, the image of the object is focused on the center of your fovea. The clearest point of vision, the fovea is the part of the retina that we use for fine detail work. Only ⅟₅₀ of an inch in diameter, the fovea contains no rods but has some 30,000 cones tightly packed together (Beatty, 1995).

The rods respond to black and white, and they encode all other visible wavelengths but encode them in shades of gray instead of in color. More sensitive to light than the cones, the rods enable us to see in very dim light and provide night vision, but they do not provide the sharp, clear images that the cones make possible.

Step from the bright sunlight into a darkened movie theater and at first you can hardly tell which seats are occupied and which are empty. After a few moments in the dark, your eyes begin to adapt and you can see dimly. Yet it takes about half an hour or more for your eyes to adapt completely. After complete **dark adaptation**, you can see light that is 100,000 times less bright than daylight.

When you leave a movie theater, your eyes are dark-adapted, and the return to the bright sunlight is a "blinding" experience. However, it takes only about 60 seconds, not half an hour, to become light-adapted again. In light adaptation, a reflexive action occurs; the pupils immediately become smaller, permitting less light to enter the eyes.

What path does the neural impulse take from the retina to the primary visual cortex?

From the Retina to the Brain: From Visual Sensation to Visual Perception
In the initial stages of visual information processing, the rods and cones transduce, or change, light waves into neural impulses that are fed to the bipolar cells, which in turn pass the impulses along to the ganglion cells. The approximately 1 million axon-like extensions of the ganglion cells are bundled together in a pencil-sized cable that extends through the wall of the retina, leaving the eye on its way to the brain. Where the cable runs through the retinal wall, there can be no rods or cones, and so this point is a *blind spot* in each eye. Beyond the retinal wall, the cable becomes the **optic nerve**.

Leaving each eye at the blind spot, the optic nerve cables come together at the *optic chiasma*, a point where some of the nerve fibers cross to the opposite side of the brain. The visual fibers from the right half of each retina go to the right hemisphere, and the visual fibers from the left half of each retina go to the left hemisphere. This switching is important because it allows visual information from a single eye to be represented in the primary visual cortex of both hemispheres of the brain. Moreover, it plays an important part in depth perception.

From the optic chiasma, the optic nerve travels to the thalamus (specifically, to its lateral geniculate nucleus). There it synapses with neural fibers that transmit the impulses to the primary visual cortex. Approximately one-fourth of the primary visual cortex is dedicated exclusively to analyzing input from the fovea.

Color Vision: A Multicolored World

What are the three dimensions that combine to provide the colors people perceive?

Some light waves striking an object are absorbed by it, and others are reflected from it. We see only the wavelengths that are reflected, not those that are absorbed. Why does an apple look red? If you hold a red apple in bright light, light waves of all the different wavelengths are striking the apple, but more of the longer red wavelengths of light are reflected from the apple's skin. The shorter wavelengths are absorbed, so you see only the reflected red. Bite into the apple and it looks white. Why? You see white because, rather than being absorbed, all the wavelengths of the visible spectrum are reflected from the inside part of the apple. The presence of all visible wavelengths gives the sensation of white.

Our everyday visual experience goes far beyond the colors in the rainbow. We can detect thousands of subtle color shadings. What produces these fine color distinctions? Researchers have identified three dimensions that combine to provide the rich world of color we experience: (1) The chief dimension is **hue**, which refers to the specific color perceived—red, green, and so forth. (2) **Saturation** refers to the purity of a color. A color becomes less saturated, or less pure, as other wavelengths of light are mixed with it. (3) **Brightness** refers to the intensity of the light energy that is perceived.

Theories of Color Vision: How the Eyes Sense Color   Two major theories have been offered to explain color vision, and both were formulated before the development of laboratory technology capable of testing them. The **trichromatic theory**, first proposed by Thomas Young in 1802, was modified by Hermann von Helmholtz about 50 years later. This theory states that there are three kinds of cones in the retina and that each kind makes its maximum chemical response to one of three colors—blue, green, or red. Research in the 1950s and the 1960s by Nobel Prize winner George Wald (1964; Wald et al., 1954) supports the trichromatic theory. Wald discovered that even though all cones have basically the same structure, the retina does indeed contain three kinds of cones.

The trichromatic theory alone, however, cannot explain how we are able to perceive such a rich variety of colors. Researchers now know that there must be color-coding processes that combine color information in a more complex way than occurs in the cones.

The other major attempt to explain color vision is the **opponent-process theory**, which was first proposed by physiologist Ewald Hering in 1878 and revised in 1957 by researchers Leon Hurvich and Dorthea Jamison. According to the opponent-process theory, three classes of cells respond by increasing or decreasing their rate of firing when different colors are present. The red/green cells increase their firing rate when red is present and decrease it when green is present. The yellow/blue cells have an increased response to yellow and a decreased response to blue. Another type of cell increases its response rate for white light and decreases it in the absence of light. Think of the opponent-process theory as opposing pairs of cells on a see-saw. As one goes up, the other goes down, and vice versa. The relative firing positions of the three pairs of cells transmit color information to the brain.

Does the opponent process operate in the cones, or elsewhere? Researchers now believe that the cones pass on information about wavelengths of light to higher levels of visual processing. Researchers De Valois and De Valois (1975) proposed that the opponent processes might operate at the ganglion cells in the retina and in the higher brain centers rather than at the level of the receptors, the cones.

If you look long enough at one color in the opponent-process pair and then look at a white surface, your brain will give you the sensation of the opposite color—a negative **afterimage**. After you have stared at one color in an opponent-process pair (red/green, yellow/blue, black/white), the cell responding to that color tires and the opponent cell begins to fire, producing the afterimage. Demonstrate this for yourself in the *Try It!* on page 72.

Color Blindness: Weakness for Sensing Some Colors   Not everyone sees the world in the same colors. If normal genes for the three color pigments are not present, a person will experience some form of **color blindness**—the inability to distinguish some colors or, in rare cases, the total absence of color vision.

What two major theories attempt to explain color vision?

brightness: The dimension of visual sensation that is dependent on the intensity of light reflected from a surface and that corresponds to the amplitude of the light wave.

trichromatic theory: The theory of color vision suggesting that there are three types of cones, which are maximally sensitive to red, green, or blue, and that varying levels of activity in these receptors can produce all of the colors.

opponent-process theory: The theory that three classes of cells increase their firing rate to signal one color and decrease their firing rate to signal the opposing color (red/green, yellow/blue, white/black).

afterimage: The visual sensation that remains after a stimulus is withdrawn.

color blindness: The inability to distinguish some or all colors, resulting from a defect in the cones.

Stare at the dot in the green, black, and yellow flag for approximately 1 minute. Then shift your gaze to the dot in the blank rectangle. You will see the American flag in its true colors—red, white, and blue, which are the opponent-process opposites of green, black, and yellow.

Link It!

Researchers discovered what the world looks like to a color-blind person by studying people who have normal vision in one eye but some form of color blindness in the other.

Until recently, scientists believed that in order to have normal color vision, a person must inherit three genes for color—one gene for blue on chromosome 7 and one gene each for red and green on the X chromosome. However, recent DNA evidence from a group of men with normal color vision revealed that the number of genes for red and green on the X chromosome ranged from two to nine (Neitz & Neitz, 1995). This study suggests that people's ability to perceive color ranges over a continuum from red-green color blindness in those missing one or both of the color genes on the X chromosome to exceptional red-green color vision in those with multiple color genes on that chromosome. Some form of red-green color blindness is found in about 5% of males, compared to less than 1% of females (Neitz et al., 1996). The large difference is due to the fact that males have only one X chromosome.

Before leaving the topic of vision, let us dispel the myth that some mammals, especially dogs, generally lack color vision. Research has confirmed that some form of color vision is present in all species of mammals (Jacobs, 1993).

On the left a hot air balloon is shown as it would appear to a person with normal color vision; on the right is the same balloon as it would appear to a person with red-green color blindness.

HEARING

Years ago, the frightening science fiction movie *Alien* was advertised this way: "In space no one can hear you scream!" Although the movie was fiction, the statement is true. Light can travel through the vast nothingness of space, a vacuum, but sound cannot. In this section, you will learn why.

Sound: What We Hear

Sound requires a medium through which to move, such as air, water, or a solid object. This fact was first demonstrated by Robert Boyle in 1660 when he suspended a ringing pocket watch by a thread inside a specially designed jar. When Boyle pumped all the air out of the jar, he could no longer hear the watch ring. But when he pumped the air back into the jar, he could again hear the watch ringing.

If you attend a very loud rock concert, you not only hear but actually feel the mechanical vibrations. The pulsating speakers may cause the floor, your seat, the walls, and the air around you to seem to shake or vibrate. What you feel are the moving air molecules being pushed toward you in waves as the speakers blast their vibrations outward.

Frequency is an important characteristic of sound and is determined by the number of cycles completed by a sound wave in one second. The unit used to measure frequency, or the cycles per second, is known as the hertz (Hz). The pitch, how high or low the sound is, is chiefly determined by frequency—the higher the frequency (the more vibrations per second), the higher the sound. The human ear can hear sound frequencies from low bass tones of around 20 Hz up to high-pitched sounds of about 20,000 Hz. Many mammals—dogs, cats, bats, and rats—can hear tones much higher in frequency than 20,000 Hz. Amazingly, dolphins can respond to sounds up to 100,000 Hz.

The loudness of a sound is determined largely by a measure called **amplitude**. Amplitude depends on the energy of the sound wave. The force or pressure with which air molecules move chiefly determines loudness. The sound pressure level (loudness) of sounds is measured using a unit called the *bel*, named for Alexander Graham Bell. Because the bel is a rather large unit, sound levels are expressed in tenths of a bel, or **decibels** (dB). The threshold of human hearing is set at 0 dB, which does not mean the absence of sound but the softest sound that can be heard in a very quiet setting. Each increase of 10 decibels makes a sound 10 times louder. A whisper is about 20 dB, but that is 100 times louder than 0 dB. A normal conversation, around 60 dB, is 10,000 times louder than a soft whisper at 20 dB. Figure 3.3 (on page 74) shows comparative decibel levels for a variety of sounds.

If pitch and loudness were the only perceptual dimensions of sound, we could not tell the difference between two instruments if both were playing exactly the same note at the same decibel level. A third characteristic of sound, **timbre**, refers to the distinct quality of a sound that distinguishes it from other sounds of the same pitch and loudness.

The Ear: More to It Than Meets the Eye

The part of the body called the ear plays only a minor role in human **audition**. In fact, even if your visible outer ears were cut off, your hearing would suffer very little. Let's see how each part of the ear contributes to the ability to hear.

The oddly shaped, curved flap of cartilage and skin called the *pinna* is the visible part of the **outer ear** (see Figure 3.4 on page 74). Inside the ear, the *auditory canal* is about 1 inch long, and its entrance is lined with hairs. At the end of the auditory canal is the *eardrum* (or tympanic membrane), a thin, flexible membrane about ⅓ inch in diameter. The eardrum moves in response to the sound waves that strike it.

frequency: Measured in the unit called the hertz, the number of sound waves or cycles a second, determining the pitch of a sound.

amplitude: Measured in decibels, the magnitude or intensity of a sound wave, determining the loudness of the sound.

decibel (DES-ih-bel): A unit of measurement of the intensity or loudness of sound based on the amplitude of the sound wave.

timbre (TAM-burr): The distinctive quality of a sound that distinguishes it from other sounds of the same pitch and loudness.

audition: The sensation of hearing; the process of hearing.

outer ear: The visible part of the ear, consisting of the pinna and the auditory canal.

What determines the pitch and the loudness of sound, and how is each quality measured?

How do the outer, middle, and inner ears function in hearing?

Figure 3.3

Decibel Levels of Various Sounds

The loudness of a sound (its amplitude) is measured in decibels. Each increase of 10 decibels makes a sound 10 times louder. A normal conversation at 3 feet measures about 60 decibels, which is 10,000 times louder than a soft whisper of 20 decibels. Any exposure to sounds of 130 dB or higher puts a person at immediate risk for hearing damage.

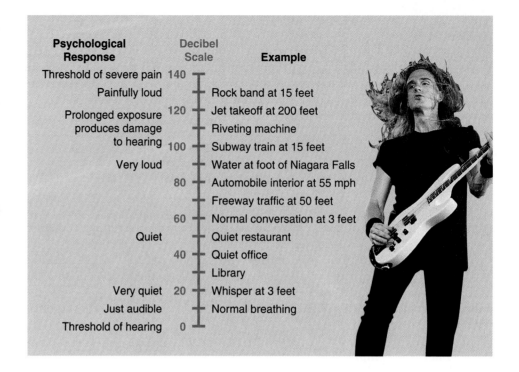

Psychological Response	Decibel Scale	Example
Threshold of severe pain	140	
Painfully loud		Rock band at 15 feet
Prolonged exposure produces damage to hearing	120	Jet takeoff at 200 feet
		Riveting machine
	100	Subway train at 15 feet
Very loud		Water at foot of Niagara Falls
	80	Automobile interior at 55 mph
		Freeway traffic at 50 feet
	60	Normal conversation at 3 feet
Quiet		Quiet restaurant
	40	Quiet office
		Library
Very quiet	20	Whisper at 3 feet
Just audible		Normal breathing
Threshold of hearing	0	

The **middle ear** is no larger than an aspirin tablet. Inside its chamber are the *ossicles*, the three smallest bones in your body, each "about the size of a grain of rice" (Strome & Vernick, 1989). Named for their shapes, the three connected ossicles—the hammer, the anvil, and the stirrup—link the eardrum to the oval window (see Figure 3.4). The ossicles amplify the sound some 22 times (Békésy, 1957).

The **inner ear** begins at the inner side of the oval window on the base of the **cochlea**—a fluid-filled, snail-shaped, bony chamber. When the stirrup pushes against the oval window, it sets up vibrations that move the fluid in the cochlea

Figure 3.4

Anatomy of the Human Ear

Sound waves pass through the auditory canal to the eardrum, causing it to vibrate and set in motion the ossicles in the middle ear. When the stirrup pushes against the oval window, it sets up vibrations in the inner ear. This moves the fluid in the cochlea back and forth and sets in motion the hair cells, causing a message to be sent to the brain via the auditory nerve.

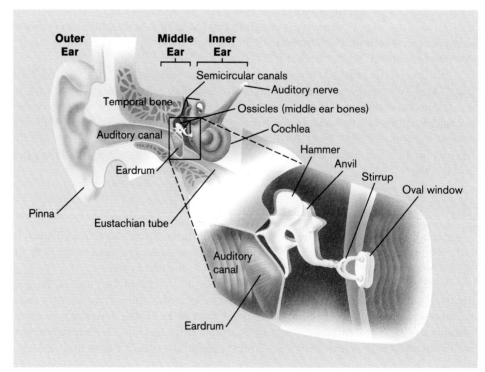

back and forth in waves. The movement of the fluid sets in motion the thin *basilar membrane* that runs through the cochlea. Attached to the basilar membrane are about 15,000 sensory receptors called **hair cells**, each with a bundle of tiny hairs protruding from it. The tiny hair bundles are pushed and pulled by the motion of the fluid inside the cochlea. If the tip of the hair bundle is moved only as much as the width of an atom, an electrical impulse is generated, which is transmitted to the brain by way of the auditory nerve (Hudspeth, 1983).

Theories of Hearing: How Hearing Works

In the 1860s Hermann von Helmholtz helped develop **place theory**, one of the two major theories of hearing. This theory holds that each individual pitch a person hears is determined by the particular spot or place along the basilar membrane of the cochlea that vibrates the most. By observing the living basilar membrane, researchers have verified that different locations do indeed vibrate in response to differently pitched sounds (Ruggero, 1992). Even so, place theory cannot explain how humans perceive the low frequencies below 150 Hz.

Another attempt to explain hearing is **frequency theory**. According to this theory, the hair cell receptors vibrate the same number of times per second as the sounds that reach them. Thus, a tone of 500 Hz would stimulate the hair cells to vibrate 500 times per second as well. Frequency theory seems valid for low-pitched tones, but it cannot account for frequencies higher than 1,000 Hz. Individual neurons cannot fire more than about 1,000 times per second. Therefore, they could not signal to the brain the higher-pitched tones exceeding 1,000 Hz.

The *volley principle* was put forth to suggest that groups, or volleys, of neurons, if properly synchronized, could together produce the firing rate required for tones somewhat higher than 1,000 Hz (Wever, 1949). Today, however, researchers believe that frequency theory best explains how we perceive low frequencies and place theory best accounts for how we perceive the remaining frequencies (Matlin & Foley, 1997).

Hearing Loss: Kinds and Causes

About 28 million people in the United States suffer from hearing loss (Kalb, 1997), and almost 15% of American children have low- or high-frequency hearing loss (Niskan et al., 1998). Hearing loss and deafness can be caused by disease, birth defects, injury, excessive noise, and old age. Conductive hearing loss, or *conduction deafness*, is usually caused by disease or injury to the eardrum or the bones of the middle ear, which prevents sound waves from being conducted to the cochlea. Almost all conductive hearing loss can be repaired medically or surgically. And in rare cases, a person can be fitted with a hearing aid that bypasses the middle ear.

Most adults with hearing loss suffer from *sensorineural hearing loss*, which involves damage to either the cochlea or the auditory nerve. Large numbers of the cochlea's delicate hair cells, which transduce sound waves into neural impulses, may be damaged or destroyed. If the damage is not too severe, a conventional hearing aid may reduce the effects of this type of hearing loss (Bramblett, 1997). But hearing aids are useless if the damage is to the auditory nerve, which connects the cochlea to the brain; in such cases the hearing loss is usually total. Although hearing loss occurs most often in older people, about 75% of the cases of hearing loss appear to be caused by lifelong exposure to excessive noise rather than by aging (Kalb, 1997).

middle ear: The portion of the ear containing the ossicles, which connect the eardrum to the oval window and amplify the vibrations as they travel to the inner ear.

inner ear: The innermost portion of the ear, containing the cochlea, the vestibular sacs, and the semicircular canals.

cochlea (KOK-lee-uh): The snail-shaped, fluid-filled chamber in the inner ear that contains the hair cells (the sound receptors).

hair cells: Sensory receptors for hearing, found in the cochlea.

place theory: The theory that sounds of different frequency or pitch cause maximum activation of hair cells at certain locations along the basilar membrane.

frequency theory: The theory that hair cell receptors vibrate the same number of times as the sounds that reach them, thereby accounting for how variations in pitch are transmitted to the brain.

What two major theories attempt to explain hearing?

What are some major causes of hearing loss?

Link It!

SMELL AND TASTE

You have been reading about the importance of the abilities to sense light and sound. Now let's explore the chemical senses, smell and taste.

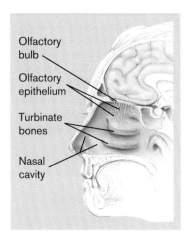

Figure 3.5

The Olfactory Sense

Odor molecules travel up the nostrils to the olfactory epithelium, which contains the receptor cells for smell. Olfactory receptors are special neurons whose axons form the olfactory nerve. The olfactory nerve relays smell messages to the olfactory bulbs, which pass them on to the olfactory cortex.

What path does a smell message take from the nose to the brain?

Smell: Sensing Scents

Consider what it would be like to live in a world without smell. "Not really so bad," you might say. "Although I could not smell flowers, perfume, or my favorite foods, I would never again have to endure the foul odors of life. It's a trade-off, so what's the difference?"

The difference is large indeed. Our ability to detect odors close at hand and at a distance is an aid to survival. We smell smoke and can escape before the flames of a fire envelop us. Our noses broadcast an odor alarm to the brain when certain poisonous gases or noxious fumes are present. But the survival value of odor detection in humans does not stop there. Smell, aided by taste, is the last line of defense—our final chance to avoid putting spoiled food or drink into our bodies.

Odors have a powerful ability to call forth old memories and rekindle strong feelings, even decades after the experiences originally occurred. This is not surprising since the olfactory system sends information to the limbic system, an area in the brain that plays an important role in emotions and memories as well (Horwitz, 1997).

Olfaction—the sense of smell—is a chemical sense. We cannot smell a substance unless some of its molecules vaporize—pass from a solid or liquid into a gaseous state. Heat speeds up the evaporation of molecules, which is why food that is cooking has a stronger and more distinct odor than uncooked food. When odor molecules vaporize, they become airborne and make their way up each nostril to the olfactory epithelium. The **olfactory epithelium** consists of two 1-square-inch patches of tissue, one at the top of each nasal cavity, which together contain about 10 million olfactory neurons—the receptor cells for smell. Each of these neurons contains only one of the 1,000 different types of odor receptors (Bargmann, 1996). Because humans are able to detect some 10,000 odors, each of the 1,000 types of odor receptors must be able to respond to more than one kind of odor molecule. Moreover, some odor molecules trigger more than one type of odor receptor (Axel, 1995). The intensity of a smell stimulus—how strong or weak it is—is apparently determined by the number of olfactory neurons firing at the same time (Freeman, 1991). Figure 3.5 shows a diagram of the human olfactory system.

Olfactory neurons are different from all other sensory receptors. They are special types of neurons that both come into direct contact with sensory stimuli and reach directly into the brain. Unlike all other neurons, olfactory neurons have a short life span, between 30 and 60 days, and they are continuously being replaced (Buck, 1996). The axons of the olfactory neurons relay a smell message directly to the **olfactory bulbs**. From the olfactory bulbs, the message is relayed to the olfactory cortex, which distinguishes the odor and relays that information to other parts of the brain.

Pheromones   Many animals excrete chemicals called **pheromones**, which can have a powerful effect on the behavior of other members of the same species. Animals use pheromones to mark off territories and to signal sexual receptivity. "When in heat, dogs, wolves, coyotes, foxes, and a host of others discharge a scent that is virtually irresistible to able-bodied males" (Dobb, 1989, p. 51).

Studies conducted by Viennese researcher Karl Grammer (cited in Holden, 1996) suggest that humans, although not consciously aware of it, respond to pheromones when it comes to mating. In his research, Grammer analyzed the saliva of 66 young men who had used an inhalant to sniff copulines—pheromones found in female vaginal secretions. The ovulatory secretions were the only ones to cause a rise in testosterone levels in the men's saliva. The men apparently recognized, though not consciously, which of the women were most likely to be fertile. A later study also indicates that humans can communicate by pheromones (Stern & McClintock, 1998).

Taste: What the Tongue Can Tell

What are the four primary taste sensations, and how are they detected?

A sizzling steak, hot buttered popcorn, chocolate cake—does the sense of taste alone tell us what these foods taste like? Surprisingly, no. **Gustation**, or the sense of taste, provides only four distinct kinds of sensations—sweet, sour, salty, and bitter. When

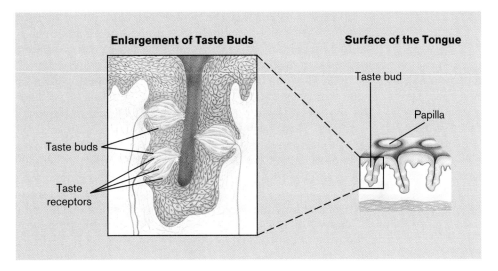

Enlargement of Taste Buds

Surface of the Tongue

Taste buds

Taste receptors

Taste bud

Papilla

Figure 3.6
The Tongue's Taste Buds

Taste buds are sensitive to only four tastes: bitter, sour, salty, and sweet. The vertical cross-section enlargement shows one of the papillae. The taste buds are in the small trenches around the papillae.

we say that a food tastes good or bad, we are actually referring to flavor—the combined sensory experience of the taste, smell, and touch. As we taste, we feel the texture and temperature of foods we put in the mouth. But most of the pleasure we attribute to the sense of taste actually arises from smells, which are due to odor molecules forced up the nasal cavity by the action of the tongue, cheeks, and throat when we chew and swallow.

If you look at your tongue in a mirror, you will see many small bumps called *papillae*. There are four different types of papillae, and three of them contain **taste buds**, which cluster around the cracks and crevices between the papillae (see Figure 3.6). Each taste bud is composed of from 60 to 100 receptor cells, which resemble the petals of a flower (Kinnamon, 1988). But even a person with no tongue could still taste to some extent, thanks to the taste receptors found in the palate, in the mucous lining of the cheeks and lips, and in parts of the throat, including the tonsils. The life span of the receptor cells for taste is very short, only about 10 days, and they are continually replaced.

Taste buds are most densely packed on the tip of the tongue, less densely packed on the rear edges, and absent from the center of the tongue (Bartoshuk, 1989). But taste is poorly localized, and taste sensations appear to come from all over the mouth. Even people with damage over large areas of the mouth are usually unaware of the loss of taste buds, because very intense sensations can be produced by rather small areas of normal tissue (Bartoshuk et al., 1987).

olfaction (ol-FAK-shun): The sensation of smell; the process of smelling.

olfactory epithelium: Two 1-inch-square patches of tissue, one at the top of each nasal cavity, which together contain about 10 million olfactory neurons, the receptors for smell.

olfactory bulbs: Two matchstick-sized structures above the nasal cavities, where smell sensations first register in the brain.

pheromones: Chemicals excreted by humans and other animals that act as signals to and elicit certain patterns of behavior from members of the same species.

gustation: The sensation of taste.

taste buds: Structures composed of 60 to 100 sensory receptors for taste.

THE OTHER SENSES

Our other senses are the sense of touch (the tactile sense), the kinesthetic sense, and the sense of balance (the vestibular sense).

The Skin Senses: Information from the Natural Clothing

Our natural clothing, the skin, is the largest organ of the body. It performs many important biological functions while also providing much of what is known as sen-

How does the skin provide sensory information?

Have someone touch the palm of your hand with two toothpicks held about 1½ inches apart. Do you feel one point or two? How far apart do the toothpicks have to be before you perceive them as two separate touch sensations? How far apart do they have to be on your face? On your forearm? On your fingers? On your toes? Which of these body parts are the most sensitive? Which are the least sensitive?

What beneficial purpose does pain serve?

tactile: Pertaining to the sense of touch.

gate-control theory: The theory that the pain signals transmitted by slow-firing nerve fibers can be blocked at the spinal gate if fast-firing fibers get their messages to the gate first, or if the brain itself inhibits transmission of the pain messages.

endorphins (en-DOR-fins): Chemicals, produced naturally by the pituitary gland, that reduce pain and positively affect mood.

naloxone: A drug that blocks the action of endorphins.

kinesthetic sense: The sense providing information about relative position and movement of body parts.

sual pleasure. Our skin can detect heat, cold, pressure, pain, and a vast range of touch sensations—caresses, pinches, punches, pats, rubs, scratches, and the feel of many different textures, from silk to sandpaper.

Tactile information is conveyed to the brain when an object touches and depresses the skin, stimulating one or more of the several distinct types of receptors found in the nerve endings. These sensitive nerve endings in the skin send the touch message through nerve connections to the spinal cord. The message travels up the spinal cord and through the brainstem and the lower brain centers, finally reaching the brain's somatosensory cortex. Only then do we become aware of where and how hard we have been touched. Remember from Chapter 2 that the somatosensory cortex is the strip of tissue at the front of the parietal lobes where touch, pressure, temperature, and pain register.

If you could examine the skin from the outermost to the deepest layer, you would find a variety of nerve endings that differ markedly in appearance. Most or all of these nerve endings appear to respond in some degree to all different types of tactile stimulation. The more densely packed a part of the body's surface with such sensory receptors, the more sensitive it is to tactile stimulation.

In the 1890s one of the most prominent researchers of the tactile sense, Max von Frey, discovered the two-point threshold that measures how far apart two points must be before they are felt as two separate touches. Demonstrate the two-point threshold for yourself with the *Try It!*

Touch is the sense we use to express our most intimate feelings. Lovers kiss, embrace, cuddle. Touch has the power to comfort and reassure. A pat on the back may motivate someone. Even social greetings and partings are punctuated by touching— the handshake and the more intimate embrace. But touch is not simply a means of communicating emotion—it is vitally important to human growth and development.

Research in the mid-1980s established the importance of touch in human development. Premature infants who were massaged for 15 minutes three times a day gained weight 47% faster than other premature infants who received only regular intensive care treatment (Field et al., 1986). The massaged infants were more responsive and were able to leave the hospital about 6 days earlier on average than those who were not massaged. And 8 months later they scored higher on tests of motor and mental ability.

Pain: Physical Hurts

Although the tactile sense delivers a great deal of pleasure, it brings us pain as well.

> He has never had a headache or a toothache, never felt the pain of a cut, a bruise, or a burn. If you are thinking, "How lucky!" you are completely wrong. His arms and legs are twisted and bent. Some of his fingers are missing. A large, bloody wound covers one of his knees, and his lips are chewed raw.
>
> A battered child? No. Born with a very rare genetic defect, he is totally insensitive to pain. He does not even notice a deep cut, a burn, or a broken bone when it happens, so he continues whatever he is doing and injures himself severely. (Adapted from Wallis, 1984.)

This story shows that pain functions as a valuable warning and protective mechanism. It motivates us to tend to injuries, to restrict activity, and to seek medical help. Pain also teaches us to avoid pain-producing circumstances in the future. Chronic pain, however, persists long after it serves any useful function and is itself a serious medical problem for some 34 million Americans (Brownlee & Schrof, 1997). The three major types of chronic pain are low-back pain, headache, and arthritis pain. For its victims, chronic pain is like a fire alarm that no one can turn off.

The Gate-Control Theory   Pain is probably the least understood of all the sensations. Scientists are not certain how pain works, but one major theory seeks to explain it—the **gate-control theory** of Melzack and Wall (1965, 1983). They contend that there is an area in the spinal cord that can act like a "gate" and either inhibit pain messages or transmit them to the brain. Only so many messages can go through the gate at any one time. We feel pain when pain messages carried by the small, slow-conducting nerve fibers reach the gate and cause it to open. Large, fast-conducting nerve fibers carry other sensory messages from the body, and these can effectively tie up traffic at the gate so that it will close and keep many of the pain messages from getting through. What is the first thing you do when you stub your toe or pound your finger with a hammer? If you rub or apply gentle pressure to the injury, you are stimulating the large, fast-conducting nerve fibers, which get their message to the spinal gate first and block some of the pain messages from the slower nerve fibers. Applying ice, heat, or electrical stimulation to the painful area also stimulates the large nerve fibers and closes the spinal gate.

Americans spend over $40 billion each year on treatments for chronic pain ranging from over-the-counter medications to surgery and psychotherapy (Brownlee & Schrof, 1997). The body produces its own natural painkillers, the **endorphins**, which block pain and produce a feeling of well-being. Endorphins are released when we are injured, when we experience stress or extreme pain, and when we laugh, cry, or exercise.

The drug **naloxone** blocks the action of endorphins. When naloxone is injected into patients, it binds to the endorphin receptor sites, thereby preventing the endorphins from having their pain-relieving effect. Joggers who normally experience runner's high will not experience it if they are injected with naloxone before they run, an indication that jogging stimulates the release of endorphins.

Acupuncture, the ancient Chinese technique for relieving pain, appears to work because the fine needles that are inserted at specific points on the body seem to stimulate the release of endorphins, thereby relieving pain. But endorphins do not account for other methods of pain relief, such as meditation, relaxation, distraction, and hypnosis, which we will discuss in Chapter 4. The next time you experience pain, you may want to try the techniques in the *Try It!*.

The other two senses we will explore may seem minor, but they too make important contributions to our sensory world.

What is the gate-control theory of pain?

What are endorphins?

 Link It!

 Try It!

If you experience pain, you can try any of the following techniques for controlling it:

■ Distraction can be particularly effective for controlling brief or mild pain. Generally, activities or thoughts that require a great deal of attention will provide more relief than passive distractions.

■ Counterirritation—stimulating or irritating one area of the body in order to mask or diminish pain in another area—can be accomplished with ice packs, heat, massage, mustard packs, or electrical stimulation.

■ Relaxation techniques are useful for reducing the stress and muscular tension that usually accompany pain.

■ Positive thoughts can help you cope with pain, whereas negative thoughts tend to increase your anxiety.

■ Attention and sympathy from family members and friends should be kept at a moderate level; too much attention may prove to be so reinforcing that it serves to prolong pain.

The Kinesthetic Sense: Keeping Track of the Body's Parts

The **kinesthetic sense** provides information about (1) the position of body parts in relation to each other and (2) the movement of various body parts. This information is detected by receptors in the joints, ligaments, and muscles. The other senses, especially vision, provide additional information about body position and movement, but the kinesthetic sense works well on its own. Thanks to the kinesthetic sense, we are able to perform smooth and skilled body movements without visual feedback or a studied, conscious effort. A companion sense, the vestibular sense, involves equilibrium, or the sense of balance.

What kind of information does the kinesthetic sense provide, and how is this sensory information detected?

Figure 3.7
Sensing Balance and Movement

You sense the rotation of your head in any direction because the movement sends fluid coursing through the tubelike semicircular canals in the inner ear. The moving fluid bends the hair cell receptors—which, in turn, send the message to the brain.

What is the vestibular sense, and where are its sensory receptors located?

---

vestibular sense (ves-TIB-yu-ler): Sense that provides information about the body's movement and orientation in space through sensory receptors in the semicircular canals and the vestibular sacs, which detect changes in the movement and orientation of the head.

semicircular canals: Three fluid-filled tubular canals in the inner ear that provide information about rotating head movements.

perception: The process by which sensory information is actively organized and interpreted by the brain.

Gestalt (geh-SHTALT): A German word roughly meaning "form" or "pattern."

What are the Gestalt principles of perceptual organization?

The Vestibular Sense: Sensing Up and Down and Changes in Speed

The **vestibular sense** detects movement and provides information about the body's orientation in space. The vestibular sense organs are located in the semicircular canals and the *vestibular sacs* in the inner ear. The **semicircular canals** sense the rotation of your head, such as when you are turning your head from side to side or when you are spinning around (see Figure 3.7). Because the canals are filled with fluid, rotating movements of the head in any direction send the fluid coursing through the tubelike semicircular canals. In the canals the moving fluid bends the hair cells, which act as receptors and send neural impulses to the brain. Because there are three canals, each positioned on a different plane, the hair cells in one canal will bend more than the hair cells in the other canals, depending on the direction of rotation.

PERCEPTION: WAYS OF PERCEIVING

In the first part of this chapter, you learned how the senses detect visual, auditory, and other sensory information and transmit it to the brain. Now we will explore **perception**—the process by which this sensory information is actively organized and interpreted by the brain. Humans *sense* sounds in hertz and decibels, but *perceive* melodies. They *sense* light of certain wavelengths and intensities, but *perceive* a multicolored world of objects and people. Sensations are the raw materials of human experiences; perceptions are the finished products.

Scientists can analyze physical objects down to their smallest parts, even to the atoms that make up an object. But can perception be analyzed and understood in the same way—broken down into its smallest sensory elements? The answer is no, according to Gestalt psychology, a school of thought that began in Germany early in the 20th century.

The Gestalt Principles of Perceptual Organization

The Gestalt psychologists maintained that people cannot understand the perceptual world by breaking down experiences into tiny parts and analyzing them separately. When sensory elements are brought together, something new is formed. The whole is more than just the sum of its parts, insisted the Gestalt psychologists. The German word **Gestalt** has no exact English equivalent, but it roughly refers to the whole form, pattern, or configuration that a person perceives.

How do human beings organize the world of sights, sounds, and other sensory stimuli in order to perceive the way they do? The Gestalt psychologists claimed that sensory experience is organized according to certain basic principles of perceptual organization. The principles include the figure-ground relationship and other principles of perceptual grouping.

Figure and Ground   The **figure-ground** relationship is the most fundamental principle of perceptual organization and is, therefore, the best place to start analyzing how we perceive. As we view our world, some object (the figure) seems to stand out from the background (the ground).

Many psychologists believe that the figure-ground perceptual ability is **innate**, that is, does not have to be learned. Figure-ground perception is present very early in life. It is also the first ability to appear in patients blind from birth who have received their sight as adults, like S.B., whose case study opened this chapter. Figure-ground perception is not limited to vision. If you listen to a symphony orchestra or a rock band, the melody line tends to stand out as figure, while the chords and the rest of the accompaniment are heard as background.

How can scientists be sure that knowing the difference between figure and ground is achieved by the perceptual system rather than being part of the sensory stimulus itself? The best proof is represented by reversible figures, where figure and ground seem to shift back and forth between two equal possibilities, as shown in Figure 3.8.

Gestalt Principles of Grouping   The Gestalt psychologists believed that when people see figures or hear sounds, they organize or integrate them according to the simplest, most basic arrangement possible. The following are the Gestalt principles of grouping: similarity, proximity, continuity, and closure (Wertheimer, 1958).

We tend to group visual, auditory, or other stimuli according to the principle of *similarity*. Objects that have similar characteristics are perceived as a unit. In Figure 3.9(a), dots of a similar color are perceived as belonging together to form horizontal rows on the left and vertical columns on the right. Objects that are close together in space or time are usually perceived as belonging together, because of a principle of grouping called *proximity*. Because of their spacing, the lines in Figure 3.9(b) are perceived as four pairs of lines rather than as eight separate lines. The principle of *continuity* means that we tend to perceive figures or objects as belonging together if they appear to form a continuous pattern, as in Figure 3.9(c). The principle of *closure* attempts to explain the tendency to complete figures with gaps in them. Even though parts of the figure in Figure 3.9(d) are missing, we use closure and perceive it as a triangle.

figure-ground: A principle of perceptual organization whereby the visual field is perceived in terms of an object (figure) standing out against a background (ground).

innate: Inborn, unlearned.

Figure 3.8
Reversing Figure and Ground

In this illustration, you can see a white vase as figure against a black background, or two black faces in profile on a white background. Exactly the same visual stimulus produces two opposite figure-ground perceptions.

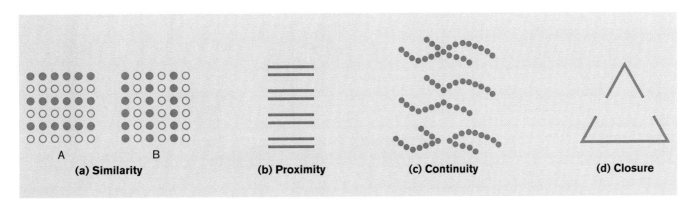

(a) Similarity   (b) Proximity   (c) Continuity   (d) Closure

Figure 3.9

Gestalt Principles of Grouping

Gestalt psychologists proposed four principles of perceptual grouping: similarity, proximity, continuity, and closure.

perceptual constancy: The tendency to perceive objects as maintaining stable properties, such as size, shape, brightness, and color, despite differences in distance, viewing angle, and lighting.

size constancy: The tendency to perceive an object as the same size regardless of changes in the retinal image.

retinal image: The image of objects in the visual field projected onto the retina.

shape constancy: The tendency to perceive an object as having a stable or unchanging shape regardless of differences in viewing angle.

brightness constancy: The tendency to see an object as maintaining the same brightness regardless of differences in lighting conditions.

color constancy: The tendency to see an object as about the same color regardless of differences in lighting conditions.

Perceptual Constancy

Even though we view objects or other people from different angles and distances and under different lighting conditions, we tend to see them as maintaining the same size, shape, brightness, and color. Scientists call this phenomenon **perceptual constancy**.

When you say good-bye to friends and watch them walk away, the image they cast on your retina grows smaller and smaller until they finally disappear in the distance. But the shrinking-size information that the retina sends to the brain (the sensation) does not confuse the perceptual system. As objects or people move farther away, we continue to perceive them as being about the same size.

This perceptual phenomenon is known as **size constancy**. We do not make a literal interpretation about the size of objects from the **retinal image**—the image projected onto the retina of objects in the visual field. Some evidence suggests that size constancy is learned. Recall that S.B. had trouble perceiving visual sensations he had never experienced. He so grossly misjudged distances that he perceived the automobiles 60 feet below his hospital window as toy cars nearby.

Our perceptual ability includes **shape constancy**—the tendency to perceive objects as having a stable or unchanging shape regardless of changes in the retinal image resulting from differences in viewing angle. In other words, we perceive a door as rectangular and a plate as round from whatever angle we view them (see Figure 3.10).

People normally see objects as maintaining a constant level of brightness regardless of differences in lighting conditions—a phenomenon known as **brightness constancy**. Nearly all objects reflect some part of the light that falls on them. We learn to infer the brightness of objects by comparing them to the brightness of all other objects viewed at the same time.

Colors can change considerably under different lighting conditions. But when objects are familiar, they appear to look about the same color under different conditions of illumination. This is called **color constancy**. Like brightness constancy, color

Figure 3.10

Shape Constancy

The door projects very different images on the retina when viewed from different angles. But because of shape constancy, you continue to perceive the door as rectangular.

constancy depends on the comparisons we make between differently colored objects viewed at the same time (Brou et al., 1986).

Depth Perception: Perceiving What's Up Close and Far Away

Depth perception is the ability to perceive the visual world in three dimensions and to judge distances accurately. We judge how far away objects and other people are. We climb and descend stairs without stumbling, and perform other visual tasks too numerous to list, all requiring depth perception.

Depth perception is three-dimensional. Yet each eye is able to provide only a two-dimensional view. The images cast on the retina do not contain depth; they are flat, just like a photograph. How, then, do we perceive depth so vividly?

Binocular Depth Cues   Some cues to depth perception depend on both eyes working together. These are called **binocular depth cues**, and they include convergence and binocular disparity. **Convergence** occurs when the eyes turn inward to focus on nearby objects—the closer the object, the greater the convergence. Hold the tip of your finger about 12 inches in front of your nose and focus on it. Now slowly begin moving your finger toward your nose. Your eyes will turn inward so much that they virtually cross when the tip of your finger meets the tip of your nose. Many psychologists believe that the tension of the eye muscles as they converge conveys information to the brain that serves as a cue for distance and depth perception.

Fortunately, the eyes are just far enough apart, about 2½ inches or so, to give each eye a slightly different view of the objects focused on and, consequently, a slightly different retinal image. The difference between the two retinal images, known as **binocular disparity** (or *retinal disparity*), provides an important cue for depth and distance. The farther away from the eyes the objects being looked at (up to 20 feet or so), the less the disparity, or difference, between the two retinal images. The brain integrates the two slightly different retinal images and gives the perception of three dimensions (Wallach, 1985). Ohzawa and others (1990) suggest that there are specific neurons in the visual cortex particularly suited to detecting disparity. Ordinarily you are not aware that each eye provides a slightly different view of the objects you see, but you can prove this for yourself in the *Try It!*

depth perception: The ability to see in three dimensions and to estimate distance.

binocular depth cues: Depth cues that depend on two eyes working together; convergence and binocular disparity.

convergence: A binocular depth cue in which the eyes turn inward as they focus on nearby objects—the closer an object, the greater the convergence.

binocular disparity: A binocular depth cue resulting from differences between the two retinal images formed of an object viewed at distances up to about 20 feet.

What are the binocular depth cues?

Link It!

Try It!

Hold your forefinger or a pencil at arm's length straight in front of you. Close your right eye and focus on the pencil. Now quickly close your left eye at the same time that you open your right eye. Repeat this procedure, closing one eye just as you open the other one. The pencil will appear to move from side to side in front of your face.

Now slowly bring the pencil closer and closer until it almost reaches your nose. The closer you bring the pencil, the more it appears to move from side to side. This is because there is progressively more disparity between the two retinal images as a viewed object gets closer and closer to your eyes.

Convergence and binocular disparity provide depth or distance cues only for nearby objects. Fortunately, each eye by itself provides cues for objects at greater distances.

What are seven monocular depth cues?

Monocular Depth Cues   Close one eye and you will see that you can still perceive depth. The visual depth cues perceived by one eye alone are called **monocular depth cues**. The following is a description of seven monocular depth cues, many of which have been used by artists in Western cultures to give the illusion of depth to their paintings.

■ *Interposition.* Some psychologists consider interposition, or overlapping, to be the most powerful depth cue of all. When one object partly blocks our view of another, we perceive the partially blocked object as farther away.

■ *Linear perspective.* Linear perspective is a depth cue in which parallel lines that are known to be the same distance apart appear to grow closer together, or converge, as they recede into the distance. Linear perspective was used extensively by Renaissance artists in the 15th century.

■ *Relative size.* Larger objects are perceived as being closer to the viewer, and smaller objects as being farther away. Most adults are between 5 and 6 feet tall, so when images of the people we view are two, three, or many times smaller than their normal size, we perceive them as being two, three, or as many times farther away.

■ *Texture gradient.* Texture gradient is a depth cue in which near objects appear to have sharply defined textures, while similar objects appear progressively fuzzier as they recede into the distance.

■ *Atmospheric perspective.* Atmospheric perspective, sometimes called *aerial perspective*, is a depth cue in which objects in the distance have a bluish tint and appear more blurred than objects close at hand.

■ *Shadow or shading.* When light falls on objects, they cast shadows. We can distinguish bulges from indentions by the shadows they cast. This ability appears to be learned (Hess, 1961).

■ *Motion parallax.* When you ride in a moving vehicle and look out the side window, the objects you see outside appear to be moving in the opposite direction. The objects also seem to be moving at different speeds—those closest to you appear to be moving faster than those in the distance. This phenomenon, called *motion parallax*, provides another monocular cue to depth perception. Objects very far away, such as the moon and the sun, appear to move in the same direction as the viewer.

The texture of objects can provide depth cues. The flowers in the foreground appear sharp and well defined, while those in the distance are blurred and fuzzy.

monocular depth cues (mah-NOK-yu-ler): Depth cues that can be perceived by only one eye.

apparent motion: The perception of motion when none is occurring (as in the phi phenomenon or in stroboscopic movement).

phi phenomenon: An illusion of movement occurring when two or more stationary lights are flashed on and off in sequence, giving the impression that one light is actually moving from one spot to the next.

Perception of Motion

When we focus and concentrate on visual and other sensory information, we must disregard a great deal. We fix our attention on the information that is important to us and ignore the rest. There is, however, one universal visual attention-getter: Movement catches the attention of humans, and of practically every other animal. We notice motion, usually regardless of where in the visual field it occurs. When objects do move in the field of vision, they project images that move across the retina, but this alone does not explain the perception of movement. We can perceive movement, that is, **apparent motion**, even when objects do not move at all.

If several stationary lights are flashed on and off in sequence, the light will actually appear to move from one spot to the next. This type of apparent motion, called the **phi phenomenon**, was first discussed by Max Wertheimer (1912), one of the founders of Gestalt psychology. How many neon signs have you seen that caused you to perceive motion? The neon lights don't move; they simply flash on and off in a particular sequence.

When you watch a motion picture, you are seeing apparent motion. People and objects appear to be moving, but in reality you are seeing *stroboscopic motion*, a series of still pictures of successive phases of movement. The pictures are flashed in rapid succession to give the illusion of movement.

Extraordinary Perceptions: Puzzling Perceptions

Not only can we perceive motion that does not exist, we can also perceive ambiguous figures, impossible figures, and illusions. When we are faced for the first time with an *ambiguous figure,* we have no experience to call on. Our perceptual system is puzzled and tries to work its way out of the quandary by seeing the ambiguous figure first one way and then another, but not both at once. We never get a lasting impression of ambiguous figures because they seem to jump back and forth beyond our control.

In some ambiguous figures, two different objects or figures are seen alternately. The best known of these, "Old Woman/Young Woman," by E. G. Boring, is shown in Figure 3.11. If you direct your gaze to the left of the drawing, you are likely to see an attractive young woman, her face turned away. But the young woman disappears when you suddenly perceive the image of the old woman. Such examples of object ambiguity offer striking evidence that perceptions are more than the mere sum of sensory parts. It is hard to believe that the same drawing (the same sum of sensory parts) can convey such dramatically different perceptions.

At first glance, many *impossible figures* do not seem so unusual—not until we examine them more closely. Would you invest your money in a company that manufactured three-pronged tridents as shown in Figure 3.12? Such an object could not be made as pictured because the middle prong appears to be in two different places at the same time. However, this type of impossible figure is more likely to fool the depth-perception sensibilities of people from Western cultures. People in some African cultures do not represent three-dimensional visual space in their art, and they do not perceive depth in drawings that contain pictorial depth cues. These people see no ambiguity in drawings similar to the three-pronged trident, and they can draw the figure accurately from memory much more easily than people from Western cultures (Bloomer, 1976).

An **illusion** is a false perception or a misperception of an actual stimulus in the environment. We can misperceive size, shape, or the relationship of one element to another. We need not pay to see illusions performed by magicians. Illusions occur naturally, and we see them all the time. An oar in the water appears to be bent where it meets the water. The moon looks much larger at the horizon than it does overhead. Why? One explanation of the moon illusion involves relative size. This idea suggests that the moon looks very large on the horizon because it is viewed in comparison to trees, buildings, and other objects. When viewed overhead, the moon cannot be compared with other objects, and it appears smaller. People have been speculating about the moon illusion for 22 centuries and experimenting for 50 years to determine its cause, but there is still no agreement (Hershenson, 1989).

The Müller-Lyer illusion confuses our estimate of length. In Figure 3.13(a) (on page 86), which horizontal line is longer, the upper or the lower one? Although the two lines are the same length, the diagonals extending outward from both ends of the upper line make it look longer than the lower line, which has diagonals pointing inward. British psychologist R. L. Gregory (1978) has suggested that the Müller-Lyer illusion is actually a misapplication of size constancy. In Figure 3.13(b), the corner in the left-hand photo projects forward, toward the viewer, and is

illusion: A false perception of actual stimuli involving a misperception of size, shape, or the relationship of one element to another.

What are three types of puzzling perceptions?

Figure 3.11

"Old Woman/Young Woman" by E. G. Boring

The most famous ambiguous figure can be seen alternately as a young woman or an old woman depending on where your eyes fixate.

Figure 3.12

The Three-Pronged Trident

This is an impossible figure because the middle prong appears to be in two places at the same time.

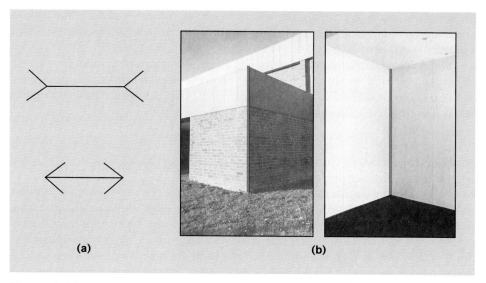

(a)   (b)

Figure 3.13

The Müller-Lyer Illusion

The two horizontal lines in (a) are identical in length. Although the two vertical lines in (b) are the same length, the line on the left seems to project forward and appears closer than the line on the right, which seems to recede in the distant corner. When two lines are the same length, the one perceived as farther away will appear longer. (Based on Gregory, 1978.)

Figure 3.14

The Ponzo Illusion

The two white bars superimposed on the railroad track are actually identical in length. But, because A appears farther away than B, you perceive it as longer.

therefore perceived to be closer. The corner in the right-hand photo appears to be more distant because it seems to recede from the viewer. When two lines are the same length, the line we perceive to be farther away will look longer.

The Ponzo illusion also plays an interesting trick on our estimation of size. Look at Figure 3.14. Which obstruction on the railroad tracks looks larger? You have undoubtedly guessed by now that, contrary to your perceptions, A and B are the same size. Again, perceptions of size and distance, which we trust and which are normally accurate in informing us about the real world, can be wrong. If you saw two obstructions like the ones in the illusion on real railroad tracks, the one that looks larger would indeed be larger. So the Ponzo illusion is not a natural illusion but rather a contrived one. In fact, all these illusions are really misapplications of principles that nearly always work properly in normal everyday experience.

Cultural Differences in the Perception of Visual Illusions   British psychologist R. L. Gregory believed that susceptibility to the Müller-Lyer and other such illusions is not inborn. Rather, the culture in which people live is responsible to some extent for the illusions they perceive.

To test whether susceptibility to the Müller-Lyer and similar illusions is due to experience, Segall and others (1966) tested 1,848 adults and children from 15 different cultures in Africa, the Philippines, and the United States. Included were a group of Zulus from South Africa and a group of Illinois residents. The study revealed that "there were marked differences in illusion susceptibility across the cultural groups included in this study" (Segall, 1994, p. 137). People in all the cultures showed some tendency to see the illusion, indicating a biological component, but experience was clearly a factor. Zulus, who have round houses and see few corners of any kind, are not fooled by the Müller-Lyer illusion. Illinois residents saw the illusion readily, while the Zulu tribespeople tended not to see it.

Some researchers suggested that race might offer an explanation for the cultural differences observed (Pollack, 1970). But a study by Stewart (1973) provides evidence to indicate that it is fundamentally culture, not race, that drives perceptions of illusions. When two groups of schoolchildren from Illinois (60 African Americans and 60

Whites) were tested with the Müller-Lyer and other illusions, no significant differences were found in susceptibility to the illusions. And in Zambia, researchers tested five different groups of Black African schoolchildren using the same illusions. Children's tendency to see the illusions had nothing to do with race but was strongly influenced by culture. Those children who lived in areas where buildings consisted of angles, edges, corners, and doors were likely to be fooled by the illusions; those who lived in remote villages with primarily round houses were not.

Pedersen and Wheeler (1983) studied Native American responses to the Müller-Lyer illusion among two groups of Navajos. The group who lived in rectangular houses and had experienced corners, angles, and edges tended to see the illusion. The other group, like the Zulus, tended not to see it because their cultural experience consisted of round houses similar to the one shown in the photo.

Some visual illusions seem to be culture-dependent. For example, Zulus and people from other cultures in which the houses lack straight sides and corners do not perceive the Müller-Lyer illusion.

Illusions of the Other Senses   Although visual illusions are the most dramatic and the easiest to demonstrate, the other senses are also subject to illusions. You can experience an illusion involving touch and temperature in the *Try It!*

Try It!

Take three large cereal bowls or small mixing bowls. Fill one with very cold water, another with hot water (*not* boiling or scalding), and the third with lukewarm water. Hold your left hand in the cold water and your right hand in the hot water for at least 1 minute. Then quickly plunge both hands into the lukewarm water at the same time.

Why do you experience the illusion that the lukewarm water feels simultaneously warmer and colder than its actual temperature? The answer is adaptation. You perceive the lukewarm water as warm on your cold-adapted left hand and as cold on your warm-adapted right hand. This illustrates that our perceptions of sensory stimuli are relative and are affected by differences between stimuli we are already adapted to and new stimuli.

ADDITIONAL INFLUENCES ON PERCEPTION

Why don't we all perceive sights, sounds, odors, and events in the same way? The reason is that our perceptions involve more than just the sensory stimuli themselves.

Bottom-Up and Top-Down Processing

Psychologists distinguish between two distinct information-processing techniques that people use in recognizing patterns: bottom-up processing and top-down processing.

Bottom-up processing begins with the individual components of a stimulus that are detected by the sensory receptors. The information is then transmitted to

In what types of situations do people rely more on bottom-up processing or top-down processing?

bottom-up processing: Information processing in which individual components or bits of data are combined until a complete perception is formed.

top-down processing: Application of previous experience and conceptual knowledge to recognize the whole of a perception and thus easily identify the simpler elements of that whole.

perceptual set: An expectation of what will be perceived, which can affect what actually is perceived.

areas in the brain where it is combined and assembled into the whole patterns that a person perceives.

In **top-down processing**, on the other hand, past experience and knowledge of the context play a role in forming a perception. In other words, what we perceive is more than the sum of the individual elements taken in by our sensory receptors.

Of course, we use both bottom-up and top-down processing to form perceptions. In unfamiliar situations, we are likely to use bottom-up processing. In familiar situations, where we have some prior knowledge and experience, we tend to use top-down processing.

The Role of Psychological Factors in Perception

What are some psychological factors that affect perceptions?

We make perceptual judgments from our own individual points of reference. Other people are perceived as tall or short, young or old, depending on one's own height or age. Words such as *intelligent, attractive, expensive, thin, successful, sensible, talented, rich, exciting, loud,* and so on are all measured from one's own perceptual point of view. Perceptions are also affected by values, needs, interests, and emotions.

The **perceptual set**—what people expect to perceive—determines, to a large extent, what they actually see, hear, feel, taste, and smell. If you ordered raspberry sherbet and it was colored green, would it still taste like raspberry, or might it taste more like lime? Once their expectations are set, people often bend reality to make it fit them. Psychologist David Rosenhan (1973) and some of his colleagues were admitted as patients to various mental hospitals with "diagnoses" of schizophrenia. Once admitted, they acted normal in every way. The purpose? They wondered how long it would take the doctors and the hospital staff to realize that they were not mentally ill. But the doctors and the staff members saw only what they expected to see and not what actually occurred. They perceived everything the pseudo-patients said and did, such as notetaking, to be symptoms of their illness. But the real patients were not deceived. They were the first to realize that the psychologists were not really mentally ill.

SUBLIMINAL PERSUASION AND EXTRASENSORY PERCEPTION

Link It!

So far we have considered perceptions that are formed above the threshold of awareness and perceptions that arise from known sensory abilities. Can people be influenced by persuasive messages below the level of awareness, through subliminal persuasion? And are people able to gain information by some means other than known sensory channels, through extrasensory perception?

Subliminal Persuasion: Does It Work?

Is subliminal persuasion effective in influencing behavior?

Decades ago, it was reported that moviegoers in a New Jersey theater were exposed to advertising messages flashed on the screen so briefly that they were not aware of them. An advertising executive claimed that the words "Eat popcorn" and "Drink Coca-Cola" were projected on the screen for only $\frac{1}{3000}$ of a second every 5 seconds during the movie. The purpose of the messages was to influence audience members to buy popcorn and Coca-Cola, not by getting their conscious attention, but by sending persuasive messages below their level of awareness, a technique called **subliminal persuasion**. During the 6-week period the messages ran, popcorn sales supposedly went up by 57.5%, and Coca-Cola sales rose by more than 18% (McConnell et al., 1958). But the advertising executive who released the story later admitted that it was a hoax—no subliminal messages had actually been flashed.

Technically, **subliminal perception** would be defined as the perception of sensory stimuli that are below the absolute threshold. But subliminal persuasion experiments are limited to messages flashed so quickly that they could *never* be perceived normally at all. Can people actually perceive information that is completely below their level of awareness? Some say they can, and today subliminal persuasion is aimed at selling much more than popcorn and Coke. Subliminal self-help tapes are so popular that Americans spend over $50 million a year on the tapes (Adams, 1991). Embedded in the recordings of soothing music or ocean waves lapping the shore are subliminal messages for those who want to lose weight ("I eat less"), reduce stress ("I am calm"), or improve their self-image ("I am capable").

Is subliminal persuasion in audiotapes effective? Researchers conducting double-blind studies found that audiotapes that claimed to influence behavior with subliminal messages were no more effective in doing so than tapes containing unrelated subliminal messages or no subliminal messages whatsoever (Greenwald, 1992; Greenwald et al., 1991; Russell et al., 1991). But if subliminal persuasion does not influence behavior, why do some users insist that the tapes have helped them to quit smoking, lose weight, and so on? Evidently the change is due to the power of suggestion or the placebo effect, and not to the messages on the tapes (Pratkanis et al., 1994; Smith & Rogers, 1994).

Extrasensory Perception: Does It Exist?

Is it possible to perceive information that does not come through the senses? Is there such a thing as **extrasensory perception (ESP)**—gaining information about objects, events, or another's thoughts through some means other than the known sensory channels? Can some people read minds or foretell the future? According to a 1990 Gallup poll, 49% of Americans believe in ESP (Gallup & Newport, 1990b). Extrasensory perception is part of a larger area of interest known as **parapsychology**, the study of psychic phenomena. Reported cases of ESP roughly fall into three categories—telepathy, clairvoyance, and precognition.

Telepathy means gaining awareness of the thoughts, the feelings, or the activities of another without the use of the senses—in other words, reading a person's mind. *Clairvoyance* means gaining information about objects or events without use of the senses, such as knowing the contents of a letter before opening it. *Precognition* refers to an awareness of an event before it occurs. Most of the reported cases of precognition in everyday life have occurred while people were dreaming.

One researcher revealed the poor record of well-known psychics who made New Year's predictions for the *National Enquirer* over a period of 8 years. Only two of their 425 predictions proved to be accurate (Strentz, 1986). Because psychic phenomena violate what is known about the real, measurable, physical world, scientists and skeptics naturally demand proof of their existence (Hansel, 1966, 1980; Randi, 1980). Time after time, investigators have discovered trickery when examining the claims of psychics who assert that they can read minds or contact and communicate with the dead. Uri Geller, well known for his ability to bend spoons and keys, to "read" the contents of sealed envelopes, and to perform other feats supposedly using his mind alone, was found to use magic tricks and fraud to deceive the public.

What is the truth about psychic phenomena? Either they exist but their existence has not yet been proven, or they may exist but might not be verifiable under laboratory conditions, or they do not exist at all. What do you believe?

Earlier we noted that sensation and perception are so closely linked in everyday experience that it is hard to see clearly where one ends and the other begins. But in this chapter you have seen many examples of what is sensed and what is perceived. Our perceptual system is continuously trying to complete what we merely sense. We are always busy filling in, organizing, and making more complete perceptual sense out of the sensory parts that we are able to see, hear, touch, taste, and smell.

subliminal persuasion: Sending persuasive messages below the recipient's level of awareness.

subliminal perception: Perceiving sensory stimulation that is below the absolute threshold.

extrasensory perception (ESP): Gaining awareness of or information about objects, events, or another's thoughts through some means other than the known sensory channels.

parapsychology: The study of psychic phenomena, including extrasensory perception (ESP).

What is extrasensory perception, and have the claims of psychics been verified scientifically?

Noise and Hearing Loss: Bad Vibrations

Hearing loss is increasing rapidly in the industrialized world, and the main reason for the increase is NOISE. Jet engines, firecrackers, motorcycles, power mowers, radios, chain saws, and other power tools are well-known sources of noise that can injure the ear.

Currently, U.S. government regulations protect employees from exposure to sound levels of more than 85 dB in the workplace during an 8-hour day (Martin, 1994). But, there are no laws to protect people outside of the workplace from hearing loss. And people are in more danger of losing their hearing off the job than at the work site. Without proper protection, a person's hearing can be more damaged by recreational hunting, rock concerts, and some sports events than by industrial noise. People would probably be more willing to wear protective devices if they were aware of their benefits (Lusk et al., 1995).

Noisy toys and other hazards. Exposure to hazardous noise can begin long before a person is old enough to listen to a Sony Walkman. Researchers Axelsson and Jerson (1985) tested seven squeaking toys that, at a distance of 10 centimeters, emitted sound levels loud enough to put toddlers at risk for hearing loss at only 2 minutes of daily exposure.

And if older children play with toy weapons, noise-induced hearing loss can occur with only seconds of exposure. Researchers tested several toy weapons and found that, at a distance of 50 centimeters, the guns produced explosive sound levels ranging from 144 to 152 dB (Axelsson & Jerson, 1985). All exceeded the 130-dB peak level that is considered the upper limit for exposure to short-lived explosive sounds if hearing loss is to be avoided.

Firecrackers pose a particular hazard if they explode close to the ear. In one study a number of firecrackers were tested at 3 meters, and sound levels were found to range from 130

dB to an unbelievable and highly dangerous 190 dB (Gupta & Vishwakarma, 1989).

The destructive effects of noise. Explosions, gun blasts, and other extremely loud noises may burst the eardrum or may fracture or dislocate the tiny ossicles in the middle ear. Often these injuries can be repaired surgically, but noise injuries to the inner ear cannot. "Extremely intense sounds can rip the delicate sensory [hair] cells completely off the basilar membrane on which they normally sit, kill the cells, or merely injure them permanently" (Bennett, 1990, p. 3). During the filming of a Western movie, former President Ronald Reagan's hearing was damaged beyond repair by a single shot from a blank pistol fired too close to his ear. Rock musician Kathy Peck lost 40% of her hearing in one evening after her band opened a stadium concert for Duran Duran.

How much noise is too much? How can you tell when noise levels are high enough to jeopardize your hearing? You are putting yourself at risk if you have difficulty talking over the noise level, or if the noise exposure leaves you with a ringing in your ears or a temporary hearing loss (Dobie, 1987).

Experts claim that exposure to noise of 90 dB (a lawn mower, for example) for more than 8 hours in a 24-hour period can damage hearing. For every increase of 5 dB, maximum exposure time should be cut in half–4 hours for 95 dB, 2 hours for 100 dB, and 1 hour for 105 dB. The Department of Labor considers 115 dB to be the maximum allowable level of exposure to steady sound levels (Catlin, 1986). And 120 decibels, what you would hear directly in front of the speakers at a rock concert, would immediately destroy some of the hair cells.

In 1986 the rock group The Who entered the *Guiness Book of World Records* as the loudest rock band on record, blasting out deafening sound intensities that measured 120 decibels at a distance of 164 feet from the speakers. Unless their ears were pro-

tected, audience members within that 164-foot radius were likely to suffer some irreversible hearing loss. And the band members? Pete Townshend of The Who has severely damaged hearing and, in addition, is plagued by tinnitus, an annoying condition that causes him to experience a continuous ringing in the ears.

In an article in *Rolling Stone*, Ted Nugent admitted his hearing problem. "My left ear is there just to balance my face, because it doesn't work at all" (Murphy, 1989, p. 101). In the early 1990s a rash of lawsuits were filed against rock musicians and promoters by fans complaining of tinnitus and hearing loss suffered after attending their concerts.

Protecting yourself from hearing loss. What can you do to protect yourself from the effects of noise?

- If you must be exposed to loud noise, use earplugs (not the kind used for swimming) or earmuffs to reduce noise by as much as 15–30 dB (Dobie, 1987).

- If you must engage in an extremely noisy activity, such as cutting wood with a chain saw, limit periods of exposure so that stunned hair cells can recover.

- Keep the volume down on your Walkman-type radio or tape player. If the volume control is numbered 1 to 10, a volume above 4 probably exceeds the federal standards for noise. If you have a ringing in your ears, if sounds seem muffled, or if you have a tickling sensation in your ears after you remove your headset, you may have sustained some hearing loss.

- Begin humming before you are exposed to loud noise. Humming will set in motion the very tiny muscles in the middle ear that dampen the sound and provide some measure of protection from the effects of noise (Borg & Counter, 1989).

- Put your fingers in your ears or leave the scene.

SUMMARY AND REVIEW

SENSATION: THE SENSORY WORLD

What is the difference between sensation and perception?

Sensation is the process through which the senses pick up sensory stimuli and transmit them to the brain. Perception is the process by which this sensory information is actively organized and interpreted by the brain.

What is the difference between the absolute threshold and the difference threshold?

The absolute threshold is the minimum amount of sensory stimulation that can be detected 50% of the time. The difference threshold is a measure of the smallest increase or decrease in a physical stimulus that can be detected 50% of the time.

How are sensory stimuli in the environment experienced as sensations?

For each of the senses, the body has sensory receptors that detect and respond to sensory stimuli. Through a process known as transduction, the receptors convert sensory stimuli into neural impulses, which are then transmitted to special locations in the brain.

Key Terms
sensation (p. 65); perception (p. 65); absolute threshold (p. 66); difference threshold (p. 66); just noticeable difference (p. 66); Weber's law (p. 66); signal detection theory (p. 67); sensory receptors (p. 67); transduction (p. 67); sensory adaptation (p. 67)

VISION

How do the cornea, the iris, and the pupil function in vision?

The cornea bends light rays inward through the pupil—the small, dark opening in the eye. The iris dilates and contracts the pupil to regulate the amount of light entering the eye.

What are the lens and the retina?

The lens changes its shape as it focuses images of objects from varying distances on the retina, a thin membrane containing the sensory receptors for vision.

What roles do the rods and cones play in vision?

The cones detect color, provide the sharpest vision, and function best in high illumination. The rods enable vision in dim light. Rods respond to black and white, and they encode all other visible wavelengths in shades of gray.

What path does the neural impulse take from the retina to the primary visual cortex?

The rods and the cones transduce light waves into neural impulses that pass from the bipolar cells to the ganglion cells, whose axons make up the optic nerve. At the optic chiasma, some of the fibers of the optic nerve cross to the opposite side of the brain, before reaching the thalamus. From the thalamus, the neural impulses travel to the primary visual cortex.

What are the three dimensions that combine to provide the colors people perceive?

The three dimensions of color are hue, saturation, and brightness.

What two major theories attempt to explain color vision?

Two major theories that attempt to explain color vision are the trichromatic theory and the opponent-process theory.

Key Terms
visible spectrum (p. 68); cornea (p. 69); lens (p. 69); accommodation (p. 69); retina (p. 69); rods (p. 70); cones (p. 70); fovea (p. 70); dark adaptation (p. 70); optic nerve (p. 70); hue (p. 71); saturation (p. 71); brightness (p. 71); trichromatic theory (p. 71); opponent-process theory (p. 71); afterimage (p. 71); color blindness (p. 71)

HEARING

What determines the pitch and the loudness of sound, and how is each quality measured?

The pitch of a sound is determined by the frequency of the sound waves, which is measured in hertz. The loudness of a sound is determined largely by the amplitude of the sound waves and is measured in decibels.

How do the outer, middle, and inner ears function in hearing?

Sound waves enter the pinna, the visible part of the outer ear, and travel to the end of the auditory canal, causing the eardrum to vibrate. This sets in motion the ossicles in the middle ear, which amplify the sound waves. The vibration of the oval window causes activity in the inner ear, setting in motion the fluid in the cochlea and moving the hair cells, which transduce the vibrations into neural impulses. The auditory nerve carries the neural impulses to the brain.

What two major theories attempt to explain hearing?

Two major theories that attempt to explain hearing are place theory and frequency theory.

What are some major causes of hearing loss?

Some major causes of hearing loss are noise, disease, birth defects, injury, and aging.

Key Terms
frequency (p. 73); amplitude (p. 73); decibel (p. 73); timbre (p. 73); audition (p. 73); outer ear (p. 73); middle ear (p. 74); inner ear (p. 74); cochlea (p. 74); hair cells (p. 75); place theory (p. 75); frequency theory (p. 75)

SMELL AND TASTE

What path does a smell message take from the nose to the brain?

The act of smelling begins when odor molecules reach the smell receptors in the olfactory epithelium at the top of the nasal cavity. The axons of these receptors form the olfactory nerve, which relays the smell message to the olfactory bulbs. From there the smell message travels to the olfactory cortex and on to other parts of the brain.

What are the four primary taste sensations, and how are they detected?

The four primary taste sensations are sweet, salty, sour, and bitter. The receptor cells for taste are found in the taste buds on the tongue and in other parts of the mouth and throat.

Key Terms
olfaction (p. 76); olfactory epithelium (p. 76); olfactory bulbs (p. 76); pheromones (p. 76); gustation (p. 76); taste buds (p. 77)

THE OTHER SENSES

How does the skin provide sensory information?

Nerve endings in the skin (the sensory receptors) respond to different kinds of stimulation, including heat and cold, pressure, pain, and a vast range of touch sensations. The neural impulses ultimately register in the somatosensory cortex.

What beneficial purpose does pain serve?

Pain can be a valuable warning and a protective mechanism, motivating people to tend to an injury, to restrict activity, and to seek medical help if needed.

What is the gate-control theory of pain?

Melzack and Wall's gate-control theory of pain holds that pain signals transmitted by slow-conducting fibers can be blocked at the spinal gate (1) if fast-conducting fibers get their message to the gate first, or (2) if the brain itself inhibits their transmission.

What are endorphins?

Endorphins are the body's natural painkillers. Released when a person is stressed or injured or exercises vigorously, they block pain and produce a feeling of well-being.

What kind of information does the kinesthetic sense provide, and how is this sensory information detected?

The kinesthetic sense provides information about the relative position of body parts and movement of those parts. The position or motion is detected by sensory receptors in the joints, ligaments, and muscles.

What is the vestibular sense, and where are its sensory receptors located?

The vestibular sense provides information about movement and the body's orientation in space. Sensory receptors in the semicircular canals and in the vestibular sacs detect changes in the movement and orientation of the head.

Key Terms
tactile (p. 78); gate-control theory (p. 79); endorphins (p. 79); naloxone (p. 79); kinesthetic sense (p. 79); vestibular sense (p. 80); semicircular canals (p. 80)

PERCEPTION: WAYS OF PERCEIVING

What are the Gestalt principles of perceptual organization?

The Gestalt principles of perceptual organization include the figure-ground relationship and four principles of perceptual grouping—similarity, proximity, continuity, and closure.

What is perceptual constancy, and what are the four types?

Perceptual constancy is the tendency to perceive objects as maintaining the same size, shape, brightness, and color despite changes in lighting conditions or changes in the retinal image that result when objects are viewed from different angles and distances.

What are the binocular depth cues?

The binocular depth cues are convergence and binocular disparity, and they depend on both eyes working together for depth perception.

What are seven monocular depth cues?

The monocular depth cues, those that can be perceived by one eye, include interposition, linear perspective, relative size, texture gradient, atmospheric perspective, shadow or shading, and motion parallax.

What are three types of puzzling perceptions?

Three types of puzzling perceptions are ambiguous figures, impossible figures, and illusions.

Key Terms
perception (p. 80); Gestalt (p. 80); figure-ground (p. 81); innate (p. 81); perceptual constancy (p. 82); size constancy (p. 82); retinal image (p. 82); shape constancy (p. 82); brightness constancy (p. 82); color constancy (p. 82); depth perception (p. 83); binocular depth cues (p. 83); convergence (p. 83); binocular disparity (p. 83); monocular depth cues (p. 84); apparent motion (p. 84); phi phenomenon (p. 84); illusion (p. 85)

ADDITIONAL INFLUENCES ON PERCEPTION

In what types of situations do people rely more on bottom-up processing or top-down processing?

People rely on bottom-up processing more in unfamiliar situations and top-down processing more in situations about which they have some prior knowledge and experience.

What are some psychological factors that affect perceptions?

People's perceptions are affected by their point of reference, by the value they attach to a stimulus, and by their perceptual set—what they expect to perceive.

Key Terms
bottom-up processing (p. 87); top-down processing (p. 88); perceptual set (p. 88)

SUBLIMINAL PERSUASION AND EXTRASENSORY PERCEPTION

Is subliminal persuasion effective in influencing behavior?

In experimental studies, subliminal persuasion has not been found to influence behavior.

What is extrasensory perception, and have the claims of psychics been verified scientifically?

Extrasensory perception refers to gaining awareness of information about objects, events, or another's thoughts through some means other than the known sensory channels. Experiments claiming to prove psychic phenomena have not been repeatable under carefully controlled conditions.

Key Terms
subliminal persuasion (p. 88); subliminal perception (p. 89); extrasensory perception (ESP) (p. 89); parapsychology (p. 89)

Study Guide for Chapter 3

Answers to all the Study Guide questions are provided at the end of the book.

Section One: Chapter Review

1. The process through which the senses detect sensory information and transmit it to the brain is called (sensation, perception).

2. The point at which you can barely sense a stimulus 50% of the time is called the (absolute, difference) threshold.

3. The difference threshold is the same for all individuals. (true/false)

4. Which of the following is not true of sensory receptors?
   a. They are specialized to detect certain sensory stimuli.
   b. They transduce sensory stimuli into neural impulses.
   c. They are located in the brain.
   d. They provide the link between the physical sensory world and the brain.

5. The process by which a sensory stimulus is converted into a neural impulse is called _____.

6. Each morning when Jackie goes to work at a dry cleaner, she smells a strong odor of cleaning fluid. After she is there for a few minutes, she is no longer aware of it. What accounts for this?
   a. signal detection theory
   b. sensory adaptation
   c. transduction
   d. the just noticeable difference

7. Match each part of the eye with its description.

   ____ (1) the colored part of the eye
   ____ (2) the opening in the iris that dilates and constricts
   ____ (3) the transparent covering of the iris
   ____ (4) the transparent structure that focuses an inverted image on the retina
   ____ (5) the thin, photosensitive membrane at the back of the eye on which the lens focuses an inverted image

   a. retina
   b. cornea
   c. pupil
   d. iris
   e. lens

8. The receptor cells in the retina that enable you to see in dim light are the (cones, rods); the cells that enable you to see color and sharp images are (cones, rods).

9. Neural impulses are carried from the retina to the thalamus by the _____ and then relayed to their final destination, the _____.
   a. optic chiasma; primary visual cortex
   b. rods and cones; optic nerve
   c. optic nerve; primary visual cortex
   d. optic nerve; optic chiasma

10. Most people who are color-blind see no color at all. (true/false)

11. Pitch is chiefly determined by _____; loudness is chiefly determined by _____.
    a. amplitude; frequency
    b. wavelength; frequency
    c. intensity; amplitude
    d. frequency; amplitude

12. Pitch is measured in (hertz, decibels); loudness is measured in (decibels, hertz).

13. Match the part of the ear with the structures it contains.

    ____ (1) ossicles   a. outer ear
    ____ (2) pinna, auditory canal   b. middle ear
    ____ (3) cochlea, hair cells   c. inner ear

14. The receptors for hearing are found in the
    a. ossicles.   c. auditory membrane.
    b. auditory canal.   d. cochlea.

15. The two major theories that attempt to explain hearing are
    a. conduction theory and place theory.
    b. hair cell theory and frequency theory.
    c. place theory and frequency theory.
    d. conduction theory and hair cell theory.

16. According to the text, lifelong exposure to excessive noise may be more of a factor in hearing loss than aging. (true/false)

17. The technical name for the process or sensation of smell is (gustation, olfaction).

18. The olfactory, or smell, receptors are located in the
    a. olfactory tract.
    b. olfactory nerve.
    c. olfactory epithelium.
    d. olfactory bulbs.

19. The four primary taste sensations are
    _____, _____,
    _____, and _____.

20. Each (papilla, taste bud) contains from 60 to 100 receptor cells.

21. Taste receptor cells have a very short life span and are continually replaced. (true/false)

22. Each skin receptor responds only to touch, pressure, warmth, or cold. (true/false)

23. People would be better off if they could not feel pain. (true/false)

24. Match the substance with the appropriate description.
    ____ (1) a sugar pill or saline injection that a person believes to be a drug
    ____ (2) pain-blocking substances produced by the body
    ____ (3) a drug that blocks the action of endorphins
    a. naloxone
    b. endorphins
    c. placebo

25. The (kinesthetic, vestibular) sense provides information about the position of body parts in relation to each other and about movement in those body parts.

26. The receptors for the (kinesthetic, vestibular) sense are located in the semicircular canals and vestibular sacs in the (middle ear, inner ear).

27. The Gestalt principle of (continuity, closure) refers to the tendency to complete figures with gaps in them.

28. Which of the perceptual constancies cause people to perceive objects as being different from the retinal image they project?
    a. brightness constancy and color constancy
    b. color constancy and shape constancy
    c. shape constancy and size constancy
    d. color constancy and size constancy

29. Which of the perceptual constancies depend on a comparison of one object with other objects viewed under the same lighting conditions?
    a. brightness constancy and color constancy
    b. color constancy and shape constancy
    c. shape constancy and size constancy
    d. color constancy and size constancy

30. Retinal disparity and convergence are two (monocular, binocular) depth cues.

31. Match the appropriate monocular depth cue with each example.
    ____ (1) one building partly blocking another
    ____ (2) railroad tracks converging in the distance
    ____ (3) closer objects appearing to move faster than objects farther away
    ____ (4) objects farther away looking smaller than near objects
    a. motion parallax
    b. linear perspective
    c. interposition
    d. relative size

32. The type of apparent motion produced by motion pictures is (motion parallax, stroboscopic motion).

33. An illusion is
    a. an imaginary sensation.
    b. an impossible figure.
    c. a misperception of a real stimulus.
    d. a figure-ground reversal.

34. In situations where you have some prior knowledge and experience, you are likely to rely more on (bottom-up, top-down) processing.

35. Perceptual set is most directly related to a person's
    a. needs.
    b. interests.
    c. expectations.
    d. emotions.

36. Subliminal advertising has been proven effective in influencing consumers to buy products. (true/false)

37. Match the type of psychic phenomenon with the description:
    ____ (1) reading someone's mind
    ____ (2) gaining awareness of events before they occur
    ____ (3) gaining information about objects or events without the use of the senses
    a. clairvoyance
    b. precognition
    c. telepathy

38. Carefully controlled and repeatable laboratory experiments have proved the existence of extrasensory perception. (true/false)

1. Perception is the process we use to
   a. organize and interpret stimuli.
   b. detect stimuli.
   c. gather information from the environment.
   d. retrieve information from memory.

2. What part of the nose serves the same function as the retina in the eye and the basilar membrane in the ear?
   a. olfactory bulbs
   b. olfactory lining
   c. olfactory neurons
   d. olfactory epithelium

3. The vestibular system is most closely related to
   a. audition.   c. gustation.
   b. olfaction.   d. kinesthetics.

4. As you look down a sandy beach, the sand seems to become more fine as it goes into the distance. This depth cue is called
   a. elevation.
   b. convergence.
   c. texture gradient.
   d. linear perspective.

5. The minimum amount of physical stimulation necessary for a person to experience a sensation 50% of the time is called the
   a. figure-to-ground ratio.
   b. blind spot.
   c. difference threshold.
   d. absolute threshold.

6. Which of the following is the correct sequence of structures encountered by light moving toward the retina?
   a. lens, cornea, pupil
   b. pupil, lens, cornea
   c. pupil, cornea, lens
   d. cornea, pupil, lens

7. Which theory suggests that color vision can be explained by the existence of three types of cones, which are maximally sensitive to red, green, or blue?
   a. opponent-process theory
   b. trichromatic theory
   c. signal detection theory
   d. gate-control theory

8. Ms. Scarpaci complains that the street noise in her apartment is much louder than the noise in her upstairs neighbor's apartment. To test her claim, you use a sound meter to check the noise in each apartment. Your meter registers 50 dB in Ms. Scarpaci's apartment and only 30 dB in her neighbor's. From these readings, how much louder is Ms. Scarpaci's apartment than her neighbor's?
   a. 20% louder
   b. 10 times louder
   c. 100 times louder
   d. not enough to be noticeable

9. When you hear a tone of 400 Hz, some of the hair cells in your ear are stimulated, but most others are not. This is the basic idea behind the
   a. place theory of hearing.
   b. volley principle of hearing.
   c. frequency theory of hearing.
   d. bone conduction theory of hearing.

10. The receptors for odors are located in the
    a. olfactory epithelium.
    b. projecting septum.
    c. turbinate mucosa.
    d. vestibular membrane.

11. Nerve endings in the skin send signals to the somatosensory cortex for processing. This area of the brain is found in the
    a. frontal lobe.   c. parietal lobe.
    b. temporal lobe.   d. occipital lobe.

12. Which of the following sensations would best be explained by the gate-control theory?
    a. the pain of a pin prick
    b. the smell of dinner cooking
    c. the taste of your favorite cookie
    d. the sound of paper rustling

13. The receptors for the kinesthetic sense are located in the
    a. middle ear.
    b. inner ear.
    c. joints, ligaments, and muscles.
    d. cortex.

14. The depth cue that occurs when your eyes "cross" to see an object that is very near your face is called
    a. convergence.   c. aerial perspective.
    b. elevation.   d. binocular disparity.

15. Weber's law applies to
    a. difference thresholds.
    b. absolute thresholds.
    c. transduction thresholds.
    d. retinal thresholds.

16. Recent research on the genetics of color blindness show that color vision is controlled by
    a. a single gene.
    b. 2 genes.
    c. from 2 to 9 genes.
    d. from 20 to 30 genes.

17. Gustation is also known as the sense of
    a. taste.   c. smell.
    b. hearing.   d. vision.

18. In the Ponzo illusion, two bars of equal length are superimposed over a picture of railroad tracks that recede into the distance and eventually converge at a single point. One reason the bars appear to be of unequal lengths is because the illusion takes advantage of
    a. binocular disparity cues.
    b. linear perspective cues.
    c. apparent motion cues.
    d. depth disparity cues.

19. Perceptual set reflects
    a. bottom-up processing.
    b. top-down processing.
    c. subliminal processing.
    d. extrasensory processing.

20. The process through which the senses detect sensory stimuli and transmit them to the brain is called
    a. consciousness.   c. sensation.
    b. perception.   d. reception.

21. If you were listening to music and your friend wanted to know how far he could turn the volume down without your noticing, he would need to know your
    a. sensory threshold for sound.
    b. absolute threshold for sound.
    c. transduction threshold for sound.
    d. difference threshold for sound.

22. Margaret is reaching middle age and is having trouble reading fine print. She did not have this problem when she was younger. Her optometrist has concluded that she has presbyopia, or "old eyes." Given this diagnosis, you know that Margaret's difficulty is due to the aging of her
    a. corneas.   c. retinas.
    b. lenses.   d. rods and cones.

23. The trichromatic theory of color is based on the idea that the retina contains three types of
    a. rods.   c. bipolar cells.
    b. cones.   d. ganglion cells.

24. When you hear a tone of 750 Hz, the hair cells in your ear begin vibrating 750 times per second. This is the basic idea behind the
    a. place theory of hearing.
    b. volley principle of hearing.
    c. frequency theory of hearing.
    d. bone conduction theory of hearing.

25. A person who suffers a major injury like a broken bone often feels very little pain at the time of the injury. This is probably because when the body suffers a traumatic injury, the pituitary gland releases
    a. serotonin.   c. pheromones.
    b. endorphins.   d. hormones.

26. Megan watches from the car as her parents drive away from her grandfather's house. Because of _____, Megan knows her grandfather's house remains the same size, even though the image gets smaller as they drive farther away.
    a. the law of good continuation
    b. the law of proximity
    c. size constancy
    d. the Müller-Lyer illusion

27. If they existed, telepathy and clairvoyance would be examples of
    a. precognition.
    b. subliminal perception.
    c. extrasensory perception.
    d. Gestalt principles of perception.

Section Three: Fill In the Blank

1. Sensation is to _____ as perception is to _____.
    a. detection of stimuli; sensory interpretation
    b. difference threshold; absolute threshold
    c. absolute threshold; difference threshold
    d. sensory interpretation; detection of stimuli

2. The _____ threshold is a measure of the smallest change in a physical stimulus required to produce a noticeable difference in sensation 50% of the time.

3. Researchers in sensory psychology and _____ study phenomena related to

sensation, such as the least amount of a stimulus required for detection.

4. _____ refers to the process by which a sensory stimulus is changed by the sensory receptors into neural impulses.

5. As part of his training in personnel relations, Ted had to spend a whole day in a very noisy factory. Though the sound seemed almost painful at first, he noticed by the end of the day that it didn't seem so loud anymore. This is an example of _____ _____.

6. One of the major parts of the eye, the _____, performs the first step in vision by bending the light rays inward through the pupil.

7. According to the _____ theory of color vision, certain cells in the visual system increase their rate of firing to signal one color and decrease their firing rate to signal the opposing color.

8. An important characteristic of sound, _____ is determined by the number of cycles completed by a sound wave in 1 second.

9. A sense influenced by the temperature, smell, color, and texture of a stimulus is _____.

10. _____ psychologists studied perception and were guided by the principle that "the whole is more than the sum of its parts."

11. That humans seem to perceive the environment in terms of an object standing out against a background is known as the _____ _____ principle.

12. Ted, an artist, creates pictures that force viewers to fill in gaps in the lines, thereby forming a whole pattern. Ted's art takes advantage of the principle of _____.

13. A person who interpreted a _____ literally would believe that Joe, who is 5 foot 7 and standing 3 feet away, is taller than John, who is 6 feet tall but is standing a block away.

14. Sometimes brilliant moonlight can seemingly change the shade of red of Alicia's horse barn. However, even under these conditions, she still perceives the barn as its usual shade of red. This tendency to perceive the correct color of familiar objects even under different lighting conditions is known as _____ _____.

15. One important contribution to three-dimensional perception is _____ _____, which results when each eye receives a slightly different view of the objects being viewed.

16. In Las Vegas, the sequential flashing of hundreds of neon lights creates the illusion of apparent motion known as the _____ _____.

Section Four: Comprehensive Practice Test

1. The process by which humans detect visual, auditory, and other stimuli is known as
   a. perception.   c. sensation.
   b. transduction.   d. threshold.

2. The process of organizing and interpreting the information gathered through vision, hearing, and the other senses is known as
   a. perception.
   b. the absolute threshold.
   c. transduction.
   d. sensory induction.

3. The _____ _____ is the minimum amount of stimulus that can be detected 50% of the time.
   a. difference reaction   c. difference threshold
   b. absolute reaction   d. absolute threshold

4. The _____ _____ is a measure of the smallest change in a stimulus required for a person to detect a change in the stimulus 50% of the time.
   a. difference reaction   c. difference threshold
   b. absolute difference   d. sensory threshold

5. You are waiting to meet a blind date at a restaurant. You are searching the faces of the people who come in for the one who matches your date's description. You hope you don't approach the wrong person. Some people (those of the wrong sex, those in groups) you don't even pay attention to. This is the process explained by
   a. the recognition threshold.
   b. signal detection theory.
   c. absolute recognition.
   d. sensory adaptation.

6. Sense organs have specialized cells called
   _____ that detect and respond to
   particular stimuli.
   a. sensory detectors
   b. sensory receptors
   c. perceptual responders
   d. perceptual receptors

7. When you see, hear, taste, smell, or feel a sensory
   stimulus, the physical energy that caused the stimulus is changed to neural impulses that are processed in your brain. This process is known as
   a. sensory adaptation.
   b. the absolute threshold
   c. perceptual organization.
   d. transduction.

8. Joe installed an in-ground pool last spring,
   although his wife thought he was crazy to do
   that when it was still cool outside. The first day it
   seemed a little warm Joe jumped in the new pool,
   but soon he realized just how cold the water really
   was. As he continued to "enjoy" the water, it
   seemed to become less cold and even comfortable. This was probably due to a process called
   a. sensory adaptation.
   b. difference threshold.
   c. sensory threshold.
   d. perceptual adaptation.

9. If someone tells you she loves the color of your
   eyes, she is actually talking about your
   a. pupils.   c. irises.
   b. corneas.   d. retinas.

10. Rods are to cones as _____ is to
    _____.
    a. dim light; color
    b. color; dim light
    c. bright light; color
    d. color; bright light

11. The blind spot in the back of the eye is where
    a. the rods and cones come together.
    b. the retina converges on the fovea.
    c. the optic nerve leaves the eye.
    d. the blood supply enters the eye.

12. When you read a book, the lenses in your eyes are
    probably a little more spherical, and when you gaze
    up at the stars at night, your lenses become flatter.
    These differences are due to a process known as
    a. retinal disparity.   c. accommodation.
    b. lens reactivity.   d. adaptation.

13. Sally tells her roommate that we see color be-
    cause three kinds of cones react to one of three

colors–blue, green, or red. Sally has been reading
about the _____ theory of color vision.
    a. opponent-process
    b. trichromatic
    c. relative disparity
    d. complementary color

14. The number of cycles completed by a sound wave
    in 1 second is the wave's
    a. decibel level.   c. amplitude.
    b. timbre.   d. frequency.

15. The job of the _____, also known as the
    hammer, the anvil, and the stirrup, is to amplify
    sound as it moves from the eardrum to the oval
    window.
    a. ossicles   c. hair cells
    b. cochlear bones   d. timbre bones

16. Tomas says that we hear different pitches depend-
    ing on which spot along the basilar membrane
    vibrates the most. He is talking about the
    _____ theory of hearing.
    a. frequency   c. cochlea
    b. position   d. place

17. Olfaction refers to
    a. the sense of taste.
    b. the sense of smell.
    c. the ability to detect skin temperature.
    d. the ability to differentiate sounds.

18. Despite what you learned in grade school, all parts
    of the tongue can detect sweet, sour, salty, and
    bitter. (true/false)

19. *Tactile* is used in reference to the sense of
    a. smell.   c. taste.
    b. balance.   d. touch.

20. The gate-control theory of pain suggests that
    slow-conducting nerve fibers carry pain messages
    and that these messages can be blocked by
    messages from fast-conducting nerve fibers.
    (true/false)

21. An athlete's ability to move gracefully on the paral-
    lel bars is due to the _____ sense.
    a. tactile   c. kinesthetic
    b. olfactory   d. eustachian

22. The vestibular sense provides information that
    allows you to know that a red door is still red even
    in a dark room. (true/false)

23. The half-time show at a football game involved a
    hundred people marching on the field—all in differ-
    ent colored uniforms. Then they took on a forma-
    tion and suddenly all the red uniforms spelled out

the initials of the home team. Gestalt psychologists would suggest that the principle of _____ explains why fans could read the initials.
a. similarity   c. closure
b. continuity   d. constancy

24. Which of the following is not a Gestalt principle of gouping?
a. closure   c. constancy
b. similarity   d. proximity

25. Painters sometimes represent familiar objects using unfamiliar or even unrealistic shapes, sizes, or perspectives. The fact that viewers can recognize the familiar object despite such distortion is known as perceptual
a. equilibrium.   c. continuity.
b. constancy.   d. reliability

26. If you move your finger closer and closer to your nose and focus on perceiving only one image of the finger even when it is almost touching the nose, your eyes begin to turn inward. This eye movement is known as
a. disparity.   c. congruity.
b. monocular adjustment.   d. convergence.

27. Cues such as interposition, linear perspective, and relative size are known as _____ depth cues.
a. binoclar   c. monocular
b. divergent   d. bimodal

28. The phi phenomenon refers to the perception of movement created by stationary lights flashing on and off in a specific sequence. (true/false)

29. Lines of the same length with diagonals at their ends pointing in or out appear to be of different lengths because of the _____ illusion.
a. Ponzo   c. trident
b. Müller-Lyer   d. ambiguous

30. Bottom-up processing is to _____ stimuli as top-down processing is to _____ stimuli.
a. unfamiliar; familiar   c. familiar; unfamiliar
b. visual; auditory   d. perceptual; subliminal

31. While visiting family friends, Josh is thrilled to find out they are having hotdogs for lunch. When lunch is served Josh is horrified to see a hotdog that is a very different color than the familiar reddish tint of his favorite brand. It tastes terrible! Given that the new hotdog is in fact as good as Josh's favorite, what would explain his distaste for this unpleasant luncheon surprise?
a. perceptual constancy
b. parapsychology
c. perceptual persuasion
d. perceptual set

Section Five: Critical Thinking

1. Using what you have learned about the factors that contribute to hearing loss, prepare a statement indicating what you think the government should do to control noise pollution, even to the extent of banning certain noise hazards. Consider the workplace, the home, automobiles and other vehicles, toys, machinery, rock concerts, and so on.

2. Polls indicate that nearly 49% of Americans believe in ESP. Prepare a sound, logical argument supporting one of the following positions:

a. There is evidence to suggest that ESP exists.
b. There is no evidence to suggest that ESP exists.

3. Vision and hearing are generally believed to be the two most highly prized senses. How would your life change if you lost your sight? How would your life change if you lost your hearing? Which sense would you find more traumatic to lose? Why?

States of Consciousness

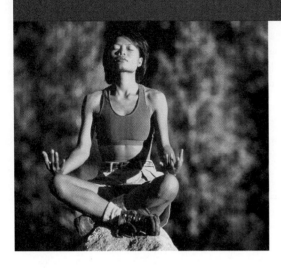

Shortly after 6:00 A.M. one day in March 1990, Northwest Airlines Flight 650, with 91 passengers on board, left Fargo, North Dakota, bound for St. Paul, Minnesota. The flight was uneventful, and the plane landed safely.

A safe landing doesn't usually make the news, but Flight 650 did. Upon arrival, all three members of the cockpit crew—the pilot, the first officer, and the second officer—were arrested. On the night before their early morning flight, all three had been out drinking until after midnight at a tavern across the street from their motel. Although there was no evidence that any of the three were drunk, tests confirmed the presence of alcohol in their blood. Having violated Federal Aviation Administration rules against drinking alcohol within 8 hours of flying, all three fliers lost their FAA licenses.

Several years before the Flight 650 incident, a Boeing 707 took off from New York en route to Los Angeles International Airport. The flight was scheduled to arrive at midnight. As the plane neared Los Angeles, the air traffic controllers were puzzled to see it maintaining its altitude of 32,000 feet. The flight tower continued to issue clearances to land, but the plane passed over Los Angeles and was soon 50 miles out over the Pacific Ocean, still at a high altitude. The air traffic controllers were alarmed as the plane continued flying 100 miles westward over the Pacific, because its fuel supply was running low.

What was wrong with the pilots? They had used neither drugs nor alcohol but were responding naturally to their biological clocks, which were synchronized with New York time. In New York, it was 3:00 A.M.—a time when most of us feel an urgent need to sleep. And indeed the flight crew had succumbed to their urgent need. They were all sound asleep, cruising on automatic pilot. Finally the tower was able to awaken them by activating a series of chimes in the cockpit, and the pilots returned to Los Angeles with just enough fuel to land safely. (Coleman, 1986)

WHAT IS CONSCIOUSNESS?

The crews of the two flights had problems because they were not flying in a state of ordinary waking consciousness. Consciousness is one of the most basic concepts in the study of psychology, and yet it remains rather elusive. You may think of **consciousness** as an awareness of one's own perceptions, thoughts, feelings, sensations, and external environment.

The first American psychologist, William James, likened consciousness to a flowing stream. This "stream of consciousness," he believed, wanders, meanders, and flows, sometimes where the person wills and sometimes not. We control the flow of consciousness when we concentrate and focus our attention. At other times we do not control it, as images, thoughts, and feelings, like uninvited guests, slip into the stream of consciousness and capture it temporarily.

Sigmund Freud extended the notion of consciousness as envisioned by James. Far beneath the stream of consciousness, Freud identified what he termed the *unconscious,* which holds wishes, ideas, and impulses, primarily sexual and aggressive in nature, of which a person is unaware. Freud advanced the notion of various levels of awareness in consciousness.

When you are at the highest level of consciousness, you are fully absorbed. Your thoughts are fixed on the object of your concentration, such as studying, taking an exam, or learning a new skill. At such times you are less conscious of other potentially competing stimuli, both external (the noise around you) and internal (whether you are hungry). Athletes at full concentration during a game may be oblivious to pains, even those that signal potentially serious injuries.

A lower level of awareness involves such mental activities as daydreaming. Daydreaming may involve fantasies and wishful thoughts, but much more often it is simply a form of mental drifting—planning for some future event, thinking about what you *should* have said or rehearsing what you are going to say to someone. Daydreams typically appear when a person is bored, lying in bed waiting to fall asleep, or engaged in activities that do not require full conscious awareness, such as driving to school or work. Sexual fantasies, too, are frequent topics of daydreaming and are far more frequent in males than in females (Leitenberg & Henning, 1995).

Is daydreaming merely a waste of time? Not according to some experts, who suggest that daydreaming may serve a variety of useful functions (Klinger, 1987). Daydreaming is a highly effective way to rehearse for some future action, to explore

What are some different states of consciousness?

consciousness: An awareness of one's own perceptions, thoughts, feelings, sensations, and external environment.

a variety of solutions for everyday problems, or even to provide motivation to achieve a goal (Singer, 1975).

A still lower level of awareness is the state of consciousness to which we descend when we sleep. But asleep or awake, a great deal of nonconscious (below the level of awareness) information processing is going on constantly. The decisions we reach, the values we embrace, the ideas we conceive, the plans we make, even the friends we choose are all heavily influenced by nonconscious information processing. Furthermore, many of the actions we perform—driving a car, riding a bicycle, walking to class—are accomplished by means of automatic processing, thus freeing conscious awareness to focus on other things.

We will now look at the various states of consciousness and examine the many ways in which consciousness may be altered. Ordinary waking consciousness can be altered by substances such as alcohol or drugs and by focused concentration as in meditation and hypnosis. This chapter will explore these **altered states of consciousness**.

The most fundamental altered state is one in which people spend about one-third of their lives, the one they visit for several hours nearly every night—sleep.

CIRCADIAN RHYTHMS: 24-HOUR HIGHS AND LOWS

What is a circadian rhythm, and which rhythms are most relevant to the study of sleep?

Do you notice changes in the way you feel throughout the day—fluctuations in your energy level, moods, or efficiency? Over 100 bodily functions and behaviors follow **circadian rhythms**—that is, they fluctuate regularly from a high to a low point over a 24-hour period (Dement, 1974). Circadian rhythms play a critical role in the timing of life-sustaining processes in virtually all organisms, from the most complex—humans and other vertebrates—to plants and even single-cell life forms (Kay, 1997). Blood pressure, heart rate, appetite, secretion of hormones and digestive enzymes, sensory acuity, elimination, and even the body's response to medication all follow circadian rhythms. Learning efficiency, ability to perform a wide range of tasks, and even moods ebb and flow according to these daily rhythms (Boivin et al., 1997; Johnson et al., 1992).

Two circadian rhythms of particular importance to the study of sleep are the sleep/wakefulness cycle and body temperature. Normal human body temperature can range from a low of about 97 or 97.5 degrees between 3:00 and 4:00 A.M. to a high of about 98.6 degrees between 5:00 and 8:00 P.M. People sleep best when their body temperature is lowest, and they are most alert when their body temperature is at its daily high point. Alertness also follows a circadian rhythm, one that is quite separate from the sleep/wakefulness rhythm (Monk, 1989). For most people, alertness decreases between 2:00 and 5:00 P.M. and between 2:00 and 7:00 A.M. (Webb, 1995).

What are the mechanisms that control or disrupt our circadian rhythms?

The Suprachiasmatic Nucleus: The Body's Timekeeper

What is the suprachiasmatic nucleus?

In their studies of circadian rhythms in mammals, researchers have found that the biological clock is the **suprachiasmatic nucleus (SCN)**, located in the brain's hypothalamus (Ginty et al., 1993; Ralph, 1989). The SCN, a tiny piece of brain tissue smaller than the head of a pin, controls the timing of circadian rhythms (Moore-Ede, 1993).

But the ebb and flow of circadian rhythms is not strictly biological. Environmental cues also play a part. The most significant environmental cue is bright light, particularly sunlight. Specialized cells (photoreceptors) in the retina at the back of each eye respond to the amount of light reaching the eye and relay this information to the SCN. The SCN acts on this information by signaling the pineal gland, located in the center of the brain. In response, the pineal gland secretes the hormone **melatonin** from dusk to shortly before dawn and suppresses secretion of melatonin dur-

Link It!

ing daylight. Melatonin acts to induce sleep, which may be a function of its ability to lower the activity of neurons in the SCN (Barinaga, 1997).

But what happens in people who have volunteered to live for weeks or months in underground caves or in laboratories where there are no cues indicating the time of day? Most of these people naturally fall into a 25-hour schedule, each day waking up and going to sleep an hour later (Moore-Ede, 1993). However, the circadian rhythms of their sleep/wakefulness cycle, body temperature, melatonin secretion, and other bodily functions become desynchronized (Mistlberger & Rusak, 1989; Welsh, 1993). When participants return to their normal environment with daylight and dark, alarm clocks, and job and school demands, their biological clock resets to a 24-hour schedule.

Circadian rhythms are slightly disrupted each year when daylight saving time begins and ends. An even greater disruption occurs when people fly across a number of time zones or work rotating shifts.

Jet Lag: Where Am I and What Time Is It?

Suppose you fly from Chicago to London, and the plane lands at 12:00 midnight Chicago time, about the time you usually go to sleep. At the same time that it is midnight in Chicago, it is 6:00 A.M. in London, almost time to get up. The clocks, the sun, and everything else in London tell you it is early morning, but you still feel like it is 12:00 midnight. You are experiencing jet lag.

The problem is not simply the result of losing a night's sleep. You are fighting your own biological clock, which is synchronized with your usual time zone and not the time zone you are visiting. It is difficult to try to sleep when our biological clock is telling us to wake up and feel alert. It is even harder to remain awake and alert when our internal clock is telling us to sleep. Some research indicates that jet lag is less troublesome for women, younger people, extroverts, and night owls (Kiester, 1997).

Some people experience a problem similar to jet lag without the benefit of a trip to Europe or Asia. These people are shift workers.

Shift Work: Working Day and Night

The United States is increasingly becoming a 24-hour society (Moore-Ede, 1993). About 20% of Americans work at night and sleep during the day (Slon, 1997). The health care, data-processing, and transportation industries are the largest employers of shift workers.

Not surprisingly, shift workers complain of sleepiness and sleeping difficulties. Shift workers average 2 to 4 hours less sleep than nonshift workers of the same age (Campbell, 1995). From 75% to 90% of workers complain of sleepiness during the night shift, and many actually fall asleep during their shift (Leger, 1994).

What about performance on the job? Alertness and performance deteriorate if people work during **subjective night**, when their biological clock is telling them to go to sleep (Åkerstedt, 1990; Folkard, 1990). During subjective night, energy and efficiency are at their lowest point, reaction time is slowest, productivity is diminished, and industrial accidents are significantly higher. If you become sleepy while driving, researchers say you should not rely on a blast of cold air or higher volume from your radio to keep you awake for more than 30 minutes (Reyner & Horne, 1998).

Many air, rail, marine, and highway accidents have occurred when the shift workers in charge suffered sleep loss and fatigue because of the disruption of their circadian rhythms (Lauber & Kayten, 1988). More errors in judgment and most accidents occur during the night shift. The failure of the nuclear reactor at Three Mile

subjective night: The time during a 24-hour period when body temperature is lowest and when the biological clock is telling a person to go to sleep.

Link It!

What are some problems experienced by people who work rotating shifts?

What are the physical and psychological effects of disturbing the normal sleep/wakefulness cycle when a person works the night shift, as this printing press operator does?

NREM sleep: Non–rapid eye movement sleep, consisting of the four sleep stages and characterized by slow, regular respiration and heart rate, an absence of rapid eye movements, and blood pressure and brain activity that are at a 24-hour low point.

REM sleep: Sleep characterized by rapid eye movements, paralysis of large muscles, fast and irregular heart rate and respiration rate, increased brain-wave activity, and vivid dreams.

Island, the Russian nuclear disaster at Chernobyl, and the Challenger disaster all occurred in the middle of the night when those directly responsible were dangerously fatigued (Moore-Ede, 1993).

However, the situation isn't hopeless. In simulated night-shift schedules, exposure to appropriately timed bright or medium-intensity light or even light of lower intensity has been found to reset young adults' biological clocks and improve their performance (Martin & Eastman, 1998). A recent study by Campbell and Murphy (1998) suggests that even light focused on the back of a person's knees can reset the biological clock.

Taking Melatonin as a Sleep Aid

Melatonin has not been approved by the FDA as a drug, but it is sold over the counter as a sleep aid or dietary supplement. Taking melatonin helps reset the biological clock in night-shift workers and in those suffering from jet lag. Low doses (0.3–1.0 milligram) taken several hours before bedtime have been found to promote sleep in healthy young males, without significantly altering the structure of sleep and without creating negative aftereffects the following morning (Zhdanova et al., 1996). Some researchers suggest that melatonin may facilitate sleep by lowering the core body temperature (Dawson et al., 1995; Hughes & Badia, 1997).

Although these sound like good reasons to take a melatonin supplement, there are even better reasons not to take it. First, a second biological clock that secretes melatonin has been found in the retinas of hamsters (Tosini & Menaker, 1996). Might a second biological clock be found in the human retina as well? Melatonin expert Alfred Lewy warns, "If we knew with certainty that melatonin has an important function in the human eye, [it] should be taken off the market immediately—no questions asked" (quoted in Raloff, 1996, p. 245). Also, since melatonin reduces the activity of neurons in the SCN, too much of it could actually shut down the biological clock (Barinaga, 1997).

Some supplements contain 2.5 or 3 milligrams of melatonin, 10 times more than is needed to promote normal sleep and enough to raise blood melatonin levels to 30 times their normal nighttime level (Zhdanova & Wurtman, 1996). The safety and long-term effects of such dosage levels are not yet known (Finkbeiner, 1998; Haimov & Lavie, 1996).

SLEEP: THAT MYSTERIOUS ONE-THIRD OF LIFE

Over a lifetime, a person spends about 25 years sleeping. Before the 1950s there was no understanding of what goes on during the state of consciousness known as sleep. Then, in the 1950s, several universities set up sleep laboratories where people's brain waves, eye movements, chin-muscle tension, heart rate, and respiration rate were monitored through a night of sleep. From analyses of sleep recordings, known as *polysomnograms*, researchers discovered the characteristics of two major categories of sleep.

NREM and REM Sleep: Watching the Eyes

How does a sleeper react physically during NREM sleep?

The two categories of sleep are NREM (non–rapid eye movement) sleep and REM (rapid eye movement) sleep. **NREM** (pronounced NON-rem) **sleep** is sleep in which there are no rapid eye movements. It is often called "quiet sleep," because heart rate and respiration are slow and regular, there is little body movement, and blood pressure and brain activity are at their lowest points of the 24-hour period. There are four stages of NREM sleep—Stages 1, 2, 3, and 4—with Stage 1 being the lightest sleep and Stage 4 being the deepest. Sleepers pass gradually rather than abruptly from one stage to the next. Each stage can be identified by its brain-wave

104

CHAPTER 4

pattern, as shown in Figure 4.1. Growth hormone is secreted primarily in Stage 3 and Stage 4 sleep (Gronfier et al., 1996).

Most of us envision sleep as a time of deep relaxation and calm. But **REM sleep,** sometimes called "active sleep," is anything but calm, and it constitutes 20–25% of a normal night's sleep in adults. During the REM state, there is intense brain activity. In fact, within 1 to 2 minutes after REM sleep begins, brain metabolism increases and brain temperature rises rapidly (Krueger & Takahashi, 1997). The body reacts as if to a daytime emergency. Epinephrine (adrenaline) shoots into the system, blood pressure rises, and heart rate and respiration become faster and irregular. In contrast to this storm of internal activity, there is an external calm during REM sleep. The large muscles of the body—arms, legs, trunk—become paralyzed. Some researchers suggest that this paralysis prevents people from acting out their dreams. But there is a rare condition known as REM sleep behavior disorder, in which individuals are not paralyzed during REM sleep. Consequently, while dreaming, they may become violent, causing injury to themselves and their bed partners and damage to their homes (Broughton & Shimizu, 1995; Moldofsky et al., 1995).

How does the body respond physically during REM sleep?

In a sleep laboratory or sleep clinic, researchers tape electrodes to a person's head to monitor brain-wave activity, eye movements, and muscle tension.

Observe a sleeper during the REM state, and you will see the eyes darting around under the eyelids. In 1952 Eugene Azerinsky first discovered these bursts of rapid eye movements, and William Dement and Nathaniel Kleitman (1957) made the connection between rapid eye movements and dreaming. It is during REM periods that most vivid dreams occur. When awakened from REM sleep, 80% of people report dreaming (Carskadon & Dement, 1989).

Almost from birth, regardless of the content of their dreams, males have a full or partial erection during REM sleep, and females experience vaginal swelling and lubrication. Because sleepers are more likely to awaken naturally at the end of a REM period than during NREM sleep, men usually wake up with an erection (Campbell, 1985). In males suffering from impotence, the presence of an erection during REM sleep indicates that the impotence is psychological; its absence indicates that the impotence is physiological in origin.

Figure 4.1

Brain-Wave Patterns Associated with Different Stages of Sleep

By monitoring brain-wave activity with the EEG throughout a night's sleep, researchers have identified the brain-wave patterns associated with different stages of sleep. As sleepers progress through the four NREM stages, the brain-wave pattern changes from faster, low-voltage waves in Stages 1 and 2 to the slower, larger delta waves in Stages 3 and 4. Notice that the brain-wave activity during REM sleep is similar to that of the person when awake.

sleep cycle: A cycle of sleep lasting about 90 minutes and including one or more stages of NREM sleep followed by a period of REM sleep.

delta wave: The slowest brain-wave pattern, associated with Stage 3 sleep and Stage 4 sleep.

slow-wave sleep: Stage 3 sleep and Stage 4 sleep.

Stage 4 sleep: The deepest stage of NREM sleep, characterized by an EEG pattern of more than 50% delta waves.

What is the progression of NREM stages and REM sleep that a person follows in a typical night?

If you awaken during REM sleep and remain awake for several minutes, you will not go back into REM sleep for at least 30 minutes. This is why most people have experienced the disappointment of waking in the middle of a wonderful dream and trying in vain to get back to sleep quickly and into the dream again.

Sleep Cycles: The Nightly Pattern of Sleep

You may be surprised to learn that sleep follows a fairly predictable pattern each night. We all sleep in cycles. During each **sleep cycle**, which lasts about 90 minutes, a person has one or more stages of NREM sleep followed by a period of REM sleep. Let's look closely at a typical night of sleep for a young adult.

The first sleep cycle begins with a few minutes in Stage 1 sleep, sometimes called "light sleep." Stage 1 is actually a transition stage between waking and sleeping. Then sleepers descend into Stage 2 sleep, in which they are somewhat more deeply asleep and harder to awaken. (About 50% of a total night's sleep is spent in Stage 2 sleep.) As sleep gradually becomes deeper, brain activity slows, and more **delta waves** (slow waves) appear in the EEG. When the EEG registers 20% delta waves, sleepers enter Stage 3 sleep, the beginning of **slow-wave sleep** (or deep sleep). Delta waves continue to increase, and when they reach more than 50%, people enter **Stage 4 sleep**—the deepest sleep, from which they are hardest to awaken (Carskadon & Rechtschaffen, 1989; Cooper, 1994). Perhaps you have taken an afternoon nap and awakened confused, not knowing whether it was morning or night, a weekday or a weekend. If so, you probably awakened during Stage 4 sleep.

In Stage 4 sleep, delta waves may reach nearly 100% on the EEG, but after about 40 minutes in this stage, brain activity increases and the delta waves begin to disappear. Sleepers ascend back through Stage 3 and Stage 2 sleep, then enter their first REM period, which lasts 10 or 15 minutes. At the end of this REM period, the first sleep cycle is complete, and the second sleep cycle begins. Unless people awaken after the first sleep cycle, they go directly from REM into Stage 2 sleep. They then follow the same progression as in the first sleep cycle, through Stages 3 and 4 and back again into REM sleep.

After the first two sleep cycles of about 90 minutes each (3 hours total), the sleep pattern changes and sleepers usually get no more Stage 4 sleep. From this point on, during each 90-minute sleep cycle, people alternate mainly between Stage 2 and REM sleep for the remainder of the night. With each sleep cycle, the REM periods (and therefore dreaming time) get progressively longer. At the end of the night, REM periods may last 30 to 40 minutes. Most people have about five sleep cycles (7½ to 8 hours) and average about 1½ hours of slow-wave sleep and 1½ hours of REM sleep. Figure 4.1 shows the progression through NREM and REM sleep during a typical night.

Variations in Sleep: How People Differ

How do sleep patterns change over the life span?

There are great individual variations in patterns of sleep; the major factor contributing to this variation is age. Infants and young children have the longest sleep time and the highest percentage of REM and slow-wave sleep, but they get even more REM sleep before birth. A fetus spends up to 80% of the time in REM sleep (Hobson, 1989). Children from age 6 to puberty are the champion sleepers and wakers. They fall asleep easily, sleep soundly for 8½ to 9 hours at night, and feel awake and alert during the day. Teenagers average 7.2 hours of sleep but need about 2 hours more than that to do well in school (Carskadon & Wolfson, 1997).

As people age, the quality and quantity of sleep usually decrease (Reyner & Horne, 1995). In one large study of 9,000 participants aged 65 and over, only 12% reported no sleep problems (Foley et al., 1995). Older adults have more difficulty falling asleep than younger people do and typically sleep more lightly. Moreover, they spend more time in bed but less time asleep, averaging about 6½ hours of sleep a night (Prinz et al., 1990). Slow-wave sleep decreases substantially from age 30 to age 50 (Mourtazaev et al., 1995). The percentage of REM sleep stays about the same (Moran & Stoudemire, 1992).

Some people awaken early every morning and leap out of bed with enthusiasm, eager to start the day. Others fumble for the alarm clock and push a snooze button to get a few more precious minutes of sleep. Early risers find it hard to keep from yawning after 10:00 P.M. and have an overwhelming urge to get to bed. But this is precisely the time when the night people come to life. Sleep researchers have names for these two types—larks and owls. There is a physical explanation for the difference in the way they feel. About 25% of people are larks, people whose body temperature rises rapidly after they awaken and stays high until about 7:30 P.M. Larks turn in early and have the fewest sleep problems. Then there are the 25% of people who are owls and the 50% who are somewhere in between. The body temperature of an owl gradually rises throughout the day, peaking in the afternoon and not dropping until later in the evening. Differences in one of the genes that run the biological clock are responsible, in part, for the differences between larks and owls (Mignot et al., 1998).

How much sleep does the average person need? More than he or she gets, according to sleep researcher William Dement. And a temporary increase in mental activity can increase the need for sleep.

What factors influence sleep needs?

How Much Sleep Do You Need? More Than You Probably Get   Maybe you have wondered how much sleep you need in order to feel good. Data from a number of studies indicate that more than 36% of the U.S. population is chronically sleep-deprived (Bonnet & Arand, 1995). When it comes to sleep, the expression "one size fits all" does *not* apply. Although adults average about 7½ hours of sleep daily with an extra hour on weekends, this is too much for some people and too little for others. Short sleepers are the 20% who require less than 6 hours of sleep; long sleepers are the 10% who require more than 9 hours. There seems to be a limit below which most people cannot go. In one study, not a single participant could get by with less than 4½ hours of sleep, and 6½ hours appears to be the minimum most people require.

What accounts for the large variation in the need for sleep? Genetics appears to play a part. Identical twins, for example, have strikingly similar sleep patterns compared to fraternal twins (Webb & Campbell, 1983). Laboratory animals have even been bred to be short or long sleepers. But genetics aside, people need more sleep when they are depressed, under stress, or experiencing significant life changes such as changing jobs or schools. Temporary increases in mental, physical, or emotional effort also increase the need for sleep (Hartmann, 1973). Contrary to popular opinion, the amount of activity required in an occupation does not affect the amount of sleep a person needs.

The Functions of Sleep: The Restorative and Circadian Theories

The very fact that people spend about one-third of their lives sleeping indicates that sleep must serve important functions. But why do we need sleep?

Two general theories have been advanced to explain the function of sleep. One, the **restorative theory**, holds that being awake produces wear and tear on the body and the brain, and sleep restores body and mind (Gökcebay et al., 1994). Yet there are many known aspects of sleep that a restorative theory alone cannot explain. For example, if you intentionally stay awake for a night, why do you find it so difficult to keep your eyes open during the middle of the night and yet are much less sleepy and more alert in the morning, without having had any restorative sleep?

A second explanation, the **circadian theory**, argues that sleepiness and alertness ebb and flow according to circadian rhythms. The circadian theory of sleep is based on the premise that sleep evolved to keep humans out of harm's way during the dark of night and possibly from becoming prey for some nocturnal predator.

Alexander Borbely (1984; Borbely et al., 1989) makes an argument that blends the circadian and restorative theories. That people feel sleepy at certain times of day

What are the two main theories that attempt to explain the function of sleep?

restorative theory: The theory that the function of sleep is to restore body and mind.

circadian theory: The theory that sleep evolved to keep humans out of harm's way during the night and that sleepiness ebbs and flows according to a circadian rhythm.

is consistent with the circadian theory. And that sleepiness increases the longer a person is awake is consistent with the restorative theory. In other words, the urge to sleep is partly a function of how long a person has been awake and partly a function of the time of day (Webb, 1995).

What happens when we are sleep-deprived and miss the restorative interval of sleep?

Sleep Deprivation: What Are Its Effects?

Link It!

What is the longest you have ever stayed awake—two days, three days? According to the *Guinness Book of World Records*, Robert McDonald stayed awake 453 hours and 40 minutes (almost 19 days) in a 1986 rocking-chair marathon. Unlike McDonald, most people have missed no more than a few consecutive nights of sleep, perhaps studying for final exams. If you have ever missed two or three nights of sleep, you may remember having had difficulty concentrating, lapses in attention, and general irritability. After 60 hours without sleep, some people even have minor hallucinations. Most people who try to stay awake for long periods of time will have **microsleeps**, 2- to 3-second lapses from wakefulness into sleep. You may have experienced a microsleep if you have ever caught yourself nodding off for a few seconds in class or on a long automobile trip.

A meta-analysis using data from over 1,900 subjects indicated that sleep deprivation seriously impairs human functioning (Pilcher & Huffcutt, 1996). It has a negative impact on mood, alertness, and performance and reduces the body's ability to warm itself, even in relatively comfortable temperatures (Bonnet & Arand, 1995; Landis et al., 1998). Even partial sleep deprivation impairs one's ability to attend to and process relevant stimuli in the environment (McCarthy & Waters, 1997). Children whose school starts around 7:00 AM get less sleep than those who begin school later, and they report difficulty in concentrating and paying attention (Epstein et al., 1998). Partial sleep loss, even for one night, can significantly reduce the effectiveness of the human immune system by lowering killer cell activity. But after one full night of sleep, the immune function appears to return to normal (Irwin et al., 1994).

But what if you cannot sleep more hours each night? Going to sleep and waking up on a regular schedule seems to increase alertness, reduce sleepiness, and improve sleep efficiency.

Dreaming: Mysterious Mental Activity during Sleep

How do REM and NREM dreams differ?

Humans have always been fascinated by dreams. The vivid dreams people remember and talk about are **REM dreams**—the type that occur almost continuously during each REM period. But people also have **NREM dreams**, dreams that occur during NREM sleep, although they are typically less frequent and less memorable than REM dreams (Foulkes, 1996). REM dreams have a storylike or dreamlike quality and are more visual, vivid, and emotional than NREM dreams (Hobson, 1989). Blind people who lose their sight before age 5 usually do not have visual dreams. Nevertheless, they have vivid dreams involving the other senses.

You may have heard that an entire dream takes place in an instant. Do you find that hard to believe? In fact, it is not true. Sleep researchers have discovered that it takes about as long to dream a dream as it would to experience the same thing in real life (Kleitman, 1960). Let's take a closer look at the dream state.

Although some people insist that they do not dream at all, sleep researchers say that all people dream unless they are drinking heavily or taking drugs that suppress REM sleep. Sleepers have the best recall of a dream if they are awakened during the dream; the more time that passes after the dream ends, the poorer the recall. If you awaken 10 minutes or more after a dream is over, you probably will not remember it. Even the dreams you remember on awakening will quickly fade from memory unless you mentally rehearse them or write them down. Very few dreams are memorable enough to be retained very long. Some researchers suggest that human brain

microsleep: A momentary lapse from wakefulness into sleep, usually occurring when a person has been sleep deprived.

REM dream: A type of dream having a dreamlike and storylike quality and occuring almost continuously during each REM period; more vivid, visual, and emotional than NREM dreams.

NREM dream: Mental activity occurring during NREM sleep that is more thoughtlike in quality than REM dreams are.

chemistry during sleep differs from that in the waking state and does not facilitate the storing of memories (Hobson, 1996; Hobson & Stickgold, 1995).

What do people dream about? You may be surprised to learn that most dreams are less bizarre and less filled with emotion than is generally believed (Cipolli et al., 1993; Hall & Van de Castle, 1966; Snyder, 1971). Because dreams are notoriously hard to remember, the features that stand out tend to be those that are bizarre or emotional.

Sleep researchers generally agree that dreams reflect a person's preoccupations in waking life—hopes and plans, worries and fears. Most dreams have rather commonplace settings with real people, half of whom are known to the dreamer. In general, dreams are more unpleasant than pleasant, and they contain more aggression than friendly interactions and more misfortune than good fortune. Fear and anxiety, often quite intense, are common in REM dreams (Hobson, 1996). Some dreams are in "living color," while others are in black and white.

Some people are troubled by unpleasant recurring dreams. The two most common themes involve being chased or falling (Stark, 1984). People who have recurring dreams seem to have more minor physical complaints, greater stress, and more anxiety and depression than other people (Brown & Donderi, 1986). Is there anything that can be done to stop recurring dreams? Some people have been taught to use **lucid dreaming** (during which they are aware that they are dreaming) to bring about satisfactory resolutions to their unpleasant recurring dreams.

In general, what have researchers found regarding the content of dreams?

Link It!

Interpreting Dreams: Are There Hidden Meanings in Dreams?

Sigmund Freud believed that dreams function to satisfy unconscious sexual and aggressive wishes. Because such wishes are unacceptable to the dreamer, they have to be disguised and therefore appear in a dream in symbolic form. Freud (1900/1953a) claimed that objects such as sticks, umbrellas, tree trunks, and guns symbolize the male sex organ; objects such as chests, cupboards, and boxes represent the female sex organ. Freud differentiated between the *manifest content* of the dream—the dream as recalled by the dreamer—and the underlying meaning of the dream, called the *latent content*, which he considered more significant.

In recent years there has been a major shift away from the Freudian interpretation of dreams. Now there is a greater focus on the manifest content, the actual dream itself. J. Allan Hobson (1988) rejects the notion that nature would equip humans with a capability and a need to dream dreams that would require a specialist to interpret. Hobson and McCarley (1977) advanced the *activation-synthesis hypothesis* of dreaming. This hypothesis suggests that dreams are simply the brain's attempt to make sense of the random firing of brain cells during REM sleep. Just as people try to make sense of input from the environment during their waking hours, they try to find meaning in the conglomeration of sensations and memories that are generated internally by this random firing of brain cells. Hobson (1989) now believes that dreams also have psychological significance, because the meaning a person imposes reflects that person's experiences, remote memories, associations, drives, and fears.

The Function of REM Sleep: Necessary, but Why?

Some researchers suggest that REM sleep aids in information processing, helping people sift through daily experience, to organize and store in memory information that is relevant to them.

Research has shown that REM sleep serves an information-processing function in humans and is involved in the consolidation of memories following learning. Karni and others (1994) found that research participants learning a new perceptual skill showed an improvement in performance, with no additional practice, 8 to 10 hours later if they had a normal night's sleep or if the researchers disturbed only their NREM sleep. Performance did not improve, however, in those who were deprived of REM sleep. Animal studies also provide strong evidence for a relationship between REM sleep and learning (Hennevin et al., 1995; Smith, 1995; Winson, 1990).

An opposite view is proposed by Francis Crick and Graeme Mitchison (1983, 1995). They suggest that REM sleep functions as mental housecleaning, erasing trivial

What function does REM sleep appear to serve, and what happens when people are deprived of REM sleep?

lucid dream: A dream during which the dreamer is aware of dreaming and is often able to influence the content of the dream while it is in progress.

REM rebound: The increased amount of REM sleep that occurs after REM deprivation; often associated with unpleasant dreams or nightmares.

sleepwalking (somnambulism) (som-NAM-bue-lism): Walking that occurs during a partial arousal from Stage 4 sleep.

sleep terror: A sleep disturbance in which a person partially awakens from Stage 4 sleep with a scream, dazed and groggy, in a panic state, and with a racing heart.

nightmare: A very frightening dream occurring during REM sleep.

What are the characteristics common to sleepwalking and sleep terrors?

What is a sleep terror?

and unnecessary memories and clearing overloaded neural circuits that might interfere with memory and rational thinking. In other words, they say, people dream in order to forget.

There is no doubt that REM sleep serves an important function, even if psychologists do not know precisely what that function is. The fact that newborns have such a high percentage of REM sleep has led to the conclusion that REM sleep is necessary for maturation of the brain in infants (Marks et al., 1995). Furthermore, when people are deprived of REM sleep as a result of general sleep loss or illness, they will make up for the loss by getting an increased amount of REM sleep after the deprivation. This increase in the percentage of REM sleep to make up for REM deprivation is called a **REM rebound**. Because the intensity of REM sleep is increased during a REM rebound, nightmares often occur. Alcohol, amphetamines, cocaine, and LSD suppress REM sleep, and withdrawal from these drugs results in a REM rebound (Porte & Hobson, 1996).

SLEEP DISORDERS

So far our discussion has centered on a typical night for a typical sleeper. But one-third of American adults report sleep problems (Rosekind, 1992), and many children also experience sleep disturbances. Sleep problems range from mild to severe and from problems that affect only sleep to those that affect a person's entire life. Yet medical schools, on average, provide less than 2 hours of instruction on sleep and sleep disorders (Rosen et al., 1993).

Parasomnias: Unusual Behaviors during Sleep

Parasomnias are sleep disturbances in which behaviors and physiological states that normally occur only in the waking state take place during sleep or the transition from sleep to wakefulness. Parasomnias include sleepwalking, sleep terrors, nightmares, and sleeptalking.

Sleepwalking (somnambulism) and sleep terrors are parasomnias that often run in families. They occur during a partial arousal from Stage 4 sleep in which the sleeper does not come to full consciousness. Typically, there is no memory of the episode the following day (Moldofsky et al., 1995). Most cases begin in childhood and are attributed primarily to a delayed development of the nervous system (Masand et al., 1995). The child usually outgrows the disturbance by adolescence.

If an EEG recording were made during a sleepwalking episode, it would show a combination of delta waves, indicating deep sleep, and alpha and beta waves, signaling the waking state. Sleepwalkers are awake enough to carry out activities that do not require their full attention, but asleep enough not to remember having done so the following day. Sleepwalkers may get up and roam through the house, or simply stand for a short time and then go back to bed. Occasionally they get dressed, eat a snack, or go to the bathroom. Some sleepwalkers have even been known to drive during an episode (Schenck & Mahowald, 1995).

Episodes of sleepwalking in adults often occur during periods of stress or major life events and are more likely to be associated with a psychiatric disorder (Masand et al., 1995). Although it is not dangerous to awaken a sleepwalker, experts suggest that it is better to simply guide the individual back to bed (Masand et al., 1995). Rare, but not unheard of, are individuals who commit violent acts while sleepwalking (Broughton & Shimizu, 1995; Moldofsky et al., 1995; Schenck & Mahowald, 1995).

Sleep terrors usually begin with a piercing scream. The sleeper springs up in a state of panic—eyes open, perspiring, breathing rapidly, with the heart pounding at two or more times the normal rate (Karacan, 1988). Episodes usually last from 5 to 15 minutes, and then the person falls back to sleep. If not awakened during a night terror, children usually have no memory of the episode the next morning. If awakened, however, they may recall a single frightening image.

Parents should not be unduly alarmed by sleep terrors in young children, but episodes that continue through adolescence into adulthood are more serious (Horne, 1992). Sleep terrors in adults often indicate extreme anxiety or other psychological problems. Up to 5% of children have sleep terrors (Keefauver & Guilleminault, 1994), but they are rare in adults (Hublin et al., 1999).

Unlike sleep terrors, **nightmares** are very frightening dreams that occur during REM sleep and are likely to be remembered in vivid detail. The most common themes are being chased, threatened, or attacked. Nightmares can be a reaction to traumatic life experiences, and they are more frequent at times of high fevers, anxiety, and emotional upheaval. REM rebound during drug withdrawal or following long periods without sleep can also produce nightmares. Sleep terrors occur early in the night during Stage 4 sleep, while anxiety nightmares occur toward morning, when the REM periods are longest.

According to the American Psychiatric Association (1994), from 10% to 50% of children between ages 3 and 5 have nightmares severe enough to worry their parents. And about 50% of adults have occasional nightmares, which are nothing to be alarmed about. But frequent nightmares may be associated with psychological maladjustment (Berquier & Aston, 1992).

Do you sometimes talk in your sleep? Are you afraid that you might confess to something embarrassing, or reveal some deep, dark secret? Relax. Sleeptalkers rarely reply to questions, and they usually mumble words or phrases that make no sense to the listener. Sleeptalking can occur during any sleep stage and is more frequent in children than in adults. There is no evidence at all that sleeptalking is related to a physical or psychological disturbance—not even to a guilty conscience.

Major Sleep Disorders

Some sleep disorders can be so debilitating that they affect a person's entire life. These disorders are narcolepsy, sleep apnea, and insomnia.

Narcolepsy: Sudden Attacks of REM Sleep   Many people complain about having difficulty falling asleep, but a more serious problem is not being able to stay awake during the day. **Narcolepsy** is an incurable sleep disorder characterized by excessive daytime sleepiness and uncontrollable attacks of REM sleep, usually lasting 10 to 20 minutes. People with narcolepsy—who number from 250,000 to 350,000 in the United States—suffer the effects of a drastically lowered quality of life. They are subject to more accidents virtually everywhere—driving automobiles, at work, and at home. There is an emotional price to pay as well. They are often stigmatized as lazy, depressed, and disinterested in their work. Anything that causes an ordinary person to be tired can trigger a sleep attack in a person with narcolepsy—a heavy meal, sunbathing at the beach, or a boring lecture. A sleep attack can also be brought on by laughter or by any situation that is exciting (such as lovemaking) or that causes a strong emotion (such as anger or elation).

Narcolepsy is a physiological disorder caused by an abnormality in the part of the brain that regulates sleep, and it appears to have a strong genetic component (Billiard et al., 1994; Partinen et al., 1994). Some dogs are subject to narcolepsy, and much has been learned about the genetics of this disorder from research on canine subjects (Lamberg, 1996). Although there is no cure for narcolepsy, stimulant medications improve daytime alertness in most patients (Guilleminault, 1993; Mitler et al., 1994). Experts also recommend scheduled naps to relieve sleepiness (Garma & Marchand, 1994).

Sleep Apnea: When Breathing Stops during Sleep   Over 1 million Americans—mostly obese men—suffer from another dangerous sleep disorder, sleep apnea. **Sleep apnea** consists of periods during sleep when breathing stops, and the

narcolepsy (NAR-co-lep-see): A serious sleep disorder characterized by excessive daytime sleepiness and sudden, uncontrollable attacks of REM sleep.

sleep apnea: A sleep disorder characterized by periods when breathing stops during sleep and the person must awaken briefly in order to breathe; major symptoms are excessive daytime sleepiness and loud snoring.

How do nightmares differ from sleep terrors?

What are the major symptoms of narcolepsy?

Sleep researcher William Dement holds a dog that is experiencing a narcoleptic sleep attack. Much has been learned about narcolepsy through research with dogs.

What is sleep apnea?

individual must awaken briefly in order to breathe (White, 1989). The major symptoms of sleep apnea are excessive daytime sleepiness and extremely loud snoring (as loud as a jackhammer), often accompanied by snorts, gasps, and choking noises.

A person with sleep apnea will drop off to sleep, stop breathing altogether, and then awaken struggling for breath. After gasping several breaths in a semi-awakened state, the person falls back to sleep and stops breathing again. People with severe sleep apnea may partially awaken as many as 800 times a night to gasp for air. Alcohol and sedatives aggravate the condition (Langevin et al., 1992).

Severe sleep apnea can lead to chronic high blood pressure, heart problems, and even death (Lavie et al., 1995). Treatments for sleep apnea include greatly reducing body weight (Strobel & Rosen, 1996) and surgically modifying the upper airway (Sher et al., 1996). The favored treatment, however, is the use of a continuous positive airway pressure (CPAP) device, which delivers air through a mask worn over the nose at night (Lévy & Robert, 1996; Rapoport, 1996).

What is insomnia?

Insomnia: The Most Common Sleep Disorder   Approximately one-third of adults in the United States suffer from **insomnia**—a sleep disorder characterized by difficulty falling or staying asleep, by waking too early, or by sleep that is light, restless, or of poor quality—any of which can lead to distress and impairment in daytime functioning (Costa E Silva et al., 1996; Roth, 1996b). Transient (temporary) insomnia, lasting 3 weeks or less, can result from jet lag, emotional highs (an upcoming wedding) or lows (losing a loved one or a job), or a brief illness or injury that interferes with sleep (Reite et al., 1995). Much more serious is chronic insomnia, which lasts for months or even years and plagues about 10% of the adult population (Roth, 1996b). The percentages are even higher for women, the elderly, and people suffering from psychiatric and medical disorders (Costa E Silva et al., 1996). Chronic insomnia may begin as a reaction to a psychological or medical problem but persist long after the problem is resolved. Individuals with chronic insomnia experience "higher psychological distress [and] greater impairments of daytime functioning, are involved in more fatigue-related accidents, take more sick leave, and utilize health care resources more often than good sleepers" (Morin & Wooten, 1996, p. 522).

The *Apply It!* at the end of this chapter offers some strategies for battling insomnia.

ALTERING CONSCIOUSNESS THROUGH CONCENTRATION AND SUGGESTION

Sleep is an altered state of consciousness and a necessary one. We must all sleep. But there are other forms of altered consciousness that we may experience only if we choose to do so. Meditation and hypnosis are two of these.

Meditation: Expanded Consciousness or Relaxation?

For what purposes is meditation used?

insomnia: A sleep disorder characterized by difficulty falling or staying asleep, by waking too early, or by light, restless, or poor sleep.

meditation (concentrative): A group of techniques that involve focusing attention on an object, a word, one's breathing, or body movement in order to block out all distractions, to enhance well-being, and to achieve an altered state of consciousness.

Meditation (the concentrative form) is a group of techniques that involve focusing attention on an object, a word, one's breathing, or body movement in order to block out all distractions, to enhance well-being, and to achieve an altered state of consciousness. Some forms of concentrative meditation—yoga, Zen, and transcendental meditation (TM)—have their roots in Eastern religions and are practiced by followers of those religions to attain a higher spiritual state. In the United States these approaches are often used to increase relaxation, reduce arousal, or expand consciousness.

In practicing yoga, a meditator typically assumes a cross-legged position known as the lotus and gazes at a visual stimulus—a mandala (a symbolic circular pattern) or an object such as a vase or a flower. During Zen meditation, the individual counts breaths or concentrates on the breathing process. In transcendental meditation, the meditator is given a *mantra*, a secret word assigned by a teacher. The meditator sits quietly with closed eyes and silently repeats the mantra over and over during meditation. With all three approaches, the meditator's goal is to block out unwanted thoughts and facilitate the meditative state. Herbert Benson (1975) suggests that any word or sound can be used for transcendental meditation. Moreover, he claims that the beneficial effects of meditation can be achieved through simple relaxation techniques. Do the *Try It!* to experience Benson's relaxation response.

Try It!

Find a quiet place and sit in a comfortable position.

1. Close your eyes.

2. Relax all your muscles deeply. Beginning with your feet and moving slowly upward, relax the muscles in your legs, buttocks, abdomen, chest, shoulders, neck, and finally your face. Allow your whole body to remain in this deeply relaxed state.

3. Now concentrate on your breathing, and breathe in and out through your nose. Each time you breathe out, silently say the word *one* to yourself.

4. Repeat this process for 20 minutes. (You can open your eyes to look at your watch periodically but don't use an alarm.) When you are finished, remain seated for a few minutes—first with your eyes closed, then with them open.

Benson recommends that you maintain a passive attitude. Don't try to force yourself to relax. Just let it happen. If a distracting thought comes to mind, ignore it and just repeat *one* each time you exhale. It is best to practice this exercise one or two times each day, but not within two hours of your last meal. Digestion interferes with the relaxation response.

Hypnosis: The Power of Suggestion

Have you ever been hypnotized? Many people are fascinated by this unusual, somewhat mysterious phenomenon. **Hypnosis** may be defined as a procedure through which one person, the hypnotist, uses the power of suggestion to induce changes in thoughts, feelings, sensations, perceptions, or behavior in another person, the subject. Under hypnosis, people suspend their usual rational and logical ways of thinking and perceiving and allow themselves to experience distortions in perceptions, memories, and thinking. They may experience positive hallucinations, in which they see, hear, touch, smell, or taste things that are not present in the environment. Or they may have negative hallucinations, in which they fail to perceive things that are actually present.

About 80–95% of people are hypnotizable to some degree, but only 5% can reach the deepest levels of the hypnotic state (Nash & Baker, 1984). The ability to become completely absorbed in imaginative activities is characteristic of highly hypnotizable people (Nadon et al., 1991). Silva and Kirsch (1992) found that individuals' fantasy-proneness and their expectation of responding to hypnotic suggestions were predictors of hypnotizability.

There are many misconceptions about hypnosis, some of which probably stem from its long association with stage entertainers. Hypnotized people are not under the complete control of the hypnotist. Subjects retain the ability to refuse to comply with the hypnotist's suggestions, and they will not do anything that is contrary to their true moral beliefs. Subjects are not stronger or more powerful under hypnosis (Druckman & Bjork, 1994). Memory is not more accurate under hypnosis. Although it is true that hypnotized subjects supply more information and are more confident of their recollections, the information is often inaccurate (Dywan & Bowers, 1983; Kihlstrom & Barnhardt, 1993; Nogrady et al., 1985; Weekes et al., 1992). And in the process of trying to help people recall certain events, hypnotists may instead create in them false memories, or pseudomemories (Lynn & Nash, 1994; Yapko, 1994).

What is hypnosis, and when is it most useful?

hypnosis: A procedure in which one person, the hypnotist, uses the power of suggestion to induce changes in thoughts, feelings, sensations, perceptions, or behavior in another person, the subject.

Hypnosis is not like a truth serum. Subjects can keep secrets or lie under hypnosis. Careful reviews of studies on hypnotic age regression have found no evidence to support the claim that people under hypnosis can relive an event as it occurred when they were children and can function mentally as if they were that age (Nash, 1987).

Link It!

Hypnosis is now recognized as a viable technique to be used in medicine, dentistry, and psychotherapy. It is accepted by the American Medical Association, the American Psychological Association, and the American Psychiatric Association. Hypnosis has been particularly helpful in the control of pain (Hilgard, 1975; Kihlstrom, 1985). It has also been used successfully to treat a wide range of disorders, including high blood pressure, bleeding, psoriasis, severe morning sickness, and the side effects of chemotherapy. Other problems that have responded well to hypnosis are asthma, severe insomnia, some phobias (Orne, 1983), and dissociative identity disorder (Kluft, 1992). Furthermore, there are studies suggesting that hypnosis can be useful in treating warts (Ewin, 1992), pain due to severe burns (Patterson & Ptacek, 1997), repetitive nightmares (Kingsbury, 1993), and sexual dysfunctions such as inhibited sexual desire and impotence (Crasilneck, 1992; Hammond, 1992). Suppose you are overweight, or you smoke or drink heavily. Would a quick trip to a hypnotist rid you of overeating or other bad habits? Hypnosis has been only moderately effective in weight control and virtually useless in overcoming drug and alcohol abuse (Orne, 1983).

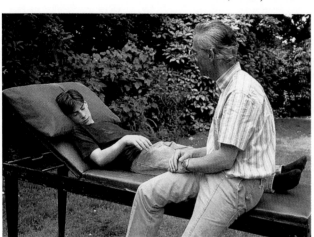

A hypnotized person is in a state of heightened suggestibility. This hypnotherapist suggested to the subject that a balloon was tied to his right hand and his arm raised accordingly.

For the most hypnotizable people, hypnosis can be used instead of a general anesthetic in surgery. In one remarkable case, a young Canadian dentist had gall bladder surgery, using only hypnosis. From the time of the first incision until the operation was over, the patient maintained a steady pulse rate and blood pressure. Unbelievably, he claimed that he felt nothing that could be described as pain, only a tugging sensation (Callahan, 1997). Did the dentist have the world's greatest hypnotist? No, most experts in hypnosis believe that "hypnotic responsiveness depends more on the efforts and abilities of the person hypnotized than on the skill of the hypnotist" (Kirsch & Lynn, 1995, p. 846).

What are the three main theories that have been proposed to explain hypnosis?

What Is Hypnosis? Is hypnosis a trancelike, altered state of consciousness? Today, most hypnosis researchers reject the notion that hypnosis is a genuinely altered state of consciousness (Kirsch & Lynn, 1995). Rather, most believe that the impressive, sometimes stunning, effects of hypnosis can be accounted for by the demands of the situation—the same social and cognitive influences that explain ordinary, nonhypnotic behavior.

According to the *sociocognitive theory of hypnosis,* the behavior of a hypnotized person is a function of that person's expectations about how subjects behave under hypnosis. People are motivated to be good subjects, to follow the suggestions of the hypnotist, and to fulfill the social role of the hypnotized person as they perceive it (Spanos, 1986, 1991, 1994). But does this mean that hypnotized people are merely acting or faking it? No. Using the single most effective and reliable indicator of deception in the laboratory, the skin conductance response, Kinnunen and others (1994) found that 89% of hypnotized people had been truly hypnotized.

More than three decades ago, Barber (1962) claimed that behavior of subjects under hypnosis is not different from behavior of other highly motivated people. But does this include *all* behavior under hypnosis? No. Although social suggestibility alone can explain the performance of less difficult actions under hypnosis, it becomes less of a factor as the difficulty of the action increases (Woody et al., 1997). It is hard to imagine how the Canadian dentist could tolerate the pain of major surgery armed with nothing more than social suggestibility and strong motivation.

Ernest Hilgard (1986, 1992) has proposed a theory to explain the accomplishment of very difficult acts under hypnosis, even undergoing surgery without anesthesia. According to his *neodissociation theory of hypnosis,* hypnosis induces a split, or dissociation, between two aspects of the control of consciousness that are ordinarily linked—the planning and the monitoring functions. Hilgard called the monitoring function, when separated from conscious awareness, "the hidden observer." In one series of experiments (Hilgard, 1979), he hypnotized a participant, had the person place one hand in ice water, and suggested that he or she would feel no discomfort. And, indeed, subjects did not report any discomfort. But, according to Hilgard, through automatic writing or talking, a subject's hidden observer was able to describe how the water felt, even though the subject was not consciously aware of having experienced the extreme cold.

Bowers and his colleagues (Bowers, 1992; Woody & Bowers, 1994) view hypnosis as an authentic altered state of consciousness. Their *theory of dissociated control* maintains that hypnosis does not induce a splitting of different aspects of consciousness, as Hilgard's model suggests. Rather, they believe that the hypnotist's suggestions weaken the control of the executive function over other parts (subsystems) of consciousness and influence the other subsystems of consciousness directly. The hypnotized person's responses are automatic and involuntary (Kirsch & Lynn, 1995). Some research supports this belief (Bowers & Woody, 1996; Hargadon et al., 1995).

Although the majority of hypnosis researchers seem to support the sociocognitive theory of hypnosis, most clinicians and some influential researchers apparently believe that hypnosis *is* a unique altered state of consciousness (Kirsch & Lynn, 1995; Nash, 1991; Woody & Bowers, 1994). Kihlstrom (1986) has suggested that a more complete picture of hypnosis would emerge from some combination of the sociocognitive approach of Spanos and the neodissociation position of Hilgard. But even though researchers have some serious theoretical differences, hypnosis is increasingly used in clinical practice and in selected areas of medicine and dentistry.

psychoactive drug: A drug that alters normal mental functioning—mood, perception, or thought; called a controlled substance if used medically.

Culture and Altered States of Consciousness

In every culture around the world, and throughout recorded history, human beings have found ways to induce altered states of consciousness. Some means of inducing altered states in other cultures may seem strange and exotic to most Westerners. Entering ritual trances and experiencing spirit possession are forms of altered states of consciousness used in many cultures in the course of religious rites and tribal ceremonies. Typically, people induce ritual trance by flooding the senses with repetitive chanting, clapping, or singing; by whirling in circles until they are moving at dizzying speed; or by burning strong, pungent incense.

The fact that so many different means of altering consciousness are practiced by members of so many varied cultures has led some experts to ask whether "there may be a universal human need to produce and maintain varieties of conscious experiences" (Ward, 1994, p. 60). Whatever the method used to induce it, the experience of an altered state of consciousness can vary greatly from one culture to another.

In Haiti the practice of voodoo includes ritual trances to induce spirit possession. Here a practitioner crushes leaves on a possessed woman during a Christmas Eve ceremony.

ALTERED STATES OF CONSCIOUSNESS AND PSYCHOACTIVE DRUGS

The altered states of consciousness we have examined thus far are natural ones. We will now explore psychoactive drugs, a wide range of substances that are used to modify natural consciousness. A **psychoactive drug** is any substance that alters mood, per-

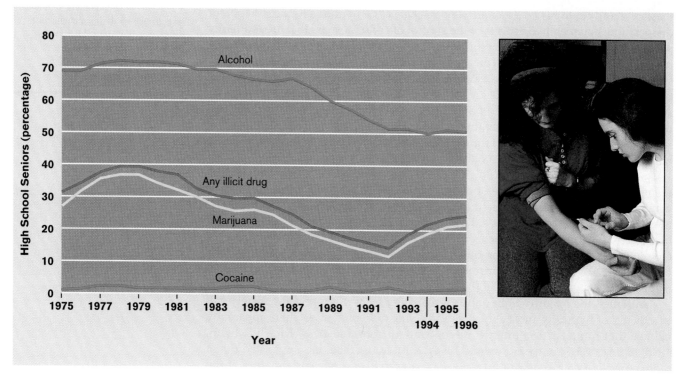

Figure 4.2

Results of a Survey on the Use of Alcohol, Marijuana, Cocaine, and Any Illicit Drug among High School Seniors

Shown for 1975 through 1996 are the percentages of high school seniors who reported using alcohol, marijuana, cocaine, or any illicit drug during the 30 days preceding the survey. After a decline in the use of marijuana and most illicit drugs from 1985 to 1992, drug use has been increasing. (Data from Johnston et al., 1997.)

ception, or thought. Some of these drugs are legal, but most are **illicit** (illegal). When psychoactive drugs are approved for medical use, they are called *controlled substances*.

Of all the industrial nations in the world, the United States has the highest rate of illicit drug use. Some 70% of Americans have tried illicit drugs, and close to 20% have used them during the past year (Gazzaniga, 1997). About 5.5 million Americans are addicted to illicit drugs (Holloway, 1991). But in terms of sheer numbers of those addicted, the most serious damage to users is caused by the legal drugs tobacco and alcohol (Goldstein & Kalant, 1990).

Why do so many Americans use psychoactive drugs? There are many reasons for taking drugs, and users often do not recognize their real motivation. Some people take drugs to cope with anxiety, depression, or boredom (Baker, 1988). Others use drugs just to feel good, for a thrill, or because of social pressures. Still others use psychoactive drugs for their medical benefits.

Every year since 1975, the University of Michigan's Institute for Social Research has conducted surveys on drug use, and on attitudes and beliefs about drug use, among high school students and young adults. These surveys show that drug use among high school seniors had been falling continuously from 1980 to 1992. But as of 1993 the 12-year decline reversed itself and drug use was on the rise again, as shown in Figure 4.2. Since 1992, the percentage of 12th graders using any illicit drug in the previous 12 months rose from 27% to 40%. And in that time period, marijuana use alone has tripled among 8th graders, doubled among 10th graders, and increased by nearly two-thirds among 12th graders. Researchers Johnston and others (1997) believe one reason for the increases may be that since 1992 there has been a decline in the perception of the harmfulness of certain drugs and less disapproval associated with their use.

illicit drug: An illegal drug.

Several protective factors tend to lower the risk of drug use by young people. These include parental support, behavioral coping skills, academic and social competence (Newcomb, 1997; Wills & Cleary, 1996; Wills et al., 1996), and traditional religious beliefs (Kendler et al., 1997).

The earlier adolescents start using drugs, the more likely they are to progress into "the most severe forms of drug use" (Kandel & Davies, 1996). Those who began early and escalated rapidly were found to have "greater life stress, lower parental support, more parental substance use, more deviant attitudes and maladaptive coping, lower self-control, and greater affiliation with peers who use substances (particularly marijuana)" (Wills et al., 1996, p. 177). Adolescents who use drugs seek out peers who also use and, in turn, are influenced by those peers (Curran et al., 1997). In a 16-year longitudinal study that followed 552 7th, 8th, and 9th graders into adulthood, Newcomb (1997) found that drug use and abuse in adolescents was associated with a number of problem behaviors, including "cigarette use, alcohol abuse, . . . precocious sexual involvement, academic problems, frequency of various sexual activities, deviant attitudes, and delinquent behavior" (Newcomb, 1997, p. 65).

Variables Influencing Individual Responses to Drugs

The effects of drugs are not always predictable. There are individual differences in the way people respond to drugs. Some differences result from the physical characteristics of the user, such as weight, gender, metabolism, and, of course, individual genetic makeup. Psychological factors also strongly influence a person's response to a drug. These factors include expectations about the effect of a drug, mood, mental or psychological health, and past experiences with the drug. Finally, the environment in which a drug is taken (the people present and the setting) and whether it is taken in combination with any other drug can profoundly influence its effect on the user.

Drug Addiction: Slavery to a Substance

The trip from first use to abuse of a drug may be a long one or a very short one. *Substance abuse* may be defined as continuing drug use that interferes with a person's major life roles at home, in school, at work, or elsewhere and contributes to legal difficulties or any psychological problems (American Psychiatric Association, 1994). Some drugs create a physical or chemical dependence; others create a psychological dependence. **Physical drug dependence** comes about as a result of the body's natural ability to protect itself against harmful substances by developing a **drug tolerance**. This means that the user becomes progressively less affected by the drug and must take larger and larger doses to get the same effect or high (Ramsay & Woods, 1997). Tolerance occurs because the brain adapts to the presence of the drug by responding less intensely to it. In addition, the liver produces more enzymes to break down the drug. The various bodily processes adjust in order to continue to function with the drug in the system.

Once drug tolerance is established, a person cannot function normally without the drug. If the drug is taken away, the user begins to suffer withdrawal symptoms. The **withdrawal symptoms**, both physical and psychological, are usually the exact opposite of the effects produced by the drug. For example, withdrawal from stimulants leaves a person exhausted and depressed; withdrawal from tranquilizers leaves a person nervous and agitated.

If physical dependence alone explained drug addiction, now termed *substance dependence*, there would be no problem with drugs long thought to be physically nonaddictive. Also, once the period of physical withdrawal was over, the desire for the drug would end along with the withdrawal symptoms. But there is more to drug addiction than physical dependence. **Psychological drug dependence** is a craving or irresistible urge for the drug's pleasurable effects, and it is more difficult to combat than physical dependence (O'Brien, 1996).

Link It!

What is the difference between physical and psychological drug dependence?

physical drug dependence: A compulsive pattern of drug use in which the user develops a drug tolerance coupled with unpleasant withdrawal symptoms when the drug use is discontinued.

drug tolerance: A condition in which the user becomes progressively less affected by the drug so that larger and larger doses are necessary to maintain the same effect.

withdrawal symptoms: The physical and psychological symptoms (usually the opposite of those produced by the drug) that occur when a regularly used drug is discontinued and that terminate when the drug is taken again.

psychological drug dependence: A craving or irresistible urge for a drug's pleasurable effects.

Four factors influence the addictive potential of a drug: (1) how fast the effects of the drug are felt, (2) how pleasurable the drug's effects are in producing euphoria or in extinguishing pain, (3) how long the pleasurable effects last, and (4) how much discomfort is experienced when the drug is discontinued (Medzerian, 1991). The pleasurable effects of the most addictive drugs are felt almost immediately, and they are short-lived. For example, the intense, pleasurable effects of crack are felt in seconds, and last only about 5 minutes. The discomfort after the pleasurable effects wear off is intense, so a user is highly motivated to take more of the drug. The addictive potential of an addictive drug is higher if it is injected rather than taken orally, and higher still if it is smoked rather than injected.

Psychoactive drugs alter consciousness in a variety of ways. Let's consider the various alterations produced by the major categories of drugs: stimulants, depressants, and hallucinogens (or psychedelics).

Stimulants: Speeding Up the Nervous System

How do stimulants affect the user?

Stimulants, often called "uppers," speed up the central nervous system, suppress appetite, and can make a person feel more awake, alert, and energetic. Stimulants increase pulse rate, blood pressure, and respiration rate, and they reduce cerebral blood flow (Mathew & Wilson, 1991). In higher doses, stimulants make people feel nervous, jittery, and restless, and they can cause shaking or trembling and interfere with sleep.

No stimulant actually delivers energy to the body. Instead, a stimulant forces the body to use some of its own stored-up energy sooner and in greater amounts than it would naturally. When the stimulant's effect wears off, the body's natural energy is depleted, leaving the person feeling exhausted and depressed.

There are legal stimulants, such as caffeine and nicotine; controlled stimulants, such as amphetamines; and illegal stimulants, such as cocaine.

Caffeine and Nicotine   Caffeine is the world's most widely used drug, and more than 85% of Americans ingest it daily in one form or another (Levinthal, 1996). Coffee, tea, cola drinks, chocolate, and more than 100 prescription and over-the-counter drugs contain caffeine. They provide a mild jolt to the nervous system that perks up the user, at least temporarily. Caffeine makes people more mentally alert and can help them stay awake. Many people use caffeine to lift their mood; but laboratory studies reveal that 1 hour after consuming medium or high doses of caffeine, participants show significantly higher levels of anxiety, depression, and hostility (Veleber & Templer, 1984).

Link It!

Few people who have ever tried to quit smoking doubt the addictive power of nicotine. A growing body of scientific evidence indicates that nicotine's addictive power is not unlike that of major abused drugs, such as amphetamines, morphine, and cocaine (Iversen, 1996).

It is estimated that 45 million Americans smoke cigarettes, cigars, or pipes, and several million more use snuff or chewing tobacco ("Nicotine dependence—Part I," 1997). Teen smoking has been steadily increasing, and in 1996 34% of high school seniors smoked, compared to 25% of adults (Johnston et al., 1997). White adolescents smoke more than their African American and Hispanic counterparts. Among 12th graders, 38.1% of Whites smoke, compared to 14.2% of African Americans and 25.4% of Hispanics. Tobacco kills 434,000 Americans every year (Raloff, 1994), and "cigarette smoking results in the premature death of approximately 50% of smokers" (Henningfield et al., 1996, p. 1857). Smoking also increases the risk of spontaneous abortion (Ness et al., 1999).

For other serious health problems associated with smoking, see Chapter 11.

What effects do amphetamines have on the user?

Amphetamines   Amphetamines are a class of stimulants that increase arousal, relieve fatigue, improve alertness, suppress the appetite, and give a rush of energy. In low to moderate doses, they may temporarily boost athletic and intellectual performance. A person who takes amphetamines becomes more alert and energetic, mildly euphoric, and usually more talkative, animated, and restless.

In high doses (100 milligrams or more) amphetamines can cause confused and disorganized behavior, extreme fear and suspiciousness, delusions and hallucinations, aggressiveness and antisocial behavior, even manic behavior and paranoia. The powerful amphetamine methamphetamine (known as "crank" or "speed") comes in smokable form—"ice," which is highly addictive and can be fatal.

Withdrawal from amphetamines leaves a person physically exhausted, sleeping for 10 to 15 hours or more, only to awaken in a stupor, extremely depressed and intensely hungry. Stimulants constrict the tiny capillaries and the small arteries. Over time, high doses can stop blood flow, causing hemorrhaging and leaving parts of the brain deprived of oxygen. In fact, victims of fatal overdoses of stimulants usually have multiple hemorrhages in the brain.

Yet some amphetamines have therapeutic value in the treatment of narcolepsy and attention-deficit/hyperactivity disorder (ADHD). Recent research suggests that amphetamines can work to stimulate brain activity in whatever brain regions are most essential in performing a specific mental task, while decreasing activity in other brain areas not required for the task (Mattay et al., 1996). This may explain why the stimulants Ritalin and Cylert are useful in treating ADHD.

Cocaine   Cocaine, a stimulant derived from coca leaves, can be sniffed as a white powder, injected intravenously, or smoked in the form of crack. The rush of well-being is dramatically intense and powerful, but it is just as dramatically short-lived. The effects of snorting cocaine are felt within 2 to 3 minutes, and the high lasts 30 to 45 minutes. With crack, however, the effects are felt in 8 to 10 seconds but last no more than 5 to 10 minutes (Julien, 1995). The euphoria from cocaine is followed by an equally intense **crash**, marked by depression, anxiety, agitation, and a powerful craving for more of the drug.

Cocaine stimulates the reward or "pleasure" pathways in the brain, which use the neurotransmitter dopamine (Landry, 1997). With continued use, the reward systems fail to function normally, and the user becomes incapable of feeling any pleasure except from the drug. The main withdrawal symptoms are psychological—the inability to feel pleasure and the craving for more cocaine.

Cocaine constricts the blood vessels, raises blood pressure, speeds up the heart, quickens respiration, and can even cause epileptic seizures in people who have no history of epilepsy (Pascual-Leone et al., 1990). Over time, or even quickly in high doses, cocaine can cause heart palpitations, an irregular heartbeat, and heart attacks, and high doses can cause strokes even in healthy young individuals.

Crack, or "rock," the most dangerous form of cocaine, can produce a powerful dependency in several weeks. Dr. Jeffrey Rosecan, a drug abuse consultant to the National Football League, called cocaine "the most addicting substance known to man"; and crack, he said, is "the most addicting form of the most addicting drug" (Lundgren, 1986, p. 7).

Depressants: Slowing Down the Nervous System

Another class of drugs, the **depressants** (sometimes called "downers") decrease activity in the central nervous system, slow down body functions, and reduce sensitivity to outside stimulation. Within this category are the sedative-hypnotics (alcohol, barbiturates, and minor tranquilizers) and the narcotics, or opiates. When different depressants are taken together, their sedative effects are additive, and thus potentially dangerous.

Alcohol   Even though **alcohol** is a depressant, the first few drinks seem to relax and enliven a person at the same time. But the more alcohol a person consumes, the more the central nervous system is depressed. As drinking increases, the symptoms of drunkenness mount—slurred speech, poor coordination, staggering. Men tend to

cocaine: A type of stimulant that produces a feeling of euphoria.

crash: The feelings of depression, exhaustion, irritability, and anxiety that occur following an amphetamine, cocaine, or crack high.

crack: A form of cocaine that is smoked; the most potent and addictive form of cocaine.

depressants: A category of drugs that decrease activity in the central nervous system, slow down bodily functions, and reduce sensitivity to outside stimulation; also called "downers."

alcohol: A central nervous system depressant.

How does cocaine affect the user?

What are some of the effects of depressants, and what drugs comprise this category?

The use of alcohol in religious rites and social celebrations is more common among some cultural, religious, and ethnic groups within the United States than others.

become more aggressive (Pihl et al., 1997) and more sexually aroused (Roehrich & Kinder, 1991) but less able to perform sexually (Crowe & George, 1989). Binge drinking is becoming widespread on college and university campuses, and fraternity parties are notorious for making a game of rapid, excessive drinking (Cohen, 1997). But excessive alcohol can cause a person to lose consciousness, and extremely large amounts can kill. Sadly, several student deaths have resulted from binge drinking parties. We will discuss the health consequences of alcohol abuse in detail in Chapter 11.

There is great cultural variation in drinking habits and styles, and in attitudes toward alcohol. Moderate drinking is prevalent in some American ethnic groups, most notably Jewish, Greek, Chinese, and Italian (Colón & Wuollet, 1994; Peele, 1984). In these cultures alcohol is used primarily in the family or larger social settings where young people are gradually included. Alcohol is rarely used excessively and is controlled by cultural norms and social customs. Alcohol use is rare or nonexistent among some religious groups in the United States, especially the Amish, Mennonites, and Mormons. The use of alcohol is forbidden for members of these three religions, as is the use of other psychoactive drugs (Trimble, 1994).

Culture, more than genes, seems to drive the patterns of use and abuse of alcohol. Certain genetic similarities have been found among Native Americans and Chinese Americans. Yet Native Americans have a high rate of alcoholism, while Chinese Americans have an unusually low rate.

Who drinks most of the alcohol consumed in the United States? A mere 2.5% of the heaviest drinkers drink slightly more than 25% of all the alcohol consumed. Most heavy drinkers are men, who drink 76% of all the alcohol consumed. And young adults (aged 18 to 29) account for 45% of it (Greenfield & Rogers, 1999).

Barbiturates and the Minor Tranquilizers   **Barbiturates** depress the central nervous system, and, depending on the dose, a barbiturate can act as a sedative or a sleeping pill. People who abuse barbiturates become drowsy and confused, their thinking and judgment suffer, and their coordination and reflexes are affected (Henningfield & Ator, 1986). Barbiturates can kill if taken in overdose, and a lethal dose can be as little as only three times the prescribed dose. Alcohol and barbiturates, when taken together, are a potentially fatal combination.

The popular **minor tranquilizers**, the benzodiazepines, came on the scene in the early 1960s and are sold under the brand names Valium, Librium, Dalmane, and, more recently, Xanax (also used as an antidepressant). About 90 million prescriptions for minor tranquilizers are filled each year. Benzodiazepines are prescribed for several medical and psychological disorders. A more detailed discussion of tranquilizers can be found in Chapter 13.

Narcotics   **Narcotics** are derived from the opium poppy and produce both a pain-relieving and a calming effect. Opium affects mainly the brain and the bowel. It paralyzes the intestinal muscles, which is why it is used medically to treat diarrhea. If you have ever taken paregoric, you have had a little tincture of opium. Because opium suppresses the cough center, it is used in some cough medicines. Both morphine and codeine, two drugs prescribed for pain, are natural constituents of opium.

A highly addictive narcotic derived from morphine is **heroin**. Heroin addicts describe a sudden "rush" of euphoria, followed by drowsiness, inactivity, and impaired concentration. Withdrawal symptoms begin about 6 to 24 hours after use, and the addict becomes physically sick. Nausea, diarrhea, depression, stomach cramps, insomnia, and pain grow worse and worse until they become intolerable—unless the person gets another fix. Heroin has become popular in Hollywood, on college campuses, and at all levels of society, and its use has doubled since the mid-1980s (Leland, 1996).

What are the general effects of narcotics, and what are several drugs in this category?

barbiturates: A class of addictive depressants used as sedatives, sleeping pills, and anesthetics; overdoses can cause coma or death.

minor tranquilizer: A central nervous system depressant that calms the user.

narcotics: A class of depressant drugs derived from the opium poppy and producing pain-relieving and calming effects.

Inhalants   Not all substances that are abused are purchased illegally. Many can be found in any household—under the kitchen sink or in kitchen cabinets, in the bathroom, or in the garage (Levinthal, 1996). And some everyday household products, if sniffed or inhaled, are capable of delivering intoxicating and euphoric highs, as dramatic and perhaps as deadly as the effects of the most dangerous street drugs.

Solvents, aerosol sprays, and commercial glues are leading products likely to be abused as inhalants because they produce a quick intoxication and a feeling of euphoria. And not only does psychological dependence often develop, but the toxic effect on body organs—heart, lungs, kidneys, and/or liver—may present major problems. The behavioral effects of inhalants can be as deadly as the physical effects. Some young abusers of inhalants, feeling indestructible, leap off rooftops attempting to fly, dash into oncoming traffic, lie down on railroad tracks, and engage in other dangerous behaviors (Levinthal, 1996). Most users of inhalants are in junior high school and have friends who also use inhalants (Yarnold, 1996).

Hallucinogens: Seeing, Hearing, and Feeling What Is Not There

The **hallucinogens**, or psychedelics, are drugs that can alter and distort perceptions of time and space, alter mood, and produce feelings of unreality. As the name implies, hallucinogens also cause hallucinations, sensations that have no basis in external reality (Andreasen & Black, 1991; Miller & Gold, 1994). Hallucinogens have been used in religious and recreational rituals and ceremonies in diverse cultures since ancient times (Millman & Beeder, 1994).

Mescaline, the psychedelic derivative from the mescal cactus, has long been used by some groups of Native Americans to produce hallucinations in their religious ceremonies. Other people have also used peyote, another mescal derivative, but typically only to get high. Is the altered state of consciousness induced by either mescaline or peyote the same for Native Americans and for nonreligious recreational users? No, the descriptions of the hallucinatory experiences of these two cultural groups tend to be so different that they do not even seem to be taking the same substance (Ward, 1994). So in these two groups, at least, the culture and the motives, more than the substance itself, seem to define the quality of the altered state.

Rather than producing a relatively predictable effect like most other drugs, hallucinogens usually magnify the mood of the user at the time the drug is taken. The hallucinogens we will discuss are marijuana, LSD, and MDMA.

Marijuana   About 20 million people in the United States use marijuana regularly, making it the most widely used illicit drug (Andreasen & Black, 1991). In general, **marijuana** tends to produce a feeling of well-being, promote relaxation, lower inhibitions, and relieve anxiety. The user may experience an increased sensitivity to sights, sounds, and touch, as well as perceptual distortions and a perceived slowing of time.

THC (tetrahydrocannabinol), the ingredient in marijuana that produces the high, remains in the body "for days or even weeks" (Julien, 1995). Marijuana impairs attention and coordination and slows reaction time, and these effects make operating complex machinery such as an automobile dangerous, even after the feeling of intoxication has passed. Marijuana can interfere with concentration, logical thinking, and the ability to form new memories. It can produce fragmentation in thought and confusion in remembering recent occurrences (Herkenham, 1992). A 17-year longitudinal study of Costa Rican men supports the claim that long-term use has a negative impact on short-term memory and the ability to focus sustained attention (Fletcher et al., 1996). Many of the receptors for marijuana are in the hippocampus, which explains why it affects memory (Matsuda et al., 1990). Chronic use of marijuana has been associated with loss of motivation, general apathy, and decline in school performance—referred to as *amotivational syndrome* (Andreasen & Black, 1991).

heroin: A highly addictive, partly synthetic narcotic derived from morphine.

hallucinogens (hal-LU-sin-o-jenz): A category of drugs, sometimes called psychedelics, that alter perception and mood and can cause hallucinations.

marijuana: A hallucinogen with effects ranging from relaxation and giddiness to perceptual distortions and hallucinations.

THC (tetrahydrocannabinol): The principal psychoactive ingredient in marijuana and hashish.

What are the main effects of hallucinogens, and what are three psychoactive drugs classified as hallucinogens?

What are some harmful effects of heavy marijuana use?

Link It!

Marijuana, the most widely used illicit drug in the United States, has been associated with loss of motivation, general apathy, and decline in school performance.

Marijuana abuse affects the reproductive system in males, causing (1) a 20% impotence rate, (2) a 44% reduction in testosterone level (Kolodny et al., 1979), (3) a 30 to 70% reduction in sperm count, and (4) an abnormal appearance of sperm cells (Hembree et al., 1979). In women, failure to ovulate, other menstrual irregularities, and lower-birthweight babies have been associated with heavy marijuana use (Hingson et al., 1982; Kolodny et al., 1979).

An advisory panel of the National Institute of Drug Abuse, after reviewing the scientific evidence, concluded that marijuana shows promise as a treatment for certain medical conditions. It has been found effective for treating the eye disease glaucoma, for controlling nausea and vomiting in cancer patients receiving chemotherapy, and for improving appetite and curtailing weight loss in some AIDS patients (Fackelmann, 1997). But there is a continuing controversy over whether marijuana should be legalized for medical purposes.

LSD and MDMA   **LSD** is lysergic acid diethylamide, sometimes referred to simply as "acid." The average LSD "trip" lasts for 10 to 12 hours and usually produces extreme perceptual changes—visual hallucinations and distortions. Emotions can become very intense and unstable, ranging from euphoria to anxiety, panic, depression, or even suicidal thoughts and actions (Miller & Gold, 1994). LSD can cause bad trips that can be terrifying and leave the user in a state of panic. On occasion, bad LSD trips have ended tragically in accidents, death, or suicide. Sometimes a person who has taken LSD in the past experiences a **flashback**, a brief recurrence of a previous trip that occurs suddenly and without warning. Flashbacks reportedly can occur for months after LSD use. The use of marijuana and some other drugs may trigger these LSD flashbacks (Gold, 1994).

MDMA (Ecstasy) is a *designer drug*—a laboratory creation—that is a cross between a hallucinogen and an amphetamine. It is a popular drug of abuse with teenagers, especially at marathon dances called "raves" (Schwartz & Miller, 1997). The drug's main appeal is its psychological effect—a feeling of relatedness and connectedness with others (Taylor, 1996). But animal experiments with MDMA have revealed some disturbing findings—irreversible destruction of serotonin-releasing neurons (Green & Goodwin, 1996). MDMA is also more toxic than most other hallucinogens, and it should be considered a dangerous drug.

Review & Reflect 4.1 provides a summary of the effects and withdrawal symptoms of the major psychoactive drugs.

How Drugs Affect the Brain

Eating, drinking, and sexual activity—in fact, all natural reinforcers—have one thing in common with all addictive drugs. They increase the availability of the neurotransmitter dopamine in a part of the brain's limbic system known as the *nucleus accumbens*. The stimulation of the nucleus accumbens by dopamine plays an important role in reinforcement and reward (Di Chiara, 1997).

There is ample evidence that a surge of dopamine is involved in the rewarding and motivational effects produced by a long list of psychoactive drugs, including alcohol, amphetamines, cocaine (Carlson, 1998), marijuana, heroin (Tanda et al., 1997), and nicotine (Pich et al., 1997; Pontieri et al., 1996). Amphetamines affect dopamine transmission directly by stimulating its release and, to some extent, by blocking its reuptake. Cocaine is highly efficient at blocking the reuptake of dopamine at the synapses, thus increasing and prolonging its reinforcing effects (Landry, 1997; Volkow et al., 1997; 1998).

Beyond affecting the dopamine system, opiates such as morphine and heroin mimic the effects of the brain's own *endorphins*, chemicals that have pain-relieving properties and produce a feeling of well-being. Opiate molecules and endorphin mol-

LSD (lysergic acid diethylamide): A powerful hallucinogen with unpredictable effects ranging from perceptual changes and vivid hallucinations to states of panic and terror.

flashback: The brief recurrence, occurring suddenly and without warning at a later time, of effects a person has experienced while taking LSD.

MDMA (Ecstasy): A designer drug that is a hallucinogen-amphetamine and can produce permanent damage of the serotonin-releasing neurons.

What effect on the brain do all addictive drugs have in common?

Review & Reflect 4.1 The Effects and Withdrawal Symptoms of Some Psychoactive Drugs

Psychoactive Drug	Effects	Withdrawal Symptoms
Stimulants		
Caffeine	Produces wakefulness and alertness; increases metabolism but slows reaction time	Headache, depression, fatigue
Tobacco (nicotine)	Effects range from alertness to calmness; lowers appetite for carbohydrates; increases pulse rate and other metabolic processes	Irritability, anxiety, restlessness, increased appetite
Amphetamines	Increase metabolism and alertness; elevate mood, cause wakefulness, suppress appetite	Fatigue, increased appetite, depression, long periods of sleep, irritability, anxiety
Cocaine	Brings on euphoric mood, energy boost, feeling of excitement; suppresses appetite	Depression, fatigue, increased appetite, long periods of sleep, irritability
Depressants		
Alcohol	First few drinks stimulate and enliven while lowering anxiety and inhibitions; higher doses have a sedative effect, slowing reaction time, impairing motor control and perceptual ability	Tremors, nausea, sweating, depression, weakness, irritability, and in some cases hallucinations
Barbiturates (e.g., phenobarbital)	Promote sleep, have calming and sedative effect, decrease muscular tension, impair coordination and reflexes	Sleeplessness, anxiety; sudden withdrawal can cause seizures, cardiovascular collapse, and death
Tranquilizers (e.g., Valium, Xanax)	Lower anxiety, have calming and sedative effect, decrease muscular tension	Restlessness, anxiety, irritability, muscle tension, difficulty sleeping
Hallucinogens		
Marijuana	Generally produces euphoria, relaxation; affects ability to store new memories	Anxiety, difficulty sleeping, decreased appetite, hyperactivity
LSD	Produces excited exhilaration, hallucinations, experiences perceived as insightful and profound	

ecules have similar shapes, and opiates bind with the same receptors in the brain as endorphins do, producing virtually the same physiological and psychological effects.

Research has shown that alcohol, barbiturates, and benzodiazepines (such as Valium and Librium) act on GABA receptors (Harris et al., 1992). GABA, an inhibitory neurotransmitter, slows down the central nervous system. Thus, stimulating the release of GABA with alcohol or tranquilizers has a calming, sedating effect. If enough GABA is released, it can shut down the brain. This is why alcohol and tranquilizers together are such a potentially deadly duo.

Unfortunately, most addicts experience a virtually irresistible compulsion to use drugs and are apparently unable to consider the likely consequences of their acts—the loss of the love and respect of family and friends, of money, of jobs, of health, and even their lives (Leshner, 1999).

Battling Insomnia

If you've ever experienced insomnia, you know the negative effects it can have on your state of mind and ability to function during the day. Sleep researchers believe that most cases are psychological in origin. The major causes include the following (Bootzin & Perlis, 1992; Costa E Silva et al., 1996; Mendelson, 1995; Morin & Ware, 1996):

- Psychological disorders such as depression, anxiety disorders, or alcohol or other drug abuse

- Medical problems such as chronic pain, breathing problems, or gastrointestinal disorders

- Circadian rhythm disturbances due to shift work, jet lag, or a chronic mismatch between clock time and a person's body time

- Use of various drugs, such as prescription drugs, caffeine, nicotine, alcohol, tranquilizers, sleeping pills, and so on

- Poor sleep environment with conditions that may be too noisy, hot, cold, or bright

- Poor sleep habits, such as spending too much nonsleep time in bed, taking too many naps, or having irregular sleep times; or association of bedtime with the frustration of not being able to get to sleep

Do sleeping pills help? When insomnia becomes a problem, many people resort to sleeping pills to help them fall asleep. But do sleeping pills really work? In general, many leading authorities on sleep disorders believe that low doses of benzodiazepine *hypnotics*—drugs approved by the FDA for the treatment of insomnia—are effective and safe to use in treating transient (temporary) insomnia (Costa E Silva et al., 1996; Dement, 1992). Short-term use of hypnotics for "a bout of stress-related insomnia or jet lag" is beneficial, according to Dement, and does not cause addiction or dependence. In fact, it may prevent an even more serious problem—chronic insomnia—from

developing. But hypnotics are recommended only for short-term use—for about 2 weeks and for 4 weeks at most. Prolonged use causes hypnotics to lose their effectiveness, and physical dependence and rebound insomnia may result after such use is discontinued (Hohagen, 1996; Morin & Wooten, 1996; Roth, 1996a).

People with insomnia may resort to a variety of sleep "aids," including tranquilizers, melatonin, other over-the-counter sleep products, and the most widely used one—alcohol. A few drinks at bedtime may get you to sleep faster, but there is a price to be paid: lighter sleep, more awakenings, less sleep overall, and increased daytime sleepiness (Hartmann, 1988; Johnson et al., 1998).

Melatonin has been found to promote sleep in healthy young males, in shift workers, in those with jet lag, and in elderly insomniacs, who typically secrete inadequate amounts of melatonin at night because the pineal gland becomes calcified with age (Dawson et al., 1995; Haimov et al., 1995; Hughes & Badia, 1997; Zhdanova et al., 1996). But there are serious questions about the safety of melatonin.

Other over-the-counter sleep aids (such as Sominex, Unisom, and Nytol) contain antihistamines. Rather than actually inducing sleep, these products simply cause grogginess. For serious cases of insomnia, they are virtually useless. Users develop a tolerance to these sleep aids rapidly and may experience significant sleepiness and cognitive and psychomotor impairments the morning after using them (Morin & Wooten, 1996). Taken in higher-than-recommended doses, these products can be dangerous (Meltzer, 1990).

Hints for getting a better night's sleep. So what can you do to fight insomnia and improve the quality of your sleep? Several meta-analyses have revealed that behavioral interventions, such as relaxation techniques to reduce physical and mental arousal and procedures to modify maladaptive sleep habits, can significantly improve sleep patterns and enhance your sleep

quality. And these changes were found to be fairly durable over time (Morin et al., 1994; Murtagh & Greenwood, 1995). Here are some strategies that may help you sleep better:

- Use your bed *only* for sleep. Don't read, study, write letters, watch television, eat, or talk on the phone from your bed.

- Go to bed only if you are sleepy. Leave the bedroom whenever you cannot fall asleep within 10 to 15 minutes. Don't return to bed to try again until you feel more tired. Repeat the process until you fall asleep within that time frame.

- Establish a consistent, relaxing ritual that you follow each night just before bedtime. For example, take a warm bath, eat a small snack, brush your teeth, and so on.

- Set your alarm and wake up at the same time every day including weekends, regardless of how much you have slept. Do not take naps during the day.

- Exercise regularly—but not within several hours of bedtime. (Exercise raises body temperature and makes it more difficult to fall asleep.)

- Establish regular mealtimes. Don't eat heavy or spicy meals close to bedtime. If you must eat then, try milk and a few crackers.

- Beware of caffeine and nicotine—they are sleep disturbers. Avoid caffeine within 6 hours and smoking within 1 or 2 hours of bedtime.

- Avoid wrestling with your problems when you go to bed. Try counting backward from 1,000 by twos. Or try a progressive relaxation exercise (see the *Try It!* on p. 113).

SUMMARY AND REVIEW

WHAT IS CONSCIOUSNESS?

What are some different states of consciousness?

Different states of consciousness include ordinary waking consciousness, daydreaming, sleep, and altered states brought about through meditation, hypnosis, or the use of psychoactive drugs.

Key Terms
consciousness (p. 101); altered state of consciousness (p. 102)

CIRCADIAN RHYTHMS: 24-HOUR HIGHS AND LOWS

What is a circadian rhythm, and which rhythms are most relevant to the study of sleep?

A circadian rhythm is the regular fluctuation in certain body functions from a high point to a low point within a 24-hour period. Two rhythms most relevant to sleep are the sleep/wakefulness cycle and body temperature.

What is the suprachiasmatic nucleus?

The suprachiasmatic nucleus is the body's biological clock, which regulates circadian rhythms and signals the pineal gland to secrete or suppress secretion of melatonin.

What are some problems experienced by people who work rotating shifts?

People working rotating shifts experience a disruption in their circadian rhythms that can cause sleep difficulties; lowered alertness, efficiency, productivity, and safety during subjective night; and a variety of psychological and physical problems.

Key Terms
circadian rhythm (p. 102); suprachiasmatic nucleus (SCN) (p. 102); melatonin (p. 102); subjective night (p. 103)

SLEEP: THAT MYSTERIOUS ONE-THIRD OF LIFE

How does a sleeper react physically during NREM sleep?

During NREM sleep, heart rate and respiration are slow and regular, blood pressure and brain activity are at a 24-hour low point, and there is little body movement and no rapid eye movements.

How does the body respond physically during REM sleep?

During REM sleep, the large muscles of the body are paralyzed, respiration and heart rate are fast and irregular, brain activity increases, and rapid eye movements and vivid dreams occur.

What is the progression of NREM stages and REM sleep that a person follows in a typical night?

During a typical night, a person sleeps in sleep cycles, each lasting about 90 minutes. The first sleep cycle contains Stages 1, 2, 3, and 4, and REM sleep; the second contains Stages 2, 3, and 4, and REM sleep. In the remaining sleep cycles, the sleeper alternates mainly between Stage 2 and REM sleep, with each sleep cycle having progressively longer REM periods.

How do sleep patterns change over the life span?

Infants and young children have the longest sleep time and the largest percentage of REM and slow-wave sleep. Children from age 6 to puberty sleep best. The elderly typically have shorter total sleep time, more awakenings, and substantially less slow-wave sleep.

What factors influence sleep needs?

Factors that influence sleep needs are heredity, the amount of stress in a person's life, and the person's emotional state.

What are the two main theories that attempt to explain the function of sleep?

The two main theories about the function of sleep are the restorative theory and the circadian theory.

How do REM and NREM dreams differ?

REM dreams have a dreamlike, story-like quality and are more vivid, visual, and emotional than the more thought-like NREM dreams.

In general, what have researchers found regarding the content of dreams?

Dreams usually reflect the dreamer's preoccupations in waking life. They tend to have commonplace settings, to be more unpleasant than pleasant, and to be less emotional and bizarre than is generally believed.

What function does REM sleep appear to serve, and what happens when people are deprived of REM sleep?

REM sleep appears to aid in learning and memory. Following REM deprivation, individuals experience a REM rebound—an increase in the percentage of REM sleep.

Key Terms
NREM sleep (p. 104); REM sleep (p. 105); sleep cycle (p. 106); delta wave (p. 106); slow-wave sleep (p. 106); Stage 4 sleep (p. 106); restorative theory (p. 107); circadian theory (p. 107); microsleep (p. 108); REM dream (p. 108); NREM dream (p. 108); lucid dream (p. 109); REM rebound (p. 110)

SLEEP DISORDERS

What are the characteristics common to sleepwalking and sleep terrors?

Sleepwalking and sleep terrors occur during a partial arousal from Stage 4 sleep, and the person does not come to full consciousness. Episodes are rarely recalled. These disorders are typically found in children, who outgrow them by adolescence, and they tend to run in families.

What is a sleep terror?

A sleep terror is a parasomnia in which the sleeper awakens from Stage 4 sleep with a scream, dazed and groggy, in a panic state, and with a racing heart.

How do nightmares differ from sleep terrors?

Nightmares are frightening dreams that occur during REM sleep and are remembered in vivid detail. Sleep terrors occur during Stage 4 sleep and are rarely remembered, but often involve a single, frightening image.

What are the major symptoms of narcolepsy?

The symptoms of narcolepsy include excessive daytime sleepiness and sudden attacks of REM sleep.

What is sleep apnea?

Sleep apnea is a serious sleep disorder in which a sleeper's breathing stops and the person must awaken briefly to breathe. Its major symptoms are excessive daytime sleepiness and loud snoring.

What is insomnia?

Insomnia is a sleep disorder that involves difficulty in falling or staying asleep, waking too early, or sleep that is light, restless, or of poor quality.

Key Terms
sleepwalking (somnambulism) (p. 110); sleep terror (p. 110); nightmare (p. 111); narcolepsy (p. 111); sleep apnea (p. 111); insomnia (p. 112)

ALTERING CONSCIOUSNESS THROUGH CONCENTRATION AND SUGGESTION

For what purposes is meditation used?

Meditation is used by some to promote relaxation and reduce arousal, and by others to expand consciousness or attain a higher spiritual level.

What is hypnosis, and when is it most useful?

Hypnosis is a procedure in which a hypnotist uses the power of suggestion to induce changes in thoughts, feelings, sensations, perceptions, or behavior of a subject. It has been used most successfully for the control of pain.

What are the three main theories that have been proposed to explain hypnosis?

The three main theories proposed to explain hypnosis are the sociocognitive theory, the neodissociation theory, and the theory of dissociated control.

Key Terms
meditation (concentrative) (p. 112); hypnosis (p. 113);

ALTERED STATES OF CONSCIOUSNESS AND PSYCHOACTIVE DRUGS

What is the difference between physical and psychological drug dependence?

With physical drug dependence, the user develops a drug tolerance so that larger and larger doses are needed to get the same effect. Withdrawal symptoms appear when the drug is discontinued and disappear when the drug is taken again. Psychological drug dependence involves an intense craving for the drug.

How do stimulants affect the user?

Stimulants speed up activity in the central nervous system, suppress appetite, and make a person feel more awake, alert, and energetic.

What effects do amphetamines have on the user?

Use of amphetamines energizes, increases arousal, and suppresses the appetite, but continued use results in exhaustion, depression, and agitation.

How does cocaine affect the user?

Cocaine energizes, causes a feeling of euphoria, and is highly addictive. Heavy use can cause heart damage, seizures, and even heart attacks.

What are some of the effects of depressants, and what drugs comprise this category?

Depressants decrease activity in the central nervous system, slow down body functions, and reduce sensitivity to outside stimulation. Depressants include sedative-hypnotics (alcohol, barbiturates, and minor tranquilizers) and narcotics (opiates).

What are the general effects of narcotics, and what are several drugs in this category?

Narcotics—which include opium, codeine, morphine, and heroin—have both pain-relieving and calming effects.

What are the main effects of hallucinogens, and what are three psychoactive drugs classified as hallucinogens?

Hallucinogens—including marijuana, LSD, and MDMA—can alter perception and mood and cause hallucinations.

What are some harmful effects of heavy marijuana use?

There is some evidence that heavy use of marijuana can cause memory problems, respiratory damage, loss of motivation, impotence, lowered testosterone level and sperm count, and irregular menstrual cycles.

What effect on the brain do all addictive drugs have in common?

All addictive drugs increase the availability of dopamine in the brain's nucleus accumbens.

Key Terms
psychoactive drug (p. 115); illicit drug (p. 116); physical drug dependence (p. 117); drug tolerance (p. 117); withdrawal symptoms (p. 117); psychological drug dependence (p. 117); stimulants (p. 118); amphetamines (p. 118); cocaine (p. 119); crash (p. 119); crack (p. 119); depressants (p. 119); alcohol (p. 119); barbiturates (p. 120); minor tranquilizers (p. 120); narcotics (p. 120); heroin (p. 120); hallucinogens (p. 121); marijuana (p. 121); THC (p. 121); LSD (p. 122); flashback (p. 122); MDMA (p. 122)

Study Guide for Chapter 4

Answers to all the Study Guide questions are provided at the end of the book.

Section One: Chapter Review

1. Which of the following best defines consciousness?
   a. awareness
   b. wakefulness
   c. receptiveness
   d. rationality

2. The two circadian rhythms most relevant to the study of sleep are the sleep/wakefulness cycle and
   a. blood pressure.
   b. secretion of hormones.
   c. body temperature.
   d. heart rate.

3. People sleep best when their body temperature is at its low point in the 24-hour cycle. (true/false)

4. The structure that serves as the body's biological clock is the _____.

5. The long-term use of melatonin to induce sleep is known to be safe. (true/false)

6. People who are suffering from jet lag or the effects of working rotating shifts or night shifts are experiencing
   a. a deficiency in melatonin production.
   b. an excess of melatonin production.
   c. a defect in their suprachiasmatic nucleus.
   d. a disturbance in their circadian rhythms.

7. The performance of shift workers is enhanced during their subjective night. (true/false)

8. State the type of sleep–NREM or REM–that corresponds to each characteristic.

   ____ (1) paralysis of large muscles   a. REM
   ____ (2) slow, regular respiration   b. NREM
            and heart rate
   ____ (3) rapid eye movements
   ____ (4) penile erection and vaginal swelling
   ____ (5) vivid dreams

9. The average length of a sleep cycle in adults is
   a. 30 minutes.   c. 90 minutes.
   b. 60 minutes.   d. 120 minutes.

10. After the first two sleep cycles, most people get equal amounts of deep sleep and REM sleep. (true/false)

11. Match the age group with the appropriate description of sleep.

   ____ (1) have most difficulty sleeping, most awakenings
   ____ (2) sleep best at night; feel best during day
   ____ (3) have highest percentage of REM and deep sleep
   ____ (4) are usually sleepy during the day regardless of the amount of sleep at night

   a. infants   c. adolescents
   b. children aged 6 to puberty   d. adults over 65

12. Which factor *least* affects the amount of sleep people need?
   a. their genetic makeup
   b. their emotional state
   c. the amount of stress in their life
   d. the amount of physical activity required by their occupation

13. The two main theories that attempt to explain the function of sleep are the _____ and the _____.

14. Compared to REM dreams, NREM dreams are
   a. more emotional.   c. more thoughtlike.
   b. more visual.   d. more vivid.

15. Dream memories usually do not persist for more than 10 minutes after a dream has ended. (true/false)

16. According to researchers, each of the following statements about the content of dreams is correct *except*
   a. dreams are generally bizarre and filled with emotion.
   b. dreams generally reflect our waking preoccupations.
   c. dreams are generally more unpleasant than pleasant.
   d. dreams contain more aggression than friendly interactions.

17. Experts tend to agree on how dreams should be interpreted. (true/false)

18. Following REM deprivation, there is usually
   a. an absence of REM sleep.
   b. an increase in REM sleep
   c. a decrease in REM sleep.
   d. no change in the amount of REM sleep.

19. Which type of sleep seems to aid learning and memory in humans and other animals?
   a. Stage 1   c. Stages 3 and 4
   b. Stage 2   d. REM sleep

20. Sleepwalking and sleep terrors occur during a partial arousal from
   a. Stage 1 sleep.   c. Stage 4 sleep.
   b. Stage 2 sleep.   d. REM sleep.

21. Sleepwalking episodes and sleep terrors are rarely recalled. (true/false)

22. Match each sleep problem with the description or associated symptom.
   ____ (1) uncontrollable sleep attacks during the day
   ____ (2) cessation of breathing during sleep
   ____ (3) difficulty falling or staying asleep
   ____ (4) very frightening REM dream

   a. sleep apnea
   b. nightmare
   c. insomnia
   d. narcolepsy

23. Which is not a proposed use of meditation?
   a. to promote relaxation
   b. to substitute for anesthesia during surgery
   c. to bring a person to a higher level of spirituality
   d. to alter consciousness

24. A special mantra is used in transcendental meditation. (true/false)

25. According to Herbert Benson, the beneficial effects of meditation cannot be duplicated with simple relaxation techniques. (true/false)

26. Which of the following statements is true of people under hypnosis?
   a. They will often violate their moral code.
   b. They are much stronger than they are in the normal waking state
   c. They can be made to experience distortions in their perceptions.
   d. Their memory is more accurate than it is during the normal waking state.

27. For a moderately hypnotizable person, which use of hypnosis would probably be most successful?
   a. for relief from pain
   b. instead of a general anesthetic during surgery
   c. for treating drug addiction
   d. for improving memory

28. The three main theories proposed to explain hypnosis are the _____, _____, and _____ theories.

29. Drug use among adolescents has been declining since the early 1990s. (true/false)

30. Which of the following does not necessarily occur with drug tolerance?
   a. The body adjusts to functioning with the drug in the system.
   b. The user needs larger and larger doses of the drug to get the desired effect.
   c. The user becomes progressively less affected by the drug.
   d. The user develops a craving for the pleasurable effects of the drug.

31. During withdrawal from a drug, the user experiences symptoms that are the opposite of the effects produced by the drug. (true/false)

32. Psychological dependence on a drug is more difficult to combat than physical dependence. (true/false)

33. Match the stimulant with the appropriate description.
   ____ (1) responsible for the most deaths
   ____ (2) used to increase arousal, relieve fatigue, and suppress appetite
   ____ (3) found in coffee, tea, chocolate, and colas
   ____ (4) snorted or injected
   ____ (5) most dangerous, potent, and addictive form of cocaine

   a. caffeine
   b. cigarettes
   c. amphetamines
   d. crack
   e. cocaine

34. Decreased activity in the central nervous system is the chief effect of
   a. stimulants.   c. hallucinogens.
   b. depressants.   d. narcotics.

35. Which of the following is a narcotic?
   a. cocaine   c. LSD
   b. heroin   d. Valium

36. Narcotics have
   a. pain-relieving effects.
   b. stimulating effects.
   c. energizing effects.
   d. perception-altering effects.

37. Which category of drugs alters perception and mood and can cause hallucinations?
   a. stimulants   c. hallucinogens
   b. depressants   d. narcotics

38. Which of the following is *not* associated with long-term use of marijuana?
    a. respiratory damage
    b. loss of motivation
    c. reproductive problems
    d. increased risk of heart attack and stroke

39. All addictive drugs increase the effect of the neurotransmitter _____ in the nucleus accumbens.
    a. acetylcholine   c. dopamine
    b. GABA   d. serotonin

Section Two: Identify the Drug

Match the description of drug effects with the drug.

_____ 1. Effects range from alertness to calmness; lowers appetite for carbohydrates; increases pulse rate

_____ 2. Promote sleep, have a sedative effect, decrease muscle tension, impair coordination and reflexes

_____ 3. Produces excited exhilaration and hallucinations

_____ 4. Produces wakefulness and alertness with increased metabolism but slowed reaction time

_____ 5. Increase metabolism and alertness, elevate mood and wakefulness and decrease appetite

_____ 6. Produce euphoria and relaxation but also affect ability to store new memories

_____ 7. Lower anxiety and decrease muscle tension

_____ 8. Produces an energy boost and feeling of excitement while suppressing appetite

_____ 9. Initial doses stimulate and enliven while lowering anxiety, but higher doses have a sedative effect

a. barbiturates
b. alcohol
c. hallucinogens
d. LSD
e. caffeine
f. cocaine
g. nicotine
h. amphetamines
i. tranquilizers

Section Three: Fill In the Blank

1. The text defined _____ as an awareness of one's own perceptions, thoughts, feelings, sensations, and external environment.

2. The _____ wave is the slowest brain wave and occurs during Stage 3 and 4 sleep.

3. After a person loses REM sleep because of illness or drug use, he or she might experience _____.

4. Luis says he is aware of his dreams as they occur and can even change the content of his dreams. This type of dream is a _____ dream.

5. A person who experiences sleepwalking or sleeptalking is suffering from one of a class of sleep disturbances collectively known as _____.

6. With regard to the differences between *larks* and *owls*, it appears that the performance of _____ declines as the day progresses, while the performance of_____ seems to improve.

7. Sleep _____ is a condition in which breathing stops during sleep.

8. _____ is characterized by daytime sleepiness and sudden REM sleep.

9. Psychoactive drugs are a group of substances that alter _____, _____, or _____.

10. _____ is a group of techniques designed to block out all distractions so as to achieve an altered state of consciousness.

11. A compulsive pattern of drug use in which the user develops a tolerance coupled with unpleasant withdrawal symptoms when drug use is discontinued is referred to as physical drug _____.

12. The use of _____ is determined more by cultural factors than by heredity.

13. The euphoric high from cocaine lasts only a short time and is followed by an equally intense _____, which is marked by depression,

anxiety, agitation, and a powerful craving for more cocaine.

14. Cocaine's action in the human brain includes blocking the reuptake of the neurotransmitter _____, thereby leading to the continual

excitatory stimulation of the reward pathways in the brain.

15. Heroin is classed as a _____; Valium is classed as a_____.

Section Four: Comprehensive Practice Test

1. People seem to sleep best when their body temperature is _____, and are more alert when their body temperature is _____.
   a. higher; lower
   b. lower; higher

2. People who work during their _____, when their biological clock is telling them it is time to sleep, can suffer lowered efficiency and productivity.
   a. REM rebound
   b. subjective night
   c. circadian rebound
   d. episodes of narcolepsy

3. REM sleep is the _____ stage of sleep in a typical sleep cycle.
   a. first
   b. second
   c. last
   d. middle

4. Delta waves appear primarily in Stages _____ sleep.
   a. 1 and 2
   b. 2 and 3
   c. 3 and 4
   d. 1 and 4

5. Another name for slow-wave sleep is
   a. light sleep.
   b. deep sleep.
   c. REM sleep.
   d. dream sleep.

6. Which of the following was *not* suggested as a possible function of REM sleep?
   a. maturation of the brain in infants
   b. information processing
   c. muscle relaxation
   d. mental housecleaning

7. As we grow older we sleep more than when we were younger; we also sleep more deeply, with more REM sleep. (true/false)

8. Freud believed dreams functioned to satisfy unconscious _____ and _____ urges.
   a. parental; childhood
   b. sexual; superego
   c. aggressive; violent
   d. sexual; aggressive

9. J. Allan Hobson believes dreams are merely the brain's attempt to make sense of the random firing of brain cells. This view is known as the

a. Hobson dream hypothesis.
b. somniloquy hypothesis.
c. activation-synthesis hypothesis.
d. physiological activation hypothesis.

10. The technical term for sleepwalking is
    a. somniloquy.
    b. mobile insomnia.
    c. narcolepsy.
    d. somnambulism.

11. People who talk in their sleep often reveal secrets or strong negative opinions. (true/false)

12. Some people suffer from a sleep disorder known as _____, which causes them to stop breathing and then to wake for a brief time in order to start breathing again.
    a. narcolepsy
    b. sleep apnea
    c. somniloquy
    d. somnambulism

13. The sleep disorder characterized by either difficulty falling asleep or frequently waking is known as
    a. sleep apnea.
    b. insomnia.
    c. somnambulism.
    d. REM rebound.

14. Jack pleaded not guilty to his public indecency charges. He claimed he would never do such a thing if he were in his right mind and that he was the victim of the effects of hypnosis. A psychologist would probably support this claim. (true/false)

15. Which of the following is *not* a factor that influences the addictive potential of a drug?
    a. how fast the drug effects are felt
    b. the degree of discomfort a user experiences after he or she stops using the drug
    c. the cost of the drug
    d. how long the pleasurable feeling lasts

16. While caffeine is considered a relatively harmless stimulant in most cases, evidence suggests that some people can experience anxiety, depression, or hostility after using it. (true/false)

17. LSD, MDMA, and marijuana are classified as
    a. narcotics.
    b. stimulants.
    c. hallucinogens.
    d. depressants.

18. One reason for the popularity of crack cocaine is its
    a. price.
    b. rapid and intense effects.
    c. reduced risk.
    d. depressant effects.

19. Which of the following drugs produces its effect by mimicking endorphins?
    a. marijuana   c. alcohol
    b. cocaine   d. heroin

20. Drugs like cocaine and amphetamines seem to produce their effects in part by _____ the reuptake of the neurotransmitter dopamine.
    a. facilitating   c. reversing
    b. mimicking   d. blocking

Section Five: Thinking Critically

1. Suppose you have been hired by a sleep clinic to formulate a questionnaire for evaluating patients' sleep habits. List 10 questions you would include in your questionnaire.

2. You hear much debate about the pros and cons of legalizing drugs. Present the most convincing argument possible to support each of these positions:
    a. Illicit drugs should be legalized.
    b. Illicit drugs should not be legalized.

3. You have been asked to make a presentation to 7th and 8th graders about the dangers of drugs. What are the most persuasive general arguments you can give to convince them not to start using drugs? What are some convincing, specific arguments against using each of these drugs: alcohol, marijuana, nicotine, and cocaine?

Learning

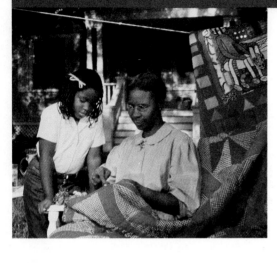

Our cat Missy's favorite food is tuna, and she always comes running when that special treat appears. Some time ago, Missy developed the habit of wanting to be put outdoors at about 3:00 A.M. She got her way by hiding somewhere in the house before we went to bed at night. Then, when the spirit moved her, she would leap on the bed or scratch at the bedroom door to awaken us. Obviously, we were motivated to put her outside for the rest of the night so that we could get back to sleep.

Wanting to avoid these unwelcome interruptions, we began a nightly ritual—going through the house looking for Missy in closets and under the beds and calling her name. But she never came when we called her at bedtime, and we were rarely able to find her then. Missy had associated our calling her at that time with being put outside before she was ready.

After many nights of interrupted sleep, we were desperate for a solution to the problem. Then one night, when we were opening a can of soup, Missy raced through the house and slid to a stop in front of her bowl, no doubt expecting delicious chunks of tuna to materialize. She had learned to associate the sound of the can opener with her favorite food.

By applying simple principles of learning, we solved our problem. Now, instead of calling Missy before bedtime, we simply turn the can opener a few times, and she comes rushing to her bowl. We must admit, though, that we feel a little guilty each time we trick her.

Our experience with Missy provides examples of two basic types of learning psychologists study: classical conditioning and operant conditioning. In *classical conditioning*, an association is formed between one stimulus and another. A **stimulus** (plural, *stimuli)* is any event or object in the environment to which an organism responds. In Missy's case, the sound of a can opener became associated with food. In *operant conditioning*, an association is formed between a behavior and its consequences. Missy learned to associate coming when her name was called late at night with being put outdoors.

Psychologists also study another form of learning, observational learning. In *observational learning*, individuals learn by observing the behavior of others and then may imitate that behavior. These three kinds of learning are powerful forces that influence human thought and behavior for good and for ill. But let's look at learning more broadly.

Learning may be defined as a relatively permanent change in behavior, knowledge, capability, or attitude that is acquired through experience and cannot be attributed to illness, injury, or maturation. Several parts of this definition warrant further explanation. First, defining learning as a "relatively permanent change" excludes temporary changes that could result from illness, fatigue, or fluctuations in mood. Second, referring to changes that are "acquired through experience" excludes some readily observable changes in behavior that occur as a result of brain injuries or certain diseases. Also, certain observable changes that occur as individuals grow and mature have nothing to do with learning. For example, a young male at puberty does not *learn* to speak in a deeper voice—his voice changes to a lower pitch because of maturation.

Psychologists cannot observe learning directly but must infer that it has occurred. They draw inferences from changes in observable behavior or in measurable capabilities and attitudes. Certainly much learning occurs that psychologists are not able to observe or measure. As a student, you might have experienced occasions when you had learned more than your test scores reflected. But learning does not always result in an immediate change in behavior. Often we learn or acquire a capability that we may not demonstrate until we are motivated to do so.

Learning is one of the most important topics in the field of psychology, and available evidence suggests that we learn through many different avenues. This chapter explores the three basic forms of learning—classical conditioning, operant conditioning, and observational learning (a type of cognitive learning).

CLASSICAL CONDITIONING: THE ORIGINAL VIEW

Classical conditioning is a form of learning that has a powerful effect on attitudes, likes and dislikes, and emotional responses. We learn to respond in specific ways to

stimulus (STIM-yu-lus): Any event or object in the environment to which an organism responds; plural is *stimuli.*

learning: A relatively permanent change in behavior, knowledge, capability, or attitude that is acquired through experience and cannot be attributed to illness, injury, or maturation.

classical conditioning: A learning process through which one stimulus comes to predict the occurrence of another stimulus and to elicit a response similar to or related to the response evoked by that stimulus.

a variety of words and symbols. Adolf Hitler, the IRS, Santa Claus, and the American flag are just sounds and symbols, but they tend to evoke strong emotional responses because of their associations. People's lives are profoundly influenced by the associations learned through classical conditioning, sometimes referred to as *respondent conditioning*, or *Pavlovian conditioning*.

Pavlov and Classical Conditioning

What was Pavlov's major contribution to psychology?

Ivan Pavlov (1849–1936) organized and directed research in physiology at the Institute of Experimental Medicine in St. Petersburg, Russia, from 1891 until his death 45 years later. There he conducted his classic experiments on the physiology of digestion, which won him a Nobel Prize in 1904—the first time this honor went to a Russian.

Like so many other important scientific discoveries, Pavlov's contribution to psychology came about quite by accident. To conduct his study of the salivary response in dogs, Pavlov made a small incision in the side of each dog's mouth. Then he attached a tube so that the flow of saliva could be diverted from inside the animal's mouth, through the tube, and into a container, where the saliva was collected and measured.

Pavlov's purpose was to collect the saliva that the dogs would secrete naturally in response to food placed inside the mouth. But he noticed that, in many cases, the dogs would begin to salivate even before the food was presented. Pavlov observed drops of saliva collecting in the containers when the dogs heard the footsteps of the laboratory assistants coming to feed them. He observed saliva collecting when the dogs heard their food dishes rattling, or saw the attendant who fed them, or merely sighted their food. How could an involuntary response such as salivation come to be associated with the sights and sounds involved in feeding? Pavlov spent the rest of his life studying this question. The type of learning he studied is known today as classical conditioning.

In Pavlov's studies, the dogs were isolated inside soundproof cubicles and placed in harnesses to restrain their movements. From an adjoining cubicle, the experimenter observed the dogs through a one-way mirror. Food and other stimuli were presented and the flow of saliva measured by remote control. What did Pavlov and his colleagues learn?

Link It!

Ivan Pavlov (1849–1936) earned fame by studying the conditioned reflex in dogs.

The Elements and Processes of Classical Conditioning

A **reflex** is an involuntary response to a particular stimulus. Two examples are the eyeblink response to a puff of air and salivation in response to food placed in the mouth. There are two kinds of reflexes—conditioned and unconditioned. Think of the term *conditioned* as meaning "learned" and the term *unconditioned* as meaning "unlearned." Salivation in response to food is an unconditioned reflex because it is an inborn, automatic, unlearned response to a particular stimulus. Unconditioned reflexes are built into the nervous system.

When Pavlov observed that his dogs would salivate at the sight of food or the sound of rattling dishes, he realized that this salivation reflex was the result of learning. He called these learned involuntary responses **conditioned reflexes**.

The Conditioned and Unconditioned Stimulus and Response   Pavlov (1927/1960) continued to investigate the circumstances under which a conditioned reflex is formed. He used tones, bells, buzzers, lights, geometric shapes, electric shocks, and metronomes in his conditioning experiments. In a typical experiment, food powder was placed in the dog's mouth, causing salivation. Because dogs do not need to be conditioned to salivate to food, salivation to food is an unlearned response, or **unconditioned response (UR)**. Any stimulus, such as food, that without learning will automatically elicit, or bring forth, an unconditioned response is called an **unconditioned stimulus (US)**.

Remember, a reflex is made up of both a stimulus and a response. Following is a list of some common unconditioned reflexes, showing their two components—the unconditioned stimulus and the unconditioned response.

Unconditioned Reflexes

Unconditioned Stimulus (US)		*Unconditioned Response (UR)*
food	$\longrightarrow$	salivation
loud noise	$\longrightarrow$	startle
light in eye	$\longrightarrow$	contraction of pupil
puff of air in eye	$\longrightarrow$	blink
touching hot stove	$\longrightarrow$	hand withdrawal

Pavlov demonstrated that dogs could be conditioned to salivate to a variety of stimuli never before associated with food. During the conditioning or acquisition process, the researcher would present a neutral stimulus such as a musical tone shortly before placing food powder in the dog's mouth. The food powder would cause the dog to salivate. Pavlov found that after the tone and food were paired many times, usually 20 or more, the tone alone would elicit salivation (Pavlov, 1927/1960, p. 385). Because dogs do not naturally salivate in response to musical tones, he concluded that this salivation was a learned response. Pavlov called the tone the learned stimulus, or **conditioned stimulus (CS)**, and salivation to the tone the learned response, or **conditioned response (CR)**. (See Figure 5.1 on p. 136.)

In a modern view of classical conditioning, the conditioned stimulus can be thought of as a signal that the unconditioned stimulus will follow (Schreurs, 1989). In Pavlov's experiment the tone became a signal that food would follow shortly. So, the signal (conditioned stimulus) gives advance warning, and an organism (animal or person) is prepared with the proper response (conditioned response) even before the unconditioned stimulus arrives.

Extinction and Spontaneous Recovery   After conditioning an animal to salivate to a tone, what would happen if you continued to sound the tone but no longer paired it with food? Pavlov found that without the food, salivation to the tone

---

reflex: An involuntary response to a particular stimulus, such as the eyeblink response to a puff of air or salivation when food is placed in the mouth.

conditioned reflex: A learned reflex rather than a naturally occurring one.

unconditioned response (UR): A response that is invariably elicited by the unconditioned stimulus without prior learning.

unconditioned stimulus (US): A stimulus that elicits a specific response without prior learning.

conditioned stimulus (CS): A neutral stimulus that, after repeated pairing with an unconditioned stimulus, becomes associated with it and elicits a conditioned response.

conditioned response (CR): That response that comes to be elicited by a conditioned stimulus as a result of its repeated pairing with an unconditioned stimulus.

How was classical conditioning accomplished in Pavlov's experiments?

How does extinction occur in classical conditioning?

Figure 5.1

Classically Conditioning a Salivation Response

A neutral stimulus (a tone) elicits no salivation until it is repeatedly paired with the unconditioned stimulus (food). After many pairings, the neutral stimulus (now called conditioned stimulus) alone produces salivation. Classical conditioning has occurred.

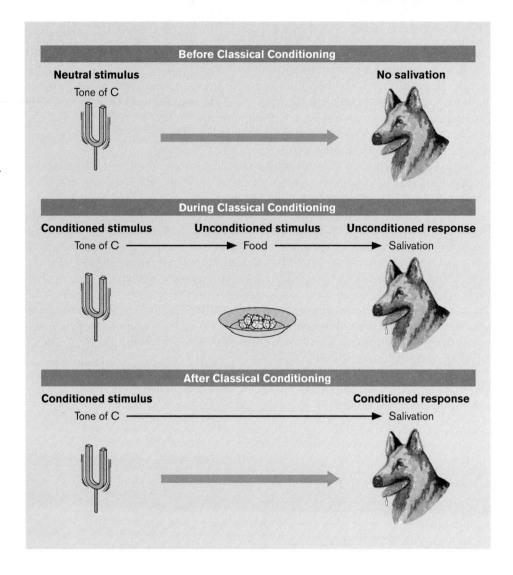

Before Classical Conditioning

Neutral stimulus
Tone of C

No salivation

During Classical Conditioning

Conditioned stimulus
Tone of C

Unconditioned stimulus
Food

Unconditioned response
Salivation

After Classical Conditioning

Conditioned stimulus
Tone of C

Conditioned response
Salivation

extinction: The weakening and often eventual disappearance of a learned response (in classical conditioning, the conditioned response is weakened by repeated presentation of the conditioned stimulus without the unconditioned stimulus).

spontaneous recovery: The reappearance of an extinguished response (in a weaker form) when an organism is exposed to the original conditioned stimulus following a rest period.

What is generalization?

became weaker and weaker and then finally disappeared altogether—a process known as **extinction**.

Pavlov learned that the conditioned response, once extinguished, had not been permanently erased or forgotten. After the response had been extinguished, Pavlov allowed the dog to rest and then brought it back to the laboratory. He found that the dog would again salivate to the tone. Pavlov called this recurrence **spontaneous recovery**. But the spontaneously recovered response was weaker and shorter in duration than the original conditioned response.

More recent research (Bouton, 1993; Bouton & Ricker, 1994) indicates that extinction is context-specific. When a conditioned response is extinguished in one setting, it can still be elicited in other settings where extinction training has not occurred. Pavlov did not discover this because his experiments were always conducted in the same setting.

Generalization and Discrimination   Assume that you have conditioned a dog to salivate when it hears the tone middle C played on the piano. Would it also salivate if you played a slightly different tone, say B or D? Pavlov found that a tone similar to the original conditioned stimulus would also produce the conditioned response (salivation), a phenomenon called **generalization**. But salivation decreased the further the tone was from the original conditioned stimulus, until it became so different that the dog would not salivate at all.

It is easy to see the value of generalization in daily life. Suppose that as a child you had been bitten by a large, gray dog. To experience fear in the future, you probably would not need to see exactly the same dog—or even one of the same breed or color—coming toward you. Your original fear would probably generalize to all large dogs of any description.

Because of generalization, we do not need to learn a conditioned response to every stimulus that may differ only slightly from an original one. Rather, we learn to approach or avoid a range of stimuli similar to the one that produced the original conditioned response.

Not only must we be able to generalize, we must also learn to distinguish between stimuli that may be very similar. Let's return to the example of a dog being conditioned to a musical tone to trace the process of **discrimination**.

Step 1: The dog is conditioned to salivate in response to the tone C.

Step 2: Generalization occurs, and the dog salivates to a range of musical tones above and below C. The dog salivates less and less as the tone moves away from C.

Step 3: The original tone C is repeatedly paired with food. Neighboring tones are also sounded, but they are not followed by food. The dog is being conditioned to discriminate. Gradually, the salivation response to the neighboring tones is extinguished, while salivation to the original tone C is strengthened.

Conditioned Stimulus	Conditioned Response
Tone C	more salivation
Tones A, B, D, E	progressively less salivation

Step 4: Discrimination is achieved.

Conditioned Stimulus	Conditioned Response
Tone C	strengthened salivation response
Tones A, B, D, E	no salivation

Like generalization, discrimination has survival value. Discriminating between the odors of fresh and spoiled milk will spare you an upset stomach. Discriminating between a rattlesnake and a garter snake could save your life.

Higher-Order Conditioning   Classical conditioning would be somewhat limited in its effect on behavior if a conditioned response could be produced only by the pairing of a conditioned stimulus with an unconditioned stimulus or through generalization. Fortunately, classical conditioning can occur in another way— through higher-order conditioning. **Higher-order conditioning** takes place when a neutral stimulus is paired with an existing conditioned stimulus, becomes associated with it, and gains the power to elicit the same conditioned response. Suppose that after Pavlov conditioned the dogs to salivate to a tone, he presented a light (a neutral stimulus) immediately before the tone a number of times. Then the light would become associated with the tone, and the dogs would learn to give the salivation response to the light alone.

Watson, Little Albert, and Peter

John Watson (1878–1958) launched a new school of thought in psychology known as *behaviorism.* Through his research and writing, Watson freed psychology from its exclusively academic setting and made it a subject of great interest to the general public. He believed that in humans all fears except those of loud noises and loss of support are classically conditioned. In 1919 Watson and his assistant, Rosalie Rayner, conducted a now-famous study to prove that fear could be classically conditioned. The subject of the study, known as Little Albert, was a healthy and emo-

Link It!

What is discrimination in classical conditioning?

A child attacked by a dog can easily develop a long-lasting fear of all dogs, through the process of generalization.

generalization: In classical conditioning, the tendency to make a conditioned response to a stimulus similar to the original conditioned stimulus.

discrimination: The learned ability to distinguish between similar stimuli so that the conditioned response occurs only to the original conditioned stimulus but not to similar stimuli.

higher-order conditioning: Conditioning that occurs when a neutral stimulus is paired with an existing conditioned stimulus, becomes associated with it, and gains the power to elicit the same conditioned response.

How did Watson demonstrate that fear could be classically conditioned?

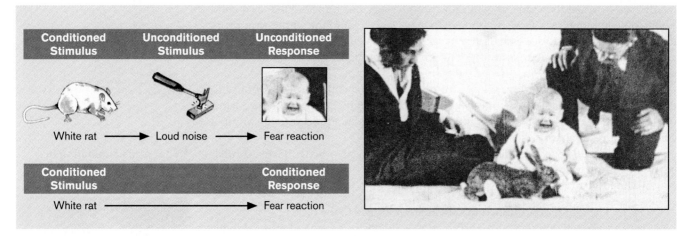

Conditioned Stimulus	Unconditioned Stimulus	Unconditioned Response
White rat →	Loud noise →	Fear reaction

Conditioned Stimulus		Conditioned Response
White rat ────────→		Fear reaction

Figure 5.2

The Conditioned Fear Response

Little Albert's fear of a white rat was a conditioned response that was generalized to other stimuli, including a rabbit.

tionally stable 11-month-old infant. When tested, he showed no fear except of the loud noise Watson made by striking a hammer against a steel bar near Albert's head. In this classic study, Watson tested whether he could condition Albert to fear a white rat by causing him to associate the rat with a loud noise.

In the laboratory, Rayner presented Little Albert with a white rat. As Albert reached for the rat, Watson struck the steel bar with a hammer just behind Albert's head. This procedure was repeated, and Albert "jumped violently, fell forward and began to whimper" (Watson & Rayner, 1920, p. 4). A week later, Watson continued the experiment, pairing the rat with the loud noise five more times. Then at the sight of the white rat alone, Albert began to cry (see Figure 5.2).

When Albert returned to the laboratory 5 days later, the fear had generalized to a rabbit and, somewhat less, to a dog, a seal coat, Watson's hair, and a Santa Claus mask. After 30 days Albert made his final visit to the laboratory, with his fears still evident but somewhat less intense. Watson concluded that conditioned fears "persist and modify personality throughout life" (Watson & Rayner, 1920, p. 12).

Link It!

Although Watson had formulated techniques for removing conditioned fears, Albert moved out of the city before they could be tried on him. Some of Watson's ideas for removing fears were excellent and laid the groundwork for some behavior therapies used today. One method consisted of pairing the feared object with a positive stimulus and conditioning a new association. In Albert's case, candy or other food could have been given just as the white rat was presented. Another procedure was a modeling technique in which Albert could have observed other children playing happily with the white rat. Since Watson apparently knew that Albert would be moving away before these fear-removal techniques could be applied, he clearly showed a disregard for the child's welfare. Fortunately, the American Psychological Association now has strict ethical standards for the use of human and animal participants in research experiments and would not sanction an experiment such as Watson's.

Some 3 years after his experiment with Little Albert, Watson and a colleague, Mary Cover Jones (1924), found 3-year-old Peter, who, like Albert, was afraid of white rats. He was also afraid of rabbits, a fur coat, feathers, cotton, and a fur rug. Peter's fear of the rabbit was his strongest fear, and this became the target of Watson's fear-removal techniques.

Peter was brought into the laboratory, seated in a high chair, and given candy to eat. A white rabbit in a wire cage was brought into the room but kept far enough away from Peter that it would not upset him. Over the course of 38 therapy sessions, the rabbit was brought closer and closer to Peter, who continued to enjoy his candy. Occasionally some of Peter's friends were brought in to play with the rabbit at a safe distance from Peter so that he could see firsthand that the rabbit did no harm. Toward the end of Peter's therapy, the rabbit was taken out of the cage and eventually put in Peter's lap. By the final session, Peter had grown fond of the rabbit. What is more, he had lost all fear of the fur coat, cotton, and feathers, and he could tolerate the white rats and the fur rug.

So far we have considered classical conditioning primarily in relation to Pavlov's dogs and Watson's human subjects. How is classical conditioning viewed today?

CLASSICAL CONDITIONING: THE CONTEMPORARY VIEW

Pavlov viewed classical conditioning as a mechanical process that resulted in a conditioned reflex more or less automatically if certain conditions were met. He believed that the critical element in classical conditioning was the repeated pairing of the conditioned stimulus and the unconditioned stimulus, with only a brief interval between the two. The most effective arrangement, according to Pavlov, was to present the conditioned stimulus slightly before the unconditioned stimulus. He thought that if these criteria were met, almost anything could act as a conditioned stimulus.

Beginning in the late 1960s, researchers began to discover exceptions to some of the general principles Pavlov identified. Today, many researchers acknowledge that classical conditioning is a much more complex phenomenon than originally thought.

The Cognitive Perspective: Prediction Is the Critical Element

More than any other single researcher, Robert Rescorla (1967, 1968, 1988; Rescorla & Wagner, 1972) is responsible for changing how psychologists view classical conditioning. Rescorla was able to demonstrate that the critical element in classical conditioning is not the repeated pairing of the conditioned stimulus and unconditioned stimulus. Rather, the important factor is whether the conditioned stimulus provides information that enables the organism to reliably predict the occurrence of the unconditioned stimulus. How was Rescorla able to prove that prediction is the critical element?

Using rats as his subjects, Rescorla used a tone as the conditioned stimulus and a shock as the unconditioned stimulus. For one group of rats the tone and shock were paired 20 times—the shock always occurred during the tone. The other group of rats also received a shock 20 times while the tone was sounding, but this group also received 20 shocks that were not paired with the tone. If the only critical element in classical conditioning were the number of pairings of the conditioned stimulus and the unconditioned stimulus, both groups of rats should have developed a conditioned fear response to the tone, because both groups experienced exactly the same number of pairings of tone and shock. But this was not the case. Only the first group, for which the tone was a reliable predictor of the shock, developed the conditioned fear response to the tone. The second group showed little evidence of conditioning, because the shock was just as likely to occur without the tone as with it. In other words, for this group the tone provided no additional information about the shock.

More evidence that a classically conditioned response depends on information provided by the conditioned stimulus about the unconditioned stimulus comes from research by Leon Kamin (1968) on a phenomenon known as *blocking*. Blocking occurs when previous conditioning to one stimulus prevents conditioning to a second stimulus with which it has been paired.

Using rats as subjects, Kamin repeatedly sounded a tone slightly before a shock was delivered. As expected, the rats developed a conditioned fear response to the

According to Rescorla, what is the critical element in classical conditioning?

tone. Then Kamin repeatedly presented a light along with the tone just before the shock was administered. Again, the rats exhibited the conditioned fear response to the tone/light combination. Next, Kamin wondered if the rats would exhibit a conditioned fear response to the light alone, but he found little evidence of such conditioning. What was Kamin's explanation? Because the tone already signaled the occurrence of the shock, the light provided no useful additional information that added to the predictability of the shock. Previous conditioning to the tone *blocked* conditioning to the light.

Both Rescorla's and Kamin's research demonstrates that the mere pairing of a second stimulus with an unconditioned stimulus will not result in a conditioned response. But if the second stimulus provides information that helps predict the occurrence of the unconditioned stimulus, a conditioned response will occur.

Rescorla (1988) takes a broader view of classical conditioning than Pavlov did. For Rescorla, classical conditioning is the learning of relations between stimuli that results when one stimulus gives information about another. And this learning goes beyond simply forming an association between the conditioned stimulus and the unconditioned stimulus. Also learned are relations between and among other stimuli in the context. In this way, humans and other animals are able construct a more complete representation of their world.

But what about Pavlov's belief that almost any neutral stimulus could serve as a conditioned stimulus? Later research revealed that organisms' biological predispositions can limit the associations they can form through classical conditioning.

Biological Predispositions: Their Role in Classical Conditioning

What two exceptions to traditional ideas about classical conditioning did Garcia and Koelling find?

Remember that Watson conditioned Little Albert to fear the white rat by pairing the presence of the rat with the loud noise of a hammer striking against a steel bar. Do you think Watson could just as easily have conditioned a fear response to a flower or a piece of ribbon?

Why do most fears and phobias people have center around a fairly limited number of stimuli—especially snakes, insects, the dark, storms, and heights? According to Martin Seligman (1972), most common fears "are related to the survival of the human species through the long course of evolution" (p. 455). Seligman (1970) has suggested that humans and other animals are *prepared* to associate only certain stimuli with particular consequences. One example of this preparedness is the tendency to develop **taste aversions**—the intense dislike and/or avoidance of particular foods that have been associated with nausea or discomfort.

Experiencing nausea and vomiting after eating a certain food is often enough to condition a long-lasting taste aversion. Taste aversions can be classically conditioned when the delay between the conditioned stimulus (food or drink) and the unconditioned stimulus (nausea) is as long as 12 hours. Researchers believe that many taste aversions begin when children are between 2 and 3 years old, so adults may not remember how they originated (Rozin & Zellner, 1985). People are more likely to develop taste aversions to "less preferred, less familiar foods," and a taste aversion can be acquired even when a person is convinced that the food did not cause the nausea (Logue, 1985). Once developed, taste aversions often generalize to similar foods. For example, an aversion to chili might extend to Sloppy Joes as well.

In a classic study on taste aversion, Garcia and Koelling (1966) exposed rats to a three-way conditioned stimulus: a bright light, a clicking noise, and flavored water. For one group of rats, the unconditioned stimulus was being exposed to either X rays or lithium chloride, either of which produces nausea and vomiting several hours after exposure; for the other group, the unconditioned stimulus was an electric shock to the feet. The rats that were made ill associated the flavored water with the nausea and avoided it at all times, but they would still drink unflavored water

Link It!

taste aversion: The dislike and/or avoidance of a particular food that has been associated with nausea or discomfort.

when the bright light and the clicking sound were present. The rats receiving the electric shock continued to prefer the flavored water over unflavored water, but they would not drink at all in the presence of the bright light or the clicking sound. The rats in one group associated nausea only with the flavored water; those in the other group associated electric shock only with the light and the sound.

Garcia and Koelling's research established two exceptions to traditional ideas of classical conditioning. First, the finding that rats formed an association between nausea and flavored water ingested several hours earlier contradicted the principle that the conditioned stimulus must be presented shortly before the unconditioned stimulus. The finding that rats associated electric shock *only* with noise and light, and nausea *only* with flavored water revealed (1) that animals are apparently biologically predisposed to make certain associations, and (2) that associations between *any* two stimuli cannot be readily conditioned.

Other research on conditioned taste aversions has led to the solution of practical problems such as helping cancer patients. One unfortunate side effect of chemotherapy treatment is that cancer patients often associate nausea with the foods they have eaten in the several hours before the treatment (Jacobsen et al., 1993). As a result, patients often develop taste aversions to foods they normally eat. This response can lead to a loss of appetite and weight at a time when good nutrition is particularly important.

Chemotherapy treatments can result in conditioned taste aversions, but providing patients with a "scapegoat" target for the taste aversion can help them maintain a proper diet.

Bernstein and others (1982; Bernstein, 1985) devised a technique to help patients avoid aversions to desirable foods. A group of cancer patients were given a novel-tasting, maple-flavored ice cream before chemotherapy. The nausea caused by the treatment resulted in a taste aversion to the ice cream. The researchers found that when an unusual or unfamiliar food becomes the "scapegoat," or target for taste aversion, other foods in the patient's diet may be protected, and the patient will continue to eat them regularly. So cancer patients should refrain from eating preferred or nutritious foods prior to chemotherapy. Instead, they should be given an unusual-tasting food shortly before treatment.

Classical Conditioning in Everyday Life

Do certain songs have special meaning because they remind you of a current or past love? Do you find the scent of a particular perfume or after-shave pleasant or unpleasant because it reminds you of a special person? Many of our emotional responses, whether positive or negative, result from classical conditioning (often higher-order conditioning). Neutral cues become associated with particular people, objects, locations, situations, or even words and develop the power to elicit the same feeling as the original stimulus.

Fears and phobias often result from classical conditioning. For example, many people who have had painful dental work develop a dental phobia. Not only do they come to fear the dentist's drill, but they develop anxiety in response to a wide range of stimuli associated with it—the dental chair, the waiting room, or even the building where the dentist's office is located.

Through classical conditioning, environmental cues associated with drug use can become conditioned stimuli and later produce the conditioned responses of drug craving or withdrawal symptoms in a former user. Such symptoms are powerful forces and may lead the individual to seek out and use the drug. For this reason, drug counselors strongly urge recovering addicts to avoid any cues associated with their past drug use—people, places, drug paraphernalia, and so on. Relapse is far more common in those who do not avoid such associated environmental cues. This observation helps explain why the American soldiers who used heroin heavily in Vietnam had only a 7% addiction rate when they returned to the United States,

What types of responses can be acquired through classical conditioning?

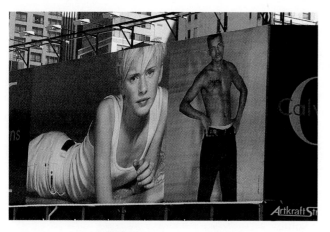

Classical conditioning has proved to be effective in advertising. Here a neutral product (clothing) has been paired with images of very attractive people.

where they no longer encountered many of the environmental cues associated with use of the drug (Basic Behavioral Science Task Force, 1996).

Businesspeople wine and dine customers, hoping that they and their product or service will elicit the same positive response as the pleasant setting and fine food. Advertisers seek to classically condition consumers when they show products along with great-looking models or celebrities or in situations where people are enjoying themselves. Advertisers reason that if the "neutral" product is associated with people, objects, or situations consumers particularly like, then in time the product will elicit a similarly positive response. Pavlov found that presenting the tone just before the food was the most efficient way to condition salivation in dogs. Television advertisements, too, are most effective when the products are presented *before* the beautiful people or situations are shown (van den Hout & Merckelbach, 1991).

You might want to get an idea of just how the principles of classical conditioning are applied in TV advertising with the *Try It!*

Try It!

Some commercials simply give information about a product or place of business. Others attempt to classically condition the viewer to form a positive association. One night while you are watching TV, keep a record of the commercials you see. What proportion rely on classical conditioning? What are the kinds of cues (people, objects, or situations) with which the products are to be associated? Are the products introduced slightly before, during, or after these cues?

Research indicates that even the immune system is subject to classical conditioning (Ader, 1985; Ader & Cohen, 1982, 1993). In the mid-1970s Robert Ader was conducting an experiment with rats, conditioning them to avoid saccharin-sweetened water. Immediately after drinking the sweet water (which rats consider a treat), the rats were injected with a tasteless drug (cyclophosphamide) that causes severe nausea. The conditioning worked, and from that time on, the rats would not drink the sweet water, with or without the drug. Attempting to reverse the conditioned response, Ader had to force-feed the sweet water to the rats for many days; but later, unexpectedly, many of them died. Ader was puzzled, because the saccharin water was in no way lethal. Checking further into the properties of the tasteless drug, Ader learned that it suppresses the immune system. A few doses of an immune-suppressing drug paired with sweetened water had produced a conditioned response. As a result, the sweet water alone continued to suppress the immune system, causing the rats to die. Ader and Cohen successfully repeated the experiment with strict controls to rule out other explanations. How far-reaching the power of classical conditioning must be if a neutral stimulus such as sweetened water can produce effects similar to those of a powerful drug!

Bovbjerg and others (1990) found that in some cancer patients undergoing chemotherapy, environmental cues in the treatment setting eventually came to elicit nausea and immune suppression. These were the same conditioned responses that the treatment alone had caused earlier. Other researchers showed that classical conditioning could be used to suppress the immune system in order to prolong the survival of heart tissue transplants in rats (Grochowicz et al., 1991). And not only can classically conditioned stimuli suppress the immune system, they can be used to boost it as well (Markovic et al., 1993).

Factors Influencing Classical Conditioning

What are four factors that influence classical conditioning?

In summary, there are four major factors that facilitate the acquisition of a classically conditioned response:

1. *How reliably the conditioned stimulus predicts the unconditioned stimulus.* Rescorla (1967, 1988) has shown that classical conditioning does not occur automatically just because a neutral stimulus is repeatedly paired with an unconditioned stimulus.

The neutral stimulus must also reliably predict the occurrence of the unconditioned stimulus. A smoke alarm that never goes off except in response to a fire will elicit more fear when it sounds than one that occasionally gives false alarms. A tone that is *always* followed by food will elicit more salivation than one that is followed by food only some of the time.

2. *The number of pairings of the conditioned stimulus and the unconditioned stimulus.* The number of pairings required to acquire a conditioned response varies considerably, depending on the individual characteristics of the person or animal being conditioned. But in general, the greater the number of pairings, the stronger the conditioned response. But one pairing is all that is needed to classically condition a taste aversion or a strong emotional response to cues associated with some traumatic event, such as an earthquake or rape.

3. *The intensity of the unconditioned stimulus.* If a conditioned stimulus is paired with a very strong unconditioned stimulus, the conditioned response will be stronger and will be acquired more rapidly than if it is paired with a weaker unconditioned stimulus (Gormezano, 1984). Striking the steel bar with the hammer produced stronger and faster conditioning in Little Albert than if Watson had merely clapped his hands behind Albert's head.

4. *The temporal relationship between the conditioned stimulus and the unconditioned stimulus.* Conditioning takes place fastest if the conditioned stimulus occurs shortly before the unconditioned stimulus. It takes place more slowly or not at all when the two stimuli occur at the same time. Conditioning rarely takes place when the conditioned stimulus follows the unconditioned stimulus (Spetch et al., 1981; Spooner & Kellogg, 1947).

The ideal time between the presentation of the conditioned and the unconditioned stimuli is about ½ second, but this varies according to the type of response being conditioned and the nature and intensity of the conditioned stimulus and the unconditioned stimulus (see Wasserman & Miller, 1997). Some studies indicate that the age of the subject may also be a variable affecting the optimal time interval (Solomon et al., 1991). In general, if the conditioned stimulus occurs too long before the unconditioned stimulus, an association between the two will not form. As we have seen, the one notable exception to this general principle is in the conditioning of taste aversions.

OPERANT CONDITIONING

Thorndike and the Law of Effect

Before Pavlov began his experiments with dogs, American psychologist Edward Thorndike (1874–1949) was designing and conducting experiments to study animal intelligence. Profoundly influenced by Darwin's theory of evolution, Thorndike attempted to answer questions about the nature of learning across animal species. He investigated **trial-and-error learning** in cats, dogs, chicks, and monkeys.

In his best-known experiments, Thorndike would place a hungry cat in a wooden box with slats called a *puzzle box*. It was designed so that the animal had to manipulate a simple mechanism—pressing a pedal or pulling down a loop—to escape and claim a food reward just outside the box. The cat would first try to squeeze through the slats; when these attempts failed, it would scratch, bite, and claw inside the box. In time, the cat would accidentally trip the mechanism, which would open the door and release it. Each time, after winning freedom and claiming the food reward, the cat was returned to the box. After many trials, the cat learned through trial and error to open the door almost immediately after being placed in the box.

What was Thorndike's major contribution to psychology?

trial-and-error learning: Learning that occurs when a response is associated with a successful solution to a problem after a number of unsuccessful responses.

law of effect: Thorndike's law of learning, which states that the connection between a stimulus and a response will be strengthened if the response is followed by a satisfying consequence and weakened if the response is followed by discomfort.

operant conditioning: A type of learning in which the consequences of behavior are manipulated in order to increase or decrease that behavior in the future.

What was Skinner's major contribution to psychology?

Link It!

How are responses acquired through operant conditioning?

How is shaping used to condition a response?

B. F. Skinner shapes a rat's bar-pressing behavior in a Skinner box.

Based on the puzzle-box experiments, Thorndike (1911/1970) formulated several laws of learning, the most important being the law of effect. The **law of effect** states that the consequence, or effect, of a response will determine whether the tendency to respond in the same way in the future will be strengthened or weakened. Responses that are closely followed by satisfying consequences are more likely to be repeated. Thorndike (1898) insisted that it was "unnecessary to invoke reasoning" to explain how the learning took place. Thorndike's law of effect formed the conceptual starting point for B. F. Skinner's work in operant conditioning.

B. F. Skinner: A Pioneer in Operant Conditioning

Like Watson before him, Burrhus Frederic Skinner (1904–1990) believed that the causes of behavior are in the environment and do not result from inner mental events such as thoughts, feelings, or perceptions. Rather, Skinner claimed that these inner mental events are themselves behaviors, and like any other behaviors, are shaped and determined by environmental forces.

After graduating from college, Skinner began reading the books of Pavlov and Watson. He became so intrigued that he entered graduate school at Harvard and completed his PhD in psychology in 1931. He conducted much of his research in operant conditioning at the University of Minnesota in the 1930s and wrote *The Behavior of Organisms* (1938), now a classic. Gaining more attention was his first novel, *Walden Two* (1948b), set in a fictional utopian community where reinforcement principles are used to produce happy, productive, and cooperative citizens. In 1948 Skinner returned to Harvard and continued his research and writing. There he wrote his book *Science and Human Behavior* (1953), which provides a description of the process of operant conditioning.

The Elements and Processes of Operant Conditioning

Recall that in classical conditioning, the organism does not learn a new response. Rather, it learns to make an old or existing response to a new stimulus. Classically conditioned responses are involuntary or reflexive, and in most cases the person or animal cannot help but respond in expected ways. In contrast, **operant conditioning** is a method for conditioning *voluntary* responses.

Operant conditioning does not begin, as does classical conditioning, with the presentation of a stimulus to elicit a response. Rather, the response comes first, and then the consequence that follows tends to modify this response in the future. In operant conditioning, the consequences of behavior are manipulated in order to increase or decrease the frequency of a response or to shape an entirely new response. Behavior that is reinforced—followed by rewarding consequences—tends to be repeated. A **reinforcer** is anything that strengthens or increases the probability of the response it follows. Behavior that is ignored or punished is less likely to be repeated.

Operant conditioning permits the learning of a broad range of new responses. A simple response can be operantly conditioned if a researcher simply waits for it to appear and then reinforces it. But this can be time-consuming. The process can be speeded up with a technique called *shaping*. Shaping also can be used to condition responses that would never occur naturally.

Shaping Behavior   **Shaping**, a technique B. F. Skinner used, is particularly effective in conditioning complex behaviors. With shaping, rather than waiting for the desired response to occur and then reinforcing it, a researcher (or parent or animal trainer) reinforces any movement in the direction of the desired response, gradually guiding the responses closer and closer to the ultimate goal.

Skinner designed a soundproof apparatus, commonly called a **Skinner box**, with which he conducted his experiments in operant conditioning. One type of box is equipped with a lever, or bar, that a rat presses to gain a reward of food pellets or water from a dispenser. A record of the animal's bar-pressing is registered on a device called a *cumulative recorder*, also invented by Skinner. Through the use of shaping, a rat in a Skinner box is conditioned to press a bar for rewards. It may be rewarded first for simply turning toward the bar. The next reward comes only when the rat moves closer to the bar. Each step closer to the bar is rewarded. Next the rat must touch the bar to receive a reward; finally, it is rewarded only when it presses the bar.

Shaping—rewarding **successive approximations** of the desired response—has been used effectively to condition complex behaviors in people as well as other animals. Parents may use shaping to help their children develop good table manners, praising them each time they show an improvement. Teachers often use shaping with disruptive children, reinforcing them at first for very short periods of good behavior and then gradually expecting them to work productively for longer and longer periods. Through shaping, circus animals have learned to perform a wide range of amazing feats, and pigeons have learned to bowl and play Ping-Pong.

Of course, the motive of the shaper is very different from that of the person or animal whose behavior is being shaped. The shaper seeks to change another's behavior by controlling its consequences. The person or animal's motive is to gain rewards or avoid unwanted consequences. You might want to try shaping your own behavior using the *Try It!*

Try It!

Use conditioning to modify your own behavior.

1. *Identify the target behavior.* It must be both observable and measurable. You might choose, for example, to increase the amount of time you spend studying.

2. *Gather and record baseline data.* Keep a daily record of how much time you spend on the target behavior for about a week. Also note where the behavior takes place and what cues (or temptations) in the environment precede any slacking off from the target behavior.

3. *Plan your behavior modification program.* Formulate a plan and set goals to either decrease or increase the target behavior.

4. *Choose your reinforcers.* Any activity you enjoy more can be used to reinforce any activity you enjoy less. For example, you could reward yourself with a movie after a specified period of studying.

5. *Set the reinforcement conditions and begin recording and reinforcing your progress.* Be careful not to set your reinforcement goals so high that it becomes nearly impossible to earn a reward. Keep in mind Skinner's concept of shaping–rewarding small steps toward the desired outcome. Be perfectly honest with yourself and claim a reward only when you meet the goals. Chart your progress as you work toward gaining more control over the target behavior.

Extinction, Generalization, and Discrimination   We have seen that responses followed by reinforcers tend to be repeated and that responses no longer followed by reinforcers will occur less and less frequently and eventually die out. In operant conditioning, **extinction** occurs when reinforcers are withheld. A rat in a Skinner box will eventually stop pressing a bar when it is no longer rewarded with food pellets.

In humans and other animals, the withholding of reinforcement can lead to frustration or even rage. If a vending machine takes your coins but fails to deliver candy or soda, you might shake the machine or even kick it before giving up. It is what we expect and don't get that makes us angry.

The process of spontaneous recovery, which we discussed in relation to classical conditioning, also occurs in operant conditioning. A rat whose bar pressing has been extinguished may again press the bar a few times when it is returned to the Skinner box after a period of rest.

Skinner conducted many of his experiments with pigeons placed in a specially designed Skinner box. The box contained small illuminated disks that the pigeons could peck to receive bits of grain from a food tray. Skinner found that **generalization** occurs in operant conditioning. A pigeon reinforced for pecking at a yellow disk is likely to peck at another disk similar in color. The less similar a disk is to the original color, the lower the rate of pecking will be.

Discrimination in operant conditioning involves learning to distinguish between a stimulus that has been reinforced and other stimuli that may be very similar. Discrimination is learned when the response to the original stimulus is reinforced but responses to similar stimuli are not reinforced. For example, to encourage discrimination, a researcher would reinforce the pigeon for pecking at the yellow disk but not for pecking at the orange or red disk. Pigeons have even been conditioned to discriminate between a cubist-style Picasso painting and a Monet with 90% accuracy. However, they weren't able to tell a Renoir from a Cezanne ("Psychologists' pigeons . . . ," 1995).

Certain cues come to be associated with reinforcement or punishment. For example, children are more likely to ask their parents for a treat when the parents are smiling than when they are frowning. A stimulus that signals whether a certain response or behavior is likely to be rewarded, ignored, or punished is called a **discriminative stimulus**. Why do children sometimes misbehave with a grandparent but not with a parent, or make one teacher's life miserable yet be model students for another? The children may have learned that in the presence of some people (the discriminative stimuli), their misbehavior will almost certainly lead to punishment, but in the presence of certain other people, it may even be rewarded.

Sometimes a reward follows a response but the two are not related. Superstitious behavior occurs if an individual falsely believes that a connection exists between an act and its consequences. A baseball player who hits a game-winning homerun with a certain bat, for example, may want to use that "lucky" bat in subsequent games.

Reinforcement: What's the Payoff?

Reinforcement, a key concept in operant conditioning, refers to any event that strengthens or increases the probability of the response that it follows. There are two types of reinforcement, positive and negative. **Positive reinforcement**, roughly the same thing as a reward, refers to any *positive* consequence that, if applied after a response, increases the probability of that response. Many employees will work hard for a raise or a promotion, salespeople will increase their efforts to get awards and bonuses, students will study to get good grades, and children will throw temper tantrums to get candy or ice cream. In these examples, the raises, promotions, awards, bonuses, good grades, candy, and ice cream are positive reinforcers.

Just as people engage in behaviors to get positive reinforcers, they also engage in behaviors to avoid or escape aversive, or unpleasant, conditions. With **negative reinforcement**, a person's or animal's behavior is reinforced by the termination or avoidance of an aversive condition. If we find that a response successfully ends an aversive condition, we are likely to repeat it. We will get out of bed to turn off a faucet and end its annoying "drip, drip, drip." Heroin addicts will do almost anything to obtain heroin to terminate their painful withdrawal symptoms. In these instances, negative reinforcement involves putting an end to a dripping faucet or to withdrawal symptoms.

Responses that end discomfort and those that are followed by rewards are likely to be strengthened or repeated because *both* lead to a more desirable outcome. Some behaviors are influenced by a combination of positive and negative reinforcement. If you eat a plateful of rather disgusting leftovers to relieve intense hunger, then you are eating solely to remove hunger, a negative reinforcer. But if your hunger is relieved by a delicious dinner at a fine restaurant, both positive and negative rein-

What is the goal of both positive reinforcement and negative reinforcement, and how is the goal accomplished with each?

generalization: In operant conditioning, the tendency to make the learned response to a stimulus similar to the one that was originally reinforced.

discriminative stimulus: A stimulus that signals whether a certain response or behavior is likely to be followed by reward or punishment.

reinforcement: An event that follows a response and increases the strength of the response and/or the likelihood that it will be repeated.

positive reinforcement: A reward or pleasant consequence that follows a response and increases the probability that the response will be repeated.

negative reinforcement: The termination of an unpleasant stimulus after a response in order to increase the probability that the response will be repeated.

forcement will have played a role. Your hunger has been removed, and the dinner has been a reward in itself.

A **primary reinforcer** is one that fulfills a basic physical need for survival and does not depend on learning. Food, water, sleep, and termination of pain are examples of primary reinforcers. And sex is a powerful reinforcer that fulfills a basic physical need for survival of the species. Fortunately, learning does not depend solely on primary reinforcers. If that were the case, people would need to be hungry, thirsty, or sex starved before they would respond at all. Much observed human behavior occurs in response to secondary reinforcers. A **secondary reinforcer** is acquired or learned by association with other reinforcers. Some secondary reinforcers (money, for example) can be exchanged at a later time for other reinforcers. Praise, good grades, awards, applause, attention, and signals of approval such as a smile or a kind word are all examples of secondary reinforcers.

Schedules of Reinforcement

Initially, Skinner conditioned rats by reinforcing each bar-pressing response with a food pellet. Reinforcing every correct response, known as **continuous reinforcement**, is the most efficient way to condition a new response. However, after a response has been conditioned, partial or intermittent reinforcement is more effective in maintaining or increasing the rate of response. **Partial reinforcement** is operating when some but not all responses are reinforced. In real life, reinforcement is almost never continuous. Partial reinforcement is the rule.

Partial reinforcement may be administered according to different **schedules of reinforcement**. Different schedules produce distinct rates and patterns of responses, as well as varying degrees of resistance to extinction when reinforcement is discontinued. The effects of reinforcement schedules can vary somewhat with humans depending on any instructions given to participants that could change their expectations (Lattal & Neef, 1996).

The two basic types of schedules are ratio and interval schedules. Ratio schedules require that a certain *number of responses* be made before one of the responses is reinforced. With interval schedules, a given *amount of time* must pass before a reinforcer is administered. These types of schedules are further subdivided into fixed and variable categories.

The Fixed-Ratio Schedule On a **fixed-ratio schedule**, a reinforcer is given after a fixed number of nonreinforced responses. If the fixed ratio is set at 30 responses (FR-30), a reinforcer is given after 30 correct responses. Examples are payments to factory workers according to the number of units produced and to migrant farm workers for each bushel of fruit they pick.

The fixed-ratio schedule is a very effective way to maintain a high response rate, because the number of reinforcers received depends directly on the response rate. The faster people or animals respond, the more reinforcers they earn and the sooner they earn them. When large ratios are used, people and animals tend to pause after each reinforcement but then return to the characteristic high rate of responding.

The Variable-Ratio Schedule Pauses after reinforcement with a high fixed-ratio schedule normally do not occur with the variable-ratio schedule. On a **variable-ratio schedule**, a reinforcer is given after a varying number of nonreinforced responses based on an average ratio. With a variable ratio of 30 responses (VR-30), people might be reinforced one time after 10 responses, another after 50, another after 30 responses, and so on. They cannot predict exactly which responses will be reinforced, but in this example, reinforcement would average 1 in 30.

Variable-ratio schedules result in higher, more stable rates of responding than fixed-ratio schedules. Skinner (1953) reports that on this schedule "a pigeon may respond as rapidly as five times per second and maintain this rate for many hours"

What are the four types of schedules of reinforcement, and which schedule yields the highest response rate and the greatest resistance to extinction?

primary reinforcer: A reinforcer that fulfills a basic physical need for survival and does not depend on learning.

secondary reinforcer: A neutral stimulus that becomes reinforcing after repeated pairings with other reinforcers.

continuous reinforcement: Reinforcement that is administered after every desired or correct response; the most effective method of conditioning a new response.

partial reinforcement: A pattern of reinforcement in which some portion, rather than 100%, of the correct responses are reinforced.

schedule of reinforcement: A systematic program for administering reinforcements that has a predictable effect on behavior.

fixed-ratio schedule: A schedule in which a reinforcer is given after a fixed number of correct responses.

variable-ratio schedule: A schedule in which a reinforcer is given after a varying number of nonreinforced responses based on an average ratio.

Migrant farm workers are paid according to a fixed-ratio schedule. Since their earnings depend on the number of bushels of tomatoes they pick, they are motivated to work quickly. Gamblers receive payoffs according to a variable-ratio schedule. They cannot predict when they will be reinforced, so they are highly motivated to keep playing.

(p. 104). According to Skinner (1988), the variable-ratio schedule is useful because "it maintains behavior against extinction when reinforcers occur only infrequently. The behavior of the dedicated artist, writer, businessman, or scientist is sustained by an occasional, unpredictable reinforcement" (p. 174).

The best example of the seemingly addictive power of the variable-ratio schedule is found in the gambling casino. Slot machines, roulette wheels, and most other games of chance pay on this type of schedule. In general, the variable-ratio schedule produces the highest response rate and the most resistance to extinction.

The Fixed-Interval Schedule   On a **fixed-interval schedule**, a specific time interval must pass before a response is reinforced. For example, on a 60-second fixed-interval schedule (FI-60), a reinforcer is given for the first correct response that occurs 60 seconds after the last reinforced response. People working on salary are reinforced on the fixed-interval schedule.

Unlike ratio schedules, reinforcement on interval schedules does not depend on the number of responses made, only on the one correct response made after the time interval has passed. Characteristic of the fixed-interval schedule is a pause or a sharp decline in responding immediately after each reinforcement and a rapid acceleration in responding just before the next reinforcer is due.

As an example of this schedule, think of a psychology test as a reinforcer (what a joke!) and studying for the test as the desired response. Suppose you have four tests scheduled during the semester. Your study responses will probably drop to zero immediately after the first test, gradually accelerate and perhaps reach a frenzied peak just before the next scheduled exam, then immediately drop to zero again, and so on. As you may have guessed, the fixed-interval schedule produces the lowest response rate.

The Variable-Interval Schedule   Variable-interval schedules eliminate the pause after reinforcement typical of the fixed-interval schedule. On a **variable-interval schedule**, a reinforcer is given after the first correct response following a varying time of nonreinforced responses based on an average time. Rather than being given every 60 seconds, for example, a reinforcer might be given after a 30-second interval with others following after 90-, 45-, and 75-second intervals. But the average time elapsing between reinforcers would be 60 seconds (VI-60). This schedule maintains remarkably stable and uniform rates of responding, but the response rate is typically lower than that of the ratio schedules, because reinforcement is not tied directly to the *number* of responses made.

fixed-interval schedule: A schedule in which a reinforcer is given following the first correct response after a fixed period of time has elapsed.

variable-interval schedule: A schedule in which a reinforcer is given after the first correct response following a varying time of nonreinforcement based on an average time.

Schedule of Reinforcement	Response Rate	Pattern of Responses	Resistance to Extinction
Fixed-ratio schedule	Very high	Steady response with low ratio. Brief pause after each reinforcement with very high ratio.	The higher the ratio, the more resistance to extinction.
Variable-ratio schedule	Highest response rate	Constant response pattern, no pauses.	Most resistance to extinction.
Fixed-interval schedule	Lowest response rate	Long pause after reinforcement, followed by gradual acceleration.	The longer the interval, the more resistance to extinction.
Variable-interval schedule	Moderate	Stable, uniform response.	More resistance to extinction than fixed-interval schedule with same average interval.

Again, a psychology test could be thought of as the reinforcer and studying for the test as the response. Rather than a regularly scheduled exam, however, pop quizzes illustrate the variable-interval schedule. Because you cannot predict when a pop quiz will be given, your study responses will be more uniform and stable. Also, the response rate tends to be higher with shorter intervals and lower with longer ones. If your professor gives a pop quiz once a week on the average, your study response will be higher than if you average only one quiz per month. Random drug testing in the workplace is an excellent example of application of the variable-interval schedule and appears to be quite effective.

Review & Reflect 5.1 summarizes the characteristics of the four schedules of reinforcement.

The Effect of Continuous and Partial Reinforcement on Extinction

One way to understand extinction in operant conditioning is to consider how consistently a response is followed by reinforcement. On a continuous schedule, a reinforcer is expected without fail after each correct response. When a reinforcer is withheld, it is noticed immediately. But on a partial-reinforcement schedule, a reinforcer is not expected after every response. Thus, no immediate difference is apparent between the partial-reinforcement schedule and the onset of extinction.

When you put money in a vending machine and pull the lever but no candy or soda appears, you know immediately that something is wrong with the machine. But if you were playing a broken slot machine, you could have many nonreinforced responses before you would suspect the machine of malfunctioning.

Partial reinforcement results in a greater resistance to extinction than does continuous reinforcement (Lerman et al., 1996). This phenomenon is known as the **partial-reinforcement effect**. There is an inverse relationship between the percentage of responses that have been reinforced and resistance to extinction. That is, the lower the percentage of responses that are reinforced, the longer extinction will take when reinforcement is withheld. The strongest resistance to extinction ever observed occurred in one experiment in which pigeons were conditioned to peck at a disk. Holland and Skinner (1961) report that "after the response had been maintained on

What is the partial-reinforcement effect?

partial-reinforcement effect: The greater resistance to extinction that occurs when a portion, rather than all, of the correct responses are reinforced.

a fixed ratio of 900 and reinforcement was then discontinued, the pigeon emitted 73,000 responses during the first 4½ hours of extinction" (p. 124).

Parents often wonder why their children continue to nag in order to get what they want, even though the parents usually do not give in to the nagging. Unwittingly, parents are reinforcing nagging on a variable-ratio schedule, which results in the most persistent behavior. This is why experts always caution parents to be consistent. If parents never reward nagging, the behavior will extinguish; if they give in occasionally, it will persist and be extremely hard to extinguish.

Factors Influencing Operant Conditioning

What three factors, in addition to the schedule of reinforcement, influence operant conditioning?

We have seen that responses are acquired more quickly with continuous rather than partial reinforcement and that the schedule of reinforcement influences both response rate and resistance to extinction. Three other factors affect response rate, resistance to extinction, and how quickly a response is acquired:

1. *The magnitude of reinforcement.* In general, as the magnitude of reinforcement increases, acquisition of a response is faster, the rate of responding is higher, and resistance to extinction is greater (Clayton, 1964). Yard crews would be motivated to work harder and faster if they were paid $30 for each yard mowed rather than only $10. Other research indicates that level of performance is also influenced by the relationship between the amount of reinforcement expected and what is actually received (Crespi, 1942). For example, your performance on the job would undoubtedly be affected if your salary were suddenly cut in half. Also, it might improve dramatically, at least temporarily, if your employer doubled your pay.

2. *The immediacy of reinforcement.* In general, responses are conditioned more effectively when reinforcement is immediate. As a rule, the longer the delay in reinforcement, the more slowly a response is acquired (Church, 1989; Mazur, 1993). In animals, little learning occurs when there is any delay at all in reinforcement, because even a short delay obscures the relationship between the behavior and the reinforcer. In humans, a reinforcer sometime in the future is usually no match for immediate reinforcement in controlling behavior. Overweight people, for example, have difficulty changing their eating habits partly because of the long delay between their behavior change and the rewarding consequences of weight loss.

3. *The level of motivation of the learner.* In general, the more highly motivated we are, the faster we learn. Skinner found that when food is the reinforcer, a hungry animal will learn faster than a full animal. To maximize motivation, he used rats that had been deprived of food for 24 hours and pigeons that were maintained at 75–80% of their normal body weight.

Comparing Classical and Operant Conditioning: What's the Difference?

In summary, the processes of generalization, discrimination, extinction, and spontaneous recovery occur in both classical and operant conditioning. Both types of conditioning depend on associative learning. In classical conditioning, an association is formed between two stimuli—for example, a tone and food, a white rat and a loud noise, a product and a celebrity. In operant conditioning, the association is established between a response and its consequences—studying hard and a high test grade, or, in the world of rats, bar pressing and food.

In classical conditioning, the focus is on what precedes the response. Pavlov focused on what led up to the salivation in his dogs, not on what happened after they salivated. In operant conditioning, the focus is on what follows the response. If

Characteristics	Classical Conditioning	Operant Conditioning
Type of association	Between two stimuli	Between a response and its consequence
State of subject	Passive	Active
Focus of attention	On what precedes response	On what follows response
Type of response typically involved	Involuntary or reflexive response	Voluntary response
Bodily response typically involved	Internal responses: emotional and glandular reactions	External responses: muscular and skeletal movement and verbal responses
Range of responses	Relatively simple	Simple to highly complex
Responses learned	Emotional reactions: fears, likes, dislikes	Goal-oriented responses

a rat's bar pressing or your studying is followed by a reinforcer, that response is more likely to occur in the future.

Generally, in classical conditioning, the subject is passive and responds to the environment rather than acting on it. In operant conditioning, the subject is active and *operates* on the environment. Children *do* something to get their parents' attention or their praise. *Review & Reflect 5.2* highlights the major differences between classical and operant conditioning.

Punishment: That Hurts!

In many ways **punishment** is the opposite of reinforcement. Punishment tends to lower the probability of a response by following it with an aversive or unpleasant consequence. Punishment can be accomplished by either adding an unpleasant stimulus or removing a pleasant stimulus. The added unpleasant stimulus might take the form of criticism, a scolding, a disapproving look, a fine, or a prison sentence. The removal of a pleasant stimulus might consist of withholding affection and attention, suspending a driver's license, or taking away a privilege such as watching television.

It is common to confuse punishment and negative reinforcement because both involve an unpleasant condition, but there is a big difference between the two. Punishment may involve adding a negative condition, but with negative reinforcement, a negative condition is terminated or avoided. Moreover, the two are designed to have opposite effects: Punishment is applied to discourage a behavior; negative reinforcement is used to encourage or strengthen a behavior. Unlike punishment, negative reinforcement *increases* the probability of a desired response by removing an unpleasant stimulus when the correct response is made. "Grounding" can be used as either punishment or negative reinforcement. If a teenager fails to clean her room after many requests to do so, her parents could ground her for the weekend—a punishment. An alternative approach would be to use negative reinforcement—to tell her she is grounded *until* the room is clean. Which approach is more likely to be effective?

How does punishment differ from negative reinforcement?

punishment: The removal of a pleasant stimulus or the application of an unpleasant stimulus, which tends to suppress a response.

There are a number of potential problems associated with the use of punishment.

1. According to Skinner, *punishment does not extinguish an undesirable behavior; rather, it suppresses that behavior when the punishing agent is present.* But the behavior is apt to continue when the threat of punishment is removed and in settings where punishment is unlikely. If punishment (imprisonment, fines, and so on) reliably extinguished unlawful behavior, there would be fewer repeat offenders in the criminal justice system.

2. *Punishment indicates that a behavior is unacceptable but does not help people develop more appropriate behaviors.* If punishment is used, it should be administered in conjunction with reinforcement or rewards for appropriate behavior.

3. *The person who is severely punished often becomes fearful and feels angry and hostile toward the punisher.* These reactions may be accompanied by a desire to retaliate or to avoid or escape from the punisher and the punishing situation. Many runaway teenagers leave home to escape physical abuse. Punishment that involves a loss of privileges is more effective than physical punishment and engenders less fear and hostility.

4. *Punishment frequently leads to aggression.* Those who administer physical punishment may become models of aggressive behavior—people who demonstrate aggression as a way of solving problems and discharging anger. Children of abusive, punishing parents are at greater risk than other children of becoming aggressive and abusive themselves (Widom, 1989).

Link It!

Because of the many disadvantages of punishment, parents and teachers should explore alternative ways of handling misbehavior. Many psychologists believe that removing the rewarding consequences of undesirable behavior is the best way to extinguish a problem behavior. According to this view, parents should extinguish a child's temper tantrums not by punishment but by never giving in to the child's demands during a tantrum. A parent might best extinguish problem behavior performed merely to get attention by ignoring it and giving attention to more appropriate behavior. Sometimes, simply explaining why certain behaviors are not appropriate is all that is required to extinguish the behavior.

Using positive reinforcement such as praise will make good behavior more rewarding for children. This approach brings with it the attention that children want and need—attention that often only comes when they misbehave. And the earlier example of grounding illustrated, negative reinforcement can often be more effective than punishment in bringing about desired outcomes.

It is probably unrealistic to believe that punishment can be dispensed with entirely. If a young child runs into the street, puts a finger near an electrical outlet, or reaches for a hot pan on the stove, a swift punishment may save the child from a potentially disastrous situation.

Review & Reflect 5.3 summarizes the differences between reinforcement and punishment.

What three factors increase
the effectiveness of
punishment?

Making Punishment More Effective: Some Suggestions   Research has revealed several factors that influence the effectiveness of punishment: its *timing*, its *intensity*, and the *consistency* of its application (Parke, 1977).

1. *Punishment is most effective when it is applied during the misbehavior or as soon afterward as possible.* Interrupting the problem behavior is most effective because doing so abruptly halts its rewarding aspects. The longer the delay between the response and the punishment, the less effective the punishment is in suppressing the response (Camp et al., 1967). When there is a delay, most animals do not make the connection between the misbehavior and the punishment. With humans, however, if the punishment must be delayed, the punisher should remind the perpetrator of the incident and explain why the behavior was inappropriate.

Review & Reflect 5.3 The Effects of Reinforcement and Punishment

Reinforcement (increases or strengthens a behavior)	Punishment (decreases or suppresses a behavior)
Adding a Positive (positive reinforcement) Presenting food, money, praise, attention, or other rewards.	**Adding a Negative** Delivering a pain-producing or otherwise aversive stimulus, such as a spanking or an electric shock.
Subtracting a Negative (negative reinforcement) Removing or terminating some pain-producing or otherwise aversive stimulus, such as an electric shock.	**Subtracting a Positive** Removing some pleasant stimulus or taking away privileges such as TV watching or use of automobile.

2. *Ideally, punishment should be of the minimum severity necessary to suppress the problem behavior.* Animal studies reveal that the more intense the punishment, the greater the suppression of the undesirable behavior (Church, 1963). But the intensity of the punishment should match the seriousness of the misdeed. Unnecessarily severe punishment is likely to produce the negative side effects mentioned earlier. Yet, if the initial punishment is too mild, it will have no effect. Similarly, gradually increasing the intensity of the punishment is not effective because the perpetrator will gradually adapt to it, and the unwanted behavior will persist (Azrin & Holz, 1966). At a minimum, if a behavior is to be suppressed, the punishment must be more punishing than the misbehavior is rewarding. In human terms, a $200 ticket is more likely to suppress the urge to speed than a $2 ticket.

A person who wishes to apply punishment must understand that the purpose of punishment is not to vent anger but rather to modify behavior. Punishment meted out in anger is likely to be more intense than necessary to bring about the desired result.

3. *To be effective, punishment must be applied consistently.* A parent cannot ignore misbehavior one day and punish the same act the next. And both parents should react to the same misbehavior in the same way. An undesired response will be suppressed more effectively when the probability of punishment is high. Would you be tempted to speed if you saw a police car in your rear-view mirror?

Culture and Punishment   Punishment has been used throughout recorded history to control and suppress people's behavior. It is administered when important values, rules, regulations, and laws are violated. But not all cultures share the same values or have the same laws regulating behavior. U.S. citizens traveling in other countries need to be aware of how different cultures view and administer punishment. For example, all crimes are punished harshly in Singapore—murder, rape, robbery, dealing drugs. Although the culture of Singapore is severely restrictive by American standards, Singaporeans have succeeded in suppressing undesirable behavior by using the threat of harsh punishment and applying punishment swiftly and surely. The extremely low crime rate in Singapore indicates that its citizens have learned to practice law-abiding behavior consistently in order to avoid punishment. Both humans and animals readily learn to escape or avoid punishing consequences.

Escape and Avoidance Learning

Learning to perform a behavior because it terminates an aversive event is called *escape learning*, and it reflects the power of negative reinforcement. Running away from a punishing situation and taking aspirin to relieve a pounding headache are examples of escape behavior. In these situations the aversive event has begun and an attempt is being made to escape it.

Avoidance learning, in contrast, depends on two types of conditioning. First, through classical conditioning, an event or condition comes to signal an aversive state. Drinking and driving may be associated with automobile accidents and death. Because of such associations, people may engage in behaviors to avoid the anticipated aversive consequences. Making it a practice to avoid riding in a car with a driver who has been drinking is sensible avoidance behavior.

Many avoidance behaviors are maladaptive, however, and occur in response to phobias. Students who have had a bad experience speaking in front of a class may begin to fear any situation that involves speaking before a group. Such students may avoid taking courses that require class presentations or taking leadership roles that necessitate public speaking. But the avoidance behavior is negatively reinforced and thus strengthened through operant conditioning. Maladaptive avoidance behaviors are very difficult to extinguish, because people never give themselves a chance to learn that the dreaded consequences probably will not occur, or that they are greatly exaggerated.

Link It!

Some students would avoid taking a class like this one in archaeology, which requires oral presentations, because they fear speaking to a group.

Learned Helplessness

There is an important exception to the ability of humans and other animals to learn to escape and avoid aversive situations. Research on learned helplessness suggests that if people or animals are exposed to repeated aversive events that they cannot escape or avoid, they may learn simply to stand helplessly and suffer the punishment. **Learned helplessness** is a passive resignation to aversive conditions learned by repeated exposure to aversive events that are inescapable and unavoidable.

The initial experiment on learned helplessness was conducted by Overmeier and Seligman (1967), who used dogs as their subjects. Dogs in the experimental group were strapped, one at a time, into a harness from which they could not escape and were exposed to electric shocks. Later, these same dogs were placed in a shuttle box with two experimental compartments separated by a low barrier. The dogs then experienced a series of trials in which a warning signal was followed by an electric shock. The floor on one side was electrified, and the dogs should have learned quickly to escape the electric shocks simply by jumping the barrier. Surprisingly, the dogs did not do so; they simply suffered as many shocks as the experimenter chose to deliver *as if* escape were impossible. Another group of dogs, the control group, had not previously experienced the inescapable shock. They quickly learned to jump the barrier when the warning signal sounded and thus to escape the shock. Seligman reported that the dogs experiencing the inescapable shock were less active than normal, suffered loss of appetite, and showed other symptoms resembling those of depression.

Seligman (1975) later reasoned that humans who have suffered painful experiences they could neither avoid nor escape may also experience learned helplessness. Then, having experienced helplessness, they may simply give up and react to disappointment in life by becoming inactive, withdrawn, and depressed (Seligman, 1991).

Applications of Operant Conditioning

What are some applications of operant conditioning?

Operant conditioning has numerous applications, from training animals, to biofeedback, to behavior modification.

The principles of operant conditioning are used effectively to train animals that help physically challenged people lead more independent lives. Dogs and monkeys have been trained to help people who are paralyzed or confined to wheelchairs, and of course, for years, seeing-eye dogs have been trained to assist the blind.

Through the use of shaping, animals at zoos, circuses, and marine parks have been conditioned to perform a wide range of amazing feats. After conditioning thousands of animals from over 38 different species to perform numerous feats for advertising and entertainment purposes, Breland and Breland (1961) concluded that biological predispositions in various species can affect how easily responses can be learned. When an animal's instinctual behavior runs counter to the behavior being conditioned, the animal will eventually resume its instinctual behavior, a phenomenon known as *instinctual drift*. For example, picking up coins and depositing them in a bank is a task that runs counter to the natural tendencies of raccoons and pigs. In time, a raccoon will hold the coins and rub them together instead of dropping them in the bank, and the pigs will drop them on the ground and push them with their snouts.

Internal responses such as heart rate, brain-wave patterns, and blood flow can be subject to operant conditioning. When people are given very precise feedback about these internal processes, they can learn, with practice, to exercise control over them. **Biofeedback** is a way of getting information about internal biological states. Biofeedback devices have sensors that can monitor slight changes in these internal responses and then amplify and convert them into visual or auditory signals. Thus, people can *see* or *hear* evidence of internal physiological processes, and by trying out various strategies (thoughts, feelings, or images), they can learn which ones routinely increase, decrease, or maintain a particular level of activity.

Biofeedback has been used to regulate heart rate and to control migraine and tension headaches, gastrointestinal disorders, asthma, anxiety tension states, epilepsy, sexual dysfunctions, and neuromuscular disorders such as cerebral palsy, spinal-cord injuries, and stroke (Kalish, 1981; Miller, 1989; Miller, 1985).

Behavior modification is a method of changing behavior through a systematic program based on the principles of learning—classical conditioning, operant conditioning, or observational learning (which we will discuss soon). Most behavior modification programs use the principles of operant conditioning.

Many institutions—schools, mental hospitals, homes for youthful offenders, prisons—have used behavior modification programs, with varying degrees of success. Institutions are well suited to the use of such techniques because they provide a restricted environment where the consequences of behavior can be more strictly controlled. Some institutions such as prisons or mental hospitals use a **token economy**—a program that motivates socially desirable behavior by reinforcing it with tokens. The tokens (poker chips or coupons) may later be exchanged for desired goods like candy or cigarettes and privileges such as weekend passes, free time, or participation in desired activities. People in the program know in advance exactly what behaviors will be reinforced and how they will be reinforced. Token economies have been used effectively in mental hospitals to encourage patients to attend to grooming, to interact with other patients, and to carry out housekeeping tasks (Ayllon & Azrin, 1965, 1968). Although the positive behaviors generally stop when the tokens are discontinued, this does not mean that the programs are not worthwhile. After all, most people who are employed would probably quit their jobs if they were no longer paid.

Many classroom teachers and parents use *time out*—a behavior modification technique in which a child who is misbehaving is removed for a short time from sources of positive reinforcement. (Remember, according to operant conditioning, a behavior that is no longer reinforced will extinguish.)

Behavior modification is also used successfully in business and industry to increase profits and to modify employee behavior related to health, safety, and learning. In order to keep their premiums down, some companies give annual rebates to employees who do not use up the deductibles in their health insurance plan. To reduce costs associated with automobile accidents and auto theft, insurance companies offer incentives in the form of reduced premiums for installing airbags and burglar alarm systems. Many companies promote sales by giving salespeople bonuses, trips, and other prizes for increasing sales. Behavior modification is also used in the

With biofeedback devices, people can see or hear evidence of internal physiological states and learn how to control them through various mental strategies.

avoidance learning: Learning to avoid events or conditions associated with dreaded or aversive outcomes.

learned helplessness: The learned response of resigning oneself passively to aversive conditions, rather than taking action to change, escape, or avoid them; learned through repeated exposure to inescapable or unavoidable aversive events.

biofeedback: The use of sensitive equipment to give people precise feedback about internal physiological processes so that they can learn, with practice, to exercise control over them.

behavior modification: The systematic application of the learning principles of operant conditioning, classical conditioning, or observational learning to individuals or groups in order to eliminate undesirable behavior and/or encourage desirable behavior.

token economy: A program that motivates and reinforces socially acceptable behaviors with tokens that can be exchanged for desired items or privileges.

cognitive processes (COG-nuh-tiv): Mental processes such as thinking, knowing, problem solving, and remembering.

insight: The sudden realization of the relationship between elements in a problem situation, which makes the solution apparent.

latent learning: Learning that occurs without apparent reinforcement but that is not demonstrated until sufficient reinforcement is provided.

What is insight, and how does it affect learning?

Link It!

What is latent learning?

treatment of psychological problems ranging from phobias to addictive behaviors. In this context, behavior modification is called *behavior therapy*, which is discussed in Chapter 13.

COGNITIVE LEARNING

Behaviorists such as Skinner and Watson believed that learning through operant and classical conditioning could be explained without reference to internal mental processes. Today, however, a growing number of psychologists stress the role of mental processes. They choose to broaden the study of learning to include such **cognitive processes** as thinking, knowing, problem solving, remembering, and forming mental representations. According to cognitive theorists, these processes are critically important in a more complete, more comprehensive view of learning.

We will consider the work of three important researchers in the field of cognitive learning: Wolfgang Köhler, Edward Tolman, and Albert Bandura.

Learning by Insight: Aha! Now I Get It

Wolfgang Köhler (1887–1967), a German psychologist, studied anthropoid apes and became convinced that they behaved intelligently and were capable of problem solving. In his book *The Mentality of Apes* (1925), Köhler describes experiments he conducted on chimpanzees confined in caged areas.

In one experiment, Köhler hung a bunch of bananas inside the caged area but overhead, out of reach of the apes; boxes and sticks were left around the cage. Köhler observed the chimps' unsuccessful attempts to reach the bananas by jumping up or swinging sticks at them. Eventually the chimps solved the problem by piling the boxes one on top of the other until they could reach the bananas.

In another experiment, Sultan, the brightest of the chimps, was given one short stick; beyond reach outside the cage was a longer stick and a bunch of bananas. After failing to reach the bananas with the short stick, Sultan used it to drag the long stick within reach. Then, finding that the long stick did not reach the bananas, Sultan finally solved the problem by fitting the two sticks together to form one long stick. With this stick, he successfully retrieved the bananas.

Köhler observed that the chimps sometimes appeared to give up in their attempts to get the bananas. However, they often returned later and came up with the solution to the problem as if it had come to them in a flash of **insight**. They seemed to have suddenly discovered the relationship between the sticks or boxes and the bananas. Köhler insisted that insight, rather than trial-and-error learning, accounted for the chimps' successes, because they could easily repeat the solution and transfer this learning to similar problems. In human terms, a solution gained through insight is more easily learned, less likely to be forgotten, and more readily transferred to new problems than solutions learned through rote memorization (Rock & Palmer, 1990).

Latent Learning and Cognitive Maps: I Might Use That Later

Like Köhler, Edward Tolman (1886–1959) held views that differed from the prevailing ideas on learning. First, Tolman (1932) believed that learning could take place without reinforcement. Second, he differentiated between learning and performance. He maintained that **latent learning** could occur, that is, learning could occur without apparent reinforcement but not be demonstrated until the organism was motivated to do so. The following experiment by Tolman and Honzik (1930) supports this position.

Three groups of rats were placed in a maze daily for 17 days. The first group always received a food reward at the end of the maze. The second group never received a reward, and the third group did not receive a food reward until the 11th day. The first group showed a steady improvement in performance over the 17-day period. The second group showed slight, gradual improvement. The third group, after being rewarded on the 11th day, showed a marked improvement the next day and from then on, outperforming the rats that had been rewarded daily. The rapid improvement of the third group indicated to Tolman that latent learning had occurred—that the rats had actually learned the maze during the first 11 days.

Skinner was still in graduate school in 1930, when Tolman provided this exception to a basic principle of operant conditioning—that reinforcement is required for learning new behavior. The rats in the learning group *did* learn something before reinforcement and without exhibiting any evidence of learning by overt, observable behavior. But what did they learn? Tolman concluded that the rats had learned to form a **cognitive map**, a mental representation or picture, of the maze but had not demonstrated their learning until they were reinforced. In later studies, Tolman showed how rats quickly learn to rearrange learned cognitive maps and find their way through increasingly complex mazes with ease.

The very notion of explaining the rats' behavior with the concept of cognitive maps is counter to Skinner's most deeply held belief—that mental processes do not explain the causes of behavior. But the concepts of cognitive maps and latent learning have a far more important place in psychology today than was true in Tolman's lifetime. They provide a cognitive perspective on operant conditioning.

Observational Learning: Watching and Learning

In the earlier discussion of operant conditioning, we saw how people and other animals learn by directly experiencing the consequences, positive or negative, of their behavior. But must people experience rewards and punishment firsthand in order to learn? Not according to Albert Bandura (1986), who contends that many behaviors or responses are acquired through observational learning. **Observational learning**, sometimes called **modeling**, results when people observe the behavior of others and note the consequences of that behavior.

The person who demonstrates a behavior or whose behavior is imitated is called the **model**. Parents, movie stars, and sports personalities are often powerful models. The effectiveness of a model is related to his or her status, competence, and power. Other important factors are the age, sex, attractiveness, and ethnicity of the model. Whether learned behavior is actually performed depends largely on whether the observed models are rewarded or punished for their behavior and whether the observer expects to be rewarded for the behavior (Bandura, 1969, 1977).

People may find their inhibitions decreasing or disappearing entirely as a result of observing the behavior of others. Adolescents can lose whatever resistance they may have to drinking, drug use, or sexual activity by seeing or hearing about peers engaging in these behaviors. There is often an overwhelming tendency to conform to the behavior and accept the values of the peer group. But inhibitions can also be strengthened through observational learning. A person does not need to experience the unfortunate consequences of dangerous behavior to avoid it.

Fears, too, can be acquired through observational learning. Muris and others (1996) found that children whose mothers expressed fears of animals, injuries, or medical problems or procedures had significantly higher levels of fear than children whose mothers did not express such fears. Conversely, children who see "a parent or peer behaving nonfearfully in a potentially fear-producing situation may be 'immunized'" to feeling fear when confronting a similar frightening situation later (Basic Behavioral Science Task Force, 1996, p. 139). And observational learning is not restricted to humans. Monkeys, for example, learn specific fears by observing other monkeys (Cook et al., 1985). An octopus can learn some responses by observing others of its species (Fiorito & Scotto, 1992), and so can pigeons (Zeutall et al., 1996).

cognitive map: A mental representation of a spatial arrangement such as a maze.

observational learning: Learning by observing the behavior of others and the consequences of that behavior; learning by imitation.

modeling: Another name for observational learning.

model: The individual who demonstrates a behavior or serves as an example in observational learning.

What is observational learning?

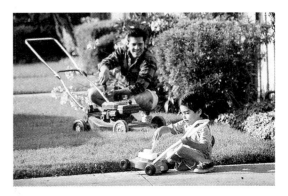

Children can learn effectively by observing and imitating others.

Apply what you know about the three basic types of learning to do the *Try It!*

Think about everything you did yesterday from the time you woke up until the time you went to sleep. List ten behaviors, and indicate whether observational learning (OL), operant conditioning (OC), and/or classical conditioning (CC) played some role in the acquisition and maintenance of each behavior. Remember, a behavior might originally have been learned by some combination of the three types of learning and then maintained by one or more of the types.

You probably learned how to brush your teeth through a combination of observational learning (watching a parent demonstrate how to brush) and operant conditioning (receiving praise as you improved—shaping).

Tooth brushing behavior may be maintained through operant conditioning, specifically negative reinforcement (getting rid of the bad taste in your mouth).

Which kind of learning had the most checks on your chart?

Behavior	Acquired through:			Maintained through:		
	OL	OC	CC	OL	OC	CC
Brushing teeth	X	X			X	

Learning Aggression: Copying What We See   Albert Bandura suspected that aggressive behavior is particularly subject to observational learning and that aggression and violence on television programs, including cartoons, tend to increase aggression in children. His pioneering work has greatly influenced current thinking on these issues. In several classic experiments, Bandura demonstrated how children are influenced by exposure to aggressive models.

One study involved three groups of preschool children. Children in one group individually observed an adult model punching, kicking, and hitting a 5-foot inflated plastic "Bobo Doll" with a mallet, while uttering aggressive phrases (Bandura et al., 1961, p. 576). Children in the second group observed a nonaggressive model who ignored the Bobo Doll and sat quietly assembling Tinker Toys. The control group was placed in the same setting with no adult present. Later, each child was observed through a one-way mirror. Children exposed to the aggressive model imitated much of the aggression and engaged in significantly more nonimitative aggression than either of the other groups. Children who had observed the nonaggressive model showed less aggressive behavior than the control group.

A further study compared the degree of aggression in children following exposure to (1) a live aggressive model, (2) a filmed version of the episode, and (3) a film depicting a cartoon character using the same aggressive behaviors in a fantasylike setting (Bandura et al., 1963). A control group was not exposed to any of the three situations of aggression. The groups exposed to aggressive models used significantly more aggression than the control group. The researchers concluded that "of the three experimental conditions, exposure to humans on film portraying aggression was the most influential in eliciting and shaping aggressive behavior" (p. 7).

Bandura's research provided the impetus for studying the effects of televised violence and aggression in both cartoons and regular programming. Although there has been some consciousness raising about the negative impact of media violence, the amount of television violence is still excessive. The problem is compounded by the fact that the average family watches more than 7 hours of television each day. Watching excessive violence gives people an exaggerated view of the pervasiveness of violence in society, while making them less sensitive to the victims of violence.

Media violence also encourages aggressive behavior in children by portraying aggression as an acceptable and effective way to solve problems and by teaching new forms of aggression (Wood et al., 1991). But just as children imitate the aggressive behavior they observe on television, they also imitate the prosocial, or helping, behavior they observe. Programs like *Mister Rogers' Neighborhood* and *Sesame Street* have been found to have a positive influence on children.

Apparently many avenues of learning are available to humans and other animals. Luckily, people's capacity to learn seems practically unlimited. Certainly advances in civilization could not have been achieved without the ability to learn.

Apply It!

How to Win the Battle against Procrastination

"So much to do, and so little time to do it in." How often have you thought that you could accomplish a great deal more if only you had more time? Such a thought is as appealing as it is irrational. Instead of wishing for the impossible, it makes more sense to use the time you *do* have wisely. And your only hope for using your time more wisely is to learn how to overcome the greatest time waster of all—procrastination.

You can use behavior modification techniques to systematically apply the following suggestions for avoiding procrastination:

- *Identify the environmental cues that habitually interfere with your studying.* What competing interests are most likely to cause you to put off or interrupt your studying? Television, sleeping, snacking, talking on the phone, visiting friends or family members?

- *Choose a good work environment.* Select a place to study that you associate only with studying, preferably away from the distracting environmental cues you have identified.

- *Schedule your study time.* Schedule your study time in advance so that your decisions about when to start work will not be ruled by the whim of the moment.

- *Get started.* The most difficult part is getting started. Give yourself an extra reward for starting on time and, perhaps, a penalty for not starting on time. Let the clock rather than your mood be the signal to begin studying.

- *Use visualization.* Visualizing the consequences of *not* studying can be an effective tool for combating procrastination. Suppose that you are considering going out of town with friends for the weekend instead of studying for a midterm test on Monday. Picture this! You walk into the classroom Monday morning unprepared; you know the answers to very few questions; you flunk the test. Now visualize the outcome if you stay home for the weekend and study. Picture how much better you will feel as you breeze through the test on Monday and get a good grade.

- *Become better at estimating how long it takes to complete an assignment.* Estimate how long it will take to complete an assignment, and then keep track of how long it actually takes. If you habitually underestimate the time involved, begin scheduling longer periods of time to accomplish your work.

- *Beware of jumping to another task when you reach a difficult part of an assignment.* This is a procrastination tactic designed to give you the feeling that you are busy and accomplishing something, but it is, nevertheless, an avoidance tactic.

- *Beware of preparation overkill.* Procrastinators may spend hours preparing for the task rather than working on the task itself. They may gather enough materials in the library to write a book rather than a five-page term paper. This enables them to postpone writing the paper.

- *Keep a record of the reasons you give yourself for postponing study-* ing or completing important assignments. If a favorite rationalization is "I'll wait until I'm in the mood to do this," count the number of times in a week you are seized with the desire to study. The mood to study typically arrives after you begin, not before.

- *Stop believing your own promises.* All too often procrastinators break their own promises to themselves. Can you relate to any of these self-promises?

"I'll do this tomorrow." Why would tomorrow be a better day? You told yourself this yesterday, and now you are not following through.

"I'll go out with my friends, but only for a few hours." As a rule, does your time with friends turn out to be a few hours or a whole day or night?

"I'll get some sleep now and set my alarm for 3:00 A.M. and then study." Are you usually able to get up at 3:00 A.M.? Is that really the ideal time for you to study?

"I'll watch TV for a few minutes and then get back to studying." Does a few minutes often turn into several hours?

"I'll rest for a few minutes and clear my mind so I can think better." Does your ability to think really improve, or do you find that you are more tired than you realized and that you need to rest longer?

Don't procrastinate! Begin today! Apply the steps outlined here to gain more control over your behavior and win the battle against procrastination.

SUMMARY AND REVIEW

CLASSICAL CONDITIONING: THE ORIGINAL VIEW

What was Pavlov's major contribution to psychology?

Pavlov's study of the conditioned reflex provided a model of learning called classical conditioning.

How was classical conditioning accomplished in Pavlov's experiments?

In Pavlov's experiments, a neutral stimulus (a tone) was presented shortly before the unconditioned stimulus (food), which naturally elicited, or brought forth, an unconditioned response (salivation). After repeated pairings, the conditioned stimulus (the tone) alone came to elicit the conditioned response (salivation).

How does extinction occur in classical conditioning?

If the conditioned stimulus (tone) is presented repeatedly without the unconditioned stimulus (food), the conditioned response (salivation) becomes progressively weaker and eventually disappears.

What is generalization?

Generalization occurs when an organism makes a conditioned response to a stimulus similar to the original conditioned stimulus.

What is discrimination in classical conditioning?

Discrimination is the ability to distinguish between similar stimuli, so that the organism makes the conditioned response only to the original conditioned stimulus.

How did Watson demonstrate that fear could be classically conditioned?

Watson showed that fear could be classically conditioned by presenting a white rat along with a loud, frightening noise, thereby conditioning Little Albert to fear the white rat.

Key Terms
stimulus (p. 133); learning (p. 133); classical conditioning (p. 133); reflex (p. 135); conditioned reflex (p. 135);

unconditioned response (p. 135); unconditioned stimulus (p. 135); conditioned stimulus (p. 135); conditioned response (p. 135); extinction (p. 136); spontaneous recovery (p. 136); generalization (p. 136); discrimination (p. 137); higher-order conditioning (p. 137)

CLASSICAL CONDITIONING: THE CONTEMPORARY VIEW

According to Rescorla, what is the critical element in classical conditioning?

The critical element in classical conditioning is whether the conditioned stimulus provides information that enables the organism to reliably predict the occurrence of the unconditioned stimulus.

What two exceptions to traditional ideas about classical conditioning did Garcia and Koelling find?

The fact that rats formed an association between nausea and the flavored water ingested several hours earlier was an exception to the principle that the conditioned stimulus must be presented shortly before the unconditioned stimulus. The finding that rats associated electric shock only with noise and light and nausea only with flavored water proved that associations cannot be readily conditioned between any two stimuli.

What types of responses can be acquired through classical conditioning?

Types of responses acquired through classical conditioning include positive and negative emotional responses (including likes, dislikes, fears, and phobias), drug cravings in former drug users, and conditioned immune responses.

What are four factors that influence classical conditioning?

Four factors influencing classical conditioning are (1) the number of pairings of conditioned stimulus and unconditioned stimulus, (2) the intensity of the unconditioned stimulus, (3) how reliably the conditioned stimulus predicts the unconditioned stimulus, and (4)

the temporal relationship between the conditioned stimulus and the unconditioned stimulus.

Key Term
taste aversion (p. 140)

OPERANT CONDITIONING

What was Thorndike's major contribution to psychology?

Thorndike formulated the law of effect, which was the conceptual starting point for Skinner's work on operant conditioning.

What was Skinner's major contribution to psychology?

Skinner's major contribution to psychology was his extensive and significant research on operant conditioning.

How are responses acquired through operant conditioning?

Operant conditioning is a method for conditioning voluntary responses. The consequences of behavior are manipulated to shape a new response or to increase or decrease the frequency of an existing response.

How is shaping used to condition a response?

In shaping, rather than waiting for the desired response to be emitted, a researcher selectively reinforces successive approximations toward the desired response until the desired response is achieved.

How does extinction occur in operant conditioning?

In operant conditioning, extinction occurs when reinforcement is withheld.

What is the goal of both positive reinforcement and negative reinforcement, and how is the goal accomplished with each?

Both positive reinforcement and negative reinforcement are used to strengthen, or increase the probability of, a response. With positive reinforcement, the desired response is followed by a reward; with negative reinforcement, it is followed by the termination of an aversive stimulus.

What are the four types of schedules of reinforcement, and which schedule yields the highest response rate and the greatest resistance to extinction?

The four types of schedules of reinforcement are the fixed-ratio, variable-ratio, fixed-interval, and variable-interval schedules. A variable-ratio schedule provides the highest response rate and the most resistance to extinction.

What is the partial-reinforcement effect?

The partial-reinforcement effect is the greater resistance to extinction that occurs when responses are maintained under partial reinforcement rather than under continuous reinforcement.

What three factors, in addition to the schedule of reinforcement, influence operant conditioning?

In operant conditioning, acquisition of a response, response rate, and resistance to extinction are influenced by the magnitude of reinforcement, the immediacy of reinforcement, and the motivation of the organism.

How does punishment differ from negative reinforcement?

Punishment is used to decrease the frequency of a response; negative reinforcement is used to increase the frequency of a response.

What are some disadvantages of punishment?

Punishment generally suppresses rather than extinguishes behavior. It does not help people develop more appropriate behaviors. And punishment can cause fear, anger, hostility, and aggression in the punished person.

What three factors increase the effectiveness of punishment?

Punishment is most effective when it is given immediately after undesirable behavior, when it is consistently applied, and when it is just intense enough to suppress the behavior.

What are some applications of operant conditioning?

Applications of operant conditioning include training animals to provide entertainment or to help physically challenged people, the use of biofeedback to gain control over internal physiological processes, and the use of behavior modification techniques to eliminate undesirable behavior and/or encourage desirable behavior in individuals or groups.

Key Terms
trial-and-error learning (p. 143); law of effect (p. 144); operant conditioning (p. 144); reinforcer (p. 144); shaping (p. 144); Skinner box (p. 144); successive approximations (p. 145); extinction (p. 145); generalization (p. 146); discriminative stimulus (p. 146); reinforcement (p. 146); positive reinforcement (p. 146); negative reinforcement (p. 146); primary reinforcer (p. 147); secondary reinforcer (p. 147); continuous reinforcement (p. 147); partial reinforcement (p. 147); schedule of reinforcement (p. 147); fixed-ratio schedule (p. 147); variable-ratio schedule (p. 147); fixed-interval schedule (p. 148); variable-interval schedule (p. 148); partial-reinforcement effect (p. 149); punishment (p. 151); avoidance learning (p. 154); learned helplessness (p. 154); biofeedback (p. 155); behavior modification (p. 155); token economy (p. 155)

COGNITIVE LEARNING

What is insight, and how does it affect learning?

Insight is the sudden realization of the relationship of the elements in a problem situation that makes the solution apparent; this solution is easily learned and transferred to new problems.

What is latent learning?

Latent learning occurs without apparent reinforcement, but it is not demonstrated in the organism's performance until the organism is motivated to do so.

What is observational learning?

Observational learning is learning by observing the behavior of others (who are called models) and the consequences of that behavior.

Key Terms
cognitive processes (p. 156); insight (p. 156); latent learning (p. 156); cognitive map (p. 157); observational learning (p. 157); modeling (p. 157); model (p. 157)

Study Guide for Chapter 5

Answers to all the Study Guide questions are provided at the end of the book.

Section One: Chapter Review

1. Classical conditioning was originally researched most extensively by _____.

2. A dog's salivation in response to a musical tone is a(n) (conditioned, unconditioned) response.

3. The weakening of a conditioned response that occurs when a conditioned stimulus is presented without the unconditioned stimulus is called _____.

4. Five-year-old Jesse was bitten by his neighbor's collie. He won't go near that dog but seems to have no fear of other dogs, even other collies. Which learning process accounts for his behavior?
   a. generalization   c. extinction
   b. discrimination   d. spontaneous recovery

5. For higher-order conditioning to occur, a neutral stimulus is typically paired repeatedly with an (existing conditioned stimulus, unconditioned stimulus).

6. In Watson's experiment with Little Albert, the white rat was the (conditioned, unconditioned) stimulus, and Albert's crying when the hammer struck the steel bar was the (conditioned, unconditioned) response.

7. Albert's fear of the white rat transferred to a rabbit, a dog, a fur coat, and a mask. What learning process did this demonstrate?
   a. generalization   c. extinction
   b. discrimination   d. spontaneous recovery

8. Garcia and Koelling's research supports Pavlov's contention that almost any neutral stimulus can serve as a conditioned stimulus. (true/false)

9. Which of the following responses contradicts the general principle of classical conditioning that the unconditioned stimulus should occur immediately after the conditioned stimulus and the two should be paired repeatedly?
   a. salivation response
   b. immune response
   c. taste aversion
   d. conditioned drug cravings

10. In everyday life, which of the following are *not* acquired through classical conditioning?
   a. positive feelings   c. skills
   b. negative feelings   d. fears and phobias

11. Classical conditioning can be used to suppress or to boost the immune system. (true/false)

12. Who researched trial-and-error learning using cats in puzzle boxes and formulated the law of effect?
   a. Watson   c. Skinner
   b. Thorndike   d. Pavlov

13. Operant conditioning was researched most extensively by
   a. Watson.   c. Skinner.
   b. Thorndike.   d. Pavlov.

14. Operant conditioning can be used effectively for all of the following except
   a. learning new responses.
   b. learning to make an existing response to a new stimulus.
   c. increasing the frequency of an existing response.
   d. decreasing the frequency of an existing response.

15. Even though the B that Billy wrote looked more like a D, his teacher, Mrs. Chen, praised him because it was better than his previous attempts. Mrs. Chen is using a procedure called _____.

16. Which of the following processes occurs in operant conditioning when reinforcers are withheld?
   a. generalization   c. spontaneous recovery
   b. discrimination   d. extinction

17. Many people take aspirin to relieve painful headaches. Taking aspirin is a behavior that is likely to continue because of the effect of (positive, negative) reinforcement.

18. (Partial, Continuous) reinforcement is most effective in conditioning a new response; once a response is acquired (partial, continuous) reinforcement results in greater resistance to extinction.

19. Jennifer and Ashley are both employed raking leaves. Jennifer is paid $1 for each bag of leaves she rakes; Ashley is paid $4 per hour. Jennifer is paid according to the _____ schedule; Ashley is paid according to the _____ schedule.
   a. fixed-interval; fixed-ratio
   b. variable-ratio; fixed-interval

c. variable-ratio; variable-interval
d. fixed-ratio; fixed-interval

20. Which schedule of reinforcement yields the highest response rate and the greatest resistance to extinction?
    a. variable-ratio schedule
    b. fixed-ratio schedule
    c. variable-interval schedule
    d. fixed-interval schedule

21. Danielle's parents have noticed that she has been making her bed every day, and they would like this to continue. Because they understand the partial-reinforcement effect, they will want to reward her *every* time she makes the bed. (true/false)

22. Recall what you have learned about classical and operant conditioning. Which of the following is descriptive of operant conditioning?
    a. An association is formed between a response and its consequence.
    b. The responses acquired are usually emotional reactions.
    c. The subject is usually passive.
    d. The response acquired is usually an involuntary or reflexive response.

23. Punishment is roughly the same as negative reinforcement. (true/false)

24. Punishment usually does *not* extinguish undesirable behavior. (true/false)

25. Depending on the circumstances, avoidance learning can be either adaptive or maladaptive. (true/false)

26. Victims of spousal abuse who have repeatedly failed to escape or avoid the abuse may eventually passively resign themselves to it, a condition known as _____ _____.

27. Using sensitive electronic equipment to monitor physiological processes in order to bring them under conscious control is called
    _____.

28. Applying learning principles to eliminate undesirable behavior and/or encourage desirable behavior is called _____ _____.

29. The sudden realization of the relationship between the elements in a problem situation that results in the solution to the problem is called (latent learning, insight).

30. Learning that is not demonstrated until one is motivated to perform the behavior is called
    a. learning by insight.
    b. observational learning.
    c. classical conditioning.
    d. latent learning.

31. Hayley has been afraid of snakes for as long as she can remember, and her mother has the same paralyzing fear. Hayley most likely acquired her fear through
    a. learning by insight.
    b. observational learning.
    c. classical conditioning.
    d. latent learning.

32. Match the researcher with the subject(s) researched.
    ____ (1) Edward Tolman
    ____ (2) Albert Bandura
    ____ (3) Wolfgang Kohler
    a. observational learning
    b. cognitive maps
    c. learning by insight
    d. latent learning

Section Two: Identify the Concept

In the blank following each statement below, list the learning principle illustrated by the statement.

1. Ben continues to play a slot machine even though he never knows when it will pay off. _____

2. Alice watched a movie about tornadoes and is now afraid of bad storms. _____

3. Joey is crying and asking for a candy bar. His mother gives in because doing so will make him stop crying for now—but Joey will most likely behave this way again. _____

4. Jan got sick eating lasagna and now never eats food containing tomato sauce. _____

5. Helen washed the dinner dishes, and her mother allowed her to watch television for 30 extra minutes that evening. _____

6. Sarah's parents are advised to stop paying attention to her crying when it is time for bed and instead ignore it. _____

7. Frank is paid for his factory job once every two weeks. _____

8. Marty is scolded for running into the road and never does it again. _____

9. Ellen watches her lab partner mix the chemicals and set up the experiment. She then repeats the same procedure and completes her assignment. _____

10. Through associations with such things as food and shelter, pieces of green paper with pictures of past U.S. presidents on them become very powerful reinforcers. _____

11. Although he studied the problem, Jack did not seem to be able to figure out the correct way to reconnect the pipes under the sink. He took a break before he became too frustrated. Later he returned and immediately saw how to do it. _____

Section Three: Fill In the Blank

1. Classical conditioning is based on the association between _____, and operant conditioning is based on the association between a _____ and its _____.

2. _____ is a relatively permanent change in behavior, knowledge, capability, or attitude that is acquired through experience and cannot be attributed to illness, injury, or maturation.

3. Ed feeds the horses on his ranch every day at the same time. He notices that the horses now run to their feed troughs and whinny as if they know dinner is on its way as soon as they hear his truck coming up the drive. In this example, the conditioned stimulus is _____.

4. In question 3, the unconditioned stimulus is _____.

5. The unconditioned response of Pavlov's dogs was _____.

6. In Pavlov's classic experiment, the bell was originally a(n) _____ stimulus.

7. To get coyotes to stop eating sheep, ranchers poison sheep carcasses in the hope that coyotes that eat the carcasses will get sick enough to avoid eating sheep from that point on. The ranchers hope that the coyotes will avoid all types and sizes of sheep—which is an example of _____ in classical conditioning.

8. The ranchers in question 7 also hope that the coyotes will be able to distinguish between sheep and other more appropriate sources of food. This is an example of _____ in classical conditioning.

9. Jimmy loved eating at a certain fast-food restaurant. After a while even the giant logo sign in front of the restaurant would make him hungry every time he saw it. The restaurant ran a TV ad showing a clown standing by the logo sign. Pretty soon, every time Jimmy saw a clown, he became hungry. Jimmy's responses are examples of _____ _____ conditioning.

10. If Watson had wanted to extinguish Little Albert's conditioned fear of white furry things, he would have presented the _____ stimulus without presenting the _____ stimulus.

11. The law of _____, developed by _____, states that a response that is followed by a satisfying consequence will tend to be repeated, while a response followed by discomfort will tend to be weakened.

12. Since researchers cannot tell rats to press the bar in a Skinner box for food or have them read "The Skinner Box Owner's Manual," they must initiate the bar-pressing response by rewarding _____ _____, an approach known as *shaping*.

13. Reinforcement is any event that follows a response and increases the probability of the response. _____ reinforcement involves the removal of a stimulus and _____ reinforcement involves the presentation of a stimulus.

14. You're driving on an interstate highway and suddenly notice that you've been going 80 miles per hour without realizing it. Immediately after you slow down, you see the flashing light of a state police car, and you know you're about to be pulled over. In this case the flashing light is a _____ stimulus.

15. Food is considered a _____ reinforcer; money is considered a _____ reinforcer.

16. If you were going to train a rat to press a bar for food, you would probably use _____ reinforcement for the initial training period and a _____-reinforcement schedule to strengthen the learned bar-pressing behavior.

17. Using learning theory in a therapeutic setting to help people overcome phobias or bad habits such as smoking is called _____ therapy.

Section Four: Comprehensive Practice Test

1. Pavlov is associated with
   a. classical conditioning.
   b. operant conditioning.
   c. cognitive conditioning.
   d. Watsonian conditioning.

2. This theorist believed that the causes of behavior are in the environment and that inner mental events are themselves shaped by environmental forces.
   a. Bandura   c. Skinner
   b. Pavlov   d. Tolman

3. Which of the following theorists developed the concepts of latent learning and cognitive mapping?
   a. Pavlov   c. Tolman
   b. Kohler   d. Skinner

4. This theorist researched observational learning and the effects of modeling on behavior.
   a. Kohler   c. Skinner
   b. Thorndike   d. Bandura

5. Which of the following is associated with research on reinforcement theory?
   a. Pavlov   c. Tolman
   b. Skinner   d. Bandura

6. The concept that is associated with cognitive learning is
   a. negative reinforcement.
   b. positive reinforcement.
   c. latent learning.
   d. the discriminative stimulus.

7. Jim has been sober since he completed a treatment program for alcoholics. He was told to stay away from his old drinking places. The danger is that he may start drinking again as a result of the conditioned stimuli in those environments. If he did, it would be a practical example of _____ in classical conditioning.
   a. extinction
   b. spontaneous recovery
   c. stimulus generalization
   d. observational response sets

8. The seductive nature of a slot machine in a gambling casino is based on its _____ schedule of reinforcement.

   a. continuous   c. variable-ratio
   b. fixed-interval d. variable-interval

9. For Little Albert, the conditioned stimulus was
   a. the white rat.
   b. a loud noise.
   c. Watson.
   d. based on negative reinforcement.

10. Positive reinforcement increases behavior; negative reinforcement
    a. decreases behavior.
    b. has no effect on behavior.
    c. removes a behavior.
    d. also increases behavior.

11. A good example of a fixed-interval schedule of reinforcement is
    a. factory piece work.
    b. a child's weekly allowance.
    c. a slot machine.
    d. turning on a light switch.

12. The nice thing about continuous reinforcement is that it creates a behavior that is very resistant to extinction. (true/false)

13. Drug tolerance and taste aversion are real-world examples of
    a. operant conditioning.
    b. classical conditioning.
    c. observational learning.
    d. cognitive mapping.

14. A major league pitcher accidentally laced his right shoe incorrectly prior to a big game, during which he pitched the best game of his career. From that day forward, he made sure to lace his right shoe in the same incorrect way before each game, believing that would make him pitch better. This is an example of
    a. generalization.   c. superstition.
    b. latent learning.   d. spontaneous recovery.

15. In _____ learning, a person or animal learns a response that _____ a negative reinforcer.
    a. escape; prevents the occurrence of
    b. escape; terminates   *(continued)*

c. avoidance; terminates
d. avoidance; initiates

16. Ms. Doe, a new teacher, is having a difficult time with her misbehaving second graders. When the principal enters the room, the children behave like perfect angels. In this case, the principal may be thought of as a(n)
a. positive reinforcer.
b. unconditioned stimulus.
c. shaping reinforcer.
d. discriminative stimulus.

17. According to Tolman, _____ _____ is defined as learning that occurs without apparent reinforcement but is not demonstrated until the organism is motivated to do so.
a. classical conditioning   c. latent learning
b. modeling behavior   d. cognitive mapping

18. Skinner asserted that classical conditioning is based on unconscious motivation while operant conditioning is based on conscious control of emotions. (true/false)

Section Five: Critical Thinking

1. Outline the strengths and limitations of classical conditioning, operant conditioning, and observational learning in explaining how behaviors are acquired and maintained.

2. The use of behavior modification has been a source of controversy among psychologists and others. Prepare arguments supporting each of these positions:
a. Behavior modification should be used in society to shape the behavior of others.
b. Behavior modification should not be used in society to shape the behavior of others.

3. Think of a behavior of a friend, family member, or professor that you would like to change. Using what you know about classical conditioning, operant conditioning, and observational learning, formulate a detailed plan for changing the behavior of the target person.

6 *Memory*

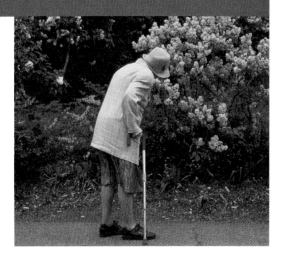

n a bizarre case involving eyewitness testimony, Australian psychologist Donald Thompson was saved by the fact that a person cannot be in two places at once. One night, Thompson was a guest with other experts, including a chief of police, on an Australian talk show about eyewitness testimony. Thompson argued that eyewitness testimony is rarely reliable, because few eyewitnesses notice and remember specific features of a face. Later, a woman who had been assaulted and raped while watching him on the show identified Thompson as the rapist. Fortunately for Thompson, the show had been broadcast live, and he had many witnesses to support his alibi. It turns out that his accuser had remembered Thompson's face rather than the face of her attacker.

Does this case simply reflect the rare and unusual in human memory, or are memory errors common occurrences? This and many other questions you may have about memory will be answered in this chapter. We will look closely at three memory systems: sensory, short-term, and long-term. You will learn how much information each system holds, for how long, and in what form. Is memory like a video cassette recorder, in which the sights and sounds we experience are captured intact and simply played back in exact detail? Or do we "reconstruct" the past when we remember, leaving out certain bits and pieces of events that actually happened and adding others that did not?

REMEMBERING

Memory is the storehouse for everything we know. It enables us to know who and where we are when we awaken each morning. Memory provides the continuity of life—the long thread to which are tied our joys and sorrows, knowledge and skills, triumphs and failures, and the people and places of our lives.

Most current efforts to understand human memory have been conducted within a framework known as the *information-processing approach* (Klatzky, 1984). This approach makes use of modern computer science and related fields to provide models that help psychologists understand the processes involved in memory.

The Three Processes in Memory: Encoding, Storage, and Retrieval

What three processes are involved in the act of remembering?

What must occur to enable you to remember a friend's name, a fact from history, or an incident from your past? The act of remembering requires the successful completion of three processes: encoding, storage, and retrieval. The first process, **encoding**, involves transforming information into a form that can be stored in memory. Sometimes we encode information automatically, without any effort, but often we must do something with the information in order to remember it. For example, if you met someone named Bill at a party, you might associate his name with Bill Clinton or Bill Cosby. Such simple associations can markedly improve your ability to recall names and other information. The careful encoding of information greatly increases the chance that you will remember it.

The second memory process, **storage**, involves keeping or maintaining information in memory. For encoded information to be stored, some physiological change in the brain must take place—a process called **consolidation**. Normally consolidation occurs automatically, but if a person loses consciousness for any reason, the process can be disrupted and a permanent memory may not form. That is why someone who has been in a serious car accident may awaken in a hospital and not remember what happened.

The final process, **retrieval**, occurs when information stored in memory is brought to mind. Calling Bill by name the next time you meet him shows that you have retrieved his name from memory. To remember, we must perform all three processes—encode the information, store it, and then retrieve it. Memory failure can result from the failure of any one of the three (see Figure 6.1).

Figure 6.1
The Processes Required in Remembering

The act of remembering requires successful completion of all three of these processes: encoding, storage, and retrieval.

Encoding	Storage	Retrieval
Transforming information into a form that can be stored in memory	Maintaining information in memory	Bringing stored material to mind

Figure 6.2

The Three Memory Systems

According to the Atkinson-Shiffrin model, there are three separate memory systems: sensory memory, short-term memory, and long-term memory.

Similar steps are required in the processing of information by computers. Information is encoded (entered in some form the computer is able to use), then stored on disk, and later retrieved on the screen. You would not be able to retrieve the material if you had failed to enter it, if a power failure occurred before you could save what you had entered, or if you forgot which disk or file contained the needed information. Of course, human memory is far more complex than even the most advanced computer systems, but computer processing provides a useful analogy to memory, if not taken too literally.

The Three Memory Systems: The Long and the Short of It

How are memories stored? According to one widely accepted view, the Atkinson-Shiffrin model, there are three different, interacting memory systems known as sensory, short-term, and long-term memory (Atkinson & Shiffrin, 1968; Broadbent, 1958). Considerable research in the biology of memory lends support to the model (Squire et al., 1993). We will examine each of these three memory systems, which are shown in Figure 6.2.

Link It!

Sensory Memory   As information comes in through the senses, virtually everything we see, hear, or otherwise sense is held in **sensory memory**, but only for the briefest period of time. Sensory memory normally holds visual images for a fraction of a second and sounds for about 2 seconds (Crowder, 1992). Visual sensory memory lasts just long enough to keep whatever you are viewing from disappearing when you blink your eyes.

What is sensory memory?

You can demonstrate visual sensory memory for yourself by doing the *Try It!*

Try It!   To prove the existence of visual sensory memory, move your forefinger back and forth rapidly in front of your face. You will see what appears to be the blurred images of many fingers. This occurs because your sensory memory briefly holds a trace of the various positions that your finger occupies as it moves.

Sensory memory holds a visual image, such as a lightning bolt, for a fraction of a second—just long enough for us to perceive a flow of movement.

Glance at the three rows of letters shown below for a fraction of a second and then close your eyes. How many of the items can you recall?

X B D F
M P Z G
L C N H

short-term memory: The second
stage of memory, which holds
about seven (a range of five to nine)
items for less than 30 seconds without rehearsal; working memory; the
mental workspace a person uses to
keep in mind tasks being thought
about at any given moment.

displacement: The event that
occurs when short-term memory
is holding its maximum and each
new item entering short-term memory pushes out an existing item.

Most people can recall correctly only four or five of the items when they are briefly presented. Does this indicate that visual sensory memory can hold only four or five items at a time? No. George Sperling (1960) reasoned that the human visual sensory capacity should enable a person to take in most or all of the 12 items at a single glance. Could it be that sensory memory is so short-lived that while someone is reporting some items, others have already faded from sensory memory? Sperling thought of an ingenious method to test this notion. He briefly flashed 12 items as shown above to participants. Immediately upon turning off the display, he sounded a high, medium, or low tone that signaled the participants to report *only* the top, middle, or bottom row of items. Before they heard the tone, the participants had no way of knowing which row they would have to report. Yet Sperling found that, when the participants could view the letters for $^{15}/_{1000}$ to $\frac{1}{2}$ second, they could report correctly all the items in any row nearly 100% of the time. But the items fade from sensory memory so quickly that during the time it takes to report three or four of the items, the other eight or nine have already disappeared.

Sensory memory for sound is similar to that for vision. We experience auditory sensory memory when the last few words someone has spoken leave a brief echo. Auditory sensory memory lasts about 2 seconds, compared with a fraction of a second for visual sensory memory (Klatzky, 1980).

It is clear that an abundance of information in raw, natural form can be stored briefly in sensory memory. This brief period is just long enough for a person to begin to process the sensory stimuli and to select the most important information for further processing in the second memory system—short-term memory.

What are the characteristics
of short-term memory?

Link It!

Short-Term Memory Whatever you are thinking about right now is in your **short-term memory** (STM). We use short-term memory when we carry on a conversation, solve a problem, or look up a telephone number and remember it just long enough to dial it.

Compared to sensory memory, which can hold vast amounts of information briefly, short-term memory has a very limited capacity—about seven (plus or minus two) different items or bits of information at one time. Test the capacity of your short-term memory in the *Try It!*

Try It!

Read aloud the digits in the first row (a) at a steady rate of about two per second. Then, from memory, write them down on a sheet of paper, being sure to cover up this page while you write.

Repeat the process, row by row.

a. 3 8 7 1

b. 9 6 4 7 3

c. 1 8 3 0 5 2

d. 8 0 6 5 9 1 7

e. 5 2 9 7 3 1 2 5

f. 2 7 4 0 1 9 6 8 3

g. 3 9 1 6 5 8 4 5 1 7

How well did you do in the *Try It*? Most people recall about seven items. This is just enough for phone numbers and ordinary zip codes. (Nine-digit zip codes strain the capacity of most people.) When short-term memory is filled to capacity, **displacement** can occur. In displacement, each new, incoming item pushes out an existing item, which is then forgotten.

One way to overcome the limitation of seven or so bits of information is to use a technique that George A. Miller (1956) calls *chunking*—organizing or grouping separate bits of information into larger units, or chunks. A *chunk* is an easily identifiable unit such as a syllable, a word, an acronym, or a number (Cowan, 1988). For example, the numbers 5 2 9 7 3 1 2 5 can be chunked as 52 97 31 25, leaving the short-term memory with the easier task of dealing with four chunks of information rather than eight separate bits. Complete the *Try It!* and see if chunking works for you.

Chunking is a very useful technique for increasing the capacity of short-term memory, but there are limits. Simon (1974) suggests that the larger the chunk, the fewer chunks we can remember.

Items in short-term memory are lost very quickly, in less than 30 seconds, unless we repeat them over and over to ourselves, silently or out loud, to retain them (Peterson & Peterson, 1959). This process is known as **rehearsal.** People rehearse telephone numbers that they have looked up to keep them in short-term memory long enough to dial the number. But short-term memory is easily disrupted. It is so fragile, in fact, that an interruption or a distraction can cause information to be lost in just a few seconds.

Allan Baddeley (1990, 1992, 1995) is of the opinion that "working memory" is a more fitting term than short-term memory. More than just a temporary way station between sensory memory and long-term memory, working memory is a kind of mental workspace that temporarily holds incoming information from sensory memory or information retrieved from long-term memory for performing some conscious cognitive task.

> Without it you couldn't understand this sentence, add up a restaurant tab in your head, or find your way home. . . . Working memory is . . . an erasable mental blackboard that allows you to hold briefly in your mind and manipulate the information—whether it be words, menu prices, or a map of your surroundings—essential for comprehension, reasoning, and planning. (Wickelgren, 1997, p. 1580)

Recent research shows that the prefrontal cortex is the primary area responsible for working memory (Courtney et al., 1997; Rao et al., 1997).

Long-Term Memory Some information from short-term memory makes its way into long-term memory. **Long-term memory** (LTM) is a person's vast storehouse of permanent or relatively permanent memories. There are no known limits to the storage capacity of long-term memory, and long-term memories last a long time, some of them for a lifetime. When people talk about memory in everyday conversation, they are usually referring to long-term memory. Long-term memory holds all the knowledge we have accumulated, the skills we have acquired, and the memories of our past experiences.

But how does this vast store of information make its way from short-term memory into long-term memory? People seem to remember some information with ease, almost automatically, but other kinds of material require great effort. Sometimes, through mere repetition or rehearsal, a person is able to transfer information into long-term memory. Your teachers may have used drill to try to cement the multiplication tables and other material in your long-term memory. This rote rehearsal, however, is not usually the best way to transfer information to long-term memory (Craik & Watkins, 1973). For better results, try **elaborative rehearsal**. Consider the meaning of new information and relate it to information already in your long-term memory, information about yourself whenever possible (Symons & Johnson, 1997). Forming multiple associations will increase your chance of retrieving the new information later.

Figure 6.3 (on page 172) summarizes the three memory systems.

Read the following letters individually at the rate of about one per second and then see if you can repeat them.

> N-F L-C-B S-U-S
> A-V-C R-F-B I

Did you have difficulty? Probably so, because there are 15 different letters.
Now try this:

> NFL CBS USA VCR FBI

Did you find that five chunks are easier to remember than 15 separate items?

What is long-term memory, and what are its subsystems?

rehearsal: The act of purposely repeating information to maintain it in short-term memory or to transfer it to long-term memory.

long-term memory: The relatively permanent memory system with a virtually unlimited capacity.

elaborative rehearsal: A technique used to encode information into long-term memory by considering its meaning and associating it with other information already stored in long-term memory.

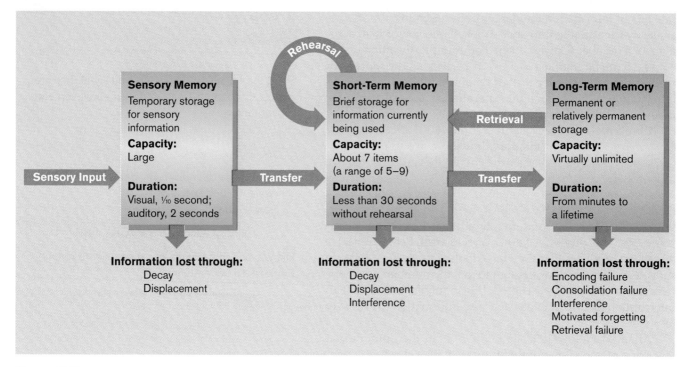

Figure 6.3

Characteristics of and Processes Involved in the Three Memory Systems

The three memory systems differ in what and how much they hold and for how long they store it. (From Peterson & Peterson, 1959.)

Some experts believe that there are two main subsystems within long-term memory—declarative memory and nondeclarative memory.

Declarative memory (also called *explicit memory*) stores facts, information, and personal life events that can be brought to mind verbally or in the form of images and then declared or stated. It holds information you can intentionally and consciously recollect. There are two types of declarative memory—episodic memory and semantic memory.

Episodic memory is the subpart of declarative memory that contains the memory of events as they have been subjectively experienced (Wheeler et al., 1997). It is somewhat like a mental diary, recording the episodes of your life—the people you have known, the places you have seen, and the personal experiences you have had.

Semantic memory, the second subpart of declarative memory, is memory for general knowledge, or objective facts and information. In other words, semantic

Declarative memory stores facts, information, and personal life events, such as a trip to a foreign country. Nondeclarative memory encompasses motor skills, such as the movements of figure skating, which once learned can be carried out with little or no conscious effort.

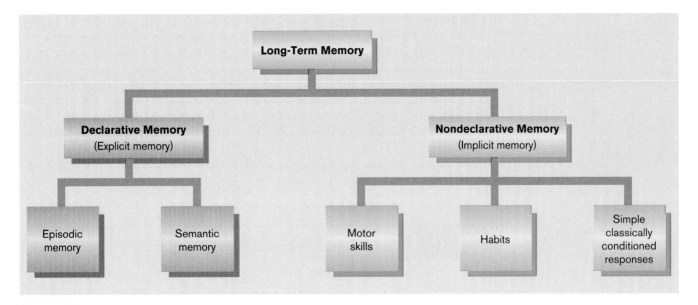

Figure 6.4

Subsystems of Long-Term Memory

Declarative memory can be divided into two subparts—episodic memory, which stores memories of personally experienced events, and semantic memory, which stores facts and information. Nondeclarative memory consists of motor skills acquired through repetitive practice, habits, and simple classically conditioned responses.

memory is a mental dictionary or encyclopedia of stored knowledge. As a rule, the facts you have stored in semantic memory are not personally referenced to time and place as episodic memories are. You probably do not remember exactly where and when you learned to spell *dictionary* or that 10 times 10 equals 100.

Nondeclarative memory (also called *implicit memory*) consists of motor skills, habits, and simple classically conditioned responses (Squire et al., 1993). Motor skills are acquired through repetitive practice and include such things as eating with a fork, riding a bicycle, or driving a car. Although acquired slowly, once learned, these skills become habit, are quite reliable, and can be carried out with little or no conscious effort.

Associated with nondeclarative, or implicit, memory is a phenomenon known as **priming**, by which an earlier encounter with a stimulus (such as a word or a picture) increases the speed or accuracy of naming that stimulus or a related stimulus at a later time. Such improvement occurs without the person's conscious awareness of having seen or heard the stimulus. For example, a researcher might flash the word *elephant* on a computer screen so briefly that it is not consciously perceived. But if asked later to name as many animals as come to mind, the person is quite likely to include *elephant* on the list (Challis, 1996).

Priming can influence not only performance, but preferences and behavior as well. People exposed briefly (even subliminally) to pictures of abstract art showed greater preferences for that type of art than others not exposed. And in one study, participants subliminally exposed to faces of real people later interacted with those people more than individuals not exposed to the photos (Basic Behavioral Science Task Force, 1996). Unlike declarative memory, nondeclarative memory does not depend on the hippocampus (Clark & Squire, 1998).

Figure 6.4 shows the subsystems of long-term memory.

The Levels-of-Processing Model: Another View of Memory

Not all psychologists support the notion of three memory systems. Craik and Lockhart (1972) propose instead a **levels-of-processing model**. They suggest that

declarative memory: The subsystem within long-term memory that stores facts, information, and personal life experiences; also called *explicit memory*.

episodic memory (ep-ih-SOD-ik): The subpart of declarative memory that contains memories of personally experienced events.

semantic memory: The subpart of declarative memory that stores general knowledge; a mental encyclopedia or dictionary.

nondeclarative memory: The subsystem within long-term memory that consists of skills acquired through repetitive practice, habits, and simple classically conditioned responses; also called *implicit memory*.

priming: The phenomenon by which an earlier encounter with a stimulus (such as a word or a picture) increases the speed or accuracy with which that stimulus or a related stimulus can be named at a later time.

levels-of-processing model: A model of memory as a single system in which retention depends on how deeply information is processed.

whether people remember an item for a few seconds or a lifetime depends on how deeply they process the information. With the shallowest levels of processing, a person is merely aware of the incoming sensory information. Deeper processing takes place only when the person does something more with the information—forms a relationship, makes an association, or attaches meaning to a sensory impression.

Craik and Tulving (1975) tested the levels-of-processing model. They had participants answer *yes* or *no* to questions asked about words just before the words were flashed to them for ⅕ of a second. The participants had to process the words in three ways: (1) visually (is the word in capital letters?); (2) acoustically (does the word rhyme with another particular word?); and (3) semantically (does the word make sense when used in a particular sentence?). Test yourself in the *Try It!*

Try It!

1. Is the word *LARK* in capital letters? ___ Yes ___ No

2. Does the word *speech* rhyme with *sleet*? ___ Yes ___ No

3. Would the word *park* make sense in this sentence?

   The woman passed a _____ on her way to work.
   ___ Yes ___ No

Wait a few minutes and see which words you can recall.

The test required shallow processing for the first question, deeper processing for the second question, and still deeper processing for the third. Later retention tests showed that the deeper the level of processing, the higher the accuracy rate of memory. But this conclusion is equally valid for the three-system model. Recent brain-imaging studies with fMRI have revealed that semantic (deeper) encoding causes greater activity in the left prefrontal cortex (Gabrieli et al., 1996).

MEASURING MEMORY

Three Methods of Measuring Memory

What are three methods of measuring retention?

Psychologists have used three main methods to measure memory: recall, recognition, and the relearning method.

In **recall** a person must produce required information by searching memory without the help of **retrieval cues**. Trying to remember someone's name, recalling items on a shopping list, memorizing a speech or a poem word for word, and remembering appointments are all recall tasks. Test items such as essay and fill-in-the-blank questions require recall. Try to answer the following question:

The three processes involved in memory are _____, _____, and _____.

To recall, you must remember information "cold." A recall task may be made a little easier if cues are provided to jog memory. Such cues might consist of providing the first letter of the required words for fill-in-the-blank questions. If you did not recall the three terms in the first question, try again with cued recall:

The three processes involved in memory are e _____, s _____, and r _____.

recall: A measure of retention that requires a person to remember material with few or no retrieval cues, as in an essay test.

retrieval cue: Any stimulus or bit of information that aids in the retrieval of particular information from long-term memory.

Sometimes serial recall is required; that is, information must be recalled in a specific order. This is the way you learned your ABCs, memorized poems, and learned any sequences that had to be carried out in a certain order. Often serial recall is easier than free recall—recalling the items in any order—because in serial recall, each letter, word, or task may serve as a cue for the one that follows.

Recognition is exactly what the word implies. A person simply recognizes something as familiar—a face, a name, a taste, a melody. Multiple-choice, matching, and true/false questions are examples of recognition test items. Answer the following question:

> Which of the following is *not* one of the processes involved in memory?
> a. encoding   b. assimilation   c. storage   d. retrieval

Was this recognition question easier than the recall version? The main difference between recall and recognition is that a recognition task does not require you to supply the information but only to recognize it when you see it. The correct answer is included along with the other items in a recognition question.

There is yet another way to measure memory that is even more sensitive than recognition. With the **relearning method** (the savings method), retention is expressed as the percentage of time saved when material is relearned compared with the time required to learn the material originally. Suppose it took you 40 minutes to memorize a list of words, and 1 month later you were tested, using recall or recognition. If you could not recall or recognize a single word, would this mean that you had absolutely no memory of anything on the test? Or could it mean that the recall and the recognition methods of testing were not sensitive enough to pick up what little information you may have stored? How could a researcher measure a remnant of this former learning? Using the relearning method, a researcher could time how long it would take you to relearn the list of words. If it took 20 minutes to relearn the list, this would represent a 50% savings over the original learning time of 40 minutes. The percentage of time saved—the **savings score**—reflects how much material remains in long-term memory.

College students demonstrate the relearning method each semester when they study for comprehensive final exams. Relearning material for the final exams takes less time than it took to learn the material originally.

Ebbinghaus and the First Experimental Studies on Learning and Memory

Hermann Ebbinghaus (1850–1909) conducted the first experimental studies on learning and memory. Realizing that some materials are easier than others to understand and remember, Ebbinghaus was faced with the task of finding materials that would all be equally difficult to memorize. So he invented the **nonsense syllable**—a consonant-vowel-consonant combination that is not an actual word. Examples are LEJ, XIZ, LUK, and ZOH. The use of nonsense syllables largely accomplished Ebbinghaus's goal. But did you notice that some of the syllables sound more like actual words than others and would, therefore, be easier to remember?

Ebbinghaus (1885/1964) memorized lists of nonsense syllables by repeating them over and over until he could recall them twice without error, a point that he called *mastery*. Ebbinghaus recorded the amount of time or the number of trials it took to memorize his lists to mastery. After different periods of time had passed and forgetting had occurred, he recorded the amount of time or number of trials needed to relearn the same list to mastery. He then compared the time or trials required for relearning with those of the original learning and computed the percentage of time saved—the *savings score*. The percentage of savings represented the percentage of the original learning that remained in memory. His famous curve of forgetting shows that the largest amount of forgetting occurs very quickly; then forgetting gradually tapers off. If Ebbinghaus retained information as long as a day or two, very little more

recognition: A measure of retention that requires a person to identify material as familiar, or as having been encountered before.

relearning method: Measuring retention in terms of the percentage of time or learning trials saved in relearning material compared with the time required to learn it originally; also called the savings method.

savings score: The percentage of time or learning trials saved in relearning material over the amount of time or number of learning trials required for the original learning.

nonsense syllable: A consonant-vowel-consonant combination that does not spell a word; used to control for the meaningfulness of the material.

What was Ebbinghaus's major contribution to psychology?

Link It!

encoding failure: A cause of forgetting resulting from material never having been put into long-term memory.

would be forgotten even a month later. But remember, this curve of forgetting applies to nonsense syllables. Meaningful material is usually forgotten more slowly, as is material that was carefully encoded, deeply processed, and frequently rehearsed.

What Ebbinghaus learned about the rate of forgetting is relevant for everyone. Do you, like most students, cram before a big exam? If so, don't assume that everything you memorize on Monday can be held intact until Tuesday. So much forgetting occurs within the first 24 hours that it is wise to spend at least some time reviewing the material on the day of the test. The less meaningful the material is to you, the more you will forget and the more necessary a review will be.

FORGETTING

Patient: Doctor, you've got to help me. I'm sure I'm losing my memory. I hear something one minute and forget it the next. I don't know what to do!
Doctor: When did you first notice this?
Patient: Notice what?

Most people think of forgetting as a problem to be overcome, but forgetting is not all bad. Wouldn't it be depressing if you were condemned to remember in stark detail all the bad things that ever happened to you?

The Causes of Forgetting

What are six causes of forgetting?

There are many reasons why people fail to remember. Among them are encoding failure, consolidation failure, decay, interference, motivated forgetting, and retrieval failure.

Encoding and Consolidation Failures   There is a distinction between forgetting and not being able to remember. Forgetting is the inability to recall something that you could recall previously. But often when people say they cannot remember, they have not actually forgotten. The inability to remember may be a result of **encoding failure**—the information never entered long-term memory in the first place. Of the many things we encounter every day, it is surprising how little we actually encode. Can you recall accurately, or even recognize, something you have seen thousands of times before? Read the *Try It!* to find out.

In your lifetime you have seen thousands of pennies, but unless you are a coin collector, you probably have not encoded the details of a penny. If you did poorly on

Try It!   On a sheet of paper, draw a sketch of a U.S. penny from memory using recall. In your drawing, show the direction in which President Lincoln's image is facing and the location of the date, and include all the words on the "heads" side of the penny. Or try the easier recognition task and see if you can recognize the real penny in the drawings below. (From Nickersen & Adams, 1979)

A   B   C   D   E

the *Try It!*, you have plenty of company. After studying a large group of participants, Nickerson and Adams (1979) reported that few people could reproduce a penny from recall. In fact, only a handful of participants could even recognize a drawing of a real penny when it was presented along with incorrect drawings. (The correct penny is labeled A in the *Try It!*)

Consolidation is the process by which encoded information is stored in memory. When a disruption in this process occurs, a long-term memory usually does not form. **Consolidation failure** can result from anything that causes a person to lose consciousness—a car accident, a blow to the head, a grand mal seizure, or an electroconvulsive shock treatment given for severe depression. Memory loss of the experiences that occurred shortly before the loss of consciousness is called **retrograde amnesia**.

Decay   **Decay theory**, probably the oldest theory of forgetting, assumes that memories, if not used, fade with time and ultimately disappear entirely. The term *decay* implies a physiological change in the neural trace that recorded the experience. According to this theory, the neural trace may decay or fade within seconds, days, or much longer periods of time.

Decay, or fading of the memory trace, is quite common in sensory and short-term memory. But there does not appear to be a gradual, inevitable decay of the long-term memory trace. In one study, Harry Bahrick and others (1975) found that after 35 years, participants could recognize 90% of their high school classmates' names and photographs—the same percentage as for recent graduates.

Interference   A major cause of forgetting that affects people every day is **interference**. Whenever someone tries to recall any given memory, two types of interference can hinder the effort. Information or associations stored either before or after an item can interfere with the ability to remember it.

Proactive interference occurs when information or experiences already stored in long-term memory hinder the ability to remember newer information (Underwood, 1957). For example, when you drive a new car, it may take a while to feel comfortable with the arrangement of the dashboard. Your earlier habits of responding to your old car's dashboard may interfere with your driving at first. This type of proactive interference is called *negative transfer*. One explanation for interference is the competition between old and new responses (Bower et al., 1994).

New learning or experience that interferes with the ability to remember information previously stored is called *retroactive interference*. The more similar the new learning or experience is to the previous learning, the more interference there is (Underwood, 1964). Is there any way to minimize interference? You may be surprised to learn that of all human activities, sleep interferes with previous learning the least.

What can you do to lessen the effects of retroactive interference on memory?

■ When possible, study before going to sleep.

■ If you can't study before going to sleep, at least review at that time the material you need to remember.

■ Try not to study similar subjects back-to-back. Better yet, after studying one subject, take a short break before beginning the next subject.

■ Schedule your classes so that courses with similar subject matter do not follow each other.

We have discussed ways to avoid forgetting, but there are occasions when people may need to avoid remembering—times when they want to forget.

Motivated Forgetting   Victims of rape or physical abuse, war veterans, and survivors of airplane crashes or earthquakes all have had terrifying experiences that may haunt them for years. These victims are certainly motivated to forget their trau-

consolidation failure: Any disruption in the consolidation process that prevents a permanent memory from forming.

retrograde amnesia (RET-ro-grade): A loss of memory affecting experiences that occurred shortly before a loss of consciousness.

decay theory: A theory of forgetting that holds that the memory trace, if not used, disappears with the passage of time.

interference: Memory loss that occurs because information or associations stored either before or after a given memory hinder the ability to remember it.

What is interference, and how can it be minimized?

motivated forgetting: Forgetting through suppression or repression in order to protect oneself from material that is too painful, anxiety- or guilt-producing, or otherwise unpleasant.

repression: Removing from one's consciousness disturbing, guilt-provoking, or otherwise unpleasant memories so that one is no longer aware that a painful event occurred.

amnesia: A partial or complete loss of memory resulting from brain trauma or psychological trauma.

matic experiences, but even people who have not suffered any trauma use **motivated forgetting** to protect themselves from experiences that are painful, frightening, or otherwise unpleasant.

With one form of motivated forgetting, *suppression,* a person makes a conscious, active attempt to put a painful, disturbing, anxiety- or guilt-provoking memory out of mind, but the person is still aware that the painful event occurred. With another type of motivated forgetting, **repression,** unpleasant memories are literally removed from consciousness, and the person is no longer aware that the unpleasant event ever occurred (Freud, 1922). People who have **amnesia** (memory loss) that is not due to loss of consciousness or brain damage have actually repressed the events they no longer remember. Motivated forgetting is probably used by more people than any other method to deal with unpleasant memories. It seems to be a natural human tendency to forget the unpleasant circumstances of life and to remember the pleasant ones (Linton, 1979; Meltzer, 1930).

Retrieval Failure   How many times have these experiences happened to you? You are with a friend when you meet an acquaintance, but you can't introduce the two because you cannot recall the name of your acquaintance. Or, while taking a test, you can't remember the answer to a question that you are sure you know. Often people are certain that they know something, but they are not able to retrieve the information when they need it. This type of forgetting is called *retrieval failure.*

A common retrieval failure experience is known as the *tip-of-the-tongue (TOT) phenomenon* (Brown & McNeil, 1966). Surely you have experienced trying to recall a name, a word, or some other bit of information, knowing what you were searching for almost as well as your own name. You were on the verge of recalling the word or name, perhaps aware of the number of syllables and the beginning or ending letter of the word. It was on the tip of your tongue, but it just wouldn't quite come out.

THE NATURE OF REMEMBERING AND FORGETTING

Memory as a Permanent Record: The Video Cassette Recorder Analogy

For hundreds of years people have speculated about the nature of memory. Aristotle suggested that the senses imprint memories in the brain like signet rings stamping impressions in wax. Sigmund Freud believed that all memories are permanently preserved, with some lying deep in the unconscious. Wilder Penfield (1969), a Canadian neurosurgeon, claimed that experiences leave a "permanent imprint on the brain . . . as though a tape recorder had been receiving it all" (p. 165). What would lead him to such a conclusion?

Penfield (1975) performed over 1,100 operations on patients with epilepsy. He found that when parts of the temporal lobes were stimulated with an electrical probe, 3.5% of patients reported flashback experiences, as though they were actually reliving parts of their past. After reviewing Penfield's findings, other researchers offered different explanations for his patients' responses. Neisser (1967) suggested that the experiences patients reported were "comparable to the content of dreams," rather than the recall of actual experiences (p. 169).

Memory as a Reconstruction: Partly Fact and Partly Fiction

What is meant by the statement "Memory is reconstructive in nature"?

Other than Penfield's work, there is no research to suggest that memory works like a video cassette recorder, capturing every part of an experience exactly as it happens.

Normally what a person recalls is not an exact replica of an event (Schachter et al., 1998). Rather a memory is a **reconstruction**—an account pieced together from a few highlights, using information that may or may not be accurate (Loftus & Loftus, 1980). Put another way, "memory is not so much like reading a book as it is like writing one from fragmentary notes" (Kihlstrom, 1995, p. 341). There is ample evidence indicating that memory is quite often inaccurate. "Critical details of an experience can be forgotten or become distorted, their source and order may be misremembered, and under certain circumstances completely new details may be incorporated into a memory" (Conway et al., 1996, p. 69). Recall is, even for people with the most accurate memories, partly truth and partly fiction. This was the finding of another pioneer in memory research, Englishman Sir Frederick Bartlett.

When people recall an event, such as a car accident, they are actually reconstructing it from memory by piecing together bits of information that may or may not be totally accurate.

While Ebbinghaus explored memory by memorizing nonsense syllables under controlled experimental conditions, Sir Frederick Bartlett (1886–1969) studied memory using rich and meaningful material learned and remembered under more lifelike conditions. Bartlett (1932) gave participants stories to read and drawings to study, and at varying time intervals he had them reproduce the original material. Accurate reports were rare. The participants seemed to reconstruct the material they had learned, rather than actually remember it. They recreated the stories, making them shorter and more consistent with their own individual viewpoints. They rationalized puzzling features of the stories to fit their own expectations and often changed details, substituting more familiar objects or events instead. Errors in memory increased with time, and Bartlett's participants were not aware that they had partly remembered and partly invented. Ironically, the parts his participants had created were often the very parts that they most adamantly claimed to have remembered. Bartlett concluded that people systematically distort the facts and the circumstances of experiences. Information already stored in long-term memory exerts a strong influence on how people remember new information and experiences.

What is Bartlett's contribution to scientists' understanding of memory?

Schemas and Memory   Bartlett suggested that his participants' inaccuracies in memory reflected their **schemas**—the integrated frameworks of knowledge and assumptions they had about people, objects, and events. Schemas aid in processing large amounts of material, because they provide frameworks into which people can incorporate new information and experience. Schemas also provide association cues that can help in retrieval.

What are schemas, and how do they affect memory?

Once formed, schemas influence what people notice and how they encode and recall information. When we encounter new information or have a new experience related to an existing schema, we try to make it fit or be consistent with that schema. To accomplish this, we may have to distort some aspects of the information and ignore or forget other aspects. Some of the distorting and ignoring occurs as the material is being encoded; more can occur when we try to remember or reconstruct the original experience.

reconstruction: A memory that is not an exact replica of an event but has been pieced together from a few highlights, using information that may or may not be accurate.

schemas: The integrated frameworks of knowledge and assumptions a person has about people, objects, and events, which affect how the person encodes and recalls information.

Distortion in Memory   When people reconstruct memories, they do not purposely try to distort the actual experience—unless, of course, they are lying. But people tend to omit some facts that actually occurred and to supply other details from their own imaginations. Distortion occurs when people alter the memory of an event or an experience in order to fit their beliefs, expectations, logic, or prejudices.

The tendency toward systematic distortion of actual events has been proven many times. The *Try It!* (on page 180) demonstrates distortion in memory.

Read this list of words aloud at a rate of about one word per second. Then close your book and write down all the words you can remember.

bed	awake	dream	snooze	nap	snore
rest	tired	wake	doze	yawn	slumber

Now check your list. Did you "remember" the word *sleep*? Many people do, even though it is not one of the words on the list (Deese, 1959).

The *Try It!* shows that we are very likely to alter or distort what we see or hear to make it fit with what we believe *should* be true. All the words on the list are related to sleep, so it seems logical that *sleep* should be one of the words. In experiments using word lists similar to the one in the *Try It!*, between 40% and 55% of the participants "remembered" the key related word that was not on the list (Roediger & McDermott, 1995).

The tendency to distort makes the world more understandable and enables people to organize their experiences into their existing systems of beliefs and expectations. But this tendency often causes gross inaccuracies in what people remember. People distort memories of their own lives in the positive direction. Bahrick and others (1996) found that 89% of college students accurately remembered the A's they earned in high school, but only 29% accurately recalled the D's. The most dramatic examples of systematic distortion may occur in eyewitness testimony.

Eyewitness Testimony: Is It Accurate?

What conditions reduce the reliability of eyewitness testimony?

When someone says, "I ought to know—I saw it with my own eyes," we might accept the statement almost without question. After all, seeing is believing. Or is it?

Traditionally, eyewitness testimony has been viewed as reliable by the legal system in the United States and elsewhere (Brigham & Wolfskeil, 1983). Recall from the opening story psychologist Donald Thompson, who was a victim of faulty eyewitness identification. Is his case just an isolated incident? According to psychologist Elizabeth Loftus (1993a), a staggering number of wrongful convictions in the United States each year are based on eyewitness testimony. And according to Huff (1995), the number is probably at least 10,000.

Studies on the accuracy of human memory suggest that eyewitness testimony is highly subject to error, and that it should always be viewed with caution (Loftus, 1979). Nevertheless, it does play a vital role in the U.S. justice system. Says Loftus (1984), "We can't afford to exclude it legally or ignore it as jurors. Sometimes, as in cases of rape, it is the only evidence available, and it is often correct" (p. 24).

Fortunately, eyewitness mistakes can be minimized. Eyewitnesses to crimes typically identify suspects from a lineup. If shown photographs of a suspect before viewing the lineup, eyewitnesses may mistakenly identify that suspect in the lineup because the person looks familiar. The familiarity may result from the mug shot, not from seeing the suspect at the scene of the crime.

Studies on the accuracy of human memory suggest that eyewitness testimony is highly subject to error and should be weighed critically.

The composition of the lineup is also important. Other subjects in a lineup must resemble the suspect in age, body build, and certainly in race. Even then, if the lineup does not contain the guilty party, eyewitnesses may identify the person who most resembles the perpetrator (Gonzalez et al., 1993). Eyewitnesses are less likely to make errors if a sequential lineup is used, that is, if the members of the lineup are viewed one after the other, rather than simultaneously (Loftus, 1993a).

Eyewitnesses are more likely to identify the wrong person if the person's race is different from their own. According to Egeth (1993), misidentifications are approximately 15% higher in cross-race than in same-race identifications. Misidentification is also somewhat more likely to occur when a weapon is used in a crime. The witnesses may pay more attention to the weapon than to the physical characteristics of the criminal (Steblay, 1992).

Even questioning witnesses after a crime can influence what they later remember. Because leading questions can substantially change a witness's memory of an event, it is critical that the interviewers ask neutral questions (Leichtman & Ceci, 1995). Misleading information supplied after the event can result in erroneous recollections of the actual event, a phenomenon known as the *misinformation effect* (Kroll et al., 1988; Loftus & Hoffman, 1989). Loftus (1997) and her students have conducted "more than 20 experiments involving over 20,000 participants that document how exposure to misinformation induces memory distortion" (p. 71). Furthermore, after eyewitnesses have repeatedly recalled information, whether accurate or inaccurate, they become even more confident when they testify in court because the information is so easily retrieved (Shaw, 1996).

Recovering Repressed Memories: A Controversy

Since the late 1980s, thousands of people, most of them adult women under the age of 50, have come forward claiming to have been sexually abused as children. Given the fact that childhood sexual abuse is widespread and underreported, a growing number of claims of sexual abuse, including incest, should not be surprising. But many of these new claims are surprising because the accusers maintain that they had repressed all memory of the abuse until they underwent therapy or read a self-help book for survivors of childhood sexual abuse. Could people endure repeated episodes of childhood sexual abuse for years, selectively repress all memory of their abuse, and then recover the repressed memories as adults? Many psychologists are doubtful, but a growing number of therapists specialize in helping people recover repressed memories.

In 1988, Ellen Bass and Laura Davis published *The Courage to Heal*, a self-help book for survivors of childhood sexual abuse. This best-selling book has become the "bible" for sex abuse victims and the leading "textbook" for some therapists who specialize in treating them. Bass and Davis not only seek to help survivors who remember having suffered sexual abuse; they reach out as well to other people who have no memory of any sexual abuse and try to help them determine whether they might have been abused. They suggest that "if you are unable to remember any specific instances . . . but still have a feeling that something abusive happened to you, it probably did" (p. 21). They offer a definite conclusion: "If you think you were abused and your life shows the symptoms, then you were" (p. 22). And they free potential victims of sexual abuse from the responsibility of establishing any proof: "You are not responsible for proving that you were abused" (p. 37). Other similar self-help books suggest that almost anything can be interpreted as a symptom of early sexual abuse—depression, loss of appetite, eating disorders, anxiety, sexual problems, problems with intimacy, phobias, low self-esteem, lack of motivation, feeling bad, feeling ashamed or powerless, or feeling the need to be perfect.

The critics of repressed-memory therapy claim that problems shown to have multiple causes, such as depression, eating disorders, sexual dysfunction, and others, should not be cited as symptoms to support the probability of abuse (Wakefield & Underveeager, 1992). Also troubling is the possibility that patients looking for a

What is the controversy regarding the therapy used to recover repressed memories of childhood sexual abuse?

cause of their problems might be inclined to accept an explanation so confidently put forth by the therapist. Critics "argue that repression of truly traumatic memories is rare" (Bowers & Farvolden, 1996, p. 355). Moreover, they maintain that "when it comes to a serious trauma, intrusive thoughts and memories of it are the most characteristic reaction" (p. 359). According to Loftus (1993b), "The therapist convinces the patient with no memories that abuse is likely, and the patient obligingly uses reconstructive strategies to generate memories that would support that conviction" (p. 528). Repressed-memory therapists believe, however, that healing hinges on their patient's being able to recover the repressed memories.

Critics charge that recovered memories of sexual abuse are suspect because of the techniques therapists usually use to uncover them—namely, hypnosis and guided imagery. Hypnosis does *not* improve the accuracy of memory, only the confidence that what one remembers is accurate.

Link It!

Can merely imagining experiences through guided imagery with a therapist lead people to believe that those experiences had actually happened to them? Yes, according to some recent studies. About 25% of participants who had imagined that a fictitious event had happened, did in fact develop a false memory of the imagined event after they had been interviewed about it several times (Hyman et al., 1995; Hyman & Pentland, 1996; Loftus & Pickrell, 1995). Garry and Loftus (1994) were able to implant a false memory of being lost in a shopping mall at 5 years of age in 25% of participants aged 18 to 53, after verification of the fictitious experience by a relative. Repeated exposure to suggestions of false memories can create those memories (Zaragoza & Mitchell, 1996).

Critics are especially skeptical of recovered memories of events that occurred in the first few years of life; in part because the hippocampus, vital in the formation of episodic memories, is not fully developed then. And neither are the areas of the cortex where memories are stored (Squire et al., 1993). Furthermore, young children, who are still limited in language ability, do not store memories in the categories that would be accessible to them later in life. The relative inability of older children and adults to recall events from the first few years of life is referred to as **infantile amnesia**.

False accusations of childhood sexual abuse are apparently widespread, and a group of parents who deny the accusations against them have formed an organization known as the False Memory Syndrome (FMS) Foundation, which had over 12,000 members as of early 1995. The foundation has received more than 1,000 reports about individuals who recovered what they believed to be repressed memories of sexual abuse during therapy but later denied that any abuse had occurred (Merskey, 1996).

The American Psychological Association (1994), the American Psychiatric Association (1993c), and the American Medical Association (1994) have all stated that current evidence supports the possibility that repressed memories exist as well as that false memories can be constructed in response to suggestions of abuse. This position suggests that recovered memories of abuse should be verified independently before they are accepted as facts.

infantile amnesia: The relative inability of older children and adults to recall events from the first few years of life.

flashbulb memory: An extremely vivid memory of the conditions surrounding one's first hearing the news of a surprising, shocking, or highly emotional event.

eidetic imagery (eye-DET-ik): The ability to retain the image of a visual stimulus several minutes after it has been removed from view.

Unusual Memory Phenomena

Flashbulb Memories: Extremely Vivid Memories   Most people over age 50 remember the assassination of President John F. Kennedy, and many claim to have unusually vivid memories of exactly when and where they received the news of the assassination. This type of extremely vivid memory is called a **flashbulb memory** (Bohannon, 1988). Brown and Kulik (1977) suggest that a flashbulb memory is formed when a person learns of an event that is very surprising, shocking, and highly emotional. You might have a flashbulb memory of when you received the news of the death or the serious injury of a close family member or a friend.

Pillemer (1990) argues that flashbulb memories do not constitute a different type of memory altogether. Rather, he suggests, all memories can vary on the dimensions of emotion, consequentiality (the importance of the consequences of the event), and rehearsal (how often people think or talk about the event afterwards). Flashbulb memories rank high in all three dimensions and thus are extremely memorable. Therefore, flashbulb memories should be the most accurate of any memories. But are they infallible? Hardly.

Several studies suggest that flashbulb memories are not as accurate as people believe them to be. Neisser and Harsch (1992) questioned first-year university students about the Challenger disaster the following morning. When the same students were questioned again 3 years later, one-third gave accounts that differed markedly from those given initially, even though they were extremely confident of their recollections. Weaver (1993) questioned students following the bombing of Iraq that signaled the beginning of the Gulf War and again 1 year later. He found that the accuracy of the students' accounts decreased, although confidence in their recollections had not.

A flashbulb memory is formed when a person learns of an event that is shocking and highly emotional, such as the tragic death of Princess Diana in a Paris car crash. Where were you when you first heard the news of her death?

Eidetic Imagery: Almost Like "Photographic Memory"   Have you ever wished that you had a photographic memory? Perhaps you have heard of someone who is able to read a page in a book and recall it word for word. More than likely, that person has developed an enviable memory by learning and applying principles of memory improvement. Psychologists doubt that there are more than a few rare cases of a truly photographic memory that captures all the details of an experience and retains them perfectly. But some studies do show that about 5% of children apparently have something akin to photographic memory that psychologists call **eidetic imagery** (Haber, 1980). This is the ability to retain the image of a visual stimulus, such as a picture, for several minutes after it has been removed from view and to use this retained image to answer questions about the visual stimulus (see Figure 6.5).

Children with eidetic imagery generally have no better long-term memory than others their age. And virtually all children with eidetic imagery lose it before adulthood. One exceptional case, however, is Elizabeth, a teacher and a skilled artist. She can create on canvas an exact duplicate of a remembered scene in all its rich detail. Just as remarkable is her ability to retain visual images of words. "Years after having read a poem in a foreign language, she can fetch back an image of the printed page and copy the poem from the bottom line to the top line as fast as she can write" (Stromeyer, 1970, p. 77).

Figure 6.5

Test for Eidetic Imagery

Researchers test children for eidetic imagery by having them stare for 30 seconds at a picture like the one in (a). A few minutes later, the drawing in (b) is shown to the children, who are asked to report what they see. Those with eidetic imagery usually claim that they see a face and describe the composite sketch in (c). The face can be perceived only if the child retains the image of the first picture and fuses it with the middle drawing. (From Haber, 1980.)

Memory and Culture

Link It!

Sir Frederick Bartlett (1932) believed that some impressive memory abilities operate within a social or cultural context. He stated that "both the manner and matter of recall are often predominantly determined by social influences" (p. 244). Bartlett (1932) described the amazing ability of the Swazi people of Africa to remember the slight differences in individual characteristics of their cows. One Swazi herdsman, Bartlett claimed, could remember details of every cow he had tended the year before. Such a feat is less surprising when you consider that the key component of traditional Swazi culture is the herds of cattle the people tend and depend on for their living. Do the Swazi people have super powers of memory? Bartlett asked young Swazi men and young European men to recall a message consisting of 25 words. The Swazi had no better recall ability than the Europeans.

Among many of the tribal peoples in Africa, the history of the tribe is preserved orally. Thus an oracle, or specialist, must be able to encode, store, and retrieve huge volumes of historical data (D'Azevedo, 1982). Elders of the Iatmul people of New Guinea are also said to have committed to memory the lines of descent for the various clans of their people stretching back generation upon generation (Bateson, 1982). The unerring memory of the elders for the kinship patterns of their people are used to resolve disputed property claims (Mistry & Rogoff, 1994).

In many traditional cultures, elders may be oral historians—remembering and passing on the details of tribal traditions and myths as well as genealogical data.

Barbara Rogoff, an expert in cultural psychology, maintains that such phenomenal, memory feats must be understood in their cultural context (Rogoff & Mistry, 1985). The tribal elders perform their impressive memory feats because it is an integral and critically important part of the culture in which they live. Most likely, their ability to remember lists of nonsense syllables would be no better than your own.

FACTORS INFLUENCING RETRIEVAL

Researchers in psychology have identified several factors that influence memory. A person can control some of these factors, but not all of them.

The Serial Position Effect: To Be Remembered, Be First or Last But Not in the Middle

What is the serial position effect?

If you were introduced to a dozen people at a party, you would most likely recall the names of the first few people you met and the last one or two, but forget more of the names in the middle. The reason is the **serial position effect**—the finding that for information learned in sequence, recall is better for items at the beginning and the end than for items in the middle of the sequence.

serial position effect: The tendency to remember the beginning and ending items of a sequence or list better than the middle items.

primacy effect: The tendency to recall the first items on a list more readily than the middle items.

recency effect: The tendency to recall the last items on a list more readily than those in the middle of the list.

Information at the beginning of a sequence is subject to the **primacy effect** and is likely to be recalled because it already has been placed in long-term memory. Information at the end of a sequence is subject to the **recency effect** and has an even higher probability of being recalled because it is still in short-term memory. The poorer recall of information in the middle of a sequence occurs because that information is no longer in short-term memory and has not yet been placed in long-term memory. The serial position effect lends strong support to the notion of separate systems for short-term and long-term memory (Postman & Phillips, 1965).

Primacy and recency effects can also have an impact on information stored for longer periods of time (Roediger, 1991). For example, children learning their ABCs are likely to remember the first and last several letters of the alphabet better than many of the letters in the middle.

Environmental Context and Memory

Have you ever stood in your living room and thought of something you needed from your bedroom, only to forget what it was when you got there? Did the item come to mind when you returned to the living room? Some research reveals that people recall information better when they are in the same location—the same environmental context—as when the information was originally encoded.

How does environmental context affect memory?

Tulving and Thompson (1973) suggest that many elements of the physical setting in which a person learns information are encoded along with the information and become part of the memory trace. If part or all of the original context is reinstated, it may serve as a retrieval cue. Then the information learned in that context may come to mind. This is why criminal investigators often bring eyewitnesses back to the crime scene or ask them to visualize it to help them recall more details of the crime.

Godden and Baddeley (1975) conducted one of the early studies of context and memory with members of a university diving club. Participants memorized a list of words when they were either 10 feet underwater or on land. They were later tested for recall of the words in the same or in a different environment. The results of the study suggest that recall of information is strongly influenced by environmental context (see Figure 6.6). Words learned underwater were best recalled underwater, and words learned on land were best recalled on land. In fact, when the scuba divers learned and recalled the words in the same context, their scores were 47% higher than when the two contexts were different. But context does not improve recognition, only recall.

Going from 10 feet underwater to dry land is a rather drastic change in context, yet some researchers find the same effects even in more subtle context changes, such as going from one room to another. Steven Smith and others (1978) had students memorize lists of words in one room. The following day, students tested in the same room recalled 50% more words than those tested in another room. Again, there were

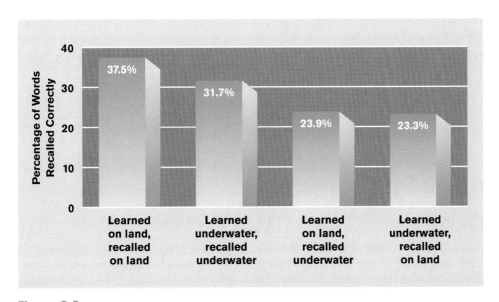

Figure 6.6

Context-Dependent Memory

Godden and Baddeley showed the strong influence of environmental context on recall. Scuba divers who memorized a list of words, either on land or underwater, had significantly better recall in the same physical context in which the learning had taken place. (Data from Godden & Baddeley, 1975.)

state-dependent memory effect:
The tendency to recall information better if one is in the same pharmacological or psychological (mood) state as when the information was encoded.

What is the state-dependent memory effect?

Link It!

What role do the hippocampus and the rest of the hippocampal region play in episodic and semantic memory?

no significant differences on recognition tests. Smith (1979) also found that students who simply visualized the room in which they had learned the words could remember almost as much when tested in a different room as students who learned and were tested in the same room.

Odors can also supply powerful and enduring retrieval cues for memory. Experimental participants who experienced a pleasant odor during learning and again when tested 5 days later had significantly higher recall than those who did not experience the odor during both learning and recall (Morgan, 1996).

The more completely and carefully people encode material to be remembered, the less dependent they are on reinstating the original context.

The State-Dependent Memory Effect

If, as we have seen, the external environment can affect memory, might a person's internal state (happy or sad, intoxicated or sober) also influence memory performance? The answer is yes. People tend to recall information better if they are in the same internal state as when the information was encoded. Psychologists call this the **state-dependent memory effect**.

Some studies have shown a state-dependent memory effect for alcohol and drugs such as marijuana, amphetamines, and barbiturates (Eich, 1980). Participants encoded material while sober or intoxicated, and later were tested in either the sober or intoxicated state. Recall was found to be best when the participants were in the same state for both learning and testing (Weingartner et al., 1976). As in other studies, the state-dependent memory effect was evident for recall but not for recognition.

Researchers have not been able to demonstrate reliably that recall is best if participants are in the same mood (happy or sad) when they encode or learn material as when they try to recall it. However, some evidence does suggest that pleasant experiences are more likely to be recalled when people are in a happy mood, and negative experiences when people are experiencing a negative mood (Eich et al., 1994; Teasdale & Fogarty, 1979). Adults who are clinically depressed tend to recall more negative life experiences (Clark & Teasdale, 1982) and are likely to recall their parents as unloving and rejecting (Lewinsohn & Rosenbaum, 1987). But as depression lifts, the tendency toward negative recall reverses itself. Seidlitz and Diener (1993) found that recall of either positive or negative life events was influenced by subjective well-being (life satisfaction and long-term happiness), rather than by current mood (momentary happiness or unhappiness). Alcohol affects memory by intensifying the processes of interference (Bruce et al., 1999).

BIOLOGY AND MEMORY

Obviously a person's vast store of memories must exist physically somewhere in the brain. But where?

Brain Damage: A Clue to Memory Formation

Researchers are finding specific locations in the brain that house and mediate functions and processes in memory. One important source of information comes from people who have suffered memory loss resulting from damage to specific brain areas. One such person is H.M., a man who has had a major influence on scientists' knowledge of human memory, not as a researcher but as a subject.

The Case of H.M.   H.M. suffered from such severe epilepsy that, out of desperation, he agreed to a radical surgical procedure. The surgeon removed the part of the brain believed to be causing H.M.'s seizures, the medial portions of both temporal lobes—the amygdala and the **hippocampal region**, which includes the hippocampus itself and the underlying cortical areas. It was 1953, and H.M. was 27 years old.

> After his surgery, H.M. remained intelligent and psychologically stable, and his seizures were drastically reduced. But unfortunately, the tissue cut from H.M.'s brain housed more than the site of his seizures. It also contained his ability to form new, conscious long-term memories. Though his short-term memory is still as good as ever and he easily remembers the events of his life stored well before the operation, H.M. suffers from **anterograde amnesia**. He has not been able to remember a single event that has occurred since the surgery. And though H.M. turned 74 in 2000, as far as his conscious long-term memory is concerned, it is still 1953 and he is still 27 years old.
>
> Surgery affected only H.M.'s declarative, long-term memory—his ability to store facts, personal experiences, names, faces, telephone numbers, and the like. But researchers were surprised to discover that he could still form nondeclarative memories; that is, he could still acquire skills through repetitive practice although he could not remember having done so. For example, since the surgery, H.M. has learned to play tennis and improve his game, but he has no memory of ever having played. (Adapted from Milner, 1966, 1970; Milner et al., 1968.)

H.M.'s case was one of the first indications that the hippocampal region is involved in forming long-term memories. The most recent research indicates that the hippocampus is critically important in forming episodic memories (Eichenbaum, 1997; Gluck & Myers, 1997). Semantic memory, however, depends not on the hippocampus itself, but on the other parts of the hippocampal region underlying it (Vargha-Khadem et al., 1997).

The Case of K.C. To support the distinction between semantic and episodic memory, Tulving and others (1988) reported the case of K.C., who sustained a severe head injury from a motorcycle accident. K.C. suffered massive damage to his frontal lobe and other parts of the brain as well. "K.C.'s case is remarkable in that he cannot remember, in the sense of bringing back to conscious awareness, a single thing that he has ever done or experienced in the past" (Tulving, 1989, p. 362).

Although his episodic memory was erased, K.C.'s semantic memory was largely spared. His storehouse of knowledge from fields such as geography, history, politics, and music is still large, enabling him to answer questions about many topics. Tulving concluded that episodic memory depends on the functioning of parts of the frontal lobe. And a number of studies using PET scans have revealed that, in addition to the hippocampus, the left prefrontal lobe plays a role in encoding episodic memories, while the right prefrontal lobe is involved in their retrieval (Nyberg, Cabeza, & Tulving, 1996; Nyberg, McIntoch, et al., 1996).

Neuronal Changes in Memory: Brain Work

Some researchers are exploring memory more minutely, by studying the actions of single neurons. Others are studying collections of neurons and their synapses, and the neurotransmitters whose chemical action begins the process of recording and storing a memory. The first close look at the nature of memory in single neurons was provided by Eric Kandel and his colleagues, who traced the effects of learning and memory in the sea snail *Aplysia* (Dale & Kandel, 1990). Using tiny electrodes implanted in several single neurons in the sea snail, the researchers mapped the neural circuits that are formed and maintained as the animal learns and remembers. They also discovered the different types of protein synthesis that facilitate short-term and long-term memory (Sweatt & Kandel, 1989).

But the studies of learning and memory in *Aplysia* reflect only simple classical conditioning, which is a type of nondeclarative memory. Other researchers studying mammals are finding that physical changes occur in the neurons and synapses in brain regions involved in declarative memory.

hippocampal region: A part of the limbic system that includes the hippocampus itself (primarily involved in the formation of episodic memories) and its underlying cortical areas (involved in the formation of semantic memories).

anterograde amnesia: The inability to form long-term memories of events occurring after a brain injury or brain surgery, although memories formed before the trauma are usually intact.

Link It!

As far back as the 1940s, Canadian psychologist Donald O. Hebb (1949) argued that the necessary neural ingredients for learning and memory must involve the enhancement of transmission at the synapses. Today the most widely studied model for learning and memory at the level of the neurons meets the requirements of the mechanism Hebb described (Fischbach, 1992). *Long-term potentiation (LTP)* is an increase in the efficiency of neural transmission at the synapses that lasts for days or even weeks (Cotman & Lynch, 1989; Martinez & Derrick, 1996; Nguyen et al., 1994; Schuman & Madison, 1994; Stein et al., 1993). Leading researchers now believe that LTP has the characteristics required of a process that is capable of forming memories (Cotman & Lynch, 1989). Increased neural activity at very fast frequencies (20–70 cycles per second) occurs at the synapses when learning and memory tasks are performed (Miltner et al., 1999).

Hormones and Memory

How do memories of threatening situations that elicit the "fight or flight response" compare with ordinary memories?

The strongest and most lasting memories are usually those fueled by emotion. Research by McGaugh and Cahill (1995) suggests that there may be two pathways for forming memories—one for ordinary information and another for memories that are fired by emotion. When a person is emotionally aroused, the adrenal glands release the hormones adrenalin (epinephrine) and noradrenalin (norepinephrine) into the bloodstream. Long known to be involved in the "fight or flight response," these hormones enable humans to survive, and they also imprint powerful and enduring memories of the circumstances surrounding threatening situations.

Such emotionally laden memories activate the amygdala (known to play a central role in emotion) and other parts of the memory system (Gabrieli, 1998). Emotional memories are lasting memories, and this may be the most important factor in explaining the intensity and durability of flashbulb memories.

Other hormones may have important effects on memory. Estrogen, the female sex hormone, appears to improve learning and memory, not only in healthy women but in patients with Alzheimer's disease as well. Estrogen appears to exert this effect by helping to build and maintain synapses between neurons in brain areas known to be involved in memory, such as the hippocampal region (Woolley et al., 1997).

IMPROVING MEMORY: SOME HELPFUL STUDY HABITS

What are four study habits that can aid memory?

There are no magic formulas for improving memory. Remembering is a skill and, like any other skill, requires knowledge and practice. In this section we will consider several study habits and techniques that can improve your memory.

Organization: Everything in Its Place

People tend to retrieve information from long-term memory according to the way they have organized it for storage. Almost anyone can name the months of the year in about 10 seconds, but how long would it take to recall them in alphabetical order? The same 12 items, all well-known, are much harder to retrieve in alphabetical order, because they are not organized that way in memory. A telephone directory would be of little use to you if the names and phone numbers were listed in random order. Similarly, you are giving your memory a task it probably will not accept if you try to remember large amounts of information in a haphazard fashion. Try to organize items you want to remember in alphabetical order, or according to categories, historical sequence, size, shape, or any other way that will make retrieval easier.

Organizing material to be learned is a tremendous aid to memory. You can prove this for yourself by completing the *Try It!*

Link It!

overlearning: Practicing or studying material beyond the point where it can be repeated once without error.

Have a pencil and a sheet of paper handy. Read the following list of items out loud and then write down as many as you can remember.

peas	ice cream	fish	perfume	bananas
toilet paper	onions	apples	cookies	ham
carrots	shaving cream	pie	grapes	chicken

If you organize this list, the items are much easier to remember. Now read each category heading and the items listed beneath it. Write down as many items as you can remember.

Desserts	Fruits	Vegetables	Meat	Toilet Articles
pie	bananas	carrots	chicken	perfume
ice cream	apples	onions	fish	shaving cream
cookies	grapes	peas	ham	toilet paper

Overlearning: Reviewing Again, and Again, and Again

Do you still remember the words to songs that were popular when you were in high school? Can you recite many of the nursery rhymes you learned as a child even though you haven't heard them in years? You probably can because of **overlearning**.

Suppose that you wanted to memorize a list of words, and you studied until you could recite them once without error. Would this amount of study or practice be sufficient? Research suggests that people remember material better and longer if they overlearn it, that is, if they practice or study beyond the minimum needed to barely learn it (Ebbinghaus, 1885/1964). A pioneering study in overlearning by Krueger (1929) showed very substantial long-term gains for participants who engaged in 50% and 100% overlearning (see Figure 6.7). Furthermore, overlearning

What is overlearning, and why is it important?

Figure 6.7
Overlearning

When a person learns material only to the point of one correct repetition, forgetting is very rapid. Just 22% is retained after 1 day, 3% after 4 days, and 2% after 14 days. When participants spend 50% more time going over the material, the retention increases to 36% after 1 day, 30% after 4 days, and 21% after 14 days. (Data from Krueger, 1929.)

massed practice: Learning in one long practice session as opposed to spacing the learning in shorter practice sessions over an extended period.

makes material more resistant to interference and is perhaps the best insurance against stress-related forgetting.

The next time you study for a test, don't stop studying as soon as you think you know the material. Spend another hour or so going over it, and you will be surprised at how much more you will remember.

Spaced Practice versus Massed Practice: A Little at a Time Beats All at Once

Most students have tried cramming for examinations, but spacing study over several different sessions generally is more effective than **massed practice**—learning in one long practice session without rest periods (Glover & Corkill, 1987). You will remember more with less total study time if you space your study over several sessions. Long periods of memorizing make material particularly subject to interference and often result in fatigue and lowered concentration. Also, when you space your practice, you probably create a new memory that may be stored in a different place, thus increasing your chance for recall. The spacing effect applies to learning motor skills as well as to learning facts and information. Music students can tell you that it is better to practice for half an hour each day, every day, than to practice many hours in a row once a week.

Recitation versus Rereading: Recitation Wins

Many students simply read and reread their textbook and notes when they study for an exam. Research over many years shows that you will recall more if you increase the amount of recitation in your study. For example, it is better to read a page or a few paragraphs and then recite or practice recalling what you have just read. Then continue reading, stop and practice reciting again, and so on. When you study for a psychology test and review the assigned chapter, try to answer each of the study questions. Then read the material that follows each question and check to see if you answered the question correctly. This will be your safeguard against encoding failure. Don't simply read each section and assume that you can answer the question. Test yourself before your professor does.

Apply It!

Improving Memory with Mnemonic Devices

Most people use external aids to help them remember. Writing notes, making lists, writing on a calendar, or keeping an appointment book is often more reliable and accurate than trusting to memory. But there are times, such as when you are taking a test, when you cannot rely on external prompts. What if you need information at some unpredictable time, when you do not have external aids handy?

Several *mnemonics*, or memory devices, have been developed over the years to aid memory (Bower, 1973; Higbee, 1977; Roediger, 1980). We

will explore rhyme, the first-letter technique, the method of loci, the pegword method, and the link method.

Rhyme. Rhymes are a common aid to remembering material that otherwise might be difficult to recall. Perhaps as a child you learned the alphabet by using a rhyming song: "A-B-C-D-E-F-G-H-I-J-K-L-M-N-O-P." You may repeat the verse "Thirty days hath September" when you try to recall the number of days in each month, or the saying "*i* before *e* except after *c*" when you are trying to spell a word. Rhymes are useful because they ensure that information is recalled in the proper sequence.

The first-letter technique. Another useful technique is to take the first letter of each item to be remembered and form a word, a phrase, or a sentence with those letters (Matlin, 1989). For example, if you had to memorize the seven colors of the visible spectrum in their proper order, you could use the first letter of each color to form the name Roy G. Biv. Three chunks are easier to remember than seven different items.

Red Orange Yellow Green
Blue Indigo Violet

As a child taking music lessons, you may have learned the saying "*Every*

---

good *boy does fine*" to remind you of the lines of the treble clef, and *FACE* to help you remember the spaces. To remember their license plate more easily, the authors think of the letters PCS as "poor civil servant."

The method of loci: "In the first place." The *method of loci* is a mnemonic device that can be used when you want to remember a list of items such as a grocery list, or when you give a speech or a class report and need to make your points in order without using notes. The word *loci* (pronounced loh'-sye) is the plural form of *locus*, which means "location" or "place."

To use the method of loci, select any familiar location (your home, for example) and then simply associate the items to be remembered with places there. Begin by picturing the first locus, for example, your driveway; the second locus, your garage; the third locus, the walk leading to your front door; and the fourth locus, perhaps the front hall closet. Progress through your house from room to room in an orderly fashion. Visualize the first item or idea you want to remember in its place on the driveway, the second item in your garage, the third at your front door, and so on until you have associated each item you want to remember with a specific place. You may find it helpful to conjure up exaggerated images of the items that you place at each location.

When you want to recall the items, take an imaginary walk starting at the first place—the first item will pop into your mind. When you think of the second place, the second item will come to mind, and so on.

Research suggests that the method of loci is very effective. In one study, college students memorized a different list of 40 nouns on each of four consecutive days. They visualized each word at specific locations on campus (Ross & Lawrence, 1968). The students were tested immediately after memorizing each list, and the average recall was 37 out of 40 words in the exact order in which they were memorized. Average recall one day later was 34 words, and average recall for all four lists was 29 words.

The pegword system. Another mnemonic that has been proven effective is the *pegword system* (Harris & Blaiser, 1997). Developed in England around 1879, it uses rhyming words:

one = bun	six = sticks
two = shoe	seven = heaven
three = tree	eight = gate
four = door	nine = wine
five = hive	ten = hen

Many children in English-speaking countries have learned these rhyming associations from the old nursery rhyme "One, two, buckle my shoe—three, four, close the door." The rhyming words are memorized in sequence and then linked through vivid associations with any items you wish to remember in order.

For example, suppose you want to remember to buy five items at the store: milk, bread, grapefruit, laundry detergent, and eggs. Begin by associating the milk with the bun (your first pegword) by picturing milk pouring over a bun. Next picture the shoe, the second pegword, kicking a loaf of bread. Then continue by associating each item on your list with a pegword. To recall the items, simply go through your list of pegwords and the associated word will immediately come to mind.

SUMMARY AND REVIEW

REMEMBERING

What three processes are involved in the act of remembering?

Three processes involved in remembering are (1) encoding—transforming information into a form that can be stored in memory; (2) storage—maintaining information in memory; and (3) retrieval—bringing stored material to mind.

What is sensory memory?

Sensory memory holds the information coming in through the senses for up to several seconds, just long enough to allow the nervous system to begin to process the information and send some of it on to short-term memory.

What are the characteristics of short-term memory?

Short-term (working) memory holds about seven unrelated items of information for less than 30 seconds without rehearsal. Short-term memory also acts as a mental workspace while the person carries out any mental activity.

What is long-term memory, and what are its subsystems?

Long-term memory is the permanent or relatively permanent memory system with a virtually unlimited capacity. Its subsystems are (1) declarative memory, which holds facts and information (semantic memory) along with personal experiences (episodic memory); and (2) nondeclarative memory, which consists of motor skills acquired by means of repetitive practice, habits, and simple classically conditioned responses.

Key Terms
encoding (p. 168); storage (p. 168); consolidation (p. 168); retrieval (p. 168); sensory memory (p. 169); short-term memory (p. 170); displacement (p. 170); rehearsal (p. 171); long-term memory (p. 171); elaborative

rehearsal (p. 171); declarative memory (p. 172); episodic memory (p. 172); semantic memory (p. 172); nondeclarative memory (p. 173); priming (p. 173); levels-of-processing model (p. 173)

MEASURING MEMORY

What are three methods of measuring retention?

Three methods of measuring retention are (1) recall, where information must be supplied with few or no retrieval cues; (2) recognition, where information must simply be recognized as having been encountered before; and (3) the relearning method, which measures retention in terms of time saved in relearning material compared with the time required to learn it originally.

What was Ebbinghaus's major contribution to psychology?

Hermann Ebbinghaus conducted the first experimental studies of learning and memory. He invented the nonsense syllable, conceived the relearning method as a test of memory, and plotted the curve of forgetting.

Key Terms
recall (p. 174); retrieval cue (p. 174); recognition (p. 175); relearning method (p. 175); savings score (p. 175); nonsense syllable (p. 175)

FORGETTING

What are six causes of forgetting?

Six causes of forgetting are encoding failure, consolidation failure, decay, interference, motivated forgetting, and retrieval failure.

What is interference, and how can it be minimized?

Interference occurs when information or associations stored either before or after a given memory hinder the ability to remember it. To minimize interference, follow a learning activity with sleep, and arrange learning so that you do not study similar subjects back to back.

Key Terms
encoding failure (p. 176); consolidation failure (p. 177); retrograde amnesia (p. 177); decay theory (p. 177); interference (p. 177); motivated for-

getting (p. 178); repression (p. 178); amnesia (p. 178)

THE NATURE OF REMEMBERING AND FORGETTING

What is meant by the statement "Memory is reconstructive in nature"?

Memory does not work like a video cassette recorder. People reconstruct memories, piecing them together from a few highlights and using information that may or may not be accurate.

What is Bartlett's contribution to scientists' understanding of memory?

Sir Frederick Bartlett found that people do not recall facts and experiences detail by detail. Rather, they systematically reconstruct and distort them to fit information already stored in memory.

What are schemas, and how do they affect memory?

Schemas are the integrated frameworks of knowledge and assumptions that people have about other people, objects, and events; schemas affect how people encode and recall information.

What conditions reduce the reliability of eyewitness testimony?

The reliability of eyewitness testimony is reduced when witnesses view a photograph of the suspect before viewing the lineup, when members of a lineup are viewed at the same time rather than one by one, when the perpetrator's race is different from that of the eyewitness, when a weapon has been used in the crime, and when leading questions are asked to elicit information.

What is the controversy regarding the therapy used to recover repressed memories of childhood sexual abuse?

Critics maintain that therapists using hypnosis and guided imagery to help their patients recover repressed memories of childhood sexual abuse are actually implanting false memories in those patients. The therapists who use these techniques believe that a number of psychiatric problems can be treated

successfully by helping patients recover repressed memories of sexual abuse.

Key Terms
reconstruction (p. 179); schemas (p. 179); infantile amnesia (p. 182); flashbulb memory (p. 182); eidetic imagery (p. 183)

FACTORS INFLUENCING RETRIEVAL

What is the serial position effect?

The serial position effect is the tendency, when recalling a list of items, to remember the items at the beginning of the list (the primacy effect) and the items at the end of the list (the recency effect) better than items in the middle.

How does environmental context affect memory?

People tend to recall material more easily if they are in the same physical location during recall as during the original learning.

What is the state-dependent memory effect?

The state-dependent memory effect is the tendency to recall information better if one is in the same pharmacological or psychological state as when the information was learned.

Key Terms
serial position effect (p. 184); primacy effect (p. 184); recency effect (p. 184); state-dependent memory effect (p. 186)

BIOLOGY AND MEMORY

What role do the hippocampus and the rest of the hippocampal region play in episodic and semantic memory?

The hippocampus is involved primarily in forming episodic memories; the rest of the hippocampal region is involved primarily in forming semantic memories.

How do memories of threatening situations that elicit the "fight or flight response" compare with ordinary memories?

Memories of threatening situations tend to be more powerful and enduring than ordinary memories.

hippocampal region (p. 186); anterograde amnesia (p. 187);

IMPROVING MEMORY: SOME HELPFUL STUDY HABITS

What are four study habits that can aid memory?

Four study habits that can aid memory
are organization, overlearning, the use
of spaced rather than massed practice,
and spending a higher percentage of
time reciting than rereading material.

What is overlearning, and why is it important?

Overlearning is practicing or studying
material beyond the point where it
can be repeated once without error.
You remember overlearned material
better and longer, and it is more resistant to interference and stress-related
forgetting.

Key Terms

overlearning (p. 189); massed practice
(p. 190)

Study Guide for Chapter 6

Answers to all the Study Guide questions are provided at the end of the book.

Section One: Chapter Review

1. Transforming information into a form that can be stored in memory is called _____; bringing to mind the material that has been stored is called _____.
   a. encoding; decoding
   b. consolidation; retrieval
   c. consolidation; decoding
   d. encoding; retrieval

2. Match the memory system with the best description of its capacity and the duration of time it holds information:
   ____ (1) sensory memory
   ____ (2) short-term memory
   ____ (3) long-term memory

   a. virtually unlimited capacity; long duration
   b. large capacity; short duration
   c. very limited capacity; short duration

3. Match each example with the appropriate memory system:
   ____ (1) semantic memory
   ____ (2) episodic memory
   ____ (3) nondeclarative memory
   ____ (4) working memory

   a. playing tennis
   b. remembering your high school graduation
   c. deciding what you will do tomorrow
   d. naming the presidents of the United States

4. Which subsystem of long-term memory does not require conscious awareness?
   a. episodic memory   c. nondeclarative memory
   b. semantic memory   d. declarative memory

5. Which of the following methods is the most sensitive way of measuring retention and can detect learning when other methods cannot?
   a. recall   c. relearning
   b. recognition   d. retrieval

6. Who invented the nonsense syllable, conceived the relearning method for testing retention, and plotted the curve of forgetting?
   a. George Sperling   c. Frederick Bartlett
   b. H. E. Burtt   d. Hermann Ebbinghaus

7. The curve of forgetting shows that memory loss
   a. occurs most rapidly at first and then levels off to a slow decline.

   b. begins to occur about 3 to 4 hours after learning.
   c. occurs at a fairly steady rate over a month's time.
   d. occurs slowly at first and increases steadily over a month's time.

8. Match the example with the corresponding method of measuring retention:
   ____ (1) identifying a suspect in a lineup
   ____ (2) answering a fill-in-the-blank question on a test
   ____ (3) having to study less for a comprehensive final exam than for all of the previous exams put together
   ____ (4) answering questions in this Study Guide
   ____ (5) reciting one's lines in a play

   a. recognition
   b. relearning
   c. recall

9. Match the example with the appropriate cause of forgetting:
   ____ (1) encoding failure
   ____ (2) consolidation failure
   ____ (3) retrieval failure
   ____ (4) repression
   ____ (5) interference

   a. failing to remember the answer on a test until after you turn in the test
   b. forgetting a humiliating childhood experience
   c. not being able to describe the back of a dollar bill
   d. calling a friend by someone else's name
   e. waking up in the hospital and not remembering you had an automobile accident

10. To minimize interference, it is best to follow learning with
    a. rest.   c. sleep.
    b. recreation.   d. unrelated study.

11. In older people, decay is the main cause of forgetting in long-term memory. (true/false)

12. According to the text, the major cause of forgetting is interference. (true/false)

13. What early memory researcher found that, rather than accurately recalling information detail by

detail, people often reconstruct and systematically distort facts to make them more consistent with past experience?
a. Hermann Ebbinghaus   c. Wilder Penfeld
b. Frederick Bartlett   d. William James

14. Which of the following is *not* true of schemas?
a. Schemas are the integrated frameworks of knowledge and assumptions a person has about people objects, and events.
b. Schemas affect the way a person encodes information.
c. Schemas affect the way a person retrieves information.
d. When a person uses schemas, memories are accurate.

15. There are few errors in eyewitness testimony if
a. eyewitnesses are identifying a person of their own race.
b. eyewitnesses view suspects' photos prior to a lineup.
c. a weapon has been used in the crime.
d. questions are phrased to provide retrieval cues for the eyewitness.

16. As a rule, people's memories are more accurate under hypnosis. (true/false)

17. The ability to retain a visual image several minutes after it has been removed is called
a. photographic memory.   c. eidetic imagery.
b. flashbulb memory.   d. sensory memory.

18. When children learn the alphabet, they often learn "A, B, C, D" and "W, X, Y, Z" before learning the letters in between. This is due to the
a. primacy effect.   c. serial position effect.
b. recency effect.   d. state-dependent memory.

19. Recall is about as good when people visualize the context in which learning occurred as it is when recall and learning occur in the same context. (true/false)

20. Scores on recognition tests (either multiple-choice or true/false) will be higher if testing and learning take place in the same physical environment. (true/false)

21. Which best explains why drugs such as alcohol and marijuana can interfere with recall if the drugs are taken during learning but not during retrieval?
a. the consistency effect
b. the state-dependent memory effect
c. context-dependent memory
d. consolidation failure

22. Compared to nondepressed people, depressed people tend to have more sad memories. (true/false)

23. The hippocampus itself is involved primarily in the formation of _____ memories; the rest of the hippocampal region is involved primarily in the formation of _____ memories.

24. H.M. retained his ability to add to his nondeclarative memory. (true/false)

25. What is the term for the long-lasting increase in the efficiency of neural transmission at the synapses that may be the basis for learning and memory at the level of the neurons?
a. long-term potentiation
b. synaptic facilitation
c. synaptic potentiation
d. presynaptic potentiation

26. Memories of circumstances surrounding threatening situations that elicit the "fight or flight response" tend to be more powerful and enduring than ordinary memories. (true/false)

27. When studying for an exam, it is best to spend
a. more time reciting than rereading.
b. more time rereading than reciting.
c. equal time rereading and reciting.
d. all of the time reciting rather than rereading.

28. The ability to recite a number of nursery rhymes from childhood is probably due mainly to
a. spaced practice.   c. mnemonics.
b. organization.   d. overlearning.

Section Two: Complete the Diagrams

Section Three: Fill In the Blank

1. The first step in the memory process is _____.

2. Short-term memory seems to have a limited life span—less than 30 seconds. If you want to keep a phone number in short-term memory, you will need to use some form of _____, such as repeating the number several times.

3. Another name for short-term memory is _____ memory.

4. When people talk about memory, they are usually talking about _____-term memory.

5. When you take a test in your psychology class, you may be asked to list the names of famous psychologists and their major contributions to psychology. For this task you would use _____ memory.

6. A fill-in-the-blank question requires you to _____ the correct answers, whereas to answer a multiple-choice question, you rely on _____ of the correct answer in a list.

7. When Jan moved to a new town, she had trouble remembering her new zip code. Every time she tried to think of her new zip code, her old zip code

seemed to interfere with her recall. This is probably an example of _____ interference.

8. A patient cannot remember the period of his life ranging from age 5 through 7. A doctor can find no physical cause for this amnesia. The patient also has no history of injury or other trauma at any age. This is very likely a case of _____.

9. Jim found himself in trouble during his physics test—he could not remember the formulas from class. He realized that he should have been paying more attention during the lectures. His current memory problem is probably due to _____ failure.

10. In a list of items, those in the _____ position are the items least easily remembered.

11. The_____ _____ memory effect is the tendency to remember best when in the same physical or phsychological state as when the information was encoded.

12. The_____ of the brain appears to be very important in the formation of long-term memory.

13. One theory of memory suggests that neural transmission becomes more efficient at certain synapses along neural paths. This increase in transmission efficiency is known as long-term _____.

14. Strategies or devices used to help memory are called _____.

15. A patient survived delicate brain surgery and displayed no signs of personality change or loss of intelligence. Days after the surgery, however, the doctor realized that the patient was unable to form long-term memories. He was, however, able to remember everything from before the surgery. The patient was diagnosed as having

_____ _____.

16. Pete started studying for his psychology test six nights ago, spending about 45 minutes per night. Jason studied for his test all in one night, in a non-stop, 6-hour study session. Pete got a better grade on the test than Jason. Jason unfortunately used a study technique called _____ practice, a strategy that is usually not as effective as spacing sessions.

17. When you study for your next psychology test, you may want to study beyond the point where you think you know the material. If you repeat or rehearse the material over and over, you will probably remember it better. This study technique is known as _____.

Section Four: Comprehensive Practice Exam

1. The first step in the memory process is known as _____, when information is transformed into a form that can be stored in short-term memory.
   a. retrieval   c. encoding
   b. storage   d. rehearsal

2. The process in which information is stored in permanent memory involves a change in the brain's physiology. This change is known as

   _____.
   a. consolidation.
   b. transformation.
   c. hippocampal transformation.
   d. recalcitration.

3. You are at a party and meet someone you are really interested in. You get that person's phone number but have no way to write it down, so you use the process of _____ in order to get it into memory.
   a. encoding   c. rehearsal
   b. latent retrieval   d. recalcitration

4. The kind of memory that has a large capacity but a very short duration is _____ memory.
   a. short-term   c. long-term
   b. sensory   d. temporary

5. Alice's ability to remember all the actions required to ride her motorcycle is due to her repetitive practice, to the point where riding it is almost reflexive. Any set of skills acquired this way is part of _____ memory.

6. Implicit memory is to explicit memory as _____ are to _____.
   a. motor skills; facts and information
   b. episodic memories; semantic memories
   c. semantic memories; episodic memories
   d. facts and information; motor skills

7. Ben and his friends were talking about some great times they had in high school. Recounting those stories as if they had happened yesterday, the friends were relying on _____ memory.
   a. semantic   c. personal
   b. implicit   d. episodic

8. You use _____ memory when you answer questions such as "What is the capital of California?"
   a. episodic   c. geographic
   b. semantic   d. flashbulb

9. An example of good recall is doing well on a multiple-choice test. (true/false)

10. An example of good recognition ability is doing well on a multiple-choice test. (true/false)

11. Sigmund Freud did extensive research on memory. He used nonsense syllables to determine forgetting curves. (true/false)

12. When she was 16 years old, Sarah was severely injured in a car accident and was unconscious for 14 days. She can remember nothing immediately preceding the accident. This is known as _____ amnesia.
    a. trauma   c. proactive
    b. retroactive d. retrograde

13. With retroactive interference, _____ information interferes with _____ information.
    a. new; old   c. unpleasant; pleasant
    b. old; new   d. factual; emotional

14. Using_____, a person removes an unpleasant memory from consciousness.
    a. regression   c. repression
    b. traumatic amnesia d. degeneration

15. Wilder Penfield believed that what patients whose temporal lobes were stimulated experienced were vivid memories; Neisser suggested that these experiences were more like the contents of _____
    a. flashbulb memories.   c. dreams.
    b. repression recall.   d. desires.

16. The concept of infantile amnesia is used to dispute the idea that people can recover repressed memories from early childhood. (true/false)

17. Experts say that overlearning is basically a waste of time—that is, after you have gone over material once, you will not benefit from further study. (true/false)

18. It appears that the _____ is important in the formation of episodic memory.
    a. hippocampus   c. amygdala
    b. cerebellum   d. temporal lobe

19. Jason's vivid memory of the day President Kennedy was shot is known as _____ memory.
    a. histrionic   c. semantic
    b. flashbulb   d. retroactive

20. Eyewitnesses are more likely to identify the wrong person if the person is of a different race. (true/false)

Section Five: Critical Thinking

1. Some studies cited in this chapter involved only one or a few participants.
   a. Select two of these studies and discuss the possible problems in drawing conclusions on the basis of studies using so few participants.
   b. Suggest several possible explanations for the findings other than those proposed by the researchers.
   c. In your view, should such limited studies be mentioned in a textbook? Why or why not?

2. Prepare an argument in favor of each of the following statements regarding therapeutic approaches for treating depression and eating disorders in patients who at the outset have no memory of childhood sexual abuse:
   a. Attempting to recover repressed memories of childhood sexual abuse through hypnosis is useful.
   b. Attempting to recover repressed memories of childhood sexual abuse through hypnosis can cause more harm than good.

3. Drawing on your knowledge, formulate a plan that you can put into operation to help improve your memory and avoid the pitfalls that cause forgetting.

7 Cognition, Language, and Creativity

Around 4 P.M. on May 11, 1997, a human conceded defeat to a machine in a contest involving a highly complex mental activity. Garry Kasparov, the Russian-born grand master widely considered to be the best chess player of all time, was defeated by a computer.

The computer, Deep Blue, had been designed and programmed by a team from IBM specifically to play chess against Kasparov. In their grueling first match a year earlier, Kasparov beat Deep Blue, as the world had expected. Then, when he faced a much improved, more powerful version of the computer in the second match and was forced to concede, the event made headlines around the world.

Can Deep Blue really think? Does this machine have cognitive abilities equal to, or even greater than, those of humans? Many experts—including cognitive psychologists, computer scientists, and even philosophers—have debated these questions almost endlessly.

The issue hinges, of course, on how "thinking" is defined. Deep Blue (technically a supercomputer with 32 nodes for parallel processing) far outclasses any human in mathematical search-and-match activity: It can evaluate 200 million chess positions a second and discard useless ones (Peterson, 1996). And some experts believe that when the computer demonstrated selectivity—looking in the right place in its stores of information for a required piece of data—it was engaging in a process analogous to human thought. But other experts claim that Deep Blue was not really thinking on its own. Computers can only do what they are programmed to do; in other words, they lack the intuition and practical experience of humans. Thus, even the sophisticated "thinking" of supercomputers is not really intelligence because, unlike humans, these machines are merely following a set of rules, no matter how complex those rules may be.

Stunned by his defeat, Kasparov disagreed with Deep Blue's critics. As the match proceeded, he felt that the computer was showing signs of human-like cognitive ability in the form of strategic understanding. Somewhere along the way, the tactics (specific rules for playing chess) that had been programmed into Deep Blue had apparently been transformed into strategy (formulation of an overall game plan). As one of Kasparov's advisers concluded, the machine's victory may have been the best evidence yet of true computer intelligence.

What is meant by cognition, and what specific processes does it include?

cognition: The mental processes that are involved in acquiring, storing, retrieving, and using information and that include sensation, perception, imagery, concept formation, reasoning, decision making, problem solving, and language.

imagery: The representation in the mind of a sensory experience—visual, auditory, gustatory, motor, olfactory, or tactile.

concept: A mental category used to represent a class or group of objects, people, organizations, events, situations, or relations that share common characteristics or attributes.

Until the modern age, who could have envisioned the development of a computer—a machine—capable of defeating a world-champion chess player? Surprisingly, the ancient Greek thinker Aristotle (384–322 B.C.), who furthered the study of human cognition by inventing laws for reasoning and stressed the importance of mental imagery, foresaw something similar:

> If every instrument could accomplish its own work, obeying or anticipating the will of others . . . if the shuttle could weave, and the pick touch the lyre, without a hand to guide them, chief workmen would not need servants, nor masters slaves.

What Aristotle envisioned when he wrote those words over 2,000 years ago—shuttles that could weave without a weaver, lyres that could play music without a musician—were machines much like the modern robots and supercomputers developed through the science of artificial intelligence. And even though a human was defeated at chess by a supercomputer, human cognitive ability—which developed and built the machine—was the victor.

Cognition refers collectively to the mental processes involved in acquiring, storing, retrieving, and using knowledge (Matlin, 1989). In earlier chapters, we looked at some specific cognitive processes, such as sensation, perception, and memory. In this chapter, we explore the cognitive processes of imagery, concept formation, reasoning, decision making, problem solving, and language, and then we examine intelligence and creativity.

IMAGERY AND CONCEPTS: TOOLS OF THINKING

In trying to prove his existence, the great French philosopher René Descartes (1596–1650) said, "I think, therefore I am." Unfortunately, he did not proceed to describe the act of thinking itself. All of us have an intuitive notion of what thinking is. We say, "I think it's going to rain" (a prediction); "I think this is the right answer" (a choice); "I think I will resign" (a decision). But our everyday use of the word *think* does not suggest the processes we use to perform the act itself. Sometimes thinking is free-flowing rather than goal-oriented. At other times it is directed and aimed at a goal such as solving a problem or making a decision. Just how is the act of thinking accomplished? There is general agreement that it makes use of at least two tools—images and concepts.

Imagery: Picture This

Can you imagine hearing a recording of your favorite song or someone calling your name? Can you picture yourself jogging, walking, or kissing someone you love? In doing these things, you take advantage of your own ability to use mental **imagery**—that is, to represent or picture a sensory experience mentally. Albert Einstein is said to have done much of his thinking in images.

In a survey of 500 adults conducted by McKellar (1972), 97% said they had visual images; 93% reported auditory images (imagine your psychology professor's voice); 74% claimed to have motor imagery (imagine raising your hand); 70%, tactile or touch images (imagine rubbing sandpaper); 67%, gustatory images (imagine the taste of a dill pickle); and 66%, olfactory images (imagine smelling a rose). Visual imagery is certainly the most common, although auditory imagery is not far behind.

Our mental images may be dimmer and less vivid than actual experiences, but the images are not limited to time and space, size, or other physical realities. You can imagine yourself flying though the air like an eagle, singing to the thundering applause of adoring fans, or performing all sorts of amazing feats. But normally our imaging is quite similar to the real world we are thinking about.

Not only can we form a mental image of an object, but we can manipulate and move it around mentally much as we would if we were actually holding and looking at the object (Cooper & Shepard, 1984; Farah, 1995; Kosslyn & Sussman, 1995). In an early study, Shepard & Metzler (1971) asked eight research participants to judge some 1,600 pairs of drawings like the ones in Figure 7.1. Participants had to rotate the objects mentally to see if they matched. The objects in Figure 7.1 (a) and (b) match; those in Figure 7.1 (c) do not. The more the objects had to be rotated mentally, the longer it took participants to decide whether they matched. This is precisely what would happen if the participants had rotated real objects—the more the objects needed to be rotated, the longer it would take to make the decision.

Concepts: A Mental Classification System (Is a Penguin a Bird?)

Fortunately, thinking is not limited to conjuring up images of sights, sounds, touches, tastes, and smells. We humans are capable of conceptualizing as well. A **concept** is a mental category used to represent a class or group of objects, people, organizations, events, situations, or relations that share common characteristics or attributes. *Furniture, tree, student, college, wedding* are all examples of concepts. As fundamental units of thought, concepts are useful tools that help us to order our world and to think and communicate with speed and efficiency.

Thanks to our ability to use concepts, we are not forced to consider and describe everything in great detail before we make an identification. We do not need a differ-

Figure 7.1

Samples of Geometric Patterns in Shepard and Metzler's Mental Rotation Study

Mentally rotate one of the patterns in each pair—(a), (b), and (c)—and decide whether the two patterns match. Do you find that the more you have to rotate the objects mentally, the longer it takes to decide if they match? (From Shepard & Metzler, 1971.)

What is imagery?

What is a concept?

ent name to identify and describe every single rock, tree, animal, or situation. If you see a hairy, brown and white, four-legged animal with its mouth open, tongue hanging out, and tail wagging, you recognize it immediately as a representative of the concept *dog*. *Dog* is a concept that stands for a class of animals that share similar characteristics or attributes, even though they may differ in significant ways. Great Danes, dachshunds, collies, Chihuahuas, and other breeds—you recognize all these varied creatures according to the concept *dog*.

What is the difference between a formal concept and a natural concept?

Formal and Natural Concepts   Psychologists identify two basic types of concepts: formal (also known as artificial) concepts and natural (also known as fuzzy) concepts.

Some concepts are learned in an orderly, systematic way, rather than in a random, informal fashion. Such a concept is generally a **formal concept**, one that is clearly defined by a set of rules, a formal definition, or a classification system. Formal concepts often arise in the sciences and other academic disciplines.

Eleanor Rosch (1973, 1978) argues that formal concepts tend to be rather artificial and not related to actual experience. Most of the concepts we form and use are **natural concepts**, acquired not from definitions but through everyday perceptions and experiences. Rosch and her colleagues studied concept formation in its natural setting and concluded that in real life, natural concepts (such as *fruit*, *vegetable*, and *bird*) are somewhat fuzzy, not clear-cut and systematic.

We acquire many natural concepts through experiences with examples, or positive instances of the concept. When children are young, parents may point out examples of a car—the family car, the neighbor's car, cars on the street, and pictures of cars in books. But if a child points to some other type of moving vehicle and says "car," the parent will say, "No, that is a truck," or "This is a bus." *Truck* and *bus* are negative instances, or nonexamples, of the concept *car*. After experience with positive and negative instances of the concept, a child begins to grasp some of the properties of a car that distinguish it from other wheeled vehicles.

In using natural concepts, we are likely to picture a **prototype** of the concept—an example that embodies its most common and typical features. What is your prototype for the concept *bird*? Chances are it is not a penguin, an ostrich, or a kiwi. All three are birds that cannot fly. A more likely bird prototype is a robin or perhaps a sparrow. Most birds can fly, but not all; most mammals cannot fly, but bats are mammals, have wings, and can fly. So not all examples of a natural concept fit it equally well. This is why natural concepts often seem less clear-cut than formal ones. Nevertheless, the prototype most closely fits a given natural concept, and other examples of the concept most often share more attributes with that prototype than with the prototype of any other concept.

A recent theory of concept formation suggests that concepts are represented by their **exemplars**—individual instances, or examples, of a concept that are stored in memory from personal experience (Estes, 1994). To decide whether an unfamiliar item belongs to a concept, we compare it with exemplars (other examples) of that concept.

A prototype is an example that embodies the most typical features of a concept. Which of the animals shown here best fits your prototype for the concept bird?

The concepts we form do not exist in isolation, but rather in hierarchies. For example, the canary and the cardinal are subsets of the concept *bird*; at a higher level, birds are subsets of the concept *animal*; and at a still higher level, animals are a subset of the concept *living things*. Thus, concept formation has a certain logic to it.

DECISION MAKING: MAKING CHOICES IN LIFE

Reasoning is a vital component of decision making. And the quality of our lives is strongly influenced by the decisions we make. Many decisions are simple and mundane—what to have for dinner or what clothes to put on in the morning. But other decisions are more far-reaching—what career to pursue or whether to remain in a relationship. **Decision making** is the process of considering alternatives and choos-

Table 7.1   Selecting an Apartment Using the Additive Strategy

Factors to Be Considered	Apartment A		Apartment B		Apartment C	
Convenience of location	+2	(+4)	+3	(+6)	+2	(+4)
Safety of neighborhood	+3	(+6)	−1	(−2)	+1	(+2)
Rent	−3	−3	+1	+1	−2	−2
Attractiveness	+3	+3	+2	+2	+3	+3
Availability of parking	+2	+2	+3	+3	+2	+2
	7	(12)	8	(10)	6	(9)

Note: Numbers in parentheses are ratings after weighting the factors.

ing among them. Decisions are influenced by many factors, including values, interests, life goals, experiences, and knowledge.

Psychologists have identified various approaches to decision making. Let's examine some of these approaches.

The Additive Strategy

Suppose you wanted to rent an apartment starting next semester. How would you go about deciding among different apartments? You could use the **additive strategy**—a decision-making approach in which each alternative is rated on each of the important factors affecting the decision and the alternative with the highest overall rating is chosen.

Suppose you decided that the important factors in choosing an apartment were those listed in Table 7.1. Having identified the factors, you would arbitrarily select a rating scale, such as −3 to +3, and rate each of the apartments on each factor. Then, you would add the ratings and select the apartment with the highest total, which in this example is apartment B.

But if you are like most people, some factors are more important than others when selecting a suitable place to live. To take the difference into account, you can weight, or give more emphasis to, the factors that are most important. In Table 7.1, a convenient location and safety are weighted as being most important, and their ratings are multiplied by 2. With this weighted additive strategy, apartment A is the best choice.

Elimination by Aspects

Another decision-making strategy is called *elimination by aspects* (Tversky, 1972). With this approach, the factors on which the alternatives are to be evaluated are ordered from most important to least important. Any alternative that does not satisfy the most important factor is automatically eliminated. The process of elimination continues as each factor is considered in order. The alternative that survives is the one chosen.

The elimination-by-aspects strategy is an example of a *noncompensatory decision strategy*—one that does not allow a high ranking on one factor to compensate for a low ranking on another. This type of approach is most useful when there are many alternatives and multiple factors to be considered. It is usually best to use the elimination-by-aspects strategy first to quickly and efficiently reduce the number of alternatives. Then the additive strategy can be used to make the best choice among the surviving alternatives.

How is the additive strategy used in decision making?

When is the elimination-by-aspects strategy most useful?

formal concept: A concept that is clearly defined by a set of rules, a formal definition, or a classification system; an artificial concept.

natural concept: A concept acquired not from a definition but through everyday perceptions and experiences; a fuzzy concept.

prototype: The example that embodies the most common and typical features of a concept.

exemplars: The individual instances of a concept that are stored in memory from personal experience.

decision making: The process of considering alternatives and choosing among them.

additive strategy: A decision-making approach in which each alternative is rated on each important factor affecting the decision and the alternative rated highest overall is chosen.

Heuristics and Decision Making

Sometimes we make decisions based on a belief that an event or a set of circumstances carries a certain probability. Such probability assumptions are often based on **heuristics**—rules of thumb that are derived from experience and used in decision making and problem solving, although there is no guarantee of their accuracy or usefulness.

What is the availability heuristic?

The Availability Heuristic   Decision making is quite likely to be influenced by how quickly and easily information bearing on the decision comes to mind—that is, how readily available that information is in memory. The cognitive rule of thumb that the probability of an event or the importance assigned to it is based on its availability in memory is known as the **availability heuristic**.

Any information affecting a decision, whether it is accurate or not, is more likely to be considered if it is readily available. In 1998, Oprah Winfrey was sued by the cattle industry for comments made on her show about "mad cow disease" and the possibility that it made eating hamburgers too risky. In other words, the cattle industry was blaming Oprah for establishing an availability heuristic that led viewers to decide *not* to eat its product.

What is the representativeness heuristic?

The Representativeness Heuristic   Another common heuristic used in decision making, in judging people, or in predicting the probability of certain events is the representativeness heuristic. The **representativeness heuristic** is a thinking strategy based on how closely a new object or situation is judged to resemble or match an existing prototype of that object or situation (Pitz & Sachs, 1984). The representativeness heuristic is an effective decision-making strategy that can lead to good decisions *if* the instance selected truly matches the appropriate prototype.

Suppose you were playing a coin-tossing game in which you had to predict whether the outcome of each toss would be heads or tails. Let's say the first five coin tosses came up heads. What would you predict the next toss to be? Many people would predict tails to be more likely on the next toss, because a sample of coin tosses should be approximately 50% heads. Thus, a tail is long overdue, they reason. Nevertheless, the next toss is just as likely to be a head as a tail. After 100 coin tosses, the proportions of heads and tails should be about equal, but for each *individual* coin toss, the probability still remains 50–50.

Framing and Decision Making

What is framing?

Words matter! The way information is "framed" tends to influence decision making. **Framing** refers to the way information is presented so as to emphasize either a potential gain or a potential loss as the outcome.

To study the effects of framing on decision making, Kahneman and Tversky (1984) presented the following options to a group of participants. Which program would you choose?

> The United States is preparing for the outbreak of a dangerous disease, which is expected to kill 600 people. There have been designed two alternative programs to combat the disease. If program A is adopted, 200 people will be saved. If program B is adopted, there is a one-third probability that all 600 will be saved and a two-thirds probability that no people will be saved.

The researchers found that 72% of the participants selected the "sure thing" of program A over the "risky gamble" of program B. Now consider the options as they were reframed:

> If program C is adopted, 400 people will die. If program D is adopted, there is a one-third probability that nobody will die and a two-thirds probability that all 600 people will die.

Which program did you choose? Of research participants given this version of the problem, 78% chose program D. A careful reading will reveal that program D has the exact same consequences as program B in the earlier version. How can this result be explained?

The first version of the problem was framed to focus attention on the number of lives that could be saved. And when people are primarily motivated to achieve gains (save lives), they are more likely to choose a safe option over a risky one, as 72% of the participants did. The second version was framed to focus attention on the 400 lives that would be lost. When trying to avoid losses, people appear much more willing to choose a risky option, as 78% of the participants were.

There are numerous practical applications of framing to decision making. Customers are more readily motivated to buy products if they are on sale than if they are simply priced lower than similar products to begin with. As a result, customers focus on what they save—a gain—rather than on what they spend—a loss. People seem more willing to purchase an $18,000 car and receive a $1,000 rebate (a gain) than to simply pay $17,000 for the same car.

Heuristics can be effective and efficient cognitive techniques, but they can also lead to errors in perceptions and decisions.

PROBLEM SOLVING: BEYOND DECISION MAKING

Approaches to Problem Solving: Helpful Basic Techniques

We all face problems that must be solved—problems both great and small. We solve many everyday problems with little difficulty and a minimum of mental effort. Some problems can be solved by insight, as described in Chapter 5. But some problems are more challenging. **Problem solving** refers to thoughts and actions required to achieve a desired goal that is not readily attainable. Three basic approaches to problem solving are trial and error, algorithms, and heuristics.

How would you go about solving the problem described in the *Try It!*?

heuristic (yur-RIS-tik): A rule of thumb that is derived from experience and used in decision making and problem solving, even though there is no guarantee of its accuracy or usefulness.

availability heuristic: A cognitive rule of thumb that says that the probability of an event or the importance assigned to it is based on its availability in memory.

representativeness heuristic: A thinking strategy based on how closely a new object or situation is judged to resemble or match an existing prototype of that object or situation.

framing: The way information is presented so as to emphasize either a potential gain or a potential loss as the outcome.

problem solving: Thoughts and actions required to achieve a desired goal that is not readily attainable.

What are three basic approaches to problem solving?

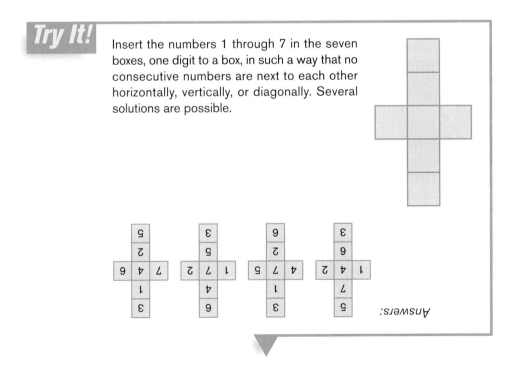

Try It!

Insert the numbers 1 through 7 in the seven boxes, one digit to a box, in such a way that no consecutive numbers are next to each other horizontally, vertically, or diagonally. Several solutions are possible.

Answers:

Trial and Error   How did you choose to solve the *Try It!* problem? Some people examine the problem carefully and devise a strategy—such as placing the 1 or the 7 in the middle box because each has only *one* forbidden consecutive number (2 or 6) to avoid. Many people, however, simply start placing the numbers in the boxes and then change them around when a combination doesn't work. This approach, called **trial and error**, involves trying one solution after another, in no particular order, until hitting upon the answer by chance. Even nonhuman animals use trial and error. However, other techniques are far more effective and less time-consuming.

What is an algorithm?

Algorithms   Another major problem-solving method is the algorithm (Newell & Simon, 1972). An **algorithm** is a systematic, step-by-step procedure that guarantees a solution to a problem of a certain type if the algorithm is appropriate and is executed properly. Formulas used in mathematics and sciences are algorithms. Another type of algorithm is a systematic strategy for exploring every possible solution to a problem until the correct one is reached. In some cases millions or even billions or more possibilities may have to be considered before the solution is found. Often computers are programmed to solve problems using such algorithms, because with a computer an accurate solution is guaranteed and millions of possible solutions can be tried in a few seconds.

Many problems do not lend themselves to solution by algorithms, however. Suppose you were a contestant on "Wheel of Fortune," trying to solve this missing-letter puzzle: P_Y_ _ _L_ _ Y. An exhaustive search algorithm would be out of the question—even Vanna White's smile would fade long before the nearly 9 billion possibilities could be considered. An easier way to solve such problems is by using a heuristic strategy.

What are three heuristics used in problem solving?

Heuristics and Problem Solving   As we have seen, using a heuristic does not guarantee success but offers a promising way to attack a problem and arrive at a solution. Chess players must use heuristics because there is not enough time in a lifetime to consider all of the moves and countermoves that would be possible in a single game of chess.

People use heuristic techniques to eliminate useless steps and to take the shortest probable path toward a solution. The missing-letter puzzle presented earlier is easily solved through a simple heuristic approach that makes use of your existing knowledge of words (prefixes, roots, suffixes). You can supply the missing letters and spell out PSYCHOLOGY.

Working Backwards   One heuristic that is effective for solving some problems is **working backwards,** sometimes called the *backward search*. This approach starts with the solution, a known condition, and works back through the problem. Once the backward search has revealed the steps to be taken and their order, the problem can be solved. Try working backwards to solve the water lily problem in the *Try It!*

Means–End Analysis   A popular heuristic strategy is **means–end analysis**, in which the current position is compared with a desired goal, and a series of steps is formulated and then taken to close the gap between the two (Sweller & Levine, 1982). Many problems are large and complex and must be broken down into smaller steps or subproblems before a solution can be reached. If your professor assigns a term paper, for example, you probably do not simply sit down and write it. You must first determine how you will deal with your topic, research the topic, make an outline, and then write the sections over a period of time. At last you are ready to assemble the complete term paper, write several drafts, and put the finished product in final form before handing it in and receiving your A.

The Analogy Heuristic   Another problem-solving strategy is the **analogy heuristic**—applying a solution used for a past problem to a current problem that shares many similar features. Situations with many features in common are said to be analogous.

trial and error: An approach to problem solving in which one solution after another is tried in no particular order until an answer is found.

algorithm: A systematic, step-by-step procedure, such as a mathematical formula, that guarantees a solution to a problem of a certain type if the algorithm is appropriate and is executed properly.

working backwards: A heuristic strategy in which a person discovers the steps needed to solve a problem by defining the desired goal and working backwards to the current condition.

means–end analysis: A heuristic strategy in which the current position is compared with the desired goal, and a series of steps are formulated and taken to close the gap between them.

analogy heuristic: A rule of thumb that applies a solution that solved a problem in the past to a current problem that shares many similar features.

Try It!

Water lilies double the area they cover every 24 hours. At the beginning of the summer there is one water lily on a pond. It takes 60 days for the pond to become covered with water lilies. On what day is the pond half covered? (From Fixx, 1978.)

Answer: The most important fact is that the lilies double in number every 24 hours. If the pond is to be completely covered on the 60th day, it has to be half covered on the 59th day.

When faced with a new problem to solve, you can look for commonalities between the new problem and other problems you have solved before and apply a strategy similar to one that has worked in the past. For example, if your car is making strange sounds and you take it to an auto mechanic, the mechanic may be able to diagnose the problem by analogy—the sounds your car is making are comparable to sounds heard before and associated with a particular problem.

Impediments to Problem Solving: Mental Stumbling Blocks

Sometimes we face problems that seem to defy solution despite our best efforts. We may lack the relevant knowledge or experience to solve some problems or sufficient material resources to solve others. Do you have any problems that could be solved if money were no object? There are other impediments to problem solving that serve as stumbling blocks for many. Two of these are functional fixedness and mental set.

Functional Fixedness   Many of us are hampered in our efforts to solve problems in daily life because of **functional fixedness**—the failure to use familiar objects in novel ways to solve problems. We tend to see objects only in terms of their customary functions. Just think of all the items you use daily—tools, utensils, and other equipment—that help you perform certain functions. Often the normal functions of objects become fixed in your thinking so that you do not consider using them in new and creative ways.

Suppose you wanted a cup of coffee, but the decanter for your coffeemaker was broken? If you suffered from functional fixedness, you might come to the conclusion that there was nothing you could do to solve your problem at that moment. But, rather than thinking about the object or utensil that you *don't* have, think about the function that will solve your problem. What you need is something to catch the coffee, rather than the specific glass decanter that came with the coffeemaker. Could you catch the coffee in a bowl or cooking utensil, or even in coffee mugs?

Mental Set   Another impediment to problem solving, similar to functional fixedness but much broader, is mental set. **Mental set** is a mental rut in one's

How do functional fixedness and mental set impede problem solving?

Link It!

functional fixedness: The failure to use familiar objects in novel ways to solve problems because of a tendency to view objects only in terms of their customary functions.

mental set: The tendency to apply a familiar strategy to the solution of a problem without carefully considering the special requirements of that problem.

approach to solving problems, the tendency to continue to use the same old method even though another approach might be better. Perhaps you hit on a way to solve a problem once in the past and continue to use the same technique in similar situations, even though it is not highly effective or efficient. People are much more susceptible to mental set when they fail to consider the special requirements of a problem. Not surprisingly, the same people who are subject to mental set are also more likely to have trouble with functional fixedness when they attempt to solve problems (McKelvie, 1984).

Humans are not the only ones on the planet able to solve problems. We mentioned that many animals can solve problems, and so can modern computers.

Artificial Intelligence

What is artificial intelligence?

Computer intelligence that rivals or surpasses human intelligence has long been the stuff of which science fiction is made. You may have heard of Hal, the uncontrollable superintelligent computer from Arthur Clarke's novel or the movie based on it, *2001: A Space Odyssey*. Although the year 2001 is fast approaching, no computer anything like the sinister Hal is on the horizon.

Nevertheless, amazing progress has been made in the field of artificial intelligence since the term was first used officially by researcher John McCarthy in 1956. **Artificial intelligence**, or AI, refers to the programming of computer systems to simulate human thinking in solving problems and in making judgments and decisions.

World champion Garry Kasparov contemplates a move against Deep Blue, an IBM computer that exhibits artificial intelligence in the area of top-level chess play.

Now *expert systems* are available that "perform a substantial number of human tasks at a professional level" (Simon, 1995, p. 507). Some expert systems use the collective knowledge and the problem-solving strategies of the top experts in a field. Today there are expert systems in medicine, psychotherapy, space technology, military defense, weather prediction, and a variety of other fields.

Expert systems have severe limitations, however. They cannot function outside of their area of expertise. Expert systems, then, are useful only as assistants to humans; they cannot stand alone. Expert systems cannot, as humans can, take exceptions into account, consider the context, or make countless other interpretations as they "think." They cannot execute many of the tasks that humans perform with ease, such as recognizing a particular face or interpreting a slurred, indistinct word in a conversation (Lenat, 1995).

How does the ability of computer systems compare with that of the human brain? These systems far surpass the human brain in their ability to retrieve accurately massive amounts of stored data and make decisions about the data based on specific facts and rules that have been programmed into the system. And computers are vastly superior to humans in carrying out complex mathematical operations, all at lightning speed. Modern computers can process millions of numbers in the span of an eyeblink.

Computer Neural Networks   Conventional computers have a single central processing unit that solves problems one step at a time. In contrast, supercomputers contain a number of processors that work in parallel. A problem can be divided into parts and handled by the various processors simultaneously; this enables the job to be completed much more quickly.

The human brain resembles the parallel-processing supercomputer in that it can carry out many functions at the same time. Researchers are devising computer systems based on their understanding of how neurons in certain parts of the brain are connected and how the connections develop (Buonomano & Merzenich, 1995; Hinton et al., 1995). Computer systems that are intended to mimic the human brain are called **neural networks**. Like those in the brain, connections in a computer neural network

artificial intelligence: The programming of computer systems to simulate human thinking in solving problems and in making judgments and decisions.

neural networks: Computer systems that are intended to mimic the human brain.

can be strengthened or weakened as a result of experience. Using neural networks, psychologists can test theories about how the brain works, and computer scientists can use the knowledge gained to develop new systems that better simulate the ability of the human brain.

For example, already in existence is a speech recognition system that can handle a 20,000-word vocabulary regardless of who the speaker is. Voice recognition systems are now used by banks and credit card companies and in other commercial settings. But unlike humans, such computer systems cannot understand the subtleties of language—tone of voice, quality of nonverbal behavior, or even level of politeness (Peterson, 1993). No computer can even approach the complexity and capability of the human brain.

The study of neural networks is being applied to the design of computerized work stations with voice recognition systems and robotic arms to allow paraplegics to perform a variety of tasks.

LANGUAGE

It is true that we can think without language. We can use imagery, picture steps in a process, think kinesthetically in terms of body movements, and so on. Yet language remains a critically important tool of thought. Language increases the ability to think abstractly, to grasp and formulate concepts, to reason by analogy, to solve problems, and to express ideas. Without language, there would be no books to read, no papers to write, no lectures to endure. Not bad so far, you may be thinking. But consider: Without language, each of us would live in a largely solitary and isolated world, unable to communicate or receive any information.

Language is a means of communicating thoughts and feelings, using a system of socially shared but arbitrary symbols (sounds, signs, or written symbols) arranged according to rules of grammar. Fortunately, language is creative and generative. Language allows us to form and comprehend a virtually infinite number of meaningful sentences. Language enables us to communicate about things that are abstract or concrete, present or not present, and about what has been, is now, or conceivably might be. Thanks to language, we can profit from the experience, the knowledge, and the wisdom of others from every corner of the world.

Truly, language is one of the most important capabilities of the human species. Whether spoken, written, or signed, it is our most important cognitive tool. In Chapter 8, we will discuss how language is acquired by infants. Here we explore the components and the structure of this amazing form of human communication.

The Structure of Language

Psycholinguistics is the study of how language is acquired, produced, and used and how the sounds and symbols of language are translated into meaning. Psycholinguists devote much effort to the study of the structure of language and the rules governing its use. The structure and rules governing language involve four different components—phonemes, morphemes, syntax, and semantics.

Phonemes   The smallest units of sound in a spoken language are known as **phonemes**. Phonemes form the basic building blocks of a spoken language. Three phonemes together form the sound of the word *cat*—the *c* (which sounds like *k*), *a*, and *t*. Phonemes sound like the letters as they are used in words, like the *b* in *boy*, the *p* in *pan*, and so on. The sound of the phoneme *c* in the word *cat* is different from the sound of the phoneme *c* in the word *city*.

Letters combined to form sounds are also phonemes, such as the *th* in *the* and the *ch* in *child*. The same sound (phoneme) may be represented by different letters in different words, as the *a* in *stay* and the *ei* in *sleigh*. And, as you saw with *c*, the same

What are the four important components of language?

language: A means of communicating thoughts and feelings, using a system of socially shared but arbitrary symbols (sounds, signs, or written symbols) arranged according to rules of grammar.

psycholinguistics: The study of how language is acquired, produced, and used, and how the sounds and symbols of language are translated into meaning.

phonemes: The smallest units of sound in a spoken language.

letter can serve as different phonemes. The letter *a*, for example, is sounded as four different phonemes in *day, cap, watch,* and *law.*

Though phonemes are the basic building blocks of language, they alone, with a few exceptions, do not provide language with meaning. Meaning is based on the next component of language, the morphemes.

Morphemes Morphemes are the smallest units of meaning in a language. In almost all cases in the English language, a morpheme is made of two or more phonemes. But a few phonemes also serve as morphemes, such as the article *a* and the personal pronoun *I.* Many words in English are single morphemes—*book, word, learn, reason,* and so on. In addition to root words, morphemes may also be prefixes (such as *re* in *relearn*) or suffixes (such as *ed* to show past tense, as in *learned*). The single morpheme *reason* becomes the dual morpheme *reasonable.* The letter *s* gives a plural meaning to a word and is thus a morpheme. The morpheme *book* (singular) becomes two morphemes, *books* (plural).

So morphemes, singly and in combination, form the words in a language and provide meaning. But sounds and single words alone are not enough. A language also requires rules for structuring or putting together words in orderly and meaningful fashion. This is where syntax enters the picture.

Syntax Syntax is the aspect of grammar that specifies the rules for arranging and combining words to form phrases and sentences. An important rule of syntax in English is that adjectives usually come before nouns. So we refer to the residence of the U.S. President as the White House. But in Spanish the noun usually comes before the adjective, and speakers would say, "la Casa Blanca," or "the House White." So the rules of word order, or syntax, differ from one language to another.

Semantics Semantics refers to the meaning derived from morphemes, words, and sentences. The same word can have different meanings depending on how it is used in sentences: "I don't mind." "Mind your manners." "He has lost his mind." Or consider another example: "Loving to read, the young girl read three books last week." Here the word *read* is pronounced two different ways and in one case is in the past tense.

Animal Language

How does language in trained chimpanzees differ from human language?

Ask people what capability most reliably sets humans apart from all other animal species, and most will answer language. And for good reason. As far as scientists know, humans are the only species to have developed this rich, varied, and complex system of communication. But even though they have never developed language, could our nearest cousins, the chimpanzees, learn to master its rudiments and complexities if humans taught them? The earliest attempts to answer this question date back almost 70 years.

As early as 1933 and 1951, researchers attempted to teach chimpanzees to speak by raising the chimps in their homes. These experiments failed because the vocal tract in chimpanzees and the other apes is not adapted to human speech. Researchers next turned to sign language.

Psychologists Allen and Beatrix Gardner (1969) took in a 1-year-old chimp named Washoe and taught her sign language. Washoe learned signs for objects, and certain commands and concepts such as "flower," "give me," "come," "open," and "more." By the end of her fifth year she had mastered about 160 signs (Fleming, 1974).

Psychologist David Premack (1971) taught another chimp, Sarah, to use an artificial language he developed. Its symbols consisted of magnetized chips of various shapes, sizes, and colors, as shown in Figure 7.2. Premack used operant conditioning techniques to teach Sarah to select the magnetic chip representing a fruit and place it on a magnetic language board. The trainer would then reward Sarah with the fruit she had requested.

Sarah mastered the concepts of similarities and differences, and eventually she could signal whether two objects were the same or different with nearly perfect accuracy (Premack & Premack, 1983). Even more remarkable, Sarah could view a whole apple and a cut apple and, even though she had not seen the apple being cut, could match the apple with the utensil needed to cut it—a knife.

At the Yerkes Primate Research Center at Emory University, a chimp named Lana participated in a computer-controlled language training program. She learned to press keys imprinted with geometric symbols that represented words in an artificial language called Yerkish. Researcher Sue Savage-Rumbaugh and a colleague (1986; Rumbaugh, 1977) varied the location, color, and brightness of the keys, so Lana had to learn which symbols to use no matter where they were located. One day her trainer Tim had an orange that she wanted. Lana had available symbols for many fruits—apple, banana, and so on—but none for an orange. Yet there was a symbol for the color orange. So Lana improvised and signaled, "Tim give apple which is orange." Impressive!

But was human-like language being displayed in these studies with primates? Not according to Herbert Terrace (1979, 1981), who examined the research of others and conducted his own. Terrace and coworkers taught sign language to a chimp they called Nim Chimpsky (after the famed linguist Noam Chomsky) and reported Nim's progress from the age of 2 weeks to 4 years. Nim learned 125 symbols, which is respectable, but does not amount to language, according to Terrace (1985, 1986). Terrace believed that chimps like Nim and Washoe were simply imitating their trainers and making responses to get reinforcers, according to the laws of operant conditioning, not the laws of language. Finally, Terrace suggested that the studies with primates were probably influenced by experimenter bias; trainers might unconsciously tend to interpret the behavior of the chimps as more indicative of progress toward developing language than it really was. However, Terrace had not heard of Kanzi when he expressed his skepticism.

The most impressive performance to date is that of a pygmy chimpanzee, Kanzi, who developed an amazing ability to communicate with his trainers without any formal training. During the mid-1980s, researchers had taught Kanzi's mother to press symbols representing words. Her progress was not remarkable; but her infant son Kanzi, who stood by and observed her during training, was learning rapidly (thanks to observational learning, discussed in Chapter 5). When Kanzi had a chance at the symbol board, his performance quickly surpassed that of his mother and of every other chimp the researchers had tested.

Kanzi demonstrated an advanced understanding (for chimps) of spoken English and could respond correctly even to new commands, such as "Throw your ball to the river," or "Go to the refrigerator and get out a tomato" (Savage-Rumbaugh, 1990; Savage-Rumbaugh et al., 1992). By the time Kanzi was 6 years old, a team of researchers who worked with him had recorded more than 13,000 "utterances" and reported that Kanzi could communicate using some 200 different geometric symbols (Gibbons, 1991). Kanzi could press symbols to ask someone to play chase with him and even ask two others to play chase while he watched. And if Kanzi signalled someone to "chase" and "hide," he was insistent that his first command, "chase," be done first (Gibbons, 1991).

Kanzi was not merely responding to nearby trainers whose actions or gestures he might have copied. He could respond just as well when requests were made over earphones so that no one else in the room could signal to him purposely or inadvertently.

Do such seemingly remarkable feats indicate that chimps are capable of using anything close to human language? Impressive as Kanzi's accomplishments seem to be, Premack firmly maintains that it is unlikely that animals are capable of language. They can be taught to signal, to choose, and to solve some problems, but mere strings

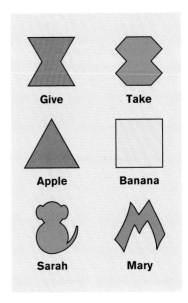

Figure 7.2

Sarah's Symbols

A chimpanzee named Sarah learned to communicate using plastic chips of various shapes, sizes, and colors to represent words in an artificial language developed by her trainer, David Premack. (From Premack, 1971.)

From their studies of communication among chimps, researchers have gained useful insights into the nature of language. Kanzi is skilled in using a special symbol board to communicate.

of words spoken, written, or signed do not amount to language unless they are structured grammatically.

Most animal species studied by language researchers are limited to motor responses, such as sign language, gestures, using magnetic symbols, or pressing keys on symbol boards. But these limitations do not extend to some bird species, such as parrots, which *are* capable of making human-like speech sounds. One remarkable case is Alex, an African grey parrot who not only mimics human speech, but seems to do so intelligently. Able to recognize and name various colors, objects, and shapes, Alex answers questions about them in English. Asked "Which object is green?" Alex easily names the green object (Pepperberg, 1991, 1994b). And he can count as well. When asked such questions as "How many red blocks?" Alex answers correctly about 80% of the time (Pepperberg, 1994a).

Research with sea mammals such as whales and dolphins has established that they apparently use complicated systems of grunts, whistles, clicks, and other sounds to communicate within their species (Herman, 1981; Savage-Rumbaugh, 1993). Researchers at the University of Hawaii have trained dolphins to respond to fairly complex commands requiring an understanding of directional and relational concepts. Dolphins can learn to pick out an object and put it on the right or left of a basket, for example, and comprehend such commands as "in the basket" and "under the basket" (Chollar, 1989).

Many of the remarkable communication feats reported for animal species are indeed impressive, especially those of chimpanzees. Clearly chimpanzees can learn to string together requests. But keep in mind that these are constructions, not sentences.

Language and Thinking

In general, does thought influence language more, or does language influence thought more?

If language is unique to humans, then does language drive human thinking? Does the fact that you speak English mean that you reason, think, and perceive your world differently than someone who speaks Spanish, or Chinese, or Swahili? According to one hypothesis presented over 40 years ago, it does.

Benjamin Whorf (1956) put forth his **linguistic relativity hypothesis** suggesting that the language a person speaks largely determines the nature of that person's thoughts. According to this hypothesis, people's worldview would be constructed primarily by the words in their language. As proof, Whorf offered his classic example. The languages used by the Eskimo people have a number of different words for snow, "*apikak*, first snow falling; *aniv*, snow spread out; *pukak*, snow for drinking water," while the English-speaking world has but one word, *snow* (Restak, 1988, p. 222). Whorf claimed that such a rich and varied selection of words for snow enabled Eskimos to think differently about it than do people whose languages lack specific words for various snow conditions.

Eleanor Rosch (1973) tested whether people whose language contains many names for colors would be better at thinking about and discriminating among colors than people whose language has only a few color names. Her subjects were English-speaking Americans and the Dani, members of a remote tribe in New Guinea whose language has only two names for colors—*mili* for dark, cool colors and *mola* for bright, warm colors.

Rosch showed members of both groups single-color chips of 11 colors—black, white, red, yellow, green, blue, brown, purple, pink, orange, and gray—for 5 seconds each. Then, after 30 seconds, she had the participants select the 11 colors they had viewed from an assortment of 40 color chips. Did the Americans outperform the Dani subjects, for whom brown, black, purple, and blue are all *mili*, or dark? No. Rosch found no significant differences between the Dani and the Americans in discriminating, remembering, or thinking about the 11 basic colors. Rosch's study did not support the linguistic relativity hypothesis.

Benjamin Whorf went too far in suggesting that language determines how people think. But we should not go too far in the opposite direction and assume that

linguistic relativity hypothesis: The notion that the language a person speaks largely determines the nature of that person's thoughts.

language has no influence on how people think. Thought both influences and is influenced by language, and language appears to *reflect* cultural differences more than it determines them (Pinker, 1994; Rosch, 1987). Language and thought have a mutually supportive relationship.

Sexism in Language   The words people use matter a great deal. Consider the generic use of the pronoun *he* to refer to people in general. If your professor says, "I expect each student in this class to do the best he can," does this announcement mean the same to males and females? Not according to research conducted by Gastil (1990) in which participants read sentences worded in three different forms. Perform Gastil's experiment yourself by completing the *Try It!*

 After reading each of these three sentences, pause and jot down any image that comes to mind.

1. The average American believes he watches too much television.

2. The average American believes he/she watches too much television.

3. Average Americans believe they watch too much television.

Whether you are male or female, the odds are high that you imaged a male after reading the first sentence in the *Try It!* Other studies confirm that the generic *he* is not interpreted very generically. It is interpreted heavily in favor of males (Hamilton, 1988; Henley, 1989; Ng, 1990). If this were not the case, then this sentence would not seem unusual at all: "Like other mammals, man bears his offspring live."

Bilingualism

Most native-born Americans speak only their native tongue, English. But in many other countries around the world, the majority of citizens speak two or even more languages (Snow, 1993). In European countries, most students learn English in addition to the languages of the countries bordering their own. Dutch is the native language of the Netherlands, but all Dutch schoolchildren learn German, French, and English. You would have to look long and hard for a native of the Netherlands who does not speak English.

   Most linguists are convinced that being bilingual has many advantages (Genesee, 1994). For example, in Canada, where most students study both French and English, bilingual students are said to score higher on aptitude and math tests than their counterparts who speak only one language (Lambert et al., 1993).

   People who are older when they learn a new language are far more likely to have an obvious accent and to make more grammatical errors than those who learn a new language as young children (McDonald, 1997). For learning to speak a second language like a native, with great fluency and no accent, apparently the younger the better is the rule. One reason for this difference between early and late language learners may have to do with slight variations in neural processing in Broca's area, the area of the brain that controls speech production. Research by Kim and others (1997) suggests that bilinguals who learn a second language early (younger than age 10 or 11) rely on the same patch of tissue in Broca's area for both of the languages they speak. But in those who were older when they learned a second language, two

What is the best time of life to learn a second language, and why?

Link It!

different sections of Broca's area are active while they are performing language tasks—one section for the native language and another for the second language. Yet the two sections were very close, only ⅛ inch apart. An earlier study by Klein and others (1995) also found that the same patch of tissue in Broca's area was activated by both the native and second languages in research participants whose mean age was 7.3 years when they learned their second language.

Americans, as noted earlier, lag far behind citizens of most other technologically advanced nations in their knowledge of languages other than their native tongue and have much catching up to do. The ability to communicate in more than one language will surely become increasingly important in the new millennium.

THE NATURE OF INTELLIGENCE

The Search for Factors Underlying Intelligence

What factors underlie intelligence, according to Spearman and Thurstone?

First, let's ask the most obvious question: What is intelligence? A task force of experts from the American Psychological Association (APA) defined **intelligence** as an individual's "ability to understand complex ideas, to adapt effectively to the environment, to learn from experience, to engage in various forms of reasoning, and to overcome obstacles by taking thought" (Neisser et al., 1996, p. 77).

No concept in psychology has been at the center of more public policy debates and more scientific disagreement than intelligence (Moffitt et al., 1993). Is intelligence a single, general capability, or are there multiple types of intelligence? Is intelligence influenced more by heredity or by environment? Is it fixed or changeable, culture-free or culture-bound? The nature of intelligence continues to be hotly debated.

English psychologist Charles Spearman (1863–1945) observed that people who are bright in one area are usually bright in other areas as well. In other words, they tend to be generally intelligent. Spearman (1927) came to believe that intelligence is composed of a general ability, or *g* **factor**, which underlies all intellectual functions. Spearman concluded that intelligence tests tap a person's *g* factor, or general intelligence, and a number of *s* factors, or specific intellectual abilities. Spearman's influence can be seen in those intelligence tests, such as the Stanford–Binet, that yield one IQ score to indicate the level of general intelligence.

Another early researcher in testing, Louis L. Thurstone (1938), rejected Spearman's notion of general intellectual ability, or *g* factor. After analyzing the scores of many subjects on some 56 separate ability tests, Thurstone identified seven **primary mental abilities**: verbal comprehension, numerical ability, spatial relations, perceptual speed, word fluency, memory, and reasoning. He maintained that all intellectual activities involve one or more of these primary mental abilities. Thurstone and his wife, Thelma G. Thurstone, developed their Primary Mental Abilities Tests to measure these seven abilities.

Thurstone believed a single IQ score obscured more than it revealed. He suggested that a profile showing relative strengths and weaknesses on the seven primary abilities would provide a more accurate picture of a person's mental ability.

Intelligence: More Than One Type?

What types of intelligence did Gardner and Sternberg identify?

Some theorists, instead of searching for the factors that underlie intelligence, propose that there are different types of intelligence. Two such modern theorists are Howard Gardner and Robert Sternberg.

Gardner's Theory of Multiple Intelligences   Harvard psychologist Howard Gardner (1983) also denies the existence of a *g* factor. Instead he proposes seven independent and equally important forms of intelligence:

1. *Linguistic* (language skills)

2. *Logical/mathematical* (math and quantitative skills)

3. *Musical*

4. *Spatial* (skills used by painters, sculptors, and architects to manipulate and create forms)

5. *Bodily kinesthetic* (body control and manual dexterity as exemplified by athletes, dancers, and carpenters)

6. *Interpersonal* (the ability to understand the behavior and read the moods, desires, and intentions of others)

7. *Intrapersonal* (the ability to understand one's own feelings and behavior)

Perhaps the most controversial aspect of Gardner's theory is his view that all seven forms of intelligence are of equal importance. In fact, different cultures assign varying importance to the types of intelligence. For example, linguistic and logical/mathematical intelligences are valued most in the United States and other Western cultures; bodily kinesthetic intelligence is more highly prized in cultures that depend on hunting for survival.

Gardner's theory "has enjoyed wide popularity, especially among educators, but [his] ideas are based more on reasoning and intuition than on the results of empirical research studies" (Aiken, 1997, p. 196). Gardner's critics doubt that all seven frames of mind are of equal value in education and in life. Robert Sternberg (1985b) claims that "the multiple intelligences might better be referred to as multiple talents" (p. 1114). He asks whether an adult who is tone-deaf and has no sense of rhythm can be considered mentally limited in the same way as one who has never developed any verbal skills. But Sternberg is not merely a critic. He has developed his own theory of intelligence.

Sternberg's Triarchic Theory of Intelligence   Robert Sternberg uses the information-processing approach to understand intelligence. This approach involves a step-by-step analysis of the cognitive processes people use as they acquire knowledge and use it to solve problems.

Sternberg (1985a; 1986a) has formulated a **triarchic theory of intelligence**, which, as the term *triarchic* implies, proposes that there are three types of intelligence—componential (analytical), experiential (creative), and contextual (practical). The first type, *componential intelligence*, refers to the mental abilities most closely related to success on conventional IQ and achievement tests. Sternberg claims that traditional IQ tests measure only componential, or analytical, intelligence.

The second type, *experiential intelligence*, is reflected in creative thinking and problem solving. People with high experiential intelligence are able to solve novel problems and deal with unusual and unexpected challenges. Another aspect of experiential intelligence is finding creative ways to perform common daily tasks more efficiently and effectively, almost automatically.

The third type, *contextual intelligence*, or practical intelligence, might be equated with common sense or "street smarts." People with high contextual intelligence are survivors who capitalize on their strengths and compensate for their weaknesses. They either adapt well to their environment, change the environment so that they can succeed, or if necessary, find a new environment. People who have succeeded in spite of hardships and adverse circumstances probably have a great deal of contextual intelligence.

Accumulating evidence suggests that performance on practical intelligence measures is related to various aspects of real-world performance but is more or less unrelated to conventional academic measures of intelligence. Sternberg and others (1995) maintain that testing both academic and practical intelligence yields more accurate predictions about real-world performance than does testing either kind alone.

intelligence: An individual's ability to understand complex ideas, to adapt effectively to the environment, to learn from experience, to engage in various forms of reasoning, and to overcome obstacles through mental effort.

***g* factor:** Spearman's term for a general intellectual ability that underlies all mental operations to some degree.

primary mental abilities: According to Thurstone, seven relatively distinct abilities that singly or in combination are involved in all intellectual activities.

triarchic theory of intelligence: Sternberg's theory that there are three types of intelligence—componential (analytical), experiential (creative), and contextual (practical).

Link It!

MEASURING INTELLIGENCE

Binet and the First Successful Intelligence Test

What is Binet's major contribution to psychology?

The first successful effort to measure intelligence resulted not from a theoretical approach, but as a practical means of solving a problem. The Ministry of Public Instruction in Paris wanted to ensure that average or brighter children would not be wrongly assigned to special classes and that children of limited ability would not be subjected to the regular program of instruction. In 1903 a commission was formed to study the problem, and one of its members was French psychologist Alfred Binet (1857–1911).

With the help of his colleague, psychiatrist Theodore Simon, Binet began testing the schoolchildren of Paris in 1904. The two men used a wide variety of tests, and they kept only those items that discriminated well between older and younger children. The Binet–Simon Intelligence Scale, first published in 1905, was an immediate success.

Working with psychiatrist Theodore Simon to develop a test for evaluating children's intelligence, Alfred Binet (shown here) began testing Parisian students in 1904.

Test items on the scale were structured according to increasing difficulty—with the easiest item first and each succeeding item becoming more difficult. Children went as far as they could, and then their progress was compared to others of the same age. Binet established the concept that mental retardation and mental superiority are a function of the difference between chronological age (actual age in years) and mental age. An 8-year-old with a mental age of 8 is normal or average. An 8-year-old with a mental age of 5 is seriously deficient; an 8-year-old with a mental age of 11 is mentally superior.

Binet believed that children with a mental age 2 years below their chronological age were retarded and should be placed in special education classes. But there was a flaw in his thinking. A 4-year-old with a mental age of 2 is far more retarded than a 12-year-old with a mental age of 10. How could a similar degree of retardation at different ages be expressed?

German psychologist William Stern (1914) provided an answer. In 1912 he devised a simple formula for calculating an index of intelligence—the *intelligence quotient*. He divided a child's mental age by his or her chronological age.

Intelligence Testing in the United States

What is the Stanford–Binet Intelligence Scale?

What does IQ mean, and how has the method for calculating it changed over time?

Lewis M. Terman, a psychology professor at Stanford University, published a thorough revision of the Binet–Simon scale in 1916. Terman revised and adapted the items for American children, added new items, and established new **norms**—standards based on the scores of a large number of people and used as bases for comparison. Within 2½ years, 4 million children had taken Terman's revision, known as the **Stanford–Binet Intelligence Scale.** It was the first test to make use of Stern's formula for the **intelligence quotient (IQ)**, but Terman improved the formula by multiplying the result by 100 to eliminate the decimal. He also introduced the abbreviation IQ.

$$\frac{\text{Mental age}}{\text{Chronological age}} \times 100 = \text{IQ}$$

For example,

$$\frac{14}{10} \times 100 = 1.40 \times 100 = \text{IQ } 140 \text{ (superior IQ)}$$

The highly regarded Stanford–Binet is an individually administered IQ test for those aged 2 to 23. It contains four subscales: verbal reasoning, quantitative reasoning, abstract visual reasoning, and short-term memory. An overall IQ score is

norms: Standards based on the range of test scores of a large group of people who are selected to provide the bases of comparison for those who take the test later.

Stanford–Binet Intelligence Scale: An individually administered IQ test for those aged 2 to 23; Terman's adaptation of the Binet– Simon Scale.

derived from scores on the four subscales, and the test scores correlate well with achievement test scores (Laurent et al., 1992).

Intelligence testing became increasingly popular in the United States in the 1920s and 1930s, but it quickly became obvious that the Stanford–Binet Intelligence Scale was not useful for testing adults. The original IQ formula could not be applied to adults, because at a certain age people achieve maturity in intelligence. According to the original IQ formula, a 40-year-old with the same IQ test score as the average 20-year-old would be considered mentally retarded, with an IQ of only 50. Obviously, something was wrong with the formula when applied to populations of all ages.

Today psychologists still use the term *IQ*, but for adults, IQ is a **deviation score** derived by comparing an individual's score to scores of others the *same age* on whom the test was normed. The deviation score is a contribution of David Wechsler, another pioneer in mental testing.

The Wechsler Intelligence Tests In 1939 psychologist David Wechsler developed the first successful individual intelligence test for adults, designed for those aged 16 and older. The original test has been revised, restandardized, and renamed the **Wechsler Adult Intelligence Scale (WAIS-R)** and is one of the most widely used psychological tests. The test contains both verbal and performance (nonverbal) subtests, which yield separate verbal and performance IQ scores as well as an overall IQ score. This test is a departure from the Stanford–Binet scale, which yields a single IQ score. Wechsler also published the Wechsler Intelligence Scale for Children (WISC-R) and the Wechsler Preschool and Primary Scale of Intelligence (WPPSI), which is normed for children aged 4 to 6½.

One advantage of the Wechsler scales is their ability to identify intellectual strengths in nonverbal as well as verbal areas. Wechsler also believed that differences in a person's scores on the various verbal and performance subtests could be used for diagnostic purposes.

Individual intelligence tests such as the Stanford–Binet and Wechsler scales must be given to one person at a time by a qualified professional. For testing large numbers of people in a short period of time on a limited budget, group intelligence tests are the answer. Group intelligence tests, such as the California Test of Mental Maturity, the Cognitive Abilities Test, and the Otis–Lennon Mental Ability Test, are widely used.

Requirements of Good Tests: Reliability, Validity, and Standardization

If your watch gains 6 minutes one day and loses 3 or 4 minutes the next day, it is not reliable. You want a watch that you can rely on to give the correct time day after day. Like a watch, an intelligence test must have **reliability**; the test must consistently yield nearly the same score when the same people are tested and then retested on the same test or an alternative form of the test. The higher the correlation between the two scores, the more reliable the test. A correlation coefficient of 1.0 would indicate perfect reliability. Most widely used tests, such as the Stanford–Binet and Wechsler scales and the Scholastic Assessment Test (SAT), boast high reliabilities of about .90.

Tests can be highly reliable but worthless if they are not valid. **Validity** is the ability or power of a test to measure what it is intended to measure. For example, a thermometer is a valid instrument for measuring temperature; a bathroom scale is valid for measuring weight. But no matter how reliable your bathroom scale is, it will not take your temperature. It is valid only for weighing.

Aptitude tests are designed to predict a person's probable achievement or performance at some future time. Selecting students for admission to college or graduate schools is based partly on the predictive validity of aptitude tests, such as the Scholastic Assessment Test (SAT), the American College Testing Program (ACT), and the Graduate Record Examination (GRE). How well do SAT scores predict success in

intelligence quotient (IQ): An index of intelligence originally derived by dividing mental age by chronological age and then multiplying by 100; now derived by comparing an individual's score to the scores of others of the same age.

deviation score: A test score calculated by comparing an individual's score to the scores of others of the same age.

Wechsler Adult Intelligence Scale (WAIS-R): An individual intelligence test for adults that yields separate verbal and performance (nonverbal) IQ scores as well as an overall IQ score.

reliability: The ability of a test to yield nearly the same score when the same people are tested and then retested on the same test or an alternative form of the test.

validity: The ability of a test to measure what it is intended to measure.

aptitude test: A test designed to predict a person's achievement or performance at some future time.

What did Wechsler's tests provide that the Stanford–Binet did not?

What do the terms *reliability*, *validity*, and *standardization* mean?

standardization: Establishing norms for comparing the scores of people who will take a test in the future; administering tests using a prescribed procedure.

college? Moderately at best. The correlation between SAT scores and the grades of college freshmen is about .40 (Linn, 1982).

Once a test is proven to be valid and reliable, the next requirement is **standardization**. There must be standard procedures for administering and scoring the test. Exactly the same directions must be given, whether written or oral, and the same amount of time must be allowed for every test taker. But even more important, standardization means establishing norms by which all scores are interpreted. A test is standardized by administering it to a large sample of people representative of those who will be taking the test in the future. The group's scores are analyzed, and then the average score, standard deviation, percentile rankings, and other measures are computed. These comparative scores become the norms used as the standard against which all other scores on that test are measured.

The Range of Intelligence

What are the ranges of IQ scores considered average, superior, and in the range of mental retardation?

When large populations are measured on intelligence or on physical characteristics such as height or weight, the test scores or results usually conform to the bell-shaped distribution known as the *normal curve*. The majority of the scores cluster around the mean (average). The farther scores deviate, or move away, from the mean, either above or below, the fewer there are.

The average IQ test score for all people in the same age group is arbitrarily assigned an IQ score of 100. On the Wechsler intelligence tests, approximately 50% of the scores are in the average range, between 90 and 110. About 68% of the scores fall between 85 and 115, and about 95% fall between 70 and 130. About 2% of the scores are above 130, which is considered superior, and about 2% fall below 70, in the range of mental retardation (see Figure 7.3).

According to the Terman study, how do the gifted differ from the general population?

Terman's Study of the Gifted   In 1921 Lewis M. Terman (1925) launched a longitudinal study, now a classic, in which 1,528 gifted students were selected and measured at different ages throughout their lives. Tested on the Stanford–Binet, the participants, 857 males and 671 females, had unusually high IQs, ranging from 135

Figure 7.3

The Normal Curve

When a large number of test scores are compiled, they are typically distributed in a normal (bell-shaped) curve. On the Wechsler scales, the average or mean IQ score is set at 100. As the figure shows, about 68% of the scores fall between 15 IQ points (1 standard deviation) above and below 100 (from 85 to 115), and about 95.5% of the scores fall between 30 points (2 standard deviations) above and below 100 (from 70 to 130).

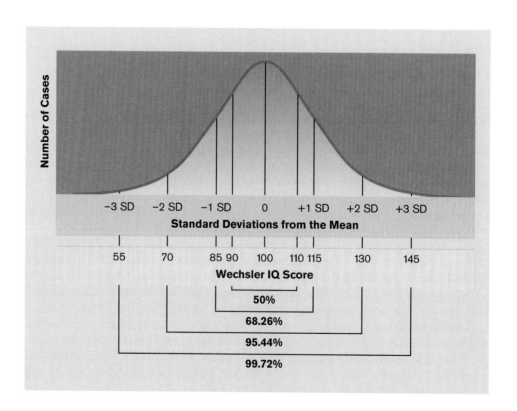

to 200, with an average of 151. Terman assumed the Stanford–Binet measured innate intelligence and that IQ was fixed at birth (Cravens, 1992).

Terman's early findings put an end to the myth that mentally superior people are more likely to be physically inferior. Terman's gifted participants excelled in almost all of the abilities he studied—intellectual, physical, emotional, moral, and social. Terman also exploded many other myths about the mentally gifted (Terman & Oden, 1947). For example, you may have heard the saying that there is a thin line between genius and madness. Actually Terman's gifted group enjoyed better mental health than the general population. Terman's participants earned more academic degrees, achieved higher occupational status and higher salaries, were better adjusted both personally and socially, and were healthier than their less mentally gifted peers. However, most women at that time did not pursue careers outside of the home, so the findings related to occupational success applied primarily to the men. Terman (1925) concluded that "there is no law of compensation whereby the intellectual superiority of the gifted is offset by inferiorities along nonintellectual lines" (p. 16).

The Terman study continues today, with most of the participants in their 80s. In a report on Terman's study, Shneidman (1989) states its basic findings—that "an unusual mind, a vigorous body, and a relatively well-adjusted personality are not at all incompatible" (p. 687).

Who Are the Gifted?   Beginning in the early 1920s, the term *gifted* was used to describe the intellectually superior—those with IQs in the upper 2–3% of the U.S. population. Today the term includes both the exceptionally creative and those who excel in the visual or performing arts.

Traditionally, special programs for the gifted have involved either acceleration or enrichment. Acceleration enables students to progress at a rate that is consistent with their ability. Students may skip a grade, progress through subject matter at a faster rate, be granted advanced placement in college courses, or enter college early. Enrichment programs aim to broaden students' knowledge by giving them special courses in foreign language, music appreciation, and the like, or by providing special experiences designed to foster advanced thinking skills.

The Mentally Retarded   At the opposite end of the continuum from the intellectually gifted are the 2% of the U.S. population whose IQ scores place them in the range of **mental retardation**. Individuals are not classified as mentally retarded unless (1) their IQ score is below 70 and (2) they have a severe deficiency in everyday adaptive functioning—the ability to care for themselves and relate to others (Grossman, 1983). There are degrees of retardation from mild to profound. Individuals with IQs ranging from 55 to 70 are considered mildly retarded; from 40 to 55, moderately retarded; from 25 to 40, severely retarded; and below 25, profoundly retarded. Table 7.2 (on page 220) shows the level of functioning expected for various categories of mental retardation.

There are many causes of mental retardation, including brain injuries, chromosomal abnormalities such as Down syndrome, chemical deficiencies, lead poisoning, and hazards present during fetal development.

Before the late 1960s, mentally retarded children in the United States were educated almost exclusively in special schools. Since then there has been a movement toward **mainstreaming**—educating mentally retarded students in regular schools. Mainstreaming may involve placing these students in classes with nonhandicapped students for part of the day or in special classrooms in regular schools.

Some mentally retarded individuals, even with low general intelligence, may have exceptional abilities in some narrow area of accomplishment. This phenomenon, known as *savant syndrome*, allows such individuals to excel, often to a remarkable degree, on arithmetic or memory tasks, or in music, art, or sculpture (Miller, 1999).

mental retardation: Subnormal intelligence reflected by an IQ below 70 and by adaptive functioning severely deficient for one's age.

mainstreaming: Educating mentally retarded students in regular rather than special schools by placing them in regular classes for part of the day or having special classrooms in regular schools.

What two criteria must a person meet to be classified as mentally retarded?

Table 7.2   Mental Retardation as Measured on the Wechsler Scales

Classification	IQ Range	Percentage of the Mentally Retarded	Characteristics of Retarded Persons at Each Level
Mild	55–70	90%	Are able to grasp learning skills up to 6th grade level. They may become self-supporting and can be profitably employed in various vocational occupations.
Moderate	40–55	6%	Probably are not able to grasp more than 2nd grade academic skills but can learn self-help skills and some social and academic skills. They may work in sheltered workshops.
Severe	25–40	3%	Can be trained in basic health habits; can learn to communicate verbally. They learn through repetitive habit training.
Profound	Below 25	1%	Rudimentary motor development. They may learn very limited self-help skills.

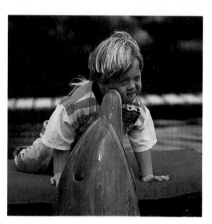

Intelligence and Neural Processing

What is the relationship between intelligence and the efficiency and speed of neural processing?

Recently, researchers have sought to understand more fully the relationships between neural processing and intelligence. Using PET scan studies, researchers are comparing the *efficiency* and *speed* of neural processing in people with a range of intelligence levels. A PET scan, as you will recall from Chapter 2, reveals the location and amount of brain activity by measuring how much glucose and oxygen are used during the performance of various mental tasks.

If a highly intelligent person and a less gifted person were monitored by PET scans while performing the same mental tasks, which person's brain would use more energy (consume more glucose and oxygen)? It may seem contrary to logic, but research shows that more intelligent people, who have the advantage of more efficient neural processing, expend less brain energy (Haier, 1993; Parks et al., 1988). Of course, you would expect a highly intelligent person who had all the answers readily in mind to use less mental effort on a test than a person who was struggling in vain to retrieve the answers. Thus, the more efficient the brain, the less effort it expends to perform mental tasks.

What about the relationship of intelligence to speed of neural processing? Researchers have found that processing speed is related to intelligence, and that processing speed accelerates as children get older (Fry & Hale, 1996; Neisser et al., 1996).

THE IQ CONTROVERSY: BRAINY DISPUTE

The Uses and Abuses of Intelligence Tests

Intelligence testing has become a major growth industry. And many Americans have come to believe that a "magical" number—an IQ score, a percentile rank, or some other derived score—unfalteringly portrays a person's intellectual capacity, ability, or potential. In many cases, the score has served as the ticket of admission or the mark of rejection to educational and occupational opportunity.

What can intelligence tests really reveal? IQ scores are fairly good predictors of academic performance. However, academic performance is also influenced by other factors. According to Neisser and others (1996), "successful school learning depends on many personal characteristics other than intelligence, such as persistence, interest in school, and willingness to study" (p. 81).

Is there a high correlation between IQ and success in life? Although the average IQ score of people in the professions (doctors, dentists, lawyers) tends to be higher than that of people in lower-status occupations, the exact relationship between IQ score and occupational status is not clearly understood. Nevertheless, studies indicate that intelligence test scores are related to a wide range of social outcomes, including job performance, income, social status, and years of education completed (Neisser et al., 1996).

Abuses occur when scores on intelligence or aptitude tests are the only or even the major criterion for admitting people to various educational programs. Intelligence tests do not measure attitude and motivation, critical ingredients of success. Many people are admitted to educational programs who probably should not be, while others are denied admission who could profit from them and possibly make significant contributions to society.

Early categorization based solely on IQ scores can doom children to slow-track educational programs that are not appropriate for them. Many poor and minority children (particularly those for whom English is a second language) and visually or hearing impaired children have been erroneously placed in special education programs. IQ tests predicted that they were not mentally able to profit from regular classroom instruction. There would be no problem if IQ test results were unfailingly accurate, but in fact they are not.

In some states IQ tests are banned altogether. In others it is now illegal to place children in classes for the mentally retarded based solely on their IQ scores without additional testing of their level of adaptive functioning in daily life. Mercer (1973) developed tests to measure performance on practical life skills, such as keeping score in baseball, reading a newspaper, and so on. She tested African American and White students, all of whom had IQ scores under 70. Her results showed that on pass-fail tests on these skills, 95% of the African American participants passed, but none of the White participants did. Such results may suggest that "IQ tests are measuring something fundamentally different for Blacks and Whites, at least for low scores" (Crane, 1994, p. 200).

Are minority children and those for whom English is a second language at a disadvantage when they are assessed on conventional tests? Attempts have been made to develop **culture-fair intelligence tests** designed to minimize cultural bias. The questions do not penalize individuals whose cultural experience or language differs from that of the middle or upper classes. See Figure 7.4 (on page 222) for an example of the type of test item found on a culture-fair test.

The Nature–Nurture Controversy: Battle of the Centuries

The most vocal area of disagreement concerning intelligence has been the **nature–nurture controversy**, the debate over whether intelligence is primarily the result of

culture-fair intelligence test: An intelligence test that uses questions that will not penalize those whose culture differs from that of the middle or upper classes.

nature–nurture controversy: The debate over whether intelligence and other traits are primarily the result of heredity or environment.

Of what are intelligence tests good predictors?

What are some abuses of intelligence tests?

How does the nature–nurture controversy apply to intelligence?

Figure 7.4

An Example of an Item on a Culture-Fair Test

This culture-fair test item does not penalize test takers whose language or cultural experiences differ from those of the urban middle or upper classes. Subjects are asked to select, from the six samples on the right, the patch that will complete the pattern. Patch number 3 is the correct answer. (Adapted from the Raven's Standard Progressive Matrices Test.)

heredity or environment. Englishman Sir Francis Galton (1874) initiated this debate and coined the term. After studying a number of prominent families in England, Galton concluded that intelligence was inherited.

The nature–nurture controversy has raged for well over 100 years. Hereditarians like Galton claim that intelligence is largely inherited—the result of nature. Environmentalists, on the other hand, insist that it is influenced primarily by one's environment—the result of nurture. Most psychologists today agree that both nature and nurture contribute to intelligence, but they continue to debate the proportions contributed by each.

What is behavioral genetics, and what are the primary methods used in the field today?

Behavioral Genetics   **Behavioral genetics** is a field of research that investigates the relative effects of heredity and environment on behavior and ability (Plomin et al., 1997). Two of the primary methods used by behavioral geneticists are the twin study method, first used by Galton (1875) in his studies of heredity, and the adoption method.

In the **twin study method**, researchers study **identical twins** (monozygotic twins) and **fraternal twins** (dizygotic twins) to determine how much they resemble each other on a variety of characteristics. Identical twins have exactly the same genes because a single sperm cell of the father fertilizes a single egg of the mother, forming a cell that then splits and forms two human beings—"carbon copies." But fraternal twins are no more alike genetically than any two siblings born to the same parents. In the case of fraternal twins, two separate sperm cells fertilize two separate eggs that happen to be released at the same time during ovulation.

Twins who are raised together, whether identical or fraternal, have similar environments. If identical twins raised together are found to be more alike than fraternal twins on a certain trait, then that trait is assumed to be more influenced by heredity. But if identical and fraternal twins from similar environments do not differ on a trait, then that trait is assumed to be influenced more by environment. The term **heritability** is an index of the degree to which a characteristic is estimated to be influenced by heredity. Figure 7.5 shows estimates of genetic and environmental factors contributing to intelligence.

In the **adoption method**, behavioral geneticists study children adopted shortly after birth. By comparing their abilities and personality traits to those of their adoptive family members with whom they live and those of their biological parents whom they may never have met, researchers can disentangle the effects of heredity and environment (Plomin et al., 1988).

How do twin studies support the view that intelligence is inherited?

A Natural Experiment: Identical Twins Reared Apart   Minnesota—home of the twin cities and the Minnesota Twins—is also, fittingly, the site of the most extensive U.S. study of identical and fraternal twins. The Minnesota Center for Twin and Adoption Research has assembled the Minnesota Twin Registry, which in 1998 included over 10,000 twin pairs (Bouchard, 1998).

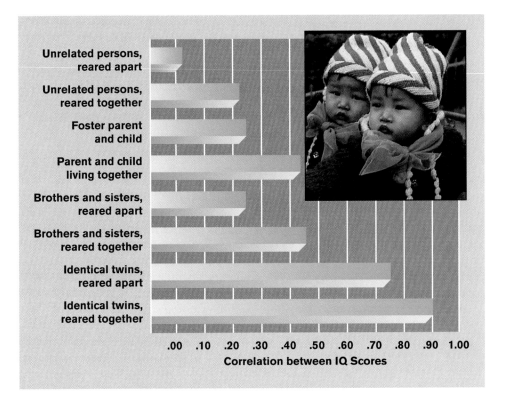

Figure 7.5

Correlations between the IQ Scores of Persons with Various Relationships

The more closely related two individuals are, the more similar their IQ scores tend to be. Thus, there is a strong genetic contribution to intelligence. (Based on data from Bouchard & McGue, 1981; Erlenmeyer-Kimling & Jarvik, 1963.)

The bar chart shows the following relationships on the vertical axis:
- Unrelated persons, reared apart
- Unrelated persons, reared together
- Foster parent and child
- Parent and child living together
- Brothers and sisters, reared apart
- Brothers and sisters, reared together
- Identical twins, reared apart
- Identical twins, reared together

With horizontal axis: .00 .10 .20 .30 .40 .50 .60 .70 .80 .90 1.00

Correlation between IQ Scores

Probably the best way to assess the relative contributions of heredity and environment is to study identical twins who have been separated at birth and raised apart. Although it seems amazing, researchers have found that identical twins who grow up in the same family are no more alike as adults than identical twins who are reared apart. When separated twins are found to have strikingly similar traits, it is assumed that heredity has been a major contributor to those traits. When separated twins differ on a given trait, the influence of the environment is thought to be greater.

Since 1979 the Minnesota researchers headed by Thomas Bouchard have studied about 60 pairs of fraternal twins and 80 pairs of identical twins who were reared apart. Of all the traits Bouchard and his colleagues studied, the most heritable trait turned out to be intelligence. Bouchard (1997) reports that various types of twin studies have consistently yielded heritability estimates of .60 to .70 for intelligence. (The heritability of some personality traits is discussed in Chapter 10.)

Not all researchers agree with Bouchard's heritability estimate for intelligence. Combining data from a number of twin studies, Plomin and others (1994) found the heritability estimate for general intelligence to be .52. Similar findings emerged from meta-analyses using dozens of adoption studies and twin studies involving over 10,000 pairs of twins. These analyses concluded that the heritability of general cognitive ability was about .50 (McClearn et al., 1997). Psychologists who consider environmental factors as the chief contributors to differences in intelligence also take issue with Bouchard's findings. They claim that most separated identical twins are raised by adoptive parents who have been matched as closely as possible to the biological parents. This fact, the critics say, could account for the similarity in IQ. In response to his critics, Bouchard (1997) points out that children who are not related biologically but are raised in the same home are no more similar in intelligence once they reach adulthood than complete strangers.

Adoption studies reveal that children adopted shortly after birth have IQs more closely resembling those of their biological parents than those of their adoptive parents. The family environment has an influence on IQ early in life, but that influence seems to diminish. Twin and adoption studies indicate that as people reach adulthood, it is genes that are most closely correlated with IQ (Loehlin et al., 1988, 1989;

behavioral genetics: A field of research that investigates the relative effects of heredity and environment on behavior and ability.

twin study method: Studying identical and fraternal twins to determine the relative effects of heredity and environment on a variety of characteristics.

identical twins: Twins with identical genes; monozygotic twins.

fraternal twins: Twins who are no more alike genetically than ordinary brothers and sisters; dizygotic twins.

heritability: An index of the degree to which a characteristic is estimated to be influenced by heredity.

adoption method: A method researchers use to study the relative effects of heredity and environment on behavior and ability in children adopted shortly after birth, by comparing them to their biological and adoptive parents.

McCartney et al., 1990; Plomin & Rende, 1991). In fact, the influence of the genes seems to increase predictably as people age: there is a heritability of .30 in infancy, .40 in childhood, .50 in adolescence, and about .60 in adulthood (McGue et al., 1993).

Bouchard and others (1990) claim that "although parents may be able to affect their children's rate of cognitive skill acquisition, they may have relatively little influence on the ultimate level attained" (p. 225). But does this mean that the degree to which intelligence is inherited is the degree to which it is absolutely fixed and immune to environmental intervention?

Intelligence: Is It Fixed or Changeable?

What kinds of evidence suggest that IQ is changeable rather than fixed?

Probably the most important issue in intelligence is whether IQ is fixed or changeable. Clearly, the high degree of similarity in the intelligence scores of identical twins who have been reared apart makes a strong case for the powerful influence of genetics. But even Bouchard and his colleagues (1990) caution against trying to generalize their findings to people raised in disadvantaged environments. Bouchard (1997) states: "A child raised in crushing poverty by illiterate parents is unlikely to score well on IQ tests, no matter what his mental inheritance. . . . Twin studies tend to attract few subjects in such dire straits, so their findings may not always apply to people exposed to extremes of deprivation or privilege" (p. 56).

Several studies indicate that IQ test scores are not fixed but can be modified with an enriched environment. More than two decades ago, Sandra Scarr and Richard Weinberg (1976) studied 130 African American and interracial children who had been adopted by highly educated, upper-middle-class White families; 99 of the children had been adopted in the first year of life. The adoptees were fully exposed to middle-class cultural experiences and vocabulary, the "culture of the tests and the school" (p. 737).

How did the children perform on IQ and achievement tests? For these children, the 15-point IQ gap between Blacks and Whites that had been observed by some researchers was bridged by an enriched environment. Compared to an average IQ score of 90, which would be expected had these children been reared by their biological parents, the average IQ score of the 130 adoptees was 106.3. And their achievement test scores were slightly above the national average, not below. On the average, the earlier the children were adopted, the higher their IQs. The mean IQ score of the 99 early adoptees was 110.4, about 10 IQ points above the average for Whites.

Studies in France also show that IQ scores and achievement are substantially higher when children from lower-class environments are adopted by middle- and upper-middle-class families (Duyme, 1988; Schiff and Lewontin, 1986).

Children's environment—whether deprived or enriched—can have a significant effect on their IQ scores and future achievement.

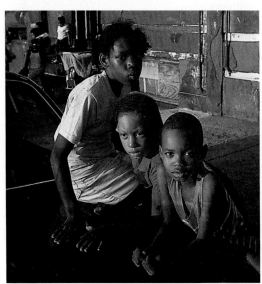

Other evidence also suggests that environmental factors have a strong influence on IQ scores. Americans and similarly advantaged populations all over the world have gained about 3 IQ points per decade since 1940. James Flynn (1987) analyzed 73 studies involving some 7,500 participants ranging in age from 12 to 48 and found that "every Binet and Wechsler sample from 1932 to 1978 has performed better than its predecessor" (p. 225). This consistent improvement in IQ scores over time is known as the *Flynn effect* (Holloway, 1999). The average IQ in Western industrialized nations is currently about 15 IQ points, or 1 standard deviation, higher than 50 years ago. Regarding the Black–White IQ gap among U.S. adults, Flynn (1987) asserts that "the environmental advantage Whites enjoy over Blacks is similar to what Whites (adults) of today enjoy over their own parents or grandparents of 50 years ago" (p. 226).

Researcher Ken Vincent (1991) presents data suggesting that the Black–White IQ gap is narrowing in younger children—to about 7 or 8 IQ points. Vincent (1993) attributes the rapid mean gains by African American children to environmental changes in economic and educational opportunity.

It should not be surprising that enriched environments alter traits that are highly heritable. Consider the fact that American and British adolescents are 6 inches taller on average than their counterparts a century and a half ago (Tanner, 1962). Height has the same heritability (.90) today as it did in the mid–19th century. So this tremendous average gain in height of 6 inches is entirely attributable to environmental influences: better health, better nutrition, and so on. The highest heritability estimates for intelligence are far lower than those for height. It seems clear then that environmental influences have the power to affect intelligence and achievement. Poverty affects nutrition. And research clearly shows that malnutrition, especially early in life, can harm intellectual development (Brown & Pollitt, 1996).

Gender Differences in Cognitive Abilities

Concerning gender differences in cognitive abilities, there are two important points to keep in mind: First, the differences within each gender are greater than the differences between the genders. Second, even though gender differences in cognitive abilities have been generally small on average, there tends to be more variation in such abilities among males than among females (that is, the range of test scores is typically greater for males).

For what cognitive abilities have gender differences been proven?

Gender Differences in Verbal Ability: Are Females Better with Words?

Using meta-analysis, researchers Janet Hyde and Marcia Linn (1988) examined 165 studies reporting test results on verbal ability for approximately 1.5 million males and females. But they found no significant gender differences in verbal ability. Hedges and Nowell (1995) analyzed the results of the National Assessment of Educational Progress, which has tested a nationally representative sample of 70,000 to 100,000 9-, 13-, and 17-year-olds annually in reading comprehension, writing, math, and science. The researchers compared the achievement of the 17-year-olds from 1971 through 1992 and reported that females outperformed males in reading and writing, while males did better in science and math. Although average gender differences were small, there was one prominent exception: "Females performed substantially better than males in writing every year" (p. 44). Furthermore, Hedges and Nowell reported that more males than females were near the bottom of the distribution, not only in writing, but in reading comprehension as well. Finally, in high school, girls are generally more fluent verbally than boys are (Halpern, 1992) and do considerably better in spelling (Lubinsky & Benbow, 1992).

Gender Differences in Math Ability: Do Males Have the Edge?

In one of the largest studies conducted to date on gender differences in mathematics, Hyde and others (1990) performed a meta-analysis of 100 studies, which together represented test results for more than 3 million participants. They found no significant gender difference in the understanding of mathematical concepts among the various age groups. Although females did slightly better in mathematical problem solving in elementary and middle school, males scored moderately higher in high school and college. Benbow and Stanley (1980, 1983) found a significant male superiority in a select segment of the population—the brightest of the bright in mathematics ability. There were twice as many boys as girls scoring above 500 on the SAT, and 13 times as many scoring above 700. Hedges and Nowell (1995) reported that twice as many boys as girls were in the top 3% of the Project Talent Mathematics total scale, and seven times as many were in the top 1%.

Parents often expect boys to do better than girls in math (Lummis & Stevenson, 1990). Such expectations may become a self-fulfilling prophecy, leading girls to lack confidence in their math ability and to decide not to pursue advanced math courses (Eccles & Jacobs, 1986). A report by the American Association of University Women Education Foundation provided evidence that many science teachers and some math teachers, as well, tend to pay noticeably more attention to boys than to girls

(Chira, 1992). Such treatment may discourage girls with math or science aptitude from choosing careers in these areas.

Gender Differences in Spatial Ability   Researchers have found that, in general, males tend to perform somewhat better than females on tests of spatial skills (Kimura, 1992; Linn & Hyde, 1989; Linn & Peterson, 1985). This gender difference has been found on some but not all of the various spatial tasks (Geary, 1996; Kimura, 1992). Some research has shown that spatial abilities appear to be enhanced by prenatal exposure to high levels of androgens (Berenbaum et al., 1995). However, this finding does not minimize the role of social experiences and expectations in shaping children's abilities and interests.

Expectations, Effort, and Academic Achievement: A Cross-Cultural Comparison

Stevenson and others (1986) compared the math ability of randomly selected elementary school children from three comparable cities—Taipei in Taiwan, Sendai in Japan, and Minneapolis in the United States. It was no contest. By the fifth grade, the Asian students were outscoring the Americans by about 15 points in math ability, roughly 1 standard deviation. And the Asian superiority held firmly from the highest to the lowest achievement levels. Of the lowest 100 students in math achievement, 67 were Americans; of the top 100, only 1 was. The Japanese children scored the highest of the three groups in fifth grade, and even the lowest-scoring Japanese classes did better than the top-scoring classes in the United States.

How can such differences in achievement in children from different cultures be explained? Researchers such as Jensen (1985) and Galton before him, and more recently Herrnstein and Murray (1994), would point to genetic differences, but there are other possibilities. Stevenson and others (1990) suggest that cultural, rather than genetic, differences may be a major factor in explaining the gap in math ability. Their study was conducted with first and fifth graders from the same three cities and included 1,440 students (480 from each of the three countries). The children were tested in reading and mathematics and interviewed along with their mothers. In a follow-up study 4 years later, the first graders (now fifth graders) were tested again, and again they and their mothers were interviewed.

The interviews revealed significant differences between the Asian and American cultures. Stevenson and others (1990) reported that the Chinese and Japanese mothers considered academic achievement to be *the most important* pursuit of their children, whereas American parents did not value it as a central concern. The Asian, but not the American, families structured their home activities to promote academic achievement as soon as their first child started elementary school.

The Asian parents downplayed the importance of innate ability but emphasized the value of hard work and persistence (Stevenson, 1992). American parents, in contrast, believed more firmly in genetic limitations on ability and achievement. Such a belief has devastating effects, according to Stevenson, who states, "When parents believe success in school depends for the most part on ability rather than effort, they are less likely to foster participation in activities related to academic achievement" (p. 73). Also, American mothers tended to overestimate the cognitive abilities of their children, but the Chinese and Japanese mothers did not. Asian mothers held their children to higher standards while giving more realistic assessments of their children's abilities (see Figure 7.6).

In follow-up studies, Stevenson and others (1993) found that the achievement gap between Asian and American students persisted over a 10-year period. Differences in high-school achievement were explained in part by the fact that the American students spent more time working at part-time jobs and socializing than their Asian counterparts did (Fuligni & Stevenson, 1995). But do Asian students pay a psychological price for their stunning academic achievement? Are they more likely than

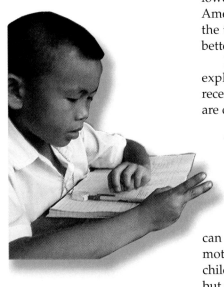

Asian students consistently score higher on math achievement tests than their American counterparts. It appears that the reasons for this difference are cultural and relate to parental expectations.

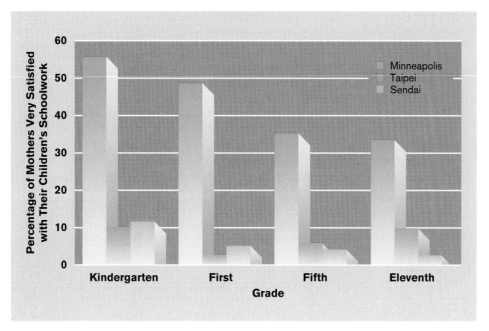

Figure 7.6

Mothers' Satisfaction with Their Children's Academic Performance

Even though American students had by far the poorest achievement record of the children studied in the United States, Taiwan, and Japan, American mothers expressed much higher satisfaction with their children's academic performance than did mothers from the two Asian countries. (From Stevenson, 1992.)

students in the United States to be depressed, nervous, stressed, and heavily burdened by pressures to maintain academic excellence? A recent, large cross-cultural study comparing 11th-grade students from Japan, Taiwan, and the United States did find a correlation between achievement in mathematics and psychological distress—but, surprisingly, for the American students, not the Asian students (Crystal et al., 1994). Moreover, contrary to popular belief, adolescent suicide rates are lower in Japan than in the United States.

Why should high-achieving American students, but not Asian students, pay a price in terms of psychological distress? The researchers found that Asian teenagers typically enjoy support and encouragement for their academic achievement from family and peers alike. In contrast, high-achieving teenagers in the United States are torn between studying harder to excel academically and pursuing nonacademic social interests. Such interests may be strongly encouraged by their peers and often by parents who want their children to be "well-rounded."

Which of these two cultural tendencies is more likely to maximize the development of one's intellectual potential, whether large or modest? Perhaps the answer to the stunning record of academic achievement of Asian students lies not in their genes, but in the cultural values that nurture them.

EMOTIONAL INTELLIGENCE

Daniel Goleman (1995) claims that success in life is more markedly influenced by emotional intelligence than by IQ. **Emotional intelligence** refers to a set of capabilities that are separate from IQ but necessary for success in life—in the workplace, in intimate personal relations, and in social interactions. Goleman (1995) has extended

emotional intelligence: A type of intelligence that includes an awareness of and an ability to manage one's own emotions, the ability to motivate oneself, empathy, and the ability to handle relationships successfully.

the work of Peter Salovey and John Mayer (1990; Mayer & Salovey, 1993, 1995, 1997), who first introduced the concept of emotional intelligence.

Personal Components of Emotional Intelligence

What are the personal components of emotional intelligence?

The foundation of emotional intelligence is self-knowledge. It involves an awareness of emotions, an ability to manage those emotions, and self-motivation.

Awareness of our own emotions—recognizing and acknowledging feelings as they happen—is at the very heart of emotional intelligence. It means being aware not only of our moods, but of thoughts about those moods, as well. Those who are able to monitor their feelings as they arise are more likely to be able to manage them rather than being ruled by them.

Managing emotions does not mean suppressing them, any more than it means giving free rein to every feeling and impulse. As Goleman (1995) puts it, "The goal is balance, not emotional suppression: every feeling has its value and significance. A life without passion would be a dull wasteland of neutrality, cut off and isolated from the richness of life itself" (p. 56).

Thus, to manage emotions is to express them in an appropriate manner and not let them run out of control. For example, if not tempered with reason, uncontrolled anger can lead to rage and violence. People high in emotional intelligence have learned how to regulate their moods and not let anger, boredom, or depression ruin their day (or their lives). You manage your emotions when you do something to cheer yourself up, soothe your own hurts, reassure yourself, or otherwise temper an inappropriate or out-of-control emotion.

Self-motivation refers to a strength of emotional self-control that enables a person to get moving and pursue worthy goals, persist at tasks even when frustrated, and resist the temptation to act on impulse. Resisting impulsive behavior is, according to Goleman (1995), "the root of all emotional self-control" (p. 81).

Of all the attributes of emotional intelligence, the ability to postpone immediate gratification and to persist in working toward some greater future gain is most closely related to success—whether one is trying to build a business, get a college degree, or even stay on a diet. One researcher has found that 4-year-old children who have mastered the art of delaying instant gratification in order to advance toward some greater future goal are "far superior as students" on high-school graduation compared to four-year-olds who are not able to resist the impulse to satisfy their immediate wishes (Shoda et al., 1990).

Interpersonal Components of Emotional Intelligence

What are the interpersonal components of emotional intelligence?

The interpersonal aspects of emotional intelligence are sensitivity to and understanding of others' emotions and the ability to handle relationships.

The ability to empathize—to recognize and understand the motives and emotions of others—is the cornerstone of successful interpersonal relations. *Empathy*, a sensitivity toward the needs and feelings of others, appears to be a higher level of development that springs from self-awareness. If we have no insight into our own emotions, it is unlikely that we will develop sensitivity and understanding of the emotions of others.

One key indicator, or hallmark, of the empathy component of emotional intelligence is the ability to read and interpret nonverbal behavior—the gestures, vocal inflections, tones of voice, and facial expressions of others. Nonverbal behavior is, in a sense, the language of the emotions, because our feelings are most genuinely expressed this way. People may fail to communicate their feelings verbally or even lie about them, but their nonverbal behavior will most often reveal their true feelings.

For most people, hardly anything in life is more important than their relationships—intimate love relationship, family, professional, and work relationships, and relationships with friends. Without rewarding relationships, life would be lonely indeed. What does emotional intelligence have to do with forming and maintaining successful relationships? Virtually everything. Some people are inept at forming and handling mutually satisfying relationships; others seem to be masters of the art. What aspects of emotional intelligence enable a person to handle relationships well?

Two components of emotional intelligence that are prerequisites for handling relationships are (1) the ability to manage one's own emotions, and (2) empathy, or the ability to perceive, understand, and relate to the emotions of others. These two components combine to produce the ability to respond appropriately to emotions in others. And this, Goleman (1995) maintains, is the very center of the art of handling relationships. But he does not mean "handling" in an autocratic, dominating sense. People who handle relationships well, says Goleman, are able to shape encounters, "to mobilize and inspire others to thrive in intimate relationships, to persuade and influence, to put others at ease" (p. 113).

A person with high emotional intelligence shows empathy— recognizing nonverbal signals from others and making appropriate responses.

Although it is not one of the five main domains of emotional intelligence identified by Salovey and Mayer (1990), *optimism* appears to be a component of emotional intelligence. People who are optimistic have a "strong expectation in general [that] things will turn out all right in life" (p. 88). The most significant aspect of optimism in the context of emotional intelligence is the way in which optimists explain their successes and failures. When optimists fail, they attribute their failure to something in the situation that can be changed. Thus, they believe that by trying harder, they can succeed the next time. But when pessimists fail, they blame themselves and attribute their failure to some personal characteristic or flaw that cannot be changed.

CREATIVITY: UNIQUE AND USEFUL PRODUCTIONS

Creativity can be thought of as the ability to produce original, appropriate, and valuable ideas and/or solutions to problems. Is creativity related to intelligence? Research to date indicates that there is a modest correlation between creativity and IQ. Highly creative people tend to be well above average in intelligence, but in the upper IQ ranges (over 120) there seems to be little correlation between IQ and creativity (Barron & Harrington, 1981).

What is creativity, and how is it related to intelligence?

The Creative Process

Where does creativity originate? Cartoonists often illustrate creative thinking as a flash of insight, a lightbulb that suddenly turns on in the mind. But research studies indicate that useful and genuine creativity rarely appears in the form of sudden flashes (Haberlandt, 1997). For the most part, creative ideas that come to conscious awareness have been incubating for some time. And most experts agree that genuine creativity "is an accomplishment born of intensive study, long reflection, persistence and interest" (Snow, 1993, p. 1033).

There are four basic stages in the creative problem-solving process (Goleman et al., 1992):

What are the four stages in the creative process?

- *Preparation*—searching for information that may help solve the problem

- *Incubation*—letting the problem "sit" while the relevant information is digested

- *Illumination*—being suddenly struck by the right solution

- *Translation*—transforming the new insight into useful action

creativity: The ability to produce original, appropriate, and valuable ideas and/or solutions to problems.

The incubation stage, perhaps the most important part of the process, takes place below the level of awareness.

Characteristics of Creative People

What are some characteristics of creative people?

Link It!

Creative people share a number of characteristics that distinguish them from less creative individuals. Among the most important of these traits are expertise, openness to experience, independence of mind, intrinsic motivation, and perseverance.

Expertise Expertise in a specific area of endeavor is built up over years of disciplined study and practice. Although expertise alone is not enough, genuine creative accomplishments are rooted in this quality (Ericsson & Charness, 1994). Benjamin Bloom (1985) and his associates studied 120 case histories of people who had made notable creative contributions in six different fields. Every one of these individuals had unquestioned expertise, based on high-quality training, as well as unyielding determination.

Openness to Experience Creative individuals are open to experience and will entertain, at least initially, even seemingly irrational thoughts that uncreative people might dismiss. Creative people are typically less close-minded and less inhibited than others in their feelings and fantasies (McCrae, 1987). Moreover, they seem to be inherently curious and inquisitive (Sternberg, 1985a). They are comfortable with ambiguity and don't seem to need immediate resolution of conflicting and contradictory ideas. During the early stages of creative work, these individuals are not on a quest for certainty, but rather a quest of discovery. And along the way they are not bothered by loose or dead ends. Rather, they work their way through failures and out of blind alleys, persisting until they succeed.

One characteristic of creative people is intrinsic motivation. They enjoy the process of creation for its own sake—the end result may be a whimsical toy rather than a practical tool.

Independence of Mind Creative people tend to be independent thinkers. They cherish this independence and, especially in their area of creative expertise, prefer to go their own way. They can easily spend long periods alone and are not influenced by the opinions of others as much as their less creative counterparts are. They will take unpopular stands if they must and are often seen as nonconformists. But then, by its very nature, creativity is unconventional and uncommon. Such unconventionality is, however, typically confined to the work of creative people. Otherwise, they do not appear to be especially eccentric or out-of-the-ordinary.

Intrinsic Motivation Unlike people who are readily influenced by the opinions of others and motivated by extrinsic rewards, the creative are more likely to be intrinsically motivated. Creative people are moved by—and sometimes carried away with—the anticipation, excitement, and enjoyment of their work, whether it is inventing, producing works of art, or advancing scientific knowledge. For creative people, the sheer joy of creative activity itself carries its own reward. In short, they "enjoy the process of creation for its own sake" (Csikszentmihalyi, 1996, p. 40).

Perseverance Creative endeavor requires intelligence and hard work. Creativity is not poured from empty vessels, nor fashioned by idle hands. Thomas A. Edison, who held 1,093 patents, claimed that his magnificently creative contributions were accomplished by 2% inspiration and 98% perspiration. Albert Einstein published 248 papers and persevered (perspired) for 10 years on his theory of relativity before it was finished. And Mozart, when he died at age 35, had created 609 musical compositions (Haberlandt, 1997).

Can creativity be learned? There is some evidence that creative abilities can be learned, or at least improved. To learn some techniques for stimulating your own creativity, read the *Apply It!*

Stimulating Creativity

Creativity is certainly not limited only to "special" people, who are naturally gifted with flair and imagination. Everyone has some potential for creativity. What can you do to become more creative? Psychologists have suggested a variety of techniques for stimulating creativity.

- *"Tune in" to your own creativity and have confidence in it.* The more you develop the habit of thinking of yourself as a creative person and the higher you value creativity as a personal goal, the more likely it is that you will come up with creative ideas and solutions to problems (Hennessey & Amabile, 1988).

- *Challenge yourself to develop your special interests.* Maybe you enjoy cooking or photography? Whatever your creative interest, set small challenges for yourself. Go beyond simply cooking a tasty meal or taking pictures of friends and family. Start inventing new recipes or taking photographs of subjects in original ways. The more you stretch yourself beyond the ordinary, the more creative you will become.

- *Broaden yourself.* The more knowledge and expertise you acquire, the greater potential for creative output you will develop (Epstein, 1996).

- *Use problem finding as a stimulus to creativity.* Instead of being upset by everyday inconveniences and annoyances, consider such problems to be opportunities for devising creative solutions (Getzels & Csikszentmihalyi, 1976).

- *Change your normal routine.* Have lunch at a different time. Take a new route to school or work. Seek out someone you've never talked to and strike up a conversation. Don't ask yourself why you're making these changes; just do them for the sake of change.

- *Spend more time with creative people.* This will stimulate whatever creativity abilities you might have (Amabile, 1983).

- *Be flexible and open to new possibilities.* Free your thoughts from arbitrary restraints. Learn to avoid *mental set,* or the failure to consider alternative solutions to common problems.

- *Avoid self-censorship.* Ignore the inner voice that tells you something can't possibly work. Don't be critical of your thoughts or efforts during the early stages of the creative process. Fretting over the correctness of the output inhibits the very process itself (Amabile, 1983).

- *Don't be afraid to make mistakes.* For the creative person, mistakes are valuable learning experiences, not something to be feared and avoided at all costs. In fact, creative people tend to make more mistakes than less imaginative people. Why? Because they make more attempts, try more experiments, and come up with more ideas to be tested (Goleman et al., 1992).

- *Capture your creative thoughts.* Become more attentive to your creative thoughts, and be prepared to preserve them no matter where you might be (Epstein, 1996). Use a notepad, sketchpad, tape recorder, or any other device or method to capture your good ideas when you get them. It is highly unlikely that they will reappear in the same form at a more convenient time.

- *Relax.* One way to stimulate creative thinking is to relax. Go for a walk, take a long shower, sit in a comfortable chair and daydream, lie on the beach. Relaxing gives the unconscious mind a chance to play with ideas and combine them in new ways. The result may be a flash of insight like the one that led Archimedes to leap from his bath and exclaim "Eureka!" (Greek for "I've found it!") when he figured out why heavy objects float in water.

In group settings, creativity appears to be fostered by humor. Groups whose members joke, kid around, and laugh easily often have been found to be more creative than groups whose members interact more formally. One technique that is used to stimulate creativity in group settings is *brainstorming*, in which group members try to generate as many ideas as possible, no matter how wild or unusual. Because anxiety and self-consciousness can inhibit the free flow of suggestions, all judgment and evaluation are prohibited until everyone's ideas have been presented.

But Margaret Matlin (1994) and other psychologists are skeptical of the value of brainstorming. She points out that the products of group brainstorming sessions are often of lower quality than the creative ideas offered by individuals working independently.

Organizations that seek to encourage creativity and innovation should allow employees more leeway in solving problems and more control over performance of their assigned tasks. Moreover, employees should be given sufficient time to allow them to do quality work, should be allowed to work independently where appropriate, and should be free of continuous monitoring.

SUMMARY AND REVIEW

What is meant by cognition, and what specific processes does it include?

Cognition refers collectively to all the mental processes involved in acquiring, storing, retrieving, and using knowledge. These mental processes include sensation, perception, imagery, concept formation, reasoning, decision making, problem solving, and language.

Key Term
cognition (p. 200)

IMAGERY AND CONCEPTS: TOOLS OF THINKING

What is imagery?

Imagery is the mental representation of a sensory experience—visual, auditory, gustatory, motor, olfactory, or tactile.

What is a concept?

A concept is a mental category that represents a class or group of objects, people, organizations, events, or relations that share common characteristics or attributes.

What is the difference between a formal concept and a natural concept?

A formal concept is one that is clearly defined by a set of rules, a formal definition or a characteristic. A natural concept is formed on the basis of everyday perceptions and experiences and is somewhat fuzzy. In using a natural concept, a person is likely to picture a prototype of the concept—an example that embodies its most common and typical features.

Key Terms
imagery (p. 201); concept (p. 201); formal concept (p. 202); natural concept (p. 202); prototype (p. 202); exemplars (p. 202)

DECISION MAKING: MAKING CHOICES IN LIFE

How is the additive strategy used in decision making?

The additive strategy is a decision-making approach in which each alternative is rated on each important factor affecting the decision and the alternative rated highest overall is chosen.

When is the elimination-by-aspects strategy most useful?

The elimination-by-aspects strategy is most useful when a decision involves many alternatives and multiple factors. With this approach, some alternatives are eliminated because they do not satisfy the most important factors. Then the additive strategy is typically used to make the best choice among the surviving alternatives.

What is the availability heuristic?

The availability heuristic is a rule of thumb that says that the probability of an event or the importance assigned to it is based on its availability in memory, that is, the ease with which the information comes to mind.

What is the representativeness heuristic?

The representativeness heuristic is a thinking strategy that is used in decision making and that assesses how closely a new object or situation matches an existing prototype of that object or situation.

What is framing?

Framing is the way information is presented so as to focus on either a potential gain or a potential loss.

Key Terms
decision making (p. 202); additive strategy (p. 203); heuristic (p. 204); availability heuristic (p. 204); representativeness heuristic (p. 204); framing (p. 204)

PROBLEM SOLVING: BEYOND DECISION MAKING

What are three basic approaches to problem solving?

Three basic approaches to problem solving are trial and error, algorithms, and heuristics.

What is an algorithm?

An algorithm is a systematic, step-by-step procedure or formula that guarantees a solution to a certain type of problem if the algorithm is appropriate and is executed properly.

What are three heuristics used in problem solving?

Three heuristics used in problem solving are working backwards, means–end analysis, and the analogy heuristic.

How do functional fixedness and mental set impede problem solving?

Functional fixedness, or the tendency to view objects only in terms of their customary functions, results in a failure to use the objects in novel ways to solve problems. Mental set is the tendency to apply a strategy that was successful in the past to solve new problems, even though the strategy may not be appropriate for the requirements of the new problem.

What is artificial intelligence?

Artificial intelligence refers to the programming of computer systems to simulate human thinking in solving problems and in making judgments and decisions.

Key Terms
problem solving (p. 205); trial and error (p. 206); algorithm (p. 206); working backwards (p. 206); means–end analysis (p. 206); analogy heuristic (p. 206); functional fixedness (p. 207); mental set (p. 207); artificial intelligence (p. 208); neural networks (p. 208)

LANGUAGE

What are the four important components of language?

The four important components of language are (1) phonemes, the smallest units of sound in a spoken language; (2) morphemes, the smallest units of meaning; (3) syntax, the grammatical rules for arranging and combining words to form phrases and sentences; and (4) semantics, the meaning derived from phonemes, morphemes, and sentences.

How does language in trained chimpanzees differ from human language?

Chimpanzees do not have a vocal tract adapted to speech, and their communication using sign language or symbols consists of constructions strung together rather than actual sentences.

In general, does thought influence language more, or does language influence thought more?

In general, thought has a greater influence on language than vice versa. Whorf's linguistic relativity hypothesis has not been supported by research.

What is the best time of life to learn a second language, and why?

People who learn a second language when they are younger than 10 or 11 usually speak without an accent, are more fluent, and make fewer grammatical errors than do those who are older when they learn another language.

Key Terms
language (p. 209); psycholinguistics (p. 209); phonemes (p. 209); morphemes (p. 210); syntax (p. 210); semantics (p. 210); linguistic relativity hypothesis (p. 212)

THE NATURE OF INTELLIGENCE

What factors underlie intelligence, according to Spearman and Thurstone?

Spearman believed that intelligence is composed of a general ability (*g* factor), which underlies all intellectual functions, and a number of specific abilities (*s* factors). Thurstone points to seven primary mental abilities, which singly or in combination are involved in all intellectual activities.

What types of intelligence did Gardner and Sternberg identify?

Gardner claims that there are seven independent and equally important types of intelligence. Sternberg's triarchic theory of intelligence identifies three types: componential (conventional intelligence), experiential (creative intelligence), and contextual (practical intelligence).

Key Terms
intelligence (p. 214); *g* factor (p. 214); primary mental abilities (p. 214); triarchic theory of intelligence (p. 215)

MEASURING INTELLIGENCE

What is Binet's major contribution to psychology?

Binet's major contribution to psychology is the concept of mental age and a

method for measuring it—the intelligence test.

What is the Stanford–Binet Intelligence Scale?

The Stanford–Binet Intelligence Scale is a highly regarded individual intelligence test for those aged 2 to 23. It yields one overall IQ score.

What does IQ mean, and how has the method for calculating it changed over time?

IQ stands for intelligence quotient, an index of intelligence originally derived by dividing a person's mental age by his or her chronological age and then multiplying by 100. Now it is derived by comparing an individual's score to the scores of others of the same age.

What did Wechsler's tests provide that the Stanford–Binet did not?

David Wechsler developed the first successful individual intelligence test for adults, the Wechsler Adult Intelligence Scale (WAIS-R). His tests for adults, for children, and for preschoolers yield separate verbal and performance (nonverbal) IQ scores as well as an overall IQ score.

What do the terms *reliability*, *validity*, and *standardization* mean?

Reliability is the ability of a test to yield nearly the same score each time a person takes the test or an alternative form of the test. Validity is the power of a test to measure what it is intended to measure. Standardization refers to prescribed procedures for administering a test and to established norms that provide a means of evaluating test scores.

What are the ranges of IQ scores considered average, superior, and in the range of mental retardation?

Fifty percent of the U.S. population have IQ scores ranging from 90 to 109, considered average; 2% have scores above 130, considered superior; and 2% have scores below 70, in the range of mental retardation.

According to the Terman study, how do the gifted differ from the general population?

Terman's longitudinal study revealed that, in general, the gifted enjoy better

physical and mental health and are more successful than the general population.

What two criteria must a person meet to be classified as mentally retarded?

To be classified as mentally retarded, an individual must have an IQ score below 70 and show severe deficiencies in everyday adaptive functioning.

What is the relationship between intelligence and the efficiency and speed of neural processing?

People who are more intelligent generally use less mental energy and have a faster neural processing speed than less intelligent people.

Key Terms
norms (p. 216); Stanford–Binet Intelligence Scale (p. 216); intelligence quotient (IQ) (p. 216); deviation score (p. 217); Wechsler Adult Intelligence Scale (WAIS-R) (p. 217); reliability (p. 217); validity (p. 217); aptitude test (p. 217); standardization (p. 218); mental retardation (p. 219); mainstreaming (p. 219)

THE IQ CONTROVERSY: BRAINY DISPUTE

Of what are intelligence tests good predictors?

IQ tests are good predictors of academic achievement and success in school.

What are some abuses of intelligence tests?

Abuses occur when IQ tests are the only criterion for admitting people to educational programs, for tracking children, or for placing them in classes for the mentally retarded. Many people claim that IQ tests are biased in favor of the urban middle or upper class.

How does the nature–nurture controversy apply to intelligence?

The nature–nurture controversy is the debate over whether intelligence is primarily determined by heredity or environment.

What is behavioral genetics, and what are the primary methods used in the field today?

Behavioral genetics is the study of the relative effects of heredity and environment on behavior and ability. The twin study method and the adoption method are the primary methods used.

How do twin studies support the view that intelligence is inherited?

Twin studies provide evidence that intelligence is primarily inherited because identical twins are more alike in intelligence than fraternal twins, even if they have been reared apart.

What kinds of evidence suggest that IQ is changeable rather than fixed?

Several adoption studies have revealed that when infants from disadvantaged environments are adopted by middle- and upper-middle-class parents, their IQ scores are higher on average than would otherwise be expected. Also, IQ scores have been rising steadily over the past 50 years in Western industrialized nations, presumably because of increases in the standard of living and educational opportunities.

For what cognitive abilities have gender differences been proven?

Females outperform males in reading and writing; males seem to do better in science, math, and some spatial tasks.

More males than females are found at the very highest levels of mathematics ability.

Key Terms
culture-fair intelligence test (p. 221); nature–nurture controversy (p. 221); behavioral genetics (p. 222); twin study method (p. 222); identical twins (p. 222); fraternal twins (p. 222); heritability (p. 222); adoption method (p. 222)

EMOTIONAL INTELLIGENCE

What are the personal components of emotional intelligence?

The personal components of emotional intelligence are an awareness of and an ability to control one's own emotions and the ability to motivate oneself.

What are the interpersonal components of emotional intelligence?

The interpersonal components of emotional intelligence are empathy and the ability to handle relationships.

Key Term
emotional intelligence (p. 227)

CREATIVITY: UNIQUE AND USEFUL PRODUCTIONS

What is creativity, and how is it related to intelligence?

Creativity is the ability to produce original, appropriate, and valuable ideas and/or solutions to problems. Highly creative people tend to have well above average intelligence, but there seems to be little correlation between very high IQ (above 120) and creativity.

What are the four stages in the creative process?

The four stages in the creative process are preparation, incubation, illumination, and translation.

What are some characteristics of creative people?

Creative people share some characteristics that distinguish them: expertise, openness to experience, independence of mind, intrinsic motivation, and perseverance.

Key Term
creativity (p. 229)

Study Guide for Chapter 7

Answers to all the Study Guide questions are provided at the end of the book.

Section One: Chapter Review

1. The two most common forms of imagery are
   a. visual and motor.
   c. visual and auditory.
   b. auditory and tactile.
   d. visual and gustatory.

2. A mental category that represents a class or group of items that share common characteristics or attributes is called a(n)
   a. image.
   c. positive instance.
   b. concept.
   d. prototype.

3. A prototype is the most _____ example of a concept.
   a. abstract
   c. recent
   b. unusual
   d. typical

4. The (additive strategy, elimination by aspects strategy) allows the more desirable aspects of a situation to compensate for other less desirable aspects.

5. _____ refers to the way information is presented so as to focus on a potential gain or loss.

6. Which of the following is guaranteed, if properly applied, to result in the correct answer to a problem?
   a. an algorithm
   c. trial and error
   b. a heuristic
   d. applying prior knowledge

7. Working backwards and means–end analysis are examples of
   a. algorithms.
   c. mental sets.
   b. heuristics.
   d. functional fixedness.

8. John uses a wastebasket to keep a door from closing. In solving his problem, he was not hindered by
   a. a heuristic.
   c. functional fixedness.
   b. an algorithm.
   d. mental set.

9. One characteristic of good problem solvers is mental set. (true/false)

10. Artificial intelligence systems surpass the problem solving ability of experts in a number of fields. (true/false)

11. Match the component of language with the appropriate description.
    ____ (1) the smallest units of meaning
    ____ (2) the meaning derived from phonemes, morphemes, and sentences

    ____ (3) grammatical rules for arranging and combining words to form phrases and sentences
    ____ (4) the smallest units of sound in a spoken language
    a. syntax
    b. morphemes
    c. semantics
    d. phonemes

12. Communication in trained chimpanzees approaches human language in form and complexity. (true/false)

13. The linguistic relativity hypothesis is not supported by research. (true/false)

14. In general, thought influences language more than language influences thought. (true/false)

15. Match the theorist with the theory of intelligence.
    ____ (1) seven primary abilities   a. Spearman
    ____ (2) multiple intelligences   b. Thurstone
    ____ (3) the g factor   c. Gardner

16. The first successful effort to measure intelligence was made by
    a. Binet and Simon.
    c. Wechsler.
    b. Spearman.
    d. Terman.

17. According to Stern's formula, as revised by Terman, what is the IQ of a child with a mental age of 12 and a chronological age of 8?
    a. 75
    c. 125
    b. 150
    d. 100

18. In which range will the scores of the largest percentage of people taking an IQ test fall?
    a. 80 to 100
    c. 100 to 130
    b. 90 to 100
    d. 65 to 90

19. What field of research investigates the relative effects of heredity and environment on behavior and ability?
    a. genetics
    c. biology
    b. behavioral genetics
    d. physiology

20. Twin studies suggest that environment is stronger than heredity as a factor in shaping IQ differences. (true/false)

21. In general, differences in cognitive abilities are greater within each gender than between the genders. (true/false)

22. For each cognitive ability, indicate whether males or females, in general, tend to score higher on tests of that ability.

   ____ (1) writing   a. males
   ____ (2) science   b. females
   ____ (3) spatial ability
   ____ (4) reading comprehension
   ____ (5) mathematics

23. Emotional intelligence means controlling and suppressing one's emotions. (true/false)

24. Which of the following does *not* demonstrate emotional intelligence?
   a. Feeling depressed and distracted, Kyra takes a break and goes to the movies.
   b. When he fails a test, Alan thinks to himself, "It was my girlfriend's fault for being so needy and demanding so much of my time."
   c. Mike notices that his boss is in a particularly bad mood and stays out of her way for the afternoon.
   d. Gisela really knows how to get her team moving to solve a problem.

25. (Pessimism, Optimism) is an important component of emotional intelligence.

26. Geniuses are typically highly creative. (true/false)

27. The stages in the creative problem-solving process occur in the following sequence:
   a. illumination, incubation, preparation, translation
   b. incubation, illumination, preparation, translation
   c. preparation, incubation, illumination, translation
   d. translation, preparation, incubation, illumination

Section Two: Important Concepts and Psychologists

On the line opposite each term, write the name of the theorist or researcher who is most closely associated with it.

1. formal concepts _____

2. elimination by aspects _____

3. algorithm _____

4. artificial intelligence _____

5. linguistic relativity hypothesis _____

6. *g* factor _____

7. triarchic theory of intelligence _____

8. Stanford–Binet Intelligence Scale _____

9. WAIS/WISC _____

10. nature–nurture controversy _____

11. emotional intelligence _____

Section Three: Fill In the Blank

1. The mental processes involved in the acquisition, storage, retrieval, and use of knowledge are known as _____.

2. _____ is defined as the representation of sensory experience in the mind.

3. If you are a member of a Western culture, your concept of food probably includes meat. Beef, pork, and chicken most likely are _____ of the concept, but whale blubber probably is not.

4. Duane decides to list the four most important features of a new car. He then rates the cars he sees based on color, price, gas mileage, and safety and selects the car that ranks highest on these factors. He is using the _____ strategy for decision making.

5. Joann must consider many alternatives and factors in making a particular decision. She decides to rank the factors from most important to least important. She then starts to eliminate alternatives as they fail to meet the highest ranked factors. This is an example of the _____ strategy for decision making.

6. The study of how language is acquired, produced, and used and how sounds and symbols of language are translated into meaning is known as _____.

7. When we speak of the rules of language use, we are talking about _____.

8. Frank asserts that the language you use determines the nature of your thoughts. Frank is a proponent of the _____ _____ hypothesis.

9. The theory proposing seven different kinds of intelligence, including linguistic intelligence and intrapersonal intelligence, was developed by _____.

10. If Sally scores very low on an IQ test and then is found to be at the top of her class in academic

performance, we can assume that the IQ test does not have very good _____.

11. Research using PET scans has indicated that people of higher intelligence tend to use _____ energy when performing mental tasks than those who are less gifted.

12. Jack is the kind of person who seems to be able to make the world work for him. He knows how to fit into a situation or change the situation to his needs, and he is very successful in business because of this talent. Sternberg would say that Jack has a high level of _____ intelligence.

13. James takes the same IQ test on two different days. His score on the second day is much higher than his score on the first day. We can assume that the test does not have good

_____.

14. The ability to produce original, appropriate, and valuable ideas and/or solutions to problems is known as _____.

Section Four: Comprehensive Practice Test

1. The mental processes involved in acquiring, storing, retrieving, and using knowledge are known collectively as
   a. conceptualization.   c. imagery.
   b. cognition.   d. thinking.

2. *Dog, car, honesty,* and *trees* are all examples of
   a. images.   c. verbal images.
   b. concepts.   d. typographs.

3. A gun would be identified by many people as a _____ of the concept *weapon*.

4. Artificial concepts are also known as fuzzy concepts. (true/false)

5. A good example of a formal concept is
   a. the periodic table of the elements.
   b. social display rules.
   c. ethical guidelines.
   d. established table manners.

6. If, while working at your computer, you forgot a command, and you then tried all the commands you could remember until you found the one that worked, this would be an example of using
   a. a syllogism.   c. inductive reasoning.
   b. the additive heuristic. d. trial and error.

7. Students who learn systematic, step-by-step procedures to solve their statistics problems are learning
   a. algorithms.   c. elimination by aspects.
   b. trial and error.   d. means–end analysis.

8. A neural network is a computer system that is designed to mimic
   a. artificial intelligence.   c. human heuristics.
   b. animal intelligence.   d. the human brain.

9. _____ are the smallest units of sound in a spoken language.
   a. Phonemes   c. Morphemes
   b. Semantics   d. Consonants

10. It is obvious that other animals have no real language or communication abilities at all. Any apparent display of such abilities has been shown to be simply a matter of operant conditioning. (true/false)

11. Research suggests that gender-specific pronouns such as "he" influence interpretation of sentences in favor of males. (true/false)

12. Thurstone believed that the single IQ score method of measuring and describing intelligence

was the most effective manner of measuring intelligence. (true/false)

13. Sternberg's experiential intelligence includes
    a. the ability to learn from past events.
    b. the ability to manipulate people's opinions.
    c. creative problem solving.
    d. basic academic skills.

14. The WAIS-R intelligence test provides two different subtest scores, in addition to an overall IQ score. The two subtests are
    a. verbal and mathematics.
    b. contextual and componential.
    c. performance and musical.
    d. verbal and performance.

15. Mike has just taken a test that is designed to predict future achievement or performance. Mike took a(n)
    a. aptitude test.
    b. projective test.
    c. intelligence test.
    d. creativity test.

16. About what percentage of IQ test scores fall between −1 and +1 standard deviation from the mean of 100 on a normal curve?
    a. 34%   b. 68%   c. 50%   d. 13%

17. Culture-fair intelligence tests were designed to represent different cultural values equally on the same test. (true/false)

18. Behavioral genetics is a field of inquiry that investigates
    a. how our behavior affects our genes.
    b. how our genes affect our behavior and ability.
    c. how our genes affect our biology.
    d. how our behavior affects our ability.

19. Intelligence is not fixed at birth; rather, evidence suggests that improved environmental factors can increase IQ scores. (true/false)

20. Although intelligence may be necessary for creativity, it is not sufficient. (true/false)

Section Five: Critical Thinking

1. Review the three basic approaches to problem solving discussed in this chapter. Which approach do you think is most practical and efficient for solving everyday problems?

2. Which of the theories of intelligence best fits your notion of intelligence? Why?

3. Prepare an argument supporting each of the following positions:
   a. English is the only language that should be taught in U.S. public schools.
   b. Bilingual education should be provided for all U.S. students for whom English is a second language.
   c. All students in U.S. public schools should be required to learn a language other than their native language.

4. Prepare an argument supporting each of the following positions:
   a. Intelligence tests should be used in the schools.
   b. Intelligence tests should not be used in the schools.

5. Give several examples of how you might bring more creativity into your educational and personal life.

8 *Human Development*

orth of Kampala, Uganda, in Africa, the jungle is dark and dense, lush with a rich variety of exotic plant life and an abundance of animal species. But civil war disturbed the peace and beauty of Uganda for many years, and brutal massacres claimed the lives of many men, women, and children.

In 1984 Ugandan soldiers retreating through the jungle came upon one of the strangest sights they had ever seen. They were accustomed to the numerous monkeys living in the jungle, hopping, chattering, and leaping from place to place and avoiding humans who alarmed them. But with one group of monkeys, the soldiers saw a larger creature who was unlike the others but was playfully hopping around with them. Intrigued, the soldiers came closer and were amazed to discover a human child.

The soldiers captured the young boy and brought him to an orphanage in Kampala, Uganda. Here staff members named him Robert, estimated him to be between 5 and 7 years old, and were amazed by his behavior. He squealed and grunted but could not speak. He didn't walk normally but jumped from one place to another the way a monkey would. He scratched people when they approached him; he ate grass or any other edible thing he could find. And he did not sit but squatted when he was not moving around. Small for his age, Robert was only 2½ feet tall when he was found and weighed only 22 pounds.

Foreign relief workers stationed in Uganda at the time were afraid that other children might be living as wild creatures in the jungle where Robert was found. They suspected this because hundreds of orphaned children had been discovered wandering around in nearby villages after the civil war ended. Those who studied Robert's case believed that his parents had been slaughtered when he was about 1 year old. Somehow he had managed to escape the massacre and make his way deep into the jungle.

---

developmental psychology: The study of how humans grow, develop, and change throughout the life span.

nature–nurture controversy: The debate concerning the relative influences of heredity and environment on development.

longitudinal study: A type of developmental study in which the same group of participants is followed and measured at different ages.

cross-sectional study: A type of developmental study in which researchers compare groups of participants of different ages on certain characteristics to determine age-related differences.

genes: The segments of DNA that are located on the chromosomes and are the basic units for the transmission of all hereditary traits.

chromosomes: Rod-shaped structures in the nuclei of body cells, which contain all the genes and carry all the hereditary information.

Link It!

Genetically, Robert is fully as human as any other human, but for most of his young life he was "adopted" by a group of monkeys whose members nurtured him as though he were one of their own. Developmental psychologists are intrigued by cases like Robert's because they show the profound effect that extreme environmental conditions can have on the course of human development.

DEVELOPMENTAL PSYCHOLOGY: BASIC ISSUES AND METHODOLOGY

Developmental psychology is the study of how humans grow, develop, and change throughout the life span. Some developmental psychologists specialize in a particular age group along the continuum from infancy, childhood, and adolescence to early, middle, and late adulthood. Others may concentrate on a specific area of interest such as physical development, language or cognitive development, or moral development.

Controversial Issues in Developmental Psychology

Developmental psychologists must consider several controversial issues as they pursue their work.

1. *To what degree do heredity and environment influence development?* For centuries thinkers have debated the influences of heredity and environment on human development—a debate called the **nature–nurture controversy**. Today the debate is not about nature *versus* nurture, but about the degree to which each influences various aspects of development.

2. *Is development continuous, or does it occur in stages?* Are aspects of development best understood in terms of gradual, continuous, cumulative change? Or does change in some aspects of development occur in spurts in the form of stages, with one stage *qualitatively* different from the next? We will explore two stage theories in this chapter: Piaget's theory of cognitive development and Erikson's theory of psychosocial development.

3. *To what extent are personal traits stable over time?* In various later chapters we will discuss whether certain personal traits (intelligence, aggression, and aspects of temperament, for example) tend to be stable or changeable over time. How do developmental psychologists study changes over the life span?

Approaches to Studying Developmental Change

Developmental psychologists use the longitudinal study and the cross-sectional study to investigate age-related changes. A **longitudinal study** is one in which the same group of participants is followed and measured at different ages, and it may take years to complete. There are some drawbacks to the longitudinal study. It is time-consuming and expensive, and participants may drop out of the study or die, possibly leaving the researcher with a biased sample.

A **cross-sectional study** is a less expensive and less time-consuming method in which researchers compare groups of participants of different ages on various characteristics to determine age-related differences. But in the cross-sectional study, differences found in age groups are based on group averages, so this approach is not able to provide answers to some questions.

Development is a fascinating and remarkable process that begins even before birth, and we will trace its course from the very beginning.

HEREDITY AND PRENATAL DEVELOPMENT

The Mechanism of Heredity: Genes and Chromosomes

Genes are the biological blueprints that determine and direct the transmission of all hereditary traits. Genes are segments of DNA located on each of the rod-shaped structures called **chromosomes** that are found in the nuclei of body cells. Normal body cells, with two exceptions, have 23 pairs of chromosomes (46 chromosomes in all). The two exceptions are the sperm cells and the mature egg cells, each of which has 23 single chromosomes. At conception the sperm adds its 23 single chromosomes to the 23 of the egg. From this union a single cell called a *zygote* is formed, with the full complement of 46 chromosomes (23 pairs), which contain about 100,000 genes—all of the genetic information needed to make a human being.

The 23rd pair of chromosomes are called **sex chromosomes** because they carry the genes that determine a person's sex; primary and secondary sex characteristics; and other sex-linked traits, such as red-green color blindness, male pattern baldness, and hemophilia. The sex chromosomes of females consist of two X chromosomes (XX); males have an X chromosome and a Y chromosome (XY). The egg cell always contains an X chromosome. Therefore, the sex of a child will depend on whether the egg is fertilized by a sperm carrying an X chromosome, which produces a female, or a sperm carrying a Y chromosome, which produces a male. Half of a man's sperm cells carry an X chromosome, and half carry a Y.

When two different genes are transmitted for the same trait, one is usually a **dominant gene**, causing the dominant trait to be expressed in the individual. The gene for brown hair, for example, is dominant over the gene for blond hair. A person having one gene for brown hair and one gene for blond hair will have brown hair. And, of course, two dominant genes will produce brown hair (see Figure 8.1 on page 242).

The gene for blond hair is recessive. A **recessive gene** will be expressed if it is paired with another recessive gene. Therefore, blond people have two recessive genes for blond hair. A recessive gene will *not* be expressed if it is paired with a dominant gene. Yet a person with such a pair can pass either the recessive gene or the dominant gene along to his or her offspring.

sex chromosomes: The 23rd pair of chromosomes, which carries the genes that determine one's sex, primary and secondary sex characteristics, and other sex-linked traits.

dominant gene: The gene that is expressed in the individual.

recessive gene: A gene that will not be expressed if paired with a dominant gene but will be expressed if paired with another recessive gene.

What are two types of studies developmental psychologists use to investigate age-related changes?

How are hereditary traits transmitted?

When are dominant or recessive genes expressed in an individual's traits?

Link It!

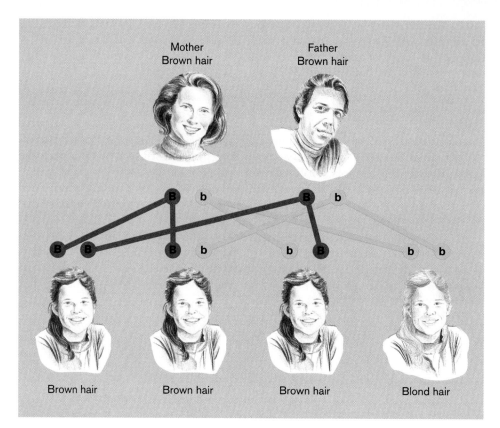

Figure 8.1

Gene Transmission for Hair Color

This figure shows all the possible combinations in children when both parents carry a gene for brown hair (B) and a gene for blond hair (b). The chance of their having a blond-haired child (bb) or a brown-haired child (BB) is 25% in each case. There is a 50% chance of having a brown-haired child who carries both the dominant gene (B) and the recessive gene (b).

What are the three stages of prenatal development?

period of the zygote: The approximately 2-week-long period between conception and the attachment of the zygote to the uterine wall.

prenatal: Occurring between conception and birth.

embryo: The developing human organism during the period (week 3 through week 8) when the major systems, organs, and structures of the body develop.

fetus: The developing human organism during the period (week 9 until birth) when rapid growth and further development of the structures, organs, and systems of the body occur.

identical (monozygotic) twins: Twins with exactly the same genes, who develop after one egg is fertilized by one sperm, and the zygote splits into two parts.

The Stages of Prenatal Development: Unfolding According to Plan

Conception occurs the moment a sperm cell fertilizes the ovum (egg cell), forming the single-celled *zygote*. Conception usually takes place in one of the fallopian tubes, and within the next 2 weeks the zygote travels to the uterus and attaches itself to the uterine wall. During this 2-week period, called the **period of the zygote**, rapid cell division occurs. At the end of this first stage of **prenatal** development, the zygote is only the size of the period at the end of this sentence.

The second stage is the period of the **embryo**, when the major systems, organs, and structures of the body develop. Lasting from week 3 through week 8, this period ends when the first bone cells form. Only 1 inch long and weighing ⅓ of an ounce, the embryo already resembles a human being, with limbs, fingers, toes, and many internal organs that have begun to function.

The final stage of prenatal development, called the period of the **fetus**, lasts from the end of the second month until birth. It is a time of rapid growth and further development of the structures, organs, and systems of the body. Table 8.1 describes the characteristics of each stage of prenatal development.

In the case of **identical twins (monozygotic twins)**, one egg is fertilized by one sperm, but the zygote splits and develops into two embryos with identical genetic codes. Thus, identical twins are always of the same sex. This splitting of the zygote seems to be a chance occurrence accounting for about 4 in 1,000 births.

Table 8.1   Stages of Prenatal Development

Stage	Time after Conception	Major Activities of the Stage
Period of the zygote	1 to 2 weeks	Zygote attaches to the uterine lining. At 2 weeks, zygote is the size of the period at the end of this sentence.
Period of the embryo	3 to 8 weeks	Major systems, organs, and structures of the body develop. Period ends when first bone cells appear. At 8 weeks, embryo is about 1 inch long and weighs ⅕ of an ounce.
Period of the fetus	9 weeks to birth (38 weeks)	Rapid growth and further development of the body structures, organs, and systems.

This sequence of photos shows the fertilization of an egg by a sperm (top), an embryo at 7 weeks (middle), and a fetus at 22 weeks (bottom).

What are some negative influences on prenatal development, and during what time is their impact greatest?

fraternal (dizygotic) twins: Twins, no more alike genetically than ordinary siblings, who develop after two eggs are released during ovulation and fertilized by two different sperm.

teratogens: Harmful agents in the prenatal environment, which can have a negative impact on prenatal development or even cause birth defects.

critical period: A period that is so important to development that a harmful environmental influence at that time can keep a bodily structure from developing normally or can impair later intellectual or social development.

fetal alcohol syndrome: A condition, caused by maternal alcohol intake during pregnancy, in which the baby is born mentally retarded, with a small head, and facial, organ, and behavioral abnormalities.

Fraternal twins (dizygotic twins) develop when two eggs are released during ovulation and are fertilized by two different sperm. The two zygotes develop into two siblings who are no more alike genetically than ordinary brothers and sisters. The likelihood of fraternal twins increases if there is a family history of multiple births, if the mother is between ages 35 and 40, or if the mother has recently stopped taking birth control pills. Also, fertility drugs often cause the release of more than one egg.

Twins are not the only type of multiple births. Triplets, quadruplets, and on up to septuplets can result when multiple eggs are released during ovulation, when one or more eggs split before or after fertilization, or when a combination of these events occurs.

Negative Influences on Prenatal Development: Sabotaging Nature's Plan

Teratogens are agents in the prenatal environment that can have a negative impact on prenatal development, causing birth defects and other problems. A teratogen's impact depends on both its intensity and the time during prenatal development when it is present. Drugs, environmental hazards such as X rays or toxic waste, and diseases such as rubella generally have their most devastating consequences during the first 3 months of development (the first trimester). During this time there are **critical periods** when certain body structures develop. If drugs or infections interfere with development during a critical period, the structure or body part will not form properly, nor will it develop later (Kopp & Kaler, 1989).

The Hazard of Drugs   Many drugs cross the placental barrier and directly affect the unborn child. Consequently, both prescription and nonprescription drugs (for example, aspirin, nasal sprays, laxatives, douches, reducing aids, baking soda, and vitamin supplements) should be taken only with the consent of a doctor (Apgar & Beck, 1982). Some prescription drugs, such as certain antibiotics, tranquilizers, and anticonvulsants, are known to cause specific damage in the unborn.

The use of heroin, cocaine, and crack during pregnancy has been linked to miscarriage, prematurity, low birthweight, breathing difficulties, physical defects, and fetal death. Alcohol also crosses the placental barrier, and alcohol levels in the fetus almost match the levels in the mother's blood (Little et al., 1989). Women who drink heavily during pregnancy risk having babies with **fetal alcohol syndrome**. Babies with this syndrome are mentally retarded and have abnormally small heads with wide-set eyes and a short nose. They also have behavioral problems such as hyper-

Drinking alcohol during pregnancy can lead to an infant's being born with fetal alcohol syndrome, a permanent condition that includes mental retardation and physical and behavioral abnormalities.

activity (Julien, 1995). Some children prenatally exposed to alcohol have fetal alcohol effects—some of the characteristics of fetal alcohol syndrome but in less severe form. The Surgeon General warns women to abstain from drinking alcohol altogether during pregnancy, but about 20% ignore the warnings (Braun, 1996).

Smoking decreases the amount of oxygen and increases the amount of carbon monoxide crossing the placental barrier. The embryo or fetus is exposed to nicotine and several thousand other chemicals as well. Smoking increases the probability that a baby will be premature or of low birthweight (McDonald et al., 1992; Nordentoft et al., 1996). Because researchers disagree as to whether heavy caffeine consumption has an adverse effect on the fetus, the wisest course of action is to restrict caffeine consumption to less than 300 milligrams (3 cups) daily.

Low-Birthweight Babies   **Low-birthweight babies** are those weighing less than 5.5 pounds. Infants of this weight born at or before the 37th week are considered **preterm infants**. The smaller and more premature the baby, the greater the risk for problems ranging from subtle learning and behavior problems, in babies closer to normal birthweight, to "severe retardation, blindness, hearing loss, and even death," in the smallest newborns (Apgar & Beck, 1982, p. 69). Poor nutrition, poor prenatal care, smoking, drug use, and maternal infection all increase the likelihood of having a low-birthweight baby with complications.

PHYSICAL DEVELOPMENT AND LEARNING IN INFANCY

The Neonate

Neonates (newborn babies) come equipped with an impressive range of **reflexes**—built-in responses to certain stimuli that are needed to ensure survival in their new world. Sucking, swallowing, coughing, and blinking are some important behaviors that newborns can perform right away. Newborns will move an arm, a leg, or other body part away from a painful stimulus and will try to remove a blanket or cloth placed over the face. Stroke a baby on the cheek and you will trigger the rooting reflex—the baby opens its mouth and actively searches for a nipple.

Perceptual Development in Infancy

What are the perceptual abilities of the newborn?

low-birthweight baby: A baby weighing less than 5.5 pounds.

preterm infant: An infant born before the 37th week and weighing less than 5.5 pounds; a premature infant.

neonate: Newborn infant up to 1 month old.

reflexes: Inborn, unlearned, automatic responses (such as blinking, sucking, and grasping) to certain environmental stimuli.

visual cliff: An apparatus used to test depth perception in infants and young animals.

The five senses, although not fully developed, are functional at birth, and the newborn already has preferences for certain odors, tastes, sounds, and visual configurations. Hearing is much better developed than vision in the neonate and is functional even before birth (Busnel et al., 1992). A newborn is able to turn the head in the direction of a sound and shows a general preference for female voices. Newborns are able to discriminate among and show preferences for certain odors and tastes (Bartoshuk & Beauchamp, 1994; Leon, 1992). They favor sweet tastes and are able to differentiate between salty, bitter, and sour solutions. Newborns are also sensitive to pain (Porter et al., 1988) and are particularly responsive to touch, reacting positively to stroking and fondling.

Robert Fantz (1961) made a major breakthrough when he realized that a baby's interest in an object can be gauged by the length of time it fixates on it. Fantz demonstrated that infants prefer the image of a human face to other images such as a black-and-white abstract pattern (see Figure 8.2). Fantz's study and others have shown that newborns have clear preferences and powers of discrimination, and even memory recognition and learning ability.

At birth, an infant's vision is about 20/600, and it typically does not reach 20/20 until the child is about 2 years old (Courage & Adams, 1990; Held, 1993). Newborns

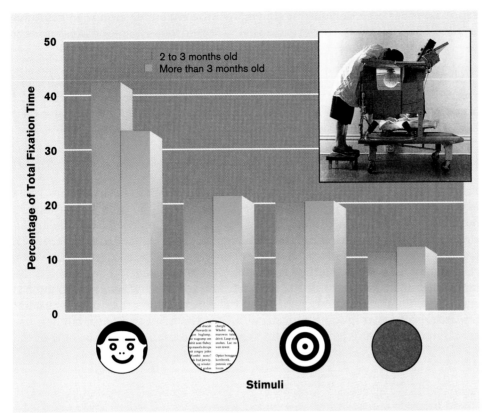

Figure 8.2
Results of Fantz's Study

Using a device called a *viewing box* to observe and record infants' eye movements, Fantz (1961) found that they preferred faces, to black-and-white abstract patterns.

focus best on objects about 9 inches away, and they can follow a slowly moving object. Infants 22 to 93 hours old already indicate a preference for their own mother's face over that of an unfamiliar female (Field et al., 1984). Although newborns prefer colored stimuli to gray ones, they can't distinguish all of the colors adults normally can until they are about 2 months old (Brown, 1990).

One famous experiment was devised to study depth perception in infants and other animals. Gibson and Walk (1960) designed an apparatus called the **visual cliff**, which is "a board laid across a sheet of heavy glass, with a patterned material directly beneath the glass on one side and several feet below it on the other" (p. 65). This arrangement made it appear that there was a sudden drop-off, or "visual cliff," on one side. Most babies aged 6 to 14 months could be coaxed by their mothers to crawl to the shallow side, but only three would crawl onto the deep side. Gibson and Walk concluded that most babies "can discriminate depth as soon as they can crawl" (p. 64).

Learning in Infancy

When are babies first capable of learning? If you say from the moment of birth, you are underestimating them. Learning begins even before birth, because infants' experiences in the womb can affect their preferences shortly after birth. DeCasper and Spence (1986) had 16 pregnant women read *The Cat in the Hat* to their developing fetuses twice a day during the final 6½ weeks of pregnancy. A few days after birth the infants could adjust their sucking on specially designed, pressure-sensitive nipples to hear their mother reading either *The Cat in the Hat* or *The King, the Mice, and the Cheese*, a story they had never heard before. Which story did the infants prefer? You guessed it—by their sucking behavior they showed a clear preference for the familiar sound of *The Cat in the Hat*.

Amazing as it may seem, Meltzoff and Moore (1977) found that babies only 42 minutes old could imitate gestures such as sticking out the tongue or opening and closing the mouth. And infants averaging 42 hours old can imitate head movements (Meltzoff & Moore, 1989). More recently, the ability of newborns to imitate facial

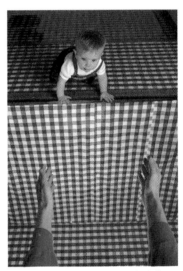

When placed on the visual cliff, most infants older than 6 months will not crawl out over the deep side, indicating that they can perceive depth.

What types of learning occur in the first few days of life?

maturation: Changes that occur according to one's genetically determined, biological timetable of development.

expressions has been demonstrated in many different ethnic groups and cultures (Meltzoff & Kuhl, 1994). However, Anisfeld (1996) reviewed nine studies and concluded that only tongue protrusion was consistently matched by newborns.

A study by Meltzoff (1988a) demonstrated observational learning in 14-month-olds. After watching an adult on television handling "a novel toy in a particular way," the babies were able to imitate the behavior when presented with the toy 24 hours later. Perhaps parents should be more particular about the TV programs their babies watch.

Motor Development in Infancy

What is the primary factor influencing attainment of the major motor milestones?

Babies undergo rapid change during the first few years of life. Some changes are due to maturation, others to learning. **Maturation** occurs naturally according to the infant's own genetically determined, biological timetable of development. Many motor milestones, such as sitting, standing, and walking (shown in Figure 8.3) are primarily a result of maturation and ultimately depend on the growth and development of the central nervous system. But the rate at which these milestones are achieved is delayed when an infant is subjected to extremely unfavorable environmental conditions such as severe malnutrition or maternal or sensory deprivation. Cross-cultural research reveals that in some African cultures in Uganda and Kenya, mothers use special motor training techniques that enable their infants to attain some of the

Figure 8.3
The Progression of Motor Development

Most infants develop motor skills in the sequence shown in the figure. The ages indicated are only averages, so normal, healthy infants may develop any of these milestones a few months earlier or several months later than the average. (From Frankenburg et al., 1992.)

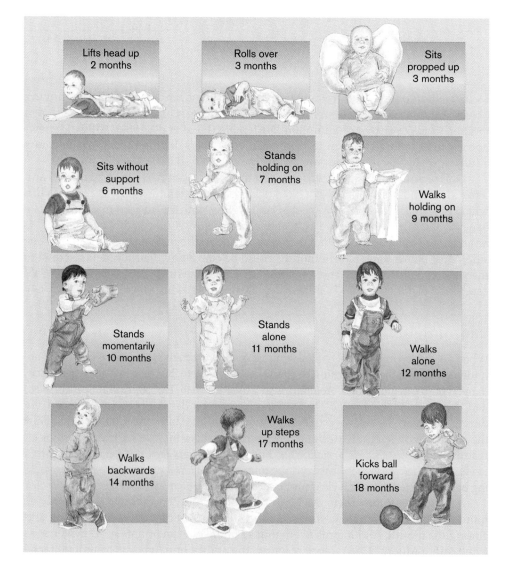

major motor milestones earlier than most infants in the United States (Kilbride & Kilbride, 1975; Super, 1981). But speeding up the attainment of motor skills has no lasting impact on development. Babies will walk, talk, and be toilet trained according to their own developmental schedules.

EMOTIONAL DEVELOPMENT IN INFANCY

Temperament: How and When Does It Develop?

Maria is usually cheerful, easygoing, and adaptable. John is always on the go, and he sticks with a problem until it is solved, but he gets upset easily. Their parents say the two children have always been that way. Is each baby born with an individual behavior style or characteristic way of responding to the environment—a particular **temperament**?

What is temperament, and what are the three temperament types identified by Thomas, Chess, and Birch?

Link It!

The New York Longitudinal Study was undertaken in 1956 to investigate temperament and its effect on development. Thomas, Chess, and Birch (1970) studied 2- to 3-month-old infants and followed them into adolescence and adulthood using observation, interviews with parents and teachers, and psychological tests. They found that "children do show distinct individuality in temperament in the first weeks of life independently of their parents' handling or personality style" (p. 104). Three general types of temperament emerged from the study.

"Easy" children—40% of the group—had generally pleasant moods, were adaptable, approached new situations and people positively, and established regular sleeping, eating, and elimination patterns. "Difficult" children—10% of the group—had generally unpleasant moods, reacted negatively to new situations and people, were intense in their emotional reactions, and showed irregularity of bodily functions. "Slow-to-warm-up" children—15% of the group—tended to withdraw, were slow to adapt, and were "somewhat negative in mood." The remaining 35% of the children studied were too inconsistent to categorize.

Thomas and others (1970) believe that personality is molded by the continuous interaction of temperament and environment. Although the environment can intensify, diminish, or modify these inborn behavioral tendencies, "the original characteristics of temperament tend to persist in most children over the years" (p. 104). Adjustment in children seems to rest in part on the fit between individual temperament and the accommodation of family and environment to behavioral style. A difficult child, may stimulate hostility and resentment in parents and others, which, in turn, may perpetuate negative behavior. On the other hand, an easy child usually elicits a positive response from the parents, which reinforces the child's behavior and increases the likelihood that the behavioral style will continue.

Several studies have revealed that children who were undercontrolled or impulsive at a young age tended to become aggressive, danger-seeking, impulsive adolescents (Hart et al., 1997) with strong negative emotions (Caspi & Silva, 1995). Overcontrolled children were found to be "more prone to social withdrawal" (Hart et al., 1997) and lacking in social potency as adolescents; that is, "they were submissive, not fond of leadership roles, and had little desire to influence others" (Caspi & Silva, 1995, p. 495).

Attachment

Human newborns are among the most helpless and dependent of all animal babies and cannot survive alone. Fortunately, infants form a strong **attachment** to their mothers or primary caregivers. Because their attachment is a two-way affair, the word *bonding* has been used to describe this mutual attachment (Brazelton et al., 1975).

What precisely is the glue that binds caregiver (usually the mother) and infant? For decades people believed that an infant's attachment to its caregiver was formed

temperament: A person's behavioral style or characteristic way of responding to the environment.

attachment: The strong affectionate bond a child forms with the mother or primary caregiver.

primarily because the caregiver provides the nourishment that sustains life. However, a series of classic studies conducted by Harry Harlow on attachment in rhesus monkeys suggests that physical nourishment alone is not enough to bind infants to their primary caregivers.

Attachment in Infant Monkeys   Harlow constructed two **surrogate** (artificial) monkey "mothers." One was a plain wire-mesh cylinder with a wooden head; the other was a wire-mesh cylinder that was padded, covered with soft terry cloth, and fitted with a somewhat more monkey-like head. A baby bottle could be attached to either surrogate mother for feeding.

Newborn monkeys were placed in individual cages where they had equal access to a cloth surrogate and a wire surrogate. The source of their nourishment (cloth or wire surrogate) was unimportant. "The infants developed a strong attachment to the cloth mothers and little or none to the wire mothers" (Harlow & Harlow, 1962, p. 141). Harlow found that it was contact comfort—the comfort supplied by bodily contact—rather than nourishment that formed the basis of the infant monkey's attachment to its mother.

The monkeys formed the same type of attachment to the cloth mothers as normal monkeys did to their real mothers. In both cases monkeys would cling to their mothers many hours each day and "run to them for comfort or reassurance when they are frightened" (Harlow, 1959, p. 73). If the cloth mother was not present when unfamiliar objects were placed in the cage, the monkey would huddle in the corner, clutching its head, rocking, sucking its thumb or toes, and crying in distress. But when the cloth mother was present, it would first cling to her and then explore and play with the unfamiliar objects.

The Development of Attachment in Humans   With humans, a strong emotional attachment between mother and infant is not present at birth but develops gradually. The mother holds, strokes, and talks to the baby, and responds to the baby's needs, and the baby gazes at and listens to the mother and even moves in synchrony with her voice (Condon & Sander, 1974; Lester et al., 1985). The baby's responses reinforce the mother's attention and care. Even crying can promote attachment, because the mother is motivated to relieve the baby's distress and feels rewarded when she is successful. Much like Harlow's monkeys, babies cling to their mothers, and when they are old enough to crawl, they use locomotion to stay near them.

Once the attachment has formed, infants show **separation anxiety**—fear and distress when the parent leaves them. Occurring from about age 8 to 24 months, separation anxiety peaks between ages 12 and 18 months (Fox & Bell, 1990). Toddlers who previously voiced no distress when their parents left them with a babysitter may now scream when their parents leave.

At about 6 or 7 months of age, infants develop a fear of strangers called **stranger anxiety**, which increases in intensity until 12½ months and then declines in the second year (Marks, 1987b). Stranger anxiety is greater in an unfamiliar setting, when the parent is not close at hand, and when a stranger abruptly approaches or touches the child. Interestingly, stranger anxiety is not directed at unfamiliar children until ages 19 to 30 months (P. K. Smith, 1979).

Stranger anxiety and separation anxiety in infants are not just Western phenomena. They are found in Israeli kibbutzim and in cultures as diverse as those of the Kung bushmen, rural Ganda, Navajo, and Guatemalan Maya (Super, 1981).

Ainsworth's Study of Attachment: The Importance of Being Securely Attached
Practically all infants reared in a family develop an attachment to a familiar caregiver by the age of 2. But there are vast differences in the quality of attachment. In a classic study of mother–child attachment, Mary Ainsworth (1973, 1979) observed mother–child interactions in the home during the infants' first year and then again at age 12 months in a laboratory using a procedure called the "strange situation." Based

What did Harlow's studies reveal about attachment in infant monkeys?

Harlow found that infant monkeys developed a strong attachment to a cloth-covered surrogate mother and little or no attachment to a wire surrogate mother—even when the wire mother provided nourishment.

When does the infant have a strong attachment to the mother?

What are the four attachment patterns identified in infants?

on infants' reactions to their mothers after brief periods of separation, Ainsworth and others (1978; Main & Solomon, 1990) identified four patterns of attachment: secure, avoidant, resistant, and disorganized/disoriented.

Securely attached infants (about 65% of American infants), although usually distressed when separated from their mother, eagerly seek to re-establish the connection and then show an interest in play. Moreover, securely attached infants use the mother as a safe base of operation from which to explore, much as Harlow's monkeys did when unfamiliar objects were placed in their cages. Securely attached infants are typically more responsive, obedient, cooperative, and content and also cry less than other infants.

Securely attached infants are likely to grow up to be more sociable, more effective with peers, more interested in exploring the environment, and generally more competent than less securely attached infants (Masters, 1981). Their interactions with friends tend to be more harmonious and less controlling (Park & Waters, 1989). Attachment style even seems to have an impact on the quality of adult love relationships (Collins, 1996).

Fathers of securely attached infants tend to be more agreeable and extroverted and to have happier marriages than fathers of insecurely attached infants (Belsky, 1996). Mothers of securely attached infants are typically more sensitive, accepting, affectionate, and responsive to their infants' cries and needs (Isabella et al., 1989; Pederson et al., 1990). This observation contradicts the notion that mothers who respond promptly to their infant's cries end up with a spoiled baby who cries more.

Infants with an avoidant attachment pattern (approximately 20% of American infants) are usually not responsive to their mother when she is present and not troubled when she leaves. When the parent returns, the infant may actively avoid contact with her or, at least, not be quick to greet her. In short, these infants do not act much more attached to a parent than to a stranger. Mothers of avoidant infants tend to show little affection and to be generally unresponsive to their infants' needs and cries.

Prior to a period of separation, infants who show resistant attachment (10–15% of American infants) seek and prefer close contact with their mother. Yet they do not tend to branch out and explore like securely attached infants. And when the mother returns to the room after a period of separation, the resistant infant displays anger and may push the mother away or hit her. When picked up, the infant is hard to comfort and may continue crying.

The disorganized/disoriented attachment pattern (5–10% of American infants) is the most puzzling and apparently the least secure pattern. When reunited with the mother, the infant exhibits contradictory and disoriented responses. Rather than looking at the mother while being held, the child may purposely look away or approach the mother with an expressionless or depressed demeanor. Also characteristic are a dazed and vacant facial expression and a peculiar, frozen posture after being calmed by the mother.

Secure attachment is the most common pattern across cultures. However, cross-cultural research revealed a higher incidence of insecure attachment patterns in Israel, Japan, and West Germany than in the United States (Collins & Gunnar, 1990). Ainsworth's procedure may not be valid for all cultures.

The Father–Child Relationship

Mother–child rather than father–child relationships have been the traditional focus of research. But this is changing because of the greater child-rearing responsibility some fathers are assuming. Some fathers even elect to stay home with the children, while the mother works outside the home (Grbich, 1994). Fathers can be as responsive and competent as mothers when they voluntarily assume child-rearing responsibilities (Parke et al., 1972; Roberts & Moseley, 1996), and their attachments can be just as strong. In the United States, mothers spend more time in caretaking and fathers generally spend more time playing with their infants (Bronstein, 1984;

surrogate: Substitute; someone or something that stands in place of someone or something else.

separation anxiety: The fear and distress shown by toddlers when their parent leaves, occurring from 8 to 24 months and reaching a peak between 12 and 18 months.

stranger anxiety: A fear of strangers common in infants at about 6 months and increasing in intensity until about 12½ months, and then declining in the second year.

What are the typical differences in the ways mothers and fathers interact with their children?

What were Piaget's claims regarding the stages of cognitive development?

 Link It!

Lamb, 1987). Fathers engage in more exciting and arousing physical play, while mothers tend to talk more to their children, provide toys, and play more conventional games with them.

There appear to be qualitative differences in the ways mothers and fathers typically interact with their infants. Mothers primarily comfort, reassure, and provide a safe harbor from which the infant may launch out and then return to. Fathers primarily stimulate, challenge, and help children develop a sense of individual identity (Moradi, cited in Adler, 1997). While a mother may instill a sense of caution in a child—"be careful"—a father may encourage the child (especially if male) to be more daring. Generally, fathers appear to be more likely than mothers to give children "a longer leash," letting them crawl farther away, up to twice as far as mothers usually allow. And fathers remain farther away as the infant explores novel stimuli and situations; mothers tend to move in closer when the child confronts the unknown.

Ideally, children need both sets of influences. Father–child interaction has many enduring positive influences on children. Children who experience regular interaction with their fathers tend to have higher IQs, be better in social situations and at coping with frustration. Also, they persist longer in solving problems and are less impulsive and less likely to become violent than children lacking father interaction (Adler, 1997; Roberts & Moseley, 1996).

PIAGET'S THEORY OF COGNITIVE DEVELOPMENT

How does a child's mind differ from an adult's? Thanks to the work of Swiss psychologist Jean Piaget (PEE-ah-ZHAY), psychologists have gained insights into the cognitive, or mental, processes of children—how they think, perceive, and gain knowledge about the world.

Piaget maintained that children are active participants in their own cognitive development. Rather than being empty vessels that can be filled with knowledge, children discover and construct knowledge through their own activity. According to Piaget, cognitive development begins with a few basic **schemas**—cognitive structures or concepts used to identify and interpret objects, events, and other information in the environment. Confronted with new objects, events, experiences, and information, children try to fit them into their existing schemas, a process known as **assimilation**. But not everything can be assimilated into the existing schemas. If children call a stranger "Daddy" or the neighbor's cat "doggie," assimilation has led them to make an error. When parents and others correct them, or when they discover for themselves that something cannot be assimilated into an existing schema, children will use a process known as accommodation. In **accommodation**, existing schemas are modified or new schemas are created to process new information. It is through the processes of assimilation and accommodation, then, that schemas are formed, differentiated, and broadened.

The Cognitive Stages of Development: Climbing the Steps to Cognitive Maturity

Piaget (1963, 1964; Piaget & Inhelder, 1969) claimed that cognitive development occurs in a sequence of four stages: the sensorimotor stage, the preoperational stage, the concrete operations stage, and the formal operations stage. Each stage reflects a qualitatively different way of reasoning and understanding the world. The stages occur in a fixed sequence in which the accomplishments of one stage provide the foundation for the next stage. Although children throughout the world seem to progress through the stages in the same order, they show individual differences in the rate at which they pass through them. And the rate is influenced by a child's

According to Piaget, this infant has not yet developed object permanence—the understanding that objects continue to exist even when they are out of sight. He makes no attempt to look for the toy behind the screen.

level of maturation and experience. The transition from one stage to another is gradual, not abrupt, and children often show aspects of two stages at the same time during these transitions.

The Sensorimotor Stage   In the first stage, the **sensorimotor stage** (ages birth to 2 years), infants gain an understanding of the world through their senses and their motor activities (actions or body movements). An infant's behavior, which is mostly reflexive at birth, becomes increasingly complex and gradually evolves into intelligent behavior. At this stage, the intelligence is one of action rather than of thought, and it is confined to objects that are present and events that are directly perceived. The child learns to respond to and manipulate objects and to use them in goal-directed activity.

At birth, infants are incapable of thought, and they are unable to differentiate themselves from others or from the environment. Living in a world of the here and now, infants are aware that objects exist only when they can actually see them. Take a stuffed animal away from a 5-month-old and it ceases to exist, as far as the child is concerned. At this age, out of sight is always out of mind.

The major achievement of the sensorimotor period is the development of **object permanence**—the realization that objects (including people) continue to exist even when they are out of sight. This concept develops gradually and is complete when the child is able to represent objects mentally in their absence. The attainment of this ability marks the end of the sensorimotor period.

The Preoperational Stage   The **preoperational stage** (ages 2 to 7 years) is a period of rapid development in language. Children become increasingly able to represent objects and events mentally with words and images. Evidence of representational thought is a child's ability to engage in imaginary play using one object to stand for another, such as using a broom to represent a horse.

Although thinking at the preoperational stage is more advanced than at the previous stage, it is still quite restricted. Thinking is dominated by perception, and children at this stage exhibit egocentrism in thought. They believe that everyone sees what they see, thinks as they think, and feels as they feel.

The preoperational stage is so named because children are not yet able to perform mental operations (manipulations) that follow logical rules. Children at this stage are not aware that a given quantity of matter (a given number, mass, area, weight, or volume of matter) remains the same if it is rearranged or changed in its appearance, as long as nothing is added or taken away. This concept is known as **conservation**.

If you know a child of preschool age, try the conservation experiment illustrated in the *Try It!* (on page 252).

What occurs during Piaget's sensorimotor stage?

What cognitive limitations characterize a child's thinking during the preoperational stage?

Show a preschooler two glasses of the same size and then fill them with the same amount of juice. After the child agrees they are the same, pour the juice from one glass into a taller, narrower glass and place that glass beside the other original one. Now ask the child if the two glasses have the same amount of juice, or if one glass has more than the other. Children at this stage will insist that the taller, narrower glass has more juice, although they will quickly agree that you neither added juice nor took any away.

Preoperational children have not developed **reversibility** in thinking—the realization that after any change in its shape, position, or order, matter can be returned mentally to its original state. In the *Try It!* the preoperational child cannot mentally return the poured juice to the original glass and realize that the two glasses of juice are equal.

What cognitive abilities do children acquire during the concrete operations stage?

The Concrete Operations Stage   In the third stage, the **concrete operations stage** (ages 7 to 11 or 12 years), children gradually overcome the obstacles to logical thought associated with the preoperational period. Their thinking is less egocentric, and they come to realize that other people have thoughts and feelings that may be different from their own. Children acquire the ability to carry out mentally the operations essential for logical thought. They are able to *decenter* their thinking, that is, to attend to two or more dimensions of a stimulus at the same time. Children can also understand the concept of reversibility and acquire the concept of conservation. However, they are able to apply logical operations only to concrete problems that they can perceive directly. They cannot apply these mental operations to verbal, abstract, or hypothetical problems. Surprisingly, the concepts of conservation of number, substance (liquid or mass), length, area, weight, and volume are not all acquired at once. They come in a certain sequence and usually at specific ages (see Figure 8.4).

What new capability characterizes the formal operations stage?

The Formal Operations Stage   The **formal operations stage** (ages 11 or 12 years and beyond) is Piaget's fourth and final stage of cognitive development. At this stage adolescents can apply reversibility and conservation to abstract, verbal, or hypothetical situations and to problems in the past, present, or future. Teenagers can comprehend abstract subjects such as philosophy and politics. They become interested in the world of ideas, and they begin to formulate theories.

Not all people attain full formal operational thinking (Kuhn, 1984; Neimark, 1981), but high school math and science experience seems to facilitate it (Sharp et al., 1979). Failure to achieve formal operational thinking has been associated with below-average scores on intelligence tests (Inhelder, 1966).

Conservation Task	Age of Acquisition	Original Presentation	Transformation
Number	6–7 years	Are there the same number of pennies in each row?	Now are there the same number of pennies in each row, or does one row have more?
Liquid	6–7 years	Is there the same amount of juice in each glass?	Now is there the same amount of juice in each glass, or does one have more?
Mass	6–7 years	Is there the same amount of clay in each ball?	Now does each piece have the same amount of clay, or does one have more?
Area	8–10 years	Does each of these two cows have the same amount of grass to eat?	Now does each cow have the same amount of grass to eat, or does one cow have more?

Figure 8.4

Piaget's Conservation Tasks

Pictured here are several of Piaget's conservation tasks. The ability to answer correctly develops over time, at approximately the ages indicated for each task. (From Berk, 1994.)

Review & Reflect 8.1 (on p. 254) provides a summary of Piaget's four stages.

An Evaluation of Piaget's Contribution

Although Piaget's genius and his monumental contribution to scientists' knowledge of mental development are rarely disputed, his methods and some of his findings and conclusions have been criticized (Halford, 1989). It now seems clear that children are more advanced cognitively and adults less competent cognitively than Piaget believed (Flavell, 1985, 1992; Mandler, 1990; Siegler, 1991).

Piaget was limited in the information he could gather about infants, because he relied on observation and on the interview technique, which depended on verbal responses. Newer techniques requiring nonverbal responses—sucking, looking, heart-rate changes, reaching, and head turning—have shown that infants and young children are more competent than Piaget proposed (Flavell, 1992). For example, there are some signs that awareness of object permanence may begin as early as 3½ months

reversibility: The realization that any change in the shape, position, or order of matter can be reversed mentally.

concrete operations stage: Piaget's third stage of cognitive development (ages 7 to 11 years), during which a child acquires the concepts of reversibility and conservation and is able to apply logical thinking to concrete objects.

formal operations stage: Piaget's fourth and final stage, characterized by the ability to apply logical thinking to abstract problems and hypothetical situations.

Review & Reflect 8.1 Piaget's Stages of Cognitive Development

Stage	Description
Sensorimotor **(0 to 2 years)**	Infants experience the world through their senses, actions, and body movements. At the end of this stage, toddlers develop the concept of object permanence and can mentally represent objects in their absence.
Preoperational **(2 to 7 years)**	Children are able to represent objects and events mentally with words and images. They can engage in imaginary play (pretend), using one object to represent another. Their thinking is dominated by their perceptions. Their thinking is also egocentric; that is, they fail to consider the perspective of others.
Concrete operational **(7 to 11 or 12 years)**	Children at this stage become able to think logically in concrete situations. They acquire the concepts of conservation and reversibility, can order objects in a series, and can classify them according to multiple dimensions.
Formal operational **(11 or 12 years and beyond)**	At this stage, adolescents learn to think logically in abstract situations, learn to test hypotheses systematically, and become interested in the world of ideas. Not all people attain full formal operational thinking.

(Baillargeon & DeVos, 1991). And whereas Piaget claimed that deferred imitation begins in the preoperational stage, some research (Heimann & Meltzoff, 1996; Meltzoff, 1988b) has demonstrated that even 9-month-olds are able to imitate actions they have observed as long as 24 hours earlier.

Few developmental psychologists believe that cognitive development takes place in the general stagelike fashion proposed by Piaget. If it did, children's cognitive functioning would be similar across all cognitive tasks and content areas (Flavell, 1992). Neo-Piagetians believe that while there are important general patterns in cognitive development, there is also more variability in how children perform on certain tasks than Piaget described (Case, 1992). This variability results from expertise children acquire in different content areas through extensive practice and experience (Flavell, 1992).

Cross-cultural studies have affirmed the universality of the types of reasoning and the sequence of stages formulated by Piaget. But cross-cultural research has also revealed differences in the rates of cognitive development in various domains. Whereas Piaget's subjects began to acquire the concept of conservation between ages 5 and 7, Australian Aboriginal children show this change between the ages of 10 and 13 (Dasen, 1994). Yet the Aboriginal children function at the concrete operations stage earlier on spatial tasks than on quantification (counting) tasks, while the reverse is true for Western children. This difference makes sense in light of the high value Aborigines place on spatial skills and the low premium they place on quantification. In the Australian desert, moving from place to place hunting, gathering, and searching for water, Aborigines have few possessions and rarely count things. Their language has words for numbers up to five, and their word for "many" applies to anything above five.

According to Flavell (1996), "Piaget's greatest contribution was to found the field of cognitive development as we currently know it" (p. 200). Piaget's work has had a profound impact on the fields of psychology and education. His influence has led teachers to arrange richer learning environments in which children gain knowledge and improve cognitive skills through exploration and discovery.

VYGOTSKY'S SOCIOCULTURAL VIEW OF COGNITIVE DEVELOPMENT

Russian psychologist Lev Vygotsky (1896–1934) strongly rejected Piaget's individualistic view of cognitive development and offered his own theory that each individual's quest for cognitive growth and development is forged within a sociocultural environment.

Vygotsky (1934/1986) maintained that human infants come equipped with basic skills such as perception, the ability to pay attention, and certain capacities of memory not unlike those of many other animal species. During the first 2 years of life, these skills grow and develop naturally through direct experiences and interactions with the child's sociocultural world. In due course, children develop the mental ability to represent objects, activities, ideas, people, and relationships in a variety of ways, but primarily through language (speech). With their new ability to represent ideas, activities, and so on through speech, children are often observed "talking to themselves." Vygotsky believed that talking to oneself—*private speech*—is a key component in cognitive development. Through private speech, children can specify the components of a problem and verbalize steps in a process to help them work through puzzling activities and situations. As young children develop greater competence, private speech fades into barely audible mumbling and muttering, and finally becomes simply thinking.

Followers of Vygotsky advocate the use of an instructional technique known as *scaffolding*—in which a teacher or parent adjusts the quality and degree of help to fit the child's present level of ability or performance. In scaffolding, more direct instruction is given, at first, for unfamiliar tasks (Maccoby, 1992). But as the child shows increasing competence, the scaffolder (teacher or parent) gradually withdraws from direct and active teaching, and the child may continue toward independent mastery of the task.

Contemporary researchers have found widespread evidence to support many of Vygotsky's ideas (Berk, 1994).

In Vygotsky's view, how do private speech and scaffolding contribute to cognitive development?

Link It!

Vygotsky maintained that, with instruction and guidance from an adult or older peer, a child can learn to perform a wide range of cognitive tasks.

LANGUAGE DEVELOPMENT

At birth, the infant's only means of communication is crying, but at age 17, the average high school graduate has a vocabulary of 80,000 words (Miller & Gildea, 1987). From age 18 months to 5 years, the child acquires about 14,000 words, an amazing average of 9 new words per day (Rice, 1989).

But children do much more than simply add new words to their vocabulary. In the first 5 years of life, they also acquire an understanding of the way words are put together to form sentences (syntax) and the way language is used in social situations. Children acquire most of their language without any formal teaching and discover the rules of language on their own—a truly remarkable feat.

Link It!

The Stages of Language Development: The Orderly Progression of Language

Infants begin to communicate long before they utter their first words. During their first few months, they communicate distress or displeasure through crying, although this is not actually their intent (Shatz, 1983). The cry is simply their innate reaction to an unpleasant internal state, such as hunger, thirst, discomfort, or pain.

What are the stages of language development from cooing through the acquisition of grammatical rules?

Cooing and Babbling   During the second or third month, infants begin cooing—repeatedly uttering vowel sounds such as "ah" and "oo." At about 6 months, infants begin **babbling**. They utter **phonemes**—the basic speech sounds of any language, which form words when combined. Consonant–vowel combinations are repeated in a string, like "ma-ma-ma" or "ba-ba-ba." During the first part of the babbling stage, infants babble all the basic speech sounds that occur in all the languages of the world. Language up to this point seems to be biologically determined, because all babies throughout the world, even deaf children, vocalize this same range of speech sounds.

At about 8 months, babies begin to focus attention on those speech sounds (phonemes) common to their native tongue and on the rhythm and intonation of the language. Gradually they cease making the sounds not found in their native language (Levitt & Wang, 1991). Deaf children who are exposed to sign language from birth babble manually by making the hand movements that represent the phonemes in sign language (Petitto & Marentette, 1991).

The One-Word Stage   At about 1 year, the babbling stage gives way to the one-word stage, and infants utter their first real words. The first words usually represent objects that move or those that infants can act on or interact with. Early words usually include food, animals, and toys—"cookie," "mama," "dada," "doggie," and "ball," to name a few (Nelson, 1973).

From 13 to 18 months of age, children markedly increase their vocabulary (Woodward et al., 1994), and by 2 years it consists of about 270 words (Brown, 1973). Initially a child's understanding of words differs from that of an adult. On the basis of some shared feature and because they lack the correct word, children may apply a word to a broader range of objects than is appropriate. This is known as **overextension**. For example, any man may be called "dada," any four-legged animal, "doggie." **Underextension** occurs, too, when children fail to apply a word to other members of the class. The family's poodle is a "doggie," but the German shepherd next door is not.

The Two-Word Stage and Telegraphic Speech   Between 18 and 20 months, when the vocabulary is about 50 words, children begin to put nouns, verbs, and adjectives together in two-word phrases and sentences. At this stage children depend to a great extent on gesture, tone, and context to convey their meaning (Slobin, 1972). Depending on intonation, their sentences may indicate questions, statements, or possession. Children adhere to a rigid word order. You might hear "mama drink," "drink milk," or "mama milk," but not "drink mama," "milk drink," or "milk mama."

At about 2½ years, children begin to use short sentences, which may contain three or more words. Labeled **telegraphic speech** by Roger Brown (1973), these short sentences follow a rigid word order and contain only essential content words, leaving out all plurals, possessives, conjunctions, articles, and prepositions. Telegraphic speech reflects the child's understanding of syntax—the rules governing how words are ordered in a sentence. When a third word is added to a sentence, it usually fills in the word missing from the two-word sentence (for example, "Mama drink milk").

Suffixes, Function Words, and Grammatical Rules   After using telegraphic speech for a time, children gradually begin to add modifiers to make words more precise. Suffixes and function words—pronouns, articles, conjunctions, and prepositions—are acquired in a fixed sequence, although the rate of acquisition varies (Brown, 1973; Maratsos, 1983).

Children pick up grammatical rules intuitively and apply them rigidly. **Overregularization** is the kind of error that results when a grammatical rule is misapplied to a word that has an irregular plural or past tense (Marcus, 1996). Thus, children who have correctly used the words "went," "came," and "did" incorrectly apply the rule for past tenses and begin to say "goed," "comed," and "doed." What the parents see as a regression in speech actually means that the child has acquired a grammatical rule.

babbling: Vocalization of the basic speech sounds (phonemes), which begins between 4 and 6 months.

phonemes: The basic speech sounds in any language that, when combined, form words.

overextension: The act of using a word, on the basis of some shared feature, to apply to a broader range of objects than appropriate.

underextension: Restricting the use of a word to only a few, rather than to all, members of a class of objects.

telegraphic speech: Short sentences that follow a strict word order and contain only essential content words.

overregularization: The act of inappropriately applying the grammatical rules for forming plurals and past tenses to irregular nouns and verbs.

Theories of Language Development: How Is Language Acquired?

There is no disagreement among theorists that children's learning of language is a truly amazing feat. But theorists do disagree about *how* children are able to accomplish such a feat. Several theories have been proposed to explain language acquisition. Some theories emphasize the role of learning and experience (nurture); some propose a biological explanation, emphasizing maturation (nature); and others suggest an interaction between maturation and experience. "There is currently no consensus of support for any one of them" (Rice, 1989, p. 150).

Learning theorists have long maintained that language is acquired in the same way as other behaviors are acquired—as a result of learning through reinforcement and imitation. B. F. Skinner (1957) asserted that parents selectively criticize incorrect speech and reinforce correct speech through praise, approval, and attention. Thus, the child's utterances are progressively shaped in the direction of grammatically correct speech. Others believe that children acquire vocabulary and sentence construction mainly through imitation (Bandura, 1977).

There are some problems, however, with learning theory as the sole explanation for language acquisition. Imitation cannot account for patterns of speech such as telegraphic speech or for systematic errors such as overregularization. Children do not hear telegraphic speech in everyday life, and "I comed" and "he goed" are not forms commonly used by parents.

There are also problems with reinforcement as an explanation for language acquisition. First, parents seem to reward children more for the content of the utterance than for the correctness of the grammar (Brown et al., 1968). And parents are much more likely to correct them for saying something untrue than for making a grammatical error. Regardless, correction has little impact on a child's grammar. But reinforcement still plays an important part in language learning. Responsiveness to infants' vocalizations increases the amount of vocalization, and reinforcement can help children with language deficits improve (Whitehurst et al., 1989).

Noam Chomsky (1957) believes that language ability is largely innate, and he has proposed a very different theory. Chomsky (1968) maintains that the brain contains a *language acquisition device (LAD)*, which enables children to acquire language and discover the rules of grammar easily and naturally. Language develops in stages that occur in a fixed order and appear at about the same time in most normal children. Lenneberg (1967) claims that biological maturation underlies language development in much the same way that it underlies physical and motor development. These views are know as the *nativist position.*

The nativist position is better able than learning theory to account for the fact that children throughout the world go through the same basic stages in language development. It can account, too, for the similar errors all children make when they are first learning to form plurals, past tenses, and negatives—errors not acquired through imitation or reinforcement. However, there are several aspects of language development that the nativist position cannot explain.

One's native language, after all, is acquired in a social setting, and experience must exert some influence on development (Bohannon & Warren-Leubecker, 1989). You remember Robert, in the chapter-opening story, who could not speak, but whose oral utterances were more like those of the monkeys he lived with. He vocalized what he heard in his own social setting.

Parents can facilitate language acquisition by adjusting their speech to their infant's level of development. Parents often use *motherese*—highly simplified speech with shorter phrases and sentences and simpler vocabulary, which is uttered slowly, at a high pitch, and with exaggerated intonation and much repetition (Fernald, 1993). Deaf mothers communicate with their infants in a similar way, signing more slowly and with exaggerated hand and arm movements and frequent repetition (Masataka, 1996).

Reading to children and with them supports language development. Parents should comment and expand on what the child says and encourage the child to say

How do learning theory and the nativist position explain the acquisition of language?

more by asking questions. According to Rice (1989), "Most children do not need to be taught language, but they do need opportunities to develop language" (p. 155).

SOCIALIZATION OF THE CHILD

To function effectively and comfortably in society, children must come to know the patterns of behavior considered to be desirable and appropriate. The process of learning socially acceptable behaviors, attitudes, and values is called **socialization**. Although parents have the major role in socialization, peers, school, the media, and religion are all important influences as well.

Erikson's Theory of Psychosocial Development

What is Erikson's theory of psychosocial development?

socialization: The process of learning socially acceptable behaviors, attitudes, and values.

psychosocial stages: Erikson's eight developmental stages through the life span, each defined by a conflict that must be resolved satisfactorily in order for healthy personality development to occur.

basic trust versus basic mistrust: Erikson's first stage (ages birth to 1 year), when infants develop trust or mistrust based on the quality of care, love, and affection provided.

autonomy versus shame and doubt: Erikson's second stage (ages 1 to 3 years), when infants develop autonomy or shame based on how parents react to their expression of will and their wish to do things for themselves.

initiative versus guilt: Erikson's third stage (ages 3 to 6 years), when children develop a sense of initiative or guilt depending on how parents react to their initiation of play, their motor activities, and their questions.

industry versus inferiority: Erikson's fourth stage (ages 6 years to puberty), when children develop a sense of industry or inferiority based on how parents and teachers react to their efforts to undertake projects.

Erik Erikson (1902–1994) proposed the only major theory of development to include the entire life span. He was the first to stress the part that society and individuals themselves play in their own personality development, rather than focusing exclusively on the influence of parents.

According to Erikson, individuals progress through eight **psychosocial stages** during the life span. Each stage is defined by a conflict involving the individual's relationship with the social environment, which must be resolved satisfactorily in order for healthy development to occur. The stages are named for a "series of alternative basic attitudes," which result depending on how the conflict is resolved (Erikson, 1980). Erikson believed that a healthy personality depends on acquiring the appropriate basic attitudes in the proper sequence. Although failure to resolve a conflict impedes later development, resolution may occur at a later stage and reverse any damage done previously.

Stage 1: Basic Trust versus Basic Mistrust (Ages Birth to 1 Year)   During the first stage, **basic trust versus basic mistrust**, infants develop a sense of trust or mistrust depending on the degree and regularity of care, love, and affection they receive from the mother or primary caregiver. Erikson (1980) considered "basic trust as the cornerstone of a healthy personality" (p. 58).

Stage 2: Autonomy versus Shame and Doubt (Ages 1 to 3 Years)   During the second stage, **autonomy versus shame and doubt**, children are developing their physical and mental abilities and want to do things for themselves. They begin to express their independence and develop a "sudden violent wish to have a choice" (Erikson, 1963, p. 252). "No!" becomes one of their favorite words. Erikson believed that parents must set appropriate limits, but at the same time facilitate the child's desire for autonomy by encouraging appropriate attempts at independence. If parents are impatient or overprotective, they may make children feel shame and doubt about their efforts to exercise their own will and explore their environment.

Stage 3: Initiative versus Guilt (Ages 3 to 6 Years)   In the third stage, **initiative versus guilt**, children go beyond merely expressing their autonomy and begin to develop initiative. Enjoying their new locomotor and mental powers, children initiate play and motor activities and ask questions. If appropriate attempts at initiative are encouraged and inappropriate attempts are handled firmly but sensitively, children will leave this stage with a sense of initiative that will form "a basis for a high and yet realistic sense of ambition and independence" (Erikson, 1980, p. 78).

Stage 4: Industry versus Inferiority (Ages 6 Years to Puberty)   During the fourth stage, **industry versus inferiority**, children begin to enjoy and take pride in making things and doing things. Children may develop a sense of inferiority if their attempts in this regard are seen as "mischief" or "making a mess" (Elkind, 1970).

Stage	Ages	Description
Trust vs. mistrust	Birth to 1 year	Infants learn to trust or mistrust depending on the degree and regularity of care, love, and affection provided by parents or caregivers.
Autonomy vs. shame and doubt	1 to 3 years	Children learn to express their will and independence, to exercise some control, and to make choices. If not, they experience shame and doubt.
Initiative vs. guilt	3 to 6 years	Children begin to initiate activities, to plan and undertake tasks, and to enjoy their developing motor and other abilities. If not allowed to initiate or if made to feel stupid and considered a nuisance, they may develop a sense of guilt.
Industry vs. inferiority	6 years to puberty	Children develop industriousness and feel pride in accomplishing tasks, making things, and doing things. If not encouraged, or if rebuffed by parents and teachers, they may develop a sense of inferiority.
Identity vs. role confusion	Adolescence	Described later in this chapter.
Intimacy vs. isolation	Young adulthood	
Generativity vs. stagnation	Middle adulthood	
Ego integrity vs. despair	Late adulthood	

The encouragement of teachers as well as parents is important for a positive resolution of this stage.

Review & Reflect 8.2 describes Erikson's first four stages. Erikson's next four stages, which cover adolescence through adulthood, are discussed later in this chapter.

The Parents' Role in the Socialization Process

The parents' role in the socialization process is to set examples, to teach, and to provide discipline. Parents are usually more successful if they are loving, warm, nurturant, and supportive (Maccoby & Martin, 1983). In fact, a longitudinal study that followed individuals from age 5 to age 41 revealed that "children of warm, affectionate parents were more likely to be socially accomplished adults who, at age 41, were mentally healthy, coping adequately, and psychosocially mature in work, relationships, and generativity" (Franz et al., 1991, p. 593). Families are dysfunctional when the roles are reversed, and the children nurture and control their parents (Maccoby, 1992).

To be effective, socialization must ultimately result in children coming to regulate their own behavior. The attainment of this goal is undermined when parents control their children's behavior by asserting power over them (Maccoby, 1992). Diane Baumrind (1971, 1980, 1991) studied the continuum of parental control and identified three parenting styles—the authoritarian, the authoritative, and the per-

In Erikson's fourth stage—industry versus inferiority—children enjoy and take pride in making things.

What are the three parenting styles identified by Baumrind, and which did she find most effective?

authoritarian parents: Parents who make arbitrary rules, expect unquestioned obedience from their children, punish transgressions, and value obedience to authority.

authoritative parents: Parents who set high but realistic standards, reason with the child, enforce limits, and encourage open communication and independence.

permissive parents: Parents who make few rules or demands and allow children to make their own decisions and control their own behavior.

How do peers contribute to the socialization process?

At a very young age, children begin to form peer relationships—learning to share and cooperate and developing social skills.

missive. She related these styles to different patterns of behavior in predominantly white, middle-class children.

Authoritarian parents make the rules, expect unquestioned obedience from their children, punish misbehavior (often physically), and value obedience to authority. Rather than giving a rationale for a rule, authoritarian parents consider "because I said so" a sufficient reason for obedience. Parents using this parenting style tend to be uncommunicative, unresponsive, and somewhat distant. Baumrind (1967) found preschool children disciplined in this manner to be withdrawn, anxious, and unhappy.

Parental failure to provide a rationale for rules makes it hard for children to see any reason for following them. Saying "Do it because I said so" may succeed in making the child do what is expected when the parent is present, but it is ineffective when the parent is not around. The authoritarian style has been associated with low intellectual performance and lack of social skills, especially in boys (Maccoby & Martin, 1983).

Authoritative parents set high but realistic and reasonable standards, enforce limits, and at the same time encourage open communication and independence. They are willing to discuss rules and supply rationales for them. Knowing why the rules are necessary makes it easier for children to internalize them and to follow them, whether in the presence of their parents or not. Authoritative parents are generally warm, nurturant, supportive, and responsive, and they show respect for their children and their opinions. Their children are the most mature, happy, self-reliant, self-controlled, assertive, socially competent, and responsible. The authoritative parenting style is associated with higher academic performance, independence, higher self-esteem, and internalized moral standards in middle childhood and adolescence (Lamborn et al., 1991; Steinberg et al., 1989).

Although they are rather warm and supportive, **permissive parents** make few rules or demands and usually do not enforce those that are made. They allow children to make their own decisions and control their own behavior. Children raised in this manner are the most immature, impulsive, and dependent, and they seem to be the least self-controlled and self-reliant.

Permissive parents also come in the indifferent, unconcerned, uninvolved variety (Maccoby & Martin, 1983). This parenting style is associated with drinking problems, promiscuous sex, delinquent behavior, and poor academic performance in adolescents.

Peer Relationships

Infants begin to show an interest in each other at a very young age. At only 6 months of age, they already demonstrate an interest in other infants by looking, reaching, touching, smiling, and vocalizing (Vandell & Mueller, 1980). Friendships begin to develop by 3 or 4 years, and relationships with peers become increasingly important. By middle childhood, membership in a peer group is central to a child's happiness. Peer groups are usually composed of children of the same race, sex, and social class (Schofield & Francis, 1982).

The peer group serves a socializing function by providing models of behavior, dress, and language. It is a continuing source of both reinforcement for appropriate behavior and punishment for deviant behavior. The peer group also provides an objective measure against which children can evaluate their own traits and abilities— how smart or how good at sports they are, for example. In their peer groups children learn how to get along with age-mates—how to share and cooperate, develop social skills, and regulate aggression.

Low acceptance by peers is an important predictor of later mental health problems (Kupersmidt et al., 1990). Most often excluded from the peer group are neglected children, who are shy and withdrawn, and rejected children, who typically exhibit aggressive and inappropriate behavior and who are likely to start fights (Dodge, Cole, et al., 1990). Children abused at home tend to be unpopular with their classmates, who typically view them as aggressive and uncooperative (Salzinger et al., 1993). Rejection by peers is linked to unhappiness, alienation, and poor achievement, and in middle childhood with delinquency and dropping out of school (Kupersmidt & Coie, 1990; Parker & Asher, 1987).

adolescence: The developmental stage that begins at puberty and encompasses the period from the end of childhood to the beginning of adulthood.

puberty: A period of rapid physical growth and change that culminates in sexual maturity.

adolescent growth spurt: A period of rapid physical growth that peaks in girls at about age 12 and in boys at about age 14.

ADOLESCENCE: PHYSICAL AND COGNITIVE DEVELOPMENT

How difficult is adolescence for most teenagers?

What comes to mind when you picture the world of the adolescent? Many people have quite negative associations to the term *adolescence* and may picture a life of rebellion, and stormy and stressful relationships with parents and family. Others picture strong peer-group conformity, which may include unorthodox dress, tattoos, piercing of unusual body parts, drug dependency, and worse.

Is this view of adolescence supported by research? The answer might surprise you. **Adolescence** is the developmental stage that spans the period from the end of childhood to the beginning of adulthood. A person does not go to sleep one night as a child and awaken as an adult the next morning, at least not in contemporary American society. But some cultures have designed elaborate ceremonies known as rites of passage or puberty rites, which publicly mark the passage from childhood to adulthood. At the end of the ceremony, the young person becomes an "instant adult," ready to assume adult responsibilities and to marry.

The concept of adolescence did not exist until psychologist G. Stanley Hall first wrote about it in his book by that name in 1904. He portrayed this stage in life as one of "storm and stress," the inevitable result of biological changes occurring during the period. Anna Freud (1958), daughter of Sigmund Freud, even considered a stormy adolescence a necessary part of normal development. But Hall and Freud were wrong.

Compelling evidence now suggests that adolescence is not typically stormy and difficult (Peterson, 1988). Although adolescence poses a great risk to healthy development for about one-fourth of teenagers, for at least one-half of them the period is marked by healthy development (Takanishi, 1993). Offer and others (1981) found that average adolescents "function well, enjoy good relationships with their families and friends, and accept the values of the larger society" (p. 116). And researchers continue to find that the majority of adolescents say they are happy and self-confident (Diener & Diener, 1996).

Contrary to popular belief, adolescence is not stormy and difficult for most teenagers.

Children at highest risk for a troubled adolescence seem to be those who have a tendency toward depression or aggressive behavior or who come from particularly negative environments, such as those filled with family conflict (Buchanan et al., 1992).

Physical Development during Adolescence: Growing, Growing, Grown

What physical changes occur during puberty?

Adolescence begins with the onset of **puberty**—a period of rapid physical growth and change that culminates in sexual maturity (Rice, 1992). Although the average onset of puberty is age 10 for girls and age 12 for boys, the normal range extends from age 7 to age 14 for girls and from 9 to 16 for boys (Chumlea, 1982). Every person's individual timetable for adolescence is influenced primarily by heredity, although environmental factors also exert some influence.

Puberty begins with a surge in hormone production, which in turn causes a number of physical changes. The most startling change during puberty is the marked acceleration in growth known as the **adolescent growth spurt**. Who doesn't remember that

What are the psychological effects of early and late maturation for boys and girls?

time in life when the girls were towering over boys of the same age? On the average, the growth spurt occurs from age 10½ to 13 in girls and about 2 years later in boys, from age 12½ to 15 (Tanner, 1961). Because various parts of the body grow at different rates, the adolescent often has a lanky, awkward appearance. Girls attain their full height between ages 16 and 17, and boys, between ages 18 and 20 (Roche & Davila, 1972).

During puberty the reproductive organs in both sexes mature, and **secondary sex characteristics** appear—those physical characteristics not directly involved in reproduction that distinguish the mature male from the mature female. In girls the breasts develop and the hips round; in boys the voice deepens, and facial and chest hair appears; and in both sexes there is growth of pubic and underarm (axillary) hair.

The major landmark of puberty for males is the first ejaculation, which occurs, on average, at age 13 (Jorgensen & Keiding, 1991). And for females it is **menarche**— the onset of menstruation—which occurs at an average age of 12½, although from 10 to 15½ is considered within the normal range (Tanner, 1990). Some recent research suggests that environmental stress, such as parental divorce or conflict, is related to an earlier onset of menarche (Belsky et al., 1991; Wierson et al., 1993).

Probably at no other time in life does physical appearance have such a strong impact on self-image and self-esteem as during adolescence. The timing of puberty can have important psychological consequences, coming as it does at a time when a sense of security is gained from being like other members of the peer group. Early-maturing boys, taller and stronger than their classmates, have an advantage in sports and are likely to have a positive body image, to feel confident, secure, independent, and happy, and to be more successful academically as well (Alsaker, 1995; Blyth et al., 1981; Peterson, 1987). Late-maturing boys are self-conscious about their size and lack the physical traits of manliness—a deep voice and a developing beard. To make matters worse, they are often teased by their peers and treated like "kids."

Early-maturing girls, who may tower over their peers, feel more self-conscious about their developing bodies and their size. In addition, they have to deal with the sexual advances of older boys before they are emotionally or psychologically mature (Peterson, 1987). In addition to having earlier sexual experiences and more unwanted pregnancies than late-maturing girls, early-maturing girls are more likely to be exposed to alcohol and drug use (Caspi et al., 1993). And, having had such experiences, early-maturing girls, not surprisingly, tend to perform less well academically than their age mates (Stattin & Magnusson, 1990). Late-maturing girls often experience considerable stress when they fail to develop physically along with their peers, but they are likely to be taller and slimmer than their early-maturing age mates.

Cognitive Development in Adolescence: Piaget's Formal Operations Stage

What cognitive abilities develop during the formal operations stage?

The most striking achievement in cognitive development during adolescence is the ability to think abstractly. Jean Piaget (1972; Piaget & Inhelder, 1969) believed that young people typically enter the final stage of cognitive development, the **formal operations stage**, at age 11 or 12, when they become able to use logical reasoning in abstract situations. Remember that, according to Piaget, preadolescents are able to apply logical thought processes only in concrete situations. With the attainment of full operational thinking, adolescents are able to attack problems by systematically testing hypotheses and drawing conclusions through deductive reasoning.

When high school students develop formal operational thinking, they are able to unravel the mysteries of algebra and to decipher analogies and metaphors in English literature. With formal operations comes the ability to explore the world of ideas, to look at religion and moral values in a new light, and to consider different philosophies and political systems. Formal operational thinking enables adolescents to think hypothetically; they can think of what *might* be. Given this new ability, it is not surprising that they begin to conceive of "perfect" solutions to the world's problems.

Formal operational thought does not develop automatically, and it may be virtually absent in some primitive cultures (Dasen, 1972). Siegler (1991) claims that it is rare to find high school or college students in the United States who can solve Piagetian formal operations tasks without training. One longitudinal study of American adolescents and adults concluded that only 30% of those studied attained formal operations (Kuhn et al., 1977). Not only do many people fail to show formal operational thinking, but those who do attain it usually apply it only in those areas in which they are most proficient (Ault, 1983; Martorano, 1977). Some studies suggest that even very intelligent, well-educated adults think best when thinking concretely (Neimark, 1975). According to John Flavell (1992), adults appear less competent, and infants and young children more competent, than developmental psychologists once believed.

David Elkind (1967, 1974) claims that the early teenage years are marked by adolescent egocentrism, which takes two forms—the imaginary audience and the personal fable. Do you remember, as a teenager, picturing how your friends would react to the way you looked when you made your grand entrance at a big party? This **imaginary audience** of admirers (or critics) that adolescents conjure up exists only in their imagination. In their minds, they are always on stage.

Teenagers also have an exaggerated sense of personal uniqueness and indestructibility that Elkind calls the **personal fable**. Many believe they are somehow indestructible and protected from the misfortunes that befall others, such as unwanted pregnancies or drug overdoses.

imaginary audience: A belief of adolescents that they are or will be the focus of attention in social situations and that others will be as critical or approving as they are of themselves.

personal fable: An exaggerated sense of personal uniqueness and indestructibility, which may be the basis for adolescent risk taking.

ADOLESCENCE: MORAL AND SOCIAL DEVELOPMENT

Kohlberg's Theory of Moral Development

How do we develop our ideas of right and wrong? As children, do we acquire our moral values from our parents, from attending church or temple, from our peer group, and from other societal influences? Most of us would agree that all these forces can influence our moral values. But Lawrence Kohlberg (1981, 1984, 1985) believed, as did Piaget before him, that moral reasoning is closely related to cognitive development and that it, too, evolves in stages.

Kohlberg (1969) studied moral development by presenting a series of moral dilemmas to male participants from the United States and other countries. Read one of his best-known dilemmas, and *Try It!*

Try It!

In Europe a woman was near death from a special kind of cancer. There was one drug the doctors thought might save her. It was a form of radium that a druggist in the same town had recently discovered. The drug was expensive to make, and the druggist was charging ten times what it cost him. He paid $200 for the radium and charged $2,000 for a small dose of the drug. The sick woman's husband, Heinz, went to everyone he knew to borrow the money, but he could only get to-gether $1,000, which was half of what the drug cost. He told the druggist that his wife was dying, and asked him to sell it cheaper or let him pay later. But the druggist said, "No, I discovered the drug, and I am going to make money from it." So Heinz got desperate and broke into the man's store to steal the drug for his wife. (Colby et al., 1983, p. 77)

What moral judgment would you make about this dilemma? Should Heinz have stolen the drug? Why or why not?

What are Kohlberg's three
levels of moral reasoning?

Levels of Moral Reasoning   Kohlberg was less interested in whether the participants judged Heinz's behavior (as described in the *Try It!*) right or wrong than in the *reasons* for their responses. He found that moral reasoning could be classified into three levels, with each level having two stages.

At the first level of moral reasoning, the **preconventional level**, moral reasoning is governed by the standards of others rather than one's own internalized standards of right and wrong. An act is judged good or bad based on its physical consequences. In Stage 1 "right" is whatever avoids punishment; in Stage 2 "right" is whatever is rewarded, benefits the individual, or results in a favor being returned. "You scratch my back and I'll scratch yours" is the thinking common at this stage. Children through age 10 usually function at the preconventional level.

At the second level of moral reasoning, the **conventional level**, the individual has internalized the standards of others and judges right and wrong in terms of those standards. At Stage 3, sometimes called the "good boy–nice girl" orientation, "good behavior is that which pleases or helps others and is approved by them" (Kohlberg, 1968, p. 26). At Stage 4 the orientation is toward "authority, fixed rules, and the maintenance of the social order. Right behavior consists of doing one's duty, showing respect for authority, and maintaining the given social order for its own sake" (p. 26). Kohlberg believed that a person must function at Piaget's concrete operations stage to reason morally at the conventional level.

Kohlberg's highest level is the **postconventional level**, which requires the ability to think at Piaget's stage of formal operations. Postconventional reasoning is most often found among middle-class, college-educated people. At this level, people do not simply internalize the standards of others. Instead, they weigh moral alternatives, realizing that at times the law may conflict with basic human rights. At Stage 5 the person believes that laws are formulated to protect both society and the individual and should be changed if they fail to do so. At Stage 6 ethical decisions are based on universal ethical principles, which emphasize respect for human life, justice, equality, and dignity for all people. People who reason morally at Stage 6 believe that they must follow their conscience even if it results in a violation of the law.

Could this kind of moral reasoning provide a convenient justification for doing anything a person feels like doing at any time? Not according to Kohlberg, who insisted that an action must be judged in terms of whether it is right and fair from the perspective of everyone involved. In other words, the person must be convinced that the action would be proper even if he or she had to change positions with any individual, from the most favored to the least favored, in the society. Later Kohlberg had second thoughts about this sixth stage and was unsure whether it exists except as a matter of theoretical speculation (Levine et al., 1985).

Review & Reflect 8.3 summarizes Kohlberg's six stages of moral development.

The Development of Moral Reasoning   Kohlberg claimed that people progress through moral stages one stage at a time in a fixed order, without skipping stages; if movement occurs, it is to the next higher stage. Postconventional reasoning is not possible, Kohlberg said, until people fully attain Piaget's level of formal operations. They must be able to think abstractly and to apply ethical principles in hypothetical situations (Kohlberg & Gilligan, 1971; Kuhn et al., 1977). As Kohlberg came to realize, discussion of moral dilemmas does not reliably improve moral behavior. He eventually agreed that direct teaching of moral values is necessary and compatible with his theory (Higgins, 1995; Power et al., 1989).

What do cross-cultural
studies reveal about the
universality of Kohlberg's
theory?

Research on Kohlberg's Theory   In a review of 45 studies of Kohlberg's theory conducted in 27 countries, Snarey (1985) found support for the virtual universality of Stages 1 through 4, and for the invariant sequence of these stages in all groups studied. Although extremely rare, Stage 5 was found in almost all samples from urban or middle-class populations and absent in all of the tribal or village folk societies studied. And Snarey's more recent research (1995) supports the conclusions he and his colleagues reached a decade earlier.

Review & Reflect 8.3 Kohlberg's Stages of Moral Development

Level	Stage
Level I: Preconventional level (Ages 4–10) Moral reasoning is governed by the standards of others; an act is good or bad depending on its physical consequences—whether it is punished or rewarded.	**Stage 1** The stage in which behavior that avoids punishment is right. Children obey out of fear of punishment. **Stage 2** The stage of self-interest. What is right is what benefits the individual or gains a favor in return. "You scratch my back and I'll scratch yours."
Level II: Conventional level (Ages 10–13) The child internalizes the standards of others and judges right and wrong according to those standards.	**Stage 3** The morality of mutual relationships. The "good boy–nice girl" orientation. Child acts to please and help others. **Stage 4** The morality of the social system and conscience. Orientation toward authority. Morality is doing one's duty, respecting authority, and maintaining the social order.
Level III: Postconventional level (After age 13, at young adulthood, or never) Moral conduct is under internal control; this is the highest level and the mark of true morality.	**Stage 5** The morality of contract; respect for individual rights and laws that are democratically agreed on. Rational valuing of the wishes of the majority and the general welfare. Belief that society is best served if citizens obey the law. **Stage 6** The highest stage of the highest social level. The morality of universal ethical principles. The person acts according to internal standards independent of legal restrictions or opinions of others.

One controversy concerns possible gender bias in Kohlberg's stages. Kohlberg indicated that the majority of women remain at Stage 3, while most men attain Stage 4. Do men typically attain a higher level of moral reasoning than women? Carol Gilligan (1982) asserts that Kohlberg's theory is sex-biased. Not only did Kohlberg fail to include females in his original research, Gilligan points out, but he limited morality to abstract reasoning about moral dilemmas. And, at his highest level, Stage 6, Kohlberg emphasized justice and equality but not mercy, compassion, love, or concern for others. Gilligan suggests that females, more than males, tend to view moral behavior in terms of compassion, caring, and concern for others. Thus, she agrees that the content of moral reasoning differs between the sexes, but she contends that males and females do not differ in the complexity of their moral reasoning. More recent evidence suggests that females do tend to emphasize care and compassion in resolving moral dilemmas, while males tend to stress justice or at least to give it equal standing with caring (Garmon et al., 1996; Wark & Krebs, 1996). Although Kohlberg's theory does emphasize rights and justice over concern for others, researchers, nevertheless, have found that females score as high as males in their moral reasoning (Walker, 1989).

Finally, some critics claim that Kohlberg's theory has a built-in liberal bias and is culture-bound, favoring Western middle-class values (Simpson, 1974; Sullivan, 1977). Yet Snarey (1985), in a review of 45 studies, found that samples from India, kibbutzim in Israel, Taiwan, and Turkey "ranked higher than parallel groups from the United States at one or more points in the life cycle" (p. 228).

preconventional level: Kohlberg's lowest level of moral reasoning, based on the physical consequences of an act; "right" is whatever avoids punishment or gains a reward.

conventional level: Kohlberg's second level of moral reasoning, in which right and wrong are based on the internalized standards of others; "right" is whatever helps or is approved of by others, or whatever is consistent with the laws of society.

postconventional level: Kohlberg's highest level of moral reasoning, in which moral reasoning involves weighing moral alternatives; "right" is whatever furthers basic human rights.

Some critics point out that moral reasoning and moral behavior are not one and the same. Kohlberg readily acknowledged that people can be capable of making mature moral judgments yet fail to live morally. But, said Kohlberg (1968), "The man who understands justice is more likely to practice it" (p. 30). Regardless of whether we agree with Kohlberg's theory, most of us would agree that moral reasoning and moral behavior are critically important aspects of human development. Moral individuals make moral societies.

Parental Relationships: Their Quality and Influence

Link It!

Some research indicates that teens at puberty begin to distance themselves from their parents and that conflict increases, particularly with the mother (Paikoff & Brooks-Gunn, 1991). But despite all the talk about the generation gap, most adolescents have good relationships with their parents (Steinberg, 1990).

Bachman (1987) found that over 70% of high school seniors believed their personal values were either "very similar" or "mostly similar" to those of their parents. Adolescents typically value their parents' advice more than that of their friends, particularly on educational and occupational goals, finances, and questions about religion, politics, morality, and the use of hard drugs (Marcia, 1980; Sebald, 1989). But on questions of dress, hairstyle, music, sex, tobacco, and alcohol, peer opinions carry more weight.

What outcomes are often associated with the authoritative, authoritarian, and permissive parenting styles?

Of the three parenting styles discussed on page 260—authoritative, authoritarian, and permissive—the authoritative parenting style is most effective and the permissive least effective for adolescents (Baumrind, 1991; Steinberg et al., 1994). In a study of about 2,300 adolescents, those with permissive parents were more likely to use alcohol and drugs and to have conduct problems and less likely to be engaged in school than were those with authoritative or authoritarian parents (Lamborn et al., 1991). The authoritarian style was related to more psychological distress and less self-reliance and self-confidence in adolescents. The authoritative parenting style was associated with psychosocial competence for adolescents of all racial and ethnic groups and with academic success for those who are White and middle-class (Steinberg et al., 1994). Adolescents with authoritative parents benefit even further when their friends' parents are also authoritative (Fletcher et al., 1995).

Most adolescents and their parents have good relationships and enjoy doing things together.

Steinberg (1992) suggests that White middle-class students benefit both from an authoritative parenting style and from peer support for academic achievement. And although Asian American adolescents typically have authoritarian parents, several factors may explain why they outperform other groups academically. First, academic achievement is highly valued by both their families and their peers, and second, they believe strongly that academic excellence is a prerequisite for future occupational success. But African American and Hispanic adolescents typically lack peer support for academic excellence and are less likely to see it as necessary for their occupational future. In fact, according to Steinberg (1992), "African American students are more likely than others to be caught in a bind between performing well in school and being popular among their peers" (p. 728). Thus, when peer values and norms do not support academic pursuits, the peer influences often negate parental influence.

The Peer Group

What are some of the useful functions of the adolescent peer group?

At a time when adolescents feel the need to become more independent from their parents, friends become a vital source of emotional support and approval. Adolescents usually choose friends of the same sex and race (Clark & Ayers, 1992), who have similar values, interests, and backgrounds (Duck, 1983; Epstein, 1983).

Interactions with peers are critical while young people are fashioning their identities. Adolescents can try out different roles and observe the reactions of their friends to their behavior and their appearance. The peer group provides teenagers with a standard of comparison for evaluating their own assets as well as a vehicle for developing social skills (Berndt, 1992).

Sexuality and Adolescence

Link It!

Before the 1960s the surging sex drive of adolescents was held in check primarily because most societal influences—parents, religious leaders, the schools, and the media—were all preaching the same message: Premarital sex is wrong. Then sexual attitudes began to change. In a 1969 national survey by Gallup, 68% of adults in the United States believed that premarital sex was wrong; but by 1991, the number had dropped to 40% (Hugick & Leonard, 1991).

According to the Centers for Disease Control (1992), the incidence of premarital intercourse among high school students is 60.8% for males and 48% for females. "Black students were significantly more likely than white or Hispanic students to ever have had intercourse (72.3%, 51.6%, and 53.4%, respectively)" (p. 885). Son-estein and others (1991) report that the typical pattern for males and females is serial monogamy—"a pattern of monogamous relationships that follow one another" (p. 166). Early premarital intercourse is associated with an increased risk of pregnancy (Morgan et al., 1995) and of sexually transmitted diseases and with a higher number of sexual partners.

Teens who tend to be less experienced sexually are those who attend religious services frequently and live with both biological parents, who are neither too permissive nor too strict in their discipline and rules (White & DeBlassie, 1992). Early intercourse is less prevalent among adolescents whose academic achievement is above average and whose parents have a harmonious relationship (Brooks-Gunn & Furstenberg, 1989).

Teenage Pregnancy: Too Much Too Soon

Teenagers in the United States are no more sexually active than those in Western Europe, yet the incidence of pregnancy among 15- to 19-year-olds is higher in this country than in any other developed nation (Ambuel, 1995; Creatsas et al., 1995; Kaufman, 1996). There are about 10 million adolescent girls in the United States, of whom approximately 1 million, or 10%, become pregnant each year ("Rate of Births," 1995). About 40% of those pregnancies are terminated by abortion and 13% by miscarriage (Jaskiewics & McAnarney, 1994). And few teenage mothers (only 5%) put their babies up for adoption (Wallis, 1985). Nearly 70% of all teenage mothers are unmarried (Children's Defense Fund, 1996), and 92% of African American teenagers who give birth are single (National Research Council, 1993). Unfortunately, almost one-third of unwed mothers find themselves in the same condition again within 2 years (Alan Guttmacher Institute, 1991). In 1994, out-of-wedlock births accounted for 32% of U.S. births (U.S. Bureau of the Census, 1997). In contrast, only 15% of American babies were born to unwed mothers in 1960 (National Research Council, 1993). Why the dramatic increase in out-of-wedlock births? One reason is that the stigma attached to unwed motherhood has largely disappeared. In fact, some unmarried teens actually want to get pregnant.

Early pregnancy can have serious physical consequences. Pregnant teens are more likely to come from poor backgrounds and less likely to receive early prenatal medical care and adequate nutrition. As a result, they are at higher risk for miscarriage, stillbirth, and complications during delivery. They are also more likely to deliver premature or low-birthweight babies, who have a higher infant mortality rate (Fraser et al., 1995; Goldenberg & Klerman, 1995; Scholl et al., 1996).

Among young women who give birth before age 18 and choose to keep their babies, half never complete high school. As a group, their earning power is about half that of their counterparts who did not have babies at this early age (National

What are some of the disturbing consequences of teenage pregnancy?

identity versus role confusion:
Erikson's fifth psychosocial stage,
when adolescents need to establish
their own identity and to form values to live by; failure can lead to
an identity crisis.

intimacy versus isolation: Erikson's sixth psychosocial stage,
when the young adult must establish intimacy in a relationship in
order to avoid feeling a sense of
isolation and loneliness.

generativity versus stagnation:
Erikson's stage for middle age,
when people become increasingly
concerned with guiding the next
generation rather than stagnating.

ego integrity versus despair: Erikson's stage for old age, when people look back on their lives with
satisfaction or with major regrets.

Research Council, 1993), and many eventually depend on welfare (Grogger &
Bronars, 1993). Because many teenage mothers are single parents living in poverty,
their children often suffer from inadequate parenting, nutrition, and health care,
and are more likely to be abused and neglected. In school, these children typically
score lower on intelligence tests, have poor achievement records, and are more
likely to exhibit disruptive behavior (Berk, 1997).

ERIKSON'S PSYCHOSOCIAL THEORY: ADOLESCENCE THROUGH ADULTHOOD

Earlier in this chapter, we presented the first four stages of Erik Erikson's psychosocial
theory of development. Recall that his was the only major theory of development to
include the entire life span, and he was the first to stress the part that society and individuals themselves play in their own personality development. Also, keep in mind
that each of Erikson's stages is built around a conflict that involves the individual's
relationship with the social environment. If healthy development is to occur, the conflict at each stage must be resolved satisfactorily. The stages themselves are named for
the two opposite basic attitudes that may be formed, depending on how the conflicts
are resolved. To preserve the continuity of the theory, we will consider the remaining
four stages together. Erikson's last four stages are described in *Review & Reflect 8.4*.

Review & Reflect 8.4 Erikson's Psychosocial Stages of Development

Stage	Ages	Description
Trust vs. mistrust	Birth to 1 year	Described earlier in this chapter.
Autonomy vs. shame and doubt	1 to 3 years	
Initiative vs. guilt	3 to 6 years	
Industry vs. inferiority	6 years to puberty	
Identity vs. role confusion	Adolescence	Adolescents must make the transition from childhood to adulthood, estab-lish an identity, develop a sense of self, and consider a future occupational identity. Otherwise, role confusion can result.
Intimacy vs. isolation	Young adulthood	Young adults must develop intimacy—the ability to share with, care for, and commit themselves to another person. Avoiding intimacy brings a sense of isolation and loneliness.
Generativity vs. stagnation	Middle adulthood	Middle-aged people must find some way of contributing to the develop-ment of the next generation. Failing this, they may become self-absorbed and emotionally impoverished and reach a point of stagnation.
Ego integrity vs. despair	Late adulthood	Individuals review their lives, and if they are satisfied and feel a sense of accomplishment, they will experience ego integrity. If dissatisfied, they may sink into despair.

Identity versus Role Confusion: Erikson's Stage for Adolescence

Erikson's fifth stage of psychosocial development, **identity versus role confusion**, is the developmental struggle of adolescence. "Who am I?" becomes the critical question at this stage, as adolescents seek to establish their identity and find values to guide their lives (Erikson, 1963). At this point, for the first time, adolescents are seriously looking to the future and considering what they will choose as their life's work. Erikson (1968) believed that "in general it is the inability to settle on an occupational identity which most disturbs young people" (p. 132). The danger at this stage, he said, is that of role confusion—not knowing who you are or where you belong.

How did Erikson explain the fifth psychosocial stage–identity versus role confusion?

Link It!

Intimacy versus Isolation: Erikson's Stage for Early Adulthood

Erikson contended that if healthy development is to continue into adulthood, it is necessary for a young adult to establish intimacy in a relationship. This sixth stage of psychosocial development he called **intimacy versus isolation**. For Erikson, intimacy meant the ability of young adults to form strong emotional attachments—that is, to share with, care for, make sacrifices for, and commit themselves to another person. He believed that avoiding intimacy results in a sense of isolation and loneliness.

Erikson (1980) argued that young adults must establish their own identity before true intimacy is possible. He said, "The condition of a true twoness is that one must first become oneself" (p. 101). Several studies support Erikson's notion that a stable identity is a necessary prerequisite for an intimate relationship (Tesch & Whitbourne, 1982; Vaillant, 1977).

What is Erikson's psychosocial task for early adulthood?

What changes did Erikson believe are essential for healthy personality development in middle age?

Generativity versus Stagnation: Erikson's Stage for Middle Adulthood

Erikson's seventh psychosocial stage is called **generativity versus stagnation**. Erikson (1980) claimed that in order to maintain good mental health into middle adulthood, individuals must develop generativity—an "interest in establishing and guiding the next generation" (p. 103). Concern extends beyond their own immediate family to ". . . the welfare of young people and with making the world a better place for them to live and work" (Elkind, 1970, p. 112).

People who do not develop generativity become self-absorbed and "begin to indulge themselves as if they were their own one and only child" (Erikson, 1980, p. 103). Personal impoverishment and a sense of stagnation often accompany such self-absorption. We enlarge ourselves when we have concern for others.

According to Erikson, in middle adulthood, people develop generativity—an interest in guiding the next generation.

Ego Integrity versus Despair: Erikson's Final Stage

Psychosocial development continues into later adulthood, but its course is usually an extension of the former life pattern. The outcome of Erikson's eighth stage, **ego integrity versus despair**, depends primarily on whether a person has resolved the conflicts at previous stages (Erikson et al., 1986). Those who have a sense of ego integrity believe their life has had meaning. They look back with satisfaction and a sense of accomplishment and do not have major regrets. A sense of despair results when individuals view their lives as a "series of missed opportunities and missed directions" (Elkind, 1970, p. 112).

What is the key to a positive resolution of Erikson's eighth psychosocial stage–ego integrity versus despair?

presbyopia (prez-bee-O-pee-uh): A condition, occurring in the mid to late 40s, in which the lenses of the eyes no longer accommodate adequately for near vision, and reading glasses or bifocals are required for reading.

menopause: The cessation of menstruation, occurring between ages 45 and 55 and signifying the end of reproductive capacity.

What are the physical changes associated with middle age?

EARLY AND MIDDLE ADULTHOOD

The long period of some 40 to 45 years known as adulthood is generally divided into three parts—young or early adulthood (ages 20 to 40 or 45), middle adulthood (ages 40 or 45 to 65), and late adulthood (after age 65 or 70). These ages are only approximate, because there are no biological or psychological events that neatly define the beginning or ending of a period. Obviously, some things change; but in many ways adults remain much the same as they were in their earlier years. The most obvious changes are usually physical ones.

Physical Changes in Adulthood

Opinions vary about what period should be called the "prime of life," but it is clear that the *physical* prime of life occurs early. Most people in their 20s and 30s enjoy good general health and vitality, but the decade of the 20s is the period of top physical condition, when physical strength, reaction time, reproductive capacity, and manual dexterity all peak. During the 30s, there is a slight decline in these physical capacities, which is barely perceptible to most people other than professional athletes.

Middle-aged people often complain about a loss of physical vigor and endurance. But such losses have to do less with aging than with exercise, diet, and health habits. Some fine professional athletes, such as star pitcher Nolan Ryan and heavyweight champion George Foreman, were competing into their 40s. Simply adopting a more physically active lifestyle is as effective for maintaining fitness as a structured exercise program (Dunn et al., 1999). One unavoidable change in the mid- to late 40s is **presbyopia**, a condition in which the lenses of the eyes no longer accommodate adequately for near vision, and reading glasses or bifocals are required for reading.

The major biological event for women during middle age is **menopause**—the cessation of menstruation, which usually occurs between ages 45 and 55 and signifies the end of reproductive capacity. The most common symptom associated with menopause and the sharp decrease in the level of estrogen is *hot flashes*—sudden feelings of being uncomfortably hot. Some women also experience symptoms such as anxiety, irritability, and/or mood swings, and about 10% become depressed. However, most women do not experience psychological problems in connection with menopause (Busch et al., 1994; Matthews, 1992).

Although men do not have a physical event equivalent to menopause, they do experience a gradual decline in testosterone from age 20 until about age 60. During late middle age, many men also experience a reduction in the functioning of the prostate gland that affects the production of semen. Usually coupled with these reductions in testosterone and semen production is a reduction in the sex drive. However, though women are not able to conceive after menopause, many men can and do father children during late adulthood.

Intellectual Capacity during Early and Middle Adulthood

In general, can adults look forward to an increase or a decrease in intellectual performance from their 20s to their 60s?

Conventional wisdom has held that intellectual ability reaches its peak in the late teens or early 20s, and that it's all downhill after that. Fortunately, conventional wisdom is wrong. It is true that younger people do better on tests requiring speed or rote memory. But on tests measuring general information, vocabulary, reasoning ability, and social judgment, older participants usually do better than younger ones because of their greater experience and education (Horn, 1982). Adults actually continue to gain knowledge and skills over the years, particularly when they lead intellectually challenging lives.

Schaie (1994, 1995) analyzed data from the Seattle Longitudinal Study, which assessed the intellectual abilities of some 5,000 participants. Many of the participants were tested six times over the course of 35 years. Schaie found that in five areas—verbal meaning, spatial orientation, inductive reasoning, number, and word fluency—

participants showed modest gains from young adulthood to the mid-40s. Decline did not occur, on average, until after age 60, and even then the decline was modest until the 80s. Half of the participants, even at age 81, showed no decline over the previous 7 years. The study also revealed several gender differences. Females performed better on tests of verbal meaning and inductive reasoning, while males tended to do better on tests of number and spatial orientation. The only ability found to show a continuous decline from the mid-20s to the 80s was perceptual speed.

Career Choice: A Critical Life Decision

Probably no other part of life is so central to identity and self-esteem as a person's occupation or profession, with the possible exception of motherhood for some women. A career often becomes a basic part of a person's definition of self and a major factor in the way others define him or her. A career can define your lifestyle—the friends you choose, the neighborhood you live in, your habits, and even your ideas and opinions. And job satisfaction affects general life satisfaction.

Although the majority of Americans seem satisfied with their jobs, job satisfaction is higher for middle-aged adults than for young adults (Kohut & DeStefano, 1989). However, young adults are probably less likely than middle-aged adults to be permanently situated in jobs and careers they will continue to follow. In fact, nearly one out of three young adults (in their 20s and 30s) will not only change jobs, but will even change occupational field (Phillips & Blustein, 1994).

One of the most profound changes in employment patterns has been the tremendous increase of women in the workplace. In 1996 women made up 46.2% of the civilian labor force (U.S. Bureau of the Census, 1997). But women are not rushing into the workplace primarily to find self-fulfillment. Most are there out of economic necessity. Figure 8.5 shows the percentage of married women in the U.S. labor force according to the age of their youngest child. In spite of lower pay, sex discrimination, and fewer opportunities for advancement, most women who have jobs find them enjoyable and express higher self-esteem than do full-time homemakers (Baruch et al., 1983; Hoffman, 1979).

Personality and Social Development in Middle Age

Many people consider middle age the prime of life. Researcher Bernice Neugarten (1968) states that society "may be oriented towards youth," but it is "controlled by the middle-aged" (p. 93). People aged 40 to 60 are the decision makers in industry,

Why is middle age often considered the prime of life?

Figure 8.5

Percentage of the U.S. Labor Force Made Up of Married Women with Children

The percentage of the U.S. labor force consisting of married women with children continues to rise. About 59% of women with children 1 year of age or under, and about 66% of women with children 3 to 5 years old, are employed. (Data from U.S. Bureau of the Census, 1997.)

government, and society. Neugarten found that very few at this age "express a wish to be young again" (p. 97). As a participant in one of her studies said, "There is a difference between wanting to *feel* young and wanting to *be* young" (p. 97).

Reaching middle age, men and women begin to express personality characteristics they had formerly suppressed. Men generally become more nurturant and women more assertive. For many women, middle age is a time of increased freedom.

Wink and Helson (1993) found that after children leave home, most women work at least part-time and tend to experience an increase in self-confidence and a heightened sense of competence and independence. Contrary to the conventional notion of the empty nest syndrome, most parents seem to be happier when their children are on their own (Norris & Tindale, 1994). Parents have more time and money to pursue their own goals and interests. "For the majority of women in middle age, the departure of teenage children is not a crisis, but a pleasure. It is when the children do *not* leave home that a crisis occurs (for both parent and child)" (Neugarten, 1982, p. 163). For most people, an empty nest is a happy nest!

LATER ADULTHOOD

Age 65 or 70 is generally considered the beginning of old age, and 12.7% of the U. S. population is now over age 65 (U.S. Bureau of the Census, 1997). What are your perceptions of life after 65? Before reading further, complete the *Try It!* by answering *true* or *false* to the statements about older adults.

Try It!

Are the following statements true (T) or false (F)?

____ 1. Older adults tend to express less satisfaction with life in general than younger adults do.

____ 2. A lack of money is a serious problem for most people over age 65.

____ 3. Marital satisfaction declines in old age.

____ 4. Mandatory retirement forces most workers out of jobs before they are ready to leave.

____ 5. The majority of retirees do not adjust well to retirement.

____ 6. A large percentage of individuals over age 85 end up in nursing homes or institutions.

Answers: All of the statements are false!

Physical Changes in Later Adulthood

What are some physical changes generally associated with later adulthood?

It was long assumed that the number of neurons declined sharply in later adulthood, but this assumption appears to be false (Gallagher & Rapp, 1997). Recent research has shown that the shrinking volume of the aging cortex is due more to breakdown of the myelin that covers the axons in the white matter than to loss of the neurons that make up the gray matter (Peters et al., 1994; Wickelgren, 1996). As you learned in Chapter 2, the myelin sheath facilitates the rapid conduction of neural impulses. The breakdown of myelin thus explains one of the most predictable characteristics of aging—the slowing of behavior (Birren & Fisher, 1995). With degeneration of the myelin, the brain takes longer to process information, and reaction time is slower.

With advancing age, the elderly typically become more farsighted, have increasingly impaired night vision, and suffer hearing loss in the higher frequencies (Long & Crambert, 1990;.Slawinski et al., 1993). Joints become stiffer, and bones lose calcium and become more brittle, increasing the risk of fractures from falls.

About 80% of Americans over age 65 have one or more chronic conditions such as arthritis, rheumatism, heart problems, or high blood pressure. For both males and females, the three leading causes of death are heart disease, cancer, and stroke. But the good news is that in spite of all of these changes, the vast majority of people over age 65 consider their health good. One-half of those aged 75 to 84 and more than one-third of those over 85 do not have to curb their activities because of health problems (Toufexis, 1988). In short, the majority of older adults are active, healthy, and self-sufficient (Schaie & Willis, 1996).

Today people are living longer. In fact, during the last half-century, average life expectancy worldwide increased by 20 years (Satcher, 1999). An interesting study of the "oldest old"—those over 95—revealed that they are often in better mental and physical condition than those 20 years younger (Perls, 1995). They often remain employed and sexually active through their 90s and carry on "as if age were not an issue" (p. 70). How do they do it? They appear to have a genetic advantage that makes them particularly resistant to the diseases that kill or disable most people at younger ages.

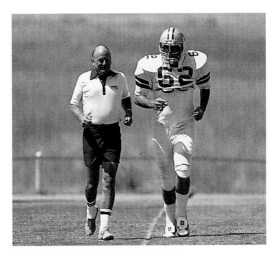

Men and women in their 60s and 70s who exercise properly and regularly can have the energy and fitness of someone 20 to 30 years younger (deVries, 1986). Recent research suggests that physical exercise even enhances the performance of older adults on tests of reaction time, working memory, and reasoning (Clarkson-Smith & Hartley, 1990). "People rust out faster from disuse than they wear out from overuse" (Horn & Meer, 1987, p. 83). In one study, 100 frail nursing-home residents, average age 87, exercised their thigh and hip muscles vigorously on exercise machines for 45 minutes three times a week. At the end of 10 weeks, they had increased their stair-climbing power by 28.4% and their walking speed by 12%, and four were able to exchange their walkers for canes (Fiatarone et al., 1994). For most of us, remaining fit and vigorous as we age lies within our power.

Masters and Johnson (1966) studied the sexual response in older men and women and found that regular sexual relations are necessary to maintain effective sexual performance. In a survey of adults aged 80 to 102 who were not taking medication, 70% of the men and 50% of the women admitted fantasizing about intimate sexual relations often or very often. But 63% of the men and 30% of the women were doing more than fantasizing—they were still having sex (McCarthy, 1989). And, remember, they were between 80 and 102.

Older adults who stay fit and active have a better chance of remaining healthy.

Cognitive Development in Later Adulthood

Intellectual decline in late adulthood is *not* inevitable. Older adults who keep mentally and physically active tend to retain their mental skills as long as their health is good (Meer, 1986). They do well on tests of vocabulary, comprehension, and general information, and their ability to solve practical problems is generally higher than that of young adults.

Researchers often distinguish between two types of intelligence (Horn, 1982). **Crystallized intelligence**—one's verbal ability and accumulated knowledge—tends to increase over the life span. **Fluid intelligence**—abstract reasoning and mental flexibility—peaks in the early 20s and declines slowly as people age. The rate at which people

crystallized intelligence: Aspects of intelligence, including verbal ability and accumulated knowledge, that tend to increase over the life span.

fluid intelligence: Aspects of intelligence involving abstract reasoning and mental flexibility, which peak in the early 20s and decline slowly as people age.

What happens to mental ability in later adulthood?

process information also slows gradually with age (Hertzog, 1991; Lindenberger et al., 1993; Salthouse, 1996). This explains, in part, why older adults perform more poorly on tests requiring speed.

Is it accurate to equate old age with forgetfulness? In laboratory memory tasks, older people do as well or almost as well as younger people on recognition tasks (Hultsch & Dixon, 1990) and on recall of information in their areas of expertise (Charness, 1989). But in tasks requiring speed of processing in short-term memory or recall of items that hold no particular meaning for them, younger participants do significantly better than older ones (Verhaeghen et al., 1993).

Several factors are positively correlated with good cognitive functioning in the elderly. They are education level (Anstey et al., 1993; Lyketsos et al., 1999), a complex work environment, a long marriage to an intelligent spouse, and a higher income (Schaie, 1990). And gender is a factor as well. Women not only outlive men, they generally show less cognitive decline during old age. But intellectual functioning can be hampered by physical problems (Manton et al., 1986) or by psychological problems such as depression. A study by Shimamura and others (1995) revealed that people who continue to lead intellectually stimulating and mentally active lives are far less likely to suffer mental decline as they age. And people with a high degree of intellectual functioning tend to live longer (Neugarten, 1976). So, "use it or lose it" is good advice if you want to remain mentally sharp as you age.

What is Alzheimer's disease?

Alzheimer's Disease and Other Types of Dementia   **Senile dementia**, or senility, is a state of severe mental deterioration marked by impaired memory and intellect, as well as by altered personality and behavior. It afflicts about 5–8% of those over age 65, 15–20% of those over 75, and 25–50% of those over 85 (American Psychiatric Association, 1997). Senility is caused by physical deterioration of the brain. It can result from such conditions as cerebral arteriosclerosis (hardening of the arteries in the brain), chronic alcoholism, and irreversible damage by a series of small strokes.

About 50–60% of all cases of senility result from Alzheimer's disease. In **Alzheimer's disease** there is a progressive deterioration of intellect and personality that results from widespread degeneration of brain cells. At present, about 4 million people in the United States suffer from this incurable disorder (Khachaturian, 1997). At first, victims show a gradual impairment in memory and reasoning, and in their efficiency in carrying out everyday tasks. Many have difficulty finding their way around in familiar locations. As the disorder progresses, Alzheimer's patients become confused and irritable, tend to wander away from home, and become increasingly unable to take care of themselves. Eventually their speech becomes unintelligible, and they become unable to control bladder and bowel functions. If they live long enough, they reach a stage where they do not respond when spoken to and no longer recognize even spouse or children.

People with Alzheimer's disease, which affects an estimated 4 million Americans, function best in a stable, structured environment.

Age and a family history of Alzheimer's disease are the two risk factors that have been consistently associated with the disorder (Farrer & Cupples, 1994; Payami et al., 1994). Can Alzheimer's disease be delayed? According to Alexander and others (1997), a high IQ coupled with life-long intellectual activity may delay or lessen the symptoms of Alzheimer's in those who are at risk for the disease. Tang and others (1996) reported that postmenopausal women who had taken estrogen supplements for 10 years reduced their risk of developing Alzheimer's by almost 40%. And certain antiinflammatory drugs (such as ibuprofen) and the antioxidant vitamin E may provide a measure of protection (Nash, 1997; Sano et al., 1997).

Social Development and Adjustment in Later Adulthood

Would you say that people are more satisfied with their marriages and with life in general when they are young adults or when they are over 65? It may surprise you to learn that in several major national surveys life satisfaction and feelings of well-being were about as high in older adults as in younger ones (Inglehart, 1990) (see Figure 8.6). Life satisfaction appears to be most strongly related to good health, as well as to a feeling of control over one's life (Schulz & Heckhausen, 1996). Levenson and others (1993) found that older couples tended to be happier in their marriages than middle-aged couples, experiencing less conflict and more sources of pleasure than their younger counterparts.

Most retirees are happy to leave the world of work; less than 12.5% of people over age 65 remain in the workforce. Generally, those most reluctant to retire are better educated, hold high-status jobs with a good income, and find fulfillment in their work. Life satisfaction after retirement also appears to be related to participation in community service and in social activities (Harlow & Cantor, 1996). Bosse and others (1991) found that only 30% of retirees reported finding retirement stressful, and of those who did, most were likely to be in poor health and to have financial problems.

Much has been said about the elderly poor. About 10.5% of Americans over age 65 live below the poverty line, and among them are disproportionately high numbers of African Americans (25.4%) and Hispanic Americans (23.5%) (U.S. Bureau of the Census, 1997). But many adults in the 65-plus group live comfortably. With homes that are paid for and no children to support, people over 65 tend to view their financial situation more positively than do younger adults.

Yet old age undoubtedly involves many losses. Health declines, friends die, and some who do not wish to retire must do so because of company policies or for health reasons. Eventually one spouse dies, and if the other lives long enough, he or she will be increasingly dependent on others. When life becomes more burdensome than enjoyable, an older person can fall victim to depression, a serious problem affecting about 15% of the elderly. This depression can even be deadly. White males over age 75 have the highest suicide rate of any age group in this society (U.S. Bureau of the Census, 1997).

For most people, losing a spouse is the most stressful event in a lifetime, and more women than men experience this loss. In 1996, 63.6% of women over age 65 had lost a spouse compared with only 32.5% of men. There were only about 69.5 males for every 100 females aged 65 and older (U.S. Bureau of the Census, 1997). Both widows and widowers are at a greater risk for health problems due to suppressed

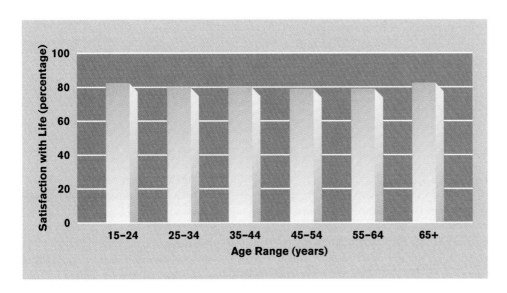

Figure 8.6

Age and Life Satisfaction

Surveys including participants from many nationalities reveal that levels of life satisfaction and happiness remain much the same and relatively high (approximately 80%) throughout life. (Data from Inglehart, 1990.)

immune function and have a higher mortality rate, particularly within the first 6 months, than their age mates who are not bereaved (Martikainen & Valkonen, 1996).

Cultural Differences in Care for the Elderly

The fastest-growing segment of the U.S. population consists of those 85 and older (Thomas, 1992). Are there cultural differences in the ways older family members are viewed, treated, and cared for? Only about 18% of older parents live in the same household with one of their adult children (Crimmins & Ingegneri, 1990). Older African Americans as well as older Asian and Hispanic Americans are more likely to live with and be cared for by their adult children than are other elderly Americans. African Americans are more likely than Whites to regard elderly persons with respect and to feel that children should help their older parents (Mui, 1992). But multigenerational households are by no means commonplace among most racial groups in the United States.

Economic and social necessity often dictate living arrangements. In many Latin American countries, the majority of elderly people live in the same household with younger generations in an extended family setting (De Vos, 1990). In Korea, 80% of the elderly are cared for by family members (Sung, 1992). And three-generation households have been the rule rather than the exception among the Japanese.

How do attitudes toward providing care for aged relatives differ between the United States and Japan? Researchers examining this question studied women's attitudes, because the care of aged relatives is typically provided by female family members in both countries (Brody et al., 1984; Campbell & Brody, 1985). The studies yielded some surprising findings. The American women expressed a stronger sense of obligation toward elderly members of their family, such as helping them with household chores, than the Japanese women did. The American women also expressed stronger agreement that their aged parents should be able to look to them for help.

Older Asian Americans, as well as older African and Hispanic Americans, are more likely than other elderly Americans to live with their adult children.

How can these differences be explained? Campbell and Brody (1985) point out that daughters typically care for their elderly parents in the United States. In Japan, daughters-in-law most often care for elderly family members, who are more likely to live in the home of their oldest son. Relations between daughters and parents are likely to be more positive than relations between daughters-in-law and parents-in-law.

Brody and others (1992) found that married daughters experienced less strain and less depression resulting from parent care than those who were single, divorced, or widowed. Also, African-Americans caring for elderly relatives suffering from Alzheimer's report less stress and depression than do their White counterparts (Hayley et al., 1996).

Death and Dying

One of the developmental tasks for every elderly person is to accept the inevitability of death and to prepare for it. At no time does this task become more critical than when an individual faces a terminal illness.

According to Kübler-Ross, what stages do terminally ill patients experience as they come to terms with death?

Kübler-Ross on Death and Dying   Elisabeth Kübler-Ross (1969) interviewed some 200 terminally ill people and found they shared common reactions to their impending death. In her book *On Death and Dying* she identifies five stages people go through in coming to terms with death.

In the first stage, denial, most patients react to the diagnosis of their terminal illness with shock and disbelief. (Surely, the doctors must be wrong.) The second stage, anger, is marked by feelings of anger, resentment, and envy of those who are young and healthy. In the third stage, bargaining, the person attempts to postpone death in return for a promise of "good behavior." An individual may offer God some special service or a promise to live a certain kind of life in exchange for an opportunity to attend a child's wedding or a grandchild's graduation. The fourth stage, depression, brings a great sense of loss and may take two forms—depression over past losses and depression over impending losses. Given enough time, patients may reach the final stage, acceptance, in which they stop struggling against death and contemplate its coming without fear or despair. Kübler-Ross claims that the family also goes through stages similar to those experienced by the patient.

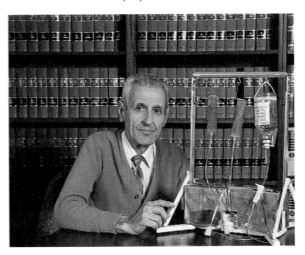

Dr. Jack Kevorkian, now serving a prison sentence, is shown here with his controversial apparatus used to help many terminally ill people commit suicide.

Critics deny the universality of Kübler-Ross's proposed stages and their invariant sequence (Butler & Lewis, 1982; Kastenbaum, 1992). Each person is unique. The reactions of all the terminally ill cannot be expected to conform to some rigid sequence of stages.

Decisions about Death   Death comes too soon for most people, but not soon enough for others. Some who are terminally ill and subject to intractable pain would welcome an end to their suffering. Should dying patients be left with no choice but to suffer to the end? In answer to this highly controversial question, Dr. Jack Kevorkian has said, "No!" Known as "Dr. Death" to those who oppose his "assisted suicides," Kevorkian has defied both laws and criticism and helped many terminally ill patients end their lives.

A rapidly growing alternative to hospitals and nursing homes is *hospice care*. Hospices are agencies that care for the needs of the dying more humanely and affordably than hospitals can and that use special facilities or, in some cases, the patient's own home. A hospice follows a set of guidelines that make it more attuned to patients' personal needs and preferences than a hospital or nursing homes typically can be.

What are some benefits of hospice care?

Bereavement: The Grieving Process   Many of us have experienced the grieving process—the period of bereavement that follows the death of a loved one and sometimes lingers long after the person has gone. Contrary to what many believe, bereaved individuals who suffer the most intense grief initially, who weep inconsolably and feel the deepest pain, do not get through their bereavement more quickly than others (Bonanno et al., 1995).

Recent research has looked at the bereavement of those who care for loved ones dying of AIDS. Folkman and her colleagues (1996) found that the grieving process for male caregivers whose partners were dying of AIDS was very similar to that experienced by spouses.

Death and dying are not pleasant subjects, but remember that life itself is a terminal condition, and each day of life should be treasured like a precious gift.

Building a Good Relationship

Decide whether each of the following statements about intimate relationships is true (T) or false (F):

____ The best relationships are free from conflict.

____ Voicing complaints to one's partner undermines happiness in the relationship.

____ Anger in all its forms is a negative emotion that is destructive in a relationship.

____ The best way to maintain a relationship is to have a realistic view of one's partner.

All of these statements are true, right? Wrong! Every one of them is false. Recent research has offered some surprising findings about the dynamics of successful relationships. Perhaps the most significant finding is that some conflict is necessary for long-term survival of a close relationship. How can this be so?

In studies of couples married 20 years or more, John Gottman (1994) and his colleagues have found that many couples equate lack of conflict with happiness and are proud that they "never fight." However, these marriages may suffer from a lack of communication. In reality, "a certain amount of conflict is necessary to help couples weed out actions and ways of dealing with each other that can harm the marriage in the long run" (p. 67). Couples who do not resolve the conflicts that are inevitable in any relationship run the risk of becoming mired in negative emotions and eventually breaking up. And since the formation of intimate relationships is a crucial task of young adulthood, it is important for couples to learn how to communicate effectively and resolve their conflicts.

Complaints, criticism, contempt, and anger. Gottman points out that a common barrier to effective communication is criticism. Although criticizing and complaining are often equated, the difference between them is crucial to any relationship. A complaint is limited to a specific situation and states how you feel: "I am upset because you didn't take out the garbage tonight." Complaints may actually make a relationship stronger. In fact, Gottman believes that complaining "is one of the healthiest activities that can occur in a marriage" (1994, p. 73). Why? Because it is better to express feelings through complaints than to let them seethe until they crystallize into deep-seated resentment.

This is not to say that all complaining is useful. *Cross-complaining*, in which you counter your partner's complaint with one of your own and ignore what your partner has said, obviously serves no useful purpose. And spouting off a lengthy list of complaints all at once—what Gottman calls *kitchen-sinking*—is not productive either.

A criticism differs from a complaint in that it heaps blame on the other person. A complaint is likely to begin with "I," but criticisms typically begin with "you": "You never remember to take out the trash. You promised you would do it, and you broke your promise again!" Criticisms also tend to be global, often including the word *always* or *never*: "You never take me out anywhere"; "You're always finding fault with me." Criticizing thus goes beyond merely stating a feeling; a criticism is an accusation, sometimes even a personal attack. Frequent criticism can destroy a relationship.

Even more damaging than criticism is contempt. As Gottman points out, "what separates *contempt* from criticism is the *intention to insult* and to *psychologically abuse* your partner" (1994, p. 79). Contempt basically adds insult to criticism. The insult can take a variety of forms, including name-calling, hostile humor, mockery, and body language such as sneering and rolling the eyes. According to Gottman, words such as *bitch, jerk, fat,* and *stupid* "are such dangerous assault weapons that they ought to be outlawed" (1994, p. 80).

While criticism and contempt definitely have negative effects on relationships, anger does not. Anger has negative effects on a relationship only if it is expressed along with criticism or contempt. In fact, according to Gottman, "expressing anger and disagreement—airing a complaint—though rarely pleasant, makes the [relationship] stronger in the long run than suppressing the complaint" (1994, p. 73).

Hints for resolving conflicts. How can you make good use of your knowledge about the varying effects of complaining, criticism, contempt, and anger? Apply the following guidelines for resolving conflicts:

- *Be gentle with complaints.* Kindness works wonders when stating a complaint. And remember to avoid criticism.

- *Don't become defensive when your partner makes requests.* Remain positive, and comply willingly and as quickly as possible.

- *Stop conflicts before they get out of hand.* Don't let negative thoughts about your partner grow into criticism or contempt. Do whatever it takes to put the brakes on negativity. Replay in memory and relish the happiest moments you and your partner have spent together.

Of course, none of this will work if you have a thoroughly negative attitude toward your partner. In fact, it helps to have a positive, even idealistic, perception of one's partner. Research by Sandra Murray and her colleagues (1996a, 1996b) has shown that in the best relationships partners overlook each other's faults as well as embellishing each other's virtues. A full and accurate assessment of one's partner's frailties leads to dissatisfaction.

Love, then, is only half-blind. Partners in intimate relationships are blind to each other's negative qualities, while magnifying each other's virtues far beyond reality (see Gottman, 1998).

SUMMARY AND REVIEW

DEVELOPMENTAL PSYCHOLOGY: BASIC ISSUES AND METHODOLOGY

What are two types of studies developmental psychologists use to investigate age-related changes?

To investigate age-related changes, developmental psychologists use the longitudinal study and the cross-sectional study.

Key Terms
developmental psychology (p. 240); nature–nurture controversy (p. 240); longitudinal study (p. 241); cross-sectional study (p. 241)

HEREDITY AND PRENATAL DEVELOPMENT

How are hereditary traits transmitted?

Hereditary traits are transmitted by the genes, which are located on each of the 23 pairs of chromosomes.

When are dominant or recessive genes expressed in an individual's traits?

When there is more than one gene for a specific trait, the dominant gene will be expressed. A recessive gene is expressed when it is paired with another recessive gene.

What are the three stages of prenatal development?

The three stages of prenatal development are the period of the zygote, the period of the embryo, and the period of the fetus.

What are some negative influences on prenatal development, and during what time is their impact greatest?

Some common negative influences on prenatal development include certain prescription and nonprescription drugs, psychoactive drugs, poor maternal nutrition, and maternal infections and illnesses. Their impact is greatest during the first trimester.

Key Terms
genes (p. 241); chromosomes (p. 241); sex chromosomes (p. 241); dominant gene (p. 241); recessive gene (p. 241); period of the zygote (p. 242); prenatal (p. 242); embryo (p. 242); fetus (p. 242); identical (monozygotic) twins (p. 242); fraternal (dizygotic) twins (p. 243); teratogens (p. 243); critical period (p. 243); fetal alcohol syndrome (p. 243); low-birthweight baby (p. 244); preterm infant (p. 244)

PHYSICAL DEVELOPMENT AND LEARNING IN INFANCY

What are the perceptual abilities of the newborn?

All of the newborn's senses are functional at birth, and he or she already shows preferences for certain odors, tastes, sounds, and visual patterns.

What types of learning occur in the first few days of life?

Newborns can acquire new responses through classical and operant conditioning and observational learning.

What is the primary factor influencing attainment of the major motor milestones?

Maturation is the primary factor influencing attainment of the major motor milestones.

Key Terms
neonate (p. 244); reflexes (p. 244); visual cliff (p. 245); maturation (p. 246)

EMOTIONAL DEVELOPMENT IN INFANCY

What is temperament, and what are the three temperament types identified by Thomas, Chess, and Birch?

Temperament refers to an individual's characteristic way of responding to the environment. The three temperament types are easy, difficult, and slow-to-warm-up.

What did Harlow's studies reveal about attachment in infant monkeys?

Harlow found that the basis of attachment in infant monkeys is contact comfort, whether with the real mother or with a cloth surrogate mother.

When does the infant have a strong attachment to the mother?

The infant has usually developed a strong attachment to the mother at age 6 to 8 months.

What are the four attachment patterns identified in infants?

The four attachment patterns identified in infants are secure, avoidant, resistant, and disorganized/disoriented.

What are the typical differences in the ways mothers and fathers interact with their children?

Mothers tend to spend more time caretaking, and fathers spend more time playing with their children.

Key Terms
temperament (p. 247); attachment (p. 247); surrogate (p. 248); separation anxiety (p. 248); stranger anxiety (p. 248)

PIAGET'S THEORY OF COGNITIVE DEVELOPMENT

What were Piaget's claims regarding the stages of cognitive development?

Piaget claimed that cognitive ability develops in four stages, each representing a qualitatively different form of reasoning and understanding. He believed the stages to be universal and sequential, although children may progress through them at different rates.

What occurs during Piaget's sensorimotor stage?

During the sensorimotor stage (ages birth to 2 years), infants gain knowledge and understanding of the world through their senses and motor activities. The major accomplishment of the stage is object permanence.

What cognitive limitations characterize a child's thinking during the preoperational stage?

Children at the preoperational stage (ages 2 to 7 years) are increasingly able to represent objects and events mentally, but they exhibit egocentrism and have not developed the concepts of reversibility and conservation.

What cognitive abilities do children acquire during the concrete operations stage?

When working on concrete problems, children at the concrete operations stage (ages 7 to 11 or 12 years) become able to decenter their thinking and to understand the concepts of reversibility and conservation.

What new capability characterizes the formal operations stage?

At the formal operations stage (ages 11 or 12 years and beyond) adolescents are able to apply logical thinking to abstract problems and hypothetical situations.

Key Terms

schema (p. 250); assimilation (p. 250); accommodation (p. 250); sensorimotor stage (p. 251); object permanence (p. 251); preoperational stage (p. 251); conservation (p. 251); reversibility (p. 252); concrete operations stage (p. 252); formal operations stage (p. 252)

VYGOTSKY'S SOCIOCULTURAL VIEW OF COGNITIVE DEVELOPMENT

In Vygotsky's view, how do private speech and scaffolding contribute to cognitive development?

Private speech, or self-guided talk, helps children to direct their actions and solve problems. Scaffolding is an instructional technique in which a teacher or parent adjusts the quality and degree of help to fit the child's ability. It allows a child gradually to become independent.

LANGUAGE DEVELOPMENT

What are the stages of language development from cooing through the acquisition of grammatical rules?

The stages of language development are cooing (age 2 to 3 months), babbling (beginning at 6 months), single words (about 1 year), two-word sentences (18 to 20 months), and telegraphic speech (2½ years), followed by the acquisition of grammatical rules.

How do learning theory and the nativist position explain the acquisition of language?

Learning theory suggests that language is acquired through imitation and reinforcement. The nativist position is that language ability is largely innate, because it is acquired in stages that occur in a fixed order at the same ages in most normal children throughout the world.

Key Terms

babbling (p. 256); phonemes (p. 256); overextension (p. 256); underextension (p. 256); telegraphic speech (p. 256); overregularization (p. 256)

SOCIALIZATION OF THE CHILD

What is Erikson's theory of psychosocial development?

Erikson believed that all individuals progress through eight psychosocial stages during the life span, and each stage is defined by a conflict with the social environment, which must be resolved. The four stages in childhood are basic trust versus basic mistrust (ages birth to 2 years), autonomy versus shame and doubt (ages 1 year to 3 years), initiative versus guilt (ages 3 to 6 years), and industry versus inferiority (ages 6 years to puberty).

What are the three parenting styles identified by Baumrind, and which did she find most effective?

The three parenting styles identified by Baumrind are the authoritarian, the permissive, and the authoritative. She found the authoritative style to be the most effective.

How do peers contribute to the socialization process?

The peer group serves a socializing function by modeling and reinforcing behaviors it considers appropriate, by punishing inappropriate behavior, and by providing an objective measure children can use to evaluate their own traits and abilities.

Key Terms

socialization (p. 258); psychosocial stages (p. 258); basic trust versus basic mistrust (p. 258); autonomy versus shame and doubt (p. 258); initiative versus guilt (p. 258); industry versus inferiority (p. 258); authoritarian parents (p. 260); authoritative parents (p. 260); permissive parents (p. 260)

ADOLESCENCE: PHYSICAL AND COGNITIVE DEVELOPMENT

How difficult is adolescence for most teenagers?

Only about one-fourth of teenagers experience a troubled adolescence; at least half enjoy a period of healthy development and good relationships with family and friends.

What physical changes occur during puberty?

Puberty is characterized by the adolescent growth spurt, further development of the reproductive organs, and the appearance of the secondary sex characteristics.

What are the psychological effects of early and late maturation for boys and girls?

Early maturation provides enhanced status for boys, because of their early advantage in sports and greater attractiveness to girls. Late maturation puts boys at a disadvantage in these areas, resulting in a lack of confidence that can persist into adulthood. Early maturation makes girls more likely to be exposed prematurely to alcohol and drug use and to have early sexual experiences and unwanted pregnancies.

What cognitive abilities develop during the formal operations stage?

During the formal operations stage, adolescents develop the ability to think abstractly, to attack problems by systematically testing hypotheses, to draw conclusions through deductive reasoning, and to think hypothetically.

Key Terms

adolescence (p. 261); puberty (p. 261); adolescent growth spurt (p. 261); secondary sex characteristics (p. 262); menarche (p. 262); formal operations stage (p. 262); imaginary audience (p. 263); personal fable (p. 263)

ADOLESCENCE: MORAL AND SOCIAL DEVELOPMENT

What are Kohlberg's three levels of moral reasoning?

At the preconventional level, moral reasoning is based on the physical consequences of an act—"right" is whatever averts punishment or brings a reward. At the conventional level, right and wrong are based on the internalized standards of others—"right" is whatever helps or is approved of by others, or whatever is consistent with the laws of society. Postconventional moral reasoning involves weighing moral alternatives—"right" is whatever furthers basic human rights.

What do cross-cultural studies reveal about the universality of Kohlberg's theory?

Cross-cultural studies support the universality of Kohlberg's moral stages 1 through 4 as well as their invariant sequence. Stage 5 was found in almost all of the urban or middle-class samples but was absent in tribal and village folk societies.

What outcomes are often associated with authoritative, authoritarian, and permissive parenting styles?

Authoritative parenting is most effective and is associated with psychosocial competence in all groups and with academic success in White middle-class youth. Adolescents with authoritarian parents are typically the most psychologically distressed and the least self-reliant and self-confident. Permissive parenting is least effective and is often associated with adolescent drug use and behavior problems.

What are some of the useful functions of the adolescent peer group?

The adolescent peer group (usually composed of teens of the same sex and race and similar social background) provides a vehicle for developing social skills and a standard of comparison against which teens' attributes can be evaluated.

What are some of the disturbing consequences of teenage pregnancy?

Teens are at higher risk for delivering premature or low-birthweight babies. Half of teenage mothers never finish high school, and many eventually depend on welfare. Their children are more likely to receive inadequate parenting, nutrition, and health care and to have behavior and academic problems in school.

Key Terms
preconventional level (p. 264); conventional level (p. 264); postconventional level (p. 264)

ERIKSON'S PSYCHOSOCIAL THEORY: ADOLESCENCE THROUGH ADULTHOOD

How did Erikson explain the fifth psychosocial stage–identity versus role confusion?

In this stage adolescents seek to establish their identity and to find values to guide their lives. Difficulty at this stage can result role confusion.

What is Erikson's psychosocial task for early adulthood?

In Erikson's sixth stage, intimacy versus isolation, young adults must establish intimacy in a relationship to avoid a sense of isolation and loneliness.

What changes did Erikson believe are essential for healthy personality development in middle age?

Erikson's seventh stage, generativity versus stagnation, occurs during middle age. To avoid stagnation, individuals must develop generativity—an interest in establishing and guiding the next generation.

What is the key to a positive resolution of Erikson's eighth stage–ego integrity versus despair?

Erikson's psychosocial stage for old age is a time for reflection. People look back on their lives with satisfaction and a sense of accomplishment, or they have major regrets about mistakes and missed opportunities.

Key Terms
identity versus role confusion (p. 269); intimacy versus isolation (p. 269); generativity versus stagnation (p. 269); ego integrity versus despair (p. 269)

EARLY AND MIDDLE ADULTHOOD

What are the physical changes associated with middle age?

Physical changes associated with middle age are a need for reading glasses, the end of reproductive capacity (menopause) in women, and decline in testosterone levels and often sex drive in men.

In general, can adults look forward to an increase or a decrease in intellectual performance from their 20s to their 60s?

Although younger people tend to do better on tests requiring speed or rote memory, the intellectual performance of adults shows modest gains until the mid-40s. A modest decline occurs from the 60s to the 80s.

Why is middle age often considered the prime of life?

The decision makers in society are usually aged 40 to 60. When children grow up and leave home, parents have more time and money to pursue their own goals and interests.

Key Terms
presbyopia (p. 270); menopause (p. 270)

LATER ADULTHOOD

What are some physical changes generally associated with later adulthood?

Physical changes generally associated with later adulthood include a general slowing, a decline in sensory capacity, and an increase in the number of chronic conditions such as arthritis, heart problems, and high blood pressure.

What happens to mental ability in later adulthood?

Crystallized intelligence shows no significant age-related decline; fluid intelligence does decline. Although older adults perform tasks more slowly, if they keep mentally and physically active, they can usually maintain their mental skills as long as their health holds out.

What is Alzheimer's disease?

Alzheimer's disease is an incurable form of dementia characterized by a progressive deterioration of intellect and personality, resulting from widespread degeneration of brain cells.

According to Kübler-Ross, what stages do terminally ill patients experience as they come to terms with death?

Kübler-Ross maintains that terminally ill patients go through five stages in coming to terms with death: denial, anger, bargaining, depression, and acceptance.

What are some benefits of hospice care?

Hospice agencies care for the needs of the dying more humanely and affordably than hospitals do, and they also provide support for family members.

Key Terms
crystallized intelligence (p. 273); fluid intelligence (p. 273); senile dementia (p. 274); Alzheimer's disease (p. 274)

Study Guide for Chapter 8

Answers to all the Study Guide questions are provided at the end of the book.

Section One: Chapter Review

1. The cross-sectional study takes longer to complete than the longitudinal study. (true/false)

2. A dominant gene cannot be expressed if the individual carries
   a. two dominant genes for the trait.
   b. one dominant gene and one recessive gene for the trait.
   c. two recessive genes for the trait.
   d. either one or two dominant genes for the trait.

3. Fraternal twins are no more alike genetically than ordinary brothers and sisters. (true/false)

4. Match the stage of prenatal development with its description.
   _____ (1) first 2 weeks of life
   _____ (2) rapid growth and further development of body structures and systems
   _____ (3) formation of major systems, organs, and structures
   a. period of the fetus
   b. period of the embryo
   c. period of the zygote

5. Which of the following statements about infant sensory development is *not* true?
   a. Vision, hearing, taste, and smell are all fully developed at birth.
   b. Vision, hearing, taste, and smell are all functional at birth.
   c. Infants can show preferences in what they want to look at, hear, and smell shortly after birth.
   d. Hearing is better developed at birth than vision.

6. The primary factor influencing the attainment of the major motor milestones is
   a. experience.   c. learning.
   b. maturation.   d. habituation.

7. Which statement best describes Thomas, Chess, and Birch's thinking about temperament?
   a. Temperament develops gradually as a result of parental handling and personality.
   b. Temperament is inborn and is not influenced by the environment.
   c. Temperament is inborn but can be modified by the family and the environment.
   d. Temperament is set at birth and is unchangeable.

8. Ainsworth found that most infants had secure attachment. (true/false)

9. Which statement reflects Piaget's thinking about the stages of cognitive development?
   a. All people pass through the same stages but not necessarily in the same manner.
   b. All people progress through the stages in the same order but not at the same rate.
   c. All people progress through the stages in the same order and at the same rate.
   d. Very bright children sometimes skip stages.

10. Three-year-old Brittany says "airplane!" when she sees a helicopter for the first time. She is using the process Piaget called (assimilation; accommodation).

11. Four-year-old Danielle rolls a ball of clay into a sausage shape to make "more" clay. Her actions demonstrate that she has *not* acquired the concept of
    a. reversibility.
    b. animism.
    c. centration.
    d. conservation.

12. Vygotsky believed that children's private speech slowed their cognitive growth. (true/false)

13. Match the linguistic stage with the example.
    _____ (1) "ba-ba-ba"
    _____ (2) "He eated the cookies"
    _____ (3) "Mama see ball"
    _____ (4) "oo," "ah"
    _____ (5) "kitty," meaning a lion
    a. telegraphic speech
    b. overregularization
    c. babbling
    d. overextension
    e. cooing

14. Learning theory is better able than the nativist position to account for how language development can be encouraged. (true/false)

15. According to Erikson, if the basic conflict of a given stage is *not* resolved satisfactorily,
    a. a person will not enter the next stage.
    b. development at the next stage will be adversely affected.

c. a person will be permanently damaged regardless of future experiences.

d. a person will revert to the previous stage.

16. Match the parenting style with the approach to discipline.

_____ (1) expecting unquestioned obedience

_____ (2) setting high standards, giving rationale for rules

_____ (3) setting few rules or limits

a. permissive

b. authoritative

c. authoritarian

17. The peer group usually has a negative influence on social development. (true/false)

18. Adolescence is a stormy time for most teenagers. (true/false)

19. The secondary sex characteristics

a. are directly involved in reproduction.

b. appear at the same time in all adolescents.

c. distinguish mature males from mature females.

d. include the testes and ovaries.

20. Which of the following provides the most advantages?

a. early maturation in girls

b. early maturation in boys

c. late maturation in girls

d. late maturation in boys

21. The teenager's personal fable includes all of the following except

a. a sense of personal uniqueness.

b. a belief that he or she is indestructible and protected from misfortunes.

c. a belief that no one has ever felt so deeply before.

d. a feeling that he or she is always on stage.

22. Match Kohlberg's level of moral reasoning with the rationale for engaging in a behavior.

_____ (1) to avoid punishment or gain a reward

_____ (2) to ensure that human rights are protected

_____ (3) to gain approval or follow the law

a. conventional

b. preconventional

c. postconventional

23. Most teenagers have good relationships with their parents. (true/false).

24. Although teen pregnancy has many negative consequences for the mother, it has relatively few for the child. (true/false).

25. Which of the following was *not* identified by Erikson as a developmental task in his psychosocial stage for adolescence?

a. forming an intimate relationship

b. planning for an occupation

c. forming an identity

d. finding values to live by

26. Erikson believed the main task in young adulthood is to

a. develop generativity.

b. forge an identity.

c. start a family.

d. form an intimate relationship.

27. During which decade do people reach their peak physically?

a. teens   c. 20s

b. 30s   d. 40s

28. Higher levels of life satisfaction are reported by (singles; married people).

29. Which of the following statements is true of adults over 65?

a. They are considerably less satisfied with life than young adults are.

b. Their financial situation is considerably worse than that of younger adults.

c. Most retirees are happy to be retired.

d. A large percentage of adults over 85 end up in nursing homes.

30. Compared to older adults who are mentally and physically active, younger adults do better on

a. tests requiring speed.

b. comprehension tests.

c. general information tests.

d. practical problem solving.

31. According to Kübler-Ross, the first stage experienced by terminally ill patients in coming to terms with death is _____; the last stage is _____.

a. anger; depression

b. denial; depression

c. bargaining; acceptance

d. denial; acceptance

Section Two: Important Psychologists and Concepts

On the line opposite each name, list the major concept or theory associated with that name.

Name   Major Concept or Theory

1. Piaget   _____

2. Erikson   _____

3. Thomas   _____

4. Ainsworth   _____

5 Vygotsky   _____

6. Chomsky   _____

7 Kohlberg   _____

8. Kübler-Ross   _____

Section Three: Fill In the Blank

1. When developmental researchers measure the same people over time, they are conducting a _____ study.

2. When developmental researchers measure people of different ages at the same time, they are conducting a _____ study.

3. The period of the _____ is the first stage of prenatal development.

4. Substances in the prenatal environment that may cause birth defects are called _____.

5. The pediatrician said that Sandra began to crawl when she did because she had achieved a sufficient degree of _____ in her genetically programmed, biological timetable of development.

6. The chapter identified four different patterns of attachment. Ainsworth would say that a child who does not seem to be responsive to his or her mother and does not seem to be troubled when she is gone demonstrates _____ attachment.

7. Piaget's term for an individual's cognitive structure or concept that is used to make sense of information is a _____.

8. Vygotsky asserted that talking to themselves is a key component in children's cognitive development. He called this activity _____.

9. Watching one of the family dogs sleeping on the couch right next to her, 2-year-old Peg says, "Doggie sleep." This is an example of _____.

10. One day, her mother asked Peg where the dog was. Peg responded, "Doggie goed outside." This is an example of _____.

11. Jennifer has mastered algebra and is fascinated by philosophical ideas. Jennifer appears to be in the _____ stage, according to Piaget's theory of cognitive development.

12. Tamara believes that pleasing others defines a good person. She is at the _____ level of moral development.

13. According the concept of the _____, adolescents may take risks such as driving fast, smoking cigarettes, or having unprotected sex because they believe they are indestructible.

14. _____ intelligence is to verbal ability as _____ intelligence is to abstract reasoning.

15. _____ is the third stage of grieving, according to Kübler-Ross's theory.

16. Charlene is at a point in her life when she is wrestling with a sense of who she is and where she will go from here. She would be considered to be in Erikson's _____ stage of psychosocial development.

Section Four: Comprehensive Practice Test

1. From the evidence presented in the book, it appears that the nature–nurture controversy has been solved: Human development is based primarily on biology. (true/false)

2. A _____ study follows the same participants over a period of time.
   a. cross-sectional   c. longitudinal
   b. multi-measurement   d. multi-factors

3. Except for sperm cells and egg cells, how many chromosomes does each body cell contain?
   a. 23
   b. 23 pairs
   c. 46 pairs
   d. different cells can have different numbers

4. The period of time from conception to birth is called the period of _____ development.
   a. neonatal   c. post-zygotic
   b. prenatal   d. post-fertilization

5. The second stage of pregnancy is known as the period of
   a. germination.   c. the fetus.
   b. the embryo.   d. the zygote.

6. Monozygotic is to dizygotic as _____ is to _____.
   a. identical; fraternal   c. male; female
   b. female; male   d. fraternal; identical

7. A baby is considered preterm if she or he is born
   a. some place other than a hospital.
   b. prior to the parents paying the doctor's bill.
   c. before the 45th week of pregnancy.
   d. before the 37th week of pregnancy.

8. June is just a few days old. She can see, but not as well as she will later. If she is a typical baby, she probably has _____ vision.
   a. 20/40   c. 40/20
   b. 20/600   d. 10/40

9. Maturation is
   a. genetically determined biological changes that follow a timetable of development.
   b. behavioral changes based on the child's interaction with the environment.
   c. behavioral changes that take place when the child enters high school.
   d. applicable only to physiology and not to cognition or psychomotor development.

10. Cindy says that her new baby's responses to things that happen in the environment are gener-

ally happy and positive. Cindy is talking about her baby's
   a. response system.   c. latent personality.
   b. temperament.   d. infant personification.

11. Assimilation is a process used with _____; accommodation is a process used with _____.
   a. new schemas; existing schemas
   b. existing schemas; new schemas
   c. positive responses; negative responses
   d. negative responses; positive responses

12. The nativist position on speech development is that language ability is basically innate. (true/false)

13. Which of the following is not an example of a secondary sex characteristic?
   a. development of breasts in females
   b. differentiation of internal reproductive organs
   c. deepening of the voice in males
   d. rounding of the hips in females

14. Piaget's final stage of cognitive development is known as the _____ stage.
   a. concrete operations   c. generativity
   b. cognitive integrity   d. formal operations

15. A child in Kohlberg's _____ level of moral reasoning is governed by the standards of others rather than by internalized ideas of right and wrong.
   a. postconventional   c. preconventional
   b. conventional   d. preadolescent

16. A person must be at Piaget's stage of formal operations in order to attain Kohlberg's _____ level of moral reasoning.
   a. conventional   c. postconventional
   b. formal conventional   d. ego integrity

17. Evidence suggests that females tend to stress care and compassion in resolving moral dilemmas, whereas males tend to stress _____ (or to give it and caring equal weight).
   a. romance   c. justice
   b. aggression   d. morality

18. The children of teenage mothers tend to display academic and/or behavioral difficulties. (true/false)

19. The most obvious changes as an individual gets older are usually
   a. cognitive.
   b. physical.
   c. social.
   d. sexual.

20. Women go to work mainly because of
    a. financial need.
    b. marital conflict.
    c. a need for personal fulfillment.
    d. increased recreational opportunities.

21. The results of current research seem to indicate that older adults are _____ younger adults.
    a. less happy and satisfied with life than
    b. as satisfied with life as
    c. as dissatisfied with life as
    d. less satisfied but more secure than

22. For the majority of those who stop working, retirement is not as stressful as popularly believed. (true/false)

23. The most stressful event faced by people in their lifetimes is
    a. retirement.
    b. losing a spouse.
    c. children leaving home.
    d. restricted physical ability due to age.

Section Five: Critical Thinking

1. Evaluate Erikson's first four stages of psychosocial development, explaining what aspects of his theory seem most convincing. Support your answer.

2. Using Baumrind's categories, classify the parenting style your mother and/or father used in rearing you.
    a. Cite examples of techniques they used that support your classification.
    b. Do you agree with Baumrind's conclusions about the effects of that parenting style on children? Why or why not?

3. Think back to your junior high school and high school years. To what degree did early or late maturation seem to affect how boys and girls were treated by their peers, their parents, or their teachers? Did early or late maturation affect their adjustment? Explain your answer.

Motivation and Emotion

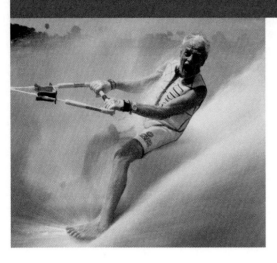

In a London subway a woman reading a newspaper account of Princess Diana's death broke down. Hearing her sobs, the other passengers burst into tears. Similar scenes occurred throughout Great Britain. The entire nation was overwhelmed by grief. The outpouring of emotion at the news of Diana's death was astonishing in a country whose people had long been famous for gritting their teeth in the face of adversity, for suppressing their feelings and keeping a "stiff upper lip." Journalists and essayists produced endless commentary trying to explain this unprecedented phenomenon.

People throughout the world viewed Diana's death as a tragedy. Immediately after the princess's death was announced, mourners began gathering outside the hospital in Paris where she had died. In London, thousands of people gathered outside Buckingham Palace and her home, Kensington Palace. More arrived every minute. Weeping, they lit candles, added bouquets to the growing mounds of flowers, and left teddy bears and other tributes at the gates. Outside St. James's Palace, people stood in line for hours, waiting to add to the books of condolence not only their signatures but personal messages full of love and grief.

What kind of person could evoke such an unprecedented outpouring of grief? Diana was described as a warm and compassionate woman whose simplicity, modesty, and natural charm touched the lives of many. She was universally acknowledged to be a devoted mother, and she was deeply committed to a variety of charities and causes. But what was most striking about her was her empathy. She loved helping people in trouble, especially children, and she had a gift for communication that went beyond words. Ordinary people called her "the people's Princess," and "Queen of our hearts"; she gave a human face to a royal family that frequently seemed remote. Women in particular felt a kinship with her because of her troubled private life, her eating disorder, and her public divorce.

The emotions of sadness and grief evoked by Diana's death motivated thousands of people to make financial contributions to the charities and causes she had championed. Other emotions emerged as well. Many mourners expressed outrage toward the news photographers who, they believed, had hounded the princess to her death, and the tabloid publishers whose willingness to purchase photos of Diana encouraged the photographers' relentless pursuit. And there was anger at some of the royal family for appearing too stoic, more interested in observing protocol than in joining in the mourning.

The emotions surrounding Diana's death and funeral, both in Britain and around the world, were both subtle and complex. Many psychologists consider motivation and emotion to be fascinating subjects of study. Some of their findings, and some of the questions that remain to be answered, are discussed in this chapter.

INTRODUCTION TO MOTIVATION

In this chapter on **motivation**, we will look at the underlying processes that initiate, direct, and sustain behavior in order to satisfy physiological and psychological needs. At any given time your behavior might be explained by one or a combination of **motives**—needs or desires that energize and direct behavior toward a goal. Motives can arise from an internal need, such as when we are hungry and are motivated to find something to eat. In this case we are pushed into action from within. Other motives originate from outside, as when some external stimulus, or **incentive**, pulls or entices us to act. After finishing a huge meal, some people yield to the temptation of a delicious dessert. At times like this, it is the enticement of the external tempter, not the internal need for food, that provides the motive.

Three primary characteristics of motivation are activation, persistence, and intensity (Geen, 1995). *Activation* is the initiation of motivated behavior; it involves taking the first steps required to achieve a goal or complete a project. *Persistence* is

What is the difference between intrinsic and extrinsic motivation?

motivation: The process that initiates, directs, and sustains behavior to satisfy physiological or psychological needs or wants.

motives: Needs or desires that energize and direct behavior toward a goal.

incentive: An external stimulus that motivates behavior (examples: money, fame).

Table 9.1   Intrinsic and Extrinsic Motivation

	Description	Examples
Intrinsic motivation	An activity is pursued as an end in itself because it is enjoyable and rewarding.	A person anonymously donates a large sum of money to a university to fund scholarships for deserving students. A child reads several books each week because reading is fun.
Extrinsic motivation	An activity is pursued to gain an external reward or to avoid an undesirable consequence.	A person agrees to donate a large sum of money to a university for the construction of a building, provided it will bear the family name. A child reads two books each week to avoid losing TV privileges.

intrinsic motivation: The desire to perform an act because it is satisfying or pleasurable in and of itself.

extrinsic motivation: The desire to perform an act to gain a reward or to avoid an undesirable consequence.

instinct: An inborn, unlearned, fixed pattern of behavior that is characteristic of an entire species.

the faithful and continued effort put forth in order to achieve a goal or finish a project. *Intensity* refers to the focused energy and attention applied in order to achieve a goal or complete a project.

Sometimes activities are pursued as ends in themselves, simply because they are enjoyable, not because any external reward is attached. This type of motivation is known as **intrinsic motivation**. On the other hand, when we act in order to gain some external reward or to avoid some undesirable consequence, we are pulled by **extrinsic motivation**. If you are working hard in this course solely because you find the subject interesting, then your motivation is intrinsic. But if you are studying only to meet a requirement or to satisfy some other external need, your motivation is extrinsic. In real life, the motives for many activities are both intrinsic and extrinsic. You may love your job, but you would probably be motivated to leave if your salary, an important extrinsic motivator, were taken away. Table 9.1 gives examples of intrinsic and extrinsic motivation.

What do researchers say about the motives for behavior? Let's consider some theories of motivation.

THEORIES OF MOTIVATION

Do we do the things we do because of our inherent nature—the inborn, biological urges that push us from within? Or, do we act because of the incentives that pull us from without? Obviously, both forces influence us, but theories of motivation differ in the relative power they attribute to each. The most thoroughly biological theories of motivation are the instinct theories.

Instinct Theories of Motivation

How do instinct theories explain motivation?

Scientists have learned much about instincts by observing animal behavior. Spiders instinctively spin their intricate webs without being taught the technique by other spiders. It is neither a choice they make nor a task they learn, but an **instinct**—an inborn, unlearned, fixed pattern of behavior that is characteristic of an entire species. Even when their web-spinning glands are removed, spiders still perform the complex spinning movements and then lay their eggs in the imaginary webs they have spun. So instincts explain much of animal behavior.

But can human motivation be explained by **instinct theory**—the notion that human behavior is motivated by certain innate, unlearned tendencies or instincts that are shared by all individuals? Instinct theory was widely accepted by William James, Sigmund Freud, and others through the early decades of the 20th century. Most psychologists today reject instinct theory as an explanation of human motivation. Human behavior is too richly diverse, and often too unpredictable, to be considered fixed and invariant across the entire species.

Drive-Reduction Theory: Striving to Keep a Balanced Internal State

Another major attempt to explain motivation is the **drive-reduction theory**, or drive theory, which was popularized by Clark Hull (1943). According to Hull, all living organisms have certain biological needs that must be met if they are to survive. A need gives rise to an internal state of tension or arousal called a **drive**, and the person or organism is motivated to reduce it. For example, when we are deprived of food or go too long without water, our biological need causes a state of tension, in this case the hunger or thirst drive. We become motivated to seek food or water to reduce the drive and satisfy our biological need.

Drive-reduction theory is derived largely from the biological concept of **homeostasis**—the tendency of the body to maintain a balanced, internal state in order to ensure physical survival. Body temperature, blood sugar, water balance, oxygen—in short, everything required for physical existence—must be maintained in a state of equilibrium, or balance. When this state is disturbed, a drive is created to restore the balance, as shown in Figure 9.1. But drive theory cannot fully account for the broad range of human motivation.

It is true that people are sometimes motivated to reduce tension, as drive-reduction theory states, but often they are just as motivated to increase it. Why do people seek activities that actually create a state of tension—hang-gliding, horror movies,

instinct theory: The notion that human behavior is motivated by certain innate tendencies, or instincts, shared by all individuals.

drive-reduction theory: A theory of motivation suggesting that a need creates an unpleasant state of arousal or tension called a drive, which impels the organism to engage in behavior that will satisfy the need and reduce tension.

drive: A state of tension or arousal brought about by an underlying need, which motivates an organism to engage in behavior that will satisfy the need and reduce the tension.

homeostasis: The tendency of the body to maintain a balanced internal state with regard to oxygen level, body temperature, blood sugar, water balance, and so forth.

How does drive-reduction theory explain motivation?

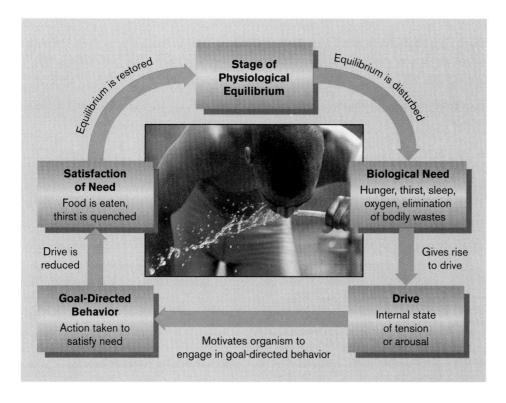

Figure 9.1
Drive-Reduction Theory

Drive-reduction theory is based on the biological concept of homeostasis—the natural tendency of a living organism to maintain a state of internal balance, or equilibrium. When the equilibrium becomes disturbed (by a biological need such as thirst), a drive (an internal state of arousal) emerges. Then the organism is motivated to take action to satisfy the need, thus reducing the drive and restoring equilibrium.

arousal theory: A theory suggesting that the aim of motivation is to maintain an optimal level of arousal.

arousal: A state of alertness and mental and physical activation.

Yerkes–Dodson law: The principle that performance on tasks is best when the arousal level is appropriate to the difficulty of the task—higher arousal for simple tasks, moderate arousal for tasks of moderate difficulty, and lower arousal for complex tasks.

How does arousal theory explain motivation?

and bungee-jumping? Why do animals and humans alike engage in exploratory behavior when it does not serve to reduce any primary drive?

Arousal Theory: Striving for an Optimal Level of Arousal

Unlike drive-reduction theory, **arousal theory** does not suggest that people are always motivated to reduce tension or **arousal** (their state of alertness and mental and physical activation). Arousal theory states that people are motivated to maintain an optimal level of arousal. If arousal is less than the optimal level, we do something to stimulate it; if arousal exceeds the optimal level, we seek to reduce the stimulation.

Biological needs, such as the need for food and water, increase arousal. But people also become aroused when they encounter new stimuli or when the intensity of stimuli is increased, as with loud noises, bright lights, or foul odors. And of course, certain kinds of drugs—stimulants such as caffeine, nicotine, amphetamines, and cocaine—also increase arousal.

People differ in the level of arousal they normally prefer. Some people are sensation seekers, who love the thrill of new experiences and adventure. Sensation seekers are easily bored, experience little fear or uncertainty, and are willing, even eager, to take risks (McCourt et al., 1993). Other people are the opposite: They enjoy the routine and the predictable, avoid risk, and fare best when arousal is relatively low.

Review & Reflect 9.1 summarizes three major motivation theories that we have discussed: instinct theory, drive-reduction theory, and arousal theory.

Arousal and Performance   There is often a close link between arousal and performance. According to the **Yerkes–Dodson law**, performance on tasks is best when arousal level is appropriate to the difficulty of the task. Performance on simple tasks is better when arousal is relatively high. Tasks of moderate difficulty are best accomplished when arousal is moderate; complex or difficult tasks when arousal is lower. But performance suffers when arousal level is either too high or too low for the task. You may have experienced too much or too little arousal when taking an exam. Perhaps your arousal was so low that your mind was sluggish and you didn't finish the test; or you might have been so keyed up that you couldn't remember much of what you had studied.

Stimulus Motives: Increasing Stimulation   When arousal is too low, **stimulus motives**, such as curiosity and the motives to explore, to manipulate objects, and to play, cause humans and other animals to increase stimulation. Young monkeys will play with mechanical puzzles for long periods just for the stimulus of doing so (Harlow, 1950). Rats will explore intricate mazes when they are neither thirsty nor hungry

Review & Reflect 9.1   Theories of Motivation

Theory	View	Example
Instinct theory	Behavior is the result of innate, unlearned tendencies. (This view has been rejected by most modern psychologists.)	Two people fighting because of their aggressive instinct
Drive-reduction theory	Behavior results from the need to reduce an internal state of tension or arousal.	Eating to reduce hunger
Arousal theory	Behavior results from the need to maintain an optimal level of arousal.	Climbing a mountain for excitement; listening to classical music for relaxation

and when no reinforcement is provided (Dashiell, 1925). Rats, and humans too, will spend more time exploring novel objects than familiar ones. People enjoy tinkering with interesting new objects, working on puzzles, and exploring.

The Effects of Sensory Deprivation: Sensory Nothingness   How do you suppose it would feel to have no stimulation at all? In an early experiment, Bexton and others (1954) at McGill University gave student volunteers the opportunity to find out when they studied the effects of **sensory deprivation**—a condition in which sensory stimulation is reduced to a minimum or eliminated.

Students had to lie motionless in a specially designed sensory deprivation chamber in which all sensory stimulation was severely restricted, as in the photograph. The participants could eat, drink, and go to the bathroom when they wanted to. Occasionally they would take tests of motor and mental function, but otherwise they were confined to their sensationless prison.

Did they enjoy the experience? Hardly! Half the participants quit the experiment after the first 2 days. Eventually the remaining participants became irritable, confused, and unable to concentrate. They began to have visual hallucinations, and some reporting hearing imaginary voices and music. Their performance on motor and cognitive tasks deteriorated, and none of the participants said they liked the experiment.

Other studies using milder forms of sensory deprivation, known as *sensory restriction*, have produced some beneficial effects. Positive results range from improved concentration (Lilly, 1956) to better control over cigarette smoking (Suedfeld, 1990) and other addictions (Borrie, 1991). Some studies have shown that sensory restriction has beneficial effects for autistic children (Harrison & Barabasz, 1991).

Sensory stimulation is reduced to the minimum for participants in sensory deprivation experiments.

Maslow's Hierarchy of Needs: Putting Human Needs in Order

Humans have a variety of needs or motives. Clearly some needs are more critical to sustaining life than others. We could live without self-esteem, but obviously we could not live long without air to breathe, water to drink, or food to eat.

Abraham Maslow (1970) proposed a **hierarchy of needs** (Figure 9.2 on page 294) to account for the range of human motivation. He placed physiological needs such as food and water at the base of the hierarchy, stating that these needs must be adequately satisfied before higher ones can be considered.

If the physiological needs (for water, food, sleep, sex, and shelter) are adequately met, then the motives at the next higher level (the safety and the security needs) come into play. When these needs are satisfied, the individual climbs another level to satisfy the needs to belong and to love and be loved. Maslow believed that inability to have one's belonging and love needs met deprives an individual of acceptance, affection, and intimacy and is the most prominent factor in human adjustment problems. Still higher in the hierarchy are the needs for self-esteem and the esteem of others. These needs involve one's sense of worth and competence, need to achieve and be recognized for it, and need to be respected.

At the top of Maslow's hierarchy is the need for **self-actualization**, the need to actualize or realize one's full potential. People may reach self-actualization through achievement in virtually any area of life. But the surest path to self-actualization is one in which a person finds significant and consistent ways to serve and contribute to the well-being of humankind.

Maslow's hierarchy of needs has been a popular notion, appealing to many, but much of it has not been verified by empirical research. And the steps on the hierarchy cannot be said to be invariant, or the same for all people (Wahba & Bridwell, 1976). For example, it is well known that in some people the desire for success and recognition is so strong that they are prepared to sacrifice safety, security, and personal relationships to achieve it. Perhaps they, too, have a hierarchy, but one in which the order of needs is somewhat different.

Link It!

How does Maslow's hierarchy of needs account for human motivation?

Link It!

stimulus motives: Motives that cause humans and other animals to increase stimulation and that appear to be unlearned (examples: curiosity and the need to explore, manipulate objects, and play).

sensory deprivation: A condition in which sensory stimulation is reduced to a minimum or eliminated.

hierarchy of needs: Maslow's theory of motivation, in which needs are arranged in order of urgency ranging from physical needs to security needs, belonging needs, esteem needs, and finally the need for self-actualization.

self-actualization: The development of one's full potential; the highest need on Maslow's hierarchy.

Figure 9.2
**Maslow's Hierarchy
of Needs**

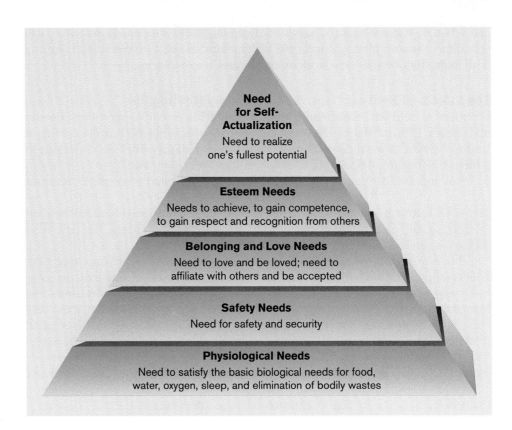

**Need
for Self-
Actualization**
Need to realize
one's fullest potential

Esteem Needs
Needs to achieve, to gain competence,
to gain respect and recognition from others

Belonging and Love Needs
Need to love and be loved; need to
affiliate with others and be accepted

Safety Needs
Need for safety and security

Physiological Needs
Need to satisfy the basic biological needs for food,
water, oxygen, sleep, and elimination of bodily wastes

primary drive: A state of tension
or arousal arising from a biological
need; one not based on learning.

lateral hypothalamus (LH): The
part of the hypothalamus that acts
as a feeding center and, when
activated, signals an animal to eat;
when the LH is destroyed, the animal refuses to eat.

**ventromedial hypothalamus
(VMH):** The part of the hypothalamus that acts as a satiety center
and, when activated, signals an
animal to stop eating; when the
VMH is destroyed, the animal
overeats, becoming obese.

There is convincing research to support Maslow's beliefs about the belonging and
love needs. Baumeister and Leary (1995) analyzed a large number of empirical studies on the need to belong. They concluded that fulfillment of this need affects health,
adjustment, and well-being. Moreover, many of the strongest emotions, whether positive or negative, are tied to the sense of belongingness. (You will learn more about
Maslow when we discuss humanistic psychology in Chapter 10.)

Rather than searching for a general theory that explains all types of motivation,
researchers today assume that a variety of factors—biological, cognitive, behavioral,
social, and cultural—in various combinations influence the motivation underlying
any given behavior.

HUNGER: A PRIMARY DRIVE

Drive-reduction theory suggests that motivation is based largely on the **primary
drives**, those that are unlearned and that serve to satisfy biological needs. One of
the most important primary drives is hunger.

The Biological Basis of Hunger: Internal Hunger Cues

Hunger is a biological drive operating in all animals. What happens in the body to
make you feel hungry, and what causes satiety—the feeling of being full or satisfied?

What are the roles of the
lateral hypothalamus and the
ventromedial hypothalamus
in the regulation of eating
behavior?

The Role of the Hypothalamus: The Feeding and Satiety Centers   Researchers have found two areas of the hypothalamus that are of central importance
in regulating eating behavior and thus affect the hunger drive (Steffens et al., 1988).
The **lateral hypothalamus (LH)** acts as a feeding center to excite eating. Stimulating
the feeding center causes animals to eat even when they are full (Delgado & Anand,

1953). And when the feeding center is destroyed, animals initially refuse to eat (Anand & Brobeck, 1951).

The **ventromedial hypothalamus (VMH)** acts as a satiety center, and when active, it inhibits eating (Hernandez & Hoebel, 1989). If the satiety center is electrically stimulated, animals stop eating (Duggan & Booth, 1986). If the VMH is surgically removed, animals soon eat their way to gross obesity (Hetherington & Ranson, 1940; Parkinson & Weingarten, 1990). One rat whose satiety center was destroyed weighed nearly six times as much as a normal rat. In human terms this would be like a 150-pound person ballooning up to 900 pounds.

Gorging to obesity or refusing to eat altogether occurs immediately after the destruction of a rat's VMH or LH. Some time after the surgery, the rat begins to establish more normal eating patterns. But the obese rats continue to maintain above-average body weight, and the noneating rats eventually establish a below-average body weight (Hoebel & Teitelbaum, 1966). Some researchers believe that destruction of the VMH causes animals to lose the ability to adjust their metabolism and thereby stabilize their body weight (Vilberg & Keesey, 1990).

Other organs and substances in the body also play a role in our feelings of hunger and satiety.

A rat whose satiety center has been destroyed can weigh up to six times as much as a normal rat—in this case, 1080 grams, enough to exceed the capacity of the scale.

What are some of the body's hunger and satiety signals?

Hunger and Satiety Signals   How do you know when you are hungry? Do you have stomach contractions called hunger pangs? In a classic experiment, Cannon and Washburn (1912) demonstrated a close correlation between stomach contractions and the perception of hunger.

Yet animals and humans who have had their stomachs removed entirely continue to experience hunger and satiety. So there must be other hunger and satiety signals besides stomach contractions. The search for these signals moved from the stomach to the blood, because the bloodstream is the means of transporting the products of digestion to sustain all the cells of the body.

Templeton and Quigley (1930) found that the blood of an animal that has eaten its fill is different from the blood of an excessively hungry animal. What was in the blood that signaled hunger and satiety? Researchers began investigating factors such as the blood levels of glucose—a simple sugar resulting from the digestion of carbohydrates.

Glucose and Hunger   Blood levels of glucose are monitored by nutrient detectors in the liver that send this information to the brain (Friedman et al., 1986). Hunger is stimulated when the brain receives the message that blood levels of glucose are low.

Insulin Levels in the Blood   Insulin, a hormone produced by the pancreas, chemically converts glucose into energy that is usable by the cells. Elevations in insulin cause an increase in hunger, in food intake, and in a desire for sweets (Rodin et al., 1985). Chronic oversecretion of insulin stimulates hunger and often leads to obesity.

Satiety Signals Released from the Gastrointestinal Tract   Some of the substances secreted by the gastrointestinal tract during digestion are released into the blood and act as satiety signals (Flood et al., 1990). The hormone cholecystokinin (CCK) is one satiety signal that causes people to limit the amount of food they eat during a meal (Bray, 1991; Woods & Gibbs, 1989).

But we are motivated to eat not only by the internal hunger drive. There are also external factors that stimulate hunger.

Other Factors Influencing Hunger: External Eating Cues

Apart from internal hunger, there are external factors influencing what, where, and how much people eat. Sensory cues such as the taste, smell, and appearance of food stimulate the appetite. For many, the hands of the clock alone, signaling mealtime, are enough to prompt a quest for food. Even eating with other people can tend to

What are some nonbiological factors that influence what and how much people eat?

Table 9.2   Biological and Environmental Factors That Inhibit and Stimulate Eating

	Biological	**Environmental**
Factors that inhibit eating	Activity in ventromedial hypothalamus	Unappetizing smell, taste, or appearance of food
	Raised blood glucose levels	Acquired taste aversions
	Distended (full) stomach	Learned eating habits
	CCK (hormone that acts as satiety signal)	Desire to be thin
	Sensory-specific satiety	Reaction to stress, unpleasant emotional state
Factors that stimulate eating	Activity in lateral hypothalamus	Appetizing smell, taste, or appearance of food
	Low blood levels of glucose	Acquired food preferences
	Increase in insulin	Being around others who are eating
	Stomach contractions	Foods high in fat and sugar
	Empty stomach	Learned eating habits
		Reaction to boredom, stress, unpleasant emotional state

Just the sight of mouth-watering foods can make us want to eat, even when we aren't actually hungry.

What are some factors that account for variations in body weight?

stimulate people to eat more than they would if they were eating alone (de Castro & de Castro, 1989).

External cues *can* trigger internal processes that motivate a person to eat. The sight and smell of appetizing food can trigger the release of insulin, particularly in those who are externally responsive (Rodin et al., 1977). Even in rats, environmental cues previously associated with food cause an increase in insulin level (Detke et al., 1989). For some individuals, simply seeing or thinking about food can cause an elevated level of insulin, and such people have a greater tendency to gain weight (Rodin, 1985).

Foods that are sweet and high in fat tend to stimulate the human appetite (Ball & Grinker, 1981), even when the sweetness is provided by artificial sweeteners (Blundell et al., 1988; Tordoff, 1988). In fact, even artificially sweetened chewing gum has been found to increase hunger (Tordoff & Alleva, 1990).

Table 9.2 summarizes the factors that stimulate and inhibit eating.

Understanding Body Weight: Why Does It Vary So Widely?

Pencil-thin models seen in TV commercials and fashion magazines have come to represent the ideal body for many American women. But most of these models have only 10–15% body fat, far below the 22–26% considered normal for women (Brownell, 1991). Fat has become a negative term, even though some body fat is necessary. Men need 3% and women, 12%, just to survive. And in order for a woman's reproductive system to function properly, she must maintain 20% body fat.

Extremes in either fatness or thinness can pose health risks. An abnormal desire for thinness can result in eating disorders such as the self-starvation of anorexia nervosa and the pattern of binging and purging seen with bulimia nervosa. At the other extreme are a full one-third of American adults aged 20 and older who are overweight (Flegal, 1996; Kuczmarski et al., 1994). Obesity—excessive fatness—increases the risk of high blood pressure, coronary heart disease, stroke, and cancer (Whelan & Stare, 1990). Approximately 300,000 of those obese Americans die annually as a result of the damaging effects of eating too much and moving too little

(Gibbs, 1996). People who have excess fat in the waist and stomach (the so-called apple pattern) are at much greater risk than those whose fat is deposited in the hips and thighs (the pear pattern) (Shapiro, 1997).

Although both excessive thinness and obesity result from a long-term imbalance between energy intake and energy expenditure, the cause is not necessarily insufficient or excessive food intake. Obesity is usually caused by a combination of factors that include heredity, metabolic rate, activity level, number of fat cells, and eating habits.

The Role of Genetic Factors in Body Weight

How strong is the genetic influence on body mass? When results from twin, adoption, and family studies are combined, heritability estimates for the genetic influence on body mass range from 25% to 40% (Bouchard, 1996). Genes are particularly likely to be involved when obesity begins before age 10 (Price et al., 1990). Across all weight classes, from very thin to very obese, children adopted from birth tend to resemble their biological parents more than their adoptive parents in body size. In adoptees, thinness seems to be even more influenced by genes than obesity (Costanzo & Schiffman, 1989). Also, people may inherit their resting metabolic rate, their tendency to store surplus calories primarily as muscle or fat, and even the pattern of where fat is deposited (Bouchard et al., 1990). Nevertheless, Bouchard (1997) found evidence "that environmental conditions and lifestyle characteristics make an even stronger contribution than the genes" to overall body mass (p. S25).

Different genes in some strains of mice and rats, when mutated, lead to gross obesity (Roberts & Greenberg, 1996). Mice with two copies of the obese (ob) gene lack leptin, a protein that suppresses appetite, increases metabolic rate, and regulates fat stores (Pelleymounter et al., 1995). But when the leptin level is increased sufficiently, energy expenditure exceeds food intake, and the mice lose weight (Friedman, 1997). Obese mice injected with leptin lose 30% of their body weight within 2 weeks (Halaas et al., 1995). In humans, a mutation of the leptin receptor gene can cause obesity as well as pituitary abnormalities (Clément et al., 1998).

Metabolic Rate: Burning Energy—Slow or Fast

Metabolism refers to all the physical and chemical processes that are carried out in the body to sustain life. The rate at which the body burns calories to produce energy is called the **metabolic rate**. Physical activity uses up only about one-third of our energy intake; the other two-thirds is consumed by the maintenance processes that keep us alive. When there is an imbalance between energy intake (how much we eat) and output (how much energy we use), our weight changes. Generally, if our caloric intake exceeds our daily energy requirement, we gain weight. If our daily energy requirement exceeds our caloric intake, we lose weight. But there are significant individual differences in the efficiency with which energy is burned. Even if two people are the same age and weight and have the same build and level of activity, one may be able to consume many more calories each day without gaining weight.

Fat-Cell Theory: Tiny Storage Tanks for Fat

Fat-cell theory proposes that fatness is related to the number of **fat cells** (adipose cells) in the body. It is estimated that people of normal weight have between 25 and 35 billion fat cells, while those whose weight is twice normal may have between 100 and 125 billion fat cells (Brownell & Wadden, 1992). The number is determined by both genes and eating habits (Grinker, 1982). Fat cells serve as storehouses for liquefied fat. When you lose weight, you do not lose the fat cells themselves. You lose the fat that is stored in them, and the cells simply shrink (Dietz, 1989). Also, researchers now believe that when people overeat beyond the fat cells' capacity, the number of fat cells continues to increase (Rodin & Wing, 1988).

Set-Point Theory: Thin/Fat Thermostat

Set-point theory suggests that humans are genetically programmed to carry a certain amount of body weight (Keesey,

metabolic rate (meh-tuh-BALL-ik): The rate at which the body burns calories to produce energy.

fat cells: Cells that serve as storehouses for liquefied fat in the body and that number from 25 to 35 billion in normal-weight individuals; with weight loss, they decrease in size but not in number.

How does set point affect body weight?

set point: The weight the body normally maintains when one is trying neither to gain nor to lose weight; if weight falls below the normal level, appetite increases and metabolic rate decreases; if weight is gained, appetite decreases and metabolic rate increases to its original level.

Why is it almost impossible to maintain weight loss by cutting calories alone?

1988). **Set point**—the weight the body maintains when one is trying neither to gain nor to lose weight—is affected by the number of fat cells in the body and by metabolic rate, both of which are influenced by the genes (Gurin, 1989). Yet people with a genetic propensity to be thin can become overweight if they continually overeat, because they will gradually develop a high set point for body fat.

According to set-point theory, an internal homeostatic system functions to maintain set-point weight, much as a thermostat works to keep temperature near the point at which it is set. Whether an individual is lean, overweight, or average, when body weight falls below set point, appetite increases. When weight climbs above set point, appetite decreases so as to restore the original weight. The rate of energy expenditure is also adjusted to maintain the body's set-point weight (Keesey & Powley, 1986). When people gain weight, metabolic rate increases (Dietz, 1989). But when they restrict calories to lose weight, the metabolic rate lowers, causing the body to burn fewer calories and thus making further weight loss more difficult. Increasing the amount of physical activity—exercising during and after weight loss—is the one method recommended for lowering the set point so that the body will store less fat (Foreyt et al., 1996).

Dieting: A National Obsession

At any given time, one out of five adults in the United States is on some kind of reducing diet, but a far larger number—51% of women and 43% of men—perceive themselves as overweight (Gallup & Newport, 1990a). Most diets do produce an initial weight loss—but not a permanent one (Serdula et al., 1993; Wadden, 1993). In fact, little of the weight lost in diet programs is kept off over the long term (Williams et al., 1996). The one behavior that separates those who keep the pounds off from those who regain them is regular exercise (Wadden et al., 1997). Furthermore, dieters who are self-motivated to participate in weight loss programs are much more likely to maintain their lower weight than those who feel pressured or coerced to lose weight (Williams et al., 1996). Sometimes exercise alone, without a restriction in diet, can result in weight loss (Frey-Hewitt et al., 1990).

Why Diets Don't Work   To lose weight, a person must decrease calorie intake, increase exercise, or do both. Unfortunately, most people who are trying to lose weight focus only on cutting calories. But as the calorie restriction continues, the rate of weight loss begins to decrease. The dieter's metabolic rate slows down as if to conserve the remaining fat store because fewer calories are being consumed (Hirsch, 1997).

What can overweight people do to reach their desired weight and then maintain it? The answer, according to Bouchard (1996), is to adopt a physically active lifestyle coupled with a diet containing no more than 30% fat. Reasonable calorie restriction must be coupled with increased exercise and activity to counteract the body's tendency to maintain a lower metabolic rate when fewer calories are consumed (Blair, 1993). Starvation diets are self-defeating in the long run. When a person restricts calories too severely, even exercise cannot reverse the body's drastic lowering of metabolism and its natural tendency to conserve remaining fat (Ballor et al., 1990). Women should consume at least 1,000 calories a day, and men 1,500 calories a day, unless they are under a doctor's supervision.

Changing Eating Habits: A Long-Term Solution   Dieting is not a long-term solution to the problem of being overweight. Many people believe that once the weight is lost, the diet is no longer necessary and old eating habits can be resumed. But because the old habits caused much of the weight problem, returning to those habits is a sure-fire formula for weight gain.

Some evidence suggests that successful weight loss involves more than simply counting calories. It seems that calories eaten in the form of fat are more likely to be stored as body fat than calories eaten as carbohydrates. Miller and others (1990) found that even when obese and thin people have the same caloric intake, thin people derive about 29% of their calories from fats, while obese people average 35% from fat. The composition of the diet may have as much to do with weight gain as the amount of food eaten and the lack of exercise. Counting and limiting the grams of fat may be more beneficial than counting calories to help a person achieve and maintain a desirable body weight. Low-fat diets are healthier, too!

Eating Disorders: The Tyranny of the Scale

Over the past quarter century, the "ideal" female figure, as portrayed in the media and by the fashion and entertainment industries, has become ever thinner, often to the point of emaciation. Accompanying this trend has been an increase in the incidence of eating disorders, such as anorexia nervosa and bulimia nervosa (Halmi, 1996).

Anorexia Nervosa   Anorexia nervosa is characterized by an overwhelming, irrational fear of gaining weight or becoming fat, compulsive dieting to the point of self-starvation, and excessive weight loss. Some anorexics lose as much as 20–25% of their original body weight. Anorexia typically begins in adolescence, and 90% of those afflicted are females (American Psychiatric Association, 1994). About 1% of females between ages 12 and 40 suffer from this disorder (Johnson et al., 1996).

Anorexia often begins with dieting, which gradually develops into an obsession. Anorexic individuals continue to feel hunger and are strangely preoccupied with food. And their perceptions of their body size are grossly distorted. No matter how emaciated they become, they continue to perceive themselves as fat. Frequently, they not only starve themselves but also exercise relentlessly in an effort to accelerate the weight loss. Among young women, progressive and significant weight loss eventually results in *amenorrhea* (cessation of menstruation). Anorexics may also develop low blood pressure, impaired heart function, dehydration, electrolyte disturbances, and/or sterility (American Psychiatric Association, 1993a), as well as decreases in the gray matter volume in the brain, which are thought to be irreversible (Lambe et al., 1997).

Unfortunately, up to 20% of those suffering from anorexia nervosa eventually die of starvation or complications from organ damage (Brotman, 1994). One casualty of the battle against anorexia and bulimia was gymnast Christy Heinrich (shown in the photo), who died in 1994 at the age of 22.

It is difficult to pinpoint the cause of this disorder. Most anorexic individuals are well-behaved and academically successful (Vitousek & Manke, 1994). Some investigators believe that young women who refuse to eat are attempting to control a portion of their lives, which they may feel unable to control in other respects.

Anorexia is very difficult to treat. Most anorexics are steadfast in their refusal to eat, while insisting that nothing is wrong with them. The main thrust of treatment, therefore, is to get the anorexic individual to gain weight. The patient may be admitted to a hospital, fed a controlled diet, and given rewards for small weight gains and

anorexia nervosa: An eating disorder characterized by an overwhelming, irrational fear of being fat, compulsive dieting to the point of self-starvation, and excessive weight loss.

What are the symptoms of anorexia nervosa?

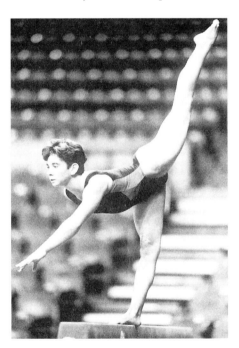

Top-rated gymnast Christy Heinrich was one of the many young victims of the eating disorders anorexia and bulimia.

What are the symptoms of bulimia nervosa?

increases in food intake. The treatment usually includes some type of psychotherapy and/or a self-help group.

Bulimia Nervosa   Up to 50% of anorexics also develop **bulimia nervosa**, a chronic disorder characterized by repeated and uncontrolled (and often secretive) episodes of binge eating (American Psychiatric Association, 1993a). An episode of binge eating has two main features: (1) the consumption of much larger amounts of food than most people would eat during the same period of time, and (2) a feeling that one cannot stop eating or control the amount eaten. Binges—which generally involve foods that are rich in carbohydrates, such as cookies, cake, and candy—are frequently followed by purging. Purging consists of self-induced vomiting and/or the use of large quantities of laxatives and diuretics. Bulimics may also engage in excessive dieting and exercise. Athletes are especially susceptible to this disorder. But many bulimics are of average size and purge after an eating binge simply to maintain their weight.

Bulimia nervosa can cause a number of physical problems. The stomach acid in vomit eats away at the teeth and may cause them to rot, and the delicate balance of body chemistry is destroyed by excessive use of laxatives and diuretics. The bulimic may have a chronic sore throat as well as a variety of other symptoms, including dehydration, swelling of the salivary glands, kidney damage, and hair loss. Recent evidence suggests that decreased function of the neurotransmitter serotonin appears to be a contributing factor (Jimerson et al., 1997).The disorder also has a strong emotional component; the bulimic person is aware that the eating pattern is abnormal and feels unable to control it. Depression, guilt, and shame accompany both bingeing and purging.

Bulimia nervosa tends to appear in the late teens and affects about 1 in 25 women (Kendler et al., 1991). An even larger number of young women regularly binge and purge, but not frequently enough to warrant the diagnosis of bulimia nervosa (Drewnowski et al., 1994). About 10–15% of all bulimics are males, and homosexuality or bisexuality seems to be a risk factor for bulimia in males (Carlat et al., 1997).

Bulimia, like anorexia, is difficult to treat. Cognitive-behavioral therapy has been used successfully to help bulimics modify their eating habits and their abnormal attitudes about body shape and weight (Halmi, 1996; Johnson et al., 1996). Certain antidepressant drugs have been found to reduce the frequency of binge eating and purging and to result in significant attitudinal change (Agras et al., 1994; "Eating disorders," 1997).

SEXUAL MOTIVES

Few would disagree that society's attitudes about sexual behavior are more liberal now than in decades past. In the 1940s and 1950s, virtually all societal institutions officially frowned on sex before marriage. Sex was not considered an appropriate subject for serious investigation, nor was it discussed openly in polite society. But all that began to change when Alfred Kinsey came on the scene.

The Kinsey Surveys: The First In-Depth Look at Sexual Behavior

What were the famous Kinsey surveys?

In the 1940s Alfred Kinsey and his associates undertook a monumental survey that helped to bring the subject of sex out in the open. They interviewed thousands of men and women about their sexual behaviors and attitudes, and their results were published in a two-volume report—*Sexual Behavior in the Human Male* (1948) and *Sexual Behavior in the Human Female* (1953). The public was stunned by what Kinsey's participants said they had done and were doing. And there was a great gulf between what people were practicing in private and what they were admitting openly.

Kinsey's interviews revealed that about 50% of the females and nearly 90% of the males reported having sexual intercourse, **coitus**, before marriage. Over 40% of the college-educated couples said that they engaged in oral sex. And the majority of women and virtually all males reported that they had masturbated. Finally some 26% of the married women and half of the married men admitted having had extra-marital affairs.

But was Kinsey's study valid? Was it scientific? People attacked the findings for a variety of reasons. Unfortunately, Kinsey's sample was not broadly representative. He reported no information on African Americans. Elderly people, rural residents, and those with only grade school educations were underrepresented; Protestants, the college-educated, the middle class, and urban residents were overrepresented.

Have sexual attitudes and behavior changed much since Kinsey's surveys half a century ago?

Sexual Attitudes and Behavior Today: The New Sexual Revolution

The most comprehensive survey of sexual behavior since Kinsey was published in 1994. *The Social Organization of Sexuality* by Laumann and others (1994) is believed to be the most valid and reliable survey of its kind to date. The findings were based on interviews of a nationwide representative sample composed of 3,432 males and females aged 18 to 59. The major findings are summarized below and in Figure 9.3.

■ People with one sexual partner are happier than people with none or more than one.

■ Married people have sex more frequently and are more likely to have orgasms than noncohabiting men and women.

■ On average, over the course of a lifetime, men have six sex partners and women have two.

■ Almost 75% of men and 90% of women reported that they had been faithful to their spouses.

■ About 54% of men and 19% of women reported thinking about sex every day or several times a day; 4% of men and 14% of women reported either never thinking of sex or thinking of it less than once a month.

■ About 27% of men and 8% of women said that they had masturbated at least once a week during the previous 12 months; 37% of men and 58% of women said they had not masturbated.

coitus (KOeh-tis): Penile-vaginal intercourse.

Figure 9.3

Some Results of a 1994 U.S. Sex Survey

Contrary to what is generally portrayed in the media, most Americans are having sex a few times a month or less. Of the respondents to the survey, 83% reported having either one or no sex partner during the past 12 months.

- Of women, 22.8% reported having been forced to do something sexual that they did not want to do, while only 2.8% of men reported forcing a woman to engage in a sexual act.

Throughout all age groups in the United States today, men report having had more sex partners and express a more permissive attitude toward casual premarital sex than women (Oliver & Hyde, 1993). According to Sprecher and Hatfield (1996), African American students tend to have more permissive premarital sexual standards than White students, while Mexican American students have more conservative sexual standards than White students do.

In general, males are likely to be more interested in purely physical sex, and "females tend to be more interested . . . in love, nurturant relationships, and lasting social bonds" (Baldwin & Baldwin, 1997, p. 182). Males tend to be less inhibited than females of the same age about masturbation—and to do it far more often. Perhaps this explains, in part, why males, more than females, can think of sex as a quick, easy, casual release without any emotional commitment (Baldwin & Baldwin, 1997).

In a study of first-year college students, Cohen and Shotland (1996) found that the men expected sexual intercourse to become part of a dating relationship far sooner than the women did. Nearly all of the men in the study expressed a willingness to have sex on a basis of physical attraction only, with no emotional involvement, while women were far less willing to do so. And approximately one-third of the men but only 5% of the women admitted to having had sex with someone they were neither attracted to nor emotionally involved with. Another interesting finding was that the research participants reported believing that "the average person of their gender was considerably more permissive" in sexual matters than they were (p. 291). Another study found that college men with numerous sex partners tend to have a positive attitude toward sexual activities, to be physically attractive, to have high testosterone levels, to be sensation-seekers, and even to have antisocial tendencies (Bogaert & Fisher, 1995).

From 1990 to 1995, researchers Sprecher and Regan (1996) surveyed college students who were virgins to determine their reasons for and feelings about their virginity. For both men and women, it was not lack of sexual desire that prompted their decision to remain virgins. The main reason given was not having found the "right" person, followed by fear of pregnancy or other possible negative consequences of sexual activity, including AIDs and other sexually transmitted diseases. Moral and religious beliefs also influenced the decision for some of the students. The women surveyed felt more pride and happiness about being virgins, while the men were more inclined to experience embarrassment or guilt. But in the more recent years of the study, the men reported greater pride in their status. This, the researchers suggest, might be a response to the "greater number of publicly visible virginal role models to emulate" (p. 12), such as the well-known male athletes in the group Athletes for Abstinence.

Sexual Desire and Arousal: Driving the Sex Drive

Masters and Johnson and the Human Sexual Response Cycle   Kinsey conducted the first major survey of sexual behavior, and Dr. William Masters and Virginia Johnson conducted the first laboratory investigations of the human sexual response. They monitored their volunteer participants, who engaged in sex while connected to electronic sensing devices.

Masters and Johnson (1966) concluded that the human sexual response is quite similar for males and females. Two major physiological changes occur in both sexes—the flow of blood into the genitals (and the breasts in females) and an increase in neuromuscular tension.

Both males and females experience a **sexual response cycle** with four phases: (1) the excitement phase, (2) the plateau phase, (3) the orgasm, and (4) the resolution

According to Masters and Johnson, what are the four phases of the human sexual response cycle?

sexual response cycle: The four phases—excitement, plateau, orgasm, and resolution—that Masters and Johnson found are part of the human sexual response in both males and females.

excitement phase: The first stage in the sexual response cycle, characterized by an erection in males and a swelling of the clitoris and vaginal lubrication in females.

plateau phase: The second stage of the sexual response cycle, during which muscle tension and blood flow to the genitals increase in preparation for orgasm.

orgasm: The third phase in the sexual response cycle, marked by rhythmic muscular contractions and a sudden discharge of accumulated sexual tension.

phase. Masters and Johnson (1966) found that these phases apply not only to sexual intercourse but also to other types of sexual activity.

The **excitement phase** is the beginning of the sexual response. It can be triggered by direct physical contact as well as by psychological arousal—thoughts, emotions, and a variety of sensory stimuli. This phase is characterized by penile erection in males and swelling of the clitoris and vaginal lubrication in females. During the second stage, the **plateau phase,** muscle tension and blood flow to genitals increase in preparation for orgasm.

The **orgasm**, the shortest of the phases, is the highest point of sexual pleasure, marked by a sudden discharge of accumulated sexual tension. Involuntary muscle contractions may seize the entire body during orgasm, and the genitals contract rhythmically. Marked by powerful, rhythmic contractions, the female's orgasm usually lasts longer than that of the male. About 40–50% of women regularly experience orgasm during intercourse (Wilcox & Hager, 1980). Although vaginal orgasms and clitoral orgasms may feel different, according to Masters and Johnson (1966), the actual physiological response in the female is the same.

The orgasm gives way to the **resolution phase**, a tapering-off period, when the body returns to its unaroused state. Men experience a *refractory period* in the resolution phase, during which they cannot have another orgasm. The refractory period may last from only a few minutes for some men to as much as several hours for others. Women do not have a refractory period and may, if restimulated, experience another orgasm right away.

William Masters and Virginia Johnson were pioneers in the study of the human sexual response.

The Role of Hormones in Sexual Desire and Arousal: Sexual Substances

In most animal species, sexual activity does not occur unless the female is "in heat." Thus, most animals behave sexually in response to hormones, odors, and biologically determined sexual cycles. But human sexual desire can be aroused at practically any time, independent of rhythmic biological cycles. And humans engage in far more sex than is required to continue the species.

The sex glands themselves manufacture hormones—**estrogen** and **progesterone** in the ovaries, and androgens in the testes. The adrenal glands in both sexes also produce small amounts of these hormones. Females have considerably more estrogen and progesterone than males do, so these are known as the female sex hormones. Males have considerably more androgens—the male sex hormones. **Testosterone**, the most important androgen, influences the development and maintenance of male sex characteristics as well as sexual motivation.

Testosterone and Sexual Desire   Males must have a sufficient level of testosterone in order to maintain sexual interest and have an erection. It is more than coincidence that at puberty, when testosterone levels increase dramatically, sexual thoughts and fantasies, masturbation, and nocturnal emissions also increase significantly.

As men age, the level of testosterone declines, and usually there is also a decline in sexual interest and activity and in sexual fantasies (Leitenberg & Henning, 1995). Castration (removal of the testes, which produce 95% of the male's androgens) usually lowers sexual desire and activity dramatically.

Females, too, need small amounts of testosterone circulating in the bloodstream to maintain sexual interest and responsiveness (Anderson & Cyranowski, 1995).

SEXUAL ORIENTATION

So far we have discussed many aspects of human sexual response and sexual arousal, but we have not considered **sexual orientation**—the direction of an individual's sexual preference, erotic feelings, and sexual activity. In heterosexuals, the

---

What are the male and female sex hormones, and how do they affect sexual desire and activity in males and females?

resolution phase: The final stage of the sexual response cycle, during which the body returns to an unaroused state.

estrogen (ES-truh-jen): A female sex hormone that promotes the secondary sex characteristics in females and controls the menstrual cycle.

progesterone (pro-JES-tah-rone): A female sex hormone that plays a role in the regulation of the menstrual cycle and prepares the lining of the uterus for possible pregnancy.

testosterone (tes-TOS-tah-rone): The most powerful androgen secreted by the testes and adrenal glands in males and by the adrenal glands in females; influences the development and maintenance of male sex characteristics and sexual motivation; associated with male aggressiveness.

sexual orientation: The direction of one's sexual preference—toward members of the opposite sex (heterosexuality), toward one's own sex (homosexuality), or toward both sexes (bisexuality).

What is meant by sexual orientation?

A gay rights demonstration gives lesbians and gay men and their supporters the chance to show pride and solidarity.

human sexual response is oriented toward members of the opposite sex; in homosexuals, toward those of the same sex; and in bisexuals, toward members of both sexes.

Homosexuality has been reported in all societies throughout recorded history (Carrier, 1980; Ford & Beach, 1951). Kinsey and his associates (1948, 1953) estimated that 4% of the male participants had nothing but homosexual relations throughout life, and about 2–3% of the female participants had been in mostly or exclusively lesbian relationships. Gay and lesbian rights groups, however, claim that about 10% of the U.S. population is predominantly homosexual. Laumann and others (1994) reported that the percentages of people who identified themselves as homosexual or bisexual were 2.8% of men and 1.4% of women. But 5.3% of men and 3.5% of women said that they had had a sexual experience with a person of the same sex at least once since puberty. And even larger percentages of those surveyed—10% of males and 8–9% of females—said that they had felt some same-sex desires. Notably, all estimates suggest that homosexuality is twice as prevalent in males as in females.

Determinants of Sexual Orientation: Physiological or Psychological?

What are the various biological factors that have been suggested as possible determinants of a gay or lesbian sexual orientation?

Link It!

Psychologists continue to debate whether sexual orientation is biologically fixed or acquired through learning and experience. A few decades ago, many experts believed that a homosexual orientation is learned (Gagnon & Simon, 1973; Masters & Johnson, 1979). Many now believe that biological factors largely determine sexual orientation (Bailey & Pillard, 1994; Isay, 1989; LeVay, 1993). And still others lean toward an interaction—the theory that both nature and nurture play their parts (Breedlove, 1994; Byne, 1994; Patterson, 1995). Could hormones play a role?

Some have suggested that abnormal levels of androgens during prenatal development might influence sexual orientation (Collaer & Hines, 1995). Too much or too little androgen at critical periods of brain development might masculinize or feminize the brain of the developing fetus, making a homosexual orientation more likely (Berenbaum & Snyder, 1995). A few studies have revealed an increase in the incidence of lesbianism among females who had been exposed prenatally to synthetic estrogen (Meyer-Bahlburg et al., 1995) or to an excess of androgens (Ehrhardt et al., 1968; Money & Schwartz, 1977).

Definitive answers to nature–nurture questions are always elusive, but some recent research suggests that biological factors may play a part in homosexuality. Neuroscientist Simon LeVay (1991) reported that an area in the hypothalamus governing sexual behavior is about twice as large in heterosexual men as in homosexual men. This part of the hypothalamus, no larger than a grain of sand, is about the same size in heterosexual females as in homosexual males. LeVay admits that his research offers no direct evidence that the brain differences he found cause homosexuality (LeVay & Hamer, 1994).

In researching the influence of heredity on sexual orientation, Bailey and Pillard (1991) studied gay males who had twin brothers. They found that 52% of the gay identical twins and 22% of the gay fraternal twins had a gay twin brother. Of the gay twins who had adoptive brothers, however, only 11% shared a homosexual orientation. In a similar study, Whitam and others (1993) found that 66% of the identical twins and 30% of the fraternal twins of gay males studied were also gay. Such studies indicate a substantial genetic influence on sexual orientation, but suggest that nongenetic influences are at work as well.

According to Bailey and Benishay (1993), "female homosexuality appears to run in families" (p. 277). They found that 12.1% of their lesbian participants had a sister who was also lesbian, compared to 2.3% of heterosexual female participants. Bailey and others (1993) report that in a study of lesbians, 48% of their identical twins, 16% of their fraternal twins, 14% of their nontwin biological sisters, and 6% of their adopted sisters were also lesbian. Bailey and Pillard (1994) claim that, according to their statistical analysis, the heritability of sexual orientation is about 50%.

Do the findings of LeVay and of Bailey and Pillard provide convincing evidence that sexual orientation is biologically determined? Some researchers (Byne, 1993; Byne & Parsons, 1993, 1994) maintain that, in the absence of studies of identical twins reared *apart*, the influence of environment cannot be ruled out as the cause of a higher incidence of homosexuality in certain families. Furthermore, they suggest that if one or more genes are involved, they may not be genes directly influencing sexual orientation. Rather, they could be genes affecting personality or temperament that could influence how people react to environmental stimuli (Byne, 1994). Let's explore early environmental influences.

The Developmental Experiences of Gay Men and Lesbians

Some evidence suggests that sexual orientation, whether homosexual or heterosexual, is established by early childhood (Marmor, 1980; Money, 1987). Bell, Weinberg, and Hammersmith (1981) questioned 979 homosexual participants and 477 heterosexual controls about their childhood, adolescence, and sexual experiences. No single condition of family life in and of itself appeared to be a factor in either homosexual or heterosexual development. The only experience common to homosexuals was that as children they did not feel they were like others of their sex. For this reason, these researchers assume there is a biological predisposition toward homosexuality.

Some researchers have suggested that boys and girls who do not show typical gender-role behavior, but rather are seen as sissies or tomboys, may be more likely to be homosexual (Green, 1985, 1987; Green & Money, 1961). Zuger (1990) believes that, in many cases, early and extreme effeminate behavior in boys is an early stage of homosexuality. Such effeminate behavior might include a boy's cross-dressing, expressing the desire to be a girl or insisting that he is in fact a girl, and/or preferring girls as playmates and girls' games over boys' games and sports. Boys with these effeminate characteristics often are very close to their mothers but spend little time with their fathers (Zuger, 1990).

This early effeminate pattern is not characteristic of all gay males by any means. In a study of sexual orientation and childhood memories of gender-conforming and nonconforming behaviors, Bailey and others (1995) found a strong association between sexual orientation and sex-typed behavior in childhood as recalled by both gay men and their mothers. Although the relationship between sexual orientation and early sex-typed behavior was found to be strong, there were exceptions. Some gay men exhibited masculine sex-typed behavior, while some heterosexual men were "feminine" boys.

In another study of recalled childhood experiences and sexual orientation, Phillips and Over (1995) found that heterosexual women could be distinguished from lesbian women with 80% accuracy, on the basis of recalled childhood experiences. The lesbian women were more likely to recall imagining themselves as males, preferring boy's games, and being called "tomboys." Using meta-analysis, Bailey and Zucker (1995) found that cross-gender behavior could be a predictor of homosexuality for both females and males.

Researchers continue to disagree on the genesis of sexual orientation. Psychologist Charlotte Patterson (1995) suggests that the relationship between sexual orientation and human development can be studied most profitably as a complex interaction of nature and nurture.

What does the study by Bell, Weinberg, and Hammersmith reveal about the developmental experiences of gay men and lesbians?

SOCIAL MOTIVES

Do you have a strong need to be with other people (affiliation) or a need for power or achievement? These needs are three examples of **social motives**, which we learn or acquire through social and cultural experiences. We differ in the strength of various social motives and in the priorities we assign to them. Our highest aspirations, the professions we choose, the partners we are drawn to, and the methods we use to achieve a sense of importance result primarily from social motives.

Henry Murray (1938) identified and defined a list of social motives, or needs, such as the need for achievement, recognition, affiliation, dominance, or order. Murray believed that people have social motives in differing degrees. To investigate the strength of various needs, Murray developed the **Thematic Apperception Test (TAT)**, which consists of a series of pictures of ambiguous situations. The person taking the test is asked to write a story about each picture—to describe what is going on in the picture, what the person or persons pictured are thinking about, what they may be feeling, and what is likely to be the outcome of the situation. The stories are presumed to reveal the test taker's needs and the strength of those needs. (The TAT has also been used as a more general personality test, as described in Chapter 10.)

What is Murray's contribution to the study of motivation?

Link It!

The Need for Achievement: The Drive to Excel

What is the need for achievement?

Murray (1938) defined the **need for achievement** (abbreviated n Ach) as the motive "to accomplish something difficult. . . . To overcome obstacles and attain a high standard. To excel one's self. To rival and surpass others. To increase self-regard by the successful exercise of talent" (p. 164). The need for achievement, rather than being satisfied with accomplishment, seems to grow as it is fed, not to diminish.

The need for achievement has been researched more vigorously than any other of Murray's needs, and researchers David McClelland and John Atkinson have conducted many of these studies using the TAT (McClelland et al., 1953; McClelland, 1958, 1961, 1985). Unfortunately, the participants in these studies were almost exclusively male.

Complete the *Try It!* which describes a game that is said to reveal high or low achievement motivation.

Try It!

Imagine yourself involved in a ring-toss game. You have three rings to toss at any of the six pegs pictured here. You will be paid a few pennies each time you are able to ring a peg.

Which peg would you try to ring with your three tosses—peg 1 or 2 nearest you, peg 3 or 4 at a moderate distance, or peg 5 or 6 at the far end of the row?

Characteristics of Achievers: Successful People Possess Them McClelland and others (1953) found that high achievers differ from low achievers in several ways. People with a high *n* Ach tend to set goals of moderate difficulty. They pursue goals that are challenging, yet attainable through hard work, ability, determination, and persistence. Goals that are too easy, those anyone can reach, offer no challenge and hold no interest, because success would not be rewarding (McClelland, 1985). Impossibly high goals and high risks are also not pursued, because they offer little chance of success and are considered a waste of time. People high in *n* Ach enjoy taking moderate risks in situations that depend on their ability, but they are not gamblers. To become wealthy, businesspeople high in achievement motivation often take moderate risks, which are more likely to pay off, rather than very high risks offering little or no chance of success.

People with low *n* Ach, the researchers claim, are not willing to take chances when it comes to testing their own skills and abilities. They are motivated more by their fear of failure than by their hope and expectation of success. This is why they set either ridiculously low goals, which anyone can attain, or else impossibly high goals (Geen, 1984). After all, who can fault a person for failing to reach a goal that is impossible for almost anyone?

In view of this description, which peg in the ring-toss game in the *Try It!* would people low in achievement motivation try for? If you guessed peg 1 or 2, or peg 5 or 6, you are right. People low in achievement motivation are likely to stand right over peg 1 so they can't possibly fail. Or they may toss the rings at peg 6, hoping that they might be lucky. If they failed, no one could blame them for not attaining a nearly impossible goal. People with a high need for achievement tend to toss their rings at peg 3 or 4, an intermediate distance that offers some challenge. Which pegs did you choose?

People with high *n* Ach see their success as a result of their own talents, abilities, persistence, and hard work (Kukla, 1972). They typically do not credit luck or the influence of other people for their successes, or blame luck or others for their failures. When people with low *n* Ach fail, they usually give up quickly and attribute failure to their lack of ability. They believe that luck or fate, rather than effort and ability, is responsible for accomplishment (Weiner, 1974).

Developing Achievement Motivation: Can You Learn It? If achievement motivation, like the other social motives, is primarily learned, how is it learned? Some experts believe that child-rearing practices and values in the home are important factors in developing achievement motivation (McClelland & Pilon, 1983). Parents can foster *n* Ach if they give their children responsibilities, teach them to think and act independently from the time they are very young, stress excellence, persistence, and independence, and praise them sincerely for their accomplishments (Ginsburg & Bronstein, 1993; Gottfried et al., 1994). Birth order appears to be related to achievement motivation, with first-born and only children showing higher *n* Ach than younger siblings (Falbo & Polit, 1986). Younger siblings, however, tend to be more sociable and likable than first-born or only children, and this has its rewards, too.

THE WHAT AND WHY OF EMOTIONS

Motivation and Emotion: What Is the Connection?

Motivation does not occur in a vacuum. Much of our motivation to act is fueled by emotional states. In fact, the root of the word **emotion** means "to move," indicating the close relationship between motivation and emotion. For example, fear motivates us either to flee to escape danger or to take actions that will provide security and

People with a high need for achievement can overcome even serious disabilities in their efforts to succeed.

What are some characteristics shared by people who are high in achievement motivation?

social motives: Motives acquired through experience and interaction with others.

Thematic Apperception Test (TAT): A projective test consisting of drawings of ambiguous situations, which the test taker describes; thought to reveal inner feelings, conflicts, and motives.

need for achievement (*n* Ach): The need to accomplish something difficult and to perform at a high standard of excellence.

emotion: A feeling state involving physiological arousal, a cognitive appraisal of the situation arousing the state, and an outward expression of the state.

safety (Izard, 1992). Furthermore, emotions enable us to communicate feelings and intentions more effectively than just words alone and thus make it more likely that others will respond. But what, precisely, are emotions?

The Components of Emotions: The Physical, the Cognitive, and the Behavioral

What are the three components of emotion?

Nothing more than feelings—is that what emotions are? We may say that we feel lonely or sad, happy or content, embarrassed or afraid. We normally describe emotions in terms of feeling states, but psychologists study emotions according to their three components—the physical, the cognitive, and the behavioral.

The physical component is the physiological arousal (the internal body state) that accompanies the emotion. Without the physiological arousal, the emotion would not be felt in all its intensity. The surge of powerful feeling we know as emotion is due largely to the physiological arousal we experience.

The cognitive component—the way we perceive or interpret a stimulus or situation—determines the specific emotion we feel. If you are home alone and the wind is banging a tree limb on your roof, you may become fearful if you perceive the knocking and the banging as a burglar trying to break into your house. An emotional response to an imaginary threat is every bit as powerful as a response to a real threat. Perceptions make it so. Have you ever worked yourself into a frenzy before a first date, a job interview, or an oral presentation for one of your classes? If so, you have experienced the powerful influence your own thinking has on your emotional state.

The behavioral component of emotions is the outward expression of the emotions. Facial expressions, gestures, body posture, and tone of voice stem from and convey the emotions felt within. Some of the facial expressions that accompany emotions are innate and are the same across cultures. But some emotional expressions are more influenced by culture and its rules for displaying emotion.

Theories of Emotion: Which Comes First, the Thought or the Feeling?

According to the James–Lange theory, what sequence of events occurs when an individual experiences an emotion?

There is no doubt that we react to certain experiences with emotion. For example, if you think you are making a fool of yourself in front of your friends, the emotion you feel is embarrassment, which triggers a physiological response that may cause you to blush. This explanation of your embarrassed reaction seems logical—it seems to fit with everyday experience. But is this sequence of events the course that an emotional experience really follows? Not according to psychologist William James.

The James–Lange Theory   American psychologist William James (1884) argued that the sequence of events in an emotional experience is exactly the reverse of what subjective experience tells us. James claimed that first an event causes physiological arousal and a physical response. Only then does the individual perceive or interpret the physical response as an emotion. In other words, saying something stupid causes you to blush, and you interpret your physical response, blushing, as an emotion, embarrassment. James (1890) went on to suggest that "we feel sorry *because* we cry, angry *because* we strike, afraid *because* we tremble" (p. 1066).

At about the same time that James proposed his theory, a Danish physiologist and psychologist, Carl Lange, independently formulated nearly the same theory. The **James–Lange theory** of emotion (Lange & James, 1922) suggests that different patterns of arousal in the autonomic nervous system produce the different emotions people feel, and that the physiological arousal appears before the emotion is perceived. See Figure 9.4.

But if the physical arousal itself causes what we know as emotion, there would have to be distinctly different bodily changes associated with each emotion. Otherwise, you wouldn't know whether you were sad, embarrassed, frightened, or happy.

James–Lange theory of emotion: The theory that emotional feelings result when an individual becomes aware of a physiological response to an emotion-provoking stimulus (for example, feeling fear because of trembling).

Cannon–Bard theory of emotion: The theory that an emotion-provoking stimulus is transmitted simultaneously to the cortex, providing the feeling of an emotion, and to the sympathetic nervous system, causing the physiological arousal.

Schachter–Singer theory of emotion: A two-stage theory stating that for an emotion to occur, there must be (1) physiological arousal and (2) an explanation for the arousal.

Lazarus theory of emotion: The theory that an emotion-provoking stimulus triggers a cognitive appraisal, which is followed by the emotion and the physiological arousal.

Figure 9.4

The James–Lange Theory of Emotion

The James–Lange theory of emotion is the exact opposite of what subjective experience tells us. If a dog growls at you, the James–Lange interpretation is that the dog growls, your heart begins to pound, and only after perceiving that your heart is pounding do you conclude that you must be afraid.

Labels in figure: Stimulus situation — Physiological arousal, action — Experience of emotion based on interpretation of arousal and action

Fear

A dog growls at you. — Your heart pounds; you run. — "My heart is racing and I'm running. I must be afraid."

The Cannon–Bard Theory   An early theory of emotion that challenged the James–Lange theory was proposed by Walter Cannon (1927), who claimed that the bodily changes caused by the various emotions are not sufficiently distinct to allow people to distinguish one emotion from another.

Cannon's original theory was later expanded by physiologist Philip Bard (1934). The **Cannon–Bard theory** suggests that the following chain of events occurs when we feel an emotion: Emotion-provoking stimuli are received by the senses and are then relayed simultaneously to the cerebral cortex, which provides the conscious mental experience of the emotion, and to the sympathetic nervous system, which produces the physiological state of arousal. In other words, your feeling of emotion (fear, for example) occurs at about the same time that you experience physiological arousal (a pounding heart). One does not cause the other.

What is the Cannon–Bard theory of emotion?

The Schachter–Singer Theory   Stanley Schachter believed that the early theories of emotion left out a critical component—the subjective cognitive interpretation of why a state of arousal has occurred. Schachter and Singer (1962) proposed a two-factor theory. According to the **Schachter–Singer theory**, two things must happen in order for a person to feel an emotion: (1) The person must first experience physiological arousal. (2) Then there must be a cognitive interpretation or explanation of the physiological arousal so that the person can label it as a specific emotion. Thus, Schachter concluded, a true emotion can occur only if a person is physically aroused *and* can find some reason for it.

According to the Schachter–Singer theory, what two factors must occur in order for a person to experience an emotion?

The Lazarus Theory   The theory of emotion that most heavily emphasizes the cognitive aspect has been proposed by Richard Lazarus (1991a, 1991b, 1995). According to the **Lazarus theory**, a cognitive appraisal is the first step in an emotional response, and all other aspects of an emotion, including physiological arousal, depend on the cognitive appraisal. This theory is most compatible with the subjective experience of an emotion's sequence of events—the sequence that William James reversed long ago. Faced with a stimulus—an event—a person first appraises it. This cognitive appraisal determines whether the person will have an emotional response and, if so, what type of

According to Lazarus, what sequence of events occurs when an individual feels an emotion?

Theory	View	Example
James–Lange theory	An event causes physiological arousal. You experience an emotion only *after* you interpret the physical response.	You are walking home late at night and hear footsteps behind you. Your heart pounds and you begin to tremble. You interpret these physical responses as *fear*.
Cannon–Bard theory	An event causes a physiological *and* an emotional response simultaneously. One does not cause the other.	You are walking home late at night and hear footsteps behind you. Your heart pounds, you begin to tremble, *and* you feel afraid.
Schachter–Singer theory	An event causes physiological arousal. You must then be able to identify a reason for the arousal in order to label the emotion.	You are walking home late at night and hear footsteps behind you. Your heart pounds and you begin to tremble. You know that walking alone at night can be dangerous, and so you feel afraid.
Lazarus theory	An event occurs, a cognitive appraisal is made, and then the emotion and physiological arousal follow.	You are walking home late at night and hear footsteps behind you. You think it could be a mugger. So you feel afraid, and your heart starts to pound and you begin to tremble.

response. The physiological arousal and all other aspects of the emotion flow from the appraisal. In short, Lazarus contends that emotions are provoked when cognitive appraisals of events or circumstances are positive or negative—but not neutral.

Critics of the Lazarus theory point out that some emotional reactions are instantaneous—occurring too rapidly to pass through a cognitive appraisal (Zajonc, 1980, 1984). Lazarus (1984, 1991b) responds that some mental processing occurs without conscious awareness. And there must be some form of cognitive realization, however brief, or else a person would not know what he or she is responding to or what emotion to feel—fear, happiness, embarrassment, and so on.

Review & Reflect 9.2 summarizes the four major theories of emotion: James–Lange, Cannon–Bard, Schachter–Singer, and Lazarus.

THE EXPRESSION OF EMOTION

Expressing emotions comes as naturally to humans as breathing. No one has to be taught how to smile or frown, or how to express fear, sadness, surprise, or disgust. And the facial expressions of the basic emotions are much the same in cultures all over the world.

The Range of Emotion: How Wide Is It?

What are basic emotions?

How many emotions are there? The number of emotions people list depends on their culture, the language they speak, and other factors. Two leading researchers on emotion, Paul Ekman (1993) and Carroll Izard (1992), insist that there are a limited number of basic emotions. **Basic emotions** are unlearned and universal; that is, they are found in all cultures, are reflected in the same facial expressions, and emerge in children according to their own biological timetable of development. Fear, anger, disgust, surprise, joy or happiness, and sadness or distress are usually considered basic emotions. Izard (1992, 1993) suggests that there are distinct neural circuits that underlie each of the basic emotions, and Levenson and others (1990) point to specific autonomic nervous system activity associated with the basic emotions. Panksepp (1992) believes there is strong evidence for emotional systems in the brain that, at a minimum, underlie rage, fear, expectancy, and panic. Not all researchers, however, subscribe to the notion of basic emotions (Turner & Ortony, 1992).

In studying the range of emotion, Ekman (1993) has suggested considering emotions as families. Clearly there are gradients, or degrees, of intensity within a single emotion. A person could experience fear, for example, in various degrees, from being mildly apprehensive to being afraid, scared, or terrified.

Research continues to show that people have stronger emotional reactions to negative stimuli than to positive ones (National Advisory Mental Health Council, 1995). For example, in social interactions, a person's feelings about another individual are typically influenced more by a single negative attribute than by a collection of positive qualities. And some research suggests that positive emotional experiences in a marriage must outnumber negative ones by about 5 to 1 for a satisfactory relationship to be sustained (Gottman, 1994).

From the vantage point of evolution, such findings are logical. Survival may depend on avoiding noxious stimuli and dangerous situations that provoke negative emotions. But with respect to one's mental health, it is important to guard against the power of negative emotions by balancing them with positive ones.

But how do we learn to express emotions? Or do we learn? There is considerable evidence that the basic emotions (fear, anger, sadness, happiness, disgust, and surprise), or at least the facial expressions we make when we feel them, are biologically rather than culturally determined.

The Development of Facial Expressions in Infants: Smiles and Frowns Come Naturally

Like the motor skills of crawling and walking, facial expressions of emotions develop naturally, according to a biological timetable of maturation. Even newborns are capable of expressing certain emotions—specifically, distress, pleasure, and interest in the environment. By 3 months, babies can express happiness and sadness (Lewis, 1995), and laughter appears somewhere around 3½ to 4 months (Provine, 1996). Between the ages of 4 and 6 months, the emotions of anger and surprise appear, and by about 7 months, infants show fear. The self-conscious emotions do not emerge until later. Between 18 months and 3 years, children begin to show first empathy, envy, and embarrassment, followed by shame, guilt, and pride (Lewis, 1995).

How does the development of facial expressions of different emotions in infants suggest a biological basis for emotional expression?

Another strong indication that the facial expressions of emotion are biologically determined, rather than learned, results from research on children who were blind and deaf since birth. Their smiles and frowns, laughter and crying, and facial expressions of anger, surprise, and pouting were the same as those of children who could hear and see (Eibl-Eibesfeldt, 1973).

Although recent studies have contributed much to scientists' understanding of facial expressions, the biological connection between emotions and facial expressions was proposed many years ago.

Facial Expressions for the Basic Emotions: A Universal Language

The relationship between emotions and facial expressions was first studied by Charles Darwin (1872/1965). He believed that the facial expression of emotion was an aid to survival, because it enabled people to communicate their internal states and react to emergencies before they developed language. Darwin maintained that most emotions and the facial expressions that convey them are genetically inherited and characteristic of the entire human species. To test his belief, he asked missionaries and people of different cultures around the world to record the facial expressions that accompany the basic emotions. Based on those data, he concluded that facial expressions were similar across cultures. Modern researchers agree that Darwin was right.

Convincing evidence that the facial expressions of emotion are universal was provided by Ekman and Friesen (1971). They showed photographs portraying facial expressions of the primary emotions—sadness, surprise, happiness, anger, fear, and disgust—to members of the Fore tribe in a remote area in New Guinea. The Fore people were able to identify the emotional expressions of happiness, sadness, anger, and disgust, although they had difficulty distinguishing fear and surprise.

In later research Ekman and others (Ekman, 1982; Ekman & Friesen, 1975; Ekman et al., 1987) used participants from the United States, Argentina, Japan, Brazil, and Chile, who viewed photographs showing the same basic emotions. Could people from widely diverse cultures name the emotions conveyed by the facial expressions of Americans? Yes, to an amazing degree. Ekman (1992) believes that such research results provide strong support for a biological explanation of facial expression. Russell (1994) reviewed 11 cross-cultural studies spanning a period of 12 years (1980–1992), and all of the studies concluded that the human face reveals emotions that are universally recognized.

Other research finds evidence for universality, as Darwin and Ekman and others did, but evidence for cultural variations as well. Scherer and Wallbott (1994) found very extensive overlap in the patterns of emotional experiences reported across cultures in 37 different countries on 5 continents. They also found important cultural differences in the ways emotions are elicited and regulated and in how they are shared socially. These findings are reminders that even though we acknowledge and appreciate cultural differences and human diversity, people are, after all, one species. And facial expressions of basic emotion are much the same around the world.

Try Ekman's test and see if you can identify the faces of emotion in the *Try It!*

Try It!

Look carefully at the six photographs. Which basic emotion is portrayed in each? Match the number of the photograph with the basic emotion it conveys:

a. happiness   b. sadness   c. fear   d. anger   e. surprise   f. disgust

1. _____   2. _____   3. _____   4. _____   5. _____   6. _____

Answers: 1.d 2.c 3.f 4.e 5.a 6.b

You had to identify the emotions associated with the facial expressions in the photographs in the *Try It!* without any help from context. But in real life you use information provided by the situation or context in addition to the facial expression itself to help determine the emotion being conveyed (Carroll & Russell, 1996).

Cultural Rules for Displaying Emotion

While the facial expressions of the basic emotions are much the same in cultures around the world, each culture can have very different **display rules**—cultural rules that dictate how emotions should generally be expressed and where and when their expression is appropriate (Ekman, 1993; Ekman & Friesen, 1975; Scherer & Wallbott, 1994). Often a society's display rules require people to give evidence of certain emotions that they may not actually feel or to disguise their true feelings. For example, we are expected to look sad at funerals, to hide disappointment when we lose, and to refrain from making facial expressions of disgust if the food we are served tastes bad. In one study, Cole (1986) found that 3-year-old girls, when given an unattractive gift, smiled nevertheless. They had already learned a display rule and signaled an emotion they very likely did not feel. Davis (1995) found that among first to third graders, girls were better able to hide disappointment than boys were.

The stern faces of these two young Masai warriors from Kenya reflect their culture's display rules banning the public expression of emotion.

Different cultures, neighborhoods, and even families may have very different display rules. Display rules in Japanese culture dictate that negative emotions must be disguised when other people are present (Ekman, 1972; Triandis, 1994). In many societies in the West, women are expected to smile often, whether they feel happy or not. And in East Africa, young males from traditional Masai society are expected to appear stern and stony-faced and to "produce long, unbroken stares" (Keating, 1994). So it appears that much emotion that is displayed is not authentic, not truly felt, but merely reflects compliance with display rules.

Most of us learn display rules very early and abide by them most of the time. Yet we may not be fully aware that the rules we have learned dictate where, when, how, and even how long certain emotions should be expressed. You will learn more about reading emotions and detecting the probable motives of others when we explore nonverbal behavior—the language of facial expressions, gestures, and body positions—in Chapter 14.

EXPERIENCING EMOTION

How is the expression of emotion related to the experience of emotion? Some researchers go so far as to suggest that the facial expression alone can actually produce the experience.

The Facial-Feedback Hypothesis: Does the Face Cause the Feeling?

Researcher Sylvan Tomkins (1962, 1963), like Darwin, agreed that facial expressions of the basic emotions are genetically programmed. But Tomkins went a step further. He claimed that the facial expression itself—that is, the movement of the facial muscles producing the expression—triggers both the physiological arousal and the conscious feeling associated with the emotion. The notion that the muscular movements involved in certain facial expressions produce the corresponding emotion is called the **facial-feedback hypothesis** (Izard, 1971, 1977, 1990; Strack et al., 1988).

In an extensive review of research on the facial-feedback hypothesis, Adelmann and Zajonc (1989) found impressive evidence to support the association between facial expression and the subjective experience of an emotion. In addition, they found considerable support for the notion that simply making the facial expression can initiate the subjective feeling of the emotion. If this is true, we should be able to feel more understanding and empathy for others if we mirror their facial expressions with our own.

What is the facial-feedback hypothesis?

facial-feedback hypothesis: The idea that the muscular movements involved in certain facial expressions trigger the corresponding emotions (for example, smiling makes one feel happy).

The Simulation of Facial Expressions: Put On a Happy Face   Nearly 125 years ago Darwin wrote, "Even the simulation of an emotion tends to arouse it in our minds" (1872/1965, p. 365). Ekman and colleagues (1983) put this notion to the test using 16 participants (12 professional actors and 4 scientists). The participants were guided to contract specific muscles in the face so that they could assume the facial expressions of six basic emotions—surprise, disgust, sadness, anger, fear, and happiness. They were never actually told to smile, frown, or put on an angry face, however.

The participants were monitored by electronic instruments, which recorded physiological changes in heart rate, galvanic skin response (to measure perspiring), muscle tension, and hand temperature. Measurements were taken as the participants made each facial expression. The participants were also asked to imagine or relive an experience in which they had felt each of the six emotions.

Ekman reported that a distinctive physiological response pattern emerged for the emotions of fear, sadness, anger, and disgust, whether the participants relived one of their emotional experiences or simply made the corresponding facial expression (Ekman et al., 1983). The researchers found that both anger and fear accelerate heart rate, but fear produces colder fingers than does anger.

Do you think that making particular facial expressions can affect your emotions? A simple experiment you can try alone or with friends or classmates is described in the *Try It!* In the *Try It!* activity, when you hold a pencil between your teeth, you activate the facial muscles used to express happiness. When you hold it between your lips, you activate the muscles involved in the expression of anger.

Try It!   Hold a pencil between your lips with your mouth closed, as shown in the left-hand drawing, for about 15 seconds. Pay attention to your feelings. Now hold the pencil between your teeth, letting your teeth show, as shown in the right-hand drawing, for about 15 seconds.

Did you have more pleasant feelings with the pencil between your lips or between your teeth? Why do you think that was so? (Adapted from Strack et al., 1988.)

Controlling Facial Expressions to Regulate Feelings   If facial expressions can activate emotions, than intensifying or weakening a facial expression might intensify or weaken the corresponding feeling state. Izard (1990) believes that learning to self-regulate emotional expression can help in controlling emotions. You might learn to change the intensity of an emotion by inhibiting, weakening, or amplifying its expression. Or you might change the emotion itself by simulating the expression of another emotion. Izard proposes that this approach to the regulation of emotion might be a useful adjunct to psychotherapy.

Gender Differences in Experiencing Emotion

Do females and males differ significantly in the ways they experience their emotions? Some research suggests that the answer may be yes.

In surveys of happiness, women report greater happiness and life satisfaction than men report (Wood et al., 1989). Paradoxically, women also report more sadness than men, are twice as likely to report being depressed, and admit to greater fear than men (Scherer et al., 1986). How can women be both happier and sadder than men? Another gender difference may explain it. Researchers have found sex differences in the intensity of emotional response. Grossman and Wood (1993) tested male and female participants for the intensity of emotional responses on five basic emotions— joy, love, fear, sadness, and anger. They found that "women reported more intense and more frequent emotions than men did, with the exception of anger" (p. 1013).

More joy, more sadness, more fear, more love! But these were self-reports. How did Grossman and Wood know that the female participants actually *felt* four of the five emotions more intensely than the males? The researchers also measured physiological arousal. The participants viewed slides depicting the various emotions while they were hooked up to an electromyograph to measure tension in the facial muscles. The researchers found that "women not only reported more intense emotional experience than men, but they also generated more extreme physiological reactions" (p. 1020). Other researchers agree that, in general, women respond with greater emotional intensity than men and thus can experience both greater joy and greater sorrow (Fujita et al., 1991).

An AIDS Memorial Quilt display evoked strong feelings of grief and sadness in both of these people, but the woman's visible emotional reaction is more intense.

Apply It!

The Quest for Happiness

"Life, Liberty and the pursuit of Happiness"—these ringing words from the Declaration of Independence are familiar to most of us, and most of us would agree that happiness is a desirable goal. But what exactly is happiness, and how can a person attain it? These questions are not as easily answered as you might expect.

Psychologists usually equate happiness with the feeling of well-being, the pervasive sense that life is good. As David G. Myers, a leader in the field of happiness research, puts it, well-being "is an ongoing perception that this time of one's life, or even life as a whole, is fulfilling, meaningful, and pleasant" (1992, p. 23). Happiness is closely related to life satisfaction—people who feel happy also tend to believe that their lives are satisfying.

Happiness does not appear to be associated with age, gender, race, or geographical location. Instead, it is related to self-satisfaction. Researchers have found that happy people tend to be energetic, decisive, flexible, creative, and sociable. Happy people are more trusting, loving, and responsive than sad people, tend to look at the brighter side of life, and are more willing to help those in need. They have high self-esteem and a sense of personal control, are optimistic, and enjoy social support—that is, they have a large circle of friends and often engage in rewarding social activities.

Although it is commonly believed that money can't buy happiness, there is a connection between money and a sense of well-being. When asked what would improve their quality of life, most people answer, "More money." It is true that many poor people are far from happy, but there are limits to the amount of happiness that money can buy. A survey of 49 wealthy Americans, all with net worths well over $100 million,

found them to be only slightly happier than average (Diener et al., 1985).

An important factor affecting happiness is the tendency to compare one's situation with that of other people. If you see yourself as struggling to make ends meet while everyone around you appears to be living in comfort and security, you will feel less joy and more stress. Indeed, surveys have shown that perceived wealth matters more than absolute wealth. As Myers points out, "actual income doesn't much influence happiness; how *satisfied* we are with our income does. If we're content with our income, regardless of how much it is, we're likely to say we're happy." To put it another way, "satisfaction isn't so much getting what you want as wanting what you have" (1992, p. 39).

If good fortune in the form of wealth cannot buy certain and enduring happiness, does a life-shattering experience destroy all hope of future happiness?

Surprisingly, no. People who have suffered a tragic accident leading to blindness or paralysis (such as Christopher Reeve) tend to return to a near-normal state of day-to-day happiness after a period of adjustment.

What can you do to make yourself happier from day to day? For one thing, you can smile more. Smiling really does induce feelings of happiness. Start with the *Try It!* on page 314. Then smile at other people—even people you don't like a lot. As the song goes, "Put on a happy face." Don't worry if it feels like pretending; after a while it will come naturally. "Act as if you like someone and soon you may," Myers notes (1992, p. 125).

Another way to make your life happier is to make the most of social occasions—phone calls, visits, meals with friends. Such occasions often require you to behave as if you were happy, which can actually serve to free you from unhappiness.

There are inevitably times when happiness seems far removed from life in the real world—times when we feel bored or anxious, overwhelmed by work, relationships, or life in general. However, there are also times when we are so caught up in an activity that we become oblivious to our surroundings and time seems to fly by. Psychologists refer to this feeling as *flow*. To be in flow is to be unselfconsciously absorbed (Csikszentmihalyi, 1990). People who are involved in some activity that engages their skills—whether it is work, play, or simply driving a car—report more positive feelings. "To experience flow," says Myers, "we need to find challenge and meaning in our work, and to seek experiences that fully engage our talents" (1992, p. 134). So, pursue happiness by living more *intentionally*—devoting more time to the things you do best and find most meaningful, while avoiding activities that waste time and bring little satisfaction, such as sleeping late, hanging out, and watching television.

In short, there are many things you can do to try to become happier. Myers sums them up in these words:

> You and I can *decide* to exercise, to allow enough hours for sleep, to make comparisons that remind us of our blessings, to manage our time in ways that boost our sense of control, . . . to initiate relationships, to devote effort to maintaining love rather than taking it for granted, to plan involving rather than passive leisure activities, . . . and even to begin working at reshaping our culture in ways that will promote the well-being that fame and fortune can't buy. (1992, p. 207; emphasis added)

SUMMARY AND REVIEW

INTRODUCTION TO MOTIVATION

What is the difference between intrinsic and extrinsic motivation?

With intrinsic motivation, an act is performed because it is satisfying or pleasurable in and of itself; with extrinsic motivation, an act is performed to bring a reward or to avert an undesirable consequence.

Key Terms
motivation (p. 289); motives (p. 289); incentive (p. 289); intrinsic motivation (p. 290); extrinsic motivation (p. 290)

THEORIES OF MOTIVATION

How do instinct theories explain motivation?

Instinct theories suggest that human behavior is motivated by certain innate, unlearned tendencies—or instincts—which are shared by all people.

How does drive-reduction theory explain motivation?

Drive-reduction theory suggests that a biological need creates an unpleasant state of arousal or tension called a drive, which impels the organism to engage in behavior that will satisfy the need and reduce the tension.

How does arousal theory explain motivation?

Arousal theory suggests that the aim of motivation is to maintain an optimal level of arousal. If arousal is less than optimal, a person engages in activities that stimulate arousal; if arousal exceeds the optimal level, the person seeks to reduce stimulation.

How does Maslow's hierarchy of needs account for human motivation?

Maslow's hierarchy of needs arranges needs in order of urgency—from physical needs (food, water, air, and shelter) to security needs, belonging and love needs, esteem needs, and finally the need for self-actualization (developing to one's full potential) at the top. Theoretically, the needs at the lower levels of the hierarchy must be satisfied adequately before a person will be motivated to fulfill the higher needs.

Key Terms
instinct (p. 290); instinct theory (p. 291); drive-reduction theory (p. 291); drive (p. 291); homeostasis (p. 291); arousal theory (p. 292); arousal (p. 292); Yerkes–Dodson law (p. 292); stimulus motives (p. 292); sensory deprivation (p. 293); hierarchy of needs (p. 293); self-actualization (p. 293)

HUNGER: A PRIMARY DRIVE

What are the roles of the lateral hypothalamus and the ventromedial hypothalamus in the regulation of eating behavior?

The lateral hypothalamus (LH) apparently acts as a feeding center—when it is activated, it signals the animal to eat; when it is destroyed, the animal refuses to eat. The ventromedial hypothalamus (VMH) evidently acts as a satiety center—when it is activated, it signals the animal to stop eating; when it is destroyed, the animal overeats, becoming obese.

What are some of the body's hunger and satiety signals?

Some of the body's hunger signals are stomach contractions, low blood glucose levels, and high insulin levels. Some satiety signals are high blood glucose levels and the presence in the blood of other satiety substances (such as CCK), secreted by the gastrointestinal tract during digestion.

What are some nonbiological factors that influence what and how much people eat?

External eating cues such as the taste, smell, and appearance of food, the variety of food offered, as well as the time of day, can cause people to eat more food than they actually need.

What are some factors that account for variations in body weight?

Variations in body weight are influenced by genes, metabolic rate, activity level, number of fat cells, and eating habits.

How does set point affect body weight?

Set-point theory suggests an internal homeostatic system that functions to maintain body weight by adjusting appetite and metabolic rate.

Why is it almost impossible to maintain weight loss by cutting calories alone?

It is almost impossible to maintain weight loss by cutting calories alone because a dieter's metabolic rate slows down to compensate for the lower intake of calories. Exercise both prevents the lowering of metabolic rate and burns up additional calories.

What are the symptoms of anorexia nervosa?

The symptoms of anorexia nervosa are an overwhelming, irrational fear of be-

ing fat, compulsive dieting to the point of self-starvation, and excessive weight loss.

What are the symptoms of bulimia nervosa?

The symptoms of bulimia nervosa are repeated and uncontrolled episodes of binge eating, usually followed by purging, that is, self-induced vomiting and/or the use of large quantities of laxatives and diuretics.

Key Terms
primary drive (p. 294); lateral hypothalamus (LH) (p. 294); ventromedial hypothalamus (VMH) (p. 295); metabolic rate (p. 297); fat cells (p. 297); set point (p. 298); anorexia nervosa (p. 299); bulimia nervosa (p. 300)

SEXUAL MOTIVES

What were the famous Kinsey surveys?

In the 1940s and 1950s Alfred Kinsey and his associates conducted the first major surveys of the sexual attitudes and behaviors of American men and women.

According to Masters and Johnson, what are the four phases of the human sexual response cycle?

The sexual response cycle consists of four phases: excitement phase, plateau phase, orgasm, and resolution phase.

What are the male and female sex hormones, and how do they affect sexual desire and activity in males and females?

The female sex hormones are estrogen and progesterone; the male sex hormones are the androgens, the most important of which is testosterone. Testosterone affects sexual interest and the ability to have an erection in males, and small amounts are necessary for females to maintain sexual interest and responsiveness.

Key Terms
coitus (p. 301); sexual response cycle (p. 302); excitement phase (p. 303); plateau phase (p. 303); orgasm (p. 303); resolution phase (p. 303); estrogen (p. 303); progesterone (p. 303); testosterone (p. 303)

SEXUAL ORIENTATION

What is meant by sexual orientation?

Sexual orientation refers to the direction of a person's sexual preference—toward members of the opposite sex (heterosexuality), toward members of the same sex (homosexuality), or toward both sexes (bisexuality).

What are the various biological factors that have been suggested as possible determinants of a gay or lesbian sexual orientation?

The biological factors suggested as possible causes of a gay or lesbian sexual orientation are (1) abnormal levels of androgens during prenatal development, which could masculinize or feminize the brain of the developing fetus; (2) structural differences in an area of the hypothalamus of gay men; and (3) genetic factors.

What does the study by Bell, Weinberg, and Hammersmith reveal about the developmental experiences of gay men and lesbians?

In comparing gay men and lesbians to heterosexual controls, Bell, Weinberg, and Hammersmith were unable to trace differences between the two groups to problems in parental relationships. The only commonality was that as children, gays did not feel that they were like others of their sex.

Key Terms
sexual orientation (p. 303)

SOCIAL MOTIVES

What is Murray's contribution to the study of motivation?

Murray developed a list of social motives, or needs, and developed the Thematic Apperception Test (TAT) to assess a person's level of these needs.

What is the need for achievement?

The need for achievement (*n* Ach) is the need to accomplish something difficult and to perform at a high standard of excellence.

What are some characteristics shared by people who are high in achievement motivation?

People high in achievement motivation enjoy challenges and like to compete. They tend to set goals of moderate difficulty, are more motivated by hope of success than fear of failure, and attribute their success to their ability and hard work.

Key Terms
social motives (p. 306); Thematic Apperception Test (TAT) (p. 306); need for achievement (*n* Ach) (p. 306)

THE WHAT AND WHY OF EMOTIONS

What are the three components of emotion?

An emotion is a feeling state that involves physiological arousal, cognitive appraisal of the arousing situation, and outward expression of the emotion.

According to the James–Lange theory, what sequence of events occurs when an individual experiences an emotion?

According to the James–Lange theory, environmental stimuli produce a physiological response, and then awareness of this response causes the emotion to be experienced.

What is the Cannon–Bard theory of emotion?

The Cannon–Bard theory suggests that emotion-provoking stimuli received by the senses are relayed simultaneously to the cortex, providing the mental experience of the emotion, and to the sympathetic nervous system, producing the physiological arousal.

According to the Schachter–Singer theory, what two factors must occur in order for a person to experience an emotion?

The Schachter–Singer theory states that for an emotion to occur (1) there must be physiological arousal, and (2) the person must perceive some reason for the arousal in order to label the emotion.

According to Lazarus, what sequence of events occurs when an individual feels an emotion?

An emotion-provoking stimulus triggers a cognitive appraisal, which is followed by the emotion and the physiological arousal.

Key Terms
emotion (p. 307); James–Lange theory (p. 308); Cannon–Bard theory (p. 309); Schachter–Singer theory (p. 309); Lazarus theory (p. 309)

THE EXPRESSION OF EMOTION

What are basic emotions?

The basic emotions (happiness, sadness, disgust, and so on) are those that are unlearned and that are reflected in the same facial expressions in all cultures.

How does the development of facial expressions of different emotions in infants suggest a biological basis for emotional expression?

The facial expressions develop in a particular sequence in infants and seem to be the result of maturation rather than learning. The same sequence occurs even in children who have been blind and deaf since birth.

Key Terms
basic emotions (p. 311); display rules (p. 312)

EXPERIENCING EMOTION

What is the facial-feedback hypothesis?

The facial-feedback hypothesis suggests that the muscular movements involved in certain facial expressions trigger the corresponding emotion (for example, smiling triggers happiness).

Key Terms
facial-feedback hypothesis (p. 313)

Study Guide for Chapter 9

Answers to all the Study Guide questions are provided at the end of the book.

Section One: Chapter Review

1. When you engage in an activity in order to gain a reward or to avoid an unpleasant consequence, your motivation is (intrinsic, extrinsic).

2. In its original form, drive-reduction theory focused primarily on which of the following needs and the drives they produce?
   a. cognitive
   b. psychological
   c. biological
   d. emotional

3. Which theory suggests that human behavior is motivated by certain innate, unlearned tendencies that are shared by all individuals?
   a. arousal theory
   b. instinct theory
   c. Maslow's theory
   d. drive-reduction theory

4. According to arousal theory, people seek _____ arousal.
   a. minimized
   b. increased
   c. decreased
   d. optimal

5. According to Maslow's hierarchy of needs, which needs must be satisfied before a person will try to satisfy the belonging and love needs?
   a. safety and self-actualization needs
   b. self-actualization needs and esteem needs
   c. physiological and safety needs
   d. physiological and esteem needs

6. The lateral hypothalamus (LH) acts as a (feeding, satiety) center; the ventromedial hypothalamus (VMH) acts as a (feeding, satiety) center.

7. All of the following are hunger signals except
   a. activity of the lateral hypothalamus.
   b. low levels of glucose in the blood.
   c. the hormone CCK.
   d. a high insulin level.

8. Foods that are sweet and high in fat tend to stimulate the appetite. (true/false)

9. Which factor is most responsible for how fast your body burns calories to produce energy?
   a. calories consumed
   b. fat cells
   c. eating habits
   d. metabolic rate

10. According to set-point theory, the body works to (increase, decrease, maintain) body weight.

11. Fat cells never decrease in number. (true/false)

12. Adopted children are more likely to be very thin or obese if their (biological, adoptive) parents are very thin or obese.

13. Increased exercise during dieting is important to counteract the body's tendency to
    a. increase the fat in the fat cells.
    b. increase the number of fat cells.
    c. lower its metabolic rate.
    d. raise its metabolic rate.

14. Compulsive dieting to the point of self-starvation is the defining symptom of _____; binge eating followed by purging is the main symptom of _____.

15. Who conducted the first major surveys of sexual attitudes and behaviors of American males and females?
    a. Alfred Kinsey
    b. Masters and Johnson
    c. George Gallup
    d. Laumann and others

16. Men and women have equally permissive attitudes toward premarital sex. (true/false)

17. Which of the following statements about the human sexual response is false?
    a. It consists of four phases.
    b. It occurs in sexual intercourse and can occur in other types of sexual activity.
    c. It is quite different in males and females.
    d. It was researched by Masters and Johnson.

18. Androgens, estrogen, and progesterone are present in both males and females. (true/false)

19. Testosterone plays a role in maintaining sexual interest in males and females. (true/false)

20. The direction of one's sexual preference—toward members of the opposite sex or members of one's own sex—is termed one's
    a. sexual role.
    b. sexual orientation.
    c. sexual desire.
    d. sexual motive.

21. Statistics suggest that homosexuality is twice as common in males as in females. (true/false)

22. Which of the following did Bell, Weinberg, and Hammersmith's study reveal about their gay and lesbian participants?
    a. They were likely to have been seduced or molested by adult homosexuals.
    b. As adolescents, they did not have normal opportunities for dating.
    c. As children, they did not feel that they were like others of their gender.
    d. As children, they had disturbed relationships with their parents.

23. Social motives are mostly unlearned. (true/false)

24. According to McClelland, which of the following is *not* a major factor in determining whether a person high in *n* Ach approaches a goal?
    a. the strength of the need for achievement
    b. the expectation of success
    c. how much pride would result from achieving the goal as opposed to how upsetting failure would be
    d. the financial reward attached to the goal

25. Which statement is *not* true of people high in *n* Ach?
    a. They set very high goals, which will be extremely difficult to attain.
    b. They set goals of moderate difficulty.
    c. They attribute their success to their talents, abilities, and hard work.
    d. They are not gamblers.

26. According to the text, emotions have all of the following *except* a _____ component.
    a. physical   c. sensory
    b. cognitive   d. behavioral

27. Which theory of emotion holds that you feel a true emotion only when you become physically aroused and can identify some cause for the arousal?
    a. Schachter–Singer theory
    b. James–Lange theory
    c. Cannon–Bard theory
    d. Lazarus theory

28. Which theory of emotion suggests that you would feel fearful because you were trembling?
    a. Schachter–Singer theory
    b. James–Lange theory
    c. Cannon–Bard theory
    d. Lazarus theory

29. Which theory suggests that the feeling of emotion and the physiological response to an emotional situation occur at about the same time?
    a. Schachter–Singer theory
    b. James–Lange theory
    c. Cannon–Bard theory
    d. Lazarus theory

30. Which theory suggests that the physiological arousal and the emotion flow from a cognitive appraisal of an emotion-provoking event?
    a. Schachter–Singer theory
    b. James–Lange theory
    c. Cannon–Bard theory
    d. Lazarus theory

31. Which of the following is *not* true of the basic emotions?
    a. They are reflected in distinctive facial expressions.
    b. They are found in all cultures.
    c. There are several hundred known to date.
    d. They are unlearned.

32. Which of the following is not one of the emotions represented by a distinctive facial expression?
    a. happiness   c. surprise
    b. hostility   d. sadness

33. Facial expressions associated with the basic emotions develop naturally according to a child's own biological timetable of maturation. (true/false)

34. People show stronger emotional reactions to positive stimuli than to negative stimuli. (true/false)

35. All of the following are true of display rules *except* that they
    a. are the same in all cultures.
    b. dictate when and where emotions should be expressed.
    c. dictate what emotions should not be expressed.
    d. often cause people to display emotions they do not feel.

36. The idea that making a happy, sad, or angry face can actually trigger the psychological response and feeling associated with the emotion is called the
    a. emotion production theory.
    b. emotion and control theory.
    c. facial-feedback hypothesis.
    d. facial expression theory.

Section Two: Important Psychologists and Concepts

On the line opposite each name, list the major concept or theory discussed in this chapter.

Name	Major Concept or Theory
1. Hull	_____
2. Maslow	_____
3. Murray	_____
4. James and Lange	_____
5 Cannon and Bard	_____
6. Lazarus	_____
7. Tomkins	_____

Section Three: Fill In the Blank

1. _____ are needs or desires that energize and direct behavior toward a goal.

2. Jeffery mows his parents' lawn and, in the winter, shovels his own and his elderly neighbor's sidewalk. He does this because he enjoys helping others. Jeffery is responding to _____ motivation.

3. Fred will only help around the house if he receives a financial reward or special privilege. Fred responds to _____ motivation.

4. Your dog walks around her bed three times before she lies down, and other dog owners tell you similar stories about their pets. This behavior seems to be inborn, unlearned, and fixed, and is thus an example of an _____.

5. Jack always wants to ride the wildest rides at the amusement park . He also seems to get bored very easily and then finds a way to create action in his environment. His behavior would probably best be explained by the _____ theory of motivation.

6. The _____ hypothalamus acts as the feeding center, and the _____ hypothalamus acts as the satiety center.

7. The most important factor in successful long-term weight loss is _____.

8. _____ nervosa involves rigid restriction of calorie intake; _____ nervosa involves a cycle of bingeing and purging.

9. Needs for affiliation, power, or achievement are _____ motives.

10. The _____ theory of emotion says that we experience emotion as a result of becoming aware of our physical response to a situation.

11. The _____ theory of emotion says that our physical response to a stimulus and our emotional response occur at the same time.

12. The _____ theory of emotion says that we experience a physical response to a stimulus and then give it meaning; from this comes our emotional response.

13. Feelings of fear, anger, disgust, surprise, joy, or happiness have been identified as _____ emotions.

14. Research suggests that people have stronger reactions to _____ stimuli than to _____ stimuli.

15. The _____ phase is the beginning of the human sexual response cycle.

16. Males must have a sufficient level of _____ in order to maintain sexual interest and have an erection.

17. The tendency of the body to maintain a balanced internal state with regard to oxygen level, body temperature, blood sugar, water balance, and so forth is called _____.

18. Simon LeVay, a neuroscientist, reported that an area in the hypothalamus governing sexual behavior is about twice as large in _____ men as in _____ men.

Section Four: Comprehensive Practice Test

1. If James is responding to an incentive, he is responding to an _____ stimulus.
   a. external   c. explicit
   b. internal   d. intrinsic

2. Dan reads books on research and statistics because these subjects fascinate him; he really enjoys learning about new approaches to research and the results of major research projects. Dan is being driven by _____ motivation.
   a. intrinsic   c. academic
   b. intellectual   d. extrinsic

3. Jill studies chemistry every night because she wants to excel in this field; she believes she will make a great deal of money as a chemist. Jill is being driven mainly by _____ motivation.
   a. career   c. extrinsic
   b. intrinsic   d. academic

4. The primary characteristics of motivation are
   a. activation, persistence, and goal.
   b. activation, persistence, and reward.
   c. activation, persistence, and focus.
   d. activation, persistence, and intensity.

5. Research by Laumann and others (1994) indicated that people with one sexual partner are less happy than people with more than one partner. (true/false)

6. A _____ is a state of tension or arousal brought about by an underlying need, which motivates one to engage in behavior that will satisfy the need and reduce the tension.
   a. drive   c. tension stimulus
   b. balance stimulus d. homeostatic condition

7. Angel's behavior sometimes scares his friends. He drives his motorcycle fast, he loves bungee jumping, and he can't wait for his first parachute jump. These interests could be explained by the _____ theory of motivation.
   a. instinct   c. arousal
   b. risky shift   d. homeostasis

8. According to Maslow, the need for love and affiliation is satisfied _____ basic biological needs and the need for safety.
   a. instead of   c. at the same time as
   b. before   d. after

9. Jim realizes that the goals he has set for himself are going to take too much time and effort so he decides to compromise and go for what he considers less difficult but more rational goals. Jim is a good example of a high achiever. (true/false)

10. When you are hungry, you experience the effects of the _____ hypothalamus; when you have eaten and feel full, you experience the effects of the _____ hypothalamus.
    a. proximal; distal
    b. distal; proximal
    c. ventromedial; lateral
    d. lateral; ventromedial

11. The orgasm is the shortest phase in the sexual response cycle. (true/false)

12. Murray developed the Thematic Apperception Test as a way to measure
    a. anger.
    b. personal perceptions of success.
    c. personal needs.
    d. social needs.

13. A person with a _____ n Ach is likely to set either very low goals or impossibly high goals.
    a. high   c. low
    b. moderate   d. borderline

14. Masters and Johnson concluded that the sexual response cycle is _____ for males and females.
    a. quite similar
    b. different
    c. variable
    d. instinctive

15. Surprisingly, boys who display early effeminate behavior spend more time with their fathers than their mothers. (true/false)

16. Which of the following theories asserts that, when presented with an emotion-producing stimulus, we feel the physiological effects and the subjective experience of emotion at about the same time?
    a. James–Lange
    b. Lazarus
    c. Cannon–Bard
    d. Schachter–Singer

17. All researchers who are doing work in the physiology of emotions agree that humans experience both basic emotions and instinctual responses such as fear, rage, and joy. (true/false)

18. Children need to be at least _____ months old before they show emotions such as empathy, envy, or embarrassment.
    a. 3   c. 9
    b. 6   d. 13

19. Diane smiled and thanked her friend for a birthday gift that she really did not like. Diane has learned the _____ of her culture.

    a. social rules   c. display rules
    b. interpersonal rules   d. expressive rules

20. The facial-feedback hypothesis states that the muscular movements that cause facial expressions trigger the corresponding emotions. (true/false)

Section Five: Critical Thinking

1. In your view, which theory or combination of theories best explains motivation: drive-reduction theory, arousal theory, or Maslow's hierarchy of needs? Which theory do you find least convincing? Support your answers.

2. Using what you have learned about body weight and dieting, select any well-known weight-loss plan (for example, Weight Watchers, Jenny Craig, Slim Fast) and evaluate it, explaining why it is or is not an effective way to lose weight and keep it off.

3. Which level of Maslow's hierarchy provides the strongest motivation for your behavior in general? Give specific examples to support your answer.

Personality Theory and Assessment

10

What makes us the way we are? Are the personality characteristics we exhibit influenced more markedly by genes or by the environment in which we live, grow, and develop? Environments can be strikingly different. Consider the environments described in the next two paragraphs.

Oskar Stohr was raised as a Catholic by his grandmother in Nazi Germany. As part of Hitler's youth movement, Oskar was expected to be an obedient Nazi. Book burnings, military parades, hatred of Jews, and the right hand raised with the salute "Heil Hitler" were all part of Oskar's early environment. How did this environment affect his personality?

Jack Yufe, the same age as Oskar, was raised by his Jewish father on the island of Trinidad. Far removed from the goose-stepping storm troopers in Nazi Germany, Jack enjoyed all of the educational advantages and social supports of a middle-class Jewish upbringing. How did Jack's environment affect his personality?

Though raised in starkly different environments, Oskar and Jack are amazingly alike. They have quick tempers, are domineering toward women, enjoy surprising people by faking sneezes in elevators, and flush the toilet before using it. They both read magazines from back to front, store rubber bands on their wrists, like spicy foods and sweet liqueurs, and dip buttered toast in their coffee.

The list of similarities between Oskar and Jack is much longer, but there is a good reason for them. The men are identical twins. They were separated shortly after birth when their father took Jack with him to the island of Trinidad, and their maternal grandmother raised Oskar in Germany.

Researchers at the Minnesota Center for Twin and Adoption Research are studying the effects of genetics and environment on identical twins reared apart. When Oskar and Jack first arrived at the center to take part in the study, they looked almost exactly alike physically, and both of them were wearing double-breasted blue shirts with epaulets, identical neatly trimmed mustaches, and wire-rimmed glasses. How powerfully the genes influence personality!

Joan Gardiner and Jean Nelson are another pair of identical twins in the Minnesota study. They were also raised apart, but their environments did not differ so markedly. Joan's adoptive mother and Jean's adoptive father were sister and brother, so the twins were together quite often.

Like Oskar and Jack, Joan and Jean have many similarities and a few differences. But one difference between the twins is so unusual that researchers are especially intrigued by it. Joan is musical; Jean is not. Although her adoptive mother was a piano teacher, Jean does not play. But Joan, whose adoptive mother was not a musician, plays piano very well—so well, in fact, that she has performed with the Minnesota Symphony Orchestra. Joan's mother made her practice piano several hours every day, while Jean's mother allowed her to pursue whatever interests she chose.

Duplicate genes but differences in musical ability—how do the researchers explain this? David Lykken of the Minnesota Center suggests that both twins have the same genetic musical capability, but the reason one plays and the other does not shows the effects produced by the environment. How powerfully the environment influences personality!

You have often heard it said that no two people are exactly alike, that each of us is unique. When most people talk about someone's uniqueness, they are referring to the personality. **Personality** is defined as an individual's characteristic patterns of behaving, thinking, and feeling (Carver & Scheier, 1996). And personalities are indeed different—consider Mother Theresa and Madonna, Howard Stern and Billy Graham, Eddie Murphy and Bill Cosby. What makes these people so different?

There are a number of theories that attempt to account for personality differences and explain how people come to be the way they are. In this chapter we explore some

personality: A person's characteristic patterns of behavior, thinking, and feeling.

psychoanalysis (SY-co-ah-NAL-ih-sis): Freud's term for his theory of personality and his therapy for treating psychological disorders.

of the major personality theories and a variety of tests and inventories used to assess personality.

SIGMUND FREUD AND PSYCHOANALYSIS

To what two aspects of Freud's work does the term *psychoanalysis* apply?

Most textbooks begin their exploration of personality theory with Sigmund Freud, and for good reason. Freud created one of the first and most controversial personality theories. Using information gained while treating his patients and from his own life experiences, Freud developed the theory of **psychoanalysis**. When you hear the term *psychoanalysis*, you may picture a psychiatrist treating a troubled patient on a couch. But psychoanalysis is much more than that. The term refers not only to a therapy for treating psychological disorders (which we will explore in Chapter 13) but also to a personality theory.

Link It!

Freud's theory of psychoanalysis is neither the extension of an earlier theory nor a reaction against one. It is largely original, and it was revolutionary and shocking to the 19th- and early 20th-century European audience to which it was introduced. The major components of Freud's theory, and perhaps the most controversial, are (1) the central role of the sexual instinct, (2) the concept of infantile sexuality, and (3) the dominant part played by the unconscious in moving and shaping human thought and behavior. Freud's theory assumes a psychic determinism, the view that there is a cause for every thought, idea, feeling, action, or behavior. Nothing happens by chance or accident; everything we do and even everything we forget to do has a cause behind it.

A married man vacationing alone in Hawaii sends his wife a postcard and writes, "Having a wonderful time! Wish you were her." The husband, no doubt, would protest that he was writing hurriedly and accidentally left off the *e*. His wife might suspect otherwise, and Freud would agree. The "her" was no accident. It was a Freudian slip. Slips of the tongue, slips of the pen, and forgetting appointments—incidents we often call accidental—are not accidental at all, according to Freud (1901/1960).

The Conscious, the Preconscious, and the Unconscious: Levels of Awareness

What are the three levels of awareness in consciousness?

Freud believed that there are three levels of awareness in consciousness: the conscious, the preconscious, and the unconscious. The **conscious** consists of whatever a person is aware of at any given moment—a thought, a feeling, a sensation, or a memory. When attention shifts, there is a change in the content of the conscious.

conscious (KON-shus): The thoughts, feelings, sensations, or memories of which a person is aware at any given moment.

preconscious: The thoughts, feelings, and memories that a person is not consciously aware of at the moment but that may be brought to consciousness.

unconscious (un-KON-shus): For Freud, the primary motivating force of behavior, containing repressed memories as well as instincts and wishes that have never been conscious.

Freud's **preconscious** is very much like long-term memory. It contains all the memories, feelings, experiences, and perceptions that you are not consciously thinking about at the moment, but that may be brought to consciousness. Where did you go to high school? In what year were you born?

The most important of the three levels is the **unconscious,** which Freud believed to be the primary motivating force of human behavior. The unconscious holds memories that once were conscious but were so unpleasant or anxiety-provoking that they were repressed (involuntarily removed from consciousness). The unconscious also contains all of the instincts (sexual and aggressive), wishes, and desires that have never been allowed into consciousness. Freud traced the roots of psychological disorders to these impulses and repressed memories.

The Id, the Ego, and the Superego: Warring Components of the Personality

What are the roles of the id, the ego, and the superego?

In 1920, Freud (1923/1961) proposed a new conception of the personality, one that contained three systems—the id, the ego, and the superego. These systems do not exist physically; they are only concepts, or ways of looking at personality.

The **id** is the only part of the personality that is present at birth. It is inherited, primitive, inaccessible, and completely unconscious. The id contains (1) the life instincts, which are the sexual instincts and the biological urges such as hunger and thirst, and (2) the death instinct, which accounts for aggressive and destructive impulses (Freud, 1933/1965). The id operates according to the **pleasure principle**; that is, it tries to seek pleasure, avoid pain, and gain immediate gratification of its wishes. The id is the source of the **libido**, the psychic energy that fuels the entire personality; yet the id cannot act on its own. It can only wish, image, fantasize, demand.

The **ego** is the logical, rational, realistic part of the personality. The ego evolves from the id and draws its energy from the id. One of the ego's functions is to satisfy the id's urges. But the ego, which is mostly conscious, acts according to the reality principle. It must consider the constraints of the real world in determining appropriate times, places, and objects for gratification of the id's wishes.

When a child is age 5 or 6, the **superego**—the moral component of the personality—is formed. The superego has two parts: (1) The "conscience" consists of all the behaviors for which the child has been punished and about which he or she feels guilty; (2) the "ego ideal" contains the behaviors for which the child has been praised and rewarded and about which he or she feels pride and satisfaction. At first the superego reflects only the parents' expectations of what is good and right, but it expands over time to incorporate teachings from the broader social world. In its quest for moral perfection, the superego sets guidelines that define and limit the ego's flexibility. A harsher judge than any external authority, including one's parents, the superego judges not only behavior, but also thoughts, feelings, and wishes.

Figure 10.1 describes the three systems of the personality.

Defense Mechanisms: Protecting the Ego

The id's demands for sensual pleasure are often in direct conflict with the superego's desire for moral perfection. So at times the ego needs some way to defend itself against the anxiety created by the excessive demands of the id, by the harsh judgments of the superego, or by the sometimes threatening conditions in the environment. Often the ego can relieve anxiety by solving its problems rationally and

id (IHD): The unconscious system of the personality, which contains the life and death instincts and operates on the pleasure principle.

pleasure principle: The principle by which the id operates to seek pleasure, avoid pain, and obtain immediate gratification.

libido (lih-BEE-doe): Freud's name for the psychic or sexual energy that comes from the id and provides the energy for the entire personality.

ego (EE-go): In Freudian theory, the rational, largely conscious system of personality, which operates according to the reality principle.

superego (sue-per-EE-go): The moral system of the personality, which consists of the conscience and the ego ideal.

What is a defense mechanism?

Structure	Level of Consciousness	Characteristics
Id	Unconscious	Primitive component containing the sexual instincts, biological urges, and aggressive and destructive impulses. Source of the libido. Operates according to the pleasure principle, seeking immediate gratification. Impulsive, amoral, and selfish.
Ego	Largely conscious, partly unconscious	Logical, rational component, which functions to satisfy the id's urges and carry out transactions in the real world. Acts according to the reality principle.
Superego	Both conscious and unconscious	The moral component, consisting of the conscience and the ego ideal. Sets moral guidelines, which limit the flexibility of the ego.

Figure 10.1

Freud's Conception of Personality

According to Freud, personality is composed of three structures, or systems: the id, the ego, and the superego. Their characteristics are diagrammed and described here.

Review & Reflect 10.1 Defense Mechanisms

Defense Mechanism	Description	Example
Repression	Involuntarily removing an unpleasant memory from consciousness or barring disturbing sexual and aggressive impulses from consciousness	Jill forgets a traumatic incident from childhood.
Projection	Attributing one's own undesirable traits or impulses to another	A very lonely divorced woman accuses all men of having only one thing on their minds.
Denial	Refusing to acknowledge consciously the existence of danger or a threatening situation	Amy fails to take a tornado warning seriously and is severely injured.
Rationalization	Supplying a logical, rational reason rather than the real reason for an action or event	Fred tells his friend that he didn't get the job because he didn't have connections.
Regression	Reverting to a behavior characteristic of an earlier stage of development	Susan bursts into tears whenever she is criticized.
Reaction formation	Expressing exaggerated ideas and emotions that are the opposite of disturbing, unconscious impulses and desires	A former purchaser of pornography, Bob is now a tireless crusader against it.
Displacement	Substituting a less threatening object for the original object of an impulse	After being spanked by his father, Bill hits his baby brother.
Sublimation	Rechanneling sexual and aggressive energy into pursuits that society considers acceptable or even admirable	Tim goes to a gym to work out when he feels hostile and frustrated.

defense mechanism: An unconscious, irrational means used by the ego to defend against anxiety; involves self-deception and the distortion of reality.

repression: Involuntarily removing an unpleasant memory or barring disturbing sexual and aggressive impulses from consciousness.

directly. When it cannot do so, it must resort to irrational defenses against anxiety, called *defense mechanisms*. Freud's daughter Anna (1966), also a psychoanalyst, contributed much to the understanding of defense mechanisms.

A **defense mechanism** is a technique used to defend against anxiety and to maintain self-esteem, but it involves self-deception and an altering of "perception of both internal and external reality" (Vaillant, 1994). People use defense mechanisms to protect themselves from failure and from guilt-producing desires or actions. Defense mechanisms are like painkillers. They lessen the pain of anxiety, but do not cure the problem; and if they are to work, they must be unconscious. All people use defense mechanisms to some degree; it is only their overuse that is considered abnormal. *Review & Reflect 10.1* summarizes the defense mechanisms.

What are two ways in which repression operates?

Repression: Out of Mind, Out of Sight   According to Freud, **repression** is the most important and the most frequently used defense mechanism, and it is present to some degree in all other defense mechanisms. Repression operates in two ways: (1) It can remove painful or threatening memories, thoughts, ideas, or perceptions from consciousness and keep them in the unconscious; (2) it can prevent unconscious but disturbing sexual and aggressive impulses from breaking into consciousness.

Even though they are repressed, the memories lurk in the unconscious and exert an active influence on personality and behavior. In fact, Freud (1933/1965) said repressed memories are "virtually immortal; after the passage of decades, they behave as though they had just occurred" (p. 74). This is why repressed traumatic events of childhood can cause psychological disorders (neuroses) in adults. Freud believed that the way to cure such disorders is to bring the repressed material back to consciousness. This was what he tried to accomplish through his system of therapy, psychoanalysis.

Other Defense Mechanisms: Excuses, Substitutions, and Denials   There are several other defense mechanisms that people may use from time to time. They use **projection** when they attribute their own undesirable impulses, thoughts, personality traits, or behavior to others, or when they minimize the undesirable in themselves and exaggerate it in others. Projection allows people to avoid acknowledging unacceptable traits and thereby to maintain self-esteem, but it seriously distorts their perception of the external world. For example, a sexually promiscuous husband or wife may accuse the partner of being unfaithful.

Denial is a refusal to acknowledge consciously or to believe that a danger or a threatening condition exists. Many people who abuse alcohol and drugs deny that they have a problem. Yet denial is sometimes useful as a temporary means of getting through a crisis until a more permanent adjustment can be made, such as when people initially deny the existence of a terminal illness.

Rationalization occurs when a person unconsciously supplies a logical, rational, or socially acceptable reason rather than the real reason for an action or event. Rationalization can be used to justify past, present, or future behaviors or to soften the disappointment connected with not attaining a desired goal. When people rationalize, they make excuses for, or justify, failures and mistakes. A student who did not study and then failed a test might complain, "The test was unfair."

Sometimes, when frustrated or anxious, people may use **regression** and revert to behavior that might have reduced anxiety at an earlier stage of development. A 5-year-old child with a new baby sister or brother may regress and suck her thumb or drag a blanket around the house. An adult may have a temper tantrum, rant and rave, or throw things.

Reaction formation is at work when people express exaggerated ideas and emotions that are the opposite of their disturbing, unconscious impulses and desires. In reaction formation the conscious thought or feeling masks the unconscious one. Unconscious hatred may be expressed as love and devotion, cruelty as kindness. A reaction formation may be suspected when a behavior is extreme, excessive, and compulsive, as when a former chain smoker becomes irate and complains loudly at the faintest whiff of cigarette smoke. Reaction formation can be viewed as a barrier a person unconsciously erects to keep from acting on an unacceptable impulse.

Displacement occurs when a person substitutes a less threatening object or person for the original object of a sexual or aggressive impulse. If your boss makes you angry, you may take out your hostility on your boyfriend or girlfriend, husband or wife.

With **sublimation**, people rechannel sexual or aggressive energy into pursuits or accomplishments that society considers acceptable or even praiseworthy. An aggressive person may rechannel the aggression and become a football or hockey player, a boxer, a surgeon, or a butcher. Freud viewed sublimation as the only completely healthy ego defense mechanism. In fact, Freud (1930/1962) considered all advancements in civilization to be the result of sublimation.

The Psychosexual Stages of Development: Centered on the Erogenous Zones

The sex instinct, Freud said, is the most important factor influencing personality; but it does not suddenly appear full-blown at puberty. It is present at birth and then develops through a series of **psychosexual stages**. Each stage centers on a particular eroge-

What are some other defense mechanisms?

projection: Attributing one's own undesirable thoughts, impulses, traits, or behaviors to others.

denial: Refusing to acknowledge consciously the existence of danger or a threatening condition.

rationalization: Supplying a logical, rational, socially acceptable reason rather than the real reason for an action.

regression: Reverting to a behavior characteristic of an earlier stage of development.

reaction formation: Denying an unacceptable impulse, often a sexual or aggressive one, by giving strong conscious expression to its opposite.

displacement: Substituting a less threatening object for the original object of an impulse.

sublimation: Rechanneling sexual or aggressive energy into pursuits that society considers acceptable or admirable.

psychosexual stages: A series of stages through which the sexual instinct develops; each stage is defined by an erogenous zone that becomes the center of new pleasures and conflicts.

What are the psychosexual stages, and why did Freud consider them so important in personality development?

nous zone, a part of the body that provides pleasurable sensations and around which a conflict arises (1905/1953b; 1920/1963b). If the conflict is not resolved without undue difficulty, the child may develop a **fixation**. This means that a portion of the libido (psychic energy) remains invested at that stage, leaving less energy to meet the challenges of future stages. Overindulgence at a stage may leave a person unwilling psychologically to move on to the next stage. But too little gratification may leave the person trying to make up for previously unmet needs. Freud believed that certain personality characteristics develop as a result of difficulty at one or another of the stages.

The Oral Stage (Birth to 12 or 18 Months)   During the **oral stage**, the mouth is the primary source of an infant's sensual pleasure, which Freud (1920/1963b) considered to be an expression of infantile sexuality. The conflict at this stage centers on weaning. Too much or too little gratification may result in an oral fixation—an excessive preoccupation with oral activities such as eating, drinking, smoking, gum chewing, nail biting, and even kissing. Freud claimed that difficulties at the oral stage can result in personality traits such as either excessive dependence, optimism, and gullibility (tendency to "swallow" anything) or extreme pessimism, sarcasm, hostility, and aggression.

The Anal Stage (1 or 1½ to 3 Years)   During the **anal stage**, children derive sensual pleasure, Freud believed, from expelling and withholding feces. But a conflict arises when toilet training begins, because this is one of the parents' first attempts to have children postpone gratification. When parents are harsh in their approach, children may rebel openly, defecating whenever and wherever they please. This may lead to an anal expulsive personality—someone who is sloppy, irresponsible, rebellious, hostile, and destructive. Other children may defy their parents and gain attention by withholding feces. They may develop anal retentive personalities, gaining security through what they possess and becoming stingy, stubborn, rigid, excessively neat and clean, orderly, and precise (Freud, 1933/1965).

The Phallic Stage (3 to 5 or 6 Years)   During the **phallic stage**, children learn that they can derive pleasure from touching their genitals, and masturbation is common. They become aware of the anatomical differences in males and females and may begin to "play doctor."

The conflict that develops at this stage is a sexual desire for the parent of the opposite sex and a hostility toward the same-sex parent, a conflict Freud called the **Oedipus complex** (after the central character in the Greek tragedy *Oedipus Rex*, by Sophocles). "Boys concentrate their sexual wishes upon their mother and develop hostile impulses against their father as being a rival" (1925/1963a, p. 61). But the young boy eventually develops castration anxiety—an intense fear that his father might retaliate and harm him by cutting off his penis, the offending organ (1933/1965). This fear becomes so intense, Freud believed, that the boy usually resolves the Oedipus complex by identifying with his father and repressing his sexual feelings for his mother. With identification, the child takes on his father's behaviors, mannerisms, and superego standards, and in this way the superego develops (Freud, 1930/1962).

Girls experience a similar internal Oedipal conflict that is often referred to as the Electra complex, although Freud did not use that term. When young girls discover they have no penis, they develop "penis envy," Freud claimed, and they turn to their father because he has the desired organ (1933/1965). They feel sexual desires for him and develop jealousy and rivalry toward their mother. But eventually girls, too, experience anxiety as a result of their hostile feelings. They repress their sexual feelings toward the father and identify with the mother, leading to the formation of their superego (Freud, 1930/1962).

According to Freud, failure to resolve these conflicts can have serious consequences for both boys and girls. Freud thought that tremendous guilt and anxiety

Freud believed that a fixation at the anal stage, resulting from harsh parental pressure, could lead to an anal retentive personality—characterized by excessive stubbornness, rigidity, and neatness.

What is the Oedipus complex?

fixation: Arrested development at a psychosexual stage occurring because of excessive gratification or frustration at that stage.

oral stage: Freud's first psychosexual stage (birth to 1 or 1½ years), in which sensual pleasure is derived mainly through stimulation of the mouth.

anal stage: Freud's second psychosexual stage (ages 1 or 1½ to 3 years), in which the child derives sensual pleasure mainly from expelling and withholding feces.

phallic stage: Freud's third psychosexual stage (ages 3 to 5 or 6 years), during which sensual pleasure is derived mainly through touching the genitals, and the Oedipus complex arises.

could be carried over into adulthood and cause sexual problems, great difficulty relating to members of the opposite sex, and even homosexuality.

The Latency Period (5 or 6 Years to Puberty)   Following the stormy phallic stage, the **latency period** is one of relative calm. The sex instinct is repressed and temporarily sublimated in school and play activities, hobbies, and sports. And children prefer same-sex friends and playmates.

The Genital Stage (from Puberty On)   In the **genital stage**, the focus of sexual energy gradually shifts to the opposite sex for the vast majority of people, culminating in heterosexual love and the attainment of full adult sexuality. Freud believed that the few who reach the genital stage without having fixations at earlier stages can achieve the state of psychological health that he equated with the ability to love and work.

Review & Reflect 10.2 provides a summary of Freud's psychosexual stages.

Freud's Explanation of Personality

According to Freud, personality is almost completely formed at age 5 or 6, when the Oedipal conflict is resolved and the superego is formed. He believed that there are two primary sources of influence on personality: (1) the traits that develop because of fixations at any of the psychosexual stages, and (2) the relative strengths of the id, the ego, and the superego. In psychologically healthy people, there is a balance among the three components. If the id is too strong and the superego too weak, people will

Oedipus complex (ED-uh-pus): Occurring in the phallic stage, a conflict in which the child is sexually attracted to the opposite-sex parent and feels hostility toward the same-sex parent.

latency period: The period following Freud's phallic stage (ages 5 or 6 years to puberty), in which the sex instinct is largely repressed and temporarily sublimated in school and play activities.

genital stage: Freud's final psychosexual stage (from puberty on), in which for most people the focus of sexual energy gradually shifts to the opposite sex, culminating in the attainment of full adult sexuality.

According to Freud, what are the two primary sources of influence on the personality?

Review & Reflect 10.2   Freud's Psychosexual Stages of Development

Stage	Erogenous Zone	Conflicts/Experiences	Adult Traits Associated with Problems at This Stage
Oral (birth to 12–18 months)	Mouth	Weaning Oral gratification from sucking, eating, biting	Optimism, gullibility, dependency, pessimism, passivity, hostility, sarcasm, aggression
Anal (12–18 months to 3 years)	Anus	Toilet training Gratification from expelling and withholding feces	Excessive cleanliness, orderliness, stinginess, messiness, rebelliousness, destructiveness
Phallic (3 to 5–6 years)	Genitals	Oedipal conflict Sexual curiosity Masturbation	Flirtatiousness, vanity, promiscuity, pride, chastity
Latency (5–6 years to puberty)	None	Period of sexual calm Interest in school, hobbies, same-sex friends	
Genital (puberty onward)	Genitals	Revival of sexual interests Establishment of mature sexual relationships	

take pleasure and gratify desires, no matter who is hurt or what the cost, and not feel guilty. But a tyrannical superego will leave people with perpetual guilt feelings, unable to enjoy sensual pleasure.

Evaluating Freud's Contribution

Freud's theory is so comprehensive (he wrote more than 24 volumes) that its elements must be evaluated separately. His beliefs that women are inferior to men sexually, morally, and intellectually and that they suffer penis envy seem ridiculous today. However, psychology is indebted to him for emphasizing the influence of early childhood experiences on later development.

Critics charge that much of Freud's theory defies scientific testing. How, they ask, can a conceptual framework based on Freud's analysis of his own life and the case histories of his disturbed patients provide a theory of personality generalizable to the larger population? The most serious flaw critics find is that Freud's theory interprets and explains behavior after the fact and lacks the power to predict behavior (Stanovich, 1989). Some critics even go so far as to say that Freud's entire theory can be neither supported scientifically nor justified therapeutically (Crews, 1996; Erwin, 1996; Webster, 1995).

Freud believed that his concepts of the unconscious and the principles by which it operated were his most important work. In fact the primary aim of psychoanalysis is to bring unconscious thoughts, wishes, and desires to consciousness. Leading scholars today do not dispute the existence of unconscious processes (Loftus & Klinger, 1992). However, they do not see the unconscious as envisioned by Freud. Rather, unconscious mental activity is viewed more broadly as information processing that takes place below the level of awareness. For example, certain aspects of stereotypic thinking, though unconscious, strongly influence the way people process information related to themselves and others (Bargh, 1997). And research by Motley (1985) indicates that although the unconscious is sometimes at work in Freudian slips, most slips of the tongue should be attributed to misfirings in the brain and its verbal mechanisms.

Although Freud does not loom as large today as in decades past, his standing as a pioneer in psychology cannot be denied. In fact, when members of the general public are asked to name a famous psychologist, Freud's is still the name that comes most readily to mind (Stanovich, 1996).

THE NEO-FREUDIANS

Several personality theorists, referred to as *neo-Freudians*, started their careers as followers of Freud but began to disagree on certain basic principles of psychoanalytic theory. They modified aspects of the theory and presented their own original ideas about personality. We will discuss Carl Jung (analytical psychology), Alfred Adler (individual psychology), and Karen Horney.

Carl Gustav Jung: Delving into the Collective Unconscious

Carl Gustav Jung (1875–1961)

Carl Jung (1875–1961) differed with Freud on many major points. He did not consider the sexual instinct to be the main factor in personality; nor did he believe that the personality is almost completely formed in early childhood. For Jung (1933), middle age was an even more important period for personality development. He also disagreed with Freud on the basic structure of personality.

Jung's View of the Personality: A Different View of the Unconscious   Jung conceived of the personality as consisting of three parts: the ego, the personal unconscious, and the collective unconscious. He saw the ego as the conscious component of

Link It!

Link It!

According to Jung, what are the three components of personality?

332

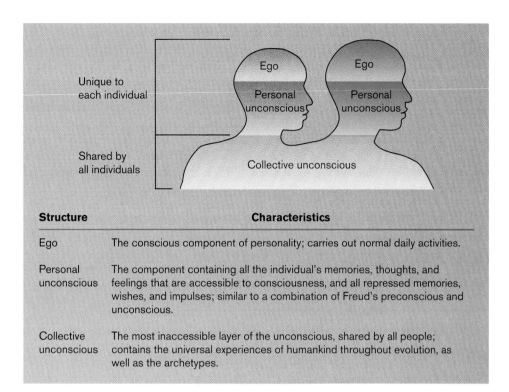

Figure 10.2

Jung's Conception of Personality

Like Freud, Carl Jung saw three components in personality. The ego and the personal unconscious are unique to each individual. The collective unconscious accounts for the similarity of myths and beliefs in diverse cultures.

Structure	Characteristics
Ego	The conscious component of personality; carries out normal daily activities.
Personal unconscious	The component containing all the individual's memories, thoughts, and feelings that are accessible to consciousness, and all repressed memories, wishes, and impulses; similar to a combination of Freud's preconscious and unconscious.
Collective unconscious	The most inaccessible layer of the unconscious, shared by all people; contains the universal experiences of humankind throughout evolution, as well as the archetypes.

personality, which carries out normal daily activities. Like Freud, he believed the ego to be secondary in importance to the unconscious.

The **personal unconscious** develops as a result of one's own experience and is therefore unique to each person. It contains all the experiences, thoughts, and perceptions accessible to the conscious, as well as repressed memories, wishes, and impulses. The personal unconscious resembles a combination of Freud's preconscious and unconscious.

The **collective unconscious** is the deepest and most inaccessible layer of the unconscious. Jung thought that the universal experiences of humankind throughout evolution are transmitted to each of us and reside in the collective unconscious. This is how he accounted for the similarity of certain myths, dreams, symbols, and religious beliefs in cultures widely separated by distance and time.

The collective unconscious contains what Jung called *archetypes*. An **archetype** is an inherited tendency to respond to universal human situations in particular ways. Jung would say that the tendencies of people to believe in a god, a devil, evil spirits, and heroes, and to have a fear of the dark and of snakes, all result from inherited archetypes that reflect the shared experience of humankind.

Figure 10.2 provides a summary of Jung's conception of the personality.

personal unconscious: In Jung's theory, the layer of the unconscious containing all of the thoughts and experiences that are accessible to the conscious, as well as repressed memories and impulses.

collective unconscious: In Jung's theory, the most inaccessible layer of the unconscious, which contains the universal experiences of humankind transmitted to each individual.

archetype (AR-keh-type): Existing in the collective unconscious, an inherited tendency to respond in particular ways to universal human situations.

Alfred Adler: Overcoming Inferiority

Alfred Adler (1870–1937) disagreed with most of Freud's basic beliefs; on many points his views were the exact opposite. Adler emphasized the unity of the personality rather than the separate warring components of id, ego, and superego. Adler (1927, 1956) maintained that people are driven by the need to compensate for inferiority and to strive for superiority or significance.

According to Adler (1956), people at an early age develop a "style of life"—a unique way in which the child and later the adult will go about the struggle to achieve superiority. Sometimes inferiority feelings are so strong that they prevent personal development, and Adler originated a term to describe this condition—the "inferiority complex" (Dreikurs, 1953). Adler (1964/1933) also maintained that *birth*

What did Adler consider to be the driving force of the personality?

order influences personality, making first-born children more likely than their younger siblings to be high achievers.

Karen Horney: Championing Feminine Psychology

Why is Horney considered a pioneer in psychology?

Karen Horney insisted that, rather than envying the penis, as Freud believed, women really want the same opportunities and privileges as men—to play sports at the Olympic and professional levels, for example.

The work of Karen Horney (1885–1952) centered on two main themes—the neurotic personality (Horney, 1937, 1945, 1950) and feminine psychology (Horney, 1967). Horney considered herself a disciple of Freud, accepting his emphasis on unconscious motivation and the basic tools of psychoanalysis. However, she disagreed with many of his basic beliefs. She did not accept his division of personality into id, ego, and superego, and she flatly rejected his psychosexual stages and the concepts of the Oedipus complex and penis envy.

Horney insisted that, rather than envying the male's penis, women really want the same opportunities, the same rights and privileges society grants to males. She argued convincingly that women must be free to find their own personal identities, to develop their abilities, and to pursue careers if they choose.

Horney (1945) believed that in order to be psychologically healthy, we all need safety and satisfaction. But these needs can be frustrated in early childhood by parents who are indifferent, unaffectionate, rejecting, or hostile. Such early experiences may cause a child to develop basic anxiety—"the feeling a child has of being isolated and helpless in a potentially hostile world" (p. 41). To minimize this basic anxiety and satisfy the need for safety, children develop coping strategies that form their basic attitude toward life—either moving toward people, moving against people, or moving away from people. Normal people move in all three ways as different situations demand. But a neurotic person will use only one way to reduce anxiety, and will use it excessively and inappropriately. Horney's influence may be seen in modern cognitive-behavioral therapies, which we will explore in Chapter 13.

TRAIT THEORIES

What are trait theories of personality?

How would you describe yourself—cheerful, moody, talkative, quiet, shy, friendly, outgoing? When you describe your personality or that of someone else, you probably list several relatively consistent personal characteristics called **traits**. **Trait theories** are attempts to explain personality and differences between people in terms of their personal characteristics.

Gordon Allport: Personality Traits in the Brain

How did Allport differentiate between cardinal and central traits?

Gordon Allport (1897–1967) claimed that personality traits are real entities, physically located somewhere in the brain (Allport & Odbert, 1936). Each person inherits a unique set of raw materials for given traits, which are then shaped by experiences. Traits describe the particular way an individual responds to the environment and the consistency of that response.

Allport (1961) identified two main categories of traits—common traits and individual traits. Common traits are those we share or hold in common with most others in our own culture. More important to Allport were three types of individual traits: cardinal, central, and secondary traits.

A **cardinal trait** is so strong a part of a person's personality that he or she may become identified with or known for that trait. **Central traits** are those, said Allport (1961), that we would "mention in writing a careful letter of recommendation" (p. 365).

People also have secondary traits, but these are not as critical in defining personality as the cardinal and central traits. Secondary traits are such things as food and music preferences and specific attitudes. Each of us has many more secondary traits than cardinal or central traits.

Raymond Cattell's 16 Personality Factors

Raymond Cattell (1950) considered personality to be a pattern of traits providing the key to understanding and predicting a person's behavior. Cattell identified two types: surface traits and source traits.

If you were asked to describe your best friend, you might say that she is kind, honest, helpful, generous, and so on. These observable qualities of personality Cattell called **surface traits**. (Allport called these qualities central traits.) Using observations and questionnaires, Cattell studied thousands of people and found certain clusters of surface traits that appeared together time after time. Using factor analysis, a statistical technique, Cattell tried to identify underlying personality factors, which he called *source traits*.

Source traits make up the most basic personality structure and, according to Cattell, cause behavior. Even though these traits are common to everyone, people differ in the degree to which they possess each trait. Intelligence is a source trait, and every person has a certain amount of it, but obviously not exactly the same amount or the same kind. How intelligent people are can influence their choice of friends, activities, and profession.

Cattell found 23 source traits in normal individuals, 16 of which he studied in great detail. Cattell's Sixteen Personality Factor Questionnaire, commonly called *the 16 PF*, yields a personality profile (Cattell et al., 1950, 1977). A Cattell personality profile can be used to provide a better understanding of a single individual or to compare one person's traits with those of others. When later researchers tried to confirm Cattell's 16 factors, however, no one could find more than 7 factors, and most found 5 (Digman, 1990). You can chart your own source traits in the *Try It!*

trait: A personal characteristic that is used to describe or explain personality.

trait theories: Theories that attempt to explain personality and differences between people in terms of their personal characteristics.

cardinal trait: Allport's name for a personal quality that is so strong a part of a person's personality that he or she may become identified with that trait.

central trait: Allport's name for the type of trait that might be mentioned in an accurate letter of recommendation.

surface traits: Cattell's name for observable qualities of personality, such as those used to describe a friend.

source traits: Cattell's name for the traits that make up the most basic personality structure and cause behavior.

How did Cattell differentiate between surface and source traits?

Try It!

This hypothetical personality profile is based on Cattell's Sixteen Personality Factor Questionnaire. Along each of the 16 dimensions of bipolar traits, circle the point you think would apply to you if you took the 16 PF. (From Cattell, 1993.)

Reserved	Warm
Concrete	Abstract
Reactive	Emotionally stable
Avoids conflict	Dominant
Serious	Lively
Expedient	Rule-conscious
Shy	Socially bold
Utilitarian	Sensitive
Trusting	Suspicious
Practical	Imaginative
Forthright	Private
Self-assured	Apprehensive
Traditional	Open to change
Group-oriented	Self-reliant
Tolerates disorder	Perfectionistic
Relaxed	Tense

Hans Eysenck: Stressing Two Factors

British psychologist Hans Eysenck (1990) has always believed that personality is largely determined by the genes, and that environmental influences are slight at

What does Eysenck consider to be the two most important dimensions of personality?

best. Although Eysenck claims that three higher-order factors, or dimensions, are needed to capture the essence of personality, he places particular emphasis on two of those dimensions—Extroversion (extroversion versus introversion) and Neuroticism (emotional stability versus instability). Extroverts are sociable, outgoing, and active, whereas introverts are withdrawn, quiet, and introspective. Emotionally stable people are calm, even-tempered, and often easygoing, while emotionally unstable people are anxious, excitable, and easily distressed.

Eysenck (1981) believes that extroverts have a lower level of cortical arousal than introverts and as a result actively seek out more stimulation to increase arousal. Introverts are more easily aroused and thus more likely to show emotional instability.

The Five-Factor Theory of Personality: The Big Five

What are the Big Five personality dimensions in the five-factor theory as described by McCrae and Costa?

Today, the most talked-about personality theory is the **five-factor theory**, also known as the Big Five (Wiggins, 1996). Each of the five broad personality factors is composed of a constellation of traits. The five-factor theory seeks to provide a scientifically accurate framework for organizing the many individual differences that characterize humankind (Goldberg, 1993; Goldberg & Saucier, 1995).

Some researchers who accept these five broad dimensions of personality still disagree as to what they should be named. We will consider the Big Five dimensions using the names assigned by Robert McCrae and Paul Costa (1987; McCrae, 1996), the most influential proponents of the five-factor theory:

- *Extroversion*. This dimension contrasts such traits as sociable, outgoing, talkative, assertive, persuasive, decisive, and active with more introverted traits such as withdrawn, quiet, passive, retiring, and reserved.

- *Neuroticism*. People high on Neuroticism are prone to emotional instability. They tend to experience negative emotions and to be moody, irritable, nervous, and inclined to worry. Neuroticism differentiates people who are anxious, excitable, and easily distressed from those who are emotionally stable and thus calm, even-tempered, easygoing, and relaxed.

- *Conscientiousness*. This factor differentiates individuals who are dependable, organized, reliable, responsible, thorough, hard-working, and persevering from those who are undependable, disorganized, impulsive, unreliable, irresponsible, careless, negligent, and lazy.

- *Agreeableness*. This factor is composed of a collection of traits that range from compassion to antagonism toward others. A person high on Agreeableness would be a pleasant person, good-natured, warm, sympathetic, and cooperative; one low on Agreeableness would tend to be unfriendly, unpleasant, aggressive, argumentative, cold, even hostile and vindictive.

According to the five-factor theory of personality, people who are extroverts are sociable, outgoing, and active. What are some characteristics of introverts?

- *Openness to Experience*. This factor contrasts individuals who seek out varied experiences and who are imaginative, intellectually curious, and broad-minded with those who are concrete-minded and practical and whose interests are narrow. Researchers have found that being high on Openness to Experience is a requirement for creative accomplishment (King et al., 1996).

To measure the Big Five dimensions of personality, Costa and McCrae (1985, 1992, 1997) developed the NEO Personality Inventory (NEO-PI) and, more recently, the Revised NEO Personality Inventory (NEO-PI-R).

Researchers from many different traditions have found five factors when they have subjected self-ratings, observer ratings, and peer ratings to factor analysis. Five factors have emerged, as well, from studies in many different languages; across different age groups; with females and males; and in various cultures, including the German, Chinese, Korean, Hebrew, and Portuguese (McCrae & Costa, 1997). Still

five-factor theory: A trait theory that attempts to explain personality using five broad dimensions, each of which is composed of a constellation of personality traits.

more support for the five-factor theory comes from cross-cultural studies involving participants from Canada, Finland, Poland, Germany, Russia, and Hong Kong (Paunonen et al., 1996). One study suggests that the Big Five factors are relevant across 20 different cultures (Williams et al., 1998). Based on studies of a wide variety of cultures, McCrae and Costa (1997) "strongly suggest that personality trait structure is universal" (p. 509).

Using meta-analysis, Sulloway (1996, 1997) found evidence of a relationship between birth order and the Big Five traits. First-borns were more likely than later-borns to be extroverted and conscientious, but less likely to be emotionally stable, agreeable, and open to experience.

Arguing from the evolutionary perspective, Buss (1991) suggests that humans have evolved who were able to pay attention to, interpret, and act upon dimensions of their social world related to these traits and thus gain a better chance of survival.

Although acceptance for it is growing, the five-factor model has its critics. Block (1995) maintains that there is inconsistency in "the way the five-factor advocates represent the Big Five or say the factors ought to be understood" (p. 208). McAdams (1992) argues that the model fails to address "core constructs of personality functioning beyond the level of traits" and to provide "compelling causal explanations for human behavior and experience" (p. 329). Because the five-factor theory describes personality on a very general level, knowing how high or low a person scored on the five dimensions would not enable one to predict that person's behavior in a specific situation. But the Big Five may be helpful in predicting general trends of behavior in a wide variety of situations. It has proved useful in predicting job performance in the United States (Costa, 1996) and Europe (Salgado, 1997).

Evaluating the Trait Perspective

Do people possess stable and enduring traits that predictably guide the way they will act over time and across changing situations? Critics of trait theories say no and maintain that there is very little consistency of behavior across situations and that behavior is not predictable on the basis of personality traits. Mischel (1973, 1977) believes that behavior is influenced by both the person *and* the situation. He views a trait as a conditional probability that a particular action will occur in response to a particular situation (Wright & Mischel, 1987).

Support for trait theories has come from longitudinal studies. McCrae and Costa (1990) studied personality traits of participants over time and found them to be stable for periods of 3 to 30 years. Typically, personality changes very little with age. As McCrae (1993) puts it, "Stable individual differences in basic dimensions are a universal feature of adult personality" (p. 577).

The weight of evidence supports the view that there are internal traits that strongly influence behavior across situations (Carson, 1989; McAdams, 1992). Characteristic traits, say the trait theorists, determine how we behave *most* of the time, not *all* of the time. Even the most optimistic, happy, and outgoing people have "down" days, fall ill, and frown occasionally.

LEARNING THEORIES AND PERSONALITY

According to the learning perspective, personality consists of the learned tendencies that have been acquired over a lifetime.

The Behaviorist View of B. F. Skinner

B. F. Skinner and other strict behaviorists have an interesting view of personality. They deny that there is any such thing. What people call personality, they believe, is nothing more or less than a collection of learned behaviors or habits that have been

How did Skinner account for what most people refer to as personality?

reinforced in the past. Skinner denied that a personality or self initiates and directs behavior. The causes of behavior, he stated, lie outside the person, and they are based on past and present rewards and punishments. Thus, Skinner did not use the term *personality*. He simply described the variables in the environment that shape an individual's observable behavior. Skinner (1953) believed that healthy experiences in a healthy environment make a healthy person and that psychologically unhealthy people have been reinforced by the environment for behaving abnormally.

The Social-Cognitive Theorists: Expanding the Behaviorist View

Much of human behavior can be traced to classical and operant conditioning; but can all of personality, or even all of learning, be explained in this way? Not according to social-cognitive theorists, who consider both the environment *and* personal/cognitive factors in their attempts to understand personality and behavior. Personal/cognitive factors include personal dispositions, feelings, expectations, perceptions, and cognitions, such as thoughts, beliefs, and attitudes.

Albert Bandura's Views on Personality   The chief advocate of the social-cognitive theory is Albert Bandura (1977, 1986). He maintains that personal/cognitive factors, one's behavior, and the external environment all influence each other and are influenced by each other (Bandura, 1989). This mutual relationship Bandura calls **reciprocal determinism** (see Figure 10.3).

One of the personal/cognitive factors Bandura (1997a; 1997b) considers especially important is self-efficacy. **Self-efficacy** is the perception people hold of their ability to perform competently and successfully in whatever they attempt. People high in self-efficacy will approach new situations confidently, set high goals, and persist in their efforts because they believe success is likely. They are less likely to suffer stress and depression because they believe they can handle threatening or difficult situations. People low in self-efficacy, on the other hand, will expect failure and avoid challenges, will "give up in the face of difficulty, recover slowly from setbacks, and easily fall victim to stress and depression" (Bandura, 1997a, p. 5).

Julian Rotter and Locus of Control   Julian Rotter proposes another concept—**locus of control.** Some people see themselves as primarily in control of their behavior and its consequences. This perception Rotter (1966, 1971, 1990) defines as an *internal* locus of control. Others perceive that whatever happens to them is in the hands of fate, luck, or chance. They exhibit an *external* locus of control and may claim that it does not matter what they do because "whatever will be, will be." Rotter contends that people

---

reciprocal determinism: Bandura's concept that behavior, personal/cognitive factors, and environment all influence and are influenced by each other.

self-efficacy: A person's belief in his or her ability to perform competently in whatever is attempted.

locus of control: A concept used to explain how people account for what happens in their lives—people with an *internal* locus of control see themselves as primarily in control of their behavior and its consequences; those with an *external* locus of control perceive what happens to be in the hands of fate, luck, or chance.

What are the components of Bandura's concept of reciprocal determinism, and how do they interact?

What does Rotter mean by the terms *internal* and *external locus of control?*

Figure 10.3
Bandura's Reciprocal Determinism

Albert Bandura takes a social-cognitive view of personality. He suggests that three components—the environment, behavior, and personal/cognitive factors such as beliefs, expectancies, and personal dispositions—play reciprocal roles in determining personality and behavior.

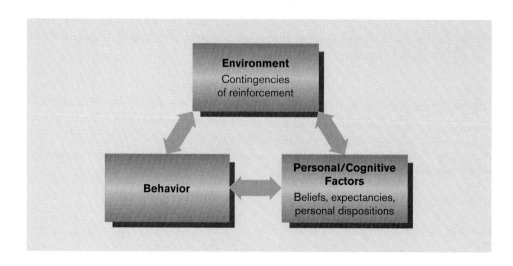

with an external locus of control are less likely to change their behavior as a result of reinforcement, because they do not see reinforcers as being tied to their own actions.

Evaluating the Social-Cognitive Perspective   The social-cognitive perspective cannot be criticized for lacking a strong research base. Yet some of its critics claim that the social-cognitive perspective continues to weigh the situation too heavily. These critics ask: What about unconscious motives or internal dispositions (traits) that people exhibit fairly consistently across many different situations? Other critics point to mounting evidence of a genetic influence on personality, which may explain 40–50% or more of the variation in personality characteristics (Bouchard, 1994).

humanistic psychology: An approach to psychology that stresses the uniquely human attributes and a positive view of human nature.

self-actualization: Developing to one's fullest potential.

HUMANISTIC PERSONALITY THEORIES

Humanistic psychology seeks to give a more complete and positive picture of the human personality than the two other major forces in psychology—behaviorism and psychoanalysis. Humanistic psychologists developed their own unique view of human nature, a view that is very positive. Human nature is seen as innately good, and people are assumed to have a natural tendency toward growth and the realization of their fullest potential. The humanists largely deny a dark or evil side of human nature. They do not believe that we are shaped strictly by the environment or ruled by mysterious unconscious forces. Rather, as creative beings with an active, conscious free will, we can chart our own course in life.

Humanistic psychology is sometimes called the "third force" in psychology. (Behaviorism and psychoanalysis are the other two forces.) The pioneering humanistic psychologists were Abraham Maslow and Carl Rogers.

Who were the two pioneers in humanistic psychology, and how did they view human nature?

Abraham Maslow: The Self-Actualizing Person

For Abraham Maslow (1970), motivational factors were at the root of personality. As we saw in Chapter 9, Maslow constructed a hierarchy of needs, ranging from physiological needs at the bottom upward to safety needs, belonging and love needs, esteem needs, and finally to the highest need—for self-actualization. **Self-actualization** means developing to one's fullest potential. A healthy person is ever growing and becoming all that he or she can be.

Maslow studied people he believed were using their talents and abilities to their fullest—in other words, those who exemplified self-actualization. He studied some historical figures, such as Abraham Lincoln and Thomas Jefferson, and figures who made significant contributions during his own lifetime—Albert Einstein, Eleanor Roosevelt, and Albert Schweitzer. After examining the lives of such people, Maslow identified characteristics that self-actualizing persons seem to share.

Maslow found self-actualizers to be comfortable with life; they accept themselves and others, and nature as well, with good humor and tolerance. Most of them believe they have a mission to accomplish or the need to devote their life to some larger good. Self-actualizers tend not to depend on external authority or other people but seem to be inner-driven, autonomous, and independent. They feel a strong fellowship with humanity, and their relationships with others are characterized by deep and loving bonds. They can laugh at themselves, and their sense of humor, though well developed, never involves hostility or criticism of others. Finally, the most telling mark of self-actualizers are frequently occurring *peak experiences*—experiences of deep meaning, insight, and harmony within and with the universe.

Maslow concluded that each of us has the capacity for self-actualization. If we apply our talent and energy to doing our best in whatever endeavor we choose, then we, too, can lead creative lives and be self-actualizing.

What is self-actualization, and how did Maslow study it?

Abraham Maslow (1908–1970)

Carl Rogers: The Fully Functioning Person

According to Rogers, why don't all people become fully functioning persons?

Link It!

Like Freud, Carl Rogers (1951, 1961), developed his theory of personality through insights gained from his patients in therapy sessions. Yet he saw something very different from what Freud and the psychoanalysts observed. Rogers viewed human nature as basically good. If left to develop naturally, he thought, people would be happy and psychologically healthy.

According to Rogers, we each live in our own subjective reality, which he called the *phenomenological field*. It is in this personal, subjective field (rather than in the objective, real, physical environment) that we act and think and feel. In other words, the way we see things is the way they are—for us. Gradually a part of the phenomenological field becomes differentiated as the self. The self concept emerges as a result of repeated experiences involving such terms as "I," "me," and "mine." With the emerging self comes the need for positive regard. We need warmth, love, acceptance, sympathy, and respect from the people who are significant in our lives. But there are usually strings attached to positive regard from others.

Our parents do not view us positively regardless of our behavior. They set up **conditions of worth**—conditions on which their positive regard hinges. Conditions of worth force us to live and act according to someone else's values rather than our own. In our efforts to gain positive regard, we deny our true self by inhibiting some of our behavior, denying and distorting some of our perceptions, and closing ourselves to parts of our experience. In so doing, we experience stress and anxiety, and our whole self-structure may be threatened.

For Rogers, a major goal of psychotherapy is to enable people to begin to live according to their own values rather than according to the values of others in order to gain positive regard. He calls his therapy "person-centered therapy," (Rogers's therapy will be discussed in Chapter 13). Rogers believes that the therapist must give the client **unconditional positive regard**, that is, positive regard no matter what the client says, does, has done, or is thinking of doing. Unconditional positive regard is designed to reduce threat, eliminate conditions of worth, and bring the person back in tune with his or her true self. If successful, the therapy helps the client become what Rogers calls a *fully functioning person*—one who is functioning at an optimal level and living fully and spontaneously according to his or her own inner value system.

Evaluating the Humanistic Perspective

Humanism has become much more than a personality theory and an approach to therapy. Its influence has spread significantly as a social movement in the schools and in society in general. Some of its severest critics charge that an all-consuming personal quest for self-fulfillment can lead to a self-centered, self-serving, self-indulgent personality, lacking moral restraint or genuine concern for others (Campbell & Sprecht, 1985; Wallach & Wallach, 1983).

Humanistic psychologists do not accept such criticisms as valid. By and large, they trust in the inherent goodness of human nature, and their perspective on personality is consistent with that trust. But how do humanists explain the evil we see around us—assaults, murder, rape? Where does this originate? Carl Rogers (1981) replied, "I do not find that this evil is inherent in human nature " (p. 16). Of psychological environments that nurture growth and choice, Rogers said, "I have never known an individual to choose the cruel or destructive path. . . . So my experience leads me to believe that it is cultural influences which are the major factors in our evil behaviors" (p. 16).

Though humanists have been criticized for being unscientific and for seeing, hearing, and finding no evil within the human psyche, they have inspired the study of the positive qualities—altruism, cooperation, love, and acceptance of self and others.

conditions of worth: Conditions on which the positive regard of others rests.

unconditional positive regard: Unqualified caring and nonjudgmental acceptance of another.

PERSONALITY: IS IT IN THE GENES?

Behavioral genetics is a field of research that investigates the relative effects of heredity and environment on behavior and ability.

The Twin Study Method: Studying Identical and Fraternal Twins

When identical twins who were reared apart have strikingly similar traits, as in the case of Oskar and Jack, introduced at the beginning of this chapter, it is assumed that heredity has been a major contributor. When twins differ on a given trait, as Joan and Jean do, the influence of the environment is thought to be greater.

In the Minnesota twin study, Tellegen and others (1988) found that identical twins are quite similar on several personality factors regardless of whether they are raised together or apart. The term **heritability** refers to the degree to which a characteristic is estimated to be influenced by heredity. After studying heritability of traits in 573 adult twin pairs, Rushton and colleagues (1986) found that nurturance, empathy, and assertiveness are substantially influenced by heredity. Even altruism and aggressiveness, traits one would expect to be strongly influenced by parental upbringing, were actually more heavily influenced by heredity. A meta-analysis by Miles and Carey (1997) revealed that the heritability of aggressiveness may be as high as .50 (or 50%). Twin studies also reveal a genetic influence on alcoholism in males (Prescott & Kendler, 1999b) and on social attitudes such as traditionalism—whether a person endorses traditional moral values and follows rules and authority (Finkel & McGue, 1997).

Evidence from behavioral genetics suggests that the average heritability of the Big Five personality factors is about .41 to .42, somewhat less than the earlier twin study estimates of around .50 (Bouchard, 1994). Figure 10.4 (on page 342) shows the heritability estimates for the Big Five from the Minnesota studies of twins reared apart and the Loehlin twin studies (Loehlin, 1992).

Taken together, these data show that personality factors are significantly influenced by heredity. But even with a heritability estimate as high as .50, the remaining 50% of the variance has to be attributed to nongenetic (environmental) factors plus measurement error. The behavioral genetics studies, then, leave a great deal of room for environmental forces to shape personality. Plomin and others (1994) claim that "nongenetic factors generally account for as much variance as genetic factors" (p. 1736). So personality is a product of nature and nurture working together.

The Shared and Nonshared Environment

Have you ever wondered why siblings raised in the same household often seem to have totally different personalities? To explain why, researchers point out that environmental influences are produced in two different forms: through the shared environment and through the nonshared environment. The shared environment consists of those environmental influences that tend to make family members similar. If the shared environmental influences were high, then you would expect siblings raised in the same household to be more alike than different. But the shared environmental influences on personality are modest at best, about 7% (Bouchard, 1994; Loehlin, 1992).

The nonshared environment consists of influences that operate in different ways among children in the same family (Rowe, 1994). These influences "cause family members to differ regardless of whether the locus of influence is the family (such as differential treatment by parents) or outside the family (such as different experiences at school or with peers)" (Plomin & Daniels, 1987, p. 7). Nonshared influences can occur because individual children tend to elicit different responses from their parents for a variety of reasons—their temperament, gender, or birth order, or accidents and

What has research in behavioral genetics revealed about the influence of the genes and the environment on personality?

behavioral genetics: The field of research that investigates the relative effects of heredity and environment on behavior and ability.

heritability: An index of the degree to which a characteristic is estimated to be influenced by heredity.

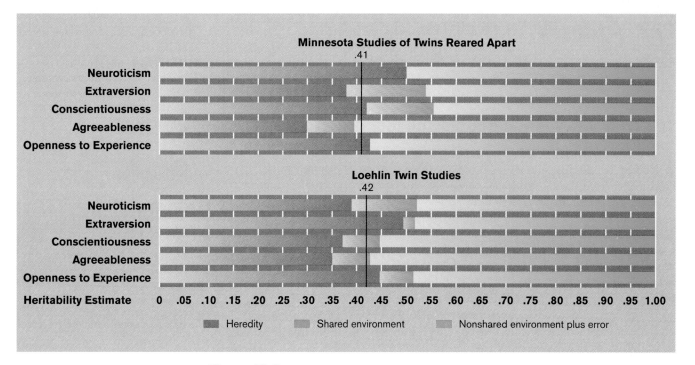

Figure 10.4

Estimated Influence of Heredity and Environment on the Big Five Personality Factors

The Minnesota studies of twins reared apart yield an average heritability estimate of .41 (41%) for the Big Five personality factors; the Loehlin twin studies, a heritability estimate of .42 (42%). Both studies found the influence of the shared environment to be only about .07 (7%). The remaining percentage represents a combination of nonshared environmental influences and measurement error. (Adapted from Bouchard, 1994.)

illnesses they may have had (Plomin, 1989). Bouchard claims that twins can experience nonshared environmental influences even in the womb if the positioning of the twin embryos in the uterus leads to differences in fetal nutrition (Aldhous, 1992).

The Adoption Method

Another method used to disentangle the effects of heredity and environment is to study children adopted shortly after birth. Loehlin and others (1987) assessed the personalities of 17-year-olds who had been adopted at birth and came to this startling conclusion: "Adopted children do not resemble their adoptive family members in personality, despite having lived with them from birth, but they do show a modest degree of resemblance to their genetic mothers, whom they had never known" (p. 968). When the adopted children were compared to other children in the family, the researchers found that the shared family environment had virtually no influence on their personalities. Other researchers studying adopted children have come to the same basic conclusion (Scarr et al., 1981). Loehlin and colleagues (1990) measured change in personality of adoptees over a 10-year period and found that children tended "to change on the average in the direction of their genetic parents' personalities" (p. 221). The prevailing thinking in behavioral genetics, then, is that the shared environment plays a negligible role in the formation of personality (Loehlin et al., 1988), although there have been a few dissenting voices (Rose et al., 1988).

To learn that most psychological traits are significantly heritable does not lessen the value or reduce the importance of environmental factors such as family influences, parenting, culture, and education (Bouchard et al., 1990). Furthermore,

Bouchard and colleagues (1990) state that their findings "do not imply that parenting is without lasting effects" (p. 227).

Personality and Culture

There is general agreement that nature and nurture together influence the formation of personality. Important among the influences of nurture are the diverse cultures in which humans live and work.

Hofstede (1980, 1983) analyzed questionnaire responses measuring the work-related values of more than 100,000 IBM employees in 53 countries around the world. Factor analysis revealed four separate dimensions related to culture and personality, but one factor, the individualism/collectivism dimension, is of particular interest here. In individualist cultures, more emphasis is placed on individual achievement than on group achievement, and high-achieving individuals are accorded honor and prestige. People in collectivist cultures, on the other hand, tend to be more interdependent and define themselves and their personal interests in terms of their group membership.

Hofstede rank-ordered the 53 countries on each of the four dimensions. It should hardly be surprising that the United States ranked as the most individualist culture in the sample; however there are many distinct minority cultural groups in the United States, which may be decidedly less individualistic.

Native Americans number close to 2 million, but even within this relatively small cultural group, there are over 200 different tribes, and no single language, religion, or culture (Bennett, 1994). Yet Native Americans have many shared values—collectivist values—such as the importance of family, community, cooperation, and generosity. Native Americans value a generous nature as evidenced by gift giving and helpfulness. Such behaviors bring more honor and prestige than accumulating property and building individual wealth.

Hispanic Americans, who number almost 28.3 million (U.S. Bureau of the Census, 1997), also tend to be more collectivist than individualist. While there are significant cultural differences among various Hispanic American groups, there are striking similarities as well. The clearest shared cultural value is a strong identification with and attachment to the extended family. Another important value is *simpatía*—the desire for smooth and harmonious social relationships, which include respect for the dignity of others, avoidance of confrontation, and avoidance of words or actions that might hurt the feelings of another (Marín, 1994).

Keep in mind that members of Native American or Hispanic American cultures may value both orientations, being individualistic at work, for example, and collectivistic in the home and community (Kagitcibasi, 1992).

The influences of culture on personality become more important social considerations as societies become more multicultural and economies become increasingly global.

For these native Alaskans, participating in the traditional blanket toss ceremony is one manifestation of their culture's values related to community and cooperation.

PERSONALITY ASSESSMENT

Just as there are many different personality theories, there are many different methods for measuring personality. Various personality tests are used by clinical and counseling psychologists, psychiatrists, and counselors in the diagnosis of patients and in the assessment of progress in therapy. Personality assessment is also used in business and industry to aid in hiring decisions and by counselors for vocational and educational counseling.

What are the three major methods used in personality assessment?

inventory: A paper-and-pencil test with questions about a person's thoughts, feelings, and behaviors, which can be scored according to a standard procedure.

Minnesota Multiphasic Personality Inventory (MMPI): The most extensively researched and widely used personality test; used to screen and diagnose psychiatric problems and disorders; revised as MMPI-2.

Personality assessment methods can be grouped in a few broad categories: (1) observation, interviews, and rating scales, (2) personality inventories, and (3) projective tests.

Observation, Interviews, and Rating Scales

Observation   Psychologists use observation in personality assessment and evaluation in a variety of settings—hospitals, clinics, schools, and workplaces.

Behaviorists, in particular, prefer observation to other methods of personality assessment. Using an observational technique known as *behavioral assessment*, psychologists can count and record the frequency of particular behaviors. This method is often used in behavior modification programs in settings such as mental hospitals, where psychologists may chart the patients' progress in reducing aggressive acts or other undesirable or abnormal behaviors.

Although much can be learned from observation, it is time-consuming and expensive. What is observed may be misinterpreted, and two observers can view the same event and interpret it differently. Probably the most serious limitation is that the very presence of the observer can alter the behavior being observed.

The Interview   Another personality assessment technique is the interview. Clinical psychologists and psychiatrists use interviews to help in the diagnosis and treatment of patients. Counselors use interviews to screen applicants for admission to college or other special programs, and employers use them to evaluate job applicants and employees for job promotions.

Interviewers consider not only a person's answers to questions but the person's tone of voice, speech, mannerisms, gestures, and general appearance as well. Interviewers often use a structured interview, in which the content of the questions and even the manner in which they are asked are carefully planned ahead of time. The interviewer tries not to deviate in any way from the structured format so that more reliable comparisons can be made between different subjects.

Rating Scales   Sometimes examiners use rating scales to record data from interviews or observations. Rating scales are useful because they provide a standardized format, including a list of traits or behaviors to evaluate. The rating scale helps to focus the rater's attention on all the relevant traits to be considered so that none is overlooked or weighed too heavily.

But there is sometimes little agreement among raters in their evaluation of the same individual. If you have watched Olympic events such as figure skating on television, you have sometimes noticed wide variations in the several judges' scoring of the same performance. One way to overcome this problem is to train the judges or raters to a point where high agreement can be achieved when rating the same person or event.

Personality Inventories: Taking Stock

What is an inventory, and what are the MMPI-2 and the CPI designed to reveal?

There is an objective method for measuring personality, a method in which the personal opinions and ratings of observers or interviewers do not unduly influence the results. This method is the **inventory**, a paper-and-pencil test with questions about an individual's thoughts, feelings, and behaviors, which measures several dimensions of personality and can be scored according to a standard procedure. Psychologists favoring the trait approach prefer the inventory because it reveals where people fall on various dimensions of personality and yields a personality profile. Of the many personality inventories available, none has been more widely used than the Minnesota Multiphasic Personality Inventory.

The MMPI and MMPI-2   The **Minnesota Multiphasic Personality Inventory (MMPI)** and its revision, the **MMPI-2**, for years have been the most popular, the most heavily researched, and the most widely used personality tests for screening and diagnosing psychiatric problems and disorders, and for use in psychological research (Butcher & Rouse, 1996). However, it does not reveal differences among normal personalities very well.

There have been more than 115 recognized translations of the MMPI, and it is used in more than 65 countries (Butcher & Graham, 1989). Published in 1943 by researchers McKinley and Hathaway, the MMPI was originally intended to identify tendencies toward various types of psychiatric disorders. The researchers administered over 1,000 questions about attitudes, feelings, and specific psychiatric symptoms to selected groups of psychiatric patients who had been clearly diagnosed with various specific disorders and to a control group of normal men and women. They retained the 550 items that differentiated the specific groups of psychiatric patients from the group of participants considered to be normal.

Because the original MMPI had become outdated, the MMPI-2 was published in 1989 (Butcher et al., 1989). Most of the original test items were retained, but new items were added to more adequately cover areas such as alcoholism, drug abuse, suicidal tendencies, eating disorders, and Type A personality. New norms were established to reflect national census data and thus achieve a better geographical, racial, and cultural balance (Ben-Porath & Butcher, 1989).

Following are examples of questions on the test, which are to be answered "true," "false," or "cannot say."

I wish I were not bothered by thoughts about sex.
When I get bored I like to stir up some excitement.
In walking I am very careful to step over sidewalk cracks.
If people had not had it in for me, I would have been much more successful.

A high score on any of the scales does not necessarily mean that a person has a problem or a psychiatric symptom. Rather, the psychologist looks at the individual's MMPI profile—the pattern of scores on all the scales—and then compares it to the profiles of normal individuals and those with various psychiatric disorders.

But what if someone lies on the test in order to appear mentally healthy? Embedded in the test to provide a check against lying are questions such as these:

Once in a while I put off until tomorrow what I ought to do today.
I gossip a little at times.
Once in a while, I laugh at a dirty joke.

Most people would almost certainly have to answer "true" in response to such items—unless, of course, they were lying. Another scale controls for people who are faking psychiatric illness, as in the case of someone hoping to be judged not guilty of a crime by reason of insanity. Research seems to indicate that the validity scales in the MMPI-2 are effective in detecting test takers who were instructed to fake psychological disturbance or to lie to make themselves appear more psychologically healthy (Bagby et al., 1994; Butcher et al., 1995). Even when given specific information about various psychological disorders, test takers could not produce profiles similar to those of people who actually suffered from the disorder (Wetter et al., 1993).

The California Psychological Inventory　　What instruments are available for assessing the personality of a normal person? The **California Psychological Inventory (CPI)** is a highly regarded personality test developed especially for normal populations aged 13 and older.

Similar to the MMPI, the CPI even has many of the same questions, but it does not include any questions designed to reveal psychiatric illness (Gough, 1987). The CPI is valuable for predicting behavior, and it has been "praised for its technical competency, careful development, cross-validation and follow-up, use of sizable samples and sep-

California Psychological Inventory (CPI): A highly regarded personality test used to assess the normal personality.

Myers–Briggs Type Indicator (MBTI): An inventory for classifying personality types based on Jung's theory of personality.

projective test: A personality test in which people respond to inkblots, drawings of ambiguous human situations, incomplete sentences, and the like, by projecting their own inner thoughts, feelings, fears, or conflicts onto the test materials.

Rorschach Inkblot Method (ROR-shok): A projective test composed of 10 inkblots to which a test taker responds; used to reveal unconscious functioning and the presence of psychiatric disorders.

How do projective tests provide insight into personality, and what are several of the most commonly used projective tests?

arate sex norms" (Domino, 1984, p. 156). The CPI was revised in 1987, to make it provide "a picture of the subject's life-style and the degree to which his or her potential is being realized" (McReynolds, 1989, p. 101). The CPI is particularly useful in predicting school achievement in high school and beyond; leadership and executive success; and effectiveness of police, military personnel, and student teachers (Gregory, 1996).

The Myers–Briggs Type Indicator (MBTI)   The **Myers–Briggs Type Indicator (MBTI)** is a personality inventory based on Jung's theory. The MBTI is a forced-choice, self-report inventory that is scored on four separate bipolar dimensions:

Extraversion (E) .... Introversion (I)

Sensing (S) .... Intuition (N)

Thinking (T) .... Feeling (F)

Judging (J) .... Perceptive (P)

A person could score anywhere along each continuum of the four bipolar dimensions, and these individual scores are usually summarized according to a typology. Sixteen types of personality profile can be derived from the possible combinations of the four bipolar dimensions. For example, a person whose scores were more toward the Extraversion, Intuition, Feeling, and Perceptive poles would be labeled an ENFP personality type, which is described as follows:

> Relates more readily to the outer world of people and things than to the inner world of ideas (E); prefers to search for new possibilities over working with known facts and conventional ways of doing things (N); makes decisions and solves problems on the basis of personal values and feelings rather than relying on logical thinking and analysis (F); and prefers a flexible, spontaneous life to a planned and orderly existence (P). (Gregory, 1996)

The MBTI is growing in popularity, especially in business and industry and in schools. Critics point to the absence of rigorous, controlled validity studies of the inventory (Pittenger, 1993). And it has been criticized for being interpreted too often by unskilled examiners, who have been accused of making overly simplistic interpretations (Gregory, 1996). However, sufficiently sophisticated methods for interpreting the MBTI do exist, as revealed by almost 500 research studies to date. And interest in this tool continues to be strong (Allen, 1997).

Projective Tests: Projections from the Unconscious

Responses on interviews and questionnaires are conscious responses and, for this reason, are less useful to therapists who wish to probe the unconscious. Such therapists may choose a completely different technique called a projective test. A **projective test** is a personality test consisting of inkblots, drawings of ambiguous human situations, or incomplete sentences for which there are no obvious correct or incorrect responses. People respond by projecting their own inner thoughts, feelings, fears, or conflicts into the test materials. Just as a movie projector projects the images on the film outward and onto a screen, so do people project their inner thoughts, feelings, fears, and conflicts into the analysis and description of inkblots and other vague or ambiguous projective test materials.

The Rorschach Inkblot Method: What Do You See?   One of the oldest and most popular projective tests is the **Rorschach Inkblot Method** developed by Swiss psychiatrist Hermann Rorschach (ROR-shok) in 1921. It consists of 10 inkblots, which the test taker is asked to describe (see Figure 10.5).

To develop his test, Rorschach put ink on paper and then folded the paper so that symmetrical patterns would result. Earlier, psychologists had used standardized series of inkblots to study imagination and other variables, but Rorschach was the first to use inkblots to investigate personality. He experimented with thousands of inkblots on different groups of people and found that 10 of the inkblots could be used to discriminate among different diagnostic groups, such as manic depressives, paranoid schizophrenics, and so on. These 10 inkblots—5 black and white, and 5 with color—were standardized and are still widely used.

The Rorschach can be used to describe personality, make differential diagnoses, plan and evaluate treatment, and predict behavior (Ganellen, 1996; Weiner, 1997). For the last 20 years, it has been second in popularity to the MMPI for use in research and clinical assessment (Butcher & Rouse, 1996).

Figure 10.5
An Inkblot Similar to One Used for the Rorschach Inkblot Method

The Thematic Apperception Test: Seeing Oneself in Scenes of Others

Another projective test is the **Thematic Apperception Test (TAT)** developed by Henry Murray and his colleagues in 1935 (Morgan & Murray, 1935; Murray, 1938). The TAT consists of 1 blank card and 19 other cards showing vague or ambiguous black-and-white drawings of human figures in various situations. "The test is based upon the well-recognized fact that when a person interprets an ambiguous social situation he is apt to expose his own personality as much as the phenomenon to which he is attending" (Morgan & Murray, 1962, p. 531). Test takers are asked to create a story about the people or situations shown in the cards and answer questions such as "what might the individuals be thinking and feeling?"

What does the story you write have to do with your personality or your problems or motives? Murray (1965) stresses the importance of "an element or theme that recurs three or more times in the series of stories" (p. 432). For example, if many of a person's story themes are about illness, sex, fear of failure, aggression, power, or interpersonal conflict, such a recurring theme is thought to reveal a problem in the person's life. Murray (1965) also claims that the strength of the TAT is "its capacity to reveal things that the patient is unwilling to tell or is unable to tell because he [or she] is unconscious of them" (p. 427).

Although the TAT has been used extensively in research, it relies heavily on the interpretation skills of the examiner. Also, it may reflect too strongly a person's temporary motivational and emotional state and not get at the more permanent aspects of personality. Because Murray was trained as a Freudian and Jungian analyst, it is not surprising that he developed an instrument to assess unconscious motivation (Triplet, 1992).

The Sentence Completion Method: Filling in the Blanks

Another projective technique, the sentence completion method, may be one of the most valid projective techniques of all. It consists of a number of incomplete sentences to be completed by the test taker, such as these:

In a comprehensive review, Goldberg (1965) summarized 50 validity studies and concluded that sentence completion is a valuable technique appropriate for widespread clinical and research use.

Review & Reflect 10.3 (on page 348) summarizes the various personality tests.

Thematic Apperception Test (TAT): A projective test consisting of drawings of ambiguous human situations, which the test taker describes; thought to reveal inner feelings, conflicts, and motives, which are projected onto the test materials.

Review&Reflect 10.3   Three Approaches to Personality Assessment

Method	Examples	Description
Observation and rating	Observation Interviews Rating scales	Performance (behavior) is observed in a specific situation, and personality is assessed based on observation. In interviews, the responses to questions are taken to reveal personality characteristics. Rating scales are used to score or rate test takers on the basis of traits, behaviors, or results of interviews. Assessment is subjective, and accuracy depends largely on the ability and experience of the evaluator.
Inventories	Minnesota Multiphasic Personality Inventory–2 (MMPI-2) California Personality Inventory (CPI) Myers–Briggs Type Indicator (MBTI)	Test takers reveal their beliefs, feelings, behavior, and/or opinions on paper-and-pencil tests. Scoring procedures are standardized and responses are compared to group norms.
Projective tests	Rorschach Inkblot Method Thematic Apperception Test (TAT) Sentence completion method	Test takers respond to ambiguous test materials and presumably reveal elements of their own personalities by what they describe in inkblots, by themes they write about scenes showing possible conflict, or by how they complete sentences. Scoring is subjective, and accuracy depends largely on the ability and experience of the evaluator.

Apply It!

Learning to Be Optimistic

Optimistic people are often derided as "pollyannas"–a reference to the heroine of the novel *Pollyanna,* who was famous for her blind, even foolish, optimism. But it would be a mistake to dismiss optimism altogether. An optimistic outlook appears to be conducive to achievement. Optimists do better in school, succeed more often at work, and win more elections than pessimists do. What's the connection? According to Martin Seligman, who has conducted extensive studies of optimistic and pessimistic people, "Success requires persistence, the ability to not give up in the face of failure. I believe that optimistic explanatory style is the key to persistence" (1990, p. 101).

Optimists versus pessimists. By "explanatory style," Seligman means the way people explain what happens to them. Pessimists tend to believe that bad events will last a long time, will undermine everything they do, and are their own fault; that is, they see bad events as permanent, pervasive, and personal. Optimists, in contrast, tend to believe that a bad event is just a temporary setback, that its causes are unique, and that it is due to circumstances, bad luck, or other people.

This difference can have profound consequences. In Seligman's words,

> Life inflicts the same setbacks and tragedies on the optimist as on the pessimist, but the optimist bounces back from defeat, and, with his [or her] life somewhat poorer, . . . picks up and starts again. The pessimist gives up and falls into depression. . . . Even when things go well for the pessimist, he [or she] is haunted by forebodings of catastrophe. (1990, p. 207)

Pessimism can thus stand in the way of achievement and a happy and productive life.

The ABC method. If you get discouraged easily, get depressed more often than you would like, and fail more than you think you should, you may need to change your explanatory style. In other words, you may need to become more optimistic.

Seligman believes that an individual can *learn* to be more optimistic and thereby improve his or her general health and sense of well-being. But contrary to what you might expect, this is not a matter of learning to say positive things to yourself. "What *is* crucial," Seligman notes, "is what you think when you fail. . . . Changing the destructive things you say to yourself when you experience the setbacks that life deals all of us is the central skill of optimism" (1990, p. 15).

Seligman has developed a method for learning optimism that he calls the *ABC method*, for adversity, beliefs, and consequences. Adversity is anything that causes you to become discouraged; it can range from a leaky faucet or a crying baby to a failed exam or a fight with your lover. Beliefs are how you explain the adversity: Do you think this particular setback is permanent or temporary? Pervasive or unique? Your own fault or the result of outside factors? And consequences are the way you feel about the adverse

event and what you do about it. Here is an example:

- *Adversity:* I decided to join a gym, and when I walked into the place I saw nothing but firm, toned bodies all around me.

- *Belief:* What am I doing here? I look like a beached whale compared to these people! I should get out of here while I still have my dignity.

- *Consequences:* I felt totally self-conscious and ended up leaving after 15 minutes. (Seligman, 1990, pp. 214-215)

What you can do. If your reactions to adversity consistently follow a pessimistic pattern, you can do several specific things to alter your thought patterns. Seligman has identified three useful techniques: distraction, disputation, and distancing.

- *Distraction.* Start by attempting to distract yourself—slap your hand against the wall and shout "Stop!" Then try to think about something else.

- *Disputation.* Argue with yourself about the adverse event. Take a close look at the facts. "The most convincing way of disputing a nega-

tive belief is to show that it is factually incorrect" (1990, p. 221). An advantage of this technique is that it is realistic. Learned optimism is based on accuracy, not merely on making positive statements. For example, a student whose grades are somewhat below expectations might say, "I'm blowing things out of proportion. I hoped to get all As, but I got a B, a B+, and a B−. Those aren't awful grades. I may not have done the best in the class, but I didn't do the worst in the class either" (Seligman, 1990, p. 219).

- *Distancing.* Still another way of dealing with pessimistic beliefs is distancing. Try to dissociate yourself from your pessimistic thoughts, at least long enough to judge their accuracy objectively. Recognize that simply believing something doesn't make it so.

Once you have challenged your pessimistic beliefs and have convinced yourself that bad events are temporary and will not affect everything you do for the rest of your life, you will be able to look forward to better times in the future. Along with Little Orphan Annie, you will be confident that "The sun will come out tomorrow!"

SUMMARY AND REVIEW

SIGMUND FREUD AND PSYCHOANALYSIS

To what two aspects of Freud's work does the term *psychoanalysis* apply?

Psychoanalysis is the term Freud used for both his theory of personality and his therapy for the treatment of psychological disorders.

What are the three levels of awareness in consciousness?

The three levels of awareness in consciousness are the conscious, the preconscious, and the unconscious.

What are the roles of the id, the ego, and the superego?

The id is the primitive, unconscious part of the personality, which contains the instincts and operates on the pleasure principle. The ego is the rational, largely conscious system, which operates according to the reality principle. The superego is the moral system of the personality, consisting of the conscience and the ego ideal.

What is a defense mechanism?

A defense mechanism is an unconscious, irrational means that the ego uses to defend against anxiety and to

maintain self-esteem; it involves self-deception and the distortion of reality.

What are two ways in which repression operates?

Through repression, (1) painful memories, thoughts, ideas, or perceptions are involuntarily removed from consciousness, and (2) disturbing sexual or aggressive impulses are prevented from breaking into consciousness.

What are some other defense mechanisms?

Other defense mechanisms include projection, denial, rationalization, regression, reaction formation, displacement, and sublimation.

What are the psychosexual stages, and why did Freud consider them so important in personality development?

Freud believed that the sexual instinct is present at birth, develops through a series of psychosexual stages, and provides the driving force for thought and activity. The psychosexual stages are the oral stage, anal stage, phallic stage (followed by the latency period), and genital stage.

What is the Oedipus complex?

The Oedipus complex, occurring in the phallic stage, is a conflict in which the child is sexually attracted to the opposite-sex parent and feels hostility toward the same-sex parent.

According to Freud, what are the two primary sources of influence on the personality?

Freud believed that differences in personality are the result of the relative strengths of the id, the ego, and the superego and of the personality traits that develop as a result of problems during the psychosexual stages.

Key Terms
personality (p. 325); psychoanalysis (p. 326); conscious (p. 326); preconscious (p. 326); unconscious (p. 326); id (p. 327); pleasure principle (p. 327); libido (p. 327); ego (p. 327); superego (p. 327); defense mechanism (p. 328); repression (p. 328); projection (p. 329); denial (p. 329); rationalization (p. 329); regression (p. 329); reaction formation (p. 329); displacement (p. 329); sublimation (p. 329); psychosexual stages (p. 329); fixation (p. 330); oral stage (p. 330); anal stage (p. 330); phallic stage (p. 330); Oedipus complex (p. 330); latency period (p. 331); genital stage (p. 331)

THE NEO-FREUDIANS

According to Jung, what are the three components of personality?

Jung conceived of the personality as having three parts: the ego, the personal unconscious, and the collective unconscious.

What did Adler consider to be the driving force of the personality?

Adler claimed that the predominant force of the personality is the drive to overcome and compensate for feelings of weakness and inferiority and to strive for superiority or significance.

Why is Horney considered a pioneer in psychology?

Horney took issue with Freud's sexist view of women and added the feminine dimension to the world of psychology.

Key Terms
personal unconscious (p. 333); collective unconscious (p. 333); archetype (p. 333);

TRAIT THEORIES

What are trait theories of personality?

Trait theories of personality are attempts to explain personality and differences between people in terms of their personal characteristics.

How did Allport differentiate between cardinal and central traits?

Allport defined a cardinal trait as a personal quality that is so strong a part of a person's personality that he or she may become identified with that trait or known for it. A central trait is the type you might mention when writing a letter of recommendation.

How did Cattell differentiate between surface and source traits?

Cattell used the term *surface traits* to refer to observable qualities of personality, which you might use in describing a friend. *Source traits* underlie the surface traits, exist in all of us in varying degrees, make up the most basic personality structure, and cause behavior.

What does Eysenck consider to be the two most important dimensions of personality?

Eysenck considers the two most important dimensions of personality to be Extroversion (extroversion versus introversion) and Neuroticism (emotional stability versus emotional instability).

What are the Big Five personality dimensions in the five-factor theory described by McCrae and Costa?

According to McCrae and Costa, the Big Five factors are Neuroticism, Extroversion, Conscientiousness, Agreeableness, and Openness to Experience.

Key Terms
trait (p. 334); trait theories (p. 334); cardinal trait (p. 334); central trait (p. 334); surface traits (p. 335); source traits (p. 335); five-factor theory (p. 336)

LEARNING THEORIES AND PERSONALITY

How did Skinner account for what most people refer to as personality?

B. F. Skinner viewed personality as simply a collection of behaviors and habits that have been reinforced in the past.

What are the components of Bandura's concept of reciprocal determinism, and how do they interact?

The external environment, behavior, and personal/cognitive factors are the three components of reciprocal determinism, each influencing and being influenced by the others.

What does Rotter mean by the terms *internal* and *external locus of control*?

According to Rotter, people with an internal locus of control see themselves as primarily in control of their behavior and its consequences; those with an external locus of control believe their destiny is in the hands of fate, luck, or chance.

Key Terms
reciprocal determinism (p. 338); self-efficacy (p. 338); locus of control (p. 338)

HUMANISTIC PERSONALITY THEORIES

Who were the two pioneers in humanistic psychology, and how did they view human nature?

Abraham Maslow and Carl Rogers, the two pioneers in humanistic psychology, believed that human nature is innately good and that people have free will and a tendency toward growth and realization of their potential.

What is self-actualization, and how did Maslow study it?

Self-actualization means developing to one's fullest potential. Maslow studied people who had made significant contributions in their lifetimes and who exemplified self-actualization to determine what characteristics they shared.

According to Rogers, why don't all people become fully functioning persons?

Individuals often do not become fully functioning persons because in childhood they did not receive unconditional positive regard from their parents. To gain positive regard, they had to meet their parents' conditions of worth.

Key Terms
humanistic psychology (p. 339); self-actualization (p. 339); conditions of worth (p. 340); unconditional positive regard (p. 340)

PERSONALITY: IS IT IN THE GENES?

What has research in behavioral genetics revealed about the influence of the genes and the environment on personality?

Research in behavioral genetics has revealed that about 40–50% of personality can be attributed to the genes, and that the environmental influences on personality are mainly from the non-shared environment.

Key Terms
behavioral genetics (p. 341); heritability (p. 341)

PERSONALITY ASSESSMENT

What are the three major methods used in personality assessment?

The three major methods used in personality assessment are (1) observation, interviews, and rating scales, (2) inventories, and (3) projective tests.

What is an inventory, and what are the MMPI-2 and the CPI designed to reveal?

An inventory is a paper-and-pencil test posing questions about a person's thoughts, feelings, and behaviors; it can be scored according to a standard procedure. The MMPI-2 is designed to screen and diagnose psychiatric problems, and the CPI is designed to assess the normal personality.

How do projective tests provide insight into personality, and what are some of the most commonly used projective tests?

In a projective test, people respond to inkblots, drawings of ambiguous human situations, incomplete sentences, and the like by projecting their own inner thoughts, feelings, fears, or conflicts onto the test materials. Examples are the Rorschach Inkblot Method, the Thematic Apperception Test (TAT), and the sentence completion method.

Key Terms
inventory (p. 344); Minnesota Multiphasic Personality Inventory (MMPI) (p. 344); California Psychological Inventory (CPI) (p. 345); Myers–Briggs Type Indicator (MBTI) (p. 346); projective test (p. 346); Rorschach Inkblot Method (p. 346); Thematic Apperception Test (TAT) (p. 347)

Study Guide for Chapter 10

Answers to all the Study Guide questions are provided at the end of the book.

Section One: Chapter Review

1. Psychoanalysis is both a theory of personality and a therapy for the treatment of psychological disorders. (true/false)

2. Freud considered the (conscious, unconscious) to be the primary motivating force of human behavior.

3. The part of the personality that would make you want to eat, drink, and be merry is your
   a. id.   c. superego.
   b. ego.   d. ego ideal.

4. You just found a gold watch in a darkened movie theater. Which part of your personality would urge you to turn it in to the lost and found?
   a. id   c. superego
   b. ego   d. ego ideal

5. The part of the personality that determines appropriate ways to satisfy biological urges is the
   a. id.   c. superego.
   b. ego.   d. ego ideal.

6. Defense mechanisms are used only by psychologically unhealthy individuals. (true/false)

7. Match the defense mechanism and the example.

   ____ (1) sublimation
   ____ (2) repression
   ____ (3) displacement
   ____ (4) rationalization

   a. forgetting a traumatic childhood experience
   b. supplying a logical reason for arriving late
   c. creating a work of art
   d. venting anger on a friend or spouse after getting a speeding ticket

8. According to Freud, the sex instinct arises at (birth, puberty).

9. Which of the following lists presents Freud's stages in the order in which they occur?
   a. anal, oral, genital, phallic
   b. genital, anal, oral, phallic
   c. oral, phallic, anal, genital
   d. oral, anal, phallic, genital

10. Matt's excessive concern with cleanliness and order could indicate a fixation at the _____ stage.
    a. oral   b. anal   c. phallic   d. genital

11. When a young boy develops sexual feelings toward his mother and hostility toward his father, he is said to have a conflict called the
    _____.

12. According to Freud, which of the following represents a primary source of influence on personality?
    a. heredity
    b. life experiences after beginning school
    c. the relative strengths of the id, ego, and superego
    d. the problems experienced during adolescence

13. In Jung's theory, the inherited part of the personality that stores the experiences of humankind is the (collective, personal) unconscious.

14. Which personality theorist believed that the basic human drive is to overcome and compensate for inferiority and strive for superiority and significance?
    a. Sigmund Freud   c. Alfred Adler
    b. Carl Jung   d. Karen Horney

15. Horney traced the origin of psychological maladjustment to
    a. the inferiority feelings of childhood.
    b. basic anxiety resulting from the parents' failure to satisfy the child's needs for safety and satisfaction.
    c. excessive frustration or overindulgence of the child at early stages of development.
    d. the failure to balance opposing forces in the personality.

16. According to Allport, the kind of trait that is a defining characteristic of one's personality is a _____ trait.
    a. common   c. secondary
    b. source   d. cardinal

17. According to Cattell, the differences between people are explained by the number of source traits they possess. (true/false)

18. Who claimed that psychologists can best understand personality by assessing people on two major dimensions, extroversion and neuroticism?
    a. Hans Eysenck
    b. Gordon Allport
    c. Raymond Cattell
    d. Carl Jung

19. This chapter suggests that, according to a growing consensus among trait theorists, there are _____ major dimensions of personality.
    a. 3   c. 7
    b. 5   d. 16

20. According to Skinner, behavior is initiated by inner forces called personality. (true/false)

21. Bandura's concept of reciprocal determinism refers to the mutual effects of
    a. a person's behavior, personality, and thinking.
    b. a person's feelings, attitudes, and thoughts.
    c. a person's behavior, personal/cognitive factors, and the environment.
    d. classical and operant conditioning and observational learning.

22. Which statement is *not* true of people low in self-efficacy?
    a. They persist in their efforts.
    b. They lack confidence.
    c. They expect failure.
    d. They avoid challenge.

23. Who proposed the concept of locus of control?
    a. B. F. Skinner   c. Hans Eysenck
    b. Albert Bandura   d. Julian Rotter

24. Humanistic psychologists would *not* say that
    a. human nature is innately good.
    b. human beings have a natural tendency toward self-actualization.
    c. human beings have free will.
    d. researchers should focus primarily on observable behavior.

25. Which psychologist studied individuals he believed exemplified self-actualization in order to identify characteristics that self-actualized persons share?
    a. Carl Rogers   c. Abraham Maslow
    b. Gordon Allport   d. Hans Eysenck

26. Which psychologist believed that individuals often do not become fully functioning persons because, in childhood, they fail to receive unconditional positive regard from their parents?
    a. Carl Rogers   c. Abraham Maslow
    b. Gordon Allport   d. Hans Eysenck

27. Many behavioral geneticists believe that personality may be as much as _____ inherited.
    a. 10–20%   c. 40–50%
    b. 25–35%   d. 65–75%

28. Behavioral geneticists have found that the (shared, nonshared) environment has the greater effect on personality.

29. Children adopted at birth are more similar in personality to their adoptive parents than to their biological parents. (true/false)

30. (All, The majority of) individuals in a collectivist society have a collectivist orientation.

31. Match each personality test with its description.
    ____ (1) MMPI-2
    ____ (2) Rorschach
    ____ (3) TAT
    ____ (4) CPI
    ____ (5) MBTI
    a. inventory used to diagnose psychopathology
    b. inventory used to assess normal personality
    c. projective test using inkblots
    d. projective test using drawings of ambiguous human situations
    e. inventory used to assess personality types

32. Two experts in personality assessment would be most likely to agree on interpreting results from the
    a. Rorschach.
    b. MMPI-2.
    c. TAT.
    d. sentence completion method.

33. George has an unconscious resentment toward his father. Which test might best detect this?
    a. MMPI-2   c. Rorschach
    b. CPI   d. TAT

34. Which of the following items might appear on the MMPI-2?
    a. What is happening in the picture?
    b. Hand is to glove as foot is to _____.
    c. My mother was a good person.
    d. What is your favorite food?

Section Two: Complete the Table

Approach	Key Theorist(s)	Major Assumption about Behavior
1. Psychoanalytic	_____	_____
2. Trait	_____	_____
3. Learning-behaviorist	_____	_____
4. Social-cognitive	_____	_____
5. Humanistic	_____	_____

Section Three: Fill In the Blank

1. According to Freud, the _____ is the personality structure that is completely unconscious and operates on the pleasure principle.

2. According the Freud, the _____ is the logical and rational part of the personality.

3. Freud's _____ is very much like long-term memory.

4. The stages of psychosexual development, in the proper order, are _____, _____, _____, _____, and _____.

5. Mother Teresa would be said to possess the _____ trait of altruism.

6. According to Cattell, _____ traits are the observable qualities of personality, whereas _____ traits make up the most basic personality structure and cause behavior.

7. Bandura asserted that personal/cognitive factors, one's behavior, and the external environment all influence each other and are influenced by each other. He called this relationship _____ _____.

8. According to Jung, the _____ _____ accounts for the similarity of certain myths, dreams, symbols, and religious beliefs in different cultures.

9. According to Eysenck, _____ are more important in determining personality than is the _____.

10. Psychologists who adopt a behavioral perspective on personality usually prefer the _____ method to other methods of personality assessment.

11. The Myers–Briggs Type Indicator is a personality inventory that is based on_____ theory of personality.

12. The Rorschach Inkblot Method is an example of a _____ test.

13. The _____ is the most widely used of the many different personality inventories.

14. The defense mechanism called _____ involves rechanneling sexual or aggressive energy into pursuits that society considers acceptable or admirable.

15. _____ refers to a person's belief that he or she can perform competently in what is attempted.

16. Cattell defined _____ traits as those traits that make up the most basic personality structure and cause behavior.

17. In Jung's view, an _____ exists in the collective unconscious and is an inherited tendency to respond in particular ways to universal human situations.

Section Four: Comprehensive Practice Test

1. A person's unique pattern of behaving, thinking, and feeling is his or her
   a. motivation.
   c. personality.
   b. emotion.
   d. cognition.

2. Freud's theory of personality and his therapy for the treatment of psychological disorders are both known as
   a. behaviorism.
   c. psychoanalysis.
   b. psychosocialism.
   d. humanism.

3. Of Freud's three conceptual systems of personality, the _____ is mainly in the conscious, the _____ is split between the conscious and the unconscious, and the _____ is completely unconscious.
   a. id; ego; superego
   c. superego; ego; id
   b. ego; superego; id
   d. ego; id; superego

4. The libido is Freud's name for the psychic or sexual energy that comes from the superego and provides the energy for the entire personality. (true/false)

5. Anna is 13 months old, and whatever she can pick up is likely to go into her mouth. Anna is in Freud's _____ stage of psychosexual development.
   a. anal
   c. phallic
   b. oral
   d. genital

6. Art is 5 years old, and he thinks his mother is as beautiful as a princess; he would rather spend time with her than with his father. Art is in Freud's _____ stage of psychosexual development.
   a. anal
   c. phallic
   b. oral
   d. genital

7. A central theme in Adler's theory is the individual's quest for feelings of
   a. superiority.
   c. adequacy.
   b. the collective unconscious.
   d. ego integrity.

8. A central theme in Horney's theory is the concept of
   a. ego integrity.
   c. basic anxiety.
   b. penis envy.
   d. introversion/extroversion.

9. Allport and Cattell were proponents of the _____ theory of personality.
   a. stage
   c. biological
   b. trait
   d. humanistic

10. Which of the following Big Five personality factors has been found to be a requirement for creative accomplishment?
    a. extroversion
    b. conscientiousness
    c. neuroticism
    d. openness to experience

11. Based on meta-analysis, Sulloway concluded that _____ are more likely to be extroverted and conscientious.
    a. twins raised together
    c. later borns
    b. first borns
    d. twins raised apart

12. Bandura's theory includes the concept of _____, the belief a person has regarding his or her ability to perform competently whatever is attempted.
    a. reciprocal determinism
    b. self-efficacy
    c. extroversion
    d. conditions of worth

13. Rick believes that what happens to him is based on fate, luck, or chance, and his philosophy of life is "whatever will be will be." Rotter would say that Rick has a(n) _____ locus of control.
    a. internal
    c. external
    b. explicit
    d. regressed

14. Rogers's theory included the concept of conditions of worth—the idea that our parents teach us important values in life and that we as individuals will be motivated to seek out those values. (true/false)

15. The MMPI-2 is a good example of a projective personality test. (true/false)

16. The California Psychological Inventory was developed to evaluate the personalities of
    a. the mentally ill.
    c. normal people.
    b. males.
    d. females.

17. You are shown a black and white scene and asked to tell a story about it. You are probably responding to
    a. the Rorschach Inkblot Method.
    b. the CPI.
    c. the Myers-Briggs Type Indicator.
    d. the TAT.

Section Five: Critical Thinking

1. In your opinion, which of the major personality theories discussed in this chapter is the most accurate, reasonable, and realistic? Which is the least accurate, reasonable, and realistic? Give reasons to support your answers.

2. Are personality characteristics mostly learned? Or are they mostly transmitted through the genes? Using what you have learned in this chapter and other evidence you can gather, make a case for each position. Support your answers with research and expert opinion.

3. Consider your own behavior and personality attributes from the standpoint of each of these theories: psychoanalysis, trait theory, and the learning, humanistic, and genetic perspectives. Which theory or theories best explain your personality? Why?

Health and Stress

April 19, 1995. Throughout the world people stopped what they were doing to listen in shocked disbelief to news of the bombing of the Murrah Federal Building in Oklahoma City. More than 160 people, many of them children, were killed in the blast. Hundreds more were injured, and many of those victims died in the next few days.

Thousands of doctors, nurses, medics, ambulance drivers, psychologists, and other professionals poured into the city to offer assistance. Some came to help the rescue workers who were risking their lives combing through the rubble to save the living and retrieve the bodies of the dead. All of those who were trying to give assistance needed relief from the unbearable stress they had to endure. Although there are many techniques for relieving tension and stress, one that proved highly effective in Oklahoma City was massage therapy.

Robin Devine, a massage therapist, worked at one of several city mortuaries, where morticians did the grim work of piecing together and identifying bodies. Although the morticians did not receive much media attention, their job was as emotionally draining as that of the rescue workers. "Some were in 'business as usual' mode," Devine remembers. "Some 'locked down,' not allowing what was just beneath the surface to come out. When some were massaged, tears would break through, and feelings would emerge and be released" (Devine, 1998).

Devine also worked with ambulance drivers and medics who pulled bodies from the building in the hours and days after the bombing. These workers were on full alert, 24 hours a day, for days on end. Said Devine, "All of these rescue workers carried incredible tension in their bodies and into the massage room with them. Their bodies were stiff as boards when they came in. After a 15- to 20-minute massage, though, [their muscles] became [less tight], and they left less stressed physically and mentally."

Fortunately, few of us will ever have to endure such a traumatic experience as the Oklahoma City bombing, but it does dramatically illustrate the relationship between stress and both physical and mental health. And the relief provided to the morticians and rescue workers by Robin Devine and other professional therapists suggests that the body is not simply an isolated physical system that is unaffected by psychological and social influences.

TWO APPROACHES TO HEALTH AND ILLNESS

How do the biomedical and biopsychosocial models differ in their approaches to health and illness?

The predominant view in medicine is the **biomedical model**, which focuses on illness rather than on health. It explains illness in terms of biological factors without considering psychological and social factors that might contribute to the condition.

Another approach that is growing in importance is the **biopsychosocial model** of health and wellness (see Figure 11.1). This approach focuses on health as well as illness, and it holds that both are determined by a combination of biological, psychological, and social factors (Engel, 1977, 1980; Schwartz, 1982). Endorsed by most health psychologists, this model goes beyond disease prevention to include health promotion (Breslow, 1999).

But first, what is health psychology? **Health psychology** is "the field within psychology devoted to understanding psychological influences on how people stay healthy, why they become ill, and how they respond when they do get ill" (Taylor, 1991, p. 6). Health psychologists study psychological factors associated with health and illness, and they promote interventions that foster good health and aid recovery from illness.

Why do people become ill in the modern age? At the beginning of the 20th century, the primary causes of death in the United States were pneumonia and infectious diseases such as diphtheria and tuberculosis. Medical research has virtually conquered these diseases, with the exception of some new strains of tuberculosis. The health menaces of modern times are diseases related to unhealthy lifestyle and stress (Taylor & Repetti, 1997). The price of an unhealthy lifestyle coupled with the added burden of stress is high indeed—heart attack, stroke, hardening of the arteries, cancer, and cirrhosis of the liver. In this chapter we discuss stress, disease, and behaviors that promote and compromise health.

biomedical model: A perspective that focuses on illness rather than on health, explaining illness in terms of biological factors without regard to psychological and social factors.

biopsychosocial model: A perspective that focuses on health as well as illness and holds that both are determined by a combination of biological, psychological, and social factors.

health psychology: The field concerned with the psychological factors that contribute to health, illness, and recovery.

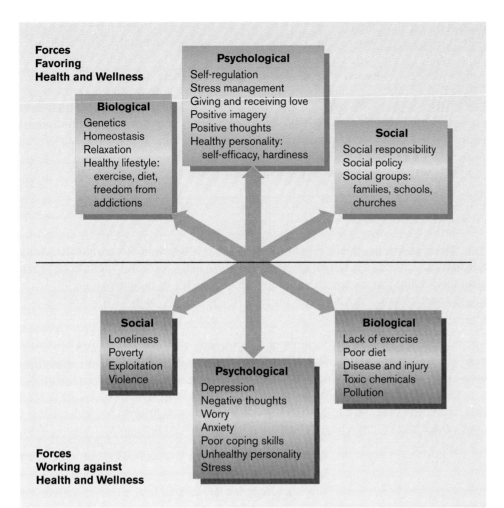

Figure 11.1

The Biopsychosocial Model of Health and Wellness

The biopsychosocial model focuses on health as well as on illness and holds that both are determined by a combination of biological, psychological, and social factors. Most health psychologists endorse the biopsychosocial model. (From Green & Shellenberger, 1990.)

THEORIES OF STRESS

How would you define stress? Is stress something in the environment? Is it a physiological or psychological reaction that occurs within a person? Is it something we should avoid at all costs? As with most issues in psychology, there are different ways to view stress. Some researchers emphasize the physiological effects of stress, while others focus on the role that thinking plays in stress (Carpi, 1996). Most psychologists define **stress** as the physiological and psychological response to a condition that threatens or challenges the individual and requires some form of adaptation or adjustment.

Selye and the General Adaptation Syndrome

An early, classic contribution to stress research was made by Walter Cannon (1932), who described the fight-or-flight response. Cannon discovered that when an organism (animal or human) perceives a threat, the sympathetic nervous system and the endocrine glands prepare the body to fight the threat or flee from it. Cannon considered the fight-or-flight response wonderfully adaptive, because it helps the organism respond rapidly to threats. He also considered it potentially harmful in the long run, if an organism is not able to fight or flee and experiences prolonged stress and continuing physical arousal (Sapolsky, 1994).

Hans Selye (1907–1982), the researcher most prominently associated with the effects of stress on health, established the field of stress research. Selye initially con-

stress: The physiological and psychological response to a condition that threatens or challenges a person and requires some form of adaptation or adjustment.

ducted research on the effects of sex hormones. In one experiment, he injected rats with hormone-rich extracts of cow ovaries. What happened to the rats? To Selye's amazement, (1) their adrenal glands became swollen, (2) their immune systems were weakened, and (3) they developed bleeding ulcers in their stomachs and intestines. Never before had a hormone been shown to cause such clear physical symptoms. But further experiments proved that the same symptoms could be produced by almost anything he tried on the rats, including a wide variety of toxic chemicals and exposure to freezing cold temperatures. Even extreme muscle fatigue caused the same symptoms.

Selye realized that the body responds in much the same way to all harmful agents (toxic substances, injuries, electric shock) and a host of other stressors. The physical response was so predictable, so general, that Selye named it the *general adaptation syndrome.*

What is the general adaptation syndrome?

The General Adaptation Syndrome: A General Physical Response to Many Stressors   Selye knew that all living organisms are constantly confronted with **stressors**—stimuli or events that place a demand on the organism to adapt or read-just. Each stressor causes both specific and nonspecific responses. Extreme cold, for example, causes the specific response of shivering. Apart from the specific response, the body makes a common, or nonspecific, response to a wide variety of stressors. The heart of Selye's concept of stress is the **general adaptation syndrome (GAS)**, his term for the nonspecific response to stress. The syndrome consists of three stages: the alarm stage, the resistance stage, and the exhaustion stage (Selye, 1956). (See Figure 11.2.)

The body's first response to a stressor is the **alarm stage**, when emotional arousal occurs and the defensive forces of the body are prepared to meet the threat. In the alarm stage the sympathetic nervous system, through the release of hormones, mobilizes the body to fight or flee. If the stressor cannot be quickly conquered or avoided, the organism enters the **resistance stage**, characterized by intense physiological efforts to either resist or adapt to the stressor. During the resistance stage the adrenal cortex releases hormones known as *glucocorticoids* to help the body resist stressors. Resistance may last a long time, but according to Selye, the length of the resistance stage depends both on the strength or intensity of the stressor and on the body's power to adapt.

If the organism finally fails in its efforts to resist, it reaches the **exhaustion stage**. Selye (1974) wrote, "The stage of exhaustion after a temporary demand upon the body, is reversible, but the complete exhaustion of all stores of deep adaptation

Figure 11.2

The General Adaptation Syndrome

The three stages in Hans Selye's general adaptation syndrome are (1) the alarm stage, during which there is emotional arousal and the defensive forces of the body are mobilized for fight or flight; (2) the resistance stage, in which intense physiological efforts are exerted to resist or adapt to the stressor; and (3) the exhaustion stage, when the organism fails in its efforts to resist the stressor. (Based on Selye, 1956.)

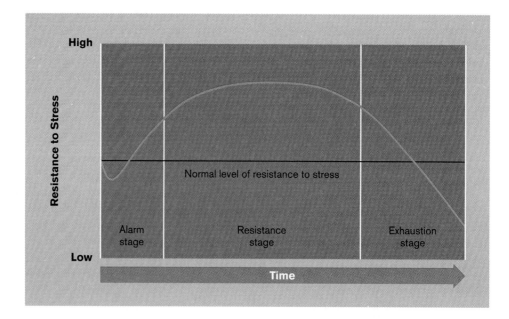

energy is not" (p. 29). If exposure to the stressor continues, all the stores of deep energy are depleted, and disintegration and death follow.

Selye claimed that any event requiring a readjustment, positive or negative, will produce stress in an organism. He did, however, differentiate between the positive and negative aspects of stress. "Eustress" is positive or good stress, including exhilaration, excitement, and the thrill of accomplishment. "Distress" is damaging or unpleasant stress, such as frustration, inadequacy, loss, disappointment, insecurity, helplessness, or desperation.

Criticisms of Selye's Theory: A Missing Cognitive Factor   Thanks to Selye, the connection between extreme, prolonged stress and certain diseases is now widely accepted by medical experts. But criticism is directed at Selye's claim that the intensity of the stressor determines one's physical reaction to it. His theory does not provide for a psychological component—how a person perceives and evaluates the stressor. This criticism led to the development of the cognitive theory of stress.

Lazarus's Cognitive Theory of Stress

Richard Lazarus (1966; Lazarus & Folkman, 1984) contends that it is not the stressor itself that causes stress, but a person's perception of the stressor. Because Lazarus emphasizes the importance of perceptions and appraisal of stressors, his is a cognitive theory of stress and coping. Lazarus (1993) asserts that the stress process can be understood in terms of four phases. First, there is a causal agent, either external or internal, that is commonly referred to as stress or the stressor. Second, the mind or the body evaluates the stressor as either threatening or benign. Third, the mind or the body uses coping processes to deal with the stressor. Finally, there is the stress reaction—the "complex pattern of effects on mind and body" (p. 4). Lazarus believes that physiological and psychological stress must be analyzed differently. Selye's model describes how the body copes with physiological stress; Lazarus's model focuses on how people cope with psychological stressors.

The Cognitive Appraisal of Stressors: Evaluating the Stressor and Considering the Options   According to Lazarus, when people are confronted with a potentially stressful event, they engage in a cognitive process that involves a primary and a secondary appraisal. A **primary appraisal** is an evaluation of the meaning and significance of a situation—whether its effect on one's well-being is positive, irrelevant, or negative. An event appraised as stressful could involve (1) harm or loss—damage that has already occurred; (2) threat—the potential for harm or loss; or (3) challenge—the opportunity to grow or to gain. An appraisal of threat, harm, or loss can occur in relation to anything important to you—a friendship, a part of your body, your property, your finances, or your self-esteem.

The same event can be appraised differently by different people. Some students may welcome the opportunity to give an oral presentation in class, seeing it as a challenge and a chance to impress their professor and raise their grade. Other students may feel threatened, fearing that they may embarrass themselves in front of their classmates and lower their grade in the process. Still others may view the assignment as both a challenge and a threat. When people appraise a situation as involving harm, loss, or threat, they experience negative emotions such as anxiety, fear, anger, or resentment (Folkman, 1984). A challenge appraisal, on the other hand, is usually accompanied by positive emotions such as excitement, hopefulness, and eagerness. Stress for younger people is more likely to take the form of challenges; for older people, losses and threats are more common (El-Shiekh et al., 1989).

When people assess an event as stressful, they engage in a **secondary appraisal**. During secondary appraisal, if they judge the situation to be within their control, they make an evaluation of available coping resources—physical (health, energy, stamina), social (support network), psychological (skills, morale, self-esteem), material (money, tools, equipment), and time. Then they consider the options and decide

What are the roles of primary and secondary appraisal when a person is confronted with a potentially stressful event?

stressor: Any stimulus or event capable of producing physical or emotional stress.

general adaptation syndrome (GAS): The predictable sequence of reactions (alarm, resistance, and exhaustion stages) that organisms show in response to stressors.

alarm stage: The first stage of the general adaptation syndrome, when there is emotional arousal and the defensive forces of the body are prepared for fight or flight.

resistance stage: The second stage of the general adaptation syndrome, when there are intense physiological efforts to either resist or adapt to the stressor.

exhaustion stage: The final stage of the general adaptation syndrome, occurring if the organism fails in its efforts to resist the stressor.

primary appraisal: An evaluation of the significance of a potentially stressful event according to how it will affect one's well-being—whether it is perceived as irrelevant or as involving harm or loss, threat, or challenge.

secondary appraisal: An evaluation of one's coping resources prior to deciding how to deal with a stressful event.

Figure 11.3

Lazarus and Folkman's Psychological Model of Stress

Lazarus and Folkman emphasize the importance of a person's perceptions and appraisal of stressors. The stress response depends on the outcome of the primary and secondary appraisals, whether the person's coping resources are adequate to cope with the threat, and how severely the resources are taxed in the process. (From Folkman, 1984.)

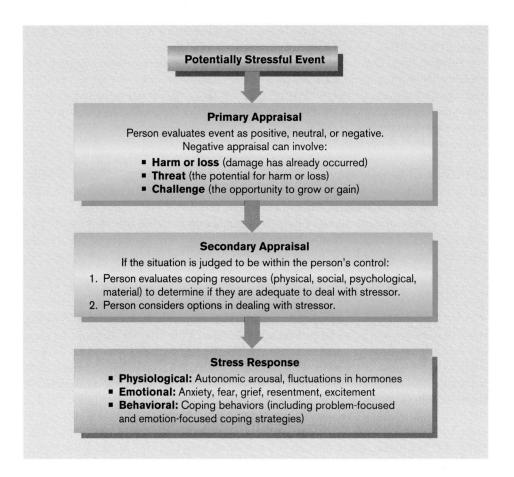

how to deal with the stressor. The level of stress they feel is largely a function of whether their resources are adequate to cope with the threat, and how severely those resources will be taxed in the process.

Figure 11.3 summarizes the Lazarus and Folkman psychological model of stress. There is research support for Lazarus and Folkman's claim that the physiological, emotional, and behavioral reactions to stressors depend partly on whether the stressors are appraised as challenging or threatening. Tomaka and others (1993) found that active coping with stressors appraised as challenging was associated with increased heart rate, better performance, and positive emotions. Active coping with stressors appraised as threatening was related to increased blood pressure, poorer performance, and negative emotional tone.

SOURCES OF STRESS: THE COMMON AND THE EXTREME

Some stressors produce temporary stress, while others produce chronic stress—a state of stress that continues unrelieved over time. Chronic health problems, physical handicaps, poverty, and unemployment are sources of chronic stress. The burden of chronic stress is disproportionately heavy for the poor, for minorities, and for the elderly.

Everyday Sources of Stress

Everyday sources of stress can range from the need to make choices to the perception of a lack of control over one's life. And some people experience added stress from being a member of a minority group within the the larger culture.

How do approach–approach, avoidance–avoidance, and approach–avoidance conflicts differ?

Making Choices: Should I or Shouldn't I?   Sometimes conflicting motives can be sources of stress. When a person must make a choice between two desirable alternatives, known as an **approach–approach conflict**, stress may be the result. Some approach–approach conflicts are minor, such as deciding which movie to see. Others can have major consequences, such as the conflict between building a promising career or interrupting the career to raise a child. In approach–approach conflicts, both choices are desirable.

In an **avoidance–avoidance conflict** a person must choose between two undesirable alternatives. You may want to avoid studying for an exam, but at the same time you want to avoid failing the test. **Approach–avoidance conflicts** include both desirable and undesirable features in the same choice. The person facing this type of conflict is simultaneously drawn to and repelled by a choice—wanting to take a wonderful vacation but having to empty a savings account to do so.

Unpredictability and Lack of Control   Unpredictable stressors are more difficult to cope with than predictable stressors. Laboratory tests have shown that rats receiving electric shocks without warning develop more ulcers than rats given shocks just as often but only after a warning (Weiss, 1972). Likewise, humans who are warned of a stressor before it occurs and have a chance to prepare themselves for it experience less stress than those who must cope with an unexpected stressor.

Our physical and psychological well-being is profoundly influenced by the degree to which we feel a sense of control over our lives (Rodin & Salovey, 1989). Langer and Rodin (1976) studied the effects of control on nursing-home residents. Residents in one group were given some measure of control over their lives, such as choices in arranging their rooms and in the times they could see movies. They showed improved health and well-being and had a lower death rate than another group who were not given control. Within 18 months, 30% of the residents given no choices had died, compared to only 15% of those who had been given some control over their lives. Control is important for cancer patients, too. Some researchers suggest that for cancer patients a sense of control over their daily physical symptoms and emotional reactions may be even more important than control over the course of the disease itself (Thompson et al., 1993).

Several studies suggest that we are less subject to stress when we have the power to do something about it, whether we exercise that power or not. Glass and Singer (1972) subjected two groups of participants to the same loud noise, but one group was told that they could, if necessary, terminate the noise by pressing a switch. The group that had the control suffered less stress even though they never did exercise the control they were given. Friedland and others (1992) suggest that when people experience a loss of control because of a stressor, they are motivated to try to reestablish control in the stressful situation. Failing this, they often attempt to increase their sense of control in other areas of their lives.

Racial Stress   A significant source of everyday stress is being a member of a minority group in a majority culture. A study of White and Black participants' responses to a questionnaire about ways of coping revealed that a person may experience *racial stress* from simply being one of the few or only members of a particular race in any of a variety of settings, such as a classroom, the workplace, or a social situation. The feeling of stress experienced in such situations can be intense, even in the absence of racist attitudes, discrimination, or any other overt evidence of racism (Plummer & Slane, 1996).

Stress in the Workplace

In the modern workplace, too many people find their jobs a source of chronic stress. Assembly-line workers and piece-goods workers must endure boring and repetitive jobs; doctors, nurses, and emergency ambulance personnel must deal with life and death every day. Even workers who hold more ordinary jobs can be subject to

approach–approach conflict: A conflict arising from having to choose between desirable alternatives.

avoidance–avoidance conflict: A conflict arising from having to choose between undesirable alternatives.

approach–avoidance conflict: A conflict arising when the same choice has both desirable and undesirable features.

How do the unpredictability of and lack of control over a stressor affect its impact?

intense stress—the salesperson struggling to reach a quota, the manager fretting over the bottom line for the upcoming quarterly financial report. And employees in any field working under managers who hassle or threaten them may suffer from excessive work-related stress.

For people to function effectively and find satisfaction on the job, what nine variables should fall within their comfort zone?

Variables in Work Stress   Everyone who works is subject to certain amounts of job-related stress, but the amount and sources of stress differ, depending on the type of job and the kind of organization. Albrecht (1979) suggests that if people are to function effectively and find satisfaction on the job, the following nine variables must fall within their comfort zone (see Figure 11.4):

- *Workload.* An overload of work—too much to do and too little time to do it in—causes people to feel anxious, frustrated, and unrewarded. Interestingly, just the opposite—work underload—produces the same feelings.

- *Clarity of job description and evaluation criteria.* The lack of a clearly defined role or confusion about performance criteria often causes anxiety and stress in workers. At the other extreme, a role that is too rigidly defined may leave insufficient room for creativity or individual initiative and may result in worker stress.

- *Physical variables.* Temperature, noise, humidity, pollution, and amount of work space should fall within a person's comfort zone. Being confined to a desk or having to work in fatiguing positions can also create stress.

- *Job status.* Extremes in job status can produce stress. People with very low status—garbage collectors, or janitors, for example—may feel psychological discomfort. At the other extreme, those with celebrity status often cannot handle the stress that fame brings.

- *Accountability.* Accountability underload occurs when workers perceive their jobs as meaningless. Extreme overload occurs when people have responsibility for the physical or psychological well-being of others but only a limited degree of control, such as air-traffic controllers and emergency-room nurses and doctors.

Figure 11.4

Variables in Work Stress

For a person to function effectively and find satisfaction on the job, these nine variables should fall within the person's comfort zone. (Based on Albrecht, 1979.)

- *Task variety.* Jobs can be deadly boring, repetitive, and monotonous. To function well, people need a comfortable amount of variety and stimulation.

- *Human contact.* Some workers have virtually no human contact on the job (forest-fire lookouts); others have almost continuous contact with others (welfare and

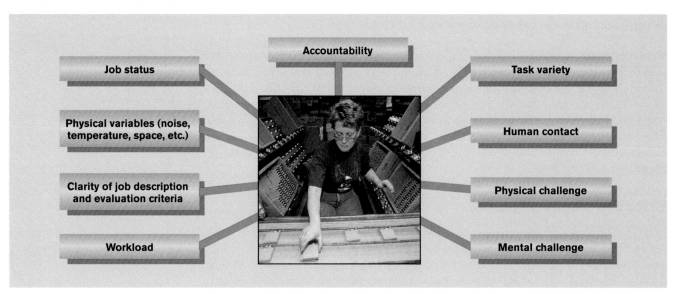

employment-office workers). People vary greatly in how much interaction they enjoy or even tolerate.

■ *Physical challenge.* Jobs range from physically demanding (construction work, professional sports) to those requiring no physical activity. Some jobs (fire fighting, police work) involve physical risk as well.

■ *Mental challenge.* Jobs that tax people beyond their mental capability or training cause feelings of inadequacy and frustration. Yet jobs that require too little mental challenge are also frustrating.

Decision Latitude: A Critical Factor in Job Stress   Whether occupational stress is the spice of life or the kiss of death depends largely on the amount of decision latitude a job offers (Levi, 1990). **Decision latitude** refers to the degree to which employees may exercise initiative and use their skills to control their working conditions. Jobs that involve a large workload but little latitude in or control over the pace and manner in which the work will be completed are highly stressful (Karasek & Theorell, 1990). According to Sauter and others (1990), machine-paced assembly workers report "the highest levels of anxiety, depression, and irritation, as well as more frequent somatic [bodily] complaints" (p. 1150).

In contrast are jobs like those of executives and professionals, in which high demand is coupled with a high degree of control over how the work will be done. In this case high demand is likely to be viewed as challenging and rewarding.

How much stress have you experienced in jobs you have had? Rate your stress in the *Try It!*

Try It!

What are the sources of stress in a job you have now or have had in the past? Rate the job by indicating whether there is or was too little, too much, or about the right amount of each of the job dimensions listed. (Adapted from Albrecht, 1979.)

Job Dimension	Too Little	About Right	Too Much
Workload	_____	_____	_____
Decision latitude	_____	_____	_____
Clarity of job description	_____	_____	_____
Task variety	_____	_____	_____
Mental challenge	_____	_____	_____
Physical demand	_____	_____	_____
Human contact	_____	_____	_____
Job status	_____	_____	_____
Job security	_____	_____	_____

Psychological and Health Consequences of Job Stress   Job stress can have a variety of consequences. Perhaps the most frequent is reduced effectiveness on the job. But stress can also lead to absenteeism, tardiness, accidents, substance abuse, and lower morale (Smith, 1993). Workers who are experiencing stress often become

What are some of the psychological and health consequences of job stress?

alienated from their coworkers and may also suffer from headaches, exhaustion, back problems, insomnia, and indigestion. Stress can even lead to more serious illnesses, such as depression, high blood pressure, and cardiovascular disease. And job-related stress can have even more negative consequences in people with high levels of job involvement (Frone et al., 1995).

What is burnout?

Burnout   When job stress is intense and unrelieved, many people suffer from **burnout**, a condition in which they become pessimistic, dissatisfied, inefficient on the job, and debilitated psychologically. Energy reserves are depleted, resistance to illness is lowered, and interest in work wanes. In the final stages of burnout, people may be unable to function. "Job burnout is not a symptom of work stress, it is the end of unmanaged work stress" (Rice, 1987, p. 223). A strong relationship exists between number of hours worked per week and the likelihood of burnout. Workers putting in 80 or more hours per week generally run a much higher risk of depleting their energy stores.

Catastrophic Events and Chronic Intense Stress

How do people typically react to catastrophic events?

Environmental, social, physical, and emotional stressors are a fact of life for most people, but some people also experience catastrophic events such as plane crashes, fires, or earthquakes. Panic reactions are rare, except in situations such as fires in which people feel that they will survive only if they escape immediately. Many victims of catastrophic events react initially with such shock that they appear dazed, stunned, and emotionally numb. They seem disoriented and may wander about aimlessly, often unaware of their own injuries, attempting to help neither themselves nor others. Following this stage, victims show a concern for others, and although unable to act efficiently on their own, they are willing to follow the directions of rescue workers. You may have observed these reactions in TV coverage of the Oklahoma City bombing.

As victims begin to recover, the shock is replaced by generalized anxiety. Recovering victims typically have recurring nightmares and feel a compulsive need to talk about the event repeatedly. Reexperiencing the event through dreaming and retelling helps desensitize them to the horror of the experience. Crisis-intervention therapy can provide victims with both coping strategies and realistic expectations about the problems they may face in connection with the trauma.

What is posttraumatic stress disorder?

Posttraumatic Stress Disorder: The Trauma Is Over, but the Stress Remains
Posttraumatic stress disorder (PTSD) is a prolonged and severe stress reaction to a catastrophic event (such as a plane crash or an earthquake) or to chronic intense stress (such as occurs in combat or imprisonment as a hostage or POW). Breslau and others (1991) found that 9% of a random sample of 1,007 adults aged 20 to 30 in metropolitan Detroit had suffered from posttraumatic stress disorder from a variety of events; 80% of the women with PTSD had been raped. Some researchers estimate that between 1% and 2% of Americans meet the diagnostic criteria for PTSD (Foa & Meadows, 1997). The disorder may show up immediately, or it may not occur until 6 months or more after the traumatic experience, in which case it is called *delayed posttraumatic stress disorder*. People who suffer a traumatic experience early in life are much more vulnerable to PTSD than those who are older when the trauma occurs ("Post-traumatic stress," 1996). More than 400,000 Vietnam veterans were found to suffer from PTSD (Goldberg et al., 1990). And for female veterans, not only war trauma, but sexual trauma as well, was a contributing factor (Fontana et al., 1997). The most serious cases of PTSD have resulted from witnessing brutal atrocities, whether among Vietnam veterans (Yehuda et al., 1992), Cambodian refugees (Carlson & Rosser-Hogan, 1991), Holocaust survivors (Kuch & Cox, 1992), or victims of state-sanctioned terrorism and torture (Bloche & Eisenberg, 1993).

People with posttraumatic stress disorder often have flashbacks, nightmares, or intrusive memories that make them feel as though they are actually reexperiencing

burnout: The result of intense, unrelieved, and unmanaged job stress; a condition in which an individual becomes pessimistic, dissatisfied, inefficient on the job, and debilitated psychologically.

posttraumatic stress disorder (PTSD): A prolonged and severe stress reaction to a catastrophic event or to chronic intense stress.

366   CHAPTER 11 the traumatic event. They suffer increased anxiety and startle easily, particularly in response to anything that reminds them of the trauma (Green et al., 1985). Many survivors of war or catastrophic events experience survivor guilt because they lived while others died. Some feel that perhaps they could have done more to save others. Extreme combat-related guilt in Vietnam veterans is a risk factor for suicide or preoccupation with suicide (Hendin & Haas, 1991). And a study of women with PTSD revealed that they were twice as likely as women without PTSD to experience first-onset depression and three times as likely to develop alcohol use disorder (Breslau et al., 1997).

Research on 4,042 identical and fraternal twin pairs who were Vietnam veterans suggests a genetic susceptibility to posttraumatic stress symptoms. Identical twins were much more similar than fraternal twins in the posttraumatic stress symptoms they had in response to similar combat experiences (True et al., 1993). Moreover, some research has revealed that high intelligence seems to protect against symptoms of PTSD (McNally & Shin, 1995).

Can anything lessen the stress that follows a major trauma? According to Bloche and Eisenberg (1993), "Belief systems that give life a sense of purpose and meaning can prevent emotional damage" (p. 5).

When writer Pico Iyer's home was destroyed by arson, he saved only his cat and his manuscript. A fairly common reaction to such catastrophic events is posttraumatic stress disorder.

COPING WITH STRESS

When we encounter stressful situations, we try either to alter or to reinterpret them to make them seem more favorable. **Coping** refers to a person's efforts through action and thought to deal with demands perceived as taxing or overwhelming.

Problem-Focused and Emotion-Focused Coping

Coping strategies fall into two categories—problem-focused and emotion-focused (Lazarus & Folkman, 1984). **Problem-focused coping** is direct; it consists of reducing, modifying, or eliminating the source of stress itself. If you are getting a poor grade in history and appraise this as a threat, you may study harder, talk over your problem with your professor, form a study group with other class members, get a tutor, or drop the course.

But what can people do when they face stress that they cannot fight, escape from, avoid, or modify in any way? They can use **emotion-focused coping** to change the way they respond emotionally. Emotion-focused coping may involve reappraising a stressor. If you lose your job, you may decide that it isn't a major tragedy and instead view it as a challenge—an opportunity to find a better job with a higher salary. To cope emotionally, people may use anything from religious faith, wishful thinking, humor, or denial, to alcohol, drugs, or promiscuous sex (Lazarus & DeLongis, 1983). But misguided emotion-focused coping efforts can themselves become additional sources of stress.

Well-functioning people use a combination of problem-focused and emotion-focused coping in almost every stressful situation. Folkman and Lazarus (1980) studied the coping patterns of 100 participants over a 12-month period and found that both types of coping were used in 98% of the 1,300 stressful life events the participants had confronted. Not surprisingly, problem-focused coping strategies increased in situations participants appraised as changeable, and emotion-focused coping techniques increased in situations appraised as not changeable.

The two types of coping are summed up well in an ancient prayer you may have heard: "Lord, grant me the strength to change those things that I can change

Link It!

What is the difference between problem-focused and emotion-focused coping?

coping: Efforts through action and thought to deal with demands that are perceived as taxing or overwhelming.

problem-focused coping: A response aimed at reducing, modifying, or eliminating a source of stress.

emotion-focused coping: A response aimed at reducing the emotional impact of a stressor.

proactive coping: Efforts or actions taken in advance of a potentially stressful situation to prevent its occurrence or to minimize its consequences.

Social Readjustment Rating Scale (SRRS): Holmes and Rahe's stress scale, which ranks 43 life events from most to least stressful and assigns a point value to each.

hassles: Little stressors that include the irritating demands and troubled relationships that can occur daily and that, according to Lazarus, cause more stress than do major life changes.

[problem-focused coping], the grace to accept those things that I cannot change [emotion-focused coping], and the wisdom to know the difference."

Religion and Coping with Negative Life Events

According to one of the largest surveys of religious affiliation ever conducted in the United States, more than 92% of Americans reported that they considered themselves religious (Goldman, 1991). Does religious faith help people cope with negative life events? Several studies indicate that in the majority of cases, it does. Koenig and others (1992) studied a large sample of hospitalized elderly men who had been suffering from a range of serious medical problems. They found that religious coping was inversely related to depression. That is, the more these patients turned to religious coping, the less likely they were to be depressed. One longitudinal study (conducted over a period of 28 years) revealed that frequent attendance at religious services is correlated with better health habits (Strawbridge et al., 1997). And another study found that the chances of surviving at least 6 months after heart surgery are greatly improved for religious people whose beliefs are a source of comfort and strength and who have an active social life (Oxman et al., 1995).

McIntosh and others (1993) evaluated 124 parents who had lost a child to sudden infant death syndrome. When they evaluated participants 3 weeks and 18 months after the death of their infants, the researchers found that the parents who participated in religious services were better able to cope with their loss. The researchers suggested that religious participation had provided social support, enabled the parents to view death as less threatening, and helped them find meaning in the death.

Proactive Coping: Dealing with Stress in Advance

Most of our discussion of coping has explored ways of coping once stress has begun. Although stress is inevitable in life, many of the stressful situations people must endure are self-imposed, a result of a lack of planning. Some stressful situations can be anticipated in advance, allowing active measures to be taken to avoid or minimize stress. Such active measures are known as *proactive coping* (Aspinwall & Taylor, 1997). **Proactive coping** consists of efforts or actions taken in advance of a potentially stressful situation to prevent its occurrence or to minimize its consequences.

The important feature of proactive coping is action itself. Proactive copers anticipate and then prepare for upcoming stressful events and situations, including those that are certain and those that are only likely. Worrying and dread are not ingredients of proactive coping. Worrying is useful only if it moves a person to plan and to act—that is, to use proactive coping.

EVALUATING LIFE STRESS: MAJOR LIFE CHANGES, HASSLES, AND UPLIFTS

There are two major approaches to evaluating life stress and its relation to illness. One approach focuses on major life events, which cause life changes that require adaptation. A second approach focuses on life's daily hassles.

Holmes and Rahe's Social Readjustment Rating Scale: Adding Up the Stress Score

What was the Social Readjustment Rating Scale designed to reveal?

Interested in the relationship between life changes and illness, researchers Thomas Holmes and Richard Rahe (1967) developed the **Social Readjustment Rating Scale (SRRS)**. The SRRS is designed to measure stress by ranking different life events from most to least stressful and assigning a point value to each event. Life events that produce the greatest life changes and require the greatest adaptation are considered the most stressful, regardless of whether the events are positive or negative. The 43 life events range from death of a spouse (assigned 100 stress points), to such items as divorce (73 points), death of a close family member (63 points), marriage (50 points), and pregnancy (40 points), to minor law violations such as getting a traffic ticket (11 points).

Even positive life events, such as getting married, can cause stress.

Holmes and Rahe claim that there is a connection between the degree of life stress and major health problems. After analyzing more than 5,000 medical case histories, they concluded that major life changes often precede serious illness (Rahe et al., 1964). However, one of the main shortcomings of the SRRS is that it assigns a point value to each life change without taking into account whether the change is for better or worse. For example, life changes such as divorce, pregnancy, retirement from work, and changing jobs or residences may be either welcome or unwelcome events.

The Hassles of Life: Little Things Stress a Lot

Richard Lazarus disagrees with the rationale behind Holmes and Rahe's scale. He contends that life events cannot be assessed and assigned a numerical value for stressfulness without considering their meaning to the individual. Furthermore, he believes that the little stressors, which he calls **hassles**, add up to more stress than major life events.

Daily hassles are the "irritating, frustrating, distressing demands and troubled relationships that plague us day in and day out" (Lazarus & DeLongis, 1983, p. 247). Kanner and others (1981) developed the Hassles Scale to assess various categories of hassles. Unlike the Holmes and Rahe scale, the Hassles Scale takes into account that items may or may not represent stressors and that the amount of stress produced by an item varies from person to person. People completing the scale indicate the items that have been a hassle for them and rate the items for severity on a 3-point scale. Table 11.1 shows the ten hassles most frequently reported by college students.

What roles do hassles and uplifts play in the stress of life, according to Lazarus?

Table 11.1 The Ten Most Common Hassles for College Students

Hassle	Percentage of Times Checked
1. Troubling thoughts about future	76.6
2. Not getting enough sleep	72.5
3. Wasting time	71.1
4. Inconsiderate smokers	70.7
5. Physical appearance	69.9
6. Too many things to do	69.2
7. Misplacing or losing things	67.0
8. Not enough time to do the things you need to do	66.3
9. Concerns about meeting high standards	64.0
10. Being lonely	60.8

Source: From Kanner et al., 1981.

sedentary lifestyle: A lifestyle that includes less than 20 minutes of exercise three times a week.

Type A behavior pattern: A behavior pattern marked by a sense of time urgency, impatience, excessive competitiveness, hostility, and anger; considered a risk factor in coronary heart disease.

Type B behavior pattern: A behavior pattern marked by a relaxed, easygoing approach to life; not associated with coronary heart disease.

More recent research indicates that minor hassles that accompany stressful major life events are better predictors of the level of psychological distress than the major life events themselves (Pillow et al., 1996).

According to Lazarus, "a person's morale, social functioning, and health don't hinge on hassles alone, but on a balance between the good things that happen to people—that make them feel good—and the bad" (quoted in Goleman, 1979, p. 52). Fortunately, the **uplifts**, or positive experiences in life, may neutralize or cancel out the effect of many of the hassles. Lazarus and his colleagues also constructed an Uplifts Scale. As with the Hassles Scale, people completing the scale make a cognitive appraisal of what they consider an uplift. Items viewed as uplifts by some people may actually be stressors for other people. Kanner and others (1981) found that for middle-aged people, uplifts were often health- or family-related, whereas for college students uplifts often came in the form of having a good time.

HEALTH AND DISEASE

Three topics are of high interest to psychologists who focus on health and disease: (1) heart disease and cancer; (2) the varying quality of health and the leading health risk factors for different cultural and ethnic groups; and (3) the immune system and AIDS.

Coronary Heart Disease: The Leading Cause of Death

Link It!

The leading cause of death in the United States is coronary heart disease, which accounts for approximately 33% of all deaths (U.S. Bureau of the Census, 1994). In order to survive, the heart muscle requires a steady, sufficient supply of oxygen and nutrients carried by the blood. Coronary heart disease is caused by the narrowing or the blockage of the coronary arteries—the arteries that supply blood to the heart muscle.

A health problem of modern times, coronary heart disease is largely attributable to lifestyle and is therefore an important field of study for health psychologists. A **sedentary lifestyle**—one that includes less than 20 minutes of exercise three times per week—is the primary modifiable risk factor contributing to death from coronary heart disease. High levels of stress and job strain have also been associated with increased risk for coronary heart disease and stroke (Rosengren et al., 1991; Siegrist et al., 1990). Other risk factors are high serum cholesterol levels, cigarette smoking, obesity, high blood pressure, and diabetes. Though not modifiable, another important risk factor is a family history of heart disease.

What are the Type A and Type B behavior patterns?

The Type A and Type B Behavior Patterns: In a Hurry or Laid Back   Is personality related to heart disease? After extensive research, cardiologists Meyer Friedman and Ray Rosenman (1974) concluded that there are two types of personality—Type A, associated with a high rate of coronary heart disease, and Type B, commonly found in persons unlikely to develop heart disease. Are your characteristics more like those of a Type A or a Type B person? Before reading further, complete the *Try It!* and find out.

People with the **Type A behavior pattern** have a strong sense of time urgency and are impatient, excessively competitive, hostile, and easily angered. They are "involved in a *chronic, incessant* struggle to achieve more and more in less and less time" (Friedman & Rosenman, 1974, p. 84). Type A's would answer "true" to most or all of the questions in the *Try It!* The Type A person may be a driven executive, a competitive mortician, or a stressed blue collar employee.

In stark contrast to Type A's, people with the **Type B behavior pattern** are relaxed and easygoing and do not suffer from a sense of time urgency. They are not impatient or hostile and are able to relax without guilt. They play for fun and relax-

Try It! Answer true (T) or false (F) for each of the statements below. (Adapted from Friedman and Rosenman, 1974.)

_____ 1. I forcefully emphasize key words in my everyday speech.

_____ 2. I usually walk and eat quickly.

_____ 3. I get irritated and restless around slow workers.

_____ 4. When talking to others, I get impatient and try to hurry them along.

_____ 5. I get very irritated, even hostile, when the car in front of me drives too slowly.

_____ 6. When others are talking, I often think about my own concerns.

_____ 7. I usually think of or do at least two things at the same time.

_____ 8. I get very impatient when I have to wait.

_____ 9. I usually take command and move the conversation to topics that interest me.

_____ 10. I usually feel guilty when I relax and do nothing.

_____ 11. I am usually too absorbed in my work to notice my surroundings.

_____ 12. I keep trying to do more and more in less time.

_____ 13. I sometimes punctuate my conversation with forceful gestures such as clenching my fists or pounding the table.

_____ 14. My accomplishments are due largely to my ability to work faster than others.

_____ 15. I don't play games just for fun. I play to win.

_____ 16. I am more concerned with acquiring things than with becoming a better person.

_____ 17. I usually use numbers to evaluate my own activities and the activities of others.

ation rather than to exhibit superiority over others. Yet the Type B individual may be as bright and ambitious as the Type A, and more successful as well. Type B's would answer "false" to most or all of the *Try It!* questions.

Research on Behavior Pattern and Heart Disease Using meta-analysis, Miller and others (1991) found that 70% of middle-aged men with coronary heart disease were Type A. Some researchers speculate that it may not be the whole Type A behavior pattern that leads to heart disease. Dembroski and others (1985) point to anger and hostility as the toxic components. Redford Williams of Duke University Medical School also suggests that hostility is the real culprit, particularly a cynical, distrustful attitude (Barefoot et al., 1983; Williams, 1989). More recent research supports earlier findings that the lethal core of the Type A personality is not time urgency but anger and hostility, which fuel an aggressive, reactive temperament (Miller et al., 1996; Williams, 1993). Hostility is not only highly predictive of coronary heart disease but also associated with ill health in general (Miller et al., 1996).

What aspect of the Type A behavior pattern is most clearly linked to coronary heart disease?

The Type A personality has a lethal core of anger and hostility. These qualities may manifest themselves as "road rage," a behavior pattern becoming all too common among American drivers.

While anger and hostility clearly place male heart-attack survivors at greater risk of dying from heart disease, just the opposite may be the case for females. Powell and others (1993) found that among women who have survived a heart attack, those who suppress unpleasant emotions such as anger, resentment, loneliness, and dissatisfaction tend to be at greatest risk of death. Women who died of heart disease were also more likely to be divorced, to lack a college education, and to be working full-time but earning less than $20,000. Financial and emotional stress and the lack of an intimate relationship appeared to be associated with increased risk of dying of coronary heart disease.

Moser and Dracup (1996) found that of patients who had suffered heart attacks, those who had high levels of anxiety were almost five times more likely to experience further complications than those with lower levels of anxiety. Apparently the effects of stress may enter the bloodstream almost as if they were injected intravenously. Malkoff and others (1993) report that after an experimental group of participants had experienced laboratory-induced stress, their blood platelets (special clotting cells) released large amounts of a substance that promotes the buildup of plaque in blood vessels and may lead to heart attack and stroke. No changes were found in the blood platelets of unstressed control-group participants.

Cancer: A Dreaded Disease

Link It!

Cancer. The word alone is frightening. Second only to heart disease as the leading cause of death, cancer is responsible for 23.4% of deaths in the United States (U.S. Bureau of the Census, 1997). Cancer strikes frequently in the adult population, and about 30% of Americans—over 75 million people—will develop cancer at some time in their lives. The young are not spared the scourge of cancer, for it takes the lives of more children aged 3 to 14 than any other disease.

We speak of cancer as a single disease, but actually it is a complicated collection of diseases. It can invade cells in any part of a living organism—humans, other animals, and even plants. It always starts small, because it is a disease of the body's cells. Normal cells in all parts of the body divide, but fortunately they have built-in instructions about when to stop dividing. If they did not, every part of the body would continue to grow throughout life. Unlike normal cells, cancer cells do not stop dividing. And unless caught in time and destroyed, they continue to grow and spread, eventually killing the organism.

Health psychologists warn that an unhealthy diet, smoking, excessive alcohol consumption, promiscuous sexual behavior, or becoming sexually active in the early teens (especially for females) are all behaviors that increase the risk of cancer. Many cancer patients report experiencing more high-stress situations before their cancer was diagnosed.

The 1 million people in the United States who are diagnosed with cancer each year have the difficult task of adjusting to a potentially life-threatening disease and the chronic stressors associated with it. Patients must cope with difficult therapies, "continued emotional distress, disrupted life tasks, social and interpersonal turmoil and fatigue and low energy" (Anderson et al., 1994, p. 390). Patients need more than medical treatment for cancer, say researchers. Their therapy should include help with psychological and behavioral factors that can influence their quality of life. Patients should be free to discuss their fears and anxieties, be given information about their disease and treatment, and be taught coping strategies and relaxation techniques to lower their arousal.

What behaviors and attitudes help cancer patients lessen psychological distress and improve quality of life? Carver and others (1993) found that 3 months and 6 months after surgery, breast-cancer patients who maintained an optimistic outlook, accepted the reality of their situation, and maintained a sense of humor experienced less distress. Patients who used denial—refusal to accept the reality of their situation—and had thoughts of giving up experienced much higher levels of distress. Dunkel-Schetter and others (1992) found that the most effective elements of a strategy for coping with cancer were social support (such as through self-help groups), a focus on the positive, and distraction. Avoidant coping strategies such as fantasizing, denial, and social withdrawal were associated with more emotional distress.

Health in the United States

The quality of health and the leading health risk factors are not the same for all Americans. They differ among various cultural and ethnic groups and according to gender, age, and socioeconomic status as well. The mortality rate is higher among people from lower socioeconomic levels for virtually all major causes of death (Schrijvers et al., 1999; Taylor & Repetti, 1997). And quality of life, even in the last years, is better for those from higher socioeconomic levels (Liao et al., 1999).

African Americans As the largest minority group in the United States, African Americans make up 12.6% of the population and are represented in every socioeconomic group from the poorest to the richest. But their overall poverty rate is about three times higher than that of the White population. As a result, many African Americans are at higher risk for disease and death and are more likely to suffer from inadequate health care. Their life expectancy has trailed behind that of the total U.S. population throughout the 20th century. African American infants are at twice the risk of death within their first year of life as White infants.

Compared to White Americans, African Americans have higher rates of diabetes, arthritis, and high blood pressure (Cooper et al., 1999; Kington & Smith, 1997). And as of 1998, 45% of the new AIDS cases in the United States were African American (Laurence, 1999).

Hispanic Americans By 1996, Hispanic Americans, the fastest-growing and second-largest of U.S. minority groups, had increased to about 10.7% of the total population (U.S. Bureau of the Census, 1997). While many Hispanic Americans are immigrants, over 70% are native-born. Most Hispanics, about 63%, are Mexican Americans.

Hypertension and diabetes are more prevalent among Hispanic Americans than they are among non-Hispanic Whites, whereas heart problems are less prevalent (Kington & Smith, 1997). Cigarette smoking and alcohol abuse are more common among Hispanic teenagers than among other teenagers, White or Black. Hispanic Americans are at high risk of death from accidental injuries (from automobile accidents and other causes), homicide, cirrhosis and other chronic liver diseases, and AIDS (Laurence, 1999; Public Health Service, 1991).

Partly because of a lower average socioeconomic level, Hispanic Americans and other minorities often have less access than White Americans to adequate health care.

Native Americans Native Americans, the smallest of the defined minority groups in the United States, number about 2 million. A large proportion of Native Americans die before the age of 45. This fact partly accounts for their statistically low rates of heart disease and cancer, which are more common among older people.

Alcohol represents a serious risk factor for Native Americans and is a leading factor in their high homicide and suicide rates. Native Americans under age 35 are at least 10 times more likely than other Americans to die from diseases directly related to alcoholism (Sandfur et al., 1996).

Obesity is common among many Native American tribes and contributes to extremely high rates of diabetes. According to the Indian Health Service (1988), over one-fifth of the members of some tribes suffer from diabetes. Among members of the Pima tribe over age 35, the rate is more than 50% (Sandfur et al., 1996).

The Gender Gap in America's Health Care American society also has significant health disparities that are related neither to poverty nor to racial or ethnic differences (Holloway, 1994). There has been a serious gender gap in health care and medical research in the United States. Most medical research in the past, much of it funded by the U.S. government, rejected women as participants in favor of men (Matthews et al., 1997). Women are slighted as well in health care and treatment (Rodin & Ickovics, 1990). Physicians are more likely to see women's health complaints as "emotional" in nature rather than due to physical causes (Council on Ethical and Judicial Affairs, AMA, 1991). The American Medical Association released a major report in 1991 revealing that of men and women who received an abnormal reading on a heart scan, 40% of the men but only 4% of the women were referred for further testing and possible bypass surgery. Women are less likely than men to receive kidney dialysis and 30% less likely to receive a kidney transplant (Council on Ethical and Judicial Affairs, AMA, 1991).

The good news is that efforts to erase the gender and race disparities in medical research and treatment are now underway. The National Institutes of Health created offices of Research on Women's Health and of Minority Programs. Every application for research funding from the National Institutes of Health must now include women and minorities unless there is a good rationale for not doing so. Studies of hypertension and coronary disease in African Americans have been funded. And a study of 164,000 postmenopausal women is examining the effects of estrogen replacement therapy and nutrition on cardiovascular health and the prevention of breast cancer and osteoporosis (Matthews et al., 1997). Such efforts are long overdue.

The Immune System: An Army of Cells to Fight Off Disease

Today most researchers do not question the notion that stress and health are closely related (Kiecolt-Glaser & Glaser, 1992). People who experience stress may indeed be more susceptible to coronary heart disease, stroke, and poorer pregnancy outcomes (Adler & Matthews, 1994). But even more ominous is the growing evidence that stress can impair the functioning of the immune system itself.

The immune system, known to be one of the most complex systems of the body, protects against infection and disease. An army of highly specialized cells and organs, the immune system works to identify and search out and destroy bacteria, viruses, fungi, parasites, and any other foreign matter that may enter the body. And the immune system can identify a previously encountered pathogen later, sometimes for the person's lifetime (Ahmed & Gray, 1996). Cells of the immune system can distinguish instantly between self and nonself. Virtually every cell in the body carries distinctive molecules that mark it as self (Schindler, 1988). Nonself cells also carry their own distinctive molecules, which mark them as foreign invaders to be attacked and destroyed. This is why organ transplants—foreign, or nonself, tissue to the recipient—are rejected by the immune system unless powerful immune-suppressing drugs are administered.

The key components of the immune system are white blood cells known as **lymphocytes**, which include B cells and T cells. B cells are so named because they are produced in the bone marrow. T cells derive their name from the thymus gland (a spongy organ located behind the breastbone) where they grow to maturity (von Boehmer & Kisielow, 1991). B cells carry on their surface large protein molecules known as *antibodies*. Each B cell carries only one kind of antibody, which is specific to only one type of invading cell. All cells foreign to the body, such as bacteria, viruses, and so on, are known as *antigens*. When an antigen enters the body, it will eventually confront a B cell whose antibody has a matching receptor. This encounter will chemically stimulate that B cell to divide and immediately begin mass production of its antibody. And B cells are prolific producers. "One B cell can pump out more than 10 billion antibody molecules an hour" (Nossal, 1993, p. 58). The antibodies produced by B cells are highly effective in destroying antigens that live outside the body's cells, such as in the bloodstream and in the fluid surrounding other body tissues (Paul, 1993). But for defeating harmful foreign invaders that have taken up residence inside the body's cells, T cells are critically important.

One class of T cells assists the B cells, and thus are known as "helper" cells. These T cells attack and defeat bacteria and other parasites living inside the body's cells, beyond the reach of B cells. The other class of T cells, known as "killer" cells, root out and destroy pathogens, such as viruses, that have more deeply invaded the body's cells (Paul, 1993). The killer T cells are indeed deadly. To kill cells infected by

lymphocytes: The white blood cells—B cells, T cells, and macrophages—that are key components of the immune system.

bacteria or viruses, they punch holes in the infected cells and release "chemicals that destroy the entire cell" (Janeway, 1993, p. 78).

Other large lymphocytes in the immune system are known as *macrophages* ("big eaters"). Found throughout the body, macrophages roam around, gobble up infected cells, and digest them. Particles of the digested invading cells are then "presented" to T cells, which recognize and remember them as antigens. The T cells will then find these antigen-marked cells and kill them on contact.

During wartime, when recognition and communication systems fail, troops may attack and kill their own soldiers—a phenomenon referred to as "friendly fire." Likewise, the immune system may turn on healthy self cells or specific organs and attack them, as happens in autoimmune diseases such as juvenile diabetes, multiple sclerosis, rheumatoid arthritis, and lupus.

Acquired Immune Deficiency Syndrome (AIDS)   The most feared disease related to the immune system is **acquired immune deficiency syndrome (AIDS)**. Although the first case was diagnosed in this country in 1981, there is still no cure for AIDS and no vaccine to protect against it. By the end of 1996, 581,429 cases of AIDS and 362,000 deaths from AIDS had been reported to the Centers for Disease Control (1997). Worldwide, over 6 million people have died from AIDS, and by 1999, 33.4 million people were infected with HIV (Laurence, 1999; Mertens & Low-Beer, 1996).

AIDS is caused by **HIV**, the **human immunodeficiency virus**, often referred to as the *AIDS virus*. When a person is first infected, HIV enters the bloodstream. This initial infection usually causes no symptoms, and the immune system begins to produce HIV antibodies. It is these antibodies that are detected in the AIDS test. Individuals then progress to the asymptomatic *carrier state*, in which they experience no symptoms whatsoever and thus can unknowingly infect others.

HIV attacks the immune system until it becomes essentially nonfunctional. The diagnosis of AIDS is made when the immune system is so damaged that victims develop rare forms of cancer or pneumonia or other so-called opportunistic infections. Such infections would not usually be serious in people with normal immune responses, but in those with a very impaired immune system, these infections can be serious and even life-threatening. At this point patients typically experience progressive weight loss, weakness, fever, swollen lymph nodes, and diarrhea, and 25% develop a rare cancer that produces reddish-purple spots on the skin. Other infections develop as the immune system weakens further.

Before developing a full-blown case of AIDS, some people develop less severe immune-system symptoms such as unexplained fevers, chronic diarrhea, and weight loss. The average time from infection with HIV to advanced AIDS is about 10 years, but the time may range from 2 years to as long as 15 years or more (Nowak & McMichael, 1995). The disease progresses faster in smokers, in the very young, in people over 50, and apparently, in women. AIDS also progresses faster in those who are repeatedly exposed to the virus and in those who were infected by someone in an advanced stage of the disease.

Currently researchers are testing drugs on people infected with HIV, and early detection of HIV infection can lead to life-prolonging medical intervention. Researchers have discovered that drugs known as *protease inhibitors*, in combination with some drugs such as AZT, can cause significant reductions in blood levels of HIV (Collier et al., 1996).

The Transmission of AIDS   Researchers believe that HIV is transmitted primarily through the exchange of blood, semen, or vaginal secretions during sexual contact or when IV (intravenous) drug users share contaminated needles or syringes. In the United States about 22.6% of those with AIDS are IV drug users (U.S. Bureau of the Census, 1997). An estimated 50% of IV drug users are infected with HIV, whereas 20% of gay men carry the virus ("AIDS and Mental Health," 1994).

acquired immune deficiency syndrome (AIDS): A devastating and incurable illness that is caused by HIV and progressively weakens the body's immune system, leaving the person vulnerable to opportunistic infections that usually cause death.

HIV (human immunodeficiency virus): The virus that causes AIDS.

What happens to a person from the time of infection with HIV to the development of full-blown AIDS?

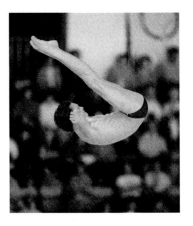

Greg Louganis, winner of an Olympic gold medal for diving in 1988, announced in 1995 that he is HIV-positive.

How is AIDS transmitted?

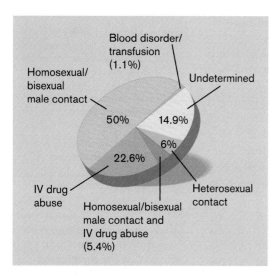

The rate of AIDS among gay men is high because many gay men have multiple sex partners, and because gay men are likely to have anal intercourse. Anal intercourse is more dangerous than coitus, because rectal tissue often tears during penetration, allowing HIV ready entry into the bloodstream.

It is a mistake to view AIDS as a disease confined to gay men, however. About 25% of the AIDS cases reported in the United States in 1996 were females, 40% of whom contracted it through heterosexual contact and 35.4% through IV drug abuse (U.S. Bureau of the Census, 1997). In Africa, where AIDS is believed to have originated, it strikes men and women equally, and heterosexual activity is believed to be the primary means of transmission (Abramson & Herdt, 1990). AIDS is transmitted 12 times more easily from infected men to women than vice versa (Padian et al., 1991).

Figure 11.5 summarizes the means of transmission for male AIDS cases in the United States.

Figure 11.5

How HIV Was Transmitted in Adult/Adolescent AIDS Cases Reported in the United States

The primary means of transmission of HIV is through homosexual/bisexual male contact (50%). IV drug abuse (sharing needles) accounts for 22.6% of the AIDS cases in the United States. (U.S. Bureau of the Census, 1997.)

What are the effects of stress and depression on the immune system?

The Psychological Impact of HIV Infection and AIDS   Consider the devastating psychological impact—the anxiety, fear, and depression—of learning that one is infected with HIV. A death sentence, alone, is traumatic enough, with one's time left to live measured in a few years, but there is more. Added to the fear of rapidly declining health when full-blown AIDS arrives is the ugly stigma paralleled by few other diseases in history.

To cope psychologically, AIDS patients and those infected with HIV need education and information about the disease. They can be helped by psychotherapy, self-help groups, and medications such as antidepressants and antianxiety drugs. Self-help groups and group therapy may serve as a substitute family for some patients. An ever-present concern voiced by patients in psychotherapy is whether to tell others, and if so, what to tell them and how. Patients may feel a compelling need to confide in others and, at the same time, to conceal their condition.

Stress and the Immune System   A relatively new field of study is known as **psychoneuroimmunology**. This nine-syllable word describes the work of psychologists, biologists, and medical researchers who combine their expertise to learn the effects of psychological factors (emotions, thinking, and behavior) on the immune system (Cohen, 1996; Cohen & Herbert, 1996; Maier et al., 1994). Researchers now know that the immune system is not merely a separate system to fight off foreign invaders. Rather, it is an incredibly complex, interconnected defense system working with the brain to keep the body healthy (Pennisi, 1997).

Several studies provide evidence that psychological factors, emotions, and stress are related to immune system functioning (O'Leary, 1990). Moreover, the immune system exchanges information with the brain, and what goes on in the brain can apparently influence the immune system for good or ill. In one study researchers gave volunteers nasal drops containing a cold virus. Within the next few days, symptoms of the viral infection rose sharply in some of the 151 women and 125 men who participated in the study, but less so or not at all in others. Participants with a rich social life in the form of frequent interactions with others—spouses, children, parents, coworkers, friends, and volunteer and religious groups—seemed to enjoy a powerful shield of protection against the virus infection (Cohen et al., 1997). And this pattern of protection held across age and racial groups, for both sexes, at all educational levels, and at every season of the year (Cohen et al., 1997).

Close social ties—to family, friends, and others—apparently have good effects on the immune system. Ill effects often come from stress. High periods of stress are correlated with increased symptoms of many infectious diseases, including oral and genital herpes, mononucleosis, colds, and flu (Jemmott & Locke, 1984). And stress has caused decreased levels of the immune system's B and T cells (Schindler, 1988). Kiecolt-Glaser and others (1996) found that elderly men and women experiencing

psychoneuroimmunology (sye-ko-NEW-ro-IM-you-NOLL-oh-gee): A field in which psychologists, biologists, and medical researchers study the effects of psychological factors on the immune system.

chronic stress due to years of caring for a spouse with Alzheimer's disease showed an impaired immune response to flu shots. Reviews of studies show that stress is associated with an increase in illness behaviors—reporting physical symptoms and seeking medical care (Cohen & Herbert, 1996; Cohen & Williamson, 1991). Moreover, physicians have long observed that stress and anxiety can worsen autoimmune diseases. And "if fear can produce relapses [in autoimmune diseases], then even the fear of a relapse may become a self-fulfilling prophecy" (Steinman, 1993, p. 112).

Personal Factors Reducing the Impact of Stress and Illness

Researchers have identified three personal factors that may contribute to better health: optimism, psychological hardiness, and social support.

Optimism and Pessimism   People who are generally optimistic tend to cope more effectively with stress, and this in turn may reduce their risk of illness (Seligman, 1990). An important characteristic optimists share is that they generally expect good outcomes. And such positive expectations help make them more stress-resistant than pessimists, who tend to expect bad outcomes. Optimists adjust better to stress (Chang, 1998).

Optimists are more likely to use problem-focused coping, to seek social support, and to find the positive aspects of a stressful situation (Carver et al., 1993; Scheier & Carver, 1992). Pessimists, on the other hand, are more likely to use denial or to focus on their stressful feelings (Scheier et al., 1986). In a study of college students, Scheier and Carver (1985) found that at the end of the semester, optimistic students reported fewer physical symptoms than those who were pessimistic. And another study, of patients who had undergone coronary bypass surgery, revealed that optimists recovered faster during their hospitalization and were able to resume their normal activities sooner after discharge than pessimists (Scheier et al., 1989). "Optimists, who readily take matters into their own hands, are more likely to take action that prevents illness or get it treated once illness strikes" (Seligman, 1990, p. 173). Apparently, happy thoughts are healthy thoughts.

Psychological Hardiness: Commitment, Challenge, and Control   Suzanne Kobasa (1979; Kobasa et al., 1982) wondered why some people under great stress succumb to illness while others do not. Studying male executives with high levels of stress, she found three psychological characteristics that distinguished those who remained healthy from those who had a high incidence of illness. The three qualities, which she referred to collectively as **hardiness**, were *commitment, control,* and *challenge.*

Hardy individuals feel a strong sense of commitment to both their work and their personal life. They see themselves not as victims of whatever life brings, but as people who have control over consequences and outcomes. They act to solve their own problems. And they welcome challenges in life, viewing them not as threats but as opportunities for growth and improvement.

Florian and others (1995) found that commitment and control alone are apparently sufficient to produce hardiness. Commitment ensures a continuing involvement in the situation and provides the staying power to see it through. A person who is committed does not give up. Control provides the confidence that the person is in charge of the situation and capable of finding the right solution to solve the problems at hand.

Social Support: Help in Time of Need   Another factor contributing to better health is **social support** (Cohen, 1988; Kaplan et al., 1994). Social support is support provided, usually in time of need, by a spouse or other family members or by friends, neighbors, colleagues, support groups, or others. It can involve tangible aid, information, and advice, as well as emotional support. It can also be viewed as the feeling

What three personal factors are associated with health and resistance to stress?

hardiness: A combination of three psychological qualities shared by people who can undergo high levels of stress yet remain healthy: a sense of control over one's life, commitment to one's personal goals, and a tendency to view change as a challenge rather than as a threat.

social support: Tangible support, information, advice, and/or emotional support provided in time of need by family, friends, and others; the feeling of being loved, valued, and cared for.

A strong social support network can help a person recover faster from an illness.

of being loved, valued, and cared for by those for whom we feel a mutual obligation (Cobb, 1976).

Social support appears to have positive effects on the body's immune system as well as on the cardiovascular and endocrine systems (Uchino et al., 1996). Social support may help encourage health-promoting behaviors and reduce the impact of stress so that people will be less likely to resort to unhealthy methods of coping, such as smoking or drinking (Adler & Matthews, 1994).

Social support has been shown to reduce the impact of stress from unemployment, long-term illness, retirement, and bereavement (Krantz et al., 1985). People with social support recover more quickly from illnesses and lower their risk of death from specific diseases (House et al., 1988). Social support may even increase the probability of surviving a heart attack, help moderate the effects of high blood pressure, and influence the length of survival for those stricken with cancer (Turner, 1983). A longitudinal study of 4,775 people over a 9-year period found that those low in social support died at twice the rate of those high in social support (Berkman & Syme, 1979). Research on natural disasters reveals that initial social support is common but that the support tends to deteriorate, because the needs of victims overwhelm the tangible and emotional resources of friends and family (Kaniasty & Norris, 1993).

LIFESTYLE AND HEALTH

What constitutes an unhealthy lifestyle, and how important a factor is lifestyle in illness and disease?

For most Americans, health enemy number one is their own habits. As Figure 11.6 shows, 53.5% of all deaths in the United States are attributable to unhealthy behavior or lifestyle (Powell et al., 1986). What are these unhealthy behaviors? The culprits are all well known—lack of exercise, too little sleep, alcohol or drug abuse, an unhealthy diet, and overeating. A longitudinal study on the health consequences of certain lifestyle factors tracked nearly 117,000 female nurses from 1976 through 1992. The study showed that the overweight nurses were from 2 to 2.5 times more likely to suffer a stroke than were their leaner counterparts. But the most dangerous unhealthy behavior of all is smoking.

Smoking: Hazardous to Your Health

Why is smoking considered the single most preventable cause of death?

Every year in the economically developed countries of the world, smoking claims the lives of some 3 million people, most of whom are below the age of 70 (Iversen, 1996). A 1996 Gallup poll revealed that 27% of Americans aged 18 and over are smokers, and the percentages are about the same for both men and women (Newport, 1996). Even worse is that every day 3,000 more teenagers become regular smokers (Novello, 1990). The Centers for Disease Control (1991) calls smoking "the single most preventable cause of death in the United States." According to current estimates, smoking is directly related to 434,000 deaths annually in the United States (Raloff, 1994). Countless other millions who must breathe smoke-filled air suffer the ill effects of passive smoking. Recent studies indicate that nonsmokers who are regularly exposed to passive smoke have twice the risk of heart attack of those who are not exposed (Kawachi et al., 1997). And think of the suffering of millions from chronic bronchitis, emphysema, and other respiratory diseases; the deaths and injuries from fires caused by smoking; and the low birthweight and retarded fetal development in babies born to smoking mothers. The American Cancer Society claims that compared to the death rates of nonsmokers, the death rate increases 60% for men who smoke less than half a pack of cigarettes a day, 90% for those who smoke one to two packs a day, and 120% for those smoking more than two packs a day. Among women who smoke, lung cancer claims more lives than breast cancer. But the risk of cancer, particularly lung cancer, can be greatly reduced if a person quits smoking (Chyou et al., 1992).

The increased risk for lung cancer in nonsmoking adults who live with smokers averages 24%. For nonsmokers exposed at work, the increased risk is 39%; and those exposed to smoke for at least 2 hours a week in social settings have a 50% greater risk for lung cancer (Fontham et al., 1994).

Most smokers acquire the habit during adolescence, when peer pressure is strong. Adolescents tend to emulate the behavior of others to gain social acceptance (Taylor, 1991). And teens with parents and friends who smoke are at greater risk of taking up smoking themselves.

Now for the good news: The percentage of smokers in the U.S. population is declining. There are now about 45 million ex-smokers, and 80% of current smokers claim they want to quit, an indication that a strong antismoking sentiment is building (Sherman, 1994).

Why do adult smokers continue the habit when the majority admit that they would prefer to be nonsmokers? There seems little doubt that smoking is an addiction, and the U.S. Surgeon General declared in 1988 that tobacco is as addictive as cocaine and heroin. Nicotine is a powerful substance that increases the release of acetylcholine, norepinephrine, dopamine, and other neurotransmitters, which improve mental alertness, sharpen memory, and reduce tension and anxiety (Pomerleau & Pomerleau, 1989). According to Parrott (1993), some people smoke primarily to increase arousal, while others smoke primarily to reduce stress and anxiety. Thus, smoking becomes a coping mechanism used to regulate moods.

Because smoking is so addictive, smokers have great difficulty breaking the habit. Even so, 90% of ex-smokers quit smoking on their own (Novello, 1990). The average smoker makes five or six attempts to quit before finally succeeding (Sherman, 1994). Some aids, such as nicotine gum and the nicotine patch, help many people kick the habit. A meta-analysis involving 17 studies and over 5,000 participants revealed that 22% of people who used the nicotine patch were smoke-free compared to only 9% of those who received a placebo. And 27% of those receiving the nicotine patch plus antismoking counseling or support remained smoke-free (Fiore, cited in Sherman, 1994). But even with the patch, quitting is difficult, because the patch only lessens withdrawal symptoms, which typically last 2 to 4 weeks (Hughes, 1992). Half of all relapses occur within the first 2 weeks after people quit, and relapses are most likely when people are experiencing negative emotions or are using alcohol. It takes just one cigarette, sometimes only one puff, to cause a relapse.

Alcohol: A Problem for Millions

Although smoking is directly related to a greater number of deaths, alcohol abuse undoubtedly causes more misery. The health and social costs of alcohol abuse are staggering—fatalities, medical bills, lost work, family problems. According to Rodin and Salovey (1989), alcohol is one of the three main causes of death in modern societies. Some 18 million Americans have a serious drinking problem (Lord et al., 1987), and about 10 million are alcoholics (Neimark et al., 1994). Alcohol abuse and dependence is three times more prevalent in males than in females (Grant et al., 1991). And people who begin drinking before age 15 are more likely than those who begin later to become dependent on alcohol (Grant & Dawson, 1998; Prescott & Kendler, 1999a). Although a higher percentage of white-collar workers use alcohol, the percentage of problem drinkers is higher among blue-collar workers (Harford et al., 1992). For many, alcohol provides a method of coping with life stresses they feel powerless to control (Seeman & Seeman, 1992).

As many as 80% of men and women who are alcoholics complain of episodes of depression. A large study of almost 3,000 alcoholics concluded that some depressive

Figure 11.6
Factors Contributing to Death before Age 65

The number one factor leading to premature death in the United States is unhealthy lifestyle. Fortunately your own lifestyle is more completely under your control than are any of the other factors contributing to premature death. (Based on Powell et al., 1986.)

What are some health risks of alcohol abuse?

Link It!

episodes are independent of alcohol, whereas others are substance-induced (Schuckit et al., 1997).

Alcohol can damage virtually every organ in the body, but it is especially harmful to the liver and is the major cause of cirrhosis, which kills 26,000 people each year (Neimark et al., 1994). Alcohol can also cause stomach problems—indigestion, nausea, diarrhea, and ulcers. One-half of long-term, heavy drinkers suffer damage to their skeletal muscles, and one-third sustain damage to their heart muscle (Urbano-Marquez et al., 1989). Alcohol increases the risk of many cancers, including cancer of the liver, mouth, throat, tongue, and voice box. Pregnant women should avoid all alcohol because of its potentially disastrous effects on the developing fetus. (See Chapter 8 for a discussion of fetal alcohol syndrome.)

Heavy drinking can cause cognitive impairment (Goldman, 1983) and seizures (Ng et al., 1988). MRI studies have revealed shrinkage of the cerebral cortex and reduced volume of the hippocampus among alcoholics (Agartz et al., 1999; Jernigan et al., 1991; Korbo, 1999). CT scans also show brain shrinkage in a high percentage of alcoholics, even in young subjects and in those who appear to be intact mentally (Lishman, 1990). The only good news in recent studies is that some of the effects of alcohol on the brain seem to be partially reversible with prolonged abstinence.

Alcoholism's toll goes beyond the physical damage to the alcoholic. In 1995 alcohol was involved in 41% of the traffic fatalities in the United States, which numbered almost 17,300 (National Safety Council, 1997). Alcohol has been implicated in 40% of criminal victimization cases ("Alcoholism: A factor," 1998), 20–36% of suicides, 53% of falls, and 48% of burns (U.S. House, Committee on Energy and Commerce, 1991).

Alcoholism: Causes and Treatment   The American Medical Association maintains that alcoholism is a disease, and once an alcoholic, always an alcoholic. According to this view, even a small amount of alcohol is believed to cause an irresistible craving for more, leading alcoholics to lose control of their drinking (Jellinek, 1960). Thus, total abstinence is seen as the only acceptable and effective method of treatment. The medical establishment and Alcoholics Anonymous endorse both the disease concept and the total abstinence approach to treatment. And a new drug may make abstinence somewhat easier. German researchers report that the drug acamprosate helps prevent relapse in recovering alcoholics (Sass et al., 1996).

Some studies suggest a genetic factor in alcoholism and lend support to the disease model. According to Goodwin (1985), about one-half of hospitalized alcoholics have a family history of alcohol abuse. Adoption studies have revealed that "sons of alcoholics were three or four times more likely to be alcoholic than were sons of nonalcoholics, whether raised by their alcoholic biologic parents or by nonalcoholic adoptive parents" (Goodwin, 1985, p. 172).

A large study by McGue and others (1992) involving 356 pairs of identical and fraternal twins revealed a substantial genetic influence for males when the first symptoms of alcoholism appear before age 20. And a study of 1,000 pairs of female identical and fraternal twins by Kendler, Neale, and others (1994) found that alcoholism in women has a heritability of 50–60%, a rate similar to that for male alcoholics.

Is alcoholism a disease? Some experts reject the disease concept and contend that alcoholism can take various forms and have various causes (Pattison, 1982). Even in people who are genetically predisposed, researchers caution against overlooking the environmental contribution to alcoholism (Searles, 1988). Family and cultural influences are apparently the dominant factors in men whose drinking problems appear after adolescence.

Some experts stress the role of behavioral, social, and cultural factors in alcoholism and advocate various approaches to treatment. One approach—*cue exposure*—systematically exposes the problem drinker to cues that have stimulated a craving for alcohol and triggered drinking in the past (Neimark et al., 1994). The person is prevented from drinking in the presence of those cues and gradually becomes less responsive to them.

Whatever treatment approach is used, social support is essential. It can be provided by friends, family members, therapists, or self-help groups. Abstinence remains the surest solution to alcoholism (Nathan, 1992).

Exercise: Keeping Fit Is Healthy

For years medical experts, especially health psychologists, have promoted regular exercise. Yet most Americans exercise irregularly, if at all (Hurrell, 1997). Some 60% of the U.S. population does not engage in enough physical activity to remain healthy, according to a 1996 Surgeon General's report. Many studies show that regular **aerobic exercise** pays rich dividends in the form of physical and mental fitness. Aerobic exercise (such as running, swimming, brisk walking, bicycling, rowing, and jumping rope) is exercise that uses the large muscle groups in continuous, repetitive action and increases oxygen intake and breathing and heart rates. To improve cardiovascular fitness and endurance and to lessen the risk of heart attack, aerobic exercise should be performed regularly. This means three or four times a week for 20–30 minutes, with additional 5–10 minute warm-up and cool-down periods (Alpert et al., 1990; Shepard, 1986). Less than 20 minutes of aerobic exercise 3 times a week has "no measurable effect on the heart," and more than 3 hours per week "is not known to reduce cardiovascular risk any further" (Simon, 1988, p. 3).

Regular aerobic exercise is beneficial for people of all ages. Even preschoolers have been shown to receive cardiovascular benefits from planned exercise (Alpert et al., 1990). At the other end of the age spectrum, regular, planned exercise yields dramatic increases in muscle and bone strength in older people. Exercisers between the ages of 87 and 96 who were on a weight-lifting program for only 2 months showed the same absolute gains in rate of muscular strength as younger people (Allison, 1991). Strenuous workouts would not have transformed George Burns into Arnold Schwarzenegger, but significant increases in muscle strength have been recorded even in people pushing 100.

A large study on the health benefits of physical fitness is compelling enough to convince couch potatoes of all ages to get up and get moving. Steven Blair and colleagues (1989) studied 13,344 men and women of different age groups, 20 years and older. The participants were tested for physical fitness and then assigned to one of five physical fitness levels based on age, sex, and performance on a treadmill test. Follow-up continued for a little more than 8 years, and during that time 283 participants (240 men and 43 women) died. And the number of deaths from all causes was significantly related to fitness level for both men and women.

But there is some encouraging news from this large study. You do not need to become a marathon runner or spend several hours a day sweating and grunting in a fitness center in order to enjoy the maximum benefits of health and longevity. Exercise need not be strenuous. Low-intensity physical training improves physical fitness in older adults (De Vito et al., 1997). Even a brisk daily walk of 30 minutes or more helps to reduce stress and yields the fitness standard associated with a much lower death rate.

According to Brown (1991), "People who are physically fit are less vulnerable to the adverse effects of life stress than are those who are less fit" (p. 560). In a study of 137 stressed male business executives, Kobasa and her colleagues (1982) found that those who exercised had lower rates of illness. The more stress the men suffered, the more important exercise was in the prevention of illness.

In case you are not yet convinced, consider the following benefits of exercise:

- Increases the efficiency of the heart, enabling it to pump more blood with each beat; reduces the resting pulse rate and improves circulation

- Raises HDL (the good blood cholesterol) levels, which (1) helps rid the body of LDL (the bad blood cholesterol) and (2) removes plaque buildup on artery walls

- Burns up extra calories, enabling you to lose weight or maintain your weight

What are some benefits of regular aerobic exercise?

Regular aerobic exercise improves cardiovascular fitness in people of all ages.

aerobic exercise (ay-RO-bik): Exercise that uses the large muscle groups in continuous, repetitive action and increases oxygen intake and breathing and heart rates.

- Makes bones denser and stronger, helping to prevent osteoporosis in women
- Moderates the effects of stress
- Gives you more energy and increases your resistance to fatigue
- Benefits the immune system by increasing natural killer cell activity (Fiatarone et al., 1988)

Managing Stress

Everyone who is alive is subject to stress, but some people are more negatively affected by it than others.

If stress leaves you fretting and fuming with your muscles in knots, the following relaxation techniques might spell relief.

Progressive relaxation. The fight-or-flight response is the body's way of preparing a person to deal with a threat. But if you can neither fight nor flee, you are left with intense physiological arousal, or stress. There are several relaxation techniques that you can use to calm yourself and relieve your muscular tension. Probably the most widely used relaxation technique in the United States is *progressive relaxation* (Rice, 1987). It consists of flexing and then relaxing the different muscle groups throughout the body from the head to the toes. Here's how to do it:

1. Loosen or remove any tight-fitting clothing, take off your shoes, and situate yourself comfortably in an armchair with your arms resting on the chair's arms. Sit straight in the chair, but let your head fall forward so that your chin rests comfortably on your chest. Place your feet flat on the floor with your legs slightly apart in a comfortable position.

2. Take a deep breath. Hold it for a few seconds, and then exhale slowly and completely. Repeat several times. Notice the tension in your chest as you hold the breath, and the relaxation as you let the breath out.

3. Flex the muscles in your right upper arm (in your left arm if you are left-handed). Hold the muscles as tight as you can for about 10 seconds. Observe the feeling of tension. Now relax the muscles completely and observe the feeling of relaxation. Repeat the flexing and the relaxing several times. Then do the same with the other arm.

4. After completing the opening routine with your arms, use the same procedure, tensing and then relaxing a group of muscles, starting with the muscles in the forehead. Progressively work your way down through all the muscle groups in the body, ending with your feet.

Another excellent relaxation technique is Herbert Benson's relaxation response, described in Chapter 4 (on p. 113).

Managing mental stress. Many people stress themselves almost to the breaking point by their own thinking. When people become angry, hostile, fearful, worried, or upset by things they think are going to happen, they cause the heart to pound and the stomach to churn. How often have you done this to yourself only to find that what you had imagined never actually materialized? The next time you begin to react to something that you *think* will happen, stop yourself. Remember all the times you have become upset about things that never came to pass. Learn to use your own thinking to reduce stress, not create it. Give your body a break!

Stress-inoculation training, a program that was designed by Donald Meichenbaum (1977), helps people cope with stressors that are troubling them. Test anxiety, stress over personal and social relationships, and some types of performance anxiety have been successfully treated with stress inoculation. Individuals are taught to recognize their own negative thoughts ("I'll never be able to do this" or "I'll probably make a fool of myself") and to replace negative thoughts with positive ones. They learn how to talk to themselves using positive coping statements to dispel worry and provide self-encouragement. Here are some examples of these coping statements (adapted from Meichenbaum, 1977):

Preparing for the Stressor

"I can come up with a plan to handle the problem."
"I refuse to worry about it. Worry doesn't help anything."

Facing or Confronting the Stressor

"If I take one step at a time, I know I can handle this situation."
"I will take a few slow, deep breaths and relax."

Coping with the Stressor

"If I feel fear, I will simply pause."
"I will keep my mind focused on the present, on what is happening now, and just concentrate on what I have to do."

Following the Coping Attempt

"This was easier than I thought it would be."
"I am really making progress."

To counteract the shallow, rapid breathing that occurs when you are stressed, you need to take deep, abdominal breaths. To learn how, place one hand on your chest and the other on your abdomen. Practice inhaling in such a way that your abdomen, not your chest, expands. Once you are able to accomplish this, you are ready to learn how to "take a breather" to counteract stress.

1. Slowly exhale through your mouth to remove the stale air from your lungs. Repeat until your lungs feel empty.

2. Inhale through your nose until your abdomen (not your lungs) begins to expand, hold for 5 seconds, and then exhale.

3. Repeat four or five times whenever you feel tense and irritable.

When your body is reacting with the fight-or-flight response in a situation where you can neither fight nor flee, what can you do? You can blow off steam physically by exercising or engaging in physical work (raking leaves, gardening, or cleaning the house). Physical activity provides a "flight" outlet for your mental stress.

You may have been told after you have had a major hassle or mishap that some day you would look back and laugh about it. And it is true that much of what we laugh about has an element of pain. Kathleen Passanisi suggests that "humor is pain removed from pain," and that a key to well-being is to shorten the time between experiencing the pain and being able to laugh at it (quoted in M. Harris, 1993, p. 1C).

Other stress-reducing measures. Here are some additional suggestions for reducing the negative effects of stress.

- Engage in regular exercise.
- Eat a balanced diet and get enough sleep.
- Use caffeine in moderation.
- Make time for relaxation and activities you enjoy.
- Rely on social support to moderate the effects of stress.
- Don't expect perfection from yourself or from other people.
- If you suffer from "hurry sickness," slow down.
- Learn patience.
- Don't respond to stress with behaviors that will increase stress in the long run, such as overeating, drinking, or using drugs.

SUMMARY AND REVIEW

TWO APPROACHES TO HEALTH AND ILLNESS

How do the biomedical and biopsychosocial models differ in their approaches to health and illness?

The biomedical model focuses on illness rather than on health and explains illness in terms of biological factors. The biopsychosocial model focuses on health as well as on illness and holds that both are determined by a combination of biological, psychological, and social factors.

Key Terms
biomedical model (p. 358); biopsychosocial model (p. 358); health psychology (p. 358)

THEORIES OF STRESS

What is the general adaptation syndrome?

The general adaptation syndrome is the predictable sequence of reactions that organisms show in response to stressors. It consists of the alarm stage, the resistance stage, and the exhaustion stage.

What are the roles of primary and secondary appraisal when a person is confronted with a potentially stressful event?

Lazarus maintains that when a person is confronted with a potentially stressful event, he or she engages in a cognitive appraisal process consisting of (1) a primary appraisal, to evaluate the relevance of the event to one's well-being (whether it will be positive; will be irrelevant; or will involve harm or loss, threat, or challenge); and (2) a secondary appraisal to determine how to cope with the stressor.

Key Terms
stress (p. 359); stressor (p. 360); general adaptation syndrome (GAS) (p. 360); alarm stage (p. 360); resistance stage (p. 360); exhaustion stage (p. 360);

primary appraisal (p. 361); secondary appraisal (p. 361)

SOURCES OF STRESS: THE COMMON AND THE EXTREME

How do approach–approach, avoidance–avoidance, and approach–avoidance conflicts differ?

In an approach–approach conflict, a person must decide between equally desirable alternatives; in an avoidance–avoidance conflict, the choice is between two undesirable alternatives. In an approach–avoidance conflict, a person is both drawn to and repelled by a choice.

How do the unpredictability of and lack of control over a stressor affect its impact?

Stressors that are unpredictable and uncontrollable are more stressful than those that are predictable and controllable.

For people to function effectively and find satisfaction on the job, what nine variables should fall within their comfort zone?

Nine variables that should fall within a worker's comfort zone are workload, clarity of job description and evaluation criteria, physical variables, job status, accountability, task variety, human contact, and physical and mental challenge.

What are some of the psychological and health consequences of job stress?

Job stress can cause serious illnesses, such as depression, high blood pressure, and cardiovascular disease; it can also cause headaches, exhaustion, back problems, insomnia, and indigestion. Other consequences may include absenteeism, reduced productivity, tardiness, accidents, substance abuse, low morale, and alienation from co-workers.

What is burnout?

Burnout is the result of intense, unrelieved, and unmanaged job stress; a person experiencing burnout becomes pessimistic, dissatisfied, inefficient on the job, and debilitated psychologically.

How do people typically react to catastrophic events?

Victims of catastrophic events are initially dazed and stunned. When they begin to recover from the shock, they typically experience anxiety, nightmares, and a compulsive need to recount the event over and over.

What is posttraumatic stress disorder?

Posttraumatic stress disorder (PTSD) is a prolonged, severe stress reaction to a catastrophic event.

Key Terms
approach–approach conflict (p. 363); avoidance–avoidance conflict (p. 363); approach–avoidance conflict (p. 363); decision latitude (p. 365); burnout (p. 366); posttraumatic stress disorder (PTSD) (p. 366)

COPING WITH STRESS

What is the difference between problem-focused and emotion-focused coping?

Problem-focused coping is a response aimed at reducing, modifying, or elim-

inating the source of stress; emotion-focused coping is aimed at reducing the emotional impact of the stressor.

Key Terms
coping (p. 367); problem-focused coping (p. 367); emotion-focused coping (p. 367); proactive coping (p. 368)

EVALUATING LIFE STRESS: MAJOR LIFE CHANGES, HASSLES, AND UPLIFTS

What was the Social Readjustment Rating Scale designed to reveal?

The SRRS assesses stress in terms of life events that necessitate life change. Holmes and Rahe found a relationship between degree of life stress (as measured on the scale) and major health problems.

What roles do hassles and uplifts play in the stress of life, according to Lazarus?

According to Lazarus, daily hassles typically cause more stress than major life changes. The positive experiences in life—the uplifts—can neutralize the effects of many of the hassles.

Key Terms
Social Readjustment Rating Scale (SRRS) (p. 368); hassles (p. 369); uplifts (p. 370)

HEALTH AND DISEASE

What are the Type A and Type B behavior patterns?

The Type A behavior pattern, often cited as a risk factor for coronary heart disease, is characterized by a sense of time urgency, impatience, excessive competitive drive, hostility, and easily aroused anger. The Type B behavior pattern is characterized by a relaxed, easygoing approach to life.

What aspect of the Type A behavior pattern is most clearly linked to coronary heart disease?

Hostility is the aspect of the Type A pattern most clearly linked to coronary heart disease.

What happens to a person from the time of infection with HIV to the development of full-blown AIDS?

When a person is initially infected with HIV, the body begins to produce HIV antibodies, eventually detectable

in a blood test. For a period of time the victim is without symptoms, but HIV gradually renders the immune system nonfunctional. The diagnosis of AIDS is made when the person succumbs to various opportunistic infections.

How is AIDS transmitted?

AIDS is transmitted primarily through the exchange of blood or semen during sexual contact or through the sharing of contaminated needles and syringes among IV drug users.

What are the effects of stress and depression on the immune system?

Both stress and depression have been associated with lowered immune response, and stress has been linked with increased symptoms of various infectious diseases.

What three personal factors are associated with health and resistance to stress?

Personal factors related to health and resistance to stress are optimism, psychological hardiness, and social support.

Key Terms
sedentary lifestyle (p. 370); Type A behavior pattern (p. 370); Type B behavior pattern (p. 370); lymphocytes (p. 374); acquired immune deficiency syndrome (AIDS) (p. 375); HIV (human immunodeficiency virus) (p. 375); psychoneuroimmunology (p. 376); hardiness (p. 377); social support (p. 377)

LIFESTYLE AND HEALTH

What constitutes an unhealthy lifestyle, and how important a factor is lifestyle in illness and disease?

Slightly over 50% of all deaths in this country can be attributed to unhealthy lifestyle factors, which include smoking, overeating, an unhealthy diet, too much coffee or alcohol, drug abuse, and/or too little exercise and rest.

Why is smoking considered the single most preventable cause of death?

Smoking is considered the single most preventable cause of death because it is directly related to 434,000 deaths each year, including deaths from heart disease, cancer, lung disease, and stroke.

What are some health risks of alcohol abuse?

Alcohol abuse can damage virtually every organ in the body, including the liver, stomach, skeletal muscles, heart, and brain; and it is involved in over 50% of motor vehicle accidents.

What are some benefits of regular aerobic exercise?

Regular aerobic exercise reduces the risk of cardiovascular disease, increases muscular strength, moderates the effects of stress, makes bones denser and stronger, and helps one maintain a desirable weight.

Key Term
aerobic exercise (p. 381)

Study Guide for Chapter 11

Answers to all the Study Guide questions are provided at the end of the book.

Section One: Chapter Review

1. The biomedical model focuses on _____; the biopsychosocial model focuses on _____.
   a. illness; illness
   b. health and illness; illness
   c. illness; health and illness
   d. health and illness; health and illness

2. The stage of the general adaptation syndrome marked by intense physiological efforts to adapt to the stressor is the (alarm, resistance) stage.

3. Susceptibility to illness increases during the (alarm, exhaustion) stage of the general adaptation syndrome.

4. During secondary appraisal, a person
   a. evaluates his or her coping resources and considers options for dealing with the stressor.
   b. determines whether an event is positive, neutral, or negative.
   c. determines whether an event involves loss, threat, or challenge.
   d. determines whether an event causes physiological or psychological stress.

5. Selye focused on the (psychological, physiological) aspects of stress; Lazarus focused on the (psychological, physiological) aspects of stress.

6. Rick cannot decide whether to go out or stay home and study for his test. What kind of conflict does he have?
   a. approach–approach
   b. avoidance–avoidance
   c. approach–avoidance
   d. ambivalence–ambivalence

7. What factor or factors increase stress, according to research on the topic?
   a. predictability of the stressor
   b. unpredictability of the stressor
   c. predictability of and control over the stressor
   d. unpredictability of and lack of control over the stressor

8. In general, an assembly-line worker suffers more stress than a business executive because
   a. the workload is higher.
   b. the workload is lower.
   c. the decision latitude is higher.
   d. the decision latitude is lower.

9. Victims of catastrophic events typically want to talk about their experience. (true/false)

10. Posttraumatic stress disorder is a prolonged and severe stress reaction that results when a number of common sources of stress occur simultaneously. (true/false)

11. Coping aimed at reducing, modifying, or eliminating a source of stress is called (emotion-focused, problem-focused) coping; that aimed at reducing an emotional reaction to stress is called (emotion-focused, problem-focused) coping.

12. People typically use a combination of problem-focused and emotion-focused coping when dealing with a stressful situation. (true/false)

13. Proactive coping involves taking action (before, after) a stressor occurs.

14. On the Social Readjustment Rating Scale, only negative life changes are considered stressful. (true/false)

15. The Social Readjustment Rating Scale takes account of the individual's perceptions of the stressfulness of the life change in assigning stress points. (true/false)

16. According to Lazarus, hassles typically account for more life stress than major life changes. (true/false)

17. Lazarus's approach to measuring hassles and uplifts considers individual perceptions of stressful events. (true/false)

18. HIV eventually causes a breakdown in the _____ system.
    a. circulatory   c. immune
    b. vascular   d. respiratory

19. The incidence of AIDS in the United States is highest among
    a. homosexuals and IV drug users.
    b. homosexuals and hemophiliacs.
    c. homosexuals and bisexuals.
    d. heterosexuals, IV drug users, and hemophiliacs.

20. Recent research suggests that the most toxic component of the Type A behavior pattern is
    a. hostility.   c. a sense of time urgency.
    b. impatience.   d. perfectionism.

21. Most research has pursued the connection between the Type A behavior pattern and
    a. cancer.   c. stroke.
    b. coronary heart disease.   d. ulcers.

22. Lowered immune response has been associated with
    a. stress.
    b. depression.
    c. stress and depression.
    d. neither stress nor depression.

23. Some research suggests that optimists are more stress-resistant than pessimists. (true/false)

24. Which of the following is *not* a dimension of psychological hardiness?
    a. a feeling that adverse circumstances can be controlled and changed
    b. a sense of commitment and deep involvement in personal goals
    c. a tendency to look on change as a challenge rather than a threat
    d. close, supportive relationships with family and friends

25. Social support tends to reduce stress but is unrelated to health outcomes. (true/false)

26. Which is the most important factor leading to disease and death?
    a. unhealthy lifestyle
    b. a poor health care system
    c. environmental hazards
    d. genetic disorders

27. Which health-compromising behavior is responsible for the most deaths?
    a. overeating   c. lack of exercise
    b. smoking   d. excessive alcohol use

28. (Alcohol, Smoking) damages virtually every organ in the body.

29. To improve cardiovascular fitness, aerobic exercise should be done
    a. 15 minutes daily.
    b. 1 hour daily.
    c. 20 to 30 minutes daily.
    d. 20 to 30 minutes three or four times a week.

Section Two: The Biopsychosocial Model of Health and Illness

List at least two forces for each of the following:

1. Biological forces favoring health and wellness

2. Biological forces working against health and wellness

3. Psychological forces favoring health and wellness

4. Psychological forces working against health and wellness

5. Social forces favoring health and wellness

6. Social forces working against health and wellness

Section Three: Fill In the Blank

1. Medicine has been dominated by the _____ model, which focuses on illness rather than on health, whereas the _____ model asserts that both health and illness are determined by a combination of biological, psychological, and social factors.

2. The field of psychology that is concerned with the psychological factors that contribute to health, illness, and recovery is known as_____ _____.

3. The fight-or-flight response is controlled by the _____ and the endocrine glands.

4. The first stage of the general adaptation syndrome is the _____ stage.

5. The stage of the general adaptation syndrome during which the adrenal glands release hormones to help the body resist stressors is called the _____ stage.

6. Lazarus's theory is considered a _____ theory of stress and coping.

7. Laura knew that her upcoming job interview would be difficult, so she tried to anticipate the kinds of questions she would be asked and practiced the best possible responses. Laura was practicing _____ coping.

8. The most feared disease related to the immune system is _____.

9. The primary means of transmission of HIV is through sexual contact between _____ _____.

10. Daily _____ are the "irritating, frustrating, distressing demands and troubled relationships that plague us day in and day out."

11. Jan is a psychologist who works with biologists and medical researchers to determine the effects of psychological factors on the immune system. Jan works in the field of _____.

12. People with the Type _____ behavior pattern have a strong sense of time urgency and are impatient, excessively competitive, hostile, and easily angered.

13. One approach to treatment of alcoholism is _____ _____ therapy, in which the alcohol abuser is systematically exposed to the cues that have stimulated alcohol craving and consumption in the past.

14. _____ appraisal is an evaluation of the significance of a potentially stressful event according to how it will affect one's well-being—whether it is perceived as irrelevant or as involving harm, loss, threat, or challenge.

15. _____ is the result of intense, unrelieved, and unmanaged job stress, which causes an individual to become pessimistic, dissatisfied, inefficient on the job, and debilitated psychologically.

16. A _____ is any event capable of producing physical or emotional stress.

17. Jason wants to get a flu shot, but he is also very afraid of needles. He is faced with an _____–_____ conflict.

Section Four: Comprehensive Practice Test

1. Stress consists of the threats and problems we encounter in life. (true/false)

2. Hans Selye developed the
   a. diathesis stress model.
   b. general adaptation syndrome model.
   c. cognitive stress model.
   d. conversion reaction model.

3. The fight-or-flight response is seen in the _____ stage of the general adaptation syndrome.
   a. alarm   c. resistance
   b. exhaustion   d. arousal

4. Which of the following is not one of the four phases of the stress response, as described by Lazarus?
   a. a causal agent
   b. the stress reaction
   c. mind/body evaluates the stressor
   d. the outcome evaluation

5. Lack of exercise, poor diet, and disease and injury are considered to be _____ forces that work against health and wellness.
   a. environmental   c. biological
   b. psychological   d. social

6. Patricia has been looking for new bedroom furniture and has found two styles that she really likes. She is trying to decide which one she will purchase. Patricia is experiencing an _____ conflict.
   a. approach–approach
   b. approach–avoidance
   c. avoidance–avoidance
   d. avoidance–approach

7. People's sense of control over a situation can have an important beneficial influence on how a stressor affects them even if they do not exercise that control. (true/false)

8. Posttraumatic stress leaves some people more vulnerable for future mental health problems. (true/false)

9. Which of the following is not a variable in work stress?
   a. workload
   b. clarity of job description
   c. perceived equity of pay for work
   d. task variety

10. Decision latitude refers to the extent to which an employee can challenge his or her supervisor's orders or decisions. (true/false)

11. Religious faith helps people cope with negative life events? (true/false)

12. Lazarus's term for the positive experiences that can serve to cancel out the effects of day-to-day hassles is
    a. stress assets.   c. uplifts.
    b. coping mechanisms.   d. appraisals.

13. Type B behavior patterns seem to be more correlated with heart disease than do Type A behavior patterns. (true/false)

14. B cells produce antibodies that are effective in destroying antigens that live _____ the body cells; T cells are important in the destruction of antigens that live _____ the body cells.
    a. outside; inside
    b. inside; outside

15. AIDS is caused by HIV, often called the AIDS virus. (true/false)

16. A class of chemicals called protease inhibitors seem to be responsible for the immune deficiencies in AIDS. (true/false)

17. African Americans have a (higher/ lower) rate of diabetes than White Americans.

Section Five: Critical Thinking

1. In your view, which is more effective for evaluating stress—the Social Readjustment Rating Scale or the Hassle Scale? Explain the advantages and disadvantages of each.

2. Prepare two arguments—one supporting the position that alcoholism is a genetically inherited disease, and the other supporting the position that alcoholism is not a medical disease but results from learning.

3. Choose several stress-producing incidents from your life and explain what problem-focused and emotion-focused coping strategies you used. From the knowledge you have gained in this chapter, list other coping strategies that might have been more effective.

Psychological Disorders

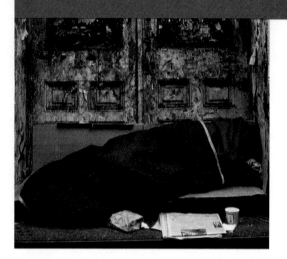

It was early in January, and Sybil Dorsett was working with other students in the chemistry lab at Columbia University in New York. Suddenly the loud crash of breaking glass made her heart pound and her head throb. The room seemed to be whirling around, and the acrid smell of chemicals filled the air, stinging her nostrils.

That smell—so like the old drugstore back in her native Wisconsin—and the broken glass—like a half-forgotten, far-off memory of being at home in her dining room when she was a little girl. Again Sybil heard the accusing voice, "You broke it." Frantically she seized her chemistry notes, stuffed them into her brown zipper folder, and ran for the door with the eyes of the professor and the other students following her in astonishment.

Sybil ran down the long, dark hall on the third floor of the chemistry building, pushed the elevator button, and waited. Seconds seemed like hours.

The next thought that entered Sybil's awareness was that of clutching for her folder, but it was gone. Gone, too, were the elevator she was waiting for and the long, dark hallway. She found herself walking down a dark, deserted street in a strange city. An icy wind whipped her face, and thick snowflakes filled the air. This wasn't New York. Where could she be? And how could she have gotten here in the few seconds between waiting for the elevator and now? Sybil walked on, bewildered, and finally came to a newsstand, where she bought a local paper. She was in Philadelphia. The date on the newspaper told her that five days had passed since she stood waiting for the elevator. Where had she been? What had she done?

A victim of sadistic physical abuse since early childhood, Sybil had experienced blackouts—missing days, weeks, and even longer periods, which seemed to have been taken from her life. Unknown to Sybil, other, very different personalities emerged during those periods to take control of her mind and body. Sixteen separate selves, 14 female and 2 male, lived within Sybil, each with different talents and abilities, emotions, ways of speaking and acting, moral values, and ambitions.

After many years of working with a talented psychiatrist, Sybil's 16 personalities were integrated into one. At last she was herself alone. (Adapted from Schreiber, 1973.)

What you have just read is not fiction. These and even stranger experiences are part of the real-life story of Sybil Isabel Dorsett, who suffered from an unusual condition, dissociative identity disorder, better known as multiple personality. Her life story, told in the book *Sybil*, and the life story of Chris Sizemore, told in *The Three Faces of Eve*, are two of the best-known cases of this disorder.

How can we know whether our own behavior is normal or abnormal? At what point do fears, thoughts, mood changes, and actions move from normal to mentally disturbed? This chapter explores many psychological disorders, their symptoms, and their possible causes. But first let's ask the obvious question: What is abnormal?

WHAT IS ABNORMAL?

Virtually everyone would agree that Sybil's behavior was abnormal. But most abnormal behavior is not so extreme and clear-cut. Behavior lies along a continuum, with most of us fairly well adjusted and experiencing only occasional maladaptive thoughts or behavior. At one end of the continuum are the unusually mentally healthy; at the other end are the seriously disturbed, like Sybil.

But where along the continuum does behavior become abnormal? Several questions can help determine what behavior is abnormal:

- *Is the behavior considered strange within the person's own culture?* What is considered normal and abnormal in one culture is not necessarily considered so in another. The culture generally defines what behaviors are acceptable. But even within the same culture, conceptions about what is normal can change from time to time.

- *Does the behavior cause personal distress?* When people experience considerable emotional distress without any life experience that warrants it, they may be diagnosed as having a psychological or mental disorder. Some people may be sad and depressed, some anxious; others may be agitated or excited, and still others fright-

What criteria might be used to differentiate normal from abnormal behavior?

Link It!

Abnormal behavior is defined by each culture. For example, homelessness is considered abnormal in some cultures and completely normal in others.

ened, or even terrified by delusions and hallucinations. But not all persons with psychological disorders feel distress.

■ *Is the behavior maladaptive?* Some experts believe that the best way to differentiate between normal and abnormal behavior is to consider whether the behavior is adaptive or maladaptive. Maladaptive behavior interferes with the quality of people's lives and can cause a great deal of distress to family members, friends, and coworkers.

■ *Is the person a danger to self or others?* Another consideration is whether people are a danger to themselves or others. To be committed to a mental hospital, a person must be judged both mentally ill and a danger to self or others.

■ *Is the person legally responsible for his or her acts?* Often the term *insanity* is used to label those who behave abnormally, but mental health professionals do not use this term. It is a legal term used by the courts to declare people not legally responsible for their acts. Mass murderer Jeffrey Dahmer was ruled legally responsible for his acts, yet his behavior was clearly abnormal.

Perspectives on the Causes and Treatment of Psychological Disorders

What are five current perspectives that attempt to explain the causes of psychological disorders?

Several different perspectives on psychological disorders attempt to explain their causes and to recommend the best methods of treatment. The five current perspectives are the biological, psychodynamic, learning, cognitive, and humanistic perspectives.

The Biological Perspective   The biological perspective views abnormal behavior as a symptom of an underlying physical disorder. Just as doctors look for an organic cause of physical illness, those who hold the biological view believe that psychological disorders have a physical cause, such as genetic inheritance, biochemical abnormalities or imbalances, structural abnormalities within the brain, and/or infection. Consequently, those taking the biological perspective generally favor biological treatments, which may include drugs, electroconvulsive therapy (shock treatment), or psychosurgery.

There are two points to keep in mind as you read this chapter. First, even when there is strong evidence of a genetic factor in a psychological disorder, people do not inherit the disorder directly. They inherit a predisposition toward the disorder.

Whether they actually develop the disorder will depend on other conditions in their lives. Second, when certain structural or biochemical abnormalities are associated with a psychological disorder, there is the possibility that such abnormalities could be the result rather than the cause of the disorder.

The Psychodynamic Perspective Originally proposed by Freud, the psychodynamic perspective maintains that psychological disorders stem from early childhood experiences and unresolved, unconscious conflicts, usually of a sexual or aggressive nature. The cause assumed by the psychodynamic approach also suggests the cure—psychoanalysis—which Freud developed to uncover and resolve such unconscious conflicts.

The Learning Perspective According to the learning perspective, psychological disorders are not symptoms of an underlying disorder; the behavioral symptoms *are* the disorder. Get rid of the symptoms (the abnormal behavior), and the problem is solved. According to this view, people who exhibit abnormal behavior either are victims of faulty learning or have failed to learn appropriate patterns of thinking and acting. Behavior therapists use learning principles to eliminate distressing behavior and to establish new, more appropriate behavior in its place.

The Cognitive Perspective The cognitive perspective suggests that faulty thinking or distorted perceptions can contribute to some types of psychological disorders. For example, negative thinking is intimately involved in depression and anxiety. Treatment consistent with this perspective is aimed at changing thinking and perceptions, which presumably will lead to a change in behavior.

The Humanistic Perspective The humanistic perspective views human nature as inherently good and rational and as naturally moving toward self-actualization (the fulfillment of each person's potential). According to this view, psychological disorders result when a person's natural tendency toward self-actualization is blocked (Maslow, 1970; Rogers, 1961). Remove the psychological blocks, and the person can move toward self-actualization.

Review & Reflect 12.1 (on page 394) summarizes the five perspectives on psychological disorders. Each perspective has its place in the description, analysis, and treatment of certain psychological disorders.

Although mental health professionals often disagree about the causes of abnormal behavior and the best treatments, there is less disagreement about diagnosis. A standard set of criteria has been established and is used by the majority of mental health professionals to diagnose psychological disorders.

Defining and Classifying Psychological Disorders

Published by the American Psychiatric Association, the *Diagnostic and Statistical Manual of Mental Disorders,* Fourth Edition, commonly known as the **DSM-IV,** is a diagnostic system for describing and classifying psychological disorders. It contains descriptions of about 290 specific psychological disorders and lists criteria that must be met in order to make a particular diagnosis. The *DSM-IV,* the most widely accepted diagnostic system in the United States, is used by researchers, therapists, mental health workers, and most insurance companies. It enables professionals to speak the same language when diagnosing, treating, researching, and conversing about a variety of psychological disorders (Clark et al., 1995).

Review & Reflect 12.2 (on page 395) summarizes the major categories of disorders in the *DSM-IV.*

You have heard the terms *neurotic* and *psychotic* used in relation to mental disturbances. Although now obsolete, the term **neurosis** was applied to disorders that cause people considerable personal distress and some impairment in functioning, without causing them to lose contact with reality or to violate important social

DSM-IV: The *Diagnostic and Statistical Manual of Mental Disorders,* Fourth Edition, a manual published by the American Psychiatric Association, which describes about 290 mental disorders and their symptoms.

neurosis (new-RO-sis): An obsolete term for a disorder causing personal distress and some impairment in functioning but not causing loss of contact with reality or violation of important social norms.

Link It!

What is the *DSM-IV?*

Perspective	Cause of Psychological Disorders	Treatment
Biological perspective	A psychological disorder is a symptom of an underlying physical disorder caused by a structural or biochemical abnormality in the brain, by genetic inheritance, or by infection.	Diagnose and treat like any other physical disorder Drugs, electroconvulsive therapy, or psychosurgery
Psychodynamic perspective	Psychological disorders stem from early childhood experiences; unresolved, unconscious sexual or aggressive conflicts; and/or imbalance among id, ego, and superego.	Bring disturbing repressed material to consciousness and help patient work through unconscious conflicts Psychoanalysis
Learning perspective	Abnormal thoughts, feelings, and behaviors are learned and sustained like any other behaviors, or there is a failure to learn appropriate behaviors.	Use classical and operant conditioning and modeling to extinguish abnormal behaviors and to increase adaptive behavior Behavior therapy, behavior modification
Cognitive perspective	Faulty and negative thinking can cause psychological disorders.	Change faulty, irrational, and/or negative thinking Beck's cognitive therapy, rational-emotive therapy
Humanistic perspective	Psychological disorders result from blocking of normal tendency toward self-actualization.	Increase self-acceptance and self-understanding; help patient become more inner-directed Client-centered therapy, Gestalt therapy

norms. In contrast, a **psychosis** is a more serious disturbance that greatly impairs the ability to function in everyday life. It can cause people to lose touch with reality, possibly suffer from delusions and/or hallucinations, and sometimes require hospitalization. The term *psychosis* is still used by mental health professionals, most often in discussing the most serious psychological disorder, schizophrenia.

SCHIZOPHRENIA

Schizophrenia is so far removed from common, everyday experience that it is all but impossible for most of us to imagine what it is like to be schizophrenic. Consider the case of Eric, whose normal childhood and youth turned into a nightmare when he lost touch with reality during his senior year in high school:

> He lives in his parents' wood-paneled basement and usually sits with a blanket covering his head. His world consists of the voices he hears inside his head and the visual hallucinations he takes to be real. Eric insists that he talks to God and to

psychosis (sy-CO-sis): A severe psychological disorder, marked by loss of contact with reality and a seriously impaired ability to function.

Review & Reflect 12.2   Major *DSM-IV* Categories of Mental Disorders

Disorder	Symptoms	Examples
Schizophrenia and other psychotic disorders	Disorders characterized by the presence of psychotic symptoms including hallucinations, delusions, disorganized speech, bizarre behavior, or loss of contact with reality	Schizophrenia, paranoid type Schizophrenia, disorganized type Schizophrenia, catatonic type Delusional disorder, jealous type
Mood disorders	Disorders characterized by periods of extreme or prolonged depression or mania or both	Major depressive disorder Bipolar disorder
Anxiety disorders	Disorders characterized by anxiety and avoidance behavior	Panic disorder Social phobia Obsessive compulsive disorder Posttraumatic stress disorder
Somatoform disorders	Disorders in which physical symptoms are present that are psychological in origin rather than due to a medical condition	Hypochondriasis Conversion disorder
Dissociative disorders	Disorders in which one handles stress or conflict by forgetting important personal information or one's whole identity, or by compartmentalizing the trauma or conflict into a split-off alter personality	Dissociative amnesia Dissociative fugue Dissociative identity disorder
Personality disorders	Disorders characterized by long-standing, inflexible, maladaptive patterns of behavior beginning early in life and causing personal distress or problems in social and occupational functioning	Antisocial personality disorder Histrionic personality disorder Narcissistic personality disorder Borderline personality disorder
Substance-related disorders	Disorders in which undesirable behavioral changes result from substance abuse, dependence, or intoxication	Alcohol abuse Cocaine abuse Cannabis dependence
Disorders usually first diagnosed in infancy, childhood, or adolescence	Disorders that include mental retardation, learning disorders, communication disorders, pervasive developmental disorders, attention-deficit and disruptive behavior disorders, tic disorders, and elimination disorders	Conduct disorder Autistic disorder Tourette's syndrome Stuttering
Eating disorders	Disorders characterized by severe disturbances in eating behavior	Anorexia nervosa Bulimia nervosa

Source: Based on *DSM-IV* (American Psychiatric Association, 1994).

Satan, and at times he believes that he is Jesus Christ. If he refuses to take his anti-psychotic medication, he is likely to become violent, and two times he has tried to take his own life. For his parents, there is rarely a stress-free moment or an hour with peace of mind. (Bartimus, 1983)

Link It!

Schizophrenia is the most serious and devastating of all the psychological disorders because of the social disruption and misery it causes for both the people who suffer from it and their families. It affects about 1 person in 100, and one-half of all the mental hospital beds in this country are occupied by schizophrenic patients. Many people who develop schizophrenia showed significant behavioral dysfunction as children (Neumann et al., 1995; Torrey et al., 1994). Schizophrenia usually begins in adolescence or early adulthood, but it can appear later in life. More men than women suffer from this disorder, and they develop it at an earlier age. Men generally do not respond as well to treatment, spend more time in mental hospitals, and are more likely to relapse (Castle et al., 1995; Szymanski et al., 1995). To further complicate the problem, about 50% of schizophrenic patients have substance abuse problems at some point in their illness (Kosten & Ziedonis, 1997).

The Symptoms of Schizophrenia: Many and Varied

What are some of the major positive and negative symptoms of schizophrenia?

Any given individual with schizophrenia may have one or more of its major symptoms, yet there is not one single symptom or brain abnormality shared by all people with the disorder (see Andreasen, 1999). The symptoms of schizophrenia are classified into two categories—positive symptoms and negative symptoms.

Positive Symptoms   Positive symptoms are the abnormal behaviors that are present in people with schizophrenia. They include hallucinations and delusions, as well as disorganized thinking and speech and grossly disorganized or bizarre behavior (McGlashan & Fenton, 1992).

Hallucinations   One of the clearest positive symptoms of schizophrenia is the presence of **hallucinations**—imaginary sensations. Schizophrenic patients may see, hear, feel, taste, or smell strange things in the absence of any stimulus in the environment, but hearing voices is the most common type of hallucination. Patients may think they hear the voice of God or Satan, the voices of family members or friends, unknown voices, and even their own voice broadcasting aloud what they are thinking. Most often the voices accuse or curse the patients or engage in a running commentary on their behavior. Sometimes there are *command hallucinations*, in which the voices give instructions such as "Go outside" (Zisook et al., 1995). At other times a menacing voice may order the patient to kill someone or take his or her own life.

Visual hallucinations, less common than auditory hallucinations, are usually in black and white and commonly take the form of friends, relatives, God, Jesus, or the devil. Schizophrenics also may experience exceedingly frightening and painful bodily sensations and feel they are being beaten, burned, or sexually violated.

Delusions   Imagine how upset you would be if you believed that your every thought was being broadcast aloud for everyone to hear. What if you were convinced that some strange agent was stealing your thoughts or inserting other thoughts in your head? These are examples of **delusions**—false beliefs not generally shared by others in the culture. Usually patients cannot be persuaded that their beliefs are false, even in the face of strong evidence.

Delusions may take different forms. Schizophrenics with **delusions of grandeur** may believe they are a famous person, such as Jesus Christ, or an important person with great knowledge, ability, or authority. Those with **delusions of persecution** falsely believe that some person or agency is trying to harass, cheat, spy on, conspire against, injure, kill, or in some other way harm them.

schizophrenia (SKIT-soh-FREE-nee-ah): A severe psychological disorder characterized by loss of contact with reality, hallucinations, delusions, inappropriate or flat affect, some disturbance in thinking, social withdrawal, and/or other bizarre behavior.

hallucination: A sensory perception in the absence of any external sensory stimulus; an imaginary sensation.

delusion: A false belief, not generally shared by others in the culture, that cannot be changed despite strong evidence to the contrary.

delusion of grandeur: A false belief that one is a famous person or a person who has some great knowledge, ability, or authority.

delusion of persecution: A false belief that a person or group is trying in some way to harm one.

Disturbances in the Form of Speech or Thought The speech of schizophrenics is often difficult or even impossible to understand. The content of the message may be extremely vague, or the person may invent words or use them inappropriately (Chaika, 1985). There is often a disturbance in the form of thought. Most common is the loosening of associations, or *derailment*, when a person does not follow one line of thought to completion, but on the basis of vague connections shifts from one subject to another.

> The pen I am using is from a factory called "Perry & Co." This factory is in England. . . . The city of London is in England. I know this from my school-days. Then, I always liked geography. My last teacher in that subject was . . . a man with black eyes. I also like black eyes. There are also blue and gray eyes and other sorts, too. I have heard it said that snakes have green eyes. All people have eyes. There are some, too, who are blind. (Bleuler, 1911/1950, p. 17)

Grossly Disorganized Behavior and Inappropriate Affect Grossly disorganized behavior can include such things as childlike silliness, inappropriate sexual behavior (masturbating in public), disheveled appearance, and peculiar dress. There may also be unpredictable agitation, including shouting and swearing, and unusual or inappropriate motor behavior, including strange gestures, facial expressions, or postures.

Schizophrenics may display **inappropriate affect**; that is, they may exhibit facial expressions, tone of voice, and gestures that do not reflect the emotion that would be expected under the circumstances. A person might cry when watching a TV comedy and laugh when watching a news story showing bloody bodies at the scene of a fatal automobile accident.

inappropriate affect: A symptom common in schizophrenia in which a person's behavior (including facial expression, tone of voice, and gestures) does not reflect the emotion that would be expected under the circumstances; for example, a person laughs at a tragedy or cries at a joke.

Negative Symptoms A negative symptom of schizophrenia is a loss of or deficiency in thoughts and behaviors that are characteristic of normal functioning. Negative symptoms include social withdrawal, apathy, loss of motivation, lack of goal-directed activity, very limited speech, slowed movements, and poor hygiene and grooming (McGlashan & Fenton, 1992). Some schizophrenic patients have *flat affect*—showing practically no emotional response at all, even though they often report feeling the emotion. These patients may speak in a monotone, have blank and emotionless facial expressions, and act and move more like robots than humans.

Negative symptoms are predictors of impaired overall social and vocational functioning, and those with negative symptoms seem to have the poorest outcomes (Fenton & McGlashan, 1994). They tend to withdraw from others and retreat into their own world. Often their functioning is too impaired for them to hold a job or even to care for themselves.

Brain Abnormalities in Some Schizophrenics Several abnormalities in brain structure and function have been found in schizophrenic patients. Among these are defects in the neural circuitry of the cerebral cortex (Andreasen, 1999) and abnormally low neural activity in the frontal lobes and the thalamus (Benes, 1996; Buchsbaum et al., 1996). Other studies have revealed a decreased volume of the hippocampus, the amygdala (Nelson et al., 1998), and the thalamus (Andreasen et al., 1994; Buchsbaum et al., 1996). In many schizophrenics, there is a deficit in cortical gray matter (Lim et al., 1996), and the ventricles—fluid-filled cavities in the brain—are larger than in a normal brain (Lieberman et al., 1992; Zipursky et al., 1992). This particular abnormality was found in the brain of John Hinckley, Jr., the man who tried to assassinate Ronald Reagan.

Types of Schizophrenia

Even though various symptoms are commonly shared by schizophrenics, certain features distinguish one type of schizophrenia from another. The four types of schizophrenia are paranoid, disorganized, catatonic, and undifferentiated.

What are the four types of schizophrenia?

A person with catatonic schizophrenia may become frozen in an unusual position, like a statue, for hours at a time.

What are some suggested causes of schizophrenia?

paranoid schizophrenia (PAIR-uh-nnoid): A type of schizophrenia characterized by delusions of grandeur or persecution.

disorganized schizophrenia: The most serious type of schizophrenia, marked by inappropriate affect, silliness, laughter, grotesque mannerisms, and bizarre behavior.

catatonic schizophrenia (KAT-uh-TAHN-ik): A type of schizophrenia characterized by complete stillness or stupor and/or periods of great agitation and excitement; patients may assume an unusual posture and remain in it for long periods.

People with **paranoid schizophrenia** usually suffer from delusions of grandeur or persecution. They may be convinced that they have an identity other than their own—that they are the president, the Virgin Mary, or God—or that they possess great ability or talent. Paranoid schizophrenics often show exaggerated anger and suspiciousness. If they have delusions of persecution and feel that they are being harassed or threatened, they may become violent in an attempt to defend themselves against their imagined persecutors.

Disorganized schizophrenia, the most serious type, tends to occur at an earlier age than the other types and is marked by extreme social withdrawal, hallucinations, delusions, silliness, inappropriate laughter, grimaces, grotesque mannerisms, and other bizarre behavior. These patients show flat or inappropriate affect and are frequently incoherent. They often exhibit obscene behavior, may masturbate openly, and swallow almost any kind of object or material. Disorganized schizophrenia results in the most severe disintegration of the personality (Beratis et al., 1994), and its victims have the poorest chance of recovery (Fenton & McGlashan, 1991; Kane, 1993).

Persons with **catatonic schizophrenia** may display complete stillness and stupor, or great excitement and agitation. Frequently they alternate rapidly between the two. They may become frozen in a strange posture or position, as shown in the photograph, and remain there for hours without moving.

Undifferentiated schizophrenia is the general catchall category used when schizophrenic symptoms either do not conform to the criteria of any schizophrenia type or conform to more than one type.

The Causes of Schizophrenia

There is no convincing evidence that unhealthy patterns of communication and interaction in the family are the breeding ground for schizophrenia, as many psychiatrists claimed in the 1950s and 1960s (Bateson et al., 1956; Lidz et al., 1965; Torrey, 1983). However, research evidence that suggests a biological factor in many cases of schizophrenia continues to mount.

Genetic Inheritance   Schizophrenia does tend to run in families, and genetic factors play a major role (Cannon et al., 1998; Gottesman, 1991; Mortensen et al., 1999). The chance of a person in the United States developing schizophrenia is about 1 in 100 (Jeste, 1994). However, people with one schizophrenic parent have about a 13% chance of developing the disorder; those with two schizophrenic parents have roughly a 46% chance. If one identical twin develops schizophrenia, the other twin has about a 46% chance of having it as well (Nicol & Gottesman, 1983). Figure 12.1 shows how the chance of developing schizophrenia varies with the degree of relationship to a schizophrenic person. Still more evidence for a genetic factor comes from adoption studies showing that adoptees have ten times the risk of developing schizophrenia if their biological parent rather than their adoptive parent is schizophrenic (Kendler et al., 1994; Kety et al., 1994).

According to genetic theorists, what is inherited is not schizophrenia itself, but a predisposition or tendency to develop it (Zubin & Spring, 1977). According to the **diathesis–stress model**, schizophrenia develops when there is *both* a genetic predisposition toward the disorder (diathesis) and more stress than a person can handle (Fowles, 1992). The excessive stress can occur in the womb or during childhood, adolescence, or adulthood.

Whether predisposed people develop the disorder may depend on their life circumstances (Fowles, 1992; Johnson, 1989). Torrey and Bowler (1990) speculated that schizophrenia is more common in highly urbanized areas of the United States than in rural areas because of the greater stress of city life coupled with higher exposure to pollutants, toxins, and infectious diseases.

Excessive Dopamine Activity   Abnormal activity in the brain's dopamine systems is found in many schizophrenics, particularly in the limbic system, which is

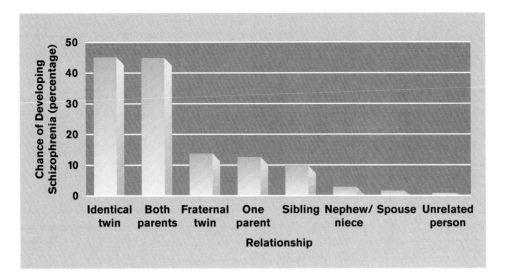

Figure 12.1

Genetic Similarity and Probability of Developing Schizophrenia

Research strongly indicates a genetic factor operating in many cases of schizophrenia. Identical twins have identical genes, and if one twin develops schizophrenia, the other twin has a 46% chance of developing it also. In fraternal twins the chance is only 14%. A person with one schizophrenic parent has a 13% chance of developing schizophrenia, but a 46% chance if both parents are schizophrenic. (Data from Nicol & Gottesman, 1983.)

involved in human emotions (Davis et al., 1991; Winn, 1994). Drugs that are effective in reducing the symptoms of schizophrenia block dopamine action, although about one-third of the patients who are given these drugs do not show improvement (Iverson, 1979; Torrey, 1983; Wolkin et al., 1989).

MOOD DISORDERS

Mood disorders involve moods or emotions that are extreme and unwarranted. In the most serious of these disorders, mood ranges from the depths of severe depression to the heights of extreme elation. Mood disorders fall into two broad categories: depressive disorders and bipolar disorders.

Depressive Disorders and Bipolar Disorder: Emotional Highs and Lows

Major Depressive Disorder   It is normal to feel blue, sad, or depressed in response to many of life's common experiences—death of a loved one, loss of a job, or an unhappy ending to a long-term relationship. Major depression, however, is not normal. People with **major depressive disorder** feel an overwhelming sadness, despair, and hopelessness, and they usually lose their ability to experience pleasure. They may have changes in appetite, weight, or sleep patterns, loss of energy, and difficulty in thinking or concentrating. Key symptoms of major depressive disorder are psychomotor disturbances (Sobin & Sackheim, 1997). For example, body movements, reaction time, and speech may be so slowed that some depressed people seem to be doing everything in slow motion. Others experience the opposite extreme and are constantly moving and fidgeting, wringing their hands, and pacing. Depression can be so severe that its victims suffer from delusions or hallucinations, which are symptoms of psychotic depression (Coryell, 1996). The most common of all serious mental disorders, depression strikes people of all social classes, cultures, and nations around the world.

Women are reported to be twice as likely as men to suffer from depression with one notable exception (Culbertson, 1997). Among Jews, males are equally as likely as females to have major depression (Levav et al., 1997). In the United States, about 21.3% of women and 12.7% of men have had a major depressive episode at some time in their lives (Kessler et al., 1994). In recent years there has been an increase in depression among adolescents, particularly in adolescent girls, and perhaps in

What are the symptoms of major depressive disorder?

diathesis–stress model: The idea that people with a constitutional predisposition (diathesis) toward a disorder, such as schizophrenia, may develop the disorder if they are subjected to sufficient environmental stress.

mood disorders: Disorders characterized by extreme and unwarranted disturbances in feeling or mood.

major depressive disorder: A mood disorder marked by feelings of great sadness, despair, guilt, worthlessness, and hopelessness.

Native American and homosexual young people as well (Peterson et al., 1993). Studies have also revealed high rates of mood disorders in writers and artists (Jamison, 1995; Schildkraut et al., 1994), composers, and entertainers (Ludwig, 1995, 1996), and among patients experiencing chronic pain (Banks & Kerns, 1996).

Some people suffer only one major depressive episode, but 50–60% will have a recurrence. Risk of recurrence is greatest for females (Winokur et al., 1993), for those with an onset of depression before age 20 (Brown, 1996; Giles et al., 1989), and for those with a family history of mood disorders (Akiskal, 1989). Recurrences may be frequent or infrequent, and recurring episodes tend to be increasingly more severe and long-lasting (Greden, 1994; Maj et al., 1992). According to the American Psychiatric Association (1994), 1 year after their initial diagnosis of major depressive disorder, 40% of patients are without symptoms; 40% are still suffering from major depression; and 20% are depressed, but not enough to warrant a diagnosis of major depression. Unfortunately, about 80% of those suffering from depression never even receive treatment (Holden, 1986), and about 15% of people with major depressive disorder commit suicide (Coppen, 1994).

Many people suffer from a milder form of depression called *dysthymia*, which is nonetheless chronic (lasting 2 years or longer). People with dysthymia experience depressed mood but have fewer of the associated symptoms common in major depressive disorder.

Seasonal Depression   Many people find that their moods seem to change with the seasons, but people suffering from **seasonal affective disorder (SAD)** experience a significant depression that tends to come and go with the seasons (Wehr & Rosenthal, 1989). A spring/summer depression that remits in winter does exist, but the more common type, winter depression, seems to be triggered by light deficiency. During the winter months, when the days are shorter, some people become very depressed and tend to sleep and eat more, gain weight, and crave carbohydrates (Rosenthal et al., 1986; Wurtman & Wurtman, 1989). Molin and others (1996) found a correlation between the depression ratings of SAD patients and the minutes of sunshine and of daylight from September through May.

Rosenthal and colleagues (1985) exposed patients with winter depression to bright light, which simulated the longer daylight hours of summer. After several days of the light treatment, most of the subjects improved. Figure 12.2 shows the difference in mood fluctuations between seasonal-affective-disorder patients and a random sample of New York residents.

Bipolar Disorder   Another type of mood disorder is **bipolar disorder**, in which patients experience two radically different moods—extreme highs called *manic episodes* (or *mania*) and the extreme lows of major depression—usually with relatively normal periods in between. A **manic episode** is marked by excessive euphoria, inflated self-esteem, wild optimism, and hyperactivity. During a manic episode people are wound up and full of energy. They frantically engage in a flurry of activity, rarely sleep, and talk loud and fast, skipping from one topic to another.

What is wrong with being euphoric, energetic, and optimistic? Obviously nothing, as long as the state is warranted. But people in a manic state have temporarily lost touch with reality and frequently have delusions of grandeur along with their euphoric highs. They may go on wild spending sprees or waste large sums of money on grand get-rich-quick schemes. If family members try to stop them or to convince them to abandon their irrational plans, they are likely to become irritable, hostile, enraged, or even dangerous. Quite often patients must be hospitalized during manic episodes to protect them and others from the disastrous consequences of their poor judgment.

The excessive euphoria, boundless energy, and delusions of grandeur are all apparent in this description of a manic episode experienced by Edward O, a 27-year-old high school teacher:

Link It!

The depressed moods of seasonal affective disorder (SAD) usually occur during the winter, when days are short, and can be improved using light therapy.

What are the extremes of mood suffered by those with bipolar disorder?

seasonal affective disorder (SAD): A mood disorder in which depression comes and goes with the seasons.

bipolar disorder: A mood disorder in which manic episodes alternate with periods of depression, usually with relatively normal periods in between.

manic episode (MAN-ik): A period of extreme elation, euphoria, and hyperactivity, often accompanied by delusions of grandeur and by hostility if activity is blocked.

One day Edward O's behavior suddenly became bizarre. He charged into the principal's office and outlined his plan for tearing down the school building and having his students rebuild it from the ground up over the weekend. The school principal called the police and had Edward taken to a hospital. There Edward paced up and down for two days, would not sleep or eat, and spoke excitedly about his plans to take over administration of the hospital. On the third day he demanded paper and pens and, in a frenzy, wrote 100 letters, one to each U.S. senator. . . . When staff members tried to stop him, Edward flew into a rage, so they decided to let him "run out of steam." After the fourth day he collapsed, totally exhausted. (Adapted from Goldenberg, 1977)

Bipolar disorder is much less common than major depressive disorder, and the lifetime prevalence rates are about the same for males (1.6%) and females (1.7%) (Kessler et al., 1994). Unfortunately, 89% of those with bipolar disorder have recurrences, and half of bipolar patients experience another episode within a year of recovering from one. In 60–70% of cases, the manic episodes either directly precede or directly follow major depressive episodes. The good news is that 70–80% of the patients return to normal after an episode (American Psychiatric Association, 1994). But some are "rapid cyclers" who experience four or more episodes per year. And like depression, bipolar disorder can follow a seasonal pattern (Faedda et al., 1993).

Causes of Major Depressive Disorder and Bipolar Disorder

The biological and cognitive perspectives offer some insight into the causes of mood disorders and suggest treatments that have proven helpful to many people suffering from these disorders.

The Biological Perspective   Biological factors such as genetic inheritance and abnormal brain chemistry play a major role in bipolar disorder and major depressive disorder. PET scans have revealed abnormal patterns of brain activity in both of these disorders (Drevets et al., 1992; George et al., 1993).

The Role of Genetic Inheritance   People who have relatives with mood disorders are at higher risk of developing mood disturbances, and this risk is due to shared genetic factors rather than shared environmental factors (Kendler, Walters, et al., 1994). Earlier onset and more severe depression is more heavily influenced by genetic factors. Based on a study of 1,721 identical and fraternal female twins, Kendler and others (1993) estimated the heritability of a lifetime history of major depression to be 70% and the contribution of environment to be 30%. In a later study of the female twins, Kendler and others (1995) concluded that a genetic predisposition to depression increases the risk of an episode of major depression by heightening a person's sensitivity to stressful life events. Several recent twin studies have found genetic influences on depression to be similar in male twins and female twins (Kendler & Prescott, 1999; Lyons et al., 1998).

Adoption studies have shown that among adult adoptees who had developed depression, there was 8 times more major depression and 15 times more suicide in biological than in adoptive family members (Wender et al., 1986). And the genetic link is even stronger for bipolar disorder than for depression. The odds of developing bipolar disorder are 24 times greater in persons who have **first-degree relatives** (parents, children, or siblings) with the disorder (Weissman et al., 1984).

The Role of Serotonin and Norepinephrine   It is common knowledge that substances can alter mood—alcohol, caffeine, other uppers and downers, and a host of addi-

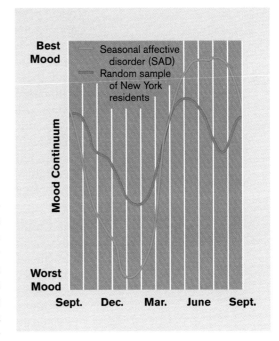

Figure 12.2

Seasonal Mood Changes

Many people report feeling best during May and June and worst during January and February. People with seasonal affective disorder (SAD) experience wider mood fluctuations—higher highs in June, July, and August and lower lows in December, January, and February. (Based on data from Wurtman & Wurtman, 1989.)

What are some suggested causes of major depressive disorder and bipolar disorder?

first-degree relatives: A person's parents, children, or siblings.

tional psychoactive substances. Researchers now know that moods are also altered and regulated by biochemicals occurring naturally in the body. Norepinephrine and serotonin are two neurotransmitters thought to play important roles in mood disorders. Both are localized in the limbic system and the hypothalamus, parts of the brain that help regulate emotional behavior. Too little norepinephrine is associated with depression, and too much is related to mania (Schildkraut, 1970). Amphetamines, which cause an emotional "high," are reported to stimulate the release of both serotonin and norepinephrine. And hypersecretion of cortisol in response to stress can cause suppression of norepinephrine and serotonin (Dinan, 1996).

An important unanswered question remains. Do these biochemical differences in the brain *cause* psychological changes or *result* from them? Theorists who emphasize psychological causes see biochemical changes as results, not causes, of mood disorders.

The Cognitive Perspective   Cognitive explanations hold that depression results from distortions in thinking. According to Beck (1967, 1991), depressed individuals view themselves, their world, and their future all in negative ways. They see their interactions with the world as a series of burdens and obstacles that usually end in failure. Depressed persons believe they are deficient, unworthy, and inadequate, and they attribute their perceived failures to their own physical, mental, or moral inadequacies. Finally, according to the cognitive theory, depressed patients believe that their future holds no hope. They may reason: "Everything always turns out wrong." "I never win." "Things will never get better." "It's no use."

The cognitive perspective offers a great deal of insight that can be applicable in daily life. Read the *Apply It!* at the end of this chapter to learn more.

The Psychodynamic Explanation   Psychodynamic theorists propose another cause for mood disorders. They suggest that when people cannot effectively express aggressive or negative feelings, they may turn those feelings inward (repress them) and thus experience depression.

Stress   Even though heredity is the best predictor of depression over a lifetime, Kendler and others (1995) found stressful life events such as getting divorced or losing a job to be the best short-term predictors of depression. And for those who are genetically predisposed, the risk is much greater. The vast majority of first episodes of depression strike after major life stress (Brown et al., 1994; Frank et al., 1994). Cui and Vaillant (1996), in a longitudinal study of Harvard graduates that continued for over 40 years, found that negative life events as well as family history played significant roles in the development of mood disorders. This seems particularly true of women, who are more likely to have experienced a severe negative life event just prior to the onset of depression (Spangler et al., 1996). Yet recurrences of depression, at least in people who are biologically predisposed, often occur without significant life stress (Brown et al., 1994).

Why are women so much more likely to suffer from depression than men? Are they somehow more biologically predisposed? The National Task Force on Women and Depression suggests that the higher rate of depression in women is largely due to social and cultural factors. In fulfilling her many roles—mother, wife, lover, friend, daughter, neighbor—a woman is likely to put the needs of others ahead of her own. Having young children poses a particular risk, and women suffer other stresses disproportionately, such as poverty and physical and sexual abuse. In fact, Pribor and Dinwiddie (1992) found an alarming incidence of depression, 88.5%, among female incest victims.

Stressful life events may leave some people simply feeling bad, but others become clinically depressed. What accounts for the difference? Genes? Brain chemistry? Early childhood experiences? Or is it the way people interpret life events,

Women raising children in conditions of extreme poverty are at higher risk of developing depression.

whether optimistically or pessimistically? There is some evidence to suggest that each explanation may play a part in the puzzle of depression.

Some depressed people commit the ultimate act of desperation—suicide. What are some of the risk factors for suicide, and what can be done to help prevent a person from committing suicide?

Suicide and Gender, Race, and Age

On April 5, 1994, Kurt Cobain, lead singer of the rock group Nirvana, committed suicide by shooting himself. He was 27 years old. Why would any person commit this final act of desperation?

Who Commits Suicide?   There were more than 31,000 suicides reported in the United States in 1994, and more than 81% were males (U.S. Bureau of the Census, 1997). Females are at least three times more likely than males to *attempt* suicide, but men are four times more likely to *succeed* at taking their own lives (Garland & Zigler, 1993). Up to 40% of those who attempt suicide will try again (Garland & Zigler, 1993), and 5–15% will eventually succeed (Rudd et al., 1996).

Regardless of age group, suicide rates are lowest for married persons, lower in women who have children (Hoyer & Lund, 1993), and lower still for pregnant women (Marzuk et al., 1997). And the suicide rate is highest for persons who have made a previous suicide attempt (Beck et al., 1990). People suffering from psychiatric disorders, particularly depression, schizophrenia, panic disorder, and alcoholism or drug abuse, are at higher risk (Lesage et al., 1994; Meltzer, 1998; Mościcki, 1995). In fact, 70% of suicides are associated with depression (Coppen, 1994).There is also evidence that suicidal behavior runs in families (Brent et al., 1996).

People experiencing major depression feel overwhelming sadness, despair, and hopelessness, which may lead them to commit suicide.

White males of all age groups have the highest suicide rate, about 10 times higher than the rate among African American males. For teenagers and young adults aged 15 through 24, suicide is now the third leading cause of death, and for college students, suicide ranks second. The rate of suicide among 15- to 19-year-olds has nearly doubled over the last few decades, an increase that may be due to increases in alcohol and drug abuse, psychiatric disorders, antisocial behavior, and disturbed home life. Or a precipitating circumstance such as the breakup of a relationship, family conflict, a disciplinary crisis, or school problems may push a teenager "over the edge" (Gould et al., 1996; Heikkinen et al., 1993). According to Garland and Zigler (1993), 6–13% of adolescents and 10.4% of college students have made a suicide attempt.

Older Americans are at far greater risk for suicide than younger people. White males aged 85 and over have the highest recorded suicide rate, more than six times the average national rate. Poor general health, serious illness, loneliness (often due to the death of a spouse), and decline in social and economic status are conditions that may push many older Americans, especially those aged 75 and over, to commit suicide.

Figure 12.3 (on page 404) shows the differences in U.S. suicide rates according to race, gender, and age.

Preventing Suicide   Although there are cultural differences in the rates, the reasons for committing suicide, and the methods used, the warning signs are very similar across racial, gender, and age groups.

Most suicidal persons communicate their intent; in fact, about 90% of them leave clues (Shneidman, 1994). They may communicate verbally: "You won't be seeing me again." "You won't have to worry about me any more." They may show behavioral clues, such as giving away their most valued possessions, withdrawing

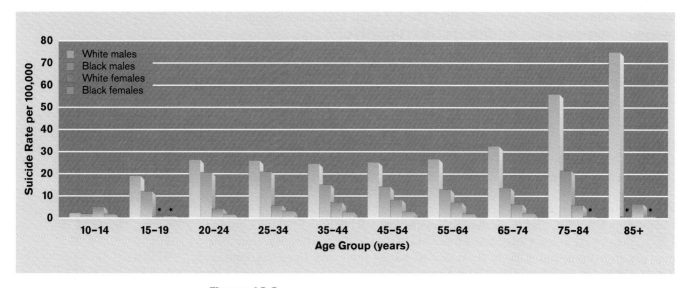

Figure 12.3

Differences in Suicide Rate According to Race, Gender, and Age

In every age group the suicide rate is highest for White males and second highest for Black males. The general conclusion is that males are more likely to commit suicide than females, and Whites are more likely than Blacks. Suicide rates indicated by asterisks (*) are too low to be statistically reliable. (Data from U.S. Bureau of the Census, 1994.)

from friends and family, taking unnecessary risks, or acting and looking depressed. These warning signs should always be taken seriously. Suicidal individuals need compassion, emotional support, and the opportunity to express the feelings and problems that are the source of their psychological pain.

Hopelessness is a common characteristic of suicidal individuals (Beck et al., 1993). Most people contemplating suicide are not totally committed to self-destruction. This may explain why many potential victims leave warnings or use less lethal means in attempting suicide.

But you should not try to be an amateur psychologist if you are dealing with a suicidal person. Probably the best service you can render is to encourage the person to get professional help. There are 24-hour suicide hotlines all over the country. A call might save a life.

ANXIETY DISORDERS: WHEN ANXIETY IS EXTREME

When is anxiety normal, and when is it abnormal?

The most commonly occurring psychological disorders (other than substance abuse disorders) are the **anxiety disorders**. **Anxiety** is a vague, general uneasiness or an ominous feeling that something bad is about to happen. It may be associated with a particular situation or object or may be free-floating—not associated with anything specific. None of us is a stranger to anxiety. We have all felt it.

Some anxiety is normal and appropriate. Imagine driving on a highway late at night and noticing that your gas gauge is on empty. The anxiety you would feel in this situation is normal anxiety—a response to a real threat. Normal anxiety would prompt you to take useful action—to look for a gas station. But anxiety serves no useful purpose and is abnormal if it is all out of proportion to the seriousness of the situation, if it does not soon fade once the danger is past, or if it occurs in the absence of real danger (Goodwin, 1986).

The neurotransmitter serotonin plays an important role in anxiety disorders (Greist, 1996), but it works in concert with other neurotransmitters, particularly norepinephrine and dopamine (Lucki, 1996). Unfortunately, half of psychiatric patients with anxiety disorders are not appropriately diagnosed (Zajecka, 1997).

Psychological disorders characterized by severe anxiety are generalized anxiety disorder, panic disorder, phobias, and obsessive compulsive disorder.

Generalized Anxiety Disorder

How many people do you know who are chronic worriers? **Generalized anxiety disorder** is the diagnosis given to those who experience *excessive* anxiety and worry, which they find difficult to control. They may be unduly worried about their finances, their own health or that of family members, their performance at work, or their ability to function socially. They may feel tense, tired, and irritable, and have difficulty concentrating and sleeping. Other symptoms may include trembling, palpitations, sweating, dizziness, nausea, diarrhea, or frequent urination. About 5.1% of the population will suffer from generalized anxiety disorder at some time in their lives—3.6% of men and 6.6% of women (Kessler et al., 1994). Kendler and others (1992) estimate the heritability of generalized anxiety disorder to be about 30%. Leading researchers consider it to be a common chronic disorder that affects twice as many women as men and one that leads to considerable distress and impairment (Brawman-Mintzer & Lydiard, 1996, 1997; Kranzler, 1996). But, as troubling as this disorder is, it is less severe than panic disorder.

Panic Disorder

> Mindy Markowitz is young, attractive, and successful. An art director for a trade magazine, she came seeking treatment for panic attacks she had suffered over the past year. Now occurring as often as two or three times a day, the panic attacks would appear, seemingly out of nowhere, as a sudden, intense wave of terrible fear, sometimes during the day and sometimes at night, waking her from sleep. During the attacks Mindy would begin to tremble, feel nauseated, and sweat profusely. She "feels as though she is gagging," she said, but even worse is the horrible fear that "she will lose control and do something crazy, like run screaming into the street." (Spitzer et al., 1989, p. 154)

During **panic attacks**—attacks of overwhelming anxiety, fear, or terror—people commonly report a pounding heart, trembling or shaking, and sensations of choking or smothering. Some say they are afraid they are going to die or are "going crazy."

Mindy Markowitz was diagnosed with **panic disorder**—a disorder characterized by recurrent, unpredictable panic attacks that cause apprehension about the occurrence and consequences of further attacks. This apprehension can lead people to avoid situations that have been associated with previous panic attacks. About 2% of men and 5% of women in the United States suffer from panic disorder (Kessler et al., 1994). For most patients, panic disorder is "a chronic condition characterized by intermittent remissions and relapses over many years" (Rosenbaum et al., 1996, p. 44).

The biological perspective sheds some light on panic disorder. PET scans reveal that even in a nonpanic state, many panic-disorder patients show a greatly increased blood flow to parts of the right hemisphere of the limbic system—the part of the brain involved in emotion (Reiman et al., 1989). And family and twin studies suggest that genetic factors play a role in panic disorder (Goldstein et al., 1994).

High life stress, particularly significant losses or threatening events, may be the precipitating factor in the first panic attack (Faravelli & Pallanti, 1989). And once people have had an attack, they may develop extreme anxiety about the possibility that it will happen again (Gorman et al., 1989). A cognitive theory suggests that panic attacks are associated with excessive vigilance toward and catastrophic misinterpretation of internal bodily sensations (Clark et al., 1997; Schmidt et al., 1997). Roth and

anxiety disorders: Psychological disorders characterized by severe anxiety (e.g., panic disorder, phobias, general anxiety disorder, obsessive compulsive disorder).

anxiety: A general uneasiness or ominous feeling that may be associated with a particular object or situation or may be free-floating (not associated with anything specific).

generalized anxiety disorder: An anxiety disorder in which people experience excessive anxiety or worry that they find difficult to control.

panic attack: An attack of overwhelming anxiety, fear, or terror.

panic disorder: An anxiety disorder in which a person experiences recurrent unpredictable attacks of overwhelming anxiety, fear, or terror.

What are the symptoms of panic disorder?

others (1992) maintain that when panic-disorder patients know a stressor is coming, their anticipatory anxiety itself may set the stage for a panic attack.

Panic disorder can have significant social and health consequences (Sherbourne et al., 1996). Panic-disorder patients tend to overuse the health-care system (Katon, 1996) and are at increased risk for abuse of alcohol and other drugs (Marshall, 1997).

Phobias: Persistent, Irrational Fears

What are the characteristics of the three categories of phobias?

A person suffering from a **phobia** experiences a persistent, irrational fear of some specific object, situation, or activity that poses no real danger (or whose danger is blown all out of proportion). Phobics realize their fears are irrational, but they nevertheless feel compelled to avoid the feared objects or situations. There are three classes of phobias—agoraphobia, social phobia, and specific phobia.

Agoraphobia   The phobia most likely to drive people to seek professional help is **agoraphobia**. Agoraphobics have an intense fear of being in a situation from which immediate escape is not possible or in which help would not be available if the person should become overwhelmed by anxiety or experience a panic attack or panic-like symptoms. In some cases a person's entire life must be planned around avoiding feared situations such as busy streets, crowded stores, restaurants, and/or public transportation. An agoraphobic often will not leave home unless accompanied by a friend or family member and, in severe cases, not even then. Women are four times more likely than men to be diagnosed with agoraphobia (Bekker, 1996).

Although agoraphobia can occur without panic attacks, it typically begins during the early adult years with repeated panic attacks (Horwath et al., 1993). Some researchers believe that agoraphobia is actually an extreme form of panic disorder (Sheehan, 1983). *Panic disorder with agoraphobia (PDA)* is one of the most debilitating of psychological disorders and is more common in women than in men (Yonkers et al., 1998). It can affect most areas of life—physical, psychological, social, occupational, interpersonal, and economic (Michelson et al., 1996).

People are at greater risk of developing agoraphobia when other family members have it—the closer the relative, the higher the risk (Rosenbaum et al., 1994). Some agoraphobics have been treated successfully with psychotherapy (Shear & Weiner, 1997); others have responded well to antidepressants (Marshall, 1997c).

People with agoraphobia have an intense fear of public places and are often reluctant to leave home.

Social Phobia   Those who suffer from **social phobia** are intensely afraid of any social or performance situation in which they might embarrass or humiliate themselves in front of others—where they might shake, blush, sweat, or in some other way appear clumsy, foolish, or incompetent. About one-third of social phobics fear only speaking publicly (Kessler et al., 1998). The rest may fear speaking, performing, or writing in public, eating with others, or using public restrooms (Greist, 1995). Can you imagine being unable to cash a check or even take notes or a written exam in class because you feared writing in front of others?

Social phobia typically develops by adolescence (Hirschfeld, 1995; Jefferson, 1996) and may have its origins in childhood shyness and a traumatic event such as a very embarrassing social evaluation (Stemberger et al., 1995). It affects 11.1% of males and 15.5% of females at some time during their lives (Kessler et al., 1994), and genetic factors appear to play a role (Fyer, 1993).

Social phobia may take the form of specific performance anxiety, commonly experienced by musicians (Jefferson, 1996), as well as many successful politicians, actors, comedians, and singers. Barbra Streisand's extreme performance anxiety kept her from appearing live in concert for many years. Even many people who have not been diagnosed as social phobics fear speaking in public. In fact, one-third of 449 survey respondents said they would experience excessive anxiety if they had to speak in front of a large audience (Stein et al., 1996).

Social phobia in its extreme form can seriously affect people's performance at work, prevent them from advancing in their careers or pursuing an education, and

phobia (FO-bee-ah): A persistent, irrational fear of an object, situation, or activity that the person feels compelled to avoid.

agoraphobia (AG-or-uh-FO-bee-uh): An intense fear of being in a situation from which immediate escape is not possible or in which help is not immediately available in case of incapacitating anxiety.

social phobia: An irrational fear and avoidance of social situations in which one might embarrass or humiliate oneself by appearing clumsy, foolish, or incompetent.

severely restrict their social lives (Greist, 1995). And often those with social phobia turn to alcohol and tranquilizers to lessen their anxiety in social situations. Mickey Mantle, for example, used alcohol to calm himself when making public appearances.

Specific Phobia   Specific phobia—a marked fear of a specific object or situation—is a catchall category for any phobias other than agoraphobia and social phobia. This type usually begins in childhood. The categories of specific phobias, in order of frequency of occurrence, are (1) situational phobias (fear of elevators, airplanes, enclosed places, public transportation, tunnels, or bridges); (2) fear of the natural environment (storms, water, or heights); (3) animal phobias (fear of dogs, snakes, insects, or mice); and (4) blood–injection–injury phobia (fear of seeing blood or an injury, or of receiving an injection) (Fredrikson et al., 1996). Two types of situational phobias— claustrophobia (fear of closed spaces) and acrophobia (fear of heights)—are the specific phobias treated most often by therapists.

People with specific phobias usually fear the same things others fear, but their fears are greatly exaggerated. To be considered a phobia, a fear must cause great distress or interfere with a person's life in a major way.

Phobics experience intense anxiety, even to the point of shaking or screaming and will go to great lengths to avoid the feared object or situation. Some people with blood–injection–injury phobia will even risk their lives, rather than seek medical care (Marks, 1988). And those with a severe dental phobia will actually let their teeth rot rather than visit the dentist.

Causes of Phobias   Most specific and social phobias probably are learned through direct conditioning, modeling, or the transmission of information (Rachman, 1977). Virtually all dog phobias can be attributed to one or the other of these learning pathways (King et al., 1997). Frightening experiences set the stage for phobias, although not all phobics recall the experience producing the phobia. A person with a dental phobia may be able to trace its beginning to a previous traumatic experience during a visit to the dentist (de Jongh et al., 1995). Or a person humiliated by performing poorly in front of others may develop a social phobia (Rosenbaum et al., 1994).

Phobias may be acquired, as well, through observational learning. For example, children who hear their parents talk about frightening experiences with the dentist or with bugs or snakes or thunderstorms may develop similar fears themselves. In many cases phobias are acquired through a combination of conditioning and observational learning (Merckelbach et al., 1996; Milgrom et al., 1995).

Genes appear to play a role in all classes of phobias. A person has three times the risk of developing a phobia if a close relative suffers from one (Fyer et al., 1993).

From the psychodynamic perspective, people develop phobias primarily as a defense against the anxiety they feel when sexual or aggressive impulses threaten to break into consciousness. For example, a single person who has strong repressed sexual urges may develop a fear of going out at night as an unconscious defense against acting on these urges.

Obsessive Compulsive Disorder

What is wrong with people who are endlessly counting, checking, or performing other time-consuming rituals over and over? The answer is **obsessive compulsive disorder (OCD)**, another form of anxiety disorder in which people suffer from recurrent obsessions or compulsions, or both.

Obsessions   If you have ever had a tune or the words of a song run through your mind over and over without being able to stop it, you have experienced obsessive thinking in a mild form. But imagine how miserable you would be if every time you touched something you thought you were being contaminated. **Obsessions** are persistent, recurring, involuntary thoughts, images, or impulses that invade consciousness and cause a person great distress.

specific phobia: A marked fear of a specific object or situation; a catchall category for any phobia other than agoraphobia and social phobia.

obsessive compulsive disorder (OCD): An anxiety disorder in which a person suffers from obsessions and/or compulsions.

obsession: A persistent, recurring, involuntary thought, image, or impulse that invades consciousness and causes great distress.

What do psychologists see as probable causes of phobias?

What is obsessive compulsive disorder?

Table 12.1 *DSM-IV* Categories of Sexual Disorders

Type of Disorder	Symptoms
Sexual dysfunctions	Disorders involving low sexual desire; the inability to attain or maintain sexual arousal; a delay or absence of orgasm; premature ejaculation; or genital pain associated with sexual activity
Paraphilias	Disorders in which recurrent sexual urges, fantasies, and behavior involve objects, children, other nonconsenting persons, or the suffering or humiliation of the individual or his/her partner
Fetishism	A disorder in which sexual urges, fantasies, and behavior involve an inanimate object, such as women's undergarments or shoes
Pedophilia	A disorder in which sexual urges, fantasies, and behavior involve sexual activity with a prepubescent child or children
Exhibitionism	A disorder in which sexual urges, fantasies, and behavior involve exposing one's genitals to an unsuspecting stranger
Voyeurism	A disorder in which sexual urges, fantasies, and behavior involve watching unsuspecting people naked, undressing, or engaging in sexual activity
Sexual masochism	A disorder in which sexual urges, fantasies, and behavior involve being beaten, humiliated, bound, or otherwise made to suffer
Sexual sadism	A disorder in which sexual urges, fantasies, and behavior involve inflicting physical or psychological pain and suffering on another
Other paraphilias	Disorders in which sexual urges, fantasies, and behavior involve, among other things, animals, feces, urine, corpses, filth, or enemas
Sexual identity disorders	Problems accepting one's identity as male or female

Source: Based on the *DSM-IV* (American Psychiatric Association, 1994).

---

sexual dysfunction: A persistent or recurrent problem that causes marked distress and interpersonal difficulty and that may involve any or some combination of the following: sexual desire, sexual arousal, or the pleasure associated with sex or orgasm.

paraphilia: A sexual disorder in which sexual urges, fantasies, and behavior generally involve children, other nonconsenting partners, objects, or the suffering and humiliation of oneself or one's partner.

gender identity disorders: Disorders characterized by a problem accepting one's identity as male or female.

What characteristics are shared by most people with personality disorders?

tions and paraphilias. **Sexual dysfunctions** are persistent, recurrent, and distressing problems involving sexual desire, sexual arousal, or the pleasure associated with sex or orgasm. **Paraphilias** are disorders in which a person experiences recurrent sexual urges, fantasies, or behaviors involving children, other nonconsenting partners, objects, or the suffering or humiliation of the individual or a partner. To be diagnosed as having a paraphilia, the person must experience considerable psychological distress or an impairment in functioning in an important area of his or her life. **Gender identity disorders** involve a problem accepting one's identity as male or female; children either express a desire to be or insist that they are the other gender. They show a preference for the clothes, games, pastimes, and playmates of the opposite sex.

Table 12.1 shows a number of the sexual disorders listed in the *DSM-IV*. Please note that homosexuality is *not* considered a sexual disorder.

Personality Disorders: Troublesome Behavior Patterns

Do you know people who are impossible to get along with—people who always seem to be at odds with themselves, their environment, their family, and others? Such a person may have a **personality disorder**—a long-standing, inflexible, maladaptive pattern of behaving and relating to others, which usually begins early in childhood or adolescence (Widiger et al., 1988). People with personality disorders tend to have problems in their social relationships and at work, and may experience personal dis-

Table 12.2 Examples of *DSM-IV* Categories of Personality Disorders

Type of Disorder	Symptoms
Antisocial personality	Person shows callous disregard for the rights and feelings of others; is manipulative, impulsive, selfish, aggressive, irresponsible, reckless; is willing to break the law, lie, cheat, or exploit others for personal gain, without remorse; fails to hold job.
Paranoid	Person is highly suspicious, untrusting, guarded, hypersensitive, easily slighted, lacking in emotion; holds grudges.
Histrionic	Individual seeks attention and approval; is overly dramatic, self-centered, shallow; is demanding, manipulative, easily bored, suggestible; craves excitement; often, is attractive and sexually seductive.
Narcissistic	Person has exaggerated sense of self-importance and entitlement and is self-centered, arrogant, demanding, exploitive, envious; craves admiration and attention; lacks empathy.
Borderline	Individual is unstable in mood, behavior, self-image, and social relationships; has intense fear of abandonment; exhibits impulsive and reckless behavior, inappropriate anger; makes suicidal gestures and performs self-mutilating acts.

Source: Based on the *DSM-IV* (American Psychiatric Association, 1994).

tress as well. Some of these people know that their behavior causes problems in their lives, yet they seem unable to change. But more commonly, they are self-centered and do not see themselves as responsible for their difficulties. Instead, they tend to blame other people or situations for their problems.

The *DSM-IV* lists ten categories of personality disorders; five are explained briefly in Table 12.2. Of particular interest is antisocial personality disorder.

People with **antisocial personality disorder** have a "pervasive pattern of disregard for, and violation of, the rights of others that begins in childhood or early adolescence and continues into adulthood" (American Psychiatric Association, 1994, p. 645). As children they lie, steal, vandalize, initiate fights, skip school, run away from home, and may be physically cruel to others. By early adolescence they usually drink excessively, use drugs, and engage in promiscuous sex. And in adulthood they cannot keep a job, act as a responsible parent, honor financial commitments, or obey the law.

Many antisocial types are intelligent and may seem charming and very likable at first. They are good con men, and they are more often men—as many as 5.8% of the U.S. male population, compared to less than 1.3% of the female population (Kessler et al., 1994). Checkley (1941), one of the first to study antisocial personality, revealed that persons with the disorder seem to lack the ability to love or feel loyalty and compassion toward others. They do not appear to have a conscience and feel little or no guilt or remorse no matter how cruel or despicable their actions might be. As Hare (1995) puts it, they "use charm, manipulation, intimidation, and violence to control others and satisfy their own selfish needs" (p. 4). Ted Bundy, the infamous serial killer executed in 1990, was thought to have antisocial personality disorder.

Although the *DSM-IV* does not include this characteristic, some experts believe that antisocial types fail to experience anxiety as normal people do. They seem fearless, oblivious to danger to themselves and unconcerned about the possible, even likely, consequences of their actions; and they appear to be unable to profit from experience (Chesno & Kilmann, 1975; Hare, 1970, 1995). Several adoption studies indicate a genetic factor in antisocial personality disorder (Loehlin et al., 1988). Other studies of adoptees have provided strong evidence of an interaction between heredity and environment accounting for this disorder (Rutter, 1997).

personality disorder: A continuing, inflexible, maladaptive pattern of inner experience and behavior that causes great distress or impaired functioning and differs significantly from the patterns expected in the person's culture.

antisocial personality disorder: A disorder marked by lack of feeling for others; selfish, aggressive, irresponsible behavior; and willingness to break the law, lie, cheat, or exploit others for personal gain.

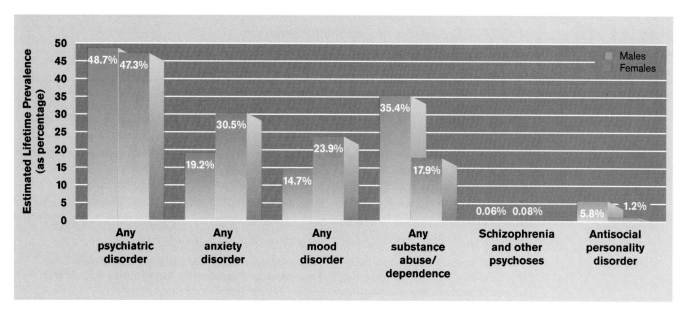

Figure 12.4

Lifetime Prevalence of Psychological Disorders

The percentages of males and females in the United States who suffer from various psychological disorders during their lifetime are based on the findings of the National Comorbidity Survey. Almost 50% of the respondents interviewed in this large national survey suffered from at least one psychological disorder in their lifetime. Males and females had about the same rate for experiencing some type of disorder. Males had higher rates for substance abuse and dependence and antisocial personality disorder. Females had higher rates for anxiety disorders and mood disorders. (Data from Kessler et al., 1994.)

Years ago people with antisocial personality disorder were referred to as *psychopaths* or *sociopaths*. Con men, quack doctors, impostors, and today many drug pushers, pimps, delinquents, and criminals could be diagnosed as having this disorder. Some come to the attention of the authorities and end up serving time (about 15–20% of U.S. prisoners); others do not (Hare, 1995).

Figure 12.4 shows the estimated lifetime prevalence in the United States of antisocial personality disorder and other disorders we have discussed.

By now, you should know a great deal about psychological disorders. Apply your knowledge in the *Try It!*

Try It!

Make a list of movies, TV shows, or plays you have seen or heard about in which a character with a psychological disorder plays a prominent role. One example is given to get you started.

As Good As It Gets	Jack Nicholson	Obsessive compulsive disorder
_____	_____	_____
_____	_____	_____
_____	_____	_____

Depression—Bad Thoughts, Bad Feelings

Did you know that you can cause your own moods? Consider these thoughts: "I'll never pass this course." "He/she would never go out with me." "I'm a failure." Where mental health is concerned, to a large extent, "You are what you think." Depression and other forms of mental misery can be fueled by negative or irrational thoughts.

Depression is so widespread that it is often called the "common cold" of psychological problems. Everyone feels "down" or "blue" once in a while, but depression goes beyond such feelings. According to the American Psychiatric Association (1994), the most frequent symptoms of depression are:

- Feeling depressed, sad, hopeless, empty, or tearful most of the time

- Losing interest in and pleasure from most activities

- Feeling tired or without energy for no reason most of the time

- Feeling worthless or inappropriately guilty most of the time

- Experiencing difficulty concentrating and making decisions

- Experiencing a change in appetite—either eating more or less than usual

- Having difficulty sleeping or sleeping much more than usual

The cognitive approach to depression. Many psychologists and psychiatrists take a cognitive approach to depression and believe that, in many cases, negative and irrational thoughts are directly responsible for a person's depressed mood. David Burns (1980) even says:

> *All* your moods are created by your "cognitions," or thoughts. . . . You *feel* the way you do right now because of the *thoughts you are thinking at this moment.* . . . The moment you have a certain thought and believe it, you will experience an immediate emotional response. Your thought actually *creates* the emotion. (pp. 11–12)

One step toward healthy thinking is to recognize and avoid five cognitive traps.

- *Cognitive Trap 1: The "Tyranny of the Should."* One sure path to unhappiness is to set unrealistic, unachievable standards for yourself. Karen Horney (1950) called this cognitive trap the "tyranny of the should." Unrealistic and unachievable standards are characterized by such words as *always, never, all, everybody,* and *everything.* Have you ever been tyrannized by any of these "shoulds"?

  > I "should always be the perfect friend, lover, spouse, parent, student, teacher, [or] employee."

  > I "should never feel hurt" and "should always be calm."

  > I "should be able to solve all of my problems and the problems of others in no time."

  > (Adapted from Horney, 1950, pp. 64–66.)

- *Cognitive Trap 2: Negative, "What If" Thinking.* Much unhappiness stems from a preoccupation with what might be. These are examples of "what if" thinking: "What if she/he turns me down for a date?" "What if I lose my job?" "What if I flunk this test?" "What if I can't pay my bills?" And if a "what if" comes to pass, the third cognitive trap may be sprung.

- *Cognitive Trap 3: Making Mountains Out of Molehills.* A molehill becomes a mountain when a single negative event is perceived as catastrophic or allowed to become a definition of total worth. "I failed this test" might become "I'll never pass this course," "I'm a failure," or "I'm too dumb to be in college."

- *Cognitive Trap 4: The Perfection–Failure Dichotomy.* Only on very rare occasions can anyone's performance be considered absolutely perfect or a total failure. In reality, outcomes will fall somewhere on a continuum between these two extremes. But people who fall into this cognitive trap judge anything short of perfection as total failure.

- *Cognitive Trap 5: Setting Impossible Conditions for Happiness.* Don't let your happiness hinge on perfection in yourself or in others. Not everyone will love you or even like you, approve of you, or agree with you. If any of these are conditions on which your happiness depends, you are setting the stage for disappointment or even depression.

How to develop healthier thinking habits. Albert Ellis developed rational-emotive therapy to help people change irrational thinking. (You will read more about Ellis's approach in Chapter 13.) Here are a few suggestions that may help you:

> Instead of thinking "It would be *the end of everything* if I lost my job!" think "I would not want to lose my job, but I could find another."

> Instead of thinking "I am a *failure* because this turned out so badly" substitute "I am embarrassed about how this turned out, but I'll do better the next time."

The next time you notice yourself entertaining negative thoughts or self-doubts, write them down and analyze them objectively and unemotionally. But don't go to the opposite extreme and substitute equally distorted positive thinking or mindless "happy talk." Self-delusion in either direction is not healthy.

Your goal should be to monitor your thinking and systematically make it less distorted, more rational, more accurate, and more logical. We must live in the "real" world, and in order to enjoy happiness and mental health, we must think realistically. When our expectations, goals, and desires are unrealistic and unachievable, we are setting ourselves up for unhappiness, disappointment, and misery.

Depression is a complex psychological disorder with both physiological and psychological causes. All depression cannot be controlled simply by a change in thinking. If symptoms such as those listed at the beginning of this section persist, seek professional treatment.

SUMMARY AND REVIEW

WHAT IS ABNORMAL?

What criteria might be used to differentiate normal from abnormal behavior?

Behavior might be considered abnormal if it deviates radically from what is considered normal in one's own culture, if it leads to personal distress or impaired functioning, or if it results in one's being a danger to self and/or others.

What are five current perspectives that attempt to explain the causes of psychological disorders?

Five current perspectives on the causes of psychological disorders are (1) the biological perspective, which views abnormal behavior as a symptom of an underlying physical disorder; (2) the psychodynamic perspective, which maintains that psychological disorders are caused by unconscious and unresolved conflicts; (3) the learning perspective, which claims that psychological disorders are learned and sustained in the same way as other behavior; (4) the cognitive perspective, which suggests that psychological disorders result from faulty thinking; and (5) the humanistic perspective, which views psychological disorders as a result of the blocking of one's natural tendency toward self-actualization.

What is the *DSM-IV*?

The *DSM-IV*, published by the American Psychiatric Association, is the system most widely used in the United States to diagnose psychological disorders.

Key Terms
DSM-IV (p. 393); neurosis (p. 393); psychosis (p. 394)

SCHIZOPHRENIA

What are some of the major positive and negative symptoms of schizophrenia?

The positive symptoms of schizophrenia are abnormal behaviors and characteristics—including hallucinations, delusions, disorganized thinking and speech, bizarre behavior, and inappro-

priate affect. The negative symptoms represent deficiencies in thoughts and behavior; these include social withdrawal, apathy, loss of motivation, very limited speech, slowed movements, flat affect, and poor hygiene and grooming.

What are the four types of schizophrenia?

The four types of schizophrenia are paranoid, disorganized, catatonic, and undifferentiated schizophrenia.

What are some suggested causes of schizophrenia?

Some suggested causes of schizophrenia are a genetic predisposition, sufficient stress in people who are predisposed to the disorder, and excessive dopamine activity in the brain.

Key Terms
schizophrenia (p. 396); hallucination (p. 396); delusion (p. 396); delusion of grandeur (p. 396); delusion of persecution (p. 396); inappropriate affect (p. 397); paranoid schizophrenia (p. 398); disorganized schizophrenia (p. 398); catatonic schizophrenia (p. 398); diathesis–stress model (p. 398)

MOOD DISORDERS

What are the symptoms of major depressive disorder?

Major depressive disorder is characterized by feelings of great sadness, despair, guilt, worthlessness, hopelessness, and, in extreme cases, suicidal intentions.

What are the extremes of mood suffered by those with bipolar disorder?

Bipolar disorder is a mood disorder in which a person suffers from manic episodes (periods of extreme elation, euphoria, and hyperactivity) alternating with major depression, usually with relatively normal periods in between.

What are some suggested causes of major depressive disorder and bipolar disorder?

Some of the proposed causes are (1) a genetic predisposition; (2) an imbalance in the neurotransmitters norepi-

nephrine and serotonin; (3) a tendency to turn hostility and resentment inward rather than expressing it; (4) distorted and negative views of oneself, the world, and the future; and (5) stress.

Key Terms
mood disorders (p. 399); major depressive disorder (p. 399); seasonal affective disorder (SAD) (p. 400); bipolar disorder (p. 400); manic episode (p. 400); first-degree relatives (p. 401)

ANXIETY DISORDERS: WHEN ANXIETY IS EXTREME

When is anxiety normal, and when is it abnormal?

Anxiety—a generalized feeling of apprehension, fear, or tension—is healthy if it is a response to a real danger or threat, and it is unhealthy if it is inappropriate or excessive.

What are the symptoms of panic disorder?

Panic disorder is marked by recurrent, unpredictable panic attacks—attacks of overwhelming anxiety, fear, or terror, during which people experience palpitations, trembling or shaking, choking or smothering sensations, and the feeling that they are going to die or lose their sanity.

What are the characteristics of the three categories of phobias?

The three categories of phobias are (1) agoraphobia, fear of being in situations where escape is impossible or help is not available in case of incapacitating anxiety; (2) social phobia, fear of social situations where one might be embarrassed or humiliated by appearing clumsy or incompetent; and (3) specific phobia, a marked fear of a specific object or situation and a catchall category for all phobias other than agoraphobia or social phobia.

What do psychologists see as probable causes of phobias?

Phobias result primarily from frightening experiences or through observational learning. Genes may also play a role.

What is obsessive compulsive disorder?

Obsessive compulsive disorder is characterized by obsessions (persistent, recurring, involuntary thoughts, images, or impulses that cause great distress) and/or compulsions (persistent, irresistible, irrational urges to perform an act or ritual repeatedly).

Key Terms
anxiety disorders (p. 404); anxiety (p. 404); generalized anxiety disorder (p. 405); panic attack (p. 405); panic disorder (p. 405); phobia (p. 406); agoraphobia (p. 406); social phobia (p. 406); specific phobia (p. 407); obsessive compulsive disorder (OCD) (p. 407); obsession (p. 407); compulsion (p. 408)

SOMATOFORM AND DISSOCIATIVE DISORDERS

What are two somatoform disorders, and what symptoms do they share?

Somatoform disorders involve bodily symptoms that cannot be identified as any of the known medical conditions. Hypochondriasis involves a persistent fear that bodily symptoms are the sign of some serious disease, and conversion disorder involves a loss of motor or sensory functioning in some part of the body, such as paralysis or blindness.

What are dissociative amnesia and dissociative fugue?

People with dissociative amnesia have a loss of memory for limited periods of their life or for their entire personal identity. In dissociative fugue people forget their entire identity, travel away from home, and may assume a new identity somewhere else.

What are some of the identifying symptoms of dissociative identity disorder?

Dissociative identity disorder (often called multiple personality) is one in which there are two or more distinct, unique personalities in the same person, each taking over at different times. Most patients are female and victims of early, severe physical and/or sexual abuse.

Key Terms
somatoform disorders (p. 409); hypochondriasis (p. 409); conversion disorder (p. 409); dissociative disorder (p. 410); dissociative amnesia (p. 410); dissociative fugue (p. 410); dissociative identity disorder (p. 410)

OTHER PSYCHOLOGICAL DISORDERS

What are the sexual and gender identity disorders?

There are three categories of sexual disorders: sexual dysfunctions (problems with sexual desire, sexual arousal, or orgasm); paraphilias (needing unusual or bizarre objects, conditions, or acts for sexual gratification); and gender identity disorders (having a problem accepting one's identity as male or female).

What characteristics are shared by most people with personality disorders?

People who have personality disorders have longstanding, inflexible, maladaptive patterns of behavior that cause problems in their social relationships and at work and often cause personal distress. Such people seem unable to change and blame others for their problems.

Key Terms
sexual dysfunction (p. 412); paraphilia (p. 412); gender identity disorders (p. 412); personality disorder (p. 412); antisocial personality disorder (p. 413)

Study Guide for Chapter 12

Answers to all the Study Guide questions are provided at the end of the book.

Section One: Chapter Review

1. It is relatively easy to differentiate normal behavior from abnormal behavior. (true/false)

2. The *DSM-IV* is a manual that is published by the American Psychiatric Association and is used to
   a. diagnose psychological disorders.
   b. explain the causes of psychological disorders.
   c. outline the treatments for various psychological disorders.
   d. assess the effectiveness of treatment programs.

3. Match the perspective with its suggested cause of abnormal behavior.
   ____ (1) faulty learning
   ____ (2) unconscious, unresolved conflicts
   ____ (3) blocking of the natural tendency toward self-actualization
   ____ (4) genetic inheritance or biochemical or structural abnormalities in the brain
   ____ (5) faulty thinking
   a. psychodynamic
   b. biological
   c. learning
   d. humanistic
   e. cognitive

4. Match the symptom of schizophrenia with the example.
   ____ (1) Joe believes he is Moses.
   ____ (2) Elena thinks her family is spreading rumors about her.
   ____ (3) Peter hears voices cursing him.
   ____ (4) Marco laughs at tragedies and cries when he hears a joke.
   a. delusions of grandeur
   b. hallucinations
   c. inappropriate affect
   d. delusions of persecution

5. There is substantial research evidence that all of the following have roles as causes of schizophrenia *except*
   a. genetic factors.
   b. stress in people predisposed to the disorder.
   c. excessive dopamine activity.
   d. unhealthy family interaction patterns.

6. Match the subtype of schizophrenia with the example.
   ____ (1) Louise stands for hours in the same strange position.
   ____ (2) Ron believes the CIA is plotting to kill him.
   ____ (3) Harry makes silly faces, laughs a lot, and masturbates openly.
   ____ (4) Sue has the symptoms of schizophrenia but does not fit any one type.
   a. paranoid schizophrenia
   b. disorganized schizophrenia
   c. catatonic schizophrenia
   d. undifferentiated schizophrenia

7. Monteil has periods in which he is so depressed that he becomes suicidal. At other times he is energetic and euphoric. He would probably receive the diagnosis of
   a. dysthymia.
   b. seasonal mood disorder.
   c. bipolar disorder.
   d. major depressive disorder.

8. Match the theory of depression with the proposed cause:
   ____ (1) negative thoughts about oneself, the world and one's future
   ____ (2) hereditary predisposition or biochemical imbalance
   ____ (3) turning resentment and hostility inward
   a. psychodynamic perspective
   b. cognitive perspective
   c. biological perspective

9. Stress appears to be unrelated to depression. (true/false)

10. The suicide rate is lower for
    a. males than for females.
    b. African Americans than for White Americans.
    c. the elderly than for teenagers.
    d. people who suffer psychological disorders than for those who do not.

11. Match the psychological disorder with the example.

_____ (1) René refuses to eat in front of others for fear her hand will shake.

_____ (2) John is excessively anxious about his health and his job, even though there is no concrete reason to be.

_____ (3) Betty has been housebound for 4 years.

_____ (4) Jackson gets hysterical when a dog approaches him.

_____ (5) Laura has incapacitating attacks of anxiety that come on her suddenly.

_____ (6) Max repeatedly checks his doors, windows, and appliances before he goes to bed.

a. panic disorder
b. agoraphobia
c. specific phobia
d. generalized anxiety disorder
e. social phobia
f. obsessive compulsive disorder

12. Anxiety serves no useful function. (true/false)

13. Most phobias result from frightening experiences and observational learning. (true/false)

14. Obsessive compulsive disorder appears to be caused primarily by psychological rather than biological factors. (true/false)

15. Match the psychological disorder with the example.

_____ (1) Mark is convinced he has some serious disease, although his doctors can find nothing physically wrong.

_____ (2) David is found far away from his home town, calling himself by another name and having no memory of his past.

_____ (3) Theresa suddenly loses her sight, but doctors can find no physical reason for the problem.

_____ (4) Larry has no memory of being in the boat with other family members the day his older brother drowned.

_____ (5) Nadine has no memory for blocks of time in her life and often finds clothing in her closet that she cannot remember buying.

a. dissociative identity disorder
b. dissociative fugue
c. dissociative amnesia
d. hypochondriasis
e. conversion disorder

16. Somatoform disorders have physiological rather than psychological causes. (true/false)

17. Dissociative disorders are psychological in origin. (true/false)

18. (Sexual dysfunctions, Paraphilias) are disorders in which sexual urges, fantasies, and behaviors involve children, other nonconsenting partners, or objects.

19. Which statement is true of personality disorders?
a. Personality disorders usually begin in adulthood.
b. Persons with these disorders usually realize that they have a problem.
c. Personality disorders typically cause problems in social relationships and at work.
d. Persons with these disorders typically seek professional help.

20. Tim lies, cheats, and exploits others without feeling guilty. His behavior best fits the diagnosis of _____ personality disorder.
a. avoidant
b. histrionic
c. antisocial
d. narcissistic

Section Two: Identify the Disorder

Name the disorder characterized by each set of symptoms.

Symptoms	Disorder
1. Markedly diminished interest or pleasure in all or most activities, combined with psychomotor disturbances, fatigue, insomnia, feelings of worthlessness, and recurrent thoughts of death	_____

Symptoms	Disorder
2. Grossly disorganized behavior combined with inappropriate affect, disturbed speech and loose associations, and delusions of grandeur—for example, a belief that one is working for a secret government agency and is being followed by foreign spies	_____
3. Intense mood swings, ranging from euphoric and hyperactive highs marked by delusions of grandeur to extreme depression	_____
4. Intense fear of being in a situation from which immediate escape is not possible or help is not available in the case of panic	_____
5. Complete loss of the ability to recall personal information or past experiences, with no physical explanation for the problem	_____
6. A pattern of unstable and intense interpersonal relationships combined with impulsivity, inappropriate and intense anger, a poor self-image, and recurrent thoughts of suicide	_____
7. Deriving sexual gratification from watching unsuspecting people undressing and engaging in sexual activity	_____
8. Spending excessive amounts of time engaged in daily rituals such as counting and cleaning, accompanied by obsessions	_____

Section Three: Fill In the Blank

1. The _____ perspective views abnormal behavior as a symptom of an underlying physical disorder.

2. The most serious psychological disorder is _____.

3. Hallucinations, delusions, and disorganized speech are considered to be _____ symptoms of schizophrenia.

4. Fred believes that there are three men who follow him around and whisper messages in his ear, telling him to do bad things. Fred's false belief is called a _____.

5. Symptoms such as social withdrawal, apathy, slowed movements, and limited speech are examples of the _____ symptoms of schizophrenia.

6. SAD refers to a kind of depression known as _____ _____ _____.

7. Frank called his best friend one night at 2 A.M., extremely excited about his great idea: He was going to have the Rolling Stones perform in his backyard for his birthday. He planned to call the Rolling Stones in London as soon as he got off the phone with his friend. Frank was probably having a _____ episode.

8. Hypochondriasis is an example of a _____ disorder.

9. Sarah experiences sudden and unexplained waves of fear that seem to come out of nowhere. She is suffering from _____ disorder.

10. An obsession is characterized by _____ _____; a compulsion involves an _____ _____ _____ _____ _____.

11. There seems to be no physical reason for Robert's paralysis. It is likely that he is suffering from a _____ disorder.

12. Dissociative identity disorder is the new term for what used to be called _____ _____ disorder.

13. Histrionic, borderline, antisocial, and narcissistic disorders are collectively known as _____ disorders.

14. Cherie has never felt comfortable with her gender and believes she should have been a male. According to the *DSM-IV* she has _____ _____ disorder.

15. _____ are sensory perceptions in the absence of any external stimulation, for example, seeing things that are not really there.

16. A _____ is a persistent, irrational fear of an object, situation, or activity that a person feels compelled to avoid.

17. The _____ personality disorder is marked by a lack of feeling for others, selfishness, aggressive and irresponsible behavior, and a willingness to break the law or exploit others for personal gain.

Section Four: Comprehensive Practice Test

1. Which perspective sees abnormal behavior as a symptom of an underlying physical disorder?
   a. cognitive   c. biological
   b. psychoanalytic d. behavioral

2. Which perspective sees abnormal behavior as the result of faulty and negative thinking?
   a. psychoanalytic c. behavioral
   b. cognitive   d. biological

3. Which perspective sees abnormal behavior as the result of early childhood experiences and unconscious sexual and aggressive conflicts?
   a. cognitive   c. humanistic
   b. biological   d. psychoanalytic

4. Which perspective sees psychological disorders as resulting from a blocking of one's tendency toward self-actualization?
   a. humanistic   c. biological
   b. cognitive   d. behavioral

5. Psychosis is a serious disorder, but not as serious as neurosis. (true/false)

6. Panic disorder, phobia, and obsessive compulsive disorder are all examples of _____ disorders.
   a. neurotic   c. personality
   b. anxiety   d. somatoform

7. Dawn is convinced that she has a disease and goes from one doctor to another searching for a diagnosis; however, every doctor she consults says there is nothing physically wrong with her. Dawn is suffering from
   a. hypochondriasis.
   b. seasonal affective disorder.
   c. a conversion disorder.
   d. body dysmorphic disorder.

8. Dissociative amnesia, characterized by loss of memory of one's identity, is generally brought on by physical trauma. (true/false)

9. A common early experience of patients with dissociative identity disorder is
   a. drug use by their mother while pregnant.
   b. measles or mumps when young.
   c. parental divorce.
   d. early physical or sexual abuse.

10. Hallucinations, delusions, and disorganized thinking and speech are _____ symptoms of schizophrenia.
    a. negative   c. dissociative
    b. positive   d. psychotic

11. Jackson's belief that he is a secret agent for the devil is a good example of a delusion. (true/false)

12. A patient who sits completely still for hours as if he were in a stupor and sometimes experiences periods of great agitation and excitement is suffering from _____ schizophrenia.
    a. disorganized   c. paranoid
    b. undifferentiated d. catatonic

13. Major depression, SAD, bipolar disorder, and dysthymia are all examples of _____ disorders.
    a. personality   c. mood
    b. psychotic   d. emotional

14. Depression is diagnosed more often in women than in men. (true/false)

15. _____ is characterized by periods of inflated self-esteem, wild optimism, and hyperactivity known as manic episodes.
    a. Schizophrenia
    b. Major depression
    c. Borderline personality disorder
    d. Bipolar disorder

16. The risk of suicide is especially high in patients who suffer from
    a. catatonic schizophrenia.   c. depression.
    b. paraphilia.   d. simple phobia.

17. The psychoanalytic approach asserts that depression stems from faulty thinking and distorted perceptions. (true/false)

18. Depression seems to be the result of
    a. genetic and biological factors only.
    b. both biological and environmental factors.
    c. environmental factors only.
    d. poor parenting in early childhood.

19. Sexual masochism, sexual sadism, and exhibitionism are all examples of
    a. paraphilias.
    b. gender identity disorders.
    c. sexual dysfunctions.
    d. pedophilias.

Section Five: Critical Thinking

1. Some psychological disorders are more common in women (depression, agoraphobia, and simple phobia), and some are more common in men (antisocial personality disorder and substance abuse). Give some possible reasons for such gender differences in the prevalence of these disorders. Support your answer.

2. There is continuing controversy over whether specific psychological disorders are chiefly biological in origin (nature) or result primarily from learning and experience (nurture). Select any two disorders from this chapter, and prepare arguments for both the nature and nurture positions for both disorders.

3. Formulate a specific plan for your own life that will help you recognize and avoid the five cognitive traps that contribute to unhealthy thinking. You might enlist the help of a friend to monitor your negative statements.

13 *Therapies*

Bill, a 21-year-old college student, suffers from a debilitating phobia, an intense fear of any kind of sudden loud noise—fireworks, gunshots, cars backfiring, and especially the sound of popping balloons. His fear of the sound of balloons bursting has extended to balloons themselves, and he cannot bear to touch or even stand within several feet of a balloon.

One day two people lead Bill into a small room that is filled with 100 large balloons of every imaginable color. Already Bill is visibly shaking, and he huddles near the door. One person stands close to Bill, while the other person explains that he is going to begin popping the balloons. While some 50 balloons are popped with a pin, Bill shakes uncontrollably. Tears stream down his face, he turns pale, and his legs shake so hard that a chair has to be provided so he can sit down. The remaining balloons are popped, making even more frightening sounds as the person steps on them. This upsets Bill even more, but he must endure the popping of another 250 balloons before he is allowed to leave. And he must return for the next 2 days for still more balloon popping.

What is going on here? Torture? An initiation? A sadistic ritual? No—it is a therapy session. Bill is undergoing treatment for his phobia, and the therapists are using a rapid treatment technique known as *flooding*. Flooding is a form of behavior therapy in which the patient agrees to be instantly and totally immersed in the feared situation or surrounded by the feared object—in Bill's case, balloons.

Although Bill was doing well in college—he maintained a respectable B average—he hardly had a social life at all. Because of his phobia, Bill avoided all social situations where there was even the remotest possibility that balloons might be present—parties, dances, weddings, athletic events, concerts. But he did have a girlfriend, and it was she who referred him to the therapists who treated his phobia.

During the course of the 3 days, Bill became progressively less fearful in the presence of balloons and was even able to join in stepping on hundreds of balloons and popping them. In a 1-year follow-up, Bill reported that he experienced no distress in the presence of balloons and no longer avoided situations where he might encounter them. In fact, according to his girlfriend, balloons were on the table at one formal event they attended, yet it didn't bother Bill. Neither was he ill at ease when he sat relatively near a fireworks display on the Fourth of July. (Adapted from Houlihan et al., 1993.)

Surely Bill would agree that enduring 3 rather torturous days of flooding therapy was a small price to pay to be free of his debilitating phobia. And flooding is only one of the many effective therapies you will learn about in this chapter.

Psychotherapy uses psychological rather than biological means to treat emotional and behavioral disorders, and it usually involves a conversation between the patient (or client) and a therapist. But psychotherapy has grown and changed enormously since its beginnings in the days of Freud, more than 100 years ago. Now it seems that there is a therapy for every trouble, a technique for every taste—400 different psychotherapies (Kingsbury, 1996). Today, for the most part, instead of involving years of treatment, psychotherapy is usually relatively brief in this era of managed care. Furthermore, psychotherapy today is not completely dominated by men, as more women are becoming therapists.

In this chapter we will explore insight therapies, which use talk, thought, reasoning, understanding, and analysis to treat psychological problems. Next we will look at behavior therapies, which are based on principles of learning theory. Finally, we will examine biological therapies—drug therapy, electroconvulsive therapy, and psychosurgery.

psychotherapy: The treatment for psychological disorders that uses psychological rather than biological means and primarily involves conversations between patient and therapist.

insight therapy: Any type of psychotherapy based on the notion that psychological well-being depends on self-understanding.

INSIGHT THERAPIES

Some forms of psychotherapy are collectively referred to as **insight therapies** because their assumption is that psychological well-being depends on self-understanding—understanding of one's own thoughts, emotions, motives, behavior, and coping mechanisms. The major insight therapies are psychoanalysis, person-centered therapy, and Gestalt therapy.

Psychodynamic Therapies: Freud Revisited

Freud originally proposed the psychodynamic perspective on abnormal behavior, which maintains that the cause of psychological disorders lies in early childhood experiences and in unresolved, unconscious conflicts, usually of a sexual or aggressive nature. **Psychoanalysis**, the treatment approach developed by Freud, was the first formal psychotherapy, and it was the dominant influence in psychotherapy in the 1940s and 1950s. The goals of psychoanalysis are to uncover repressed memories and to bring to consciousness the buried, unresolved conflicts believed to lie at the root of a person's problem.

Psychoanalysis: From the Couch of Freud   Freudian psychoanalysis uses four basic techniques: free association, analysis of resistance, dream analysis, and analysis of transference.

Free Association   The central technique of psychoanalytic therapy is **free association**, in which the patient is asked to reveal whatever thoughts, feelings, or images come to mind no matter how trivial, embarrassing, or terrible they might appear. Freud believed that free association allows important unconscious material to surface, such as repressed memories, threatening impulses, and traumatic episodes of childhood. The analyst pieces together the free-flowing associations, explains their meaning, and helps patients gain insight into the thoughts and behavior that are troubling them.

Analysis of Resistance   How do you think you would react if an analyst told you to express *everything* that came into your mind? Would you try to avoid revealing certain painful or embarrassing thoughts? Freud's patients did, and he called this **resistance**.

If the patient hesitates, balks, or becomes visibly upset about any topic, the analyst assumes the topic is emotionally significant for him or her. Freud also pointed out other forms of resistance, such as "forgetting" appointments with the analyst or arriving late.

Dream Analysis   Freud believed that areas of emotional concern repressed in waking life are sometimes expressed in symbolic form in dreams. He called dreams "the royal road to the unconscious" because they often convey hidden meanings and identify important repressed thoughts, memories, and emotions.

Analysis of Transference   Freud claimed that at some point during psychoanalysis, the patient inevitably begins to react to the analyst with the same feelings and attitudes that were present in another significant relationship—usually with the mother or father. This reaction he called **transference**. Transference allows the patient to relive or reenact troubling experiences from the past with the analyst as parent substitute. Then the unresolved childhood conflicts can be replayed in the present, but this time with a parent figure who does not reject, provoke guilt, or punish as the actual parent did.

Psychodynamic Therapy Today: The New View   Traditional psychoanalysis can be a long and costly undertaking. Patients attend four or five therapy sessions per week for 2 to 4 years. But by the mid-1980s, only about 2% of people undergoing psychotherapy chose classical psychoanalysis (Goode, 1987). And today the number appears to be steadily declining (Grünbaum, 1994).

Many psychoanalysts practice brief psychodynamic therapy, which is also aimed at gaining insight into unconscious conflicts. The therapist and patient decide on the issues to explore at the outset rather than waiting for them to emerge in the course of treatment. The therapist assumes a more active role and places more emphasis on the present than in traditional psychoanalysis. Brief psychodynamic therapy may require only one or two visits per week for as few as 12 to 20 weeks (Altshuler, 1989). In

Link It!

What are the four basic techniques of psychoanalysis, and how are they used to help disturbed patients?

Freud had his patients lie on this couch in his office during psychoanalysis, because relaxation aids free association.

psychoanalysis (SY-ko-uh-NAL-uh-sis): The psychotherapy that uses free association, dream analysis, and analysis of resistance and transference to uncover repressed memories, impulses, and conflicts thought to cause psychological disorders.

free association: A psychoanalytic technique used to explore the unconscious by having patients reveal whatever thoughts or images come to mind.

resistance: In psychoanalytic therapy, the patient's attempts to avoid expressing or revealing painful or embarrassing thoughts or feelings.

transference: An intense emotional reaction during psychoanalysis, when the patient displays feelings and attitudes toward the analyst that were present in a significant relationship in the past.

person-centered therapy: A non-directive, humanistic therapy in which the therapist creates a warm, accepting climate, freeing clients to be themselves and releasing their natural tendency toward positive growth.

self-actualization: Developing to one's fullest potential.

nondirective therapy: An approach in which the therapist acts to facilitate growth, giving understanding and support rather than proposing solutions, answering questions, or actively directing the course of therapy.

What are the role and the goal of the therapist in person-centered therapy?

a meta-analysis of 11 well-controlled studies, Crits-Christoph (1992) found brief psychodynamic therapy to be as effective as other psychotherapies.

Criticisms of Psychoanalytic Therapy   Traditional psychoanalysis has been criticized for its emphasis on the unconscious and the past and its virtual neglect of the conscious and the present. Furthermore, the focus on unconscious motives as the major determinants of behavior minimizes patients' responsibility for their behavior and their choices. And from a practical standpoint, research does not suggest that the tremendous cost of psychoanalysis yields results superior to briefer, less costly therapy.

Humanistic Therapies

Based on a more optimistic and hopeful picture of human nature and human potential, humanistic therapies stand in stark contrast to psychoanalysis. Individuals are viewed as unique and basically self-determining, with the ability and freedom to lead rational lives and make rational choices. Humanistic therapists encourage personal growth and seek to teach clients how to fulfill their potential and to take responsibility for their behavior and for what they become in life. The focus is primarily on current relationships and experiences.

Person-Centered Therapy: The Patient Becomes the Person   Person-centered therapy, developed by Carl Rogers (1951) (and formerly called *client-centered therapy*), is based on the humanistic view of human nature. According to this view, people are innately good and if allowed to develop naturally, they will grow toward **self-actualization**—the realization of their fullest potential.

The humanistic perspective suggests that psychological disorders result when a person's natural tendency toward self-actualization is blocked. Rogers (1959) insisted that individuals themselves block their natural tendency toward growth and self-actualization when they act in ways inconsistent with their true selves in order to gain the positive regard of others.

In person-centered therapy the focus is on conscious thoughts and feelings. The therapist attempts to create a warm, accepting climate in which clients are free to be themselves so that their natural tendency toward growth can be released. Person-centered therapy is a **nondirective therapy**; that is, the direction of the therapy sessions is controlled by the client. The therapist acts as a facilitator of growth, giving understanding, support, and encouragement rather than proposing solutions, answering questions, or actively directing the course of therapy.

Carl Rogers (at upper right) facilitates discussion in a therapy group.

According to Rogers, there are only three conditions required of therapists. First, they must have unconditional positive regard for, or total acceptance of, the client, regardless of the client's feelings, thoughts, or behavior. In this atmosphere of unconditional positive regard, clients will feel free to reveal their weakest points, to relax their defenses, and to begin to accept and value themselves. Second, therapists' expressions of their feelings toward their clients must be genuine, or congruent—no facade, no putting up a professional front. Third, therapists must have empathy with the clients—the ability to put themselves in the clients' place. Therapists must show that they comprehend the clients' feelings, emotions, and experiences, and that they understand and see the clients' world as the clients see it. When clients speak, the therapist follows by restating or reflecting back their ideas and feelings. In this way clients begin to see themselves more clearly and eventually resolve their own conflicts and make positive decisions about their lives. The following is an excerpt from a 21-year-old woman's first session of person-centered therapy.

> *Client:* It is a long story. I can't find myself. Everything I do seems to be wrong. . . .
>   If there is any criticism or anyone says anything about me I just can't take it. . . .

Therapist: You feel things are all going wrong and that you're just crushed by criticism.

Client: Well, it doesn't even need to be meant as criticism. It goes way back. In grammar school I never felt I belonged. . . .

Therapist: You feel the roots go back a long way but that you have never really belonged, even in grammar school. (Rogers, 1977, p. 199)

In the 1940s and 1950s, person-centered therapy enjoyed a strong following among psychologists. In the early 1980s, a survey of 400 psychologists and counselors revealed that Carl Rogers was considered the most influential figure in counseling and psychotherapy (Smith, 1982).

Gestalt Therapy: Getting in Touch with Your Feelings **Gestalt therapy**, developed by Fritz Perls (1969), emphasizes the importance of clients' fully experiencing, in the present moment, their feelings, thoughts, and actions and then taking responsibility for them.

Gestalt therapy is a **directive therapy**, one in which the therapist takes an active role in determining the course of therapy sessions. The well-known phrase "getting in touch with your feelings" is an ever-present objective of the Gestalt therapist, who helps, prods, or badgers clients to experience their feelings as deeply and genuinely as possible and then admit responsibility for them.

Perls suggested that those of us who are in need of therapy carry around a heavy load of unfinished business, which may be in the form of resentment toward or conflicts with parents, siblings, lovers, employers, or others. If not resolved, these conflicts are carried forward into our present relationships.

The goal of Gestalt therapy is not merely to relieve symptoms, but to help clients achieve a more integrated self and become more authentic and self-accepting. In addition, they must learn to assume personal responsibility for their behavior rather than blame society, past experiences, parents, or others.

Therapies Emphasizing Interaction with Others

Some therapies look not only at the individual's internal struggles but also at interpersonal relationships.

Interpersonal Therapy: Short Road to Recovery **Interpersonal therapy (IPT)** is a brief psychotherapy that has proven very effective in the treatment of depression (Elkin et al., 1989, 1995; Klerman et al., 1984). IPT is designed specifically to help patients cope with four types of problems commonly associated with major depression:

   1. *Unusual or severe responses to the death of a loved one.* The therapist and patient discuss the patient's relationship with the deceased person and feelings (such as guilt) that may be associated with the death. The therapist tries to help the patient release the past and develop an active interest in the present.

   2. *Interpersonal role disputes.* Depression is often associated with mutually incompatible expectations about roles or responsibilities between patients and their spouses, children, parents, friends, coworkers, or employers. These may be a source of conflict, resentment, and even hostility in that neither party discusses the problem openly and honestly or really tries to understand the other's point of view. The therapist helps the patient to understand what is at stake for those involved and to explore options for bringing about change.

   3. *Difficulty in adjusting to role transitions such as divorce, career change, and retirement.* Role transitions may involve a loss, such as a life change resulting from an illness or injury or the loss of a job. Other role transitions involve positive events, such

Gestalt therapy: A therapy that was originated by Fritz Perls and that emphasizes the importance of clients' fully experiencing, in the present moment, their feelings, thoughts, and actions and taking personal responsibility for their behavior.

directive therapy: An approach to therapy in which the therapist takes an active role in determining the course of therapy sessions and provides answers and suggestions to the patient.

interpersonal therapy (IPT): A brief psychotherapy designed to help depressed people better understand and cope with problems relating to their interpersonal relationships.

What is the major emphasis in Gestalt therapy?

What four problems commonly associated with major depression is interpersonal therapy designed to treat?

family therapy: Therapy involving an entire family, based on the assumption that an individual's problem is caused and/or maintained in part by problems within the family unit.

group therapy: A form of therapy in which several clients (usually 7–10) meet regularly with one or more therapists to resolve personal problems.

as marriage, a new baby, or a promotion. Patients are helped to see the change not as a threat but as a challenge and an opportunity for growth that they can master.

4. *Deficits in interpersonal skills.* Some people lack the skills to make friends and to sustain intimate relationships. Through role-playing and analysis of the patient's communication style, the therapist tries to help the patient develop the interpersonal skills necessary to initiate and sustain relationships.

Interpersonal therapy is brief, consisting of 12 to 16 weekly sessions. A large study conducted by the National Institute of Mental Health found IPT to be an effective treatment even for severe depression and one with a low dropout rate (Elkin et al., 1989, 1995). Research also indicates that patients who recover from major depression can enjoy a longer period without relapse when they continue with monthly sessions of IPT (Frank et al., 1991).

Family and Couple Therapy: Healing Interpersonal Relationships   Families may come to therapists for help with troubled or troublesome teenagers, alcoholic parents, abusive situations, or other problems. In **family therapy**, parents and children enter therapy as a group with one or more family therapists (called *conjoint therapy*). Sometimes therapists work with only one or a few family members at a time.

Therapists working with couples pay attention to the dynamics between the two people—how they communicate, act toward each other, and view each other.

The therapist pays attention to the dynamics of the family unit—how family members communicate, how they act toward one another, and how they view each other. The goal of the therapist is to help the family members reach agreement on certain changes that will help heal the wounds of the family unit, improve communication patterns, and create more understanding and harmony within the group. Some therapists work with couples to help them resolve their difficulties and stay together; or they may work to ease the emotional turmoil if a break-up is the best answer for the couple.

Family or couple therapy appears to have positive effects in treating a number of disorders and clinical problems (Lebow & Gurman, 1995). As an adjunct to medication, family therapy can be beneficial in the treatment of schizophrenia and can reduce relapse rates (Carpenter, 1996). Family therapy can help other family members modify their behavior toward the patient. Family therapy also seems to be the most favorable setting in which to treat adolescent drug abuse (Lebow & Gurman, 1995).

What are some advantages of group therapy?

Group Therapy: Helping One at a Time, Together   Group therapy is a form of therapy in which several clients (usually 7–10) meet regularly with one or more therapists to resolve personal problems. Besides being less expensive than individual therapy, group therapy has other advantages. It gives the individual a sense of belonging and an opportunity to express feelings, to get feedback from other members, and to give and receive help and emotional support. Learning that others also share their problems leaves people feeling less alone and ashamed. The American Psychiatric Association (1993b) has endorsed group therapy as particularly useful for depression associated with bereavement or chronic illness.

Self-help groups are groups of people who share a common problem and meet to give and receive support. They are usually not led by professional therapists. About 12 million people in the United States participate in roughly 500,000 self-help groups.

One of the oldest and best-known self-help groups is Alcoholics Anonymous, which claims 1.5 million members worldwide. Other self-help groups patterned after

Alcoholics Anonymous have been formed to help individuals overcome many other addictive behaviors, from overeating (Overeaters Anonymous) to gambling (Gamblers Anonymous). There are self-help groups for people with a variety of physical and mental illnesses, and groups to help people deal with crises, from divorce and bereavement to victimization. In addition, there are groups to help relatives and friends of people having such problems.

Self-help groups offer comfort because people can talk about their problems with others who have "been there" and learn that their painful emotional reactions are normal. They can exchange useful information, discuss their coping strategies, and gain hope by seeing people who are coping with the same problems successfully. After reviewing a number of studies of self-help groups, Lieberman (1986) concluded that the results tend to be positive. For problems such as alcoholism and obesity, self-help groups are often as effective as psychotherapy (Zilbergeld, 1986).

BEHAVIOR THERAPIES: UNLEARNING THE OLD, LEARNING THE NEW

Behavior therapies are treatment approaches consistent with the learning perspective on psychological disorders—that abnormal behavior is learned. According to the behaviorists, unless people are suffering from some physiological disorder, such as brain pathology, those who seek therapy need it for one of two reasons: (1) they have learned inappropriate or maladaptive responses, or (2) they never had the opportunity to learn appropriate behavior in the first place. Instead of viewing the maladaptive behavior as a symptom of some underlying disorder, the behavior therapist sees the behavior itself as the disorder. If a person comes to a therapist with a fear of flying, that fear of flying is seen as the problem.

Behavior therapies use the principles of operant conditioning, classical conditioning, and/or observational learning theory to eliminate inappropriate or maladaptive behaviors and replace them with more adaptive responses. Sometimes this type of approach is referred to as **behavior modification**. The goal is to change the troublesome behavior, not to change the individual's personality structure or to search for the origin of the problem behavior. "Behavior therapy is educational rather than 'healing'" (Thorpe & Olson, 1990, p. 15). The therapist's role is active and directive.

Behavior Modification Techniques Based on Operant Conditioning

Behavior modification techniques based on operant conditioning seek to control the consequences of behavior. Extinction of an undesirable behavior is accomplished by terminating, or withholding, the reinforcement that is maintaining that behavior (Lerman & Iwata, 1996). Behavior therapists also seek to reinforce any desirable behavior in order to increase its frequency, and they use reinforcement, as well, to shape entirely new behaviors. The process works best when it is applied consistently. Institutional settings such as hospitals, prisons, and school classrooms are well suited to these techniques, because they provide a restricted environment where the consequences of behavior can be more strictly controlled.

Token Economies: What Would You Do for a Token?   Some institutions use behavior modification programs called **token economies** that reward appropriate behavior with tokens such as poker chips, play money, gold stars, or the like. These tokens can later be exchanged for desired goods (candy, gum, cigarettes) and/or privileges (weekend passes, free time, participation in desirable activities). For decades mental hospitals have successfully used token economies with chronic

behavior therapy: A treatment approach employing the principles of operant conditioning, classical conditioning, and/or observational learning theory to eliminate inappropriate or maladaptive behaviors and replace them with more adaptive responses.

behavior modification: The systematic application of learning principles to help a person eliminate undesirable behaviors and/or acquire more adaptive behaviors; also called behavior therapy.

token economy: A behavior modification technique that reinforces desirable behaviors with tokens that can be exchanged later for desired objects, activities, and/or privileges.

What is a behavior therapy?

How do behavior therapists modify behavior using operant conditioning techniques?

schizophrenics to improve their self-care skills and social interaction (Ayllon & Azrin, 1965, 1968). Patients tend to perform chores when reinforced but not when reinforcement is discontinued. Schizophrenic symptoms such as delusions and hallucinations, of course, are not affected.

Time Out: All Alone with No Reinforcers   Another effective method used to eliminate undesirable behavior, especially in children and adolescents, is **time out** (Brantner & Doherty, 1983). The principle is simple. Children are told in advance that if they engage in certain undesirable behaviors, they will be removed calmly from the situation and will have to pass a period of time (usually no more than 15 minutes) in a place containing no reinforcers (no television, books, toys, friends, and so on). Theoretically, the undesirable behavior will stop if it is no longer followed by attention or any other positive reinforcers.

Stimulus Satiation: Too Much of a Good Thing   Another behavior modification technique, **stimulus satiation**, attempts to change problem behaviors by giving people too much of whatever they find reinforcing. The idea is that the reinforcer will lose its attraction and become something to be avoided.

The stimulus satiation technique was used successfully with a 47-year-old chronic schizophrenic woman who, during her 9 years of hospitalization, would collect and hoard large numbers of towels.

> At the beginning of treatment, the nurses would bring a towel to the patient in her room several times throughout the day, and without any comment, simply hand it to her. "The first week she was given an average of 7 towels daily, and by the third week this number was increased to 60." (Ayllon, 1977, p. 358)
>
> At first, she seemed to enjoy folding and stacking her towels, but finally, when the patient had 625 towels in her room, she could stand it no longer and began saying to the nurses: "Don't give me no more towels. I've got enough." "Take them towels away. . . . I can't sit here all night and fold towels." . . . Within a few weeks the patient was angrily demanding, "Get these dirty towels out of here." (p. 359)

During the following 12 months, no more than one or two towels could be found in the patient's room.

The Effectiveness of Operant Approaches: Do They Work?   Behavior therapies based on operant conditioning have been particularly effective in modifying some behaviors of seriously disturbed people (Paul & Lentz, 1977). Although these techniques do not presume to cure schizophrenia, autism, or mental retardation, they can increase the frequency of desirable behaviors and decrease the frequency of undesirable behaviors. Sometimes modifying some of the more extreme and bizarre behaviors enables family members to accept and care for the patient themselves.

Behavior modification techniques can also be used by people who want to break bad habits such as smoking and overeating or to develop good habits such as a regular exercise regime. If you want to modify any of your behaviors, devise a reward system for desirable behaviors, and remember the principles of shaping. Reward gradual changes in the direction of your ultimate goal. If you are trying to develop better eating habits, don't try to change a lifetime of bad habits all at once. Begin with a small step such as substituting frozen yogurt for ice cream. Set realistic weekly goals that you are likely to be able to achieve.

Therapies Based on Classical Conditioning

What behavior therapies are based on classical conditioning?

Some behavior therapies are based mainly on the principles of classical conditioning, which can account for how we acquire many of our emotional reactions. In classical conditioning, a neutral stimulus—some object, person, or situation that initially does not elicit any strong positive or negative emotional reaction—is paired with either a very positive or a very negative stimulus. After conditioning, the person's strong feeling toward the positive or negative stimulus is transferred to the original, neutral stimulus.

Therapies based on classical conditioning can be used to rid people of fears and other undesirable behaviors. We will discuss four types of therapy based primarily on classical conditioning: systematic desensitization, flooding, exposure and response prevention, and aversion therapy.

Systematic Desensitization: Overcoming Fears One Step at a Time   Have you ever been both afraid and relaxed at the same time? Psychiatrist Joseph Wolpe (1958, 1973) came to the conclusion that these two responses are incompatible; that is, one inhibits the other. On the basis of this idea, Wolpe developed a therapy to treat fears and phobias. He reasoned that if he could get people to relax and stay relaxed while they thought about a feared object, person, place, or situation, they could conquer their fear or phobia.

In Wolpe's therapy, **systematic desensitization**, clients are trained in deep muscle relaxation. Then they confront a hierarchy of fears—a graduated series of anxiety-producing situations—either *in vivo* (in real life) or in imagination, until they can remain relaxed even in the presence of the most feared situation. The technique can be used for everything from fear of animals to claustrophobia, test anxiety, and social and other situational fears.

What do you fear most? Many college students would say that they fear speaking in front of a group. If that were your fear and you went to a behavior therapist who used systematic desensitization, this is what would happen. First the therapist would ask you to identify the fear causing your anxiety and everything connected with it. Then all the aspects of the fear would be arranged on a hierarchy from least to most anxiety-producing.

After preparing the hierarchy, you would be taught deep muscle relaxation, progressively relaxing parts of your body until you achieved a completely relaxed state. During the actual desensitization procedure, you would be asked to picture, as vividly as possible, the least fear-producing item on your hierarchy—for example, reading in your course syllabus that an oral presentation will be assigned. When you were able to remain relaxed while visualizing this item, the therapist would have you move one step up the hierarchy and picture the next item—having your professor assign the oral presentation. This procedure would be followed until you reached the top of the hierarchy and could remain calm and relaxed while you imagined vividly the most fear-producing stimulus—actually making your presentation in class. If, during the desensitization process, anxiety should creep in as you imagined items on the hierarchy, you would signal the therapist. The therapist would instruct you to stop thinking about that item. You would then clear your mind, come back to a state of complete relaxation, and begin again. Try creating your own hierarchy in the *Try It!* (on page 432).

How effective is systematic desensitization? Many experiments, demonstrations, and case reports confirm that systematic desensitization is a highly successful treatment for eliminating fears and phobias in a relatively short time (Kalish, 1981; Rachman & Wilson, 1980). It has proved effective for specific problems such as test anxiety, stage fright, and anxiety related to sexual disorders. Wolpe (1981) claims that skilled behavior therapists using systematic desensitization report marked improvement in about 80% of their patients.

The critical element in systematic desensitization is the patient's exposure to the feared stimulus. Even the relaxation, an important part of Wolpe's treatment, is apparently not essential. But relaxation does help to keep especially fearful patients from jumping up and running away from the fear-provoking stimulus.

There are several other therapies that use exposure as the key therapeutic element to treat phobias and obsessive compulsive disorder.

How do therapists use systematic desensitization to rid people of fears?

Link It!

systematic desensitization: A behavior therapy that is used to treat phobias and that involves training clients in deep muscle relaxation and then having them confront a graduated series of anxiety-producing situations (real or imagined) until they can remain relaxed while confronting even the most feared situation.

Use what you have learned about systematic desensitization to create a step-by-step approach to help someone overcome a fear of making a class presentation. The person's hierarchy of fears begins with reading in the syllabus that an oral presentation will be assigned and culminates in actually making the oral presentation. Fill in successive steps, according to a possible hierarchy of fears, that will lead to the final step. One set of possible steps is given below.

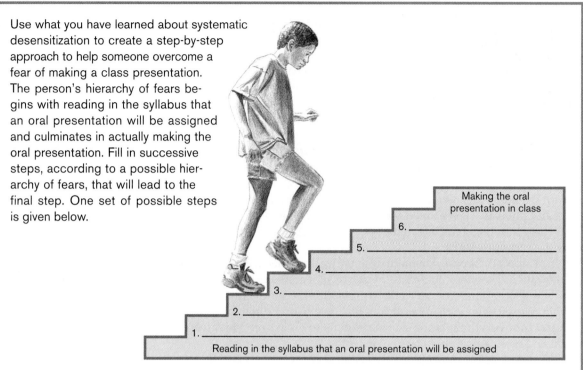

Making the oral presentation in class

6. _____

5. _____

4. _____

3. _____

2. _____

1. _____

Reading in the syllabus that an oral presentation will be assigned

Answer: (1) Being assigned the oral presentation and given a due date. (2) Preparing the oral presentation. (3) Practicing the oral presentation one week before it is due. (4) Practicing the oral presentation the night before it is due. (5) Waiting to give the presentation. (6) Walking to the front of the room to give the presentation.

What is flooding?

Flooding: Confronting Fears All at Once   **Flooding** is a behavior therapy used in the treatment of phobias. It involves exposing clients to the feared object or event (or asking them to vividly imagine it) for an extended period until their anxiety decreases. Flooding is almost the opposite of systematic desensitization. The person is exposed to the fear all at once, not gradually and certainly not while in a state of relaxation. An individual with a fear of heights, for example, might have to go onto the roof of a tall building and remain there until the fear subsided. A person with a cat phobia might be told: "Visualize the cat all over you, perhaps scratching you, its eyes right up against yours, its hair all over you" (Sheehan, 1983, pp. 158–159).

What is the key to success in flooding? It is not that a person must be scared to death in order for flooding to work. The key is keeping the patients in the feared situation long enough that they can see that none of the dreaded consequences they fear actually come to pass (Marks, 1978a). If the exposure is too brief, anxiety simply intensifies, and patients get worse instead of better. Flooding sessions typically last from 30 minutes to 2 hours and should not be terminated until patients are markedly less afraid than they were at the beginning of the session. It is rare for a patient to need more than six treatment sessions (Marshall & Segal, 1988).

In vivo flooding, the real-life experience, works faster and is more effective than simply imagining the feared object (Chambless & Goldstein, 1979; Marks, 1972). Flooding may be quite painful for the patient, as it was for Bill in the chapter's opening story. But flooding often works where other therapies have failed and works faster as well.

How does exposure and response prevention help people with obsessive compulsive disorder?

Exposure and Response Prevention: Cutting the Tie That Binds Fears and Rituals   **Exposure and response prevention** has been successful in treating obsessive compulsive disorder (Baer, 1996; Foa, 1995). The therapy consists of two com-

An acrophobic client wears a virtual-reality headset, which exposes him to the view from a high balcony (right) but allows him to experience moving toward or away from the railing. Such a realistic but safe exposure to the feared stimulus allows many people to overcome their phobias.

ponents. The first involves *exposure*—exposing patients to objects or situations they have been avoiding because they trigger obsessions and compulsive rituals. The second component is *response prevention*, in which patients agree to resist performing their compulsive rituals for progressively longer periods of time.

Initially the therapist identifies the thoughts, objects, or situations that trigger the compulsive ritual. For example, touching a doorknob, a piece of unwashed fruit, or garbage might ordinarily send people with a fear of contamination to the nearest bathroom to wash their hands. Patients are gradually exposed to stimuli they find more and more distasteful and anxiety-provoking. They must agree not to perform the normal ritual (hand washing, bathing, or the like) for a specified period of time after exposure. Gradually patients learn to tolerate the anxiety evoked by the various "contaminants."

A typical treatment course—about 10 sessions over a period of 3 to 7 weeks—can bring about considerable improvement in 60–70% of patients (Jenike, 1990). And patients treated with exposure are less likely to relapse after treatment than those treated with drugs alone (Greist et al., 1995).

Systematic desensitization, flooding, and exposure help people stop avoiding feared objects or situations. Even treatments using *virtual reality* as the means of exposure have been successful. Virtual reality has been proven effective in treating spider phobias (Carlin et al., 1997) and fear of flying (Rothbaum et al., 1996). But what if the person's problem is just the opposite—bad habits, addictions, and other such behaviors that *should* be avoided? Aversion therapy is designed to help people break bad habits, overcome addictions, and learn to avoid situations that trigger harmful behavior.

Aversion Therapy: Making Clients Sick to Make Them Better

Aversion **therapy** is used to rid clients of a harmful or socially undesirable behavior by pairing it with a painful, sickening, or otherwise aversive stimulus. Electric shock, emetics (which cause nausea and vomiting), or other unpleasant stimuli are paired with the undesirable behavior time after time until a strong negative association is formed and the person comes to avoid that behavior, habit, or substance. Treatment continues until the bad habit loses its appeal and becomes associated with pain or discomfort.

Alcoholics are sometimes given a nausea-producing substance such as Antabuse, which reacts violently with alcohol and causes a person to retch and vomit until the stomach is empty. But for most problems, aversion therapy need not be so intense as to make a person physically ill. A controlled comparison of treatments for chronic nail biting revealed that mild aversion therapy—painting a bitter-tasting substance on the fingernails—yielded significant improvement (Allen, 1996).

Therapies Based on Observational Learning Theory: Just Watch *This!*

A great deal of what we learn in life, we learn from watching others and then copying or imitating the behaviors modeled for us. Much positive behavior is learned this way; but so are bad habits, aggressive behaviors, and fears or phobias. Thera-

flooding: A behavioral therapy used to treat phobias, during which clients are exposed to the feared object or event (or asked to imagine it vividly) for an extended period until their anxiety decreases.

exposure and response prevention: A behavior therapy that exposes patients with obsessive compulsive disorder to stimuli generating increasing anxiety; patients must agree not to carry out their normal rituals for a specified period of time after exposure.

aversion therapy: A behavior therapy in which an aversive stimulus is paired with an undesirable behavior until the behavior becomes associated with pain and discomfort.

How does aversion therapy rid a person of a harmful or undesirable behavior?

How does participant modeling help people overcome fears?

Most simple phobias, such as fear of snakes, can be extinguished after only a few hours of participant modeling, a technique in which the therapist demonstrates the desired unfearful behavior in steps.

pies derived from Albert Bandura's work on observational learning are based on the belief that people can overcome fears and acquire social skills through modeling.

Therapists have effectively treated fears and phobias by having clients watch a model (on film or in real life) responding to a feared situation in appropriate ways with no dreaded consequences. Usually the model approaches the feared object in gradual steps. Bandura (1967) describes how nursery school children lost their fear of dogs after watching a film depicting a child who was not afraid of dogs first approach a dog, then play with it, pet it, and so on. Modeling films have been used to reduce the fears of children who must undergo surgery (Melamed & Siegel, 1975) and to reduce children's fear of the dentist (Shaw & Thoresen, 1974).

The most effective type of therapy based on observational learning theory is called **participant modeling** (Bandura, 1977; Bandura et al., 1975, 1977). In this therapy, not only does the model demonstrate the appropriate response in graduated steps, but the client attempts to imitate the model step by step, while the therapist gives encouragement and support. This technique provides the additional benefit of exposure to the feared stimulus.

Most specific phobias can be extinguished in only 3 or 4 hours of modeling therapy when the client participates. Participant modeling has proved more effective in treating snake phobias than simple observation of a filmed or live model, and more effective than systematic desensitization (Bandura et al., 1969).

COGNITIVE THERAPIES: IT'S THE THOUGHT THAT COUNTS

We have seen that behavior therapies based on classical and operant conditioning and modeling are effective in eliminating many types of troublesome behavior. But what if the problem is in a person's thinking, attitudes, false beliefs, or poor self-concept? There are therapies for these problems as well. *Cognitive therapies*, based on the cognitive perspective, assume that maladaptive behavior can result from irrational thoughts, beliefs, and ideas, which the therapist tries to change. The emphasis of cognitive therapies is on conscious rather than unconscious processes and on the present rather than the past. We will explore rational-emotive therapy and cognitive therapy.

Rational-Emotive Therapy: Challenging False Beliefs

What is the aim of rational-emotive therapy?

participant modeling: A behavior therapy in which an appropriate response is modeled in graduated steps and the client attempts each step, encouraged and supported by the therapist.

rational-emotive therapy: A directive, confrontational therapy developed by Albert Ellis and designed to challenge and modify the irrational beliefs thought to cause personal distress.

Picture this scenario: Harry received two free tickets to a Saturday-night concert. Excited, Harry called Sally, whom he had dated a couple of times, to ask her to go to the concert with him. To his surprise, she turned him down without even giving a reason. He was shocked and became dejected. "How could she do this to me?" he wondered. As the week dragged on, he became more and more depressed.

What caused Harry's depression? Sally's turning him down? Not according to Albert Ellis (1961, 1977, 1993), a clinical psychologist who developed **rational-emotive therapy** in the 1950s. Rational-emotive therapy is based on Ellis's ABC theory. The A refers to the *activating event*, the B to the person's *belief* about the event, and the C to the emotional *consequence* that follows. Ellis claims that it is not the event itself that causes the emotional consequence, but rather the person's belief about the event. In other words, A does not cause C; B causes C. If the belief is irrational, then the emotional consequence can be extreme distress.

Irrational beliefs cause people to see an undesirable event as a catastrophe rather than as a disappointment or an inconvenience. Irrational beliefs cause people to feel depressed, worthless, or enraged instead of simply disappointed or annoyed.

Rational-emotive therapy is a directive, confrontational form of psychotherapy designed to challenge clients' irrational beliefs about themselves and others. As clients begin to replace irrational beliefs with rational ones, their emotional reactions become more appropriate, less distressing, and more likely to lead to constructive behavior. Try challenging an irrational belief of your own in the *Try It!*

Most clients in rational-emotive therapy see a therapist individually, once a week, for 5 to 50 sessions. In stark contrast to person-centered therapists (and most other therapists, for that matter), "rational-emotive therapists do not believe a warm relationship between counselee and counselor is a necessary or a sufficient condition for effective personality change" (Ellis, 1979, p. 186). In Ellis's view, "Giving a client RET with a good deal of warmth, approval and reassurance will tend to help this client 'feel better' rather than 'get better'" (p. 194).

One meta-analysis of 28 studies showed that patients receiving rational-emotive therapy did better than those receiving no treatment or a placebo, and about the same as those receiving systematic desensitization (Engles et al., 1993).

Cognitive Therapy: Overcoming "The Power of Negative Thinking"

"In order to be happy, I have to be successful in whatever I undertake."
"To be happy, I must be accepted (liked, admired) by all people at all times."
"If people disagree with me, it means they don't like me."

How does cognitive therapy help people overcome depression and anxiety disorders?

If you agree with all of these statements, you probably spend a good part of your time upset and unhappy. Psychiatrist Aaron T. Beck (1976) claims that much of the misery endured by a depressed and anxious person can be traced to **automatic thoughts**— unreasonable but unquestioned ideas that rule the person's life. Beck (1991) believes that depressed persons hold "a negative view of the present, past, and future experiences" (p. 369). They tend to view themselves as "deficient, defective, and/or undeserving"; their environment as "unduly demanding, depriving, and/or rejecting"; and their future as "without promise, value, or meaning" (Karasu, 1990a, p. 138).

automatic thoughts: Unreasonable and unquestioned ideas that rule a person's life and lead to depression and anxiety.

Aaron T. Beck

These persons notice only negative, unpleasant things and jump to upsetting conclusions. Anxious people expect the worst; they see negative events as catastrophes and at the same time underestimate their coping ability.

The goal of **cognitive therapy** is to help patients stop their negative thoughts as they occur and replace them with more objective thoughts. The focus is on the present rather than on the past, and no attempt is made to uncover hidden meanings in the patients' thoughts and responses. Patients are given homework assignments, such as keeping track of automatic thoughts and the feelings evoked by them and substituting more rational thoughts. When cognitive therapy is combined with behavioral techniques such as relaxation training or exposure, it is called *cognitive-behavioral therapy*.

Cognitive therapy is brief, usually lasting only 10 to 20 sessions, and is therefore less expensive than many other types of therapy (Beck, 1976). This therapy has been researched extensively and is reported to be highly successful in the treatment of mild to moderately depressed patients (Antonuccio et al., 1995; Thase et al., 1991). There is some evidence that depressed people who have received cognitive therapy are less likely to relapse than those who have been treated with antidepressant drugs (Evans et al., 1992; Scott, 1996).

Cognitive therapy has also been shown to be effective for treating panic disorder (Barlow, 1997; Jacobson & Hollon, 1996). If patients with panic disorder misinterpret bodily sensations associated with anxiety as signs of mental or physical collapse, their anxiety builds and causes panic (Michelson et al., 1990). Cognitive therapy teaches them to change their catastrophic interpretations of these symptoms and thereby prevent the symptoms from escalating into panic. Recent studies have shown that after 3 months of cognitive therapy, about 90% of patients with panic disorder are panic-free (Robins & Hayes, 1993). Not only does cognitive therapy have a low dropout rate and a low relapse rate, but often patients continue to improve even after treatment is completed (Öst & Westling, 1995). Also, cognitive therapy has proved effective for generalized anxiety disorder (Beck, 1993), OCD (Abramowitz, 1997), cocaine addiction (Carroll et al., 1994), posttraumatic stress disorder (Marks et al., 1999), bulimia, and, when coupled with exposure, social phobia (Marks, 1995).

THE BIOLOGICAL THERAPIES

What are the three main biological therapies?

Professionals who favor the biological perspective—the view that psychological disorders are symptoms of underlying physical disorders—usually favor a **biological therapy**. The three main biological therapies are drug therapy, electroconvulsive therapy, and psychosurgery.

Drug Therapy: Pills for Psychological Ills

The favorite and by far the most frequently used biological treatment is drug therapy. Capable of relieving the debilitating symptoms of schizophrenia, depression, bipolar disorder, and some anxiety disorders, modern drug therapy has had a tremendous impact on the treatment of psychological disorders.

How do antipsychotic drugs help schizophrenic patients?

Antipsychotic Drugs   Historically, efforts to treat schizophrenia have been woefully inadequate. Mental hospitals confined many patients to locked wards, and padded cells, straitjackets, and other restraints were widely used. Then, shortly after the introduction of antipsychotic drugs in 1955, the picture suddenly changed. The breakthrough in drug therapy, coupled with the federal government's effort to reduce involuntary hospitalization of mental patients, enabled many schizophrenics who had been locked in mental institutions to be discharged into the community. In fact, the mental hospital patient population decreased from about 559,000 in 1955, when the drugs were introduced, to slightly over 100,000 by 1990.

cognitive therapy: A therapy designed to change maladaptive behavior by changing the person's irrational thoughts, beliefs, and ideas.

Antipsychotic drugs, or *neuroleptics* (sometimes called *major tranquilizers*), are drugs prescribed mainly for schizophrenia to control severe psychotic symptoms, such as hallucinations, delusions, and other disorders in thinking. They are also effective in reducing restlessness, agitation, and excitement. You may have heard of these drugs under their brand names—Thorazine, Stelazine, Compazine, and Mellaril. These drugs apparently work by inhibiting the activity of the neurotransmitter dopamine. About 50% of patients have a good response to the standard antipsychotics (Kane, 1996). But many patients, particularly those with an early onset of schizophrenia, are not helped by them (Meltzer et al., 1997), and others show only slight or modest improvement in symptoms. The earlier a patient begins treatment with antipsychotics, the better the long-term outcome is likely to be (McGlashan & Johannessen, 1996; Wyatt & Henter, 1997). However, many patients who are helped by these drugs stop taking them because of their very unpleasant side effects—restless pacing and fidgeting, muscle spasms and cramps, and tremors in the arms and legs (Green & Patel, 1996). The long-term use of antipsychotic drugs carries a high risk of the most severe side effect, *tardive dyskinesia*—almost continual twitching and jerking movements of the face and tongue, and squirming movements of the hands and trunk (Glazer et al., 1993).

Several newer "atypical" neuroleptics are now being used. Atypical neuroleptics affect certain dopamine receptors differently than do the standard neuroleptics, and they also block serotonin receptors (Michels & Marzuk, 1993). One such drug, clozapine, has been found to help patients who have benefited too little or not at all from standard neuroleptics (Kane, 1996; Rosenheck et al., 1997). About 10% of patients who take clozapine find the results so dramatic that they almost feel as though they have been reborn (Wallis & Willwerth, 1992). Clozapine produces fewer side effects than standard neuroleptics (Casey, 1996). However, without careful monitoring it can cause a fatal blood defect in 1–2% of patients who take it. A more recent drug, risperidone, is much more effective than other neuroleptics in treating the negative symptoms of schizophrenia—apathy, emotional unresponsiveness, and social withdrawal (Marder, 1996).

Schizophrenics who were hospitalized in the past could expect to stay for weeks or months. Now, thanks to the antipsychotics, the average stay of such patients is usually a matter of days. But even though antipsychotic drugs help two-thirds of the patients who take them, they do not cure schizophrenia. The drugs reduce and control many of the major symptoms so that patients are able to function, but most patients must continue to take them in order to avoid relapse (Carpenter, 1996; Schooler et al., 1997).

Antidepressant Drugs   Not long after the antipsychotic drugs came on the scene, the **antidepressants** were introduced. Antidepressants act effectively as mood elevators for people who are severely depressed (Elkin et al., 1995) and are also helpful in the treatment of certain anxiety disorders. About 65–75% of patients who take antidepressants find themselves significantly improved, and 40–50% of those are essentially completely recovered (Frazer, 1997). But this leaves 25–35% who show only minimal improvement.

Tricyclics Imbalances in the neurotransmitters serotonin and norepinephrine often accompany symptoms of depression. The tricyclic antidepressants, which include amitriptyline (Elavil) and imipramine (Tofranil), work against depression by blocking the reuptake of norepinephrine and serotonin into the axon terminals, thus enhancing the action of these neurotransmitters in the synapses. The tricyclics are the drug treatment of first choice for major depression (Perry, 1996), proving effective for over 60% of depressed patients (Karasu, 1990b). Imipramine is also effective in relieving the symptoms of generalized anxiety disorder (Rickels, Downing et al., 1993) and panic disorder and agoraphobia (Clum et al., 1993). But tricyclics can have some unpleasant side effects—sedation, dizziness, nervousness, fatigue, dry mouth, forgetfulness, and weight gain (Frazer, 1997).

Link It!

For what conditions are antidepressants prescribed?

biological therapy: A therapy (drug therapy, ECT, or psychosurgery) that is based on the assumption that most mental disorders have physical causes.

antipsychotic drugs: Drugs used to control severe psychotic symptoms, such as the delusions and hallucinations of schizophrenics; also known as neuroleptics or major tranquilizers.

antidepressants: Drugs that are prescribed to treat depression and some anxiety disorders.

Serotonin-Selective Reuptake Inhibitors (SSRIs) A category of antidepressants known as *serotonin-selective reuptake inhibitors (SSRIs)* block the reuptake of serotonin, increasing its effect at the synapses (Goodwin, 1996). SSRIs have fewer side effects (Nelson, 1997) and are safer in overdose than tricyclics (Thase & Kupfer, 1996). SSRIs have been found to be promising in treating obsessive compulsive disorder (Goodwin, 1996), social phobia (Jefferson, 1995), panic disorder (Coplan et al., 1997; Jefferson, 1997; Sheehan & Harnett-Sheehan, 1996), and binge eating (Hudson et al., 1996). SSRIs include such drugs as fluoxetine (sold as Prozac) and clomipramine (Anafranil). By 1994 more than 28 million people worldwide had used Prozac, making it the most widely used antidepressant (Avenoso, 1997). Prozac's popularity is due not to greater effectiveness than the tricyclics but to milder side effects (Pen et al., 1994). But Prozac can cause sexual dysfunction, although normal sexual functioning returns when the drug is discontinued.

Prozac has been proved to be an effective treatment for less severe depression, with 50–60% of patients showing improvement (Nelson, 1991). It is also effective in the treatment of obsessive compulsive disorder, which has been associated with a serotonin imbalance (Rapoport, 1989).

Monoamine Oxidase Inhibitors (MAO Inhibitors) Another line of treatment for depression is the monoamine oxidase inhibitors. By blocking the action of an enzyme that breaks down norepinephrine and serotonin in the synapses, MAO inhibitors increase the availability of norepinephrine and serotonin. MAO inhibitors (sold under the names Marplan, Nardil, and Parnate) are usually prescribed for depressed patients who do not respond to other antidepressants (Thase et al., 1992). They are also effective in treating panic disorder (Sheehan & Raj, 1988) and social phobia (Marshall et al., 1994). But MAO inhibitors have many of the same unpleasant side effects as tricyclic antidepressants, and patients taking MAO inhibitors must avoid certain foods or run the risk of stroke.

How does lithium help patients with bipolar disorder?

Lithium: A Natural Salt That Evens Moods **Lithium**, a naturally occurring salt, is considered a wonder drug for 40–50% of patients suffering from bipolar disorder (Thase & Kupfer, 1996). If a proper maintenance dose of lithium is initiated early, it yields reductions in both depression and mania (Tondo et al., 1998). It also lessens the severity of episodes of both mania and depression. But 40–60% of those who take a maintenance dose will experience a recurrence (Thase & Kupfer, 1996). Careful monitoring of the lithium level in the patient's system is necessary every 2 to 6 months to guard against lithium poisoning and permanent damage to the nervous system (Schou, 1997).

The Minor Tranquilizers The family of minor tranquilizers called *benzodiazepines* includes, among others, the well-known drugs sold as Valium and Librium and the high-potency drug Xanax (pronounced ZAN-ax). Used primarily to treat anxiety, benzodiazepines are prescribed more often than any other class of psychoactive drugs (Medina et al., 1993). They have been found to be an effective treatment for panic disorder (Davidson, 1997; Noyes et al., 1996) and generalized anxiety disorder (Lydiard et al., 1996).

Xanax, the largest selling psychiatric drug (Famighetti, 1997), appears to be particularly effective in relieving anxiety, depression, and panic disorder (Noyes et al., 1996). But many patients, once they are panic-free, find themselves unable to discontinue the drug because they experience moderate to intense withdrawal symptoms, including intense anxiety (Otto et al., 1993). Valium seems to be just as effective as Xanax for treating panic disorder, and withdrawal is easier.

What are some of the problems with drug therapy?

Some Problems with Drug Therapy Having read this far, you might conclude that drug therapy is the simplest and possibly the most effective way of treating schizophrenia, depression, panic disorder, and obsessive compulsive disorder. There are, however, a number of potential problems with the use of drugs. Antipsychotics and antidepressants have side effects that can be so unpleasant that a number of patients stop treatment before they experience a reduction in symptoms.

Antipsychotics, antidepressants, and lithium do not cure psychological disorders, so patients usually experience a relapse if they stop taking the drugs when their symptoms lift. Maintenance doses of antidepressants following a major depression reduce the probability of recurrences of depression and anxiety disorders (Prien & Kocsis, 1995). Maintenance doses are usually required, or symptoms are likely to return (Rasmussen et al., 1993).

The main problem with antidepressants is that they are relatively slow-acting. In addition, more often than not, depressed patients have to try several different antidepressants before finding one that is effective. A severely depressed patient would need at least 2 to 6 weeks to obtain relief, and 30% don't respond at all. This can be too risky for suicidal patients. Thus, antidepressant drugs are not the treatment of choice if suicide is an imminent danger. In such cases many experts consider electroconvulsive therapy the preferred treatment.

Electroconvulsive Therapy: The Controversy Continues

Electroconvulsive therapy (ECT), or electric shock, was widely used as a treatment for several mental disorders until the introduction of the antipsychotic and antidepressant drugs in the 1950s. ECT developed a bad reputation, partly because it was misused and overused in the 1940s and 1950s. Today ECT is an effective treatment for severe depression (Coryell, 1998) and also yields marked improvement or remission in 80% of manic patients who have not been helped by lithium (Fink, 1997).

If you were to have electroconvulsive therapy, what could you expect? Two electrodes would be placed on your head, and a mild electric current would be passed through your brain for 1–2 seconds. Immediately after the shock was administered, you would lose consciousness and experience a seizure lasting about 30 seconds to 1 minute. Apparently the seizure is necessary if ECT is to have any effect. The complete ECT procedure takes about 5 minutes, and medical complications following the procedure are said to be rare (Abrams, 1988). Usually there is no pain associated with the treatment, and patients have no memory of the experience when they wake up. Normally ECT is given three times per week for 2 to 4 weeks (Sackeim, 1985).

Although ECT can cut depression short, it is not a cure. Experts think that the seizure temporarily changes the biochemical balance in the brain, which in turn results in a lifting of depression. When ECT is effective, cerebral blood flow in the prefrontal cortex is reduced (Nobler et al., 1994), and delta waves (usually associated with slow-wave sleep) appear (Sackeim et al., 1996).

For what purpose is electroconvulsive therapy (ECT) used, and what is its major side effect?

Link It!

In electroconvulsive therapy a mild electric current is passed through the brain for 1–2 seconds, causing a brief seizure.

The Side Effects of ECT   Some psychiatrists and neurologists have spoken out against the use of ECT, claiming that it causes pervasive brain damage and memory loss (Breggin, 1979; Friedberg, 1977). However, no structural brain damage from ECT has been revealed in studies comparing MRI or CT scans before and after a series of treatments (Devanand et al., 1994).

Even advocates of ECT acknowledge that there are side effects, the most disturbing of which is memory loss. The memory loss appears to result from a temporary disruption of memory consolidation that, in most cases, lasts for only a few weeks. Some patients have a spotty memory loss of events that happened before ECT (Sackeim et al., 1993). But in a few patients the memory loss may last longer than 6 months (Sackeim, 1992). According to the National Institute of Mental Health (1985), a majority of psychiatrists believe that there is a legitimate place for ECT in the treatment of severely depressed patients who are suicidal or who have not been helped by any other therapy.

Psychosurgery: Cutting to Cure

What is psychosurgery, and for what problems is it used?

An even more drastic procedure than ECT is **psychosurgery**—brain surgery performed strictly to alleviate serious psychological disorders, such as severe depression, severe anxiety, or obsessions, or to provide relief from unbearable chronic pain. Psychosurgery is *not* the same as other brain surgery performed to correct a physical problem, such as removing a tumor or blood clot.

The first experimental brain surgery for human patients was developed by Portuguese neurologist Egas Moniz in 1935 to treat severe phobias, anxiety, and obsessions. In his technique, the **lobotomy**, surgeons severed the neural connections between the frontal lobes and the deeper brain centers involved in emotion. But no brain tissue was removed. At first the procedure was considered a tremendous contribution, and it won for Moniz the Nobel Prize in Medicine in 1949. Not everyone considered it a positive contribution, however. One of Moniz's lobotomized patients curtailed the surgeon's activities by shooting him in the spine, leaving him paralyzed on one side.

Neurosurgeons performed tens of thousands of frontal lobotomies in the United States and elsewhere from 1935 until 1955. Although the surgery was effective in calming many patients, it often left them in a severely deteriorated condition. Apathy, impaired intellect, loss of motivation, and a change in personality kept many from resuming a normal life.

In the mid-1950s, when antipsychotic drugs came into use, psychosurgery virtually stopped. Since that time there has been a "second wave" of psychosurgical procedures that are far less drastic than the lobotomies of decades past. Some of the most modern procedures result in less intellectual impairment because, rather than using conventional surgery, surgeons deliver electric currents through electrodes to destroy a much smaller, more localized area of brain tissue. In one procedure, called a *cingulotomy*, electrodes are used to destroy the cingulum, a small bundle of nerves connecting the cortex to the emotional centers of the brain. Several procedures, including cingulotomy, have been helpful for some extreme cases of obsessive compulsive disorder (Baer et al., 1995; Trivedi, 1996).

But even today the results of psychosurgery are still not predictable, and for better or for worse, the consequences are irreversible. For this reason, the treatment is considered experimental and absolutely a last resort.

THERAPIES AND THERAPISTS: MANY CHOICES

Evaluating the Therapies: Do They Work?

psychosurgery: Brain surgery to treat some severe, persistent, and debilitating psychological disorder or severe chronic pain.

lobotomy: A psychosurgery technique in which the nerve fibers connecting the frontal lobes to the deeper brain centers are severed.

How effective is psychotherapy? Several hundred studies have compared the effectiveness of psychotherapies against no treatment at all. Researchers Smith, Glass, and Miller (1980) reanalyzed 475 studies involving 25,000 patients. Using meta-analysis, they were able to combine the findings of the studies and compare various psychotherapies against no treatment. They concluded that "the average person who receives therapy is better off at the end of it than 80% of the persons who do not" (p. 87). Figure 13.1 shows the comparative effectiveness of various psychotherapies as reported by Smith and others (1980). Although this study revealed that psychotherapy is better than no treatment, it did not indicate that one type of therapy was clearly more effective than another. In other words, the different types of therapy—behavioral, psychodynamic, and cognitive—appeared to be more or less equally effective. Moreover, neither the length of treatment nor the therapists' years of experience appeared to be related to the effectiveness of treatment.

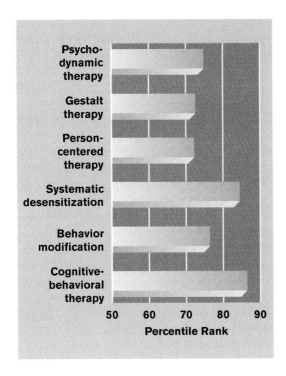

Figure 13.1

The Effectiveness of Different Types of Psychotherapy

Using meta-analysis, Smith, Glass, and Miller were able to combine the results of 475 studies involving 25,000 patients. These researchers compared the results of various psychotherapies against no treatment and concluded that, on the average, the people who received therapy were better off than about 80% of the people who received no therapy. The percentile ranks indicate how much better off those patients who received each type of therapy were than those who did not receive any therapy. (Data from Smith et al., 1980.)

Hans Eysenck (1994) takes issue with the conclusion that Smith and others (1980) reached in their meta-analysis. According to Eysenck's analysis of the data, psychodynamic, person-centered, Gestalt, and rational-emotive therapies were not significantly more effective than a placebo treatment. He found them to be significantly less effective than systematic desensitization, flooding, behavior modification, and cognitive therapy.

An even larger meta-analysis—a combined study of 302 other meta-analyses—revealed that psychological, educational, and behavioral treatment generally had "a strong, dramatic pattern of positive overall effects" (Lipsey & Wilson, 1993).

It is one thing for researchers to assess the comparative value of different therapies, but how do the patients themselves rate the therapies? To answer this question, *Consumer Reports* (1995) conducted the largest survey to date on patient attitudes toward psychotherapy. Martin Seligman (1995, 1996), a consultant for the study, summarized its findings:

■ Overall, patients believed that they benefited substantially from psychotherapy.

■ Patients seemed equally satisfied with their therapy, whether it was provided by a psychologist, a psychiatrist, or a social worker.

■ Specifically, patients who were in therapy for more than 6 months did considerably better; generally, the longer patients stayed in therapy, the more they improved.

■ Patients who took a drug such as Prozac or Xanax believed they were helped, but overall, psychotherapy alone seemed to work about as well as psychotherapy plus drugs.

According to Seligman (1995), under some conditions patients did not fare so well. "Patients whose length of therapy or choice of therapist was limited by insurance and managed care did worse" (p. 965).

Factors other than the type of therapy contribute to patient outcomes. One is the *therapeutic alliance*—the quality of the relationship between the individual patient and the therapist (Blatt et al., 1996). This factor affected treatment outcomes even when the patient received only drugs with no additional psychotherapy, according to one large study of depression (Krupnick et al., 1996). This study also revealed that 20% of individual differences in treatment outcome were accounted for by a close and positive relationship between patient and therapist.

Mental Health Professionals: How Do They Differ?

What different types of mental health professionals conduct psychotherapy?

According to one of the most comprehensive studies of the use of mental health services in the United States, 15 million people sought help during a recent year for substance use and mental health problems (Horgan, 1996). Troubled people turned to a variety of sources for help. As shown in Figure 13.2, 37.5% of all visits to professional or volunteer sources were made to psychiatrists, clinical psychologists, psychiatric social workers, and other trained mental health counselors. Practicing in the United States are 60,000 psychologists, 40,000 psychiatrists, 75,000 social workers, and relatively few who call themselves psychoanalysts (Horgan, 1996). Who are these mental health professionals, and for what problems are their services most appropriate?

For serious psychological disorders, a clinical psychologist or psychiatrist is the best source of help. A **clinical psychologist** specializes in the assessment, treatment, and/or research of psychological problems and behavioral disturbances, and usually has a PhD in clinical psychology. Clinical psychologists use various types of psychotherapy to treat a variety of psychological disorders and adjustment problems. Although clinical psychologists are not allowed to prescribe medications, the American Psychological Association is working toward gaining them this privilege (Kingsbury, 1996). While many psychologists applaud the APA's effort (DeLeon & Wiggins, 1996; Klein, 1996), others do not (DeNelsky, 1996; Hayes & Heiby, 1996).

A **psychiatrist** is a medical doctor with a specialty in the diagnosis and treatment of mental disorders. Psychiatrists can prescribe drugs and other biological treatments, and many also provide psychotherapy. A **psychoanalyst** is usually, but not always, a psychiatrist with specialized training in psychoanalysis from a psychoanalytic institute.

For clients with other psychological problems, such as adjustment disorders, substance abuse, and marital or family problems, the choice of mental health professionals widens and includes counseling psychologists, counselors, and psychiatric social workers. A counseling psychologist usually has a PhD in clinical or counseling psychology or a doctor of education degree (EdD) with a major in counseling. A counselor typically has a master's degree in psychology or counselor education. Often employed

clinical psychologist: A psychologist, usually with a PhD, whose training is in the diagnosis, treatment, or research of psychological and behavioral disorders.

psychiatrist: A medical doctor with a specialty in the diagnosis and treatment of mental disorders.

psychoanalyst (SY-ko-AN-ul-ist): A professional, usually a psychiatrist, with special training in psychoanalysis.

Figure 13.2
Where People Go for Help

People with mental health and substance use problems seek help from a variety of professional or volunteer sources. (Adapted from Narrow et al., 1993.)

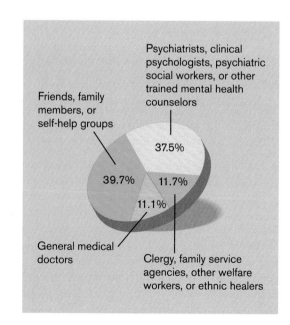

by colleges and universities, counseling psychologists and counselors help students with personal problems and/or test or counsel them in academic or vocational areas. A psychiatric social worker usually has a master's degree in social work (MSW) with specialized training in psychiatric problems, and may practice psychotherapy.

The entire range of mental health professionals may be found in private practice, in social agencies, or in hospital or clinic settings. There are hundreds of types of therapy, and in the past two decades there has been a trend among therapists toward *eclecticism*—incorporating techniques from many different therapies as appropriate, rather than practicing only one type of therapy exclusively.

Selecting a Therapy: Finding One That Fits

Is one therapy really better, on average, than other therapies? It seems obvious to ask which therapy, if any, is likely to be best for a specific person with a particular disorder, under the given circumstances. Therapists do not treat "average" persons; they treat people individually, and some therapies are more effective than others for treating certain disorders.

What therapy, if any, has proved to be the most effective in treating psychological disorders?

Insight therapies are often more effective for general feelings of unhappiness and interpersonal problems. Various types of behavior therapy are usually best for people with a specific problem behavior they want to change, such as a fear, phobia, bad habit, or some socially undesirable behavior. Specific phobias are successfully treated with flooding and systematic desensitization. Social phobia is better treated with either cognitive-behavioral therapy or exposure therapy (DeRubeis & Crits-Christoph, 1998), a high-potency benzodiazepine such as Xanax (Marshall et al., 1994), or an SSRI (Jefferson, 1995). Tricyclic antidepressants and benzodiazepines such as Xanax and Valium often relieve the symptoms of panic disorder (Davidson, 1997; Noyes et al., 1996). Cognitive or behavioral therapy also works well for panic disorder, and patients are less likely to relapse when therapy is complete than are patients treated with drugs alone (Pollack & Otto, 1997; Sharp et al., 1996). Obsessive compulsive disorder is best treated with exposure and response prevention (Foa, 1995) and/or SSRIs (Goodwin, 1996).

For depression, a variety of treatments have proved successful—tricyclic antidepressants, SSRIs, MAO inhibitors, cognitive therapy, and interpersonal therapy (DeRubeis & Crits-Christoph, 1998; Stahl, 1998). ECT is often effective for severely depressed people for whom other treatments have not worked and for suicidal individuals who need immediate help and cannot wait for the standard treatments to take effect. For bipolar disorder, lithium is the treatment of choice.

Conventional antipsychotics (neuroleptics) are prescribed for people suffering from schizophrenia. When these drugs are not effective or the patient cannot tolerate the side effects, atypical neuroleptics such as clozapine and resperidone are often helpful (Daniel & Whitcomb, 1998).

Review & Reflect 13.1 (on page 444) summarizes and compares major approaches to therapy.

Therapy and Race, Ethnicity, and Gender

There is a growing awareness that psychotherapists need to consider multicultural variables such as race, ethnicity, and gender in diagnosing and treating psychological disorders (Bernal & Castro, 1994). According to Kleinman and Cohen (1997), people experience and suffer from psychological and biological disorders within a cultural context in which the meaning of symptoms, outcomes, and responses to therapy may differ dramatically. The APA (1993) has issued "Guidelines for Providers of Psychological Services to Ethnic, Linguistic, and Culturally Diverse Populations." And for the first time, the American Psychiatric Association's *Diagnostic and Statistical Manual of Mental Disorders (Fourth Edition) (DSM-IV)* includes a section headed "Specific Culture,

Why is it important to consider multicultural variables in the therapeutic setting?

Type of Therapy	Perceived Cause of Disorder	Goals of Therapy	Methods Used	Primary Disorders Treated
Psycho-analysis	Unconscious sexual and aggressive urges or conflicts; fixations; weak ego	Help patient bring disturbing, repressed material to consciousness and work through unconscious conflicts; strengthen ego functions	Psychoanalyst analyzes and interprets dreams, free associations, resistances, and transference.	General feelings of unhappiness; unresolved problems from childhood
Person-centered therapy	Blocking of normal tendency toward self-actualization; incongruence between real and desired self; overdependence on positive regard of others	Increase self-acceptance and self-understanding; help patient become more inner-directed; increase congruence between real and desired self; enhance personal growth	Therapist shows empathy, unconditional positive regard, and genuineness, and reflects client's expressed feelings back to client.	General feelings of unhappiness; interpersonal problems
Behavior therapy	Learning of maladaptive behaviors or failure to learn appropriate behaviors	Extinguish maladaptive behaviors and replace with more adaptive ones; help patient acquire needed social skills	Therapist uses methods based on classical and operant conditioning and modeling, which include systematic desensitization, flooding, exposure and response prevention, aversion therapy, and reinforcement.	Fears, phobias, panic disorder, obsessive compulsive disorder, bad habits
Cognitive therapy	Irrational and negative assumptions and ideas about self and others	Change faulty, irrational, and/or negative thinking	Therapist helps client identify irrational and negative thinking and substitute rational thinking.	Depression, anxiety, panic disorder, general feelings of unhappiness
Biological therapies	Underlying physical disorder caused by structural or biochemical abnormality in the brain; genetic inheritance	Eliminate or control biological cause of abnormal behavior; restore balance of neurotransmitters	Physician prescribes drugs such as antipsychotics, antidepressants, lithium, or tranquilizers; ECT; or psychosurgery.	Schizophrenia, depression, bipolar disorder, anxiety disorders

Age, and Gender Features" for most psychological disorders and a description of disorders specific to particular cultures. Nevertheless, most graduate students in clinical and counseling psychology are not adequately trained to work with minority clients (Allison et al., 1994; Bernal & Castro, 1994).

When the cultures of the therapist and patient (client) differ markedly, behavior that is normal for the patient can be misinterpreted as abnormal by the therapist (Lewis-Fernández & Kleinman, 1994). Psychologists Sue and Sue (1990) identified four cultural barriers that hinder effective counseling: *cultural values*, *social class*, *language*, and *nonverbal communications* (gestures, facial expressions, and the like). For example, "an Asian American client who values restraint of strong feelings may be viewed by a counselor as repressed, inhibited, or unassertive" (Sue, 1994, p. 293).

There is dramatic evidence that language can pose a problem in both diagnosis and treatment. When a group of Puerto Rican patients took the Thematic Apperception Test (TAT) in English, their pauses and the choices of words they used to describe the TAT pictures were interpreted as indications of psychological problems. In fact, the patient's "problems" were with the language, which was not their native tongue (Suarez, 1983). A group of Mexican Americans interviewed in English were perceived as having more disorders in thinking and more emotional disorders than when they were interviewed in Spanish (Martinez, 1986).

When therapist and client have the same racial or ethnic background, they are more likely to share cultural values and communication styles, which can facilitate the counseling process.

Nonverbal behavior has different meanings for different cultural and ethnic groups. For example, making direct eye contact, which is presumed by many in the U.S. majority culture to connote honesty, interest, and self-confidence, is a gesture of disrespect among many Native Americans. The misinterpretation of this and other nonverbal communications partly helps to explain why so many Native Americans (over 50%) never return to non–Native American therapists after the first visit (Heinrich et al., 1990).

Race also accounts for some differences in the diagnosis and treatment of psychological disorders. Strakowski and others (1995) found that "Black patients were significantly more likely to be diagnosed with schizophrenia and substance abuse than similar White patients" (p. 101). And Blacks are more likely to be hospitalized involuntarily than their White counterparts under similar circumstances (Lawson et al., 1994).

The ability to generalize treatments to minority populations is compromised by the high volume of research studies that use only White populations in controlled settings (Matt & Navarro, 1997). For example, there are significant racial and gender differences in optimal therapeutic doses of some drugs used to treat mental disorders, including schizophrenia and bipolar disorder. Researcher Ken-Ming Lin discovered that a 2-milligram dose of the antipsychotic haloperidol relieved symptoms of schizophrenia in Asian patients, whereas 10 times that dose was required for White patients (Holden, 1991). And women generally need lower doses of most psychiatric drugs than men do (Yonkers & Hamilton, 1995). In spite of this difference, research to establish the dosage of drugs has been conducted largely on men, even though women use the drugs more often.

In therapy, one size does *not* fit all.

Apply It!

Finding a Therapist

People are often embarrassed to seek professional help for their psychological problems or are afraid that friends and relatives will think less of them if they do. Sometimes they are afraid of the therapy itself or afraid that seeking help means there is something funda-

mentally wrong with them. Such feelings may be understandable, but going to a psychotherapist when you are feeling anxious or depressed is no different from going to a doctor when you are feeling sick. When people have problems that have made them unhappy for a significant length of time, they should probably seek help from a trained pro-

fessional—a clinical or counseling psychologist, psychiatrist, psychiatric social worker, or mental health counselor. Such professionals are trained and licensed to work with people who are experiencing mental and emotional difficulties. (However, only psychiatrists, who are also medical doctors, can prescribe medication.)

According to the National Institute of Mental Health, asking three basic questions will determine whether a person is in need of professional help:

1. Is the person acting differently than usual?

2. Does the person complain of episodes of extreme, almost uncontrollable, anxiety or "nervousness"?

3. Does the person become aggressive, rude, and abusive over minor incidents?

Where to turn for help. Suppose that a friend agrees to seek help or that you feel you need therapy yourself. How would you go about finding a therapist? Don't just go to any therapist who happens to be nearby. Professional training and academic credentials are important, but they do not guarantee that you will receive high-quality treatment. A good place to start when searching for a therapist is to ask family members, friends, your doctor, or your psychology professor for recommendations. Another place to look is the psychology department or counseling center at your college or the psychiatry department of a local hospital or medical school. Many cities also have community mental health centers and human services agencies that can recommend therapists. In addition, some companies have employee assistance programs, which will offer counseling to employees or will refer them to an appropriate therapist.

Choosing a therapist. In considering a particular therapist, you should ask about his or her educational background, supervised experience, types of therapy practiced, length of treatment, and fees. The therapist must be one who is professionally trained to listen in a supportive fashion and to help you understand and interpret your thoughts and feelings. Bear in mind that many states place no restrictions on the use of the title "therapist." People who call themselves therapists may not actually be qualified to provide the kind of therapy you need. You can usually find out about a therapist's credentials by simply asking.

Take your time when choosing a therapist. A "good" therapist is one who is able to create an atmosphere of acceptance and sympathy. Because the relationship between client and therapist is an extremely important ingredient of successful therapy, it is essential to have a therapist whom you like and trust. The first step is to arrange for a brief consultation. If, during that initial interview, you find that you do not feel comfortable with the therapist, you should say so. Usually the therapist will be willing to recommend someone else.

Cost and other considerations. Like doctors, dentists, and other professionals, private therapists receive fees for their services. Some health insurance plans cover those fees; others do not. If you have insurance that covers psychotherapy, check to make sure that your policy covers the type of therapy you will be receiving. Also note any restrictions contained in the policy, such as limits on the number of sessions allowed.

Group therapy tends to be less expensive than individual therapy because several people share the cost. You can also receive less expensive therapy at public facilities such as community mental health centers. These are usually supported by tax revenues and therefore can charge clients on a sliding scale–that is, according to ability to pay. The services of a student counseling center are usually provided free or at a low cost.

Most forms of therapy that have been shown to be successful (for example, cognitive therapy for depression) do not require more than 20 sessions. Lengthy therapy is more expensive and has not been shown to be more effective than brief therapy. In a study of 854 psychotherapy outpatients, Kopta and others (1994) found that 50% had recovered after 2.5 months of therapy (11 sessions) and 75% had recovered after 58 sessions. Howard and others (1986) found that the greatest benefits of psychotherapy are gained within the first 6 months.

Therapy in an emergency. Some therapy needs cannot wait for an appointment. Many communities have hotlines that allow a person who needs immediate help to arrange counseling at any time–day or night. If a crisis does not involve violence, a mental health center or hospital emergency room may offer help. But if the crisis is more urgent–for example, if a friend is threatening to commit suicide–call the police.

SUMMARY AND REVIEW

INSIGHT THERAPIES

What are the four basic techniques of psychoanalysis, and how are they used to help disturbed patients?

The four basic techniques of psychoanalysis are free association, analysis of resistance, dream analysis, and analysis of transference. They are used to uncover the repressed memories, impulses, and conflicts presumed to be the cause of the patient's problems.

What are the role and the goal of the therapist in person-centered therapy?

Person-centered therapy is a nondirective therapy in which the therapist provides a climate of unconditional positive regard where clients are free to be themselves so that their natural tendency toward positive growth will be released.

What is the major emphasis in Gestalt therapy?

Gestalt therapy emphasizes the importance of clients' fully experiencing, in the present moment, their feelings, thoughts, and actions, and taking personal responsibility for their behavior.

What four problems commonly associated with major depression is interpersonal therapy designed to treat?

Interpersonal therapy (IPT) is designed to help depressed patients cope with severe responses to the death of a loved one, interpersonal role disputes, difficulties in adjusting to role transitions, and deficits in interpersonal skills.

What are some advantages of group therapy?

Group therapy is less expensive than individual therapy and gives people an opportunity to express feelings and get feedback from other group members and to give and receive help and emotional support.

Key Terms
psychotherapy (p. 424); insight therapy (p. 424); psychoanalysis (p. 425); free association (p. 425); resistance (p. 425); transference (p. 425); person-centered therapy (p. 426); self-actualization (p. 426); nondirective therapy (p. 426); Gestalt therapy (p. 427); directive therapy (p. 427); interpersonal therapy (IPT) (p. 427); family therapy (p. 428); group therapy (p. 428)

BEHAVIOR THERAPIES: UNLEARNING THE OLD, LEARNING THE NEW

What is a behavior therapy?

A behavior therapy is a treatment approach that employs the principles of operant conditioning, classical conditioning, and/or observational learning theory to replace inappropriate or maladaptive behaviors with more adaptive responses.

How do behavior therapists modify behavior using operant conditioning techniques?

Operant conditioning techniques involve the withholding of reinforcement to eliminate undesirable behaviors, as in time out, or the use of reinforcement to shape or increase the frequency of desirable behaviors, as in token economies.

What behavior therapies are based on classical conditioning?

Behavior therapies based on classical conditioning are systematic desensitization, flooding, exposure and response prevention, and aversion therapy.

How do therapists use systematic desensitization to rid people of fears?

Therapists using systematic desensitization train clients in deep muscle relaxation and then have them confront a series of graduated anxiety-producing situations, either real or imagined, until they can remain relaxed even when in the presence of the most feared situation.

What is flooding?

With flooding, clients are exposed to the feared object or event or asked to imagine it vividly for an extended period until their anxiety decreases and they realize that none of the dreaded consequences come to pass.

How does exposure and response prevention help people with obsessive compulsive disorder?

In exposure and response prevention, people with OCD are exposed to the anxiety-generating stimulus but gradually increase the time before they begin their compulsive rituals and thus learn to tolerate their anxiety.

How does aversion therapy rid a person of a harmful or undesirable behavior?

Aversion therapy pairs the unwanted behavior with an aversive stimulus until the bad habit becomes associated with pain or discomfort.

How does participant modeling help people overcome fears?

In participant modeling, an appropriate response is modeled in graduated steps and the client is asked to imitate each step with the encouragement and support of the therapist.

Key Terms
behavior therapy (p. 429); behavior modification (p. 429); token economy (p. 429); time out (p. 430); stimulus satiation (p. 430); systematic desensitization (p. 431); flooding (p. 432); exposure and response prevention (p. 432); aversion therapy (p. 433); participant modeling (p. 434)

COGNITIVE THERAPIES: IT'S THE THOUGHT THAT COUNTS

What is the aim of rational-emotive therapy?

Rational-emotive therapy is a directive form of therapy designed to challenge and modify the client's irrational beliefs, which are believed to be the cause of personal distress.

How does cognitive therapy help people overcome depression and anxiety disorders?

Cognitive therapy helps people overcome depression and anxiety disorders by pointing out the irrational thoughts causing them misery and by helping them learn other, more realistic ways of looking at themselves and their experience.

Key Terms
rational-emotive therapy (p. 434); automatic thoughts (p. 435); cognitive therapy (p. 436)

THE BIOLOGICAL THERAPIES

What are the three main biological therapies?

The three main biological therapies are drug therapy, ECT, and psychosurgery.

How do antipsychotic drugs help schizophrenic patients?

Antipsychotic drugs control the major symptoms of schizophrenia by inhibiting the activity of dopamine.

For what conditions are antidepressants prescribed?

Antidepressants are prescribed for depression, generalized anxiety disorder, panic disorder, agoraphobia, and obsessive compulsive disorder.

How does lithium help patients with bipolar disorder?

Lithium is used to control the symptoms in a manic episode and to even out the mood swings in bipolar disorder.

What are some of the problems with drug therapy?

Some problems are the drugs' unpleasant or dangerous side effects, the difficulty in establishing the proper dosages, and the fact that relapse is likely if the drug therapy is discontinued.

For what purpose is electroconvulsive therapy (ECT) used, and what is its major side effect?

ECT is a treatment of last resort for people with severe depression, and it is most often reserved for those who are in imminent danger of committing suicide. Some memory loss is its major side effect.

What is psychosurgery, and for what problems is it used?

Psychosurgery is brain surgery performed strictly to relieve some severe, persistent, and debilitating psychological disorder; it is considered experimental and highly controversial.

Key Terms

biological therapy (p. 436); antipsychotic drugs (p. 437); antidepressants (p. 437); lithium (p. 438); electroconvulsive therapy (ECT) (p. 439); psychosurgery (p. 440); lobotomy (p. 440)

THERAPIES AND THERAPISTS: MANY CHOICES

What different types of mental health professionals conduct psychotherapy?

Professionals trained to conduct psychotherapy fall into these categories: clinical psychologists, psychiatrists, psychoanalysts, counseling psychologists, counselors, and psychiatric social workers.

What therapy, if any, has proved to be the most effective in treating psychological disorders?

Although, overall, no one therapeutic approach has proved generally superior, specific therapies have proven effective in treating particular disorders.

Why is it important to consider multicultural variables in the therapeutic setting?

Multicultural variables such as race, ethnicity, and gender have a profound influence on patients' responses to the therapy and the therapist and on therapists' responses to patients.

Key Terms

clinical psychologist (p. 442); psychiatrist (p. 442); psychoanalyst (p. 442)

Study Guide for Chapter 13

Answers to all the Study Guide questions are provided at the end of the book.

Section One: Chapter Review

1. In psychoanalysis the technique whereby a patient reveals every thought, idea, or image that comes to mind is called _____; the patient's attempt to avoid revealing certain thoughts is called _____.
   a. transference; resistance
   b. free association; transference
   c. revelation; transference
   d. free association; resistance

2. (Person-centered, Gestalt) therapy is the directive therapy that emphasizes the importance of the client's fully experiencing, in the present moment, his or her thoughts, feelings, and actions.

3. (Person-centered, Gestalt) therapy is the nondirective therapy developed by Carl Rogers in which the therapist creates a warm, accepting climate so that the client's natural tendency toward positive change can be released.

4. (Psychodynamic, Humanistic) therapy presumes that the cause of the patient's problems are repressed memories, impulses, and conflicts.

5. Which depressed person would be least likely to be helped by interpersonal therapy (IPT)?
   a. Kirk, who is unable to accept the death of his wife
   b. Martha, who has been depressed since she was forced to retire
   c. Sharon, who was sexually abused by her father
   d. Tony, who feels isolated and alone because he has difficulty making friends

6. Which of the following is *not* true of group therapy?
   a. It allows people to get feedback from other members.
   b. It allows individuals to receive help and support from other members.
   c. It is not conducted by trained therapists.
   d. It is less expensive than individual therapy.

7. Self-help groups are generally ineffective, because they are not led by professionals. (true/false)

8. Techniques based on (classical, operant) conditioning are used to change behavior by reinforcing desirable behavior and removing reinforcers for undesirable behavior.

9. Behavior therapies based on classical conditioning are used mainly to
   a. shape new, more appropriate behaviors.
   b. rid people of fears and undesirable behaviors or habits.
   c. promote development of social skills.
   d. demonstrate appropriate behaviors.

10. Exposure and response prevention is a treatment for people with
    a. panic disorder.
    b. phobias.
    c. generalized anxiety disorder.
    d. obsessive compulsive disorder.

11. Match the description with the therapy.
    ____ (1) flooding
    ____ (2) aversion therapy
    ____ (3) systematic desensitization
    ____ (4) participant modeling
    a. practicing deep muscle relaxation during gradual exposure to feared object
    b. imagining painful or sickening stimuli associated with undesirable behavior
    c. being exposed directly to a feared object without relaxation
    d. imitating a model responding appropriately in a feared situation

12. Cognitive therapists believe that, for the most part, emotional disorders
    a. have physical causes.
    b. result from unconscious conflict and motives.
    c. result from faulty and irrational thinking.
    d. result from environmental stimuli.

13. Rational-emotive therapy is a nondirective therapy that requires a warm, accepting therapist. (true/false)

14. The goal of cognitive therapy is best described as helping people
    a. develop effective coping strategies.
    b. replace automatic thoughts with more objective thoughts.
    c. develop an external locus of control.
    d. develop realistic goals and aspirations.

15. Cognitive therapy has proved very successful in the treatment of
    a. depression and mania.
    b. schizophrenia.
    c. fears and phobias.
    d. anxiety disorders and depression.

16. For the most part, advocates of biological therapies assume that psychological disorders have a physical cause. (true/false)

17. Match the disorder with the drug most often used for its treatment.
    ____ (1) panic disorder and agoraphobia
    ____ (2) schizophrenia
    ____ (3) bipolar disorder
    ____ (4) depression
    ____ (5) obsessive compulsive disorder
    a. lithium
    b. antipsychotics
    c. antidepressants

18. Medication that relieves the symptoms of schizophrenia is thought to work by blocking the action of
    a. serotinin.   c. norepinephrine.
    b. dopamine.   d. epinephrine.

19. Which of the following is *not* true of drug therapy for psychological disorders?
    a. It is often difficult to determine the proper dose.
    b. Drugs often have unpleasant side effects.
    c. Patients often relapse if they stop taking the drugs.
    d. Drugs are usually not very effective.

20. For which disorder is ECT typically used?
    a. severe depression   c. anxiety disorders
    b. schizophrenia   d. panic disorder

21. The major side effect of ECT is tardive dyskinesia. (true/false)

22. Psychosurgery techniques are now so precise that the exact effects of the surgery can be predicted in advance. (true/false)

23. What is true regarding the effectiveness of therapies?
    a. All are equally effective for any disorder.
    b. Specific therapies have proved effective in treating particular disorders.
    c. Insight therapies are consistently best.
    d. Therapy is no more effective than no treatment for emotional and behavioral disorders.

24. Match the problem with the most appropriate therapy.
    ____ (1) fears, bad habits
    ____ (2) schizophrenia
    ____ (3) general unhappiness, interpersonal problems
    ____ (4) severe depression
    a. behavior therapy
    b. insight therapy
    c. drug therapy

25. One must have a medical degree to become a
    a. clinical psychologist.
    b. sociologist.
    c. psychiatrist.
    d. clinical psychologist, psychiatrist, or psychoanalyst.

26. The responses and outcomes of patients in therapy are (significantly, slightly) influenced by multicultural factors.

Section Two: Identify the Therapy

Indicate which type of therapy each sentence is describing: (a) psychoanalytic, (b) behavioral, (c) humanistic, (d) cognitive, (e) Gestalt, (f) interpersonal, or (g) biological.

____ 1. This is a directive therapy that has as an important objective "getting in touch with your feelings"; clients are encouraged to fully experience the present moment.

____ 2. This approach emphasizes early childhood experience and the conflicts one encounters in different stages of development; important concepts include free association and transference.

____ 3. Practitioners of this approach believe that faulty and irrational thinking results in emotional distress; a popular application of this approach is rational-emotive therapy.

____ 4. This therapy is considered a brief psychotherapy and is used in cases of depression due to problems such as the death of a loved one or deficits in interpersonal skills.

____ 5. This approach is based on the principles of learning theory and includes treatment strategies that use operant conditioning, classical conditioning, and observational learning.

_____ 6. This approach sees psychological problems as symptoms of underlying physical disorders and uses medical treatments such as drug therapy and electroconvulsive therapy.

_____ 7. This approach, often seen as being in direct opposition to psychoanalytic theory, views people as having free choice; clients are encouraged to seek personal growth and fulfill their potential.

Section Three: Fill In the Blank

1. Psychotherapy uses _____ rather than _____ means to treat emotional and behavioral disorders.

2. Helen begins to behave toward her therapist the same way she behaved toward a significant person in her past. The analyst would say that Helen is experiencing _____.

3. A therapy approach in which the therapist takes an active role in determining the course of therapy sessions and provides answers and suggestions to the client is known as _____ therapy.

4. One approach to treating depression is _____ therapy, which has been shown to be especially helpful for people dealing with problems such as severe bereavement and difficulty in adjusting to role transitions.

5. An approach that has been shown to be helpful for problems such as troubled or troublesome teenagers, alcoholic parents, and abusive family situations is _____ therapy.

6. Alcoholics Anonymous is the prototypical example of a _____ _____ _____.

7. The techniques of token economy, time out, and stimulus satiation are all based on _____ conditioning.

8. Jon acts out in class by throwing spitballs, making funny noises, and passing notes to classmates. The teacher decides to ignore Jon when he behaves this way, in the hope that withholding attention will reduce the behavior. The teacher is using a _____ _____ technique.

9. Rational-emotive therapy is a type of _____ therapy.

10. The class of drugs known as neuroleptics is mainly used to treat _____.

11. SSRIs and MAO inhibitors are drugs that are used mainly to treat _____.

12. Lithium is used to treat _____ _____.

13. Electroconvulsive therapy, although an extremely controversial method of therapy, may be the treatment of choice for patients suffering from _____ _____.

14. A _____ psychologist specializes in the assessment, treatment, and/or researching of psychological problems and behavioral disturbances.

15. The psychoanalytic technique that involves having patients reveal whatever thoughts or images come to mind is known as_____ _____.

16. Janet sends her son to his room for 20 minutes each time he misbehaves. Janet is using the behavior modification technique known as _____ _____.

17. A surgical technique known as _____ involves severing the nerve fibers connecting the frontal lobes and the deeper brain.

18. A _____ is usually a psychiatrist, with special training in psychoanalysis.

Section Four: Comprehensive Practice Test

1. On the first visit, your therapist asks you to reveal whatever thoughts, feelings, or images come to mind, no matter how trivial, embarrassing, or terrible they might seem. Your therapist is using a technique known as

   a. analysis of resistance.
   b. psychodrama.
   c. free association.
   d. stimulus satiation.

2. Which of the following is *not* considered an insight therapy?
   a. psychoanalysis
   c. rational-emotive therapy
   b. Gestalt therapy
   d. person-centered therapy

3. Which of the following is *not* one of the three conditions that Carl Rogers believed are required of therapists?
   a. unconditional positive regard
   b. sympathy
   c. genuineness
   d. empathy

4. Person-centered therapy is most effective when the therapist proposes valuable solutions and offers solid advice while directing the therapeutic process. (true/false)

5. In this directive form of therapy, the therapist helps, prods, or badgers clients to experience their feelings as deeply and genuinely as possible, and then to admit responsibility for them.
   a. behavioral modification
   b. psychodynamic therapy
   c. rational-emotive therapy
   d. Gestalt therapy

6. Which type of therapy seems to offer the most effective setting for treating adolescent drug abuse?
   a. family therapy
   c. person-centered therapy
   b. Gestalt therapy
   d. behavioral therapy

7. This therapy involves the application of principles of classical and operant conditioning.
   a. Gestalt therapy
   c. psychoanalysis
   b. behavior modification
   d. humanistic therapy

8. A therapist treating you for fear of heights takes you to the top floor of a tall building and asks you to look out the window toward the ground until she can see that your fear is significantly diminished. What technique is she using?
   a. flooding
   c. systematic desensitization
   b. psychodrama
   d. stimulus satiation

9. Which therapy emphasizes acceptance and unconditional positive regard?
   a. person-centered therapy
   b. cognitive therapy
   c. rational-emotive therapy
   d. psychoanalysis

10. A technique based on Bandura's observational learning theory is
    a. flooding.
    b. participant modeling.

    c. systematic desensitization.
    d. implosive therapy.

11. A type of therapy used to treat phobias that uses relaxation training techniques is called
    a. cognitive-behavioral therapy.
    b. systematic desensitization.
    c. psychoanalysis.
    d. client-centered therapy.

12. Which therapy style was developed by Fritz Perls?
    a. Gestalt therapy
    b. rational-emotive therapy
    c. client-centered therapy
    d. psychoanalysis

13. This biological therapy treatment procedure helps reduce symptoms of severe depression by producing a seizure in the patient.
    a. psychosurgery
    c. electroconvulsive therapy
    b. lobotomy
    d. chemotherapy

14. This biological therapy uses an electrical current to destroy a localized section of brain cells.
    a. psychosurgery
    b. prefrontal lobotomy
    c. electroconvulsive therapy
    d. chemotherapy

15. This group of drugs includes tricyclics, MOA inhibitors, and SSRIs.
    a. antimania drugs
    b. antidepressant drugs
    c. antianxiety drugs
    d. antipsychotic drugs

16. This group of drugs is used to treat symptoms including hallucinations and delusions.
    a. antimania drugs
    b. antidepressant drugs
    c. antianxiety drugs
    d. antipsychotic drugs

17. The most severe side effect of typical antipsychotic drugs is
    a. cramps.
    c. tardive dyskinesia.
    b. muscle spasms.
    d. mania.

18. In a major meta-analysis, researchers concluded that people who received therapy were better off than those who did not. (true/false)

19. The main problem with interpersonal therapy is the fact that it is so time-consuming. (true/false)

20. The B in Albert Ellis's ABC theory of rational-emotive therapy stands for *behavior.* (true/false)

Section Five: Critical Thinking

1. What are the major strengths and weaknesses of the following approaches to therapy: psychoanalysis, person-centered therapy, behavior therapy, cognitive therapy, and drug therapy?

2. From what you have learned in this chapter, prepare a strong argument to support each of these positions:
   a. Psychotherapy is generally superior to drug therapy in the treatment of psychological disorders.
   b. Drug therapy is generally superior to psychotherapy in the treatment of psychological disorders.

3. In selecting a therapist for yourself or advising a friend or family member, what are some important questions you would ask a therapist in order to determine whether he or she would be a good choice?

Social Psychology

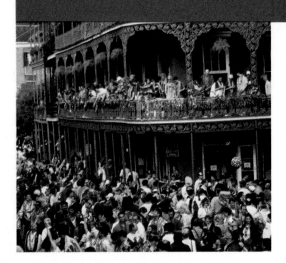

S unday mornings were usually quiet and peaceful in this college town, but not this particular Sunday morning. The scream of sirens split the air as the police conducted a surprise mass arrest, rounding up nine male college students. The students were searched, handcuffed, read their constitutional rights, and hauled off to jail. Here they were booked and fingerprinted, then transported to "Stanford County Prison." At the prison each student was stripped naked, searched, deloused, given a uniform and a number, and placed in a cell with two other prisoners. All of this was more than sufficiently traumatic, but then there were the guards in their khaki uniforms, wearing reflector sunglasses that made eye contact impossible and carrying clubs that resembled small baseball bats.

The prisoners had to get permission from the guards for the most simple, routine matters, such as writing a letter, smoking a cigarette, or even using the toilet. And the guards imposed severe punishments. Prisoners were made to do pushups while the guards sometimes stepped on them or forced another pris-

Section Five: Critical Thinking

oner to sit on them. Some prisoners were placed in solitary confinement. (Adapted from Zimbardo, 1972.)

But wait a minute! Something is wrong with this little scenario. People are not arrested, charged, and thrown into prison without a trial. What happened? In truth the guards were not guards and the prisoners were not prisoners. All were college students who had been selected to participate in a 2-week experiment on prison life conducted by Philip Zimbardo and colleagues (1973) at Stanford University. Guards and prisoners were selected randomly from a final pool of volunteers who had been judged mature, healthy, psychologically stable, law-abiding citizens. Those who were to be prisoners were not aware of their selection until they were "arrested" on that quiet Sunday morning.

This was only an experiment, but it became all too real—to the guards and especially to the prisoners. How could some of the guards, though mild-mannered pacifists as students, so quickly become sadistic, heartless tormentors in their new role? As one guard remembered it, surprised at his own behavior, he made prisoners clean the toilets with their bare hands and virtually viewed them as cattle. The prisoners fell into their roles quickly as well. How could autonomous, self-respecting students allow themselves to become debased and subservient in their captivity, to suffer physical and mental abuse, and to behave as if they were real prisoners? The experiment was to be run for 2 weeks but had to be called off after only 6 days.

"Only an experiment"—but do real-life roles affect people's behavior so dramatically? We will explore this and many other interesting questions in our study of social psychology.

INTRODUCTION TO SOCIAL PSYCHOLOGY

Social psychology is the area of study that attempts to explain how the actual, imagined, or implied presence of others influences the thoughts, feelings, and behavior of individuals. No human being lives in a vacuum, alone and apart from other people. We are truly social animals, and our social nature—how we think about, respond to, and interact with other people—provides the territory that social psychology explores. Research in social psychology yields some surprising and provocative answers to puzzling human behavior, from the atrocious to the altruistic.

This chapter explores social perception—how people form impressions of others and try to understand why they behave as they do. What are the factors involved in attraction? What draws people to one another, and how do friendships and romantic relationships develop? We will look at factors influencing conformity and obedience and will examine groups and their influence on performance and decision making. We will also discuss attitudes and learn how they can be changed,

social psychology: The study of how the actual, imagined, or implied presence of others influences the thoughts, feelings, and behavior of individuals.

and then we will explore prejudice and discrimination. Finally, we will look at the conditions under which people are likely to help each other (prosocial behavior) and hurt each other (aggression).

To start, let's consider how social psychologists conduct their studies. You may have seen the TV show *Candid Camera*, which showed people "caught in the act of being themselves." Secretly videotaped by a hidden camera, ordinary individuals caught in various social situations provided the humorous, sometimes hilarious, material for the show. This is precisely what researchers in social psychology must do in most of their studies—catch people in the act of being themselves. For this reason deception has traditionally played a prominent part in their research. To accomplish this deception, the researcher often must use one or more **confederates**—people who pose as participants in a psychology experiment but who are actually assisting the experimenter. A **naive subject** is an actual participant who has agreed to participate but is not aware that deception is being used to conceal the real purpose of the experiment. You will see why it is often necessary to conceal the purpose of an experiment as you read about some classic studies in social psychology.

SOCIAL PERCEPTION

We spend a significant portion of our lives in contact with other people. Not only do we form impressions of others, but we also attempt to understand why they behave as they do.

Impression Formation: Sizing Up the Other Person

What first impression have you formed of the person shown here?

Why are first impressions so important and enduring?

When we meet people for the first time, we begin forming impressions about them right away, and, of course, they are busily forming impressions of us. Naturally we notice the obvious attributes first—gender, race, age, dress, and how physically attractive or unattractive someone appears. Physical attractiveness, as shallow as it might seem, has a definite impact on first impressions. Beyond noticing physical appearance, we may wonder: What is her occupation? Is he married? Answers to such questions, combined with a conscious or an unconscious assessment of the person's verbal and nonverbal behavior, all play their part in forming a first impression. Moods also play a part—when we are happy, our impressions of others are usually more positive than when we are unhappy (Forgas & Bower, 1987). Even how frequently people blink their eyes has an impact on the impression they make. Those who blink frequently tend to be rated as more nervous and less intelligent (Omori & Miyata, 1996). First impressions are powerful and can color many of the later impressions we form about people.

A number of studies reveal that an overall impression or judgment of another person is influenced more by the first information received about the person than by information that comes later (Luchins, 1957; Park, 1986). This phenomenon is called the **primacy effect**. It seems that we attend to initial information more carefully, and once an impression is formed, it provides the framework through which we interpret later information. Any information that is consistent with the first impression is likely to be accepted, thus strengthening the impression. Information that does not fit with the earlier information is more likely to be disregarded.

Remember, any time you list your personal traits or qualities, always list your most positive qualities first. It pays to put your best foot forward—first.

Expectancies: Seeing What We Expect to See Sometimes expectations about how other persons will act in a situation become self-fulfilling prophecies and actually influence the way they do act. Expectations may be based on a person's gender, age, racial or ethnic group, social class, role or occupation, personality traits, past behavior, relationship to us, and so on. Once formed, our expectancies affect how we perceive the behavior of others—what we pay attention to and ignore. But expectations may also color our attitude, manner, and treatment of that person in such a way that we partly bring about the very behavior we expect (Jones, 1986; Miller & Turnbull, 1986).

Attribution: Explaining Behavior

Why do people do the things they do? To answer this question, we all make **attributions**—that is, we assign or attribute causes to explain the behavior of others and to explain our own behavior as well. People are particularly interested in the causes of behaviors when the behaviors are unexpected, when goals are not attained (Weiner, 1985), or when actions are not socially desirable (Jones & Davis, 1965).

Although we can actually observe others' behavior, we can usually only infer its cause or causes. In trying to determine why we or someone else behaved in a certain way, we might make a **situational attribution** (an external attribution) and attribute the behavior to some external cause or factor operating within the situation. After failing an exam, we might say, "The test was unfair" or "The professor didn't teach the material well." Or we might make a **dispositional attribution** (an internal attribution) and attribute the behavior to some internal cause such as a personal trait, motive, or attitude. We might attribute a poor grade to our own lack of ability or to a poor memory.

Attributional Biases: Different Attributions for Self and Others   There are basic differences in the way people make attributions about their own behavior and that of others (Jones, 1976, 1990; Jones & Nisbett, 1971). We tend to use situational attributions to explain our own behavior, because we are aware of factors in the situation that influenced us to act as we did. Also, being aware of our past behavior, we know whether our present actions are typical or atypical.

In explaining the behavior of others, however, people have a consistent tendency to focus more on personal factors than on the factors operating within the situation (Gilbert & Malone, 1995; Leyens et al., 1996). Not knowing how a person has behaved in different situations in the past, we assume a consistency in the behavior. Thus, we are likely to attribute the behavior to some personal quality. The tendency to overemphasize internal factors and underemphasize situational factors when we explain other people's behavior is so fundamental, so commonplace, that it has been named the **fundamental attribution error** (Ross, 1977).

In the United States, the plight of the homeless and of people on welfare is often attributed to laziness, an internal attribution, rather than to factors in their situation that might explain their condition. The fundamental attribution error is not universal, however. In India, for example, middle-class adults tend to make situational attributions for deviant behavior, attributing it to "role, status, or caste, and kin structures" rather than to internal dispositions (Pepitone & Triandis, 1987, p. 492).

There is one striking inconsistency in the way we view our own behavior: the self-serving bias. We use the **self-serving bias** when we attribute our successes to internal or dispositional causes and blame our failures on external or situational causes (Baumgardner et al., 1986; Brown & Rogers, 1991). If we interview for a job and get it, it is probably because we have the right qualifications. If someone else gets the job, it is probably because he or she knew the right people. The self-serving bias allows us to take credit for our successes and shift the blame for our failures to the situation.

Roesch and Amirkhan (1997) analyzed statements by professional athletes quoted in newspaper articles for evidence of the self-serving bias. And, indeed, athletes did tend to credit their wins to internal factors (their own skills) and to attribute their losses to situational factors (bad luck, poor referees).

What is the difference between a situational attribution and a dispositional attribution for a specific behavior?

 Link It!

How do the kinds of attributions people tend to make about themselves differ from those they make about other people?

attribution: An inference about the cause of one's own or another's behavior.

situational attribution: Attribution of a behavior to some external cause or factor operating in the situation; an external attribution.

dispositional attribution: Attribution of a behavior to some internal cause, such as a personal trait, motive, or attitude; an internal attribution.

fundamental attribution error: The tendency to overemphasize internal causes and underemphasize situational factors when explaining the behavior of others.

self-serving bias: The tendency to attribute personal successes to dispositional causes and failures to situational causes.

ATTRACTION

Think for a moment about the people you consider to be your closest friends. What causes you to like or even love one person yet ignore or react negatively to someone else? What factors influence interpersonal attraction—the degree to which people are drawn to or like one another?

Factors Influencing Attraction: Magnets That Draw People Together

Some of the factors influencing attraction are within the situation and some are within the person.

Why is proximity an important factor in attraction?

Proximity: Closeness Counts   One major factor influencing the choice of friends is physical **proximity**, or geographic closeness. If you live in an apartment complex, you are probably more friendly with people who live next door or only a few doors away (Festinger et al., 1950). The same is true in a dormitory (Priest & Sawyer, 1967). What about the people you like best in your classes? Do they sit next to you or not more than a seat or two away?

Why is proximity so important? It is much less trouble to make friends or even fall in love with people who are close at hand. Physical proximity also increases the frequency of interaction, and mere exposure to people, objects, and circumstances usually increases our liking for them (Zajonc, 1968). The **mere-exposure effect** is the tendency to feel more positively toward stimuli with repeated exposure. People, food, songs, and styles become more acceptable the more we are exposed to them. Advertisers rely on the positive effects of repeated exposure to increase people's liking for products and even for political candidates.

There are exceptions to the mere-exposure effect, however. If your initial reaction to a person is highly negative, frequent exposure can make you feel even more negatively toward the person (Swap, 1977). In addition, those who value privacy may react less favorably when proximity results in repeated contacts with people (Larson & Bell, 1988).

Liking through Association: A Case of Classical Conditioning   Our moods and emotions, whether positive or negative, can influence how much we are attracted to people we meet (Cunningham, 1988). And sometimes we may develop positive or negative feelings toward others simply because they are present when very good or very bad things happen to us. Then through classical conditioning, other people can become associated with the pleasant or unpleasant event and the resulting good or bad feelings may rub off on them (Riordan & Tedeschi, 1983).

Reciprocal Liking: Liking Those Who Like Us   We tend to like the people who also like us—or who we *believe* like us. Curtis and Miller (1986) falsely led participants to believe that another person either liked or disliked them after an initial encounter. This false information became a self-fulfilling prophecy. When the participants met the person again, those who believed they were liked "self-disclosed more, disagreed less, expressed dissimilarity less, and had a more positive tone of voice and general attitude than subjects who believed they were disliked" (p. 284). These positive behaviors, in turn, actually caused the other person to view them positively. The moral of this story seems easy to grasp: If you want others to like you, like them first!

How important is physical attractiveness in attraction?

Attractiveness: Good Looks Attract   Although people are quick to deny that mere physical appearance is the main factor that attracts them to someone initially, a substantial body of evidence indicates that it is. People of all ages have a strong tendency to prefer physically attractive people. Even 6-month-old infants, when given the chance to look at a photograph of an attractive or an unattractive woman, man, or infant, will spend more time looking at the attractive face (Langlois et al., 1991). More than 2,000 years ago Aristotle said, "Beauty is a greater recommendation than any letter of introduction." Apparently, it still is.

Link It!

What constitutes physical beauty? Researchers Langlois and Roggman (1990) reported that physical beauty consists not of rare physical qualities but of facial features that are approximately the mathematical average of the features in a given general population. And the more faces the researchers averaged, the more attractive the computer-generated composite representing the average face became. But Perrett and others (1994) found that simply averaging facial features can only partially account for facial beauty. These researchers generated two composite images, one of 60 White female faces and another of the most attractive 15 of the 60 faces. Then, by exaggerating the differences between the two composite images, they derived the most attractive image, with larger eyes, higher cheekbones, and a thinner jaw. Averaging faces tends to make them more symmetrical. And symmetrical faces and bodies are seen as more attractive and sexually appealing (Singh, 1995; Thornhill & Gangestad, 1994).

Do males from different cultures have similar ideas about the physical attractiveness of females? Cunningham and others (1995) found that, for the most part, they do. When native Asian, Hispanic, and White American male students rated photographs of Asian, Hispanic, Black, and White females on attractiveness, the researchers reported a very high mean correlation (.93) among the groups in attractiveness ratings. When Black and White American men rated photos of Black women, their agreement on facial features was also very high—a correlation of .94. But Black and White men differed on attractiveness from the neck down; Black men were more attracted than White men to women with heavier figures.

A meta-analysis by Vicki Ritts and others (1992) "indicated that physically attractive students are usually judged more favorably by teachers on a number of dimensions, including intelligence, academic potential, grades, and various social skills" (p. 413).

Why is physical attractiveness so important? When people have one trait or quality that we either admire or dislike very much, we often assume that they also have other admirable or negative traits—a phenomenon known as the **halo effect** (Nisbett & Wilson, 1977; Thorndike, 1920). Dion and others (1972) found that people generally attribute other favorable qualities to those who are attractive. Attractive people are seen as more exciting, personable, interesting, and socially desirable than unattractive people.

The halo effect—the attribution of other favorable qualities to those who are attractive—helps explain why physical attractiveness is so important.

Feingold (1992) conducted several meta-analyses that shed more light on the relationship between physical attractiveness and certain personality characteristics and social behaviors. One meta-analysis confirmed that positive characteristics are, indeed, attributed to physically attractive people. Feingold also discovered a positive correlation between a person's *self-rated* physical attractiveness and many attributes—self-esteem, popularity with the opposite sex, social comfort, extroversion, mental health, and sexual experience. The moral of this story seems to be that if you believe you are physically attractive, others will also perceive you as attractive.

Other than "believing" you are physically attractive, what else can you do to increase your attractiveness to others? Try smiling more. A study by Reis and others (1990) revealed that smiling increases the perceived attractiveness of others and makes them appear more sincere, sociable, and competent.

Eagly and others (1991) analyzed 76 studies of the physical attractiveness stereotype. They found that physical attractiveness has its greatest impact on judgments of popularity and sociability and less impact on judgments of adjustment and intellectual competence. They did find one negative, however. Attractive people are perceived as more vain and less modest than less attractive people.

Job interviewers are more likely to recommend highly attractive people (Dipboye et al., 1975), and attractive people have their written work evaluated more

halo effect: The tendency to infer generally positive or negative traits in a person as a result of observing one major positive or negative trait.

favorably (Landy & Sigall, 1974). Even the evaluation of the attractiveness of a person's voice is affected by the person's physical appearance (Zuckerman et al., 1991).

Being attractive is an advantage to children and adults, to males and females; but according to some studies, women's looks contribute more to how they are judged on other personal qualities than do men's looks (Bar-Tal & Saxe, 1976; Feingold, 1990). Physical attractiveness seems to have its greatest impact in the context of romantic attraction, particularly in initial encounters (Hatfield & Sprecher, 1986; Feingold, 1988). Attractiveness is even an advantage for infants. According to Langlois and others (1995), mothers of attractive infants are more playful and affectionate with them than are mothers of less attractive infants. Mothers with less attractive infants have more negative attitudes toward them than do mothers with attractive infants.

Does this mean that unattractive people don't have a chance? Fortunately not. Eagly and her colleagues (1991) suggest that the impact of physical attractiveness is strongest in the perception of strangers. But once we get to know people, other qualities assume more importance. In fact, as we come to like people, they begin to look more attractive to us, while people with undesirable personal qualities begin to appear less attractive.

Are people, as a rule, more attracted to those who are opposite or to those who are similar to them?

Similarity: A Strong Basis of Attraction   To sum up research on attraction, the saying "Birds of a feather flock together" is more accurate than "Opposites attract." Beginning in elementary school and continuing through life, people are more likely to pick friends of the same age, gender, race, and socioeconomic class. Choosing friends who are similar to us could be related to proximity—the fact that we tend to come into contact with people who are similar to us in a variety of ways.

Liking people who have similar attitudes begins early in childhood and continues throughout life in both sexes (Griffitt et al., 1972). We are likely to choose friends and lovers who have similar views on most things that are important to us. Similar interests and attitudes toward leisure-time activities make it more likely that time spent together is rewarding. Not only is similarity in attitudes an important ingredient in attraction (Newcomb, 1956), but people often have negative feelings toward others whose attitudes differ from their own (Byrne et al., 1986; Smeaton et al., 1989). People who share our attitudes validate our judgments; those who disagree with us suggest the possibility that we are wrong and arouse negative feelings in us. It is similarities, then, not differences, that usually stimulate liking and loving (Alicke & Largo, 1995).

Romantic Attraction

The Matching Hypothesis: Peas in a Pod   Can you imagine reading this ad in the personals column of your newspaper?

> Moderately attractive, unskilled, unemployed, 50-year-old divorced man with 7 children seeks beautiful, wealthy, exciting woman between ages of 20 and 30 for companionship, romance, and possible marriage. No smokers or drinkers, please.

Even though most of us may be attracted to handsome or beautiful people, the **matching hypothesis** suggests that we are likely to end up with someone similar to ourselves in attractiveness and other assets (Berscheid et al., 1971; Feingold, 1988; Walster & Walster, 1969). Furthermore, couples mismatched in attractiveness are more likely to end the relationship (Cash & Janda, 1984).

It has been suggested that we estimate our social assets and realistically expect to attract someone with approximately equal assets. In terms of physical attractiveness, some people might consider a movie star or supermodel to be the ideal man or woman, but they do not seriously consider the ideal to be a realistic, attainable possibility. Fear of rejection keeps many people from pursuing those who are much more attractive than they are. But instead of marrying an extremely handsome man,

matching hypothesis: The notion that people tend to have spouses, lovers, or friends who are approximately equivalent in social assets such as physical attractiveness.

a very beautiful woman may sacrifice physical attractiveness for money and social status. Extremely handsome men have been known to make similar "sacrifices."

What about same-sex friendships? The matching hypothesis is generally applicable to such friendships (Cash & Derlega, 1978), although it is more true of males than of females (Feingold, 1988). A person's perceived attractiveness seems to be affected in part by the attractiveness of his or her friends (Geiselman et al., 1984).

Mate Selection: The Mating Game

Robert Winch (1958) proposes that men and women tend to choose mates with needs and personalities that are complementary rather than similar to their own. Winch sees complementary needs not necessarily as opposite, but as needs that supply what the partner lacks. A talkative person may seek a quiet mate who prefers to listen. There is some support for this view (Dryer & Horowitz, 1997).

The weight of research, however, indicates that similarity in needs is mainly what attracts (Buss, 1984; Phillips et al., 1988). Similarity in personality and in "physical characteristics, cognitive abilities, age, education, religion, ethnic background, attitudes and opinions, and socioeconomic status" is related to marital choice (O'Leary & Smith, 1991, p. 196). And similarity in needs and in personality appears to be related to marital success as well as to marital choice (O'Leary & Smith, 1991). Similarities wear well.

If you were to select a marriage partner, what qualities would attract you? Complete the *Try It!* to evaluate your own preferences.

Link It!

Try It!

In your choice of a mate, which qualities are most and least important to you? Rank these 18 qualities of a potential mate from most important (1) to least important (18) to you.

_____ Ambition and industrious- ness

_____ Chastity (no previous sexual intercourse)

_____ Desire for home and children

_____ Education and intelligence

_____ Emotional stability and ma- turity

_____ Favorable social status or rating

_____ Good cooking and house- keeping skills

_____ Similar political background

_____ Similar religious background

_____ Good health

_____ Good looks

_____ Similar education

_____ Pleasing disposition

_____ Refinement/neatness

_____ Sociability

_____ Good financial prospects

_____ Dependable character

_____ Mutual attraction/love

How do your selections in the *Try It!* compare with those of men and women from 33 countries and 5 major islands around the world? Generally men and women across cultures rate these four qualities as most important in mate selection: (1) mutual attraction/love, (2) dependable character, (3) emotional stability and maturity, and (4) pleasing disposition (Buss et al., 1990). Aside from these first four choices, however, women and men differ somewhat in the attributes they prefer. According to Buss (1994), "Men prefer to mate with beautiful young women, whereas women prefer to mate with men who have resources and social status" (p. 239). These preferences, he claims, have been adaptive in human evolutionary history. To a male, beauty and youth suggest health and fertility—the best opportunity to send his genes into the next generation. To a female, resources and social status provide security for her and her children (Buss, 1997).

conformity: Changing or adopting an attitude or behavior to be consistent with the norms of a group or the expectations of others.

norms: The attitudes and standards of behavior expected of members of a particular group.

What did Asch find in his famous experiment on conformity?

Figure 14.1

Asch's Classic Study of Conformity

If you were one of eight participants in the Asch experiment who were asked to pick the line (1, 2, or 3) that matched the standard line shown above them, which line would you choose? If the other participants all chose line 3, would you conform and answer line 3? (Based on Asch, 1955.)

CONFORMITY, OBEDIENCE, AND COMPLIANCE

Conformity: Going Along with the Group

To conform or not to conform—that is not the question for most of us. Rather, the question is, to *what* will we conform? **Conformity** is changing or adopting a behavior or an attitude in order to be consistent with the norms of a group or the expectations of other people. **Norms** are the standards of behavior and the attitudes that are expected of members of the group. Some conformity is necessary if we are to have a society at all. We cannot drive on any side of the street we please, park any place we want, or drive as fast as we choose when in a hurry.

Because we need other people, we must conform to their expectations, to some extent, in order to have their esteem, their love, or even their company. It is easy to see why people conform to norms and standards of groups that are important to them, such as their family, peer group, social group, or team. But to an amazing degree, people also conform to the majority opinion, even when they are among a group of strangers.

Asch's Experiment: The Classic on Conformity The best-known experiment on conformity was conducted by Solomon Asch (1951, 1955), who designed the simple test shown in Figure 14.1. Look at the standard line, and then pick the line—1, 2, or 3—that is the same length. Did you pick line 2? Can you imagine any circumstances in which a person might tell the experimenter that either line 1 or line 3 matched the standard line? This is exactly what happened in Asch's classic experiment, even with tests so simple that participants could pick the correct line over 99% of the time.

Eight male participants were seated around a large table and were asked, one by one, to tell the experimenter which of the three lines matched the standard line as in Figure 14.1. But only one of the eight was an actual participant; the others were confederates assisting the experimenter. There were 18 trials—18 different lines to be matched. During 12 of these trials, the confederates all gave the same wrong answer, which of course puzzled the naive participant. Would that participant continue to believe his eyes and select the correct line, or would he feel pressure to conform to the group selections and give the wrong answer himself?

Asch found that 5% of the subjects conformed to the incorrect, unanimous majority *all* of the time, 70% conformed *some* of the time, but 25% remained completely independent and were *never* swayed by the group.

In this scene from Asch's experiment on conformity, all but one of the "subjects" were really confederates of the experimenter. They deliberately chose the wrong line to try to influence the naive subject (second from right) to go along with the majority.

Asch wondered how group size would influence conformity. Varying the experiment with groups of 2, 3, 4, 8, and 10–15, he found that unanimous majorities of 15 produced no higher conformity rate than did those of 3. Asch also discovered that when just one confederate in the group disagreed with the incorrect majority, the naive subjects' errors dropped drastically, from 32% to 10.4%.

Other research on conformity reveals that people of low status are more likely to conform than those of high status (Eagly, 1987); but, contrary to the conventional wisdom, women are no more likely to conform than men (Eagly & Carli, 1981). And conformity is even greater if the sources of influence are perceived as belonging to one's own group (Abrams et al., 1990).

According to Wood and others (1994), those who hold minority opinions on an issue have more influence in changing a majority view if they present a well-organized, clearly stated argument. And minorities who are especially consistent in advocating their views are more influential.

Obedience: Following Orders

Some obedience is necessary if civilized society is to function, but unquestioned obedience can cause humans to commit unbelievably horrible acts. During World War II, the civilized world was stunned and sickened by the revelations of the Nazi death camps, and nearly everyone wondered what type of person could be capable of committing such atrocities. Stanley Milgram, a young researcher at Yale University in 1961, wondered, too. He designed a study to investigate how far ordinary citizens would go to obey orders, even if obedience meant the injury or possible death of a fellow human being.

The Milgram Study: The Classic on Obedience   Back in the 1960s, an advertisement appeared in newspapers in New Haven, Connecticut, and other communities near Yale University.

> Wanted: Volunteers to serve as subjects in a study of memory and learning at Yale University.

Many people responded to the ad, and 40 male participants between the ages of 20 and 50 were selected, among them "postal clerks, high school teachers, salesmen, engineers, and laborers" (Milgram, 1963, p. 372). Yet no experiment on memory and learning was to take place. Instead, a staged drama was planned in which only one actual participant would be involved at a time. Imagine that you are one of the naive participants selected for the experiment.

The researcher actually wants to know how far you will go in obeying orders to administer what you believe to be increasingly painful electric shocks to a "learner" who misses questions on a test. The cast of characters is as follows:

> *The Experimenter:* A 31-year-old high school biology teacher dressed in a gray laboratory coat who assumes a stern and serious manner
> *The Learner:* A pleasant, heavyset accountant about 50 years of age (an accomplice of the experimenter)
> *The Teacher:* You—the only naive member of the cast

The experimenter leads you and the learner into one room, where the learner is strapped into an electric-chair apparatus. You, the teacher, are delivered a sample shock of 45 volts, which stings you and is supposedly for the purpose of testing the equipment and showing you what the learner will feel. The learner complains of a heart condition and says that he hopes the electric shocks will not be too painful. The experimenter admits that the stronger shocks will hurt but hastens to add, "Although the shocks can be extremely painful, they cause no permanent tissue damage" (p. 373).

What did Milgram find in his classic study of obedience?

At top is the shock generator used by Milgram in his famous experiment. Below is the learner (actually an accomplice) being strapped into his chair by the experimenter and the unsuspecting participant.

compliance: Acting in accordance with the wishes, the suggestions, or the direct request of another person.

foot-in-the-door technique: A strategy designed to secure a favorable response to a small request at first, with the aim of making the person more likely to agree later to a larger request.

door-in-the-face technique: A strategy in which someone makes a large, unreasonable request with the expectation that the person will refuse but will then be more likely to respond favorably to a smaller request at a later time.

low-ball technique: A strategy to gain compliance by making a very attractive initial offer to get a person to agree to an action and then making the terms less favorable.

Then the experimenter takes you to an adjoining room, out of sight of the learner. The experimenter seats you in front of an instrument panel (shown in the photograph), with 30 lever switches arranged horizontally across the front. The first switch on the left, you are told, delivers only 15 volts, but each successive switch is 15 volts stronger than the last—30 volts, 45 volts, and so on up to the last switch, which carries 450 volts. The switches on the instrument panel are labeled with designations ranging from "Slight Shock" to "Danger: Severe Shock."

The experimenter explains that you are to read a list of word pairs to the learner and then test his memory. When the learner makes the right choice, you go on to the next pair. If the learner misses a question, you are to flip a switch and shock him, moving one switch to the right—delivering 15 additional volts—each time he misses a question. The learner does well at first but then begins missing about three out of every four questions. You begin flipping the switches, which you believe are delivering stronger and stronger shocks for each incorrect answer. When you hesitate, the experimenter urges you, "Please continue" or "Please go on." If you still hesitate, the experimenter orders you, "The experiment requires that you continue," or more strongly, "You have no other choice, you *must* go on" (p. 374).

At the 20th switch, 300 volts, the learner pounds on the wall and screams, "Let me out of here, let me out, my heart's bothering me, let me out!" (Meyer, 1972, p. 461). From this point on, the learner answers no more questions. Alarmed, you protest to the experimenter that the learner, who is pounding the wall frantically, does not want to continue. The experimenter answers, "Whether the learner likes it or not, you must go on" (Milgram, 1963, p. 374). Even if the learner fails to respond, you are told to count that as an incorrect response and shock him again.

Do you continue? If so, you flip the next switch—315 volts—and hear only groans from the learner. You look at the experimenter, obviously distressed, your palms sweating, your heart pounding. The experimenter states firmly, "You have no other choice, you *must* go on" (p. 374). If you refuse at this point, the experiment is ended. Would you refuse, or would you continue to shock a silent learner nine more times until you delivered the maximum of 450 volts?

How many of the 40 participants do you think obeyed the experimenter to the end—450 volts? Not a single participant stopped before the 20th switch, supposedly 300 volts, when the learner began pounding the wall. Amazingly, 26 participants—65% of the sample—obeyed the experimenter to the bitter end, as shown in Figure 14.2. But this experiment took a terrible toll on the participants. They "were observed to sweat, tremble, stutter, bite their lips, groan, and dig their fingernails into their flesh. These were characteristic rather than exceptional responses to the experiment" (p. 375).

Would the same results have occurred if the experiment had not been conducted at a famous university like Yale? The same experiment was carried out in a three-room office suite in a run-down building identified by a sign, "Research Associates of Bridgeport." Even there, 48% of the participants administered the maximum shock compared to 65% in the Yale setting (Meyer, 1972).

Compliance: Giving In to Requests

There are many times when people act, not out of conformity or obedience, but in accordance with the wishes, suggestions, or direct requests of another person. This type of action is called **compliance**. Almost daily we are confronted with people who make requests of one sort or another. Do we comply with requests and yield to appeals? Often the answer is yes, and people use several techniques to gain our compliance.

What are three techniques used to gain compliance?

The Foot-in-the-Door Technique: Upping the Ante   One strategy, the **foot-in-the-door technique**, is designed to gain a favorable response to a small request first. The intent is to make the person more likely to agree later to a larger request (the result desired from the beginning). In one study a researcher claiming to represent a consumers' group called a number of homes and asked whether the people answering the phone would mind answering a few questions about the soap products they

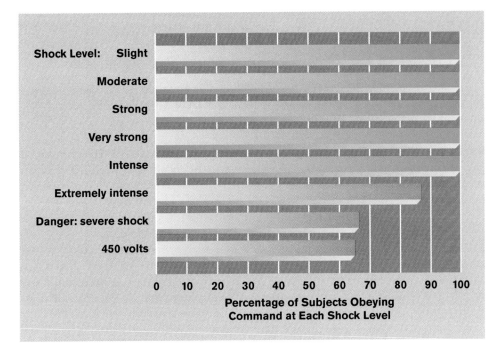

Figure 14.2
The Results of Milgram's Classic Experiment on Obedience

In his classic study, Stanley Milgram showed that a large majority of participants would obey authority even if obedience caused great pain or was life-threatening to another. Milgram reported that 87.5% of the participants continued to administer what they thought were painful electric shocks of 300 volts to a victim who complained of a heart condition. Amazingly, 65% of the participants obeyed authority to the bitter end and continued to deliver what they thought were dangerous, severe shocks to the maximum of 450 volts. (Data from Milgram, 1963.)

used. Then a few days later, the same person called those who had agreed to the first request and asked if he could send five or six of his assistants to conduct an inventory of the products in their home. The researcher told the people that the inventory would take about 2 hours, and that the inventory team would have to search all drawers, cabinets, and closets in the house. Would you agree to such an imposition?

Nearly 53% of those asked preliminary questions agreed to the larger request, compared to 22% of a control group who were contacted only once with the request (Freedman & Fraser, 1966). A review of many studies on the foot-in-the-door approach suggests that it is highly effective (Beaman et al., 1983; DeJong, 1979). But, strangely enough, exactly the opposite approach works just as well.

The Door-in-the-Face Technique: An Unreasonable Request First   With the **door-in-the-face technique**, a large, unreasonable request is made first. The expectation is that the person will refuse but will then be more likely to respond favorably to a smaller request later (the result desired from the beginning). In one of the best-known studies on the door-in-the-face technique, college students were approached on campus. They were asked to agree to serve without pay as counselors to juvenile delinquents for 2 hours each week for a minimum of 2 years. As you would imagine, not a single person agreed (Cialdini et al., 1975). Then the experimenters countered with a much smaller request, asking if the students would agree to take a group of juveniles on a 2-hour trip to the zoo. Half the students agreed, a fairly high compliance rate. The researchers used another group of college students as controls, asking them to respond only to the smaller request, the zoo trip. Only 17% agreed when the smaller request was presented alone.

The Low-Ball Technique: Not Telling the Whole Truth Up Front   Another method used to gain compliance is the **low-ball technique**. A very attractive initial offer is made to get people to commit themselves to an action, and then the terms are made less favorable. College students were asked to enroll in an experimental course for which they would receive credit. But they were low-balled: Only after the students had agreed to participate were they informed that the class would meet at 7:00 A.M. But 55% of the low-balled group agreed to participate anyway. When another group of students were told up front that the class would meet at 7:00 A.M., only about 25% agreed to take the class (Cialdini et al., 1978).

Link It!

GROUP INFLUENCE

The Effects of the Group on Individual Performance

A person's performance on tasks can be enhanced or impaired by the mere presence of others, and the decisions the person reaches as part of a group can be quite different from those she or he would make if acting alone.

Under what conditions does social facilitation have either a positive or a negative effect on performance?

Social Facilitation: Performing in the Presence of Others   The term **social facilitation** refers to any effect on performance, whether positive or negative, that can be attributed to the presence of others. Research on this phenomenon has focused on two types of effects: (1) **audience effects**—the impact of passive spectators on performance; and (2) **coaction effects**—the impact on performance caused by the presence of other people engaged in the same task.

In one of the first studies in social psychology, Norman Triplett (1898) tested whether people would work faster and harder in the presence of others than when performing alone. He set up a study in which he had 40 children wind fishing reels as quickly as possible under two conditions: (1) alone, or (2) in the presence of other children performing the same task. Triplet found that the children worked faster when other reel turners were present than when they performed alone.

Later studies on social facilitation found just the opposite effect—that the presence of others, whether coacting or just watching, could hurt or diminish individual performance. Robert Zajonc (1965; Zajonc & Sales, 1966) proposed an explanation for these seemingly contradictory effects. He found that we become aroused by the presence of others and that arousal facilitates the dominant response—the one most natural to us. On simple tasks and on tasks at which we are skilled, the dominant response is to perform effectively. However, on tasks that are difficult or tasks we are just learning, the incorrect response (making a mistake) is dominant. In other words, in the presence of others, performance improves on tasks that people can do easily, but suffers on tasks that are difficult for them (Michaels et al., 1982). See Figure 14.3. Other researchers have suggested that concern over the observers' evaluation is what most affects people's performance, particularly if they expect a negative evaluation (Sanna & Shotland, 1990).

What is social loafing, and what factors lessen or eliminate it?

Social Loafing: Not Pulling Your Weight   Researcher Bibb Latané used the term **social loafing** to refer to people's tendency to exert less effort when working with others on a common task than when they are working alone. Social loafing occurs in situations where no one person's contribution to the group can be identified and individuals are neither praised for a good performance nor blamed for a poor one (Williams et al., 1981).

Figure 14.3

Social Facilitation: Performing in the Presence of Others

The presence of others (either as an audience or as co-actors engaged in the same task) may have opposite effects, either helping or hindering an individual's performance. Why? Robert Zajonc explained that (1) the presence of others heightens arousal, and (2) heightened arousal leads to better performance on tasks we are good at and worse performance on tasks that are difficult for us. (Based on Zajonc & Sales, 1966.)

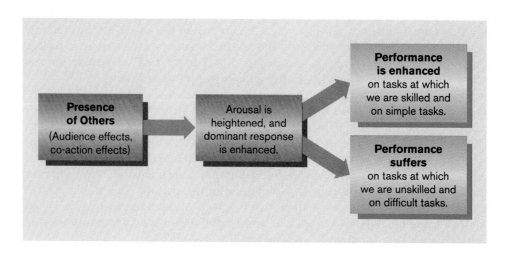

Harkins and Jackson (1985) found that social loafing disappeared when participants in a group were led to believe that each person's output could be monitored and his or her performance evaluated. Social loafing is not likely to occur when participants can evaluate their own individual contribution (Szymanski & Harkins, 1987), when they have a personal stake in the outcome, when they feel that the task is challenging (Brickner et al., 1986), or when they are working with close friends or teammates (Karau & Williams, 1993). Social loafing is apparently not peculiar to any single culture but is typical of the human species.

The Effects of the Group on Decision Making

A group can have profound and predictable effects on decision making, depending on the group's attitudes before a discussion begins.

Group Polarization: When Group Decisions Become More Extreme   It is commonly believed that groups tend to make more moderate, conservative decisions than individuals make, but some research in social psychology suggests otherwise.

Group discussion often causes members of a group to shift to a more extreme position in whatever direction the group was leaning initially—a phenomenon known as **group polarization** (Isenberg, 1986; Lamm, 1988). The group members, it seems, will decide to take a greater risk if they were leaning in a risky direction to begin with, but they will shift toward a more cautious position if they were, on the average, somewhat cautious at the beginning of the discussion (Myers & Lamm, 1975).

Groupthink: When Group Cohesiveness Leads to Bad Decisions   Group cohesiveness refers to the degree to which group members are attracted to the group and experience a feeling of oneness. **Groupthink** is the term social psychologist Irving Janis (1982) applies to the decisions often reached by overly cohesive groups. When a tightly knit group is more concerned with preserving group solidarity and uniformity than with objectively evaluating all possible alternatives in decision making, individual members may hesitate to voice any dissent. The group may also discredit opposing views from outsiders and begin to believe it is incapable of making mistakes. Even plans bordering on madness can be hatched and adopted when groupthink prevails. To guard against groupthink, Janis suggests that the group encourage an open discussion of alternative views and encourage the expression of any objections and doubts.

Groups exert an even more powerful influence on individuals through their prescribed social roles.

Social Roles

The group is indispensable to human life. We are born into a family group, a culture, a racial and ethnic group, and usually a religious group. And as we grow and mature, there are many other groups that we may choose to join, such as social groups and professional groups.

Social roles are socially defined behaviors that are considered appropriate for individuals occupying certain positions within a given group. Roles are useful because they tell us beforehand how people are likely to act toward us in many situations, even people we have never met before. If you have ever been stopped for speeding by a police officer, you were at that moment unwillingly cast in the role of speeder, and you had few doubts about the role the officer would play. But both you and the police officer assume many different roles in life—family roles, social roles, work roles, and so on—and your behavior can differ dramatically as you shift from role to role.

Roles can indeed shape human behavior, even to an alarming degree. Zimbardo's prison study, which introduced this chapter, makes this point quite dramatically. This study helps us to understand how, during some fraternity initiations, college students can assume roles that are reminiscent of those of Zimbardo's guards and prisoners.

Social loafing is people's tendency to exert less effort when working with others on a common task, such as pedaling a multiperson cycle.

How are the initial attitudes of group members likely to affect group decision making?

social facilitation: Any positive or negative effect on performance due to the presence of others, either as an audience or as co-actors.

audience effects: The impact of passive spectators on performance.

coaction effects: The impact on performance of the presence of others engaged in the same task.

social loafing: The tendency to put forth less effort when working with others on a common task than when working alone.

group polarization: The tendency of members of a group, after group discussion, to shift toward a more extreme position in whatever direction they were leaning initially—either more risky or more cautious.

groupthink: The tendency for members of a very cohesive group to feel such pressure to maintain group solidarity and to reach agreement on an issue that they fail to weigh available evidence adequately or to consider objections and alternatives.

social roles: Socially defined behaviors considered appropriate for individuals occupying certain positions within a group.

ATTITUDES AND ATTITUDE CHANGE

Attitudes: Cognitive, Emotional, and Behavioral Patterns

What are the three components of an attitude?

What is your attitude toward abortion? Gun control? Premarital sex? Essentially, **attitudes** are relatively stable evaluations of persons, objects, situations, or issues along a continuum ranging from positive to negative (Petty et al., 1997). Most attitudes have three components: (1) a cognitive component—thoughts and beliefs about the attitudinal object; (2) an emotional component—feelings toward the attitudinal object; and (3) a behavioral component—predispositions concerning actions toward the object (Breckler, 1984). Figure 14.4 shows these three components of an attitude.

Attitudes enable us to appraise people, objects, and situations, and provide structure and consistency in the social environment (Fazio, 1989). Attitudes also help us process social information (Pratkanis, 1989), guide our behavior (Sanbonmatsu & Fazio, 1990), and influence our social judgments and decisions (Jamieson & Zanna, 1989).

How do people form attitudes? Some attitudes are acquired through firsthand experience with people, objects, situations, and issues. Others are acquired vicariously. When children hear parents, family, friends, and teachers express positive or negative attitudes toward certain issues or people, they may adopt the same attitudes as their own. The mass media, including advertising, influence people's attitudes and reap billions of dollars annually for their efforts. As you might expect, however, the attitudes that people form through their own direct experience are stronger than those they acquire vicariously, and they are also more resistant to change (Wu & Shaffer, 1987).

Some research indicates that attitudes may have a partly genetic basis (Lykken et al., 1993). Tesser (1993) found that the greater the degree to which particular attitudes could be attributed to genetic influence, the more resistant those attitudes were to conformity pressures. But the controversial claim for a genetic influence on attitudes contradicts more conventional findings that emphasize the roles of learning and experience in attitude formation (Petty et al., 1997).

Children can learn attitudes from their parents and other significant adults. As a member of a Michigan-based militia group, this boy is likely to adopt attitudes held by the adult members.

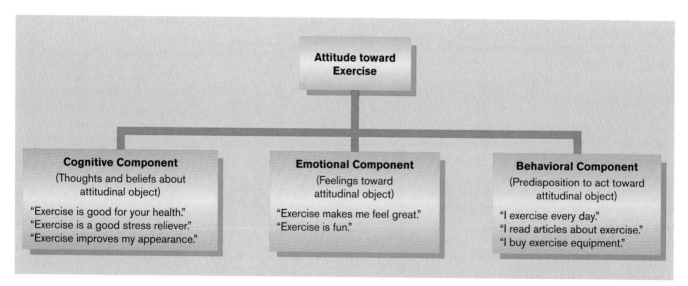

Figure 14.4

The Three Components of an Attitude

An attitude is a relatively stable evaluation of a person, object, situation, or issue. Most of our attitudes have (1) a cognitive component, (2) an emotional component, and (3) a behavioral component.

The Relationship between Attitudes and Behavior   In the first half of the 20th century, the general consensus among social scientists was that attitudes govern behavior (Allport, 1935). But toward the end of the 1960s, one study after another failed to reveal a strong relationship between people's beliefs as reported on attitude measurement scales and their actual behavior. Attitudes seemed to predict observed behavior only about 10% of the time (Wicker, 1969).

Why aren't attitude measures better predictors of behavior? Attitude measures may often be too general to predict specific behaviors. People may express strong attitudes in favor of protecting the environment and conservation of resources, yet not take their aluminum cans to a recycling center or join carpools. But when attitude measures correspond very closely to specific behaviors of interest, they actually become good predictors of that behavior (Ajzen & Fishbein, 1977). Finally, attitudes are better predictors of behavior if they are strongly held, are readily accessible in memory (Bassili, 1995; Fazio & Williams, 1986; Kraus, 1995), and vitally affect the holder's interests (Sivacek & Crano, 1982). Attitudes toward a social category (politicians or media stars, for example) and attitude–behavior consistency are affected by the specific exemplars (members of that social category) that most readily come to mind (Sia et al., 1997).

Cognitive Dissonance: The Mental Pain of Inconsistency   If people discover that some of their attitudes are in conflict with others or that their attitudes are not consistent with their behavior, they are likely to experience an unpleasant state. Leon Festinger (1957) called this **cognitive dissonance**. People usually try to reduce the dissonance by changing the behavior or the attitude, or by somehow explaining away the inconsistency or reducing its importance (Aronson, 1976; Festinger, 1957). A change in attitudes does seem to reduce the discomfort caused by dissonance (Elliot & Devine, 1994).

Smoking is a perfect situation for cognitive dissonance. What are smokers to do? The healthiest, but perhaps not the easiest, way to reduce cognitive dissonance is to change the behavior—quit smoking. Another way is to change the attitude—to convince themselves that smoking is not as dangerous as it is said to be. Smokers can also tell themselves that they will stop smoking long before any permanent damage is done, or that medical science is advancing so rapidly that a cure for cancer is just around the corner. Figure 14.5 illustrates the methods a smoker can use to reduce cognitive dissonance.

attitude: A relatively stable evaluation of a person, object, situation, or issue.

cognitive dissonance: The unpleasant state that can occur when people become aware of inconsistencies between their attitudes or between their attitudes and their behavior.

What is cognitive dissonance, and how can it be resolved?

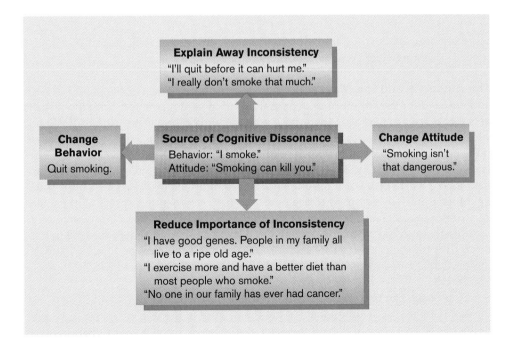

Figure 14.5

Methods of Reducing Cognitive Dissonance

Cognitive dissonance can occur when people become aware of inconsistencies in their attitudes or between their attitudes and their behavior. People try to reduce dissonance by (1) changing their behavior, (2) changing their attitude, (3) explaining away the inconsistency, or (4) reducing its importance. Here are examples of how a smoker might use these methods to reduce the cognitive dissonance created by his or her habit.

persuasion: A deliberate attempt to influence the attitudes and/or behavior of another.

Researchers have found that if people voluntarily make a statement or take a position that is counter to what they believe, they will experience cognitive dissonance because of the inconsistency. To resolve this dissonance, they are likely to change their belief to make it more consistent with their behavior (Festinger & Carlsmith, 1959). Cognitive dissonance can also be reduced by trivializing or minimizing the dissonant cognitions instead of changing one's attitudes (Simon et al., 1995).

Persuasion: Trying to Change Attitudes

What are the four elements of persuasion?

Persuasion is a deliberate attempt to influence the attitudes and/or the behavior of another person. Attempts at persuasion are pervasive parts of work experience, social experience, and even family life.

Researchers have identified four elements of persuasion: (1) the source of the communication (who is doing the persuading), (2) the audience (who is being persuaded), (3) the message (what is being said), and (4) the medium (the means by which the message is transmitted). The attitudes people hold are instrumental in their resistance to persuasion. And resistance is stronger if attitudes are infused with intense feeling (the affective component) as well as being based on sufficient, accurate knowledge (the cognitive component) (Zuwerink & Devine, 1996).

Persuasion is a deliberate attempt to influence the attitudes and/or behavior of another person. What tactics do you use when trying to persuade others?

What qualities make a source most persuasive?

The Source: Look Who's Talking Some factors that make the source (the communicator) more persuasive are credibility, attractiveness, and likability. Credibility refers to how believable a source is. A credible communicator is one who has expertise (knowledge of the topic at hand) and trustworthiness (truthfulness and integrity). The influence of a credible source is even greater if the audience knows the communicator's credentials beforehand. Moreover, people attach greater credibility to sources who have nothing to gain from persuading them or, better yet, who seem to be arguing against their own best interest. For example, arguments against pornography are more persuasive if they are made by a source known to be generally opposed to censorship.

Movie and TV stars, athletes, and even unknown but attractive fashion models have long been used by advertisers to persuade consumers to buy certain products. But likable, down-to-earth, ordinary people who are perceived to be similar to the audience are sometimes even more effective persuaders than famous experts, attractive models, or movie stars. Political candidates attempt to appear more likable and more like the voters when they don hard hats and visit construction sites and coal mines, kiss babies, and pose with farmers.

The Audience and the Message Persuaders must consider the nature of their audience before they attempt to use persuasion. In general, people with low intelligence are easier to persuade than those who are highly intelligent (Rhodes & Wood, 1992). Research evidence suggests that a one-sided message is usually most persuasive if the audience is not well informed on the issue, is not overly intelligent, or already agrees with the point of view. A two-sided message (in which both sides of an issue are mentioned) works best when the audience is well informed on the issue, is fairly intelligent, or is initially opposed to the point of view. A two-sided appeal will usually sway more people than a one-sided appeal (Hovland et al., 1949; McGuire, 1985).

People tend to scrutinize arguments that are contrary to their existing beliefs more carefully and exert more effort refuting them; they are also more likely to judge such arguments as weaker than those that support their beliefs (Edwards & Smith, 1996).

A message can be well reasoned, logical, and unemotional ("just the facts"); a message can be strictly emotional ("scare the hell out of them"); or it can be a combination of the two. Which type of message works best? Arousing fear seems to be an

Link It!

effective method for persuading people to adopt healthier attitudes and behaviors (Robberson & Rogers, 1988). Appeals based on fear are most effective when the presentation outlines definite actions the audience can take to avoid the feared outcomes (Leventhal et al., 1965).

Another important factor in persuasion is repetition. The more often a product or a point of view is presented, the more people will be persuaded to buy it or embrace it. Advertisers apparently believe in the mere-exposure effect, for they repeat their messages over and over (Bornstein, 1989).

PREJUDICE AND DISCRIMINATION

Increasing cultural diversity is a fact of life in the United States. Can we learn to live and work peacefully with our fellow Americans, no matter what racial, ethnic, cultural, or other differences exist among us? The answer is a conditional yes—if we can learn how to combat prejudice and discrimination.

The Roots of Prejudice and Discrimination

Prejudice consists of attitudes (usually negative) toward others based on their gender, religion, race, or membership in a particular group. Prejudice involves beliefs and emotions (not actions) that can escalate into hatred. **Discrimination** consists of behavior—actions (usually negative) toward members of a group. Many Americans have experienced prejudice and discrimination—minority racial groups (racism), women (sexism), the elderly (ageism), the handicapped, homosexuals, religious groups, and others. What are the roots of prejudice and discrimination?

The Realistic Conflict Theory: When Competition Leads to Prejudice   One of the oldest explanations offered for the genesis of prejudice is competition among various social groups who must struggle against each other for scarce resources—good jobs, homes, schools, and so on. Commonly called the **realistic conflict theory**, this view suggests that as competition increases, so do prejudice, discrimination, and hatred among the competing groups. Some historical evidence supports the realistic conflict theory. Prejudice and hatred were high between the American settlers and the Native Americans who struggled over land during the westward expansion. The multitudes of Irish and German immigrants who came to the United States in the 1830s and 1840s felt the sting of prejudice and hatred from other Americans who were facing economic scarcity. But prejudice and discrimination are attitudes and actions too complex to be explained solely by economic conflict and competition. What are some other causes?

Us versus Them: Dividing the World into In-Groups and Out-Groups   Prejudice can also spring from the distinct social categories into which people divide the world—*us versus them* (Turner et al., 1987). An **in-group** is a social group with a strong feeling of togetherness and from which others are excluded. Members of college fraternities and sororities often exhibit strong in-group feelings. The **out-group** consists of individuals or groups specifically identified by the in-group as not belonging. Us-versus-them thinking can lead to excessive competition, hostility, prejudice, discrimination, and even war. Prejudiced individuals who most strongly identify with their racial in-group are most reluctant to admit others to the group if there is the slightest doubt about their racial purity (Blasovich et al., 1997).

A famous study by Sherif and Sherif (1967) shows how in-group/out-group conflict can escalate into prejudice and hostility rather quickly, even between groups that are very much alike. The researchers set up their experiment at the Robber's Cave summer camp. Their subjects were 22 bright, well-adjusted, 11- and 12-year-old white middle-class boys from Oklahoma City. Divided into two groups and housed

prejudice: Negative attitudes toward others based on their gender, religion, race, or membership in a particular group.

discrimination: Behavior, usually negative, directed toward others based on their gender, religion, race, or membership in a particular group.

realistic conflict theory: The notion that prejudices arise when social groups must compete for scarce resources and opportunities.

in-group: A social group with a strong sense of togetherness and from which others are excluded.

out-group: A social group specifically identified by the in-group as not belonging.

What is the difference between prejudice and discrimination?

Link It!

What is meant by the terms *in-group* and *out-group?*

social cognition: Mental processes that people use to notice, interpret, understand, remember, and apply information about the social world and that enable them to simplify, categorize, and order that world.

stereotypes: Widely shared beliefs about the characteristic traits, attitudes, and behaviors of members of various social groups (racial, ethnic, religious), including the assumption that the members of such groups are usually all alike.

in separate cabins, the boys were kept apart for all their daily activities and games. During the first week, in-group solidarity, friendship, and cooperation developed within each of the groups. One group called itself "the Rattlers"; the other group took the name "Eagles."

During the second week of the study, competitive events were purposely scheduled so that the goals of one group could be achieved "only at the expense of the other group" (Sherif, 1958, p. 353). The groups were happy to battle each other, and intergroup conflict quickly emerged. Name-calling began, fights broke out, and accusations were hurled back and forth. During the third week of the experiment, the researchers tried to put an end to the hostility and to turn rivalry into cooperation. They simply brought the groups together for pleasant activities such as eating meals and watching movies. "But far from reducing conflict, these situations only served as opportunities for the rival groups to berate and attack each other. . . . They threw paper, food and vile names at each other at the tables" (Sherif, 1956, pp. 57–58).

Finally, the last stage of the experiment was set in motion. The experimenters manufactured a series of crises that could be solved only if all the boys combined their efforts and resources and cooperated. The water supply, sabotaged by the experimenters, could be restored only if all the boys worked together. After a week of several activities requiring cooperation, cut-throat competition gave way to cooperative exchanges. Friendships developed between groups, and before the end of the experiment, peace was declared. Working together toward shared goals had turned hostility into friendship.

How does prejudice develop, according to the social learning theory?

The Social Learning Theory: Acquiring Prejudice through Modeling and Reinforcement   According to the social learning theory, people learn attitudes of prejudice and hatred the same way they learn other attitudes. If children hear their parents, teachers, peers, and others openly express prejudices toward different racial, ethnic, or cultural groups, they may be quick to learn such attitudes. And if parents, peers, and others reward children with smiles and approval for parroting their own prejudices (operant conditioning), children may learn these prejudices even more quickly.

Phillips and Ziller (1997) suggest that people learn to be nonprejudiced. These researchers conceptualize *nonprejudice* as a set of attitudes about interpersonal relations that lead people to selectively pay attention to and emphasize the similarities between themselves and others, rather than the differences.

What are stereotypes?

Social Cognition: Natural Thinking Processes Can Lead to Prejudice   Emotion- and learning-based views help explain how prejudice develops. But a more recent view suggests that social cognition plays a role in giving birth to prejudice. **Social cognition** refers to the ways in which people typically process social information— the natural thinking processes used to notice, interpret, and remember information about the social world. The very processes we use to simplify, categorize, and order our social world are the same processes that distort our views of it. So prejudice may arise not only from heated negative emotions and hatred toward other social groups, but also from cooler cognitive processes that govern how we think and process social information (Kunda & Oleson, 1995).

One way people simplify, categorize, and order their world is by using stereotypes. **Stereotypes** are widely shared beliefs about the characteristics of members of various social groups (racial, ethnic, religious), which include the assumption that "they" are usually all alike. Macrae and colleagues (1994) suggest that stereotyping requires less mental energy than trying to understand others as individuals. Stereotyping allows people to make quick, automatic (thoughtless) judgments about others and apply their mental resources to other activities (Forgas & Fiedler, 1996). Research by Anderson and others (1990) showed that participants could process information more efficiently and answer questions faster when they were using stereotypes.

Do you use stereotypes in your thinking? To find out, complete the *Try It!*

Can you list characteristics for each of the following groups?

African Americans	Hispanic Americans
White, male top-level executives	Jews
Native Americans	Arabs
Homosexuals	Italians
Members of fundamentalist religious groups	Germans

Once developed, stereotypes strongly influence the way we attend to and evaluate incoming information about specific groups. Consequently the stereotypes we hold can powerfully affect how we react to and make judgments about persons in various groups.

In the *Try It!*, how many group characteristics could you list? If you can list traits thought to represent any group, you are probably demonstrating stereotypic thinking. We know that not *all* members of a group possess the same traits or characteristics, but we tend to use stereotypic thinking nonetheless.

Some research has revealed that social stereotypes involve more than overgeneralization about the traits or characteristics of members of certain groups (Judd et al., 1991). People tend to perceive more diversity, more variability, within the groups to which they belong (in-groups), but they see more similarity among members of other groups (out-groups) (Ostrom et al., 1993). Whites see more diversity among themselves but more sameness within groups of African Americans or Asians. This tendency in thinking can extend from race to gender to age or any other category of persons. Another study showed that young college students believed there was much more variability or diversity in 100 of their group than in a group of 100 elderly Americans, whom the students perceived to be much the same (Linville et al., 1989). What about the elderly subjects? They perceived even more variability within their own group and less variability among 100 college students. Age stereotypes can be even more pronounced and negative than gender stereotypes (Kite et al., 1991).

Some research indicates that prejudice and stereotyping (whether conscious or not) may be a means of bolstering one's self-image by disparaging others (Fein & Spencer, 1997). Moreover, some minority group members may protect their self-esteem by attempting to minimize discrimination or by denying its significance (Ruggiero & Taylor, 1997).

Stereotypes can be positive or negative, but all are distortions of reality. And stereotypic thinking can result in discrimination.

Discrimination in the Workplace

Word and others (1974) found that stereotypic thinking can govern people's expectancies. And often what we expect is what we get, regardless of whether our expectancies are high or low. Participants in one study were White undergraduates who were to interview White and African American job applicants (actually confederates of the experimenters). The researchers secretly videotaped the interviews and studied the tapes to see if the student interviewers had treated the African American and White applicants differently. The researchers found substantial differences in the interviews based on the race of the applicants. The interviewers spent less time with the African American applicants, maintained a greater physical distance from

One form of discrimination in the workplace that African Americans may face as job applicants is a tendency for White interviewers to use an interviewing style based on stereotypic thinking.

Link It!

What are two strategies for reducing prejudice and discrimination?

---

contact hypothesis: The notion that prejudice can be reduced through increased contact among members of different social groups.

---

them, and generally were less friendly and outgoing. During interviews with these applicants, the interviewers' speech deteriorated—they made more errors in grammar and pronunciation.

In a follow-up study the same researchers trained White confederates to copy the two different interview styles used in the first study. The confederates then used the different styles to interview a group of White job applicants. These interviews were videotaped as well, and later a panel of judges evaluated the tapes. The judges agreed that applicants who were subjected to the interview style for African Americans were more nervous and performed more poorly than applicants interviewed according to the "White" style. The experimenters concluded that as a result of the interview style they experienced, the African American confederates from the first study were not given the opportunity to demonstrate their skills and qualifications to the best of their ability. Thus they were subjected to a subtle form of discrimination in which their performance was hampered by the expectancies of the original interviewers.

Discrimination is also evident after the job interviews have been completed and people take their positions in the workplace. How do women and minorities fare in today's world of work? Even though federal legislation forbids hiring, promoting, laying off, or awarding benefits to workers on the basis of sex, race, color, national origin, or religion, studies continue to show discrimination exists (Renzetti & Curran, 1992). A considerable body of research refutes the notion that gender and race deficiencies explain why so few women and minorities are in upper management (Morrison & Von Glinow, 1990). Nevertheless, the mere perception of deficiencies, if held by the dominant corporate leaders, is sufficient to produce bias and discrimination.

Morrison and Von Glinow (1990) claim that "discrimination occurs in part because of the belief by White men that women and people of color are less suited for management than White men" (p. 202). The dominant group's belief that customers, employees, and others are more comfortable dealing with or working for White male managers may lead to discrimination. In such cases these managers may be less willing to promote women and minorities to sensitive, responsible management positions.

Tokenism is a subtle form of discrimination in which people are hired or promoted primarily because they represent a specific group or category rather than strictly on the basis of their qualifications. But no matter how eminently qualified an employee may be, if the employee perceives that he or she is a token, the individual suffers and so does the organization.

Combating Prejudice and Discrimination

Given that prejudice and discrimination may grow from many roots, are there effective ways to reduce them? Many experts believe there are. One way is through education. To the extent that prejudice is learned, it can also be unlearned. Sustained educational programs designed to increase teachers' and parents' awareness of the damage caused by prejudice and discrimination can be very effective (Aronson, 1990).

Direct Contact: Bringing Diverse Groups Together   Can we reduce our prejudices and stereotypic thinking by increasing our contact and interaction with others from diverse groups? Yes, according to the **contact hypothesis**.

Increased contacts with members of groups that we view stereotypically can teach us that members of those groups are not all alike. But the contact hypothesis works to reduce prejudice *only* under certain conditions. In fact, if people from diverse groups are simply thrown together, prejudice and even hostility are likely to increase rather than decrease, as you learned from Sherif's Robber's Cave experiment. Sherif outlined the conditions under which intergroup contact reduces prejudice, and his findings have been confirmed and extended by others (Aronson, 1990; Finchilescu, 1988).

The contact hypothesis will work to reduce prejudice most effectively under the following conditions:

- Interacting groups should be approximately equal in social and economic status and in their ability on the tasks to be performed.

- The intergroup contact must be cooperative (not competitive) in nature, and work should be confined to shared goals.

- The contact should be informal, so friendly interactions develop more easily and group members get to know each other individually.

- The contact situation should be one in which conditions favor group equality.

- The individuals involved should perceive each other as typical members of the groups to which they belong.

When these conditions are met, intergroup friendships can form and prejudice can be reduced. Fortunately, people tend to generalize reduced prejudice toward one group to other groups (Pettigrew, 1997). Moreover, feelings of empathy for a particular member of a stigmatized group, such as a young woman with AIDS or a homeless man, can improve feelings for the group as a whole (Batson et al., 1997).

Prejudice: Is It Increasing or Decreasing?

Few people would readily admit to being prejudiced. Gordon Allport (1954), a pioneer in research on prejudice, said, "Defeated intellectually, prejudice lingers emotionally" (p. 328). Even those who are sincerely intellectually opposed to prejudice may still harbor some prejudiced feelings (Devine, 1989).

Is there any evidence that prejudice is decreasing in U.S. society? Gallup polls reveal that Whites in the United States are becoming more racially tolerant than they were in decades past (Gallup & Hugick, 1990). When Whites were asked in 1990 whether they would move if African Americans were to move next door to them, 93% said no, compared to 65% 25 years earlier. Even if African Americans were to move into their neighborhood in great numbers, 68% of Whites still said they would not move.

School integration, which in the past created a storm of controversy, seems to be less of an issue for most Whites today. Only 10% of Gallup's White respondents said they would object to sending their children to an integrated school in which up to one-half of the children were African American. Also, the majority of African Americans polled (two-thirds) believed that their children have the same opportunity as White children to get a good education.

Prejudice has no virtues. It immediately harms those who feel its sting and ultimately harms those who practice it.

PROSOCIAL BEHAVIOR: BEHAVIOR THAT BENEFITS OTHERS

Kitty Genovese was returning home alone late one night. But this was no ordinary night. Nearly 40 of her neighbors who lived in the apartment complex nearby watched as she was attacked and stabbed, but they did nothing. The attacker left. Kitty was still screaming, begging for help, and then . . . he returned. He dragged her around, stabbing her again while her neighbors watched. Some of them turned off their bedroom lights to see more clearly, pulled up chairs to the window, and watched. Someone yelled, "Leave the girl alone," and the attacker fled again. But even then, no one came to her aid. A third time the attacker returned, more stabbing and screaming, and they watched. Finally, Kitty Genovese stopped screaming. When he had finally killed her, the attacker fled for the last time. (Adapted from Rosenthal, 1964.)

This actual event might not seem so unusual today, but it was a rare occurrence back in the early 1960s. So rare, in fact, that people wondered how her neighbors could have been so callous and cold-hearted, to do nothing but watch as Kitty Genovese begged for help that never came. Social psychologists Bibb Latané and John Darley looked deeper for an explanation. Perhaps certain factors in the situation itself would help explain why so many people just stood or sat there.

The Bystander Effect: The More Bystanders, the Less Likely They Are to Help

What is the bystander effect, and what factors have been suggested to explain why it occurs?

If you were injured or ill and needed help, would you feel safer if one or two other people were near, or if a large crowd of onlookers were present? You may be surprised to learn of the **bystander effect**: As the number of bystanders at an emergency increases, the probability that the victim will receive help from them decreases, and the help, if given, is likely to be delayed.

Why should this be? Darley and Latané (1968a) set up a number of experiments to study helping behavior. In one study, participants were placed one at a time in a small room and told that they would be participating in a discussion group by means of an intercom system. Some participants were told that they would be communicating with only one other participant, some believed that two other participants would be involved, and some were told that five other people would participate. There really were *no* other participants in the study—only the prerecorded voices of confederates assisting the experimenter.

Shortly after the discussion began, the voice of one confederate was heard over the intercom calling for help, indicating that he was having an epileptic seizure. Of the participants who believed that they alone were hearing the victim, 85% went for help before the end of the seizure. When participants believed that one other person heard the seizure, 62% sought help. But when they believed that four other people were aware of the emergency, only 31% tried to get help before the end of the seizure. Figure 14.6 shows how the number of bystanders affects both the number of people who try to help and the speed of response.

Latané and Darley suggest two possible explanations for the bystander effect—diffusion of responsibility and the influence of apparently calm bystanders.

Figure 14.6

The Bystander Effect

In their intercom experiment, Darley and Latané showed that the more people a subject believed were present during an emergency, the longer it took the subject to respond and help a person in distress. (Data from Darley & Latané, 1968a.)

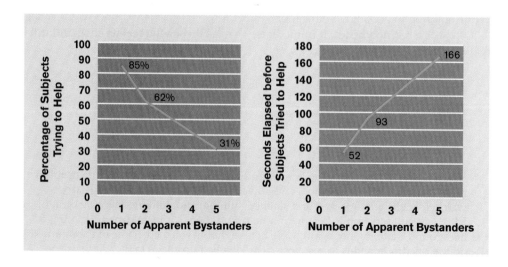

Diffusion of Responsibility: An Explanation for the Bystander Effect   When bystanders are present in an emergency, they generally feel that the responsibility for helping is shared by the group, a phenomenon known as **diffusion of responsibility**. Consequently each person feels less compelled to act than if she or he were alone and felt the total responsibility. Kitty Genovese's neighbors were aware that other people were watching because they saw lights go off in the other apartments. They did not feel that the total responsibility for action rested only on their shoulders, or they may have thought that "somebody else must be doing something" (Darley & Latané, 1968a).

The Influence of Apparently Calm Bystanders: When Faces Deceive   Sometimes real emergencies occur in rather ambiguous situations. Bystanders may not be sure if an actual emergency exists. At the risk of appearing foolish, they often hesitate to react with alarm until they are sure that intervention is appropriate (Clark & Word, 1972). So the bystanders may stand there watching other calm-appearing bystanders and conclude that nothing is really wrong and no intervention is necessary (Darley & Latané, 1968b).

Picture an orthopedic surgeon's large waiting room in which eight patients are waiting to see the doctor. In one chair a middle-aged man sits slumped over, yet he does not appear to be sleeping. His position resembles that of a person who is unconscious. If you were a patient in such a setting, would you check on the man's condition or just continue sitting?

This was the actual scene one of the authors entered a few years ago as a patient. She sat down and immediately noticed the man slumped in his chair. She scanned the faces of the other waiting patients but saw no sign of alarm or even concern. Was there really no emergency, or was this a case of the bystander effect? Knowing that the reaction of onlookers is a poor indicator of the seriousness of a situation, she quickly summoned the doctor, who found that the man had suffered a heart attack. Fortunately, the doctor's office was attached to a large hospital complex, and almost immediately a hospital team appeared and rushed the victim to the emergency room.

People Who Help in Emergencies

There are many kinds of **prosocial behavior**—behavior that benefits others, such as helping, cooperation, and sympathy. Prosocial impulses arise early in life. Researchers agree that children respond sympathetically to companions in distress at least by their second birthday (Hay, 1994; Kochanska, 1993). The term **altruism** is usually reserved for behavior aimed at helping others that requires some self-sacrifice and is not performed for personal gain. What motivates us to help or not to help in an emergency? Batson and colleagues (1989) believe that we help out of *empathy*—the ability to feel what another feels.

Cultures vary in their norms for helping others—that is, their social responsibility norms. According to Miller and others (1990), people in the United States tend to feel an obligation to help family, friends, and even strangers in life-threatening circumstances, but only family in moderately serious situations. In contrast, in India the social responsibility norm extends to strangers whose needs are only moderately serious or even minor.

In spite of the potentially high costs of helping, accounts of people who have risked their lives to help others are numerous. During World War II, thousands of Christians risked their lives to protect Jews from extermination in Nazi Germany. Are there common factors that might explain such uncommon risks in the service of others? A study of 406 of these rescuers revealed that they did not consider themselves heroes, and that different motives led to their altruistic behavior. Some rescuers were motivated by strong convictions about how human beings should be treated; others, by empathy for the particular person or persons they rescued (Fogelman & Wiener, 1985; Oliner & Oliner, 1988). Still others were acting based on norms of their family or social group that emphasized helping others.

Why do people often ignore someone who is unconscious on the sidewalk? Diffusion of responsibility is one possible explanation.

diffusion of responsibility: The feeling among bystanders at an emergency that the responsibility for helping is shared by the group, so each person feels less compelled to act than if he or she alone bore the total responsibility.

prosocial behavior: Behavior that benefits others, such as helping, cooperation, and sympathy.

altruism: Behavior aimed at helping another, requiring some self-sacrifice and not designed for personal gain.

In what conditions or circumstances might a person be more likely to receive help? People are more likely to receive help if they are physically attractive (Benson et al., 1976), if they are perceived by potential helpers as similar to them (Dovidio, 1984), and if they are not considered responsible for their plight (Schmidt & Weiner, 1988). Potential helpers are more likely to help if they have specialized training in first aid or police work, if they are not in a hurry, if they have been exposed to a helpful model (Bryan & Test, 1967), if they are in a positive mood (Carlson et al., 1988), and if the weather is good (Cunningham, 1979).

AGGRESSION: INTENTIONALLY HARMING OTHERS

Humanity has a long history of **aggression**—intentionally inflicting physical or psychological harm on others. Consider the tens of millions of people killed by other humans in wars and even in times of peace. In 1996, in the United States alone, there were reported almost 20,000 homicides, 96,000 rapes, 540,000 robberies, and 1.03 million assaults (Famighetti, 1997).

What causes aggression? One of the earliest explanations of aggression was the *instinct theory*—that human beings, along with other animal species, are genetically programmed for such behavior. Sigmund Freud believed that humans have an aggressive instinct that can be turned inward as self-destruction or outward as aggression or violence toward others. A Nobel Prize–winning researcher in animal behavior, Konrad Lorenz (1966) claimed that aggression springs from an inborn fighting instinct common in many animal species. Most social psychologists, however, consider human behavior too complex to attribute to instincts.

Biological Factors in Aggression: Genes, Hormones, and Brain Damage

What biological factors are thought to be related to aggression?

While rejecting the instinct theory of aggression, many psychologists do concede that biological factors are involved. A meta-analysis of 24 twin and adoption studies of several personality measures of aggression revealed a heritability estimate of about .50 for aggression (Miles & Carey, 1997). And twin and adoption studies have revealed a genetic link for criminal behavior (DiLalla & Gottesman, 1991). Cloninger and others (1982) found that adoptees with a criminal biological parent were four times as likely as members of the general population to commit crimes, while adoptees with a criminal adoptive parent were at twice the risk of committing a crime. But adoptees with both a criminal biological and a criminal adoptive parent were 14 times as likely to commit crimes.

One biological factor that seems very closely related to aggression is low arousal level of the autonomic nervous system (Raine, 1996). Low arousal level (low heart rate and lower reactivity) has been linked to antisocial and violent behavior (Brennan et al., 1997). People with low arousal levels tend to seek stimulation, excitement, and exhibit fearlessness, even in the face of danger.

Men are more physically aggressive than women (Green et al., 1996), and the male hormone testosterone is thought to be involved. Harris and colleagues (1996) found testosterone levels in male and female college students to be positively correlated with aggression and negatively correlated with prosocial behavior. But very low testosterone levels have also been linked to aggression (Angier, 1995). And violent behavior has been linked to low levels of the neurotransmitter serotonin (Brown & Linnoila, 1990; Gartner & Whitaker-Azmitia, 1996).

Brain damage, brain tumors, and temporal lobe epilepsy have all been related to aggressive and violent behavior (Mednick et al., 1988). A study of 15 death row inmates revealed that all had histories of severe head injuries (Lewis et al., 1986).

According to Eronen and others (1996), homicide rates are eight times higher in men with schizophrenia and ten times higher in men with antisocial personality disorder. The risk of violence is even greater when individuals with these disorders abuse alcohol (Hodgins et al., 1996; Tiihonen et al., 1997). In children, high levels of lead exposure (Needleman et al., 1996) and low IQ and problems paying attention (Loeber & Hay, 1997) are related to aggressive behavior and delinquency.

Ito and others (1996) found that alcohol intoxication is particularly likely to lead to aggression in response to frustration. People who are intoxicated commit the majority of murders, spouse beatings, stabbings, and instances of physical child abuse.

Aggression in Response to Frustration: Sometimes, but Not Always

Does **frustration**—the blocking of an impulse, or interference with the attainment of a goal—lead to aggression? The **frustration–aggression hypothesis** suggests that frustration produces aggression (Dollard et al., 1939; Miller, 1941). Frustration doesn't always cause aggression, but it is especially likely to if it is intense and seems to be unjustified (Doob & Sears, 1939; Pastore, 1950). Berkowitz (1988) points out that even if frustration is justified and not aimed specifically at an individual, it can cause aggression if it arouses negative emotions.

Aggression in response to frustration is not always aimed at the people causing it. If the preferred target is too threatening or not available, the aggression may be displaced. For example, children who are angry with their parents may take out their frustrations on a younger sibling. Sometimes minorities and others who have not been responsible for a frustrating situation become targets of displaced aggression, a practice known as **scapegoating** (Koltz, 1983).

Aggression in Response to Aversive Events: Pain, Heat, Noise, and Crowding

Aggression in response to frustration is only one special case of a broader phenomenon—aggression resulting from unpleasant or aversive events in general, says a leading researcher on aggression, Leonard Berkowitz (1988, 1989). People often become aggressive when they are in pain (Berkowitz, 1983) or are exposed to loud noise, foul odors (Rotton et al., 1979), irritating cigarette smoke, or crowding. Extreme heat has been linked to aggression in several studies (Anderson, 1989; Anderson & Anderson, 1996).

These and other studies lend support to the cognitive–neoassociationistic model proposed by Berkowitz (1990). He has suggested that anger and aggression result from aversive events and from unpleasant emotional states such as sadness, grief, and depression. "The core notion in this model is that negative affect is the basic source of anger and angry aggression" (Berkowitz, 1990, p. 494). Negative emotions (negative affect) tend to activate angry feelings, thoughts, and memories, as well as tendencies toward aggression or escape. The cognitive component of Berkowitz's model occurs when the angered person makes an appraisal of the aversive situation and makes attributions about the motives of the people involved. As a result of the cognitive appraisal, the initial reaction of anger can be intensified or reduced or suppressed. This process will make the person either more or less likely to act on the aggressive tendency.

Crowding   **Personal space** is an area surrounding each individual, much like an invisible bubble, that the person considers part of himself or herself and uses to regulate the closeness of interactions with others. Personal space serves to protect personal privacy and to regulate the level of intimacy with others. The size of personal space varies according to the person or persons with whom an individual is interacting and the nature of the interaction. And when personal space is reduced, aggression can result.

frustration: Interference with the attainment of a goal, or the blocking of an impulse.

frustration–aggression hypothesis: The hypothesis that frustration produces aggression.

scapegoating: Displacing aggression onto minority groups or other innocent targets not responsible for the frustrating situation.

personal space: An area surrounding each individual, much like an invisible bubble, that is considered to belong to the person and used to regulate the closeness of interactions with others.

What is the frustration–aggression hypothesis?

What kinds of aversive events and unpleasant emotions have been related to aggression?

What is the difference between density and crowding?

Figure 14.7
Social and Spatial Density

Social density increases as the number of people in a given space increases, as illustrated in (a). Spatial density increases as the amount of space for a given number of people decreases, as shown in (b).

Most psychologists draw a distinction between **density**—the number of people occupying a defined physical space—and crowding. **Crowding** is subjective and refers to the perception that there are too many people in a defined space. A hermit would probably feel crowded if one other person was anywhere in sight.

Psychologists further differentiate between social density and spatial density (Baum & Valins, 1977), and a sense of crowding is affected by both. Social density increases as the number of people in a fixed space increases. If five relatives came to live in your house for several weeks, social density would increase and you might feel crowded. Conversely, social density decreases as the number of people in a fixed space decreases. With spatial density, the number of people remains constant, but the space they occupy increases or decreases. If you have ever taken a family vacation in a car, you have felt the effects of increasing spatial density. Figure 14.7 illustrates the difference between social density and spatial density.

Does crowding lead to increased aggression? Comparing records from four state prisons, Paulus and others (1988) found that death rates, suicides, disciplinary actions, and psychological problems resulting in psychiatric commitment all increased as the prison population increased. The more inmates per cell, the greater the number of problems. But keep in mind that a prison is an atypical environment with an atypical population.

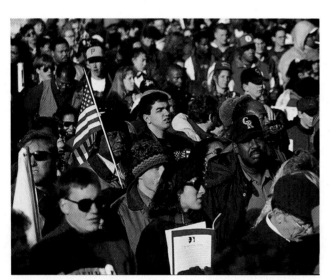

Crowding may or may not be stressful depending on the situation—waiting in a crowded airport terminal is more likely to be perceived as stressful than being part of a large crowd at a rally on Martin Luther King, Jr. Day.

Crowding often leads to higher physiological arousal, and males typically experience its effects more negatively than females do. The effects of crowding also vary across cultures and situations. Researchers have studied its effects on such diverse populations as male heads of households in India and middle-class male and female college students in the United States (Evans & Lepore, 1993). In both of these studies psychological distress was linked to household crowding.

The Social Learning Theory of Aggression: Learning to Be Aggressive

According to social learning theory, what causes aggressive behavior?

The social learning theory of aggression holds that people learn to behave aggressively by observing aggressive models and by having their own aggressive responses reinforced (Bandura, 1973). Aggression is higher in groups and subcultures that condone violent behavior and accord high status to aggressive members. A leading advocate of the social learning theory of aggression, Albert Bandura (1976), claims that aggressive models in the subculture, the family, and the media all play a part in increasing the level of aggression in society.

Abused children certainly experience aggression and see it modeled day after day. And the rate of physical abuse is seven times greater in families where there is a step-parent (Daly & Wilson, 1996). "One of the most commonly held beliefs in both the scholarly and popular literature is that adults who were abused as children are more likely to abuse their own children" (Widom, 1989, p. 6). There is some truth to this belief. On the basis of original research and an analysis of 60 other studies, Oliver (1993) concludes that one-third of people who are abused go on to become abusers, one-third do not, and the final third may become abusers if the social stress in their lives is sufficient.

Most abusive parents, however, were not abused as children (Widom, 1989b). Although abused and neglected children are at higher risk of becoming delinquent, criminal, or violent, the majority do not (Widom & Maxfield, 1996). Several researchers suggest that the higher risk for aggression may not be due solely to an abusive family environment but may be partly influenced by the genes (DiLalla & Gottesman, 1991). Some abused children become withdrawn and isolated rather than aggressive (Dodge, Bates, & Pettit, 1990).

The Media and Aggression: Is There a Connection?   By the time the average American child completes elementary school, he or she will have watched over 8,000 murders and more than 100,000 various other acts of violence (Huston et al., 1992). But is there a causal link between viewing aggressive acts and committing them? Some studies say no (Freedman, 1996; Milavsky et al., 1982), but the evidence overwhelmingly reveals a relationship between TV violence and viewer aggression (Huesmann & Moise, 1996). And the negative effects of TV violence are even worse for individuals who are, by nature, highly aggressive (Bushman, 1995).

Participants in a longitudinal study of 600 7- to 9-year-old boys launched in 1960 were reinterviewed at age 19 and again at age 30 (Eron, 1987). The males who were most aggressive at age 8 were still aggressive at ages 19 and 30, many of them showing antisocial behavior ranging from traffic violations to criminal convictions and aggressiveness toward their spouses and children (Huesmann et al., 1984). Did media influence play a part? "One of the best predictors of how aggressive a young man would be at age 19 was the violence of the TV programs he preferred when he was 8 years old" (Eron, 1987, p. 438). And the more frequently the subjects had watched TV violence at that age, "the more serious were the crimes for which they were convicted by age 30" (p. 440). A longitudinal study conducted in Finland also found that the viewing of TV violence was related to criminality in young adulthood (Viemerö, 1996).

A review of 28 studies of the effects of media violence on children and adolescents revealed that "media violence enhances children's and adolescents' aggression in interactions with strangers, classmates, and friends" (Wood et al., 1991, p. 380). Media violence may stimulate physiological arousal, lower inhibitions, cause unpleasant feelings, and decrease sensitivity to violence and make it more acceptable to people (Wood et al., 1991).

Are violent episodes of TV shows in which the "good guys" finally get the "bad guys" less harmful? Not according to Berkowitz (1964), who claims that justified aggression is the type most likely to encourage the viewer to express aggression.

Can aggression be reduced in American society? The best hope is to find ways to reduce aggression in families, eliminate reinforcement for aggression, and remove excessive violence from the media (Eron, 1980).

density: A measure referring to the number of people occupying a unit of space.

crowding: A subjective perception that there are too many people in a defined space.

Link It!

Nonverbal Behavior– The Silent Language

He that has eyes to see and ears to hear may convince himself that no mortal can keep a secret. If his lips are silent, he chatters with his fingertips; betrayal oozes out of him at every pore.

–Sigmund Freud

There is some truth to the old saying "It's not what you say, it's how you say it." When you speak, what emotional impact does the verbal message alone, the words themselves, have on your listeners? Very little, according to Albert Mehrabian (1968). He claims that the emotional impact of a communication is influenced only slightly (about 7%) by the verbal message itself. More than five times as powerful is what he calls the vocal message–tone of voice, pronunciation, stress on words, vocal inflections, and the length and frequency of pauses–which provides 38% of the impact. If you were 30 minutes late for class and your professor said in a sarcastic tone, "We're so happy that you could join us today," would you believe the vocal message (the sarcastic tone) or the verbal message?

The most powerful impact of a message comes not from the verbal or the vocal aspect, but from *nonverbal behavior*–facial expressions, gestures, posture, and so on–which provides an amazing 55% of the emotional impact of a message. If the nonverbal behavior and the verbal message do not match, which one is more likely to be attended to? Almost every time, the nonverbal message comes across as the real one.

Communicating feelings through nonverbal cues. Nonverbal behavior reveals a great deal about how we feel about others and how others feel about us. It can communicate anger, liking, love, happiness, sadness, anxiety, impatience, deception, and difference in status among people. But it is important to avoid attributing meaning to an isolated clue apart from its context.

People are best at reading nonverbal behavior that signals anger and a possible threat to their well-being. Cold stares will make almost anyone tense and uncomfortable.

Nonverbal behavior often reveals attitudes toward others. Encountering people or objects we like, we tend to move closer to them, lean toward them, and look directly at them. Our pupils dilate as if to take in more of them. The opposite occurs when we confront something or someone we dislike. Our pupils constrict, we tend to stand farther away or look away, and we often assume a closed position with arms and/or legs crossed.

Two people who are romantically involved cannot easily conceal their feelings. Their nonverbal behavior usually sends a clear message. They often gaze into each other's eyes and generally position themselves closer to each other than do friends or acquaintances. They exchange touches, lean toward one another, and often mirror each other's body language. When two people meet at a party and find each other attractive, they usually communicate their feelings to each other, although often unconsciously. Dilated pupils, extended eye contact, bodies leaning toward each other, and preening behavior–stroking the hair, readjusting the clothes–are all signs of interest.

Nonverbal behavior also communicates self-esteem or lack thereof, and whether we are relaxed or ill at ease. And gestures even signal social status relative to the person with whom we are interacting.

Touch can be a sign of warmth and intimacy, a sign of sexual interest, or a means of conveying higher status (Major et al., 1990). Higher-status persons are more likely to touch lower-status persons than vice versa (Henley, 1973). In nonintimate settings, men are more likely to touch women than the reverse (Major et al., 1990).

Nonverbal behavior can reveal deceit. In his book *Telling Lies*, Ekman (1985) states that failure to look you in the eye is not necessarily a sign of lying but can indicate that a person is uncomfortable under scrutiny. More telling cues are overly long smiles, frowns, or looks of disbelief. Genuine expressions don't last longer than 4 or 5 seconds. Furthermore, genuine smiles are usually symmetrical, in contrast to phony smiles, which tend to be lopsided. True feelings often slip through in the form of fleeting microexpressions that are quickly replaced by the expression meant to deceive (Ekman et al., 1988). In deception there are discrepancies among the verbal, vocal, and nonverbal messages. Finally, when people are lying, they often have more pauses in their speech and begin sentences, stop, then begin again (Stiff et al., 1989).

Gestures–different meanings in different countries. When traveling in another country, most tourists find a phrase book indispensable, and some even make an effort to learn another language. But even if tourists learn to speak a foreign language like natives, few will recognize that the gestures they use in communicating may convey something entirely different in another country.

For instance, after a wonderful dinner in Naples, Italy, an American, wishing to thank his waiter for fine food and expert service, flashed a big smile and the A-okay sign. The stunned waiter turned pale and rushed to the restaurant manager, and the two of them discussed excitedly whether they should call the police and have the American arrested for obscene and vulgar behavior in a public place. The A-okay gesture is not a friendly one in all cultures. The smiling American tourist had unwittingly used a sign that called his waiter a name that is a crude and vulgar reference to the anal opening. In Turkey and Greece the same gesture signals a lewd, insulting sexual invitation.

Ironically, if we are trying to communicate with people who speak a different language, we are even more likely to use an abundance of gestures. Gestures can be powerful communication tools, but travelers should be careful when using them in cultures other than their own.

SUMMARY AND REVIEW

INTRODUCTION TO SOCIAL PSYCHOLOGY

Key Terms

social psychology (p. 455); confederate (p. 456); naive subject (p. 456)

SOCIAL PERCEPTION

Why are first impressions so important and enduring?

First impressions are important because people attend more carefully to the first information that they receive about another person; and because, once formed, an impression acts as a framework through which later information is interpreted.

What is the difference between a situational attribution and a dispositional attribution for a specific behavior?

An attribution is an inference about the cause of one's own or another's behavior. In making situational attributions, people attribute the cause of behavior to some factor in the environment. With dispositional attributions, the inferred cause is internal—some personal trait, motive, or attitude.

How do the kinds of attributions people tend to make about themselves differ from those they make about other people?

People tend to overemphasize dispositional factors when making attributions about the behavior of other people and to overemphasize situational factors in explaining their own behavior.

Key Terms

primacy effect (p. 456); attribution (p. 457); situational attribution (p. 457); dispositional attribution (p. 457); fundamental attribution error (p. 457); self-serving bias (p. 457)

ATTRACTION

Why is proximity an important factor in attraction?

Proximity influences attraction because it is easier to develop relationships with people who are close at hand. Also, proximity increases the likelihood that there will be repeated contacts, and

mere exposure tends to increase attraction (the mere-exposure effect).

How important is physical attractiveness in attraction?

Physical attractiveness is a major factor in attraction for people of all ages. People attribute positive qualities to those who are physically attractive—a phenomenon called the halo effect.

Are people, as a rule, more attracted to those who are opposite or to those who are similar to them?

People are generally attracted to those who have similar attitudes and interests, and who are similar in economic status, race, and age.

Key Terms

proximity (p. 458); mere-exposure effect (p. 458); halo effect (p. 459); matching hypothesis (p. 460)

CONFORMITY, OBEDIENCE, AND COMPLIANCE

What did Asch find in his famous experiment on conformity?

In Asch's classic study on conformity, 5% of the participants went along with the incorrect, unanimous majority all the time; 70% went along some of the time; and 25% remained completely independent.

What did Milgram find in his classic study of obedience?

In Milgram's classic study of obedience, 65% of the participants obeyed the experimenter's orders to the end of the experiment and administered what they believed to be increasingly painful shocks to the learner, up to the maximum of 450 volts.

What are three techniques used to gain compliance?

Three techniques used to gain compliance are the foot-in-the-door technique, the door-in-the-face technique, and the low-ball technique.

Key Terms

conformity (p. 462); norms (p. 462); compliance (p. 464); foot-in-the-door

technique (p. 464); door-in-the-face technique (p. 465); low-ball technique (p. 465)

GROUP INFLUENCE

Under what conditions does social facilitation have either a positive or a negative effect on performance?

When others are present, either as an audience or as co-actors, a person's performance on easy tasks is usually improved, but performance on difficult tasks is usually impaired.

What is social loafing, and what factors lessen or eliminate it?

Social loafing is people's tendency to put forth less effort when they are working with others on a common task than when working alone. It is less likely to occur when individual output can be monitored or when people have a personal stake in the outcome.

How are the initial attitudes of group members likely to affect group decision making?

Following group discussions, group decisions usually shift to a more extreme position, in whatever direction the members were leaning toward initially—a phenomenon known as group polarization.

Key Terms

social facilitation (p. 466); audience effects (p. 466); coaction effects (p. 466); social loafing (p. 466); group polarization (p. 467); groupthink (p. 467); social roles (p. 467)

ATTITUDES AND ATTITUDE CHANGE

What are the three components of an attitude?

An attitude usually has a cognitive, an emotional, and a behavioral component.

What is cognitive dissonance, and how can it be resolved?

Cognitive dissonance is an unpleasant state that can occur when people become aware of inconsistencies among their attitudes or between their attitudes and their behavior. People can resolve cognitive dissonance by rationalizing away the inconsistency or by changing the attitude or the behavior.

What are the four elements of persuasion?

The four elements of persuasion are the source, the audience, the message, and the medium.

What qualities make a source most persuasive?

Persuasive attempts are most successful when the source is credible (expert and trustworthy), attractive, and likable.

Key Terms
attitude (p. 468); cognitive dissonance (p. 469); persuasion (p. 470)

PREJUDICE AND DISCRIMINATION

What is the difference between prejudice and discrimination?

Prejudice consists of attitudes (usually negative) toward others based on their gender, religion, race, or membership in a particular group. Discrimination consists of actions against others based on the same factors.

What is meant by the terms in-group and out-group?

An in-group is a social group with a strong sense of togetherness and from which others are excluded; an out-group consists of individuals or groups specifically identified by the in-group as not belonging.

How does prejudice develop, according to the social learning theory?

According to this theory, prejudice is learned the same way other attitudes are—through modeling and reinforcement.

What are stereotypes?

Stereotypes are widely shared beliefs about the characteristics of members of various social groups (racial, ethnic, religious), including the assumption that the members of such groups are usually all alike.

What are two strategies for reducing prejudice and discrimination?

Several strategies for reducing prejudice include arranging appropriate educational experiences for children and providing situations in which diverse social groups can interact under certain favorable conditions.

Key Terms
prejudice (p. 471); discrimination (p. 471); realistic conflict theory (p. 471); in-group (p. 471); out-group (p. 471); social cognition (p. 472); stereotypes (p. 472); contact hypothesis (p. 474)

PROSOCIAL BEHAVIOR: BEHAVIOR THAT BENEFITS OTHERS

What is the bystander effect, and what factors have been suggested to explain why it occurs?

The bystander effect means that as the number of bystanders at an emergency increases, the probability that the victim will receive help decreases, and help, if given, is likely to be delayed. The bystander effect may be due in part to diffusion of responsibility or, in ambiguous situations, to the assumption that no emergency exists.

Key Terms
bystander effect (p. 476); diffusion of responsibility (p. 477); prosocial behavior (p. 477); altruism (p. 477)

AGGRESSION: INTENTIONALLY HARMING OTHERS

What biological factors are thought to be related to aggression?

Biological factors thought to be related to aggression are a genetic link in criminal behavior, high testosterone levels, low levels of serotonin, and brain damage.

What is the frustration–aggression hypothesis?

The frustration–aggression hypothesis holds that frustration produces aggression and that this aggression may be directed at the frustrater or displaced onto another target, as in scapegoating.

What kinds of aversive events and unpleasant emotions have been related to aggression?

Aggression has been associated with aversive conditions such as pain, heat, loud noise, foul odors, and crowding, and with unpleasant emotional states such as sadness, grief, and depression.

What is the difference between density and crowding?

Density is an objective measure of the number of people occupying a defined physical space. Crowding is subjective and refers to the perception that there are too many people in a defined space.

According to social learning theory, what causes aggressive behavior?

According to social learning theory, people acquire aggressive responses by observing aggressive models in the family, the subculture, and the media, and by having aggressive responses reinforced.

Key Terms
aggression (p. 478); frustration (p. 479); frustration–aggression hypothesis (p. 479); scapegoating (p. 479); personal space (p. 479); density (p. 480); crowding (p. 480)

Study Guide for Chapter 14

Answers to all the Study Guide questions are provided at the end of the book.

Section One: Chapter Review

1. Which of the following statements about first impressions is *false*?
   a. People usually pay closer attention to early information they receive about a person than to later information.
   b. Early information forms a framework through which later information is interpreted.
   c. First impressions often serve as self-fulfilling prophecies.
   d. The importance of first impressions is greatly overrated.

2. People tend to make _____ attributions to explain their own behavior and _____ attributions to explain the behavior of others.
   a. situational; situational
   b. situational; dispositional
   c. dispositional; situational
   d. dispositional; dispositional

3. The tendency of people to overemphasize dispositional causes and underemphasize situational causes when they explain the behavior of others is called the
   a. fundamental attribution error.
   b. false consensus error.
   c. self-serving bias.
   d. external bias error.

4. Attributing Mike's poor grade to his lack of ability is a dispositional attribution. (true/false)

5. Match each term with a description.
   ____ (1) Brian sees Susan at the library often and begins to like her.
   ____ (2) Liane assumes that because Boyd is handsome, he must be popular and sociable.
   ____ (3) Alan and Carol are going together and are both very attractive.
   a. matching hypothesis
   b. halo effect
   c. mere-exposure effect

6. Physical attractiveness is a very important factor in initial attraction. (true/false)

7. People are usually drawn to those who are more opposite than similar to themselves. (true/false)

8. Match the technique for gaining compliance with the appropriate example.
   ____ (1) Julie agrees to sign a letter supporting an increase in taxes for road construction. Later she agrees to make 100 phone calls urging people to vote for the measure.
   ____ (2) Rick refuses a phone request for a $24 donation to send four needy children to the circus but does agree to give $6.
   ____ (3) Linda agrees to babysit for her next-door neighbors' two girls and then is informed that their three nephews will be there, too.
   a. door-in-the-face technique
   b. low-ball technique
   c. foot-in-the-door technique

9. What percentage of subjects in the Asch study never conformed to the majority's unanimous incorrect response?
   a. 70%   c. 25%
   b. 33%   d. 5%

10. What percentage of the subjects in Milgram's original obedience experiment administered what they thought was the maximum 450-volt shock?
    a. 85%   c. 45%
    b. 65%   d. 25%

11. Which of the following statements regarding the effects of social facilitation (the presence of other people) is true?
    a. Performance improves on all tasks.
    b. Performance worsens on all tasks.
    c. Performance improves on easy tasks and worsens on difficult tasks.
    d. Performance improves on difficult tasks and worsens on easy tasks.

12. Social loafing is most likely to occur when
    a. individual output is monitored.
    b. individual output is evaluated.
    c. a task is challenging.
    d. individual output cannot be identified.

13. What occurs when members of a very cohesive group are more concerned with preserving group solidarity than with evaluating all possible alternatives in making a decision?
    a. groupthink
    c. social facilitation
    b. group polarization
    d. social loafing

14. Which of the following is *not* one of the three components of an attitude?
    a. cognitive component
    b. emotional component
    c. physiological component
    d. behavioral component

15. All of the following are ways to reduce cognitive dissonance *except*
    a. changing an attitude.
    b. changing a behavior.
    c. explaining away the inconsistency.
    d. strengthening the attitude and behavior.

16. People who have made a great sacrifice to join a group usually decrease their liking for the group. (true/false)

17. Credibility relates most directly to the communicator's
    a. attractiveness.
    b. expertise and trustworthiness.
    c. likability.
    d. personality.

18. With a well-informed audience, two-sided messages are more persuasive than one-sided messages. (true/false)

19. High-fear appeals are more effective than low-fear appeals if they provide definite actions that people can take to avoid dreaded outcomes. (true/false)

20. Match the example with the term.
    ____ (1) José was promoted because the firm needed one Hispanic manager.
    ____ (2) Darlene thinks all Whites are racists.
    ____ (3) Betty's salary is $5,000 less than that of her male counterpart.
    ____ (4) Bill can't stand Jews.
    a. stereotypic thinking
    b. discrimination
    c. prejudice
    d. tokenism

21. Members of an in-group often like out-group members as individuals. (true/false)

22. The social learning theory suggests that prejudice develops and is maintained through

    a. competition and ambition.
    b. us-versus-them thinking.
    c. modeling and reinforcement.
    d. genetic inheritance.

23. Researchers have found that bringing diverse social groups together almost always decreases hostility and prejudice. (true/false)

24. The bystander effect is influenced by all of the following *except*
    a. the number of bystanders.
    b. the personalities of bystanders.
    c. whether the bystanders appear calm.
    d. whether the situation is ambiguous.

25. Altruism is one form of prosocial behavior. (true/false)

26. As the number of bystanders at an emergency increases, the probability that the victim will receive help decreases. (true/false)

27. In an ambiguous situation, a good way to determine if an emergency exists is to look at the reactions of other bystanders. (true/false)

28. The social learning theory of aggression emphasizes all of the following *except* that
    a. aggressive responses are learned from the family, the subculture, and the media.
    b. aggressive acts are learned through modeling.
    c. most aggression results from frustration.
    d. when aggression responses are reinforced, they are more likely to continue.

29. Pain, extreme heat, loud noise and foul odors have all been associated with an increase in aggressive responses. (true/false)

30. Social psychologists generally believe that aggression stems from an aggressive instinct. (true/false)

31. According to the frustration–aggression hypothesis, frustration _____ leads to aggression.
    a. always
    c. rarely
    b. often
    d. never

32. Which of the following statements is *not* true of personal space?
    a. It functions to protect privacy and regulate intimacy.
    b. How much personal space a person requires is affected by culture, race, gender, and personality.
    c. The size of a person's personal space is fixed.
    d. Invasions of personal space are usually perceived as unpleasant.

33. Research tends to support the notion that a person can drain off aggressive energy by watching others behave aggressively in sports or on television. (true/false)

34. Research suggests that media violence is probably related to increased aggression. (true/false)

Section Two: Match Terms with Definitions

_____ (1) effect of one major positive or negative trait

_____ (2) as more viewers gather at the scene of an emergency, a victim's chances of help are reduced

_____ (3) geographic closeness

_____ (4) the blocking of an impulse

_____ (5) attitudes and standards of a group

_____ (6) relatively stable evaluation of a person, object, situation, or issue

_____ (7) impact of passive spectators on performance

_____ (8) number of people occupying a unit of space

_____ (9) the tendency of individuals to go along with the group even if they disagree

_____ (10) widely shared beliefs about traits of members of certain groups

_____ (11) the fact that one's overall impression is influenced by a first impression

_____ (12) displacing aggression onto innocent people

_____ (13) making a large request in the hope of gaining compliance with a subsequent small request

_____ (14) the intentional infliction of harm on another

a. frustration

b. proximity

c. aggression

d. scapegoating

e. bystander effect

f. halo effect

g. door-in-the-face technique

h. norms

i. attitude

j. groupthink

k. stereotypes

l. audience effect

m. primacy effect

n. density

Section Three: Fill In the Blank

1. A(n) _____ is a relatively stable evaluation of a person, object, situation, or issue.

2. Research reveals that our overall impression of another person is more influenced by the first information we have about the individual than by later information about the person. This tendency is called the _____ _____.

3. Jaime explained his poor grade on his math test by saying that he is a right-brained person and, therefore, more the artistic type than the analytical type. He is making a _____ attribution.

4. We tend to use _____ factors to explain our own behavior and _____ factors to explain the behavior of others.

5. Sue tends to attribute her successes to internal factors and her failure to situational factors. This tendency is known as the _____ _____.

6. People tend to infer generally positive or negative traits in a person as a result of observing one major positive or negative trait. This tendency is known as the _____ effect.

7. A classic study in social psychology is Milgram's research on _____. His experiment revealed that most participants were willing to follow orders and deliver the strongest possible shock to a confederate for giving wrong answers in a memory test.

8. Individual performance may be affected by the mere physical presence of others. This effect is known as _____ _____.

9. Group polarization refers to the tendency of group members, following a discussion, to take a more _____ position on the issue at hand.

10. A(n) _____ is a widely shared belief about the characteristics of members of various social groups and includes the assumption that all members of a social group are alike.

11. The _____ hypothesis suggests that we can reduce prejudice and stereotypical thinking by increasing our contact and interaction with people from other groups.

12. As the number of bystanders at an emergency increases, the probability that anyone will help a victim decreases. This phenomenon is known as the _____ effect.

13. Jim suffered serious injury while attempting to save a child from being run over by a car. Jim's action is an example of _____.

14. One of the earliest explanations for aggression was the _____ theory. Although most current psychologists reject this theory, many agree that biological factors can play a role in aggression.

15. The _____ hypothesis suggests that frustration can result in aggression.

16. _____ occurs when a person is the undeserving victim of someone else's displaced aggression, which is due to that person's frustration.

17. A(n) _____ is an inference about the cause of our own or another's behavior.

18. _____ is changing or adopting an attitude or behavior to be consistent with the norms of a group or the expectations of others.

Section Four: Comprehensive Practice Test

1. Dispositional attribution is to _____ as situational attribution is to _____.
   a. external factors; internal factors
   b. others; self
   c. self; others
   d. internal factors; external factors

2. Jan attributed Bill's poor oral presentation to his basic lack of motivation to be a good student and to be prepared for class. Assuming Jan was wrong and Bill's poor performance was due to some other, external factor, Jan was making an error called the self-serving bias. (true/false)

3. Jan's own oral presentation was also poor. She explained that the students in the front row were goofing off and distracting her. Jan was excusing her performance with the
   a. primary attribution error.
   b. fundamental self-bias error.
   c. self-serving bias.
   d. error of external factors.

4. The concept of proximity relates to
   a. attribution.   c. aggression.
   b. attraction.   d. prejudice.

5. In the past few decades people have become less influenced by physical attractiveness and more influenced by internal factors such as personality. (true/false)

6. Jesse's mother reminded him to check his tie and comb his hair prior to meeting the interviewer at his college admissions interview. Jesse's mother was probably concerned about the _____ effect.
   a. attenuation   c. Harvard
   b. Soloman   d. halo

7. The old adage "Birds of a feather flock together" summarizes the concept of _____, one of the factors that influence attraction.
   a. attribution   c. similarity
   b. social influence   d. proximity

8. Research reveals that low autonomic nervous system arousal levels seem to be related to aggressive behavior. (true/false)

9. The _____ hypothesis suggests that under certain conditions, people can reduce prejudice and stereotypical thinking through increased contact and interaction between different groups.
   a. social interaction   c. social contract
   b. proximity   d. contact

10. The terms *stereotype* and *prejudice* are actually different words for the same thing. (true/false)

11. A negative attitude toward a person based on gender, religion, race, or membership in a certain group is known as
    a. discrimination.   c. a stereotype.
    b. prejudice.   d. social dissonance.

12. Strategies such as changing a behavior, changing an attitude, explaining away an inconsistency, or minimizing the importance of an inconsistency are all used to reduce
    a. cognitive distortion bias.
    b. relative attribution frustration.
    c. cognitive dissonance.
    d. inconsistency anxiety.

13. _____ are the attitudes and standards of behavior expected of members of a particular group.
    a. Values   c. Norms
    b. Social rules   d. Social postures

14. Wood and others would suggest that those who hold a minority opinion have more influence on a majority group if
    a. the opinion is stated vaguely so its departure from the majority opinion is disguised.
    b. the opinion is clearly stated and well organized.
    c. the opinion is stated as a question.
    d. the opinion is stated with qualifications that complement the majority opinion.

15. One strategy to induce compliance to a request is known as the _____ technique. In this strategy, the person making the request secures a favorable response to a small request with the aim of making the person more likely to agree to a larger request later.
    a. door-in-the-face   c. foot-in-the-door
    b. low-ball   d. risky shift

16. A good example of the door-in-the-face technique is to ask $10,000 for your used car, hoping that the buyer, who is likely to refuse to pay that much, will then be willing to agree to pay $8,000, the price you wanted in the first place. (true/false)

17. Social loafing refers to
    a. the tendency to avoid social contact and interpersonal relationships.
    b. the tendency to exert less effort when working with others on a common task.
    c. the tendency to be less productive when working alone than with others.
    d. the tendency to see others' work as more externally motivated than one's own.

18. A common finding on audience effects is that when we are being watched, we tend to do better on easy tasks and on more difficult tasks at which we are more proficient. (true/false)

19. Which of the following is not listed as a component of an attitude?
    a. social component
    b. behavioral component
    c. cognitive component
    d. emotional component

Section Five: Critical Thinking

1. Many Americans were surprised when the majority of people in the Soviet Union rejoiced at the downfall of the Communist system. Using what you have learned about attribution bias and conformity, explain why many Americans had mistakenly believed that the Soviet masses preferred Communism.

2. Prepare a convincing argument supporting each of these positions:
   a. Aggression results largely from biological factors (nature).
   b. Aggression is primarily learned (nurture).

3. Review the factors influencing impression formation and attraction discussed in this chapter. Prepare a dual list of behaviors indicating what you should and should not do if you wish to make a better impression on other people and to increase their liking for you.

Appendix: Statistical Methods

Comedian Tim Conway, who appeared on the Carol Burnett show many years ago, once did a humorous skit as an inept sports announcer. Reporting the daily baseball scores, he said, "And now here are the scores in the National League: 6 to 4, 3 to nothing, 2 to 1, 8 to 3, and 5 to 2." Conway's report of baseball scores may have been humorous, but it was not very informative. Numbers alone tell us very little.

Psychologists must deal with mountains of data in conducting their studies. The data they compute would be just as meaningless as Conway's baseball scores unless some methods were available to organize and describe the data. Fortunately, there are such methods. *Statistics*, a branch of mathematics, enables psychologists and other scientists to organize, describe, and draw conclusions about the quantitative results of their studies. We will explore the two basic types of statistics that psychologists use—descriptive statistics and inferential statistics.

DESCRIPTIVE STATISTICS

Descriptive statistics are statistics used to organize, summarize, and describe data. Descriptive statistics include measures of central tendency, variability, and relationship.

Measures of Central Tendency

A **measure of central tendency** is a measure or score that describes the center, or middle, of a distribution of scores. The most widely used and the most familiar measure of central tendency is the mean, which is short for arithmetic mean. The **mean** is the arithmetic average of a group of scores. One computes the mean by adding up all the single scores and dividing the sum by the number of scores.

Carl is a student who sometimes studies and does well in his classes, but occasionally he procrastinates and fails a test. Table A.1 shows how Carl performed on the seven tests in his psychology class last semester. Carl computes his mean score by adding up all his test scores and dividing the sum by the number of tests. Carl's mean, or average, score is 80.

The mean is an important and widely used statistical measure of central tendency, but it can be misleading when a group of scores contains one or several extreme scores. For example, in one group of 10 people, the mean annual income last year was $124,700. In this case, the figure for the mean income alone covers up more than it reveals. Table A.2 lists the annual incomes of the 10 people in rank order. When a million-dollar income is averaged with several other, more modest incomes, the mean does not provide a true picture of the group.

Therefore, when one or a few individuals score far above or below the middle range of a group, a different measure of central tendency should be used. The **median** is the middle value or score when a group of scores are arranged from highest to lowest. When there are an odd number of scores, the score in the middle is the median. When there are an even number of scores, the median is the average of the two middle scores.

For the 10 incomes arranged from highest to lowest in Table A.2, the median is $27,000, which is the average of the middle incomes, $28,000 and $26,000. The median

Table A.1   Carl's Psychology Test Scores

Test 1	98
Test 2	74
Test 3	86
Test 4	92
Test 5	56
Test 6	68
Test 7	86
Sum:	560

Mean: 560 ÷ 7 = 80

descriptive statistics: Statistics used to organize, summarize, and describe information gathered from actual observations.

measure of central tendency: A measure or score that describes the center, or middle, of a distribution of scores (example: mean, median, or mode).

mean: The arithmetic average of a group of scores; calculated by adding up all the single scores and dividing the sum by the number of scores.

median: The middle value or score when a group of scores are arranged from highest to lowest.

Table A.2 Annual Income for 10 People

Subject	Annual Income
1	$1,000,000
2	$50,000
3	$43,000
4	$30,000
5	$28,000
6	$26,000
7	$22,000
8	$22,000
9	$16,000
10	$10,000
Sum:	$1,247,000

$28,000 and $26,000 → $27,000 = Median

$22,000 and $22,000 → Mode

Mean: $1,247,000 ÷ 10 = $124,700

Median: $27,000

Mode: $22,000

income—$27,000—is a truer reflection of the comparative income of the group than is the $124,700 mean. It is important to select the measure of central tendency that most accurately reflects the group being studied.

Another measure of central tendency is the mode. The **mode** is easy to find, because it is the score that occurs most frequently in a group of scores. The mode of the annual-income group is $22,000.

Link It!

Describing Data with Tables and Graphs

A researcher tested 100 students for recall of 20 new vocabulary words. The students were tested 24 hours after they had memorized the list. The raw scores (number of words recalled), arranged from lowest to highest, for the 100 students are as follows.

2	4	4	5	5	6	6	6	6	7
7	7	7	7	7	7	7	8	8	8
8	8	8	8	8	8	8	9	9	9
9	9	9	9	9	9	9	10	10	10
10	10	10	10	10	10	10	10	10	10
11	11	11	11	11	11	11	11	11	11
11	11	12	12	12	12	12	12	12	12
12	12	12	13	13	13	13	13	13	13
13	13	14	14	14	14	14	14	14	14
15	15	15	15	15	16	16	16	17	19

We can tell from the raw data that one student remembered only 2 words (the lowest score) and that one student remembered 19 words (the highest score). We can also observe that the most frequently occurring score, the mode, is 10.

mode: The score that occurs most frequently in a group of scores.

Table A.3   Frequency Distribution of 100 Vocabulary Test Scores

Class Interval	Tally of Scores in Each Class Interval	Number of Scores in Each Class Interval (Frequency)
1–2	|	1
3–4	||	2
5–6	ⅢⅡ |	6
7–8	ⅢⅡ ⅢⅡ ⅢⅡ |||	18
9–10	ⅢⅡ ⅢⅡ ⅢⅡ ⅢⅡ |||	23
11–12	ⅢⅡ ⅢⅡ ⅢⅡ ⅢⅡ |||	23
13–14	ⅢⅡ ⅢⅡ ⅢⅡ ||	17
15–16	ⅢⅡ |||	8
17–18	|	1
19–20	|	1

frequency distribution: An arrangement showing the numbers of scores that fall within equal-sized class intervals.

histogram: A bar graph that depicts the number of scores within each class interval in a frequency distribution.

frequency polygon: A line graph that depicts the frequency or number of scores within each class interval in a frequency distribution.

variability: How much the scores in a distribution spread out, away from the mean.

range: The difference between the highest score and the lowest score in a distribution of scores.

The researcher organized the scores in a **frequency distribution**—an arrangement showing the numbers of scores that fall within equal-sized class intervals. To organize the 100 test scores, the researcher decided to use intervals of two points each. (A different class interval—three points, for example—could have been chosen instead.) Next the researcher tallied the frequency (number of scores) within each two-point interval. Table A.3 presents the resulting frequency distribution.

The researcher then made a histogram, a more graphic representation of the frequency distribution. A **histogram** is a bar graph that depicts the number of scores within each class interval in the frequency distribution. The intervals are plotted along the horizontal axis, and the frequency of scores in each interval is plotted along the vertical axis. Figure A.1 shows the histogram for the 100 test scores.

Another common method for representing frequency data is the **frequency polygon**. As in a histogram, the class intervals are plotted along the horizontal axis and the frequencies are plotted along the vertical axis. However, in a frequency polygon, each graph point is placed at the middle (midpoint) of a class interval so that its vertical distance above the horizontal axis shows the frequency of that interval. Lines are drawn to connect the points, as shown in Figure A.2. The histogram and the frequency polygon are simply two different ways of presenting data.

Figure A.1

A Frequency Histogram

Vocabulary test scores from the frequency distribution in Table A.3 are plotted here in the form of a frequency histogram. Class intervals of 2 points each appear on the horizontal axis. Frequencies of the scores in each class interval are plotted on the vertical axis.

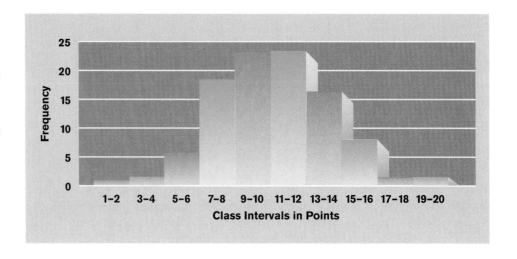

Measures of Variability

Researchers usually need more information than measures of central tendency can provide. Often they need to know the **variability** of a set of scores—how much the scores spread out, away from the mean. There can be tremendous differences in variability even when the mean and the median of two sets of scores are exactly the same, as you can see in Table A.4.

Both groups in Table A.4 have a mean and a median of 80. However, the scores in Group II cluster tightly around the mean, while the scores in Group I vary widely from the mean. Just looking at the data is not sufficient for determining variability. Fortunately researchers have statistical techniques available for measuring variability with great precision.

The Range   The simplest measure of variability is the **range**—the difference between the highest and lowest scores in a distribution of scores. Table A.4 reveals that Group I has a range of 47, indicating high variability, while Group II has a range of only 7, showing low variability. Unfortunately the range is as limited as it is simple. It reveals the difference between the lowest score and the highest score but tells nothing about the scores in between. A more sophisticated measure of variability is the standard deviation.

The Standard Deviation   The **standard deviation** is a descriptive statistic reflecting the average amount that scores in a distribution deviate, or vary, from their mean. The larger the standard deviation, the greater the variability in a distribution of scores. Refer to Table A.4 and note the standard deviations for the two distributions of test scores. In Group I the relatively large standard deviation of 18.1 reflects the wide variability in that distribution. By contrast, the small standard

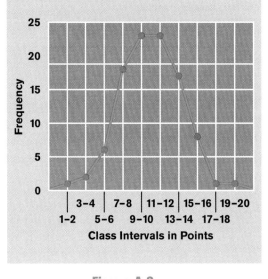

Figure A.2

A Frequency Polygon

Vocabulary test scores from the frequency distribution in Table A.3 are plotted here in the form of a frequency polygon. Class intervals of 2 points each appear on the horizontal axis. Frequencies of the scores in each class interval are plotted on the vertical axis.

Table A.4   Comparison of Range and Standard Deviation for Two Small Groups of Scores Having Identical Means and Medians

Group I			Group II		
Test	Score		Test	Score	
1	99		1	83	
2	99		2	82	
3	98		3	81	
4	80	Median	4	80	Median
5	72		5	79	
6	60		6	79	
7	52		7	76	
Sum:	560		Sum:	560	
Mean:	$\frac{560}{7} = 80$		Mean:	$\frac{560}{7} = 80$	
Median:	80		Median:	80	
Range:	$99 - 52 = 47$		Range:	$83 - 76 = 7$	
Standard deviation:	18.1		Standard deviation:	2.14	

standard deviation: A descriptive statistic reflecting the average amount that scores in a distribution deviate, or vary, from their mean.

normal curve: A symmetrical,
bell-shaped frequency distribution
that represents how scores are
normally distributed in a population; most scores fall near the
mean, and fewer and fewer scores
occur in the extremes either above
or below the mean.

deviation of 2.14 in Group II indicates that the variability is low, and you can see that the scores cluster tightly around the mean.

The Normal Curve

Psychologists and other scientists use descriptive statistics most often in connection with an important type of frequency distribution known as the normal curve, pictured in Figure A.3. The **normal curve** is a symmetrical, bell-shaped theoretical curve that represents how scores are normally distributed in a population.

If a large number of people are measured on any of a wide variety of traits, the majority of scores will fall near the mean of the distribution. There will be progressively fewer and fewer scores toward the extremes either above or below the mean. Even the small distribution of the 100 test scores in the histogram in Figure A.1 would yield a roughly bell-shaped curve. With increasingly larger numbers of scores in a distribution, the shape of the curve will more strongly resemble the ideal normal curve. On most variables researchers might measure (height or IQ score, for example), the great majority of values will cluster in the middle, with fewer and fewer individuals measuring extremely low or high on these variables. The normal distribution with its bell-shaped curve is a potent statistical concept with many very useful, practical applications.

Using the properties of the normal curve and knowing the mean and the standard deviation of a normal distribution, we can tell where any score stands (how high or low) in relation to all the other scores in the distribution. Look again at Figure A.3. You will note that slightly over 68% of the scores in a normal distribution fall within 1 standard deviation of the mean (34.13% within 1 standard deviation above the mean, and 34.13% within 1 standard deviation below the mean). Almost 95.5% of the scores in a normal distribution lie between 2 standard deviations above and below the mean. Theoretically the tails of the bell-shaped curve extend indefinitely, never touching the base line of the curve. Yet the vast majority of scores in a normal distribution, almost 99.75%, fall between 3 standard deviations above and below the mean.

On the Wechsler intelligence scales, the mean IQ is 100 and the standard deviation is 15. Thus, 99.72% of the population would have an IQ score within 3 standard deviations above and below the mean, ranging from an IQ of 55 to an IQ of 145. Recall from Chapter 7 that the highest IQ score ever recorded was an unbelievable 230 on the Stanford–Binet Intelligence Scale, scored by Marilyn Mach vos Savant. To plot her score on the normal curve, you would have to count 8½ standard deviations

Figure A.3
The Normal Curve

The normal curve is a symmetrical, bell-shaped curve that represents how scores are normally distributed in a population. Slightly over 68% of the scores in a normal distribution fall within 1 standard deviation above and below the mean. Almost 95.5% of the scores lie between 2 standard deviations above and below the mean, and about 99.75% fall between 3 standard deviations above and below the mean.

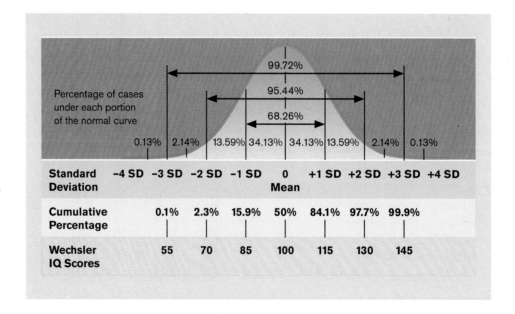

above the mean, so far up the right tail of the curve that her score would be in a standard deviation of its own. The nearest competing score of 210 was almost 7 standard deviations above the mean.

The statistical methods we have discussed so far, the measures of central tendency and the measures of variation, are designed to consider only one variable, such as test scores. What if researchers are interested in knowing whether two or more different variables are related to each other? The descriptive statistic used to show relationships between variables is the correlation coefficient.

The Correlation Coefficient

A **correlation coefficient** is a number that indicates the degree and direction of relationship between two variables. Correlation coefficients can range from +1.00 (a perfect positive correlation) to .00 (no correlation) to –1.00 (a perfect negative correlation). (See Figure A.4.) A **positive correlation** indicates that two variables vary in the same direction. An increase in one variable is associated with an increase in the other variable, or a decrease in one variable is associated with a decrease in the other. There is a positive correlation between the number of hours college students spend studying and their grades. The more hours they study, the higher their grades are likely to be.

A **negative correlation** means that an increase in one variable is associated with a decrease in the other variable. As we saw in Chapter 1, there is a negative correlation between cigarette smoking and life expectancy. When cigarette smoking increases, the number of years the smoker lives tends to decrease, and vice versa. There may be a negative correlation between the number of hours you spend watching television and studying. The more hours you spend watching TV, the fewer hours you may spend studying, and vice versa.

The sign + or – merely tells whether the two variables vary in the same or opposite directions. (If no sign appears, the correlation is assumed to be positive.) The number in a correlation coefficient indicates the relative strength of the relationship between two variables—the higher the number, the stronger the relationship. For example, a correlation of –.70 is higher than a correlation of +.56; a correlation of –.85 is just as strong as one of +.85. A correlation of .00 indicates that no relationship exists between the variables. IQ and shoe size are examples of two variables that are not correlated.

correlation coefficient: A numerical value indicating the strength and direction of relationship between two variables, which ranges from +1.00 (a perfect positive correlation) to -1.00 (a perfect negative correlation).

positive correlation: A relationship between two variables in which both vary in the same direction.

negative correlation: A relationship between two variables in which an increase in one variable is associated with a decrease in the other variable.

Negative Correlation / Positive Correlation

| Class absences | Course grade | Class absences | Course grade | SAT score | College GPA | SAT score | College GPA |

| Perfect negative correlation −1.00 | | | | No correlation .00 | | | Perfect positive correlation +1.00 |

Strength of Correlation

Increasing to −1.00 ◄──── .00 ────► Increasing to +1.00

Figure A.4

Understanding Correlation Coefficients

Correlation coefficients can range from −1.00 (a perfect negative correlation) through .00 (no correlation) to +1.00 (a perfect positive correlation). As the arrows indicate, a negative correlation exists when an increase in one variable is associated with a decrease in the other variable, and vice versa. A positive correlation exists when both variables tend to either increase or decrease together.

Table A.5　High School and College GPAs for 11 Students

Student	High School GPA (Variable X)	College GPA (Variable Y)
1	2.0	1.8
2	2.2	2.5
3	2.3	2.5
4	2.5	3.1
5	2.8	3.2
6	3.0	2.2
7	3.0	2.8
8	3.2	3.3
9	3.3	2.9
10	3.5	3.2
11	3.8	3.5

Figure A.5

A Scatterplot

A scatterplot reveals a relatively high positive correlation between the high school and college GPAs of the 11 students listed in Table A.5. One dot is plotted for each of the 11 students at the point where high school GPA (plotted on the horizontal axis) and college GPA (plotted on the vertical axis) intersect.

Table A.5 shows the measurements of two variables—high school GPA and college GPA for 11 college students. Most college and university admissions officers use high school grades along with standardized tests and other criteria to predict academic success in college.

Looking at the scores in Table A.5, we can observe that 6 of the 11 students had a higher GPA in high school, while 5 of the students had a higher GPA in college. A clearer picture of the actual relationship is shown by the scatterplot in Figure A.5. High school GPA (variable X) is plotted on the horizontal axis, and college GPA (variable Y) is plotted on the vertical axis.

One dot is plotted for each of the 11 students at the point where high school GPA, variable X, and college GPA, variable Y, intersect. For example, the first student's high school and college GPAs intersect at 2.0 on the horizontal (x) axis and at 1.8 on the vertical (y) axis. The scatterplot in Figure A.5 reveals a relatively high correlation between high school and college GPAs because the dots cluster near the diagonal line. It also shows that the correlation is positive because the dots run diagonally upward from left to right. The correlation coefficient for the high school and college GPAs of these 11 students is .71. If the correlation were perfect (1.00), all the dots would fall exactly on the diagonal line.

A scatterplot shows whether a correlation is low, moderate, or high and whether it is positive or negative. Scatterplots that run diagonally up from left to right reveal a positive correlation. Scatterplots that run diagonally down from left to right indicate a negative correlation. The closer the dots are to the diagonal line, the higher the correlation. The scatterplots in Figure A.6 depict a variety of correlations.

It is important to remember that correlation does not demonstrate cause and effect. Even a perfect correlation (+1.00 or –1.00) does not mean that one variable causes or is caused by the other. Correlation shows only that two variables are related.

Not all relationships between variables are positive or negative. The relationships between some variables are said to be *curvilinear*. A curvilinear relationship exists when two variables correlate positively (or negatively) up to a certain point and then change direction. For example, there is a positive correlation between physical strength

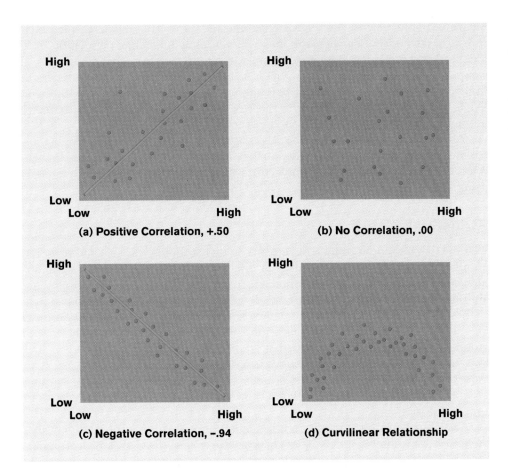

A Variety of Scatterplots

Scatterplots moving diagonally up from left to right as in (a) indicate a positive correlation. Scatterplots moving diagonally down from the left to right as in (c) indicate a negative correlation. The more closely the dots cluster around a diagonal line, the higher the correlation. Scatterplot (b) indicates no correlation. Scatterplot (d) shows a curvilinear relationship that is positive up to a point and then becomes negative. Age and strength of handgrip have a curvilinear relationship: Handgrip increases in strength up to about age 40, and then it decreases with continued aging.

(a) Positive Correlation, +.50

(b) No Correlation, .00

(c) Negative Correlation, −.94

(d) Curvilinear Relationship

and age up to about 40 or 45 years of age. As age increases from childhood to middle age, so does the strength of handgrip pressure. But beyond middle adulthood, the relationship becomes negative, and increasing age is associated with decreasing handgrip strength. Figure A.6(d) shows a scatterplot of this curvilinear relationship.

INFERENTIAL STATISTICS

We have seen that measures of central tendency, variability, and correlation are important in describing characteristics of data and in describing relationships between sets of data. Often, however, investigators wish to make inferences beyond the relatively small groups of subjects they actually measure. **Inferential statistics** allow researchers (1) to make inferences about the characteristics of the larger population from their observations and measurements of a sample, and (2) to derive estimates of how much faith or confidence can be placed in those inferences.

In statistical theory a **population** is the entire group that is of interest to researchers—the group to which they wish to apply their findings. For example, a population could be all the registered voters in the United States, all the members of a religious denomination or political party, and so on. On a smaller scale, a population might consist of all the female students, the entire senior class, or all the psychology professors at your college or university. A population need not consist of persons. It can be all the chihuahuas in California, all the automobile tires manufactured in the United States, or all the oranges grown in Florida in a given year. In short, a population is all members of any group a researcher may define for study.

Usually researchers cannot directly measure and study the entire population of interest, because the population may be extremely large or inaccessible, or studying

inferential statistics: Statistical procedures that allow researchers (1) to make inferences about the characteristics of the larger population from observations and measurements of a sample, and (2) to derive estimates of how much confidence can be placed in those inferences.

population: The entire group of interest to researchers and to which they wish to generalize their findings; the group from which a sample is selected.

sample: The portion of any population that is selected for study and from which generalizations are made about the entire population.

random sample: A sample of subjects selected in such a way that every member of the population has an equal chance of being included in the sample; its purpose is to obtain a sample that is representative of the population of interest.

the whole population may be too costly in time and money. But thanks to inferential statistical methods, researchers can make inferences about a large population from the direct observations of a relatively small sample selected from that population. A **sample** is the part of a population that is selected and studied. For researchers to draw conclusions about the larger population, the sample must be representative; that is, its characteristics must mirror those of the larger population. (See Chapter 1 for more information about representative samples.)

A **random sample** is selected in such a way that every member of the population has an equal chance of being included in the sample. To accomplish this, researchers select the sample using a chance procedure, such as pulling names out of a hat or using a table of random numbers generated by a computer.

Statistical Significance

Assume that a random sample of 200 psychology students was selected from the population of students at your college or university. Then the 200 students are randomly assigned to either the experimental group or the control group so that there are 100 students in each of these groups. Random assignment is accomplished by a chance procedure such as drawing names out of a hat. The experimental group is taught psychology with innovative learning materials for one semester. The control group receives the traditional instruction. At the end of the semester, researchers find that the mean test scores of the experimental group are considerably higher than those of the control group. Can the researchers conclude that the innovative learning program worked? No, not until they can show that the experimental results were not simply due to chance.

The researchers must use inferential statistical procedures to be confident that the results they observe are real (not chance occurrences). Tests of statistical significance yield an estimate of how often the experimental results could have occurred by chance alone. The estimates derived from tests of statistical significance are stated as probabilities. A probability of .05 means that the experimental results would be expected to occur by chance no more than 5 times out of 100. The .05 level of significance is usually required as a minimum for researchers to conclude that their findings are statistically significant. Often the level of significance reached is even more impressive, such as the .01 level. The .01 level means that the probability is no more than 1 in 100 that the results occurred by chance.

The inferences researchers make are not absolute. They are based on probability, and there is always a possibility, however small, that experimental results could occur by chance. For this reason replication of research studies is recommended.

Answers to Study Guide Questions

Chapter 1 (page 29)

Section One: Chapter Review 1. scientific method 2. description, explanation, prediction, control 3. false 4. (1) d (2) a (3) b (4) c 5. false 6. true 7. (1) d (2) c (3) a (4) b 8. d 9. true 10. c 11. false 12. b 13. positive 14. valid 15. true 16. d 17. b 18. c 19. d 20. true 21. false 22. (1) f (2) a (3) d (4) b (5) e (6) c (7) g 23. (1) c (2) d (3) e (4) b (5) a 24. (1) b (2) c (3) d (4) a (5) e (6) g (7) f

Section Two: Who Said This? 1. Skinner 2. Wundt 3. James 4. Watson 5. Maslow 6. Sumner 7. Calkins

Section Three: Fill In the Blank 1. theory 2. naturalistic observation 3. population; representative sample 4. hypothesis 5. independent; dependent 6. control 7. predictions; cause; effect 8. structuralism 9. functionalism 10. psychoanalysis 11. cognitive 12. clinical 13. psychoanalytic

Section Four: Comprehensive Practice Test 1. b 2. b 3. d 4. c 5. c 6. b 7. a 8. d 9. c 10. a 11. false 12. false 13. true 14. false 15. true 16. true 17. true 18. false 19. false 20. false

Chapter 2 (page 59)

Section One: Chapter Review 1. a 2. c 3. d 4. action 5. b 6. c 7. b 8. false 9. b 10. hippocampus 11. (1) b (2) a (3) f (4) c (5) e (6) d 12. b 13. a 14. (1) d (2) c (3) a (4) b 15. (1) d (2) a (3) e (4) g (5) b (6) f (7) c 16. (1) a (2) b (3) a (4) a (5) b 17. c 18. b 19. a 20. c 21. c 22. (1) b (2) c (3) a 23. d 24. false 25. b 26. c 27. a 28. (1) d (2) a (3) e (4) c (5) b

Section Two: Label the Brain 1. frontal lobe 2. motor cortex 3. parietal lobe 3. occipital lobe 5. cerebellum 6. pons 7. medulla 8. corpus callosum 9. pituitary gland

Section Three: Fill In the Blank 1. dendrite 2. neurotransmitters 3. limbic 4. primary visual cortex 5. parietal 6. frontal 7. left 8. axon 9. brain; spinal cord 10. sympathetic 11. hypothalamus 12. action potential 13. Broca's 14. hippocampus 15. temporal 16. cerebellum 17. peripheral

Section Four: Comprehensive Practice Test 1. b 2. d 3. a 4. a 5. c 6. b 7. c 8. b 9. d 10. b 11. a 12. c 13. b 14. c 15. d 16. true 17. false 18. a 19. true

Chapter 3 (page 93)

Section One: Chapter Review 1. sensation 2. absolute 3. false 4. c 5. transduction 6. b 7. (1) d (2) c (3) b (4) e (5) a 8. rods; cones 9. c 10. false 11. d 12. hertz; decibels 13. (1) b (2) a (3) c 14. d 15. c 16. true 17. olfaction 18. c 19. sweet, salty, sour, bitter 20. taste bud 21. true 22. false 23. false 24. (1) c (2) b (3) a 25. kinesthetic 26. vestibular; inner ear 27. closure 28. c 29. a 30. binocular 31. (1) c (2) b (3) a (4) d 32. stroboscopic motion 33. c 34. top-down 35. c 36. false 37. (1) c (2) b (3) a 38. false

Section Two: Multiple Choice 1. a 2. d 3. d 4. c 5. d 6. d 7. b 8. c 9. a 10. a 11. c 12. a 13. c 14. a 15. a 16. c 17. a 18. b 19. b 20. c 21. d 22. b 23. b 24. b 25. b 26. c 27 c

Section Three: Fill In the Blank 1. a 2. difference 3. psychophysics 4. transduction 5. sensory adaptation 6. cornea 7. opponent-process 8. frequency 9. taste 10. Gestalt 11. figure-ground 12. closure 13. retinal image 14. color constancy 15. binocular disparity 16. phi phenomenon

Section Four: Comprehensive Practice Test 1. c 2. a 3. d 4. c 5. b 6. b 7. d 8. a 9. c 10. a 11. c 12. c 13. b 14. d 15. a 16. d 17. b 18. true 19. d 20. true 21. c 22. false 23. a 24. c 25. b 26. d 27. c 28. true 29. b 30. a 31. d

Chapter 4 (page 127)

Section One: Chapter Review 1. a 2. c 3. true 4. suprachiasmatic nucleus 5. false 6. d 7. false 8. (1) a (2) b (3) a (4) a (5) a 9. c 10. false 11. (1) d (2) b (3) a (4) c 12. d 13. restorative theory; circadian theory 14. c 15. true 16. a 17. false 18. b 19. d 20. c 21. true 22. (1) a (2) b (3) c (4) d 23. b 24. true 25. false 26. c 27. a 28. sociocognitive; neodissociation; dissociated control 29. false

30. d   31. true   32. true   33. (1) b   (2) c   (3) a   (4) e
(5) d   34. b   35. b   36. a   37. c   38. d   39. c

Section Two: Identify the Drug   1. g   2. a   3. d
4. e   5. h   6. c   7. i   8. f   9. b

Section Three: Fill In the Blank   1. consciousness
2. delta   3. REM rebound   4. lucid   5. parasomnias
6. larks; owls   7. apnea   8. narcolepsy   9. mood; perception; thought   10. meditation   11. dependence   12. alcohol   13. crash   14. dopamine   15. narcotic; minor
tranquilizer

Section Four: Comprehensive Practice Test   1. b
2. b   3. c   4. c   5. b   6. c   7. false   8. d   9. c   10. d
11. false   12. b   13. b   14. false   15. c   16. true   17. c
18. b   19. d   20. d

Chapter 5 (page 162)

Section One: Chapter Review   1. Ivan Pavlov
2. conditioned   3. extinction   4. b   5. existing conditioned stimulus   6. conditioned; unconditioned   7. a   8. false
9. c   10. c   11. true   12. b   13. c   14. b   15. shaping
16. d   17. negative   18. continuous; partial   19. d
20. a   21. false   22. a   23. false   24. true   25. true
26. learned helplessness   27. biofeedback   28. behavior
modification   29. insight   30. d   31. b   32. (1) b, d
(2) a   (3) c

Section Two: Identify the Concept   1. variable-ratio
reinforcement   2. classical conditioning of emotions
3. negative reinforcement   4. generalization   5. positive
reinforcement   6. extinction in operant conditioning
7. fixed-interval reinforcement   8. punishment   9. observational learning   10. secondary reinforcement   11. insight

Section Three: Fill In the Blank   1. stimuli; response;
consequences   2. Learning   3. the sound of the truck
4. the food   5. salivation   6. neutral   7. generalization
8. discrimination   9. higher-order   10. conditioned; unconditioned   11. effect; Edward Thorndike   12. successive
approximations   13. Negative; positive   14. discriminative
15. primary; secondary   16. continuous; partial   17. behavior

Section Four: Comprehensive Practice Test   1. a
2. c   3. c   4. d   5. b   6. c   7. b   8. c   9. a   10. d
11. b   12. false   13. b   14. c   15. b   16. d   17. c
18. false

Chapter 6 (page 194)

Section One: Chapter Review   1. d   2. (1) b   (2) c
(3) a   3. (1) d   (2) b   (3) a   (4) c   4. c   5. c   6. d
7. a   8. (1) a   (2) c   (3) b   (4) a   (5) c   9. (1) c   (2) e
(3) a   (4) b   (5) d   10. c   11. false   12. true   13. b
14. d   15. a   16. false   17. c   18. c   19. true   20. false
21. b   22. true   23. episodic; semantic   24. true   25. a
26. true   27. a   28. d

Section Two: Complete the Diagrams   1. large
2. visual, ¹⁄₁₀ second; auditory, 2 seconds   3. about seven
items   4. less than 30 seconds   5. unlimited   6. from
minutes to a lifetime   7. declarative   8. episodic   9. motor
skills   10. classically

Section Three: Fill In the Blank   1. encoding
2. rehearsal   3. working   4. long   5. semantic   6. recall;
recognition   7. proactive   8. repression   9. encoding
10. the middle   11. state dependent   12. hippocampal
region   13. potentiation   14. mnemonics   15. anterograde amnesia   16. massed   17. overlearning

Section Four: Comprehensive Practice Test   1. c
2. a   3. c   4. b   5. nondeclarative   6. a   7. d   8. b
9. false   10. true   11. false   12. d   13. a   14. c   15. c
16. true   17. false   18. a   19. b   20. true

Chapter 7 (page 235)

Section One: Chapter Review   1. c   2. b   3. d
4. additive strategy   5. Framing   6. a   7. b   8. c   9. false
10. false   11. (1) b   (2) c   (3) a   (4) d   12. false
13. true   14. true   15. (1) b   (2) c   (3) a   16. a   17. b
18. b   19. b   20. false   21. true   22. (1) b   (2) a   (3) a
(4) b   (5) a   23. false   24. b   25. optimism   26. false
27. c

**Section Two: Important Concepts and Psycholo-
gists**   1. Rosch   2. Tversky   3. Newell & Simon
4. McCarthy   5. Whorf   6. Spearman   7. Sternberg
8. Terman   9. Wechsler   10. Galton   11. Goleman

Section Three: Fill In the Blank   1. cognition   2. imagery   3. exemplar   4. additive   5. elimination by aspects
6. psycholinguistics   7. syntax   8. linguistic relativity
9. Howard Gardner   10. validity   11. less   12. contextual
13. reliability   14. creativity

Section Four: Comprehensive Practice Test   1. b
2. b   3. prototype   4. false   5. a   6. d   7. a   8. d   9. a
10. false   11. true   12. true   13. c   14. d   15. a   16. b
17. false   18. b   19. true   20. true

Chapter 8 (page 283)

Section One: Chapter Review   1. false   2. c
3. true   4. (1) c   (2) a   (3) b   5. a   6. b   7. c   8. true
9. b   10. assimilation   11. d   12. false   13. (1) c   (2) b
(3) a   (4) e   (5) d   (6) b   14. true   15. b   16. (1) c
(2) b   (3) a   17. false   18. false   19. c   20. b   21. d
22. (1) b   (2) c   (3) a   23. true   24. false   25. a   26. d
27. c   28. married people   29. c   30. a   31. d

**Section Two: Important Psychologists and Con-
cepts**   1. cognitive development   2. psychosocial development   3. temperament   4. attachment   5. sociocultural
cognitive development   6. nativist view of language development   7. moral reasoning   8. death and dying

Section Three: Fill In the Blank   1. longitudinal
2. cross-sectional   3. zygote   4. teratogens   5. maturation   6. avoidant   7. schema   8. private speech   9. telegraphic speech   10. overregularization   11. formal operations   12. conventional   13. personal fable   14. crystallized; fluid   15. Bargaining   16. fifth

Section Four: Comprehensive Practice Test
1. false   2. c   3. b   4. b   5. b   6. a   7. d   8. b   9. a
10. b   11. b   12. true   13. b   14. d   15. c   16. c   17. c
18. true   19. b   20. a   21. b   22. true   23. b

Chapter 9 (page 319)

Section One: Chapter Review   1. extrinsic   2. c
3. b   4. d   5. c   6. feeding; satiety   7. c   8. true   9. d
10. maintain   11. true   12. biological   13. c   14. anorexia
nervosa; bulimia nervosa   15. a   16. false   17. c   18. true
19. true   20. b   21. true   22. c   23. false   24. d   25. a
26. c   27. a   28. b   29. c   30. d   31. c   32. b   33. true
34. false   35. a   36. c

**Section Two: Important Psychologists and Con-
cepts**   1. drive-reduction theory   2. hierarchy of needs
3. need for achievement   4. event creates physical arousal,
which is identified as an emotion   5. event creates physical arousal plus emotion   6. cognitive appraisal of a stimulus results in emotion   7. facial-feedback hypothesis

Section Three: Fill In the Blank   1. Motives   2. intrinsic   3. extrinsic   4. instinct   5. arousal   6. lateral;
ventromedial   7. exercise   8. Anorexia; bulimia   9. social
10. James–Lange   11. Cannon–Bard   12. Schachter–
Singer   13. basic   14. negative; positive   15. excitement
16. testosterone   17. homeostasis   18. heterosexual;
homosexual

Section Four: Comprehensive Practice Test   1. a
2. a   3. c   4. d   5. false   6. a   7. c   8. d   9. false
10. d   11. true   12. d   13. c   14. a   15. false   16. c
17. false   18. d   19. c   20. true

Chapter 10 (page 352)

Section One: Chapter Review   1. true   2. unconscious   3. a   4. c   5. b   6. false   7. (1) c   (2) a   (3) d
(4) b   8. birth   9. d   10. b   11. Oedipus complex   12. c
13. collective   14. c   15. b   16. d   17. false   18. a
19. b   20. false   21. c   22. a   23. d   24. d   25. c
26. a   27. c   28. nonshared   29. false   30. The majority
of   31. (1) a   (2) c   (3) d   (4) b   (5) e   32. b   33. d
34. c

Section Two: Complete the Table   1. Freud; Behavior arises mostly from unconscious conflict between plea-
sure-seeking id and moral-perfectionistic superego, with
ego as mediator.   2. Allport, Cattell, Eysenck; Behavior
springs from personality traits that may be influenced by
both heredity and environment.   3. Skinner; Behavior is

determined strictly by environmental influences.   4. Bandura, Rotter; Behavior results from an interaction between
internal cognitive factors and environmental factors.
5. Maslow, Rogers; Behavior springs from the person's
motivation to become self-actualized or fully functioning
and reflects the person's unique perception of reality and
conscious choices.

Section Three: Fill In the Blank   1. id   2. ego
3. preconscious   4. oral, anal, phallic, genital   5. cardinal
6. surface; source   7. reciprocal determinism   8. collective
unconscious   9. genes; environment   10. observation
11. Jung's   12. projective   13. Minnesota Multiphasic
Personality Inventory   14. sublimation   15. self-efficacy
16 source   17. archetype

Section Four: Comprehensive Practice Test   1. c
2. c   3. b   4. false   5. b   6. c   7. a   8. c   9. b   10. d
11. b   12. b   13. c   14. false   15. false   16. c   17. d

Chapter 11 (page 386)

Section One: Chapter Review   1. c   2. resistance
3. exhaustion   4. a   5. physiological; psychological   6. c
7. d   8. d   9. true   10. false   11. problem-focused; emotion-focused   12. true   13. before   14. false   15. false
16. true   17. true   18. c   19. a   20. a   21. b   22. c
23. true   24. d   25. false   26. a   27. b   28. Alcohol
29. d

**Section Two: The Biopsychosocial Model of Health
and Illness**   1. genetics, relaxation, healthy lifestyle
2. lack of exercise, poor diet, disease and injury, toxic
chemicals, pollution   3. stress management skills, giving
and receiving love, optimism   4. depression, pessimism,
worry, anxiety, poor coping skills, stress   5. social responsibility, social policy, social groups   6. loneliness, poverty,
exploitation, violence

Section Three: Fill In the Blank   1. biomedical;
biopsychosocial   2. health psychology   3. sympathetic
nervous system   4. alarm 5. resistance   6. cognitive
7. proactive   8. AIDS   9. homosexual and bisexual males
10. hassles   11. psychoneuroimmunology   12. A   13. cue
exposure   14. Primary   15. Burnout   16. stressor
17. approach–avoidance

Section Four: Comprehensive Practice Test
1. false   2. b   3. a   4. d   5. c   6. a   7. true   8. true
9. c   10. false   11. true   12. c   13. false   14. a   15. true
16. false   17. higher

Chapter 12 (page 418)

Section One: Chapter Review   1. false   2. a   3.
(1) c   (2) a   (3) d   (4) b   (5) e   4. (1) a   (2) d   (3) b
(4) c   5. d   6. (1) c   (2) a   (3) b   (4) d   7. c   8. (1) b
(2) c   (3) a   9. false   10. b   11. (1) e   (2) d   (3) b

(4) c   (5) a   (6) f   12. false   13. true   14. false
15. (1) d   (2) b   (3) e   (4) c   (5) a   16. false   17. true
18. Paraphilias   19. c   20. c

Section Two: Identify the Disorder   1. major depression   2. paranoid schizophrenia   3. bipolar disorder
4. agoraphobia   5. dissociative amnesia   6. borderline
personality disorder   7. voyeurism   8. obsessive compulsive disorder

Section Three: Fill In the Blank   1. biological
2. schizophrenia   3. positive   4. delusion   5. negative
6. seasonal affective disorder   7. manic   8. somatoform
9. panic   10. involuntary thoughts; urge to perform a certain act   11. conversion   12. multiple personality   13. personality   14. sexual identity   15. Hallucinations   16. phobia
17. antisocial

Section Four: Comprehensive Practice Test   1. c
2. b   3. d   4. a   5. false   6. b   7. a   8. false   9. d
10. b   11. true   12. d   13. c   14. true   15. d   16. c
17. false   18. b   19. a

Chapter 13 (page 449)

Section One: Chapter Review   1. d   2. Gestalt
3. Person-centered   4. Psychodynamic   5. c   6. c
7. false   8. operant   9. b   10. d   11. (1) c   (2) b   (3) a
(4) d   12. c   13. false   14. b   15. d   16. true   17. (1) c
(2) b   (3) a   (4) c   (5) c   18. b   19. d   20. a   21. false
22. false   23. b   24. (1) a   (2) c   (3) b   (4) c   25. c
26. significantly

Section Two: Identify the Therapy   1. e   2. a   3. d
4. f   5. b   6. g   7. c

Section Three: Fill In the Blank   1. psychological;
biological   2. transference   3. directive   4. interpersonal

5. family   6. self-help group   7. operant   8. behavior
modification   9. cognitive   10. schizophrenia   11. depression   12. bipolar disorder   13. suicidal depression
14. clinical 15. free association   16. time out   17. lobotomy   18. psychoanalyst

Section Four: Comprehensive Practice Test   1. c
2. c   3. b   4. false   5. d   6. a   7. b   8. a   9. a   10. b
11. b   12. a   13. c   14. a   15. b   16. d   17. c
18. true   19. false   20. false

Chapter 14 (page 485)

Section One: Chapter Review   1. d   2. b   3. a
4. true   5. (1) c   (2) b   (3) a   6. true   7. false   8. (1) c
(2) a   (3) b   9. c   10. b   11. c   12. d   13. a   14. c
15. d   16. false   17. b   18. true   19. true   20. (1) d
(2) a   (3) b   (4) c   21. false   22. c   23. false   24. b
25. true   26. true   27. false   28. c   29. true   30. false
31. b   32. c   33. false   34. true

Section Two: Glossary Matching   1. f   2. e   3. b
4. a   5. h   6. i   7. l   8. n   9. j   10. k   11. m   12. d
13. g   14. c

Section Three: Fill In the Blank   1. attitude   2. primacy effect   3. dispositional   4. situational; personality
5. self-serving bias   6. halo   7. obedience   8. social
facilitation   9. extreme   10. stereotype   11. contact
12. bystander   13. altruism   14. instinct   15. frustration–
aggression   16. Scapegoating   17. attribution   18. Conformity

Section Four: Comprehensive Practice Test   1. d
2. false   3. c   4. b   5. false   6. d   7. c   8. true   9. d
10. false   11. b   12. c   13. c   14. b   15. c   16. true
17. b   18. true   19. a

Note: Bracketed numbers following references indicate chapter(s) in which they are cited.

Abramowitz, J. S. (1997). Effectiveness of psychological and pharmacological treatments for obsessive-compulsive disorder: A quantitative review. *Journal of Consulting and Clinical Psychology, 65,* 44–52. [13]

Abrams, D., Wetherell, M., Cochrane, S., Hogg, M. A., & Turner, J. C. (1990). Knowing what to think by knowing who you are: Self-categorization and the nature of norm formation, conformity and group polarization. *British Journal of Social Psychology, 29* (Pt. 2), 97–119. [14]

Abrams, R. (1988). *Electroconvulsive therapy.* New York: Oxford University Press. [13]

Abramson, P., & Herdt, G. (1990). The assessment of sexual practices relevant to the transmission of AIDS: A global perspective. *Journal of Sex Research, 27,* 215–232. [11]

Adams, J. M. (1991, August 5). The clearest message may be: "Buy this tape." *Boston Globe,* 37–40. [3]

Adelmann, P. K., & Zajonc, R. B. (1989). Facial efference and the experience of emotion. *Annual Review of Psychology, 40,* 249–280. [9]

Ader, D. N., & Johnson, S. B. (1994). Sample description, reporting, and analysis of sex in psychological research: A look at APA and APA division journals in 1990. *American Psychologist, 49,* 216–218. [1]

Ader, R. (1985). CNS immune systems interactions: Conditioning phenomena. *Behavioral and Brain Sciences, 9,* 760–763. [5]

Ader, R., & Cohen, N. (1982). Behaviorally conditioned immunosuppression and murine systemic Lupus erythematosus. *Science, 215,* 1534–1536. [5]

Ader, R., & Cohen, N. (1993). Psychoneuroimmunology: Conditioning and stress. *Annual Review of Psychology, 44,* 53–85. [5]

Adler, A. (1927). *Understanding human nature.* New York: Greenberg. [10]

Adler, A. (1956). In H. L. Ansbacher & R. R. Ansbacher (Eds.), *The individual psychology of Alfred Adler: A systematic presentation in selections from his writings.* New York: Harper & Row. [10]

Adler, A. (1964). *Social interest: A challenge to mankind.* New York: Capricorn. (Originally published 1933). [10]

Adler, J. (1997, Spring/Summer). It's a wise father who knows . . . . *Newsweek* [Special Edition], p. 73. [8]

Adler, N., & Matthews, K. (1994). Health psychology: Why do some people get sick and some stay well? *Annual Review of Psychology, 45,* 229–259. [11]

Agartz, I., Momenan, R., Rawlings, R. R., Kerich, M. J., & Hommer, D. W. (1999). Hippocampal volume in patients with alcohol dependence. *Archives of General Psychiatry, 56,* 356–363. [11]

Agras, W. S., Rossiter, E. M., Arnow, B., Telch, C. F., Raeburn, S. D., Bruce, B., & Koran, L. M. (1994). One-year follow-up of psychosocial and pharmacologic treatments for bulimia nervosa. *Journal of Clinical Psychiatry, 55,* 179–183. [9]

Ahmed, R., & Gray, D. (1996). Immunological memory and protective immunity: Understanding their relation. *Science, 272,* 54–60. [11]

AIDS and Mental Health—Part II. (1994). *Harvard Mental Health Letter, 10*(8), 1–4. [11]

Aiken, L. R. (1997). *Psychological testing and assessment* (9th ed.). Boston: Allyn & Bacon. [7]

Ainsworth, M. D. S. (1973). The development of infant-mother attachment. In B. Caldwell & H. Ricciuti (Eds.), *Review of child development research* (Vol. 3). Chicago: University of Chicago Press. [8]

Ainsworth, M. D. S. (1979). Infant-mother attachment. *American Psychologist, 34,* 932–937. [8]

Ainsworth, M. D. S., Blehar, M. C., Walters, E., & Wall, S. (1978). *Patterns of attachment.* Hillsdale, NJ: Erlbaum. [8]

Ajzen, I., & Fishbein, M. (1977). Attitude-behavior relations: A theoretical analysis and review of empirical research. *Psychological Bulletin, 84,* 888–918. [14]

Åkerstedt, T. (1990). Psychological and psychophysiological effects of shift work. *Scandinavian Journal of Work and Environmental Health, 16,* 67–73. [4]

Akiskal, H. S. (1989). New insights into the nature and heterogeneity of mood disorders. *Journal of Clinical Psychiatry, 50*(5, Suppl.), 6–10. [12]

Alan Guttmacher Institute. (1991). *Facts in brief.* New York: Author. [8]

Albrecht, K. (1979). *Stress and the manager: Making it work for you.* Englewood Cliffs, NJ: Prentice-Hall. [11]

Aldhous, P. (1992). The promise and pitfalls of molecular genetics. *Science, 257,* 164–165. [10]

Aldridge-Morris, R. (1989). *Multiple personality disorder: An exercise in deception.* London: Lawrence Erlbaum Associates. [12]

Alexander, G. E., Furey, M. L., Grady, C. L., Pietrini, P., Brady, D. R., Mentis, M. J., & Schapiro, M. B. (1997). Association of premorbid intellectual function with cerebral metabolism in Alzheimer's disease: Implications for the cognitive reserve hypothesis. *American Journal of Psychiatry, 154,* 165–172. [8]

Alicke, M. D., & Largo, E. (1995). The role of the self in the false consensus effect. *Journal of Experimental Social Psychology, 31,* 28–47. [14]

Allen, B. P. (1997). *Personality theories: Development, growth, and diversity* (2nd ed.). Boston: Allyn & Bacon. [10]

Allen, G., Buxton, R. B., Wong, E. C., & Courchesne, E. (1997). Attentional activation of the cerebellum independent of motor involvement. *Science, 275,* 1940–1943. [2]

Allen, K. W. (1996). Chronic nailbiting: A controlled comparison of competing response and mild aversion treatments. *Behaviour Research and Therapy, 34,* 269–272. [13]

Allison, K. W., Crawford, I., Echemendia, R., Robinson, L., & Knepp, D. (1994). Human diversity and professional competence: Training in clinical and counseling psychology revisited. *American Psychologist, 49,* 792–796. [13]

Allison, M. (1991, February). Improving the odds. *Harvard Health Letter, 16,* 4–6. [11]

Allport, G. W. (1935). Attitudes. In C. Murchison (Ed.), *Handbook of social psychology.* Worcester, MA: Clark University Press. [14]

Allport, G. W. (1954). *The nature of prejudice.* Reading, MA: Addison-Wesley. [14]

Allport, G. W. (1961). *Pattern and growth in personality.* New York: Holt, Rinehart & Winston. [10]

Allport, G. W., & Odbert, J. S. (1936). Trait names: A psycho-lexical study. *Psychological Monographs, 47*(1, Whole No. 211), 1–171. [10]

Alpert, B., Field, T., Goldstein, S., & Perry, S. (1990). Aerobics enhances cardiovascular fitness and agility in preschoolers. *Health Psychology, 9,* 48–56. [11]

Alsaker, F. D. (1995). Timing of puberty and reactions to pubertal changes. In M. Rutter (Ed.), *Psychosocial disturbances in young people* (pp. 37–82). New York: Cambridge University Press. [8]

Altshuler, K. Z. (1989). Will the psychotherapies yield different results? A look at assumptions in therapy trials. *American Journal of Psychotherapy, 43*, 310–320. [13]

Amabile, T. M. (1983). *The social psychology of creativity.* New York: Springer-Verlag. [7]

Ambuel, B. (1995). Adolescents, unintended pregnancy, and abortion: The struggle for a compassionate social policy. *Current Directions in Psychological Science, 4*, 1–5. [8]

American Medical Association. (1994). Report of the Council on Scientific Affairs: Memories of childhood abuse. CSA Report 5-A–94. [6]

American Psychiatric Association. (1993a). Practice guideline for eating disorders. *American Journal of Psychiatry, 150*, 212–228. [9]

American Psychiatric Association. (1993b). Practice guideline for major depressive disorder in adults. *American Journal of Psychiatry, 150*(4, Suppl.), 1–26. [13]

American Psychiatric Association. (1993c). *Statement approved by the Board of Trustees, December 12, 1993.* Washington, DC: Author. [6]

American Psychiatric Association. (1994). *Diagnostic and statistical manual of mental disorders* (4th ed.). Washington DC: Author. [9, 12]

American Psychiatric Association. (1997). Practice guideline for the treatment of patients with Alzheimer's disease and other dementias of late life. *American Journal of Psychiatry, 154*, 1–39. [8]

American Psychological Association. (1992a). *Demographic characteristics of APA members by membership status, 1991.* Washington, DC: Office of Demographic, Employment, and Educational Research, APA Education Directorate. [1]

American Psychological Association. (1992b). Ethical principles of psychologists and code of conduct. *American Psychologist, 47*, 1597–1611. [1]

American Psychological Association. (1993). Guidelines for providers of psychological services to ethnic, linguistic, and culturally diverse populations. *American Psychologist, 48*, 45–48. [13]

American Psychological Association. (1994). *Interim report of the APA Working Group on Investigation of Memories of Childhood Abuse.* Washington, DC: Author. [6, 12]

American Psychological Association. (1995). *Demographic characteristics of APA members by membership status, 1993.* Washington, DC: Office of Demographic, Employment, and Educational Research, APA Education Directorate. [1]

Anand, B. K., & Brobeck, J. R. (1951). Hypothalamic control of food intake in rats and cats. *Yale Journal of Biological Medicine, 24*, 123–140. [9]

Andersen, B. L., & Cyranowski, J. M. (1995). Women's sexuality: Behaviors, responses, and individual differences. *Journal of Consulting and Clinical Psychology, 63*, 891–906. [9]

Anderson, B. L., Kiecolt-Glaser, J. K., & Glaser, R. (1994). A biobehavioral model of cancer stress and disease course. *American Psychologist, 49*, 389–404. [11]

Anderson, C. A. (1989). Temperature and aggression: Ubiquitous effects of heat on occurrence of human violence. *Psychological Bulletin, 106*, 74–96. [14]

Anderson, C. A., & Anderson, K. B. (1996). Violent crime rate studies in philosophical context: A destructive testing approach to heat and southern culture of violence effects. *Journal of Personality and Social Psychology, 70*, 740–756. [14]

Anderson, S. M., Klatzky, R. L., & Murray, J. (1990). Traits and social stereotypes: Efficiency differences in social information processing. *Journal of Personality and Social Psychology, 59*, 192–201. [14]

Andreasen, N. C. (1999). Understanding the causes of schizophrenia. *New England Journal of Medicine, 340*, 645–647. [12]

Andreasen, N. C., Arndt, S., Swayze, V., II, Cizadlo, T., Flaum, M., O'Leary, D., Ehrhardt, J. C., & Yuh, W. T. C. (1994). Thalamic abnormalities in schizophrenia visualized through magnetic resonance image averaging. *Science, 266*, 294–298. [12]

Andreasen, N. C., & Black, D. W. (1991). *Introductory textbook of psychiatry.* Washington, DC: American Psychiatric Press. [4]

Angeleri, F., Angeleri, V. A., Foschi, N., Giaquinto, S., Nolfe, G., Saginario, A., & Signorino, M. (1997). Depression after stroke: An investigation through catamnesis. *Journal of Clinical Psychiatry, 58*, 261–265. [2]

Anisfeld, M. (1996). Only tongue protrusion modeling is matched by neonates. *Developmental Review, 16*, 149–161. [8]

Annett, M. (1985). *Left, right hand and brain: The right shift theory.* London: Lawrence Erlbaum Associates. [2]

Anstey, K., Stankov, L., & Lord, S. (1993). Primary aging, secondary aging, and intelligence. *Psychology and Aging, 8*, 562–570. [8]

Antonuccio, D. O., Danton, W. G., & DeNelsky, G. Y. (1995). Psychotherapy versus medication for depression: Challenging the conventional wisdom with data. *Professional Psychology: Research and Practice, 26*, 574–585. [13]

Apgar, V., & Beck, J. (1982). A perfect baby. In H. E. Fitzgerald & T. H. Carr (Eds.), *Human Development 82/83* (pp. 66–70). Guilford, CT: Dushkin. [8]

Archer, J. (1996). Sex differences in social behavior: Are the social role and evolutionary explanations compatible? *American Psychologist, 51*, 909–917. [1]

Aronson, E. (1976). Dissonance theory: Progress and problems. In E. P. Hollander & R. C. Hunt (Eds.), *Current perspectives in social psychology* (4th ed., pp. 316–328). New York: Oxford University Press. [14]

Aronson, E. (1990). Applying social psychology to desegregation and energy conservation. *Personality and Social Psychology Bulletin, 16*, 118–132. [14]

Asch, S. E. (1951). Effects of group pressure upon the modification and distortion of judgments. In H. Guetzkow (Ed.), *Groups, leadership, and men.* Pittsburgh, PA: Carnegie Press. [14]

Asch, S. E. (1955). Opinions and social pressure. *Scientific American, 193*, 31–35. [14]

Aspinwall, L. G., & Taylor, S. E. (1997). A stitch in time: Self-regulation and proactive coping. *Psychological Bulletin, 121*, 417–436. [11]

Atkinson, R. C., & Shiffrin, R. M. (1968). Human memory: A proposed system and its controlled processes. In K. W. Spence & J. T. Spence (Eds.), *The psychology of learning and motivation* (Vol. 2, pp. 89–195). New York: Academic. [6]

Ault, R. L. (1983). *Children's cognitive development* (2nd ed.). Oxford: Oxford University Press. [8]

Avenoso, K. (1997, September 14). A decade of Prozac. *The Boston Globe,* pp. 12–13, 25–35. [13]

Axel, R. (1995, October). The molecular logic of smell. *Scientific American, 273*, 154–159. [3]

Axelsson, A., & Jerson, T. (1985). Noisy toys: A possible source of sensorineural hearing loss. *Pediatrics, 76*, 574–578. [3]

Ayllon, T. (1977). Intensive treatment of psychotic behaviour by stimulus satiation and food reinforcement. In S. J. Morse & R. I. Watson, Jr. (Eds.), *Psychotherapies: A comparative casebook* (pp. 355–362). New York: Holt, Rinehart & Winston. [13]

Ayllon, T., & Azrin, N. H. (1965). The measurement and reinforcement of behavior of psychotics. *Journal of the Experimental Analysis of Behavior, 8*, 357–383. [5, 13]

Ayllon, T., & Azrin, N. (1968). *The token economy: A motivational system for therapy and rehabilitation.* New York: Appleton-Century-Crofts. [5, 13]

Azrin, N. H., & Holz, W. C. (1966). Punishment. In W. K. Honig (Ed.), *Operant behavior: Areas of research and application.* New York: Appleton-Century-Crofts. [5]

Bachman, J. G. (1987, July). An eye on the future. *Psychology Today,* pp. 6–8. [8]

Baddeley, A. (1990). *Human memory.* Boston: Allyn & Bacon. [6]

Baddeley, A. (1992). Working memory. *Science, 255*, 556–559. [6]

Baddeley, A. D. (1995). Working memory. In M. S. Gazzaniga (Ed.), *The cognitive neurosciences.* Cambridge, MA: MIT Press. [6]

Baer, L. (1996). Behavior theory: Endogenous serotonin therapy? *Journal of Clinical Psychiatry, 57*(6, Suppl.), 33–35. [13]

Baer, L., Rauch, S. L., Ballantine, T., Jr., Martuza, R., Cosgrove, R., Cassem, E., Giriunas, I., Manzo, P. A., Dimino, C., & Jenike, M. A.

(1995). Cingulotomy for intractable obsessive-compulsive disorder. *Archives of General Psychiatry, 52,* 384–392. [13]

Bagby, R. M., Rogers, R., & Buis, T. (1994). Detecting malingered and defensive responding on the MMPI-2 in a forensic inpatient sample. *Journal of Personality Assessment, 62,* 191–203. [10]

Bahrick, H. P., Bahrick, P. O., & Wittlinger, R. P. (1975). Fifty years of memory for names and faces: A cross-sectional approach. *Journal of Experimental Psychology: General, 104,* 54–75. [6]

Bahrick, H. P., Hall, L. K., & Berger, S. A. (1996). Accuracy and distortion in memory for high school grades. *Psychological Science, 7,* 265–271. [6]

Bailey, J. M., & Benishay, D. S. (1993). Familial aggregation of female sexual orientation. *American Journal of Psychiatry, 150,* 272–277. [9]

Bailey, J. M., Nothnagel, J., & Wolfe, M. (1995). Retrospectively measured individual differences in childhood sex-typed behavior among gay men: Correspondence between self- and maternal reports. *Archives of Sexual Behavior, 24,* 613–622. [9]

Bailey, J. M., & Pillard, R. C. (1991). A genetic study of male sexual orientation. *Archives of General Psychiatry, 48,* 1089–1096. [9]

Bailey, J. M., & Pillard, R. C. (1994). The innateness of homosexuality. *Harvard Mental Health Letter, 10*(7), 4–6. [9]

Bailey, J. M., Pillard, R. C., Neale, M. C., & Agyei, Y. (1993). Heritable factors influence sexual orientation in women. *Archives of General Psychiatry, 50,* 217–223. [9]

Bailey, J. M., & Zucker, K. J. (1995). Childhood sex-typed behavior and sexual orientation: A conceptual analysis and quantitative review. *Developmental Psychology, 31,* 43–55. [9]

Baillargeon, R., & DeVos, J. (1991). Object permanence in young infants: Further evidence. *Child Development, 62,* 1227–1246. [8]

Baker, T. B. (1988). Models of addiction: Introduction to the special issue. *Journal of Abnormal Psychology, 97,* 115–117. [4]

Baldwin, J. D., & Baldwin, J. I. (1997). Gender differences in sexual interest. *Archives of Sexual Behavior, 26,* 181–210. [9]

Ball, C. G., & Grinker, J. A. (1981). Overeating and obesity. In S. J. Mule (Ed.), *Behavior in excess* (pp. 194–220). New York: The Free Press. [9]

Ball, S. G., Baer, L., & Otto, M. W. (1996). Symptom subtypes of obsessive-compulsive disorder in behavioral treatment studies: A quantitative review. *Behaviour Research and Therapy, 34,* 47–51. [12]

Ballor, D. L., Tommerup, L. J., Thomas, D. P., Smith, D. B., & Keesey, R. E. (1990). Exercise training attenuates diet-induced reduction in metabolic rate. *Journal of Applied Physiology: Respiratory, Environmental, and Exercise Physiology, 68,* 2612–2617. [9]

Bandura, A. (1967). Behavioral psychotherapy. *Scientific American, 216,* 78–82. [13]

Bandura, A. (1969). *Principles of behavior modification.* New York: Holt, Rinehart & Winston. [5]

Bandura, A. (1973). *Aggression: A social learning analysis.* Englewood Cliffs, NJ: Prentice-Hall. [14]

Bandura, A. (1976). On social learning and aggression. In E. P. Hollander & R. C. Hunt (Eds.), *Current perspectives in social psychology* (4th ed., pp. 116–128). New York: Oxford University Press. [14]

Bandura, A. (1977). *Social learning theory.* Englewood Cliffs, NJ: Prentice-Hall. [5, 8, 10, 13]

Bandura, A. (1986). *Social functions of thought and action: A social-cognitive theory.* Englewood Cliffs, NJ: Prentice-Hall. [5, 10]

Bandura, A. (1989). Social cognitive theory. *Annals of Child Development, 6,* 1–60. [10]

Bandura, A. (1997a, March). Self-efficacy. *Harvard Mental Health Letter, 13*(9), 4–6. [10]

Bandura, A. (1997b). *Self-efficacy: The exercise of control.* New York: Freeman. [10]

Bandura, A., Adams, N. E., & Beyer, J. (1977). Cognitive processes mediating behavioral change. *Journal of Personality and Social Psychology, 35,* 125–139. [13]

Bandura, A., Blanchard, E. B., & Ritter, B. J. (1969). The relative efficacy of desensitization and modeling therapeutic approaches for inducing behavioral, affective and attitudinal changes. *Journal of Personality and Social Psychology, 13,* 173–199. [13]

Bandura, A., Jeffery, R. W., & Gajdos, E. (1975). Generalizing change through participant modeling with self-directed mastery. *Behaviour Research and Therapy, 13,* 141–152. [13]

Bandura, A., Ross, D., & Ross, S. A. (1961). Transmission of aggression through imitation of aggressive models. *Journal of Abnormal and Social Psychology, 63,* 575–582. [5]

Bandura, A., Ross, D., & Ross, S. A. (1963). Imitation of film-mediated aggressive models. *Journal of Abnormal and Social Psychology, 66,* 3–11. [5]

Banks, S. M., & Kerns, R. D. (1996). Explaining high rates of depression in chronic pain: A diathesis-stress framework. *Psychological Bulletin, 119,* 95–110. [12]

Barber, T. X. (1962). Hypnotic age regression: A critical review. *Psychosomatic Medicine, 24,* 181–193. [4]

Bard, P. (1934). The neurohumoral basis of emotional reactions. In C. A. Murchison (Ed.), *Handbook of general experimental psychology.* Worcester, MA: Clark University Press. [9]

Barefoot, J. C., Dahlstrom, W. D., & Williams, R. B. (1983). Hostility, CHD incidence, and total mortality: A 25-year follow-up study of 255 physicians. *Psychosomatic Medicine, 45,* 59–63. [11]

Bargh, J. A. (1997). The automaticity of everyday life. In R. S. Wyer, Jr. (Ed.), *Advances in social cognition,* vol. 10. Mahwah, NJ: Erlbaum. [10]

Bargmann, C. (1996). From the nose to the brain. *Nature, 384,* 512–513. [3]

Barinaga, M. (1997). How jet-lag hormone does double duty in the brain. *Science, 277,* 480. [4]

Barlow, D. H. (1997). Cognitive-behavioral therapy for panic disorder: Current status. *Journal of Clinical Psychiatry, 58*(6, Suppl.), 32–36. [13]

Barron, F., & Harrington, D. M. (1981). Creativity, intelligence, and personality. *Annual Review of Psychology, 32,* 439–476. [7]

Barsky, A. J. (1993, August). How does hypochondriasis differ from normal concerns about health? *Harvard Mental Health Letter, 10*(3), 8. [12]

Bar-Tal, D., & Saxe, L. (1976). Perceptions of similarly and dissimilarly attractive couples and individuals. *Journal of Personality and Social Psychology, 33,* 772–781. [14]

Bartimus, T. (1983, March 1). One man's descent into schizophrenia. *St. Louis Post-Dispatch,* pp. D1, 7. [12]

Bartlett, F. C. (1932). *Remembering: A study in experimental and social psychology.* London: Cambridge University Press. [6]

Bartoshuk, L. (1989). Taste: Robust across the age span? *Annals of the New York Academy of Sciences, 561,* 65–75. [3]

Bartoshuk, L. M., & Beauchamp, G. K. (1994). Chemical senses. *Annual Review of Psychology, 45,* 419–449. [3, 8]

Bartoshuk, L., Desnoyers, S., Hudson, C., Marks, L., O'Brien, M., Catalanotto, F., Gent, J., Williams, D., & Ostrum, K. M. (1987). Tasting on localized areas. *Annals of the New York Academy of Sciences, 510,* 166–168. [3]

Baruch, G., Barnett, R., & Rivers, C. (1983). *Lifeprints.* New York: McGraw-Hill. [8]

Basic Behavioral Science Task Force of the National Advisory Mental Health Council. (1996). Basic behavioral science research for mental health: Perception, attention, learning, and memory. *American Psychologist, 51,* 133–142. [5, 6]

Bass, E., & Davis, L. (1988). *The courage to heal.* New York: Harper & Row. [6]

Bassili, J. N. (1995). Response latency and the accessibility of voting intentions: What contributes to accessibility and how it affects vote choice. *Personality and Social Psychology Bulletin, 21,* 686–695. [14]

Bateson, G. (1982). Totemic knowledge in New Guinea. In U. Neisser (Ed.), *Memory observed: Remembering in natural contexts.* San Francisco: W. H. Freeman. [6]

Bateson, G., Jackson, D. D., Haley, J., & Weakland, J. (1956). Toward a theory of schizophrenia. *Behavioral Science, 1,* 214–264. [12]

Batson, C. D., Batson, J. G., Griffitt, C. A., Barrientos, S., Brandt, J. R., Sprengelmeyer, P., & Bayly, M. J. (1989). Negative-state relief and the empathy-altruism hypothesis. *Journal of Personality and Social Psychology, 56,* 922–933. [14]

Batson, C. D., Polycarpou, M. R., Harmon-Jones, E., Imhoff, H. J., Mitchener, E. C., Bednar, L. L., Klein, T. R., & Highberger, L. (1997). Empathy and attitudes: Can feeling for a member of a stigmatized group improve feelings toward the group? *Journal of Personality and Social Psychology, 72,* 105–118. [14]

Baum, A., & Valins, S. (1977). *Architecture and social behavior: Psychological studies of social density.* Hillsdale, NJ: Erlbaum. [14]

Baumeister, R. F., & Leary, M. R. (1995). The need to belong: Desire for interpersonal attachments as a fundamental human motivation. *Psychological Bulletin, 117,* 497–529. [9]

Baumgardner, A. H., Heppner, P. P., & Arkin, R. M. (1986). Role of causal attribution in personal problem solving. *Journal of Personality and Social Psychology, 50,* 636–643. [14]

Baumrind, D. (1967). Child care practices anteceding three patterns of preschool behavior. *Genetic Psychology Monographs, 75,* 43–88. [8]

Baumrind, D. (1971). Current patterns of parental authority. *Developmental Psychology Monographs, 4*(1, Pt. 2). [8]

Baumrind, D. (1980). New directions in socialization research. *American Psychologist, 35,* 639–652. [8]

Baumrind, D. (1985). Research using intentional deception: Ethical issues revisited. *American Psychologist, 40,* 165–174. [1]

Baumrind, D. (1991). The influence of parenting style on adolescent competence and substance use. *Journal of Early Adolescence, 11,* 56–95. [8]

Beaman, A. L., Cole, C. M., Preston, M., Klentz, B., & Steblay, N. M. (1983). Fifteen years of foot-in-the-door research: A meta-analysis. *Personality and Social Psychology Bulletin, 9,* 181–196. [14]

Beatty, J. (1995). *Principles of behavioral neuroscience.* Dubuque, IA: Brown & Benchmark. [3]

Beck, A. T. (1967). *Depression: Causes and treatment.* Philadelphia: University of Pennsylvania Press. [12]

Beck, A. T. (1976). *Cognitive therapy and the emotional disorders.* New York: New American Library. [13]

Beck, A. T. (1991). Cognitive therapy: A 30-year retrospective. *American Psychologist, 46,* 368–375. [12, 13]

Beck, A. T. (1993). Cognitive therapy: Past, present, and future. *Journal of Consulting and Clinical Psychology, 61,* 194–198. [13]

Beck, A. T., Brown, G., Berchick, R. J., Stewart, B. L., & Steer, R. A. (1990). Relationship between hopelessness and ultimate suicide: A replication with psychiatric outpatients. *American Journal of Psychiatry, 147,* 190–195. [12]

Beck, A. T., Steer, R. A., Beck, J. S., & Newman, C. R. (1993). Hopelessness, depression, suicidal ideation, and clinical diagnosis of depression. *Suicide and Life-Threatening Behavior, 23,* 139–145. [12]

Beilin, H. (1992). Piaget's enduring contribution to developmental psychology. *Developmental Psychology, 28,* 191–204. [8]

Békésy, G. von (1957). The ear. *Scientific American, 197,* 66–78. [3]

Bekker, M. H. J. (1996). Agoraphobia and gender: A review. *Clinical Psychology Review, 16,* 129–146. [12]

Bell, A. P., Weinberg, M. S., & Hammersmith, S. K. (1981). *Sexual preference: Its development in men and women.* Bloomington: Indiana University Press. [9]

Bell, J. (1991). *Evaluating psychological information: Sharpening your critical thinking skills.* Boston: Allyn & Bacon. [1]

Belsky, J. (1996). Parent, infant, and social-contextual antecedents of father-son attachment security. *Developmental Psychology, 32,* 905–913. [8]

Belsky, J., Steinberg, L., & Draper, P. (1991). Childhood experience, interpersonal development, and reproductive strategy: An evolutionary theory of socialization. *Child Development, 62,* 647–670. [8]

Benbow, C. P., & Stanley, J. C. (1980). Sex differences in mathematical ability: Fact or artifact? *Science, 210,* 1262–1264. [9]

Benbow, C. P., & Stanley, J. C. (1983). Sex differences in mathematical reasoning ability: More facts. *Science, 222,* 1029–1031. [2, 9]

Benes, F. M. (1996). Altered neural circuits in schizophrenia. *Harvard Mental Health Letter, 13*(5), 5–7. [12]

Benjafield, J. G. (1996). *A history of psychology.* Boston: Allyn & Bacon. [1]

Bennett, S. K. (1994). The American Indian: A psychological overview. In W. J. Lonner & R. Malpass (Eds.), *Psychology and culture* (pp. 35–39). Boston: Allyn & Bacon. [10]

Bennett, W. I. (1990, November). Boom and doom. *Harvard Health Letter, 16,* 1–4. [3]

Ben-Porath, Y. S., & Butcher, J. N. (1989). The comparability of MMPI and MMPI–2 scales and profiles. *Psychological Assessment: A Journal of Consulting and Clinical Psychology, 1,* 345–347. [10]

Benson, H. (1975). *The relaxation response.* New York: Avon. [4]

Benson, P. L., Karabenick, S. A., & Lerner, R. M. (1976). Pretty pleases: The effects of physical attractiveness, race, and sex on receiving help. *Journal of Personality and Social Psychology, 12,* 409–415. [14]

Beratis, S., Gabriel, J., & Holdas, S. (1994). Age at onset in subtypes of schizophrenic disorders. *Schizophrenia Bulletin, 20,* 287–296. [12]

Berenbaum, S. A., Korman, K., & Leveroni, C. (1995). Early hormones and sex differences in cognitive abilities. *Learning and Individual Differences, 7,* 303–321. [9]

Berenbaum, S. A., & Snyder, E. (1995). Early hormonal influences on childhood sex-typed activity and playmate preferences: Implications for the development of sexual orientation. *Developmental Psychology, 31,* 31–42. [9]

Berk, L. E. (1994). *Child development* (3rd ed.). Boston: Allyn & Bacon. [8]

Berk, L. E. (1997). *Child development* (4th ed.). Boston: Allyn & Bacon. [8]

Berkman, L. F., & Syme, S. L. (1979). Social networks, host resistance, and mortality: A nine-year followup study of Alameda County residents. *American Journal of Epidemiology, 109,* 184–204. [11]

Berkowitz, L. (1964). The effects of observing violence. *Scientific American, 210,* 35–41. [14]

Berkowitz, L. (1983). Aversively stimulated aggression: Some parallels and differences in research with animals and humans. *American Psychologist, 38,* 1135–1144. [14]

Berkowitz, L. (1988). Frustrations, appraisals, and aversively stimulated aggression. *Aggressive Behavior, 14,* 3–11. [14]

Berkowitz, L. (1989). Frustration-aggression hypothesis: Examination and reformulation. *Psychological Bulletin, 106,* 59–73. [14]

Berkowitz, L. (1990). On the formation and regulation of anger and aggression: A cognitive-neoassociationistic analysis. *American Psychologist, 45,* 494–503. [14]

Bernal, M. E., & Castro, F. G. (1994). Are clinical psychologists prepared for service and research with ethnic minorities? Report of a decade of progress. *American Psychologist, 49,* 797–805. [13]

Berndt, T. J. (1992). Friendship and friends' influence in adolescence. *Current Directions in Psychological Science, 1,* 156–159. [8]

Bernstein, I. L. (1985). Learned food aversions in the progression of cancer and its treatment. *Annals of the New York Academy of Sciences, 443,* 365–380. [5]

Bernstein, I. L., Webster, M. M., & Bernstein, I. D. (1982). Food aversions in children receiving chemotherapy for cancer. *Cancer, 50,* 2961–2963. [5]

Berquier, A., & Aston, R. (1992). Characteristics of the frequent nightmare sufferer. *Journal of Abnormal Psychology, 101,* 246–250. [4]

Berscheid, E., Dion, K., Walster, E., & Walster, G. W. (1971). Physical attractiveness and dating choice: A test of the matching hypothesis. *Journal of Experimental Social Psychology, 7,* 173–189. [14]

Bexton, W. H., Herron, W., & Scott, T. H. (1954). Effects of decreased variation in the sensory environment. *Canadian Journal of Psychology, 8,* 70–76. [9]

Billiard, M., Pasquiré-Magnetto, V., Heckman, M., Carlander, B., Besset, A., Zachariev, Z., Eliaou, J. F., & Malafosse, A. (1994). Family studies in narcolepsy. *Sleep, 17,* S54–S59. [4]

Birren, J. E., & Fisher, L. M. (1995). Aging and speed of behavior: Possible consequences for psychological functioning. *Annual Review of Psychology, 46,* 329–353. [8]

Bisiach, E. (1996). Unilateral neglect and the structure of space representation. *Current Directions in Psychological Science, 5,* 62–65. [2]

Blair, S. N. (1993). Evidence for success of exercise in weight loss and control. *Annals of Internal Medicine, 119*, 702–706. [9]

Blair, S. N., Kohl, H. W., III, Paffenbarger, R. S., Jr., Clark, D. G., Cooper, K. H., & Gibbons, L. W. (1989). Physical fitness and all-cause mortality: A prospective study of healthy men and women. *Journal of the American Medical Association, 262*, 2395–2401. [11]

Blascovich, J., Wyer, N. A., Swart, L. A., & Kibler, J. L. (1997). Racism and racial categorization. *Journal of Personality and Social Psychology, 72*, 1364–1372. [14]

Blatt, S. J., Sanislow, C. A., III, Zuroff, D. C., & Pilkonis, P. A. (1996). Characteristics of effective therapists: Further analyses of data from the National Institute of Mental Health Treatment of Depression Collaborative Research Program. *Journal of Consulting and Clinical Psychology, 64*, 1276–1284. [13]

Blau, A. (1946). *The master hand*. New York: American Ortho-Psychiatric Association. [2]

Bleuler, E. (1950). *Dementia praecox, or the group of schizophrenias*. (J. Zinkin & N. D. C. Lewis, Trans.). New York: International Universities Press, 1950. (Original work published 1911). [12]

Bliss, E. L., & Jeppsen, E. A. (1985). Prevalence of multiple personality among inpatients and outpatients. *American Journal of Psychiatry, 142*, 250–251. [12]

Bloche, M. G., & Eisenberg, C. (1993). The psychological effects of state-sanctioned terror. *Harvard Mental Health Letter, 10*(5), 4–6. [11]

Block, J. (1995). A contrarian view of the five-factor approach to personality description. *Psychological Bulletin, 117*, 187–215. [10]

Bloom, B. S. (Ed.). (1985). *Developing talent in young people*. New York: Ballantine. [7]

Bloomer, C. M. (1976). *Principles of visual perception*. New York: Van Nostrand Reinhold. [3]

Blundell, J. E., Rogers, P. J., & Hill, A. J. (1988). Uncoupling sweetness and calories: Methodological aspects of laboratory studies on appetite control. *Appetite, 11*(Suppl.), 54–61. [9]

Blyth, D. A., Simmons, R. G., Bulcroft, R., Felt, D., VanCleave, E. F., & Bush, D. M. (1981). The effects of physical development on self-image and satisfaction with body-image for early adolescent males. In R. G. Simmons (Ed.), *Research in community and mental health* (Vol. 2). Greenwich, CT: JAI. [8]

Bogaert, A. F., & Fisher, W. A. (1995). Predictors of university men's number of sexual partners. *Journal of Sex Research, 32*, 119–130. [9]

Bogen, J. E., & Vogel, P. J. (1963). Treatment of generalized seizures by cerebral commissurotomy. *Surgical Forum, 14*, 431. [2]

Bohannon, J. N., III. (1988). Flashbulb memories for the Space Shuttle disaster: A tale of two theories. *Cognition, 29*, 179–196. [6]

Bohannon, J. N., & Warren-Leubecker, A. (1989). Theoretical approaches to language acquisition. In J. B. Gleason (Ed.), *The development of language* (pp. 167–223). Columbus, OH: Merrill. [8]

Boivin, D. B., Czeisler, C. A., Dijk, D-J., Duffy, J. F., Folkard, S., Minors, D. S., Totterdell, P., & Waterhouse, J. M. (1997). Complex interaction of the sleep-wake cycle and circadian phase modulates mood in healthy subjects. *Archives of General Psychiatry, 54*, 145–152. [4]

Bonanno, G. A., Keltner, D., Holen, A., & Horowitz, M. J. (1995). When avoiding unpleasant emotions might not be such a bad thing: Verbal-autonomic response dissociation and midlife conjugal bereavement. *Journal of Personality and Social Psychology, 69*, 975–989. [8]

Bonnet, M. H., & Arand, D. L. (1995). We are chronically sleep deprived. *Sleep, 18*, 908–911 [4]

Bootzin, R. R., & Perlis, M. L. (1992). Nonpharmacologic treatments of insomnia. *Journal of Clinical Psychiatry, 53*(6, Suppl.), 37–41. [4]

Borbely, A. A. (1984). Sleep regulation: Outline of a model and its implications for depression. In A. A. Borbely & J. L. Valatx (Eds.), *Sleep mechanisms*. Berlin: Springer-Verlag. [4]

Borbely, A. A., Achermann, P., Trachsel, L., & Tobler, I. (1989). Sleep initiation and initial sleep intensity: Interactions of homeostatic and circadian mechanisms. *Journal of Biological Rhythms, 4*, 149–160. [4]

Borg, E., & Counter, S. A. (1989). The middle-ear muscles. *Scientific American, 261*, 74–80. [3]

Bormann, J., & Feigenspan, A. (1995). GABAc receptors. *Trends in Neurosciences, 18*, 515–519. [2]

Bornstein, R. F. (1989). Exposure and affect: Overview and meta-analysis of research, 1968–1987. *Psychological Bulletin, 106*, 265–289. [14]

Borod, J. C. (1992). Interhemispheric and intrahemispheric control of emotion: A focus on unilateral brain damage. *Journal of Consulting and Clinical Psychology, 60*, 339–348. [2]

Borrie, R. A. (1991). The use of restricted environmental stimulation therapy in treating addictive behaviors. *International Journal of the Addictions, 25*, 995–1015. [9]

Bouchard, C. (1996). Can obesity be prevented? *Nutrition Reviews, 54*, S125–S130. [9]

Bouchard, C. (1997). Human variation in body mass: Evidence for a role of the genes. *Nutrition Reviews, 55*, S21–S30. [9]

Bouchard, C., Tremblay, A., Despres, J-P., Nadeau, A., Lupien, P. J., Theriault, G., Dussault, J., Moorjani, S., Pinault, S., & Fournier, G. (1990). The response to long-term overfeeding in identical twins. *New England Journal of Medicine, 322*, 1477–1482. [9]

Bouchard, T. J., Jr. (1994). Genes, environment, and personality. *Science, 264*, 1700–1701. [10]

Bouchard, T. J., Jr. (1997, September/October). Whenever the twain shall meet. *The Sciences, 37*, 52–57. [7, 8, 10]

Bouchard, T. J., Jr. (1998, May 13). Personal communication. [7]

Bouchard, T. J., Jr., Lykken, D. T., McGue, M., Segal, N. L., & Tellegen, A. (1990). Sources of human psychological differences: The Minnesota study of twins reared apart. *Science, 250*, 223–228. [7, 10]

Bouchard, T. J., Jr., & McGue, M. (1981). Familial studies of intelligence: A review. *Science, 212*, 1055–1058. [7]

Bouton, M. E. (1993). Context, time, and memory retrieval in the interference paradigms of Pavlovian learning. *Psychological Bulletin, 114*, 80–89. [5]

Bouton, M. E., & Ricker, S. T. (1994) Renewal of extinguished responding in a second context. *Animal Learning and Behavior, 22*, 317–324. [5]

Bovbjerg, D. H., Redd, W. H., Maier, L. A., Holland, J. C., Lesko, L. M., Niedzwiecki, D., Rubin, S. C., & Hakes, T. B. (1990). Anticipatory immune suppression and nausea in women receiving cyclic chemotherapy for ovarian cancer. *Journal of Consulting and Clinical Psychology, 58*, 153–157. [5]

Bower, G. H. (1973, October). How to . . . uh . . . remember! *Psychology Today*, pp. 63–70. [6]

Bower, G. H., Thompson-Schill, S., & Tulving E. (1994). Reducing retroactive interference: An interference analysis. *Journal of Experimental Psychology: Learning, Memory, and Cognition, 20*, 51–66. [6]

Bowers, K. S. (1992). Imagination and dissociative control in hypnotic responding. *International Journal of Clinical and Experimental Hypnosis, 40*, 253–275. [4]

Bowers, K. S., & Farvolden, P. (1996). Revisiting a century-old Freudian slip—from suggestion disavowed to the truth repressed. *Psychological Bulletin, 119*, 355–380. [6]

Bowers, K. S., & Woody, E. Z. (1996). Hypnotic amnesia and the paradox of intentional forgetting. *Journal of Abnormal Psychology, 105*, 381–390. [4]

Brain imaging and psychiatry—Part I. (1997, January). *Harvard Mental Health Letter, 13*(7), 1–4. [2]

Bramblett, D. A. (1997, October). Personal communication. [3]

Brantner, J. P., & Doherty, M. A. (1983). A review of time out: A conceptual and methodological analysis. In S. Axelrod & J. Apsche (Eds.), *The effects of punishment on human behavior* (pp. 87–132). New York: Academic Press. [13]

Braun, S. (1996). New experiments underscore warnings on maternal drinking. *Science, 273*, 738–739. [8]

Brawman-Mintzer, O., & Lydiard, R. B. (1996). Generalized anxiety disorder: Issues in epidemiology. *Journal of Clinical Psychiatry, 57*(7, Suppl.), 3–8. [12]

Brawman-Mintzer, O., & Lydiard, R. B. (1997). Biological basis of generalized anxiety disorder. *Journal of Clinical Psychiatry*, *58*(3, Suppl.), 16–25. [12]

Bray, G. A. (1991). Weight homeostasis. *Annual Review of Medicine*, *42*, 205–216. [9]

Brazelton, T. B., Tronick, E., Adamson, L., Als, H., & Wise, S. (1975). Early mother-infant interaction. In *Parent-infant interaction, Ciba symposium 33*. Amsterdam: Assoc. Science Publ. [8]

Breckler, S. J. (1984). Empirical validation of affect, behavior, and cognition as distinct attitude components. *Journal of Personality and Social Psychology*, *47*, 1191–1205. [14]

Breedlove, S. M. (1994). Sexual differentiation of the human nervous system. *Annual Review of Psychology*, *45*, 389–418. [9]

Breggin, P. R. (1979). *Electroshock: Its brain-disabling effects*. New York: Springer. [13]

Breland, K., & Breland, M. (1961). The misbehavior of organisms. *American Psychologist*, *16*, 681–684. [5]

Brennan, P. A., Raine, A., Schulsinger, F., Kirkegaard-Sorensen, L., Knop, J., Hutchings, B., Rosenberg, R., & Mednick, S. A. (1997). Psychophysiological protective factors for male subjects at high risk for criminal behavior. *American Journal of Psychiatry*, *154*, 853–855. [14]

Brent, D. A., Bridge, J., Johnson, B. A., & Connolly, J. (1996). Suicidal behavior runs in families: A controlled family study of adolescent suicide victims. *Archives of General Psychiatry*, *53*, 1145–1152. [12]

Breslau, N., Davis, G. C., Andreski, P., & Peterson, E. (1991). Traumatic events and posttraumatic stress disorder in an urban population of young adults. *Archives of General Psychiatry*, *48*, 216–222. [11]

Breslau, N., Davis, G. C., Peterson, E. L., & Schultz, L. (1997). Psychiatric sequelae of posttraumatic stress disorder in women. *Archives of General Psychiatry*, *54*, 81–87. [11]

Breslow, L. (1999). From disease prevention to health promotion. *Journal of the American Medical Association*, *281*, 1030–1033. [11]

Brickner, M. A., Harkins, S. G., & Ostrom, T. M. (1986). Effects of personal involvement: Thought-provoking implications for social loafing. *Journal of Personality and Social Psychology*, *51*, 763–769. [14]

Brigham, J. C., & Wolfskeil, M. P. (1983). Opinions of attorneys and law enforcement personnel on the accuracy of eyewitness identifications. *Law and Human Behavior*, *7*, 337–349. [6]

Broadbent, D. E. (1958). *Perception and communication*. New York: Pergamon Press. [6]

Brody, E. M., Johnson, P. T., & Fulcomer, M. C. (1984). What should adult children do for elderly parents? Opinions and preferences of three generations of women. *Journal of Gerontology*, *39*, 736–746. [8]

Brody, E. M., Litvin, S. J., Hoffman, C., & Kleban, M. H. (1992). Differential effects of daughters' marital status on their parent care experiences. *The Gerontologist*, *32*, 58–67. [8]

Bronstein, P. (1984). Differences in mothers' and fathers' behaviors toward children: A cross-cultural comparison. *Developmental Psychology*, *20*, 995–1003. [8]

Brooks-Gunn, J., & Furstenberg, F. F. (1989). Adolescent sexual behavior. *American Psychologist*, *44*, 249–257. [8]

Brotman, A. W. (1994). What works in the treatment of anorexia nervosa? *Harvard Mental Health Letter*, *10*(7), 8. [9]

Brou, P., Sciascia, T. R., Linden, L., & Lettvin, J. Y. (1986). The colors of things. *Scientific American*, *255*, 84–91. [3]

Broughton, R. J., & Shimizu, T. (1995). Sleep-related violence: A medical and forensic challenge. *Sleep*, *18*, 727–730. [4]

Brown, A. (1996, Winter). Mood disorders in children and adolescents. *NARSAD Research Newsletter*, pp. 11–14. [12]

Brown, A. M. (1990). Development of visual sensitivity to light and color vision in human infants: A critical review. *Vision Research*, *30*, 1159–1188. [8]

Brown, G. L., & Linnoila, M. I. (1990). CSF serotonin metabolite (5-HIAA) studies in depression, impulsivity, and violence. *Journal of Clinical Psychiatry*, *51*(Suppl.), 42–43. [14]

Brown, G. W., Harris, T. O., & Hepworth, C. (1994). Life events and endogenous depression: A puzzle reexamined. *Archives of General Psychiatry*, *51*, 525–534. [12]

Brown, J. D. (1991). Staying fit and staying well: Physical fitness as a moderator of life stress. *Journal of Personality and Social Psychology*, *60*, 555–561. [11]

Brown, J. D., & Rogers, R. J. (1991). Self-serving attributions: The role of physiological arousal. *Personality and Social Psychology Bulletin*, *17*, 501–506. [14]

Brown, J. L., & Pollitt, E. (1996). Malnutrition, poverty and intellectual development. *Scientific American*, *274*, 38–43. [7]

Brown, R. (1973). *A first language: The early stages*. Cambridge, MA: Harvard University Press. [8]

Brown, R., Cazden, C., & Bellugi, U. (1968). The child's grammar from I to III. In J. P. Hill (Ed.), *Minnesota symposium on child psychology* (Vol. 2, pp. 28–73). Minneapolis: University of Minnesota Press. [8]

Brown, R., & Kulik, J. (1977). Flashbulb memories. *Cognition*, *5*, 73–99. [6]

Brown, R., & McNeil, D. (1966). The "tip of the tongue" phenomenon. *Journal of Verbal Learning and Verbal Behavior*, *5*, 325–337. [6]

Brown, R. J., & Donderi, D. C. (1986). Dream content and self-reported well-being among recurrent dreamers, past-recurrent dreamers, and nonrecurrent dreamers. *Journal of Personality and Social Psychology*, *50*, 612–623. [4]

Brownell, K. (1991). Dieting and the search for the perfect body: Where physiology and culture collide. *Behavior Therapy*, *22*, 1–12. [9]

Brownell, K. D., & Wadden, T. A. (1992). Etiology and treatment of obesity: Understanding a serious, prevalent, and refractory disorder. *Journal of Consulting and Clinical Psychology*, *60*, 505–517. [9]

Brownlee, S., & Schrof, J. M. (1997, March 17). The quality of mercy. *U.S. News & World Report*, pp. 54–67. [3]

Bruce, K. R., Pihl, R. O., Mayerovitch, J. I., & Shestowsky, J. S. (1999). Alcohol and retrograde memory effects: Role of individual differences. *Journal of Studies on Alcohol*, *60*, 130–136. [6]

Bryan, J. H., & Test, M. A. (1967). Models and helping: Naturalistic studies in aiding behavior. *Journal of Personality and Social Psychology*, *6*, 400–407. [14]

Buchanan, C. M., Eccles, J. S., & Becker, J. B. (1992). Are adolescents the victims of raging hormones? Evidence for activational effects of hormones on moods and behavior at adolescence. *Psychological Bulletin*, *111*, 62–107. [8]

Buchsbaum, M. S., Someya, T., Teng, C. Y., Abel, L., Chin, S., Najafi, A., Haier, R. J., Wu, J., & Bunney, W. E., Jr. (1996). PET and MRI of the thalamus in never-medicated patients with schizophrenia. *American Journal of Psychiatry*, *153*, 191–199. [12]

Buck, L. B. (1996). Information coding in the vertebrate olfactory system. *Annual Review of Neuroscience*, *19*, 517–544. [3]

Buonomano, D. V., & Merzenich, M. M. (1995). Temporal information transformed into a spatial code by a neural network with realistic properties. *Science*, *267*, 1028–1030. [7]

Busch, C. M., Zonderman, A. B., & Costa, P. T. (1994). Menopausal transition and psychological distress in a nationally representative sample: Is menopause associated with psychological distress? *Journal of Aging and Health*, *6*, 209–228. [8]

Bushman, B. J. (1995). Moderating role of trait aggressiveness in the effects of violent media on aggression. *Journal of Personality and Social Psychology*, *69*, 950–960. [14]

Busnel, M. C., Granier-Deferre, C., & Lecanuet, J. P. (1992). Fetal audition. *Annals of the New York Academy of Sciences*, *662*, 118–134. [8]

Buss, D. M. (1984). Marital assortment for personality dispositions: Assessment with three different data sources. *Behavioral Genetics*, *14*, 111–123. [14]

Buss, D. M. (1991). Evolutionary personality psychology. *Annual Review of Psychology*, *42*, 459–491. [10]

Butcher, J. N., Dahlstrom, W. G., Graham, J. R., Tellegen, A., & Kaemmer, B. (1989). *Manual for the restandardized Minnesota Multiphasic Personality Inventory: MMPI–2. An administrative and interpretive guide*. Minneapolis: University of Minnesota Press. [10]

Butcher, J. N., & Graham, J. R. (1989). *Topics in MMPI–2 interpretation.* Minneapolis: Department of Psychology, University of Minnesota. [10]

Butcher, J. N., Graham, J. R., & Ben-Porath, Y. S. (1995). Methodological problems and issues in MMPI, MMPI-2, and MMPI-A research. *Psychological Assessment, 7,* 320–329. [10]

Butcher, J. N., & Rouse, S. V. (1996). Personality: Individual differences and clinical assessment. *Annual Review of Psychology, 47,* 89–111. [10]

Butler, R., & Lewis, M. (1982). *Aging and mental health* (3rd ed.). St. Louis: Mosby. [8]

Byne, W. (1993a). Human sexual orientation: The biologic theories reappraised. *Archives of General Psychiatry, 50,* 228–239. [9]

Byne, W. (1994). The biological evidence challenged. *Scientific American, 270,* 50–55. [9]

Byne, W., & Parsons, B. (1993). Human sexual orientation: The biologic theories reappraised. *Archives of General Psychiatry, 50,* 228–239. [9]

Byne, W., & Parsons, B. (1994). Biology and human sexual orientation. *Harvard Mental Health Letter, 10*(8), 5–7. [9]

Byrne, D., Clore, G. L., & Smeaton, G. (1986). The attraction hypothesis: Do similar attitudes affect anything? *Journal of Personality and Social Psychology, 51,* 1167–1170. [14]

Cahill, L., Babinsky, R., Markowitsch, H. J., & McGaugh, J. L. (1995). The amygdala and emotional memory. *Nature, 377,* 295–296. [2, 6]

Callahan, J. (1997, May–June). Hypnosis: Trick or treatment? You'd be amazed at what modern doctors are tackling with an 18th century gimmick. *Health, 11,* 52–54. [4]

Camp, D. S., Raymond, G. A., & Church, R. M. (1967). Temporal relationship between response and punishment. *Journal of Experimental Psychology, 74,* 114–123. [5]

Campbell, D. T., & Sprecht, J. C. (1985). Altruism: Biology, culture, and religion. *Journal of Social and Clinical Psychology, 3,* 33–42. [10]

Campbell, R., & Brody, E. M. (1985). Women's changing roles and help to the elderly: Attitudes of women in the United States and Japan. *The Gerontologist, 25,* 584–592. [8]

Campbell, S. S. (1985). Spontaneous termination of ad libitum sleep episodes with special reference to REM sleep. *Electroencephalography & Clinical Neurophysiology, 60,* 237–242. [4]

Campbell, S. S. (1995). Effects of timed bright-light exposure on shift-work adaptation in middle-aged subjects. *Sleep, 18,* 408–416. [4]

Campbell, S. S., & Murphy, P. J. (1998). *Science, 2,* [4] [FIND]

Cannon, T. D., Kaprio, J., Lönnqvist, J., Huttunen, M., & Koskenvuo, M. (1998). The genetic epidemiology of schizophrenia in a Finnish twin cohort: A population-based modeling study. *Archives of General Psychiatry, 55,* 67–74. [12]

Cannon, W. B. (1927). The James-Lange theory of emotions: A critical examination and an alternative theory. *American Journal of Psychology, 39,* 106–112. [9]

Cannon, W. B. (1929). *Bodily changes in pain, hunger, fear and rage* (2nd ed.). New York: Appleton. [3]

Cannon, W. B. (1932). *The wisdom of the body.* New York: Norton. [11]

Cannon, W. B. (1935). Stresses and strains of homeostasis. *American Journal of Public Health, 189,* 1–14. [3]

Cannon, W. B., & Washburn, A. L. (1912). An explanation of hunger. *American Journal of Physiology, 29,* 441–454. [11]

Carlat, D. J., Camargo, C. A., Jr., & Herzog, D. B. (1997). Eating disorders in males: A report on 135 patients. *American Journal of Psychiatry, 154,* 1127–1132. [9]

Carlin, A. S., Hoffman, H. G., & Weghorst, S. (1997). Virtual reality and tactile augmentation in the treatment of spider phobia: A case report. *Behaviour Research and Therapy, 35,* 153–158. [13]

Carlson, E. B., & Rosser-Hogan, R. (1991). Trauma experiences, post-traumatic stress, dissociation, and depression in Cambodian refugees. *American Journal of Psychiatry, 148,* 1548–1551. [11]

Carlson, M., Charlin, V., & Miller, N. (1988). Positive mood and helping behavior: A test of six hypotheses. *Journal of Personality and Social Psychology, 55,* 211–229. [14]

Carlson, N. R. (1998). *Foundations of physiological psychology* (4th ed.). Boston: Allyn & Bacon. [4]

Carpenter, W. T., Jr. (1996). Maintenance therapy of persons with schizophrenia. *Journal of Clinical Psychiatry, 57*(9, Suppl.), 10–18. [13]

Carpi, J. (1996, January/February). Stress: It's worse than you think. *Psychology Today, 29,* 34–42, 68–76. [11]

Carrier, J. (1980). Homosexual behavior in cross-cultural perspective. In J. Marmor (Ed.), *Homosexual behavior* (pp. 100–122). New York: Basic Books. [9]

Carroll, J. M., & Russell, J. A. (1996). Do facial expressions signal specific emotions? Judging emotion from the face in context. *Journal of Personality and Social Psychology, 70,* 205–218. [9]

Carroll, K. M., Rounsaville, B. J., Nich, C., Gordon, L. T., Wirtz, P. W., & Gawin, F. (1994). One-year follow-up of psychotherapy and pharmacotherapy for cocaine dependence: Delayed emergence of psychotherapy effects. *Archives of General Psychiatry, 51,* 989–997. [13]

Carskadon, M. A., & Dement, W. C. (1989). Normal human sleep: An overview. In M. H. Kryger, T. Roth, & W. C. Dement (Eds.), *Principles and practice of sleep medicine* (pp. 3–13). Philadelphia: W. B. Saunders. [4]

Carskadon, M. A., & Rechtschaffen, A. (1989). Monitoring and staging human sleep. In M. H. Kryger, T. Roth, & W. C. Dement (Eds.), *Principles and practice of sleep medicine* (pp. 665–683). Philadelphia: W. B. Saunders. [4]

Carson, R. C. (1989). Personality. *Annual Review of Psychology, 40,* 227–248. [10]

Carver C. S., Pozo, C., Harris, S. D., Noriega, V., Scheier, M. F., Robinson, D. S., Ketcham, A. S., Moffat, F. L., Jr., & Clark, K. C. (1993). How coping mediates the effect of optimism on distress: A study of women with early stage breast cancer. *Journal of Personality and Social Psychology, 65,* 375–390. [11]

Carver, C. S., & Scheier, M. F. (1996). *Perspectives on personality* (3rd ed.). Boston: Allyn & Bacon. [10]

Case, R. (Ed.). (1992). *The mind's staircase: Exploring the conceptual underpinnings of children's thought and knowledge.* Hillsdale, NJ: Erlbaum. [8]

Casey, D. E. (1996). Side effect profiles of new antipsychotic agents. *Journal of Clinical Psychiatry, 57*(11, Suppl.), 40–45. [13]

Cash, T. F., & Derlega, V. J. (1978). The matching hypothesis: Physical attractiveness among same-sexed friends. *Personality and Social Psychology Bulletin, 4,* 240–243. [14]

Cash, T. F., & Janda, L. H. (1984, December). The eye of the beholder. *Psychology Today,* pp. 46–52. [14]

Caspi, A., Lynam, D., Moffitt, T. E., & Silva, P. A. (1993). Unraveling girls' delinquency: Biological, dispositional, and contextual contributions to adolescent misbehavior. *Developmental Psychology, 29,* 19–30. [8]

Castle, D. J., Abel, K., Takei, N., & Murray, R. M. (1995). Gender differences in schizophrenia: Hormonal effect or subtypes? *Schizophrenia Bulletin, 21,* 1–12. [12]

Catlin, F. I. (1986). Noise-induced hearing loss. *American Journal of Otology, 7,* 141–149. [3]

Cattell, R. B. (1950). *Personality: A systematic, theoretical, and factual study.* New York: McGraw-Hill. [10]

Cattell, R. B. (1993). *16PF® fifth edition profile sheet.* Champaign, IL: Institute for Personality and Ability Testing. [10]

Cattell, R. B., Eber, H. W., & Tatsuoka, M. M. (1977). *Handbook for the 16 personality factor questionnaire.* Champaign, IL: Institute of Personality and Ability Testing. [10]

Cattell, R. B., Saunders, D. R., & Stice, G. F. (1950). *The 16 personality factor questionnaire.* Champaign, IL: Institute of Personality and Ability Testing. [10]

Centers for Disease Control. (1991). Tobacco use among high school students—United States, 1990. *Morbidity and Mortality Weekly Report, 40,* 617–619. [11]

Centers for Disease Control. (1992). Sexual behavior among high school students—United States, 1990. *Morbidity and Mortality Weekly Report*, 40(51, 52), 885–888. [8]

Chaika, E. (1985, August). Crazy talk. *Psychology Today*, pp. 30–35. [12]

Challis, B. H. (1996). Implicit memory research in 1996: Introductory remarks. *Canadian Journal of Experimental Psychology*, 50, 1–4. [6]

Chambless, D. L., & Goldstein, A. J. (1979). Behavioral psychotherapy. In R. J. Corsini (Ed.), *Current psychotherapies* (2nd ed., pp. 230–272). Itasca, IL: F. E. Peacock. [13]

Chang, E. C. (1998). Dispositional optimism and primary and secondary appraisal of a stressor: Controlling for confounding influences and relations to coping and psychological and physical adjustment. *Journal of Personality and Social Psychology*, 74, 1109–1120. [11]

Changeux, J-P. (1993). Chemical signaling in the brain. *Scientific American*, 269, 58–62. [2]

Charness, N. (1989). Age and expertise: Responding to Talland's challenge. In L. W. Poon, D. C. Rubin, & B. A. Wilson (Eds.), *Everyday cognition in adulthood and old age*. New York: Cambridge University Press. [8]

Checkley, H. (1941). *The mask of sanity*. St. Louis: Mosby. [12]

Chesno, F. A., & Killman, P. R. (1975). Effects of stimulation on sociopathic avoidance learning. *Journal of Abnormal Psychology*, 84, 144–150. [12]

Children's Defense Fund. (1996). *The state of America's children yearbook, 1996*. Washington, DC: Author. [8]

Chira, S. (1992, February 12). Bias against girls is found rife in schools, with lasting damage. *The New York Times*, pp. A1, A23. [7]

Chodoff, P. (1987). More on multiple personality disorder. *American Journal of Psychiatry*, 144, 124. [12]

Chollar, S. (1989). Conversation with the dolphins. *Psychology Today*, 23, 52–57. [7]

Chomsky, N. (1957). *Syntactic structures*. The Hague: Mouton. [8]

Chomsky, N. (1968). *Language and mind*. New York: Harcourt, Brace & World. [8]

Christensen, L. B. (1997). *Experimental methodology* (7th ed.). Boston: Allyn & Bacon. [1]

Chumlea, W. C. (1982). Physical growth in adolescence. In B. B. Wolman (Ed.), *Handbook of developmental psychology*. Englewood Cliffs, NJ: Prentice-Hall. [8]

Church, R. M. (1963). The varied effects of punishment on behavior. *Psychological Review*, 70, 369–402. [5]

Church, R. M. (1989). Theories of timing behavior. In S. P. Klein &R. Mowrer (Eds.), *Contemporary learning theories: Instrumental conditioning theory and the impact of biological constraints on learning*. Hillsdale, NJ: Erlbaum. [5]

Chyou, P. H., Nomura, A. M. Y., & Stemmermann, G. N. (1992). A prospective study of the attributable risk of cancer due to cigarette smoking. *American Journal of Public Health*, 82, 37–40. [11]

Cialdini, R. B., Cacioppo, J. T., Basset, R., & Miller, J. A. (1978). Lowball procedure for producing compliance: Commitment then cost. *Journal of Personality and Social Psychology*, 36, 463–476. [14]

Cialdini, R. B., Vincent, J. E., Lewis, S. K., Catalan, J., Wheeler, D., & Darby, B. L. (1975). Reciprocal concessions procedure for inducing compliance: The door-in-the-fact technique. *Journal of Personality and Social Psychology*, 31, 206–215. [14]

Cicirelli, V. G. (1993). Attachment and obligation as daughters' motives for caregiving behavior and subsequent effect on subjective burden. *Psychology and Aging*, 8, 144–155. [8]

Cipolli, C., Bolzani, R., Cornoldi, C., De Beni, R., & Fagioli, I. (1993). Bizarreness effect in dream recall. *Sleep*, 16, 163–170. [4]

Clark, D. M., Salkovskis, P. M., Öst, L-G., Breitholtz, E., Koehler, K. A., Westling, B. E., Jeavons, A., & Gelder, M. (1997). Misinterpretation of body sensations in panic disorder. *Journal of Consulting and Clinical Psychology*, 65, 203–213. [12]

Clark, D. M., & Teasdale, J. D. (1982). Diurnal variation in clinical depression and accessibility of memories of positive and negative experiences. *Journal of Abnormal Psychology*, 91, 87–95. [6]

Clark, L. A., Watson, D., & Reynolds, S. (1995). Diagnosis and classification of psychopathology: Challenges to the current system and future directions. *Annual Review of Psychology*, 46, 121–153. [12]

Clark, M. L., & Ayers, M. (1992). Friendship similarity during early adolescence: Gender and racial patterns. *Journal of Psychology*, 126, 393–405. [8]

Clark, R. D., III, & Word, L. E. (1972). Why don't bystanders help? Because of ambiguity? *Journal of Personality and Social Psychology*, 24, 392–400. [14]

Clark, R. E., & Squire, L. R. (1998). Classical conditioning and brain systems: The role of awareness. *Science*, 280, 77–81. [6]

Clarkson-Smith, L., & Hartley, A. A. (1990). Structural equation models of relationships between exercise and cognitive abilities. *Psychology and Aging*, 5, 437–446. [8]

Clayton, K. N. (1964). T-maze choice learning as a joint function of the reward magnitudes for the alternatives. *Journal of Comparative and Physiological Psychology*, 58, 333–338. [38]

Clément, K., Vaisse, C., Lahlou, N., Cabrol, S., Pelloux, V., Cassuto, D., Gourmelen, M., Dina, C., Chambaz, J., Lacorte, J-M., Basdevant, A., Bougnères, P., Lubouc, Y., Froguel, P., & Guy-Grand, B. (1998). A mutation in the human leptin receptor gene causes obesity and pituitary dysfunction. *Nature*, 392, 398–401. [9]

Cloninger, C. R., Sigvardsson, S., Bohman, M., & von Knorring, A. L. (1982). Predispositions to petty criminality in Swedish adoptees, II. Cross-fostering analysis of gene-environment interaction. *Archives of General Psychiatry*, 39, 1242–1249. [14]

Clum, G. A., Clum, G. A., & Surls, R. (1993). A meta-analysis of treatments for panic disorder. *Journal of Consulting and Clinical Psychology*, 61, 317–326. [13]

Cobb, S. (1976). Social support as a moderator of life stress. *Psychosomatic Medicine*, 38, 300–314. [11]

Cohen, A. (1997, September 8). Battle of the binge. *Time*, p. 54–56. [4]

Cohen, L. L., & Shotland, R. L. (1996). Timing of first sexual intercourse in a relationship: Expectations, experiences, and perceptions of others. *Journal of Sex Research*, 33, 291–299. [9]

Cohen, S. (1988). Psychosocial models of the role of social support in the etiology of physical disease. *Health Psychology*, 7, 269–297. [11]

Cohen, S. (1996). Psychological stress, immunity, and upper respiratory infections. *Current Directions in Psychological Science*, 5, 86–89. [11]

Cohen, S., Doyle, W. J., Skoner, D. P., Rabin, B. S., & Gwaltney, J. M., Jr. (1997). Social ties and susceptibility to the common cold. *Journal of the American Medical Association*, 277, 1940–1944. [11]

Cohen, S., & Herbert, T. B. (1996). Health psychology: Psychological factors and physical disease from the perspective of human psychoneuroimmunology. *Annual Review of Psychology*, 47, 113–142. [11]

Cohen, S., & Williamson, G. M. (1991). Stress and infectious disease in humans. *Psychological Bulletin*, 109, 5–54. [11]

Colasanto, D., & Shriver, J. (1989, May). Mirror of America: Middle-aged face marital crisis. *Gallup Report*, No. 284, 34–38. [8]

Colby, A., Kohlberg, L., Gibbs, J., & Lieberman, M. (1983). A longitudinal study of moral judgment. *Monographs of the Society for Research in Child Development*, 48(1–2, Serial No. 200). [8]

Cole, P. M. (1986). Children's spontaneous control of facial expression. *Child Development*, 57, 1309–1321. [9]

Coleman, M., & Ganong, L. H. (1985). Love and sex role stereotypes: Do macho men and feminine women make better lovers? *Journal of Personality and Social Psychology*, 49, 170–176. [11]

Coleman, R. M. (1986). *Wide awake at 3:00 a.m.: By choice or by chance*. New York: W. H. Freeman. [4]

Collaer, M. L., & Hines, M. (1995). Human behavioral sex differences: A role for gonadal hormones during early development. *Psychological Bulletin*, 118, 55–107. [9]

Collier, A. C., Coombs, R. W., Schoenfeld, D. A., Bassett, R. L., Timpone, J., Baruch, A., Jones, M., Facey, K., Whitacre, C., McAuliffe, V. J., Friedman, H. M., Merigan, T. C., Reichman, R. C., Hooper, C., & Corey, L. (1996). Treatment of human immunodeficiency virus infection with saquinavir, zidovudine, and zalcitabine. *New England Journal of Medicine*, 334, 1011–1017. [11]

Collins, W. A., & Gunnar, M. R. (1990). Social and personality development. *Annual Review of Psychology, 41,* 387–416. [8, 9]

Colón, I., & Wuollet, C. A. (1994). Homeland, gender and Chinese drinking. *Journal of Addictive Diseases, 13,* 59–67. [4]

Comstock, G. (1990). Television violence: Is there enough evidence that it is harmful? *Harvard Mental Health Letter, 6*(1), 8. [8]

Condon, W. S., & Sander, L. W. (1974). Neonatal movement is synchronized with adult speech: Interactional participation and language acquisition. *Science, 183,* 99–101. [8]

Consumer Reports. (1995, Novmber) Mental health: Does therapy help? pp. 734–739. [13]

Conway, M. A., Collins, A. F., Gathercole, S. E., & Anderson, S. J. (1996). Recollections of true and false autobiographical memories. *Journal of Experimental Psychology: General, 125,* 69–95. [6]

Cook, M., Mineka, S., Wolkenstein, B., & Laitsch, K. (1985). Observational conditioning of snake fear in unrelated rhesus monkeys. *Journal of Abnormal Psychology, 94,* 591–610. [5]

Coons, P. M. (1994). Confirmation of childhood abuse in child and adolescent cases of multiple personality disorder and dissociative disorder not otherwise specified. *Journal of Nervous and Mental Disease, 182,* 461–464. [12]

Coons, P. M., Bowman, E. S., Kluft, R. P., & Milstein, V. (1991). The cross-cultural occurrence of MPD: Additional cases from a recent survey. *Dissociation, 4,* 124–128. [12]

Cooper, L. A., & Shepard, R. N. (1984). Turning something over in the mind. *Scientific American, 251,* 106–114. [7]

Cooper, R. (1994). Normal sleep. In R. Cooper (Ed.), *Sleep.* New York: Chapman & Hall. [4]

Cooper, R. S., Rotimi, C. N., & Ward, R. (1999, February). The puzzle of hypertension in African-Americans. *Scientific American, 280,* 56–62. [11]

Coplan, J. D., Papp, L. A., Pine, D., Marinez, J., Cooper, T. Rosenblum, L. A., Klein, D. F., & Gorman, J. M. (1997). Clinical improvement with fluoxetine therapy and noradrenergic function in patients with panic disorder. *Archives of General Psychiatry, 54,* 643–648. [13]

Coppen, A. (1994). Depression as a lethal disease: Prevention strategies. *Journal of Clinical Psychiatry, 55*(4, Suppl.), 37–45. [12]

Coren, S. (1989). Left-handedness and accident-related injury risk. *American Journal of Public Health, 79,* 1–2. [2]

Corina, D. P., Vaid, J., & Bellugi, U. (1992). The linguistic basis of left hemisphere specialization. *Science, 255,* 1058–1060. [2]

Cork, L. C., Clarkson, T. B., Jacoby, R. O., Gaertner, D. J., Leary, S. L., Linn, J. M., Pakes, S. P., Ringler, D. H., Strandberg, J. D., & Swindle, M. M. (1997). The costs of animal research: Origins and options. *Science, 276,* 758–759. [1]

Coryell, W. (1996). Psychotic depression. *Journal of Clinical Psychiatry, 57*(3, Suppl.), 27–31. [12]

Coryell, W. (1998). The treatment of psychotic depression. *Journal of Clinical Psychiatry, 59*(1, Suppl.), 22–27. [13]

Costa, P. T., Jr. (1996). Work and personality: Use of the NEO-PI-R in industrial/organisational psychology. *Applied Psychology: An International Review, 45,* 225–241. [10]

Costa, P. T., Jr., & McCrae, R. R. (1985). *The NEO Personality Inventory.* Odessa, FL: Psychological Assessment Resources. [10]

Costa, P. T., Jr., & McCrae, R. R. (1992). *NEO-PI-R: Revised NEO Personality Inventory (NEO-PI-R).* Odessa, FL: Psychological Assessment Resources. [10]

Costa, P. T., Jr., & McCrae, R. R. (1997). Stability and change in personality assessment: The Revised NEO Personality Inventory in the year 2000. *Journal of Personality Assessment, 68,* 8694. [10]

Costa E Silva, J. A., Chase, M., Sartorius, N., & Roth, T. (1996). Special report from a symposium held by the World Health Organization and the World Federation of Sleep Research Societies: An overview of insomnias and related disorders—recognition, epidemiology, and rational management. *Sleep, 19,* 412–416. [4]

Costanzo, P. R., & Schiffman, S. S. (1989). Thinness—not obesity—has a genetic component. *Neuroscience and Biobehavioral Reviews, 13,* 55–58. [9]

Cotman, C. W., & Lynch, G. S. (1989). The neurobiology of learning and memory. *Cognition, 33,* 201–241. [6]

Council on Ethical and Judicial Affairs, American Medical Association. (1991). Gender disparities in clinical decision making. *Journal of the American Medical Association, 266,* 559–562. [11]

Courage, M. L., & Adams, R. J. (1990). Visual acuity assessment from birth to three years using the acuity card procedures: Cross-sectional and longitudinal samples. *Optometry and Vision Science, 67,* 713–718. [8]

Courtney, S. M., Ungerleider, L. G., Keil, K., & Haxby, J. V. (1997). Transient and sustained activity in a distributed neural system for human working memory. *Nature, 386,* 608–611. [6]

Cowan, N. (1988). Evolving conceptions of memory storage, selective attention, and their mutual constraints within the human information-processing system. *Psychological Bulletin, 104,* 163–191. [6]

Coyle, J., & Draper, E. S. (1996). What is the significance of glutamate for mental health? *Harvard Mental Health Letter, 13*(6), 8. [2]

Craik, F. I. M., & Lockhart, R. S. (1972). Levels of processing: A framework for memory research. *Journal of Verbal Learning and Verbal Behavior, 11,* 671–684. [6]

Craik, F. I. M., & Tulving, E. (1975). Depth of processing and the retention of words in episodic memory. *Journal of Experimental Psychology: General, 104,* 268–294. [6]

Crane, J. (1994). Exploding the myth of scientific support for the theory of Black intellectual inferiority. *Journal of Black Psychology, 20,* 189–209. [7]

Crasilneck, H. B. (1992). The use of hypnosis in the treatment of impotence. *Psychiatric Medicine, 10,* 67–75. [4]

Cravens, H. (1992). A scientific project locked in time: The Terman genetic studies of genius, 1920s–1950s. *American Psychologist, 47,* 183–189. [7]

Creatsas, G. K., Vekemans, M., Horejsi, J., Uzel, R., Lauritzen, C., & Osler, M. (1995). Adolescent sexuality in Europe: A multicentric study. *Adolescent and Pediatric Gynecology, 8,* 59–63. [8]

Crespi, G. K., Vekemans, M., Horejsi, J., Uzel, R., Lauritzen, C., & Osler, M. (1995). Adolescent sexuality in Europe: A multicentric study. *Adolescent and Pediatric Gynecology, 8,* 59–63. [8]

Crews, F. (1996). The verdict on Freud. *Psychological Science, 7,* 63–68. [10]

Crick, F., & Mitchison, G. (1983). The function of dream sleep. *Nature, 304,* 408–416. [4]

Crick, F., & Mitchison, G. (1995). REM sleep and neural nets. *Behavioural Brain Research, 69,* 147–155. [4]

Crimmins, E. M., & Ingegneri, D. G. (1990). Interaction and living arrangements of older parents and their children: Past trends, present determinants, future implications. *Research on Aging, 12,* 3–35. [8]

Crits-Christoph, P. (1992). The efficacy of brief dynamic psychotherapy: A meta-analysis. *American Journal of Psychiatry, 149,* 151–158. [13]

Crowder, R. G. (1992) Sensory memory. In L. R. Squire (Ed.), *Encyclopedia of learning and memory.* New York: Macmillan. [6]

Crowe, L. C., & George, W. H. (1989). Alcohol and human sexuality: Review and integration. *Psychological Bulletin, 105,* 374–386. [4]

Crystal, D. S., Chen, C., Fulligni, A. J., Stevenson, H. W., Hsu, C-C., Ko, H-J., Kitamura, S., & Kimura, S. (1994). Psychological maladjustment and academic achievement: A cross-cultural study of Japanese, Chinese, and American high school students. *Child Development, 65,* 738–753. [7]

Csikszentmihalyi, M. (1990). Flow: *The psychology of optimal experience.* Cambridge, England: Cambridge University Press. [9]

Csikszentmihalyi, M. (1996, July/August). The creative personality. *Psychology Today, 29,* 36–40. [7]

Cui, X-J., & Vaillant, G. E. (1996). Antecedents and consequences of negative life events in adulthood: A longitudinal study. *American Journal of Psychiatry, 153,* 21–26. [12]

Culbertson, F. M. (1997). Depression and gender: An international review. *American Psychologist, 52,* 25–31. [12]

Cunningham, M. R. (1979). Weather, mood, and helping behavior: Quasi experiments with the sunshine Samaritan. *Journal of Personality and Social Psychology, 37*, 1947–1956. [14]

Cunningham, M. R. (1988). Does happiness mean friendliness? Induced mood and heterosexual self-disclosure. *Personality and Social Psychology Bulletin, 14*, 283–297. [14]

Cunningham, M. R., Roberts, A. R., Barbee, A. P., Druen, P. B., & Wu, C-H. (1995). "Their ideas of beauty are, on the whole, the same as ours": Consistency and variability in the cross-cultural perception of female physical attractiveness. *Journal of Personality and Social Psychology, 68*, 261–279. [14]

Curran, P. J., Stice, E., & Chassin, L. (1997). The relation between adolescent alcohol use and peer alcohol use: A longitudinal random coefficients model. *Journal of Consulting and Clinical Psychology, 65*, 130–140. [4]

Curtis, R. C., & Miller, K. (1986). Believing another likes or dislikes you: Behaviors making the beliefs come true. *Journal of Personality and Social Psychology, 51*, 284–290. [14]

Dale, N., & Kandel, E. R. (1990). Facilitatory and inhibitory transmitters modulate spontaneous transmitter release at cultured Aplysia sensorimotor synapses. *Journal of Physiology, 421*, 203–222. [6]

Daly, M., & Wilson, M. I. (1996). Violence against stepchildren. *Current Directions in Psychological Science, 5*, 77–81. [14]

Daniel, D. G., & Whitcomb, S. R. (1998). Treatment of the refractory schizophrenic patient. *Journal of Clinical Psychiatry, 59*(1, Suppl.), 13–19. [13]

Darley, J. M., & Latané, B. (1968a). Bystander intervention in emergencies: Diffusion of responsibility. *Journal of Personality and Social Psychology, 8*, 377–383. [14]

Darley, J. M., & Latané, B. (1968b, December). When will people help in a crisis? *Psychology Today*, pp. 54–57, 70–71. [14]

Darwin, C. (1965). *The expression of emotion in man and animals.* Chicago: University of Chicago Press. (Original work published 1872). [9]

Dasen, P. R. (1972). Cross-cultural Piagetian research: A summary. *Journal of Cross-Cultural Psychology, 3*, 23–29. [8]

Dasen, P. R. (1994). Culture and cognitive development from a Piagetian perspective. In W. J. Lonner & R. Malpass (Eds.), *Psychology and culture* (pp. 145–149). Boston: Allyn & Bacon. [8]

Dashiell, J. F. (1925). A quantitative demonstration of animal drive. *Journal of Comparative Psychology, 5*, 205–208. [9]

Davidson, J. R. T. (1997). Use of benzodiazepines in panic disorder. *Journal of Clinical Psychiatry, 58*(2, Suppl.), 26–28. [13]

Davis, K. L., Kahn, R. S., Ko, G., & Davidson, M. (1991). Dopamine in schizophrenia: A review and reconceptualization. *American Journal of Psychiatry, 148*, 1474–1486. [12]

Davis, T. L. (1995). Gender differences in masking negative emotions: Ability or motivation? *Developmental Psychology, 31*, 660–667. [9]

Dawson, D., Encel, N., & Lushington, K. (1995). Improving adaptation to simulated night shift: Timed exposure to bright light versus daytime melatonin administration. *Sleep, 18*, 11–21. [4]

D'Azevedo, W. A. (1982). Tribal history in Liberia. In U. Neisser (Ed.), *Memory observed: Remembering in natural contexts.* San Francisco: W. H. Freeman. [6]

DeCasper, A. J., & Spence, M. J. (1986). Prenatal maternal speech influences newborns' perception of speech sounds. *Infant Behavior and Development, 9*, 133–150. [8]

de Castro, J. M., & de Castro, E. S. (1989). Spontaneous meal patterns of humans: Influence of the presence of other people. *Journal of Clinical Nutrition, 50*, 237–247. [9]

Deese, J. (1959). On the prediction of occurrence of particular verbal intrusions in immediate recall. *Journal of Experimental Psychology, 58*, 17–22. [6]

DeJong, W. (1979). An examination of self-perception mediation of the foot-in-the-door effect. *Journal of Personality and Social Psychology, 37*, 2221–2239. [14]

de Jongh, A., Muris, P., Ter Horst, G., & Duyx, M. P. M. A. (1995). Acquisition and maintenance of dental anxiety: The role of conditioning experiences and cognitive factors. *Behaviour Research and Therapy, 33*, 205–210. [12]

DeLeon, P. H., & Wiggins, J. G., Jr. (1996). Prescription privileges for psychologists. *American Psychologist, 51*, 225–229. [13]

Delgado, J. M. R. (1969). *Physical control of the mind: Toward a psychocivilized society.* New York: Harper & Row. [2]

Delgado, J. M. R., & Anand, B. K. (1953). Increased food intake induced by electrical stimulation of the lateral hypothalamus. *American Journal of Physiology, 172*, 162–168. [9]

Dembroski, T. M., MacDougall, J. M., Williams, R. B., Haney, T. I., & Blumenthal, J. A. (1985). Components of Type A hostility and anger in relationship to angiographic findings. *Psychosomatic Medicine, 47*, 219–233. [11]

Dement, W. C. (1974). *Some must watch while some must sleep.* San Francisco: W. H. Freeman. [4]

Dement, W. C. (1992). The proper use of sleeping pills in the primary care setting. *Journal of Clinical Psychiatry, 53*(12, Suppl.), 50–56. [4]

Dement, W., & Kleitman, N. (1957). The relation of eye movements during sleep to dream activity: An objective method for the study of dreaming. *Journal of Experimental Psychology, 53*, 339–346. [4]

DeNelsky, G. Y. (1996). The case against prescription privileges for psychologists. *American Psychologist, 51*, 207–212. [13]

DeRubeis, R. J., & Crits-Christoph, P. (1998). Empirically supported individual and group psychological treatments for adult mental disorders. *Journal of Consulting and Clinical Psychology, 66*, 37–52. [13]

Detke, M. J., Brandon, S. E., Weingarten, H. P., Rodin, J., & Wagner, A. R. (1989). Modulation of behavioral and insulin responses by contextual stimuli paired with food. *Physiology and Behavior, 45*, 845–851. [9]

De Valois, R. L., & De Valois, K. K. (1975). Neural coding of color. In E. C. Carterette & M. P. Friedman (Eds.), *Handbook of perception* (Vol. 5). New York: Academic. [3]

Devanand, D. P., Dwork, A. J., Hutchinson, M. S. E., Bolwig, T. G., & Sackeim, H. A. (1994). Does ECT alter brain structure? *American Journal of Psychiatry, 151*, 957–970. [13]

Devine, P. G. (1989). Stereotypes and prejudice: Their automatic and controlled components. *Journal of Personality and Social Psychology, 56*, 5–18. [14]

De Vito, G., Hernandez, R., Gonzalez, V., Felici, F., & Figura, F. (1997). Low intensity physical training in older subjects. *Journal of Sports Medicine and Physical Fitness, 37*, 72–77. [11]

De Vos, S. (1990). Extended family living among older people in six Latin American countries. *Journal of Gerontology: Social Sciences, 45*, S87–94. [8]

deVries, H. A. (1986). *Fitness after 50.* New York: Scribner's. [8]

Di Chiara, G. (1997). Alcohol and dopamine. *Alcohol Health & Research World, 21*, 108–114. [4]

Diener, E., & Diener, C. (1996). Most people are happy. *Psychological Science, 7*, 181–185. [8]

Diener, E., Horwitz, J., & Emmons, R. A. (1985). Happiness of the very wealthy. *Social Indicators, 16*, 263–274. [9]

Dietz, W. H. (1989). Obesity. *Journal of the American College of Nutrition, 8*(Suppl.), 139–219. [9]

Digman, J. M. (1990). Personality structure: Emergence of the five-factor model. *Annual Review of Psychology, 41*, 417–440. [10]

DiLalla, L. F., & Gottesman, I. I. (1991). Biological and genetic contributors to violence—Widom's untold tale. *Psychological Bulletin, 109*, 125–129. [14]

Dinan, T. G. (1996). Noradrenergic and serotonergic abnormalities in depression: Stress-induced dysfunction? *Journal of Clinical Psychiatry, 57*(4, Suppl.), 14–18. [12]

Dion, K., Berscheid, E., & Walster, E. (1972). What is beautiful is good. *Journal of Personality and Social Psychology, 24*, 285–290. [14]

Dipboye, R. L., Fromkin, H. L., & Wilback, K. (1975). Relative importance of applicant sex, attractiveness, and scholastic standing in evaluation of job applicant resumes. *Journal of Applied Psychology, 60*, 39–43. [14]

Dobb, E. (1989, November/December). The scents around us. *The Sciences, 29*, 46–53. [3]

Dobbin, M. (1987, October 12). Loud noise from little headphones. *U.S. News & World Report*, pp. 77–78. [3]

Dobie, R. A. (1987, December). Noise-induced hearing loss: The family physician's role. *American Family Physician*, pp. 141–148. [3]

Dodge, K. A., Bates, J. E., & Pettit, G. S. (1990). Mechanisms in the cycle of violence. *Science, 250*, 1678–1683. [14]

Dodge, K. A., Cole, J. D., Pettit, G. S., & Price, J. M. (1990). Peer status and aggression in boys' groups: Developmental and contextual analyses. *Child Development, 61*, 1289–1309. [8]

Dollard, J., Doob, L. W., Miller, N., Mowrer, O. H., & Sears, R. R. (1939). *Frustration and aggression*. New Haven: Yale University Press. [14]

Domjan, M, & Purdy, J. E. (1995). Animal research in psychology: More than meets the eye of the general psychology student. *American Psychologist, 50*, 496–503. [1]

Doob, L. W., & Sears, R. R. (1939). Factors determining substitute behavior and the overt expression of aggression. *Journal of Abnormal and Social Psychology, 34*, 293–313. [14]

Dovidio, J. F. (1984). Helping behavior and altruism: An empirical and conceptual overview. In L. Berkowitz (Ed.), *Advances in experimental social psychology* (Vol. 17, pp. 361–427). New York: Academic Press. [14]

Dreikurs, R. (1953). *Fundamentals of Adlerian psychology*. Chicago: Alfred Adler Institute. [10]

Drevets, W. C., Price, J. L., Simpson, J. R., Jr., Todd, R. D., Reich, T., Vannier, M., & Raichle, M. E. (1997). Subgenual prefrontal cortex abnormalities in mood disorders. *Nature, 386*, 824–827. [2, 12]

Drevets, W. C., Videen, T. O., Price, J. L., Preskorn, S. H., Carmichael, S. T., & Raichle, M. E. (1992). A functional anatomical study of unipolar depression. *Journal of Neuroscience, 12*, 3628–3641. [12]

Drewnowski, A., Yee, D. K., Kurth, C. L., & Krahn, D. D. (1994). Eating pathology and DSM-III-R bulimia nervosa: A continuum of behavior. *American Journal of Psychiatry, 151*, 1217–1219. [9]

Druckman, D., & Bjork, R. A. (Eds.) (1994). *Learning, remembering, believing: Enhancing human performance*. Washington, DC: National Academy Press. [4]

Dryer, D. C., & Horowitz, L. M. (1997). When do opposites attract? Interpersonal complementarity versus similarity. *Journal of Personality and Social Psychology, 72*, 592–603. [14]

Duck, S. (1983). *Friends for life: The psychology of close relationships*. New York: St. Martin's Press. [8]

Duggan, J. P., & Booth, D. A. (1986). Obesity, overeating, and rapid gastric emptying in rats with ventromedial hypothalamic lesions. *Science, 231*, 609–611. [9]

Dunkel-Schetter, C., Feinstein, L. G., Taylor, S. E., & Falke, R. L. (1992). Patterns of coping with cancer. *Health Psychology, 11*, 79–87. [11]

Dunn, A. L., Marcus, B. H., Kampert, J. B., Garcia, M. E., Kohl, H. W., III, & Blair, S. N. (1999). Comparison of lifestyle and structured interventions to increase physical activity and cardiorespiratory fitness: A randomized trial. *Journal of the American Medical Association, 281*, 327–334. [8]

Duyme, M. (1988). School success and social class: An adoption study. *Developmental Psychology, 24*, 203–209. [7]

Dywan, J., & Bowers, K. (1983). The use of hypnosis to enhance recall. *Science, 222*, 184–185. [4, 6]

Eagly, A. H. (1987). *Sex differences in social behavior: A social-role interpretation*. Hillsdale, NJ: Erlbaum. [14]

Eagly, A. H., Ashmore, R. D., Makhijani, M. G., & Longo, L. C. (1991). What is beautiful is good . . . : A meta-analytic review of research on the physical attractiveness stereotype. *Psychological Bulletin, 110*, 109–128. [14]

Eagly, A. H., & Carli, L. (1981). Sex of researchers and sex-typed communications as determinants of sex differences in influence-ability: A meta-analysis of social influence studies. *Psychological Bulletin, 90*, 1–20. [14]

Eating disorders—part II. (1997, November). *Harvard Mental Health Letter, 14*(5), 1–5. [9]

Ebbinghaus, H. E. (1964). *Memory: A contribution to experimental psychology* (H. A. Ruger & C. E. Bussenius, Trans.). New York: Dover. (Original work published 1885). [6]

Eccles, J. S., & Jacobs, J. E. (1986). Social forces shape math attitudes and performance. *Signs, 11*, 367–389. [7]

Edwards, K., & Smith, E. E. (1996). A disconfirmation bias in the evaluation of arguments. *Journal of Personality and Social Psychology, 71*, 5–24. [14]

Egeth, H. E. (1993). What do we not know about eyewitness identification? *American Psychologist, 48*, 577–580. [6]

Ehrhardt, A. A., Evers, K., & Money, J. (1968). Influence of androgen and some aspects of sexual dimorphic behavior in women with the late-treated adrenogenital syndrome. *Johns Hopkins Medical Journal, 123*, 115–122. [9]

Eibl-Eibesfeldt, I. (1973). The expressive behavior of the deaf-and-blind-born. In M. von Cranach & I. Vine (Eds.), *Social communication and movement*. New York: Academic Press. [9]

Eich, E., Macaulay, D., & Ryan, L. (1994). Mood dependent memory for events of the personal past. *Journal of Experimental Psychology: General, 123*, 201–215. [6]

Eich, J. E. (1980). The cue dependent nature of state-dependent retrieval. *Memory and Cognition, 8*, 157–173. [6]

Eichenbaum, H. (1997). Declarative memory: Insights from cognitive neurobiology. *Annual Review of Psychology, 48*, 547–572. [2, 6]

Ekman, P. (1972). Universals and cultural differences in facial expression of emotion. In J. Cole (Ed.), *Nebraska symposium on motivation* (Vol. 19). Lincoln: University of Nebraska Press. [9]

Ekman, P. (1982). *Emotion and the human face* (2nd ed.). New York: Cambridge University Press. [9]

Ekman, P. (1985). *Telling lies: Clues to deceit in the marketplace, marriage, and politics*. New York: Norton. [14]

Ekman, P. (1992). Are there basic emotions? *Psychological Review, 99*, 550–553. [9]

Ekman, P. (1993). Facial expression and emotion. *American Psychologist, 48*, 384–392. [9]

Ekman, P., & Friesen, W. V. (1971). Constants across cultures in the face and emotion. *Journal of Personality and Social Psychology, 17*, 124–129. [9]

Ekman, P., & Friesen, W. V. (1975). *Unmasking the face: A guide to recognizing emotions from facial clues*. Englewood Cliffs, NJ: Prentice-Hall. [9]

Ekman, P., Friesen, W. V., & O'Sullivan, M. (1988). Smiles when lying. *Journal of Personality and Social Psychology, 54*, 414–420. [14]

Ekman, P., Friesen, W. V., O'Sullivan, M., Chan, A., Diacoyanni-Tarlatzis, I., Heider, K., Krause, R., LeCompte, W. A., Pitcairn, T., Ricci-Bitti, P. E., Scherer, K., Tomita, M., & Tzavaras, A. (1987). Universals and cultural differences in the judgments of facial expressions of emotion. *Journal of Personality and Social Psychology, 53*, 712–717. [9]

Ekman, P., Levenson, R. W., & Friesen, W. V. (1983). Autonomic nervous system activity distinguishes among emotions. *Science, 221*, 1208–1210. [9]

Elkin, I., Gibbons, R. D., Shea, M. T., Sotsky, S. M., Watkins, J. T., Pikonis, P. A., & Hedeker, D. (1995). Initial severity and differential treatment outcome in the National Institute of Mental Health Treatment of Depression Collaborative Research Program. *Journal of Consulting and Clinical Psychology, 63*, 841–847. [13]

Elkin, I., Shea, M. T., Watkins, J. T., et al. (1989). National Institute of Mental Health Treatment of Depression Collaborative Research Program: General effectiveness of treatments. *Archives of General Psychology, 46*, 971–982. [13]

Elkind, D. (1970, April 5). Erik Erikson's eight ages of man. *The New York Times Magazine*, pp. 25–27, 84–92, 110–119. [8]

Ellason, J. W., & Ross, C. A. (1997). Two-year follow–up of inpatients with dissociative identity disorder. *American Journal of Psychiatry, 154*, 832–839. [12]

Elliot, A. J., & Devine, P. G. (1994). On the motivational nature of cognitive dissonance: Dissonance as psychological discomfort. *Journal of Personality and Social Psychology, 67*, 382–394. [14]

Ellis, A. (1961). *A guide to rational living*. Englewood Cliffs, NJ: Prentice-Hall. [13]

Ellis, A. (1977). The basic clinical theory of rational-emotive therapy. In A. Ellis & R. Grieger (Eds.), *Handbook of rational-emotive therapy* (pp. 3–33). New York: Springer. [13]

Ellis, A. (1979). Rational-emotive therapy. In R. J. Corsini (Ed.), *Current psychotherapies* (2nd ed., pp. 185–229). Itasca, IL: F. E. Peacock. [13]

Ellis, A. (1993). Reflections on rational-emotive therapy. *Journal of Consulting and Clinical Psychology, 61*, 199–201. [13]

El-Shiekh, M., Klacynski, P. A., & Valaik, M. E. (1989). Stress and coping across the life course. *Human Development, 32*, 113–117. [11]

Engel, G. L. (1977). The need for a new medical model: A challenge for biomedicine. *Science, 196*, 126–129. [11]

Engel, G. L. (1980). The clinical application of the biopsychosocial model. *American Journal of Psychiatry, 137*, 535–544. [11]

Engles, G. I., Garnefski, N., & Diekstra, R. F. W. (1993). Efficacy of rational-emotive therapy: A quantitative analysis. *Journal of Consulting and Clinical Psychology, 61*, 1083–1090. [13]

Epstein, J. (1983). Examining theories of adolescent friendships. In J. Epstein & N. Karweit (Eds.), *Friends in school*. New York: Academic Press. [8]

Epstein, R. (1996, July/August). Capturing creativity. *Psychology Today, 29*, 41–43, 75–78. [7]

Epstein, R., Chillag, N., & Lavie, P. (1998). Starting times of school: Effects on daytime functioning of fifth-grade children in Israel. *Sleep, 21*, 250–256. [4]

Ericsson, K. A., & Charness, N. (1994). Expert performance: Its structure and acquisition. *American Psychologist, 49*, 725–747. [14]

Erikson, E. H. (1963). *Childhood and society* (2nd ed.). New York: Norton. [8]

Erikson, E. H. (1968). *Identity: Youth and crisis*. New York: Norton. [8]

Erikson, E. H. (1980). *Identity and the life cycle*. New York: Norton. [8]

Erikson, E. H., Erikson, J. M., & Kivnick, H. Q. (1986). *Vital involvement in old age: The experience of old age in our time*. New York: W. W. Norton. [8]

Erlenmeyer-Kimling, L., & Jarvik, L. F. (1963). Genetics and intelligence: A review. *Science, 142*, 1477–1479. [7]

Eron, L. D. (1980). Prescription for reducing aggression. *American Psychologist, 35*, 244–252. [14]

Eron, L. D. (1987). The development of aggressive behavior from the perspective of a developing behaviorism. *American Psychologist, 42*, 435–442. [14]

Eronen, M., Hakola, P., & Tiihonen, J. (1996). Mental disorders and homicidal behavior in Finland. *Journal of Personality and Social Psychology, 53*, 497–501. [14]

Erwin, E. (1996). *A final accounting: Philosophical and empirical issues in Freudian psychology*. Cambridge, MA: MIT Press. [10]

Estes, W. K. (1994). *Classification and cognition*. New York: Oxford University Press. [7]

Evans, G. W., & Lepore, S. J. (1993). Household crowding and social support: A quasiexperimental analysis. *Journal of Personality and Social Psychology, 65*, 308–316. [14]

Evans, M. D., Hollon, S. D., DeRubeis, R. J., Piasecki, J. M., Grove, W. M., Garvey, M. J., & Tuason, V. B. (1992). Differential relapse following cognitive therapy and pharmacotherapy for depression. *Archives of General Psychiatry, 49*, 802–808. [13]

Ewin, D. M. (1992). Hypnotherapy for warts (Verruca vulgaris): 41 consecutive cases with 33 cures. *American Journal of Clinical Hypnosis, 35*, 1–10. [4]

Eysenck, H. J. (1981). *A model for personality*. Berlin: Springer-Verlag. [10]

Eysenck, H. J. (1990). Genetic and environmental contributions to individual differences: The three major dimensions of personality. *Journal of Personality, 58*, 245–261. [10]

Eysenck, H. J. (1994). The outcome problem in psychotherapy: What have we learned? *Behaviour Research and Therapy, 32*, 477–495. [13]

Fackelmann, K. (1997). Marijuana on trial: Is marijuana a dangerous drug or a valuable medicine? *Science News, 151*, 178–179, 183. [4]

Faedda, G. L., Tondo, L., Teicher, M. H., Baldessarini, R. J., Gelbard, H. A., & Floris, G. F. (1993). Seasonal mood disorders: Patterns of seasonal recurrence in mania and depression. *Archives of General Psychiatry, 50*, 17–23. [12]

Falbo, T., & Polit, D. F. (1986). Quantitative review of the only child literature: Research evidence and theory development. *Psychological Bulletin, 100*, 176–189. [9]

Famighetti, R. (Ed.). (1997). *The world almanac and book of facts 1998*. Mahwah, NJ: World Almanac Books. [13]

Fantz, R. L. (1961). The origin of form perception. *Scientific American, 204*, 66–72. [8]

Farah, M. J. (1995). The neural bases of mental imagery. In M. S. Gazzaniga (Ed.), *The cognitive neurosciences*. Cambridge, MA: MIT Press. [7]

Faravelli, C., & Pallanti, S. (1989). Recent life events and panic disorder. *American Journal of Psychiatry, 146*, 622–626. [12]

Farde, L. (1996). The advantage of using positron emission tomography in drug research. *Trends in Neurosciences, 19*, 211–214. [2]

Farrer, L. A., & Cupples, A. (1994). Estimating the probability for major gene Alzheimer disease. *American Journal of Human Genetics, 54*, 374–383. [8]

Fawcett, J. C. (1992). Intrinsic neuronal determinants of regeneration. *Trends in Neurosciences, 15*, 5–8. [2]

Fazio, R. H. (1989). On the power and functionality of attitudes: The role of attitude accessibility. In A. R. Pratkanis, S. J. Breckler, & A. G. Greenwald (Eds.), *Attitude structure and function* (pp. 153–179). Hillsdale, NJ: Erlbaum. [14]

Fazio, R. H., & Williams, C. J. (1986). Attitude accessibility as a moderator of the attitude perception and attitude-behavior relations: An investigation of the 1984 presidential election. *Journal of Personality and Social Psychology, 51*, 505–514. [14]

Fein, S., & Spencer, S. J. (1997). Prejudice as self-image maintenance: Affirming the self through derogating others. *Journal of Personality and Social Psychology, 73*, 31–44. [14]

Feingold, A. (1988). Matching for attractiveness in romantic partners and same-sex friends: A meta-analysis and theoretical critique. *Psychological Bulletin, 104*, 226–235. [14]

Feingold, A. (1990). Gender differences in effects of physical attractiveness on romantic attraction: A comparison across five research paradigms. *Journal of Personality and Social Psychology, 59*, 981–993. [14]

Feingold, A. (1992). Good-looking people are not what we think. *Psychological Bulletin, 111*, 304–341. [14]

Fenton, W. S., & McGlashan, T. H. (1991). Natural history of schizophrenia subtypes: I. Longitudinal study of paranoid, hebephrenic, and undifferentiated schizophrenia. *Archives of General Psychiatry, 48*, 969–977. [12]

Fenton, W. S., & McGlashan, T. H. (1994). Antecedents, symptom progression, and long-term outcome of the deficit syndrome in schizophrenia. *American Journal of Psychiatry, 151*, 351–356. [12]

Fernald, A. (1993). Approval and disapproval: Infant responsiveness to vocal affect in familiar and unfamiliar languages. *Child Development, 64*, 637–656. [8]

Festinger, L. (1957). *A theory of cognitive dissonance*. Evanston, IL: Row, Peterson. [14]

Festinger, L., & Carlsmith, J. M. (1959). Cognitive consequences of forced compliance. *Journal of Abnormal and Social Psychology, 58*, 203–210. [14]

Festinger, L., Schachter, S., & Back, K. (1950). *Social pressures in informal groups: A study of a housing community*. New York: Harper & Row. [14]

Fiatarone, M. A., Morley, J. E., Bloom, E. T., Benton, D., Makinodan, T., & Solomon, G. F. (1988). Endogenous opioids and the exercise-induced augmentation of natural killer cell activity. *Journal of Laboratory and Clinical Medicine, 112*, 544–552. [11]

Fiatarone, M. A., O'Neill, E. F., Ryan, N. D., Clements, K. M., Solares, G. R., Nelson, M. E., Roberts, S. B., Kehayias, J. J., Lipsitz, L. A., & Evans, W. J. (1994). Exercise training and nutritional supplementation for physical frailty in very elderly people. *New England Journal of Medicine, 330,* 1769–1775. [8]

Field, T. M., Cohen, D., Garcia, R., & Greenberg, R. (1984). Mother-stranger face discrimination by the newborn. *Infant Behavior and Development, 7,* 19–25. [8]

Field, T., Schanberg, S. M., Scfidi, F., Bauer, C. R., Vega-Lahr, N., Garcia, R., Nystrom, J., & Kuhn, C. (1986, May). Tactile/kinesthetic stimulation effects on preterm neonates. *Pediatrics, 77,* 654–658. [3]

Fiez, J. A. (1996). Cerebellar contributions to cognition. *Neuron, 16,* 13–15. [2]

Finchilescu, G. (1988). Interracial contact in South Africa within the nursing context. *Journal of Applied Social Psychology, 18,* 1207–1221. [14]

Fink, M. (1997, June). What is the role of ECT in the treatment of mania? *Harvard Mental Health Letter, 13*(12), 8. [13]

Finkbeiner, A. K. (1998, September/October). Getting through the sleep gate. *The Sciences, 38,* 14–18. [4]

Finkel, D., & McGue, M. (1997). Sex differences and nonadditivity in heritability of the Multidimensional Personality Questionnaire scales. *Journal of Personality and Social Psychology, 72,* 929–938. [10]

Fiorito, G., & Scotto, P. (1992). Observational learning in Octopus vulgaris. *Science, 256,* 545–547. [5]

Fischbach, G. D. (1992). Mind and brain. *Scientific American, 267,* 48–56. [2, 6]

Fixx, J. F. (1978). *Solve It! A perplexing profusion of puzzles.* New York: Doubleday. [7]

Flavell, J. H. (1985). *Cognitive development.* Englewood, NJ: Prentice-Hall. [8]

Flavell, J. H. (1992). Cognitive development: Past, present, and future. *Developmental Psychology, 28,* 998–1005. [8]

Flavell, J. H. (1996). Piaget's legacy. *Psychological Science, 7,* 200–203. [8]

Flegal, K. M. (1996). Trends in body weight and overweight in the U.S. population. *Nutrition Reviews, 54,* S97–S100. [9]

Fleming, J. D. (1974, July). Field report: The state of the apes. *Psychology Today,* pp. 31–46. [7]

Fletcher, A. C., Darling, N. E., Steinberg, L., & Dornbusch, S. M. (1995). The company they keep: Relation of adolescents' adjustment and behavior to their friends' perceptions of authoritative parenting in the social network. *Developmental Psychology, 31,* 300–311. [8]

Fletcher, J. M., Page, B., Francis, D. J., Copeland, K., Naus, M. J., Davis, C. M., Morris, R., Krauskopf, D., & Satz, P. (1996). Cognitive correlates of long-term cannabis use in Costa Rican men. *Archives of General Psychiatry, 53,* 1051–1057. [4]

Flood, J. F., Silver, A. J., & Morley, J. E. (1990). Do peptide-induced changes in feeding occur because of changes in motivation to eat? *Peptides, 11,* 265–270. [9]

Florian, V., Mikulincer, M., & Taubman, O. (1995). Does hardiness contribute to mental health during a stressful real-life situation? The roles of appraisal and coping. *Journal of Personality and Social Psychology, 68,* 687–695. [11]

Foa, E. B. (1995). How do treatments for obsessive-compulsive disorder compare? *Harvard Mental Health Letter, 12*(1), 8. [13]

Foa, E. B., & Kozack, M. J. (1995). DSM-IV Field Trial: Obsessive-compulsive disorder. *American Journal of Psychiatry, 152,* 90–96. [12]

Foa, E. B., & Meadows, E. A. (1997). Psychosocial treatments for post-traumatic stress disorder: A critical review. *Annual Review of Psychology, 48,* 449–480. [11]

Fogelman, E., & Wiener, V. L. (1985, August). The few, the brave, the noble. *Psychology Today,* pp. 60–65. [14]

Foley, D. J., Monjan, A. A., Brown, S. L., Simonsick, E. M., Wallace, R. B., & Blazer, D. G. (1995). Sleep complaints among elderly persons: An epidemiologic study of three communities. *Sleep, 18,* 425–432. [4]

Folkard, S. (1990). Circadian performance rhythms: Some practical and theoretical implications. *Philosophical Transactions of the Royal Society of London. Series B: Biological Sciences, 327,* 543–553. [4]

Folkman, S. (1984). Personal control and stress and coping processes: A theoretical analysis. *Journal of Personality and Social Psychology, 46,* 839–852. [11]

Folkman, S., Chesney, M., Collette, L., Boccellari, A., & Cooke, M. (1996). Postbereavement depressive mood and its prebereavement predictors in HIV+ and HIV- gay men. *Journal of Personality and Social Psychology, 70,* 336–348. [8]

Folkman, S., & Lazarus, R. S. (1980). An analysis of coping in a middle-aged community sample. *Journal of Health and Social Behavior, 21,* 219–239. [11]

Fontana, A., Schwartz, L. S., & Rosenheck, R. (1997). Posttraumatic stress disorder among female Vietnam veterans: A causal model of etiology. *American Journal of Public Health, 87,* 169–175. [11]

Fontham, E. T. H., Correa, P., Reynolds, P., Wu-Williams, A., Buffler, P. A., Greenberg, R. S., Chen, V. W., Alterman, T., Boyd, P., Austin, D. F., & Liff, J. (1994). Environmental tobacco smoke and lung cancer in nonsmoking women: A multicenter study. *Journal of the American Medical Association, 271,* 1752–1759. [11]

Ford, C. S., & Beach, F. A. (1951). *Patterns of sexual behavior.* New York: Harper & Row. [9]

Foreyt, J. P., Walker, S., Poston, C., II, & Goodrick, G. K. (1996). Future directions in obesity and eating disorders. *Addictive Behaviors, 21,* 767–778. [9]

Forgas, J. P., & Bower, G. H. (1987). Mood effects on person-perception judgments. *Journal of Personality and Social Psychology, 53,* 53–60. [14]

Forgas, J. P., & Fiedler, K. (1996). Us and them: Mood effects on intergroup discrimination. *Journal of Personality and Social Psychology, 70,* 28–40. [14]

Foulkes, D. (1996). Sleep and dreams: Dream research: 1953–1993. *Sleep, 19,* 609–624. [4]

Fowles, D. C. (1992). Schizophrenia: Diathesis-stress revisited. *Annual Review of Psychology, 43,* 303–336. [12]

Fox, N. A., & Bell, M. A. (1990). Electrophysiological indices of frontal lobe development: Relations to cognitive and affective behavior in human infants over the first year of life. *Annals of the New York Academy of Sciences, 608,* 677–698. [8]

Frank, E., Anderson, B., Reynolds, C. F., III, Ritenour, A., & Kupfer, D. J. (1994). Life events and the research diagnostic criteria endogenous subtype. *Archives of General Psychiatry, 51,* 519–524. [12]

Frank, E., Kupfer, D. J., Wagner, E. F., McEachran, A. B., & Cornes, C. (1991). Efficacy of interpersonal psychotherapy as a maintenance treatment of recurrent depression: Contributing factors. *Archives of General Psychiatry, 48,* 1053–1059. [13]

Frankenburg, W. K., Dodds, J. B., Archer, P., et al. (1992). *Denver II Training Manual.* Denver: Denver Developmental Materials. [8]

Franz, C. E., McClelland, D. C., & Weinberger, J. (1991). Childhood antecedents of conventional social accomplishment in midlife adults: A 36-year prospective study. *Journal of Personality and Social Psychology, 60,* 586–595. [8]

Fraser, A. M., Brockert, J. E., & Ward, R. H. (1995). Association of young maternal age with adverse reproductive outcomes. *New England Journal of Medicine, 332,* 1113–1117. [8]

Frazer, A. (1997). Antidepressants. *Journal of Clinical Psychiatry, 58*(6, Suppl.), 9–25. [13]

Fredrikson, M., Annas, P., Fischer, H., & Wik, G. (1996). Gender and age differences in the prevalence of specific fears and phobias. *Behaviour Research and Therapy, 34,* 33–39. [12]

Freedman, J. (1996, May). Violence in the mass media and violence in society: The link is unproven. *Harvard Mental Health Letter, 12*(11), 4–6. [14]

Freedman, J. L., & Fraser, S. C. (1966). Compliance without pressure: The foot-in-the-door technique. *Journal of Personality and Social Psychology, 4,* 195–202. [14]

Freeman, W. J. (1991). The physiology of perception. *Scientific American, 264,* 78–85. [3]

Freud, A. (1958). *Adolescence: Psychoanalytic study of the child* (Vol. 13). New York: Academic Press. [8]

Freud, A. (1966). *The ego and the mechanisms of defense* (rev. ed.). New York: International Universities Press. [10]

Freud, S. (1922). *Beyond the pleasure principle*. London: International Psychoanalytic Press. [6]

Freud, S. (1953a). The interpretation of dreams. In J. Strachey (Ed. and Trans.), *The standard edition of the complete psychological works of Sigmund Freud* (Vols. 4 and 5). London: Hogarth Press. (Original work published 1900). [4, 10]

Freud, S. (1953b). Three essays on the theory of sexuality. In J. Strachey (Ed. and Trans.), *The standard edition of the complete psychological works of Sigmund Freud* (Vol. 7). London: Hogarth Press. (Original work published 1905). [10]

Freud, S. (1960). Psychopathology of everyday life. In J. Strachey (Ed. and Trans.), *The standard edition of the complete psychological works of Sigmund Freud* (Vol. 6). London: Hogarth Press. (Original work published 1901). [10]

Freud, S. (1961). The ego and the id. In J. Strachey (Ed. and Trans.), *The standard edition of the complete psychological works of Sigmund Freud* (Vol. 19). London: Hogarth Press. (Original work published 1923). [10]

Freud, S. (1962). *Civilization and its discontents* (J. Strachey, Trans.). New York: W.W. Norton. (Original work published 1930). [10]

Freud, S. (1963a). *An autobiographical study* (J. Strachey, Trans.). New York: W.W. Norton. (Original work published 1925). [10, 16]

Freud, S. (1963b). *A general introduction to psycho-analysis* (J. Riviere, Trans.). New York: Simon & Schuster. (Original work published 1920). [10, 16]

Freud, S. (1965). *New introductory lectures on psychoanalysis* (J. Strachey, Trans.). New York: W. W. Norton. (Original work published 1933). [10]

Frey-Hewitt, B., Vranizan, K. M., Dreon, D. M., & Wood, P. D. (1990). The effect of weight loss by dieting or exercise on resting metabolic rate in overweight men. *International Journal of Obesity, 14,* 327–334. [9]

Friedberg, J. M. (1976). *Shock treatment is not good for your brain*. San Francisco: Glide. [13]

Friedland, N., Keinan, G., & Regev, Y. (1992). Controlling the uncontrollable: Effects of stress on illusory perceptions of controllability. *Journal of Personality and Social Psychology, 63,* 923–931. [11]

Friedman, J. M. (1997). The alphabet of weight control. *Nature, 385,* 119–120. [9]

Friedman, M., & Rosenman, R. H. (1974). *Type A behavior and your heart*. New York: Fawcett. [11]

Friedman, M. I., Tordoff, M. G., & Ramirez, I. (1986). Integrated metabolic control of food intake. *Brain Research Bulletin, 17,* 855–859. [9]

Frone, M. R., Russell, M., & Cooper, M. L. (1995). Job stressors, job involvement and employee health: A test of identity theory. *Journal of Occupational and Organizational Psychology, 68,* 1–11. [11]

Fry, A. F., & Hale, S. (1996). Processing speed, working memory, and fluid intelligence. *Psychological Science, 7,* 237–241. [8]

Fujita, F., Diener, E., & Sandvik, E. (1991). Gender differences in negative affect and well-being: The case for emotional intensity. *Journal of Personality and Social Psychology, 61,* 427–434. [9]

Fuligni, A. J., & Stevenson, H. W. (1995). Time use and mathematics achievement among American, Chinese, and Japanese high school students. *Child Development, 66,* 830–842. [7]

Fyer, A. J. (1993). Heritability of social anxiety: A brief review. *Journal of Clinical Psychiatry, 54*(12, Suppl.), 10–12. [12]

Gabrieli, J. D. E. (1998). Cognitive neuroscience of human memory. *Annual Review of Psychology, 49,* 87–115. [6]

Gabrieli, J. D. E., Desmond, J. E., Demb, J. B., Wagner, A. D., Stone, M. V., Viadya, C. J., & Glover, G. H. (1996). Functional magnetic resonance imaging of semantic memory processes in the frontal lobes. *Psychological Science, 7,* 278–283. [6]

Gagnon, J. H, & Simon, W. (1973). *Sexual conduct: The social origins of human sexuality*. Chicago: Aldine. [9]

Gallagher, M., & Rapp, P. R. (1997). The use of animal models to study the effects of aging on cognition. *Annual Review of Psychology, 48,* 339–370. [8]

Gallup, G., Jr., & Hugick, L. (1990). Racial tolerance grows, progress on racial equality less evident. *Gallup Poll Monthly, No. 297,* 23–32. [14]

Gallup, G., Jr., & Newport, F. (1990a). The battle of the bulge: Americans continue to fight it. *Gallup Poll Monthly, No. 303,* 23–34. [9]

Gallup, G., Jr., & Newport, F. (1990b). Belief in psychic and paranormal phenomena widespread among Americans. *Gallup Poll Monthly, No. 299,* 35–43. [3]

Gallup, G. G., Jr., & Suarez, S. D. (1985). Alternatives to the use of animals in psychological research. *American Psychologist, 40,* 1104–1111. [1]

Galton, F. (1874). *English men of science: Their nature and nurture*. London: Macmillan. [7]

Galton, F. (1875). The history of twins as a criterion of the relative powers of nature and nurture. *Journal of the Royal Anthropological Institute, 5,* 391–406. [7]

Ganellen, R. J. (1996). Comparing the diagnostic efficiency of the MMPI, MCMI-II, and Rorschach: A review. *Journal of Personality Assessment, 67,* 219–243. [10]

Gannon, L., Luchetta, R., Rhodes, K., Paradie, L., & Segrist, D. (1992). Sex bias in psychological research: Progress or complacency? *American Psychologist, 47,* 389–396. [1]

Garcia, J., & Koelling, A. (1966). Relation of cue to consequence in avoidance learning. *Psychonomic Science, 4,* 123–124. [5]

Gardner, H. (1983). *Frames of mind: The theory of multiple intelligence*. New York: Basic Books. [7]

Gardner, R. A., & Gardner, B. T. (1969). Teaching sign language to a chimpanzee. *Science, 165,* 664–672. [7]

Garland, A. F., & Zigler, E. (1993). Adolescent suicide prevention: Current research and social policy implications. *American Psychologist, 48,* 169–182. [12]

Garma, L., & Marchand, F. (1994). Non-pharmacological approaches to the treatment of narcolepsy. *Sleep, 17,* S97–S102. [4]

Garmon, L. C., Basinger, K. S., Gregg, V. R., & Gibbs, J. C. (1996). Gender differences in stage and expression of moral judgment. *Merrill-Palmer Quarterly, 42,* 418–437. [8]

Garry, M., & Loftus, E. R. (1994). Pseudomemories without hypnosis. *International Journal of Clinical and Experimental Hypnosis, 42,* 363–373. [6]

Gartner, J., & Whitaker-Azimitia, P. M. (1996). Developmental factors influencing aggression: Animal models and clinical correlates. *Annals of the New York Academy of Sciences, 794,* 113–120. [14]

Gastil, J. (1990). Generic pronouns and sexist language: The oxymoronic character of masculine generics. *Sex Roles, 23,* 629–643. [7]

Gazzaniga, M. S. (1970). *The bisected brain*. New York: Appleton-Century-Crofts. [2]

Gazzaniga, M. S. (1983). Right hemisphere language following brain bisection: A 20-year perspective. *American Psychologist, 38,* 525–537. [2]

Gazzaniga, M. S. (1989). Organization of the human brain. *Science, 245,* 947–952. [2]

Gazzaniga, M. S. (1997). Brain, drugs, and society. *Science, 275,* 459. [4]

Geary, D. C. (1996). Sexual selection and sex differences in mathematical abilties. *Behavioral and Brain Sciences, 19,* 229–284. [7]

Geen, R. G. (1984). Human motivation: New perspectives on old problems. In A. M. Rogers & C. J. Scheier (Eds.), *The G. Stanley Hall lecture series* (Vol. 4). Washington, DC: American Psychological Association. [9]

Geen, R. G. (1995). *Human motivation: A social psychological approach*. Pacific Grove, CA: Brooks/Cole. [9]

Geiselman, R. E., Haight, N. A., & Kimata, L. G. (1984). Context effects on the perceived physical attractiveness of faces. *Journal of Experimental Social Psychology, 20,* 409–424. [14]

Genesee, F. (1994). Bilingualism. In V. S. Ramachandran (Ed.), *Encyclopedia of human behavior* (Vol. 1, pp. 383–393). San Diego, CA: Academic. [7]

Gergen, K. J., Gulerce, A., Lock, A., & Misra, G. (1996). Psychological science in cultural context. *American Psychologist, 51*, 496–503. [1]

Geschwind, N. (1979). Specializations of the human brain. *Science, 241*, 180–199. [2]

Geschwind, N., & Behan, P. O. (1982). Left handedness: Association with immune disease, migraine, and developmental learning disorders. *Proceedings of the National Academy of Sciences, 79*, 5097–5100. [2]

Getzels, J. W., & Csikszentmihalyi, M. (1976). *The creative vision: A longitudinal study of problem finding in art.* New York: Wiley. [7]

Gevins, A., Leong, H., Smith, M. E., Le, J., & Du, R. (1995). Mapping cognitive brain function with modern high-resolution electroencephalography. *Trends in Neurosciences, 18*, 429–436. [2]

Gibbons, A. (1991). Déjà vu all over again: Chimp-language wars. *Science, 251*, 1561–1562. [7]

Gibbs, W. W. (1996, August). Gaining on fat. *Scientific American, 275*, 88–94. [9]

Gibson, E., & Walk, R. D. (1960). The "visual cliff." *Scientific American, 202*, 64–71. [7]

Giedd, J. (1999). Human brain growth. *American Journal of Psychiatry, 156*, 4. [2]

Gilbert, D. T., & Malone, P. S. (1995). The correspondence bias. *Psychological Bulletin, 117*, 21–38. [14]

Giles, D. E., Jarrett, R. B., Biggs, M. M., Guzick, D. S., & Rush, A. J. (1989). Clinical predictors of recurrence in depression. *American Journal of Psychiatry, 146*, 764–767. [12]

Gilligan, C. (1982). *In a different voice: Psychological theory and women's development.* Cambridge, MA: Harvard University Press. [8]

Ginsberg, G., & Bronstein, P. (1993). Family factors related to children's intrinsic/extrinsic motivational orientation and academic performance. *Child Development, 64*, 1461–1474. [9]

Ginty, D. D., Kornhauser, J. M., Thompson, M. A., Bading, H., Mayo, K. E., Takahashi, J. S., & Greenberg, M. E. (1993). Regulation of CREB phosphorylation in the suprachiasmatic nucleus by light and a circadian clock. *Science, 260*, 238–241. [4]

Glass, D. C., & Singer, J. E. (1972). *Urban stress: Experiments in noise and social stressors.* New York: Academic Press. [11]

Glazer, W. M., Morgenstern, H., & Doucette, J. T. (1993). Predicting the long-term risk of tardive dyskinesia in outpatients maintained on neuroleptic medications. *Journal of Clinical Psychiatry, 54*, 133–139. [13]

Gleaves, D. J. (1996). The sociocognitive model of dissociative identity disorder: A reexamination of the evidence. *Psychological Bulletin, 120*, 42–59. [12]

Glover, J. A., & Corkill, A. J. (1987). Influence of paraphrased repetitions on the spacing effect. *Journal of Educational Psychology, 79*, 198–199. [6]

Gluck, M. A., & Myers, C. E. (1997). Psychobiological models of hippocampal function in learning and memory. *Annual Review of Psychology, 48*, 481–514. [2, 6]

Godden, D. R., & Baddeley, A. D. (1975). Context-dependent memory in two natural environments: On lard and underwater. *British Journal of Psychology, 66*, 325–331. [6]

Gökcebay, N., Cooper, R., Williams, R. L., Hirshkowitz, M., & Moore, C. A. (1994). Function of sleep. In R. Cooper (Ed.), *Sleep.* New York: Chapman & Hall. [4]

Gold, M. S. (1994). The epidemiology, attitudes, and pharmacology of LSD use in the 1990s. *Psychiatric Annals, 24*, 124–126. [4]

Goldberg, J., True, W. R., Eisen, S. A., & Henderson, W. G. (1990). A twin study of the effects of the Vietnam War on posttraumatic stress disorder. *Journal of the American Medical Association, 263*, 1227–1232. [11]

Goldberg, L. R. (1993). The structure of phenotypic personality traits. *American Psychologist, 48*, 26–34. [10]

Goldberg, L. R., & Saucier, G. (1995). So what do you propose we use instead? A reply to Block. *Psychological Bulletin, 117*, 221–225. [10]

Goldberg, P. A. (1965). A review of sentence completion methods in personality. In B. I. Murstein (Ed.), *Handbook of projective techniques.* New York: Basic Books. [10]

Goldenberg, H. (1977). *Abnormal psychology: A social/community approach.* Monterey, CA: Brooks/Cole. [12]

Goldenberg, R. L., & Klerman, L. V. (1995). Adolescent pregnancy— another look. *New England Journal of Medicine, 332*, 1161–1162. [8]

Goldman, A. L. (1991, April 10). Portrait of religion in U.S. holds dozens of surprises. *The New York Times*, pp. A1, A11. [11]

Goldman, M. S. (1983). Cognitive impairment in chronic alcoholics: Some cause for optimism. *American Psychologist, 38*, 1045–1054. [11]

Goldstein, A., & Kalant, H. (1990). Drug policy: Striking the right balance. *Science, 249*, 1513–1521. [11]

Goldstein, R. B., Weissman, M. M., Adams, P. B., Horwath, E., Lish, J. D., Charney, D., Woods, S. W., Sobin, C., & Wickramaratne, P. J. (1994). Psychiatric disorders in relatives of probands with panic disorder and/or major depression. *Archives of General Psychiatry, 51*, 383–394. [12]

Goleman, D. (1979, November). Positive denial: The case for not facing reality. *Psychology Today*, pp. 13, 44–60. [11]

Goleman, D. (1995). *Emotional intelligence.* New York: Bantam. [7]

Goleman, D., Kaufman, P., & Ray, M. (1992). *The creative spirit.* New York: Dutton. [7]

Gonzalez, R., Ellsworth, P. C., & Pembroke, M. (1993). Response biases in lineups and showups. *Journal of Personality and Social Psychology, 64*, 525–537. [6]

Goode, E. E. (1987, September 28). For a little peace of mine. *U.S. News & World Report*, pp. 98–102. [13]

Goodwin, D. W. (1985). Alcoholism and genetics: The sins of the fathers. *Archives of General Psychiatry, 42*, 171–174. [11]

Goodwin, D. W. (1986). *Anxiety.* New York: Oxford University Press. [12]

Goodwin, G. M. (1996). How do antidepressants affect serotonin receptors? The role of serotonin receptors in the therapeutic and side effect profile of the SSRIs. *Journal of Clinical Psychiatry, 57*(4, Suppl.), 9–13. [13]

Gorman, C. (1996, Fall). Damage control. *Time* [special issue], 31–35. [2]

Gorman, J. M., Liebowitz, M. R., Fyer, A. J., & Stein, J. (1989). A Neuroanatomical hypothesis for panic disorder. *American Journal of Psychiatry, 146*, 148–161. [12]

Gormezano, I. (1984). The study of associative learning with CS-CR paradigms. In D. L. Alkon & J. Farley (Eds.), *Primary neural substrates of learning and behavioral change* (pp. 5–24). New York: Cambridge University Press. [5]

Gottesman, I. I. (1991). *Schizophrenia genesis: The origins of madness.* New York: W. H. Freeman. [12]

Gottfried, A. E., Fleming, J. S., & Gottfried, A. W. (1994). Role of parental motivational practices in children's academic intrinsic motivation and achievement. *Journal of Educational Psychology, 86*, 104–113. [9]

Gottman, J. (with Silver, N.). (1994). *Why marriages suceed or fail and how you can make yours last.* New York: Simon & Schuster. [8, 9]

Gottman, J. M. (1998). Psychology and the study of marital processes. *Annual Review of Psychology, 49*, 169–197. [8]

Gough, H. (1987). *California Psychological Inventory: Administrator's Guide.* Palo Alto: Consulting Psychologists Press. [10]

Gould, M. S., Fisher, P., Parides,, M., Flory, M., & Shaffer, D. (1996). Psychosocial risk factors of child and adolescent completed suicide. *Archives of General Psychiatry, 53*, 1155–1162. [12]

Graham, S. (1992). "Most of the subjects were white and middle class": Trends in published research on African Americans in selected APA journals, 1970–1989. *American Psychologist, 47*, 629–639. [1]

Grant, B. F., & Dawson, D. A. (1998). Age at onset of alcohol use and its association with *DSM-IV* alcohol abuse and dependence: Results from the National Longitudinal Alcohol Epidemiologic Survey. *Journal of Substance Abuse, 9*, 103–110. [11]

Grant, B. F., Harford, T. C., Chou, P., Pickering, M. S., Dawson, D. A., Stinson, F. S., & Noble, J. (1991). Prevalence of DSM-III-R alcohol abuse and dependence: United States, 1988. *Alcohol Health & Research World, 15*, 91–96. [11]

Grbich, C. (1994). Women as primary breadwinners in families where men are primary caregivers. *Australian New Zealand Journal of Sociology, 30,* 105–118. [8]

Greden, J. F. (1994). Introduction Part III. New agents for the treatment of depression. *Journal of Clinical Psychiatry, 55*(2, Suppl.), 32–33. [2, 12]

Green, A. L., & Patel, J. K. (1996, December). The new pharmacology of schizophrenia. *Harvard Mental Health Letter, 13*(6), 5–7. [13]

Green, A. R., & Goodwin, G. M. (1996). Ecstasy and neurodegeneration: Ecstasy's long-term effects are potentially more damaging than its acute toxicity. *British Medical Journal, 312,* 1493–1494. [4]

Green, B. L., Lindy, J. D., & Grace, M. C. (1985). Post-traumatic stress disorder: Toward DSM-IV. *Journal of Nervous and Mental Disorders, 173,* 406–411. [11]

Green, J., & Shellenberger, R. (1990). *The dynamics of health and wellness: A biopsychosocial approach.* Fort Worth: Holt, Rinehart & Winston. [11]

Green, L. R., Richardson, D. R., & Lago, T. (1996). How do friendship, indirect, and direct aggression relate? *Aggressive Behavior, 22,* 81–86. [14]

Green, R. (1985). Gender identity in childhood and later sexual orientation: Follow-up of 78 males. *American Journal of Psychiatry, 142,* 339. [9]

Green, R. (1987). *The "sissy boy syndrome" and the development of homosexuality.* New Haven: Yale University Press. [9]

Green, R., & Money, J. (1961). Effeminacy in pubertal boys. *Pediatrics, 27,* 236. [9]

Greenfield, T. K., & Rogers, J. D. (1999). Who drinks most of the alcohol in the U.S.? The policy implications. *Journal of Studies on Alcohol, 60,* 78–89. [11]

Greenwald, A. G. (1992). New look 3: Unconscious cognition reclaimed. *American Psychologist, 47,* 766–779. [3]

Greenwald, A. G., Spangenberg, E. R., Pratkanis, A. R., & Eskenazi, J. (1991). Double-blind tests of subliminal self-help audiotapes. *Psychological Science, 2,* 119–122. [3]

Gregory, R. J. (1996). *Psychological testing: History, principles, and applications* (2nd ed.). Boston: Allyn & Bacon. [8, 10]

Gregory, R. L. (1978). *Eye and brain: The psychology of seeing* (3rd ed.). New York: McGraw-Hill. [3]

Greist, J. H. (1992). An integrated approach to treatment of obsessive compulsive disorder. *Journal of Clinical Psychiatry, 53*(4, Suppl.), 38–41. [12]

Greist, J. H. (1995). The diagnosis of social phobia. *Journal of Clinical Psychiatry, 56*(5, Suppl.), 5–12. [12]

Greist, J. H. (1996). Anxiety disorders: The role of serotonin. *Journal of Clinical Psychiatry, 57*(6, Suppl.), 3–4. [12]

Griffitt, W., Nelson, J., & Littlepage, G. (1972). Old age and response to agreement-disagreement. *Journal of Gerontology, 27,* 269–274. [14]

Grinker, J. A. (1982). Physiological and behavioral basis for human obesity. In D. W. Pfaff (Ed.), *The physiological mechanisms of motivation.* New York: Springer-Verlag. [9]

Grochowicz, P., Schedlowski, M., Husband, A., King, M., Hibberd, A., & Bowen, K. (1991). Behavioral conditioning prolongs heart allograft survival in rats. *Brain, Behavior, and Immunity, 5,* 349–356. [5]

Grogger, J., & Bronars, S. (1993). The socioeconomic consequences of teenage childbearing: Findings from a natural experiment. *Family Planning Perspectives, 25,* 156–161. [8]

Gronfier, C., Luthringer, R., Follenius, M., Schaltenbrand, N., Macher, J. P., Muzet, A., & Brandenberger, G. (1996). A quantitative evaluation of the relationships between growth hormone secretion and delta wave electroencephalographic activity during normal sleep and after enrichment in delta waves. *Sleep, 19,* 817–824. [4]

Grossman, H. J. (Ed.). (1983). *Manual on terminology and classification in mental retardation.* Washington, DC: American Association on Mental Deficiency. [7]

Grossman, M., & Wood, W. (1993). Sex differences in intensity of emotional experience: A social role interpretation. *Journal of Personality and Social Psychology, 65,* 1010–1022. [9]

Grünbaum, A. (1994). Does psychoanalysis have a future? Doubtful. *Harvard Mental Health Letter, 11*(4), 3–6. [13]

Guilleminault, C. (1993). 1. Amphetamines and narcolepsy: Use of the Stanford database. *Sleep, 16,* 199–201. [4]

Gupta, D., & Vishwakarma, M. S. (1989). Toy weapons and firecrackers: A source of hearing loss. *Laryngoscope, 99,* 330–334. [3]

Gurin, J. (1989, June). Leaner, not lighter. *Psychology Today,* pp. 32–36. [9]

Guthrie, R. V. (1998). *Even the rat was white* (2nd ed.). Boston: Allyn & Bacon. [1]

Haber, R. N. (1980). How we perceive depth from flat pictures. *American Scientist, 68,* 370–380. [3]

Haberlandt, D. (1997). *Cognitive psychology* (2nd ed.). Boston: Allyn & Bacon. [1, 7]

Haier, R. J. (1993). Cerebral glucose metabolism and intelligence. In P. A. Vernon (Ed.), *Biological approaches to the study of human intelligence* (pp. 317–332). Norwood, NJ: Ablex. [7]

Haimov, I., & Lavie, P. (1996). Melatonin—a soporific hormone. *Current Directions in Psychological Science, 5,* 106–111. [4]

Haimov, I., Lavie, P., Laudon, M., Herer, P., Vigder, C., & Zisapel, N. (1995). Melatonin replacement therapy of elderly insomniacs. *Sleep, 18,* 598–603. [4]

Halaas, J. L., Gajiwala, K. S., Maffei, M., Cohen, S. L., Chait, B. T., Rabinowitz, D., Lallone, R. L., Burley, S. K., & Friedman, J. M. (1995). Weight-reducing effects of the plasma protein encoded by the obese gene. *Science, 269,* 543–546. [9]

Halford, G. S. (1989). Reflections on 25 years of Piagetian cognitive developmental psychology, 1963–1988. *Human Development, 32,* 325–327. [8]

Halligan, P. W., & Marshall, J. C. (1994). Toward a principled explanation of unilateral neglect. *Cognitive Neuropsychology, 11,* 167–206. [2]

Halmi, K. A. (1996). Eating disorder research in the past decade. *Annals of the New York Academy of Sciences, 789,* 67–77. [9]

Halpern, D. F. (1992). *Sex differences in cognitive abilities* (2nd ed.). Hillside, NJ: Erlbaum. [7]

Hamilton, M. C. (1988). Using masculine generics: Does generic "he" increase male bias in the user's imagery? *Sex Roles, 19,* 785–789. [7]

Hammond, D. C. (1992). Hypnosis with sexual disorders. *American Journal of Preventive Psychiatry & Neurology, 3,* 37–41. [4]

Hansel, C. E. M. (1966). *ESP: A scientific evaluation.* New York: Charles Scribner's Sons. [3]

Hansel, C. E. M. (1980). *ESP and parapsychology: A critical reevaluation.* Buffalo, NY: Prometheus. [3]

Hare, R. D. (1970). *Psychopathy: Theory and research.* New York: Wiley. [12]

Hare, R. D. (1995, September). Psychopaths: New trends in research. *Harvard Mental Health Letter, 12*(3), 4–5. [12]

Harford, T. C., Parker, D. A., Grant, B. F., & Dawson, D. A. (1992). Alcohol use and dependence among employed men and women in the United States in 1988. *Alcoholism: Clinical and Experimental Research, 16,* 146–148. [11]

Hargadon, R., Bowers, K. S., & Woody, E. Z. (1995). Does counterpain imagery mediate hypnotic analgesia? *Journal of Abnormal Psychology, 104,* 508–516. [4]

Harkins, S. G., & Jackson, J. M. (1985). The role of evaluation in eliminating social loafing. *Personality and Social Psychology Bulletin, 11,* 456–465. [14]

Harlow, H. F. (1950). Learning and satiation of response in intrinsically motivated complex puzzle performance by monkeys. *Journal of Comparative and Physiological Psychology, 43,* 289–294. [9]

Harlow, H. F. (1959). Love in infant monkeys. *Scientific American, 200,* 68–74. [8]

Harlow, H. F., & Harlow, M. K. (1962). Social deprivation in monkeys. *Scientific American, 207,* 137–146. [8]

Harlow, J. M. (1848). Passage of an iron rod through the head. *Boston Medical and Surgical Journal, 39,* 389–393. [2]

Harlow, R. E., & Cantor, N. (1996). Still participating after all these years: A study of life task participation in later life. *Journal of Personality and Social Psychology, 71,* 1235–1249. [8]

Harris, J. A., Rushton, J. P., Hampson, E., & Jackson, D. N. (1996). Salivary testosterone and self-report aggressive and pro-social personality characteristics in men and women. *Aggressive Behavior, 22,* 321–331. [14]

Harris, L. J., & Blaiser, M. J. (1997). Effects of a mnemonic peg system on the recall of daily tasks. *Perceptual and Motor Skills, 84,* 721–722. [6]

Harris, M. (1993). The best medicine. *West County Journal,* p. 1C. [11]

Harris, R. A., Brodie, M. S., & Dunwiddie, T. V. (1992). Possible substrates of ethanol reinforcement: GABA and dopamine. *Annals of the New York Academy of Sciences, 654,* 61–69. [4]

Harrison, J. R., & Barabasz, A. F. (1991). Effects of restricted environmental stimulation therapy on the behavior of children with autism. *Child Study Journal, 21,* 153–166. [9]

Hartmann, E. L. (1973). *The functions of sleep.* New Haven: Yale University Press. [4]

Hartmann, E. (1988). Insomnia: Diagnosis and treatment. In R. L. Williams, I. Karacan, & C. A. Moore (Eds.), *Sleep disorders: Diagnosis and treatment* (pp. 29–46). New York: John Wiley. [4]

Hasselmo, M. E., & Bower, J. M. (1993). Acetylcholine and memory. *Trends in Neurosciences, 16,* 218–222. [2]

Hatfield, E., & Sprecher, S. (1986). *Mirror, mirror . . . The importance of looks in everyday life.* Albany, NY: State University of New York Press. [14]

Hay, D. F. (1994). Prosocial development. *Journal of Child Psychology and Psychiatry, 35,* 29–71. [14]

Hayes, S. C., & Heiby, E. (1996). Psychology's drug problem: Do we need a fix or should we just say no? *American Psychologist, 51,* 198–206. [13]

Hebb, D. O. (1949). *The organization of behavior.* New York: John Wiley & Sons. [6]

Hedges, L. B., & Nowell, A. (1995). Sex differences in mental test scores, variability, and numbers of high-scoring individuals. *Science, 269,* 41–45. [7]

Heikkinen, M., Aro, H., & Lönnqvist, J. (1993). Life events and social support in suicide. *Suicide and Life-Threatening Behavior, 23,* 343–358. [12]

Heilman, K. M., Scholes, R., & Watson, R. T. (1975). Auditory affective agnosia: Disturbed comprehension of affective speech. *Journal of Neurology, Neurosurgery and Psychiatry, 38,* 69–72. [2]

Heimann, M., & Meltzoff, A. N. (1996). Deferred imitation in 9- and 14-month-old infants: A longitudinal study of a Swedish sample. *British Journal of Developmental Psychology, 14,* 55–64. [8]

Heinrich, R. K., Corbine, J. L., & Thomas, K. R. (1990). Counseling Native Americans. *Journal of Counseling and Development, 69,* 128–133. [13]

Held, R. (1993). What can rates of development tell us about underlying mechanisms? In C. E. Granrud (Ed.), *Visual perception and cognition in infancy* (pp. 75–89). Hillsdale, NJ: Erlbaum. [8]

Hellige, J. B. (1990). Hemispheric asymmetry. *Annual Review of Psychology, 41,* 55–80. [2]

Hellige, J. B. (1993). *Hemispheric asymmetry: What's right and what's left.* Cambridge, MA: Harvard University Press. [2]

Hellige, J. B., Bloch, M. I., Cowin, E. L., Eng, T. L., Eviatar, Z., & Sergent, V. (1994). Individual variation in hemispheric asymmetry: Multitask study of effects related to handedness and sex. *Journal of Experimental Psychology: General, 123,* 235-256. [2]

Hembree, W. C., III, Nahas, G. G., Zeidenberg, P., & Huang, H. F. S. (1979). Changes in human spermatozoa associated with high dose marihuana smoking. In G. G. Nahas & W. D. M. Paton (Eds.), *Marihuana: Biological effects* (pp. 429–439). Oxford: Pergamon Press. [4]

Hendin, H., & Haas, A. P. (1991). Suicide and guilt as manifestations of PTSD in Vietnam combat veterans. *American Journal of Psychiatry, 148,* 586-591. [11]

Henley, N. M. (1973). Status and sex: Some touching observations. *Bulletin of the Psychonomic Society, 2,* 91–93. [14]

Henley, N. M. (1989). Molehill or mountain? What we know and don't know about sex bias in language. In M. Crawford & M. Gentry (Eds.), *Gender and thought: Psychological perspectives.* New York: Springer-Verlag. [7]

Hennessey, B. A., & Amabile, T. M. (1988). The conditions of creativity. In R. J. Sternberg (Ed.), *The nature of creativity: Contemporary psychological perspectives.* New York: Cambridge University Press. [7]

Hennevin, E., Hars, B., Maho, C., & Bloch, V. (1995). Processing of learned information in paradoxical sleep: Relevance for memory. *Behavioural Brain Research, 69,* 125–135. [4]

Henningfield, J. E., & Ator, N. A. (1986). *Barbiturates: Sleeping potion or intoxicant?* New York: Chelsea House. [4]

Henningfield, J. E., Hariharan, M., & Kozlowski, L. T. (1996). Nicotine content and health risks of cigars. *Journal of the American Medical Association, 276,* 1857–1858. [4]

Hepper, P. G., Shahidullah, S., & White, R. (1990). Origins of fetal handedness. *Nature, 347,* 431. [2]

Herkenham, M. (1992). Cannabinoid receptor localization in brain: Relationship to motor and reward systems. *Annals of the New York Academy of Sciences, 654,* 19–32. [4]

Herman, L. (1981). Cognitive characteristics of dolphins. In L. Herman (Ed.), *Cetacean behavior.* New York: Wiley. [7]

Hernandez, L., & Hoebel, B. G. (1989). Food intake and lateral hypothalamic self-stimulation covary after medial hypothalamic lesions or ventral midbrain 6-hydroxydopamine injections that cause obesity. *Behavioral Neuroscience, 103,* 412–422. [9]

Herrnstein, R. J., & Murray, C. (1994). *The bell curve: Intelligence and class structure in American life.* New York: Free Press. [7]

Hershenson, M. (1989). *The moon illusion.* Hillsdale, NJ: Erlbaum. [3]

Hertzog, C. (1991). Aging, information processing speed, and intelligence. In K. W. Schaie & M. P. Lawton (Eds.), *Annual Review of Gerontology and Geriatrics* (Vol. 11, pp. 55–79). [8]

Hess, E. H. (1961). Shadows and depth perception. *Scientific American, 204,* 138–148. [3]

Hetherington, A. W., & Ranson, S. W. (1940). Hypothalamic lesions and adiposity in the rat. *Anatomical Record, 78,* 149–172. [9]

Higbee, K. L. (1977). *Your memory: How it works and how to improve it.* Englewood Cliffs, NJ: Prentice-Hall. [6]

Higgins, A. (1995). Educating for justice and community: Lawrence Kohlberg's vision of moral education. In W. M. Kurtines & J. L. Gerwirtz (Eds.), *Moral development: An introduction* (pp. 49–81). Boston: Allyn & Bacon. [8]

Hilgard, E. R. (1975). Hypnosis. *Annual Review of Psychology, 26,* 19–44. [4]

Hilgard, E. R. (1979). Divided consciousness in hypnosis: Implications of the hidden observer. In E. Fromm & R. E. Shor (Eds.), *Hypnosis: Developments in research and new perspectives* (2nd ed.). Chicago: Aldine. [4]

Hilgard, E. R. (1986). *Divided consciousness: Multiple controls in human thought and action.* New York: Wiley. [4]

Hilgard, E. R. (1992). Dissociation and theories of hypnosis. In E. Fromm & M. R. Nash (Eds.), *Contemporary hypnosis research.* New York: Guilford. [4]

Hingson, R., Alpert, J. J., Day, N., Dooling, E., Kayne, H., Morelock, S., Oppenheimer, E., & Zuckerman, B. (1982). Effects of maternal drinking and marijuana use on fetal growth and development. *Pediatrics, 70,* 539–546. [4]

Hinton, G. E., Dayan, P., Frey, B. J., & Neal, R. M. (1995). The "wake-sleep" algorithm for unsupervised neural networks. *Science, 268,* 1158–1161. [7]

Hirsch, J. (1997). Some heat but not enough light. *Nature, 387,* 27–28. [9]

Hirschfeld, M. A. (1995). The impact of health care reform on social phobia. *Journal of Clinical Psychiatry, 56*(5, Suppl.), 13–17. [12]

Hobson, J. A. (1988). *The dreaming brain.* New York: Basic Books. [4]

Hobson, J. A. (1989). *Sleep.* New York: Scientific American Library. [4]

Hobson, J. A. (1996, February). How the brain goes out of its mind. *Harvard Mental Health Letter, 12*(8), 3–5. [4]

Hobson, J. A., & McCarley, R. W. (1977). The brain as a dream state generator: An activation-synthesis hypothesis of the dream process. *American Journal of Psychiatry, 134*, 1335–1348. [2, 4]

Hobson, J. A., & Stickgold, R. (1995). The conscious state paradigm: A neurological approach to waking, sleeping, and dreaming. In M. S. Gazzaniga (Ed.), *The cognitive neurosciences*. Cambridge, MA: MIT Press. [4]

Hodgins, S., Mednick, S. A., Brennan, P. A., Schulsinger, F., & Engberg, M. (1996). Mental disorder and crime: Evidence from a Danish birth cohort. *Journal of Personality and Social Psychology, 53*, 489–496. [14]

Hoebel, B. G., & Teitelbaum, P. (1966). Weight regulation in normal and hypothalamic hyperphagic rats. *Journal of Comparative and Physiological Psychology, 61*, 189–193. [9]

Hoffman, L. (1979). Maternal employment. *American Psychologist, 34*, 859–865. [8]

Hofstede, G. (1980). *Culture's consequences: International differences in work-related values*. Beverly Hills, CA: Sage. [10]

Hofstede, G. (1983). Dimensions of national cultures in fifty countries and three regions. In J. Deregowski, S. Dzuirawiec, and R. Annis (Eds.), *Explications in cross-cultural psychology*. Lisse: Swets and Zeitlinger. [10]

Hohagen, F. (1996). Nonpharmacological treatment of insomnia. *Sleep, 19*, S50–S51. [4]

Holden, C. (1986). Depression research advances, treatment lags. *Science, 233*, 723–726. [12]

Holden, C. (1991). New center to study therapies and ethnicity. *Science, 251*, 748. [13]

Holden, C. (1996). Sex and olfaction. *Science, 273*, 313. [3]

Holland, J. G., & Skinner, B. F. (1961). *The analysis of behavior*. New York: McGraw-Hill. [5]

Holloway, M. (1991). Rx for addiction. *Scientific American, 264*, 94–103. [4]

Holloway, M. (1994). Trends in women's health: A global view. *Scientific American, 271*, 76–83. [11]

Holloway, M. (1999, January). Flynn's effect. *Scientific American, 280*, 37–38. [7]

Holmes, T. H., & Rahe, R. H. (1967). The social readjustment rating scale. *Journal of Psychosomatic Research, 11*, 213–218. [11]

Horgan, J. (1996, December). Why Freud isn't dead. *Scientific American, 275*, 106–111. [13]

Horn, J. C., & Meer, J. (1987, May). The vintage years. *Psychology Today*, pp. 76–90. [8]

Horn, J. L. (1982). The theory of fluid and crystallized intelligence in relation to concepts of cognitive psychology and aging in adulthood. In F. I. M. Craik & S. Trehub (Eds.), *Aging and cognitive processes* (pp. 201–238). New York: Plenum Press. [8]

Horne, J. (1992). Annotation: Sleep and its disorders in children. *Journal of Child Psychology and Psychiatry, 33*, 473–487. [4]

Horney, K. (1937). *The neurotic personality of our time*. New York: W. W. Norton. [10]

Horney, K. (1945). *Our inner conflicts*. New York: W. W. Norton. [10]

Horney, K. (1950). *Neurosis and human growth*. New York: W. W. Norton. [10, 12]

Horney, K. (1967). *Feminine psychology*. New York: W. W. Norton. [10]

Horvitz, L. A. (1997, November 10). Aromachologists nose out the secret powers of smell. *Insight on the News, 13*, pp. 36–37. [3]

Horwath, E., Lish, J. D., Johnson, J., Hornig, C. D., & Weissman, M. M. (1993). Agoraphobia without panic: Clinical reappraisal of an epidemiologic finding. *American Journal of Psychiatry, 150*, 1496–1501. [12]

Houlihan, D., Schwartz, C., Miltenberger, R., & Heuton, D. (1993). The rapid treatment of a young man's balloon (noise) phobia using in vivo flooding. *Journal of Behavior Therapy and Experimental Psychiatry, 24*, 233–240. [13]

House, J. S., Landis, K. R., & Umberson, D. (1988). Social relationships and health. *Science, 241*, 540–544. [11]

Hovland, C. I., Lumsdaine, A. A., & Sheffield, F. D. (1949). *Experiments on mass communication*. Princeton, NJ: Princeton University Press. [14]

Howard, A., Pion, G. M., Gottfredson, G. D., Flattau, P. E., Oskamp, S., Pfafflin, S. M., Bray, D. W., & Burnstein, A. G. (1986). The changing face of American psychology: A report from the committee on employment and human resources. *American Psychologist, 41*, 1311–1327. [3]

Hoyer, G., & Lund, E. (1993). Suicide among women related to number of children in marriage. *Archives of General Psychiatry, 50*, 134–137. [12]

Hublin, C., Kaprio, J., Partinen, M., & Koskenvuo, M. (1999). Limits of self-report in assessing sleep terrors in a population survey. *Sleep, 22*, 89–93. [4]

Hudson, J. I., Carter, W. P., & Pope, H. G., Jr. (1996). Antidepressant treatment of binge-eating disorder: Research findings and clinical guidelines. *Journal of Clinical Psychiatry, 57*(8, Suppl.), 73–79. [13]

Hudspeth, A. J. (1983). The hair cells of the inner ear. *Scientific American, 248*, 54–64. [3]

Huesmann, L. R., Eron, L. D., Lefkowitz, M. M., & Walder, L. O. (1984). The stability of aggression over time and generations. *Developmental Psychology, 20*, 1120–1134. [14]

Huesmann, L. R., & Moise, J. (1996, June). Media violence: A demonstrated public health threat to children. *Harvard Mental Health Letter, 12*(12), 5–7. [14]

Huff, C. R. (1995). *Convicted but innocent*. Thousand Oaks, CA: Sage. [6]

Hughes, J. R. (1992). Tobacco withdrawal in self-quitters. *Journal of Consulting and Clinical Psychology, 60*, 689–697. [11]

Hughes, R. J., & Badia, P. (1997). Sleep-promoting and hypothermic effects of daytime melatonin administration in humans. *Sleep, 20*, 124–131. [4]

Hugick, L., & Leonard, J. (1991). Sex in America. *Gallup Poll Monthly, No. 313*, 60–73. [8]

Hull, C. L. (1943). *Principles of behavior*. New York: Appleton-Century-Crofts. [9]

Hultsch, D. F., & Dixon, R. A. (1990). Learning and memory in aging. In J. E. Birren & K. W. Schaie (Eds.), *Handbook of the psychology of aging* (3rd ed., pp. 359–374). San Diego: Academic Press. [8]

Hurrell, R. M. (1997). Factors associated with regular exercise. *Perceptual and Motor Skills, 84*, 871–874. [11]

Huston, A. C., Donnerstein, E., Fairchild, H., Feshbach, N. D., Katz, P. A., Murray, J. P., Rubinstein, E. A., Wilcox, B. L., & Zuckerman, D. (1992). *Big world, small screen: The role of television in American society*. Lincoln: University of Nebraska Press. [14]

Hyde, J. S., Fenema, E., & Lamon, S. J. (1990). Gender differences in mathematics performance: A meta-analysis. *Psychological Bulletin, 107*, 139–155. [7]

Hyde, J. S., & Linn, M. C. (1988). Gender differences in verbal ability: A meta-analysis. *Psychological Bulletin, 104*, 53–69. [1, 7]

Hyman, I. E., Jr., Husband, T. H., & Billings, E. J. (1995). False memories of childhood. *Applied Cognitive Psychology, 9*, 181–197. [6]

Hyman, I. E., Jr., & Pentland, J. (1996). The role of mental imagery in the creation of false childhood memories. *Journal of Memory and Language, 35*, 101–117. [6]

Indian Health Service. (1988). *Indian health service chart series book*. Washington, DC: U.S. Department of Health and Human Services. [11]

Inglehart, R. (1990). *Culture shift in advanced industrial society*. Princeton, NJ: Princeton University Press. [8]

Inhelder, B. (1966). Cognitive development and its contribution to the diagnosis of some phenomena of mental deficiency. *Merrill-Palmer Quarterly, 12*, 299–319. [8]

Insel, T. R. (1990). Phenomenology of obsessive compulsive disorder. *Journal of Clinical Psychiatry, 51*(2, Suppl.), 4–8. [12]

Irwin, M., Mascovich, A., Gillin, C., Willoughby, R., Pike, J., & Smith, T. L. (1994). Partial sleep deprivation reduces natural killer cell activity in humans. *Psychosomatic Medicine, 56*, 493–498. [4]

Isabella, R. A., Belsky, J., & von Eye, A. (1989). Origins of infant-mother attachment: An examination of interactional synchrony during the infant's first year. *Developmental Psychology, 25*, 12–21. [8]

Isay, R. A. (1989). *Being homosexual: Gay men and their development.* New York: Farrar, Straus, & Giroux. [9]

Isenberg, D. J. (1986). Group polarization: A critical review and meta-analysis. *Journal of Personality and Social Psychology, 50,* 1141–1151. [14]

Ito, T. A., Miller, N., & Pollock, V. E. (1996). Alcohol and aggression: A meta-analysis on the moderating effects of inhibitory cues, triggering events, and self-focused attention. *Psychological Bulletin, 120,* 60–82. [14]

Iverson, L. L. (1979). The chemistry of the brain. *Scientific American, 241,* 134–147. [12]

Iversen, L. L. (1996). Smoking . . . harmful to the brain. *Nature, 382,* 206–207. [4, 11]

Izard, C. E. (1971). *The face of emotion.* New York: Appleton-Century-Crofts. [9]

Izard, C. E. (1977). *Human emotions.* New York: Plenum Press. [9]

Izard, C. E. (1990). Facial expressions and the regulation of emotions. *Journal of Personality and Social Psychology, 58,* 487–498. [9]

Izard, C. E. (1992). Basic emotions, relations among emotions, and emotion-cognition relations. *Psychological Review, 99,* 561–565. [9]

Izard, C. E. (1993). Four systems for emotion activation: Cognitive and noncognitive processes. *Psychological Review, 100,* 68–90. [9]

Jacobs, G. H. (1993). The distribution and nature of colour vision among the mammals. *Biological Review, 68,* 413–471. [3]

Jacobsen, P. B., Bovbjerg, D. H., Schwartz, M. D., Andrykowski, M. A., Futterman, A. D., Norton, L., & Redd, W. H. (1993). Formation of food aversions in cancer patients receiving repeated infusions of chemotherapy. *Behavior Research and Therapy, 31,* 739–748. [5]

Jacobson, N. S., & Hollon, S. D. (1996). Cognitive-behavior therapy versus pharmacotherapy: Now that the jury's returned its verdict, it's time to present the rest of the evidence. *Journal of Consulting and Clinical Psychology, 64,* 74–80. [13]

James, W. (1884). What is an emotion? *Mind, 9,* 188–205. [9]

James, W. (1890). Principles of psychology. New York: Holt. [1, 9]

Jamieson, D. W., & Zanna, M. P. (1989). Need for structure in attitude formation and expression. In A. R. Pratkanis, S. J. Breckler, & A. G. Greenwald (Eds.), *Attitude structure and function* (pp. 383–406). Hillsdale, NJ: Erlbaum. [14]

Jamison, K. R. (1995). Manic-depressive illness and creativity. *Scientific American, 272,* 62–67. [12]

Janeway, C. A., Jr. (1993). How the immune system recognizes invaders. *Scientific American, 269,* 72–79. [11]

Janis, I. L. (1982). *Groupthink: Psychological studies of policy decisions and fiascoes* (2nd ed.). Boston: Houghton Mifflin. [14]

Jaskiewicz, J. A., & McAnarney, E. R. (1994). Pregnancy during adolescence. *Pediatrics in Review, 15,* 32–38. [8]

Jaynes, J. (1976). *The origin of consciousness and the breakdown of the bicameral mind.* Boston: Houghton Mifflin. [2]

Jefferson, J. W. (1995). Social phobia: A pharmacologic treatment overview. *Journal of Clinical Psychiatry, 56*(5, Suppl.), 18–24. [13]

Jefferson, J. W. (1996). Social phobia: Everyone's disorder? *Journal of Clinical Psychiatry, 57*(6, Suppl.), 28–32. [12]

Jefferson, J. W. (1997). Antidepressants in panic disorder. *Journal of Clinical Psychiatry, 58*(2, Suppl.), 20–24. [13]

Jellinek, E. M. (1960). *The disease concept of alcoholism.* New Brunswick, NJ: Hillhouse Press. [11]

Jemmott, J. B., III, & Locke, S. E. (1984). Psychosocial factors, immunologic mediation, and human susceptibility to infectious diseases: How much do we know? *Psychological Bulletin, 95,* 78–108. [11]

Jenike, M. A. (1989). Obsessive-compulsive and related disorders: A hidden epidemic. *New England Journal of Medicine, 321,* 539–541. [12]

Jenike, M. A. (1990, April). Obsessive-compulsive disorder. *Harvard Medical School Health Letter, 12,* 4–8. [13]

Jenkins, J. J., Jimenez-Pabon, E., Shaw, R. E., & Sefer, J. W. (1975). *Schuell's aphasia in adults: Diagnosis, prognosis, and treatment* (2nd ed.). Hagerstown, MD: Harper & Row. [2]

Jensen, A. R. (1985). The nature of the black-white difference on various psychometric tests: Spearman's hypothesis. *Behavioral and Brain Sciences, 8,* 193–263. [7]

Jernigan, T. L., Butters, N., DiTraglia, G., Schafer, K., Smith, T., Irwin, M., Grant, I., Schuckit, M., & Cermak, L. S. (1991). Reduced cerebral grey matter observed in alcoholics using magnetic resonance imaging. *Alcoholism: Clinical and Experimental Research, 15,* 418–427. [11]

Jeste, D. V. (1994). How does late-onset compare with early-onset schizophrenia? *Harvard Mental Health Letter, 10*(8), 8–9. [12]

Jimerson, D. C., Wolfe, B. E., Metzger, E. D., Finkelstein, D. M., Cooper, T. B., & Levine, J. M. (1997). Decreased serotonin function in bulimia nervosa. *Archives of General Psychiatry, 54,* 529–534. [9]

Johnson, D. L. (1989). Schizophrenia as a brain disease: Implications for psychologists and families. *American Psychologist, 44,* 553–555. [12]

Johnson, E. O., Roehrs, T., Roth, T., & Breslau, N. (1998). Epidemiology of alcohol and medication as aids to sleep in early adulthood. *Sleep, 21,* 178–186. [4]

Johnson, L. A. (1996, June 5). Eye witness: New ATM technology identifies a customer by the iris. *St. Louis Post-Dispatch,* p. C5. [3]

Johnson, M. P., Duffy, J. F., Dijk, D-J., Ronda, J. M., Dyal, C. M., & Czeisler, C. A. (1992). Short-term memory, alertness and performance: A reappraisal of their relationship to body temperature. *Journal of Sleep Research, 1,* 24–29. [4]

Johnson, W. G., Tsoh, J. Y., & Varnado, P. J. (1996). Eating disorders: Efficacy of pharmacological and psychological interventions. *Clinical Psychology Review, 16,* 457–478. [9]

Johnston, L. D., O'Malley, P. M., & Bachman, J. G. (1997). *National survey results on drug use from the Monitoring the Future Study, 1975–1996/97: Vol. 1. Secondary school students.* The University of Michigan Institute for Social Research; National Institute on Drug Abuse, 5600 Fishers Lane, Rockville, MD 20857; USDHHS, Public Health Service, National Institutes of Health. [1, 4]

Jones, D. (1999). Cogito in vitro. *Nature, 397,* 216. [2]

Jones, E. E. (1976). How do people perceive the causes of behavior? *American Scientist, 64,* 300–305. [14]

Jones, E. E. (1986). Interpreting interpersonal behavior: The effects of expectancies. *Science, 234,* 41–46. [14]

Jones, E. E. (1990). *Interpersonal perception.* New York: Freeman. [14]

Jones, E. E., & Davis, K. E. (1965). A theory of correspondent inferences: From acts to dispositions. In L. Berkowitz (Ed.), *Advances in experimental social psychology* (Vol. 2, pp. 219–266). New York: Academic Press. [14]

Jones, E. E., & Nisbett, R. E. (1971). *The actor and the observer: Divergent perceptions of the causes of behavior.* New York: General Learning. [14]

Jones, M. C. (1924). A laboratory study of fear: The case of Peter. *Pedagogical Seminary, 31,* 308–315. [5]

Jorgensen, M., & Keiding, N. (1991). Estimation of spermarche from longitudinal spermaturia data. *Biometrics, 47,* 177–193. [8]

Judd, C. M., Ryan, C. S., & Park, B. (1991). Accuracy in the judgment of in-group and out-group variability. *Journal of Personality and Social Psychology, 61,* 366–379. [14]

Julien, R. M. (1995). *A primer of drug action* (7th ed.). New York: W.H. Freeman. [4, 8]

Jung, C. G. (1933). *Modern man in search of a soul.* New York: Harcourt Brace Jovanovich. [10]

Kagitcibasi, C. (1992). A critical appraisal of individualism-collectivism: Toward a new formulation. In U. Kim, H. C. Triandis, and G. Yoon (Eds.), *Individualism and collectivism: Theoretical and methodological issues.* Newbury Park, CA: Sage. [10]

Kahneman, D., & Tversky, A. (1984). Choices, values, and frames. *American Psychologist, 39,* 341–350. [7]

Kalb, C. (1997, August 25). Our embattled ears: Hearing loss once seemed a normal part of aging, but experts now agree that much of it is preventable. How to protect yourself. *Newsweek, 130,* 75–76. [3]

Kalish, H. I. (1981). *From behavioral science to behavior modification.* New York: McGraw-Hill. [5, 13]

Kamin, L. (1968). "Attention-like" processes in classical conditioning. In M. R. Jones (Ed.), *Miami symposium on the prediction of behavior: Aversive stimulation*. Miami: University of Miami Press. [5]

Kandel, D. B., & Davies, M. (1996). High school students who use crack and other drugs. *Archives of General Psychiatry, 53,* 71–80. [4]

Kane, J. M. (1993). Understanding and treating psychoses: Advances in research and therapy. *Journal of Clinical Psychiatry, 54,* 445–452. [12]

Kane, J. M. (1996). Treatment-resistant schizophrenic patients. *Journal of Clinical Psychiatry, 57*(9, Suppl.), 35–40. [13]

Kaniasty, K., & Norris, F. H. (1993). A test of the social support deterioration model in the context of natural disaster. *Journal of Personality and Social Psychology, 64,* 395–408. [11]

Kanner, A. D., Coyne, J. C., Schaefer, C., & Lazarus, R. S. (1981). Comparison of two modes of stress measurement: Daily hassles and uplifts versus major life events. *Journal of Behavioral Medicine, 4,* 1–39. [11]

Kaplan, G. A., Wilson, T. W., Cohen, R. D., Kauhanen, J., Wu, M., & Salomen, J. T. (1994). Social functioning and overall mortality: Prospective evidence from the Kuopio Ischemic Heart Disease Risk Factor Study. *Epidemiology, 5,* 495–500. [11]

Karacan, I. (1988). Parasomnias. In R. L. Williams, I. Karacan, & C. A. Moore (Eds.), *Sleep disorders: Diagnosis and treatment* (pp. 131–144). New York: John Wiley. [4]

Karasek, R. A., & Theorell, T. (1990). *Healthy work*. New York: Basic Books. [11]

Karasu, T. B. (1990a). Toward a clinical model of psychotherapy for depression, I: Systematic comparison of three psychotherapies. *American Journal of Psychiatry, 147,* 133–147. [13]

Karasu, T. B. (1990b). Toward a clinical model of psychotherapy for depression, II: An integrative and selective treatment approach. *American Journal of Psychiatry, 147,* 269–278. [13]

Karni, A., Tanne, D., Rubenstein, B. S., Askenasy, J. J. M., & Sagi, D. (1994). Dependence on REM sleep of overnight improvement of a perceptual skill. *Science, 265,* 679–682. [4]

Kastenbaum, R. (1992). *The psychology of death*. New York: Springer-Verlag. [8]

Katon, W. (1996). Panic disorder: Relationship to high medical utilization, unexplained physical symptoms, and medical costs. *Journal of Clinical Psychiatry, 57*(10, Suppl.), 11–18. [12]

Katzenberg, D., Young, T., Finn, L., Lin, L., King, D. P., Takahashi, J. S., & Mignot, E. (1998). A CLOCK polymorphism associated with human diurnal preference. *Sleep, 21,* 569. [4]

Kaufman, J. (1996). Teenage parents and their offspring. *Annals of the New York Academy of Sciences, 789,* 17–30. [8]

Kawachi, I., Colditz, G. A., Speizer, F. E., Manson, J. E., Stampfer, M. J., Willett, W. C., & Hennekens, C. H. (1997). A prospective study of passive smoking and coronary heart disease. *Circulation, 95,* 2374–2379. [11]

Kay, S. A. (1997). PAS, present, and future: Clues to the origins of circadian clocks. *Science, 276,* 753–754. [4]

Keating, C. R. (1994). World without words: Messages from face and body. In W. J. Lonner & R. Malpass (Eds.), *Psychology and culture* (pp. 175–182). Boston: Allyn & Bacon. [9]

Keefauver, S. P., & Guilleminault, C. (1994). Sleep terrors and sleepwalking. In M. Kryger, T. Roth, & W. C. Dement (Eds.), *Principles and practice of sleep medicine* (pp. 567–573). Philadelphia: W.B. Saunders. [4]

Keesey, R. E. (1988). The body-weight set point. What can you tell your patients? *Postgraduate Medicine, 83,* 114–118, 121–122, 127. [9]

Keesey, R. E., & Powley, T. L. (1986). The regulation of body weight. *Annual Review of Psychology, 37,* 109–133. [9]

Kelner, K. L. (1997). Seeing the synapse. *Science, 276,* 547. [2]

Kendler, K. S., & Diehl, S. R. (1993). The genetics of schizophrenia: A current genetic-epidemiologic perspective. *Schizophrenia Bulletin, 19,* 261–285. [12]

Kendler, K. S., Gardner, C. O., & Prescott, C. A. (1997). Religion, psychopathology, and substance use and abuse: A multimeasure, genetic-epidemiologic study. *American Journal of Psychiatry, 154,* 322–329. [4, 10]

Kendler, K. S., Gruenberg, A. M., & Kinney, D. K. (1994). Independent diagnoses of adoptees and relatives as defined by DSM-III in the provincial and national samples of the Danish Adoption Study of Schizophrenia. *Archives of General Psychiatry, 51,* 456–468. [12]

Kendler, K. S., Kessler, R. C., Walters, E. E., MacLean, C., Neale, M. C., Heath, A. C., & Eaves, L. J. (1995). Stressful life events, genetic liability, and onset of an episode of major depression in women. *American Journal of Psychiatry, 152,* 833–842. [12]

Kendler, K. S., MacLean, C., Neale, M., Kessler, R., Heath, A., & Eaves, L. (1991). The genetic epidemiology of bulimia nervosa. *American Journal of Psychiatry, 148,* 1627–1637. [9]

Kendler, K. S., Neale, M. C., Heath, A. C., Kessler, R. C., & Eaves, L. J. (1994). A twin-family study of alcoholism in women. *American Journal of Psychiatry, 151,* 707–715. [11]

Kendler, K. S., Neale, M. C., Kessler, R. C., Heath, A. C., & Eaves, L. J. (1992). The genetic epidemiology of phobias in women. *Archives of General Psychiatry, 49,* 273–281. [12]

Kendler, K. S., Neale, M. C., Kessler, R. C., Heath, A. C., & Eaves, L. J. (1993). The lifetime history of major depression in women: Reliability of diagnosis and heritability. *Archives of General Psychiatry, 50,* 863–870. [12]

Kendler, K. S., & Prescott, C. A. (1999). A population-based twin study of lifetime major depression in men and women. *Archives of General Psychiatry, 56,* 39–44. [12]

Kendler, K. S., Walters, E. E., Truett, K. R., Heath, A. C., Neale, M. C., Martin, N. G., & Eaves, L. J. (1994). Sources of individual differences in depressive symptoms: Analysis of two samples of twins and their families. *American Journal of Psychiatry, 151,* 1605–1614. [12]

Kessler, R. C., McGonagle, K. A., Zhao, S., Nelson, C. B., Hughes, M., Eshleman, S., Wittchen, H-U., & Kendler, K. S. (1994). Lifetime and 12-month prevalence of DSM-III-R psychiatric disorders in the United States: Results from the National Comorbidity Survey. *American Journal of Psychiatry, 51,* 8–19. [12]

Kessler, R. C., Stein, M. B., & Berglund, P. (1998). Social phobia subtypes in the National Comorbidity Survey. *American Journal of Psychiatry, 155,* 613–619. [12]

Khachaturian, Z. S. (1997, July/August). Plundered memories. *The Sciences, 37,* 20–25. [8]

Kiecolt-Glaser, J. K., & Glaser, R. (1992). Psychoneuroimmunology: Can psychological interventions modulate immunity. *Journal of Consulting and Clinical Psychology, 60,* 569–575. [11]

Kiecolt-Glaser, J. K., Glaser, R., Gravenstein, S., Malarkey, W. B., & Sheridan, J. (1996). Chronic stress alters the immune response to influenza virus vaccine in older adults. *Proceedings of the National Academy of Science, 93,* 3043–3047. [11]

Kiester, E., Jr. (1997, April). "Traveling light" has new meaning for jet laggards. *Smithsonian, 28,* 110–119. [4]

Kihlstrom, J. F. (1985). Hypnosis. *Annual Review of Psychology, 26,* 557–591. [4]

Kihlstrom, J. F. (1986). Strong inferences about hypnosis. *Behavioral and Brain Sciences, 9,* 474–475. [4]

Kihlstrom, J. F. (1995). The trauma-memory argument. *Consciousness and Cognition, 4,* 65–67. [6]

Kihlstrom, J. F., & Barnhardt, T. M. (1993). The self-regulation of memory: For better and for worse, with and without hypnosis. In D. M. Wegner & J. W. Pennebaker (Eds.), *Handbook of mental control*. Englewood Cliffs, NJ: Prentice Hall. [4]

Kilbride, J. E., & Kilbride, P. L. (1975). Sitting and smiling behavior of Baganda infants. *Journal of Cross-Cultural Psychology, 6,* 88–107. [8]

Kim, K. H. S., Relkin, N. R., Lee, K-M., & Hirsch, J. (1997). Distinct cortical areas associated with native and second languages. *Nature, 388,* 171–174. [7]

Kimura, D. (1992). Sex differences in the brain. *Scientific American, 267,* 118–125. [7]

King, L. A., Walker, L. M., & Broyles, S. J. (1996). Creativity and the five-factor model. *Journal of Research on Personality, 30,* 189–203. [10]

King, N. J., Clowes-Hollins, V., & Ollendick, T. H. (1997). The etiology of childhood dog phobia. *Behaviour Research and Therapy, 35,* 77. [12]

Kingsbury, S. J. (1993). Brief hypnotic treatment of repetitive nightmares. *American Journal of Clinical Hypnosis, 35,* 161–169. [4]

Kingsbury, S. J. (1996, October). Prescriptions by psychologists. *Harvard Mental Health Letter, 13*(4), 8. [13]

Kington, R. S., & Smith, J. P. (1997). Socioeconomic status and racial and ethnic differences in functional status associated with chronic diseases. *American Journal of Public Health, 87,* 805–810. [11]

Kinnamon, S. C. (1988). Taste transduction: A diversity of mechanisms. *Trends in Neurosciences, 11,* 491–496. [3]

Kinnunen, T., Zamansky, H. S., & Block, M. L. (1994). Is the hypnotized subject lying?. *Journal of Abnormal Psychology, 103,* 184–191. [4]

Kinomura, S., Larsson, J., Gulyás, B., & Roland, P. E. (1996). Activation by attention of the human reticular formation and thalamic intralaminar nuclei. *Science, 271,* 512–515. [2]

Kinsella, G., Prior, M. R., & Murray, G. (1988). Singing ability after right- and left-sided brain damage. A research note. *Cortex, 24,* 165–169. [2]

Kinsey, A. C., Pomeroy, W. B., & Martin, C. E. (1948). *Sexual behavior in the human male.* Philadelphia: W. B. Saunders. [9]

Kinsey, A. C., Pomeroy, W. B., Martin, C. E., & Gebhard, P. H. (1953). *Sexual behavior in the human female.* Philadelphia: W. B. Saunders. [9]

Kirsch, I., & Lynn, S. J. (1995). The altered state of hypnosis: Changes in the theoretical landscape. *American Psychologist, 50,* 846–858. [4]

Kite, M. E., Deaux, K., & Miele, M. (1991). Stereotypes of young and old: Does age outweigh gender? *Psychology and Aging, 6,* 19–27. [14]

Klatzky, R. L. (1980). *Human memory: Structures and processes* (2nd ed.). New York: W. H. Freeman. [6]

Klatzky, R. L. (1984). *Memory and awareness: An information-processing perspective.* New York: W. H. Freeman. [6]

Klein, D., Milner, B., Zatorre, R. J., Meyer, E., & Evans, A. C. (1995). The neural substrates underlying word generation: A bilingual functional-imaging study. *Proceedings of the National Academy of Science, 92,* 2899–2930. [7]

Klein, R. G. (1996). Comments on expanding the clinical role of psychologists. *American Psychologist, 51,* 216–218. [13]

Kleinman, A., & Cohen, A. (1997, March). Psychiatry's global challenge. *Scientific American, 276,* 86–89. [13]

Kleitman, N. (1960). Patterns of dreaming. *Scientific American, 203,* 82–88. [4]

Klerman, G. L., Weissman, M. N., Rounsaville, B. J., & Chevron, E. S. (1984). *Interpersonal therapy of depression.* New York: Academic Press. [13]

Klinger, E. (1987, October). The power of daydreams. *Psychology Today,* 36–44. [4]

Kluft, R. P. (1984). An introduction to multiple personality disorder. *Psychiatric Annals, 14,* 19–24. [12]

Kluft, R. P. (1992). Hypnosis with multiple personality disorder. *American Journal of Preventative Psychiatry & Neurology, 3,* 19–27. [4]

Kluft, R. P. (1993). Multiple personality disorder: A contemporary perspective. *Harvard Mental Health Letter, 10*(4), 5–7. [12]

Knight, R. T. (1996). Contribution of human hippocampal region to novelty detection. *Nature, 383,* 256–259. [2]

Kobasa, S. (1979). Stressful life events, personality, and health: An inquiry into hardiness. *Journal of Personality and Social Psychology, 37,* 1–11. [11]

Kobasa, S. C., Maddi, S. R., & Kahn, S. (1982). Hardiness and health: A prospective study. *Journal of Personality and Social Psychology, 42,* 168–177. [11]

Kochanska, G. (1993). Toward a synthesis of parental socialization and child temperament in early development of conscience. *Child Development, 64,* 325–347. [14]

Koenig, H. G., Cohen, H. J., Blazer, D. G., Pieper, C., Meador, K. G., Shelp, F., Goli, V., & DiPasquale, B. (1992). Religious coping and depression among elderly, hospitalized medically ill men. *American Journal of Psychiatry, 149,* 1693–1700. [11]

Kohlberg, L. (1968, September). The child as a moral philosopher. *Psychology Today,* pp. 24–30. [8]

Kohlberg, L. (1969). *Stages in the development of moral thought and action.* New York: Holt, Rinehart & Winston. [8]

Kohlberg, L. (1981). *Essays on moral development, Vol. 1. The philosophy of moral development.* New York: Harper & Row. [8]

Kohlberg, L. (1984). *Essays on moral development, Vol. 2. The psychology of moral development.* San Francisco: Harper & Row. [8]

Kohlberg, L. (1985). *The psychology of moral development.* San Francisco: Harper & Row. [8]

Kohlberg, L., & Gilligan, C. (1971). The adolescent as a philosopher: The discovery of the self in a postconventional world. *Daedalus, 100,* 1051–1086. [8]

Köhler, W. (1925). *The mentality of apes* (E. Winter, Trans.). New York: Harcourt Brace Jovanovich. [5]

Kohut, A., & DeStefano, L. (1989). Modern employees expect more from their careers: Job dissatisfaction particularly high among the young. *The Gallup Report, No. 288,* 22–30. [8]

Kolb, B., & Whishaw, I. Q. (1998). Brain plasticity and behavior. *Annual Review of Psychology, 49,* 43–64. [2]

Kolodny, R. C., Masters, W. H., & Johnson, V. E. (1979). *Textbook of sexual medicine.* Boston: Little, Brown. [4]

Koltz, C. (1983, December). Scapegoating. *Psychology Today,* pp. 68–69. [14]

Kopp, C. P., & Kaler, S. R. (1989). Risk in infancy: Origins and implications. *American Psychologist, 44,* 224–230. [8]

Kopta, S. M., Howard, K. I., Lowry, J. L., & Beutler, L. E. (1994). Patterns of symptomatic recovery in psychotherapy. *Journal of Consulting and Clinical Psychology, 62,* 1009–1016. [13]

Korbo, L. (1999). Glial cell loss in the hippocampus of alcoholics. *Alcoholism: Clinical and Experimental Research, 23,* 164–168. [11]

Korn, J. H., Davis, R., & Davis, S. F. (1991). Historians' and chairpersons' judgments of eminence among psychologists. *American Psychologist, 46,* 789–792. [1]

Kosslyn, S. M., & Sussman, A. L. (1995). Roles of imagery in perception: Or, there is no such thing as immaculate perception. In M. S. Gazzaniga (Ed.), *The cognitive neurosciences.* Cambridge, MA: MIT Press. [7]

Kosten, T. R., & Ziedonis, D. M. (1997). Substance abuse and schizophrenia: Editors' introduction. *Schizophrenia Bulletin, 23,* 181–186. [12]

Kozak, M. J., Foa, E. B., & McCarthy, P. R. (1988). Obsessive-compulsive disorder. In C. G. Last & M. Herson (Eds.), *Handbook of anxiety disorders* (pp. 87–108). New York: Pergamon Press. [12]

Krantz, D. S., Grunberg, N. E., & Baum, A. (1985). Health psychology. *Annual Review of Psychology, 36,* 349–383. [11]

Kranzler, H. R. (1996). Evaluation and treatment of anxiety symptoms and disorders in alcoholics. *Journal of Clinical Psychiatry, 57*(6, Suppl.). [12]

Kraus, S. J. (1995). Attitudes and the prediction of behavior: A meta-analysis of the empirical literature. *Personality and Social Psychology Bulletin, 21,* 58–75. [14]

Kroll, N. E. A., Ogawa, K. H., & Nieters, J. E. (1988). Eyewitness memory and the importance of sequential information. *Bulletin of the Psychonomic Society, 26,* 395–398. [6]

Krueger, J. M., & Takahashi, S. (1997). Thermoregulation and sleep: Closely linked but separable. *Annals of the New York Academy of Sciences, 813,* 281–286. [4]

Krueger, W. C. F. (1929). The effect of overlearning on retention. *Journal of Experimental Psychology, 12,* 71–81. [6]

Krupnick, J. L., Sotsky, S. M., Simmens, S., Moyer, J., Elkin, I., Watkins, J., & Pilkonis, P. A. (1996). The role of the therapeutic alliance in psychotherapy and pharmacotherapy outcome: Findings in the National Institute of Mental Health Treatment of Depression Collaborative Research Program. *Journal of Consulting and Clinical Psychology, 64,* 532–539. [13]

Kübler-Ross, Elisabeth. (1969). *On death and dying.* New York: Macmillan. [8]

Kuch, K., & Cox, B. J. (1992). Symptoms of PTSD in 124 survivors of the Holocaust. *American Journal of Psychiatry, 149,* 337–340. [11]

Kuczmarski, R. J., Flegal, K. M., Campbell, S. M., & Johnson, C. L. (1994). Increasing prevalence of overweight among U.S. adults: The National Health and Nutrition Examination Surveys, 1960 to 1991. *Journal of the American Medical Association, 272*, 205–211. [9]

Kuhn, D. (1984). Cognitive development. In M. H. Bernstein & M. E. Lamb (Eds.), *Developmental psychology*. Hillsdale, NJ: Erlbaum. [8]

Kuhn, D., Kohlberg, L., Langer, J., & Haan, N. (1977). The development of formal operations in logical and moral judgment. *Genetic Psychology Monographs, 95*, 97–188. [8]

Kukla, A. (1972). Foundations of an attributional theory of performance. *Psychological Review, 79*, 454–470. [9]

Kunda, Z., & Oleson, K. C. (1995). Maintaining stereotypes in the face of disconfirmation: Construction grounds for subtyping deviants. *Journal of Personality and Social Psychology, 68*, 565–579. [14]

Kupersmidt, J. B., & Coie, J. D. (1990). Preadolescent peer status, aggression, and school adjustment as predictors of externalizing problems in adolescence. *Child Development, 61*, 1350–1362. [8]

Kupersmidt, J. B., Coie, J. D., & Dodge, K. A. (1990). Predicting disorder from peer social problems. In S. R. Asher & J. D. Coie (Eds.), *Peer rejection in childhood*. New York: Cambridge University Press. [8]

Lalonde, R., & Botez, M. I. (1990). The cerebellum and learning processes in animals. *Brain Research Reviews, 15*, 325–332. [2]

Lamb, M. E. (1987). *The father's role: Cross-cultural perspectives*. Hillsdale, NJ: Erlbaum [8]

Lambe, E. K., Katzman, D. K., Mikulis, D. J., Kennedy, S. H., & Zipursky, R. B. (1997). Cerebral gray matter volume deficits after weight recovery from anorexia nervosa. *Archives of General Psychiatry, 54*, 537–542. [9]

Lamberg, L. (1996). Some schools agree to let sleeping teens lie. *Journal of the American Medical Association, 276*, 859. [4]

Lambert, W. E., Genesee, F., Holobow, N., & Chartrand, L. (1993). Bilingual education for majority English-speaking children. *European Journal of Psychology Education, 8*, 3–22. [7]

Lamborn, S. D., Mounts, N. S., Steinberg, L., & Dornbusch, S. M. (1991). Patterns of competence and adjustment among adolescents from authoritative, authoritarian, indulgent, and neglectful families. *Child Development, 62*, 1049–1065. [8]

Lamm, H. (1988). A review of our research on group polarization: Eleven experiments on the effects of group discussion on risk acceptance, probability estimation, and negotiation positions. *Psychological Reports, 62*, 807–813. [14]

Landis, C. A., Savage, M. V., Lentz, M. J., & Brengelmann, G. L. (1998). Sleep deprivation alters body temperature dynamics to mild cooling and heating, not sweating threshold, in women. *Sleep, 21*, 101–108. [4]

Landry, D. W. (1997, February). Immunotherapy for cocaine addiction. *Scientific American, 276*, 42–45. [4]

Landy, D., & Sigall, H. (1974). Beauty is talent: Task evaluation as a function of the performer's physical attractiveness. *Journal of Personality and Social Psychology, 29*, 299–304. [14]

Lang, A. R., Goeckner, D. J., Adesso, V. J., & Marlatt, G. A. (1975). Effects of alcohol on aggression in male social drinkers. *Journal of Abnormal Psychology, 84*, 508–518. [1]

Lange, C. G., & James, W. (1922). *The emotions* (I. A. Haupt, Trans.). Baltimore: Williams and Wilkins. [9]

Langer, E. J., & Rodin, J. (1976). The effects of choice and enhanced personal responsibility for the aged: A field experiment in an institutional setting. *Journal of Personality and Social Psychology, 34*, 191–198. [11]

Langevin, B., Sukkar, F., Léger, P., Guez, A., & Robert, D. (1992). Sleep apnea syndromes (SAS) of specific etiology: Review and incidence from a sleep laboratory. *Sleep, 15*, S25–S32. [4]

Langlois, J. H., Ritter, J. M., Casey, R. J., & Sawin, D. B. (1995). Infant attractiveness predicts maternal behaviors and attitudes. *Developmental Psychology, 31*, 464–472. [14]

Langlois, J. H., Ritter, J. M., Roggman, L. A., & Vaughn, L. S. (1991). Facial diversity and infant preferences for attractive faces. *Developmental Psychology, 27*, 79–84. [14]

Langlois, J. H., & Roggman, L. A. (1990). Attractive faces are only average. *Psychological Science, 1*, 115–121. [14]

Larson, J. H., & Bell, N. J. (1988). Need for privacy and its effect upon interpersonal attraction and interaction. *Journal of Social and Clinical Psychology, 6*, 1–10. [14]

Lattal, K. A., & Neef, N. A. (1996). Recent reinforcement-schedule research and applied behavior analysis. *Journal of Applied Behavior Analysis, 29*, 213–230. [5]

Lauber, J. K., & Kayten, P. J. (1988). Keynote address: Sleepiness, circadian dysrhythmia, and fatigue in transportation system accidents. *Sleep, 11*, 503–512. [4]

Laumann, E. O., Gagnon, J. H., Michael, R. T., & Michaels, S. (1994). *The social organization of sexuality*. Chicago: University of Chicago Press. [9]

Laurence, J. (1999). The usual state of emergency. *AIDS Patient Care and STDs, 13*, 3–5. [11]

Laurent, J., Swerdik, M., & Ryburn, M. (1992). Review of validity research on the Stanford-Binet Intelligence Scale: Fourth Edition. *Psychological Assessment, 4*, 102–112. [7]

Lavie, P., Herer, P., Peled, R., Berger, I., Yoffe, N., Zomer, J., & Rubin, A-H. (1995). Mortality in sleep apnea patients: A multivariate analysis of risk factors. *Sleep, 18*, 149–157. [4]

Lawson, W. B., Hepler, N., Holiday, J., et al. (1994). Race as a factor in inpatient and outpatient admissions and diagnosis. *Hospital & Community Psychiatry, 45*, 72–74. [13]

Lazarus, R. S. (1966). *Psychological stress and the coping process*. New York: McGraw-Hill. [11]

Lazarus, R. S. (1984). On the primacy of cognition. *American Psychologist, 39*, 124–129. [9]

Lazarus, R. S. (1991a). Cognition and motivation in emotion. *American Psychologist, 46*, 352–367. [9]

Lazarus, R. S. (1991b). Progress on a cognitive-motivational-relational theory of emotion. *American Psychologist, 46*, 819–834. [9]

Lazarus, R. S. (1993). From psychological stress to the emotions: A history of changing outlooks. *Annual Review of Psychology, 44*, 1–21. [11]

Lazarus, R. S. (1995). Vexing research problems inherent in cognitive-mediational theories of emotion—and some solutions. *Psychological Inquiry, 6*, 183–187. [9]

Lazarus, R. S., & DeLongis, A. (1983). Psychological stress and coping in aging. *American Psychologist, 38*, 245–253. [11]

Lazarus, R. S., & Folkman, S. (1984). *Stress, appraisal, and coping*. New York: Springer. [11]

Lebow, J. L., & Gurman, A. S. (1995). Research assessing couple and family therapy. *Annual Review of Psychology, 46*, 27–57. [13]

Leckman, J. F., Grice, D. E., Boardman, J., Zhang, H., Vitale, A., Bondi, C., Alsobrook, J., Peterson, B. S., Cohen, D. J., Rasmussen, S. A., Goodman, W. K., McDougle, C. J., & Pauls, D. L. (1997). Symptoms of obsessive-compulsive disorder. *American Journal of Psychiatry, 154*, 911–917. [12]

LeDoux, J. E. (1994). Emotion, memory, and the brain. *Scientific American, 270*, 50–57. [2]

LeDoux, J. E. (1995). Emotion: clues from the brain. *Annual Review of Psychology, 46*, 209–235. [2]

Leger, D. (1994). The cost of sleep-related accidents: A report for the National Commission on Sleep Disorders Research. *Sleep, 17*, 84–93. [5]

Leichtman, M. D., & Ceci, S. J. (1995). The effects of stereotypes and suggestions on preschoolers' reports. *Developmental Psychology, 31*, 568–578. [6]

Leitenberg, H., & Henning, K. (1995). Sexual fantasy. *Psychological Bulletin, 117*, 469–496. [4, 9]

Leland, J. (1996, August 26). The fear of heroin is shooting up. *Newsweek*, pp. 55–56. [4]

Lenat, D. B. (1995, September). Artificial intelligence. *Scientific American, 273*, 80–82. [7]

Lenneberg, E. (1967). *Biological foundations of language*. New York: Wiley. [8]

Leon, M. (1992). The neurobiology of filial learning. *Annual Review of Psychology, 43*, 337–398. [8]

Lerman, D. C., & Iwata, B. A. (1996). Developing a technology for the use of operant extinction in clinical settings: An examination of basic and applied research. *Journal of Applied Behavior Analysis, 29*, 345–382. [13]

Lerman, D. C., Iwata, B. A. , Shore, B. A., & Kahng, S. W. (1996). Responding maintained by intermittent reinforcement: Implications for the use of extinction with problem behavior in clinical settings. *Journal of Applied Behavior Analysis, 29*, 153–171. [5]

Lesage, A. D., Boyer, R., Grunberg, F., Vanier, C., Morissette, R., Ménard-Buteau, C., & Loyer, M. (1994). Suicide and mental disorders: A case-control study of young men. *American Journal of Psychiatry, 151*, 1063–1068. [12]

Leshner, A. I. (1999). Science is revolutionizing our view of addiction—and what to do about it. *American Journal of Psychiatry, 156*, 1–3. [4]

Lester, B. M., Hoffman, J., & Brazelton, T. B. (1985). The rhythmic structure of mother-infant interaction in term and preterm infants. *Child Development, 56*, 15–27. [8]

Levav, I., Kohn, R., Golding, J. M., & Weissman, M. M. (1997). Vulnerability of Jews to affective disorders. *American Journal of Psychiatry, 154*, 941–947. [12]

LeVay, S. (1991). A difference in hypothalamic structure between heterosexual and homosexual men. *Science, 253*, 1034–1037. [9]

LeVay, S. (1993). *The sexual brain*. Cambridge, MA: MIT Press. [9]

LeVay, S., & Hamer, D. H. (1994). Evidence for a biological influence in male homosexuality. *Scientific American, 270*, 44–49. [9]

Levenson, R. W., Carstensen, L. L., & Gottman, J. M. (1993). Long-term marriage: Age, gender, and satisfaction. *Psychology and Aging, 8*, 301–313. [8]

Levenson, R. W., Ekman, P., & Friesen, W. (1990). Voluntary facial action generates emotion-specific autonomic nervous system activity. *Psychophysiology, 27*, 363–385. [9]

Leventhal, H., Singer, R. P., & Jones, S. (1965). The effects of fear and specificity of recommendation upon attitudes and behavior. *Journal of Personality and Social Psychology, 2*, 20–29. [14]

Levi, L. (1990). Occupational stress: Spice of life or kiss of death? *American Psychologist, 45*, 1142–1145. [11]

Levine, C., Kohlberg, L., & Hewer, A. (1985). The current formulation of Kohlberg's theory and a response to critics. *Human Development, 28*, 94–100. [8]

Levinthal, C. F. (1996). *Drugs, behavior, and modern society*. Boston: Allyn & Bacon. [4]

Levitt, A. G., & Wang, Q. (1991). Evidence for language-specific rhythmic influences in the reduplicative babbling of French- and English-learning infants. *Language and Speech, 34*, 235–249. [8]

Levy, J. (1985, May). Right brain, left brain: Fact and fiction. *Psychology Today*, pp. 38–44. [2]

Levy, J., & Nagylaki, T. (1972). A model for the genetics of handedness. *Genetics, 72*, 117–128. [2]

Lévy, P., & Robert, D. (1996). From snoring to sleep apnea syndrome: Therapeutic approach. *Sleep, 19*, S55–S56. [4]

Lewinsohn, P. M., & Rosenbaum, M. (1987). Recall of parental behavior by acute depressives, remitted depressives, and nondepressives. *Journal of Personality and Social Psychology, 52*, 611–619. [6]

Lewis, D. O., Pincus, J. H., Feldman, M., Jackson, L., & Bard, B. (1986). Psychiatric, neurological, and psychoeducational characteristics of 15 death row inmates in the United States. *American Journal of Psychiatry, 143*, 838–845. [14]

Lewis, M. (1995, January/February). Self-conscious emotions. *American Scientist, 83*, 68–78. [9]

Lewis-Fernández, R., & Kleinman, A. (1994). Culture, personality, and psychopathology. *Journal of Abnormal Psychology, 103*, 67–71. [13]

Leyens, J-P., Yzerbyt, V., & Olivier, C. (1996). The role of applicability in the emergence of the overattribution bias. *Journal of Personality and Social Psychology, 70*, 219–229. [14]

Liao, Y., McGee, D. L., Kaufman, J. S., Cao, G., & Cooper, R. S. (1999). Socioeconomic status and morbidity in the last years of life. *American Journal of Public Health, 89*, 569–572. [11]

Lidz, T., Fleck, S., & Cornelison, A. R. (1965). *Schizophrenia and the family*. New York: International Universities Press. [12]

Lieberman, J., Bogerts, B., Degreef, G., Ashtari, M., Lantos, G., & Alvir, J. (1992). Qualitative assessment of brain morphology in acute and chronic schizophrenia. *American Journal of Psychiatry, 149*, 784–794. [12]

Lieberman, M. (1986). Self-help groups and psychiatry. *American Psychiatric Association Annual Review, 5*, 744–760. [13]

Lilly, J. C. (1956). Mental effects of reduction of ordinary levels of physical stimuli in intact, healthy persons. *Psychiatric Research Reports, 5*, 1–5. [9]

Lim, K. O., Tew, W., Kushner, M., Chow, K., Matsumoto, B., & DeLisi, L. E. (1996). Cortical gray matter volume deficit in patients with first-episode schizophrenia. *American Journal of Psychiatry, 153*, 1548–1553. [12]

Lindenberger, U., Mayr, U., & Kliegl, R. (1993). Speed and intelligence in old age. *Psychology and Aging, 8*, 207–220. [8]

Linn, M. C., & Hyde, J. S. (1989). Gender, mathematics, and science. *Educational Researcher, 18*, 17–27. [7]

Linn, M. C., & Peterson, A. C. (1985). Emergence and characterization of sex differences in spatial ability: A meta-analysis. *Child Development, 56*, 1479–1498. [7]

Linn, R. L. (1982). Ability testing: Individual differences, prediction, and differential prediction. In A. K. Wigdor & W. R. Garner (Eds.), *Ability testing: Uses, consequences, and controversies* (Part II). Washington, DC: National Academy Press. [7]

Linton, M. (1979, July). I remember it well. *Psychology Today*, pp. 80–86. [6]

Linville, P. W., Fischer, G. W., & Salovey, P. (1989). Perceived distributions of the characteristics of in-group and out-group members: Empirical evidence and a computer simulation. *Journal of Personality and Social Psychology, 57*, 165–188. [14]

Lipsey, M. W., & Wilson, D. B. (1993). The efficacy of psychological, educational, and behavioral treatment: Confirmation from meta-analysis. *American Psychologist, 48*, 1181–1209. [13]

Lishman, W. A. (1990). Alcohol and the brain. *British Journal of Psychiatry, 156*, 635–644. [11]

Little, R. E., Anderson, K. W., Ervin, C. H., Worthington-Roberts, B., & Clarren, S. K. (1989). Maternal alcohol use during breast-feeding and infant mental and motor development at one year. *New England Journal of Medicine, 321*, 425–430. [8]

Livingstone, M. S. (1988). Art, illusion and the visual system. *Scientific American, 258*, 78–85. [3]

Loeber, R., & Hay, D. (1997). Key issues in the development of aggression and violence from childhood to early adulthood. *Annual Review of Psychology, 48*, 371–410. [14]

Loehlin, J. C. (1992). *The limits of family influence: Genes, experience, and behavior*. New York: Guilford. [10]

Loehlin, J. C., Horn, J. M., & Willerman, L. (1989). Modeling IQ change: Evidence from the Texas Adoption Project. *Child Development, 60*, 993–1004. [7]

Loehlin, J. C., Horn, J. M., & Willerman, L. (1990). Heredity, environment, and personality change: Evidence from the Texas Adoption Project. *Journal of Personality, 58*, 221–243. [10]

Loehlin, J. C., Willerman, L., & Horn, J. M. (1987). Personality resemblance in adoptive families: A 10-year follow-up. *Journal of Personality and Social Psychology, 53*, 961–969. [10]

Loehlin, J. C., Willerman, L., & Horn, J. M. (1988). Human behavior genetics. *Annual Review of Psychology, 39*, 101–133. [10, 12]

Loftus, E. F. (1979). *Eyewitness testimony*. Cambridge, MA: Harvard University Press. [6]

Loftus, E. F. (1984, February). Eyewitnesses: Essential but unreliable. *Psychology Today*, pp. 22–27. [6]

Loftus, E. F. (1993a). Psychologists in the eyewitness world. *American Psychologist, 48*, 550–552. [6]

Loftus, E. F. (1993b). The reality of repressed memories. *American Psychologist, 48*, 518–537. [6]

Loftus, E. F. (1997). Creating false memories. *Scientific American, 277*, 71–75. [6]

Loftus, E. F., & Hoffman, H. G. (1989). Misinformation and memory: The creation of new memories. *Journal of Experimental Psychology: General, 118*, 100–104. [6]

Loftus, E. F., & Klinger, M. R. (1992). Is the unconscious smart or dumb? *American Psychologist, 47*, 761–765. [10]

Loftus, E. F., & Loftus, G. R. (1980). On the permanence of stored information in the human brain. *American Psychologist, 35*, 409–420. [6]

Loftus, E. F., & Pickrell, J. (1995). The formation of false memories. *Psychiatric Annals, 25*, 720–725. [6]

Logue, A. W. (1985). Conditioned food aversion learning in humans. *Annals of the New York Academy of Sciences, 443*, 316–329. [5]

Long, G. M., & Crambert, R. F. (1990). The nature and basis of age-related changes in dynamic visual acuity. *Psychology and Aging, 5*, 138–143. [8]

Lord, L. J., Goode, E. E., Gest, T., McAuliffe, K., Moore, L. J., Black, R. F., & Linnon, N. (1987, November 30). Coming to grips with alcoholism. *U.S. News & World Report*, pp. 56–62. [11]

Lorenz, K. (1966). *On aggression*. New York: Harcourt, Brace, & World. [14]

Lubinsky, D., & Benbow, C. P. (1992). Gender differences in abilities and preferences among the gifted: Implications for the math science pipeline. *Current Directions in Psychological Science, 1*, 61–66. [7]

Luchins, A. S. (1957). Experimental attempts to minimize the impact of first impressions. In C. I. Hovland (Ed.), *Yale studies in attitude and communication: Vol. 1. The order of presentation in persuasion* (pp. 62–75). New Haven, CT: Yale University Press. [14]

Lucki, I. (1996). Serotonin receptor specificity in anxiety disorders. *Journal of Clinical Psychiatry, 57*(6, Suppl.), 5–10. [12]

Ludwig, A. M. (1995). *The price of greatness: Resolving the creativity and madness controversy*. New York: Guilford. [12]

Ludwig, A. M. (1996). Mental disturbance and creative achievement. *Harvard Mental Health Letter, 12*(9), 4–6. [12]

Lummis, M., & Stevenson, H. W. (1990). Gender differences in beliefs about achievement: A cross-cultural study. *Developmental Psychology, 26*, 254–263. [7]

Lundgren, C. B. (1986, August 20). Cocaine addiction: A revolutionary new treatment. *St. Louis Jewish Light*, p. 7. [4]

Lusk, S. L., Ronis, D. L., & Kerr, M. J. (1995). Predictors of hearing protection use among workers: Implications for training programs. *Human Factors, 37*, 635–640. [3]

Lydiard, R. B., Brawman-Mintzer, O., & Ballenger, J. C. (1996). Recent developments in the psychopharmacology of anxiety disorders. *Journal of Consulting and Clinical Psychology, 64*, 660–668. [13]

Lyketsos, C. G., Chen, L-S., & Anthony, J. C. (1999). Cognitive decline in adulthood: An 11.5-year follow-up of the Baltimore Epidemiologic Catchment Area Study. *American Journal of Psychiatry, 156*, 56–58. [8]

Lykken, D. T., Bouchard, T. J., Jr., McGue, M., & Tellegen, A. (1993). Heritability of interests: A twin study. *Journal of Applied Psychology, 78*, 649–661. [14]

Lynn, S. J., & Nash, M. R. (1994). Truth in memory: Ramifications for psychotherapy and hypnotherapy. *American Journal of Clinical Hypnosis, 36*, 194–208. [4]

Lyons, M. J., Eisen, S. A., Goldberg, J., True, W., Lin, N., Meyer, J. M., Toomey, R., Faraone, S. V., Merla-Ramos, M., & Tsuang, M. T. (1998). A registry-based twin study of depression in men. *Archives of General Psychiatry, 55*, 468–472. [12]

Maccoby, E. E. (1992). The role of parents in the socialization of children: An historical overview. *Developmental Psychology, 28*, 1006–1017. [8]

Maccoby, E. E., & Martin, J. A. (1983). Socialization in the context of the family: Parent-child interaction. In P. H. Mussen (Ed.), *Handbook of child psychology* (4th ed., Vol. 4). New York: John Wiley. [8]

Macrae, C. N., Milne, A. B., & Bodenhausen, G. V. (1994). Stereotypes as energy-saving devices: A peek inside the cognitive toolbox. *Journal of Personality and Social Psychology, 66*, 37–47. [14]

Magee, J. C., & Johnston, D. (1997). A synaptically controlled, associative signal for Hebbian plasticity in hippocampal neurons. *Science, 275*, 209–213. [2]

Maier, S. F., Watkins, L. R., & Fleshner, M. (1994). Psychoneuroimmunology: The interface between behavior, brain, and immunity. *American Psychologist, 49*, 1004–1017. [11]

Main, M., & Solomon, J. (1990). Procedures for identifying infants as disorganized/disoriented during the Ainsworth Strange Situation. In M. Greenberg, D. Cicchetti, & M. Cummings (Eds.), *Attachment in the preschool years: Theory, research, and intervention* (pp. 121–160). Chicago: University of Chicago Press. [8]

Maj, M., Veltro, F., Pirozzi, R., Lobrace, S., & Magliano, L. (1992). Pattern of recurrence of illness after recovery from an episode of major depression: A prospective study. *Journal of Personality and Social Psychology, 62*, 795–800. [12, 16]

Major, B., Schmidlin, A. M., & Williams, L. (1990). Gender patterns in social touch: The impact of setting and age. *Journal of Personality and Social Psychology, 58*, 634–643. [14]

Malkoff, S. B., Muldoon, M. F., Zeigler, Z. R., & Manuck, S. B. (1993). Blood platelet responsivity to acute mental stress. *Psychosomatic Medicine, 55*, 477–482. [11]

Mandler, J. M. (1990). A new perspective on cognitive development in infancy. *American Scientist, 78*(3), 236–243. [8]

Manton, K. G., Siegler, I. C., & Woodbury, M. A. (1986). Patterns of intellectual development in later life. *Journal of Gerontology, 41*, 486–499. [8]

Maratsos, M. (1983). Some current issues in the study of the acquisition of grammar. In P. H. Mussen (Ed.), *Handbook of child psychology* (Vol. 3). New York: Wiley. [8]

Maratsos, M., & Matheny, L. (1994). Language specificity and elasticity: Brain and clinical syndrome studies. *Annual Review of Psychology, 45*, 487–516. [2]

Marcia, J. (1980). Identity in adolescence. In J. Adelson (Ed.), *Handbook of adolescent psychology*. New York: Wiley. [8]

Marcus, G. F. (1996). Why do children say "breaked"? *Current Directions in Psychological Science, 5*, 81–85. [8]

Marder, S. R. (1996). Clinical experience with risperidone. *Journal of Clinical Psychiatry, 57*(9, Suppl.), 57–61. [13]

Marín, G. (1994). The experience of being a Hispanic in the United States. In W. J. Lonner & R. Malpass (Eds.), *Psychology and culture* (pp. 23–27). Boston: Allyn & Bacon. [10]

Markovic, B. M., Dimitrijevic, M., & Jankovic, B. D. (1993). Immunomodulation by conditioning: Recent developments. *International Journal of Neuroscience, 71*, 231–249. [5]

Marks, G. A., Shatfery, J. P., Oksenberg, A., Speciale, S. G., & Roffwarg, H. P., (1995). A functional role for REM sleep in brain maturation. *Behavioural Brain Research, 69*, 1–11. [4]

Marks, I. (1987b). The development of normal fear: A review. *Journal of Child Psychology and Psychiatry, 28*, 667–697. [8]

Marks, I. (1988). Blood-injury phobia: A review. *American Journal of Psychiatry, 145*, 1207–1213. [12]

Marks, I., Lovell, K., Noshirvani, H., Livanou, M., & Thrasher, S. (1998). Treatment of posttraumatic stress disorder by exposure and/or cognitive restructuring: A controlled study. *Archives of General Psychiatry, 55*, 317–325. [8, 12]

Marks, I. M. (1972). Flooding (implosion) and allied treatments. In W. S. Agras (Ed.), *Behavior modification*. New York: Little, Brown. [13]

Marks, I. M. (1978a). Behavioral psychotherapy of adult neurosis. In S. Garfield & A. E. Bergin (Eds.), *Handbook of psychotherapy and behavior change* (2nd ed.). New York: Wiley. [13]

Marks, I. M. (1995). Advances in behavioral-cognitive therapy of social phobia. *Journal of Clinical Psychiatry, 56*(5, Suppl.), 25–31. [13]

Marlatt, G. A., & Rohsenow, D. J. (1981, December). The think-drink effect. *Psychology Today*, pp. 60–69, 93. [1]

Marmor, J. (Ed.). (1980). *Homosexual behavior: A modern reappraisal.* New York: Basic Books. [12]

Marshall, J. R. (1997). Alcohol and substance abuse in panic disorder. *Journal of Clinical Psychiatry, 58*(2, Suppl.), 46–49. [12]

Marshall, R. D., Schneier, F. R., Fallon, B. A., Feerick, J., & Liebowitz, M. R. (1994). Medication therapy for social phobia. *Journal of Clinical Psychiatry, 56*(6, Suppl.), 33–37. [13]

Marshall, W. L., & Segal, Z. (1988). Behavior therapy. In C. G. Last & M. Hersen (Eds.), *Handbook of anxiety disorders* (pp. 338–361). New York: Pergamon. [13]

Martikainen, P., & Valkonen, R. (1996). Mortality after the death of a spouse: Rates and causes of death in a large Finnish cohort. *American Journal of Public Health, 86*, 1087–1093. [8]

Martin, F. N. (1994). *Introduction to audiology* (5th ed.). Englewood Cliffs, NJ: Prentice-Hall. [3]

Martin, S. K., & Eastman, C. I. (1998). Medium-intensity light produces circadian rhythm adaptation to simulated night-shift work. *Sleep, 21*, 154–165. [4]

Martinez, C. (1986). Hispanics: Psychiatric issues. In C. B. Wilkinson (Ed.), *Ethnic psychiatry* (pp. 61–88). New York: Plenum. [13]

Martinez, J. L., Jr., & Derrick, B. E. (1996). Long-term potentiation and learning. *Annual Review of Psychology, 47*, 173–203. [6]

Martinez-Taboas, A. (1991). Multiple personality in Puerto Rico: Analysis of fifteen cases. *Dissociation, 4*, 189–192. [12]

Martorano, S. C. (1977). A developmental analysis of performance on Piaget's formal operations tasks. *Developmental Psychology, 13*, 666–672. [8]

Marzuk, P. M., Tardiff, K., Leon, A. C., Hirsch, C. S., Portera, L., Hartwell, N., & Iqbal, M. I. (1997). Lower risk of suicide during pregnancy. *American Journal of Psychiatry, 154*, 122–123. [12]

Masand, P., Popli, A. P., & Weilburg, J. B. (1995). Sleepwalking. *American Family Physician, 51*, 649–654. [4]

Masataka, N. (1996). Perception of motherese in a signed language by 6-month-old deaf infants. *Developmental Psychology, 32*, 874–879. [8]

Masland, R. H. (1996). Unscrambling color vision. *Science, 271*, 616–617. [3]

Maslow, A. H. (1970). *Motivation and personality* (2nd ed.). New York: Harper & Row. [9, 10, 12]

Masters, J. C. (1981). Developmental psychology. *Annual Review of Psychology, 32*, 117–151. [8]

Masters, W. H., & Johnson, V. E. (1966). *Human sexual response.* Boston: Little, Brown. [8, 11]

Masters, W. H., & Johnson, V. E. (1979). *Homosexuality in perspective.* Boston: Little, Brown. [9]

Mathew, R. J., & Wilson, W. H. (1991). Substance abuse and cerebral blood flow. *American Journal of Psychiatry, 148*, 292–305. [4]

Matlin, M. W. (1989). *Cognition* (2nd ed.). New York: Holt, Rinehart & Winston. [6]

Matlin, M. (1994). *Cognition* (3rd ed.). Fort Worth, TX: Harcourt. [7]

Matlin, M. W., & Foley, H. J. (1997). *Sensation and perception* (4th ed.). Boston: Allyn & Bacon. [3]

Matsuda, L., Lolait, S. J., Brownstein, M. J., Young, A. C., & Bonner, T. I. (1990). Structure of a cannabinoid receptor and functional expression of the cloned CDNA. *Nature, 346*, 561–564. [4]

Matt, G. E., & Navarro, A. M. (1997). What meta-analyses have and have not taught us about psychotherapy effects: A review and future directions. *Clinical Psychology Review, 17*, 1–32. [13]

Mattay, V. S., Berman, K. F., Ostrem, J. L., Esposito, G., Van Horn, J. D., Bigelow, L. B., & Weinberger, D. R. (1996). Dextroamphetamine enhances "neural network-specific" physiological signals: A positron-emission tomography rCBF study. *Journal of Neuroscience, 16*, 4816–4822. [4]

Matthews, K. A. (1992). Myths and realities of the menopause. *Psychosomatic Medicine, 54*, 1–9. [8]

Matthews, K. A., Shumaker, S. A., Bowen, D. J., Langer, R. D., Hunt, J. R., Kaplan, R. M., Klesges, R. C., & Ritenbaugh, C. (1997). Women's health initiative: Why now? What is it? What's new? *American Psychologist, 52*, 101–116. [11]

Mayer, J. D., & Salovey, P. (1993). The intelligence of emotional intelligence. *Intelligence, 17*, 433–442. [7]

Mayer, J. D., & Salovey, P. (1995). Emotional intelligence and the construction and regulation of feelings. *Applied and Preventive Psychology, 4*, 197–208. [7]

Mayer, J. D., & Salovey, P. (1997). What is emotional intelligence? In P. Salovey & D. Sluyter (Eds.), *Emotional development, emotional literacy, and emotional intelligence.* New York: Basic Books. [7]

Mazur, J. E. (1993). Predicting the strength of a conditioned reinforcer: Effects of delay and uncertainty. *Current Directions in Psychological Science, 2*(3), 70–74. [5]

McAdams, D. P. (1992). The five-factor model in personality: A critical appraisal. *Journal of Personality, 60*, 329–361. [10]

McAneny, L. (1992). Number of drinkers on the rise again. *Gallup Poll Monthly, No. 317*, 43–47. [4]

McCarthy, M. E., & Waters, W. F. (1997). Decreased attentional responsivity during sleep deprivation: Orienting response latency, amplitude, and habituation. *Sleep, 20*, 115–123. [4]

McCarthy, P. (1989, March). Ageless sex. *Psychology Today*, p. 62. [8]

McCartney, K., Harris, M. J., & Bernieri, F. (1990). Growing up and growing apart: A developmental meta-analysis of twin studies. *Psychological Bulletin, 107*, 226–237. [7]

McClearn, G. E., Johansson, B., Berg, S., Pedersen, N. L., Ahern, F., Petrill, S. A., & Plomin, R. (1997). Substantial genetic influence on cognitive abilities in twins 80 or more years old. *Science, 276*, 1560–1563. [7]

McClelland, D. C. (1958). Methods of measuring human motivation. In J. W. Atkinson (Ed.), *Motives in fantasy, action and society: A method of assessment and study.* Princeton, NJ: Van Nostrand. [9]

McClelland, D. C. (1961). *The achieving society.* Princeton, NJ: Van Nostrand. [9]

McClelland, D. C. (1985). *Human motivation.* New York: Cambridge University Press. [9]

McClelland, D. C., Atkinson, J. W., Clark, R. W., & Lowell, E. L. (1953). *The achievement motive.* New York: Appleton-Century-Crofts. [9]

McClelland, D. C., & Pilon, D. A. (1983). Sources of adult motives in patterns of parent behavior in early childhood. *Journal of Personality and Social Psychology, 44*, 564–574. [9]

McConnell, J. V., Cutler, R. L., & McNeil, E. B. (1958). Subliminal stimulation: An overview. *American Psychologist, 13*, 229–242. [3]

McCourt, W. F., Gurrera, R. J., & Cutter, H. S. G. (1993). Sensation seeking and novelty seeking: Are they the same? *Journal of Nervous and Mental Disease, 181*, 309–312. [9]

McCrae, R. R. (1987). Creativity, divergent thinking, and openness to experience. *Journal of Personality and Social Psychology, 52*, 1258–1265. [7]

McCrae, R. R. (1993). Moderated analyses of longitudinal personality stability. *Journal of Personality and Social Psychology, 65*, 577–583. [10]

McCrae, R. R. (1996). Social consequences of experiential openness. *Psychological Bulletin, 120*, 323–337. [10]

McCrae, R. R., & Costa, P. T., Jr. (1987). Validation of the five-factor model of personality across instruments and observers. *Journal of Personality and Social Psychology, 52*, 81–90. [10]

McCrae, R. R., & Costa, P. T., Jr. (1990). *Personality in adulthood.* New York: Guilford. [10]

McCrae, R. R., & Costa, P. T., Jr. (1997). Personality trait structure as a human universal. *American Psychologist, 52*, 509–516. [10]

McDonald, A. D., Armstrong, B. G., & Sloan, M. (1992). Cigarette, alcohol, and coffee consumption and prematurity. *American Journal of Public Health, 82*, 87–90. [8]

McDonald, J. L. (1997). Language acquisition: The acquisition of linguistic structure in normal and special populations. *Annual Review of Psychology, 48*, 215–241. [7]

McGee, A-M., & Skinner, M. (1987). Facial asymmetry and the attribution of personality traits. *British Journal of Social Psychology, 26*, 181–184. [2]

McGlashan, T. H., & Fenton, W. S. (1992). The positive-negative distinction in schizophrenia: Review of natural history validators. *Archives of General Psychiatry, 49,* 63–72. [12]

McGlashan, T. H., & Johannessen, J. O. (1996). Early detection and intervention with schizophrenia: Rationale. *Schizophrenia Bulletin, 22,* 201–222. [16]. [13]

McGue, M., Bouchard, T. J., Jr., Iacono, W. G., & Lykken, D. T. (1993). Behavioral genetics of cognitive ability: A life-span perspective. In R. Plomin & G. E. McClearn (Eds.), *Nature, nurture and psychology* (pp. 59–76). Washington, DC: American Psychological Association. [7]

McGue, M., Pickens, R. W., & Svikis, D. S. (1992). Sex and age effects on the inheritance of alcohol problems: A twin study. *Journal of Abnormal Psychology, 101,* 3–17. [11]

McGuire, W. J. (1985). Attitudes and attitude change. In G. Lindzey & E. Aronson (Ed.), *Handbook of social psychology* (Vol. 2, 3rd ed.). New York: Random House. [14]

McHugh, P. R. (1993). Multiple personality disorder. *Harvard Mental Health Letter, 10*(3), 4–6. [12]

McIntosh, D. N., Silver, R. C., & Wortman, C. B. (1993). Religion's role in adjustment to a negative life event: Coping with the loss of a child. *Journal of Personality and Social Psychology, 65,* 812–821. [11]

McKellar, P. (1972). Imagery from the standpoint of introspection. In P. W. Sheehan (Ed.), *The function and nature of imagery* (pp. 36–63). New York: Academic Press. [7]

McKelvie, S. J. (1984). Relationship between set and functional fixedness: A replication. *Perceptual and Motor Skills, 58,* 996–998. [7]

McNally, R. J., & Shin, L. M. (1995). Association of intelligence with severity of posttraumatic stress disorder symptoms in Vietnam combat veterans. *American Journal of Psychiatry, 152,* 936–938. [11]

McReynolds, P. (1989). Diagnosis and clinical assessment: Current status and major issues. *Annual Review of Psychology, 40,* 83–108. [10]

Medina, J. H., Paladini, A. C., & Izquierdo, I. (1993). Naturally occurring benzodiazepines and benzodiazepine-like molecules in brain. *Behavioural Brain Research, 58,* 1–8. [13]

Mednick, S. A., Brennan, P., & Kandel, E. (1988). Predisposition to violence. *Aggressive Behavior, 14,* 25–33. [14]

Medzerian, G. (1991). *Crack: Treating cocaine addiction.* Blue Ridge Summit, PA: Tab Books. [4, 5]

Meer, J. (1986, June). The age of reason. *Psychology Today,* pp. 60–64. [8]

Mehrabian, A. (1968, September). Communication without words. *Psychology Today,* pp. 53–55. [14]

Meichenbaum, D. (1977). *Cognitive behavior modification: An integrative approach.* New York: Plenum. [11]

Melamed, B. G., & Siegal, L. J. (1975). Reduction of anxiety in children facing hospitalization and surgery by use of filmed modeling. *Journal of Consulting and Clinical Psychology, 43,* 511–521. [13]

Meltzer, E. O. (1990). Performance effects of antihistamines. *Journal of Allergy & Clinical Immunology, 86,* 613–619. [4]

Meltzer, H. (1930). Individual differences in forgetting pleasant and unpleasant experiences. *Journal of Educational Psychology, 21,* 399–409. [6]

Meltzer, H. Y. (1998). Suicide in schizophrenia: Risk factors and clozapine treatment. *Journal of Clinical Psychiatry, 59*(3, Suppl.), 15–20. [12]

Meltzer, H. Y., Rabinowitz, J., Lee, M. A., Cola, P. A., Ranjan, R., Findling, R. L., & Thompson, P. A. (1997). Age at onset and gender of schizophrenic patients in relation to neuroleptic resistance. *American Journal of Psychiatry, 154,* 475–482. [13]

Meltzoff, A. N. (1988a). Imitation of televised models by infants. *Child Development, 59,* 1221–1229. [8]

Meltzoff, A. N. (1988b). Infant imitation and memory: Nine-month-olds in immediate and deferred tests. *Child Development, 59,* 217–255. [8]

Meltzoff, A. N., & Kuhl, P. K. (1994). Faces and speech: Intermodal processing of biologically relevant signals in infants and adults. In D. J. Lewkowicz & R. Lickliter (Eds.), *The development of intersensory perception: Comparative perspectives* (pp. 335–369). Hillsdale, NJ: Erlbaum. [8]

Meltzoff, A. N., & Moore, M. K. (1977). Imitation of facial and manual gestures by human neonates. *Science, 198,* 75–78. [8]

Meltzoff, A. N., & Moore, M. K. (1989). Imitation in newborn infants: Exploring the range of gestures imitated and the underlying mechanisms. *Developmental Psychology, 25,* 954–962. [8]

Melzack, R., & Wall, P. D. (1965). Pain mechanisms: A new theory. *Science, 150,* 971–979. [3]

Melzack, R., & Wall, P. D. (1983). *The challenge of pain.* New York: Basic Books. [3]

Mendelson, W. B. (1995). Long-term follow-up of chronic insomnia. *Sleep, 18,* 698–701. [4]

Mercer, J. R. (1973). *Labelling the mentally retarded.* Berkeley: University of California Press. [7]

Merckelbach, H., de Jong, P. J., Muris, P., & van den Hout, M. A. (1996). The etiology of specific phobias: A review. *Clinical Psychology Review, 16,* 337–361. [12]

Merskey, H. (1996). Ethical issues in the search for repressed memories. *American Journal of Psychotherapy, 50,* 323–335. [6]

Mertens, T. E., & Low-Beer, D. (1996). HIV and AIDS: Where is the epidemic going? *WHO Bulletin OMS, 74,* 121–128. [11]

Metter, E. J. (1991). Brain-behavior relationships in aphasia studied by positron emission tomography. *Annals of the New York Academy of Sciences, 620,* 153–164. [2]

Meyer, P. (1972). If Hitler asked you to electrocute a stranger, would you? In R. Greenbaum & H. A. Tilker (Eds.), *The challenge of psychology* (pp. 456–465). Englewood Cliffs, NJ: Prentice-Hall. [14]

Meyer-Bahlburg, H. F. L., Ehrhardt, A. A., Rosen, L. R., & Gruen, R. S. (1995). Prenatal estrogens and the development of homosexual orientation. *Developmental Psychology, 31,* 12–21. [9]

Michaels, J. W., Bloomel, J. M., Brocato, R. M., Linkous, R. A., & Rowe, J. S. (1982). Social facilitation and inhibition in a natural setting. *Replications in Social Psychology, 2,* 21–24. [14]

Michels, R., & Marzuk, P. M. (1993). Progress in psychiatry (First of two parts). *New England Journal of Medicine, 329,* 552–560. [13]

Michelson, L., Marchione, K., Greenwald, M., Glanz, L., Testa, S., & Marchione, N. (1990). Panic disorder: Cognitive-behavioral treatment. *Behaviour Research and Therapy, 28,* 141–151. [13]

Michelson, L. K., Marchione, K. E., Greenwald, M., Testa, S., & Marchione, N. J. (1996). A comparative outcome and follow-up investigation of panic disorder with agoraphobia: The relative and combined efficacy of cognitive therapy, relaxation training, and therapist-assisted exposure. *Journal of Anxiety Disorders, 10,* 297–330. [12]

Miesenböck, G., & Rothman, J. E. (1997). Patterns of synaptic activity in neural networks recorded by light emission from synaptolucins. *Proceedings of the National Academy of Science, 94,* 3402–3407. [2]

Migot, E. et al. (1998). *Sleep, 21.* [4]

Milavsky, J. R., Kessler, R., Stipp, H., & Rubens, W. S. (1982). Television and aggression: Results of a panel study. In D. Pearl, L. Bouthilet, & J. Lazar (Eds.), *Television and behavior: Ten years of scientific progress and implications for the eighties* (Vol. 2). Washington, DC: U.S. Government Printing Office. [14]

Miles, D. R., & Carey, G. (1997). Genetic and environmental architecture of human aggression. *Journal of Personality and Social Psychology, 72,* 207–217. [10, 14]

Miles, R. (1999). A homeostatic switch. *Nature, 397,* 215–216. [2]

Milgram, S. (1963). Behavioral study of obedience. *Journal of Abnormal and Social Psychology, 67,* 371–378. [14]

Milgrom, P., Mancl, L., King, B., & Weinstein, P. (1995). Origins of childhood dental fear. *Behaviour Research and Therapy, 33,* 313–319. [12]

Miller, D. T., & Turnbull, W. (1986). Expectancies and interpersonal processes. *Annual Review of Psychology, 37,* 233–256. [14]

Miller, G. A. (1956). The magical number seven, plus or minus two: Some limits on our capacity for processing information. *Psychological Review, 63,* 81–97. [6]

Miller, G. A., & Gildea, P. M. (1987). How children learn words. *Scientific American, 257,* 94–99. [8]

Miller, J. G., Bersoff, D. M., & Harwood, R. L. (1990). Perceptions of social responsibilities in India and in the United States: Moral imperatives or personal decisions? *Journal of Personality and Social Psychology, 58*, 33–47. [14]

Miller, L. (1989, November). What biofeedback does (and doesn't) do. *Psychology Today*, pp. 22–23. [5]

Miller, L. K. (1999). The savant syndrome: Intellectual impairment and exceptional skill. *Psychological Bulletin, 125*, 31–46. [7]

Miller, N. E. (1941). The frustration-aggression hypothesis. *Psychological Review, 48*, 337–342. [14]

Miller, N. E. (1985, February). Rx: Biofeedback. *Psychology Today*, pp. 54–59. [5]

Miller, N. S., & Gold, M. S. (1994). LSD and Ecstasy: Pharmacology, phenomenology, and treatment. *Psychiatric Annals, 24*, 131–133. [4]

Miller, T. Q., Smith, T. W., Turner, C. W., Guijarro, M. L., & Hallet, A. J. (1996). A meta-analytic review of research on hostility and physical health. *Psychological Bulletin, 119*, 322–348. [11]

Miller, T. Q., Turner, C. W., Tindale, R. S., Posavac, E. J., & Dugoni, B. L. (1991). Reasons for the trend toward null findings in research on Type A behavior. *Psychological Bulletin, 110*, 469–485. [11]

Miller, W. C., Lindeman, A. K., Wallace, J., & Niederpruem, M. (1990). Diet composition, energy intake, and exercise in relation to body fat in men and women. *American Journal of Clinical Nutrition, 52*, 426–430. [9]

Millman, R. B., & Beeder, A. B. (1994). The new psychedelic culture: LSD, Ecstasy, "rave" parties and The Grateful Dead. *Psychiatric Annals, 24*, 148–150. [4]

Milner, B. (1970). Memory and the medial temporal regions of the brain. In K. H. Pribram & D. E. Broadbent (Eds.), *Biology of memory*. New York: Academic Press. [6]

Milner, B. R. (1966). Amnesia following operation on the temporal lobes. In C. W. M. Whitty & O. L. Zangwill (Eds.), *Amnesia* (pp. 109–133). London: Butterworth. [6]

Milner, B., Corkin, S., & Teuber, H. L. (1968). Further analysis of the hippocampal amnesic syndrome: 14-year follow-up study of H. M. *Neuropsychologia, 6*, 215–234. [6]

Miltner, W. H. R., Braun, C., Arnold, M., Witte, H., & Taub, E.. (1999). Coherence of gamma-band EEG activity as a basis for associative learning. *Nature, 397*, 434–436. [6]

Mischel, W. (1973). Toward a cognitive social learning reconceptualization of personality. *Psychological Review, 80*, 252–283. [10]

Mischel, W. (1977). The interaction of person and situation. In D. Magnusson & N. S. Endler (Eds.), *Personality at the crossroads: Current issues in interactional psychology*. Hillsdale, NJ: Lawrence Erlbaum. [10]

Mistlberger, R. E., & Rusak, B. (1989). Mechanisms and models of the circadian timekeeping system. In M. H. Kryger, T. Roth, & W. C. Dement (Eds.), *Principles and practice of sleep medicine* (pp. 141–152). Philadelphia: W. B. Saunders. [4]

Mistry, J., & Rogoff, B. (1994). Remembering in cultural context. In W. J. Lonner & R. Malpass (Eds.), *Psychology and culture* (pp. 139–144). Boston: Allyn & Bacon. [6]

Mitler, M. M., Aldrich, M. S., Koob, G. F., & Zarcone, V. P. (1994). Narcolepsy and its treatment with stimulants. *Sleep, 17*, 352–371. [4]

Modestin, J. (1992). Multiple personality disorder in Switzerland. *American Journal of Psychiatry, 148*, 88–92. [12]

Moffitt, T. E., Caspi, A., Harkness, A. R., & Silva, P. A. (1993). The natural history of change in intellectual performance: Who changes? How much? Is it meaningful? *Journal of Child Psychology and Psychiatry, 34*, 455–506. [7]

Moldofsky, H., Gilbert, R., Lue, F. A., & MacLean, A. W. (1995). Sleep-related violence. *Sleep, 18*, 731–739. [4]

Molin, J., Mellerup, E., Bolwig, T., Scheike, T., & Dam, H. (1996). The influence of climate on development of winter depression. *Journal of Affective Disorders, 37*, 151–155. [12]

Money, J. (1987). Sin, sickness, or status? Homosexual gender identity and psychoneuroendocrinology. *American Psychologist, 42*, 384–399. [9]

Money, J., & Schwartz, M. (1977). Dating, romantic and nonromantic friendships, and sexuality in 17 early-treated adrenogenital females, aged 16–25. In P. A. Lee et al. (Eds.), *Congenital adrenal hyperplasia*. Baltimore: University Park Press. [9]

Monk, T. H. (1989). Circadian rhythms in subjective activation, mood, and performance efficiency. In M. H. Kryger, T. Roth, & W. C. Dement (Eds.), *Principles and practice of sleep medicine* (pp. 163–172). Philadelphia: W. B. Saunders. [4]

Moore-Ede, M. (1993). *The twenty-four hour society*. Reading, MA: Addison-Wesley. [4]

Moran, M. G., & Stoudemire, A. (1992). Sleep disorders in the medically ill patient. *Journal of Clinical Psychiatry, 53*(6, Suppl.), 29–36. [4]

Morgan, C. D., & Murray, H. A. (1935). A method for investigating fantasies: The Thematic Apperception Test. *Archives of Neurology and Psychiatry, 34*, 289–306. [10]

Morgan, C. D., & Murray, H. A. (1962). Thematic Apperception Test. 530–545. In H. A. Murray et al. (Eds.), *Explorations in personality: A clinical and experimental study of fifty men of college age*. New York: Science Editions. [10]

Morgan, C. L. (1996). Odors as cues for the recall of words unrelated to odor. *Perceptual and Motor Skills, 83*, 1227–1234. [6]

Morgan, C., Chapar, G. N., & Fisher, M. (1995). Psychosocial variables associated with teenage pregnancy. *Adolescence, 118*, 277–289. [8]

Morin, C. M., & Ware, C. (1996). Sleep and psychopathology. *Applied and Preventive Psychology, 5*, 211–224. [4]

Morin, C. M., & Wooten, V. (1996). Psychological and pharmacological approaches to treating insomnia: Critical issues in assessing their separate and combined effects. *Clinical Psychology Review, 16*, 521–542. [4]

Morris, J. S., Frith, C. D., Perrett, D. I., Rowland, D., Young, A. W., Calder, A. J., & Dolan, R. J. (1996). A differential neural response in the human amygdala to fearful and happy facial expressions. *Nature, 383*, 812–815. [2]

Morrison, A. M., & Von Glinow, M. S. (1990). Women and minorities in management. *American Psychologist, 45*, 200–208. [14]

Mortensen, P. B., Pedersen, C. B., Westergaard, T., et al. (1999). Effects of family history and place and season of birth on the risk of schizophrenia. *New England Journal of Medicine, 340*, 603–608. [12]

Móscicki, E. K. (1995). Epidemiology of suicidal behavior. *Suicide and Life-Threatening Behavior, 25*, 22–31. [12]

Moser, D., & Dracup, K. (1996). Is anxiety early after myocardial infarction associated with subsequent ischemic and arrhythmic events? *Psychosomatic Medicine, 58*, 395–401. [11]

Motley, M. T. (1985). Slips of the tongue. *Scientific American, 253*, 116–127. [10]

Mourtazaev, M. S., Kemp, B., Zwinderman, A. H., & Kamphuisen, H. A. C. (1995). Age and gender affect different characteristics of slow waves in the sleep EEG. *Sleep, 18*, 557–564. [4]

Mui, A. C. (1992). Caregiver strain among black and white daughter caregivers: A role theory perspective. *The Gerontologist, 32*, 203–212. [8]

Mukerjee, M. (1997). Trends in animal research. *Scientific American, 276*, 86–93. [1]

Muris, R., Steerneman, P., Merckelbach, H., & Meesters, C. (1996). The role of parental fearfulness and modeling in children's fear. *Behaviour Research and Therapy, 34*, 265–268. [5]

Murphy, D. L., & Pigott, T. A. (1990). A comparative examination of a role for serotonin in obsessive compulsive disorder, panic disorder, and anxiety. *Journal of Clinical Psychiatry, 51*(4, Suppl.), 53–58. [12]

Murphy, E. (1989, July 13–27). Townshend. Tinnitus and rock & roll. *Rolling Stone*, pp. 101. [3]

Murray, D. W. (1995, July/August). Toward a science of desire. *The Sciences, 35*, 244–249 . [2]

Murray, H. (1938). *Explorations in personality*. New York: Oxford University Press. [9, 10]

Murray, H. A. (1965). Uses of the Thematic Apperception Test. In B. I. Murstein (Ed.), *Handbook of projective techniques* (pp. 425–432). New York: Basic Books. [10]

Murray, S. L., Holmes, J. G., & Griffin, D. W. (1996a). The benefits of positive illusions: Idealization and the construction of satisfaction in close relationships. *Journal of Personality and Social Psychology, 70*(1), 79–98. [8]

Murray, S. L., Holmes, J. G., & Griffin, D. W. (1996b). The self-fulfilling nature of positive illusions in romantic relationships: Love is not blind, but prescient. *Journal of Personality and Social Psychology 71*(6), 1155–1180. [8]

Murtagh, D. R. R., & Greenwood, K. M. (1995). Identifying effective psychological treatments for insomnia: A meta-analysis. *Journal of Consulting and Clinical Psychology, 63*, 79–89. [4]

Myers, D. A. (1992). *The pursuit of happiness: Discovering the pathway to fulfillment, well-being, and enduring personal joy.* New York: Avon. [9]

Myers, D. G., & Lamm, H. (1975). The polarizing effect of group discussion. *American Scientist, 63*, 297–303. [14]

Nadon, R., Hoyt, I. P., Register, P. A., & Kilstrom, J. F. (1991). Absorption and hypnotizability: Context effects reexamined. *Journal of Personality and Social Psychology, 60*, 144–153. [4]

Narrow, W. E., Regier, D. A., & Rae, D. S. (1993). Use of services by persons with mental and addictive disorders: Findings from the National Institute of Mental Health Epidemiologic Catchment Area Program. *Archives of General Psychiatry, 50*, 95–107. [13]

Nash, J. M. (1997, March 24). Gift of love. *Time*, pp. 80–82. [8]

Nash, M. (1987). What, if anything, is regressed about hypnotic age regression? A review of the empirical literature. *Psychological Bulletin, 102*, 42–52. [4]

Nash, M. R. (1991). Hypnosis as a special case of psychological regression. In S. J. Lynn & J. W. Rhue (Eds.), *Theories of hypnosis: Current models and perspectives* (pp. 171–194). New York: Guilford. [4]

Nash, M., & Baker, E. (1984, February). Trance encounters: Susceptibility to hypnosis. *Psychology Today*, pp. 18, 72–73. [4]

Nathan, P. E. (1992). Peele hasn't done his homework—again: A response to "Alcoholism, politics, and bureaucracy: The consensus against controlled-drinking therapy in America." *Addictive Behaviors, 17*, 63–65. [11]

Nathans, J. (1989). The genes for color vision. *Scientific American, 260*, 42–49. [3]

National Advisory Mental Health Council. (1995). Basic behavioral science research for mental health. *American Psychologist, 50*, 838–845. [9]

National Institute of Mental Health. (1985, June 10–12). *Consensus development conference statement: Electroconvulsive therapy: Program and abstracts.* Washington, DC: National Institute of Mental Health. [13]

National Research Council. (1993). *Losing generations: Adolescents in high risk settings.* Washington, DC: National Academy Press. [8]

National Safety Council. (1997). *Accident facts.* Chicago: Author. [11]

Needleman, H. L., Riess, J. A., Tobin, M. J., Biesecker, G. E., & Greenhouse, J. B. (1996). Bone lead levels and delinquent behavior. *Journal of the American Medical Association, 275*, 363–369. [14]

Neimark, E. (1975). Intellectual development during adolescence. In F. Horowitz (Ed.), *Review of child development research* (Vol. 4). Chicago: University of Chicago Press. [8]

Neimark, E. D. (1981). Confounding with cognitive style factors: An artifact explanation for the apparent nonuniversal incidence of formal operations. In I. Sigel, D. Brodzinsky, & R. Golinkoff (Eds.), *New directions in Piagetian research and theory.* Hillsdale, NJ: Erlbaum. [8]

Neimark, J., Conway, C., & Doskoch, P. (1994, September/October). Back from the drink. *Psychology Today*, pp. 46–53. [11]

Neisser, U. (1967). *Cognitive psychology.* New York: Appleton-Century-Crofts. [6]

Neisser, U., Boodoo, G., Bouchard, T. J., Jr., Boykin, A. W., Brody, N., Ceci, S. J., Halpern, D. F., Loehlin, J. C., Perloff, R., Sternberg, R. J., & Urbina, S. (1996). Intelligence: Knowns and unknowns. *American Psychologist, 51*, 77–101. [7]

Neisser, U., & Harsch, N. (1992). Phantom flashbulbs: False recollections of hearing the news about Challenger. In E. Winograd & U. Neisser (Eds.), *Affect and accuracy in recall: Studies of "flashbulb" memories* (pp. 9–31). New York: Cambridge University Press. [6]

Neitz, J., Neitz, M., & Kainz, M. (1996). Visual pigment gene structure and the severity of color vision defects. *Science, 274*, 801–804. [3]

Neitz, M., & Neitz, J. (1995). Numbers and ratios of visual pigment genes for normal red-green color vision. *Science, 267*, 1013–1016. [3]

Nelson, J. C. (1991). Current status of tricyclic antidepressants in psychiatry: Their pharmacology and clinical applications. *Journal of Clinical Psychiatry, 52*, 193–200. [13]

Nelson, K. (1973). Structure and strategy in learning to talk. *Monographs of the Society for Research in Child Development, 38*(1–2, Serial No. 149). [8]

Nelson, M. D., Saykin, A. J., Flashman, L. A., & Riordan, H. J. (1998). Hippocampal volume reduction in schizophrenia as assessed by magnetic resonance imaging: A meta-analytic study. *Archives of General Psychiatry, 55*, 433–440. [12]

Ness, R. B., Grisso, J. A., Hirschinger, N., Markovic, N., Shaw, L., Day, N. L., & Kline, J. (1999). Cocaine and tobacco use and the risk of spontaneous abortion. *New England Journal of Medicine, 340*, 333–339. [4]

Neugarten, B. L. (1968). The awareness of middle age. In B. Neugarten (Ed.), *Middle age and aging* (pp. 93–98). Chicago: University of Chicago Press. [8]

Neugarten, B. L. (1976). *The psychology of aging: An overview. Master lectures on developmental psychology.* Washington, DC: American Psychological Association. [8]

Neugarten, B. L. (1982). Must everything be a midlife crisis? In T. H. Carr & H. E. Fitzgerald (Eds.), *Human development 82/83* (pp. 162–163). (Reprinted from Prime Time, February 1980, 45–48). Guilford, CT: Dushkin. [8]

Neumann, C. S., Grimes, K., Walker, E. F., & Baum, K. (1995). Developmental pathways to schizophrenia: Behavioral subtypes. *Journal of Abnormal Psychology, 104*, 558–566. [12]

Neville, H. J., Bavelier, D., Corina, D., Rauschecker, J., Karni, A., Lalwani, A., Braun, A., Clark, V., Jezzard, P., & Turner, R. (1998). Cerebral organization for language in deaf and hearing subjects: Biological constraints and effects of experience. *Proceedings of the National Academy of Sciences, 95*, 922–929. [2]

Newcomb, M. D. (1997). Psychosocial predictors and consequences of drug use: A developmental perspective within a prospective study. *Journal of Addictive Diseases, 16*, 51–89. [4]

Newcomb, T. M. (1956). The prediction of interpersonal attraction. *American Psychologist, 11*, 575–587. [14]

Newell, A., & Simon, H. A. (1972). *Human problem solving.* Englewood Cliffs, NJ: Prentice-Hall. [7]

Newport, F. (1996, June). One-fourth of Americans still smoke, but most want to give up the habit. *Gallup Poll Monthly, No. 369*, 2–6. [11]

Ng, S. H. (1990). Androcentric coding of man and his in memory by language users. *Journal of Experimental Social Psychology, 26*, 455–464. [7]

Ng, S. K. C., Hauser, W. A., Brust, J. C. M., & Susser, M. (1988). Alcohol consumption and withdrawal in new onset seizures. *New England Journal of Medicine, 319*, 665–672. [11]

Nguyen, P. V., Abel, T., & Kandel, E. R. (1994). Requirement of a critical period of transcription for induction of a late phase of LTP. *Science, 265*, 1104–1107. [6]

Nicholl, C. S., & Russell, R. M. (1990). Analysis of animal rights literature reveals the underlying motives of the movement: Ammunition for counter offensive by scientists. *Endocrinology, 127*, 985–989. [1]

Nickerson, R. S., & Adams, M. J. (1979). Long-term memory for a common object. *Cognitive Psychology, 11*, 287–307. [6]

Nicol, S. E., & Gottesman, I. I. (1983). Clues to the genetics and neurobiology of schizophrenia. *American Scientist, 71*, 398–404. [12]

Nicotine dependence—Part I. (1997, May). *Harvard Mental Health Letter, 13*(11), 1–4. [4]

Nisbett, R. E., & Wilson, T. D. (1977). The halo effect: Evidence for unconscious alteration of judgments. *Journal of Personality and Social Psychology, 35*, 250–256. [14]

Nishimura, H., Hashikawa, K., Doi, K., Iwaki, T., Watanabe, Y., Kusuoka, H., Nishimura, T., & Kubo, T. (1999). Sign language "heard" in the auditory cortex. *Nature, 397*, 116. [2]

Niskar, A. S., Kieszak, S. M., Holmes, A., Esteban, E., Rubin, C., & Brody, D. J. (1998). Prevalence of hearing loss among children 6 to 19 years of age: The Third National Health and Nutrition Examination Survey. *Journal of the American Medical Association, 279*, 1071–1075. [3]

Nobler, M. S., Sackeim, H. A., Prohovnik, I, Moeller, J. R., Mukherjee, S., Schnur, D. B., Prudic, J., & Devanand, D. P. (1994). Regional cerebral blood flow in mood disorders, III: Treatment and clinical response. *Archives of General Psychiatry, 15*, 884–897. [13]

Nogrady, H., McConkey, K. M., & Perry, C. (1985). Enhancing visual memory: Trying hypnosis, trying imagination, and trying again. *Journal of Abnormal Psychology, 94*, 195–204. [4, 6]

Nordentoft, M., Lou, H. C., Hansen, D., Nim, J., Pryds, O., Rubin, P., & Hemmingsen, R. (1996). Intrauterine growth retardation and premature delivery: The influence of maternal smoking and psychosocial factors. *American Journal of Public Health, 86*, 347–354. [8]

Nordström, P., Samuelsson, M., Åsberg, M., Träskman-Bendz, L., Åberg-Wistedt, A., Nordin, C., & Bertilsson, L. (1994). CSF 5-HIAA predicts suicide risk after attempted suicide. *Suicide and Life-Threatening Behavior, 24*, 1–9. [2]

Norris, J. E., & Tindale, J. A. (1994). *Among generations: The cycle of adult relationships.* New York: Freeman. [8]

Nossal, G. J. V. (1993). Life, death and the immune system. *Scientific American, 269*, 52–62. [11]

Novello, A. C. (1990). The Surgeon General's 1990 report on the health benefits of smoking cessation: Executive summary. *Morbidity and Mortality Weekly Report, 39* (No. RR–12). [11]

Nowak, M. A., & McMichael, A. J. (1995). How HIV defeats the immune system. *Scientific American, 273*, 58–65. [11]

Noyes, R., Jr., Burrows, G. D., Reich, J. H., Judd, F. K., Garvey, M. J., Norman, T. R., Cook, B. L., & Marriott, P. (1996). Diazepam versus alprazolam for the treatment of panic disorder. *Journal of Clinical Psychiatry, 57*, 344–355. [13]

Nyberg, L., Cabeza, R., & Tulving, E. (1996). PET studies of encoding and retrieval: The HERA model. *Psychonomic Bulletin and Review, 2*, 134–147. [6]

Nyberg, L., McIntoch, A., Cabeza, R., Harib, R., Houle, S., & Tulving, E. (1996). General and specific brain regions involved in encoding and retrieval of events: What, where, and when. *Proceedings of the National Academy of Science, 93*, 11280–11285. [6]

O'Brien, C. P. (1996). Recent developments in the pharmacotherapy of substance abuse. *Journal of Consulting and Clinical Psychology, 64*, 677–686. [4]

Offer, D., Ostrov, E., & Howard, K. I. (1981). *The adolescent: A psychological self-portrait.* New York: Basic Books. [8]

Ohzawa, I., DeAngelis, G. C., & Freeman, R. D. (1990). Stereoscopic depth discrimination in the visual cortex: Neurons ideally suited as disparity detectors. *Science, 249*, 1037–1041. [3]

O'Leary, A. (1990). Stress, emotion, and human immune function. *Psychological Bulletin, 108*, 363–382. [11]

O'Leary, K. D., & Smith, D. A. (1991). Marital interactions. *Annual Review of Psychology, 42*, 191–212. [14]

Olds, J. (1956). Pleasure centers in the brain. *Scientific American, 195*, 105–116. [2]

Oliner, S. P., & Oliner P. M. (1988). *The altruistic personality: Rescuers of Jews in Nazi Europe.* New York: Free Press. [14]

Oliver, J. E. (1993). Intergenerational transmission of child abuse: Rates, research, and clinical implications. *American Journal of Psychiatry, 150*, 1315–1324. [14]

Oliver, M. B., & Hyde, J. S. (1993). Gender differences in sexuality: A meta-analysis. *Psychological Bulletin, 114*, 29–51. [9]

Omori, Y., & Miyata, Y. (1996). Eyeblinks in formation of impressions. *Perceptual and Motor Skills, 83*, 591–594. [14]

Orlans, F. B., Beauchamp, T. L., Dresser, R., Morton, D. B., & Gluck, J. P. (1998). *The human use of animals: Case studies in ethical choice.* New York: Oxford University Press. [1]

Orne, M. (1983, December 12). Hypnosis "useful in medicine, dangerous in court." *U.S. News & World Report*, pp. 67–68. [4]

Öst, L-G., & Westling, B. E. (1995). Applied relaxation vs. cognitive behavior therapy in the treatment of panic disorder. *Behavior Research and Therapy, 33*, 145–158. [13]

Ostrom, T. M., Carpenter, S. L., Sedikides, C., & Li, F. (1993). Differential processing of in-group and out-group information. *Journal of Personality and Social Psychology, 64*, 21–34. [14]

Otto, M. W., Pollack, M. H., Sachs, G. S., Reiter, S. R., Meltzer-Brody, S., & Rosenbaum, J. F. (1993). Discontinuation of benzodiazepine treatment: Efficacy of cognitive-behavioral therapy for patients with panic disorder. *American Journal of Psychiatry, 150*, 1485–1490. [13]

Overmeier, J. B., & Seligman, M. E. P. (1967). Effects of inescapable shock upon subsequent escape and avoidance responding. *Journal of Comparative and Physiological Psychology, 67*, 28–33. [5]

Oxman, T. E., Freeman, D. H., Jr., & Manheimer, E. D. (1995). Lack of social participation or religious strength and comfort as risk factors for death after cardiac surgery in the elderly. *Psychosomatic Medicine, 57*, 5–15. [11]

Padian, N. S. et al. (1991). Female-to-male transmission of human immunodeficiency virus. *Journal of the American Medical Association, 266*, 1664–1667. [11]

Paikoff, R. L., & Brooks-Gunn, J. (1991). Do parent-child relationships change during puberty? *Psychological Bulletin, 110*, 47–66. [8]

Panksepp, J. (1992). A critical role for "affective neuroscience" in resolving what is basic about basic emotions. *Psychological Review, 99*, 554–560. [9]

Park, B. (1986). A method for studying the development of impressions of real people. *Journal of Personality and Social Psychology, 51*, 907–917. [14]

Park, K. A., & Waters, E. (1989). Security of attachment and preschool friendships. *Child Development, 60*, 1076–1081. [8]

Parke, R. D. (1977). Some effects of punishment on children's behavior–revisited. In E. M. Heterington, E. M. Ross, & R. D. Parke (Eds.), *Contemporary readings in child psychology.* New York: McGraw-Hill. [5]

Parke, R. D., O'Leary, S. E., & West, S. (1972). Mother-father-newborn interaction: Effects of maternal mediation, labor and sex of infant. *Proceedings of the American Psychological Association, 7*, 85–86. [8]

Parker, J. G., & Asher, S. R. (1987). Peer relations and later personal adjustment: Are low-accepted children at risk? *Psychological Bulletin, 102*, 357–389. [8]

Parkinson, W. L., & Weingarten, H. P. (1990). Dissociative analysis of ventromedial hypothalamic obesity syndrome. *American Journal of Physiology, 259*, 829–835. [9]

Parks, R. W., Loewenstein, D. A., Dodrill, K. L., Barker, W. W., Yoshi, F., Chang, J. Y., Emran, A., Apicella, A., Shermata, W. A., & Duara, R. (1988). Cerebral metabolic effects of a verbal fluency test: A PET scan study. *Journal of Clinical and Experimental Neuropsychology, 10*, 565–575. [7]

Parrott, A. C. (1993). Cigarette smoking: Effects upon self-rated stress and arousal over the day. *Addictive Behaviors, 18*, 389–395. [11]

Partinen, M. (1994). *Epidemiology* of sleep disorders. In M. Kryger, T. Roth, & W. C. Dement (Eds.), *Principles and practice of sleep medicine* (pp. 437–453). Philadelphia: W.B. Saunders. [4]

Partinen, M., Hublin, C., Kaprio, J., Koskenvuo, M., & Guilleminault, C. (1994). Twin studies in narcolepsy. *Sleep, 17*, S13–S16. [4]

Pascual-Leone, A., Dhuna, A., Altafullah, I., & Anderson, D. C. (1990). Cocaine-induced seizures. *Neurology, 40*, 404–407. [4]

Pastore, N. (1950). The role of arbitrariness in the frustration-aggression hypothesis. *Journal of Abnormal and Social Psychology, 47*, 728–731. [14]

Patterson, C. J. (1995). Sexual orientation and human development: An overview. *Developmental Psychology, 31*, 3–11. [9]

Patterson, D. R., & Ptacek, J. T. (1997). Baseline pain as a moderator of hypnotic analgesia for burn injury treatment. *Journal of Consulting and Clinical Psychology, 65,* 60–67. [4]

Pattison, E. M. (1982). The concept of alcoholism as a syndrome. In E. M. Pattison (Ed.), *Selection of treatment for alcoholics.* New Brunswick, NJ: Rutgers Center of Alcohol Studies. [11]

Paul, G. L., & Lentz, R. J. (1977). *Psychosocial treatment of chronic mental patients.* Cambridge, MA: Harvard University Press. [13]

Paul, W. E. (1993). Infectious diseases and the immune system. *Scientific American, 269,* 90–99. [11]

Paulus, P. B., Cox, V. C., & McCain, G. (1988). *Prison crowding: A psychological perspective.* New York: Springer-Verlag. [14]

Paunonen, S. V., Keinonen, M., Trzebinski, J., Forsterling, F., Grishenko-Roze, N., Kouznetsova, L., & Chan, D. W. (1996). The structure of personality in six cultures. *Journal of Cross-Cultural Psychology, 27,* 339–353. [10]

Pavlov, I. P. (1960). *Conditioned reflexes: An investigation of the physiological activity of the cerebral cortex* (G. V. Anrep, Trans.). New York: Dover. (Original translation published 1927). [5]

Payami, H., Montee, K., & Kaye, J. (1994). Evidence for familial factors that protect against dementia and outweigh the effect of increasing age. *American Journal of Human Genetics, 54,* 650–657. [8]

Pedersen, D. M., & Wheeler, J. (1983). The Müller-Lyer illusion among Navajos. *Journal of Social Psychology, 121,* 3–6. [3]

Pederson, D. R., Moran, G., Sitko, C., Campbell, K., Ghesquire, K., & Acton, H. (1990). Maternal sensitivity and the security of infant-mother attachment: A Q-sort study. *Child Development, 61,* 1974–1983. [8]

Peele, S. (1984). The cultural context of psychological approaches to alcoholism: Can we control the effects of alcohol? *American Psychologist, 39,* 1337–1351. [4]

Pelleymounter, M. A., Cullen, M. J., Baker, M. B., Hecht, R., Winters, D., Boone, T., & Collins. (1995). Effects of the obese gene product on body weight regulation in ob/ob mice. *Science, 269,* 540–543. [9]

Pen, C. L., Levy, E., Ravily, V., Beuzen, J. N., & Meurgey, F. (1994). The cost of treatment dropout in depression: A cost-benefit analysis of fluoxetine vs. tricyclics. *Journal of Affective Disorders, 31,* 1–18. [13]

Penfield, W. (1969). Consciousness, memory, and man's conditioned reflexes. In K. Pribram (Ed.), *On the biology of learning* (pp. 129–168). New York: Harcourt Brace Jovanovich. [6]

Penfield, W. (1975). *The mystery of the mind: A critical study of consciousness and the human brain.* Princeton, NJ: Princeton University Press. [6]

Pennisi, E. (1997). Tracing molecules that make the brain-body connection. *Science, 275,* 930–931. [11]

Pepitone, A., & Triandis, H. C. (1987). On the universality of social psychological theories. *Journal of Cross-Cultural Psychology, 18,* 471–498. [14]

Pepperberg, I. M. (1991, Spring). Referential communication with an African grey parrot. *Harvard Graduate Society Newsletter,* 1–4. [7]

Pepperberg, I. M. (1994a). Numerical competence in an African gray parrot (Psittacus erithacus). *Journal of Comparative Psychology, 108,* 36–44. [7]

Pepperberg, I. M. (1994b). Vocal learning in grey parrots (Psittacus erithacus): Effects of social interaction, reference, and context. *The Auk, 111,* 300–314 . [7]

Perls, F. S. (1969). *Gestalt therapy verbatim.* Lafayette, CA: Real People Press. [13]

Perls, T. T. (1995). The oldest old. *Scientific American, 272,* 70–75. [8]

Perrett, D. I., May, K. A., & Yoshikawa, S. (1994). Facial shape and judgements of female attractiveness. *Nature, 368,* 239–242. [14]

Perry, P. J. (1996). Pharmacotherapy for major depression with melancholic features: Relative efficacy of tricyclic versus selective serotonin reuptake inhibitor antidepressants. *Journal of Affective Disorders, 39,* 1–6. [13]

Pert, C. B., Snowman, A. M., & Snyder, S. H. (1974). Localization of opiate receptor binding in presynaptic membranes of rat brain. *Brain Research, 70,* 184–188. [2]

Peters, A., Leahu, D., Moss, M. B., & McNally, J. (1994). The effects of aging on area 46 of the frontal cortex of the rhesus monkey. *Cerebral Cortex, 6,* 621–635. [8]

Peterson, A. C. (1987, September). Those gangly years. *Psychology Today,* pp. 28–34. [8]

Peterson, A. C. (1988). Adolescent development. *Annual Review of Psychology, 39,* 583–607. [8]

Peterson, A. C., Compas, B. E., Brooks-Gunn, J., Stemmier, M., Ey, S., & Grant, K. E. (1993). Depression in adolescence. *American Psychologist, 48,* 155–168. [12]

Peterson, I. (1993). Speech for export: Automating the translation of spoken words. *Science News, 144,* 254–255. [7]

Peterson, I. (1996). The soul of a chess machine. *Science News, 149,* 200–201. [7]

Peterson, L. R., & Peterson, M. J. (1959). Short-term retention of individual verbal items. *Journal of Experimental Psychology, 58,* 193–198. [6]

Pettigrew, T. E. (1997). Generalized intergroup contact effects on prejudice. *Personality and Social Psychology Bulletin, 23,* 175–185. [14]

Petty, R. E., Wegener, D. T., & Fabrigar, L. R. (1997). Attitudes and attitude change. *Annual Review of Psychology, 48,* 609–647. [14]

Phillips, G. P., & Over, R. (1995). Differences between heterosexual, bisexual, and lesbian women in recalled childhood experiences. *Archives of Sexual Behavior, 24,* 1–20. [9]

Phillips, K., Fulker, D. W., Carey, G., & Nagoshi, C. T. (1988). Direct marital assortment for cognitive and personality variables. *Behavioral Genetics, 18,* 347–356. [14]

Phillips, S. D., & Blustein, D. L. (1994). Readiness for career choices: Planning, exploring, and deciding. *The Career Development Quarterly, 43,* 63–75. [8]

Phillips, S. T., & Ziller, R. C. (1997). Toward a theory and measure of the nature of nonprejudice. *Journal of Personality and Social Psychology, 72,* 420–434. [14]

Piaget, J. (1963). *Psychology of intelligence.* Patterson, NJ: Littlefield, Adams. [8]

Piaget, J. (1964). *Judgment and reasoning in the child.* Patterson, NJ: Littlefield, Adams. [8]

Piaget, J. (1972). Intellectual evolution from adolescence to adulthood. *Human Development, 15,* 1–12. [8]

Piaget, J., & Inhelder, B. (1969). *The psychology of the child.* New York: Basic Books. [8]

Pich, E. M., Pagliusi, S. R., Tessari, M., Talabot-Ayer, D., van Huijsduijnen, R. H., & Chiamulera, C. (1997). Common neural substrates for the addictive properties of nicotine and cocaine. *Science, 275,* 83–86. [4]

Pigott, T. A. (1996). OCD: Where the serotonin selectivity story begins. *Journal of Clinical Psychiatry, 57*(6, Suppl.), 11–20. [12]

Pihl, R. O., Lau, M. L., & Assaad, J-M. (1997). Aggressive disposition, alcohol, and aggression. *Aggressive Behavior, 23,* 11–18. [4]

Pilcher, J. J., & Huffcutt, A. I. (1996). Effects of sleep deprivation on performance: A meta-analysis. *Sleep, 19,* 318–326. [4]

Pillemer, D. B. (1990). Clarifying the flashbulb memory concept: Comment on McCloskey, Wible, and Cohen (1988). *Journal of Experimental Psychology: General, 119,* 92–96. [6]

Pillow, D. R., Zautra, A. J., & Sandler, I. (1996). Major life events and minor stressors: Identifying mediational links in the stress process. *Journal of Personality and Social Psychology, 70,* 381–394. [11]

Pinel, J. P. J. (1997). *Biopsychology* (3rd ed.). Boston: Allyn & Bacon. [2]

Pinker, S. (1994). *The language instinct: How the mind creates language.* New York: Morrow. [7]

Pittenger, D. J. (1993). The utility of the Myers-Briggs Type Indicator. *Review of Educational Research, 63,* 467–488. [10]

Pitz, G. F., & Sachs, N. J. (1984). Judgment and decision: Theory and application. *Annual Review of Psychology, 35,* 139–163. [7]

Plomin, R. (1989). Environment and genes: Determinants of behavior. *American Psychologist, 44,* 105–111. [7, 10]

Plomin, R., & Daniels, D. (1987). Why are children in the same family so different from one another? *Behavioral and Brain Sciences, 10,* 1–60. [10]

Plomin, R., DeFries, J. C., & Fulker, D. W. (1988). *Nature and nurture during infancy and early childhood.* New York: Cambridge University Press. [7]

Plomin, R., DeFries, J. C., McClearn, G. E., & Rutter, M. (1997). *Behavioral genetics* (3rd ed.). New York: Freeman. [7]

Plomin, R., Owen, M. J., & McGuffin, P. (1994). The genetic basis of complex human behaviors. *Science, 264,* 1733–1739. [10]

Plomin, R., & Rende, R. (1991). Human behavioral genetics. *Annual Review of Psychology, 42,* 161–190. [7, 10]

Plous, S. (1996). Attitudes toward the use of animals in psychological research and education: Results from a national survey of psychologists. *American Psychologist, 51,* 1167–1180. [1]

Plummer, D. L., & Slane S. (1996). Patterns of coping in racially stressful situations. *Journal of Black Psychology, 22,* 302–315. [11]

Pollack, M. H., & Otto, M. W. (1997). Long-term course and outcome of panic disorder. *Journal of Clinical Psychiatry, 58*(2, Suppl.), 57–60. [13]

Pollack, R. H. (1970). Müller-Lyer illusion: Effect of age, lightness, contrast and hue. *Science, 179,* 93–94. [3]

Pomerleau, O. F., & Pomerleau, C. S. (1989). A biobehavioral perspective on smoking. In T. Ney & A. Gale (Eds.), *Smoking and human behavior* (pp. 69–93). New York: Wiley. [11]

Pontieri, F. C., Tanda, G., Orzi, F., & Di Chiara, G. (1996). Effects of nicotine on the nucleus accumbens and similarity to those of addictive drugs. *Nature, 382,* 255–257. [2, 4]

Porte, H. S., & Hobson, J. A. (1996). Physical motion in dreams: One measure of three theories. *Sleep, 105,* 3329–3335. [4]

Porter, F. L., Porges, S. W., & Marshall, R. E. (1988). Newborn pain cries and vagal tone: Parallel changes in response to circumcision. *Child Development, 59,* 495–505. [8]

Posner, M. I. (1996, September). Attention and psychopathology. *Harvard Mental Health Letter, 13*(3), 5–6. [2]

Postman, L., & Phillips, L. W. (1965). Short-term temporal changes in free recall. *Quarterly Journal of Experimental Psychology, 17,* 132–138. [6]

Post-traumatic stress disorder—Part I. (1996, June). *Harvard Mental Health Letter, 12*(12), 1–4. [11]

Powell, K. E., Spain, K. G., Christenson, G. M., & Mollenkamp, M. P. (1986). The status of the 1990 objectives for physical fitness and exercise. *Public Health Reports, 101,* 15–21. [11]

Powell, L. H., Shaker, L. A., Jones, B. A., Vaccarino, L. V., Thoresen, C. E., & Pattillo, J. R. (1993). Psychosocial predictors of mortality in 83 women with premature acute myocardial infarction. *Psychosomatic Medicine, 55,* 426–433. [11]

Power, F. C., Higgins, A., & Kohlberg, L. (1989). *Lawrence Kohlberg's approach to moral education.* New York: Columbia University Press. [8]

Pratkanis, A. R., Eskenazi, J., & Greenwald, A. G. (1994). What you expect is what you believe (but not necessarily what you get): A test of the effectiveness of subliminal self-help audiotapes. *Basic and Applied Social Psychology, 15,* 251–276. [3]

Premack, D. (1971). Language in chimpanzees. *Science, 172,* 808–822. [7]

Premack, D., & Premack, A. J. (1983). *The mind of an ape.* New York: Norton. [7]

Prescott, C. A., & Kendler, K. S. (1999a). Age at first drink and risk for alcoholism: A noncausal association. *Alcoholism: Clinical and Experimental Research, 23,* 101–107. [11]

Prescott, C. A., & Kendler, K. S. (1999b). Genetic and environmental contributions to alcohol abuse and dependence in a population-based sample of male twins. *American Journal of Psychiatry, 156,* 34–40. [10]

Pribor, E. F., & Dinwiddie, S. H. (1992). Psychiatric correlates of incest in childhood. *American Journal of Psychiatry, 148,* 52–56. [12]

Price, R. A., Stunkard, A. J., Ness, R., Wadden, T., Heshka, S., Kanders, B., & Cormillot, A. (1990). Childhood onset (age less than 10) obesity has a high familial risk. *International Journal of Obesity, 14,* 185–195. [9]

Prien, R. F., & Kocsis, J. H. (1995). Long-term treatment of mood disorders. In F. E. Bloom & D. J. Kupfer (Eds.), *Psychopharmacology: The fourth generation of progress* (pp. 1067–1079). New York: Raven. [13]

Priest, R. F., & Sawyer, J. (1967). Proximity and peership: Bases of balance in interpersonal attraction. *American Journal of Sociology, 72,* 633–649. [14]

Prinz, P. N., Vitiello, M. V., Raskind, M. A., & Thorpy, M. J. (1990). Geriatrics: Sleep disorders and aging. *New England Journal of Medicine, 323,* 520–526. [4]

Provine, R. R. (1996, January/February). Laughter. *American Scientist, 84,* 38–45. [9]

Provins, K. A. (1997). Handedness and speech: A critical reappraisal of the role of genetic and environmental factors in the cerebral lateralization of function. *Psychological Review, 104,* 544–571. [2]

Psychologists' pigeons score 90 pct. picking Picasso. (1995, May 7). *St. Louis Post-Dispatch,* p. 2A. [5]

Public Health Service. (1991). *Healthy people 2000: National health promotion and disease prevention objectives* [Summary]. (DHHS Publication No. PHS 91–50213). Washington, DC: U.S. Department of Health and Human Services. [11]

Putnam, F. W. (1989). *Diagnosis and treatment of multiple personality disorder.* New York: Guilford Press. [12]

Putnam, F. W. (1992). Altered states: Peeling away the layers of a multiple personality. *The Sciences, 32,* 30–36. [12]

Putnam, F. W., Guroff, J. J., Silberman, E. K., Barban, L., & Post, R. M. (1986). The clinical phenomenology of multiple personality disorder: Review of 100 recent cases. *Journal of Clinical Psychiatry, 47,* 285–293. [12]

Putnam, F. W., & Loewenstein, R. J. (1993). Treatment of multiple personality disorder: A survey of current practices. *American Journal of Psychiatry, 150,* 1048–1052. [12]

Rachman, S. (1977). The conditioning theory of fear acquisition: A critical examination. *Behavior Research and Therapy, 15,* 375–387. [12]

Rachman, S. J., & Wilson, G. T. (1980). *The effects of psychological therapy* (2nd ed.). New York: Pergamon. [13]

Rahe, R. J., Meyer, M., Smith, M., Kjaer, G., & Holmes, T. H. (1964). Social stress and illness onset. *Journal of Psychosomatic Research, 8,* 35–44. [11]

Raichle, M. E. (1994). Visualizing the mind. *Scientific American, 270,* 58–64. [2]

Raine, A. (1996). Autonomic nervous system factors underlying disinhibited, antisocial, and violent behavior: Biosocial perspectives and treatment implications. *Annals of the New York Academy of Sciences, 794,* 46–59. [14]

Raloff, J. (1994). The great nicotine debate: Are cigarette recipes 'cooked' to keep smokers hooked? *Science News, 145,* 314–317. [4, 11]

Raloff, J. (1996). Eyes possess their own biological clocks. *Science News, 149,* 245. [4]

Ralph, M. R. (1989, November/December). The rhythm maker: Pinpointing the master clock in mammals. *The Sciences, 29,* 40–45. [4]

Ramsay, D. S., & Woods, S. C. (1997). Biological consequences of drug administration: Implications for acute and chronic tolerance. *Psychological Review, 104,* 170–193. [4]

Randi, J. (1980). *Flim-flam: The truth about unicorns, parapsychology, and other delusions.* New York: Lippincott & Crowell. [3]

Rao, S. C., Rainer, G., & Miller, E. K. (1997). Integration of what and where in the primate prefrontal cortex. *Science, 276,* 821–824. [6]

Rapoport, D. M. (1996). Methods to stabilize the upper airway using positive pressure. *Sleep, 19,* S123–S130. [4]

Rapoport, J. L. (1989). The biology of obsessions and compulsions. *Scientific American, 260,* 83–89. [13]

Rasmussen, S. A., & Eisen, J. L. (1990). *Epidemiology* of obsessive compulsive disorder. *Journal of Clinical Psychiatry, 51*(2, Suppl.), 10–13. [12]

Rasmussen, S. A., & Eisen, J. L. (1992). The epidemiology and differential diagnosis of obsessive compulsive disorder. *Journal of Clinical Psychiatry, 53*(4, Suppl.), 4–10. [12]

Rasmussen, S. A., Eisen, J. L., & Pato, M. T. (1993). Current issues in the pharmacologic management of obsessive compulsive disorder. *Journal of Clinical Psychiatry, 54*(6, Suppl.), 4–9. [13]

Rate of births for teen-agers drops again. (1995, September 22). *The New York Times*, p. A18. [8]

Rauch, S. L., Jenike, M. A., Alpert, N. M., Baer, L., Breiter, H. C. R., Savage, C. R., & Fischman, A. J. (1994). Regional cerebral blood flow measured during symptom provocation in obsessive-compulsive disorder using oxygen 15–labeled carbon dioxide and positron emission tomography. *Archives of General Psychiatry, 51*, 62–70. [12]

Reiman, E. M., Fusselman, M. J., Fox, P. T., & Raichle, M. E. (1989). Neuroanatomical correlates of anticipatory anxiety. *Science, 243*, 1071–1074. [12]

Reis, H. T., Wilson, I. M., Monestere, C., Bernstein, S., Clark, K., Seidl, E., Franco, M., Gioioso, E., Freeman, L., & Radoane, K. (1990). What is smiling is beautiful and good. *European Journal of Social Psychology, 20*, 259–267. [14]

Reite, M., Buysse, D., Reynolds, C., & Mendelson, W. (1995). The use of polysomnography in the evaluation of insomnia. *Sleep, 18*, 58–70. [4]

Renzetti, C. M., & Curran, D. J. (1992). *Women, men, and society.* Boston: Allyn & Bacon. [14]

Rescorla, R. A. (1967). Pavlovian conditioning and its proper control procedures. *Psychological Review, 74*, 71–80. [5]

Rescorla, R. A. (1968). Probability of shock in the presence and absence of CS in fear conditioning. *Journal of Comparative and Physiological Psychology, 66*, 1–5. [5]

Rescorla, R. A. (1988). Pavlovian conditioning: It's not what you think it is. *American Psychologist, 43*, 151–160. [5]

Rescorla, R. A., & Wagner, A. R. (1972). A theory of Pavlovian conditioning: Variations in the effectiveness of reinforcement and nonreinforcement. In A. Black & W. F. Prokasy (Eds.), *Classical conditioning: II. Current research and theory.* New York: Appleton. [5]

Restak, R. (1988). *The mind.* Toronto: Bantam. [7]

Restak, R. (1993, September/October). Brain by design. *The Sciences*, pp. 27–33. [4]

Reyner, A., & Horne, J. A. (1995). Gender- and age-related differences in sleep determined by home-recorded sleep logs and actimetry from 400 adults. *Sleep, 18*, 127–134. [4]

Reyner, L. A., & Horne, J. A. (1998). Evaluation of 'in-car' countermeasures to sleepiness: Cold air and radio. *Sleep, 21*, 46–50. [4]

Rhodes, N., & Wood, W. (1992). Self-esteem and intelligence affect influenceability: The mediating role of message reception. *Psychological Bulletin, 111*, 156–171. [14]

Rice, F. P. (1992). *Intimate relationships, marriages, and families.* Mountain View, CA: Mayfield. [8]

Rice, M. L. (1989). Children's language acquisition. *American Psychologist, 44*, 149–156. [8]

Rice, P. L. (1987). *Stress and health: Principles and practice for coping and wellness.* Monterey, CA: Brooks/Cole. [11]

Rickels, K., Downing, R., Schweizer, E., & Hassman, H. (1993). Antidepressants for the treatment of generalized anxiety disorder. *Archives of General Psychiatry, 50*, 884–895. [13]

Riedel, G. (1996). Function of metabotropic glutamate receptors in learning and memory. *Trends in Neurosciences, 19*, 219–224. [2, 6]

Riordan, C. A., & Tedeschi, J. T. (1983). Attraction in aversive environments: Some evidence for classical conditioning and negative reinforcement. *Journal of Personality and Social Psychology, 44*, 683–692. [14]

Ritts, V., Patterson, M. L., & Tubbs, M. E. (1992). Expectations, impressions, and judgments of physically attractive students: A review. *Review of Educational Research, 62*, 413–426. [14]

Robberson, M. R., & Rogers, R. W. (1988). Beyond fear appeals: Negative and positive persuasive appeals to health and self-esteem. *Journal of Applied Social Psychology, 18*, 277–287. [14]

Roberts, P., & Moseley, B. (1996, May/June). Fathers' time. *Psychology Today, 29*, 48–55, 81. [8]

Roberts, S. B., & Greenberg, A. S. (1996). The new obesity genes. *Nutrition Reviews, 54*, 41–49. [9]

Robins, C. J., & Hayes, A. M. (1993). An appraisal of cognitive therapy. *Journal of Consulting and Clinical Psychology, 61*, 205–214. [13]

Robins, R. W., Gosling, S. D., & Craik, K. H. (1999). An empirical analysis of trends in psychology. *American Psychologist, 54*, 117–128. [1]

Roche, A. F., & Davila, G. H. (1972). Late adolescent growth in stature. *Pediatrics, 50*, 874–880. [8]

Rock, I., & Palmer, S. (1990). The legacy of Gestalt psychology. *Scientific American, 263*, 84–90. [5]

Rodin, J. (1985). Insulin levels, hunger, and food intake: An example of feedback loops in body weight regulation. *Health Psychology, 4*, 1–24. [9]

Rodin, J., & Ickovics, J. R. (1990). Women's health: Review and research agenda as we approach the 21st century. *American Psychologist, 45*, 1018–1034. [11]

Rodin, J., & Salovey, P. (1989). Health psychology. *Annual Review of Psychology, 40*, 533–579. [11]

Rodin, J., Slochower, J., & Fleming, B. (1977). The effects of degree of obesity, age of onset, and energy deficit on external responsiveness. *Journal of Comparative and Physiological Psychology, 91*, 586–597. [9]

Rodin, J., Wack, J., Ferrannini, E., & DeFronzo, R. A. (1985). Effect of insulin and glucose on feeding behavior. *Metabolism, 34*, 826–831. [9]

Rodin, J., & Wing, R. R. (1988). Behavioral factors in obesity. *Diabetes/Metabolism Reviews, 4*, 701–725. [9]

Roediger, H. L., III. (1980). The effectiveness of four mnemonics in ordering recall. *Journal of Experimental Psychology: Human Learning and Memory, 6*, 558–567. [6]

Roediger, H. L., III. (1991). They read an article? A commentary on the everyday memory controversy. *American Psychologist, 46*, 37–40. [6]

Roediger, H. L., III, & McDermott, K. B. (1995). Creating false memories: Remembering words not presented in lists. *Journal of Experimental Psychology: Learning, Memory, and Cognition, 21*, 803–814. [6]

Roehrich, L., & Kinder, B. N. (1991). Alcohol expectancies and male sexuality: Review and implications for sex therapy. *Journal of Sex and Marital Therapy, 17*, 45–54. [4]

Roesch, S. C., & Amirkhan, J. H. (1997). Boundary condition for self-serving attributions: Another look at the sports pages. *Journal of Applied Social Psychology, 27*, 245–261. [14]

Rogers, C. R. (1951). *Client-centered therapy: Its current practice, implications, and theory.* Boston: Houghton Mifflin. [10, 13]

Rogers, C. R. (1959). A theory of therapy, personality, and interpersonal relationships, as developed in the client-centered framework. In S. Koch (Ed.), *Psychology: A study of a science, Vol. III. Formulations of the person and the social context* (pp. 184–256). New York: McGraw-Hill. [13]

Rogers, C. R. (1961). *On becoming a person: A therapist's view of psychotherapy.* Boston: Houghton Mifflin. [10, 12]

Rogers, C. R. (1977). The case of Mary Jane Tilden. In S. J. Morse & R. I. Watson, Jr. (Eds.), *Psychotherapies: A comparative casebook* (pp. 197–222). New York: Holt, Rinehart & Winston. [13]

Rogers, C. R. (1981). Notes on Rollo May. *Perspectives, 2*(1), 16. [10]

Rogoff, B., & Mistry, J. (1985). Memory development in cultural context. In M. Pressley & C. Brainerd (Eds.), *The cognitive side of memory development.* New York: Springer-Verlag. [6]

Roorda, A., & Williams, D. R. (1999). The arrangement of the three cone classes in the living human eye. *Nature, 397*, 520–521. [3]

Rosch, E. H. (1973). Natural categories. *Cognitive Psychology, 4*, 328–350. [7]

Rosch, E. H. (1978). Principles of categorization. In E. H. Rosch & B. Lloyd (Eds.), *Cognition and categorization.* Hillsdale, NJ: Erlbaum. [7]

Rosch, E. H. (1987). Linguistic relativity. *Et Cetera, 44*, 254–279. [7]

Rose, R. J., Koskenvuo, M., Kaprio, J., Sarna, S., & Langinvainio, H. (1988). Shared genes, shared experiences, and similarity of personality: Data from 14,288 adult Finnish co-twins. *Journal of Personality and Social Psychology, 54*, 161–171. [10]

Rosekind, M. R. (1992). The epidemiology and occurrence of insomnia. *Journal of Clinical Psychiatry, 53*(6, Suppl.), 4–6. [4]

Rosen, R. C., Rosekind, M., Rosevear, C., Cole, W. E., & Dement, W. C. (1993). Physician education in sleep and sleep disorders: A national survey of U.S. medical schools. *Sleep, 16*, 249–254. [4]

Rosenbaum, J. F., Biederman, J., Pollock, R. A., & Hirshfeld, D. R. (1994). The etiology of social phobia. *Journal of Clinical Psychiatry, 55*(6, Suppl.), 10–16. [12]

Rosenbaum, J. F., Pollack, M. H., & Pollock, R. A. (1996). Clinical issues in the long-term treatment of panic disorder. *Journal of Clinical Psychiatry, 57*(10, Suppl.), 44–48 [12]

Rosengren, A., Tibblin, G., & Wilhelmsen, L. (1991). Self-perceived psychological stress and incidence of coronary artery disease in middle-aged men. *American Journal of Cardiology, 68*, 1171–1175. [11]

Rosenhan, D. L. (1973). On being sane in insane places. *Science, 179*, 250–258. [3]

Rosenheck, R., Cramer, J., Xu, W., et al. (1997). A comparison of clozapine and haloperidol in hospitalized patients with refractory schizophrenia. *New England Journal of Medicine, 337*, 809–815. [13]

Rosenthal, A. M. (1964). *Thirty-eight witnesses*. New York: McGraw-Hill. [14]

Rosenthal, N. E., Carpenter, C. J., James, S. P., Parry, B. L., Rogers, S. L. B., & Wehr, T. A.. (1986). Seasonal affective disorder in children and adolescents. *American Journal of Psychiatry, 143*, 356–358. [12]

Rosenthal, N. E., Sack, D. A., Carpenter, C. J., et al. (1985). Anti-depressant effects of light in seasonal affective disorder. *American Journal of Psychiatry, 142*, 163–170. [12]

Ross, C. A., Anderson, G., Fleisher, W. P., & Norton, G. R. (1991). The frequency of multiple personality disorder among psychiatric inpatients. *American Journal of Psychiatry, 148*, 1717–1720. [12]

Ross, C. A., Norton, G. R., & Wozney, K. (1989). Multiple personality disorder: An analysis of 236 cases. *Canadian Journal of Psychiatry, 34*, 413–418. [12]

Ross, J., & Lawrence, K. A. (1968). Some observations on memory artifice. *Psychonomic Science, 13*, 107–108. [6]

Ross, L. (1977). The intuitive psychologist and his shortcomings: Distortions in the attribution process. In L. Berkowitz (Ed.), *Advances in experimental social psychology* (Vol. 10). New York: Academic Press. [14]

Roth, T. (1996a). Management of insomniac patients. *Sleep, 19*, S52–S53. [4]

Roth, T. (1996b). Social and economic consequences of sleep disorders. *Sleep, 19*, S46–S47. [4]

Roth, W. T., Margraf, J., Ehlers, A., Taylor, B., Maddock, R. J., Davies, S., & Argras, W. S. (1992). Stress test reactivity in panic disorder. *Archives of General Psychiatry, 49*, 301–310. [12]

Rothbaum, B. O., Hodges, L., Watson, B. A., Kessler, G. D., & Opdyke, D. (1996). Virtual reality exposure therapy in the treatment of fear of flying: a case report. *Behaviour Research and Therapy, 34*, 477–481. [13]

Rotter, J. B. (1966). Generalized expectancies for internal versus external control of reinforcement. *Psychological Monographs, 80*(1, Whole No. 609). [10]

Rotter, J. B. (1971, June). External control and internal control. *Psychology Today*, pp. 37–42, 58–59. [10]

Rotter, J. B. (1990). Internal versus external control of reinforcement: A case history of a variable. *American Psychologist, 45*, 489–493. [10]

Rotton, J., Frey, J., Barry, T., Milligan, M., & Fitzpatrick, M. (1979). The air pollution experience and physical aggression. *Journal of Applied Social Psychology, 9*, 397–412. [14]

Rowe, D. (1994). The limits of family influence: Genes, experience, and behavior. New York: Guilford. [10]

Rozin, P., & Zellner, D. (1985). The role of Pavlovian conditioning in the acquisition of food likes and dislikes. *Annals of the New York Academy of Sciences, 443*, 189–202. [5]

Rudd, M. D., Joiner, T., & Rajab, M. H. (1996). Relationships among suicide ideators, attempters, and multiple attempters in a young-adult sample. *Journal of Abnormal Psychology, 105*, 541–550. [12]

Ruggero, M. A. (1992). Responses to sound of the basilar membrane of the mammalian cochlea. *Current Opinion in Neurobiology, 2*, 449–456. [3]

Ruggiero, K. M., & Taylor, D. M. (1997). Why minority group members perceive or do not perceive the discrimination that confronts them: The role of self-esteem and perceived control. *Journal of Personality and Social Psychology, 72*, 373–389. [14]

Rumbaugh, D. M. (1977). *Language learning by a chimpanzee: The Lana project*. New York: Academic Press. [7]

Rushton, J. P., Fulker, D. W., Neale, M. C., Nias, D. K. B., & Eysenck, H. J. (1986). Altruism and aggression: The heritability of individual differences. *Journal of Personality and Social Psychology, 50*, 1192–1198. [10, 14]

Russell, J. A. (1994). Is there universal recognition of emotion from facial expression? A review of the cross-cultural studies. *Psychological Bulletin, 115*, 102–141. [9]

Russell, T. G., Rowe, W., & Smouse, A. D. (1991). Subliminal self-help tapes and academic achievement: An evaluation. *Journal of Counseling and Development, 69*, 359–362. [3]

Rutter, M. L. (1997). Nature-nuture integration: The example of antisocial behavior. *American Psychologist, 52*, 390–398. [12]

Ryan, M. (1997, July 6). She helps others to fight their way back. *Parade Magazine*, p. 10. [2]

Sackeim, H. A. (1985, June). The case for ECT. *Psychology Today*, pp. 36–40. [13]

Sackeim, H. A. (1992). The cognitive effects of electroconvulsive therapy. In W. H. Moos, E. R. Gamzu, & L. J. Thal (Eds.), *Cognitive disorders: Pathophysiology and treatment*. New York: Marcel Dekker. [13]

Sackeim, H. A., Luber, B., Katzman, G. P., Moeller, J. R., Prudic, J., Devanand, D. P., & Nobler, M. S. (1996). The effects of electroconvulsive therapy on quantitative electroencephalograms. *Archives of General Psychiatry, 53*, 814–824. [13]

Sackeim, H. A., Prudic, J., Devanand, D. P., Kiersky, J. E., Fitzsimmons, L., Moody, B. J., McElhiney, M. C., Coleman, E. A., & Settembrino, J. M. (1993). Effects of stimulus intensity and electrode placement on the efficacy and cognitive effects of electroconvulsive therapy. *New England Journal of Medicine, 328*, 839–846. [13]

Salgado, J. F. (1997). The five factor model of personality and job performance in the European community. *Journal of Applied Psychology, 82*, 30–43. [10]

Salovey, P., & Mayer, J. D. (1990). Emotional intelligence. *Imagination, cognition, and personality, 9*, 185–211. [7]

Salthouse, T. A. (1996). The processing-speed theory of adult age differences in cognition. *Psychological Review, 103*, 403–428. [8]

Salzinger, S., Feldman, R. S., Hammer, M., & Rosario, M. (1993). The effects of physical abuse on children's social relationships. *Child Development, 64*, 169–187. [8]

Sanbonmatsu, D. M., & Fazio, R. H. (1990). The role of attitudes in memory-based decision making. *Journal of Personality and Social Psychology, 59*, 614–622. [14]

Sandfur, G. D., Rindfuss, R. R., & Cohen, B. (Eds.). (1996). *American Indian demography and public health*. Washington, DC: National Academy Press. [11]

Sandou, F., Amara, D. A., Dierich, A., LeMeur, M., Ramboz, S., Segu, L., Buhot, M-C., & Hen, R. (1994). Enhanced aggressive behavior in mice lacking 5-HT1B receptor. *Science, 265*, 1875–1878. [2]

Sanna, L. J., & Shotland, R. L. (1990). Valence of anticipated evaluation and social facilitation. *Journal of Experimental Social Psychology, 26*, 82–92. [14]

Sano, M., Ernesto, C., Thomas, R. G., Kauber, M. R., Schafer, K., Grundman, M., Woodbury, P., Growdon, J., Cotman, C. W., Pfeiffer, E., Schneider, L. S., & Thal, L. J. (1997). A controlled trial of selegiline, alpha-tocopherol, or both as treatment for Alzheimer's disease. *New England Journal of Medicine, 336*, 1216–1222. [8]

Sapolsky, R. M. (1994). *Why zebras don't get ulcers: A guide to stress, stress-related diseases, and coping.* San Francisco: W. H. Freeman. [11]

Şar, V., Yargic, L. I., & Tutkun, H. (1996). Structured interview data on 35 cases of dissociative identity disorder in Turkey. *American Journal of Psychiatry, 153,* 1329–1333. [12]

Sass, H., Soyha, M., Mann, K., & Zieglgänsberger, W. (1996). Relapse prevention by acamprosate: Results from a placebo-controlled study on alcohol dependence. *Archives of General Psychiatry, 53,* 673–680. [11]

Satcher, D. (1999). Global health at the crossroads: Surgeon General's report on the 50th World Health Assembly. *Journal of the American Medical Association, 281,* 942–943.

Sauter, S. L., Murphy, L. R., & Hurrel, J. J., Jr. (1990). Prevention of work-related psychological disorders: A national strategy proposed by the National Institute for Occupational Safety and Health (NIOSH). *American Psychologist, 45,* 1146–1158. [11]

Savage-Rumbaugh, E. S. (1986). Ape language. New York: Columbia University Press. [7]

Savage-Rumbaugh, E. S. (1990). Language acquisition in a nonhuman species: Implications for the innateness debate. *Developmental Psychology, 26,* 599–620. [7]

Savage-Rumbaugh, E. S. (1993). Language learnability in man, ape, and dolphin. In H. L. Roitblat, L. M. Herman, & P. E. Nachtigall (Eds.), *Language and communication: Comparative perspectives. Comparative cognition and neuroscience* (pp. 457–484). Hillsdale, NJ: Erlbaum. [7]

Savage-Rumbaugh, E. S., Sevcik, R. A., Brakke, K. E., & Rumbaugh, D. M. (1992). Symbols: Their communicative use, communication, and combination by bonobos (Pan paniscus). In L. P. Lipsitt & C. Rovee-Collier (Eds.). *Advances in infancy research* (Vol. 7, pp. 221–278). Norwood, NJ: Ablex. [7]

Scarr, S., Pakstis, A., Katz, S., & Barker, W. (1977). Absence of a relationship between degree of White ancestry and intellectual skills within a Black population. *Human Genetics, 39,* 69–86. [7]

Scarr, S., Webber, P. L., Weinberg, R. A., & Wittig, M. A. (1981). Personality resemblance among adolescents and their parents in biologically related and adoptive families. *Journal of Personality and Social Psychology, 40,* 885–898. [10]

Schachter, S., & Singer, J. E. (1962). Cognitive, social, and physiological determinants of emotional state. *Psychological Review, 69,* 379–399. [9]

Schachter, D. L., Norman, K. A., & Koutstaal, W. (1998). The cognitive neuroscience of constructive memory. *Annual Review of Psychology, 49,* 289–318. [6]

Schaie, K. W. (1990). Late life potential and cohort differences in mental abilities. In M. Perlmutter (Ed.), *Late life potential* (pp. 43–61). Washington, DC: Gerontological Society. [8]

Schaie, K. W. (1993). Ageist language in psychological research. *American Psychologist, 48,* 49–51. [1]

Schaie, K. W. (1994). The course of adult intellectual development. *American Psychologist, 49,* 304–313. [8]

Schaie, K. W. (1995). *Intellectual development in adulthood: The Seattle Longitudinal Study.* New York: Cambridge University Press. [8]

Schaie, K. W., & Willis, S. L. (1996). *Adult development and aging* (4th ed.). New York: HarperCollins. [8]

Scheier, M. F., & Carver, C. S. (1985). Optimism, coping, and health: Assessment and implications of generalized outcome expectancies. *Health Psychology, 4,* 219–247. [11]

Scheier, M. F., & Carver, C. S. (1992). Effects of optimism on psychological and physical well-being: Theoretical overview and empirical update. *Cognitive Research and Therapy, 16,* 201–228. [11]

Scheier, M. F., Matthews, K. A., Owens, J., Magovern, G. J., Sr., Lefebvre, R. C., Abbott, R. A., & Carver, C. S. (1989). Dispositional optimism and recovery from coronary artery bypass surgery: The beneficial effects on physical and psychological well-being. *Journal of Personality and Social Psychology, 57,* 1024–1040. [11]

Scheier, M. F., Weintraub, J. K., & Carver, C. S. (1986). Coping with stress: Divergent strategies of optimists and pessimists. *Journal of Personality and Social Psychology, 51,* 1257–1264. [11]

Schenck, C. H., & Mahowald, M. W. (1995). A polysomnographically documented case of adult somnambulism with long-distance automobile driving and frequent nocturnal violence: Parasomnia with continuing danger as a noninsane automatism? *Sleep, 18,* 765–772. [4]

Scherer, K. R., Wallbott, H. G., & Summerfield, A. B. (1986). *Experiencing emotion: A cross-cultural study.* Cambridge, England: Cambridge University Press. [9]

Schiff, M., & Lewontin, R. (1986). *Education and class: The irrelevance of IQ genetic studies.* Oxford, England: Clarendon. [7]

Schildkraut, J. (1970). *Neuropsychopharmacology of the affective disorders.* Boston: Little, Brown. [12]

Schildkraut, J. J., Hirshfeld, A. J., & Murphy, J. M. (1994). Mind and mood in modern art, II: Depressive disorders, spirituality, and early deaths in the abstract expressionist artists of the New York school. *American Journal of Psychiatry, 151,* 482–488. [12]

Schindler, L. W. (1988). *Understanding the immune system* (NIH Publication No. 88–529). Washington, DC: Department of Health and Human Services. [11]

Schlaug, G., Jäncke, L., Huang, Y., & Steinmetz, H. (1995). In vivo evidence of structural brain asymmetry in musicians. *Science, 267,* 699–700. [2]

Schmidt, G., & Weiner, B. (1988). An attributional-affect-action theory of behavior: Replications of judgments of helping. *Personality and Social Psychology Bulletin, 14,* 610–621. [14]

Schmidt, N. B., Lerew, D. R., & Trakowski, J. H. (1997). Body vigilance in panic disorder: Evaluating attention to bodily perturbations. *Journal of Consulting and Clinical Psychology, 65,* 214–220. [12]

Schmitz, A. (1991, November). How to spot front-page fallacies. *Health,* pp. 43–45. [1]

Schofield, J. W., & Francis, W. D. (1982). An observational study of peer interaction in racially mixed "accelerated" classrooms. *Journal of Educational Psychology, 74,* 722–732. [8]

Scholl, T. O., Heidiger, M. L., & Belsky, D. H. (1996). Prenatal care and maternal health during adolescent pregnancy: A review and meta-analysis. *Journal of Adolescent Health, 15,* 444–456. [8]

Schooler, N. R., Keith, S. J., Severe, J. B., Matthews, S. M., Bellack, A. S., Glick, I. D., Hargreaves, W. A., Kane, J. M., Ninan, P. T., Frances, A., Jacobs, M., Lieberman, J. A., Mance R., Simpson, G. M., & Woerner, M. G. (1997). Relapse and rehospitalization during maintenance treatment of schizophrenia: The effects of dose reduction and family treatment. *Archives of General Psychiatry, 54,* 453–463. [13]

Schou, M. (1997). Forty years of lithium treatment. *Archives of General Psychiatry, 54,* 9–13. [13]

Schreiber, F. R. (1973). Sybil. Chicago: Henry Regnery. [12]

Schreurs, B. G. (1989). Classical conditioning of model systems: A behavioral review. *Psychobiology, 17,* 145–155. [5]

Schrijvers, C. T. M., Stronks, K., van de Mheen, D., & Mackenbach, J. P. (1999). Explaining educational differences in mortality: The role of behavioral and material factors. *American Journal of Public Health, 89,* 535–540. [11]

Schuckit, M. A., Tipp, J. E., Bergman, M., Reich, W., Hesselbrock, V. M., & Smith, T. L. (1997). Comparison of induced and independent major depressive disorders in 2,945 alcoholics. *American Journal of Psychiatry, 154,* 948–957. [11]

Schulz, R., & Heckhausen, J. (1996). A life span model of successful aging. *American Psychologist, 51,* 702–714. [8]

Schuman, E. M., & Madison, D. V. (1994). Locally distributed synaptic potentiation in the hippocampus. *Science, 263,* 532–536. [6]

Schwartz, G. E. (1982). Testing the biopsychosocial model: The ultimate challenge facing behavioral medicine? *Journal of Consulting and Clinical Psychology, 50,* 1040–1052. [10]

Schwartz, R. H., & Miller, N. S. (1997). MDMA (Ecstasy) and the rave: A review. *Pediatrics, 100,* 705–708. [4]

Schwarz, N. (1999). Self-reports: How the questions shape the answers. *American Psychologist, 54,* 93–105. [1]

Scott, J. (1996). Cognitive therapy of affective disorders: a review. *Journal of Affective Disorders, 37,* 1–11. [13]

Scott, S. K., Young, A. W., Calder, A. J., Hellawell, D. J., Aggleton, J. P., & Johnson, M. (1997). Impaired auditory recognition of fear and anger following bilateral amygdala lesions. *Nature, 385*, 254–257. [2]

Searles, J. S. (1988). The role of genetics in the pathogenesis of alcoholism. *Journal of Abnormal Psychology, 97*, 153–167. [11]

Sebald, H. (1989). Adolescents' peer orientation: Changes in the support system during the past three decades. *Adolescence, 24*, 936–946. [8]

Seeman, M., & Seeman, A. Z. (1992). Life strains, alienation, and drinking behavior. *Alcoholism: Clinical and Experimental Research, 16*, 199–205. [11]

Segall, M. H. (1994). A cross-cultural research contribution to unraveling the nativist/empiricist controversy. In J. Lonner & R. Malpass (Eds.), *Psychology and culture* (pp. 135–138). Boston: Allyn & Bacon. [3]

Segall, M. H., Campbell, D. T., & Herskovitz, M. J. (1966). *The influence of culture on visual perception*. Indianapolis: Bobbs-Merrill. [3]

Seidlitz, L., & Diener, E. (1993). Memory for positive versus negative life events: Theories for the differences between happy and unhappy persons. *Journal of Personality and Social Psychology, 64*, 654–664. [6]

Sejnowski, T. J. (1997). The year of the dendrite. *Science, 275*, 178–179. [2]

Seligman, M. E. P. (1970). On the generality of the laws of learning. *Psychological Review, 77*, 406–418. [5]

Seligman, M. E. P. (1972). Phobias and preparedness. In M. E. P. Seligman & J. L. Hager (Eds.), *Biological boundaries of learning*. Englewood Cliffs, NJ: Prentice Hall. [5]

Seligman, M. E. P. (1975). *Helplessness: On depression, development and death*. San Francisco: Freeman. [5]

Seligman, M. E. P. (1990). *Learned optimism: How to change your mind and your life*. New York: Simon & Schuster. [10, 11]

Seligman, M. E. P. (1991). *Learned optimism*. New York: Knopf. [5]

Seligman, M. E. P. (1995). The effectiveness of psychotherapy: The Consumer Reports Study. *American Psychologist, 50*, 965–974. [13]

Seligman, M. E. P. (1996). Science as an ally of practice. *American Psychologist, 51*, 1072–1079. [13]

Selye, H. (1956). *The stress of life*. New York: McGraw-Hill. [11]

Selye, H. (1974). *Stress without distress*. Philadelphia: Lippincott. [11]

Serdula, M. K., Collins, M. E., Williamson, D. F., Anda, R. F., Pamuk, E. P., & Byers, T. E. (1993). Weight control practices of U.S. adolescents and adults. *Annals of Internal Medicine, 119*, 667–671. [9]

Shapiro, L. (1997, April 21). Is fat that bad? *Newsweek*, pp. 58–64. [9]

Sharp, D., Cole, M., & Lave, C. (1979). Education and cognitive development: The evidence from experimental research. *Monographs of the Society for Research in Child Development, 44*(1–2, Serial No. 178). [8]

Sharp, D. M., Power, K. G., Simpson, R. J., & Swanson, V. (1996). Fluvoxamine, placebo, and cognitive behaviour therapy used alone and in combination in the treatment of panic disorder and agoraphobia. *Journal of Affective Disorders, 10*, 219–242. [13]

Shatz, M. (1983). Communication. In P. H. Mussen (Ed.), *Handbook of child psychology* (Vol. 3). New York: Wiley. [8]

Shaw, D. W., & Thoresen, C. E. (1974). Effects of modeling and desensitization in reducing dentist phobia. *Journal of Counseling Psychology, 21*, 415–420. [13]

Shaw, J. S., III. (1996). Increases in eyewitness confidence resulting from postevent questioning. *Journal of Experimental Psychology: Applied, 2*, 126–146. [6]

Shear, M. K., & Weiner, K. (1997). Psychotherapy for panic disorder. *Journal of Clinical Psychiatry, 58*(2, Suppl.), 38–43. [12]

Sheehan, D. V. (1983). *The anxiety disease*. New York: Scribner's. [12, 13]

Sheehan, D. V., & Harnett-Sheehan, K. (1996). The role of SSRIs in panic disorder. *Journal of Clinical Psychiatry, 57*(10, Suppl.), 51–58. [13]

Sheehan, D. V., & Raj, A. B. (1988). Monoamine oxidase inhibitors. In C. G. Last & M. Hersen (Eds.), *Handbook of anxiety disorders* (pp. 478–506). New York: Pergamon. [13]

Shepard, R. N., & Metzler, J. (1971). Mental rotation of three-dimensional objects. *Science, 171*, 701–703. [7]

Shepard, R. J. (1986). Exercise in coronary heart disease. *Sports Medicine, 3*, 26–49. [11]

Sher, A. E., Schechtman, K. B., & Piccirillo, J. F. (1996). The efficacy of surgical modifications of the upper airway in adults with obstructive sleep apnea syndrome. *Sleep, 19*, 156–177. [4]

Sherbourne, C. D., Wells, K. B., & Judd, L. L. (1996). Functioning and well-being of patients with panic disorder. *American Journal of Psychiatry, 153*, 213–218. [12]

Sherif, M. (1956). Experiments in group conflict. *Scientific American, 195*, 53–58. [14]

Sherif, M. (1958). Superordinate goals in the reduction of intergroup conflict. *American Journal of Sociology, 63*, 349–358. [14]

Sherif, M., & Sherif, C. W. (1967). The Robbers' Cave study. In J. F. Perez, R. C. Sprinthall, G. S. Grosser, & P. J. Anastasiou, *General psychology: Selected readings* (pp. 411–421). Princeton, NJ: D. Van Nostrand. [14]

Sherman, C. (1994, September/October). Kicking butts. *Psychology Today*, 41–45. [11]

Shimamura, A. P., Berry, J. M., Mangela, J. A., Rusting, C. L., & Jurica, P. J. (1995). Memory and cognitive abilities in university professors: Evidence for successful aging. *Psychological Science, 6*, 271–277. [8]

Shneidman, E. (1989). The Indian summer of life: A preliminary study of septuagenarians. *American Psychologist, 44*, 684–694. [7]

Shneidman, E. S. (1994). Clues to suicide, reconsidered. *Suicide and Life-Threatening Behavior, 24*, 395-397. [12]

Shoda, Y., Mischel, W., & Peake, P. K. (1990). Predicting adolescent cognitive and self-regulatory competencies from preschool delay of gratification. *Developmental Psychology, 26*, 978–986. [7]

Sia, T. L., Lord, C. G., Blessum, K. A., Ratcliff, C. D., & Lepper, M. R. (1997). Is a rose always a rose? The role of social category exemplar change in attitude stability and attitude-behavior consistency. *Journal of Personality and Social Psychology, 72*, 501–514. [14]

Siegler, R. S. (1991). *Children's thinking* (2nd ed.). Englewood Cliffs, NJ: Prentice-Hall. [8]

Siegrist, J., Peter, R., Junge, A., Cremer, P., & Seidel, D. (1990). Low status control, high effort at work and ischemic heart disease: Prospective evidence from blue-collar men. *Social Science and Medicine, 31*, 1127–1134. [11]

Silva, C. E., & Kirsch, I. (1992). Interpretive sets, expectancy, fantasy proneness, and dissociation as predictors of hypnotic response. *Journal of Personality and Social Psychology, 63*, 847–856. [4]

Simon, H. A. (1974). How big is a chunk? *Science, 183*, 482–488. [6]

Simon, H. A. (1995). The information-processing theory of mind. *American Psychologist, 50*, 507–508. [7]

Simon, H. B. (1988, June). Running and rheumatism. *Harvard Medical School Health Letter, 13*, 2–4. [11]

Simon, L., Greenberg, J., & Brehm, J. (1995). Trivialization: The forgotten mode of dissonance reduction. *Journal of Personality and Social Psychology, 68*, 247–260. [14]

Simpson, E. L. (1974). Moral development research. *Human Development, 17*, 81–106. [8]

Singer, J. L. (1975). Navigating the stream of consciousness: Research on daydreaming and related inner experiences. *American Psychologist, 30*, 727–738. [4]

Singh, D. (1995). Female health, attractiveness, and desirability for relationships: Role of breast asymmetry and waist-hip ratio. *Ethology and Sociobiology, 16*, 445–481. [14]

Sivacek, J., & Crano, W. D. (1982). Vested interest as a moderator of attitude-behavior consistency. *Journal of Personality and Social Psychology, 43*, 210–221. [14]

Skinner, B. F. (1938). *The behavior of organisms*. New York: Appleton-Century-Crofts. [5]

Skinner, B. F. (1948). *Walden Two*. New York: Macmillan. [5]

Skinner, B. F. (1953). *Science and human behavior*. New York: Macmillan. [5, 10]

Skinner, B. F. (1957). *Verbal behavior*. New York: Appleton Century. [7]

Skinner, B. F. (1971). *Beyond freedom and dignity*. New York: Knopf. [5]

Skinner, B. F. (1988). The operant side of behavior therapy. *Journal of Behavior Therapy and Experimental Psychiatry, 19*, 171–179. [5]

Slawinski, E. B., Hartel, D. M., & Kline, D. W. (1993). Self-reported hearing problems in daily life throughout adulthood. *Psychology and Aging, 8*, 552–561. [8]

Slobin, D. (1972, July). Children and language: They learn the same all around the world. *Psychology Today*, pp. 71–74, 82. [8]

Slon, S. (1997, June). Night moves. *Prevention, 49*, 106–113. [4]

Smeaton, G., Byrne, D., & Murnen, S. K. (1989). The repulsion hypothesis revisited: Similarity irrelevance or dissimilarity bias? *Journal of Personality and Social Psychology, 56*, 54–59. [14]

Smith, C. (1995). Sleep states and memory processes. *Behavioural Brain Research, 69*, 137–145. [4]

Smith, D. (1982). Trends in counseling and psychotherapy. *American Psychologist, 37*, 802–809. [13]

Smith, J. C. (1993). *Understanding stress and coping.* New York: Macmillan. [11]

Smith, K. H., & Rogers, M. (1994). Effectiveness of subliminal messages in television commercials: Two experiments. *Journal of Applied Psychology, 79*, 866–874. [3]

Smith, M. L., Glass, G. V., & Miller, T. I. (1980). *The benefits of psychotherapy.* Baltimore: Johns Hopkins University Press. [13]

Smith, P. K. (1979). The ontogeny of fear in children. In W. Sluckin (Ed.), *Fears in animals and man* (pp. 164–168). London: Von Nostrand Reinhold. [8]

Smith, S. M. (1979). Remembering in and out of context. *Journal of Experimental Psychology: Human Learning and Memory, 5*, 460–471. [6]

Smith, S. M., Glenberg, A., & Bjork, R. A. (1978). Environmental context and human memory. *Memory & Cognition, 6*, 342–353. [6]

Snarey, J. R. (1985). Cross-cultural universality of social-moral development: A critical review of Kohlbergian research. *Psychological Bulletin, 97*, 202–232. [8]

Snarey, J. R. (1995). In communitarian voice: The sociological expansion of Kohlbergian theory, research, and practice. In W. M. Kurtines & J. L. Gerwirtz (Eds.), *Moral development: An introduction* (pp. 109–134). Boston: Allyn & Bacon. [8]

Snow, C. E. (1993). Bilingualism and second language acquisition. In J. B. Gleason & N. B. Ratner (Eds.), *Psycholinguistics*. Fort Worth, TX: Harcourt. [7]

Snyder, F. (1971). *Psychophysiology* of human sleep. *Clinical Neurosurgery, 18*, 503–536. [4]

Sobin, C., & Sackeim, H. A. (1997). Psychomotor symptoms of depression. *American Journal of Psychiatry, 154*, 4–17. [12]

Söderfeldt, B., Rönnberg, J., & Risberg, J. (1994). Regional cerebral blood flow in sign language users. *Brain and Language, 46*, 59–68. [2]

Solomon, P. R., Blanchard, S., Levine, E., Velazquez, E., & Groccia-Ellison, M-E. (1991). Attenuation of age-related condition deficits in humans by extension of the interstimulus interval. *Psychology and Aging, 6*, 36–42. [5]

Sonenstein, F. L., Pleck, J. H., & Ku, L. C. (1991) Levels of sexual activity among adolescent males in the United States. *Family Planning Perspectives, 23*, 162–167. [8]

Spangler, D. L., Simons, A. D., Monroe, S. M., & Thase, M. E. (1996). Gender differences in cognitive diathesis-stress domain match: Implications for differential pathways to depression. *Journal of Abnormal Psychology, 105*, 653–657. [12]

Spanos, N. P. (1986). Hypnotic behavior: A social-psychological interpretation of amnesia, analgesia, and "trance logic." *Behavioral and Brain Sciences, 9*, 499–502. [4]

Spanos, N. P. (1991). A sociocognitive approach to hypnosis. In S. J. Lynn & J. W. Rhue (Eds.), *Theories of hypnosis: Current models and perspectives* (pp. 324–361). New York: Guilford. [4]

Spanos, N. P. (1994). Multiple identity enactments and multiple personality disorder: A sociocognitive perspective. *Psychological Bulletin, 116*, 143–165. [4, 12]

Spearman, C. (1927). *The abilities of man*. New York: Macmillan. [7]

Sperling, G. (1960). The information available in brief visual presentations. *Psychological Monographs: General and Applied, 74*, Whole No. 498, 1–29. [6]

Sperry, R. W. (1964). The great cerebral commissure. *Scientific American, 210*, 42–52. [2]

Sperry, R. W. (1968). Hemisphere deconnection and unity in conscious experience. *American Psychologist, 23*, 723–733. [2]

Spetch, M. L., Wilkie, D. M., & Pinel, J. P. J. (1981). Backward conditioning: A reevaluation of the empirical evidence. *Psychological Bulletin, 89*, 163–175. [5]

Spitzer, R. L., Gibbon, M., Skodol, A. E., Williams, J. B. W., & First, M. B. (1989). *DSM-III-R casebook.* Washington, DC: American Psychiatric Press. [12]

Spooner, A., & Kellogg, W. N. (1947). The backward conditionig curve. *American Journal of Psychology, 60*, 311–324.

Sprecher, S., & Regan, P. C. (1996). College virgins: How men and women perceive their sexual status. *Journal of Sex Research, 33*, 3–15. [9]

Squire, L. R., Knowlton, B., & Musen, G. (1993). The structure and organization of memory. *Annual Review of Psychology, 44*, 453–495. [6]

Stahl, S. M. (1998). Basic psychopharmacology of antidepressants, part 1: Antidepressants have seven distinct mechanisms of action. *Journal of Clinical Psychiatry, 59*(4, Suppl.), 5–14. [13]

Stanovich, K. (1996). *How to think straight about psychology.* New York: HarperCollins. [10]

Stanovich, K. E. (1989). *How to think straight about psychology* (2nd ed.). Glenview, IL: Scott, Foresman. [10]

Stark, E. (1984, October). Answer this question: Responses: To sleep, perchance to dream. *Psychology Today*, p. 16. [4]

Stattin, H., & Magnusson, D. (1990). *Pubertal maturation in female development.* Hillsdale, NJ: Erlbaum. [8]

Steblay, N. M. (1992). A meta-analytic review of the weapon focus effect. *Law and Human Behavior, 16*, 413–424. [6]

Steffens, A. B., Scheurink, A. J., & Luiten, P. G. (1988). Hypothalamic food intake regulating areas are involved in the homeostasis of blood glucose and plasma FFA levels. *Physiology and Behavior, 44*, 581–589. [9]

Stein, L., Xue, B. G., & Belluzzi, J. D. (1993). Cellular targets of brain reinforcement systems. *Annals of the New York Academy of Sciences, 702*, 41–45. [6]

Stein, M. B., Walker, J. R., & Forde, D. R. (1996). Public-speaking fears in a community sample: Prevalence, impact on functioning, and diagnostic classification. *Archives of General Psychiatry, 53*, 169–174. [12]

Steinberg, L. (1990). Autonomy, conflict, and harmony in the family relationship. In S. S. Feldman & R. E. Glen (Eds.), *At the threshold: The developing adolescent.* Cambridge, MA: Harvard University Press. [8]

Steinberg, L. (1992). Ethnic differences in adolescent achievement: An ecological perspective. *American Psychologist, 47*, 723–729. [8]

Steinberg, L., Elman, J. D., & Mounts, N. S. (1989). Authoritative parenting, psychosocial maturity, and academic success among adolescents. *Child Development, 60*, 1424–1436. [8]

Steinberg, L., Lamborn, S. D., Darling, N., Mounts, N. S., & Dornbusch, S. M. (1994). Over-time changes in adjustment and competence among adolescents from authoritative, authoritarian, indulgent, and neglectful families. *Child Development, 65*, 754–770. [8]

Steinman, L. (1993). Autoimmune disease. *Scientific American, 269*, 106–114. [11]

Stemberger, R. T., Turner, S. M., Beidel, D. C., & Calhoun, K. S. (1995). Social phobia: An analysis of possible developmental factors. *Journal of Abnormal Psychology, 104*, 526–531. [12]

Steriade, M. (1996). Arousal: Revisiting the reticular activating system. *Science, 272*, 225–226. [2]

Stern, K., & McClintock, M. K. (1998). Regulation of ovulation by human pheromones. *Nature, 392*, 177–179. [3]

Stern, W. (1914). *The psychological methods of testing intelligence.* Baltimore: Warwick and York. [7]

Sternberg, R. J. (1985a). *Beyond IQ: A triarchic theory of human intelligence.* New York: Cambridge University Press. [7]

Sternberg, R. J. (1985b). Human intelligence: The model is the message. *Science, 230*, 1111–1118. [7]

Sternberg, R. J. (1986). *Intelligence applied: Understanding and increasing your intellectual skills.* San Diego: Harcourt Brace Jovanovich. [7]

Sternberg, R. J., Wagner, R. K., Williams, W. M., & Horvath, J. A. (1995). Testing common sense. *American Psychologist, 50*, 912–927. [7]

Stevenson, H. W. (1992). Learning from Asian schools. *Scientific American, 267*, 70–76. [7]

Stevenson, H. W., Chen, C., & Lee, S. Y. (1993). Mathematics achievement of Chinese, Japanese, and American children: Ten years later. *Science, 259*, 53–58. [7]

Stevenson, H. W., Lee, S. Y., Chen, C., Stigler, J. W., Hsu, C. C., & Kitamura, S. (1990). Contexts of achievement. *Monographs of the Society for Research in Child Development, 55*(1–2, Serial No. 221). [7]

Stevenson, H. W., Lee, S. Y., & Stigler, J. W. (1986). Mathematics achievement of Chinese, Japanese, and American children. *Science, 231*, 693–699. [7]

Stewart, V. M. (1973). Tests of the "carpentered world" hypothesis by race and environment in America and Zambia. *International Journal of Psychology, 8*, 83–94. [3]

Stiff, J. B., Miller, G. R., Sleight, C., Mongeau, P. L., Garlick, R., & Rogan, R. (1989). Explanations for visual cue primacy in judgments of honesty and deceit. *Journal of Personality and Social Psychology, 56*, 555–564. [14]

Strack, F., Martin, L. L., & Stepper, S. (1988). Inhibiting and facilitating conditions of facial expressions: A nonobtrusive test of the facial feedback hypothesis. *Journal of Personality and Social Psychology, 54*, 768–777. [9]

Strakowski, S. M., Lonczak, H. S., Sax, K. W., West, S. A., Crist, A., Mehta, R., & Thienhaus, O. J. (1995). The effects of race on diagnosis and disposition from a psychiatric emergency service. *Journal of Clinical Psychiatry, 56*, 101–107. [13]

Strawbridge, W. J., Cohen, R. D., Shema, S. J., & Kaplan, G. A. (1997). Frequent attendance at religious services and mortality over 28 years. *American Journal of Public Health, 87*, 957–961. [11]

Strentz, H. (1986, January 1). Become a psychic and amaze your friends! *Atlanta Journal*, p. 15A. [3]

Strobel, R. J., & Rosen, R. C. (1996). Obesity and weight loss in obstructive sleep apnea: A critical review. *Sleep, 19*, 104–115. [4]

Strome, M., & Vernick, D. (1989, April). Hearing loss and hearing aids. *Harvard Medical School Health Letter, 14*, pp. 5–8. [3]

Stromeyer, C. F., III. (1970, November). Eidetikers. *Psychology Today*, pp. 76–80. [6]

Stuss, D. T., Gow, C. A., & Hetherington, C. R. (1992). "No longer Gage": Frontal lobe dysfunction and emotional changes. *Journal of Consulting and Clinical Psychology, 60*, 349–359. [2]

Suarez, M. G. (1983). Implications of Spanish-English bilingualism in the TAT stories. Unpublished doctoral dissertation, University of Connecticut. [13]

Sue, D. W. (1994). Asian-American mental health and help-seeking behavior: Comment on Solbert et al. (1994), Tata and Leong (1994), and Lin (1994). *Journal of Counseling Psychology, 41*, 292–295. [13]

Sue, D. W., & Sue, D. (1990). *Counseling the culturally different: Theory and practice.* New York: Wiley. [13]

Suedfeld, P. (1990). Restricted environmental stimulation and smoking cessation: A 15-year progress report. *International Journal of the Addictions, 25*, 861–888. [9]

Sullivan, E. V. (1977). A study of Kohlberg's structural theory of moral development: A critique of liberal social science ideology. *Human Development, 20*, 352–376. [8]

Sulloway, F. J. (1996). *Born to rebel: Birth order, family dynamics, and creative lives.* New York: Pantheon. [10]

Sulloway, F. J. (1997, September). Birth order and personality. *Harvard Mental Health Letter, 14*(3), 5–7. [10]

Summerfeldt, L. J., Richter, M. A., Antony, M. M., & Swinson, R. P. (1999). Symptom structure in obsessive-compulsive disorder: A confirmatory factor-analytic study. *Behaviour Research and Therapy, 37*, 297–311. [12]

Sung, K-T. (1992). Motivations for parent care: The case of filial children in Korea. *International Journal of Aging and Human Development, 34*, 109–124. [8]

Super, C. W. (1981). Behavioral development in infancy. In R. H. Munroe, R. L. Munroe, & B. B. Whiting (Eds.), *Handbook of cross-cultural human development* (pp. 181–269). Chicago: Garland. [8]

Swanson, L. W. (1995). Mapping the human brain: past, present, and future. *Trends in Neurosciences, 18*, 471–474. [2]

Swap, W. C. (1977). Interpersonal attraction and repeated exposure to rewarders and punishers. *Personality and Social Psychology Bulletin, 3*, 248–251. [14]

Sweatt, J. D., & Kandel, E. R. (1989). Persistent and transcriptionally dependent increase in protein phosphorylation in long-term facilitation of Aplysia sensory neurons. *Nature, 339*, 51–54. [6]

Swedo, S. E., Rapoport, J. L., Leonard, H., Lenane, M., & Cheslow, D. (1989). Obsessive-compulsive disorder in children and adolescents: Clinical phenomenology of 70 consecutive cases. *Archives of General Psychiatry, 46*, 335–341. [12]

Sweller, J., & Levine, M. (1982). Effects of goal specificity on means-end analysis and learning. *Journal of Experimental Psychology: Learning, Memory, and Cognition, 8*, 463–474. [7]

Swets, J. A. (1992). The science of choosing the right decision threshold in high-stakes diagnostics. *American Psychologist, 47*, 522–532. [3]

Szymanski, K., & Harkins, S. G. (1987). Social loafing and self-evaluation with a social standard. *Journal of Personality and Social Psychology, 53*, 891–897. [14]

Szymanski, S., Lieberman, J. A., Alvir, J. M., et al. (1995). Gender differences in onset of illness, treatment response, course, and biologic indexes in first-episode schizophrenic patients. *American Journal of Psychiatry, 152*, 698–703. [12]

Takanishi, R. (1993). The opportunities of adolescence—research, interventions, and policy: Introduction to the special issue. *American Psychologist, 48*, 85–87. [8]

Tamminga, C. A., & Conley, R. R. (1997). The application of neuroimaging techniques to drug development. *Journal of Clinical Psychiatry, 58*(10, Suppl.), 3–6. [2]

Tanda, G., Pontieri, F. E., & Di Chiara, G. (1997). Cannabinoid and heroin activation of mesolimbic dopamine transmission by a common µ1 opioid receptor mechanism. *Science, 276*, 2048–2050. [4]

Tang, M-X., Jacobs, D., Stern, Y., Marder, K., Schofield, P., Gurland, B., Andrews, H., & Mayeux, R. (1996). Effect of oestrogen during menopause on risk and age at onset of Alzheimer's disease. *Lancet, 348*, 429–432. [8]

Tanner, J. M. (1961). *Education and physical growth.* London: University of London Press. [8]

Tanner, J. M. (1962). *Growth at adolescence* (2nd ed.). Oxford: Blackwell. [8]

Tanner, J. M. (1990). *Fetus into man* (2nd ed.). Cambridge MA: Harvard University Press. [8]

Taylor, E. (1996, July/August). Peace Timothy Leary. *Psychology Today, 29*, 56–59, 84. [4]

Taylor, S. E. (1991). *Health psychology* (2nd ed.). New York: McGraw-Hill. [11]

Taylor, S. E., & Repetti, R. L. (1997). Health psychology: What is an unhealthy environment and how does it get under the skin? *Annual Review of Psychology, 48*, 411–447. [11]

Teasdale, J. D., & Fogarty, S. J. (1979). Differential effects of induced mood on retrieval of pleasant and unpleasant events from episodic memory. *Journal of Abnormal Psychology, 88*, 248–257. [6]

Tellegen, A., Lykken, D. T., Bouchard, T. J., Jr., Wilcox, K. J., Segal, N. L., & Rich, S. (1988). Personality similarity in twins reared apart and together. *Journal of Personality and Social Psychology, 54*, 1031–1039. [10]

Templeton, R. D., & Quigley, J. P. (1930). The action of insulin on the motility of the gastrointestinal tract. *American Journal of Physiology, 91*, 467–474. [9]

Terman, L. M. (1925). *Genetic studies of genius, Vol. 1: Mental and physical traits of a thousand gifted children.* Stanford, CA: Stanford University Press. [7]

Terman, L. M., & Oden, M. H. (1947). *Genetic studies of genius, Vol. 4: The gifted child grows up.* Stanford, CA: Stanford University Press. [7]

Terrace, H. S. (1979, November). How Nim Chimpski changed my mind. *Psychology Today,* 65–76. [7]

Terrace, H. S. (1981). A report to an academy. *Annals of the New York Academy of Sciences, 364,* 115–129. [7]

Terrace, H. S. (1985). In the beginning was the "name." *American Psychologist, 40,* 1011–1028. [7]

Terrace, H. S. (1986). *Nim: A chimpanzee who learned sign language.* New York: Columbia University Press. [7]

Tesch, S. A., & Whitbourne, S. K. (1982). Intimacy and identity status in young adults. *Journal of Personality and Social Psychology, 43,* 1041–1051. [8]

Tesser, A. (1993). The importance of heritability in psychological research: The case of attitudes. *Psychological Review, 100,* 129–142. [14]

Thase, M. E., Frank, E., Mallinger, A. G., Hammer, T., & Kupfer, D. J. (1992). Treatment of imipramine-resistant recurrent depression, III: Efficacy of monoamine oxidise inhibitors. *Journal of Clinical Psychiatry, 53*(1, Suppl.), 5–11. [13]

Thase, M. E., & Kupfer, D. J. (1996). Recent developments in the pharmacotherapy of mood disorders. *Journal of Consulting and Clinical Psychology, 64,* 646–659. [13]

Thase, M. E., Simons, A. D., Cahalane, J. F., & McGeary, J. (1991). Cognitive behavior therapy of endogenous depression: Part 1: An outpatient clinical replication series. *Behavior Therapy, 22,* 457–467. [13]

Thigpen, C. H., & Cleckley, H. M. (1984). On the incidence of multiple personality disorder. International *Journal of Clinical and Experimental Hypnosis, 32,* 63–66. [12]

Thomas, A., Chess, S., & Birch, H. G. (1970). The origin of personality. *Scientific American, 223,* 102–109. [8]

Thomas, J. L. (1992). *Adulthood and aging.* Boston: Allyn & Bacon. [8]

Thompson, S. C., Sobolew-Shubin, A., Galbraith, M. E., Schwankovsky, L., & Cruzen, D. (1993). Maintaining perceptions of control: Finding perceived control in low-control circumstances. *Journal of Personality and Social Psychology, 64,* 293–304. [11]

Thorndike, E. (1898). Some experiments on animal intelligence. *Science, 7*(181), 818–824. [5]

Thorndike, E. L. (1920). A constant error in psychological ratings. *Journal of Applied Psychology, 4,* 25–29. [12]

Thorndike, E. L. (1970). *Animal intelligence: Experimental studies.* New York: Macmillan. (Original work published 1911). [5]

Thornhill, R., & Gangestad, G. W. (1994). Human fluctuating asymmetry and sexual behavior. *Psychological Science, 5,* 297–302. [14]

Thorpe, G. L., & Olson, S. L. (1990). *Behavior therapy: Concepts, procedures, and applications.* Boston: Allyn & Bacon. [13]

Thurstone, L. L. (1938). *Primary mental abilities.* Chicago: University of Chicago Press. [7]

Tiihonen, J., Isohanni, M., Räsänen, P., Koiranen, M., & Moring, J. (1997). Specific major mental disorders and criminality: A 26-year prospective study of the 1966 northern Finland birth cohort. *American Journal of Psychiatry, 154,* 840–845. [14]

Tolman, E. C. (1932). *Purposive behavior in animals and men.* New York: Appleton-Century-Crofts. [5]

Tolman, E. C., & Honzik, C. H. (1930). Introduction and removal of reward, and maze performance in rats. *University of California Publications in Psychology, 4,* 257–275. [5]

Tomaka, J., Blascovich, J., Kelsey, R. M., & Leitten, C. L. (1993). Subjective, physiological, and behavioral effects of threat and challenge appraisal. *Journal of Personality and Social Psychology, 65,* 248–260. [11]

Tomkins, S. (1962). *Affect, imagery, and consciousness: The positive effects* (Vol. 1). New York: Springer. [9]

Tomkins, S. (1963). *Affect, imagery, and consciousness: The negative effects* (Vol. 2). New York: Springer. [9]

Tondo, L., Baldessarini, R. J., Hennen, J., & Floris, G. (1998). Lithium maintenance treatment of depression and mania in bipolar I and bipolar II disorders. *American Journal of Psychiatry, 155,* 638–645. [13]

Tordoff, M. G. (1988). Sweeteners and appetite. In G. M. Williams (Ed.), *Sweeteners: Health effects* (pp. 53–60). Princeton, NJ: Princeton Scientific. [9]

Tordoff, M. G., & Alleva, A. M. (1990). Oral stimulation with aspartame increases hunger. *Physiology and Behavior, 47,* 555–559. [9]

Torrey, E. F. (1983). *Surviving schizophrenia: A family manual.* New York: Harper & Row. [12, 13]

Torrey, E. F., & Bowler, A. (1990). Geographical distribution of insanity in America: Evidence for an urban factor. *Schizophrenia Bulletin, 16,* 591–604. [12]

Torrey, E. F., Bowler, A. E., Taylor, E. H., & Gottesman, I. I. (1994). *Schizophrenia and manic-depressive disorder.* New York: Basic Books. [12, 16]

Tosini, G., & Menaker, M. (1996). Circadian rhythms in cultured mammalian retina. *Science, 272,* 419–421. [4]

Toufexis, A. (1988, February 22). Older—but coming on strong. *Time,* pp. 76–79. [8]

Tourangeau, R., Smith, T. W., & Rasinski, K. A. (1997). Motivation to report sensitive behaviors on surveys: Evidence from a bogus pipeline experiment. *Journal of Applied Social Psychology, 27,* 209–222. [1]

Travis, J. (1996). Brains in space. *Science News, 149,* 28–29. [2]

Triandis, H. C. (1994). *Culture and social behavior.* New York: McGraw-Hill. [9]

Trimble, J. E. (1994). Cultural variations in the use of alcohol and drugs. In W. J. Lonner & R. Malpass (Eds.), *Psychology and culture* (pp. 79–84). Boston: Allyn & Bacon. [4]

Triplet, R. G. (1992). Henry A. Murray: The making of a psychologist? *American Psychologist, 47,* 299–307. [10]

Triplett, N. (1898). The dynamogenic factors in pacemaking and competition. *American Journal of Psychology, 9,* 507–533. [14]

Trivedi, M. J. (1996). Functional neuroanatomy of obsessive-compulsive disorder. *Journal of Clinical Psychiatry, 57*(8, Suppl.), 26–36. [12, 13]

True, W. R., Rice, J., Eisen, S. A., Heath, A. C., Goldberg, J., Lyons, M. J., & Nowak, J. (1993). A twin study of genetic and environmental contributions to liability for posttraumatic stress symptoms. *Archives of General Psychiatry, 50,* 257–264. [11]

Tulving, E. (1989). Remembering and knowing the past. *American Scientist, 77,* 361–367. [6]

Tulving, E., Schacter, D. L., McLachlan, D. R., & Moscovitch, M. (1988). Priming of semantic autobiographical knowledge: A case study of retrograde amnesia. *Brain and Cognition, 8,* 3–20. [6]

Tulving, E., & Thompson, D. M. (1973). Encoding specificity and retrieval processes in episodic memory. *Psychological Review, 80,* 352–373. [6]

Turner, J. C., Hogg, M. A., Oakes, P. J., Reicher, S. D., & Wetherell, M. S. (1987). *Rediscovering the social group: A self-categorization theory.* Oxford, England: Blackwell. [14]

Turner, R. J. (1983). Direct, indirect, and moderating effects of social support on psychological distress and associated conditions. In H. B. Kaplan (Ed.), *Psychosocial stress: Trends in theory and research* (pp. 105–155). New York: Academic. [11]

Turner, T. J., & Ortony, A. (1992). Basic emotions: Can conflicting criteria converge? *Psychological Review, 99,* 566–571. [9]

Tversky, A. (1972). Elimination by aspects: A theory of choice. *Psychological Review, 79,* 281–299. [7]

Uchino, B. N., Cacioppo, J. T., & Kiecolt-Glaser, J. K. (1996). The relationship between social support and physiological processes: A review with emphasis on underlying mechanisms and implications for health. *Psychological Bulletin, 119,* 488–531. [11]

Underwood, B. J. (1957). Interference and forgetting. *Psychological Review, 64,* 49–60. [6]

Underwood, B. J. (1964). Forgetting. *Scientific American, 210,* 91–99. [6]

Urbano-Marquez, A., Estruch, R., Navarro-Lopez, F., Grau, J. M., Mont, L., & Rubin, E. (1989). The effects of alcoholism on skeletal and cardiac muscle. *New England Journal of Medicine, 320,* 409–415. [11]

U.S. Bureau of the Census. (1994). *Statistical abstract of the United States 1994* (114th ed.). Washington, DC: U.S. Government Printing Office. [11, 12]

U.S. Bureau of the Census. (1997). *Statistical abstract of the United States 1997* (117th ed.). Washington, DC: U.S. Government Printing Office. [8, 12]

Vaillant, G. E. (1977). *Adaptation to life.* Boston: Little, Brown. [8]

Vaillant, G. E. (1994). Ego mechanisms of defense and personality psychopathology. *Journal of Abnormal Psychology, 103,* 44–50. [10]

Vandell, D. L., & Mueller, E. C. (1980). Peer play and friendships during the first two years. In H. C. Foot, A. J. Chapman, & J. R. Smith (Eds.), *Friendship and social relations in children.* New York: Wiley. [8]

van den Hout, M., & Merckelbach, H. (1991). Classical conditioning: Still going strong. *Behavioural Psychotherapy, 19,* 59–79. [5]

Van Lancker, D. (1987, November). Old familiar voices. *Psychology Today,* pp. 12–13. [2]

Vargha-Khadem, F., Gadian, D. G., Watkins, D. E., Connelly, A., Van Paesschen, W., & Mishkin, M. (1997). Differential effects of early hippocampal pathology on episodic and semantic memory. *Science, 277,* 376–380. [2, 6]

Veleber, D. M., & Templer, D. I. (1984). Effects of caffeine on anxiety and depression. *Journal of Abnormal Psychology, 93,* 120–122. [4]

Verhaeghen, P., Marcoen, A., & Goossens, L. (1993). Facts and fiction about memory aging: A quantitative integration of research findings. *Journal of Gerontology, 48,* 157–171. [8]

Viemerö, V. (1996). Factors in childhood that predict later criminal behavior. *Aggressive Behavior, 22,* 87–97. [14]

Vilberg, T. R., & Keesey, R. E. (1990). Ventromedial hypothalamic lesions abolish compensatory reduction in energy expenditure to weight loss. *American Journal of Physiology, 258,* 476–480. [9]

Vincent, K. R. (1991). Black/white IQ differences: Does age make the difference? *Journal of Clinical Psychology, 47,* 266–270. [7]

Vincent, K. R. (1993, Fall). On the perfectibility of the human species: Evidence using fixed reference groups. *TCA Journal,* pp. 60–63. [7]

Vincent, M., & Pickering, M. R. (1988). Multiple personality disorder in childhood. *Canadian Journal of Psychiatry, 33,* 524–529. [12]

Viney, W. (1993). *A history of psychology: Ideas and context.* Boston: Allyn & Bacon. [1]

Vitousek, K., & Manke, F. (1994). Personality variables and disorders in anorexia nervosa and bulimia nervosa. *Journal of Abnormal Psychology, 103,* 137–147. [9]

Volkow, N. D., Wang, G. J., Fischman, M. W., Foltin, R. W., Fowler, J. S., Abumrad, N. N., Vitkun, S., Logan, J., Gatley, S. J., Pappas, N., Hitzemann, R., & Shea, C. E. (1997). Relationship between subjective effects of cocaine and dopamine transporter occupancy. *Nature, 386,* 827–830. [4]

Volkow, N. D., Wang, G.-J., Fowler, J. S., Logan, J., Gatley, S. J., Hitzemann, R., Chen, A. D., Dewey, S. L., & Pappas, N. (1997). Decreased striatal dopaminergic responsiveness in detoxified cocaine-dependent subjects. *Nature, 386,* 830–833. [4]

von Boehmer, H., & Kisielow, P. (1991). How the immune system learns about self. *Scientific American, 265,* 74–81. [11]

Vygotsky, L. S. (1986). Thought and language (A. Kozulin, Trans.). Cambridge, MA: MIT Press. (Original work published 1934.) [8]

Wadden, T. A. (1993). Treatment of obesity by moderate and severe caloric restriction: Results of clinical research trials. *Annals of Internal Medicine, 119,* 688–693. [9]

Wadden, T. A., Vogt, R. A., Andersen, R. E., Bartlett, S. J., Foster, G. D., Kuehnel, R. H., Wilk, J., Weinstock, R., Buckenmeyer, P., Berkowitz, R. I., & Steen, S. N. (1997). Exercise in the treatment of obesity: Effects of four interventions on body composition, resting energy expenditure, appetite, and mood. *Journal of Consulting and Clinical Psychology, 65,* 269–277. [9]

Wahba, M. A., & Bridwell, L. G. (1976). Maslow reconsidered: A review of research on the need hierarchy theory. *Organization Behavior and Human Performance, 15,* 212–240. [9]

Wakefield, H., & Underveeger, R. (1992). Recovered memories of alleged sexual abuse: Lawsuits against parents. *Behavioral Sciences and the Law, 10,* 483–507. [6]

Wald, G. (1964). The receptors of human color vision. *Science, 145,* 1007–1017. [3]

Wald, G., Brown, P. K., & Smith, P. H. (1954). Iodopsin. *Journal of General Physiology, 38,* 623–681. [3]

Walker, L. (1989). A longitudinal study of moral reasoning. *Child Development, 60,* 157–166. [8]

Wallach, H. (1985). Learned stimulation in space and motion perception. *American Psychologist, 40,* 399–404. [3]

Wallach, M. A., & Wallach, L. (1983). *Psychology's sanction for selfishness: The error of egoism in theory and therapy.* New York: W. H. Freeman. [10]

Wallis, C. (1984, June 11). Unlocking pain's secrets. *Time,* pp. 58–66. [3]

Wallis, C. (1985, December 9). Children having children. *Time,* pp. 79–90. [8]

Wallis, C., & Willwerth, J. (1992, July 6). Awakenings: Schizophrenia, a new drug brings patients back to life. *Time,* pp. 52–57. [13]

Walster, E., & Walster, G. W. (1969). The matching hypothesis. *Journal of Personality and Social Psychology, 6,* 248–253. [14]

Ward, C. (1994). Culture and altered states of consciousness. In W. J. Lonner & R. Malpass (Eds.), *Psychology and culture* (pp. 59–64). Boston: Allyn & Bacon. [4]

Wark, G. R., & Krebs, D. L. (1996). Gender and dilemma differences in real-life moral judgment. *Developmental Psychology, 32,* 220–230. [8]

Wasserman, E. A., & Miller, R. R. (1997). What's elementary about associative learning? *Annual Review of Psychology, 48,* 573–607. [5]

Watson, J. B. (1913). Psychology as the behaviorist views it. *Psychological Review, 20,* 158–177. [1, 5]

Watson, J. B., & Rayner, R. (1920). Conditioned emotional reactions. *Journal of Experimental Psychology, 3,* 1–14. [5]

Weaver, C. A., III. (1993). Do you need a "flash" to form a flashbulb memory? *Journal of Experimental Psychology: General, 122,* 39–46. [6]

Webb, W. (1995). The cost of sleep-related accidents: A reanalysis. *Sleep, 18,* 276–280. [4]

Webb, W. B., & Campbell, S. S. (1983). Relationships in sleep characteristics of identical and fraternal twins. *Archives of General Psychiatry, 40,* 1093–1095. [4]

Webster, R. (1995). *Why Freud was wrong: Sin, science, and psychoanalysis.* New York: Basic Books. [10]

Weekes, J. R., Lynn, S. J., Green, J. P., & Brentar, J. T. (1992). Pseudomemory in hypnotized and task-motivated subjects. *Journal of Abnormal Psychology, 101,* 356–360. [4]

Wehr, T. A., & Rosenthal, N. E. (1989). Seasonality and affective illness. *American Journal of Psychiatry, 146,* 829–839. [12]

Weiner, B. (Ed.). (1974). *Achievement motivation and attribution theory.* Norristown, NJ: General Learning Press. [9]

Weiner, B. (1985). "Spontaneous" causal thinking. *Psychological Bulletin, 97,* 74–84. [14]

Weiner, I. B. (1997). Current status of the Rorschach Inkblot Method. *Journal of Personality Assessment, 68,* 5–19. [10]

Weingartner, H., Adefris, W., Eich, J. E., & Murphy, D. L. (1976). Encoding-imagery specificity in alcohol state-dependent learning. *Journal of Experimental Psychology: Human Learning and Memory, 2,* 83–87. [6]

Weiss, J. M. (1972). Psychological factors in stress and disease. *Scientific American, 226,* 104–113. [11]

Weissman, M. M., Bland, R. C., Canino, G. J., Greenwald, S., Hwu, H-G., Lee, C. K., Newman, S. C., Oakley-Browne, M. A., Rubio-Stipec, M., Wickramaratne, P. J., Wittchen, H-U., & Yeh, E-K. (1994). The cross national epidemiology of obsessive compulsive disorder. *Journal of Clinical Psychiatry, 55*(3, Suppl.), 5–10. [12]

Weissman, M. M., Gershon, E. S., Kidd, K. K., et al. (1984). Psychiatric disorders in the relatives of probands with affective disorders: The Yale University-National Institute of Mental Health Collaborative Study. *Archives of General Psychiatry, 41,* 13–21. [12]

Welsh, D. K. (1993). Timing of sleep and wakefulness. In M. A. Carskadon (Ed.), *Encyclopedia of sleep and dreaming.* New York: Macmillan. [4]

Wender, P. H., Kety, S. S., Rosenthal, D., et al. (1986). Psychiatric disorders in the biological and adoptive families of adoptive individuals with affective disorders. *Archives of General Psychiatry, 43,* 923–929. [12]

Wertheimer, M. (1912). Experimental studies of the perception of movement. *Zeitschrift fur Psychologie, 61,* 161–265. [3]

Wertheimer, M. (1958). Principles of perceptual organization. In D. C. Beardslee & M. Wertheimer (Eds.), *Readings in perception* (pp. 115–135). Princeton, NJ: D. Van Nostrand. [3]

Wetter, M. W., Baer, R. A., Berry, T. R., Robison, L. H., & Sumpter, J. (1993). MMPI-2 profiles of motivated fakers given specific symptom information: A comparison to matched patients. *Psychological Assessment, 5,* 317–323. [10]

Wever, E. G. (1949). *Theory of hearing.* New York: Wiley. [3]

Whelan, E. M., & Stare, F. J. (1990). Nutrition. *Journal of the American Medical Association, 263,* 2661–2663. [9]

Whitam, F. L., Diamond, M., & Martin, J. (1993). Homosexual orientation in twins: A report on 61 pairs and three triplet sets. *Archives of Sexual Behavior, 22,* 187–296. [9]

White, D. P. (1989). Central sleep apnea. In M. H. Kryger, T. Roth, & W. C. Dement (Eds.), *Principles and practice of sleep medicine* (pp. 513–524). Philadelphia: W. B. Saunders. [4]

White, S. D., & DeBlassie, R. R. (1992). Adolescent sexual behavior. *Adolescence, 27,* 183–191. [8]

Whitehurst, G. J., Fischel, J. E., Caulfield, M. B., DeBaryshe, B. D., & Valdez-Menchaca, M. C. (1989). Assessment and treatment of early expressive language delay. In P. R. Zelazo & R. Barr (Eds.), *Challenges to developmental paradigms: Implications for assessment and treatment* (pp. 113–135). Hillsdale, NJ: Erlbaum. [8]

Whorf, B. L. (1956). Science and linguistics. In J. B. Carroll (Ed.), *Language, thought, and reality: Selected writings of Benjamin Lee Whorf.* Cambridge, MA: MIT Press. [7]

Wickelgren, I. (1996). For the cortex, neuron loss may be less than thought. *Science, 273,* 48–50. [8]

Wickelgren, I. (1997). Getting a grasp on working memory. *Science, 275,* 1580–1582. [6]

Wicker, A. W. (1969). Attitudes versus action: The relationship of verbal and overt behavioral responses to attitude objects. *Journal of Social Issues, 25,* 41–78. [14]

Widiger, T. A., Frances, A., Spitzer, R. L., & Williams, J. B. W. (1988). The DSM-III-R personality disorders: An overview. *American Journal of Psychiatry, 145,* 786–795. [12]

Widom, C. S. (1989). Does violence beget violence? A critical examination of the literature. *Psychological Bulletin, 106,* 3–28. [5, 14]

Widom, C. S., & Maxfield, M. G. (1996). A prospective examination of risk for violence among abused and neglected children. *Annals of the New York Academy of Sciences, 794,* 224–237. [14]

Wierson, M., Long, P. J., & Forehand, R. L. (1993). Toward a new understanding of early menarche: The role of environmental stress in pubertal timing. *Adolescence, 28,* 13–24. [8]

Wiggins, J. S. (Ed.) (1996). *The five-factor model of personality: Theoretical perspectives.* New York: Guilford. [10]

Wilcox, D., & Hager, R. (1980). Toward realistic expectation for orgasmic response in women. *Journal of Sex Research, 16,* 162–179. [9]

Williams, G. C., Grow, V. M., Freedman, Z. R., Ryan, R. M., & Deci, E. L. (1996). Motivational predictors of weight loss and weight-loss maintenance. *Journal of Personality and Social Psychology, 70,* 115–126. [9]

Williams, J. E., Satterwhite, R. C., & Saiz, J. L. (1998). *The importance of psychological traits: A cross-cultural study.* New York: Plenum. [10]

Williams, K., Harkins, S. G., & Latané, B. (1981). Identifiability as a deterrent to social loafing: Two cheering experiments. *Journal of Personality and Social Psychology, 40,* 303–311. [14]

Williams, R. (1989, January/February). Curing Type A: The trusting heart. *Psychology Today,* pp. 36–42. [11]

Williams, R. (1993). *Anger kills.* New York: Times Books. [11]

Wills, T. A., & Cleary, S. D. (1996). How are social support effects mediated? A test with parental support and adolescent substance use. *Journal of Personality and Social Psychology, 71,* 937–952. [4]

Wills, T. A., McNamara, G., Vaccaro, D., & Hirky, A. E. (1996). Escalated substance use: A longitudinal grouping analysis from early to middle adolescence. *Journal of Abnormal Psychology, 105,* 166–180. [4]

Wilson, M. A., & McNaughton, B. L. (1993). Dynamics of the hippocampal ensemble code for space. *Science, 261,* 1055–1058. [2]

Winch, R. F. (1958). *Mate selection: A study of complementary needs.* New York: Harper & Row. [14]

Wink, P., & Helson, R. (1993). Personality change in women and their partners. *Journal of Personality and Social Psychology, 65,* 597–605. [8]

Winn, P. (1994). Schizophrenia research moves to the prefrontal cortex. *Trends in Neurosciences, 17,* 265–268. [12]

Winokur, G., Coryell, W., Keller, M., Endicott, J., & Akiskal, H. S. (1993). A prospective follow-up of patients with bipolar and primary unipolar affective disorder. *Archives of General Psychiatry, 50,* 457–465. [12]

Winson, J. (1990). The meaning of dreams. *Scientific American, 263,* 86–96. [4]

Witelson, S. F. (1985). The brain connection: The corpus callosum is larger in left-handers. *Science, 229,* 665–668. [2]

Wolfe, L. (1981). *The Cosmo report.* New York: Arbor House. [1]

Wolkin, A., Barouche, F., Wolf, A. P., Rotrosen, J., Fowler, J. S., Shiue, C-Y., Cooper, T. B., & Brodie, J. D. (1989). Dopamine blockade and clinical response: Evidence for two biological subgroups of schizophrenia. *American Journal of Psychiatry, 146,* 905–908. [12]

Wolpe, J. (1958). *Psychotherapy by reciprocal inhibition.* Stanford, CA: Stanford University Press. [13]

Wolpe, J. (1973). *The practice of behavior therapy* (2nd ed.). New York: Pergamon. [13]

Wolpe, J. (1981). Behavior therapy versus psychoanalysis: Therapeutic and social implications. *American Psychologist, 36,* 159–164. [13]

Wood, W., Lundgren, S., Ovellette, J. A., Busceme, S., & Blackstone, T. (1994). Minority influence: A meta-analytic review of social influence processes. *Psychological Bulletin, 115,* 323–345. [14]

Wood, W., Rhodes, N., & Whelan, M. (1989). Sex differences in positive well-being: A consideration of emotional style and marital status. *Psychological Bulletin, 106,* 249–264. [8, 9]

Wood, W., Wong, F. Y., & Chachere, J. G. (1991). Effects of media violence on viewers' aggression in unconstrained social interaction. *Psychological Bulletin, 109,* 371–383. [5, 14]

Woods, S. C., & Gibbs, J. (1989). The regulation of food intake by peptides. *Annals of the New York Academy of Sciences, 575,* 236–243. [9]

Woodward, A. L., Markman, E. M., & Fitzsimmons, C. M. (1994). Rapid word learning in 13- and 18-month-olds. *Developmental Psychology, 30,* 553–566. [8]

Woody, E. Z., & Bowers, K. S. (1994). A frontal assault on dissociated control. In S. J. Lynn & J. W. Rhue (Eds.), *Dissociation: Clinical, theoretical and research perspectives* (pp. 52–79). New York: Guilford. [4]

Woody, E. Z., Drugovic, M., & Oakman, J. M. (1997). A reexamination of the role of nonhypnotic suggestibility in hypnotic responding. *Journal of Personality and Social Psychology, 72,* 399–407. [4]

Woolley, C. S., Weiland, N. G., McEwen, B. S., & Schwartzkroin, P. A. (1997) Estradiol increases the sensitivity of hippocampal CA1 pyramidal cells to NMDA receptor-mediated synaptic input: Correlation with dendritic spine density. *Journal of Neuroscience, 17,* 1848–1859. [6]

Word, C. O., Zanna, M. P., & Cooper, J. (1974). The nonverbal mediation of self-fulfilling prophecies in interracial interaction. *Journal of Experimental Social Psychology, 10,* 109–120. [14]

Wright, J. C., & Mischel, W. (1987). A conditional approach to dispositional constructs: The local predictability of social behavior. *Journal of Personality and Social Psychology, 53,* 1159–1177. [10]

Wu, C., & Shaffer, D. R. (1987). Susceptibility to persuasive appeals as a function of source credibility and prior experience with the attitude object. *Journal of Personality and Social Psychology, 52,* 677–688. [14]

Wurtman, R. J., & Wurtman, J. J. (1989). Carbohydrates and depression. *Scientific American, 260,* 68–75. [12]

Wyatt, R. J., & Henter, I. D. (1997, July). Schizophrenia: The need for early treatment. *Harvard Mental Health Letter, 14*(1), 4–6. [13]

Yapko, M. D. (1994). Suggestibility and repressed memories of abuse: A survey of psychotherapists' beliefs. *American Journal of Clinical Hypnosis, 36,* 163–171. [4]

Yarnold, B. M. (1996). Use of inhalants among Miami's public school students, 1992. *Psychological Reports, 79,* 1155–1161. [4]

Yehuda, R., Southwick, S. M., & Giller, E. L., Jr. (1992). Exposure to atrocities and severity of chronic posttraumatic stress disorder in Vietnam combat veterans. *American Journal of Psychiatry, 149,* 333–336. [11]

Yonkers, K. A., & Hamilton, J. A. (1995, May). Do men and women need different doses of psychotropic drugs? *Harvard Mental Health Letter, 11*(11), 8. [13]

Yonkers, K. A., Zlotnick, C., Allsworth, J., Warshaw, M., Shea, T., & Keller, M. B. (1998). Is the course of panic disorder the same in women and men? *American Journal of Psychiatry, 155,* 596–602. [12]

Zajecka, J. (1997). Importance of establishing the diagnosis of persistent anxiety. *Journal of Clinical Psychiatry, 58*(3, Suppl.), 9–13. [12]

Zajonc, R. B. (1965). Social facilitation. *Science, 149,* 269–274. [14]

Zajonc, R. B. (1968). Attitudinal effects of mere exposure. *Journal of Personality and Social Psychology, Monographs Supplement, 9*(Pt. 2), 1–27. [14]

Zajonc, R. B. (1980). Feeling and thinking: Preferences need no inferences. *American Psychologist, 35,* 151–175. [9]

Zajonc, R. B. (1984). On the primacy of affect. *American Psychologist, 39,* 117–123. [9]

Zajonc, R. B., & Sales, S. M. (1966). Social facilitation of dominant and subordinate responses. *Journal of Experimental Social Psychology, 2,* 160–168. [14]

Zaragoza, M. S., & Mitchell, K. J. (1996). Repeated exposure to suggestion and the creation of false memories. *Psychological Science, 7,* 294–300. [6]

Zhdanova, I., & Wurtman, R. (1996, June). How does melatonin affect sleep? *Harvard Mental Health Letter, 12*(12), 8. [4]

Zhdanova, I. V., Wurtman, R. J., Morabito, C., Piotrovska, V. R., & Lynch, H. J. (1996). Effects of low oral doses of melatonin given 2–4 hours before habitual bedtime, on sleep in normal young humans. *Sleep, 19,* 423–431. [4]

Zilbergeld, B. (1986, June). Psychabuse. *Science, 86,* 48–52. [13]

Zimbardo, P. G. (1972). Pathology of imprisonment. *Society, 9,* 4–8. [14]

Zimbardo, P. G., Haney, C., & Banks, W. C. (1973, April 8). A Pirandellian prison. *The New York Times Magazine,* pp. 38–60. [14]

Zipursky, R. B., Lim, K. O., Sullivan, E. V., Brown, B. W., & Pfefferbaum, A. (1992). Widespread cerebral gray matter volume deficits in schizophrenia. *Archives of General Psychiatry, 49,* 195–205. [12]

Zisook, S., Byrd, D., Kuck, J., & Jeste, D. V. (1995). Command hallucinations in outpatients with schizophrenia. *Journal of Clinical Psychiatry, 56*(10, Suppl.), 462–465. [12]

Zivin, J. A., & Choi, D. W. (1991). Stroke therapy. *Scientific American, 265,* 56–63. [2]

Zubin, J., & Spring, B. J. (1977). Vulnerability: A new view of schizophrenia. *Journal of Abnormal Psychology, 86,* 103–126. [12]

Zuckerman, M., Miyake, K., & Hodgins, H. S. (1991). Cross-channel effects of vocal and physical attractiveness and their implications for interpersonal perception. *Journal of Personality and Social Psychology, 60,* 545–554. [14]

Zuger, B. (1990, August). Changing concepts of the etiology of male homosexuality. *Medical Aspects of Human Sexuality, 24,* 73–75. [9]

Zuwerink, J. R., & Devine, P. G. (1996). Attitude importance and resistance to persuasion: It's not just the thought that counts. *Journal of Personality and Social Psychology, 70,* 931–944. [14]

Glossary

absolute threshold: The minimum amount of sensory stimulation that can be detected 50% of the time.

accommodation: In vision, the action of the lens in changing shape as it focuses objects on the retina, becoming more spherical for near objects and flatter for far objects; in learning, the process by which existing schemas are modified and new schemas are created to incorporate new objects, events, experiences, or information.

acetylcholine: A neurotransmitter that plays a role in learning, memory, and rapid eye movement (REM) sleep and causes the skeletal muscle fibers to contract.

acquired immune deficiency syndrome (AIDS): A devastating and incurable illness that is caused by HIV and progressively weakens the body's immune system, leaving the person vulnerable to opportunistic infections that usually cause death.

action potential: The firing of a neuron that results when the charge within the neuron becomes more positive than the charge outside the cell's membrane.

additive strategy: A decision-making approach in which each alternative is rated on each important factor affecting the decision and the alternative rated highest overall is chosen.

adolescence: The developmental stage that begins at puberty and encompasses the period from the end of childhood to the beginning of adulthood.

adolescent growth spurt: A period of rapid physical growth that peaks in girls at about age 12 and in boys at about age 14.

adoption method: A method researchers use to study the relative effects of heredity and environment on behavior and ability in children adopted shortly after birth, by comparing them to their biological and adoptive parents.

adrenal glands (ah-DREE-nal): A pair of endocrine glands that release hormones that prepare the body for emergencies and stressful situations and also release small amounts of the sex hormones.

aerobic exercise (ay-RO-bik): Exercise that uses the large muscle groups in continuous, repetitive action and increases oxygen intake and breathing and heart rates.

afterimage: The visual sensation that remains after a stimulus is withdrawn.

aggression: The intentional infliction of physical or psychological harm on another.

agoraphobia (AG-or-uh-FO-bee-uh): An intense fear of being in a situation from which immediate escape is not possible or in which help is not immediately available in case of incapacitating anxiety.

alarm stage: The first stage of the general adaptation syndrome, when there is emotional arousal and the defensive forces of the body are prepared for fight or flight.

alcohol: A central nervous system depressant.

algorithm: A systematic, step-by-step procedure, such as a mathematical formula, that guarantees a solution to a problem of a certain type if the algorithm is appropriate and is executed properly.

alpha wave: The brain wave associated with deep relaxation.

altered state of consciousness: A mental state other than ordinary waking consciousness, such as sleep, meditation, hypnosis, or a drug-induced state.

altruism: Behavior aimed at helping another, requiring some self-sacrifice and not designed for personal gain.

Alzheimer's disease (ALZ-hye-merz): An incurable form of dementia characterized by progressive deterioration of intellect and personality, resulting from widespread degeneration of brain cells.

amnesia: A partial or complete loss of memory resulting from brain trauma or psychological trauma.

amphetamines: A class of stimulants that increase arousal, relieve fatigue, improve alertness, and suppress the appetite.

amplitude: Measured in decibels, the magnitude or intensity of a sound wave, determining the loudness of the sound.

amygdala (ah-MIG-da-la): A structure in the limbic system that plays an important role in emotion, particularly in response to aversive stimuli.

anal stage: Freud's second psychosexual stage (ages 1 or 1½ to 3 years), in which the child derives sensual pleasure mainly from expelling and withholding feces.

analogy heuristic: A rule of thumb that applies a solution that solved a problem in the past to a current problem that shares many similar features.

anorexia nervosa: An eating disorder characterized by an overwhelming, irrational fear of being fat, compulsive dieting to the point of self-starvation, and excessive weight loss.

anterograde amnesia: The inability to form long-term memories of events occurring after a brain injury or brain surgery, although memories formed before the trauma are usually intact.

antidepressants: Drugs that are prescribed to treat depression and some anxiety disorders.

antipsychotic drugs: Drugs used to control severe psychotic symptoms, such as the delusions and hallucinations of schizophrenics; also known as neuroleptics or major tranquilizers.

antisocial personality disorder: A disorder marked by lack of feeling for others; selfish, aggressive, irresponsible behavior; and willingness to break the law, lie, cheat, or exploit others for personal gain.

anxiety: A general uneasiness or ominous feeling that may be associated with a particular object or situation or may be free-floating (not associated with anything specific).

anxiety disorders: Psychological disorders characterized by severe anxiety (e.g., panic disorder, phobias, general anxiety disorder, obsessive compulsive disorder).

aphasia (uh-FAY-zyah): A loss or impairment of the ability to understand or communicate through the written or spoken word, which results from damage to the brain.

apparent motion: The perception of motion when none is occurring (as in the phi phenomenon or in stroboscopic movement).

applied research: Research conducted to solve practical problems.

approach–approach conflict: A conflict arising from having to choose between desirable alternatives.

approach–avoidance conflict: A conflict arising when the same choice has both desirable and undesirable features.

aptitude test: A test designed to predict a person's achievement or performance at some future time.

archetype (AR-keh-type): Existing in the collective unconscious, an inherited tendency to respond in particular ways to universal human situations.

arousal: A state of alertness and mental and physical activation.

arousal theory: A theory suggesting that the aim of motivation is to maintain an optimal level of arousal.

artificial intelligence: The programming of computer systems to simulate human thinking in solving problems and in making judgments and decisions.

assimilation: The process by which new objects, events, experiences, or information are incorporated into existing schemas.

association areas: Areas of the cerebral cortex that house memories and are involved in thought, perception, learning, and language.

attachment: The strong affectionate bond a child forms with the mother or primary caregiver.

attitude: A relatively stable evaluation of a person, object, situation, or issue.

attribution: An inference about the cause of one's own or another's behavior.

audience effects: The impact of passive spectators on performance.

audition: The sensation of hearing; the process of hearing.

authoritarian parents: Parents who make arbitrary rules, expect unquestioned obedience from their children, punish transgressions, and value obedience to authority.

authoritative parents: Parents who set high but realistic standards, reason with the child, enforce limits, and encourage open communication and independence.

automatic thoughts: Unreasonable and unquestioned ideas that rule a person's life and lead to depression and anxiety.

autonomy versus shame and doubt: Erikson's second stage (ages 1 to 3 years), when infants develop autonomy or shame based on how parents react to their expression of will and their wish to do things for themselves.

availability heuristic: A cognitive rule of thumb that says that the probability of an event or the importance assigned to it is based on its availability in memory.

aversion therapy: A behavior therapy in which an aversive stimulus is paired with an undesirable behavior until the behavior becomes associated with pain and discomfort.

avoidance–avoidance conflict: A conflict arising from having to choose between two undesirable alternatives.

avoidance learning: Learning to avoid events or conditions associated with dreaded or aversive outcomes.

axon (AK-sahn): The slender, tail-like extension of the neuron that transmits signals to the dendrites or cell body of other neurons or to the muscles or glands.

babbling: Vocalization of the basic speech sounds (phonemes), which begins between 4 and 6 months.

barbiturates: A class of addictive depressants used as sedatives, sleeping pills, and anesthetics; overdoses can cause coma or death.

basic emotions: Emotions that are found in all cultures, that are reflected in the same facial expressions across cultures, and that emerge in children according to their biological timetable; fear, anger, disgust, surprise, happiness, and distress are usually considered basic emotions.

basic research: Research conducted to advance knowledge rather than for its practical application.

basic trust versus basic mistrust: Erikson's first stage (ages birth to 1 year), when infants develop trust or mistrust based on the quality of care, love, and affection provided.

behavior modification: The systematic application of the learning principles of operant conditioning, classical conditioning, or observational learning to individuals or groups in order to eliminate undesirable behavior and/or encourage desirable behavior; also called behavior therapy.

behavior therapy: A treatment approach employing the principles of operant conditioning, classical conditioning, and/or observational learning theory to eliminate inappropriate or maladaptive behaviors and replace them with more adaptive responses.

behavioral genetics: The field of research that investigates the relative effects of heredity and environment on behavior and ability.

behavioral perspective: A perspective that emphasizes the role of environment in shaping behavior.

behaviorism: The school of psychology founded by John B. Watson that views observable, measurable behavior as the appropriate subject matter for psychology and emphasizes the key role of environment as a determinant of behavior.

beta wave (BAY-tuh): The brain wave associated with mental or physical activity.

binocular depth cues: Depth cues that depend on two eyes working together; convergence and binocular disparity.

binocular disparity: A binocular depth cue resulting from differences between the two retinal images formed of an object viewed at distances up to about 20 feet.

biofeedback: The use of sensitive equipment to give people precise feedback about internal physiological processes so that they can learn, with practice, to exercise control over them.

biological perspective: A perspective that emphasizes the role of biological processes and heredity as the key to understanding behavior.

biological therapy: A therapy (drug therapy, ECT, or psychosurgery) that is based on the assumption that most mental disorders have physical causes.

biomedical model: A perspective that focuses on illness rather than on health, explaining illness in terms of biological factors without regard to psychological and social factors.

biopsychosocial model: A perspective that focuses on health as well as illness and holds that both are determined by a combination of biological, psychological, and social factors.

bipolar disorder: A mood disorder in which manic episodes alternate with periods of depression, usually with relatively normal periods in between.

bottom-up processing: Information processing in which individual components or bits of data are combined until a complete perception is formed.

brainstem: The structure that begins at the point where the spinal cord enlarges as it enters the brain and that includes the medulla, the pons, and the reticular formation.

brightness: The dimension of visual sensation that is dependent on the intensity of light reflected from a surface and that corresponds to the amplitude of the light wave.

brightness constancy: The tendency to see an object as maintaining the same brightness regardless of differences in lighting conditions.

Broca's aphasia (BRO-kuz uh-FAY-zyah): An impairment in the physical ability to produce speech sounds, or in extreme cases an inability to speak at all; caused by damage to Broca's area.

Broca's area (BRO-kuz): The area in the frontal lobe, usually in the left hemisphere, that controls the production of speech sounds.

bulimia nervosa: An eating disorder characterized by repeated and uncontrolled episodes of binge eating, usually followed by purging, that is, self-induced vomiting and/or the use of large quantities of laxatives and diuretics.

burnout: The result of intense, unrelieved, and unmanaged job stress; a condition in which an individual becomes pessimistic, dissatisfied, inefficient on the job, and debilitated psychologically.

bystander effect: The fact that as the number of bystanders at an emergency increases, the probability that the victim will receive help decreases, and help, if given, is likely to be delayed.

California Psychological Inventory (CPI): A highly regarded personality test used to assess the normal personality.

Cannon–Bard theory of emotion: The theory that an emotion-provoking stimulus is transmitted simultaneously to the cortex, providing the feeling of an emotion, and to the sympathetic nervous system, causing the physiological arousal.

cardinal trait: Allport's name for a personal quality that is so strong a part of a person's personality that he or she may become identified with that trait.

case study: An in-depth study of one or a few individuals consisting of information gathered through observation, interview, and perhaps psychological testing.

catatonic schizophrenia (KAT-uh-TAHN-ik): A type of schizophrenia characterized by complete stillness or stupor and/or periods of great agitation and excitement; patients may assume an unusual posture and remain in it for long periods.

cell body: The part of the neuron, containing the nucleus, that carries out the metabolic functions of the neuron.

central nervous system (CNS): The brain and the spinal cord.

central trait: Allport's name for the type of trait that might be mentioned in an accurate letter of recommendation.

cerebellum (sehr-uh-BELL-um): The brain structure that executes smooth, skilled body movements and regulates muscle tone and posture.

cerebral cortex (seh-REE-brul KOR-tex): The gray, convoluted covering of the cerebral hemispheres that is responsible for higher mental processes such as language, memory, and thinking.

cerebral hemispheres (seh-REE-brul): The right and left halves of the cerebrum, covered by the cerebral cortex and connected by the corpus callosum.

cerebrum (seh-REE-brum): The largest structure of the human brain, consisting of the two cerebral hemispheres connected by the corpus callosum and covered by the cerebral cortex.

chromosomes: Rod-shaped structures in the nuclei of body cells, which contain all the genes and carry all the hereditary information.

circadian rhythm (sur-KAY-dee-un): Within each 24-hour period, the regular fluctuation from high to low points of certain bodily functions.

circadian theory: The theory that sleep evolved to keep humans out of harm's way during the night and that sleepiness ebbs and flows according to a circadian rhythm.

classical conditioning: A learning process through which one stimulus comes to predict the occurrence of another stimulus and to elicit a response similar to or related to the response evoked by that stimulus.

clinical psychologist: A psychologist, usually with a PhD, whose training is in the diagnosis, treatment, or research of psychological and behavioral disorders.

coaction effects: The impact on performance of the presence of others engaged in the same task.

cocaine: A type of stimulant that produces a feeling of euphoria.

cochlea (KOK-lee-uh): The snail-shaped, fluid-filled chamber in the inner ear that contains the hair cells (the sound receptors).

cognition: The mental processes that are involved in acquiring, storing, retrieving, and using information and that include sensation, perception, imagery, concept formation, reasoning, decision making, problem solving, and language.

cognitive dissonance: The unpleasant state that can occur when people become aware of inconsistencies between their attitudes or between their attitudes and their behavior.

cognitive map: A mental representation of a spatial arrangement such as a maze.

cognitive perspective: A perspective that emphasizes the role of mental processes that underlie behavior.

cognitive processes: Mental processes such as thinking, knowing, problem solving, and remembering.

cognitive psychology: A specialty that studies mental processes such as memory, problem solving, decision making, perception, language, and other forms of cognition; often uses the information-processing approach.

cognitive therapy: A therapy designed to change maladaptive behavior by changing the person's irrational thoughts, beliefs, and ideas.

coitus: Penile-vaginal intercourse.

collective unconscious: In Jung's theory, the most inaccessible layer of the unconscious, which contains the universal experiences of humankind transmitted to each individual.

color blindness: The inability to distinguish some or all colors, resulting from a defect in the cones.

color constancy: The tendency to see an object as about the same color regardless of differences in lighting conditions.

compliance: Acting in accordance with the wishes, the suggestions, or the direct request of another person.

compulsion: A persistent, irresistible, irrational urge to perform an act or ritual repeatedly.

concept: A mental category used to represent a class or group of objects, people, organizations, events, situations, or relations that share common characteristics or attributes.

concrete operations stage: Piaget's third stage of cognitive development (ages 7 to 11 years), during which a child acquires the concepts of reversibility and conservation and is able to apply logical thinking to concrete objects.

conditioned reflex: A learned reflex rather than a naturally occurring one.

conditioned response (CR): That response that comes to be elicited by a conditioned stimulus as a result of its repeated pairing with an unconditioned stimulus.

conditioned stimulus (CS): A neutral stimulus that, after repeated pairing with an unconditioned stimulus, becomes associated with it and elicits a conditioned response.

conditions of worth: Conditions on which the positive regard of others rests.

cones: The receptor cells in the retina that enable humans to see color and fine detail in adequate light, but that do not function in dim light.

confederate: Someone who is posing as a participant in an experiment but is actually assisting the experimenter.

conformity: Changing or adopting an attitude or behavior to be consistent with the norms of a group or the expectations of others.

conscious (KON-shus): The thoughts, feelings, sensations, or memories of which a person is aware at any given moment.

consciousness: An awareness of one's own perceptions, thoughts, feelings, sensations, and external environment.

conservation: The concept that a given quantity of matter remains the same despite rearrangement or change in its appearance, as long as nothing is added or taken away.

consolidation: A physiological change in the brain that must take place for encoded information to be stored in memory.

consolidation failure: Any disruption in the consolidation process that prevents a permanent memory from forming.

contact hypothesis: The notion that prejudice can be reduced through increased contact among members of different social groups.

continuous reinforcement: Reinforcement that is administered after every desired or correct response; the most effective method of conditioning a new response.

control group: In an experiment, a group that is similar to the experimental group and is exposed to the same experimental environment but is not exposed to the independent variable; used for purposes of comparison.

conventional level: Kohlberg's second level of moral reasoning, in which right and wrong are based on the internalized standards of others; "right" is whatever helps or is approved of by others, or whatever is consistent with the laws of society.

convergence: A binocular depth cue in which the eyes turn inward as they focus on nearby objects—the closer an object, the greater the convergence.

conversion disorder: A somatoform disorder in which a person suffers a loss of motor or sensory functioning in some part of the body; the loss has no physical cause but solves some psychological problem.

coping: Efforts through action and thought to deal with demands that are perceived as taxing or overwhelming.

cornea (KOR-nee-uh): The transparent covering on the front surface of the eyeball that bends light rays inward through the pupil.

corpus callosum (KOR-pus kah-LO-sum): The thick band of nerve fibers that connects the two cerebral hemispheres and makes possible the transfer of information and the synchronization of activity between them.

correlation coefficient: A numerical value that indicates the strength and direction of the relationship between two variables; ranges from +1.00 (a perfect positive correlation) to −1.00 (a perfect negative correlation).

correlational method: A research method used to establish the degree of relationship (correlation) between two characteristics, events, or behaviors.

crack: A form of cocaine that is smoked; the most potent and addictive form of cocaine.

crash: The feelings of depression, exhaustion, irritability, and anxiety that occur following an amphetamine, cocaine, or crack high.

creativity: The ability to produce original, appropriate, and valuable ideas and/or solutions to problems.

critical period: A period that is so important to development that a harmful environmental influence at that time can keep a bodily structure from developing normally or can impair later intellectual or social development.

critical thinking: The process of objectively evaluating claims, propositions, or conclusions to determine whether they follow logically from the evidence presented.

cross-sectional study: A type of developmental study in which researchers compare groups of participants of different ages on certain characteristics to determine age-related differences.

crowding: A subjective perception that there are too many people in a defined space.

crystallized intelligence: Aspects of intelligence, including verbal ability and accumulated knowledge, that tend to increase over the life span.

CT scan (computerized axial tomography): A brain-scanning technique involving a rotating X-ray scanner and a high-speed computer analysis that produces slice-by-slice, cross-sectional images of the structure of the brain.

culture-fair intelligence test: An intelligence test that uses questions that will not penalize those whose culture differs from that of the middle or upper classes.

dark adaptation: The eye's increasing ability to see in dim light; results from the recombining of molecules of rhodopsin in the rods and the dilation of the pupils.

decay theory: A theory of forgetting that holds that the memory trace, if not used, disappears with the passage of time.

decibel (DES-ih-bel): A unit of measurement of the intensity or loudness of sound based on the amplitude of the sound wave.

decision latitude: The degree to which employees have the opportunity to exercise initiative and use their skills to control their working conditions.

decision making: The process of considering alternatives and choosing among them.

declarative memory: The subsystem within long-term memory that stores facts, information, and personal life experiences; also called *explicit memory.*

defense mechanism: An unconscious, irrational means used by the ego to defend against anxiety; involves self-deception and the distortion of reality.

delta wave: The brain wave pattern associated with Stage 4 (deep) sleep.

delusion: A false belief, not generally shared by others in the culture, that cannot be changed despite strong evidence to the contrary.

delusion of grandeur: A false belief that one is a famous person or a person who has some great knowledge, ability, or authority.

delusion of persecution: A false belief that a person or group is trying in some way to harm one.

dendrites (DEN-drytes): The branchlike extensions of a neuron that receive signals from other neurons.

denial: Refusing to acknowledge consciously the existence of danger or a threatening condition.

density: A measure referring to the number of people occupying a unit of space.

dependent variable: The variable that is measured at the end of an experiment and is presumed to vary as a result of manipulations of the independent variable.

depressants: A category of drugs that decrease activity in the central nervous system, slow down bodily functions, and reduce sensitivity to outside stimulation; also called *downers.*

depth perception: The ability to see in three dimensions and to estimate distance.

descriptive research methods: Research methods that yield descriptions of behavior rather than causal explanations.

descriptive statistics: Statistics used to organize, summarize, and describe information gathered from actual observations.

developmental psychology: The study of how humans grow, develop, and change throughout the life span.

deviation score: A test score calculated by comparing an individual's score to the scores of others of the same age.

diathesis–stress model: The idea that people with a constitutional predisposition (diathesis) toward a disorder, such as schizophrenia, may develop the disorder if they are subjected to sufficient environmental stress.

difference threshold: The smallest increase or decrease in a physical stimulus required to produce a difference in sensation that is noticeable 50% of the time.

diffusion of responsibility: The feeling among bystanders at an emergency that the responsibility for helping is shared by the group, so each person feels less compelled to act than if he or she alone bore the total responsibility.

directive therapy: An approach to therapy in which the therapist takes an active role in determining the course of therapy sessions and provides answers and suggestions to the patient.

discrimination: In classical conditioning, the learned ability to distinguish between similar stimuli so that the conditioned response occurs only to the original conditioned stimulus but not to similar stimuli; in social psychology, behavior, usually negative, directed toward others based on their gender, religion, race, or membership in a particular group.

discriminative stimulus: A stimulus that signals whether a certain response or behavior is likely to be followed by reward or punishment.

disorganized schizophrenia: The most serious type of schizophrenia, marked by inappropriate affect, silliness, laughter, grotesque mannerisms, and bizarre behavior.

displacement: In memory, the event that occurs when short-term memory is holding its maximum and each new item entering short-term memory pushes out an existing item; in behavior, substituting a less threatening object for the original object of an impulse.

display rules: Cultural rules that dictate how emotions should be expressed, and when and where their expression is appropriate.

dispositional attribution: Attribution of a behavior to some internal cause, such as a personal trait, motive, or attitude; an internal attribution.

dissociative amnesia: A dissociative disorder in which there is a loss of memory of limited periods in one's life or of one's entire identity.

dissociative disorders: Disorders in which, under stress, one loses the integration of consciousness, identity, and memories of important personal events.

dissociative fugue (FEWG): A dissociative disorder in which one has a complete loss of memory of one's entire identity, travels away from home, and may assume a new identity.

dissociative identity disorder (DID): A dissociative disorder in which two or more distinct personalities occur in the same person, each taking over at different times; also called multiple personality.

dominant gene: The gene that is expressed in the individual.

door-in-the-face technique: A strategy in which someone makes a large, unreasonable request with the expectation that the person will refuse but will then be more likely to respond favorably to a smaller request at a later time.

dopamine (DOE-pah-meen): A neurotransmitter that plays a role in learning, attention, and movement; a deficiency of dopamine is associated with Parkinson's disease, and an over-sensitivity to it is associated with some cases of schizophrenia.

double-blind technique: An experimental procedure in which neither the participants nor the experimenter knows who is in the experimental or control groups until after the results have been gathered; a control for experimenter bias.

drive: A state of tension or arousal brought about by an underlying need, which motivates an organism to engage in behavior that will satisfy the need and reduce the tension.

drive-reduction theory: A theory of motivation suggesting that a need creates an unpleasant state of arousal or tension called a drive, which impels the organism to engage in behavior that will satisfy the need and reduce tension.

drug tolerance: A condition in which the user becomes progressively less affected by the drug so that larger and larger doses are necessary to maintain the same effect.

DSM-IV: *The Diagnostic and Statistical Manual of Mental Disorders,* Fourth Edition, a manual published by the American Psychiatric Association, which describes about 290 mental disorders and their symptoms.

ego (EE-go): In Freudian theory, the rational, largely conscious system of personality, which operates according to the reality principle.

ego integrity versus despair: Erikson's stage for old age, when people look back on their lives with satisfaction or with major regrets.

eidetic imagery (eye-DET-ik): The ability to retain the image of a visual stimulus several minutes after it has been removed from view.

elaborative rehearsal: A technique used to encode information into long-term memory by considering its meaning and associating it with other information already stored in long-term memory.

electroconvulsive therapy (ECT): A treatment in which an electric current is passed through the brain, causing a seizure; usually reserved for severely depressed patients who are either suicidal or unresponsive to other treatment.

electroencephalogram (EEG) (ee-lek-tro-en-SEFF-uh-lo-gram): A record of brain-wave activity made by the electroencephalograph.

embryo: The developing human organism during the period (week 3 through week 8) when the major systems, organs, and structures of the body develop.

emotion: A feeling state involving physiological arousal, a cognitive appraisal of the situation arousing the state, and an outward expression of the state.

emotion-focused coping: A response aimed at reducing the emotional impact of a stressor.

emotional intelligence: A type of intelligence that includes an awareness of and an ability to manage one's own emotions, the ability to motivate oneself, empathy, and the ability to handle relationships successfully.

encoding: Transforming information into a form that can be stored in short-term or long-term memory.

encoding failure: A cause of forgetting resulting from material never having been put into long-term memory.

endocrine system (EN-duh-krin): A system of ductless glands in various parts of the body that manufacture and secrete hormones into the bloodstream or lymph fluids, thus affecting cells in other parts of the body.

endorphins (en-DOOR-fins): Chemicals produced naturally by the brain that reduce pain and positively affect mood.

episodic memory (ep-ih-SOD-ik): The subpart of declarative memory that contains memories of personally experienced events.

estrogen (ES-truh-jen): A female sex hormone that promotes the secondary sex characteristics in females and controls the menstrual cycle.

evolutionary perspective: A perspective that focuses on how humans have evolved and adapted behaviors required for survival against various environmental pressures over the long course of evolution.

excitement phase: The first stage in the sexual response cycle, characterized by an erection in males and a swelling of the clitoris and vaginal lubrication in females.

exemplars: The individual instances of a concept that are stored in memory from personal experience.

exhaustion stage: The final stage of the general adaptation syndrome, occurring if the organism fails in its efforts to resist the stressor.

experimental group: In an experiment, the group that is exposed to the independent variable, or the treatment.

experimental method: The research method in which researchers randomly assign participants to groups and control all conditions other than one or more independent variables, which are then manipulated to determine their effect on some behavioral measure—the dependent variable in the experiment.

experimenter bias: A phenomenon that occurs when the researcher's preconceived notions in some way influence the participants' behavior and/or the interpretation of experimental results.

exposure and response prevention: A behavior therapy that exposes patients with obsessive compulsive disorder to stimuli generating increasing anxiety; patients must agree not to carry out their normal rituals for a specified period of time after exposure.

extinction: The weakening and often eventual disappearance of a learned response (in classical conditioning, the conditioned response is weakened by repeated presentation of the conditioned stimulus without the unconditioned stimulus; in operant conditioning, the conditioned response is weakened by withholding reinforcement).

extrasensory perception (ESP): Gaining awareness of or information about objects, events, or another's thoughts through some means other than the known sensory channels.

extrinsic motivation: The desire to perform an act to gain a reward or to avoid an undesirable consequence.

facial-feedback hypothesis: The idea that the muscular movements involved in certain facial expressions trigger the corresponding emotions (for example, smiling makes one feel happy).

family therapy: Therapy involving an entire family, based on the assumption that an individual's problem is caused and/or maintained in part by problems within the family unit.

fat cells: Cells that serve as storehouses for liquefied fat in the body and that number from 25 to 35 billion in normal-weight individuals; with weight loss, they decrease in size but not in number.

fetal alcohol syndrome: A condition, caused by maternal alcohol intake during pregnancy, in which the baby is born mentally retarded, with small head, and facial, organ, and behavioral abnormalities.

fetus: The developing human organism during the period (week 9 until birth) when rapid growth and further development of the structures, organs, and systems of the body occur.

figure-ground: A principle of perceptual organization whereby the visual field is perceived in terms of an object (figure) standing out against a background (ground).

first-degree relatives: A person's parents, children, or siblings.

five-factor theory: A trait theory that attempts to explain personality using five broad dimensions, each of which is composed of a constellation of personality traits.

fixation: Arrested development at a psychosexual stage occurring because of excessive gratification or frustration at that stage.

fixed-interval schedule: A schedule in which a reinforcer is given following the first correct response after a fixed period of time has elapsed.

fixed-ratio schedule: A schedule in which a reinforcer is given after a fixed number of correct responses.

flashback: The brief recurrence, occurring suddenly and without warning at a later time, of effects a person has experienced while taking LSD.

flashbulb memory: An extremely vivid memory of the conditions surrounding one's first hearing the news of a surprising, shocking, or highly emotional event.

flooding: A behavioral therapy used to treat phobias, during which clients are exposed to the feared object or event (or asked to imagine it vividly) for an extended period until their anxiety decreases.

fluid intelligence: Aspects of intelligence involving abstract reasoning and mental flexibility, which peak in the early 20s and decline slowly as people age.

foot-in-the-door technique: A strategy designed to secure a favorable response to a small request at first, with the aim of making the person more likely to agree later to a larger request.

formal concept: A concept that is clearly defined by a set of rules, a formal definition, or a classification system; an artificial concept.

formal operations stage: Piaget's fourth and final stage of cognitive development, characterized by the ability to apply logical thinking to abstract problems and hypothetical situations.

fovea (FO-vee-uh): A small area of the retina, 1/60 of an inch in diameter, that provides the clearest and sharpest vision because it has the largest concentration of cones.

framing: The way information is presented so as to emphasize a potential gain or potential loss as the outcome.

fraternal (dizygotic) twins: Twins, no more alike genetically than ordinary siblings, who develop after two eggs are released during ovulation and fertilized by two different sperm.

free association: A psychoanalytic technique used to explore the unconscious by having patients reveal whatever thoughts or images come to mind.

frequency: Measured in the unit called the hertz, the number of sound waves or cycles per second, determining the pitch of a sound.

frequency distribution: An arrangement showing the numbers of scores that fall within equal-sized class intervals.

frequency polygon: A line graph that depicts the frequency or number of scores within each class interval in a frequency distribution.

frequency theory: The theory that hair cell receptors vibrate the same number of times as the sounds that reach them, thereby accounting for how variations in pitch are transmitted to the brain.

frontal lobes: The lobes that control voluntary body movements, speech production, and such functions as thinking, motivation, planning for the future, impulse control, and emotional responses.

frustration: Interference with the attainment of a goal, or the blocking of an impulse.

frustration–aggression hypothesis: The hypothesis that frustration produces aggression.

functional fixedness: The failure to use familiar objects in novel ways to solve problems because of a tendency to view objects only in terms of their customary functions.

functional MRI (fMRI): A brain-imaging technique that reveals both brain structure and brain activity.

functionalism: An early school of psychology that was concerned with how mental processes help humans and animals adapt to their environments.

fundamental attribution error: The tendency to overemphasize internal causes and underemphasize situational factors when explaining the behavior of others.

g factor: Spearman's term for a general intellectual ability that underlies all mental operations to some degree.

gate-control theory: The theory that the pain signals transmitted by slow-firing nerve fibers can be blocked at the spinal gate if fast-firing fibers get their messages to the gate first, or if the brain itself inhibits transmission of the pain messages.

gender identity disorders: Disorders characterized by a problem accepting one's identity as male or female.

general adaptation syndrome (GAS): The predictable sequence of reactions (alarm, resistance, and exhaustion stages) that organisms show in response to stressors.

generalization: In classical conditioning, the tendency to make a conditioned response to a stimulus similar to the original conditioned stimulus; in operant conditioning, the tendency to make the learned response to a stimulus similar to the one that was originally reinforced.

generalized anxiety disorder: An anxiety disorder in which people experience excessive anxiety or worry that they find difficult to control.

generativity versus stagnation: Erikson's stage for middle age, when people become increasingly concerned with guiding the next generation rather than stagnating.

genes: The segments of DNA that are located on the chromosomes and are the basic units for the transmission of all hereditary traits.

genital stage: Freud's final psychosexual stage (from puberty on), in which for most people the focus of sexual energy gradually shifts to the opposite sex, culminating in the attainment of full adult sexuality.

Gestalt (geh-SHTALT): A German word roughly meaning "form" or "pattern."

Gestalt psychology: The school of psychology that emphasizes that individuals perceive objects and patterns as whole units and that the perceived whole is more than the sum of its parts.

Gestalt therapy: A therapy that was originated by Fritz Perls and that emphasizes the importance of clients' fully experiencing, in the present moment, their feelings, thoughts, and actions and taking personal responsibility for their behavior.

group polarization: The tendency of members of a group, after group discussion, to shift toward a more extreme position in whatever direction they were leaning initially—either more risky or more cautious.

group therapy: A form of therapy in which several clients (usually 7–10) meet regularly with one or more therapists to resolve personal problems.

groupthink: The tendency for members of a very cohesive group to feel such pressure to maintain group solidarity and to reach agreement on an issue that they fail to weigh available evidence adequately or to consider objections and alternatives.

gustation: The sensation of taste.

hair cells: Sensory receptors for hearing, found in the cochlea.

hallucination: A sensory perception in the absence of any external sensory stimulus; an imaginary sensation.

hallucinogens (hal-LU-sin-o-jenz): A category of drugs, sometimes called *psychedelics,* that alter perception and mood and can cause hallucinations.

halo effect: The tendency to infer generally positive or negative traits in a person as a result of observing one major positive or negative trait.

hardiness: A combination of three psychological qualities shared by people who can undergo high levels of stress yet remain healthy: a sense of control over one's life, commitment to one's personal goals, and a tendency to view change as a challenge rather than as a threat.

hassles: Little stressors that include the irritating demands and troubled relationships that can occur daily and that, according to Lazarus, cause more stress than do major life changes.

health psychology: The field concerned with the psychological factors that contribute to health, illness, and recovery.

heritability: An index of the degree to which a characteristic is estimated to be influenced by heredity.

heroin: A highly addictive, partly synthetic narcotic derived from morphine.

heuristic (yur-RIS-tik): A rule of thumb that is derived from experience and used in decision making and problem solving, even though there is no guarantee of its accuracy or usefulness.

hierarchy of needs: Maslow's theory of motivation, in which needs are arranged in order of urgency ranging from physical needs to security needs, belonging needs, esteem needs, and finally the need for self-actualization.

higher-order conditioning: Conditioning that occurs when a neutral stimulus is paired with an existing conditioned stimulus, becomes associated with it, and gains the power to elicit the same conditioned response.

hippocampal region: A part of the limbic system that includes the hippocampus itself (primarily involved in the formation of episodic memories) and its underlying cortical areas (involved in the formation of semantic memories).

hippocampus (hip-po-CAM-pus): A structure in the limbic system that plays a central role in the formation of long-term memories.

histogram: A bar graph that depicts the number of scores within each class interval in a frequency distribution.

HIV (human immunodeficiency virus): The virus that causes AIDS.

homeostasis: The tendency of the body to maintain a balanced internal state with regard to oxygen level, body temperature, blood sugar, water balance, and so forth.

hormone: A substance manufactured and released in one part of the body that affects other parts of the body.

hue: The property of light commonly referred to as color (red, blue, green, etc.), determined primarily by the wavelength of light reflected from a surface.

humanistic perspective: A perspective that emphasizes the importance of an individual's subjective experience as a key to understanding behavior.

humanistic psychology: An approach to psychology that stresses the uniquely human attributes and a positive view of human nature.

hypnosis: A procedure in which one person, the hypnotist, uses the power of suggestion to induce changes in thoughts, feelings, sensations, perceptions, or behavior in another person, the subject.

hypochondriasis (HI-poh-kahn-DRY-uh-sis): A somatoform disorder in which persons are preoccupied with their health and convinced they have some serious disorder despite reassurance from doctors to the contrary.

hypothalamus (HY-po-THAL-uh-mus): A small but influential brain structure that controls the pituitary gland and regulates hunger, thirst, sexual behavior, body temperature, and a wide variety of emotional behaviors.

hypothesis: A prediction about the relationship between two or more variables.

id (IHD): The unconscious system of the personality, which contains the life and death instincts and operates on the pleasure principle.

identical (monozygotic) twins: Twins with exactly the same genes, who develop after one egg is fertilized by one sperm, and the zygote splits into two parts.

identity versus role confusion: Erikson's fifth psychosocial stage, when adolescents need to establish their own identity and to form values to live by; failure can lead to an identity crisis.

illicit drug: An illegal drug.

illusion: A false perception of actual stimuli involving a misperception of size, shape, or the relationship of one element to another.

imagery: The representation in the mind of a sensory experience—visual, auditory, gustatory, motor, olfactory, or tactile.

imaginary audience: A belief of adolescents that they are or will be the focus of attention in social situations and that others will be as critical or approving as they are of themselves.

in-group: A social group with a strong sense of togetherness and from which others are excluded.

inappropriate affect: A symptom common in schizophrenia in which a person's behavior (including facial expression, tone of voice, and gestures) does not reflect the emotion that would be expected under the circumstances; for example, a person laughs at a tragedy or cries at a joke.

incentive: An external stimulus that motivates behavior (examples: money, fame).

independent variable: In an experiment, the factor or condition that the researcher manipulates in order to determine its effect on another behavior or condition known as the dependent variable.

industry versus inferiority: Erikson's fourth stage (ages 6 years to puberty), when children develop a sense of industry or inferiority based on how parents and teachers react to their efforts to undertake projects.

infantile amnesia: The relative inability of older children and adults to recall events from the first few years of life.

inferential statistics: Statistical procedures that allow researchers (1) to make inferences about the characteristics of the larger population from observations and measurements of a sample, and (2) to derive estimates of how much confidence can be placed in those inferences.

initiative versus guilt: Erikson's third stage (ages 3 to 6 years), when children develop a sense of initiative or guilt depending on how parents react to their initiation of play, their motor activities, and their questions.

innate: Inborn, unlearned.

inner ear: The innermost portion of the ear, containing the cochlea, the vestibular sacs, and the semicircular canals.

insight: The sudden realization of the relationship between elements in a problem situation, which makes the solution apparent.

insight therapy: Any type of psychotherapy based on the notion that psychological well-being depends on self-understanding.

insomnia: A sleep disorder characterized by difficulty falling or staying asleep, by waking too early, or by light, restless, or poor sleep.

instinct: An inborn, unlearned, fixed pattern of behavior that is characteristic of an entire species.

instinct theory: The notion that human behavior is motivated by certain innate tendencies, or instincts, shared by all individuals.

intelligence: An individual's ability to understand complex ideas, to adapt effectively to the environment, to learn from experience, to engage in various forms of reasoning, and to overcome obstacles by mental effort.

intelligence quotient (IQ): An index of intelligence originally derived by dividing mental age by chronological age and then multiplying by 100; now derived by comparing an individual's score to the scores of others of the same age.

interference: Memory loss that occurs because information or associations stored either before or after a given memory hinder the ability to remember it.

interpersonal therapy (IPT): A brief psychotherapy designed to help depressed people better understand and cope with problems relating to their interpersonal relationships.

intimacy versus isolation: Erikson's sixth psychosocial stage, when the young adult must establish intimacy in a relationship in order to avoid feeling a sense of isolation and loneliness.

intrinsic motivation: The desire to perform an act because it is satisfying or pleasurable in and of itself.

inventory: A paper-and-pencil test with questions about a person's thoughts, feelings, and behaviors, which can be scored according to a standard procedure.

James–Lange theory of emotion: The theory that emotional feelings result when an individual becomes aware of a physiological response to an emotion-provoking stimulus (for example, feeling fear because of trembling).

just noticeable difference (JND): The smallest change in sensation that a person is able to detect 50% of the time.

kinesthetic sense: The sense providing information about relative position and movement of body parts.

language: A means of communicating thoughts and feelings, using a system of socially shared but arbitrary symbols (sounds, signs, or written symbols) arranged according to rules of grammar.

latency period: The period following Freud's phallic stage (ages 5 or 6 years to puberty), in which the sex instinct is largely repressed and temporarily sublimated in school and play activities.

latent learning: Learning that occurs without apparent reinforcement but that is not demonstrated until sufficient reinforcement is provided.

lateral hypothalamus (LH): The part of the hypothalamus that acts as a feeding center and, when activated, signals an animal to eat; when the LH is destroyed, the animal refuses to eat.

law of effect: Thorndike's law of learning, which states that the connection between a stimulus and a response will be strengthened if the response is followed by a satisfying consequence and weakened if the response is followed by discomfort.

Lazarus theory of emotion: The theory that an emotion-provoking stimulus triggers a cognitive appraisal, which is followed by the emotion and the physiological arousal.

learned helplessness: The learned response of resigning oneself passively to aversive conditions, rather than taking action to change, escape, or avoid them; learned through repeated exposure to inescapable or unavoidable aversive events.

learning: A relatively permanent change in behavior, knowledge, capability, or attitude that is acquired through experience and cannot be attributed to illness, injury, or maturation.

left hemisphere: The hemisphere that controls the right side of the body, coordinates complex movements, and, in 95% of people, controls the production of speech and written language.

lens: The transparent structure behind the iris that changes shape as it focuses images on the retina.

levels-of-processing model: A model of memory as a single system in which retention depends on how deeply information is processed.

libido (lih-BEE-doe): Freud's name for the psychic or sexual energy that comes from the id and provides the energy for the entire personality.

limbic system: A group of structures in the brain, including the amygdala and hippocampus, that are collectively involved in emotion, memory, and motivation.

linguistic relativity hypothesis: The notion that the language a person speaks largely determines the nature of that person's thoughts.

lithium: A drug used in bipolar disorder to control the symptoms in a manic episode and to even out the mood swings and reduce recurrence of future manic or depressive states.

lobotomy: A psychosurgery technique in which the nerve fibers connecting the frontal lobes to the deeper brain centers are severed.

locus of control: A concept used to explain how people account for what happens in their lives—people with an *internal* locus of control see themselves as primarily in control of their behavior and its consequences; those with an *external* locus of control perceive what happens to be in the hands of fate, luck, or chance.

long-term memory: The relatively permanent memory system with a virtually unlimited capacity.

longitudinal study: A type of developmental study in which the same group of participants is followed and measured at different ages.

low-ball technique: A strategy to gain compliance by making a very attractive initial offer to get a person to agree to an action and then making the terms less favorable.

low-birthweight baby: A baby weighing less than 5.5 pounds.

LSD (lysergic acid diethylamide): A powerful hallucinogen with unpredictable effects ranging from perceptual changes and vivid hallucinations to states of panic and terror.

lucid dream: A dream during which the dreamer is aware of dreaming and is often able to influence the content of the dream while it is in progress.

lymphocytes: The white blood cells—B cells, T cells, and macrophages—that are key components of the immune system.

magnetic resonance imaging (MRI): A diagnostic scanning technique that produces high resolution images of the structures of the brain.

mainstreaming: Educating mentally retarded students in regular rather than special schools by placing them in regular classes for part of the day or having special classrooms in regular schools.

major depressive disorder: A mood disorder marked by feelings of great sadness, despair, guilt, worthlessness, and hopelessness.

manic episode (MAN-ik): A period of extreme elation, euphoria, and hyperactivity, often accompanied by delusions of grandeur and by hostility if activity is blocked.

marijuana: A hallucinogen with effects ranging from relaxation and giddiness to perceptual distortions and hallucinations.

massed practice: Learning in one long practice session as opposed to spacing the learning in shorter practice sessions over an extended period.

matching hypothesis: The notion that people tend to have spouses, lovers, or friends who are approximately equivalent in social assets such as physical attractiveness.

maturation: Changes that occur according to one's genetically determined, biological timetable of development.

MDMA (Ecstasy): A designer drug that is a hallucinogen-amphetamine and can produce permanent damage of the serotonin-releasing neurons.

mean: The arithmetic average of a group of scores; calculated by adding up all the single scores and dividing the sum by the number of scores.

means–end analysis: A heuristic strategy in which the current position is compared with the desired goal, and a series of steps are formulated and taken to close the gap between them.

measure of central tendency: A measure or score that describes the center, or middle, of a distribution of scores (example: mean, median, or mode).

median: The middle value or score when a group of scores are arranged from highest to lowest.

meditation (concentrative): A group of techniques that involve focusing attention on an object, a word, one's breathing, or body movement in order to block out all distractions, to enhance well-being, and to achieve an altered state of consciousness.

medulla (muh-DUL-uh): The part of the brainstem that controls heartbeat, blood pressure, breathing, coughing, and swallowing.

melatonin: A hormone secreted by the pineal gland that acts to reduce activity and induce sleep.

menarche (men-AR-kee): The onset of menstruation.

menopause: The cessation of menstruation, occurring between ages 45 and 55 and signifying the end of reproductive capacity.

mental retardation: Subnormal intelligence reflected by an IQ below 70 and by adaptive functioning severely deficient for one's age.

mental set: The tendency to apply a familiar strategy to the solution of a problem without carefully considering the special requirements of that problem.

mere-exposure effect: The tendency of people to develop a more positive evaluation of some person, object, or other stimulus with repeated exposure to it.

meta-analysis: A complex statistical procedure used to combine the results from many studies on the same topic in order to determine the degree to which a hypothesis can be supported.

metabolic rate (meh-tuh-BALL-ik): The rate at which the body burns calories to produce energy.

microelectrode: An electrical wire so small that it can be used either to monitor the electrical activity of a single neuron or to stimulate activity within it.

microsleep: A momentary lapse from wakefulness into sleep, usually occurring when a person has been sleep deprived.

middle ear: The portion of the ear containing the ossicles, which connect the eardrum to the oval window and amplify the vibrations as they travel to the inner ear.

Minnesota Multiphasic Personality Inventory (MMPI): The most extensively researched and widely used personality test; used to screen and diagnose psychiatric problems and disorders; revised as MMPI-2.

minor tranquilizer: A central nervous system depressant that calms the user.

mode: The score that occurs most frequently in a group of scores.

model: The individual who demonstrates a behavior or serves as an example in observational learning.

modeling: Another name for observational learning.

monocular depth cues (mah-NOK-yu-ler): Depth cues that can be perceived by only one eye.

mood disorders: Disorders characterized by extreme and unwarranted disturbances in feeling or mood.

morphemes: The smallest units of meaning in a language.

motivated forgetting: Forgetting through suppression or repression in order to protect oneself from material that is too painful, anxiety- or guilt-producing, or otherwise unpleasant.

motivation: The process that initiates, directs, and sustains behavior to satisfy physiological or psychological needs or wants.

motives: Needs or desires that energize and direct behavior toward a goal.

motor cortex: The strip of tissue at the rear of the frontal lobes that controls voluntary body movement.

myelin sheath (MY-uh-lin): The white, fatty coating wrapped around some axons that acts as insulation and enables impulses to travel much faster.

Myers–Briggs Type Indicator (MBTI): An inventory for classifying personality types based on Jung's theory of personality.

naive subject: A person who has agreed to participate in an experiment but is not aware that deception is being used to conceal its real purpose.

naloxone: A drug that blocks the action of endorphins.

narcolepsy (NAR-co-lep-see): A serious sleep disorder characterized by excessive daytime sleepiness and sudden, uncontrollable attacks of REM sleep.

narcotics: A class of depressant drugs derived from the opium poppy and producing pain-relieving and calming effects.

natural concept: A concept acquired not from a definition but through everyday perceptions and experiences; a fuzzy concept.

naturalistic observation: A research method in which the researcher observes and records behavior in its natural setting, without attempting to influence or control it.

nature–nurture controversy: The debate concerning the relative influences of heredity and environment on development.

need for achievement (n Ach): The need to accomplish something difficult and to perform at a high standard of excellence.

negative correlation: A relationship between two variables in which an increase in one variable is associated with a decrease in the other variable.

negative reinforcement: The termination of an unpleasant stimulus after a response in order to increase the probability that the response will be repeated.

neonate: Newborn infant up to 1 month old.

neural networks: Computer systems that are intended to mimic the human brain.

neuron (NEW-ron): A specialized cell that conducts impulses through the nervous system and contains three major parts—a cell body, dendrites, and an axon.

neuroscience: A field that combines the work of psychologists, biologists, biochemists, medical researchers, and others in the study of the structure and function of the nervous system.

neurosis (new-RO-sis): An obsolete term for a disorder causing personal distress and some impairment in functioning but not causing loss of contact with reality or violation of important social norms.

neurotransmitter (NEW-ro-TRANS-mit-er): A chemical that is released into the synaptic cleft from the axon terminal of a sending neuron, crosses a synapse, and binds to appropriate receptor sites on the dendrites or cell body of a receiving neuron, influencing the cell either to fire or not to fire.

nightmare: A very frightening dream occurring during REM sleep.

nondeclarative memory: The subsystem within long-term memory that consists of skills acquired through repetitive practice, habits, and simple classically conditioned responses; also called *implicit memory.*

nondirective therapy: An approach in which the therapist acts to facilitate growth, giving understanding and support rather than proposing solutions, answering questions, or actively directing the course of therapy.

nonsense syllable: A consonant-vowel-consonant combination that does not spell a word; used to control for the meaningfulness of the material.

norepinephrine: A neurotransmitter affecting eating and sleep; a deficiency of norepinephrine is associated with depression.

normal curve: A symmetrical, bell-shaped frequency distribution that represents how scores are normally distributed in a population; most scores fall near the mean, and fewer and fewer scores occur in the extremes either above or below the mean.

norms: Standards based on the range of test scores of a large group of people who are selected to provide the bases of comparison for those who take the test later; the attitudes and standards of behavior expected of members of a particular group.

NREM dream: Mental activity occurring during NREM sleep that is more thoughtlike in quality than REM dreams are.

NREM sleep: Non–rapid eye movement sleep, consisting of the four sleep stages and characterized by slow, regular respiration and heart rate, an absence of rapid eye movements, and blood pressure and brain activity that are at a 24-hour low point.

object permanence: The realization that objects continue to exist even when they can no longer be perceived.

observational learning: Learning by observing the behavior of others and the consequences of that behavior; learning by imitation.

obsession: A persistent, recurring, involuntary thought, image, or impulse that invades consciousness and causes great distress.

obsessive compulsive disorder (OCD): An anxiety disorder in which a person suffers from obsessions and/or compulsions.

occipital lobes (ahk-SIP-uh-tul): The lobes that contain the primary visual cortex, where vision registers, and association areas involved in the interpretation of visual information.

Oedipus complex (ED-uh-pus): Occurring in the phallic stage, a conflict in which the child is sexually attracted to the opposite-sex parent and feels hostility toward the same-sex parent.

olfaction (ol-FAK-shun): The sensation of smell; the process of smelling.

olfactory bulbs: Two matchstick-sized structures above the nasal cavities, where smell sensations first register in the brain.

olfactory epithelium: Two 1-inch-square patches of tissue, one at the top of each nasal cavity, which together contain about 10 million olfactory neurons, the receptors for smell.

operant conditioning: A type of learning in which the consequences of behavior are manipulated in order to increase or decrease that behavior in the future.

opponent-process theory: The theory that certain cells in the visual system increase their firing rate to signal one color and decrease their firing rate to signal the opposing color (red/green, yellow/blue, white/black).

optic nerve: The nerve that carries visual information from the retina to the brain.

oral stage: Freud's first psychosexual stage (birth to 1 or 1½ years), in which sensual pleasure is derived mainly through stimulation of the mouth.

orgasm: The third phase in the sexual response cycle, marked by rhythmic muscular contractions and a sudden discharge of accumulated sexual tension.

out-group: A social group specifically identified by the in-group as not belonging.

outer ear: The visible part of the ear, consisting of the pinna and the auditory canal.

overextension: The act of using a word, on the basis of some shared feature, to apply to a broader range of objects than appropriate.

overlearning: Practicing or studying material beyond the point where it can be repeated once without error.

overregularization: The act of inappropriately applying the grammatical rules for forming plurals and past tenses to irregular nouns and verbs.

panic attack: An attack of overwhelming anxiety, fear, or terror.

panic disorder: An anxiety disorder in which a person experiences recurrent unpredictable attacks of overwhelming anxiety, fear, or terror.

paranoid schizophrenia (PAIR-uh-noid): A type of schizophrenia characterized by delusions of grandeur or persecution.

paraphilia: A sexual disorder in which sexual urges, fantasies, and behavior generally involve children, other nonconsenting partners, objects, or the suffering and humiliation of oneself or one's partner.

parapsychology: The study of psychic phenomena, including extrasensory perception (ESP).

parasympathetic nervous system: The division of the autonomic nervous system that is associated with relaxation and the conservation of energy and that brings the heightened bodily responses back to normal following an emergency.

parietal lobes (puh-RY-uh-tul): The lobes that contain the somatosensory cortex (where touch, pressure, temperature, and pain register) and other areas that are responsible for body awareness and spatial orientation.

partial reinforcement: A pattern of reinforcement in which some portion, rather than 100%, of the correct responses are reinforced.

partial-reinforcement effect: The greater resistance to extinction that occurs when a portion, rather than all, of the correct responses are reinforced.

participant modeling: A behavior therapy in which an appropriate response is modeled in graduated steps and the client attempts each step, encouraged and supported by the therapist.

perception: The process by which sensory information is actively organized and interpreted by the brain.

perceptual constancy: The tendency to perceive objects as maintaining stable properties, such as size, shape, brightness, and color, despite differences in distance, viewing angle, and lighting.

perceptual set: An expectation of what will be perceived, which can affect what actually is perceived.

period of the zygote: The approximately 2-week-long period between conception and the attachment of the zygote to the uterine wall.

peripheral nervous system (PNS) (peh-RIF-er-ul): The nerves connecting the central nervous system to the rest of the body.

permissive parents: Parents who make few rules or demands and allow children to make their own decisions and control their own behavior.

person-centered therapy: A nondirective, humanistic therapy in which the therapist creates a warm, accepting climate, freeing clients to be themselves and releasing their natural tendency toward positive growth.

personal fable: An exaggerated sense of personal uniqueness and indestructibility, which may be the basis for adolescent risk taking.

personal space: An area surrounding each individual, much like an invisible bubble, that is considered to belong to the person and used to regulate the closeness of interactions with others.

personal unconscious: In Jung's theory, the layer of the unconscious containing all of the thoughts and experiences that are accessible to the conscious, as well as repressed memories and impulses.

personality: A person's characteristic patterns of behavior, thinking, and feeling.

personality disorder: A continuing, inflexible, maladaptive pattern of inner experience and behavior that causes great distress or impaired functioning and differs significantly from the patterns expected in the person's culture.

persuasion: A deliberate attempt to influence the attitudes and/or behavior of another.

PET scan (positron-emission tomography): A brain-imaging technique that reveals activity in various parts of the brain, based on the amount of oxygen and glucose consumed.

phallic stage: Freud's third psychosexual stage (ages 3 to 5 or 6 years), during which sensual pleasure is derived mainly through touching the genitals, and the Oedipus complex arises.

pheromones: Chemicals excreted by humans and other animals that act as signals to and elicit certain patterns of behavior from members of the same species.

phi phenomenon: An illusion of movement occurring when two or more stationary lights are flashed on and off in sequence, giving the impression that one light is actually moving from one spot to the next.

phobia (FO-bee-ah): A persistent, irrational fear of an object, situation, or activity that the person feels compelled to avoid.

phonemes: The smallest units of sound in a spoken language.

physical drug dependence: A compulsive pattern of drug use in which the user develops a drug tolerance coupled with unpleasant withdrawal symptoms when the drug use is discontinued.

pituitary gland: The endocrine gland located in the brain and often called the "master gland," which releases hormones that control other endocrine glands and also releases a growth hormone.

place theory: The theory that sounds of different frequency or pitch cause maximum activation of hair cells at certain locations along the basilar membrane.

placebo (pluh-SEE-bo): Some inert substance, such as a sugar pill or an injection of saline solution, given to the control group in an experiment as a control for the placebo effect.

placebo effect: The phenomenon that occurs when a person's response to a treatment or response on the dependent variable in an experiment is due to expectations regarding the treatment rather than to the treatment itself.

plasticity: The ability of the brain to reorganize and compensate for brain damage.

plateau phase: The second stage of the sexual response cycle, during which muscle tension and blood flow to the genitals increase in preparation for orgasm.

pleasure principle: The principle by which the id operates to seek pleasure, avoid pain, and obtain immediate gratification.

population: The entire group of interest to researchers and to which they wish to generalize their findings; the group from which a sample is selected.

positive correlation: A relationship between two variables in which both vary in the same direction.

positive reinforcement: A reward or pleasant consequence that follows a response and increases the probability that the response will be repeated.

postconventional level: Kohlberg's highest level of moral reasoning, in which moral reasoning involves weighing moral alternatives; "right" is whatever furthers basic human rights.

posttraumatic stress disorder (PTSD): A prolonged and severe stress reaction to a catastrophic event or to chronic intense stress.

preconscious: The thoughts, feelings, and memories that a person is not consciously aware of at the moment but that may be brought to consciousness.

preconventional level: Kohlberg's lowest level of moral reasoning, based on the physical consequences of an act; "right" is whatever avoids punishment or gains a reward.

prejudice: Negative attitudes toward others based on their gender, religion, race, or membership in a particular group.

prenatal: Occurring between conception and birth.

preoperational stage: Piaget's second stage of cognitive development (ages 2 to 7 years), characterized by rapid development of language and thinking governed by perception rather than logic.

presbyopia (prez-bee-O-pee-uh): A condition, occurring in the mid to late 40s, in which the lenses of the eyes no longer accommodate adequately for near vision, and reading glasses or bifocals are required for reading.

preterm infant: An infant born before the 37th week and weighing less than 5.5 pounds; a premature infant.

primacy effect: In memory, the tendency to recall the first items on a list more readily than the middle items; in social psychology, the tendency for an overall impression of another to be influenced more by the first information that is received about that person than by information that comes later.

primary appraisal: An evaluation of the significance of a potentially stressful event according to how it will affect one's well-being—whether it is perceived as irrelevant or as involving harm or loss, threat, or challenge.

primary auditory cortex: The part of the temporal lobes where hearing registers in the cerebral cortex.

primary drive: A state of tension or arousal arising from a biological need; one not based on learning.

primary mental abilities: According to Thurstone, seven relatively distinct abilities that singly or in combination are involved in all intellectual activities.

primary reinforcer: A reinforcer that fulfills a basic physical need for survival and does not depend on learning.

primary visual cortex: The area at the rear of the occipital lobes where vision registers in the cerebral cortex.

priming: The phenomenon by which an earlier encounter with a stimulus (such as a word or a picture) increases the speed or accuracy with which that stimulus or a related stimulus can be named at a later time.

proactive coping: Efforts or actions taken in advance of a potentially stressful situation to prevent its occurrence or to minimize its consequences.

problem-focused coping: A response aimed at reducing, modifying, or eliminating a source of stress.

problem solving: Thoughts and actions required to achieve a desired goal that is not readily attainable.

progesterone (pro-JES-tah-rone): A female sex hormone that plays a role in the regulation of the menstrual cycle and prepares the lining of the uterus for possible pregnancy.

projection: Attributing one's own undesirable thoughts, impulses, traits, or behaviors to others.

projective test: A personality test in which people respond to inkblots, drawings of ambiguous human situations, incomplete sentences, and the like, by projecting their own inner thoughts, feelings, fears, or conflicts onto the test materials.

prosocial behavior: Behavior that benefits others, such as helping, cooperation, and sympathy.

prototype: The example that embodies the most common and typical features of a concept.

proximity: Geographic closeness; a major factor in attraction.

psychiatrist: A medical doctor with a specialty in the diagnosis and treatment of mental disorders.

psychoactive drug: A drug that alters normal mental functioning—mood, perception, or thought; called a controlled substance if used medically.

psychoanalysis (SY-ko-ah-NAL-ih-sis): The term Freud used for both his theory of personality and his therapy for the treatment of psychological disorders. The unconscious is the primary focus of psychoanalytic theory; the therapy uses free association, dream analysis, and analysis of resistance and transference to uncover repressed memories, impulses, and conflicts thought to cause psychological disorders.

psychoanalyst (SY-ko-AN-ul-ist): A professional, usually a psychiatrist, with special training in psychoanalysis.

psychoanalytic perspective (SY-ko-AN-il-IT-ik): A perspective initially proposed by Freud that emphasizes the importance of the unconscious and of early childhood experiences as the keys to understanding behavior and thought.

psycholinguistics: The study of how language is acquired, produced, and used, and how the sounds and symbols of language are translated into meaning.

psychological drug dependence: A craving or irresistible urge for a drug's pleasurable effects.

psychology: The scientific study of behavior and mental processes.

psychoneuroimmunology (sye-ko-NEW-ro-IM-you-NOLL-oh-gee): A field in which psychologists, biologists, and medical researchers study the effects of psychological factors on the immune system.

psychosexual stages: A series of stages through which the sexual instinct develops; each stage is defined by an erogenous zone that becomes the center of new pleasures and conflicts.

psychosis (sy-CO-sis): A severe psychological disorder, marked by loss of contact with reality and a seriously impaired ability to function.

psychosocial stages: Erikson's eight developmental stages through the life span, each defined by a conflict that must be resolved satisfactorily in order for healthy personality development to occur.

psychosurgery: Brain surgery to treat some severe, persistent, and debilitating psychological disorder or severe chronic pain.

psychotherapy: The treatment for psychological disorders that uses psychological rather than biological means and primarily involves conversations between patient and therapist.

puberty: A period of rapid physical growth and change that culminates in sexual maturity.

punishment: The removal of a pleasant stimulus or the application of an unpleasant stimulus, which tends to suppress a response.

random assignment: In an experiment, the assignment of participants to experimental and control groups by using a chance procedure, which guarantees that each has an equal probability of being placed in any of the groups; a control for selection bias.

random sample: A sample of subjects selected in such a way that every member of the population has an equal chance of being included in the sample; its purpose is to obtain a sample that is representative of the population of interest.

range: The difference between the highest score and the lowest score in a distribution of scores.

rational-emotive therapy: A directive, confrontational therapy developed by Albert Ellis and designed to challenge and modify the irrational beliefs thought to cause personal distress.

rationalization: Supplying a logical, rational, socially acceptable reason rather than the real reason for an action.

reaction formation: Denying an unacceptable impulse, often a sexual or aggressive one, by giving strong conscious expression to its opposite.

realistic conflict theory: The notion that prejudices arise when social groups must compete for scarce resources and opportunities.

recall: A measure of retention that requires a person to remember material with few or no retrieval cues, as in an essay test.

recency effect: The tendency to recall the last items on a list more readily than those in the middle of the list.

receptors: Protein molecules on the dendrite or cell body of a neuron that will interact only with specific neurotransmitters.

recessive gene: A gene that will not be expressed if paired with a dominant gene but will be expressed if paired with another recessive gene.

reciprocal determinism: Bandura's concept that behavior, personal/cognitive factors, and environment all influence and are influenced by each other.

recognition: Measure of retention that requires a person to identify material as familiar, or as having been encountered before.

reconstruction: A memory that is not an exact replica of an event but has been pieced together from a few highlights, using information that may or may not be accurate.

reflex: An inborn, involuntary response to a particular environmental stimulus, such as the eyeblink response to a puff of air or salivation when food is placed in the mouth.

regression: Reverting to a behavior characteristic of an earlier stage of development.

rehearsal: The act of purposely repeating information to maintain it in short-term memory or to transfer it to long-term memory.

reinforcement: An event that follows a response and increases the strength of the response and/or the likelihood that it will be repeated.

reinforcer: Anything that strengthens a response or increases the probability that it will occur.

relearning method: Measuring retention in terms of the percentage of time or learning trials saved in relearning material compared with the time required to learn it originally; also called the savings method.

reliability: The ability of a test to yield nearly the same scores when the same people are tested and then retested on the same test or an alternative form of the test.

REM dream: A type of dream having a dreamlike and storylike quality and occuring almost continuously during each REM period; more vivid, visual, and emotional than NREM dreams.

REM rebound: The increased amount of REM sleep that occurs after REM deprivation; often associated with unpleasant dreams or nightmares.

REM sleep: Sleep characterized by rapid eye movements, paralysis of large muscles, fast and irregular heart rate and respiration rate, increased brain-wave activity, and vivid dreams.

replication: The process of repeating a study with different participants and preferably a different investigator to verify research findings.

representative sample: A sample of participants selected from the larger population in such a way that important subgroups within the population are included in the sample in the same proportions as they are found in the larger population.

representativeness heuristic: A thinking strategy based on how closely a new object or situation is judged to resemble or match an existing prototype of that object or situation.

repression: Involuntarily removing from one's consciousness disturbing, guilt-provoking, or otherwise unpleasant memories so that one is no longer aware that a painful event occurred.

resistance: In psychoanalytic therapy, the patient's attempts to avoid expressing or revealing painful or embarrassing thoughts or feelings.

resistance stage: The second stage of the general adaptation syndrome, when there are intense physiological efforts to either resist or adapt to the stressor.

resolution phase: The final stage of the sexual response cycle, during which the body returns to an unaroused state.

resting potential: The membrane potential of a neuron at rest, about –70 millivolts.

restorative theory: The theory that the function of sleep is to restore body and mind.

reticular formation: A structure in the brainstem that plays a crucial role in arousal and attention and that screens sensory messages entering the brain.

retina: The membrane at the back of the eye that contains the rods and the cones and onto which the incoming image is projected by the lens.

retinal image: The image of objects in the visual field projected onto the retina.

retrieval: The act of bringing to mind material that has been stored in memory.

retrieval cue: Any stimulus or bit of information that aids in the retrieval of particular information from long-term memory.

retrograde amnesia (RET-ro-grade): A loss of memory affecting experiences that occurred shortly before a loss of consciousness.

reuptake: The process by which neurotransmitter molecules are taken from the synaptic cleft back into the axon terminal for later use, thus terminating their excitatory or inhibitory effect on the receiving neuron.

reversibility: The realization that any change in the shape, position, or order of matter can be reversed mentally.

right hemisphere: The hemisphere that controls the left side of the body and that, in most people, is specialized for visual-spatial perception and for interpreting nonverbal behavior.

rods: The light-sensitive receptors in the retina that allow humans to see in black, white, and shades of gray in dim light.

Rorschach Inkblot Method (ROR-shok): A projective test composed of 10 inkblots to which a test taker responds; used to reveal unconscious functioning and the presence of psychiatric disorders.

sample: The portion of any population that is selected for study and from which generalizations are made about the larger population.

saturation: The degree to which light waves producing a color are of the same wavelength; the purity of a color.

savings score: The percentage of time or learning trials saved in relearning material over the amount of time or number of learning trials required for the original learning.

scapegoating: Displacing aggression onto minority groups or other innocent targets not responsible for the frustrating situation.

Schachter–Singer theory: A two-stage theory stating that for an emotion to occur, there must be (1) physiological arousal and (2) an explanation for the arousal.

schedule of reinforcement: A systematic program for administering reinforcements that has a predictable effect on behavior.

schema: In memory, the integrated framework of knowledge and assumptions a person has about people, objects, or events, which affect how the person encodes and recalls information; in cognitive development, Piaget's term for a cognitive structure or concept used to identify and interpret information.

schizophrenia (SKIT-soh-FREE-nee-ah): A severe psychological disorder characterized by loss of contact with reality, hallucinations, delusions, inappropriate or flat affect, some disturbance in thinking, social withdrawal, and/or other bizarre behavior.

scientific method: The orderly, systematic procedures researchers follow as they identify a research problem, design a study to investigate the problem, collect and analyze data, draw conclusions, and communicate their findings.

seasonal affective disorder (SAD): A mood disorder in which depression comes and goes with the seasons.

secondary appraisal: An evaluation of one's coping resources prior to deciding how to deal with a stressful event.

secondary reinforcer: A neutral stimulus that becomes reinforcing after repeated pairings with other reinforcers.

secondary sex characteristics: Those physical characteristics that are not directly involved in reproduction but that distinguish the mature male from the mature female.

sedentary lifestyle: A lifestyle that includes less than 20 minutes of exercise three times a week.

selection bias: The assignment of participants to experimental or control groups in such a way that systematic differences among the groups are present at the beginning of the experiment.

self-actualization: The development of one's full potential; the highest need on Maslow's hierarchy.

self-efficacy: A person's belief in his or her ability to perform competently in whatever is attempted.

self-serving bias: The tendency to attribute personal successes to dispositional causes and failures to situational causes.

semantic memory: The subpart of declarative memory that stores general knowledge; a mental encyclopedia or dictionary.

semantics: The meaning or the study of meaning derived from morphemes, words, and sentences.

semicircular canals: Three fluid-filled tubular canals in the inner ear that provide information about rotating head movements.

senile dementia: A state of mental deterioration caused by physical deterioration of the brain and characterized by impaired memory and intellect and by altered personality and behavior; senility.

sensation: The process through which the senses pick up visual, auditory, and other sensory stimuli and transmit them to the brain; sensory information that has registered in the brain but has not been interpreted.

sensorimotor stage: Piaget's first stage of cognitive development (ages birth to 2 years), culminating with the development of object permanence and the beginning of representational thought.

sensory adaptation: The process of becoming less sensitive to an unchanging sensory stimulus over time.

sensory deprivation: A condition in which sensory stimulation is reduced to a minimum or eliminated.

sensory memory: The memory system that holds information coming in through the senses for a period ranging from a fraction of a second to several seconds.

sensory receptors: Specialized cells in each sense organ that detect and respond to sensory stimuli—light, sound, odors, etc.—and transduce (convert) the stimuli into neural impulses.

separation anxiety: The fear and distress shown by toddlers when their parent leaves, occurring from 8 to 24 months and reaching a peak between 12 and 18 months.

serial position effect: The tendency to remember the beginning and ending items of a sequence or list better than the middle items.

serotonin: A neurotransmitter that plays an important role in regulating mood, sleep, aggression, and appetite; a serotonin deficiency is associated with anxiety, depression, and suicide.

set point: The weight the body normally maintains when one is trying neither to gain nor to lose weight; if weight falls below the normal level, appetite increases and metabolic rate decreases; if weight is gained, appetite decreases and metabolic rate increases to its original level.

sex chromosomes: One of the 23 pairs of chromosomes, which carry the genes that determine one's sex, primary and secondary sex characteristics, and other sex-linked traits.

sexual dysfunction: A persistent or recurrent problem that causes marked distress and interpersonal difficulty and that may involve any or some combination of the following: sexual desire, sexual arousal, or the pleasure associated with sex or orgasm.

sexual orientation: The direction of one's sexual preference—toward members of the opposite sex (heterosexuality), toward one's own sex (homosexuality), or toward both sexes (bisexuality).

sexual response cycle: The four phases—excitement, plateau, orgasm, and resolution—that Masters and Johnson found are part of the human sexual response in both males and females.

shape constancy: The tendency to perceive an object as having a stable or unchanging shape regardless of differences in viewing angle.

shaping: An operant conditioning technique that consists of gradually molding a desired behavior (response) by reinforcing responses that become progressively closer to it.

short-term memory: The second stage of memory, which holds about seven (a range of five to nine) items for less than 30 seconds without rehearsal; working memory; the mental workspace a person uses to keep in mind those tasks being thought about at any given moment.

signal detection theory: The view that detection of a sensory stimulus involves both discriminating a stimulus from background "noise" and deciding whether the stimulus is actually present.

situational attribution: Attribution of a behavior to some external cause or factor operating in the situation; an external attribution.

size constancy: The tendency to perceive an object as the same size regardless of changes in the retinal image.

Skinner box: A soundproof chamber with a device for delivering food and either a bar for rats to press or a disk for pigeons to peck; used in operant conditioning experiments.

sleep apnea: A sleep disorder characterized by periods when breathing stops during sleep and the person must awaken briefly in order to breathe; major symptoms are excessive daytime sleepiness and loud snoring.

sleep cycle: A cycle of sleep lasting about 90 minutes and including one or more stages of NREM sleep followed by a period of REM sleep.

sleep terror: A sleep disturbance in which a person partially awakens from Stage 4 sleep with a scream, dazed and groggy, in a panic state, and with a racing heart.

sleepwalking (somnambulism) (som-NAM-bue-lism): Walking that occurs during a partial arousal from Stage 4 sleep.

slow-wave sleep: Stage 3 sleep and Stage 4 sleep.

social cognition: Mental processes that people use to notice, interpret, understand, remember, and apply information about the social world and that enable them to simplify, categorize, and order that world.

social facilitation: Any positive or negative effect on performance due to the presence of others, either as an audience or as co-actors.

social loafing: The tendency to put forth less effort when working with others on a common task than when working alone.

social motives: Motives acquired through experience and interaction with others.

social phobia: An irrational fear and avoidance of social situations in which one might embarrass or humiliate oneself by appearing clumsy, foolish, or incompetent.

social psychology: The study of how the actual, imagined, or implied presence of others influences the thoughts, feelings, and behavior of individuals.

Social Readjustment Rating Scale (SRRS): Holmes and Rahe's stress scale, which ranks 43 life events from most to least stressful and assigns a point value to each.

social roles: Socially defined behaviors considered appropriate for individuals occupying certain positions within a group.

social support: Tangible support, information, advice, and/or emotional support provided in time of need by family, friends, and others; the feeling of being loved, valued, and cared for.

socialization: The process of learning socially acceptable behaviors, attitudes, and values.

sociocultural perspective: A perspective that emphasizes social and cultural influences on human behavior and stresses the importance of understanding those influences when interpreting the behavior of others.

somatoform disorders (so-MAT-uh-form): Disorders in which physical symptoms are present that are due to psychological rather than physical causes.

somatosensory cortex (so-MAT-o-SENS-or-ee): The strip of tissue at the front of the parietal lobes where touch, pressure, temperature, and pain register in the cerebral cortex.

source traits: Cattell's name for the traits that make up the most basic personality structure and cause behavior.

specific phobia: A marked fear of a specific object or situation; a catchall category for any phobia other than agoraphobia and social phobia.

spinal cord: An extension of the brain, reaching from the base of the brain through the neck and spinal column, that transmits messages between the brain and the peripheral nervous system.

split-brain operation: An operation, performed in severe cases of epilepsy, in which the corpus callosum is cut, separating the cerebral hemispheres and usually lessening the severity and frequency of grand mal seizures.

spontaneous recovery: The reappearance of an extinguished response (in a weaker form) when an organism is exposed to the original conditioned stimulus following a rest period.

Stage 4 sleep: The deepest stage of NREM sleep, characterized by an EEG pattern of more than 50% delta waves.

standard deviation: A descriptive statistic reflecting the average amount that scores in a distribution deviate, or vary, from their mean.

standardization: Establishing norms for comparing the scores of people who will take a test in the future; administering tests using a prescribed procedure.

Stanford–Binet Intelligence Scale: An individually administered IQ test for those aged 2 to 23; Terman's adaptation of the Binet–Simon Scale.

state-dependent memory effect: The tendency to recall information better if one is in the same pharmacological or psychological (mood) state as when the information was encoded.

stereotypes: Widely shared beliefs about the characteristic traits, attitudes, and behaviors of members of various social groups (racial, ethnic, religious), including the assumption that the members of such groups are usually all alike.

stimulants: A category of drugs that speed up activity in the central nervous system, suppress appetite, and cause a person to feel more awake, alert, and energetic; also called *uppers.*

stimulus (STIM-yu-lus): Any event or object in the environment to which an organism responds; plural is *stimuli.*

stimulus motives: Motives that cause humans and other animals to increase stimulation and that appear to be unlearned (examples: curiosity and the need to explore, manipulate objects, and play).

stimulus satiation (say-she-A-shun): A behavior modification technique that involves giving a patient so much of a stimulus that it becomes something the patient wants to avoid.

storage: The act of maintaining information in memory.

stranger anxiety: A fear of strangers common in infants at about 6 months and increasing in intensity until about 12½ months, and then declining in the second year.

stress: The physiological and psychological response to a condition that threatens or challenges a person and requires some form of adaptation or adjustment.

stressor: Any stimulus or event capable of producing physical or emotional stress.

stroke: The most common cause of damage to adult brains, arising when blockage of an artery cuts off the blood supply to a particular area of the brain or when a blood vessel bursts.

structuralism: The first formal school of psychology, aimed at analyzing the basic elements, or structure, of conscious mental experience through the use of introspection.

subjective night: The time during a 24-hour period when body temperature is lowest and when the biological clock is telling a person to go to sleep.

sublimation: Rechanneling sexual or aggressive energy into pursuits that society considers acceptable or admirable.

subliminal perception: Perceiving sensory stimulation that is below the absolute threshold.

subliminal persuasion: Sending persuasive messages below the recipient's level of awareness.

successive approximations: A series of gradual steps, each of which is more like the final desired response.

superego (sue-per-EE-go): The moral system of the personality, which consists of the conscience and the ego ideal.

suprachiasmatic nucleus (SCN): A tiny structure in the brain's hypothalamus that controls the timing of circadian rhythms; the biological clock.

surface traits: Cattell's name for observable qualities of personality, such as those used to describe a friend.

surrogate: Substitute; someone or something that stands in place of someone or something else.

survey: A method in which researchers use interviews and/or questionnaires to gather information about the attitudes, beliefs, experiences, or behaviors of a group of people.

sympathetic nervous system: The division of the autonomic nervous system that mobilizes the body's resources during stress, emergencies, or heavy exertion, preparing the body for action.

synapse (SIN-aps): The junction where the axon of a sending neuron communicates with a receiving neuron across the synaptic cleft.

syntax: The aspect of grammar that specifies the rules for arranging and combining words to form phrases and sentences.

systematic desensitization: A behavior therapy that is used to treat phobias and that involves training clients in deep muscle relaxation and then having them confront a graduated series of anxiety-producing situations (real or imagined) until they can remain relaxed while confronting even the most feared situation.

tactile: Pertaining to the sense of touch.

taste aversion: The dislike and/or avoidance of a particular food that has been associated with nausea or discomfort.

taste buds: Structures composed of 60 to 100 sensory receptors for taste.

telegraphic speech: Short sentences that follow a strict word order and contain only essential content words.

temperament: A person's behavioral style or characteristic way of responding to the environment.

temporal lobes: The lobes that contain the primary auditory cortex, Wernicke's area, and association areas for interpreting auditory information.

teratogens: Harmful agents in the prenatal environment, which can have a negative impact on prenatal development or even cause birth defects.

testosterone (tes-TOS-tah-rone): The most powerful androgen secreted by the testes and adrenal glands in males and by the adrenal glands in females; influences the development and maintenance of male sex characteristics and sexual motivation; associated with male aggressiveness.

thalamus (THAL-uh-mus): The structure, located above the brainstem, that acts as a relay station for information flowing into or out of the higher brain centers.

THC (tetrahydrocannabinol): The principal psychoactive ingredient in marijuana.

Thematic Apperception Test (TAT): A projective test consisting of drawings of ambiguous human situations, which the test taker describes; thought to reveal inner feelings, conflicts, and motives, which are projected onto the test materials.

theory: A general principle or set of principles proposed to explain how a number of separate facts are related.

timbre (TAM-burr): The distinctive quality of a sound that distinguishes it from other sounds of the same pitch and loudness.

time out: A behavior modification technique used to decrease the frequency of undesirable behavior by withdrawing an individual from all reinforcement for a period of time.

token economy: A program that motivates and reinforces socially acceptable behaviors with tokens that can be exchanged for desired items or privileges.

top-down processing: Application of previous experience and conceptual knowledge to recognize the whole of a perception and thus easily identify the simpler elements of that whole.

trait: A personal characteristic that is used to describe or explain personality.

trait theories: Theories that attempt to explain personality and differences between people in terms of their personal characteristics.

transduction: The process by which sensory receptors convert sensory stimuli—light, sound, odors, etc.—into neural impulses.

transference: An intense emotional reaction during psychoanalysis, when the patient displays feelings and attitudes toward the analyst that were present in a significant relationship in the past.

trial and error: An approach to problem solving in which one solution after another is tried in no particular order until an answer is found.

trial-and-error learning: Learning that occurs when a response is associated with a successful solution to a problem after a number of unsuccessful responses.

triarchic theory of intelligence: Sternberg's theory that there are three types of intelligence—componential (analytical), experiential (creative), and contextual (practical).

trichromatic theory: The theory of color vision suggesting that there are three types of cones, which are maximally sensitive to red, green, or blue, and that varying levels of activity in these receptors can produce all of the colors.

twin study method: Studying identical and fraternal twins to determine the relative effects of heredity and environment on a variety of characteristics.

Type A behavior pattern: A behavior pattern marked by a sense of time urgency, impatience, excessive competitiveness, hostility, and anger; considered a risk factor in coronary heart disease.

Type B behavior pattern: A behavior pattern marked by a relaxed, easygoing approach to life; not associated with coronary heart disease.

unconditional positive regard: Unqualified caring and nonjudgmental acceptance of another.

unconditioned response (UR): A response that is invariably elicited by the unconditioned stimulus without prior learning.

unconditioned stimulus (US): A stimulus that elicits a specific response without prior learning.

unconscious (un-KON-shus): For Freud, the primary motivating force of behavior, containing repressed memories as well as instincts and wishes that have never been conscious.

underextension: Restricting the use of a word to only a few, rather than to all, members of a class of objects.

uplifts: The positive experiences in life, which can neutralize the effects of many of the hassles.

validity: The ability of a test to measure what it is intended to measure.

variability: How much the scores in a distribution spread out, away from the mean.

variable-interval schedule: A schedule in which a reinforcer is given after the first correct response following a varying time of nonreinforcement based on an average time.

variable-ratio schedule: A schedule in which a reinforcer is given after a varying number of nonreinforced responses based on an average ratio.

ventromedial hypothalamus (VMH): The part of the hypothalamus that acts as a satiety center and, when activated, signals an animal to stop eating; when the VMH is destroyed, the animal overeats, becoming obese.

vestibular sense (ves-TIB-yu-ler): Sense that provides information about the body's movement and orientation in space through sensory receptors in the semicircular canals and the vestibular sacs, which detect changes in the movement and orientation of the head.

visible spectrum: The narrow band of electromagnetic waves, 380–760 nm in length, that are visible to the human eye.

visual cliff: An apparatus used to test depth perception in infants and young animals.

Weber's law: The law stating that the just noticeable difference (JND) for all the senses depends on a proportion or percentage of change in a stimulus rather than on a fixed amount of change.

Wechsler Adult Intelligence Scale (WAIS-R): An individual intelligence test for adults that yields separate verbal and performance (nonverbal) IQ scores as well as an overall IQ score.

Wernicke's aphasia: Aphasia resulting from damage to Wernicke's area, in which the patient's spoken language is fluent, but the content is either vague or incomprehensible to the listener.

Wernicke's area: The language area in the temporal lobe involved in comprehension of the spoken word and in formulation of coherent speech and written language.

withdrawal symptoms: The physical and psychological symptoms (usually the opposite of those produced by the drug) that occur when a regularly used drug is discontinued and that terminate when the drug is taken again.

working backwards: A heuristic strategy in which a person discovers the steps needed to solve a problem by defining the desired goal and working backwards to the current condition.

Yerkes–Dodson law: The principle that performance on tasks is best when the arousal level is appropriate to the difficulty of the task—higher arousal for simple tasks, moderate arousal for tasks of moderate difficulty, and lower arousal for complex tasks.

Name Index

Eich, E., 186
Eich, J. E., 186
Eichenbaum, H., 43, 187
Einstein, A., 201
Eisen, J. L., 408, 409, 439
Eisenberg, C., 366, 367
Ekman, P., 310, 311, 312, 313, 314, 482
Elkin, I., 427, 428, 437
Elkind, D., 258, 263, 269
Ellason, J. W., 411
Elliot, A. J., 469
Ellis, A., 415, 434, 435
El-Shiekh, M., 361
Engel, G. L., 358
Engles, G. I., 435
Epstein, J., 266
Epstein, R., 108, 231
Ericsson, K. A., 230
Erikson, E. H., 258, 259, 268, 269, 280, 281
Erlenmeyer-Kimling, L., 223
Eron, L. D., 481
Eronen, M., 479
Erwin, E., 332
Estes, W. K., 202
Evans, G. W., 480
Evans, M. D., 436
Ewin, D. M., 114
Eysenck, H. J., 335, 336, 350, 441

Fackelmann, K., 122
Faedda, G. L., 401
Falbo, T., 307
Famighetti, R., 438, 478
Fantz, R. L., 244, 245
Farah, M. J., 201
Faravelli, C., 405
Farde, L., 50
Farrer, L. A., 274
Farvolden, P., 182
Fawcett, J. C., 52
Fazio, R. H., 468, 469
Fechner, G., 17
Feigenspan, A., 38
Fein, S., 473
Feingold, A., 459, 460, 461
Fenton, W. S., 396, 397, 398
Fernald, A., 257
Festinger, L., 458, 469, 470
Fiatarone, M. A., 273, 382
Fiedler, K., 472
Field, T. M., 245
Fiez, J. A., 41
Finchilescu, G., 475
Fink, M., 439
Finkbeiner, A. K., 104
Finkel, D., 341
Fiorito, G., 157
Fischbach, G. D., 188
Fishbein, M., 469
Fisher, L. M., 273
Fisher, W. A., 302
Fixx, J. F., 207
Flavell, J. H., 253, 254, 263
Flegal, K. M., 296
Fleming, J. D., 210
Fletcher, A. C., 266

Fletcher, J. M., 121
Flood, J. F., 295
Florian, V., 377
Flynn, J. R., 224
Foa, E. B., 366, 408, 432, 443
Fogarty, S. J., 186
Fogelman, E., 477
Foley, D. J., 106
Foley, H. J., 75
Folkard, S., 103
Folkman, S., 277, 361, 362, 367
Fontana, A., 366
Fontham, E. T. H., 379
Ford, C. S., 304
Foreyt, J. P., 298
Forgas, J. P., 456, 472
Foulkes, D., 108
Fowles, D. C., 398
Fox, N. A., 248
Francis, W. D., 260
Frank, E., 402, 428
Frankenburg, W. K., 246
Franz, C. E., 259
Fraser, A. M., 267
Fraser, S. C., 465
Frazer, A., 437
Fredrikson, M., 407
Freedman, J., 481
Freedman, J. L., 465
Freeman, W. J., 76
Freud, A., 261, 328
Freud, S., 6, 19, 20, 21, 23, 28, 101, 109, 178, 261, 291, 326, 327, 328, 329, 330, 331, 332, 333, 334, 340, 349, 350, 393, 409, 424, 425, 478, 482
Frey-Hewitt, B., 298
Friedberg, J. M., 439
Friedland, N., 363
Friedman, J. M., 297
Friedman, M., 370
Friedman, M. I., 295
Friesen, W. V., 312, 313
Frone, M. R., 366
Fry, A. F., 220
Fujita, F., 315
Fuligni, A. J., 226
Furstenberg, F. F., 267
Fyer, A. J., 406, 407

Gabrieli, J. D. E., 174, 188
Gagnon, J. H., 304
Gallagher, M., 272
Gallup, G., Jr., 89, 298, 475
Gallup, G. G., Jr., 16
Galton, F., 222
Ganellen, R. J., 347
Gangestad, G. W., 459
Gannon, L., 15
Garcia, J., 140, 141, 160
Gardner, B. T., 210
Gardner, H., 214, 215
Gardner, R. A., 210
Garland, A. F., 403
Garma, L., 111
Garmon, L. C., 265
Garry, M., 182
Gartner, J., 478

Gastil, J., 213
Gazzaniga, M. S., 48, 49, 116
Geary, D. C., 226
Geen, R. G., 289, 307
Geiselman, R. E., 461
Genesee, F., 213
George, M. S., 401
George, W. H., 120
Gergen, K. J., 23
Geschwind, N., 56
Getzels, J. W., 231
Gevins, A., 50
Gibbons, A., 211
Gibbs, J., 295
Gibbs, W. W., 297
Gibson, E., 245
Giedd, J., 43
Gilbert, D. T., 457
Gildea, P. M., 255
Giles, D. E., 400
Gilligan, C., 264, 265
Ginsburg, G., 307
Ginty, D. D., 42, 102
Glaser, R., 374
Glass, D. C., 363
Glass, G. V., 440, 441
Glazer, W. M., 437
Gleaves, D. J., 411
Glover, J. A., 190
Gluck, M. A., 43, 187
Godden, D. R., 185
Gökcebay, N., 107
Gold, M. S., 121, 122
Goldberg, J., 366
Goldberg, L. R., 336
Goldberg, P. A., 347
Goldenberg, H., 401
Goldenberg, R. L., 267
Goldman, A. L., 368
Goldman, M. S., 380
Goldstein, A., 116
Goldstein, A. J., 432
Goldstein, R. B., 405
Goleman, D., 227, 228, 229, 231, 370
Gonzalez, R., 181
Goode, E. E., 425
Goodwin, D. W., 380, 404
Goodwin, G. M., 122, 438, 443
Gorman, C., 51
Gorman, J. M., 405
Gormezano, I., 143
Gottesman, I. I., 398, 399, 478, 481
Gottfried, A. E., 307
Gottman, J. M., 278, 311
Gough, H., 345
Gould, M. S., 403
Graham, J. R., 345
Graham, S., 15
Grammer, K., 76
Grant, B. F., 379
Gray, D., 374
Grbich, C., 249
Greden, J. F., 38, 400
Green, A. L., 437
Green, A. R., 122
Green, B. L., 367

Green, J., 359
Green, L. R., 478
Green, R., 305
Greenberg, A. S., 297
Greenfield, T. K., 120
Greenwald, A. G., 89
Greenwood, K. M., 124
Gregory, R. J., 346
Gregory, R. L., 65, 85, 86
Greist, J. H., 405, 406, 407, 433
Griffitt, W., 460
Grinker, J. A., 296, 297
Grochowicz, P., 142
Grogger, J., 268
Gronfier, C., 105
Grossman, M., 315
Grünbaum, A., 425
Guilleminault, C., 111
Gunnar, M. R., 249
Gupta, D., 90
Gurin, J., 298
Gurman, A. S., 428
Guthrie, R. V., 22

Haas, A. P., 367
Haber, R. N., 183
Haberlandt, D., 229, 230
Haberlandt, K., 20
Hager, R., 303
Haier, R. J., 220
Haimov, I., 104, 124
Halaas, J. L., 297
Hale, S., 220
Halford, G. S., 253
Hall, C. S., 109
Hall, G. S., 261
Halligan, P. W., 48
Halmi, K. A., 299, 300
Halpern, D. F., 225
Hamer, D. H., 304
Hamilton, J. A., 445
Hamilton, M. C., 213
Hammersmith, S. K., 305, 317
Hammond, D. C., 114
Hansel, C. E. M., 89
Hare, R. D., 413, 414
Harford, T. C., 379
Hargadon, R., 115
Harkins, S. G., 467
Harlow, H. F., 248, 279, 292
Harlow, J. M., 34
Harlow, M. K., 248
Harlow, R. E., 275
Harnett-Sheehan, K., 438
Harrington, D. M., 229
Harris, J. A., 478
Harris, L. J., 191
Harris, M., 383
Harris, R. A., 123
Harrison, J. R., 293
Harsch, N., 183
Hart, D., 247
Hartley, A. A., 273
Hartmann, E. L., 107, 124
Hasselmo, M. E., 38
Hatfield, E., 302, 460
Hay, D., 479
Hay, D. F., 477

Aphasia *(cont.)*
    Wernicke's, 46
Apnea, sleep, 111–112
Apparent motion, 84
Applied research, 4
Appraisal, of stressors, 361–362
Approach–approach conflict, 363
Approach–avoidance conflict, 363
Approximations, successive, 145
Aptitude test, 217–218
Archetype, 333
Arousal, 292
    and aggression, 478
    and emotion, 308–310
    performance and, 292
    reticular formation and, 40
    sexual, 302–303
Arousal theory, 292
Artificial intelligence, 208–209
Asch's experiment on conformity, 462–463
Asian Americans
    academic achievement of, 266
    and alcoholism, 120
    therapy and, 445
Assessment. *See* Intelligence tests; Personal-
    ity assessment; Personality inventories;
    Tests
Assimilation, 250
Association
    free, 425
    liking through, 458
Association areas, 44, 45, 46
Atmospheric perspective, 84
Attachment, 247–249
Attention-deficit/hyperactivity disorder
    (ADHD), 119
Attitudes, 468–471
Attraction
    factors influencing, 458–460
    and mate selection, 461
    romantic, 460–461
Attractiveness, 458–460
Attribution, 457
    dispositional, 457
    situational, 457
Atypical neuroleptics, 437
Audience
    imaginary, 263
    persuasion and, 470
Audience effects, 466
Audition, 73. *See also* Hearing
Auditory aphasia, 46
Auditory canal, 73
Auditory sensory memory, 170
Authoritarian parents, 260, 266
Authoritative parents, 260, 266
Automatic thoughts, 435
Autonomic nervous system, 52–54
Autonomy versus shame and doubt, 258
Availability heuristic, 204
Aversion, taste, 140
Aversion therapy, 433
Aversive events, and aggression, 479–480
Avoidance–avoidance conflict, 363
Avoidance learning, 154
Avoidant attachment, 249
Axon, 34–35

B cells, 374
Babbling, 255–256
Babies. *See* Infants
Back propagating, 34
Backward search, 206
Balance, sense of, 79, 80
Barbiturates, 120, 123
Basic emotions, 311
Basic research, 4
Basic trust versus basic mistrust, 258
Basilar membrane, 75
Behavior. *See also* Behavior modification;
    Behavior therapy
    abnormal, 391–392
    and attitudes, 469
    attributions about, 457
    grossly disorganized, 397
    nonverbal, 228, 482
    prosocial, 475–478
    shaping of, 144–145, 155
    superstitious, 146
Behavior genetics. *See* Behavioral
    genetics
Behavior modification, 155–156, 159,
    429–430
Behavior of Organisms, The (Skinner), 144
Behavior patterns, and heart disease,
    370–371
Behavior therapy, 156, 429–434
Behavioral assessment, 344
Behavioral component
    of attitudes, 468
    of emotions, 308
Behavioral genetics, 222, 341–342
Behavioral perspective, 23
Behavioral therapy. *See* Behavior therapy
Behaviorism, 18–19
Behaviorist view, of personality, 337–338
Bel, 73
Beliefs, irrational, 434–435
Bell-shaped curve. *See* Normal curve
Benzodiazepines, 120, 123, 438
Bereavement, 277
Beta wave, 50
Bias, 15–16
    age, 15–16
    attributional, 457
    experimenter, 11
    gender, 15
    observer, 5
    race, 15
    selection, 10
    self-serving, 457
Biased sample, 6
Big Five, 336, 337
    heritability of, 341
Bilingualism, 213–214
Binet–Simon Intelligence Scale, 216
Binge drinking, 120
Binge eating, 300
Binocular depth cues, 83
Binocular disparity, 83
Biofeedback, 155
Biological perspective, 22–23
    on anxiety disorders, 405
    on memory, 186–188
    on mood disorders, 401–402

on psychological disorders, 392–393
Biological therapy, 436–440
Biomedical model, 358
Biopsychosocial model, 358
Bipolar disorder, 400–401
    lithium and, 438
Birth order, 333–334
    achievement motivation and, 307
    Big Five traits and, 337
Blind spot, 80
Blocking, 139
Body language. *See* Nonverbal behavior
Body temperature, 102
Body weight, 296–297. *See also* Dieting;
    Eating disorders
Bonding, 247
Borderline personality disorder, 413
Bottom-up processing, 87–88
Boys. *See* Gender differences
Brain. *See also* Brain damage
    effects of psychoactive drugs on, 122–123
    left hemisphere of, 46–47
    lobes of, 44–46
    major structures of, 41
    methods of studying, 49–51
    plasticity of, 52
    right hemisphere of, 47–48
    in schizophrenics, 397
    surgery, 440
    and vision, 70
Brain damage
    and aggression, 478
    causes and consequences of, 51–52
    memory and, 186–187
    recovering from, 52
Brain-imaging techniques, 20, 49–51, 174, 220
Brain-wave patterns, and sleep, 104–105
Brainstem, 40
Brainstorming, 231
Brightness, 71
Brightness constancy, 82
Broca's aphasia, 44–45
Broca's area, 44
    bilingualism and, 213, 214
Bulimia nervosa, 296, 300
Burnout, 366
Bystander effect, 476–477

Caffeine, 118
California Psychological Inventory (CPI),
    345–346
Calorie intake, 298
Cancer, 363, 372
    alcohol and, 380
    chemotherapy treatment of, 140, 142
    smoking and, 379
Cannon–Bard theory (of emotion), 309
Cardinal traits, 334
Career choice, 271
Carrier state, 375
Case history, 6
Case study, 6, 18
Catastrophic events, and stress, 366–367
Catatonic schizophrenia, 398
Cattell's Sixteen Personality Factor Ques-
    tionnaire, 335
Cell body, 34

Central nervous system (CNS), 39–42. *See also* Brain
Central tendency, measures of, 490–491
Central traits, 334, 335
Cerebellum, 41
Cerebral cortex, 43–44
Cerebral hemispheres, 43
    specialization of, 46–48
Cerebrum, 43
Challenge, 365, 377
Chemotherapy, classical conditioning and, 141, 142
Chess, 199–200, 208
Child abuse, 481
Childhood sexual abuse, 181–182
Children. *See also* Infants
    abused, 481
    cognitive development in, 250–253
    language development in, 256–258
    memory in, 182
    socialization of, 258–261
Chimpanzees
    insight in, 156
    language in, 210–211
Cholecystokinin (CCK), 295
Chromosomes, 241
Chronic pain, 78–79
Chunk, 171
Chunking, 170–171
Cigarettes. *See* Smoking
Cingulotomy, 440
Circadian rhythm, 102–104
Circadian theory (of sleep), 107
Clairvoyance, 89
Classical conditioning, 133–134, 139
    biological predispositions and, 140–141
    cognitive perspective on, 139–140
    discrimination in, 137
    elements and processes of, 135–137
    in everyday life, 141–142
    extinction in, 135–136
    factors influencing, 142–143
    of fear, 137–139
    generalization and, 136–137
    immune system and, 163–164
    versus operant conditioning, 150–151
    Pavlov and, 134–136
    reflex and, 135
    sponaneous recovery in, 136
    of taste aversions, 141
    therapies based on, 138, 430–433
Client-centered therapy, 426
Cliff, visual, 245
Clinical psychologist, 24, 442
Closure, Gestalt principle of, 81
CNS. *See* Central nervous system
Coaction effects, 466
Cocaine, 119, 122
Cochlea, 74–75
Codeine, 120
Coefficient, correlatoin, 12, 495
Cognition, 200
    social, 472–473
Cognitive abilities, gender differences in, 225–226
Cognitive-behavioral therapy, 436. *See also* Cognitive therapy

Cognitive component
    of attitudes, 468
    of emotions, 308, 309–310
Cognitive development
    in adolescence, 262–263
    in childhood, 250–253
    in later adulthood, 273–274
    Piaget's theory of, 250–254
    Vygetsky's sociocultural view of, 255
Cognitive dissonance, 469–470
Cognitive learning, 156–157
Cognitive map, 157
Cognitive–neoassociationistic model, 479
Cognitive perspective, 23
    on classical conditioning, 139–140
    on mood disorders, 393, 402, 415
    on panic disorder, 405
    on psychological disorders, 393
    on stress, 361–382
Cognitive processes, 156
Cognitive psychology, 20
Cognitive therapy, 434–436
Cognitive traps, 415
Coin-tossing game, 204
Coitus, 301
Collective unconscious, 332, 333
College students, in research studies, 15
Color blindness, 71–72
Color constancy, 82–83
Color vision, 70–72
Command hallucinations, 396
Commitment, 377
Common sense, 215
Common Sense (Paine), 21
Common traits, 334
Communication
    in animals, 212
    emotion as form of, 384–385
    nonverbal, 228, 482
Compliance, 464–465
Componential intelligence, 215
Compulsion, 408
Computerized axial tomography (CT), 50
Computers, in cognitive psychology, 20, 199–200, 206, 208–209
    and memory, 168, 169
Concentrative meditation, 112–113
Concept, 201–202
Concrete operations stage, 252
Conditioned reflex, 135
Conditioned response (CR), 135
Conditioned stimulus (CS), 135
Conditioning, higher-order, 137. *See also* Classical conditioning; Operant conditioning
Conditions of worth, 340
Conduction deafness, 75
Cones, 70, 71
Confederate, 456
Conflicts, 363
Conformity, 462–463
Confounding variables, 10
Conjoint therapy, 428
Conscience, 327
Conscientiousness, 336
Conscious, 326
Consciousness, 17, 101–102. *See also* Altered states of consciousness

Consent, informed, 13
Conservation, 251, 252
Consolidation, 168
Consolidation failure, 177
Constancy, perceptual, 82
Contact hypothesis, 474–475
Context-dependent memory, 185–186
Contextual intelligence, 215
Continuity, Gestalt principle of, 81
Continuous positive airway pressure (CPAP) device, 112
Continuous reinforcement, 147
Control
    of facial expressions, 313–314
    as goal of psychology, 4
    hardiness and, 377
    locus of, 338–339
    stress and, 363
Control group, 9
Conventional level, 264
Convergence, 83
Conversion disorder, 409–410
Convolutions, of cerebral cortex, 44
Cooing, 255–256
Coping, 367
    emotion-focused, 367–368
    proactive, 368
    problem-focused, 367–368
Copulines, 76
Cornea, 69
Coronary heart disease, 370–372
Corpus callosum, 43, 48
Correlation, 12, 495–497
Correlation coefficient, 12, 495
Correlational method, 12
Cortex
    cerebral, 43–44
    motor, 44
    primary auditory, 46
    primary visual, 46
    somatosensory, 45
Corticoids, 55
Counseling psychologist, 27, 442–443
Counselor, 24, 442–443
Couple therapy, 428
Courage to Heal, The (Bass and Davis), 181
CPAP device, 112
Crack, 119
Crash, 119
Creativity, 215, 229–231
Credibility, 470
Critical period, 243
Critical thinking, 4–5, 25–26
Cross-complaining, 278
Cross-cultural studies. *See also* Multicultural issues
    of cognitive development, 254
    of display rules, 313
    of expectations and academic achievement, 227–227, 266
    of facial expressions, 312
    of five-factor theory, 336–337
    of attachment, 248, 249
    of language, 212
    of moral reasoning, 264–265
    of motor development, 246–247
Cross-sectional study, 241

Crowding, 479–480
Crystallized intelligence, 273
CT scan, 50
Cue, retrieval, 174
Cue exposure, 380
Culture. *See also* Cross-cultural studies
    and abnormal behavior, 391
    academic achievement and, 226–227, 266
    alcohol use and, 120
    and altered states of consciousness, 115
    and caring for elderly, 276
    communication of emotion and,
        312–313
    and evaluations of physical attractive-
        ness, 459
    gesture meaning and, 482
    mate selection and, 461
    memory and, 184
    perception of visual illusions and, 85,
        86–87
    personality and, 343
    and psychological disorders, 408, 411
    punishment and, 153
    separation and stranger anxiety and, 248
    social responsibility norms and, 477
    therapy and, 443–445
    and types of intelligence, 215
Culture-fair intelligence test, 221
Cumulative recorder, 145
Curve, normal, 218, 494–495

Dalmane, 120
Dark adaptation, 70
Daydreaming, 101–102
Deafness, 75
Death, 276–277
    of spouse, 275
Decay theory, 177
Decentration, 252
Deception, in research, 13–14
Decibel, 73, 74
Decision latitude, 365
Decision making, 202–203
    additive strategy of, 203
    effects of group on, 467
    through elimination by aspects, 203
    framing and, 204
    heuristics and, 204–205
Decision strategy, noncompensatory, 203
Declarative memory, 172–173
Deep Blue, 199–200, 208
Defense mechanisms, 327–327
Delayed gratification, 228
Delayed posttraumatic stress disorder, 366
Delta wave(s), 50, 106
Delusion, 396
Delusion of grandeur, 396
Delusion of persecution, 396
Dementia, senile, 274
Dendrites, 34
Denial, 329
Density, 480
Dependence, substance, 117
Dependent variable, 9
Depressants, 119–121
Depression, 415. *See also* Major depressive
    disorder
    alcohol and, 379–380

    child sexual abuse and, 182
    cognitive therapy for, 436
    drug treatment for, 437–438
    interpersonal therapy for, 427–428
    and monoamines, 38
    seasonal, 400
Deprivation, sensory, 293
Depth perception, 83–84, 245
Derailment, 397
Description, as goal of psychology, 4
Descriptive research methods, 5–7
Descriptive statistics, 490–497
Desensitization, systematic, 431
Designer drug, 122
Detection, of sensory stimulus, 67
Determinism, reciprocal, 338
Developmental psychologists, 25
Developmental psychology, 240–241. *See also*
    specific stages and types of development
Deviation, standard, 493–494
Deviation score, 217
Diabetes, 55
*Diagnostic and Statistical Manual of Mental
    Disorders*, Fourth Edition, 393–394
Diathesis–stress model, 398
Dieting, 298–299
Difference threshold, 66
Diffusion of responsibility, 477
Directive therapy, 427
Discrimination, 471
    in classical conditioning, 137
    combating, 474–475
    in operant conditioning, 146
    in the workplace, 473–474
Discriminative stimulus, 146
Disease. *See* Alzheimer's disease; Cancer;
    Coronary heart disease; Illness
Disorders. *See* Eating disorders; Psychologi-
    cal disorders; Sleep disorders
Disorganized/disoriented attachment, 249
Disorganized schizophrenia, 398
Disparity, binocular (or retinal), 83
Displacement, 170, 329
Display rules, 313
Dispositional attribution, 457
Dissociated control, theory of, 115
Dissociative amnesia, 410
Dissociative disorders, 410–411
Dissociative fugue, 410
Dissociative identity disorder (DID),
    410–411
Dissonance, cognitive, 469–470
Distortion, in memory, 179–180
Distress, 361
Distribution, frrequency, 492
Diversity, psychological research and, 15. *See
    also* Culture; Gender; Multicultural
    issues; Race
Dizygotic twins, 222, 243
DNA. *See* Chromosomes; Genes
Dolphins, 212
Dominant gene, 241
Door-in-the-face technique, 465
Dopamine, 38, 405
    antipsychotic drugs and, 437
    psychoactive drugs and, 122
    schizophrenia and, 398–399
Double-blind technique, 11

Downers, 119
Dreams, 105, 108–110
    analysis of, 425
    lucid, 109
    NREM, 108
    REM, 108
Drift, instinctual, 155
Drive, 291
    primary, 294
    sexual, 302-303
Drive-reduction theory, 291–292
Drug abuse, 117
Drug therapy, 436–439
Drug tolerance, 117
Drugs. *See also* Drug abuse
    addiction to, 117–118, 141–142
    antidepressant, 437–438
    antipsychotic, 436–437
    designer, 122
    effect on brain of, 122–123
    illicit, 116
    prenatal development and, 243–244
    psychoactive, 115–123
DSM-IV, 393–394
Dying. *See* Death
Dyskinesia, tardive, 437
Dyslexia, 68
Dysthymia, 400

Ear, structure of, 73–74
Eardrum, 73
Early and middle adulthood, 268–269
    career in, 271
    intellectual capacity in, 270–271
    personality and social development in,
        271–272
    physical changes during, 270
Early maturation, 262
Eating cues, 295–296
Eating disorders, 299–300
Eating habits, changing, 298–299
Ebbinghaus's curve of forgetting, 175–176
Eclecticism, 443
Economy, token, 155, 429
ECT. *See* Electroconvulsive therapy
Ecstasy (MDMA), 122
Educational psychologists, 25
EEG. *See* Electroencephalogram
Effeminate behavior, 305
Efferent neurons, 34
Ego, 326, 327
Ego ideal, 327
Ego integrity versus despair, 269
Egocentrism, adolescent, 263
Eidetic imagery, 183
Elaborative rehearsal, 171
Elderly. *See* Aging; Later adulthood
Electra complex, 330
Electroconvulsive therapy (ECT), 439–440
Electroencephalogram (EEG), 50, 105, 106
Electromagnetic spectrum, 68
Elimination by aspects, 203
Embryo, 242
Emotion(s), 307
    awareness of, 228
    basic, 311
    communication of, 482
    components of, 308

experiencing of, 313–315
expression of, 310–313
facial-feedback hypothesis of, 313
management of, 228, 314
and memories, 182–183, 188
motivation and, 307–308
right hemisphere and, 48
theories of, 308–310
Emotion-focused coping, 367–368
Emotional component, of attitudes, 468
Emotional development, in infants, 247–250
Emotional intelligence, 227–229
Empathy, 228
Empty nest syndrome, 272
Encoding, 168
Encoding failure, 176
Endocrine system, 54–55
Endorphins, 39, 79, 122–123
Enrichment, 219, 224, 225
Environment, shared versus nonshared, 341–342
Environmental context, and memory, 185–186
Epilepsy, 48, 52
Epinephrine, 38, 55, 105
Episodic memory, 172, 187
Epithelium, olfactory, 76
Erikson's stages of psychosocial development, 258–259, 268–269
Error
fundamental attribution, 457
trial and, 206
Escape learning, 153–154
ESP, 89
Estrogen, 55, 303
Ethics, in research, 13–14
Ethologists, 5
Eustress, 361
Evolutionary perspective, 23, 337
Excitement phase, 302–303
Exemplars, 202
Exercise, 298, 381–382
aerobic, 381
in later adulthood, 273, 381
sleep and, 124
Exhaustion stage, 360–361
Exhibitionism, 412
Expectancies, 456–457
Expectations, and achievement, 226–227
Experiential intelligence, 215
Experiment, field, 11
Experimental group, 9
Experimental method, 8
advantages and limitations of, 11
experimental and control groups for, 9–10
generalizing findings of, 10
independent and dependent variables in, 8–9
potential problems in, 10–11
Experimental psychologists, 24–25
Experimental research. *See* Experimental method
Experimenter bias, 11
Expert systems, 208
Expertise, 230
Explanation, as goal of psychology, 4
Explicit memory, 172
Exposure and response prevention, 432–433

External locus of control, 338–339
Extinction, 135–136, 145
continuous and partial reinforcement and, 149–150
Extrasensory perception (ESP), 89
Extrinsic motivation, 390
Extroversion, 336, 346
Eye, 68–70
Eye movements, rapid, 105
Eyewitness testimony, 180–181

Fable, personal, 263
Faces, 459
Facial expressions, 311–312, 313–314, 482
Facial-feedback hypothesis, 313
Facilitation, social, 466
Failure
consolidation, 177
encoding, 176
retrieval, 178
False memories, 182
Family therapy, 428
Farsightedness, 273
Fat-cell theory, 297
Fat cells, 297
Father, relationship to child of, 249–250
Fear(s). *See also* Phobia(s)
classical conditioning of, 137–139
observational learning of, 157
overcoming, 431–433, 434
Females. *See* Gender differences; Women
Feminine psychology, 334
Fetal alcohol syndrome, 243–244
Fetishism, 412
Fetus, 242
Field experiment, 11
Fight-or-flight response, 53, 188, 359, 383
Figure-ground, 81
First-degree relatives, 401
First impressions, 456
First-letter technique (for improving memory), 190–191
Five-factor theory (of personality), 336
Fixation, 330
Fixed-interval schedule, 148
Fixed-ratio schedule, 147
Flashback, 122
Flashbulb memory, 182–183
Flat affect, 397
Flooding, 424, 432
Flow, 316
Fluid intelligence, 316
Fluoxetine. *See* Prozac
Flynn effect, 224
fMRI, 50–51
Foot-in-the-door technique, 464–465
Forgetting, 176. *See also* Amnesia
causes of, 176–178
Ebbinghaus's curve of, 175–176
Formal concept, 202
Formal operations stage, 252, 262–263
Fovea, 70
Framing, 204–205
Fraternal (dizygotic) twins, 222, 243
Free association, 425
Free recall, 175
Frequency, 73
Frequency distribution, 492

Frequency polygon, 492
Frequency theory, 75
Freud's theory of personality, 331–332
Freudian interpretation, of dreams, 109
Freudian slip, 326, 332
Frontal association areas, 45
Frontal lobes, 44–45
Frustration, 479
Frustration–aggression hypothesis, 479
Fugue, dissociative, 410
Fully functioning person, 340
Functional fixedness, 207
Functional MRI (fMRI), 50–51
Functionalism, 18
Fundamental attribution error, 457

g **factor**, 214
GABA, 38–39, 123
Gambling, 148
Gardner's theory of multiple intelligences, 214–215
Gate-control theory, 79
Gay men, 303–304
developmental experiences of, 305
rate of AIDS among, 376
Gender, 397. *See also* Gender differences
Gender bias, 15
in Kohlberg's stages of moral reasoning, 265
Gender differences
in cognitive abilities, 225–226, 271
in experiencing emotion, 315
in health care, 373–374
in interview responses, 7
in math ability, 225–226
in stroke, 52
in suicide, 403–404
in verbal ability, 225
Gender identity disorders, 412
General adaptation syndrome (GAS), 359–361
Generalization (of conditioned response), 136–137, 146
Generalization (of findings), 10
Generalized anxiety disorder, 405
Generativity versus stagnation, 269
Genes, 241. *See also* Heritability
and color blindness, 72
and body weight, 297
dominant, 241
and OCD, 409
and personality, 335, 341–343
recessive, 241
schizophrenia and, 398
sexual orientation and, 304–305
Genetics, behavioral, 222
Genital stage, 331
Gestalt, 80
Gestalt principles of perceptual organization, 80–81
Gestalt psychology, 18, 80
Gestalt therapy, 427
Gestures, in various cultures, 482
Giftedness, 218–219
Girls. *See* Gender differences
Glands, endocrine, 54–55
Glucagon, 55
Glucocorticoids, 360

Glucose, blood levels of, 295
Glutamate, 38
Goals of psychology, 4
Gonads, 55
Grammar, 256, 257
Grandeur, delusion of, 396
Gray matter, 44
Grieving, 277
Grossly disorganized behavior, 397
Group, experimental vs. control, 9–10
Group influence, 466–467
Group polarization, 467
Group therapy, 428–429
Grouping, Gestalt principles of, 81
Groupthink, 467
Guided imagery, 182
Gustation, 76

Hair cells, 75
Hallucination, 396
Hallucinogens, 121–122
Halo effect, 450
Hammer (in ear), 74
Handedness, 47, 56
Happiness, 315–316
Hardiness, 377
Harlow's studies of attachment in infant
    monkeys, 248
Hassles, 369–370
Hassles Scale, 369
Head injury, 52
Health, 358, 370–371, 375–377
    job stress and, 366–367
    lifestyle and, 307, 378–382
    in United States, 372–374
Health psychology, 358
Hearing, 73–75
    temporal lobes and, 46
Hearing loss, 75, 90
Heart disease, 370–372
    smoking and, 378–379
Heat, and aggression, 479
Hebephrenia. *See* Disorganized schizophrenia
Helper cells, 374
Helping. *See* Prosocial behavior
Helplessness, learned, 154
Hemispheres, cerebral, 43, 46–48
Heredity, 241–242. *See also* Chromosomes;
    Genes; Genetics
Heritability, 222, 341
    of aggression, 478
    of alcoholism, 480
    of anxiety disorder, 405
    of intelligence, 222–224
    of mood disorders, 401
    of phobias, 407
    of sexual orientation, 304–305
Heroin, 120, 122
Hertz (Hz), 73
Heuristic, 204
    analogy, 206–207
    availability, 204
    in problem solving, 206–207
    representativeness, 204
Hierarchy of needs, 20, 293–294
Higher-order conditioning, 137
Hippocampal region, 186–187
Hippocampus, 42–43, 182

Hispanic American psychologists, 22
Hispanic Americans
    academic achievement by, 266
    collectivist values of, 343
    health of, 373
    therapy and, 445
Histogram, 492
Histrionic personality disorder, 413
HIV (human immunodeficiency virus),
    375. *See also* AIDS
Homeostasis, 291
Homosexuality, 304–305. *See also* Gay men;
    Lesbians
Hopelessness, 404
Hormone(s), 54. *See also* specific hormones
    and aggression, 478
    and memory, 188
    sexual desire and, 303
    and stress, 360
Hospice care, 277
Host personalities, 410
Hostility, and heart disease, 371
Hot flashes, 270
Hue, 71
Human immunodeficiency virus (HIV), 375
    See also AIDS
Humanistic perspective, 23, 393
Humanistic psychology, 19–20, 339
Humanistic therapies, 426–427
Hunger, 294–296
Hypnosis, 113–115
    and repressed memories, 182
Hypnotics, 124
Hypochondriasis, 409
Hypothalamus, 42, 102
    hunger and, 294–295
    sexual orientation and, 304
Hypothesis, 8
    contact, 474–475
    matching, 460

Id, 326, 327
Identical (monozygotic) twins, 222,
    223–224, 242
Identity disorders, 410–411, 412
Identity versus role confusion, 269
Illicit drug, 116
Illness, 358, 369
    reducing impact of, 377–378
Illusion(s), 85–87
    cultural differences in perception of,
    85, 86–87
Imagery, 201
    eidetic, 183
    guided, 182
Imaginary audience, 263
Imitation, by infants, 245–246, 254
Immune system, 374–376
    classical conditioning and, 142
    stress and, 376–377
Implicit memory, 173
Impossible figures, 85
Impression formation, 456
In-group, 471–472
In vivo flooding, 432
Inappropriate affect, 397
Incentive, 289
Independent thinking, 230

Independent variable, 8
Individual traits, 334
Individualism/collectivism, 343
Industrial/organizational (I/O) psycholo-
    gists, 25
Industry versus inferiority, 258–259
Infantile amnesia, 182
Infants
    development of facial expressions in, 311
    emotional development in, 247–250
    language development in, 255–256
    learning in, 245–246
    low-birthweight, 244
    motor development in, 246–247
    newborn, 244
    perceptual development in, 244–245
    preterm, 244
    socialization of, 258
    and touch, 78
Inferential statistics, 497–498
Inferiority, in Adler's theory, 333–334
Information-processing approach, 20, 168
Informed consent, 13
Inhalants, 121
Initiative versus guilt, 258
Innate, 81
Inner ear, 74–75
Insight, 156
Insight therapies, 424–429
Insomnia, 112, 124
Instinct, 290
Instinct theory, 291, 478
Instinctual drift, 155
Insulin, 55, 295
Intellectual capacity, in adulthood, 270–271,
    273–274
Intelligence, 214. *See also* Intelligence tests
    artificial, 208–209
    and creativity, 229–231
    crystallized, 273
    emotional, 227–229
    fluid, 273
    factors underlying, 214
    heritability of, 222–224
    measurement of, 216–219
    multiple, 214–215
    and neural processing, 220
    range of, 218–219
    types of, 214–215
Intelligence quotient (IQ), 216
    effect of environment on, 224–225
    race and, 224
Intelligence tests, 216–218. *See also* specific
    tests
    culture-fair, 221
    uses and abuses of, 221
Intensity, 289–290
Interference, 177
Intermittent reinforcement, 147
Internal locus of control, 338
Interneurons, 34
Interpersonal attraction. *See* Attraction
Interpersonal relationships, 228–229, 278
Interpersonal therapy (IPT), 427–428
Interposition, 84
Interval schedules, 147, 148–149
Interview, 7, 344
    discrimination in, 473–474

Intimacy versus isolation, 269
Intrinsic motivation, 230, 290
Introspection, 17
Introversion, 336
Inventory, 344. *See also* Personality
   inventories
I/O psychologists. *See* Industrial/organiza-
   tional psychologists
IQ. *See* Intelligence quotient
Iris, 69

James–Lange theory (of emotion), 308
Jet lag, 103
Job satisfaction, 271
Job stress, 364–365
Jung's theory of personality, 332–333
Just noticeable difference (JND), 66

Killer cells, 374
Kinesthetic sense, 79
Kinsey surveys, 300–301
Kitchen-sinking, 278
Kohlberg's theory of moral development,
   263–266

Laboratory observation, 5
Language, 209. *See also* Aphasia; Language
   development
   animal, 210–212
   left hemisphere and, 46–47
   second, 249–250
   structure of, 209–210
   thinking and, 212–213
   Wernicke's area and, 46
Language acquisition device (LAD), 257
Language development, 255–258
Larks vs. owls, 107
Late maturation, 262
Latency period, 331
Latent content, of dreams, 109
Latent learning, 156–157
Later adulthood, 269
   cognitive development in, 273–274
   physical changes in, 272–273
   social development and adjustment in,
      274–275
Lateral hypothalamus (LH), 294–295
Lateralization, 46
Latitude, decision, 365
Laughter, and stress, 383
Law of effect, 144
Lazarus theory (of emotion), 309–310
Lazarus's cognitive theory of stress, 361–362
Learned helplessness, 154
Learning, 133. *See also* Classical conditioning;
   Cognitive learning; Learning theory;
   Observational learning; Operant conditioning
   and attitudes, 468
   avoidance, 154
   cognitive, 156–157
   escape, 153–154
   by insight, 156
   in infancy, 245–246
   latent, 156–157
   observational, 157–159
   of optimism, 349

of phobias, 407
   trial-and-error, 143
Learning perspective, on psychological
   disorders, 393
Learning theories
   of language development, 257
   of personality, 337–339
Left-handedness, 47, 56
Left hemisphere, 46–47
Lens, 69
Leptin, 297
Lesbians, 304, 305
Levels-of-processing model (of memory),
   173–174
Libido, 327
Librium, 120, 123, 438
Life satisfaction, age and, 275
Lifestyle, and health, 307, 378–382
Light, 68, 70
   and circadian rhythm, 102–103, 104
   and depression, 400
Liking, 458
Limbic system, 42–43
Linear perspective, 84
Lineups, 180–181
Linguistic relativity hypothesis, 212
Lithium, 438
Loafing, social, 466–467
Lobes, of the brain, 44–46
Lobotomy, 440
Loci, method of, 191
Locus of control, 338–339
Long-term memory, 171–173, 184
Long-term potentiation (LTP), 188
Longitudinal study, 241
Low-ball technique, 465
Low-birthweight babies, 244
LSD (lysergic acid diethylamide), 122
LTP, 188
Lucid dream, 109
Lymphocytes, 374

Macrophages, 375
Magnetic resonance imaging (MRI), 50
Mainstreaming, 219
Major depressive disorder, 399–400
   causes of, 401–403
Major tranquilizers, 437
Maladaptive behavior, 392
Mania, 400
Manic episode, 400
Manifest content, of dreams, 109
Mantra, 112
MAO inhibitors, 438
Map, cognitive, 157
Marijuana, 121–122
Marriage, 278, 461
Maslow's hierarchy of needs, 20, 293–294
Massed practice, 190
Masters and Johnson study, 302–303
Mastery, 175
Matching hypothesis, 460
Mate selection, 461
Math ability, gender differences in, 225–226
Maturation, 246
MDMA (Ecstasy), 122
Mean, 490
Means–end analysis, 206

Measure of central tendency, 490–491
Media, aggression and, 481
Median, 490
Meditation (concentrative), 112–113
Medulla, 40
Melatonin, 102–103, 104, 124
Memory. *See also* Amnesia; Forgetting; Long-
   term memory; Sensory memory; Short-
   term memory
   acetylcholine and, 38
   aging and, 274
   biology and, 186–188
   brain damage and, 186–187
   and culture, 184
   Ebbinghaus's studies on, 175–176
   and eyewitness testimony, 180–181
   hippocampal region and, 42–43
   hormones and, 188
   hypnosis and, 113
   improving of, 188–191
   in later adulthood, 274
   levels-of-processing model of, 173–174
   marijuana use and, 121
   measuring of, 174–175
   neuronal changes in, 187–188
   as a permanent record, 178
   processes in, 168–169
   as reconstruction, 178–180
   recovering repressed, 181–182
   retrieval in, 184–186
   systems of, 169–173
   unusual phenomena of, 182–183
Menarche, 262
Menopause, 270
Mental abilities, primary, 214
Mental health professionals, 442–443
Mental retardation, 219
Mental rotation study, 201
Mental set, 207–208
Mentality of Apes, The (Köhler), 156
Mere-exposure effect, 458
Mescaline, 121
Message, persuasiveness of, 470–471
Meta-analysis, 13
Metabolic rate, 297
Metabolism, 297
Method of loci (for improving memory), 191
Microelectrode, 50
Microsleep, 108
Middle age. *See* Early and middle adulthood
Middle ear, 74
Milgram's obedience study, 463–464
Minnesota Center for Twin and Adoption
   Research, 222
Minnesota Multiphasic Personality Inven-
   tory (MMPI and MMPI-2), 344-345
Minor tranquilizers, 120, 438
Misinformation effect, 181
Mistrust, 258
MMPI. *See* Minnesota Multiphasic Personality
   Inventory
Mnemonics, 190–191
Mode, 491
Model, 157
Modeling, 157
   participant, 434
Modification, behavior, 155–156
Monkeys, attachment in, 248

Paranoid personality disorder, 413
Paranoid schizophrenia, 398
Paraphilias, 412
Parapsychology, 89
Parasomnias, 110–111
Parasympathetic nervous system, 53
Parenting styles, 259–260, 266
Parents
  influence on adolescent development, 266
  and socialization process, 259–260
Parietal lobes, 45
Parkinson's disease, 38
Partial reinforcement, 147
Partial-reinforcement effect, 149–150
Participant modeling, 434
Pavlovian conditioning, 134. *See also* Classical conditioning
Peak experiences, 339
Pedophilia, 412
Peer relationships, 260–261, 266–267
Pegword system (for improving memory), 191
Penis envy, 330
Perception, 65, 80. *See also* Sensation
  depth, 83–84
  development of, in infancy, 244–245
  extrasensory, 89
  of illusions, 85, 86–87
  of motion, 84–85
  role of psychological factors in, 88
  social, 456–457
  subliminal, 89
Perceptual constancy, 82–83
Perceptual organization, Gestalt principles of, 80–81
Perceptual set, 88
Performance
  arousal and, 292
  effects of group on, 466–467
  job satisfaction and, 271
Performance anxiety, 406
Period, critical, 243
Period of the zygote, 242
Peripheral nervous system (PNS), 39, 52–53
Permanence, object, 251, 253–254
Permissive parents, 260, 266
Persecution, delusion of, 396
Perseverence, creativity and, 279
Persistence, 289–290
Person-centered therapy, 340, 426–427
Personal fable, 263
Personal space, 479
Personal unconscious, 332, 333
Personality, 325. *See also* Personality assessment; Personality disorder; Personality inventories; Personality theories
  alter, 410–411
  behavioral genetics and, 341–342
  culture and, 343
  and heart disease, 370–371
  host, 410
  in middle age, 271–272
  neurotic, 334
  temperament and, 247
Personality assessment, 343–347
Personality disorder, 412–414

Personality inventories, 336, 344–346
Personality theories
  of Adler, 333–334
  of Bandura, 338
  five-factor, 336–337
  of Freud, 331–332
  of Horney, 334
  humanistic, 339–340
  of Jung, 332–333
  learning, 337–339
  of Neo-Freudians, 332–334
  of Rogers, 340
  of Rotter, 338–339
  trait, 334–337
Perspective, 84
Persuasion, 470–471
  subliminal, 88
Pessimism, 229, 348–349, 377
PET scan, 50–51, 220, 401, 409
Peyote, 121
Phallic stage, 330–331
Phenomenological field, 340
Pheromones, 76
Phi phenomenon, 18, 84–85
Phobia(s), 406–407. *See also* specific phobias
  avoidance learning and, 154
  causes of, 407
  classical conditioning and, 140, 141
  therapy for, 432, 434
Phonemes, 209–210, 256
Photographic memory, 183
Photons, 68
Photoreceptors, 102
Physical attractiveness, 458–460
Physical component of emotions, 308
Physical development
  in adolescence, 261–262
  in adulthood, 270, 272–273
  in infancy, 244–247
Physical drug dependence, 117
Physiological needs, 293
Physiological psychologists, 24
Piaget's theory of cognitive development, 250–254, 262–263
Pinna, 73
Pitch, 73, 75
Pituitary gland, 54
Place theory, 75
Placebo, 11
Placebo effect, 10–11
Plasticity, 52
Plateau phase, 303
Pleasure principle, 327
PNS. *See* Peripheral nervous system
Polarization, group, 467
Polysomnograms, 104
Pons, 40
Ponzo illusion, 86
Population, 6, 497
Positive correlation, 495
Positive instances, 202
Positive regard, unconditional, 340
Positive reinforcement, 146, 152
Positive symptoms, of schizophrenia, 396–397
Positron-emission tomography (PET), 50–51, 220, 401, 409

Postconventional level, 264
Posttraumatic stress disorder (PTSD), 366–367
Potential
  action, 35
  resting, 35
Potentiation, long-term, 188
Practice, massed versus spaced, 190
Precognition, 89
Preconscious, 326
Preconventional level, 264
Prediction
  in classical conditioning, 139–140
  correlations and, 12
  as goal of psychology, 4
Prefrontal cortex, 171
Pregnancy
  in adolescence, 267–268
  hazards of drugs in, 243–244
Prejudice, 471–473. *See also* Discrimination
  combating, 474–475
Premarital sex, 267
Prenatal, 289
Prenatal development, 242–244
Preoperational stage, 251–252
Presbyopia, 69, 270
Preterm infants, 244
Primacy effect, 184–185, 456
Primary appraisal, 361
Primary auditory cortex, 46
Primary drive, 294
Primary mental abilities, 214
Primary reinforcer, 147
Primary sex characteristics, 241
Primary visual cortex, 46
Priming, 173
Principles of Psychology (James), 18
Private speech, 255
Proactive coping, 368
Proactive interference, 177
Problem-focused coping, 367–368
Problem solving, 205
  approaches to, 205–207
  artificial intelligence and, 208–209
  creative, 229–230
  impediments to, 207–208
Processing, bottom-up versus top-down, 87–88
Procrastination, 159
Progesterone, 55, 303
Progressive relaxation, 382
Projection, 329
Projective tests, 346–347
Prosocial behavior, 475–478
Protease inhibitors, 375
Prototype, 202
Proximity, 458
  Gestalt principle of, 81
Prozac, 438
Psychedelics, 121
Psychiatric social worker, 442
Psychiatrist, 442
Psychic phenomena, 89
Psychoactive drug(s), 115–123
Psychoanalysis, 19, 326–332, 425
Psychoanalyst, 442
Psychoanalytic perspective, 23

Psychodynamic perspective, on psychological disorders, 393, 402, 407, 408
Psychodynamic therapies, 425–426
Psycholinguistics, 209
Psychological disorders. *See also* specific types of disorders
  defining and classifying, 393–394
  DSM-IV categories for, 395
  and MMPI, 345
  perspectives on, 392–393
Psychological drug dependence, 117
Psychological tests, 12–13. *See also* Tests
Psychologists. *See also* Mental health professionals
  types of, 23–25
Psychology, 2
  cognitive, 20
  feminine, 334
  Gestalt, 18
  goals of, 4
  history of, 17–22
  humanistic, 19–20
  modern perspectives in, 22–23
  as a science, 3
  social, 455–456
  women and minorities in, 21–22
Psychoneuroimmunology, 376
Psychopaths, 414
Psychosexual stages, 329–331
Psychosis, 394
Psychosocial development, Erikson's theory of, 258–259, 268–269
Psychosocial stages, 258
Psychosurgery, 440
Psychotherapy, 424. *See also* Therapies
PTSD. *See* Posttraumatic stress disorder
Puberty, 261–262
Punishment, 151–153
Pupil (of eye), 69
Puzzle box, 143

Questionnaires, in survey research, 7

Race
  and barriers to therapy, 564
  IQ and, 224
  and misidentification of suspects, 181
  and perception of illusions, 86–87
  suicide and, 403–404
Race bias, 15
Racial stress, 363
Random assignment, 10
Random sample, 6, 498
Range, 493
Rapid eye movements, 105
Rating scales, 344
Ratio schedules, 147–148
Rational-emotive therapy, 415, 434–435
Rationalization, 329
Raven's Standard Progressive Matrices Test, 222
Reaction formation, 329
Reading
  to fetus, 245
  language development and, 257–258
Realistic conflict theory, 471
Reality, virtual, 433
Reality principle, 327

Rebound, REM, 109
Recall, 174–175, 185, 186
Recency effect, 184–185
Receptors, 36
  olfactory, 76
  sensory, 67, 75
  taste, 77
  touch, 78
  visual, 70
Recessive gene, 241
Reciprocal determinism, 338
Reciprocal liking, 458
Recognition, 175
Reconstruction, 179
Recorder
  cumulative, 145
  video cassette, 178
Recovery, spontaneous, 135–136
Reflex, 40, 135, 244
  conditioned, 135
Refractory period, 36, 303
Regression, 329
Rehearsal, 171, 183
  elaborative, 171
Reinforcement, 146–147
  continuous, 147
  and extinction, 149–150
  negative, 146, 151
  partial, 147
  positive, 146, 152
  schedules of, 147–149
Reinforcer, 144
  primary, 147
  secondary, 147
Relationships, interpersonal, 228–229, 278
Relative size, 84
Relatives, first-degree, 401
Relaxation techniques, 113, 382
Relearning method, 175
Reliability, 13, 217
Religion, and coping, 368
REM dreams, 108
REM rebound, 110
REM sleep, 38, 105–107, 108. *See also* Dreams; NREM sleep
  function of, 109–110
REM sleep behavior disorder, 105
Remembering. *See* Memory
Repetition, of message, 471
Replication, 13
Representative sample, 6
Representativeness heuristic, 204
Repressed memories, 181–182
Repression, 178, 328–329
Research
  animals in, 16
  applied, 4
  basic, 4
  bias in, 10–11, 15–16
  deception in, 13–14
  ethics in, 13–15
  evaluation of, 26
  participants in, 13–15
Research methods
  case study, 6
  correlational, 12
  descriptive, 5–7
  experimental, 7–11

  meta-analysis, 13
  naturalistic observation, 5
  psychological tests, 12
  survey, 6–7
Resistance, 425
Resistance stage, 425
Resistant attachment, 249
Resolution phase, 303
Respondent conditioning, 134. *See also* Classical conditioning
Response
  conditioned, 135
  unconditioned, 135
Response prevention, 432–433
Responsibility, diffusion of, 477
Resting potential, 35
Restorative theory (of sleep), 107
Retardation. *See* Mental retardation
Reticular activating system (RAS), 40
Reticular formation, 40
Retina, 69, 70, 104
Retinal disparity, 83
Retinal image, 82
Retirement, 275
Retrieval, 168, 184–186
Retrieval cue, 174
Retrieval failure, 178
Retroactive interference, 177
Retrograde amnesia, 177
Reuptake, 37
Reversibility, 252
Revised NEO Personality Inventory (NEO-PI-R), 336
Rhyme (for improving memory), 190
Rhythm, circadian, 102–104
Right hemisphere, 47–48
Rites of passage, 261
Robber's cave experiment, 471–472
Rods, 70
Rogers's theory of personality, 340
Role confusion, 269
Roles, social, 467
Romantic attraction, 460–461
Rorschach Inkblot Method, 346–347
Runner's high, 39, 79

s factors, 257
SAD. *See* Seasonal affective disorder
Sample, 6, 498
  biased, 6
  random, 6, 498
  representative, 6
Satiation, stimulus, 430
Satiety signals, 295
Saturation, 82
Savant syndrome, 219
Savings method, 175
Savings score, 175
Scaffolding, 255
Scapegoating, 479
Scatterplot, 496–497
Schachter–Singer theory (of emotion), 309
Schedule of reinforcement, 147–149
Schemas, 179, 250
Schizophrenia, 394–396
  atypical neuroleptics and, 554, 555
  causes of, 398–399
  dopamine activity and, 38

symptoms of, 396–397
treatment of, 436–437
types of, 397–398
Scholastic Assessment Test (SAT), 217–218
Science and Human Behavior (Skinner), 144
Scientific method, 3
Score
deviation, 217
savings, 175
Seasonal affective disorder (SAD), 400
Secondary appraisal, 361–362
Secondary reinforcer, 147
Secondary sex characteristics, 241, 262
Secondary traits, 334, 335
Secure attachment, 248–249
Sedentary lifestyle, 370
Selection bias, 10
Self-actualization, 293, 339, 426
Self-efficacy, 338
Self-fulfilling prophecy, 11, 458
Self-help groups, 428–429
Self-image, in adolescence, 262
Self-motivation, 228
Self-serving bias, 457
Selye's general adaptation syndrome, 359–361
Semantic memory, 172–173, 187
Semantics, 210
Semicircular canals, 74, 80
Senile dementia, 274
Sensation, 65–68. *See also* Senses
Sensation seekers, 292
Senses. *See also* individual senses; Pain; Sensation
in infants, 244–245
kinesthetic, 79
vestibular, 79–80
Sensorimotor stage, 251
Sensorineural hearing loss, 75
Sensory adaptation, 67–68
Sensory deprivation, 293
Sensory images, 201
Sensory input areas, 44
Sensory memory, 169–170
Sensory neurons, 34
Sensory receptors, 67
Sensory restriction, 293
Sentence completion method, 347
Separation anxiety, 248
Serial position effect, 184–185
Serial recall, 175
Serotonin, 38
in anxiety disorders, 405, 409
in bulimia nervosa, 300
in mood disorders, 401–402
Serotonin-selective reuptake inhibitors (SSRIs), 438
Set point, 298
Set-point theory, 297–298
Sex. *See* Gender; Sexual behavior
Sex chromosomes, 241
Sex hormones, 55. *See also* Androgens; Estrogen; Progesterone; Testosterone
Sex-role development. *See* Gender-role development
Sex typing. *See* Gender typing
Sexism, in language, 213
Sexual abuse, of children, 181–182

Sexual arousal, 302–303
Sexual attitudes, 301–302
Sexual behavior
in later adulthood, 273
surveys of, 7, 300–302
Sexual Behavior in the Human Female (Kinsey), 300
Sexual Behavior in the Human Male (Kinsey), 300
Sexual desire, 302–303
Sexual disorders, 411–412
Sexual dysfunctions, 412
Sexual masochism, 412
Sexual motives, 300–303
Sexual orientation, 303–305
and HIV transmission, 375–376
Sexual response cycle, 302–303
Sexual sadism, 412
Sexually transmitted diseases. *See* Acquired immune deficiency syndrome
Shading, 84
Shadows, 84
Shape constancy, 82
Shaping, 144–145, 155
Shared environment, 341
Shift work, 103–104
Shock treatment. *See* Electroconvulsive therapy
Short-term memory, 170–171, 184
Sign language, 210, 211, 256
Signal detection theory, 67
Similarity
attraction and, 460
Gestalt principle of, 81
Situational attribution, 457
Situational phobias, 407
Sixteen Personality Factor Questionnaire, 335
Size, relative, 84
Size constancy, 82, 85
Skin, 77–78
Skinner box, 144–145, 146
Sleep, 102. *See also* Dreams; REM sleep; Sleep disorders
brain-wave patterns of, 104–105
improving, 124
melatonin and, 104
and memory, 177
need for, 107
NREM, 104–105, 106
REM, 105–106, 107
stages of, 106
variations in, 106–107
Sleep apnea, 111–112
Sleep cycles, 106
Sleep deprivation, 108
Sleep disorders, 110–112
Sleep terrors, 110–111
Sleep/wakefulness cycle, 102, 103
Sleeping pills, 124
Sleeptalking, 111
Sleepwalking, 110
Slow-wave sleep, 106
Smell, 75–76
Smoking, 118, 378–379
cognitive dissonance and, 469
in pregnancy, 244
Social cognition, 472–473

Social-cognitive theorists, 338–339
Social density, 480
Social desirability response, 7
Social development
in later adulthood, 275–276
in middle age, 271–272
Social facilitation, 466
Social learning theory
of aggression, 480–481
and prejudice, 472
Social loafing, 466–467
Social motives, 306–307
Social Organization of Sexuality, The (Laumann), 301
Social perception, 456–457
Social phobia, 406–407
drug treatment for, 438
Social psychologists, 25
Social psychology, 455–456
Social Readjustment Rating Scale (SRRS), 368–369
Social roles, 467
Social support, 377–378
Socialization, 258–261
Sociocognitive theory of hypnosis, 114
Sociocultural perspective, 23
Sociocultural view, of cognitive development, 255
Socioeconomic level, and IQ, 224–225
Sociopaths, 414
Soma, 34
Somatic nervous system, 52
Somatoform disorders, 409–410
Somatosensory cortex, 45, 78
Somnambulism, 110
Somniloquy, 111
Sound, 73
Source traits, 335
Space, personal, 479
Spaced practice, 190
Spatial ability, gender differences in, 226
Spatial density, 480
Specialization, of cerebral hemispheres, 46–49
Specialties, in psychology, 24–25
Specific phobia, 407
Spectrum, visible, 68
Speech
Broca's area and, 44
private, 255
recognition, 209
telegraphic, 256
Wernicke's area and, 46
Spinal cord, 39–40
Split-brain operation, 48
Split-brain person, 48–49
Spontaneous recovery, 135–136, 145
SRRS. *See* Social Readjustment Rating Scale
SSRIs, 438
Stage 1 sleep, 106
Stage 2 sleep, 106
Stage 3 sleep, 106
Stage 4 sleep, 106
Stage theories. *See* specific theory
Standard deviation, 493–494
Standardization, 218
Stanford–Binet Intelligence Scale, 216–217
State-dependent memory effect, 186

Photos